CCH
a Wolters Kluwer business

Introduction to Federal Income Taxation in Canada

CCH Canadian Limited

300-90 Sheppard Avenue East
Toronto Ontario
M2N 6X1
1 800 268 4522
www.cch.ca

28th Edition, 2007-2008

By
Robert E. Beam, F.C.A.
Professor Emeritus, University of Waterloo
Stanley N. Laiken, Ph.D.
Deloitte Professor, University of Waterloo
James J. Barnett, F.C.A.
Director of the School of Accountancy,
University of Waterloo

Contributors
Ling Chu, M.Tax
Wilfrid Laurier University
Barbara Rockx, M.Acc., C.A.
University of Toronto and University of Waterloo
Michael Zender, B.Comm., LLB
Ernst & Young, Chartered Accountants, Toronto

Published by CCH Canadian Limited

Library and Archives Canada has catalogued this publication as follows:

Beam, Robert E.

Introduction to federal income taxation in Canada / by Robert E. Beam, Stanley N. Laiken.

1980/81 ed.–
ISSN 0821-5340
ISBN 978-1-55367-791-8 (28th edition, 2007/2008)

1. Income tax — Canada. 2. Income tax — Canada — Problems, exercises, etc.
I. Laiken, Stanley N., 1943– II. Barnett, James J.
III. CCH Canadian Limited IV. Title.

KE5759.B43   343.7105′2   C83-030860-1   KF6370.B43

ISBN: 978-1-55367-791-8

Typeset by CCH Canadian Limited.
Printed in the United States of America.

About This Book

The study of Canadian federal income taxation is made more complex, particularly at the introductory level, not because of the lack of good interpretive materials to guide the student, but, in the authors' opinion, because of the lack of organization in the presentation of these materials for systematic study. While the *Income Tax Act* (the Act), the statute governing the federal taxation of income in Canada, is organized generally by source of income, interpretive material available to students at the introductory level is often organized by topics which may cover elements of several sources.

Since the authors of these materials feel that it is important to the understanding of the Act that the student generally studies the major provisions of the statute in sequence, the chapters of this book generally follow the organization of the Act. The purpose of these materials is to guide the student in the study at the introductory level of the major provisions of the Act and some of the related provisions in the *Excise Tax Act* (the ETA) pertaining to the Goods and Services Tax. A copy of the Act plus the Canada Revenue Agency's (CRA's) Interpretation Bulletins, Information Circulars and Advance Tax Rulings are considered to be essential materials for the course. The purpose is to organize the student's reference to interpretive material in the order of presentation in the Act. This book is designed to encourage students to refer to the Act, case law and the CRA's publications; it is not written to be used as a completely independent text.

The commentary presented in this book highlights key areas of the Act. The textbook provides additional interpretation of particularly difficult provisions of the Act or elements of the common law or case law in the area. The basic concepts and principles underlying the rules of the legislation are emphasized throughout these materials. Most important for the study of income taxation, it provides fact situations or example problems which demonstrate the application of the provisions of the Act to realistic situations. In fact, the primary teaching approach used in this commentary is the presentation of example problems and exercises with solutions. These solutions demonstrate various methods of approaching actual problems in income taxation. The solutions also provide explanatory and interpretive notes which are an important component of these materials, often expanding a topic beyond the confines of the particular facts under discussion.

The authors must emphasize that these materials are in no way intended to be a substitute for the Act. It is essential that students obtain practice in reading the Act not only for the purpose of becoming familiar with a particular provision under study, but also for the purpose of learning how to read and interpret the legislation in general. These materials are designed to present situations which will help students to focus their attention on the reading and understanding of a particular provision or set of provisions with the objective of developing more generalized skills to be used in the interpretation of the Act.

References are provided in the outer margin of the text beside the paragraph to which they pertain. These references are to the following sources:

(1) ITA refers to the sections of the *Income Tax Act* to be discussed in the chapter;

(2) ITAR refers to the *Income Tax Application Rules, 1971*, which are found in the volume containing the Act immediately following the provisions of the Act;

(3) ITR refers to the Income Tax Regulations which are also found in the volume containing the Act;

(4) ETA refers to sections of the *Excise Tax Act* in which provisions of the Goods and Services Tax (GST) can be found; and

(5) IT, IC, TR, and ATR refer, respectively, to Interpretation Bulletins, Information Circulars, Tax Rulings and Advance Tax Rulings — Second Series and are available in a one-volume softcover edition published by CCH Canadian Limited.

An explanation of all of these references is provided at the beginning of Chapter 1. References to sections of the Act are provided for all exercises and assignment problems. It should also be understood that in the course of their use within the paragraph of the text, all references preceded by such specific terms as "section", "subsection", "paragraph", "subparagraph", etc., without any indication of the pertinent statute, refer to the provisions of the *Income Tax Act*. Similarly the provisions of the Income Tax Regulations are preceded by the term "Regulation" without specifying the relevant legislation. In the margin, these references are preceded by "ITA" and "ITR", respectively.

References to the *Excise Tax Act* are usually confined to the GST part of a chapter and are specifically indicated as being to that legislation. References in the margin are preceded by "ETA". An attempt has been made to integrate GST with relevant transactions discussed under the *Income Tax Act* in the chapters where these transactions are discussed.

A copy of the CD, containing the CCH Tax Electronic Research Library, is enclosed with student editions of this book. Thorough and accurate tax research is an important part of tax practice.

A set of review questions is provided at the end of each chapter. These short-answer questions attempt to review key points made in the text or points that are not integrated into the example problems, multiple choice questions, exercises or assignment problems in the chapter. Discussion notes on the review questions are provided in Appendix I at the end of the text.

Since multiple choice questions are common in professional examinations, this textbook provides six or seven such questions covering the material in Chapters 2 to 18 at the end of each of those chapters, for a total of over 100 questions. Annotated solutions are provided in Appendix II at the end of the book to enhance learning through self-study.

Exercises have been provided at the end of each chapter. These usually consist of short problems to highlight particular areas of the chapter. They are designed to be fairly narrow in scope, to provide the student with an opportunity to apply the material in the chapter to a specific problem situation. Solutions to these exercises have been provided in Appendix III.

Assignment problems are provided for each chapter of these materials. These problems are designed to have the student apply the material discussed in each chapter to an actual fact or problem situation. While these problems focus on the key elements of the chapter in much the same way that the solved example problems in the commentary do, the problems are not identical in their coverage or presentation. As a result, it will be necessary for the student to read the assignment problems very carefully in preparing a solution. Solutions to these problems are not available. However, similar additional problems with solutions are provided on the accompanying CD, as discussed below.

Students often request additional problems with solutions that they can use on a self-study basis for preparation for tests and examinations. For this purpose, a comprehensive compilation of problems similar to the assignment problems in this book and multiple choice questions are provided on the CD accompanying this book. There are over 150 problems and solutions on the CD, classified by coverage of chapters in this textbook. The problems, most of which have been used as examination questions, will provide students with an opportunity to deal with problems of a comprehensive nature. Since these supplemental problems may cover material from several chapters, as examination questions often do, they provide an excellent source for review in preparation for examinations.

The authors suggest the following approach to the use of these materials. First, the student should scan the headings for the references for each major heading of the commentary. Thus, the student should scan for coverage and content of the particular sections of the Act under discussion, any Income Tax Application Rules or Regulations applicable to these sections, and any Interpretation Bulletins, Information Circulars or Advance Tax Rulings applicable to these sections. Then, the student should read the commentary in this book, including the example problems. The solutions provided for these problems will demonstrate the approach that can be taken for the type of example problem under consideration. The solutions can also be used as a check on the student's understanding as well as a means of providing further interpretation and explanation of the material covered. The exercises at the end of the chapter can be used in a similar manner with the solutions provided on the accompanying CD being used as a means of self-study and reinforcement. Once the parts of a chapter have been completed in this manner, the student should be sufficiently prepared to attempt the assignment problems relevant to a particular part or to the whole chapter. When reviewing material for examination or other purposes, the multiple choice questions at the end of each chapter and the problems on the accompanying CD can be attempted. The solutions in Appendix II and on the CD can then be checked. Review might also focus on the approaches used to address the various types of problems presented.

Materials at the introductory level on Canadian income tax legislation are not easy to study. A conscientious effort to do the work and, particularly, to do problems and apply what has been read is essential to a good understanding of this material. The authors have attempted to meet the challenge of presenting the material by setting out the work that must be done and by explaining, as best they can, the major provisions of the legislation. The challenge of learning the material is, of course, left to the student.

Toronto, Ontario   Robert E. Beam

Waterloo, Ontario   Stanley N. Laiken

Waterloo, Ontario   James J. Barnett

July 2007

Acknowledgement

Over the years, many people have participated in the preparation, revision and improvement of these materials. The authors would like to acknowledge their indebtedness to all who have helped in this undertaking. The Institute of Chartered Accountants of Ontario funded the initial concept and application of these materials through its correspondence course. The Chartered Accountants Students' Association of Ontario permitted the inclusion of some of its material in the area of advanced corporate taxation in Chapters 15, 16 and 17. Miss Kathy Matthews, Secretary to the Finance and Business Economics area of the Faculty of Business at McMaster University, diligently prepared the original version of the manuscript and the revision in the first edition. The business students of both McMaster University and Ryerson Polytechnical University when we were faculty members there, the students in the accountancy and the tax programs of the University of Waterloo and C.A. finalist students in the preparation program of the Chartered Accountants Students' Association of Ontario and in the School of Accountancy of the Institute of Chartered Accountants of Ontario have constantly given invaluable assistance in revising and polishing the final manuscript for each edition. In addition, a number of our colleagues teaching either full-time or part-time at various universities and colleges and teaching at the Institute of Chartered Accountants of Ontario School of Accountancy have made most helpful comments for the improvement of this book.

In particular we are greatly indebted and most grateful to the following individuals for their efforts in making contributions of materials, in providing their comments or views on various aspects of the book and in reviewing and revising these materials.

The following past major contributors have provided text materials or problems, which were added to the book and helped with annual revisions and updates. Some provided materials on specialized areas of taxation.

Greg Boehmer	Joan A. Kitunen	Michael Robillard
Catherine Brayley	Kenneth Klassen	Wayne Rudson
Mariann Coward	John MacCulloch	Karen Wensley
Irene David	Alan Macnaughton	Susan Whitney
Kass Ebrahim	Joanne E. Magee	Karen Wilkinson
Nancy Harley	Debbie Lee Mailling	Brian Wilson
Linda Hyatt	D.L. (Del) McLennan	
Gena Katz	Jane Ritchie	

The following individuals have provided detailed and valuable comments for improvements and revisions from various perspectives of practice and education.

Seema Agarwal	Kun Huo	David Palamar
Bill Chan	Ken Hurdle	Annalee Richler
Richard Colden	Rob Innis	Rick Robertson
Brian Cookson	Paul Jarvis	Julie Robson
Austin Davey	David Lam	Martin Schwartz
Gail Drory	Michelle Ma	Ian Simpson
Jonathan Eckler	Thomas Matthews	Tari Lee Vaughan
Yingxin Gao	Alastair Murdoch	Dorothy Wright
Thomas Haddrath	Ian Niven	Allister Young

The following individuals have provided extensive reviews of the manuscript and ably provided detailed comments on readability of the text. Some participated in a painstaking proofreading of the text and methodical checking of calculations.

Rayna (Laiken) Baker	Janna (Laiken) Krieger	Terry McDowell
Howard Bergman	Jonathan Krieger	Robert Montgomery
Yingxin Gao	Adam Laiken	Kirsten Richter
Tom Kingissepp	Rob Law	

As a result of the continuous change in materials on taxation, all editions required extensive revisions. A considerable burden was placed, as usual, on the Editorial Department of CCH Canadian Limited and, in particular, Kee-Hyung Kim who was a great help in the preparation of the first 19 editions before his retirement in 1998. He, also, was enticed out of retirement, briefly, to do a thorough editorial review of the 22nd edition. We are very happy that he was willing to do so. His work in converting very messy manuscripts into final copy on all those editions has been tremendous and greatly appreciated. His editorial thoroughness has held us to high standards of writing and presentation. His pleasant manner of keeping us on schedule to ensure timely production of the materials has been a major and invaluable contribution to the work for which we are very grateful. We were greatly saddened by his passing in November 2006. For subsequent editions, the considerable editorial work was ably continued by Ann Choi, Douglas Robb, and James McColl. The tradition of invaluable editorial work was meticulously provided by Jerry D'Souza for the 25th and 26th edition. For the 27th edition, Carrie Shimkofsky provided the very careful and thorough editorial work under a tight deadline caused by a late federal budget. For this 28th edition, Carrie has painstakingly managed the tremendous detail of the major formatting changes that were implemented and has helped to improve the readability of the text.

The authors have benefited tremendously from their respective associations with Ernst & Young, Chartered Accountants, Toronto (Beam), RSM Richter, Chartered Accountants, Toronto (Laiken) and Deloitte Chartered Accountants, Toronto and London (Barnett). Our experiences with these firms have provided a practical perspective which we feel is essential as academics working in the field of income taxation.

In an undertaking of this nature our wives, Karen, Elaine and Fay, and children have had to bear a burden that is often unrecognized and certainly unrewarded. We greatly appreciate their contribution of patience and understanding to the preparation of this book, because without them there would be nothing!

July 2007   Robert E. Beam

                                                                            Stanley N. Laiken

                                                                            James. J. Barnett

Note on Legislation for
Twenty-Eighth Edition

The 28th edition of the book has been updated to include proposals in the March 19, 2007 federal budget. Many of these proposals were contained in Bill C-52, which was tabled on March 29, 2007, and received Royal Assent on June 22, 2007. This edition of the text also contains references to Bill C-33, which was tabled on November 22, 2006, but had not been passed by the Senate at the time that Parliament began its summer break in June 2007. The contents of Bill C-33 were introduced originally on July 18, 2005 as draft legislation. Also referenced in this edition are the income trust measures released one December 21, 2006 as draft legislation and contained in Bill C-52, which received Royal Assent on June 22, 2007.

Table of Contents

Chapter 1

Introduction

LEARNING GOALS

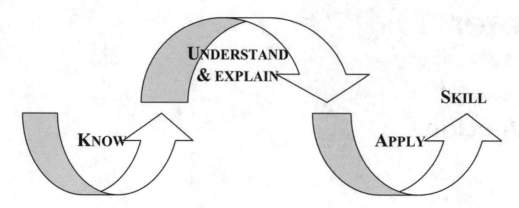

Know

By the end of this chapter you should know some of the history of income tax in Canada and how the *Income Tax Act* and the *Excise Tax Act* (pertaining to the goods and services tax) are structured, interpreted, and administered.

Understand and Explain

You should understand and be able to explain how to find things in the Act and how to put together the calculation of income for tax purposes and taxable income. In addition, you should be able to explain how to interpret tax legislation. Completing the Exercises (¶1,850) is a good way to deepen your understanding of the material.

Apply

You should be able to use your general knowledge and understanding of the calculation of income and the interpretation of tax laws to put together the calculation of income and taxable income and to find the meaning of certain words and phrases in the *Income Tax Act*. Completing the Assignment Problems (¶1,875) is an excellent way to develop your ability to apply the material in increasingly complex situations.

OVERVIEW

This chapter covers three basic areas of income taxation in Canada. First, it provides a historical, legal, and theoretical perspective. Second, it introduces the *Income Tax Act* ("ITA" or the "Act"),[1] the legal statute governing income taxation in Canada, by providing an overview of the structure of the legislation. Third, the materials present an overview of the administration and enforcement of the legislation.

This chapter also introduces, on a conceptual basis, the goods and services tax (GST). Subsequent chapters will discuss the related GST implications of the topics described in those chapters. This chapter first describes the organization of the GST in the context of its legislative authority, the *Excise Tax Act* (ETA),[2] and various interpretive sources. The balance of this material then gives an overview of the GST system and, in particular, certain basic concepts such as taxable transactions, exempt transactions, and GST refunds.

---

[1] Unless otherwise stated, all statutory references are to the *Income Tax Act*, R.S.C. 1985, c. 1 (5th Supplement), as amended (referred to as "the Act").

[2] Unless otherwise stated, the *Excise Tax Act*, R.S.C. 1985, c. E-15, will be referred to as the "ETA".

¶1,000   HISTORICAL, LEGAL, AND THEORETICAL BACKGROUND

¶1,010   Brief History of the Income Tax Act

From Confederation in 1867 through to World War I, the major sources of federal government revenue were customs and excise taxes comprising about 80% of all revenue. Remaining requirements were met largely by the issue of debt. Income tax was first imposed federally in 1917 as a temporary measure to help finance World War I. The legislation was embodied in the *Income War Tax Act*, which was a relatively simple document of some 10 pages in length. In 1948, the *Income Tax Act* was passed. Although it involved a rewording and codification of the old law, there were few changes in policy.

A major reform of federal income tax legislation began in 1962 with the setting up of the Royal Commission on Taxation under the chairmanship of the late Kenneth Carter. The Carter Commission presented its seven-volume report in 1967 recommending fundamental changes in tax legislation which would use a comprehensive tax base including capital gains. Next, the government issued a White Paper on tax reform in 1969, drawing on the Carter recommendations, but modifying them. Public hearings were held by two parliamentary committees on the White Paper proposals. This process culminated in the budget address of June 18, 1971, which proposed Bill C-259 to amend the *Income Tax Act*. This bill was given Royal Assent on December 23, 1971, effective January 1, 1972. Since that date, every budget address has presented a considerable number of amendments to the tax legislation to both "fine-tune" the existing legislation and introduce new fiscal policy.

Sixteen years later, on June 18, 1987, the government released a White Paper on Tax Reform which was to be implemented in two phases. Phase One, implemented in 1988, included changes to the personal and corporate income tax systems and interim changes to the existing federal sales tax. After consultation and recommendations made by the House of Commons Committee on Finance and Economic Affairs and the Senate Committee on Banking, Trade and Commerce, the resultant legislation was introduced as Bill C-139, which was passed on September 13, 1988. Phase Two replaced the existing federal sales tax with a broad-based multi-stage sales tax referred to as the goods and services tax (GST), effective January 1, 1991.

Currently, income taxes comprise about 64% of total federal government revenues, with personal income taxes raising over three times the amount of revenue as corporate income taxes. Sales and excise taxes, including the GST, represent about 20% of total federal government revenues. Exhibit 1-1 gives some indication of the relative importance of various taxes.

EXHIBIT 1-1
Government of Canada Budgetary Revenues
(2007-2008 Forecast)

Revenue item	Billions of dollars*	Percentage
Personal income tax	115.2	48.7
Corporate income taxes......................	36.3	15.3
Employment insurance contributions	16.2	6.9
Goods and services tax	30.1	12.7
Customs import duties.......................	3.6	1.5
Other tax revenue	15.1	6.4
Non-tax revenue	20.2	8.5
Total budgetary revenues	236.7	100.0

* Source: Table 7.4, "Revenue Outlook" in Chapter 7 "Fiscal Outlook", *The Budget Plan 2007*, Department of Finance Canada, March 19, 2007.

¶1,020 Constitutional Basis for Income Taxation

The *British North America Act, 1867*, renamed the *Constitution Act, 1867* in the process of the repatriation of the Constitution, granted authority for all taxation in Canada, separating federal and provincial powers to impose income taxes. Subsection 91(3) of the *Constitution Act, 1867* provides the federal government with unlimited powers of taxation by permitting the "raising of money by any mode or system of taxation". On the other hand, subsection 92(2) limits provincial powers to direct taxation of income earned in the province and of income of persons resident in the province. Of course, income taxation falls within both sets of these government powers. Even with a fairly liberal interpretation of the provincial powers of direct taxation, in order to meet increasing provincial requirements over the years, there has been a constant trading of tax points through federal–provincial taxation agreements. Nevertheless, intergovernmental problems of raising revenues through taxation persist.

¶1,030 Some Theoretical Concepts of Taxation

¶1,035 Classification of taxes

¶1,035.10 *Basis of the tax*

Taxes can be classified in a number of different ways. One such method is the basis of the tax, with the name of the tax reflecting to some extent the tax base or what is to be taxed.

Head tax: A tax on the existence of a particular type of taxpayer such as a tax of $X paid by all individuals over the age of 18.

Income tax: A tax on the income of the taxpayer and is exemplified by a tax on the income of individuals or corporations.

Wealth tax: A tax on capital gains or succession duties, or a tax on the accumulated capital of a taxpayer.

Commodity tax: A tax on the consumption of the commodity subject to tax as is the case of a provincial sales tax.

User tax: A toll for a bridge or road; a tax on the use of a facility or service.

Tariff: A tax or duty usually imposed on imported goods to increase the price of such goods relative to domestic goods.

Transfer tax: A tax on the value of property transferred from one owner to another, as is the case on the transfer of land under certain conditions.

Business transfer tax: A value-added tax, or a multi-stage sales tax, such as the goods and services tax, is a tax on the increase in value of a commodity created by the taxpayer in moving it from one stage of production or distribution to another.

¶1,035.20   *Incidence of the tax*

Another method of classifying taxes is by the incidence of the tax, which determines the taxpayer who ultimately bears the tax.

The incidence of a direct tax is likely to be on the initial payer of the tax. For example, the burden of the individual income tax is generally considered to be on the individual who pays the tax. On the other hand, the incidence of an indirect tax is usually not on the initial payer of the tax, but is on someone else. A sales tax imposed at the manufacturer's level is an example of such an indirect tax. While an income tax may be paid by a corporation, the incidence of the tax may be on customers, suppliers, employees, or shareholders of the corporation, depending on its economic ability to pass the tax on to the others.

¶1,035.30   *Nature of the tax*

Finally, taxes can be classified by the nature of the tax levy. A proportional or flat tax is levied at a constant percentage of the income of the payer of the tax. Under certain conditions, the corporate income tax can be considered as such a tax. A progressive tax is levied at an increasing percentage of the income of the payer, as is the case of the personal income tax. Similarly, a regressive tax is levied at a decreasing percentage of the income of the payer. A sales tax is considered to be a regressive tax to the extent that those with higher income may spend a lower proportion of that income on the item subject to the sales tax.

¶1,040   Desirable characteristics of an income tax

¶1,040.10   *Horizontal equity*

An income tax should be equitable on two dimensions. It should be equitable horizontally so that persons at the same economic level are affected by the tax to the same degree in terms of the amount of tax irrespective of the form of income generated.

¶1,040.20   *Vertical equity*

An income tax should also be equitable vertically so that persons at a higher economic level pay a greater share of the tax based on their greater ability to pay than those at a lower economic level.

¶1,040.30   *Neutral*

An income tax should be neutral so that the tax does not affect economic decisions. Thus, for the tax system to be considered neutral, a decision based on the after-tax results of an economic opportunity should not be any different than it would have been in the absence of taxation.

¶1,040.40   *Flexible*

At the same time, the income tax system must be sufficiently flexible to permit its use as an instrument of economic policy to achieve specified economic objectives. Of course, what might be considered economically desirable may not be politically feasible. For example, the Carter Commission recommendation to achieve horizontal equity by taxing all sources of economic gain equally, because "a buck is a buck", was apparently rejected for political reasons.

¶1,040.50   *Certainty*

The position of the taxpayer with respect to a tax should be certain. The taxpayer must be in a position to understand and determine with some certainty the payer of the tax, the base of the tax, the amount of the tax, the deadline for payment of the tax, and the method of payment.

¶1,040.60   *Feasible and efficient*

Administration of the tax must be feasible and efficient. Thus, the total costs, including those to the taxpayer, of administering and collecting the tax should be as low as possible. The relative costs of administration and collection of the Canadian income tax are very low when compared with those of other countries.

¶1,040.70   *How does the Canadian income tax measure up?*

Familiarity with the specifics of the Canadian income tax legislation will facilitate an evaluation of its characteristics relative to these ideal characteristics.

At the outset of its report on tax simplification,[3] the House of Commons Standing Committee on Finance and Economic Affairs made the following general observations on the current Canadian tax system.

> In addition to raising revenue efficiently, the ideal tax system is equitable and simple, and it assists the promotion of economic growth. Unfortunately, the goals of the ideal tax system often conflict. Changes made to make the system more equitable or to increase economic growth may make the system less simple. In fact since the early 1970s the tradeoffs between equity and simplicity and between growth and simplicity have been quite one-sided: if one of the goals had to give, it was always simplicity. The result, of course, is a Tax Act that even experts find confusing and a tax form for the average taxpayer that is daunting in length and complexity.

> Any tax system is defined by six characteristics:

> 1. who pays the tax,

> 2. the base to be taxed,

> 3. the rates to be applied to the base,

> 4. general exemptions,

> 5. general deductions, and

> 6. other selective measures [including how and when the tax is to be paid].

> The nature of the six characteristics determines how much revenue is produced by the tax system, as well as the equity of the system and its ability to promote growth. It is the exemptions, deductions and other selective tax measures that make modern tax systems so complicated. There are in Canada, for example, over one hundred selective tax measures dealing with personal income tax. There are even more measures dealing with corporate tax.

> The *Income Tax Act* includes the tax measures, and the tax forms must allow for them. Too often the tax system is changed — the changes rationalized in terms of improved equity or economic growth — with no attention to the possible increased complexity of the Tax Act and tax forms. The Act and forms are treated as matters that can take care of themselves — an attitude that provides no check on the ever-increasing complexity of the Tax Act and tax forms. The Committee believes that the analysis of the tax system must be realigned with attention devoted to simplifying both the Act and the forms.

¶1,045   Tax reform guidelines

Guidelines for comprehensive tax reform announced by the Minister of Finance in 1986 in a speech to the House of Commons are summarized below. These guidelines can be used as a basis for evaluating the legislation as it exists at any time.

---

[3] This report was released on June 19, 1986.

¶1,040.50

Fairness: The tax system should ensure fair sharing of the tax burden among taxpayers. People in similar circumstances should receive the same tax treatment; all high-income individuals and corporations should pay their fair share of tax; and similar products should bear the same rate of sales tax.

Simplicity and Compliance: Tax compliance should be made easier by making the system simpler and more readily understood.

Balance: Tax reform would redress the too-heavy share of tax revenues raised through the personal income tax, by requiring more of profitable corporations and by broadening the sales tax base.

Stability: Stability and dependability of tax revenues are essential for government budgeting. Raising more total tax revenues is not an objective of tax reform, but it should increase the certainty of achieving the revenue goals that the government sets itself.

International Competitiveness: The tax system should reinforce the ability of Canadians to compete internationally.

Economic Growth: The tax system should encourage growth through lower tax rates on a broader tax base. Business opportunities, rather than tax planning, should be the driving force behind business decisions.

Canadian Priorities: The tax system should help meet national social and economic needs, including regional needs, in keeping with Canadian priorities and values.

Transitional Implementation: Changes should be implemented with appropriate transitional provisions, to avoid leaving Canadians in doubt about tax rules.

Consultation: The government will consult broadly before making its final legislative proposals for tax reform.

¶1,100   INTRODUCTION TO INCOME TAX LEGISLATION

¶1,110   Note on Organization of Legislation and Availability of Interpretive Sources

¶1,115   The Income Tax Act

It is very important to the study of income taxation that one becomes thoroughly familiar with the organization, structure, and coverage of the *Income Tax Act* (the "Act"). When a tax problem arises, knowing where to find the provisions in the Act which are most likely to deal with the problem will save a considerable amount of time in the resolution of the problem. An overview of the Act can best be obtained from an inspection of the Table of Contents to the Act. A detailed sectional list of the Act is provided at the beginning of the CCH edition of the Act. References to the Act in court cases, for example, may have been changed in the *Fifth Supplement to the Revised Statutes of Canada, 1985*. A Table of Concordance is provided in the current CCH edition of the Act to relate revised provisions in the current Act to the equivalent provisions in the former Act.

CCH editions of the Act also contain several other important pieces of Canadian tax legislation, such as the Income Tax Regulations which support the Act, and the U.K. and U.S. tax treaties with Canada. The Act is divided into over 30 Parts, most of which represent specific types of tax, other than income tax. Of course, the largest Part deals with income tax and, because of its size, requires further classification into Divisions and Subdivisions. Exhibit 1-2 illustrates this structure of the Act with selected categories of provisions.

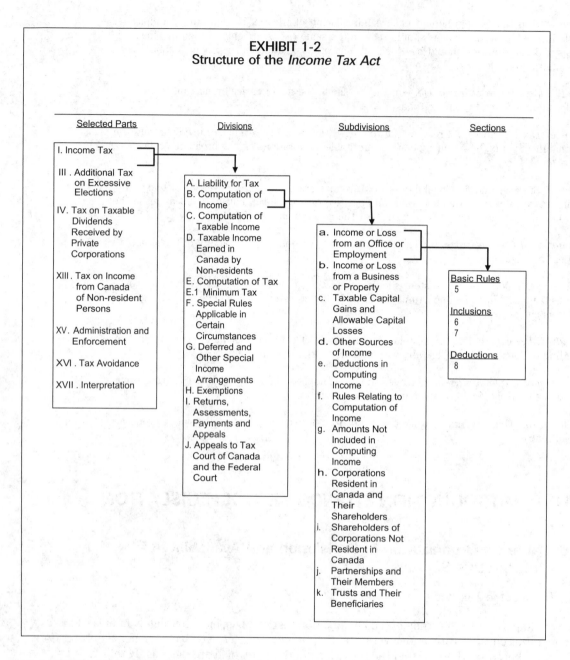

EXHIBIT 1-2
Structure of the *Income Tax Act*

¶1,115.10   *How do I reference the Act?*

For ease of reference, provisions are numbered, separating various elements of the provision. For example, consider the following reference:

$$6(1)(b)(\text{i})(A)$$

The first number refers to the section of the Act and the second number refers to the subsection. Notice that section 6 subsection (1) is a fairly lengthy sentence covering several pages of text. The letter (*b*) refers to what is called a paragraph, and the lower case Roman numeral (i) refers to a subparagraph. The upper case letter (A) refers to a clause. If necessary, a subclause would be referred to with an upper case Roman numeral, and a sub-subclause would be referred to with an Arabic numeral. The above reference would be called "clause 6(1)(*b*)(i)(A)", stating the numerals and letters in order, in normal speech. From time to time an amendment is made to the Act and it is necessary to insert it between existing provisions without renumbering the whole Act. In such a case a reference such as section 6 subsection (2.1) will be entered between subsections 6(2) and 6(3). Some sections, like section 3, have no subsections. Hence, references skip directly to paragraphs as is the case in paragraph 3(*a*). As a short-form reference in this book, the following abbreviations may be used with a provision:

Sec.   for section,

Ssec. for subsection,

Par.   for paragraph, and

Spar. for subparagraph.

¶1,115.20   *Historical footnotes*

The history footnotes to each provision of the Act are often critical to determine when the provision is applicable and what transitional rules, if any, apply in the implementation of new rules. The CCH edition provides, after each provision, a history of all changes subsequent to the enactment of the 5th Supplement in 1994. (A history of changes prior to 1994 can be found in a separate volume, "Former Income Tax Act, S.C. 1970-71-72, c. 63". In the electronic version, activate the "Former Act" link at the end of the provision and then activate the history link of that version of the ITA);

¶1,115.30   *Related matters*

After each provision there are often references to a wealth of information that may help you in your research.

- related sections;
- related regulations;
- related Interpretation Bulletins and Information Circulars divided into primary and secondary references;
- Advance Tax Rulings;
- authorized or "prescribed" forms;
- references to Income Tax Technical News issues;
- related Tax Window Files; and
- related landmark court decisions.

Some of the items listed are described below.

¶1,115.40   *Draft legislation: Pending amendments*

A federal budget may introduce draft legislation to implement new tax policy initiatives. Alternatively, technical amendments may be made to correct anomalies in the law to either close down abuses or to rectify inequalities in the law. These amendments are placed in boxes under the heading "Pending Amendment" following the specific provision of the Act which they amend. The source and application date of the amendment is also shown.

¶1,120   Income Tax Application Rules

The next major component of the CCH edition of the *Income Tax Act* is the provisions of the *Income Tax Application Rules, 1971* (ITAR). Technically, these rules appear in Part I of Chapter 2 of the *Fifth Supplement to the Revised Statutes of Canada, 1985*. These rules provide largely for the transition from the pre-1972 Act and its system of taxation to the current Act and its system of taxation including the introduction of the taxation of capital gains. These transitional rules are an important part of the law of income taxation and reference may be made to them in this book.

¶1,125   International tax conventions or treaties

The Act must be interpreted in light of International Tax Conventions which Canada has negotiated with many countries in order to reduce the impact of potential double taxation and tax avoidance. Both the Canada–United States Tax Convention (1980) and the Canada–U.K. Income Tax Convention (1978) are reproduced in the CCH edition of the Act. Over 80 others have been or are being negotiated. It is important to note that tax conventions override the provisions of the *Income Tax Act* and, hence, should be the first reference source when examining the tax implications of cross-border transactions.

¶1,130   Income Tax Regulations

The Income Tax Regulations ("Regulations") are set out to handle various specific situations and to carry on the general purposes and provisions of the Act. Unlike the Act itself, these regulations, which are part of the law, may be passed by Order-in-Council without ratification by Parliament. However, regulations must be written within the authority of a particular section of the Act and cannot be independent of the Act. Reference will also be made frequently in this book to the Regulations, which are part of the law and have assumed increasing importance in recent years.

¶1,135   Other interpretive sources

Although not part of the statute itself, a number of sources have importance in the interpretation of the Act over the years of income taxation in Canada.

¶1,135.10   *Judicial decisions (common law)*

One of these interpretive sources is case law.

- Judicial decisions, which form the common law, on income tax matters may be appealed up to the Supreme Court of Canada (S.C.C.).

- The middle-level court hearing tax cases is the Federal Court of Appeal. Prior to 1990, income tax cases went to the Federal Court, which was divided into two divisions: the Federal Court–Trial Division (F.C.T.D.) and the Federal Court of Appeal (F.C.A.); cases would first go to the F.C.T.D., and then to the F.C.A. After 1990, only the F.C.A. was used for income tax cases, with the exception of some administrative matters pertaining to income tax, which were heard by the F.C.T.D. In 2003, the *Federal Courts Act*[4] was amended, creating two separate courts: the Federal Court of Appeal and the Federal Court (F.C.). The F.C.A. continues to hear income tax cases, while the F.C. hears administrative matters pertaining to income tax. Prior to 1972, this middle level of court was called the Exchequer Court (Ex. Ct.).

- The lowest level of court hearing tax cases is now called the Tax Court of Canada (T.C.C.). Prior to 1984, the lowest level was the Tax Review Board (T.R.B.), which was called the Tax Appeal Board (T.A.B.) prior to 1972.

- Court decisions, which are almost always based on particular sets of facts, interpret the application of the law to these facts. Most tax cases heard in Canada are published by CCH in the DOMINION TAX CASES. These cases are referred to using the name of the taxpayer, a reference such as 83 DTC 5041, and the court level, as follows: *Nowegijick v. The Queen*, 83 DTC 5041 (S.C.C.). The numeral 83 refers to the 1983 volume and the letters DTC refer to the DOMINION TAX CASES set. The numeral 5041 refers to the first page of the 1983 volume on which the case report begins. The CCH electronic version of the court cases also refers to the hard copy pages — just click on the page icon in the electronic text and a pop-up box will indicate the hard copy page.

While the courts' decisions represent the law, as interpreted for a specific set of facts, and may be useful as a guide in interpreting the law more generally, it must be remembered that each set of facts differs from the previous cases in some degree and that a slight difference in the facts of a given case may materially affect the outcome.

---

[4] R.S., 1985, c. F-7.

Often a Canadian court will refer to a decision of a court outside Canada, such as a U.S. court or a court in a country with legislation and common law rooted in the British system. These decisions, at any level, made outside Canada are not binding on a Canadian court, but they may be referred to as persuasive, particularly, where principles of taxation or tax legislation are similar.

The part of a decided case that provides a binding precedent is referred to as the *ratio decidendi*, or reasons for judgment. Precedents established in previous cases create a foundation for applying principles of law (or for interpreting the law when a similar fact situation is presented to a court).

Often, a judicial decision will contain comments that are not necessary for the decision in the fact situation under consideration. These comments are known as *obiter dicta*, or comments made in passing. While these comments are not part of the precedent established by the case under consideration and, hence, not necessarily binding on other courts, they may provide insights to the interpretation of the law in different fact situations that might arise in subsequent cases.

¶1,135.20 *Forms*

Forms issued by the Canada Revenue Agency (CRA) and officially prescribed by the legislation may provide some insights to the interpretation of a provision in the legislation.

All of these forms can be obtained from the district taxation offices, the CRA's Web site (www.cra.gc.ca), or from commercial publishers either in print or electronic form.

¶1,135.30 *CRA publications*

The CRA releases some explanatory information on the official position in various taxation matters through a series of publications which are available on its Web site. The series of publications include:

Information Circulars (ICs): These deal mainly with administrative and procedural matters.

Interpretation Bulletins (ITs): These outline the CRA's interpretation of specific sections of the tax law.

Advance Tax Rulings (ATRs): These contain disguised summaries of certain advance income tax rulings given by the CRA and selected for publication. The last ruling published in the initial series was TR-101, dated December 9, 1980. Since many of the rulings in that initial series have become obsolete due to changes in the law, the CRA began with ATR-1, dated November 29, 1985, to reissue as part of a Second Series those former rulings that are still valid. The last published ATR was March 1996. The ATRs have been replaced by published technical interpretations discussed below.

Technical Interpretations: Through the *Access to Information Act* and advance income tax rulings, the CRA's responses to taxpayers' requests for technical interpretations on specific tax issues are published by commercial tax publishers. For example, CCH publishes in print form and electronically a summary, called WINDOW ON CANADIAN TAX, of the more significant interpretations. In addition, CCH publishes the full text of every one of these interpretations, referred to as TAX WINDOW FILES, but only in electronic form.

Information Booklets: In addition, the CRA publishes a number of non-technical information pamphlets for the general public and technical guides on specific topics, all of which are available at the district taxation offices, the CRA's Web site, or through the commercial tax services either in hard copy or electronic form.

Income Tax Technical News: The CRA issues this periodic newsletter, which provides timely commentary on recent tax issues and which can be found in the aforementioned sources, in particular, CCH's CANADIAN TAX REPORTER in print or electronic form.

The above publications, representing what is known as "departmental practice", or "administrative practice", are not the law, although in the case of *Nowegijick v. The Queen*, Mr. Justice Dickson of the Supreme Court of Canada stated that "administrative policy and interpretation are not determinative, but are entitled to weight and can be an 'important factor' in case of doubt about the meaning of legislation". In the case of *The Queen v. Royal Trust Corporation of Canada*, it was noted that an Interpretation Bulletin interpreted a provision in a manner which Mr. Justice Urie of the Federal Court of Appeal concluded was correct.

83 DTC 5041 (S.C.C.)

83 DTC 5172 (F.C.A.)

¶1,135.40 *Technical notes and explanations*

Technical notes are issued by the Department of Finance to explain new legislation when it is introduced. These notes are provided for an understanding of amendments and not as an official interpretation of the provisions they describe. Although the impact of the technical notes on judicial decisions is not always known, they should at least establish the general or broad intention of Parliament in respect of a particular issue.

In these Technical Notes, the Department of Finance generally indicates that:

¶1,135.50 *Generally accepted accounting principles*

Generally accepted accounting principles have been important guides in the interpretation of the Act where the statutory law was silent on a particular point. Also, an authoritative book, article, or tax service may provide a helpful source of interpretive material.

¶1,140 Structure of the Income Tax Act

Since the transitional rules, tax conventions, and regulations typically relate to specific provisions of the Act, this introduction will focus on the table of contents to the Act itself. The reader is advised to become familiar with the headings for specific sections of the Act, as listed in the table of contents mentioned previously. Refer to the table of contents for the following discussion.

¶1,145 Parts I and I.2 — Income Tax and Tax on OAS Benefits

Part I — Income Tax

ITA: 2–181.71

Part I, income tax, is the longest of the Parts of the *Income Tax Act*. This Part deals with income tax, as opposed to the variety of special transaction taxes handled in most of the other Parts. There are 11 divisions in Part I of the Act.

Part 1 - Income Tax [Sec 2 - 181.71]

Division	Subdivision	Section(s)	Comment
A - Liability for Tax		2	This short Division answers the question: Who is liable to pay tax? It is called the "charging" provision.
B - Computation of Income		3 - 108	Division B computes income for tax purposes, which is a major part of the base on which the tax is calculated.
	a - Employment	5 - 8	These subdivisions deal with the major sources of income and deductions in the calculation of Division B income for tax purposes.
	b - Business or Property	9 - 37	
	c - Capital gains and losses	38 - 55	
	d - Other sources of income	56 - 59.1	
	e - Other deductions	60 - 66.8	

f - Rules relating to the computation of income	67 - 80.5	
g - Amounts not included in income	81	
h - Canadian corporations and their shareholders	82 - 89	These subdivisions provide rules which expand the rules set out in Subdivisions a to e above. They do not provided for new sources of income or deductions.
i - Shareholders of corporations not resident in Canada	90 - 95	
j - Partnerships and their members	96 - 103	
k - Trusts and their beneficiaries	104 - 108	
C - Computation of Taxable Income	110 - 114.2	Division C contains deductions from Division B income (above) to arrive at taxable income which is the actual tax base.
D - Taxable Income Earned in Canada by Non-residents	115 - 116	Division D contains special rules for non-residents.
E - Compuation of Tax	117 - 127.41	
a - Rules applicable to individuals	117 - 122.51	Division E sets out the tax rates for individuals and corporations as well as a variety of tax credits.
a.1 - Child tax benefit	122.6 - 122.64	
b - Rules for corporations	123 - 125.5	
c - Rules for all taxpayers	126 - 127.41	
E.1 - Minimum Tax	127.5 - 127.55	
F - Special Rules	128 - 143.3	
G - Deferred and Special Income Arrangements	144 - 148.1	These Divisions deal with a variety of special situations and with procedural matters and appeals under the Act.
H - Exemptions	149 - 149.1	
I - Returns, Assessments, Payments and Appeals	150 - 168	
J - Appeals to the Courts	169 - 180	
Part I.2 - Tax on Old Age Security Benefits	180.2	

¶1,150 Special transaction taxes

The following special transaction taxes currently remain in effect. Each of these taxes is found in a separate part of the Act as follows: ITA: 182–211.91

Part II — Tobacco Manufacturers' Surtax   ITA: 182–183

Part II.1 — Tax on Corporate Distributions   ITA: 183.1–183.2

Part III — Additional Tax on Excessive Election   ITA: 184–185

Part III.1 — Additional Tax on Excessive Eligible Dividend Designations   ITA: 185.1-185.2

Part IV — Tax on Taxable Dividends Received by Private Corporations   ITA: 186–187

Part IV.1 — Taxes on Dividends on Certain Preferred Shares Received by Corporations   ITA: 187.1–187.61

Part V — Tax in Respect of Registered Charities   ITA: 187.7–189

Part VI — Tax on Capital of Financial Institutions   ITA: 190–190.211

Part VI.1 — Tax on Corporation Paying Dividends on Taxable Preferred Shares   ITA: 191–191.4

Part VII — Refundable Tax on Corporations Issuing Qualifying Shares   ITA: 192–193

Part VIII — Refundable Tax on Corporations in Respect of Scientific Research and Experimental Development Tax Credit   ITA: 194–195

Part IX — Tax on Deduction under Section 66.5   ITA: 196

Part X — Taxes on Deferred Profit Sharing Plans and Revoked Plans   ITA: 198–204

Part X.1 — Tax in Respect of Over-Contributions to Deferred Income Plans   ITA: 204.1–204.3

Part X.2 — Tax in Respect of Registered Investments   ITA: 204.4–204.7

Part X.3 — Registered Labour-Sponsored Venture Capital Corporations   ITA: 204.8–204.87

Part X.4 — Tax in Respect of Over-Payments to Registered Education Savings Plans   ITA: 204.9–204.93

Part X.5 — Payment Under a Registered Education Savings Plan   ITA: 204.94

Part XI — Tax in Respect of Certain Property Acquired by Trusts, etc. Governed by Deferred Income Plans   ITA: 205–207

Part XI.1 — Tax in Respect of Certain Property Held by Trusts Governed by Deferred Income Plans   ITA: 207.1–207.2

Part XI.2 — Tax in Respect of Certain Property Disposed of by Certain Public Authorities or Institutions   ITA: 207.3–207.4

Part XI.3 — Tax in Respect of Retirement Compensation Arrangements   ITA: 207.5–207.7

Part XII — Tax in Respect of Certain Royalties, Taxes, Lease Rentals, etc. Paid to a Government by a Tax Exempt Person   ITA: 208

Part XII.1 — Tax on Carved-out Income   ITA: 209

Part XII.2 — Tax on Designated Income of Certain Trusts   ITA: 210–210.3

Part XII.3 — Tax on Investment Income of Life Insurers   ITA: 211–211.5

Part XII.4 — Tax on Mining Reclamation Trusts   ITA: 211.6

Part XII.5 — Recovery of Labour-Sponsored Funds Tax Credit   ITA: 211.7–211.9

Part XII.6 — Tax on Flow-Through Shares   ITA: 211.91

This book will deal with several of these Parts as the need arises.

¶1,155 Non-residents

Two parts of the Act are devoted to the taxation of non-residents. These are: ITA: 212–219.3

Part XIII — Tax on Income from Canada of Non-Resident Persons   ITA: 212–218.1

Part XIII.1 — Additional Tax on Authorized Foreign Banks   ITA: 218.2

Part XIII.2 — Non-Resident investors in Canadian Mutual Funds   ITA: 218.3

Part XIV — Additional Tax on Non-Resident Corporations   ITA: 219–219.3

¶1,160 Administration and interpretation

The final three parts of the Act deal with matters of administering the Act, outlining tax evasion and interpreting the Act. These parts are: ITA: 220–260

Part XV — Administration and Enforcement   ITA: 220–244

Part XVI — Tax Avoidance   ITA: 245–246

Part XVI.I — Transfer Pricing   ITA: 247

Part XVII — Interpretation   ITA: 248–260

¶1,170 Approaches to Defining Income

There is no statutory definition of the word "income" in the Act. While section 3 might be considered as such a definition, it really provides a set of rules for aggregating a taxpayer's income from various sources once these amounts have been identified as income either by a statutory provision of the Act or by judicial decisions. In the absence of a statutory definition, it is customary to refer to prior judicial decisions which may define the term and which, in turn, may have referred to a standard dictionary to establish the ordinary meaning of the word. *The Concise Oxford Dictionary* defines "income" as "the money or other assets received, esp. periodically or in a year, from one's business, lands, work, investments, etc.".   ITA: 3

While income is usually thought of as a monetary receipt or currency, it may take the form of money's worth, that is, something of commercial value such as gold, shares, wheat, etc.

¶1,175   The economist's perspective

Adam Smith's concept of income was limited to the three sources of rent, profit and wages. Excluded from income would be capital gains, windfalls and gifts. Nevertheless, income was considered to be "net" income, that is, gross revenues less expenses incurred to produce revenues. This is a basic principle of the Canadian income tax system. In more recent years, the economist's concept of income has been broadened to include all net increases in economic power between two points in time. This would include gains of all kinds and imputed income such as the value of a tax professor's labour in preparing his or her own tax return. Obviously, there are considerable valuation and administrative problems in collecting taxes on such imputed income. However, the comprehensive tax base concept of the Carter Commission came close to this broader concept of income.

¶1,180   The role of generally accepted accounting principles

It will be seen in subsection 9(1) that income from a business is the "profit" therefrom and the computation of profit is not completely specified by provisions in the Act. Until the early 1990s, the courts have been inconsistent in their reference to generally accepted accounting principles (GAAP) as an authoritative source for interpretation of profit under the *Income Tax Act*. The Supreme Court decision in *Symes v. The Queen et al.* appears to have   94 DTC 6001 (S.C.C.)
cleared the air by the following statement:

> . . . Any reference to G.A.A.P. connotes a degree of control by professional accountants which is inconsistent with a legal test for "profit" under s. 9(1). Further, whereas an accountant questioning the propriety of a deduction may be motivated by a desire to present an appropriately conservative picture of current profitability, the *Income Tax Act* is motivated by a different purpose: the raising of public revenues. For these reasons, it is more appropriate in considering the s. 9(1) business test to speak of "well accepted principles of business (or accounting) practice" or "well accepted principles of commercial trading".

Therefore, GAAP is still to be considered but should be put into the context of overall business practices and should not stand alone. In the case of *Canderel Limited v. Her*   98 DTC 6100 (S.C.C.)
Majesty the Queen, the Supreme Court of Canada stated, as a principle, that

> well-accepted business principles, which include but are not limited to the formal codification found in G.A.A.P, are not rules of law but are interpretative aids. To the extent that they may influence the calculation of income, they will do so only in a case-by-case basis, depending on the facts of the taxpayer's financial situation.

It must be emphasized that the existence of specific statutory provisions, which are used in the computation of income for tax purposes, results in an income computation that will vary widely from income for financial accounting purposes. A major cause of this variance is the use of the capital cost allowance system for tax purposes based on a declining balance method of capital cost write-off in lieu of depreciation for financial accounting purposes often based on a straight-line method.

¶1,185   The doctrine of constructive receipt

The "constructive receipt" of income involves the inclusion of amounts which may not actually be received but are beneficially received or receivable. For example, there is a   ITA: 153(3)
provision that deems the taxpayer to have received amounts withheld as tax by his or her employer. Although the taxpayer does not receive these amounts, they are included in his or her income subject to tax. The use of the accrual system is another example of the use of the concept of constructive receipt. While amounts in accounts receivable have not actually been received they result in amounts being included in income.

In applying the doctrine of constructive receipt, one of the key determinants is that the amounts must be beneficially received or receivable by the taxpayer so that his or her use of the amounts is free and unrestricted. The test was set out in the early Canadian case of *Kenneth B.S. Robertson Ltd. v. M.N.R.* in the form of the following questions: 2 DTC 655 (Ex. Ct.)

> Is his right to it (the amount) absolute and under no restriction, contractual or otherwise, as to its disposition, use or enjoyment? To put it another way, can an amount in a taxpayer's hands be regarded as an item of profit or gain from his business as long as he holds it subject to specific and unfulfilled conditions and his right to retain it and apply it to his own use has not yet accrued and may never accrue?

As an example of an amount that is not constructively or beneficially received, consider retail sales taxes collected by retailers and passed on to the provincial government. In this case, the retailer simply acts as a conduit or transmitter of the amount and, therefore, is not taxed on it.[5]

¶1,190   Income Versus Capital

Receipts can be classified as either income or capital. As long as taxation has existed in Canada receipts of capital have received more favourable tax consequences than receipts of income. This situation continues to exist since only $\frac{1}{2}$ of capital gains is included in income.

The problem of determining whether a given receipt is one of capital or one of income has been the subject of countless court cases. In subsequent chapters, the major factors used by the courts in their determination will be examined and a number of cases will be used to illustrate these factors. One factor is the nature of the asset which is determined from its use or intended use. The classic capital asset is one which produces income from holding it or using it. A common analogy used by the courts likens a capital asset to a tree which produces income during the period of ownership in the form of fruit. Sale of the tree results in a receipt of capital and capital gains treatment whereas sale of the fruit results in a receipt of income.

¶1,200   Computation of Income

¶1,205   Aggregation formula

For Canadian taxpayers, both income and capital receipts, resulting in income subject to tax, are aggregated by the rules of section 3 irrespective of geographic source. The computation of income for tax purposes is illustrated by Exhibit 1-3. A subsequent chapter will return to these aggregation rules after all of the sources of income have been considered so that the terminology used in the section is more meaningful. Until then, a cursory examination of the section will provide an overview of the coverage of subsequent chapters.

---

[5] For two Canadian cases which illustrate situations in which constructive receipt was at issue, see *Cliffe v. M.N.R.*, 57 DTC 305 (T.A.B.), dealing with unpaid salaries left in a corporation and *Green v. M.N.R.*, 50 DTC 320 (T.A.B.), dealing with unpaid interest left in a corporation. For an application of the concept of constructive receipt to a third-party payment in a marital breakdown situation, see the case of *The Queen v. Arsenault*, 96 DTC 6131 (F.C.A.), in which the "free and unrestricted use" test was at issue. For an example of a fact situation in which it was concluded that the test that an amount must have been received by someone for the benefit of the payee was not met, see *Markman v. M.N.R.*, 89 DTC 253 (T.C.C.).

EXHIBIT 1-3
Simplified Computation of Income Under Section 3
Division B

ITA Par.	Type of income	ITA Subdivision	Chapter(s)
3(a)	Worldwide income (positive amounts only after subtracting deductible expenses) from non-capital sources including:		
	● Office or employment	a	3
	● Business	b	4 and 5
	● Property	b	5 and 6
	● Other non-capital sources	d	9
Plus			
3(b)	Net taxable capital gains (not negative)*	c	7 and 8
Less			
3(c)	General deductions not attributable to any specific source	e	9
Less			
3(d)	Negative amounts or losses from non-capital sources including:		
	● Office or employment**	a	3
	● Business**	b	4 and 5
	● Property**	b	5 and 6
Equals			
3(e), (f)	Division B income or "income for tax purposes"		

---

* If allowable capital losses exceed taxable capital gains then this net capital loss is deductible in a carryover year (i.e., the previous three years or any future year) under Division C (see Chapter 10 for individuals and Chapter 11 for corporations).

** If the losses from an office, employment, business, and property exceed the income from other sources, then it will be necessary to calculate the non-capital loss that can be carried back to previous years or forward to future years under Division C (see Chapter 10 for individuals and Chapter 11 for corporations).

Note how section 3 represents the expression of a complex formula in words contained in one very long sentence. For example, paragraph 3(a) requires the taxpayer to "determine the total of all amounts" of income from all of the non-capital sources, e.g., employment income, business income and sundry receipts. In fact, this aggregate includes only positive amounts, i.e., an excess of inclusions over deductions, from these sources. However, it is only evident that these amounts must be positive when paragraph 3(d), referring to losses from the same non-capital sources, is read.

Paragraph 3(b) requires the taxpayer to "determine the amount, if any, by which the total of" two amounts exceeds a third amount which, itself, requires a sub-calculation. In the language of the Act, the use of the words "if any", when referring to the calculation of an excess, means that if the calculated amount is negative, the amount is set at nil. That is, if the calculated amount is negative, there is no excess of the sum required in subparagraph 3(b)(i) over the amount calculated in subparagraph 3(b)(ii). In interpreting a provision of this nature, it is often helpful to determine the underlying computational formula and to substitute numbers from a particular fact situation into the formula. This procedure will be demonstrated subsequently in an example problem.

¶1,210   Sourcing or tracing of income

A taxpayer must compute his or her income or loss from each source independently by   ITA: 4
allocating deductions in amounts that can be applied reasonably to each revenue source. For
example, employment expenses cannot be deducted from business income. Similarly, in the
allocation of business income among various provinces only the deductions that can be traced
to or allowed by that particular jurisdiction can be deducted in arriving at income for tax
purposes.

Generally, no provision under the Act should be interpreted as to require an amount to   ITA: 248(28)
be included in or deducted from income more than once unless a provision is so worded to
give a contrary intention.[6]

Although income is not defined in the Act, once it has been determined that there is
income, then this income must be attached to a particular source. For example, income from
employment found in Subdivision a of Division B gathers together all of the employment
income inclusions as specifically determined in sections 5, 6 and 7 minus all of the permitted
deductions found in section 8. This sourcing of income and deductions would be continued
for:

Subdivision b — Business or Property Income

Subdivision c — Taxable Capital Gains and Allowable Capital Losses

Subdivision d — Other Income

Once the sourcing of income has been completed, then the ordering rules for Division B,
which are found in section 3 of the Act, can be applied.

¶1,220   Determination of Income and Taxable Income

The taxable income of a taxpayer is "income" for the year, plus or minus the additions   ITA: 2(2)
and deductions permitted under Division C. Hence, this provision sets out the first ordering
rule in the determination of taxable income.

This is illustrated as follows:

Division B income or "income for tax purposes"

Less:

Division C deductions

Equals:

Taxable income

Once income for tax purposes (Division B income) has been determined, adjustments are
made to this amount by the Division C additions and deductions according to the ordering   ITA: 111.1
rules (applicable to individuals) for this division (see Exhibit 1-4, which highlights some of
these deductions).

Tax credits reduce the tax computed in Division E. An ordering rule for these tax credits   ITA: 118.92
is provided (see Exhibit 1-5). All of these tax credits are often referred to as non-refundable
tax credits, because any excess of these credits over tax payable is not available for refund.

---

[6] For example, see *Joel Attis v. M.N.R.*, 92 DTC 1128 (T.C.C.), involving the repayment of shareholder loans.

EXHIBIT 1-4

Ordering Rules Applicable to Individuals for Division C
Section 111.1

Sec. 110	—Sundry deductions such as employee stock options and home relocation loan deductions
Sec. 110.2	—Lump-sum payments
Sec. 111	—Various loss carryovers arising from Division B calculations for another year such as non-capital losses and net capital losses
Sec. 110.6	—Capital gains deduction
Sec. 110.7	—Residing in prescribed zone

EXHIBIT 1-5

Ordering Rules Applicable to Individuals for Non-Refundable
Tax Credits in Division E
Section 118.92

Ssec. 118(1)	—Personal credits
Ssec. 118(2)	—Age credit
Sec. 118.7	—Employment Insurance premium and Canada Pension Plan contribution credits
Ssec. 118(3)	—Pension credit
Ssec. 118(10)	—Canada employment credit
Sec. 118.01	—Adoption expense tax credit
Sec. 118.02	—Transit pass tax credit
Sec. 118.03	—Child fitness tax credit
Sec. 118.3	—Mental or physical impairment credit
Sec. 118.61	—Unused tuition, textbook, and education credits
Sec. 118.5	—Tuition credit
Sec. 118.6	—Education and post-secondary textbook credits
Sec. 118.9	—Transfers to parent or grandparent
Sec. 118.8	—Transfer of unused credits to spouse
Sec. 118.2	—Medical expenses credit
Sec. 118.1	—Charitable gifts of individuals
Sec. 118.62	—Credit for interest on student loan
Sec. 121	—Dividend tax credit

Example Problem

The following list of income inclusions and deductions or tax credits has been determined correctly by a junior staff accountant prior to the preparation of the tax return for Ms. Beth Kelly.

Inclusions

Salary	$50,000
Canadian bank interest	1,200
Standby charge for company car	745
Taxable capital gains	7,500
Taxable benefits from employment	1,035
Pension income	5,000
Taxable amount of dividends from taxable Canadian corporations	750

Deductions, Losses, or Tax Credits:

Non-capital losses claimed	$2,000
Net capital losses carried forward	6,000
Basic personal and spousal tax credits	2,559
Registered pension plan contributions	1,000
Medical expenses tax credit	68
Interest expense to acquire Canadian shares	300
Moving expenses	600
Charitable donations tax credit	202
Pension tax credit	310
Canada Pension Plan contributions tax credit	308
Employment Insurance premiums tax credit	112
Dividend tax credit	100
Allowable capital losses	650
Business loss	3,080
Canada employment credit	155

— REQUIRED

(A) From the structural outlines and exhibits on the preceding pages, determine the income, taxable income and basic federal tax net of non-refundable tax credits based upon the above correct information using the ordering rules in sections 3, 111.1, and 118.92 for 2007. Assume federal tax before credits is $9,156 in 2007. Try to determine with logic where an item might be found.

(B) Cross-reference each amount to the appropriate section of the Act. (Refer to Sectional List of the Act.)

— SOLUTION

Division B — Section 3

Par. 3(a)	*Subdivision a*			
	Sec. 5	Salary	$ 50,000	
	Par. 6(1)(a)	Fringe benefits	1,035	
	Par. 6(1)(e), ssec. 6(2)	Standby charge	745	$ 51,780
	Less			
	Par. 8(1)(m)	Registered pension plan contributions		(1,000)
				$ 50,780

	Subdivision b			
	Business	. . . .	Nil	
	Property			
	Par. 12(1)(*c*)	Canadian bank interest	$ 1,200	
	Par. 12(1)(*j*)	Dividends (taxable amount)	750	
			$ 1,950	
	Par. 20(1)(*c*)	Interest expense	(300)	$ 1,650
	Subdivision d			
	Ssec. 56(1)	Pension income		5,000
				$ 57,430
Par. 3(*b*)	*Subdivision c*			
	Sec. 38	Taxable capital gains	$ 7,500	
	Sec. 38	Allowable capital losses	(650)	6,850
				$ 64,280
Par. 3(*c*)	*Subdivision e*			
	Sec. 62	Moving expenses		(600)
				$ 63,680
Par. 3(*d*)	Sec. 9	Business loss		(3,080)
		Division B income		$ 60,600
Division C — Section 111.1				
	Par. 111(1)(*a*)	Non-capital losses	$ (2,000)	
	Par. 111(1)(*b*)	Net capital losses	(6,000)	(8,000)
Taxable income				$ 52,600
Division E — Section 118.92				
Federal tax before credits				$ 9,156
Less tax credits:				
Sec. 118	Personal tax credits		$ 2,559	
Sec. 118.7	CPP tax credit		308	
Sec. 118.7	EI premium tax credit		112	
Ssec. 118(3)	Pension tax credit		310	
Ssec. 118(10)	Canada employment credit		155	
Sec. 118.2	Medical expense credit		68	
Sec. 118.1	Donation tax credit		202	
Sec. 121	Dividend tax credit		100	(3,814)
Basic federal tax				$ 5,342

Several other non-refundable tax credits are available in Subdivision c of Division E, but these are deductible from basic federal tax as computed in the above example. These additional non-refundable tax credits include: foreign tax credits, political contribution tax credits and investment tax credits.

ITA: 126, 127(3), 127(5)

The goods and services tax (GST) credit is a type of refundable tax credit available to individuals. This credit is actually paid separately in instalments to qualifying taxpayers.

ITA: 122.5

¶1,230   Interpretation of Tax Legislation

¶1,235   Precision

The development of tax legislation over the years has included the acceptance of rules of interpretation or construction of the income tax law. First, every attempt is made to achieve precision in the language of tax legislation so that it is clearly understood, thereby providing the taxpayer with some degree of certainty about his or her tax liability. (To see how the drafters of the Act have succeeded in this respect, try to read subsection 256(3) as an example of such language!) To quote a famous British decision heard in 1891 on the question of the drafting of legislation:

> it is not enough to attain a degree of precision which a person reading in good faith can understand, but it is necessary to attain if possible to a degree of precision which a person reading in bad faith cannot misunderstand (and) it is all the better if he cannot pretend to misunderstand it. . . .

¶1,240   Plain and obvious meaning

It has long been held that the words used in a taxing statute must be given their plain and obvious meaning, unless there is a specific definition contained in the statute or unless another meaning is required in the context of the remainder of the Act. This has become known as the "Golden Rule" of interpretation or construction (from the verb "to construe"), and it was expressed by a member of the British House of Lords as follows:

> In the construction of statutes their words must be interpreted in their ordinary grammatical sense, unless there be something in the context, or in the object of the statute in which they occur, or in the circumstances with reference to which they are used, to show that they were used in a special sense different from their ordinary grammatical sense. . . .

In an elaboration of this principle, another Lord stated:

> . . . the grammatical and ordinary sense of the word is to be adhered to, unless that would lead to some absurdity or some repugnance or inconsistency with the rest of the [statute], in which case the grammatical and ordinary sense of the words may be modified so as to avoid that absurdity and inconsistency but no farther.

Again, this principle is intended to help increase the taxpayer's certainty of his or her position.

The meaning of a provision cannot be extended by an interpretation which is not clear from the words used. A British judge expanded on this point in an 1869 case by stating:

> . . . if the person sought to be taxed comes within the letter of the law he must be taxed, however great the hardship may appear to the judicial mind to be. On the other hand, if the Crown, seeking to recover the tax, cannot bring the subject within the letter of the law, the subject is free, however apparently within the spirit of the law the case might otherwise appear to be. In other words, if there be admissible in statute, what is called an equitable construction, certainly such a construction is not admissible in a taxing statute, where you can simply adhere to the words of the statute.

To illustrate this point, the reader should refer to the case of *Witthuhn v. M.N.R.*, in which a taxpayer was denied a deduction for certain medical expenses because the patient was confined to bed or a special type of rocking chair rather than "to a bed or wheelchair" as required at the time of the facts in the case and, in fact, until the provision was amended in 1986.

57 DTC 174 (T.A.B.)

In more recent years, however, this approach appears to have been softened to some extent. For example, in the case of *Overdyck v. M.N.R.*, where the taxpayer used a leg brace to go to work and a chair with castor-like wheels while at work, the same wording was given a much more liberal interpretation on the basis that if the taxpayer had been left completely alone without external aid or assistance, he would have been in bed at all times as a result of paralysis in one leg. In fact, it has been stated in another British case that:

83 DTC 307 (T.R.B.)

... the Court's task is merely one of construction of the words used, although, in the case of ambiguity, that construction will be favoured, which seems to the Court more consonant with fairness in the circumstances. ...

¶1,245   Intention of Parliament

In interpreting or construing a taxing statute, inferences about the intention of Parliament are often made. As indicated previously, the Department of Finance now often publishes detailed explanatory notes to accompany draft legislation. These notes may be helpful in determining intention but are not binding on a court. No interpretation is allowed to defeat the plain intention of the legislation. The courts assume that what is stated in the Act is what was meant by Parliament.[7] Thus, a meaning that is consistent with the intention of Parliament is allowed to prevail.

¶1,250   Remission orders

Thus, while taxing statutes were to be interpreted strictly, according to early rules of interpretation, in the case of doubt the construction of the statute was to be resolved in favour of the taxpayer in the case of a charging provision and in favour of the Crown in the case of an exemption provision. Furthermore, while it was not possible for the Courts to render what they would consider to be an equitable decision in a particular case, relief for the taxpayer could be found under the *Financial Administration Act*. Subsection 17(1) of that Act provides for the remission of taxes and penalties when it is considered in the public interest.[8]

¶1,255   Recent developments

More recently, the Supreme Court of Canada has suggested that the strict interpretation rule is still applicable where the plain meaning of the words is straightforward. Where the provision is vague and/or confusing, it is to be interpreted within its context in the Act on a basis consistent with the object of the Act and the intention of Parliament, which may reflect political, economic, social or technological objectives. This "object and spirit" test of interpretation was used in the case of *Stubart Investments Ltd. v. The Queen* by the Supreme Court of Canada and, at least to some extent, has been codified in the general anti-avoidance rule (GAAR) of the Act.[9] The Supreme Court has often quoted the authority on the interpretation of statutes, E.E. Driedger in *Construction of Statutes* as follows:

84 DTC 6305 (S.C.C.)
ITA: 245(4)

> Today, there is only one principle or approach, namely, the words of an Act are to be read in their entire context and in their grammatical and ordinary sense harmoniously with the scheme of the Act, the object of the Act, and the intention of Parliament.

In the case of *Corporation Notre-Dame de Bon-Secours v. Communauté Urbaine de Québec*, the Supreme Court of Canada again rejected the strict rule of interpretation in cases of doubt, as outlined above, and established the following rules of interpretation:

95 DTC 5017 (S.C.C.)

(a) tax legislation should be interpreted according to ordinary rules of statutory interpretation;

(b) a legislative provision should be given a strict or liberal interpretation depending on the purpose underlying it and that purpose must be identified in the light of the context of the statute, its objective and the legislative intent (i.e., the "teleological" approach);[10]

(c) the teleological approach will favour the taxpayer or the tax department depending solely on the legislative provision in question and not on predetermined presumptions;

---

[7] This is illustrated by the case of *M.N.R. v. MacInnes*, 54 DTC 1031 (Ex. Ct.), on the meaning of "property substituted". The intention of Parliament as a means of interpretation was also raised in the case of *Duha Printers (Western) Ltd. v. The Queen*, 98 DTC 6334 (S.C.C.).

[8] For a case which refers a taxpayer to the *Financial Administration Act*, see *Bayraktaroglu v. M.N.R.*, 73 DTC 27 (T.R.B.).

[9] See *Antosko et al. v. The Queen*, 94 DTC 6314 (S.C.C.), and *Friesen v. The Queen*, 95 DTC 5551 (S.C.C.).

[10] This approach was applied in the case of *Harvey C. Smith Drugs Limited v. The Queen*, 95 DTC 5026 (F.C.A.).

(d) substance will prevail over form (see discussion below) where this is consistent with the wording and objective of the statute; and

(e) only a reasonable doubt, not resolved by ordinary rules of interpretation, will be settled by recourse to the residual presumption in favour of the taxpayer.

¶1,260 Form versus substance

The issue of form versus substance has long posed a problem in the application of the tax legislation to a taxpayer's situation. It was addressed in the often cited 1935 British case of the *Duke of Westminster* in which a member of the House of Lords stated that:

> Every man is entitled if he can to order his affairs so that the tax attaching under the appropriate Acts is less than it would otherwise be. If he succeeds in ordering them so as to secure this result, then, however unappreciative the Commissioners of Inland Revenue or his fellow taxpayers may be of his ingenuity, he cannot be compelled to pay an increased tax. This so-called doctrine of "the substance" seems to me to be nothing more than an attempt to make a man pay notwithstanding that he has so ordered his affairs that the amount of tax sought from him is not legally claimable. . . .
>
> . . . There may be, of course, cases where documents are not *bona fide* nor intended to be acted upon but are only used as a cloak to conceal a different transaction. . . .

Thus, the form or legal effect of a transaction must prevail in attempting to determine the tax effects, unless the taxing statute requires that such form be disregarded in cases where form is inconsistent with the wording and objective of the Act, or unless the form is considered to be a "sham" which misrepresents the true form, based on the facts of the case.[11] Another British case has described a "sham" as:

> . . . acts done or documents executed by the parties to the sham which were intended by them to give to third parties and to the Courts the appearance of creating between the parties legal rights and obligations different from the actual legal rights and obligations (if any) which the parties intended to create.
>
> . . . For acts and documents to be a sham, with whatever legal consequence falls from this, all the parties thereto must have a common intention that the acts or documents are not to create the legal rights and obligations which they give the appearance of creating. . . .

Furthermore, the Courts have even applied what has come to be known as a "repugnancy" or "smell" test in certain situations where substance was at considerable variance with the form of a transaction.

¶1,265 Exceptions override general

The Act contains a number of statements of general principle followed by an exception or series of exceptions to that rule. An exception or other specific provision of the legislation will override the general provision, but the former must be given a strict interpretation. This rule was followed in a Canadian case, which will be discussed in a subsequent chapter, when the judge stated that:

> . . . the subsection must in my opinion be regarded as an exception to the general rule, and while it must be given its full effect so far as it goes, it is to be strictly construed and not extended to anything beyond the scope of the natural meaning of the language used, regardless again of how much a particular case may seem to fall within its supposed spirit of intendment. . . .

Thus, a taxpayer cannot obtain an exemption from tax unless the circumstances fall squarely within the wording of the provision.

¶1,270 Specific words followed by general

A principle that has been important in the interpretation of the Act over the years is the *ejusdem generis* rule for enumerations of similar items. According to this rule, when a series of specific words in a statute is followed by general words, the general words are confined to

---

[11] This was confirmed by the Supreme Court of Canada in the case of *Stubart Investments Ltd. v. The Queen*, 84 DTC 6305.

the same scope as the specific words. This rule could be involved in the interpretation of the words "other remuneration" as used in subsection 5(1) which states that ". . . a taxpayer's income for a taxation year from an office or employment is the salary, wages and other remuneration, including gratuities, received by him in the year". The scope of the meaning of the specific words "salary", "wages" and "gratuities" might be used to constrain the meaning of the words "other remuneration".

¶1,275   Precedents

Another principle deals with the role of court decisions as precedents often referred to as the concept of *stare decisis*. This principle establishes that decisions on similar facts are to be similar. The precedent value of a case is determined by the seniority of the court. A decision of a higher Canadian court is binding on a lower Canadian court in a subsequent decision. At a given level of court, consistency in decisions on similar facts is usually attempted. If a decided case is not to apply to a given situation, the facts of the decided case must be distinguished or differentiated sufficiently from the case under consideration to justify a different decision. In the case of *B.B. Fast & Sons Distributors Ltd. v. M.N.R.*, a 82 DTC 1017 (T.R.B.) member of the Tax Review Board, as it was then, invoked the "judicial comity rule" indicating that judgments of courts of equal or co-ordinate jurisdiction should be followed in the absence of strong reasons to the contrary. However, it has been recognized that too rigid adherence to precedent might lead to injustice in a particular case and also unduly restrict the proper development of the law.

¶1,280   Interpretation Act

Finally, the effects of the *Interpretation Act*, which deals with the interpretation of Canadian statutes, should be considered. In subsection 3(3), the *Interpretation Act* recognizes rules of construction such as those discussed to the extent that they are not inconsistent with a provision of this Act. In section 14, the *Interpretation Act* sets out some rules of construction of its own regarding the use of definitions and the interpretation of exceptions to rules. Section 27 deals with the interpretation of time limits specified in a statute. For example, if such a deadline falls on a holiday, the deadline is extended to the following day that is not a holiday. Section 32 provides that deviations from a prescribed form which do not affect the substance do not invalidate a form used. Gender is dealt with in subsection 33(1) which states that "words importing female persons include male persons and corporations and words importing male persons include female persons and corporations".

¶1,290   The Role of the Professional Accountant in Tax Matters[12]

Professional accountants and others who are not qualified as lawyers very frequently play a major role in providing tax-related services to taxpayers. The basis of these services is, of course, tax law embodied in the legislation and jurisprudence discussed previously. It must be recognized that the practice of law by non-lawyers is an offence under certain provincial legislation which regulates that practice by lawyers. Often, there is a very fine and ill-defined line between an activity that constitutes the practice of law and services provided to clients by non-lawyers in the tax area. In addition to committing the foregoing offence, an adviser may be liable for the civil consequences of negligence in providing services for which the adviser is not qualified, such as drafting a will, incorporating a company, etc.

Often, the complementary nature of financial services and tax law makes the combination of the two by a single adviser most practical in providing service to clients. In these situations, the role of non-lawyers is generally recognized in most provinces and conflicts can be avoided if the non-lawyer is careful not to provide advice that can be construed as a legal opinion and not to prepare documents of a purely legal, non-tax nature arising from more general laws such as contract law and corporate law.

---

[12] For a more detailed examination of this area, see James Rossiter, "Surviving in the twilight zone", *CA Magazine*, vol. 126, no. 2, February 1993, pp. 37–41.

¶1,300   GENERAL BACKGROUND ON ADMINISTRATION AND ENFORCEMENT OF THE ACT

The purpose of this section of the chapter is to provide a broad overview of how the tax legislation is administered and enforced. A discussion of the specific details of provisions dealing with these aspects of the law is deferred until Chapter 14 where it can be related more meaningfully to material covered in the intervening chapters.

¶1,310   Onus of Proof

In tax matters, it has been established by the Supreme Court of Canada in the case of *Johnston v. M.N.R.* that the taxpayer always has the burden of proving that an assessment is incorrect. Placing the burden of proof on the taxpayer is often referred to as a "reverse onus", because the usual burden of proof is on the Crown. In tax matters, the reverse onus is justified, since it is assumed that under our self-assessment system the taxpayer has all of the basic data under his or her own control.[13] This reverse onus may be challenged someday with a Supreme Court of Canada interpretation of the Charter of Rights and Freedoms.

ITA: 163(3)
[1948] 3 DTC 1182
(S.C.C.)

In the case of *M.N.R. v. Taylor*, it was established that the standard of proof in cases dealing with the Act need only be that of the "balance of probabilities" used in civil cases rather than the more rigorous standard of "beyond reasonable doubt" used in criminal proceedings. Where penalties are assessed, the burden of proof of the facts justifying the assessment of the penalties is transferred to the Minister. The standard of proof that the Minister must demonstrate is that of the "balance of probabilities".

61 DTC 1139 (Ex. Ct.)

¶1,320   Appeals

¶1,325   Initial steps

Prior to taking any formal steps in the appeal procedure, the taxpayer may consult with officials responsible for his or her file in the appropriate Tax Services Office. Many differences can be resolved in this less formal manner. If, however, they cannot be resolved in this manner to the taxpayer's satisfaction, a notice of objection may be filed as the first formal step. There is no prescribed form at the present time. The notice of objection simply contains a statement of the facts and the reasons for objection. In the case of corporations or certain trusts, the notice of objection must be received by the CRA on or before the 90th day subsequent to the date of mailing of the notice of assessment. In the case of individuals or testamentary trusts, the deadline is the later of one year after the day the taxpayer is required to pay the balance of tax due for a year (i.e., April 30) and 90 days after the mailing of the notice of assessment for the year.

¶1,330   Tax Court of Canada

Next, the taxpayer can appeal to the Tax Court of Canada (T.C.C.) (formerly the Tax Appeal Board (T.A.B.) or the Tax Review Board (T.R.B.)). It is highly accessible, meeting in 20 cities across Canada.

The Tax Court of Canada now has exclusive jurisdiction to hear appeals under the Act and certain other federal statutes. On appeal to the Tax Court, the taxpayer is given the option of an "informal procedure" or a "general procedure".

¶1,330.10   *Informal procedure*

The informal procedure may be elected when the amount of federal tax and penalties in issue for one taxation year is $12,000 or less or when the amount of the losses is $24,000 or less. The only requirement of the informal procedure is that the appeal is submitted in writing. Court rules of evidence are flexible and hence, the taxpayer can represent himself or herself or be represented by an agent (i.e., any individual) who may be a lawyer. However, the

---

[13] This onus of proof was applied in the case of *Violi v. M.N.R.*, 80 DTC 1191 (T.R.B.).

taxpayer cannot appeal on questions of fact from a Tax Court decision reached through the informal procedure and the decision cannot be used as a precedent in subsequent cases. Judicial review of a judgment under the informal procedure lies with the Federal Court of Appeal (F.C.A.) on errors of law or erroneous findings of fact made in a perverse or capricious manner.

¶1,330.20 *General procedure*

Where the general procedure is chosen in the Tax Court of Canada, the Court will be bound by strict rules of evidence. The taxpayer can only represent himself or herself or be represented by legal counsel.

¶1,335 Federal Court of Appeal

From the general procedure, the taxpayer can appeal the decision of the Tax Court to the Federal Court of Appeal and the Tax Court decision can be used as a precedent in other cases.

¶1,340 Supreme Court of Canada

The ultimate court of appeal for tax cases in Canada is the Supreme Court of Canada (S.C.C.). According to subsections 31(2) and (3) of the *Federal Court Act*, an appeal can be made to the Supreme Court only if the Federal Court decides that the issue should be referred to the Supreme Court, or if the Supreme Court authorizes the appeal. At this level, questions of legal interpretation are raised rather than questions of fact alone. Not many cases on tax matters are given leave to appeal to the Supreme Court of Canada.

¶1,350 Administration and Enforcement

While the Department of Finance formulates tax policy, the CRA controls, regulates, manages and supervises the income tax system. Direct contact between the taxpayer and the CRA is generally made through one of the almost 30 Tax Services Offices. Trained assessors and special investigators who conduct desk audits of an individual's return or field audits of business returns are located in these offices.

The Head Office in Ottawa serves to maintain efficiency and uniformity of treatment across Canada, by supervising and directing the activities of the Tax Services Offices. In addition, a number of regional Taxation Centres are maintained to do routine operations and the initial processing of all individual income tax returns among other things.

¶1,360 Tax Evasion, Avoidance, and Planning

It is important to distinguish the terms "tax evasion", "tax avoidance" and "tax planning". Generally, tax evasion involves knowingly reporting tax that is less than the tax payable under the law with an attempt to deceive by omitting revenue, fraudulently claiming deductions or failing to use all of the true facts of a situation. This is clearly illegal and can be prosecuted as such. An Information Circular provides a description of the consequences of tax evasion.   IC 73-10R3

Tax avoidance is generally considered to arise in cases in which the taxpayer has legally circumvented the law resulting in the reduction or elimination of tax through a scheme or series of transactions which do not truly reflect the real facts. While not illegal, the CRA will challenge such tax avoidance by various means available to it.

Finally, the CRA suggests that tax planning involves cases of tax reduction or elimination that are clearly provided for or not specifically prohibited in the law in a manner that is genuine and open within the framework of the law.

Despite these statements which attempt to distinguish the terms, there are undoubtedly judgments that must be made in distinguishing between cases of tax evasion and tax avoidance and between cases of tax avoidance and tax planning.

The Act contains a general anti-avoidance rule (GAAR). In the words of the explanatory ITA: 245 notes accompanying Bill C-139 which introduced the GAAR, issued on June 30, 1988, the rule is:

> intended to prevent abusive tax avoidance transactions or arrangements, but at the same time is not intended to interfere with legitimate commercial and family transactions. Consequently, the new rule seeks to distinguish between legitimate tax planning and abusive tax avoidance and to establish a reasonable balance between the protection of the tax base and the need for certainty for taxpayers in planning their affairs.[14]

¶1,400 INTRODUCTION TO THE GOODS AND SERVICES TAX

¶1,410 Note on Organization of Legislation and Availability of Interpretive Sources

It is important in the study of the goods and services tax (GST) to become familiar with the organization, structure and coverage of the *Excise Tax Act* (ETA). This knowledge is vital to the resolution of GST problems.

The ETA is divided into 12 Parts, most of which represent specific types of tax, including the GST, and 12 Schedules.[15] As in the *Income Tax Act*, for ease of reference, provisions are numbered, separating various elements of the provision. The history footnotes to each provision of the ETA are important to determine when the provision is applicable and what transitional rules, if any, apply.

As noted above, the ETA also contains 12 Schedules, which must be read in conjunction with the other provisions of the ETA. References to the provisions of the Schedules are read somewhat differently than references to the other provisions of the ETA. For example, consider the following reference:

V, VI, 20(e)(ii)

The first upper case Roman numeral refers to a Schedule and the second upper case Roman numeral refers to a Part. The number 20 refers to a section and the letter (*e*) refers to a paragraph. The lower case Roman numeral (ii) refers to a subparagraph. The above reference would be called Schedule V, Part VI, subparagraph 20(*e*)(ii).

In addition to the ETA, the GST/HST Regulations form part of the law and are set out to handle various specific situations and to carry on the general purposes and provisions of the ETA. Unlike the ETA, though, these regulations may be passed by Order-in-Council without ratification by Parliament. Forms issued by the CRA and officially prescribed by legislation may provide some insights to the interpretation of a provision in the legislation.

Additional sources also exist to provide assistance in interpreting the legislation. First, the CRA provides some explanatory information through a series of publications. These publications include GST/HST Memoranda, which are grouped under various topic headings and contain the CRA's interpretations of specific provisions of the ETA and outline its administrative practices. In addition, the CRA issues Technical Information Bulletins (TIBs) and Policy Statements, which are intended to provide current information on new policy or policy changes on a timely basis. Draft Policy Statements are also issued by the CRA, although these statements are subject to further review before being adopted as the CRA's policy. As well, various pamphlets, booklets and guides which provide general information, often targeted for specific groups of taxpayers, are issued from time to time. Based on the income tax jurisprudence referred to earlier in this chapter, publications of this nature, although not

---

[14] Reproduced in *Technical Notes to Bill C-139*, Special Report No. 851, Extra Edition, CCH Canadian Limited, June 30, 1988, p. 313.

[15] The ETA also contains the legislation for the harmonized sales tax (HST) which was implemented by the provinces of Nova Scotia, New Brunswick and Newfoundland and Labrador on April 1, 1997. Under the HST, those provinces that are referred to as the "participating provinces" have harmonized their provincial sales tax systems with the federal GST. The HST applies at a current combined rate of 14% and includes a federal component (the 6% GST) and a provincial component (8%).

legally binding, may be considered by the courts. As taxpayers have begun to appeal decisions of the CRA through the court system, case law which provides an additional important source of interpretation for the GST is developing.

The Department of Finance issued explanatory notes to explain the new GST provisions when the legislation was first introduced as well as when amendments to the legislation have been introduced in the House of Commons. Finally, an authoritative book, article or tax service may also provide interpretive assistance.

The following discussion will focus on the structure of the ETA itself.

¶1,415   Excise Tax Act structure — Parts

Part I — Insurance Premiums Other Than Marine   ETA: 3–7

Part II — Air Transportation Tax   ETA: 8–21

Part II.1 — Telecommunication Programming Services Tax   ETA: 21.1–21.21

Part II.2 — Telecommunication Services Tax   ETA: 21.22–21.34

Part III — Excise Taxes on Cosmetics, Jewellery, Radios, etc.   ETA: 22–24

Part IV — Repealed

Part V — Repealed

Part V.1 — Repealed

Part VI — Consumption or Sales Tax   ETA: 42–58

Part VII — General   ETA: 58.1–116

Part VIII — Transitional   ETA: 117–121.1

Part IX — Goods and Services Tax   ETA: 122–368

As can be seen from the titles of the various Parts set out above, the ETA imposes a number of taxes other than GST. This text will concentrate on the GST rules which are set out in Part IX of the ETA and will not examine the other taxes imposed under the ETA. The structure of Part IX of the ETA is set out below.

¶1,420   Structure of Part IX of the Excise Tax Act — GST legislation

Division I — Interpretation   ETA: 123–164.2

This Division contains a number of definitions and basic interpretive rules that are important to an overall understanding of the GST.

Division II — Goods and Services Tax   ETA: 165–211

Division II is the longest of the Divisions in Part IX. It contains rules which set out the rate of tax, the liability for tax, and the circumstances in which tax paid on inputs used in the supply of goods and services may be recovered. This Division contains the following four subdivisions:

Subdivision a — Imposition of Tax   ETA: 165–168

Subdivision b — Input Tax Credits   ETA: 169–170

Subdivision c — Special Cases   ETA: 171–194

Subdivision d — Capital Property   ETA: 195–211

Division III — Tax on Importation of Goods   ETA: 212–216

As the title suggests, Division III sets out the rules relating to the liability for GST on the importation of goods.

Division IV — Tax on Imported Taxable Supplies Other Than Goods ETA: 217–220

This Division sets out rules for determining when GST is payable in respect of imported services and intellectual property.

Division IV.1 — Tax on Property and Services Brought into a Participating Province ETA: 220.01–220.09

This Division sets out rules for the self-assessment of the provincial component of the harmonized sales tax (HST) in certain circumstances, where property or services are brought into a participating HST province.

Division V — Collection and Remittance of Division II Tax ETA: 221–251

Division V sets out the various requirements in respect of the collection and remittance of tax. The rules relating to the requirement to register are also contained in this Division. Division V contains the following five subdivisions:

Subdivision a — Collection ETA: 221–224

Subdivision b — Remittance of Tax ETA: 225–237

Subdivision c — Returns ETA: 238–239

Subdivision d — Registration ETA: 240–242

Subdivision e — Fiscal Periods and Reporting Periods ETA: 243–251

Division VI — Rebates ETA: 252–264

Division VI sets out the rules for claiming rebates of GST paid on purchases in a variety of circumstances.

Division VII — Miscellaneous ETA: 265–274.2

Division VII sets out a number of miscellaneous provisions, including a general anti-avoidance provision. The three subdivisions in Division VII are as follows:

Subdivision a — Trustees, Receivers and Personal Representatives ETA: 265–270

Subdivision b — Amalgamations and Windings-up ETA: 271–272

Subdivision b.1 — Partnerships and Joint Ventures ETA: 272.1–273

Subdivision b.2 — Export Distribution Centres ETA: 273.1

Subdivision c — Anti-Avoidance ETA: 274–274.2

Division VIII — Administration and Enforcement ETA: 275–335

Division VIII sets out various rules for administering the Act and enforcing its provisions. The seven subdivisions in Division VIII are as follows:

Subdivision a — Administration ETA: 275–277.1

Subdivision b — Returns, Penalties and Interest ETA: 278–285.1

Subdivision c — General ETA: 286–295

Subdivision d — Assessments, Objections and Appeals ETA: 296–312

Subdivision e — Collection ETA: 313–325

Subdivision f — Offences ETA: 326–332

Subdivision g — Evidence and Procedure ETA: 333–335

Division IX — Transition ETA: 336–347

The GST came into effect on January 1, 1991. This Division contains a number of transitional rules intended to ensure an orderly transition from the federal sales tax system to the GST.

Division X — Transitional Provisions for Participating Provinces ETA: 348–363.2

The harmonized sales tax (HST) came into effect on April 1, 1997. This Division contains transitional rules to deal with the implementation of the HST. The four subdivisions of Division X are as follows:

Subdivision a — Interpretation ETA: 348

Subdivision b — Application ETA: 349

Subdivision c — Transition ETA: 350–361

Subdivision d — Special Case ETA: 362–363.2

Division XI — Tax Inclusive Pricing ETA: 364–368

This Division provides authority for the use of the tax-inclusive pricing which was required under the original HST proposals. However, the rules under tax-inclusive pricing under this Division will not come into effect until the participating provinces that represent at least 51% of Canada's total population have enacted legislation to implement HST.

¶1,425   Schedules to the Excise Tax Act

Schedule I   —[Rates of Excise Tax]

Schedule II   —Repealed

Schedule II.1   —Specific Tax Rates on Petroleum Products

Schedule III   —[Sales Tax Exemptions]

Schedule III.1   —Goods Sold by Deemed Manufacturers or Producers

Schedule IV   —[Construction Materials and Equipment for Buildings]

Schedule V   —Exempt Supplies

Schedule VI   —Zero-Rated Supplies

Schedule VII   —Non-Taxable Importations

Schedule VIII   —Participating Provinces and Applicable Tax Rates

Schedule IX   —Supply in a Province

Schedule X   —Non-Taxable Property and Services for Purposes of Division IV.I of Part IX

Schedules V through VII relate to the GST. Schedule V sets out those supplies that are exempt from GST. Schedule VI sets out those supplies that are zero-rated, i.e., subject to tax at the rate of zero per cent. Schedule VII sets out a list of imported goods that are not subject to GST.

¶1,430   Overview and Basic Concepts

The GST was implemented on January 1, 1991. The introduction of the GST at the rate of 7% culminated numerous attempts to reform the sales tax regime in Canada. The GST replaced the federal sales tax, which was riddled with inequities and inconsistent administrative practice and often led to distortions in business practices in the Canadian economy. The GST was intended to correct many of these deficiencies and to fulfill certain revenue objectives of the federal government.

Pursuant to an election promise made by the now governing Conservative Party, the federal budget of May 2, 2006 proposed to reduce the GST rate to 6%, effective July 1, 2006. The rate reduction was implemented. In the March 19, 2007 federal budget, the government confirmed that it was committed to reducing the GST to 5% no later than 2011. However, no timetable has been announced.

The discussion of GST in this book does not attempt to cover all the technical areas that are associated with the GST. The intent, rather, is to give the reader a basic working knowledge of the rules. With this grounding, readers are encouraged to do further research in this important area of taxation that affects virtually every business organization in Canada. Unlike the former federal sales tax system, in which there were few accounting professionals who became actively involved in dealing with sales tax problems, the implementation of GST has resulted in substantial work for tax and other accounting professionals.

The GST is a tax on the consumption of goods and services in Canada. The tax is collected by businesses (referred to as "registrants") who sell goods and provide services (collectively referred to as "supplies") in Canada. GST is collected by registrants throughout the production and distribution chain. Any person who is engaged in a "commercial activity" is required to register and collect GST. This includes persons who carry on business in Canada. "Business" is defined quite broadly in the legislation and does not require a profit motive. For example, charities and non-profit organizations are required to register if they engage in commercial activities, even if these entities are not subject to income tax.

The GST is intended to be a tax on final consumption. Thus, while businesses are charged GST on their purchases, they are entitled to a credit for this tax (referred to as an "input tax credit"). Input tax credits are available to the extent purchases are used in commercial activities. Businesses are required to remit to the government the difference between the amount of GST collected or collectible and the amount of any input tax credit entitlement.

Supplies of goods and services are divided into three categories. "Taxable supplies" are subject to GST at the rate of 6%, and the supplier is entitled to a full input tax credit. "Zero-rated supplies" are subject to tax at the rate of zero per cent, and the supplier may claim a full input tax credit on purchases used to provide these supplies. "Exempt supplies" do not attract GST, and the supplier is not entitled to an input tax credit in respect of purchases used to provide these supplies.

The next two sections will expand on the concepts of "supply" and "input tax credits".

¶1,440 Supplies

The concept of "supply" is essential to an understanding of GST. While in many cases the term will be synonymous with sale, it has a much broader scope for GST purposes.

The provision of a supply includes, among other things:

- sales or rentals of goods;
- rendering of services;
- leases, sales or other transfers of real property;
- licensing of copyrights or patents; and
- barter and exchange transactions and gifts.

Once it is determined that there is a supply, a further determination must be made as to the type of supply. As discussed above, there are three types of supplies under the GST: taxable, zero-rated and exempt. A taxable supply is defined as a supply made in the course of a commercial activity, but does not include an exempt supply. Taxable supplies are subject to tax each time they are sold, with no exceptions. Most goods and services are taxable. However, zero-rated and exempt status is extended to a short list of goods and services for which the government has determined that GST should not apply. Only limited relief from the tax is provided in the case of exempt supplies. Goods and services which are zero-rated are completely free of tax.

¶1,445 Zero-rated supplies

A short list of goods and services are subject to tax at the rate of 0%. These zero-rated supplies are still considered to be taxable supplies. Although this appears paradoxical, the distinction between taxable and exempt supplies is important. On taxable supplies, including zero-rated ones, the supplier is entitled to recoup the GST paid on its inputs in the form of input tax credits, since input tax credits may be claimed on inputs used in commercial activities. Thus, even though GST is not charged on the supply of zero-rated goods and services, the entitlement to input tax credits ensures that these supplies are effectively tax-free. The following are some examples of goods and services that are zero-rated:

- prescription drugs;
- medical devices;
- basic groceries; and
- exported goods and services.

¶1,450 Exempt supplies

Like suppliers of zero-rated supplies, suppliers of exempt goods and services are not required to collect GST on these supplies. However, unlike zero-rated supplies, relief from GST is not available on inputs used in the supply of exempt goods and services. The GST paid by the supplier on purchases attributable to those exempt supplies is buried in the cost of the goods or services. For income tax purposes, however, the GST paid on such inputs represents part of the cost of the inputs, and hence, is deductible.[16]

For example, when a bank purchases inputs to be used in the supply of financial services (which are exempt supplies), the bank is not entitled to recover the GST incurred in respect of those inputs. Consequently, even though the bank does not charge GST on the supply of those exempt financial services, the GST incurred on the bank's purchases is buried in the cost of those financial services. The bank will be able to deduct the GST paid on these purchases for income tax purposes as part of the cost of the purchases.

The following are some examples of exempt goods and services:

- health care and child care services;
- educational services;
- most financial services; and
- sales of used residential housing and rentals of residential premises.

¶1,460 Input Tax Credits

An integral part of the GST system is the entitlement to claim refundable input tax credits on business purchases. This relieves business inputs of GST and thus avoids the pyramiding of tax. In order to qualify for an input tax credit (ITC), the goods and services must have been purchased for use in a commercial activity. As the GST is designed to be a tax on consumption to be borne by the end user, there are certain restrictions on the claiming of ITCs. These restrictions generally mirror the restrictions on claiming expenses under the *Income Tax Act.*

Input tax credits claimed by a registrant during a reporting period are subtracted from the tax collected on goods and services during the period to arrive at the net tax payable. Where input tax credits exceed tax payable, the registrant is entitled to a refund. An important concept related to ITCs is that purchases and sales need not be matched in order to claim an ITC. The credit can be claimed when the purchase is paid for or becomes due. Similarly, GST paid on purchases of capital property need not be amortized over the life of the property (see Chapter 5).

Input tax credits are available where goods and services are purchased for use in a commercial activity. Conversely, if an input is not used at all in a commercial activity, no credit is allowed. A full credit is available where an input is used "exclusively" in a commercial activity. "Exclusively" is defined as "all or substantially all" and is interpreted by the CRA to mean 90% or more.

There will be circumstances where a purchase is used in respect of a combination of taxable and exempt activities. In these cases, except for certain capital property, registrants will be required to apportion the ITC between the taxable (including zero-rated) and exempt

---

[16] However, the May 2, 2006 federal budget announced that interest and penalties incurred in respect of GST would no longer be deductible. These measures were implemented as of April 1, 2007.

activities. For example, consider the case of a hospital that purchases an industrial dish-washer for use in its kitchen. The dishwasher will be used to clean dishes from both patients and cafeteria patrons. Because meals provided to patients are exempt and cafeteria sales are taxable, the hospital will be required to apportion the ITC between the taxable and exempt activities.

The legislation does not prescribe allocation methods for use in apportioning ITCs. As long as the allocation is reasonable and is used consistently throughout the year, it will likely not be challenged.

Registrants will be required to maintain certain documentation to support ITCs. These requirements are discussed in Chapter 14.

¶1,470   Reform of the GST and Provincial Harmonization

Pursuant to an election promise made in 1993 to replace the GST, the federal govern-ment has reviewed a number of alternatives and has had ongoing discussions with the provinces. On April 23, 1996, the federal government announced it had signed Memoranda of Understanding with the governments of Nova Scotia, New Brunswick, and Newfoundland and Labrador (referred to as the "participating provinces") to harmonize the federal goods and services tax (GST) with their respective provincial sales tax systems. Legislation to imple-ment the new harmonized sales tax (HST) received Royal Assent on March 20, 1997. The HST became effective April 1, 1997 and has an impact on businesses resident in these three Atlantic provinces, as well as businesses that make supplies to recipients in those provinces or that acquire goods and services from vendors in those provinces. It is the place where goods and services are supplied or deemed to be supplied that dictates whether GST applies at the rate of 6% or the HST at the rate of 14%. Supplies made or deemed to be made in the HST participating provinces are subject to the 14% rate. The HST applies to the same base of goods and services as the GST. The province of Quebec has already substantially harmonized its provincial sales tax with the GST through the harmonized provincial sales tax (Quebec sales tax or QST).

With the implementation of the HST by the three Atlantic provinces, the GST appears here to stay, although with additional technical amendments. Various other provinces, how-ever, have indicated that they are not interested in harmonization. The Ontario government, for example, has repeatedly stated that it is not prepared to harmonize, citing a shift in the tax burden from businesses to consumers of $2 billion to $3 billion a year as the main reason against harmonization. Under a harmonized GST–PST system, businesses would be entitled to input tax credits on purchases used in commercial activities; currently, businesses pay pro-vincial sales tax on many business inputs. Although a number of provinces appear to be opposed to harmonization, the federal government is continuing its efforts to attempt to convince the remaining provinces to harmonize.

¶1,850 EXERCISES

Exercise 1

For each of the following items, identify the appropriate provision of the Act which deals with the item listed. Be as specific as possible in citing the reference to the Act, i.e., Part, Division, Subdivision, Section, Subsection, etc. Use of the Sectional List at the beginning of CCH edition of CANADIAN INCOME TAX ACT and/or the Topical Index at the end of the book may be helpful. However, using the CD included with this text may provide faster search results.

(A) Definition of "taxable capital gain".

(B) Deduction for certain annual professional membership dues paid by an employee.

(C) Taxability of payments received as income from property acquired as personal injury award.

(D) Deductibility of an expense based on its magnitude.

(E) Definition of a "parent" under the Act.

(F) Definition of an *"inter vivos"* trust.

(G) Deadline for filing of a tax return for a deceased person.

(H) Taxability of a benefit received from a corporation by a shareholder.

(I) Transaction price in a non-arm's length disposition of property.

(J) Deductibility of fees for investment advice.

Exercise 2

ITA: Divisions B and C

Mr. Malcolm Multisource has provided you with a list of various sources of income, deductions and credits for the purpose of determining his basic federal tax.

Inclusions:

His share of tax profit from a partnership business	$10,000
Canadian bank interest	3,000
Retiring allowance from a former employer	20,000
Gross salary from new employer	60,000
Director's fee	5,000
Taxable capital gains	20,000
Imputed interest on a home relocation loan provided by employer	3,000
Rental income from a triplex	25,000

Deductions, Losses, or Tax Credits:

Mortgage interest on triplex	23,000
Canada Pension Plan contributions tax credit	308
Property taxes and insurance on triplex	4,500
Non-capital losses from a previous year	3,000
Allowable capital loss for this year	2,000
Education and textbook tax credits transfer from son	80
Net capital losses from a previous year	5,000
Home relocation interest deduction	1,000
Maintenance costs for triplex	1,500
Contribution to employer's registered pension plan	4,000
Basic personal and spousal tax credits	2,559
Fees to a professional engineering society	300
Employment Insurance premiums tax credit	112
Tuition tax credit for night course on computer applications	68
Charitable gifts tax credit	550

— REQUIRED

(A) Determine the income, taxable income and basic federal tax based on the above correct information using the ordering rules in sections 3, 111.1, and 118.92 for 2007. Assume that federal tax before credits is $21,051 in 2007.

(B) Cross-reference each amount to the appropriate section of the Act.

¶1,875 ASSIGNMENT PROBLEMS

Problem 1

Identify the provision of the Act which deals with each of the following items. Be as specific as possible in citing the reference to the Act (Part, Division, Subdivision, Section, Subsection, etc.). Use of the sectional list at the beginning of the CCH edition of the Act and/or the topical index at the end of the book may be helpful. However, using the CD included with this text may provide faster search results.

(A) Definition of a "person".

(B) Tax credit for donation made by a Canadian resident individual to a Canadian university.

(C) Definition of "balance-due day".

(D) Taxability of group term life insurance premiums paid by an employer on behalf of an employee.

(E) Definition of "capital dividend".

(F) Computation of income tax instalments for individuals.

(G) Definition of a "qualified small business corporation share".

(H) Prescribed requirement to file an information return for a corporation paying a dividend.

(I) Definition of a "testamentary trust".

(J) The calculation of a benefit associated with an interest-free loan from an employer to an employee.

(K) Definition of a "disposition" of non-depreciable capital property.

(L) Limitation on deduction of RRSP administration fees.

(M) General limitation on the amount of deductible expenses.

(N) Deduction from taxable income for taxable dividends that were received by a Canadian corporation.

(O) Tax payable on excess contributions to an RRSP.

Problem 2

ITA: Division B, C

Ms. Ichbin Verblonget had a tumultuous year in 2006. She broke her engagement early in the year and quit her job. She moved to a resort area to take a waitress job and to start up a fitness instruction business. She has had the following items correctly calculated and classified as either inclusions, deductions or tax credits for the purposes of determining her taxable income and federal tax.

Inclusions:

Benefit received from Employment Insurance program	$ 600
Board and lodging provided by employer during busy season of resort	8,000
Bonus from resort employer	500
Business revenue from fitness instruction fees	2,000
Gratuities as a waitress	12,100
Interest on Canada Savings Bonds	775
Rental revenue	6,000
Salary received as a waitress	12,000
Taxable capital gain	3,750
Retiring allowance from previous employer	800

Deductions, Losses, or Tax Credits:

Allowable capital loss	4,500
Capital cost allowance on fitness business equipment	1,300
Capital cost allowance on rental building	1,200
Charitable gifts tax credit	26
Child care expenses	1,800

Canada Pension Plan contributions tax credits on employment earnings   162

Medical expenses tax credit   9

Business expenses of earning fitness instruction fees   900

Expenses of objection to a tax assessment   65

Interest on funds borrowed to pay expenses of earning fitness instruction fees   75

Maintenance on rental property   1,100

Mortgage interest on rental property   2,500

Moving expenses   1,700

Non-capital losses from previous year   600

Personal tax credit   1,384

Property tax on rental property   1,000

Employment Insurance premiums tax credit   69

Union dues   100

Canada employment credit   155

— REQUIRED

(A) Determine the income, taxable income and basic federal tax based on the above correct information using the ordering rules in sections 3, 111.1, and 118.92 for 2007. Assume federal tax before credits is $4,717 in 2007.

(B) Cross-reference each amount to the appropriate section of the Act.

Problem 3   ITA: 2

Many words and terms used in the Act have very specific interpretations. Awareness of these interpretations is fundamental to understanding the scheme and application of the Act. These interpretations come from various sources. The primary source is statutory definition; that is, the term is explicitly defined in the Act. Common law principles also determine interpretations for terms. Many court cases have centred on the interpretation of specific words or phrases which were not explicitly defined in the statute. Once such terms are interpreted by the Courts, that interpretation becomes standard for that term. If a term is neither defined in the statute, nor the subject of a common law definition, the word or term must be assigned the meaning provided by everyday language. The definition is often that which can be found in a common dictionary.

Division A of Part I of the Act outlines who is liable for tax. This Division is a fundamental building block for the Act as it defines to whom the Act will apply. Therefore, it is essential that the terms used in this Division are clearly understood.

— REQUIRED

Identify and define those words and terms found in section 2 of the Act, in the order of their use, which you believe require definition. Indicate the references in the Act to the source of the definition for those words or terms which you have so identified. If you use the CD included with this text the words that are defined elsewhere in the Act are highlighted in red.

[For more problems and solutions thereto, see the CD accompanying this book.]

Chapter 2

Liability for Tax

LEARNING GOALS

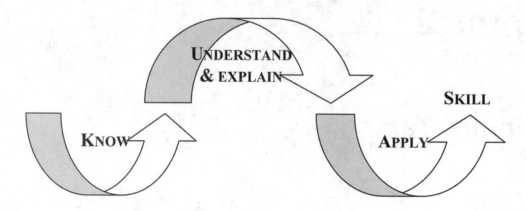

Know

By the end of this chapter you should know the basic provisions of the *Income Tax Act*, *Excise Tax Act*, and case law that relate to liability for tax and residency. Completing the Review Questions (¶2,800) and Multiple Choice Questions (¶2,825) is a good way to learn the technical provisions.

Understand and Explain

You should understand and be able to explain when an individual or a corporation is resident in Canada and whether they are liable for income tax or GST. Completing the Exercises (¶2,850) is a good way to deepen your understanding of the material.

Apply

You should be able to use your knowledge and understanding of residency and liability for income tax in a practical fact situation to determine whether a person is or is not liable for income tax. Completing the Assignment Problems (¶2,875) and the Advisory Case (¶2,880) is an excellent way to develop your ability to apply the material in increasingly complex situations.

OVERVIEW

This chapter deals with liability for Canadian income tax and the goods and services tax (GST). The chapter addresses the question of who is liable to pay the tax. Whether it is to the taxpayer's advantage or disadvantage to be a resident/non-resident will depend upon the tax laws of each jurisdiction in which the taxpayer's income is earned, the interaction of these laws and any relevant tax treaty. Many non-tax factors may also impact the choice.

The following chart provides an overview of the provisions of the *Income Tax Act* covered by this chapter.

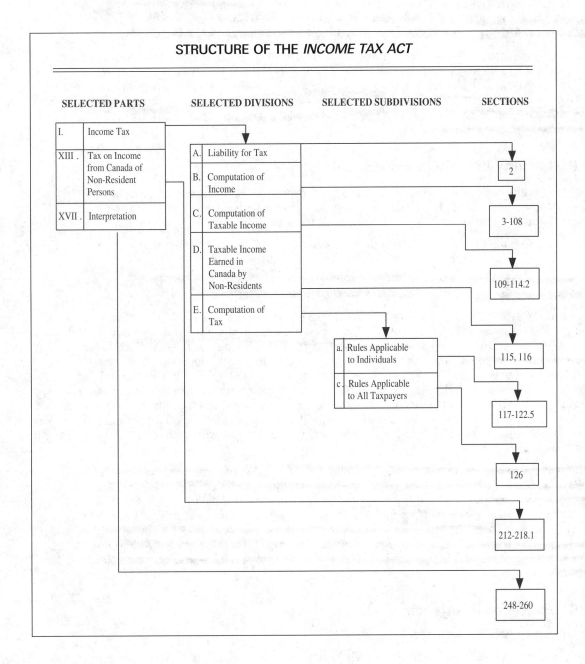

STRUCTURE OF THE *INCOME TAX ACT*

SELECTED PARTS	SELECTED DIVISIONS	SELECTED SUBDIVISIONS	SECTIONS
I. Income Tax	A. Liability for Tax		2
XIII. Tax on Income from Canada of Non-Resident Persons	B. Computation of Income		3-108
XVII. Interpretation	C. Computation of Taxable Income		109-114.2
	D. Taxable Income Earned in Canada by Non-Residents		115, 116
	E. Computation of Tax	a. Rules Applicable to Individuals	117-122.5
		c. Rules Applicable to All Taxpayers	126
			212-218.1
			248-260

¶2,000   LIABILITY OF INDIVIDUALS FOR INCOME TAX

The major issue in this area is the residence of an individual. Residency has become more and more important in recent years as taxpayers with increased mobility attempt to establish residence or non-residence to reduce their income tax liability in a variety of situations.

There are several criteria that can be used to establish income tax liability in a country including citizenship, domicile and residence. In Canada, the major criterion used is residence. Part I, Division A of the Act imposes an income tax on the income of individuals who are resident in Canada. The Act also imposes an income tax on individuals who are not resident in Canada, but only if they are employed in Canada, carry on business in Canada, or dispose of taxable Canadian property.

ITA: 2(1)
ITA: 2(3)

¶2,010   Liability of Individual Residents

The Act contains what is known as the charging provision for residents of Canada in respect of income under Part I. The provision charges taxpayers with responsibility for paying the tax by the use of the words "an income tax shall be paid".

ITA: 2(1)

Read the following provision carefully and consider some of the key terms used in that subsection:

> An income tax shall be paid as required by this Act on the *taxable income* for each *taxation year* of every *person resident* in *Canada* at any time in the year.

As indicated in Chapter 1, the word "income" is not defined in the Act. The phrase "taxable income" is a technical phrase with a limited and special meaning and the phrase "taxation year" is defined. Note that the word "person" is defined to include both an individual and a corporation. Also considered to be a person under the definition is a trust which will be discussed in Chapter 18. The word "resident" is not fully defined in the Act and, as a result, is the subject of discussion in much of this chapter. However, a definition of "Canada" is provided for the purposes of the Act. The existence of a definition for a term or phrase used in a provision like section 2 can be found by checking the "Related Sections" footnotes to the section in the CCH edition of the Act, where defined words or phrases are listed in quotation marks.

ITA: 2(2), 249(1)
ITA: 248(1)

ITA: 255

Canadian residents are taxed on their worldwide income. Thus, taxable income of a resident of Canada is subject to Canadian income tax regardless of the country in which the income is earned or generated. To avoid potential double taxation, Canada has negotiated a number of international reciprocal tax agreements which will be discussed in more detail later in this chapter. A key principle followed by these agreements is that the country in which the income is earned has priority in taxing that income and the country of which the taxpayer is a resident allows all or some part of the foreign tax paid as a credit against the domestic tax.

¶2,020   Full-Time Residence

¶2,025   Deemed full-time residence

A full-time resident is taxed on his or her worldwide income for a full year. While the Act does not define resident or residence, it does deem an individual to be a full-time resident if one of the conditions of a deeming rule is met. It is important to note the use of the word "deemed" in provisions of the Act. The effect is to establish a set of conditions and treat a taxpayer or an action in a manner desired by the legislation. In this case, a deemed resident will be treated like a full-time resident and taxed on worldwide income. Were it not for this deeming provision, the individual may not be considered to be a resident and, in fact, might be a non-resident. This provision states, among other conditions, that a person is deemed to be resident in Canada throughout the taxation year if he or she "sojourned" in Canada in the year for an aggregate of 183 days or more. The Canada Revenue Agency's (CRA's) practice is to count any part of a day as a "day" for this purpose. The word "sojourn" has the connotation of a temporary visit rather than a permanent stay. It should be noted, however, that spending

ITA: 250(1)

less than 183 days in Canada does not necessarily make an individual non-resident, if he or she is not merely visiting, but has more substantial residential ties, as discussed below.

¶2,030   Common law concept of full-time residence

It is possible for a person to be considered a full-time resident by virtue of principles of the common law or case law which have evolved over the years. Residence is determined by the application of these general principles to the facts of each case.

Consider the following fact situation presented to a British court.[1] The taxpayer had lived in England throughout her lifetime. For the year in question she stored her furniture, travelled on the Continent with no permanent abode in any one place, stayed in England only a short time, maintained a bank account in England and held no salaried position anywhere. The court held that she was resident in England. The court considered the relationship between a person's life and the place in which the taxpayer spent, at least, part of his or her time. A person's ties to a country need not be manifested in a permanent home.

In another British case,[2] the following facts were presented. A British subject gave up a leased house in England. He lived on the Continent in an apartment. He made visits of four or five months to London to obtain medical advice, to visit relatives or the graves of his parents, and to take part in certain religious observances. Again, the court held that he was resident in England. An important fact in this case was that he returned to the proximity of relatives and friends. It should be noted that the courts have determined that an individual can be resident in more than one country and that an individual must be resident in at least one country at any moment in time.

A key statement describing the residence of an individual under common law principles was made in a 1921 British decision[3] which described residence as "a continuing state of relationship between a person and a place which arises from the durable concurrence of a number of circumstances". Thus, facts must be found to establish the continuing state of relationship, that is, ties to the country. The landmark Canadian case in this area is *Thomson v. M.N.R.*, and another often cited case is that of *Meldrum v. M.N.R.* Both cases involved individuals who stayed in Canada for short periods of time on a regular basis. The courts considered facts relevant to establishing the "continuing state of relationship". 2 DTC 812 (S.C.C.)
50 DTC 232 (T.A.B.)

¶2,035   Administrative practice

An Interpretation Bulletin, "Determination of an Individual's Residence Status (Consolidated)", categorizes the type of facts that can be used for an individual to establish residential ties for a "continuing state of relationship". Many of these facts would appear to have held some importance in previous court decisions. However, it must be remembered that statements on administrative practice in an Interpretation Bulletin represent the opinion of the CRA and not the law. IT-221R3

- Maintaining a dwelling, whether owned or leased, suitable for year-round occupancy and available for occupation, would establish an important residential tie. However, the dwelling need not be vacant at all times. If it is rented to a non-arm's length person or to an arm's length person on terms and conditions that are not arm's length, then it may be considered to be available for the taxpayer's use.

- A spouse or common-law partner and other members of the immediate family remaining in Canada when an individual leaves would be regarded by the CRA as an important residential tie. A separation due to the breakdown of a relationship would, of

[1] *Reid v. C.I.R.*, [1926] 10 T.C. 673.
[2] *Levene v. C.I.R.*, [1928] A.C. 217.
[3] *Weymys v. Weymys*, [1921] Sess. Cas. 30, at p. 40.

course, reduce the significance of this factor if the individual, in leaving, severs other residential ties.

- Maintaining personal property and social ties in Canada would indicate a "continuing state of relationship" through secondary residential ties. Personal property remaining in Canada might include furniture, clothing, cars, and recreational vehicles. Maintaining provincial or territorial hospitalization and medical insurance coverage and a seasonal residence might also be an indication of residential ties. Social ties such as recreational and religious organization memberships in Canada could be used in a similar way depending on the reasons for maintaining such ties. Economic ties such as employment with a Canadian employer, active investment in a Canadian business and Canadian bank accounts, retirement savings plans, credit cards and securities accounts, are also regarded as secondary residential ties. Other such ties include: Canadian landed immigrant status or appropriate work permits, a Canadian passport, a Canadian driver's license, Canadian vehicle registration and membership in Canadian unions or professional organizations. It should be emphasized that none of the ties in this third category taken singly would be enough to determine full-time residence. However, one or more of these ties in combination with others, particularly in the first two bulleted categories above, would make a strong package of ties indicating such full-time residence. In making a determination of residence, it becomes important to give each fact an appropriate weighting according to its importance in the situation.

In order to establish that an individual is not a full-time resident, the severance of residential ties with Canada and the establishment of residential ties elsewhere is important, although an individual can be a resident of more than one country. An argument for continuing residential ties can be made, in particular, when the return could have been foreseen because of the existence of, perhaps, a contract of employment on return. No particular length of absence results in an individual becoming a non-resident. Occasional, but not regular, return visits for personal or business reasons would not likely jeopardize the severance of full-time residence.

¶2,040   Part-Time Residence

¶2,045   Applicable law

The absence of residential ties at a point in time would suggest that an individual is not a resident of Canada. Thus, at any particular point in time, an individual is either a resident of Canada, with the income tax consequences discussed above, or a non-resident, with possible income tax consequences to be discussed.

Part-time residence is a transitional position between residence and non-residence. Part-time residence can occur when an individual, having had full residential ties, leaves Canada during a year. Similarly, when an individual who did not have such ties for a prior period, comes to Canada during a year and establishes full residential ties, he or she would be considered to be a part-time resident for that year. The year of exit or entry is the year of part-time residence status.

A part-time resident is taxed in Canada on his or her worldwide income earned during the part of the year in which he or she was resident in Canada. Deductions in the computation of taxable income are allocated, if applicable, to the period of part-time residence. A similar allocation of amounts deductible as non-refundable tax credits may be made. These provisions require that during some other part of the year the taxpayer was not resident in Canada. This means that an individual will be taxed in Canada on his or her worldwide income for the period in a year during which he or she was a resident. This period constitutes the taxpayer's taxation year for the computation of income taxable in Canada during the year. Were it not for these rules, an individual might be regarded as a resident for the full year taxable on worldwide income for the whole year. Thus, the part-time residence rules provide an exception to the more general full-time residence rules.

ITA: 114

ITA: 118.91

¶2,050   Clean break or fresh start: The concept

To establish part-time residence, facts must be found to show that the person made either a "clean break" from Canada during the year or a "fresh start" in Canada during the year. An example of a "clean break" might involve a person who has resided in Canada in previous years and leaves Canada with his or her family and all of their belongings in, say, August of the year, severing all ties and indicating an intention not to return. If such a "clean break" or severing of ties can be established by the facts, then the individual becomes a non-resident after the "clean break" and the period of part-time residence. The CRA will consider a "clean break" to have been made on the latest of the date on which: IT-221R3

    (a) the individual leaves Canada,

    (b) the individual's spouse or common-law partner and/or dependants leave Canada, or

    (c) the individual becomes a resident of the country to which he or she is immigrating.

If the ties that have existed are not considered by the facts to have been severed, then the individual remains a full-time resident. An example of a "fresh start" might involve a person who has not previously or not recently resided in Canada and moves to Canada to take up residence in, say, April of the year. In both cases, the person would be in Canada for more   ITA: 250(1)(*a*) than 183 days, but his or her stay in the country for the period in question would not be temporary, as required by the rule to deem an individual to be a full-time resident.[4]

¶2,055   Liability of Non-Residents

¶2,060   General determination of liability

Subject to the provisions of an international tax agreement, a non-resident individual   ITA: 2(3) who for a taxation year was employed in Canada, carried on business in Canada or disposed of taxable Canadian property at any time in the year or a previous year, is liable to pay income tax. The base for this tax is his or her taxable income earned only in Canada. The addition of   ITA: 115 the phrase "or a previous year" means that income earned in Canada by a non-resident but not received until a later year will be taxed in that later year when the non-resident might not be employed or carrying on business in Canada. Thus, tax cannot be avoided by deferring salaries or business income until a year when no income is earned in Canada. It should be emphasized that a person who is a non-resident for the entire year cannot be a part-time   ITA: 114, 118.91 resident. To be a part-time resident, there must be a period in which the person was resident, in the sense of a full-time resident, and a period in which the person was a non-resident.

¶2,065   The meaning of carrying on business in Canada

The phrase "carrying on business" is not specifically defined in the *Income Tax Act*. The courts have tended to interpret the phrase as implying a continuous business activity.[5] A "business", on the other hand, is not required to involve a continuous business activity by   ITA: 248(1) virtue of its definition, which includes an "adventure or concern in the nature of trade". An adventure in the nature of trade can be simply described as a scheme to make a profit in the same manner as a person who is in that line of business.[6] The definition of "extended meaning of carrying on business" describes activities which, if engaged in by a non-resident   ITA: 253 person, will result in the non-resident being deemed to have been carrying on business.

Generally speaking, merely soliciting orders makes a non-resident person liable to be deemed to be carrying on business. Normally, the main determinant of carrying on business   ITA: 253 in a place is the location in which the contract in a transaction is made, not the location of the

---

[4] The cases of *Schujahn v. M.N.R.*, 62 DTC 1225 (Ex. Ct.), and *Truchon v. M.N.R.*, 70 DTC 1277 (T.A.B.), may illustrate the differences between deemed full-time and part-time residence.

[5] See *Tara Explorations & Development Co. Ltd. v M.N.R.*, 72 DTC 6288 (S.C.C.), affirming 70 DTC 6370 (Ex. Ct.).

[6] See *M.N.R. v. Taylor*, 56 DTC 1125 (Ex. Ct.), and IT-459.

offering of an item for sale as envisaged by the definition of the term "carrying on business". It should be noted that the courts have also looked beyond the place where the contract was concluded to the place where the operations occur from which the profits arise in substance. This is indicated by where payment is made or where the work is done or delivery of the goods is made. These factors indicate the place of performance of the contract. Recognize, however, that the specific activities listed in the definition of "carrying on business" override the common law principle of place of performance.

A non-resident offering something for sale in Canada through an employee who is a salesperson is carrying on business in Canada. On the other hand, a non-resident selling to an independent contractor like a Canadian-based retailer or wholesaler who resells the item in Canada is not carrying on business in Canada. Hence, the distinction between an employee and an independent contractor is important and will be explained more fully in Chapter 3. The distinction must be made on the facts of each case. These facts must establish the degree of responsibility enjoyed by the person who is soliciting orders or offering goods for sale. The courts have considered the following factors in this distinction:

(a) whether the parties describe or refer to their relationship as one of an independent contractor and a supplier;

(b) whether the alleged independent contractor carries on business in the name of the supplier or in his or her own name; and

(c) whether the independent contractor acts for other suppliers.

The greater the independence from the supplier and the greater the degree of responsibility, the greater is the likelihood that the situation involves a non-resident supplier selling to an independent contractor such that the supplier is not carrying on business in Canada and, is, therefore, not taxable in Canada on business income earned in Canada.

Note that the use of words like "carried on" or "carrying on", "solicited", and "offered" implies a continuity of activity over a period of time. The courts have indicated that an isolated transaction, even one that is described in the definition of "carrying on business", does not fit the concept of continuity over time. Hence, continuity of activity may, depending on the facts, be necessary to establish a "carrying on" of business, unless the isolated transaction in Canada is part of the normal international business activities of the non-resident. On the other hand, the CRA has expressed the view, in a memorandum obtained under Access to Information legislation, that the activity could be carried on in Canada for only a short duration and still be considered to be carrying on business. ITA: 2(3)(*b*), 253

¶2,070   International Tax Treaties and Individuals

Canada has negotiated many reciprocal tax treaties with other countries with the objective of preventing the incidence of double taxation or tax avoidance. These situations may result from the overlapping of tax provisions applicable to persons subject to tax in the two jurisdictions which are parties in the treaty. The treaty of greatest significance is probably the Canada–U.S. Tax Convention because of the considerable interrelationship of the two countries. The major provisions are described very briefly below.

¶2,075   Services

The provision in Article XV, regarding employees, in the Canada–U.S. Tax Convention is typical of many treaties that Canada has negotiated with other countries. The provision deals with the taxation of dependent personal services and exempts a resident of Canada from U.S. taxation on salaries, wages and other similar remuneration derived from an employment in the United States under certain conditions. The conditions are:

(a) that the remuneration does not exceed U.S. $10,000, or

(b) that the employee is present in the U.S. for a period not exceeding an aggregate of 183 days in the year and the remuneration is not borne by an employer who is a resident of the U.S. or by a "permanent establishment" or a "fixed base" which the employer has in the U.S.

Note, however, that as a resident of Canada, the individual would be taxable in Canada on worldwide income, including that earned in the U.S. and exempt from taxation in the U.S.

Article XIV deals with income from independent personal services, i.e., from self-employment. For example, an individual who is resident in Canada would only be taxed in the U.S. if the individual has or had a "fixed base", regularly available to him or her in the U.S. The tax in the U.S. would be limited to that on income attributable to the fixed base in the U.S. The provision is reciprocal in relation to residents of the United States performing personal services in Canada under the same conditions.

¶2,080   Resident and "tie-breaker" rules

For the purposes of the Convention, the term "resident" is defined in Article IV, paragraph 1 to mean:

> any person who, under the laws of [one country], is liable to tax therein by reason of his domicile, residence, place of management, place of incorporation or any other criterion of a similar nature. . . .

Paragraph 2 provides "tie-breaker" rules where an individual can be considered by paragraph 1 to be a resident of both countries. In this case, the individual's residence is determined as follows:

(a) he or she is deemed to be a resident of the country in which he or she has a permanent home available; if he or she has a permanent home available in both countries or in neither country, he or she is deemed to be a resident of the country with which his or her personal and economic relations are closer (i.e., centre of vital interests);

(b) if the country in which the individual has his or her centre of vital interests cannot be determined, the individual is deemed to be a resident of the country in which he or she has an habitual abode;

(c) if the individual has an habitual abode in both countries or in neither country, he or she is deemed to be a resident of the country of which he or she is a citizen; and

(d) if the individual is a citizen of both countries, or neither country, the "competent authorities" of the countries will settle the question by mutual agreement.

When these "tie-breaker rules" contained in a treaty apply and it is determined that an individual is a resident of another country, then the Act deems the individual to be a non-resident of Canada.

ITA: 250(5)

The term "competent authority" is defined in Article III, paragraph 1(*g*) to mean the Minister of National Revenue in Canada and the Secretary of the Treasury in the United States, or their designates.

¶2,085   Permanent establishment

While the term "fixed base" is not defined in the Convention, the term "permanent establishment" is defined in Article V to mean "a fixed place of business through which the business of a resident of a [country] is wholly or partly carried on". The term specifically includes a place of management, a branch, an office and a factory, among others. A person, other than an independent contractor, who has and habitually exercises an authority to conclude contracts in, say, Canada in the name of the resident of the U.S., is deemed to constitute a permanent establishment in Canada of the U.S. resident.

However, under paragraph 6 of Article V, the term "permanent establishment" does *not* include a fixed place of business in one country used solely in one or more of the following activities of the resident of the other country:

(a) the use of facilities for the purpose of storage, display or delivery of goods or merchandise belonging to the resident of the other country;

(b) the maintenance of a stock of goods or merchandise belonging to the resident of the other country for the purpose of storage, display or delivery;

(c) the maintenance of a stock of goods or merchandise belonging to the resident of the other country for the purpose of processing by another person;

(d) the purchase of goods or merchandise, or the collection of information, for the resident of the other country; and

(e) advertising, the supply of information, scientific research or similar activities which have a preparatory or auxiliary character for the resident of the other country.

¶2,090 Summary of the Residence Issue for an Individual

From the foregoing discussion, it can be concluded, generally, that an individual will be either a full-time resident of Canada or a non-resident. A full-time resident of Canada is taxable in Canada on worldwide income. A non-resident is taxable in Canada, generally, only on Canadian-source income, if any. If, in a particular year, an individual leaves Canada and severs ties to Canada, after having been a full-time resident, or enters Canada and establishes ties to Canada, after having been a non-resident, the individual will be a part-time resident for the part of that year while fully resident in Canada and a non-resident for the other part of the year. Hence, part-time residence is a transitional status. A part-time resident is taxable in Canada on worldwide income only for the part of the year while fully resident. An individual who is a non-resident of Canada can be deemed to be a full-time resident of Canada.   ITA: 250(1)

Exhibit 2-1 may provide a helpful checklist of facts to evaluate a case in which there has been a change in the residence status of an individual. In essence, it elaborates on the common law principle of "a continuing state of relationship" by establishing the existence of either continuing ties to Canada or ties elsewhere. In a transitional year, when an individual leaves Canada, having been a full-time resident, the ties to Canada may be severed (i.e., a "clean break" was made). Alternatively, when an individual moves into Canada, having been a non-resident, the ties to Canada may be established (i.e., a "fresh start" was made) and ties elsewhere may be severed. Note that full-time resident status and non-resident status are mutually exclusive. An individual cannot be a full-time resident of Canada and a non-resident at the same time. Therefore, the facts that support one status can usually be used to refute the other, although it is possible for an individual to be a resident of more than one country at the same time.

EXHIBIT 2-1
Checklist of Facts to Consider When Determining Residence
Status of an Individual
(Based on IT-221R3)

Factor	Resident	Non-resident
Significant residential ties		
(a) dwelling place		
(b) spouse or common-law partner		
(c) dependants		
Secondary residential ties		
(a) personal property in Canada		
(b) social ties with Canada		
(c) economic ties with Canada		
(d) landed immigrant status or appropriate work permits		
(e) hospitalization and medical insurance coverage from Canada		
(f) driver's license from Canada		
(g) vehicle registration in Canada		
(h) seasonal dwelling place in Canada		
(i) Canadian passport		
(j) memberships in Canadian union or professional organization		
Other residential ties of limited importance		
(a) retention of Canadian mailing address		
(b) Canadian post office box		
(c) Canadian safety deposit box		
(d) personal stationery or business cards showing Canadian address		
(e) telephone listing in Canada		
(f) Canadian newspaper and magazine subscriptions		
Nature of absence from Canada		
(a) evidence of intention to permanently sever ties with Canada		
(b) regularity and length of visits to Canada		
(c) residence ties outside of Canada		

¶2,100 Comprehensive Consideration of the Residence of an Individual

¶2,105 Stages of involvement

In any of the areas of taxation that are not resolved by a provision of the Act, there are several stages at which the tax adviser may become involved.

Appeal: At one stage, the facts of the case represent completed transactions which have been reported for income tax purposes and have been reassessed by the CRA. At this stage, the question is whether there is a sufficient basis to pursue the issue with the CRA further or to accept the reassessment as issued.

Filing: At another stage, the facts represent completed transactions, but the client has not yet filed the return which will report the transactions. Here, the issue is how to comply with the law in filing the return.

Planning: At yet another stage, the facts of the situation are in the planning phase and have not been completed. The issue at this stage is how the fact situation will be regarded for taxation purposes.

¶2,110   Consider both sides

At all stages, the type of analysis of the facts that should be done is essentially the same. If a framework of a test or a series of tests is available, as is the case in a residence situation, it should be applied to the facts to systematically evaluate the situation and enable the adviser to arrive at a logical conclusion. No matter how strongly the adviser may feel about a particular conclusion, it is important to consider both sides of the issue. A case for one particular side can be strengthened by considering the arguments for the opposing side and developing arguments against that opposing position. If this can be anticipated before actual discussions with the other side, fewer surprises will result.

¶2,115   Form of advice

While the method of analysis may be essentially the same at all stages of a tax situation, the form of the advice offered may differ, depending on the stage. At the reassessment stage, advice on whether there is a reasonably strong basis to pursue the client's position should be presented. At the initial compliance stage of filing the return, an indication of the alternatives and their tax consequences are needed to help the client decide on a filing position. The planning stage provides the greatest opportunity to help the client structure the situation to achieve the best tax result. At this stage, it is possible to modify the situation and its facts to achieve the desired outcome, because the originally planned facts have not been undertaken at this stage. However, even this stage requires a thorough evaluation of the situation and its potential tax consequences.

¶2,120   Application

The facts described in the following case situation could arise at any of the above three stages. The solution presented outlines a suggested method of systematic analysis based on the framework discussed and summarized in Exhibit 2-2.

Example Problem

Eighteen years ago, Mr. Har DeHatt, a U.S. citizen, moved to Vancouver with his parents. He went to high school in Vancouver and upon completion of his program he was employed in construction work in the Vancouver area. In time he became a construction supervisor. He married a Canadian five years ago. The couple subsequently purchased a home in Vancouver in which they lived and raised two children. He never became a Canadian citizen.

During the year in question, the state of the construction industry in Vancouver was such that he could not be employed on a regular basis although he did work on several jobs during the year. Effective August 1 of that year, he accepted an offer of employment with a construction company operating in the State of Washington and during the remainder of the year and the entire following year he worked on construction jobs in the State of Washington and in Alaska. He rented an apartment in Seattle, Washington, but maintained his home in Vancouver where his wife and children made their regular home. The household telephone listing in the Vancouver telephone directory was in his name.

He visited his family on such occasions as he was able to take time to go to Vancouver. The Vancouver address was the one to which he always returned when his duties permitted.

During the year in question, he worked a total of 800 hours on the new job, earning substantially more than U.S. $10,000.

— REQUIRED

Prepare a memo for the tax person in your firm who will advise Mr. DeHatt on his income tax liability for the year in question. Evaluate in detail the alternatives in the residence issue as they relate to this fact situation for the year in question. Discuss each possible degree of residence and its tax consequences. State your conclusion on the case after considering the relevant international tax agreement and after appropriately weighing the significance of the facts in the case. You may wish to use the framework presented in Exhibit 2-2, as it applies to individuals.

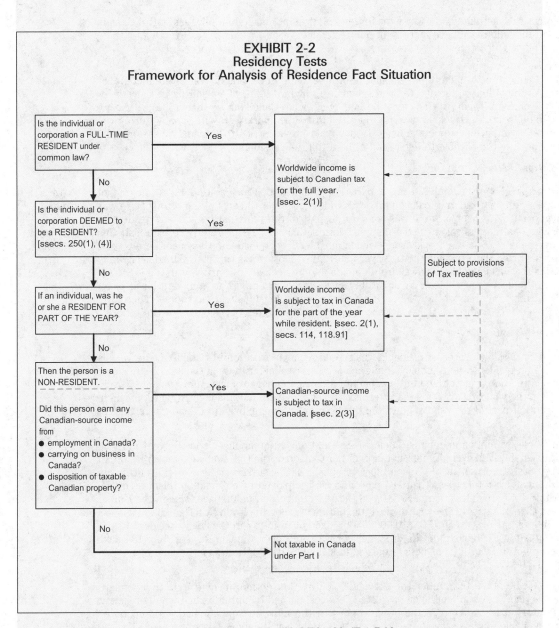

EXHIBIT 2-2
Residency Tests
Framework for Analysis of Residence Fact Situation

Is the individual or corporation a FULL-TIME RESIDENT under common law? — Yes → Worldwide income is subject to Canadian tax for the full year. [ssec. 2(1)]

No ↓

Is the individual or corporation DEEMED to be a RESIDENT? [ssecs. 250(1), (4)] — Yes → Worldwide income is subject to Canadian tax for the full year. [ssec. 2(1)]

No ↓

If an individual, was he or she a RESIDENT FOR PART OF THE YEAR? — Yes → Worldwide income is subject to tax in Canada for the part of the year while resident. [ssec. 2(1), secs. 114, 118.91]

No ↓

Then the person is a NON-RESIDENT.

Did this person earn any Canadian-source income from
● employment in Canada?
● carrying on business in Canada?
● disposition of taxable Canadian property? — Yes → Canadian-source income is subject to tax in Canada. [ssec. 2(3)]

No ↓

Not taxable in Canada under Part I

Subject to provisions of Tax Treaties

— *SOLUTION* [See *Lawrence C. Gillis v. M.N.R.*, 69 DTC 488 (T.A.B.)]

(1) *Consideration of full-time option*

ITA: 2(1)

If the taxpayer is found to be a full-time resident of Canada under the common law, he will be taxed in Canada on his worldwide income for the year. For this degree of residence to be found, "a continuing state of relationship between the person and a place" must be established. Citizenship is irrelevant to the question of residence. The facts of this case that could be used to establish the continuing relationship between the taxpayer and Canada include the following:

(a) he lived in Canada on a full-time basis for 18 years in which time he was educated in Canada, employed in Canada and married in Canada;

(b) he owned a house in Canada and the household telephone was listed in his name;

(c) his wife and children lived in Canada; and

(d) he visited his family whenever possible.

The fact that he rented an apartment in the U.S. does not make him not resident in Canada because an individual can have more than one residence.

(2) *Deemed residence option*

If the taxpayer is deemed to be resident, he will be taxed in Canada on worldwide income for the year. An individual is deemed to be resident in Canada if he or she sojourns in Canada for 183 days or more in a year. In this case, the taxpayer was in Canada more than 183 days during the year in question. However, he was not on a sojourn or temporary stay in Canada during the period of the year in question to August 1, given his previous ties to Canada. Therefore, the deeming rule is not applicable to deem him to be a full-time resident.

ITA: 2(1)

ITA: 250(1)(*a*)

(3) *Part-time residence option*

The taxpayer can be found to be a part-time resident of Canada. Under this degree of residence, he will be taxed in Canada on his worldwide income for the part of the year that he was resident in Canada as long as there was some other part of the year that he was not resident in Canada. Personal credits taken in the computation of tax must be prorated. To establish this degree of residence, a "clean break" from Canada must have been made. In this case there was no "clean break" from Canada since the taxpayer maintained most of his ties with Canada. The only change was that his job took him away from Canada and he needed an apartment in the U.S. This action is not indicative of a "clean break". Note that facts which support an argument for a "clean break" contradict an argument for "a continuing state of relationship" and *vice versa*. Therefore, it is only necessary to discuss these facts as supporting one degree of residence or the other.

ITA: 2(1), 118.91

(4) *Non-resident option*

The final possible degree of residence that could result in taxation in Canada in the year is that of the non-resident who is employed in Canada or carries on business in Canada. At this level of residence the taxpayer is taxed in Canada only on his employment or business income earned in Canada in the year or a previous year. In this case, employment in Canada must be established. During the first part of the year in question, the taxpayer was employed in Canada from time to time.

ITA: 2(3)(*a*), 2(3)(*b*)

A possible exemption under the Canada–U.S. Tax Convention applicable in the year must be checked to establish an exemption from tax in either Canada or the U.S. To be exempt from tax in the United States, a resident of Canada must establish that he or she either was present in the United States for a total of less than 184 days and was employed by a Canadian business in the United States or earned less than U.S. $10,000 there. In this case, the taxpayer was in the United States less than 184 days in the year in question, but he was not employed by a Canadian business and he did not earn less than U.S. $10,000. To be exempt from tax in Canada, a resident of the United States must establish that he or she either was present in Canada for less than 184 days and was employed by a U.S. business or earned less than C$10,000. He was in Canada more than 183 days in the year, so he could not be exempt from Canadian tax.

It should be noted that under the Canada–U.S. Tax Convention, income from independent personal services, i.e., non-employment related services, earned by an individual who is resident in one country may be taxed in the other country if the individual has or had a "fixed base" regularly available to him or her in the other country. However, the income is subject to tax in the other country only to the extent that it is attributable to the fixed base in that country. The term "fixed base" is not defined.

(5) *Conclusion*

The facts of this case indicate that the taxpayer is most likely a full-time resident of Canada. Deemed residence is not a possibility in this case, based on an evaluation of the facts. The evidence of a "clean break" is not very strong in the facts of this case. If a "clean break" is not established in the year the non-resident category is not possible in that year.

¶2,130   Non-Tax Factors Affecting Planning for the Residence of an Individual

Establishing that an individual is taxable as a full-time resident or a non-resident, or not taxable in Canada at all, is not the same as determining the best form of residency in a particular case. For example, being a full-time resident of Canada, taxed on worldwide income, is not always worse than being a non-resident who is not taxable in Canada at all and, hence, taxed completely elsewhere. The best form of residency for an individual in a particular situation depends on many factors, some of which involve tax liability and some of which do not.

Newspaper and other articles frequently appear, presenting comparisons of the net tax burden of a particular individual taxed in Canada and in another jurisdiction. As a result of different income tax rates and allowable deductions in different jurisdictions, the net income tax differences can be considerable. The implication is often that the full-time resident of Canada is better off or worse off on an after-tax basis in the other jurisdiction. These comparisons can be misleading, if they do not consider a number of non-tax factors that might have an impact on the situation. For example, differences in the cost of health care and how it is financed by an individual can offset differences in net tax. A Canadian Minister of Finance, commenting on relatively higher levels of taxation in Canada, was reported to have stated: "if taxes were the only reason [to leave Canada], the Cayman Islands would be the most populated area in the world".

While employment opportunities at the forefront of a particular field of interest or training and higher remuneration levels may be an attraction in a particular jurisdiction, quality-of-life factors should also be considered. For example, if there are differences in the cost of health care, they may result from differences in quality and in availability. On the other hand, differences in climatic conditions may solve certain health problems such as asthma or allergies. Differences in both the standard of living and the cost of living should be assessed. Cultural differences may require adjustments which may be made more difficult by geographic separation from family and social ties. Some countries may be less socially or politically stable, resulting in less personal safety and more crime. Economic differences, such as less availability of credit, may exist. Also, financial exchange risks may be encountered and exchange controls may make it difficult to remove capital from some jurisdictions.

¶2,200 LIABILITY OF CORPORATIONS FOR INCOME TAX

The liability of a corporation for income tax in Canada depends on whether it is a resident or a non-resident. The existence of a deeming rule to establish corporate residence, based on incorporation in Canada, means that contentious issues pertaining to corporate residence in Canada are limited. In recent years, there has been little litigation on the residence of corporations.

¶2,210 Charging Provision

Since the word "person" includes a corporation, the charging provision for corporations is the same as that for individuals. Also, since the taxation year of a corporation need not coincide with the calendar year and, in fact, need not be a full 12 months, there is no need for a concept of part-time residence pertaining to a corporation. When, at any time, a corporation is incorporated in Canada and commences operations, a taxation year begins. When a corporation terminates its incorporation in Canada, a taxation year ends. The appropriate rules pertaining to resident corporations are applied for those taxation years.

ITA: 2, 249

¶2,220 Residence of Corporations

¶2,225 Deemed residence

Since a corporation is an artificial legal entity, it does not "reside" anywhere in the sense that an individual does. However, a corporation incorporated in Canada after April 26, 1965, is deemed to be resident in Canada throughout a taxation year. This deeming rule clearly settles the issue of corporate residence for corporations incorporated *in Canada* in recent years. A corporation incorporated in Canada before April 27, 1965 is deemed to be resident in Canada if it was resident by the common law principle discussed below or it carried on business in Canada during any taxation year ending after April 26, 1965.[7] A corporation that is not incorporated in Canada, may still be a Canadian resident under the common law principle that its central management and control are in Canada.

ITA: 250(4)(*a*)

ITA: 250(4)(*c*)

¶2,230 Common law concept of corporate residence

A 1906 British case,[8] which established the "central management and control rule", was based on the following facts. The company was incorporated in South Africa and had its head office there. The board of directors regularly met in London and the real control was exercised in London, although no business was carried on in the United Kingdom. The corporation was held to be resident in the United Kingdom because "a corporation resides where the real business is being carried on and the real business is carried on where the central management and control actually abide". Usually central management and control exists where the board of directors meets to make decisions on company policy.

In another British case,[9] the following facts were presented. The appellant company was a wholly owned subsidiary of an English company and so were three companies registered in Kenya. The appellant had made some payments to these companies which would be tax deductible only if the companies were resident in the United Kingdom for the year in question. In addition to being registered in Kenya, the companies carried on business entirely outside the United Kingdom and their articles of association expressly provided that their directors' meetings be held anywhere except in the United Kingdom. At a certain point in time, the situation of the companies had become so serious that it was unwise to allow them to be managed in Africa any longer and it was decided that management be taken over by the parent. From that time, any decision of importance that concerned the running of the companies was made in London by the directors of the parent.

The House of Lords of the United Kingdom held the following in this case:

> . . . on these facts the seat of the "central management and control" of the subsidiaries passed from Africa to the United Kingdom. This is a straightforward case of *de facto* control being actively exercised in the United Kingdom while the local directors stood aside from their directorial duties. . . .

This case has been used as an authority for the principle that central management and control and, therefore, residence of a company is not necessarily in the country where the board of directors meets even if they have *de jure* or legal control.

The case of *The King v. British Columbia Electric Railway Company Ltd.* established the principle that the place of incorporation of a company is not relevant by itself. Of course, deemed residence of a corporation requires incorporation in Canada. *Bedford Overseas Freighters Ltd. v. M.N.R.* illustrates the application of the "central management and control" rule to a Canadian fact situation. It should be noted that if a corporation is considered to be a resident in Canada at any time in the year, it is taxed on its worldwide income for the year as if it had been resident throughout the year. Thus, there is no concept of part-time residence for corporations.

2 DTC 824 (S.C.C.)

70 DTC 6072 (Ex. Ct.)

---

[7] For the purposes of this chapter, paragraph 250(4)(*b*) can be ignored.

[8] *DeBeers Consolidated Mines Ltd. v. Howe*, [1906] A.C. 455.

[9] *Unit Construction Co. Ltd. v. Bullock*, [1959] 3 W.W.R. 1022.

¶2,240 Liability of Non-Resident Corporations

To be considered a non-resident, a corporation cannot be incorporated in Canada after April 26, 1965, subject to certain specific exceptions. A non-resident corporation may be taxable in Canada on its Canadian-source income. While a corporation cannot be "employed", it is possible for a corporation that is not incorporated in Canada to carry on business in Canada and, hence, be taxable on its Canadian-source business income. The consideration of what constitutes a carrying on of business by a corporation in Canada is generally the same as that for an individual, as discussed previously. However, one perspective on carrying on business involving a corporation may not exist in the case of an individual. A corporation may be formed for a single business purpose which, if implemented in a single transaction, would involve no continuity of activity in the carrying on of business. In the case of *Placrefid Ltd. v. M.N.R.*, the court held that a single transaction in this type of corporate situation constituted a carrying on of business. The provisions of a tax treaty may eliminate the liability for tax in Canada of a non-resident corporation carrying on business in Canada.

ITA: 250(4)
ITA: 2(3)

92 DTC 6480 (F.C.T.D.)

¶2,250 International Tax Treaties and Corporations

Most of the major treaties carry a provision similar to that in Article VII of the Canada–U.S. Income Tax Convention in which a U.S. enterprise is not subject to taxation by Canada on its "business profits" unless the enterprise carries on business in Canada through a "permanent establishment" located in Canada. If it has such a permanent establishment, it is subject to tax in Canada only on the income attributable to the permanent establishment. As indicated above, the key determinants of a permanent establishment defined in Article V are a fixed place of business or a person who habitually exercises authority to contract for his or her principal. Note that an independent agent is not considered such a person. A list of activities from Article V that do not constitute a fixed place of business is provided in the discussion of international tax treaties and individuals, above.[10] The logic used by the Exchequer Court in the *Tara Explorations* case (cited in footnote 10) is particularly noteworthy in its comprehensiveness. A similar method of analysis of a residence question is used in the following example problems. It is also illustrated in Exhibit 2-2, which sets out a framework for the analysis of a fact situation on the residence issue in terms of levels or "degrees" of residence.

The definition of the term "resident" quoted above from Article IV applies to a corporation as well as to an individual. Where that definition would determine that a corporation is a resident of both countries, then paragraph 3 of Article IV would deem the corporation to be resident in the country of its incorporation.

¶2,260 Comprehensive Consideration of the Residence of a Corporation

Example Problem

Thumbusters Corporation was incorporated in the State of New York on March 1, 1981. The head office of the corporation was established in Buffalo, New York, along with production and warehouse facilities. The directors of the company, the president, and the general manager were all U.S. citizens resident in Buffalo. Meetings necessary to maintain the corporate charter as well as major business meetings to discuss corporate strategy were held in Buffalo. The main corporation books and records were maintained at the company's head office.

One of the main reasons for locating the company facilities in Buffalo was to exploit the Canadian market for thumbusters, the company's product. As a result, immediately upon incorporation a sales office was set up in rented premises in Toronto from which orders for thumbusters could be solicited from Canadian customers. A head salesman was hired to manage the sales effort conducted through the Toronto office by himself and two subordinate salesmen. In addition, an office secretary reporting to the head salesman was hired. All of these personnel were Canadian citizens resident in Canada.

---

[10] The cases of *American Wheelabrator & Equipment Corporation v. M.N.R.*, 51 DTC 285 (T.A.B.), and *Tara Explorations and Development Company Limited v. M.N.R.*, 70 DTC 6370 (Ex. Ct.), consider the concept of a permanent establishment.

The Toronto office was identified by the company name on the door. The office telephone was listed in the company's name. The salesmen solicited orders in the Canadian market, but they had to be approved in Buffalo by the head office there. Once authorized by head office, the merchandise was shipped from the warehouses there. However, the Toronto office invoiced its Canadian customers and payments were made to the Toronto office and deposited to a bank account in the company's name in Toronto. Expenses of operating the Toronto office including the salaries of all Toronto personnel and the commissions of the salesmen were paid from the Toronto bank account by cheques signed by the head salesman in Toronto. Records of these receipts and disbursements were kept in a set of books at the Toronto office. At the end of each month, the Toronto office would remit to head office all but a nominal amount of the balance remaining in the bank account.

By the end of the last year, the Canadian market for thumbusters was such that the expense of maintaining an office in downtown Toronto was not warranted. Effective January 1 of the current year, the head salesman was instructed to carry out all of his duties from a room built to accommodate the work in the basement of his home. The two subordinate salesmen reported to him there. The home telephone with a listing in the head salesman's name was used for the business. All salesmen carried business cards printed with the company name and the number of this residence phone. It was felt that the services of the secretary were unnecessary at this location since the head salesman's wife could be paid to do the secretarial work on a part-time basis. A telephone answering service was hired to take messages when neither the head salesman nor his wife was home.

— *REQUIRED*

Prepare a memo for the tax person in your firm who will advise Thumbusters Corporation on the income tax consequences of these facts for the current year. Evaluate in detail the alternatives in the residence issue as they relate to this fact situation for the current year. Discuss each possible degree of residence and its tax consequences. State your conclusions on the case after considering the relevant international tax agreement and after appropriately weighing the significance of the facts in the case. You may wish to use the framework in Exhibit 2-1 for your analysis, as it applies to corporations.

— *SOLUTION* [See *American Wheelabrator & Equipment Corporation v. M.N.R.*, 51 DTC 285 (T.A.B.), and *Tara Explorations and Development Company Ltd. v. M.N.R.*, 70 DTC 6370 (Ex. Ct.)]

(1) *Full-time option*

Since the meaning of residence is not fully defined in the Act it is necessary to make a determination based on the specific facts of each case. A corporation can be found to be a full-time resident by common law principle. If this is the case, the corporation will be taxed in Canada on its worldwide income. The common law principle that must be in evidence by the facts is that "central management and control" are in Canada. In this case, the directors, president and general manager managed from head office in the United States. Corporate business and strategy meetings were held in the United States. Corporate books and records, with the exception of the Toronto records, were kept in the United States. The Toronto records are probably not sufficient to establish central management and control since they are subsidiary documents. Also, the management function undertaken by the head salesman would probably not be major enough to indicate central management and control of the company.

ITA: 2(1)

(2) *Deemed resident option*

A corporation can be deemed resident by meeting the conditions of subsection 250(4) and, as a result, it would be taxed in Canada on its worldwide income. To be deemed resident, the corporation must be incorporated in Canada. In this case, since the company was not incorporated in Canada, the date of incorporation is irrelevant and the questions raised in the deeming rule of residence (by common law principle) or of carrying on business in Canada need not be addressed.

ITA: 2(1)

ITA: 250(4)

(3) *Non-resident option*

Under the third degree of residence, the corporation can be considered a non-resident carrying on business in Canada. It can then be taxed in Canada on profits from its business in Canada. Carrying on business in Canada must be established by the facts of the case. Soliciting orders in Canada is enough to establish carrying on business in Canada. This raises the question as to whether the salesman was an employee of the corporation or an independent contractor. If he is an employee, then the corporation could be considered to be carrying on a business in Canada. The following facts indicate that he is an employee rather than an independent contractor operating his own business in Canada:

ITA: 2(3)(*b*), 253

(a) he carried on business in the name of the company;

(b) he acted only for the company and no one else;

(c) he had no stock of merchandise of his own; and

(d) the books and records kept in Canada were not those of an independent business, but were only enough to maintain an office in Canada.

The Canada–U.S. Tax Convention must be consulted to determine if the corporation can be exempted from tax in Canada on its profits from carrying on business in Canada. In order to be exempt, the corporation must establish that it is not operating from a "permanent establishment" in Canada. During the current year, the corporation did not have a fixed place of business in Canada. Other facts that can be used to show no permanent establishment in Canada include:

(a) the salesman did not have authority to contract, because acceptance was given only in New York;

(b) there was no stock of merchandise in Canada (note that under Article V paragraph 6(*b*) of the Canada–U.S. Tax Convention, a fixed place of business used to maintain a stock of merchandise for the purpose of storage, display or delivery will not constitute a permanent establishment);

(c) the only office used was in the house which had no company identification; and

(d) the bank account and records were not sufficient to establish a permanent establishment in Canada.

(4) *Conclusion*

In conclusion, the corporation would not likely be taxable in Canada. The tax treaty would exempt the company from tax as a non-resident on its profits since they were not earned from a permanent establishment in Canada. Also, the facts do not warrant finding either full-time residence or deemed residence.

¶2,300 REGISTRATION REQUIREMENTS AND LIABILITY FOR THE GOODS AND SERVICES TAX

¶2,310 Liability for GST

This part of the chapter deals with liability for GST and the requirements to register and charge GST under the *Excise Tax Act* (ETA). While the legal liability for payment of GST rests with the purchaser, the responsibility for collecting and remitting the tax generally lies with the supplier. These rules will also be examined in the context of the residency of the supplier, since the rules are somewhat different for resident and non-resident suppliers.

The charging provision requires that every recipient of a taxable supply made in Canada   ETA: 165(1)–(2)
to pay to Her Majesty in right of Canada a tax of 6% (0% for zero-rated supplies) of the value
of the consideration of the supply. The *recipient* of a supply is generally the person who
enters into the agreement to acquire the property or service and is liable under that agreement to pay consideration for the supply. (Special rules apply where there is no agreement or
no consideration is payable. A *taxable supply* is defined as a supply made in the course of a   ETA: 123(1)
commercial activity. The term includes both supplies taxed at the general rate of 6% and
those that are zero-rated. (A *zero-rated supply* is defined as a supply included in   ETA: 123(1)
Schedule VI). Therefore, for a person to be subject to GST, the supply must be (i) made in
Canada, and (ii) made by another person who is engaged in a commercial activity. The
definition of a commercial activity does not include activities engaged in by a business that
involve the making of an exempt supply (which in turn is defined as a supply included in
Schedule V. Rules have been introduced to determine when a supply is made in Canada and,
hence, within the scope of GST.

A relieving provision provides that if, at the time consideration is paid or becomes due for   ETA: 166
a supply, the supplier is a small supplier (who is not registered or required to be registered),
no GST is payable. However, this relieving provision does not apply to the sale of real
property. Small suppliers are discussed in greater detail below.

¶2,315   Supplies in Canada

Supplies are subject to GST only if they are made in Canada. (It should be noted that   ETA: 142(1)
imported goods and services are also subject to GST in certain circumstances.) A sale of
goods is deemed to be made in Canada if the goods are delivered or made available to the
recipient in Canada. In the case of leased goods, the supply is deemed to be made in Canada if
possession or use of the goods is given or made available to the recipient in Canada. In the
case of a supply of real property or a service in relation to real property, the supply is deemed
to be made in Canada if the real property is situated in Canada. In the case of a supply of any
other service, if the service is to be performed in whole or in part in Canada, the supply of the
service is deemed to be made in Canada.

For supplies of intangible personal property, the determination of whether a supply is
made in Canada can be more difficult. Intangible personal property is not defined in the ETA.
However, the term "property" is defined to include "any property, whether real or personal,   ETA: 123(1)
movable or immovable, tangible or intangible . . .". The main categories of property under the
ETA are real property, tangible personal property (generally referred to as goods) and
intangible personal property (movable and immovable property are terms used under civil law
in the province of Quebec). Intangible personal property includes a property that has no
intrinsic or marketable value, but is merely evidence of value, and which is enforceable by
law, such as contractual rights, stock certificates, intellectual property, etc. Intellectual
property includes patents, trademarks, industrial designs, etc. The supply of intangible per-   ETA: 142(1)(c)(i)
sonal property is deemed to be made in Canada if the property may be used in whole or in
part in Canada and the recipient is either a registrant for GST purposes or a resident of
Canada. If the intangible personal property is in respect of real property situated in Canada,   ETA: 142(1)(c)(ii)
or of goods ordinarily situated in Canada, or of a service to be performed in Canada, the
supply is also deemed to be made in Canada.

¶2,320   Supplies by non-residents

As a general rule, a supply of goods or services made in Canada by a non-resident is   ETA: 143(1)
deemed to be made in Canada if:

- the supply is made in the course of a business carried on in Canada;

- the non-resident is registered for GST purposes at the time the supply is made; or

- the supply is in respect of a place of amusement, a seminar, an activity or an event, and
  the non-resident supplies admissions directly to consumers.

Unless any of the above situations apply, supplies by a non-resident are outside the scope
of GST.

Now that the rules for determining whether a particular supply is deemed to be made in Canada have been reviewed, the issue of whether GST must be charged by the supplier will be examined. As a general rule, a supply made in Canada will only be subject to GST if it is made by a registrant.

¶2,330 Registration Requirements for Residents

¶2,335 Test for registration

A person who is engaged in a commercial activity in Canada (discussed below) is required to register for GST purposes. Persons registered or required to be registered under the legislation are referred to as *registrants*. The rights and obligations of registrants under the ETA are discussed in Chapter 14. It should be noted that as agents of the Crown, registrants are required to collect GST as required under the ETA. ETA: 240(1) ETA: 123(1)

The definition of person for the purposes of GST is broadly based to include an individual, partnership, corporation, trust or estate, or a body that is a society, union, club, association, commission, or other organization of any kind. Therefore, virtually any kind of organized unit or individual can be considered to be a person and, therefore, can be required to register. ETA: 123(1)

Unlike the *Income Tax Act*, the ETA treats partnerships as persons for purposes of the GST. Therefore, the partnership is considered to be a person for registration purposes and is liable for GST collected on taxable supplies, rather than the individual partners. Similarly, the partnership is eligible for an input tax credit for its purchases attributable to commercial activities.

¶2,340 Definition of commercial activity

Central to the determination of whether a person is required to register is the issue of whether the person is engaged in commercial activities. This topic will be discussed in greater detail in Chapter 4. However, for the purposes of the discussion of the registration requirements, it should be noted that a commercial activity is defined as: ETA: 123(1)

- a business that is carried on;

- an adventure or concern in the nature of trade; and

- the supply of real property.

Business is defined broadly to include a profession, calling, trade, manufacture, or undertaking of any kind whatever, regardless of whether the activity engaged in is for profit. This test is broader than the business test under the *Income Tax Act* in that there need not be a profit motive present for an activity to be considered a business for GST purposes. The point to remember is that the GST is a tax on consumption or value added, and not on income. Thus, many activities engaged in by non-profit organizations, charities and governments may constitute a business for GST purposes. These entities engage in activities that add value to the economy in competition with profit-motivated businesses. For example, a non-profit organization will be considered to be engaged in a commercial activity for GST purposes if it supplies taxable goods or services for consideration. Therefore, any entity that engages in an activity of a commercial nature, regardless of whether the activity is engaged in primarily for profit, will be considered to be engaged in a commercial activity. Consequently, the entity will be required to register for GST purposes.

An adventure or concern in the nature of trade, which is not defined but has the common law meaning discussed previously, also constitutes a commercial activity. This concept is discussed in Chapter 4. The supply of real property also constitutes a commercial activity unless the supply is exempt. Thus, most sales and leases of non-residential property constitute a commercial activity. Reference should be made to Chapter 7 for a discussion on supplies of real property.

¶2,345   Exclusions from commercial activity

The definition of commercial activity contains certain exclusions of which readers should be aware. First, activities that involve the making of exempt supplies do not constitute commercial activities. For example, the supply of medical services by a physician is exempt and, therefore, not a commercial activity. Consequently, physicians providing exempt medical services, only, are not able to register for GST purposes and cannot claim input tax credits in respect of GST paid on inputs. However, the GST component of these expenses can be deducted for income tax purposes.

Second, commercial activity does not include any activity engaged in by an individual (or a partnership comprised of individuals) without a reasonable expectation of profit. Thus, hobbies and recreational pastimes of individuals would not be considered to be commercial activities and, hence, registration would not be required nor permitted. The phrase "reasonable expectation of profit" is discussed in Chapter 4.

¶2,350   Exceptions from the registration requirements

The registration requirements contain an exception for *small suppliers*. The rules for determining whether a person qualifies as a small supplier are set out in the ETA. Basically, this includes persons whose revenues from taxable supplies do not exceed $30,000 in the four preceding calendar quarters. This calculation is based on the supplier's total worldwide sales including any supply made outside Canada by its "associates". Small suppliers, who are not registered, are not required to collect GST on taxable supplies. Persons who qualify as small suppliers and who are engaged in a commercial activity, however, may register on a voluntary basis. Registration would permit these persons to claim input tax credits and may be advantageous if taxable supplies are made to registrants. Since registrants are able to claim input tax credits on their purchases, they will likely prefer to deal with other registrants. Purchases from non-registrants may contain indirect GST because non-registrants are unable to recover GST paid on purchases through the input tax credit mechanism.

ETA: 148, 240(1)

In addition to the small supplier exception, a person whose only commercial activity is making supplies of real property by way of sale other than in the course of a business is not required to register. As noted above, supplies of real property are discussed in Chapter 7.

¶2,360   Registration and Collection Requirements for Non-Residents

The place of supply rules discussed earlier in this section must be read in conjunction with the registration requirements to determine when non-residents are required to register and collect GST.

¶2,365   Meaning of non-resident

For purposes of the GST, non-residents are defined as "not resident in Canada". In the absence of a definition of "resident", reference should be made to the dictionary meaning of the term and to the interpretation of the term under the *Income Tax Act*, as discussed earlier in this Chapter. The ETA does, however, contain deeming rules which provide that a corporation is deemed to be resident in Canada if it is incorporated in Canada, similar to the rules under the *Income Tax Act*. In addition, a corporation originally incorporated in a foreign jurisdiction that is continued (a special form of incorporation) in Canada and not elsewhere is deemed to be resident in Canada.

ETA: 132

In the case of a partnership or unincorporated society, club, association, or organization, or a branch thereof, the entity is deemed to be resident in Canada if a majority of its members, having management and control, are resident in Canada at that time. A labour union is deemed to be resident in Canada if it carries on its activities in Canada and has a local union or branch in Canada at that time.

Where a non-resident person has a permanent establishment in Canada, the person is deemed to be resident in Canada in respect of the activities carried on through that particular establishment. For GST purposes, a *permanent establishment* is defined as a fixed place of business, including a place of management, branch, office, factory, workshop, mine, oil or gas well, quarry, timberland, or other place of extraction of mineral resources through which supplies are made. It also includes a fixed place of business of another person (other than a broker, general commission agent, or other independent agent) making supplies on behalf of the person in the ordinary course of business. Because the definition of permanent establishment under the ETA is different from that generally found in Canada's income tax treaties, there may be situations where the existence of a permanent establishment is different for income tax and GST purposes.

¶2,370 Mandatory registration

According to the registration requirements, non-resident persons, who do not *carry on any business in Canada*, are not required to register. Thus, while the test for residents is based on engaging in a commercial activity, the test for non-residents is based on the narrower concept of carrying on business. In basic terms, the difference for a non-resident is that registration is not required if the activities undertaken in Canada are not of a regular and continuous nature. Again, reference should be made to Chapter 4 for a discussion of the distinction between commercial activity and business. ETA: 240(1)

A non-resident who directly supplies admissions to a place of amusement, a seminar, an activity or an event, must register before making any such supplies in Canada. ETA: 240(2)

The small supplier exemption, for suppliers with less than $30,000 in sales per year, is also available to non-residents, other than those who supply admissions as described above.

For individuals, an individual is deemed to be a resident of Canada at any time, if he or she meets certain conditions of the *Income Tax Act*. Thus, a deemed resident (other than a sojourner) for income tax purposes is also a resident for GST purposes. ITA: 250(1)(*a*)–(*f*)

¶2,375 Voluntary registration

Voluntary registration is available to non-residents, provided certain requirements are met. The non-resident person must, in the ordinary course of carrying on business outside Canada, ETA: 240(3)

(a) regularly solicit orders for the supply of goods for delivery in Canada; or

(b) have entered into an agreement for the supply of:

- services to be performed in Canada, or

- intangibles to be used in Canada or that relate to real property in Canada, goods ordinarily situated in Canada or services performed in Canada.

¶2,380 Imports

As the GST is a tax on consumption in Canada, it also applies to imports. The ETA imposes GST on the value of imported goods. The GST is payable by the person who is liable under the *Customs Act* to pay duty on the imported goods. The value of the goods is based on the value for customs purposes plus duties and excise taxes (excluding GST). No tax is payable on zero-rated goods, such as basic groceries and medical devices. ETA: 212 ETA: 215(1) ETA: 213

GST is imposed on the recipient of imported taxable supplies. Imported taxable supplies are defined to include intangible personal property (e.g., intellectual property) and services that are supplied outside Canada to a Canadian resident for use in Canada. However, GST is not imposed where the imported taxable supply is for use in Canada exclusively (90% or more) in a commercial activity. ETA: 217, 218

¶2,800   REVIEW QUESTIONS

(1) Canadian citizens pay tax in Canada on their world income. Comment.

(2) If a non-resident vacations in Canada for 180 days during the year, then he or she will be considered a Canadian resident for the full year. Comment.

(3) If an individual sells his or her house and then leaves the country, the person will be considered to be a non-resident. Comment.

(4) Assume that an individual resided in Buffalo and carried on a proprietorship business in St. Catharines. How would he or she pay tax on the business income earned in Canada?

(5) An individual who moves to Canada on March 31 of the year, will be considered resident in Canada throughout the year since he or she was resident here for more than 183 days. Comment.

(6) Since a corporation is an artificial legal entity, it does not "reside" anywhere in the sense that an individual does. Comment on how the residency of a corporation is determined.

(7) A company was incorporated in Canada on November 30, 1965, but has been carrying on business in Bermuda since that date and all of the officers and directors have always been resident there. Comment on the company's tax liability in Canada.

(8) A company was incorporated in Canada on November 30, 1964, but has been carrying on business in Bermuda since that date and all of the officers and directors have always been resident there. In the years from incorporation to 1971 the company actively solicited orders in Canada by telephone. It stopped this activity in Canada at the end of 1971. Comment on the company's tax liability to Canada.

(9) A Canadian executive is transferred to the U.S. with his company on a five-year contract. He and his family sell all their Canadian assets and move to the U.S. in December of the year. Due to the lower personal income tax rates in the U.S., he has the Canadian company defer the payment of the bonus of $100,000 that he earned in Canada in the year until the next year when he is resident in the U.S. Comment on whether the executive will be taxed in Canada on this bonus.

(10) If a non-resident individual were to buy and quickly resell some land in Canada and earn income of $100,000, would the non-resident be considered to be carrying on business in Canada for purposes of subsection 2(3)?

(11) If a U.S. corporation has an employee located in Canada who is selling goods on behalf of the employer, then would the U.S. company be taxable in Canada?

(12) If a U.S. corporation has an agent located in Canada who is selling goods on behalf of the U.S. company, then would the U.S. company be taxable in Canada?

(13) If a person is resident in Canada, can that same person also be resident in the U.S.?

(14) If a Canadian corporation is carrying on business in the U.S. through a permanent establishment in the U.S., will the Canadian company be considered resident in the U.S. and be subject to tax in the U.S. on the total corporate income?

(15) Mr. Smooth is an independent consultant who provides his services wherever he can get the work. He has been asked by a U.S. company to go to the U.S. to consult with them. He thinks that he will have to spend 25 days travelling to their many locations in the U.S. over the next year and that he will earn $50,000 for his efforts. His lawyer has told him that he will be taxed in the U.S. on this business income. What do you think?

¶2,825   MULTIPLE CHOICE QUESTIONS

Question 1

X Ltd. is a corporation which has always been managed by the *same* Board of Directors. The Board of Directors has always met where the directors reside. Based on these facts, X Ltd. will NOT be resident in Canada for income tax purposes if X Ltd. was:

(A) incorporated in Canada in 1968 and its directors are all U.S. residents;

(B) incorporated in the U.S. in 1970 and its directors are all U.S. residents;

(C) incorporated in the U.S. in 1968 and its directors are all Canadian residents;

(D) incorporated in Canada in 1964 and its directors are all Canadian residents.

Question 2

Joe is legally separated from his wife and has two adult children who live with his wife and are not dependent on him for support. Joe is leaving Canada to take a job in Germany on June 30 of this year. He plans to stay in Germany indefinitely and has purchased a home there. Which one of the following things is the most important for Joe to do to help ensure that he is not a resident of Canada for Canadian income tax purposes after he leaves?

(A) Take his wife and children with him to Germany.

(B) Give up his Canadian citizenship.

(C) Sell his Canadian home or rent it under a long-term lease.

(D) Put all his household furniture and personal effects into storage in Canada.

Question 3

Mr. N is *not* a resident of Canada. In the year, he had worldwide income of $200,000, including $50,000 of employment income earned in Canada (from director's fees) and $10,000 of interest on Government of Canada bonds.

What amount of taxable income must Mr. N report on his Canadian personal income tax return for the year?

(A) $10,000

(B) $50,000

(C) $60,000

(D) $200,000

Question 4

Jerry Dykopf ceased to be a resident of Canada on April 30 of the year and moved to Israel on that date. During the first four months of the year, he earned $25,000 of employment income in Canada and $1,000 of interest income from his bank accounts in Canada. While living in Israel during the remainder of the year, he earned $30,000 (Cdn. $) of employment income in Israel and received $2,000 of interest income from his Canadian bank accounts.

What amount of taxable income must Mr. Dykopf report on his Canadian personal income tax return for the year?

(A) $58,000

(B) $56,000

(C) $26,000

(D) Nil

Question 5

In which of the following situations is the person considered a non-resident of Canada for Canadian income tax purposes in the year in question?

(A) James Hill, a 25-year-old engineer living in Ottawa, accepted a six-month transfer to an office in London, England for the period July 1 to December 31, of the year in question. He returned to Canada in the following year. James is not married and has always lived at his parents' house in Ottawa.

(B) Judy Gordon, a financial analyst, lives in a house she owns in London, England. She had lived in Toronto all her life, until she started a minimum three-year contract with CS Services Inc., which started in July of the year in question. Judy is single and terminated the lease on her apartment in Toronto before moving her belongings to England when her position started in July.

(C) ERT Limited was incorporated in Canada in 1987 and, until recently, its manufacturing plant was located in Ontario. In June of the year in question, it moved all of its operations, including the manufacturing plant, to Mexico.

(D) Doug Stewart, a member of the Canadian Armed Forces, has been stationed in Germany for the last 5 years, including the year in question. Doug was born in Canada and lived in Canada prior to moving to Germany.

Question 6

CART Ltd. is registered for GST purposes. The following is a summary of the transactions for CART Ltd. for the month of December:

Account	Amount (Net of GST & PST)
Sales (Taxable at 7%)	$250,000
Exports	100,000
Purchase of supplies from a registrant	(30,000)
Salaries	(70,000)
Interest Expense	(20,000)
	$230,000

The GST that has to be remitted in respect of the above transaction is:

(A) $10,500

(B) $14,000

(C) $15,400

(D) $21,000

¶2,850 EXERCISES

Exercise 1

ITA: 2, 114, 115, 250(1)

Determine the form of residence, if any, for each of the following individuals.

(A) Alpha had lived all of his life in Vancouver until this year when he left with his family on August 27 to live in Los Angeles. RES

(B) Beta is a Canadian citizen who has lived in the United States with his family for the past nine years.

(C) Gamma lives in Niagara Falls, New York, but works Monday to Friday from 9:00 a.m. to 5:00 p.m. in an office in Niagara Falls, Ontario. NON

(D) Delta had lived all of his life in Dallas, Texas. He moved with his family to Calgary, Alberta, early this year to take a job with Dome Petroleum. He moved back to Dallas in the summer of this year. While in Canada he invested in the shares of a private corporation operating in Calgary. These shares were later sold during the year after he left Calgary.

(E) Epsilon was born in Philadelphia. He is now 10 years old and has never been to Canada but his mother has been consul in the Canadian Consulate there for the past 12 years.

(F) Mu is a German citizen who is married to a member of the Canadian forces stationed in Germany. She has been to Canada only for brief visits when her husband was on leave.

Exercise 2

ITA: 2, 114, 250; IT-221R3

This appeal concerns the appellant's place of residence in the taxation year 1964.

At the hearing on August 8, 1967 at Saint John, N.B., both counsel agreed on the following statement of facts:

(A) The appellant was about 58 years old in 1963.

(B) The appellant is and was at all material times an American citizen.

(C) The appellant is a sea captain and sails tankers around the world. His employer is the Cities Services Corporation of New York and the ships bear United States registry. He is paid in United States currency from New York and since 1956 he has been Master of the "S.S. Cities Services, Norfolk".

(D) Prior to 1962, the appellant and his wife had always lived in the United States. Until June 1962, they owned a house in Massachusetts.

(E) In September 1962, the appellant's wife and two of their children moved to Fredericton. At that time the two children were enrolled at Rothesay Collegiate School. In September 1963, a house was purchased at 146 Cambridge Crescent in Fredericton and was registered in joint tenancy in the names of the appellant and his wife.

(F) Prior to the purchase of the house in September 1963 the appellant's wife rented premises in Fredericton.

(G) The appellant filed a T1 Income Tax Return for his 1963 taxation year on which he stated, "the above taxpayer and his family are American citizens and are merely residents of Canada. He is a U.S. ship captain and is employed full-time by a U.S. company".

(H) The appellant paid $134.24 Canadian income tax for the 1963 taxation year after using his foreign tax credit.

(I) The routine into which the appellant and his wife have settled over the past years is as follows: The appellant receives his orders to sail from New York. He may be gone months at a time. He may dock at U.S. ports such as Galveston, Texas, or San Francisco.

(J) After the appellant's wife moved to Fredericton in 1963, the appellant retained two rooms in his sister's house at 48 Elm Street, Stoneham, Mass., U.S.A. The appellant gave his sister's number as his telephone number in the United States.

(K) At all material times, the appellant:

- worked for a U.S. company;

- was paid in U.S. currency;

- was a member of the First Baptist Church at Wakefield, Mass.;

- had two children living in the United States;

- had a bank account or accounts in the United States;

- had investments, including stocks and bonds, in the United States;

- had a pension plan with a U.S. company;

- intended and still intends to retire in Florida;

- banked his pay at the First National Bank in Malden, Mass. and enough to maintain his wife and children was sent to her. The rest stayed in the United States where he still retains a chequing account in Malden.

(L) The appellant, during 1964:

- had a joint bank account in Fredericton with his wife;

- had a family phone number in his wife's name;

- neither applied for nor received family allowance for his children;

- neither was employed nor carried on business in Canada;

- never belonged to a church or club in Fredericton;

- was never a member of a Canadian union;

- had no Canadian investments;

- owned a car jointly with his wife with a New Brunswick registry.

(M) The appellant's sole connections with Canada during 1964 were:

- his wife lived in Fredericton with one son;

- he visited Fredericton for a total of 166 days at the following times in the year:

January 3 to February 22	51 days
June 1 to August 7	68 days
November 14 to December 31	47 days
	166 days

(N) In June 1966 the house in Fredericton was sold and the appellant's wife moved back to the United States.

According to the appellant's wife's testimony, she moved in 1962 with their furniture from Massachusetts to the city of Fredericton, N.B., where she rented a house in her name to live nearer their two youngest sons, who were attending the Rothesay private boarding college in Saint John, N.B. Their two oldest children were married and another was attending the Springfield (Mass.) College. Upon moving, they sold their nine-room house in the United States.

On the advice of an American lawyer, the appellant and his wife tried to purchase a house in Canada within the year in order to avoid the American capital gains tax; unfortunately, they jointly bought one two months too late and had to pay the tax. As already mentioned, during the year 1964, her husband lived 166 days in Fredericton and spent the rest of the time at sea. While away, his pay cheques were sent directly from the New York office to the First National Bank in Malden, Mass., and his wife received monthly cheques of $600 for living expenditures in Canada. During his vacation, his pay cheques were deposited in a joint bank account in Fredericton. His trips usually lasted three to four months, and six months when bound for foreign ports. When he was unable to come home, his wife would visit him in New York or at his sister's home in Massachusetts. The appellant contended that, in 1964, he resided with his sister and could be reached there at any time, but did not enjoy the exclusive right to the use of rooms and furniture; during that period, his wife stayed there with him for three or four weeks.

¶2,850

— *REQUIRED*

Prepare an analysis of the residence issue. Evaluate in detail the alternatives in the residence issue as they relate to this fact situation for the year 1964. Discuss each possible degree of residence and its tax consequences. Weigh the relevance of the facts you consider and come to a conclusion on the case.

Exercise 3   ITA: 2, 250(4)

Determine the form of residence, if any, for each of the following corporations.

(A) Inch Incorporated was incorporated in 1982 in North Dakota. However, its directors are all residents of Saskatchewan where all meetings of the board of directors have been held since incorporation.

(B) Foot Limited was incorporated in Manitoba in 1972. However, it is managed in Japan where all directors' and shareholders' meetings have been held since incorporation.

(C) Yard Incorporated was incorporated in Ohio in 1967, but until five years ago all of the directors' meetings were held in Ontario and the president of the company was a resident of Ontario. However, five years ago the president moved to Ohio and from then on all directors' meetings have been held there.

(D) Mile Limited was incorporated in Nova Scotia in 1964 where all directors' meetings were held until 1971 when the directors moved to Boston where they met regularly.

¶2,875   ASSIGNMENT PROBLEMS

Problem 1

ITA: 2, 114, 250; IT-221R3

The client was born and raised in Canada. After obtaining his MBA in 1968, he began working as a consultant. In July 1976, the corporation of which he was a major shareholder entered into a contract with a Canadian Crown corporation to furnish consulting advice in Nigeria. Services were to commence July 15, 1976 and end January 14, 1978. A daily rate of fees was set, but total billings were not to exceed a specified maximum. The contract also provided for moving, travel and living expenses for the client and his dependants up to a specified maximum.

All fees and expenses were paid to the client's corporation in Toronto. He continued to be a shareholder, director and officer of the corporation and he remained very interested in its activities. The corporation paid the client and was instructed to deposit these payments in the client's Canadian bank account which he continued to maintain for this purpose and for the operation of the rental property that he owned. He felt that the Canadian bank account was necessary because of foreign exchange difficulties that he might otherwise encounter. He instructed the corporation not to withhold any income taxes on these payments because he intended to give up his Canadian residence status to establish an international consulting business abroad upon termination of the Nigerian contract.

Since the client had little time before leaving for Nigeria, he quickly rented the unit that he had been occupying in a duplex that he owned, on a month-to-month basis. He intended to sell the property when the market would provide him with a reasonable profit. He arranged to have his corporation manage the renting of this property for a fee which he paid to the corporation.

He stored his major furnishings and winter clothing in Canada. His smaller household and personal effects were shipped to Nigeria. He sold his car, cancelled his auto insurance and a gasoline company credit card and obtained an international driver's licence. He retained credit cards such as American Express, Visa and MasterCard, as well as his RRSP accounts. Under the contract he was also required to maintain his provincial health insurance coverage.

When he left Canada for Nigeria, he was accompanied by his friend, Martha, who had been a part of his life for over a year before their departure. She had obtained leave from her university program of studies for the fall 1976 term. The couple took up residence in a hotel suite that was converted into an apartment at the Holiday Inn in Lagos, Nigeria. No conventional living quarters were available, because of the housing market. During his stay in Nigeria, the client obtained a Nigerian driver's licence and maintained two bank accounts and two cars. He joined sports, dining and social clubs in Lagos. He was provided with an office by the Nigerian government and he carried business cards which identified him as a consultant with that government. He promoted the consulting business of his Toronto corporation actively in Nigeria in the hope of establishing the business abroad, but he did not generate sufficient business to stay in Nigeria beyond the period of the existing contract. He did not seek to extend his visa or pay any form of tax on his income in Nigeria.

Martha returned to Canada for the winter 1977 term, and then returned to Nigeria for the summer of 1977, but returned again to Canada in September 1977 to begin a new program.

By December 1977 the client had billed the limit under the contract. He vacated his apartment, sold his cars, packed up his possessions, including some artwork, textiles and other souvenirs that he had acquired, and returned to Canada.

— *REQUIRED*

Prepare a memo for the tax person in your firm who will advise the client on the income tax consequences of these facts. Evaluate in detail the alternatives in the residence issue as they relate to this fact situation. Discuss each possible degree of residence and its tax consequences. State your conclusions on the case after weighing the significance of the facts considered.

Problem 2

ITA: 2, 114, 250; IT-221R3

The client is an electronic engineer. He was born in Erith, England, on the 7th day of July 1946. During the relevant times the client held a valid passport for the United Kingdom of Great Britain and Northern Ireland. The passport declares him a British subject with a residence in the United Kingdom with the right of abode therein. The passport was issued on September 26, 1978 for a 10-year period.

Prior to the client's second marriage in 1981, his parents maintained a bedroom for him in Kent, England.

In 1981, the client married Cathy, a Canadian citizen residing in Canada who had no income of her own and was wholly dependent on the client. She has always resided continuously in Canada.

In June of 1981, a house near Apsley, Ontario, was purchased by Cathy with money supplied by the client. In September of 1982, Cathy borrowed money by way of a mortgage. The client guaranteed the mortgage which has an affidavit attached dated September 13, 1982 where he swore that he was not then a non-resident of Canada. For a purchase of property in Ontario, he would otherwise have had to pay a 20% non-resident land transfer tax.

During the three-year period at issue in this case, 1981 to 1983, the client regularly returned to Canada when he was not working. Each time the client entered Canada, his passport was stamped by Immigration Canada with the majority of the entries setting out a date upon which he must leave Canada. The authorized period of stay varied from five days to 45 days. On some of the stamps the word "visitor" was written in by an immigration official. Throughout the three-year period, the client was employed full-time by a non-resident corporation and all work was performed outside Canada on an oil rig at sea. All income was deposited directly into a Canadian bank.

The client indicated that he was charged in Provincial Court for failure to file an income tax return for 1981 and was acquitted (likely on the basis that he was not required to file in Canada for that year).

During the three-year period, the client indicated or claimed that he:

(a) never filed a tax return or paid income tax anywhere;

(b) was not allowed to work in Canada;

(c) was given a fixed date to leave Canada on entry (i.e., not allowed to stay in Canada);

(d) could not join OHIP, pay EI, maintain an RRSP or join a pension plan;

(e) was out of the country more than 183 days per year;

(f) had no desire to work in Canada;

(g) had a residence in Britain in the home of his mother and father;

(h) held a mortgage in Britain on his first wife's house;

(i) could not live a normal life in Canada as he had to leave every 27 days; and

(j) had a bank account with the Royal Bank of Canada both in Canada and the Caribbean.

In 1984, the client purchased a car in Canada. In 1985, the client:

(a) obtained a Canadian driver's licence;

(b) obtained a Canadian visa; and

(c) became a landed immigrant in Canada.

— REQUIRED

Prepare a memo for the tax person in your firm who will advise the client on the income tax consequences of these facts. Evaluate in detail the alternatives in the residence issue as they relate to this fact situation for the period in question. Discuss each degree of residence and its tax consequences as it applies to this fact situation. Note that in this case full-time residence under the common law principle could only result from a "fresh start" at a point in time in the period in question. Therefore, part-time residence would depend on there being a period of non-residence prior to a "fresh start", if any.

State your conclusion on this case after appropriately weighing the significance of the facts considered. Your conclusion should indicate whether the client became a full-time resident at any point in the period or remained a non-resident throughout the period. If you conclude that he became a full-time resident, indicate the point in time when the "fresh start" was made.

Problem 3

ITA: 2, 114, 250; IT-221R3

The client is a mechanical engineer, born and educated in England. The client was married in England in 1962 and he and his wife, Dawning, had three sons born in 1964, 1966 and 1969. In 1967, the client and his wife and family moved to Canada where he immediately commenced employment with Imperial Oil in Sarnia, Ontario. With Imperial Oil and/or its parent corporation, Exxon Corporation, the client and his family moved to various locations throughout Canada until 1988. In 1988, while residing and working in Edmonton, Alberta, the client was offered the position as deputy manager of the Exxon refinery at Port Dickson in Malaysia. He accepted the position because it presented the opportunity to likely become manager of this same refinery within a three-year period.

At the time of his acceptance of the above position, the client and his wife were experiencing marriage difficulties. As a result of these difficulties, it was mutually agreed that the client would go to Malaysia on his own. His wife and youngest son remained in the family home in Edmonton. His older sons were living on their own by this time.

The client and his employer undertook the following steps in preparation for his move from Canada:

- his employer obtained a work permit for him in Malaysia;

- he sold his car;

- he cancelled his provincial health plan;

- his employer obtained private health insurance for him;

- he closed all of his existing bank accounts at Royal Bank;

- he opened a savings account at the Bank of Nova Scotia because this bank had a branch in Kuala Lumpur, the capital of Malaysia;

- he allowed his membership in the Edmonton Petroleum Club to lapse; and

- he allowed his participation in the Model Guided Plane Association to lapse.

The client moved to Malaysia in the last few days of September 1988. He stayed in a hotel in Malaysia for the first few weeks and then moved into a company-provided home. His employer charged him with a monthly rent of $1,000 for his use of this house. He took the following items with him from Canada to Malaysia:

- all of his clothes and personal effects; and

- an airplane kit for model guided planes and a radio control transmitter for his hobby of model guided planes.

Once in Malaysia, the client undertook to establish Port Dickson as his home. To this end, he:

- purchased a car;

- obtained a Malaysian driver's licence;

- joined the Port Dickson yacht club which was, in fact, a social/recreational club;

- joined the petroleum club at Kuala Lumpur;

- opened a chequing account at the Bank of Nova Scotia in Kuala Lumpur;

- opened a chequing account at the Standard Chartered Bank at Port Dickson;

- acquired two Malaysian credit cards;

- became a patient at a Port Dickson medical clinic and, as well, made regular visits to a dentist in Port Dickson; and

- joined the Port Dickson Golf Club in 1991.

In accordance with Exxon corporate policy, the client remained on the payroll and in the pension plan of the Canadian subsidiary. His monthly pay was deposited into his Edmonton bank account. There was no income tax withheld at source on the client's salary because the Canadian subsidiary knew that he was working full-time outside of Canada. The total cost of his salary and related benefits (including pension) were charged by the Canadian subsidiary to Exxon Corporation International.

The client made only two visits to Canada during the period from 1989 through 1994. He visited for 14 days in 1990 and 14 days again in 1992. On each of these visits, he stayed in the family home in Edmonton. During the same period, the client's spouse made eight visits to him in Malaysia. She made no visits after January 1992, but prior to that time, the length of her visits ranged from 19 days to 32 days. On each of these visits, she stayed with the client in his Malaysian home. The client and his wife remained married throughout the relevant period.

The client maintained the following Canadian investments while he was residing in Malaysia:

- his 50% interest in the family home in Edmonton;

- a 50% investment in a rental property which his wife purchased after his move to Malaysia, because she thought it would be a good investment;

- his RRSP;

- his company savings plan; and

- a few personal shares in Canadian public companies.

He did maintain his memberships in the Canadian Society of Mechanical Engineers and the Association of Professional Engineers and Geologists of Alberta.

The client became manager of the Port Dickson plant in 1991 and eventually retired from Exxon in the summer of 1995 under the terms of an early retirement package. Upon retirement from Exxon, the client returned to Edmonton to the family home. In late 1995 the client started seeking employment in Malaysia and in January 1996 he and his wife went to Malaysia hoping that he would find employment and they would both live there. His wife returned to Canada in February 1996 and he moved on to Thailand where he stayed through July 1997 (working for the 12-month period from August 1996 through July 1997). When the Thailand employment ended, the client returned to Canada. He and his wife then worked out a plan of separation.

— REQUIRED

Prepare a memo for the tax person in your firm who will advise the client on the income tax consequences of these facts. Evaluate in detail the alternatives in the residence issue as they relate to this fact situation for the period October 1, 1988 through the summer of 1995. Discuss each possible degree of residence and its tax consequences. State your conclusions on this case after weighing the relevance of the facts you have considered.

Problem 4

ITA: 2, 250, 253

Far Eastern Airlines is a company incorporated in Korea in 1974. Its general manager and other active officers of the company are resident in Korea and have their offices there. The directors and corporate officers of the company live in Korea as well.

During the year in question, its sole business was operating an international airline which had no landing rights in Canada. However, in that year it had raised capital on the Canadian market for its international operations by selling an issue of its stock through an investment dealer in Vancouver. The vice-president–finance of the company, who believed the stock issue would sell better in Canada, travelled from the head office in Korea to Vancouver to instruct the investment dealer.

The stock issue was highly successful and the proceeds of the issue were accumulated in a bank account in Vancouver. During the several months in the year in question when these funds were being accumulated, the company became aware of an opportunity to purchase a vast quantity of aviation fuel at a very low price. A purchasing agent was dispatched from the head office in Korea to Canada to complete the purchase using some of the funds accumulated from the stock issue. The fuel was stored in Canada temporarily in rented facilities pending shipment to San Francisco, where it could be used by aircraft landing there. Subsequently, the company was unable to make suitable arrangements for shipment. The fuel was sold to a Canadian buyer at a considerable profit. All contracts involved in the purchase and sale transactions were drawn up by a Canadian lawyer under the direction of the purchasing agent who operated from a hotel room in Vancouver during the period of the transactions.

— REQUIRED

Prepare a memo for the tax person in your firm who will advise Far Eastern Airlines on the income tax consequences of these facts. Evaluate in detail the alternatives in the residence issue as they relate to this fact situation. Discuss each possible degree of residence and its tax consequences. State your conclusions on the case after considering the relevant international tax agreement and after appropriately weighing the significance of the facts considered.

Problem 5

ITA: 2, 250, 253

Wong Computer Games Inc. (WCG) was incorporated in the state of Illinois in the last decade. The founding shareholder, Mr. Andrew Wong, is an inventor of computer simulation models. His products include a wide variety of computer games as well as some programs which have industrial applications.

Mr. Wong is the controlling shareholder of WCG. His brother owns a minority interest, as does Walter Bends, a long-time associate of Mr. Wong, who often collaborates in the development of new products. All three shareholders are resident in Chicago. In addition to Mr. Wong, the WCG Board of Directors includes George Wolf, who represents the Chicago law firm, which advises WCG, and Tony

Aster who represents First National Bank of Chicago, which provides most of the financing for WCG's operations. The Board meets approximately every six months to review financial results, discuss product development and decide on strategic initiatives. The meetings are usually held in the boardroom of George Wolf's law firm.

Two years ago, Mr. Wong achieved an industry breakthrough when he developed his latest game, SuperPilot. SuperPilot is a computer game in which the operator attempts to safely land a disabled airliner. SuperPilot provided special effects which were far beyond those available in any other commercially available product. Although other WCG products were only available in the U.S. market, Wong was convinced that SuperPilot would be a global success. To ensure the competitive advantage would be maintained, Wong Computer Games Inc. took the required legal steps to ensure copyright and patent protection of the program in a variety of countries, including Canada.

By last year, SuperPilot was doing very well in the U.S. market and WCG began to launch the product in other markets. Walter Bends was assigned responsibility for the Canadian market and took a short-term lease on a Toronto apartment in March of last year. WCG established a bank account with a Toronto branch of a Canadian bank. This account was to be used by Bends for promotional expenses and other incidentals. All other expenses, including Bends' salary, continued to be paid from Chicago.

Bends attended a number of Canadian trade shows, exhibiting the SuperPilot program. Prospective purchasers were provided with SuperPilot game cartridges as a promotional item. Bends was given the authority to sign supply contracts which would permit the purchaser a one-month supply of cartridges. At the end of the one month, if the distributor was still interested, a longer-term supply contract would be required. Bends was not permitted, however, to sign any of these long-term agreements without receiving prior approval from the WCG Board. All game cartridges, including promotional cartridges, were supplied from Chicago. If the product began to sell well in Canada, the WCG Board had discussed establishing a Canadian warehouse.

By January of this year, it became obvious that SuperPilot was not going to be a Canadian success. No distributors had requested a long-term supply contract and only one, Pete's Gaming Emporium, had agreed to stock the product for one month. At the end of the month, sales had been so slow that Pete's was not interested in continuing the relationship. Bends returned to Chicago, the bank account was closed, and WCG refocussed its marketing efforts on the U.S. market.

— REQUIRED

Prepare a memo for the tax person in your firm who will advise WCG on the income tax consequences of these facts. Evaluate in detail the alternatives in the residence issue as they relate to this fact situation during last year and this year. Discuss each possible degree of residence and its tax consequences. State your conclusions on the case after appropriately weighing the significance of the facts considered.

Problem 6

ITA: 2, 250, 253

Capitol Life Insurance Company ("Capitol") was incorporated in the U.S.A. in the state of Colorado at the turn of the century. Its head office had always been in Denver, Colorado. Capitol was a subsidiary of Providence Capitol Corporation which in turn was a subsidiary of Gulf & Western Industries Inc. ("Gulf"). Gulf owned approximately 600 subsidiaries, 240 of which were in turn owned by Associates Corporation of North America ("Associates"). Six of these latter corporations were Canadian companies.

Capitol was in the business of writing individual and group life and health insurance policies. Capitol also wrote creditor's group life and health insurance policies for the 240 finance companies which were part of the Gulf group of companies. Under a creditor's group insurance policy, Capitol would pay to the finance company, upon the death or disability of the borrower, the outstanding amount of the loan in the case of death or the required instalment payments in the case of disability. The costs of the insurance were effectively passed on to the borrower, either as a separate charge or as a higher interest rate.

In the late 1960s, Capitol planned to expand into Canada and obtained licences in nearly every province and obtained federal registration under the *Foreign Insurance Companies Act* ("FICA"). The FICA registration required that Capitol name a chief agent in Canada and that he be given a power of attorney. Capitol was also required to make deposits with the insurance superintendent and maintain assets in Canada. Two bank accounts were opened in Canada. The planned expansion into Canada was cancelled. However, the licences and registration were maintained. This required that Canadian representatives and agents be retained as locations for the licensing authorities to serve legal notices. All reports to the licensing authorities and all inquiries of the licensing authorities were to be passed through the Canadian chief agent. The reports to the licensing authorities were prepared in Denver and all inquiries were passed on to Denver by the chief agent. The chief agent was required to maintain copies of records required by the superintendent of insurance. None of Capitol's representatives or agents ever solicited insurance or were expected or authorized to do any business.

The chief agent countersigned the cheques on Capitol's general bank account on the requirement of the insurance superintendent. He had no means to verify the legitimacy of the cheques; as all books and records were maintained in Denver where the cheques were prepared. The agent later deposited the premiums received in an effort to streamline the former procedure of having the premiums sent to Denver and then sent back to Canada through the bank for deposit into the Canadian general account to meet licensing requirements. All investments were administered and managed in Denver.

Capitol did not have anyone in Canada who solicited insurance business, collected premiums, processed or paid claims, administered investments or countersigned any claim cheques. Capitol had five group insurance contracts under which the lives of Canadian residents were insured. These policies were all issued to affiliated companies without solicitation in Canada. Two of these policies were creditor's group insurance policies with Associates. They were each drafted in accordance with Denver law and signed in Denver by the president of Associates, who was a resident of Indiana. Associates was shown as the insured company and paid all premiums. On the insistence of the Canadian insurance authorities, the wording of the agreements was amended to reflect "a premium collection fee". The original agreement provided for a retroactive adjustment of premiums based upon past claim experience. Capitol and Associates continued to administer, interpret and apply the agreement in the same manner as the original agreement. Blank insurance certificates were also required to be issued so that they could be provided to borrowers whose loans were insured as a way of informing them of the terms of the coverage. The coverage took place independently of the issuance of a certificate to an individual. These certificates listed the Canadian head office of Capitol as being in Don Mills, Ontario, as required by the federal insurance superintendent. This office was never used as a head office. The federal insurance superintendent also required the issuance of a brochure for the information of the Canadian borrowers whose lives and health were insured.

The income that Capitol received from the Canadian insurance and investments represented a very small proportion of its total revenue. Canadian operations were not kept separately from U.S. operations, no Denver personnel were charged with Canadian operations, and there were no special Canadian claim forms or procedures. The only separation of Canadian business from U.S. operations to be found in the accounts of Capitol was to comply with the Canadian insurance authorities. All corporate meetings as well as all levels of management took place in the U.S.A.

— REQUIRED

Prepare a memo for the tax person in your firm who will advise Capitol on the income tax consequences of these facts. Evaluate in detail the alternatives in the residence issue as they relate to this fact situation. Discuss each possible degree of residence and its tax consequences. State your conclusions on this case after weighing the relevance of the facts you have considered.

[For more problems and solutions thereto, see the CD accompanying this book.]

¶2,880 ADVISORY CASE

Transfer to France

Sally has just come to you for advice on a possible job transfer to Paris, France. She is currently working for a large private corporation located in St. Catharines, Ontario. It is now April and the president of the company has asked Sally, who is the company's computer network expert, to move to Paris for at least two years. Her time there may extend beyond two years, but that will depend on the success of the project she will be working on.

Sally is married to Harry and they have two daughters, ages six and eight. The company wants Sally to be in Paris and working by May 15, so she will have to leave by May 10 to get there and settled in time. She is planning to rent a furnished apartment when she arrives. Her children are in school and won't be done until the end of June. Harry has his own career as a school teacher and is willing to take an unpaid leave of absence for two years, but he can't leave until the end of June or middle of July at the earliest.

Sally and Harry enjoy golf and have recently joined a fairly exclusive club in the St. Catharines area, after an eight-year waiting period and after paying a large initiation fee. They do not wish to give up this membership. Their home is located just outside the city on 20 acres and they are very reluctant to sell it, as they would not be able to replace it on their return.

Both Sally and Harry grew up in the St. Catharines area and their families still live there. Sally's parents and Harry's parents are retired.

Sally and Harry both want to move to Paris, and they have come to you for tax advice on whether they could be considered non-residents of Canada, or what, if anything, they could do to achieve this result.

Chapter 3

Employment Income

LEARNING GOALS

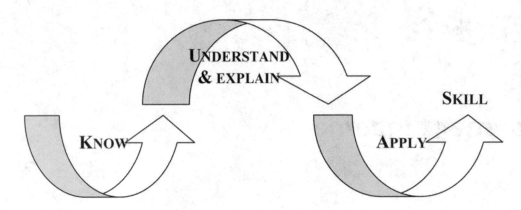

Know

By the end of this chapter you should know the basic provisions of the *Income Tax Act* that relate to employment income and expenses. Completing the Review Questions (¶3,800) and Multiple Choice Questions (¶3,825) is a good way to learn the technical provisions.

Understand and Explain

You should understand and be able to explain how employment income and expenses are calculated and why the provisions are designed the way they are. Completing the Exercises (¶3,850) is a good way to deepen your understanding of the material.

Apply

You should be able to apply your knowledge and understanding of employment income and expenses to real life situations. Completing the Assignment Problems (¶3,875) is an excellent way to develop your ability to apply the material in increasingly complex situations.

OVERVIEW

The first source of income mentioned in the income aggregation rules in Division B is employment income. Net employment income, that is, employment inclusions minus employment deductions, is determined by the rules in subdivision a of Division B in Part I of the Act. This determination, although very basic, is important because it will be used in subsequent provisions to compute the limitations on the deductibility of certain items such as retirement plan contributions and child care expenses. The following list indicates the sections and basic content of this subdivision:

ITA: 3(*a*)

Inclusions:

Sec. 5 — Salary, wages and gratuities received.

Sec. 6 — Other income inclusions arising from employment.

Sec. 7 — Stock option benefits.

Deductions:

Sec. 8 — Deductions allowed against employment income.

It is worth noting that the only expenses that can be deducted against employment income are those specifically set out in sec. 8.

ITA: 8(2)

The following chart will help locate the major provisions discussed in this chapter.

PART I — DIVISION B

SUBDIVISION a

EMPLOYMENT INCOME

DIVISION		SUBDIVISION		SECTION	
A	Liability for tax		Basic rules		
B	Computation of income	a	Office or employment	5	Basic rules
C	Computation of taxable income	b	Business or property	6-7	Inclusions
D	Taxable income earned in Canada by non-residents	c	Capital gains and losses	8	Deductions
E	Computation of tax	d	Other income		
E.1	Minimum tax	e	Other deductions		
F	Special rules	f	Rules relating to computation of income		
G	Deferred and other special income arrangements	g	Amounts not included in income		
H	Exemptions	h	Cdn corporations and shareholders		
I	Returns, Assessments, payments, appeals	i	Shareholders of non-resident corporations		
J	Appeals to the courts	j	Partnerships		
		k	Trusts		

Examine carefully the contents of these sections, especially sections 6 and 8, which contain many specific inclusions and deductions from employment sources. Note that the T1 income tax return (an individual's tax return) does not actually show net employment income as a single number, since the return separates employment inclusions from employment deductions. While the net result is, of necessity, the same as that achieved by the Act, the T1 return approach does not show a net income from employment figure that is very important for subsequent calculations.

This chapter will consider, first, whether a person is an employee or self-employed. Next, the major inclusions of employment income and the major deductions from employment income are considered. Since the system of rules that allows for deductions pertaining to the employment use of cars is extensive, these rules are considered in a separate part of this chapter. The deduction by an employee of expenditures which include GST may provide the employee with a GST rebate. The income tax implications of this rebate will be considered after the deductions for income tax purposes have been discussed.

¶3,000 BASIC RULES

¶3,010 Employed Versus Self-Employed or Independent Contractor

¶3,015 Overview

The issue of whether a person is an employee or self-employed (i.e., an independent contractor) often arises in connection with the deductibility of expenses. The issue is important because independent contractors are treated as businesses and are allowed to deduct all reasonable expenses incurred for the purpose of gaining or producing income from business, except capital outlays such as the cost of land and other fixed assets. Employees, on the other hand, are strictly limited to those deductions specifically listed in section 8. Hence, for income tax purposes, self-employed status may be preferred by both the worker and the payer. In addition, the employee versus independent contractor issue is important in determining whether the employer is required to withhold income tax, Canada Pension Plan contributions or Employment Insurance premiums from amounts paid to the individual.

ITA: 67
ITA: 18(1)(*a*)
ITA: 18(1)(*b*)
ITA: 8(2)

For labour law purposes, individuals usually prefer to be employees to gain protection for their severance, pension and injury compensation rights. While many individuals would prefer to be an employee for labour law purposes and self-employed for tax purposes this option is not available.

There is no single test that is decisive in determining whether an individual is an employee or an independent contractor. In the case of *Wiebe Door Services Ltd. v. M.N.R.* (a case dealing with Canada Pension Plan and Employment Insurance issues), the Federal Court of Appeal, a senior-level court, emphasized the need to examine the interaction of all of the facts in a situation and the following interrelated tests, which have evolved in the courts:

87 DTC 5025 (F.C.A.)

- economic reality or entrepreneur test;
- integration or organization test; and
- specific result test.

Each of the tests, which determine the nature of the relationship rather than the nature of the services, must be understood. It is important to know how the tests work to distinguish between an individual who is considered to be employed and an individual who can be considered to be self-employed.

¶3,020 The economic reality or entrepreneur test

The *economic reality or entrepreneur test* examines several economic factors and draws from them an inference as to the nature of the relationship. In particular, three dimensions have been advanced involving (a) control, (b) ownership of the tools, and (c) chance of profit/risk of loss. In a civil law case,[1] the Supreme Court of Canada added another factor to consider: the degree of responsibility for investment and management held by the worker.

¶3,020.10 *Control*

The control subtest, listed as part of the economic reality or entrepreneur test above, determines whether the individual is directed by someone who is in a position to order or require not only what is to be done but how it is to be done. Where such control is exercised over the individual, an employer–employee relationship is implied. Hence, control is evidenced by the situation of an individual who is subject to a person who has the right to give orders and instructions to the individual regarding the manner in which to carry out the work.[2] In the view of the CRA, control "exists if the person for whom services are performed has the right to control the amount, the nature, and the management of the work to be done and the manner of doing it".[3]

---

[1] *671122 Ontario Ltd. v. Sagaz Industries Canada Inc.*, [2001] 2 SCR 983 (S.C.C.).

[2] This test was applied in the cases of *Di Francesco v. M.N.R.*, 64 DTC 106 (T.A.B.), and *Compton v. M.N.R.*, 65 DTC 578 (T.A.B.).

[3] *Interpretation Bulletin* IT-525R, "Performing Artists" (Consolidated), May 16, 2001, paragraph 3.

At the turn of the twentieth century the control test was regarded as a conclusive test. However, in our increasingly complex business environment, control is no longer appropriate as a conclusive test, but is just one of the four tests which must be examined together as part of the economic reality or entrepreneur test. The shortcomings of the control test reveal themselves in circumstances where it is difficult, because of the nature of the work, to exercise any control over the manner in which the work is performed. In particular, the courts have found the test to be too inflexible in determining the issue in respect of professionals and highly skilled tradespeople who are hired for their knowledge and expertise; that is, they do not need to be told how to do a job.

The control test was considered by the Federal Court of Appeal in the case of *The Royal Winnipeg Ballet v. M.N.R.* At issue was whether the dancers of the Royal Winnipeg Ballet (RWB) were employees or self-employed independent contractors. Justice Sharlow, in finding that the dancers were independent contractors, made the following statement, at paragraph 66 of the decision: 2006 DTC 6323 (F.C.A.)

> The control factor in this case, as in most cases, requires particular attention. It seems to me that while the degree of control exercised by the RWB over the work of the dancers is extensive, it is no more than is needed to stage a series of ballets over a well planned season of performances. If the RWB were to stage a ballet using guest artists in all principal roles, the RWB's control over the guest artists would be the same as if each role were performed by a dancer engaged for the season. If it is accepted (as it must be), that a guest artist may accept a role with the RWB without becoming its employee, then the element of control must be consistent with the guest artist being an independent contractor. Therefore, the elements of control in this case cannot reasonably be considered to be inconsistent with the parties' understanding that the dancers were independent contractors.

¶3,020.20   *Ownership of tools*

In cases where the taxpayer doing the work supplies neither funds nor equipment needed to do the work, takes no financial risks and has no liability, the courts have applied the economic reality test and held that the taxpayer is an employee. On the other hand, the major tool necessary for some work is the knowledge, expertise or skill of the person doing the work, as in the case of a professional consultant. In that case, the "ownership of the tools" subtest may not be conclusive.

¶3,020.30   *Chance of profit/risk of loss*

Where the taxpayer doing the work has a chance of making a profit, risks incurring a loss from bad debts, damages to assets or delivery delays, and must cover operating costs, there is evidence of an independent contractor or self-employed status.

¶3,025   Integration or organization test

The *integration or organization test* examines whether the individual doing the work is economically dependent on the organization. The more dependent the individual is on the organization, the more he or she will appear to be an employee. In the case of *Wiebe Door Services Ltd. v. M.N.R.*, the court held that the correct perspective was that of the individual in terms of how dependent the individual is on the organization. Consideration can be given, for example, to the proportion of the individual's income derived from the organization and the availability to the individual of benefits available to employees of the organization. In applying this test, it is important to determine whether services are performed as an individual in business on his or her own account. 87 DTC 5025 (F.C.A.)

¶3,030   Specific result test

The *specific result test* has been used to distinguish an employee from an independent contractor. An employer–employee relationship usually contemplates the employee putting his or her personal services at the disposal of his or her employer during a given period of time without reference to a specified result and, generally, envisages the accomplishment of work on an ongoing basis. On the other hand, where a worker and payer agree that certain specified work will be done, possibly, with the use of assistants provided by the worker, it may be inferred that an independent contractor relationship exists. In the CRA's view, this test is satisfied where the facts suggest that "a person is engaged to achieve a defined objective and is given all the freedom to obtain the desired result".[4] The facts used in the application of the *integration or organization test* may, also, be useful in the specific result test since the tests appear to be closely related.[5]

¶3,035   Other considerations

In the *Royal Winnipeg Ballet* case, the Federal Court of Appeal considered the relevance of the intention of the parties. Justice Sharlow, at paragraph 62, indicated that "a stipulation in a contract as to the legal nature of the relationship created by the contract cannot be determinative". However, Justice Sharlow went on to state, at paragraph 64, ". . . it seems to me wrong in principle to set aside, as worthy of no weight, the uncontradicted evidence of the parties as to their common understanding of their legal relationship, even if that evidence cannot be conclusive". Justice Sharlow concluded, at paragraph 67, ". . . this is a case where the common understanding of the parties as to the nature of their legal relationship is borne out by the contractual terms and the other relevant facts".

The CRA does not have a specific Interpretation Bulletin dealing with the differences between employees and self-employed individuals. However, there is a brief description of the general principles involved in an Interpretation Bulletin, "Visual Artists and Writers". A more detailed application of the tests or factors used in the case of performing artists is provided in another Interpretation Bulletin, entitled "Performing Artists".   IT-504R2, par. 2   IT-525R, par. 3–8

Example Problem

The taxpayer, a professional pathologist, was appointed Director of the Clinical Chemistry Laboratory of a hospital for a period of five years. He reported to the hospital's Director of Laboratories who advised the taxpayer what his work involved and decided the amount to be paid to the taxpayer. The hospital supplied all the necessary laboratory facilities and equipment. The laboratory conducted tests exclusively for the patients of the hospital, although some tests were referred out by the hospital to private laboratories.

The taxpayer's main responsibility was to ensure that the output and quality of the work done in the laboratory by 15 technologists who were employees of the hospital was acceptable. He did not have the authority to hire or fire any of the technologists who worked under him, but could, if necessary, request additional help from the hospital's administration. The taxpayer did not have to arrange for or pay his replacement if he was absent from the laboratory for vacations or other lengthy periods of time. Substitute pathologists were paid directly by the hospital.

The normal deductions from employees' salaries were made by the hospital in respect of the taxpayer's remuneration. The taxpayer also participated in the group insurance plan toward which the hospital made substantial contributions.

— REQUIRED

Is the taxpayer in this case an employee or an independent contractor? In presenting your answer, discuss the tests that are applied by the courts in this type of situation and consider how the facts relate to these tests. What are the general tax consequences of your findings?

---

[4] IT-525R, *supra* note 2.

[5] The specific result test was adopted in the case of *Alexander v. M.N.R.*, 70 DTC 6006 (Ex. Ct.).

— SOLUTION

The following has been excerpted from the decision of the Chairman of the Tax Review Board in the case of *Hauser v. M.N.R.*

78 DTC 1532 (T.R.B.)

1. *The Economic Reality or Entrepreneur Test:* The control aspect of this test, which in certain circumstances is still applicable, has been found by the courts to be too inflexible in determining the issue, particularly in respect of professionals and highly trained, skilled tradespeople. In this instance, it is clear that the Director of Laboratories could not or would not interfere in the taxpayer's exercise of his professional skills. However, even though the usual strict controls of an employer over the employee's work are not found in this instance, it does not automatically rule out the possibility that an employer–employee relationship does in fact exist. The taxpayer as a staff member, therefore was under the hospital's control for the general assignment and reporting of his work and for the amount of remuneration that would be allocated to him. Although these factors would not be present if the appellant were in fact a private practitioner, the application of the control test is not, in the circumstances of this appeal, a wholly satisfactory or conclusive one.

The other aspects of the economic reality or entrepreneur test, however, are particularly revealing if we compare the economics of the taxpayer's professional activities in the hospital's chemistry laboratory with that of a private practitioner operating his own private laboratory. In the latter case, the private practitioner runs the risk of financing the equipment, supplying the help necessary to operate and administer his laboratory and he then has to ensure that he has sufficient clients to render his laboratory operation economically viable. The taxpayer, on the other hand, uses the equipment and supplies which are all furnished by the hospital. He neither hires nor fires any of the technologists who work under him but can, if necessary, request additional help from the hospital's administration and all the technologists and clerks working in the hospital's biochemistry laboratory are hired and paid directly by the hospital. The taxpayer does not seek out clients; the tests are made for patients of the hospital. The evidence is that in his absence from the laboratory the taxpayer is not obligated to arrange for or pay his replacement. Substitute pathologists are paid directly by the hospital. Note how, in this case, the "ownership of the tools" subtest pertaining to the knowledge, skills and expertise of the professional is not conclusive. These "tools" are provided by the professional, whether he acts in the capacity of an employee or of an independent contractor, in this type of situation.

On applying the Economic Reality Test to the facts, there is no valid evidence which might support the proposition that the taxpayer was under a contract for services of a self-employed individual. All the evidence tends to establish that, from an economic reality point of view, the taxpayer was under a contract of service and, therefore, an employee of the hospital.

2. *The Integration or Organization Test:* The taxpayer was appointed for a period of five years by the hospital under a contract of service. By this agreement, his knowledge and skills in pathology or in any other related field, in which the taxpayer may have been qualified, was employed in the hospital's general organization in the treatment of patients. The facts suggest an economic dependence on the organization. In such circumstances the courts have held that the taxpayer was an employee.

3. *The Specific Result Test:* This test distinguishes a contract for services of a self-employed individual from a contract of service of an employee. The taxpayer was appointed as Director of the Clinical Chemistry Laboratory of the hospital for a five-year period on a full-time basis. His income from the hospital, though paid periodically, was calculated on a yearly basis. It was the taxpayer's personal professional services which were at the disposition of the hospital and the taxpayer's work was done on a continuous day-to-day basis without there being any limited or specified amount of work that the taxpayer had, by contract, to accomplish. The taxpayer had to do the work personally and did not employ or pay substitute part-time pathologists to do his work in his absence. According to the Specific Result Test one can reasonably conclude that the taxpayer was an employee of the hospital. Note how closely related the conditions of this test are to those used in the Integration or Organization Test. In fact, the Specific Result Test might be regarded as a later stage in the evolution of the Integration or Organization Test.

As a result of applying all three tests to the facts of this case, there is nothing that supports the contention that the taxpayer was under a contract for services or was an independent contractor. All the evidence clearly indicates that the taxpayer was under a contract of service and was an employee.

The consequence of this finding is that the taxpayer's income would be taxed as employment income with the resultant restricted deductions. In this particular case, the taxpayer was allowed a deduction for professional dues in the amount of $366 in 1975, but denied deductions for property taxes, business fees, liability insurance, books and journals, telephone, accounting fees, and travels and conventions in the amount of $2,190. In addition, the payer would be required to withhold from each payment the appropriate taxes at source.

¶3,040   Salary, Wages, and Other Remuneration Including Gratuities

"Salary" and "wages" are terms in common use, but "remuneration" has a somewhat more general meaning. Remuneration includes such items as bonuses, tips, honoraria, and commissions paid to employees. However, as discussed in Chapter 1, where specific words are followed by general words, the general words are confined to the same scope as the specific words. As a result, "remuneration" must be in the same scope as "salary" and "wages".   ITA: 5

Numerous court cases have considered remuneration from employment as opposed to some other type of payment.[6] Two cases illustrate how payment by an employer for an expense incurred by the employee can be considered other remuneration or a benefit. In the case of *Pavel Bure v. The Queen*, the payment of the hockey player's agent by the hockey club was included in the player's income. In the case of *Gernhart v. The Queen*, a tax equalization payment made by an employer to compensate for higher Canadian taxes was considered to be part of the employee's compensation.   2000 DTC 1507 (T.C.C.)
98 DTC 6026 (F.C.A.)

Notice that gratuities are specifically listed for inclusion. All amounts, received by an individual in his or her capacity as an employee both from his or her employer and from others by reason of his or her employment, must be included in income. Thus, in addition to any bonus or honorarium received from an employer, an individual must include any tips received from his or her employer's customers. However, if a payment is made to such an individual without reference to his or her employment and primarily as a personal gift, it is not income. This becomes a question of fact. The magnitude and frequency of payments are also factors.[7]   ITA: 5

¶3,050   Amounts Received

The use of the word "received" in the Act means that the employee must report employment income on the cash basis. Thus, advancing or deferring a payment such as a bonus will affect the level of income of an individual for a given year. However, the voluntary deferment of an unconditional right to receive remuneration has not been accepted and, as a result, has been held to be taxable in the year it became receivable, as illustrated by the case of *Blenkarn v. M.N.R.* For example, an employee who was legally entitled to receive a bonus in December asks her employer to defer the payment until January. She would be deemed to have received the bonus in December under the principle of constructive receipt, as established in common-law court decisions. That principle would include an amount that is effectively received, or the receipt of which can be controlled by the recipient, if not actually received. In the case of *Markman v. M.N.R.*, the court held that a retroactive pay increase over a number of taxation years is included in income in the year of receipt.   ITA: 5

63 DTC 581 (T.A.B.)

89 DTC 253 (T.C.C.)

---

[6] Court cases include: *Bell v. M.N.R.*, 62 DTC 1115 (Ex. Ct.), *Grant v. M.N.R.*, 67 DTC 249 (T.A.B.), and *Curran v. M.N.R.*, 59 DTC 1247 (S.C.C.), which will be considered again under subsection 6(3).

[7] For a case on this issue see *McLuhan v. M.N.R.*, 63 DTC 211 (T.A.B.).

¶3,100   SPECIFIC INCLUSIONS

Most benefits that must be included in income from employment are specified in section 6, with section 7 limited to the benefit from employer stock options. The major list of benefits in section 6 is contained in subsection 6(1), with its many paragraphs listing different specific taxable benefits. Subsections 6(1.1) to (23) provide mostly amplification, exceptions, formulae or limits for benefits listed in subsection 6(1). Thus, when attempting to determine if a particular benefit is taxable, scanning the list of paragraph headings in subsection 6(1) should be the first step.

Note that before the rules of the paragraphs in subsection 6(1) are presented, there is a preamble which provides that amounts established to be taxable in the following paragraphs are to be "included in computing the income of a taxpayer for a taxation year as income from an office or employment". Also, each paragraph of subsection 6(1) is a continuation of the sentence commenced in the preamble. In essence, the single sentence which is subsection 6(1) covers several pages of the Act! This is a function of the particular drafting style chosen for the Act in which each subsection consists of only one sentence.

¶3,110   Value of Board and Lodging

Beyond establishing that the value of board and lodging is a taxable benefit, as was the situation in the case of *Cockerill v. M.N.R.*, the inclusion of the value of board and lodging presents a valuation problem. In pars. 4 and 28 of the Interpretation Bulletin entitled "Employees' Fringe Benefits", the CRA indicates that board and lodging must be valued for tax purposes at the fair market value less any amount charged to the employee. However, if a "reasonable amount" is recovered from the employee, then board and subsidized meals are not subject to this rule. The CRA indicates that a "reasonable amount" is one which covers costs, including food preparation and service costs. Where a lesser amount is recovered, the difference between that amount and the above total costs will be a taxable benefit.   `65 DTC 525 (T.A.B.)` `IT-470R`

As an exception to the benefit rule that requires the inclusion of the value of board and lodging, the Act excludes from the income of an employee, in carefully defined circumstances of employment at a special work site or remote location, the benefits he or she might otherwise be said to derive from board and lodging and transportation. The conditions that must be met for the exception to apply may be summarized as follows: `ITA: 6(1)(a), 6(6)`

(a) the special work site must be a distance away from the employee's ordinary residence such that he or she cannot reasonably be expected to travel daily, and the temporary nature of the duties or the remoteness of the work site must be such that it is not reasonable to establish and maintain a self-contained domestic establishment; and

(b) the board and lodging is necessary for not less than 36 hours and, if an allowance in respect of the board and lodging is paid by the employer, the allowance is not in excess of a reasonable amount.

Note that an employee's ordinary residence, referred to in part (a) above, is one in which he or she maintains a "self-contained domestic establishment" as his or her principal place of residence.   `ITA: 248(1)`

This topic is covered in more detail in the CRA Interpretation Bulletin entitled "Employment at Special Work Sites or Remote Work Locations".   `IT-91R4`

The CRA often uses a "comfort" letter, which is a letter responding to a taxpayer's adviser about a particular set of facts, to outline or explain its administrative position on an issue. As an administrative exception to including the value of lodging as a taxable benefit, the CRA has indicated that "the payment or reimbursement of monthly rental costs of an employee's personal residence in a new work location may not result in a taxable benefit to the extent that the payment or reimbursement is on account of reasonable, temporary living expenses while the employee is waiting to occupy new, permanent accommodations".[8]

¶3,120   Other Fringe Benefits

¶3,125   General rules

¶3,125.10   *Concept of a benefit*

Paragraph 6(1)(*a*) itself begins with a preamble which states the general rule for including benefits that arise in the course of or by virtue of an office or employment. This preamble is very broadly worded, as emphasized by the Supreme Court of Canada in the case of *The Queen v. Savage*, so that it would seem to catch any possible benefit which arises from employment. The Court went on to quote from its decision in *Nowegijick v. The Queen*, where it stated that:

ITA: 6(1)(*a*)

83 DTC 5409, at 5414 (S.C.C.)

83 DTC 5041 (S.C.C.)

> The words "in respect of" are . . . words of the widest possible scope. They impart such meaning as "in relation to", "with reference to" or "in connection with". The phrases "in respect of" is probably the widest of any expression intended to convey some connection between two related subject matters.

Paragraph 6(1)(*a*) includes benefits "enjoyed", as well as those benefits received, through an office or employment. A benefit enjoyed and, thereby, included in employment income by the employee-taxpayer, raises the whole question of valuation of the benefit.

The word "benefit", used on its own, is not defined in the Act. In the case of *The Queen v. Poynton*, Evans, J.A. stated, on the issue of determining whether a benefit is received or enjoyed:

72 DTC 6329, at 6355-6 (Ont. C.A.)

> . . . [a benefit] is a material acquisition which confers an *economic benefit on the taxpayer* [emphasis added] and does not constitute an exemption, e.g., loan or gift. . . .

This concept of a benefit was cited with approval by Justice Dickson in *The Queen v. Savage*. In the case of *A.G. v. Hoefele*, Linden, J.A. elaborated on that concept:

83 DTC 5409, at 5414 (S.C.C.)

95 DTC 5602, at 5604 (F.C.A.)

> According to the Supreme Court of Canada, then, to be taxable as a "benefit", a receipt must confer an economic benefit. In other words, a receipt must increase the recipient's net worth to be taxable. Conversely, a receipt which does not increase net worth is not a benefit and is not taxable.

¶3,125.20   *Statutory exclusions*

The general statement of the rule in paragraph 6(1)(*a*) is followed by specific statutory exceptions to the rule, outlined as follows:

(a) employer's contributions to:

   (i) a registered pension plan (approved by the CRA),

   (ii) a group sickness or accident insurance plan which includes all types of income protection plans,

   (iii) private health services plan premiums and provincial health tax levies, but not provincial health plan premiums,

   (iv) a supplementary unemployment benefit plan, including both public and private plans,

   (v) a deferred profit sharing plan (which is similar to a registered pension plan except that only the employer contributes and the contribution is based on profits), or

---

[8] Letter, dated November 5, 1998, from the Director, Business and Publications Division, Income Tax Rulings and Interpretations Directorate, Policy and Legislation Branch, Canada Customs and Revenue Agency, Document 9821655 reproduced in *Tax Windows Files, CCH Canadian TaxWorks.*

(vi) a group term life insurance policy (refer to subsection 6(4) for the income inclusion);

(b) benefits under a retirement compensation arrangement, an employee benefit plan or an employee trust, already included in income under other provisions;[9]

(c) benefits in respect of the use of an automobile (separate benefits for the availability of an employer-provided automobile, a standby charge and an automobile operating expense benefit are discussed later in the chapter);

(d) benefits from counselling services in respect of mental or physical health and re-employment or retirement of the employee; and

(e) benefits under a salary deferral arrangement already included in income by reason of subsection 6(11), which is discussed in supplemental notes later in the chapter.

Provincial health tax levies in part (a)(iii) above are not taxable benefits (e.g., Ontario's Employer Health Tax and similar plans in Manitoba, Northwest Territories, Nunavut, Quebec and Newfoundland and Labrador), since the basis of this tax is the total payroll amount and the liability for this tax belongs to the employer and not the employee. However, premiums paid by employers for provincial health care services plans, where the employee is liable for the premium, are taxable because, as *public* health services plans (i.e., government operated plans), they do not fit the specific wording of the exception for *private* plans (i.e., private insurance plans).

Part (c) above excludes the benefit in respect of the use of an automobile since there is a specific inclusion (discussed later in the chapter) of a standby charge for automobiles and for all operating costs paid by the employer for personal use of the automobile, such as gas, oil, maintenance, insurance, etc.

> ITA: 6(1)(*e*), 6(1)(*k*), 6(1)(*l*)

Any benefit related to parking for personal purposes is not considered to be a benefit in respect of the *use* of an automobile. As a result, any benefit related to personal parking will be included in employment income as a benefit. In the case of *Chow and Topchechka v. The Queen*, the court determined that free parking spaces were not a taxable benefit since the parking spaces were provided for the employer's advantage rather than the employee's advantage. This case rebuts the assumption that free parking spaces are automatically a taxable benefit.

> ITA: 6(1.1)
>
> 2001 DTC 164 (T.C.C.)

¶3,125.30   *Selected court decisions*

For selected court decisions on fringe benefits that were included in income in respect of:

- holiday trips and prizes,[10] see *Philp et al. v. M.N.R.* and *Arsens v. M.N.R.*;

> 70 DTC 6237 (Ex. Ct.), 69 DTC 81 (T.A.B.)

- travelling expenses paid for an employee's spouse,[11] see *Hale v. M.N.R.*; and

> 68 DTC 5326 (Ex. Ct.)

- an economic benefit from a payment made by an employer, see *The Queen v. Huffman*.

> 90 DTC 6405 (F.C.A.)

---

[9] Part (b) above became an exclusion from paragraph 6(1)(*a*) with the introduction of the following specific income inclusion provisions which prevent employees from deferring the receipt of income to subsequent years:

- retirement compensation arrangements [pars. 56(1)(*x*) and (*z*)];
- employee benefit plans[par. 6(1)(*g*)]; and
- employee trusts [par. 6(1)(*h*)].

Employee benefit plan rules were introduced to prevent a timing difference between the employer's deduction and the employee's income inclusion for non-registered income deferral plans (i.e., non-government-approved pension plans). With the introduction of even further restrictions on deferred salary arrangements in 1986, these employee benefit plan rules have limited applicability. For example, they apply to "offside" retirement compensation arrangements (RCAs), which are discussed more fully in the Supplemental Notes to Chapter 4.

[10] In the case of *Romeril v. The Queen*, 99 DTC 221 (T.C.C.), where an employee attended a convention, it was held that the trip was not taken for pleasure, but was genuinely related to employment. Hence no benefit could be assessed.

[11] In the case of *Lowe v. The Queen*, 96 DTC 6226 (F.C.A.), an account executive for an insurance company was requested to accompany a group of prize-winning brokers on a trip to New Orleans. The company paid the costs of the executive and his spouse. It was established that the executive and his spouse had little personal time on the trip and no benefit could be assessed.

¶3,125.40   *Flexible benefit programs*

An innovation in providing employee fringe benefits is a cafeteria program or flexible benefit program. These programs enable employees to select from a menu of available benefits some of which are taxable and some of which are not. In addition, some of these programs permit employees to select the quantum of the benefit within a certain defined range, e.g., group insurance plans. There is no specific provision within the Act that governs flexible benefit programs; instead each component of the flexible benefit program is governed by its own unique set of rules. However, in designing the program care must be taken to satisfy certain general conditions to ensure that there is no adverse tax consequences for all the benefits provided under the program. An Interpretation Bulletin, "Flexible employee benefit programs", discusses in great detail the various types of flexible benefit programs, overriding conditions, specific benefit provisions, and certain administrative interpretations.

IT-529

¶3,130   Housing loss and housing cost benefits

The Act addresses the income tax consequences of employer-provided compensation in respect of losses on a disposition of the employee's residence and other housing-related payments such as financing subsidies.

ITA: 6(19)–(23)

Any amount paid in respect of a housing loss is included in income. However, this general rule is modified so that only one-half the amount in excess of $15,000 of an employer-paid amount is included in employment income for an *eligible housing loss*.

ITA: 6(1)(*a*), 6(19)

ITA: 6(22)

- An eligible housing loss is the taxpayer's *housing loss* (see below) that is designated or chosen by the taxpayer as such and is in respect of an *eligible relocation* (see below) of the taxpayer or non-arm's length person.

ITA: 6(22)

- In general terms, a housing loss is the cost of the residence to the taxpayer or a non-arm's length person minus the proceeds of disposition or fair market value depending on certain circumstances.

ITA: 6(21)

- An "eligible relocation" is defined for purposes of these provisions and deductible moving expenses. This definition imposes a 40-kilometre minimum on the difference in the distance between the old residence and the new work location, and the distance between the new residence and the new work location. For example, if the distance between an employee's old residence and the new work location is 100 kilometres, and the distance between the new residence and the new work location is 20 kilometres, the difference in the two distances is 80 kilometres. The move between the two residences would qualify as an eligible relocation. This kilometre restriction is also referred to in Chapter 9, under the heading "Moving Expenses".

ITA: 6(19), 6(23), 62, 248(1) "eligible relocation"

Finally, the Act contains a catch-all provision, "for greater certainty", that includes in the income of the employee all other employer-provided payments or any other type of assistance by anyone in respect of housing.

ITA: 6(23)

¶3,135   Employee loans

¶3,135.10   *General system for inclusion and deduction*

Employment income includes a deemed interest benefit on an interest-free or low-interest loan made by an employer and received by an employee in his or her capacity as an employee. The benefit is defined as being the difference between the interest calculated at the prescribed interest rate, which may change for each quarter in the year during which the loan was outstanding, and the actual interest charged by the employer in respect of the calendar year and paid by the employee up to January 30 of the following year. Interest paid or *payable* in respect of the calendar year on behalf of the employee by the employer or related party is also included in the benefit calculation. Only the interest actually *paid* by the employee is deductible. Hence, interest not paid within the above time-frame does not reduce the benefit.

ITA: 6(9)

ITA: 80.4(1)

ITR: 4300, 4301

A deeming rule states that this deemed interest benefit is in turn deemed to be interest paid. The effect of this deeming rule is to meet a condition in the employment deduction provision which allows for a deduction of interest *paid* on funds borrowed to purchase a car for use in employment. By deeming the imputed interest benefit, which is included in employment income, to be interest *paid*, one of the conditions of the interest deduction provision is met. A similar effect is provided where funds are borrowed from an employer, for example, to purchase shares of a corporate employer. In this situation, one of the conditions, which provides for a deduction of interest paid on funds borrowed under specified circumstances, discussed in Chapter 6 under the heading "Interest", would be met by this deeming rule. However, it must be emphasized that the interest is deductible only if the amount qualifies under all of the specific provisions of these paragraphs.

ITA: 80.5
ITA: 8(1)(*j*)

ITA: 20(1)(*c*)

¶3,135.20　*Specific rules for home purchase loans*

"Home purchase loans" and "home relocation loans" are defined terms in the Act. These loans use a rate set for each quarter the loan is outstanding as the lesser of:

ITA: 80.4(7), 248(1)
ITA: 80.4(1), 80.4(4)

(a) the prescribed rate for the quarter while the loan was outstanding; and

(b) the prescribed rate in effect at the time the loan was made.

The quarter-by-quarter method described above is used by the CRA and may result in a smaller income inclusion than an annual calculation in (a) above involving the prescribed rates for all four quarters that the loan was outstanding.

Part (b) of this calculation is modified every fifth year, to use the prescribed rate on every fifth anniversary date, for home purchase loans.

ITA: 80.4(6)

Note that where the Act uses the term "prescribed" as in prescribed rate, the "prescription" will usually appear in the Income Tax Regulations. Refer to the footnotes of the provision, in the *Income Tax Act*, in which the term is used under the "Regulation" heading to locate the regulation that is applicable. Where a form is prescribed, the number of the form will usually be listed in the footnotes.

The Act contains a partial exemption for the imputed interest income inclusion, as described above, for basically the first $25,000 of a "home relocation loan". This type of loan results from any move of at least 40 kilometres by the taxpayer or his or her spouse to a new employment location in Canada. However, this exemption is deducted under Division C (deductions to arrive at taxable income) and is generally deductible during the first five years of the loan to the extent of the imputed interest net of qualified interest payments. This topic will be discussed in further detail in Chapter 10.

ITA: 248(1) "home relocation loan"

Note that the CRA computes interest on a daily basis. Following normal commercial practice, the CRA calculates interest commencing with the first day that a debt is incurred and excluding the day on which the debt is repaid, unless a provision of the Act specifies another method of calculation.

Example Problem

On May 1 of this year, Mr. Roberts borrowed from his employer, Stanley Inc., $35,000 evidenced by a 3% promissory note with principal repayable in five equal instalments on the anniversary date and interest payable monthly. Mr. Roberts spent the $35,000 on the following acquisitions:

(a) $10,000 for a second-hand car which he needs to carry out his duties of employment (approximately 60% of the time);

(b) $5,000 for acquiring dividend-paying common shares in his brother's corporation; and

(c) $20,000 as a down-payment on a new condominium which he moved into immediately.

Assume that the prescribed interest rates for this year are the following:

1st quarter 7%		3rd quarter 8%
2nd quarter 6%		4th quarter 7%

— *REQUIRED*

Discuss the tax consequences of the above transactions, supporting them with all necessary computations.

— *SOLUTION*

Income:

Mr. Roberts will have an imputed employment income inclusion for the accrued interest from May 1 to December 31[1] of this year under subsection 6(9) by virtue of subsection 80.4(1).

Car and shares portion of loan
2nd quarter: May 1 to June 30 (inclusive)

$$\frac{61}{365} \times 6\% \times \$15,000 = \text{. . . . .} \qquad \$ \ 150$$

3rd quarter: July 1 to September 30 (inclusive)

$$\frac{92}{365} \times 8\% \times \$15,000 = \text{. . . . .} \qquad 302$$

4th quarter: October 1 to December 31 (inclusive)

$$\frac{92}{365} \times 7\% \times \$15,000 = \text{. . . . .} \qquad 265 \quad \$717$$

Condominium portion of loan:[2]

May 1 to December 31 (inclusive)

$$\frac{245}{365} \times 6\% \times \$20,000 = \text{. . . . .} \qquad \$ \ 805$$

Total $1,522

Less: interest for the year paid on all loans

$$\frac{245}{365} \times 3\% \times (\$15,000 + \$20,000) = \text{. . . . .}} \qquad 705$$

Imputed interest benefit inclusion . . . . $ 817

Deductions:

Although deductions are really presented in subsequent chapters and the latter part of this chapter, a conceptual discussion of the deduction alternatives may be helpful in understanding the whole issue.

● Portion of loan used to acquire the car and shares ($15,000)

Under section 80.5, the imputed interest income in respect of both the shares and the car, in this case, is deemed to be paid and, hence, may be eligible for a deduction. However, both of these amounts must meet further tests in paragraphs 8(1)(*j*) and 20(1)(*c*), in order to qualify for a deduction.

● Portion of loan used to acquire condominium ($20,000)

There is no deduction available in connection with a home purchase loan except in Division C where the employee has moved, under certain defined conditions as described in Chapter 10.

— NOTES TO SOLUTION

(1) The days of interest were determined by counting the first day of the contractual arrangement.

(2) The condominium portion of the loan should qualify as a home purchase loan. Therefore, the imputed interest calculation would be based on the "lesser of" rule demonstrated above. Since the prescribed rate at the time the loan was made (6%) is less than the subsequent quarterly prescribed rates (8% and 7%), the 6% rate applies to all three quarters. The CRA's administrative practice is to apply these rules on a quarter-by-quarter basis, not on an annual basis.

ITA: 80.4(4) [in combination with ssec. 80.4(1)], 80.4(7)

¶3,135.30 *Forgiveness of employee loans*

The Act determines the value of an employment benefit arising on the forgiveness of an employee loan. The effect of this provision is to include in employment income the amount of the employer loan or other indebtedness net of any payments made by the employee, i.e., the forgiven amount. This treatment is logical since the principal amount of the loan is not taxed when received. If a repayment with after-tax funds is not required because the loan was forgiven, the employee receives an economic benefit.

ITA: 6(1)(a), 6(15)

¶3,140 Fringe benefits and administrative practice

As previously mentioned, Interpretation Bulletins reflect the CRA's position in interpreting a particular section of the Act. Often, the CRA uses an administratively practical interpretation of the law and, in certain cases, does not enforce the law strictly because it is simply not practical to do so.

The Interpretation Bulletin entitled "Employees' Fringe Benefits" clarifies the Agency's position on several important issues, some of which are summarized below.

IT-470R

- The exclusion from employment income of fees, paid by an employer, for an employee's membership in a social club applies to those situations "where the membership was principally for the employer's advantage rather than the employee's".

IT-470R, par. 34

- Personal-use benefits from frequent-flyer programs accumulated through employer-paid business trips are specifically included in employment income.

IT-470R, par. 14

- Financial counselling and tax return preparation provided directly or indirectly by an employer except for financial counselling in respect of re-employment or retirement are specifically included in employment income.

IT-470R, par. 26, as amended by a special release dated December 11, 1989

- The CRA's position in respect of business trips for spouses of employees indicates that there is no employment benefit to the employee if the spouse was, in fact, engaged *primarily* in the business activities on behalf of the employer as opposed to engaged primarily in personal activities.

IT-470R, par. 15

This Interpretation Bulletin is an important reference for employment benefit planning. It contains a list of items which, if received or enjoyed by an employee, must be included in employment income and a second list of items which need not be included, despite the general wording of the preamble in paragraph 6(1)(a), if the CRA's conditions outlined in the Bulletin are met. Clearly, it may be worthwhile on an after-tax basis for an employee to trade taxable salary or fringe benefits for an equivalent amount of non-taxable benefits that are desired by the employee.

IT-470R

In a change in assessing policy that is not yet reflected in this Interpretation Bulletin but was announced at a Canadian Tax Foundation Conference held in September 2001, the CRA will be assessing the taxable benefit based on the following guidelines:

IT-470R
ITA: 6(1)(a)

1. To mark special occasions, such as Christmas, Hanukkah, birthdays, or a marriage, employers can give their employees two non-cash gifts per year on a tax-free basis. In

addition, to honour employment achievements, such as years of service or meeting safety standards, employers can give their employees two non-cash awards per year on a tax-free basis.

2. The total cost to the employer, including taxes, of the two gifts or the two awards cannot be over $500 per year.

3. Employers can deduct the total cost of the gifts or awards.

4. Employees do not have to declare the cost of the gifts or awards as part of their taxable income.

5. If the cost of a gift or an award is over the $500 limit, the employer must include the full fair-market value of the gift(s) or award(s) in the employee's income.

6. If an employer gives two or more gifts — or two or more awards — in a single year and their total cost is over the $500 limit, the employer may have to include the fair market value of one or more of the gifts or awards in the employee's income.

7. This inclusion is determined by the cost of each gift or award and, also, by the number of gifts or awards given in a single year.

8. The new policy does not apply to cash or near–cash gifts and awards such as gift certificates, gold nuggets, or other items that can easily be converted into cash. The value of a cash or near–cash gift or award is considered a taxable employment benefit.

The CRA has a policy[12] on home computers supplied by an employer. According to the guidelines, there is no taxable benefit, where providing the computer is primarily to the benefit of the employer.

Income Tax Technical News, No. 13 (1999)

¶3,150 Allowances

¶3,155 Overview

First, the differences between an allowance and a reimbursement must be identified. Typically, a reimbursement involves the payment by an employee of an expense of his or her employer and the recovery from the employer of the amount paid as substantiated by vouchers or receipts. Generally, a reimbursement is not a taxable benefit to the employee. On the other hand, an allowance is a fixed amount which is paid to an employee in excess of his or her salary without the requirement that the employee substantiate the amounts expended. An Interpretation Bulletin, "Vehicle, Travel and Sales Expenses of Employees", adopts these meanings for the terms "allowance" and "reimbursement", respectively.

IT-522R, pars. 40, 50

Two precedent-setting judicial decisions on this issue are presented in *Ransom v. M.N.R.* and *Splane v. The Queen*. Both cases established a two-stage test for determining if a payment to an employee is employment income. First, a determination must be made as to whether the payment is an allowance or a reimbursement. If the payment is an allowance, then the rules in paragraph 6(1)(*b*) apply. If the payment is a reimbursement, then a further determination must be made as to whether the employee has received an "economic benefit". Normally, there is no benefit if the employee is in the same economic position as he or she was in prior to the employer-driven transaction which gave rise to payment.

67 DTC 5235 (Ex. Ct.), 92 DTC 6021 (F.C.A.)

Again, paragraph 6(1)(*b*) contains a preamble which establishes the general rule for the inclusion of allowances. The general rule is that all such allowances received must be included in the employee's income. However, there are many exceptions to this rule listed in the paragraph, some of which are discussed below. Any allowance received, that is not specifically excepted, is regarded as an allowance in respect of a personal or living expense. Since such an expense is not deductible, an amount received as an allowance for such an expense must be included in income.[13]

ITA: 6(1)(b)

---

[12] The Income Tax Technical News series is another of the CRA's interpretive publications.

[13] For a case on the topic of personal or living expenses, see *Henry v. M.N.R.*, 72 DTC 6005 (S.C.C.).

Certain allowances, reimbursements, and other payments in respect of disabled persons for transportation to and from the workplace and for the services of an attendant to assist the employee to perform his or her employment duties are excluded from employment income. In order for these exemptions to apply the disabled person must be eligible for a disability tax credit which is discussed in some detail in Chapter 10.

ITA: 6(1), 6(16)

ITA: 118.3

¶3,160 Exception of allowance for travelling expenses of sales/negotiating persons

A common exception to the taxation of allowances deals with employees who sell property or negotiate contracts. Note the conditions that must be met for the allowance to be excluded:

ITA: 6(1)(*b*)(v)

(a) the allowance must be reasonable;

(b) the allowance must be only for travelling expenses, including by implication motor vehicle expenses (this topic is covered separately, later in this chapter); and

(c) the recipient (hereinafter referred to as a "sales/negotiating person") must be involved in the selling of property or the negotiating of contracts for his or her employer.

The word "reasonable" is not defined in the Act and, therefore, must be applied to the particular facts of the situation. For example, a reasonable daily allowance for the travelling expense of the president of a large public corporation (a person who negotiates contracts) would be entirely different than a reasonable daily allowance for a salesperson for the same organization.

6(1)(*b*)(v)

In the case of *Hudema v. The Queen*, the taxpayer claimed that a car allowance was not reasonable because the allowance did not cover all of his expenses of operating the car. This was not sufficient evidence to prove that the allowance was not reasonable because the court was not convinced that the taxpayer was making a reasonable use of his vehicle. Since the taxpayer made very little personal use of the car, averaging about 15% per year over five years, he attributed most of the costs of operating his car to his work. The court indicated that the taxpayer did not establish that it was sensible to make such little personal use of the car that he used for work. The court further indicated that the employer's allowance should only be expected to pay for such reasonable use of his car as his work required. To be reasonable, the allowance should cover virtually all the costs of his car, both capital and operating. The court suggested that the taxpayer should have provided evidence of the number of hours per week for which he had to use the car for work.

94 DTC 6287 (F.C.T.D.)

In the case of *Lemire v. The Queen*, the judge suggested the type of evidence necessary to determine whether an allowance, to cover reasonable expenses of owning and maintaining a car, was inadequate. The judge indicated, at 1773, that:

94 DTC 1772 (T.C.C.)

> . . . I not only must have evidence as to how the allowance was calculated by the employer, but the intent of the employer when setting the allowance. I must also have the complete history of the vehicle such as the expenses over the years an allowance was received. Just looking at the one year, in light of the evidence before me, is not sufficient. An allowance cannot be reasonable for three years and unreasonable the fourth year. Obviously an Appellant has to demonstrate that his vehicle's expenses are reasonable for an employee in his employment.
>
> An employee earning an annual wage of $40,000 with an investment income of several hundred thousand dollars a year may choose to own and drive a $100,000 car. Obviously a normal reasonable mileage allowance would never cover the depreciation of an automobile this expensive. Even though the expense and depreciation for that car would be reasonable, it would not be reasonable for the employer or the taxpayers of Canada to subsidize this hypothetical employee.

Where a sales/negotiating person receives an allowance for the use of a motor vehicle, there are further conditions that must be satisfied in order to exclude such an allowance. These conditions and their effects will be considered separately, later in Part IV.A. of this chapter.

ITA: 6(1)(*b*)(x) or 6(1)(*b*)(xi)

¶3,165   Exception of allowance for travelling expenses of other employees

Another common income exception concerns an allowance for travelling expenses of   ITA: 6(1)(*b*)(vii)
other employees and has the following conditions:

(a) the employee (hereinafter referred to as "ordinary employee") does not sell property
   or negotiate contracts;

(b) the allowance must be reasonable in the circumstances;

(c) the allowance must be for travelling expenses, but not for the use of a motor vehicle
   (which is discussed separately, later in the chapter); and

(d) the recipient must travel away from the municipality and metropolitan area of the
   employer's establishment at which the employee ordinarily worked.

Note the difference between the conditions for sales/negotiating persons and ordinary   ITA: 6(1)(*b*)(v)
employees. First, the travelling expenses include motor vehicle expenses for sales/negotiating   ITA: 6(1)(*b*)(vii)
persons but exclude them for ordinary employees, since these are covered separately.   ITA: 6(1)(*b*)(vii.1)
Second, the ordinary employee has a geographical limitation placed on the travelling
expenses. As will be seen in the discussion later in the chapter, there is no geographical   ITA: 6(1)(*b*)(vii.1)
limitation placed on an allowance for the use of a motor vehicle for sales/negotiating
employees.

¶3,170   Director's or Other Fees

A corporate director holds an "office", as defined in the Act. As a result, fees received by   ITA: 6(1)(*c*), 248(1)
a director are received by virtue of an office and, hence, must be included as employment
income. The effect of including such fees in employment income is to limit the deductions to
those allowed against employment income.

¶3,180   Standby Charge and Operating Cost Benefit for Automobile Provided By Employer

¶3,185   Calculation of the standby charge benefit from the use of the car itself

A standby charge represents a benefit conferred upon an employee through the availability of a company-owned or leased car for any use, whether for employment or personal.
Since the employee, who has a company car made available for his or her use, does not have
to spend tax-paid dollars on either purchasing or leasing a car, the government reasoned that
this benefit should be taxed somehow, on the principle of equity.[14] The concept is not
unreasonable. Since availability rather than actual use of the company car is the basis for this
calculation, some unsuspecting employee could have an income inclusion of the rather high
minimum standby charge.

The Act provides a computational formula to establish a reasonable standby charge as: ITA: 6(1)(*a*), 6(2)

$$\frac{A}{B} \times [2\% \text{ of } (C \times D) + \tfrac{2}{3}(E - F)]$$

where A *   is the lesser of:

(a) total personal-use kilometres driven during the available
   time period, and

(b) the value determined for B (as defined below) during the
   days the automobile is available;

B **   is $1{,}667 \text{ km} \times \left(\dfrac{\text{total available days}}{30} \right)$;

C ***   is the full original cost of an employer-owned vehicle, including both
   PST and GST;

---

[14] The term "made available" was at issue in *The Queen v. Adams*, 98 DTC 6266 (F.C.A.).

D^{**} is $\dfrac{\text{the total available days when the employer owned the automobile}}{30}$

E is the lease payments, including both PST and GST, made by the employer;

F is the portion of the lease payments which pertains to insurance for loss or damages and any liability in using the automobile.

* Note that amount A above is deemed to be equal to amount B unless:

    (i) the taxpayer is required by the employer to use the automobile in respect of his or her duties of employment, and

    (ii) the automobile is used primarily (more than 50%) in his or her duties of employment.
** Rounded according to the rule in the definition (i.e., to the nearest whole number, unless the fractional part is .5, in which case round the fraction down).
*** The capital cost limitations in paragraph 13(7)(*g*) and Regulation 7307, as subsequently described, do not apply.

A separate A/B ratio must be applied to each automobile available for use by an employee in a year. Thus, if an employee had both an employer-owned automobile and an employer-leased automobile available in a year, the formula would be applied with two different A/B ratios as: ITA: 6(2)

$$\frac{A}{B} \times [2\% \text{ of } (C \times D)] + \frac{A}{B} \times [\tfrac{2}{3}\,(E - F)]$$

¶3,190 Determining the operating cost benefit

As previously mentioned, the Act specifically excludes a benefit in relation to the use of an employer-provided automobile. However, operating expenses for personal use, which are paid by an employer and not reimbursed by the employee, do give rise to a taxable benefit to the employee. Automobile operating expenses include gasoline, insurance, and maintenance costs, but not parking costs. As indicated previously, any benefit related to personal parking is included in income separately. ITA: 6(1)(*a*)(iii)
ITA: 6(1)(*k*)
ITA: 6(1)(*a*)

There are two options for computing the operating cost benefit. If the conditions for both are met, then the better option for the employee can be chosen.

¶3,190.10 *Kilometre method*

The default method (called the "kilometre method") computes the operating cost benefit to an employee whose employer pays for operating costs including those for the personal use of an employer-provided automobile. The kilometre method is required for employees who do not use their automobile primarily (more than 50%) for employment or for employees who choose not to elect the 50% calculation method, where the use is primarily for employment. ITA: 6(1)(*k*)(v),
6(1)(*k*)(iv)

The kilometre method alternative computes the amount of the operating cost benefit by reference to the number of kilometres driven for personal purposes at 22 cents per personal-use kilometre in 2007.[15] The 22-cent amount is reviewed periodically. Again, the amount computed by this method is reduced by any reimbursement paid within 45 days after the end of the year by the employee to the employer in respect of these operating costs. Again, the inclusion based on 22 cents per kilometre is considered to include a GST component and no further income inclusion is required.

¶3,190.20 *Election where use is primarily (more than 50%) employment*

If an employee notifies his or her employer in writing before the end of the particular taxation year, he or she may compute his or her operating-cost employment income inclusion as 50% of the standby charge minus any reimbursement to the employer made by the employee within 45 days after the end of the year. However, this option is only available in situations where the vehicle is used *primarily* (more than 50%) in the performance of employment duties. The resultant income inclusion is considered to include a GST component and no additional income inclusion is required. ITA: 6(1)(*k*)(iv)

IT-63R5, par. 6(d)

---

[15] Department of Finance News Release (2006-089), December 27, 2006.

¶3,200 Application of the Rules

The following examples will demonstrate how the standby charge and operating cost benefit rules should be applied.

ITA: 6(1)(e), 6(1)(k), 6(2)

Example Problem 1

Automobile owned by employer

Original cost of automobile, including PST and GST	$26,000
Operating costs for the year paid by employer, including PST and GST	$ 3,000*
Employment-use kilometres	10,000
Total kilometres for year	30,000
Number of months available	12
Reimbursement to employer for personal use (to cover operating costs and standby charge) at 10¢ per kilometre	$ 2,000

*Includes insurance of $600, but excludes parking.

— REQUIRED

Compute the standby charge and operating benefit for the use of the automobile.

— SOLUTION

Standby charge

ITA: 6(1)(e), 6(2)

$$\frac{20,004 \text{ km}^{(1)}}{20,004 \text{ km}} \times [2\% \times (\$26,000 \times 12)] = \ldots \ldots \ldots \$6,240$$

Operating benefit (20,000 km × $0.22)$^{(2)}$ 4,400 $10,640

ITA: 6(1)(k)(v)

Less: amount reimbursed 2,000

Total car benefits $8,640

— NOTES TO SOLUTION

(1) The employee does not qualify for the standby charge reduction, since the car is not used more than 50% in the performance of employment duties. Therefore, in this situation, the value of A in the formula (i.e., 20,004 km) is deemed to be equal to the value of B in the formula (i.e., 1,667 × 12 rounded).

(2) The operating benefit election method is also not available, since the car is not used more than 50% in the performance of employment duties. Since this is an employer-provided automobile, the per kilometre method must be used.

ITA: 6(1)(k)(v)

Example Problem 2

Automobile owned by employer — The facts are the same as Example Problem 1, except that the employment-use kilometres are 24,000.

— REQUIRED

Compute the standby charge and operating benefit for the use of the automobile.

— SOLUTION

Standby charge			ITA: 6(1)(*e*), 6(2)
$\frac{6{,}000 \text{ km}^{(1)}}{20{,}004 \text{ km}} \times [2\% \times (\$26{,}000 \times 12)] = \ldots\ldots\ldots\ldots$		$1,872	
Operating benefit$^{(2)}$ $\ldots\ldots\ldots\ldots\ldots\ldots\ldots\ldots\ldots$	936	$2,808	ITA: 6(1)(*k*)(v)
Less: amount reimbursed (6,000 km $\times$ 10¢) $\ldots\ldots\ldots\ldots$		600	
Total car benefit $\ldots\ldots\ldots\ldots\ldots\ldots\ldots\ldots\ldots\ldots\ldots\ldots$		$2,208	

— NOTES TO SOLUTION

$^{(1)}$ Lesser of (a) 6,000 km and (b) 1,667 km $\times$ 12 months. In this situation the employee qualifies for the standby charge reduction since the car is used primarily (i.e., more than 50%) in the performance of employment duties.

$^{(2)}$ The operating benefit election method is available to the employee, since the car is used more than 50%. This method would result in a lower income inclusion ($936 (i.e., 50% of $1,872) versus $1,320 (i.e., 6,000km $\times$ $0.22)).   ITA: 6(1)(*k*)(iv)

Example Problem 3

Automobile leased by employer	
Lease cost including $500 of insurance, PST and GST $\ldots\ldots\ldots$	$ 5,000
Operating costs for the year paid directly by the employer (includes PST and GST, but excludes parking) $\ldots\ldots\ldots\ldots\ldots$	$ 3,000
Employment-use kilometres $\ldots\ldots\ldots\ldots\ldots\ldots\ldots\ldots\ldots$	4,000
Total kilometres for the year $\ldots\ldots\ldots\ldots\ldots\ldots\ldots\ldots\ldots$	16,000
Number of months available $\ldots\ldots\ldots\ldots\ldots\ldots\ldots\ldots\ldots$	12
Reimbursement to employer for personal use (to cover operating costs and standby charge) at 5¢ per kilometre $\ldots\ldots\ldots\ldots$	$ 600

— REQUIRED

Compute the standby charge and operating benefit for the use of the automobile.

— SOLUTION

Standby charge			ITA: 6(1)(*e*), 6(2)
$\frac{20{,}004 \text{ km}^{(1)}}{20{,}004 \text{ km}} \times \frac{2}{3}\,(\$5{,}000 - \$500) \ldots\ldots\ldots\ldots\ldots$		$3,000	
Operating benefit (12,000 km $\times$ $0.22) $\ldots\ldots\ldots\ldots\ldots$	2,640	$5,640	ITA: 6(1)(*k*)(v)
Less: amount reimbursed $\ldots\ldots\ldots\ldots\ldots\ldots\ldots\ldots\ldots$		600	
Total car benefits $\ldots\ldots\ldots\ldots\ldots\ldots\ldots\ldots\ldots\ldots\ldots\ldots$		$5,040	

— NOTE TO SOLUTION

$^{(1)}$ In this situation, the employee does not qualify for the standby charge reduction or the operating benefit alternative, because he or she did not use the car more than 50% in the performance of the employment duties.

Example Problem 4

Automobile leased by employer — The facts are the same as Example Problem 3 except that the employment-use kilometres are 12,000.

— *REQUIRED*

Compute the standby charge and operating benefit for the use of the automobile.

— *SOLUTION*

Standby charge			
$\dfrac{4{,}000 \text{ km}^{(1)}}{20{,}004 \text{ km}} \times \frac{2}{3}$ ($5,000 − $500)			$ 600
Operating benefit[(2)]		300	$ 900
Less: amount reimbursed (4,000 km × 5¢)			200
Total car benefits			$ 700

ITA: 6(1)(*e*), 6(2)

ITA: 6(1)(*k*)(v)

— *NOTES TO SOLUTION*

[(1)] The employee qualifies for the standby charge reduction, since he or she used the car more than 50% (i.e., 75%) in the performance of his or her duties.

[(2)] The employee does qualify for the operating benefit alternative method of computing the operating cost benefits, since the car was used more than 50% in the performance of his or her duties. In this situation, the election would give a lower gross income inclusion of $300 (i.e., 50% of $600) versus $880 (4,000 km × $0.22).

ITA: 6(1)(*k*)(iv)

¶3,210 Employee-Owned Automobile Operating Expense Benefit

As discussed, an automobile operating expense benefit arises when an employer provides the automobile and pays for some or all of the operating costs, including costs related to the personal use of the automobile. However, a separate rule applies in cases where the automobile is provided by the employee and where an employer pays for automobile operating costs, including costs for personal use of the automobile. For example, an employee may use his or her own automobile for employment purposes, but the employer pays, through a business credit card, for all operating costs of the automobile, including costs of driving to and from work which are personal costs.

ITA: 6(1)(*k*)

ITA: 6(1)(*l*)

The value of any benefit received by an employee for automobile operating expenses attributable to personal use must be included in income. To arrive at the value of this benefit, the total costs paid by the employer should be prorated by the ratio of personal-use kilometres to total kilometres driven by the employee. Amounts paid by the employee to the employer can be deducted from the benefit. Of course, this method requires record-keeping of employment and personal kilometres in a log, but there is no simpler, alternative method allowed for an employee-provided automobile. Note that the value of this benefit is determined using GST-included operating expenses.

ITA: 6(1)(*l*)

Note the heading for paragraph 6(1)(*l*) is the single word "*idem*", which is a Latin word meaning "the same". Therefore, the heading for paragraph 6(1)(*l*) is considered to be the same as that for paragraph 6(1)(*k*) which is "automobile operating expense benefit".

¶3,220 Benefit from Employer-Paid GST

Where an employee receives a taxable benefit from his or her employer, the employer is liable for and must remit the relevant GST. The employee in turn is deemed to receive a taxable benefit which generally includes the employer-paid GST. This employment income inclusion of GST places the employee in the same economic position as if he or she acquired the goods or services on the open market. In essence, the Act includes an employer-paid GST in employment income.

ITA: 6(1)(*a*), 6(1)(*e*)

Note that the inclusion of the full GST paid by the employer in providing the benefit ignores any reimbursement by the employee for the taxable benefit/taxable supply. This is logical if the objective is to place the employee in the same position as if he or she acquired the supply on the open market and, therefore, would pay GST on the full amount rather than a partial net payment.

The general rule is that any benefit included in income under either the general benefits inclusion rule or the standby charge is subject to the GST. However, two significant exceptions are:

ITA: 6(1)(a), 6(1)(e)

(a) zero-rated supplies found in Schedule VI of the ETA (e.g., gift food baskets); and

(b) exempt supplies found in Schedule V of the ETA (e.g., day-care services, low-rent and rent-free housing, low-interest and interest-free loans, premiums for government health services and tuition fees for exempt education services).

The practical application of including GST paid by the employer in income is fairly limited. The most common applications would be:

(a) personal use of an employer's automobile by way of the standby charge; and

ITA: 6(1)(e), 6(2)

(b) other payments by the employer which would be considered taxable benefits such as automobile operating and parking costs for personal purposes, travelling expenses relating to vacations, spouse's non-business-related travelling costs, and gifts valued in excess of $500 on which the employer would have paid GST in providing the item to the employee.

ITA: 6(1)(a)

¶3,230 Employment Insurance Benefits

Section 6 excepts the inclusion in employment income of premiums paid by an employer on behalf of an employee to a group sickness or accident insurance plan. However, amounts received as a result of a disability claim by an employee in respect of a sickness or accident, disability or income maintenance plan, if the employer has made any contribution, must be taken into employment income. Hence, such plans become tainted if the employer pays all or any portion of the premium.

ITA: 6(1)(a)

ITA: 6(1)(f)

In terms of employee benefit planning, there is a basic trade-off in the tax treatment of these plans. On the one hand, all employees can receive a relatively small tax-free benefit by having the employer pay the premium. However, those relatively few employees who become disabled and receive insurance payments will be taxed on those payments. On the other hand, all employees can incur a relatively small cost by paying the premium. In this case, the relatively few employees who become disabled and receive insurance payments will receive those payments tax free.

Where an employee has paid any amount of the premiums, these amounts are deductible from the disability benefits received in arriving at the benefit.

ITA: 6(1)(f)

Non-group plans are treated in exactly the opposite manner. The premiums paid by the employer are treated as employment income. However, payments received in respect of these plans are not considered as income.

IT-428, par. 20

Summary	Sickness or Accident Insurance Plan			
	Group		Non-group	
	Premium	Disability Benefit	Premium	Disability Benefit
Employer pays all or part of premium	Not included	Included	Included	Not included
Employee pays all of premium	Not deducted	Not included	Not deducted	Not included

Example Problem

Mr. Beta is insured under a group plan which pays $3,000 per month while disabled. The premium is $25 per month, of which the employer pays one-half and has been so paying on Mr. Beta's behalf starting January 1, 1984. The employee's share of the premium is waived during the period of the disability. Mr. Beta was struck by a truck and was off work from January 1, 2006 to June 30, 2007.

— *REQUIRED*

How much must be included in Mr. Beta's income in respect of the disability payments received for the years in question?

— *SOLUTION*

2006

Total cumulative benefits received in 2006 (i.e., before end of 2006 and after 2005) (12 × $3,000)	$36,000
Less: total contributions made by employee before end of 2006 (½ × $25 × 12 × 22$^{(1)}$)	3,300
Amount to be included in income	$32,700

2007

Total benefits received in 2007 (i.e., before end of 2007 and after 2006) (6 × $3,000)	$18,000
Less: total contributions made by employee in 2007 (i.e., before end of 2007 and after 2006) (½ × $25 × 6$^{(2)}$)	75
Amount to be included in income	$17,925

— *NOTES TO SOLUTION*

$^{(1)}$ 1984 to 2005, inclusive (2006 not counted because employee's share of the premium not paid during disability).

$^{(2)}$ While no premium was paid by the employee during the six months of his disability, the premium was paid during the remaining six months in the year.

¶3,240 Payments by Employer to Employee and Other Benefits

A few payments received may be regarded as a capital receipt, not subject to tax. However, most payments, such as a signing bonus, might be considered as "other remuneration" or as part of "other benefits of any kind whatever". The payment could also be considered consideration for entering into a contract of employment. This provision basically expands employment income to include payments which are received either immediately before or after the actual employment period and which arise from the employment contract. Each of these provisions must be read very carefully to determine the conditions, if any, necessary for the provision to apply.[16] The following example problem illustrates the need for a careful interpretation.

ITA: 5
ITA: 6(1)(a)
ITA: 6(3)

[16] The case of *No. 261 v. M.N.R.*, 55 DTC 285 (T.A.B.), was heard to decide the meaning of the phrase "immediately after" used in paragraph 6(3)(b). Cases that resulted in payments which were considered taxable include *Butters v. M.N.R.*, 52 DTC 37 (T.A.B.), *Moss v. M.N.R.*, 63 DTC 1359 (Ex. Ct.), and *The Queen v. Blanchard*, 95 DTC 5479 (F.C.A.). Cases that resulted in payments which were considered not taxable include *Wilson v. M.N.R.*, 60 DTC 115 (T.A.B.), and *Segall v. M.N.R.*, 86 DTC 6486 (F.C.T.D.). Cases in which receipts were considered not to be taxable by subsection 6(3) include: *Ballard v. M.N.R.*, 87 DTC 157 (T.C.C.), and *The Queen v. Albino*, 94 DTC 6071 (F.C.T.D.).

Example Problem

The appellant, a geologist highly regarded in his field, had been employed by General Oil Limited for many years. Had he continued until retirement, he would have been entitled to a substantial pension which would be lost if he left General Oil voluntarily.

Mr. Green was a substantial shareholder and chief executive of Prairie Oil Limited which held a large number of shares of Clean Oil Limited. Under an agreement made in the year, Mr. Green paid the appellant $250,000 in consideration of the loss of pension rights, chances for advancement, and opportunities for re-employment in the oil industry. On the same day, the appellant entered into another agreement with Prairie Oil to act as its general manager at a salary of $25,000 per year, subject to the condition that he would serve as manager of another company if the director so decided.

Pursuant to this consideration, the appellant became the president and manager of Clean Oil at a salary of $25,000 per year with no superannuation benefits.

— REQUIRED

Resolve the foregoing fact situation with reference to paragraph 3(*a*), section 5 and subsection 6(3) of the current *Income Tax Act*.

— SOLUTION [see *Robert B. Curran v. M.N.R.*, 59 DTC 1247 (S.C.C.).]

The payment of $250,000 can be considered either as a non-taxable capital receipt or as income from employment. It can be argued that the payment was compensation for substantial benefits foregone, including the loss or relinquishment of a source of income which can be regarded as a capital asset. At least that part of the payment for the loss of pension rights, if such a part can be determined, could be regarded as a non-taxable capital receipt. It has been held that a lump sum paid to commute a pension is a capital payment which is substituted for a series of periodic sums in the nature of income. However, the payment did not come from General Oil to commute the pension.

On the other hand, the payment of $250,000 could be regarded as being made for personal services to be rendered by the appellant to the new employer. The mere fact that the agreement characterizes the $250,000 as a capital payment in consideration of the loss of pension rights, chances for advancement and opportunities for re-employment in the oil industry cannot change the true character of the payment as employment income. Mr. Green was seeking to acquire the skilled services of the appellant as a manager. The consideration was paid so that these services would be made available; therefore, it is income of the appellant within the meaning of paragraph 3(*a*).

Since the payment was not made by the appellant's employer as required by paragraph 6(3)(*b*), it is not *deemed*, for the purpose of section 5, to be remuneration for the appellant's services rendered during the period of employment. Although the payment is not deemed to be employment income, the more general paragraph 3(*a*) can be applied in determining income from employment from a source inside or outside Canada.

The Supreme Court of Canada held that this payment was income from employment under paragraph 3(*a*).

¶3,250 Restrictive Covenants

A proposed amendment provides that an employee may be required to include in employment income an amount that is receivable at the end of the year in respect of a covenant as to what the employee is, or is not, to do. Normally, only amounts received are included in employment income. This provision deems an amount that is receivable to be received. This provision is part of a comprehensive package of amendments related to payments received for covenants provided by individuals. For a full discussion on the treatment of payments received for restrictive covenants please refer to Chapter 9.

Bill C-33, dated Nov. 22, 2006; ITA: 6(3.1)

¶3,260 Stock Options

¶3,265 General

Stock options are a popular and important form of remuneration in some situations. Two income tax issues arise, at this stage, from an employee's perspective:

- The value of the employment income inclusion

- The timing of the inclusion

Exercising a stock option will result in employment income if the price paid under the option is less than the fair market value of the shares at the time of their purchase. However, the timing of the inclusion and the ultimate effect on taxable income will depend upon a number of factors:

- the type of corporation issuing the option;

- whether the parties involved are dealing at arm's length;

- the relationship of option price to fair market value of the shares when the option is granted; and

- the value of the shares purchased under the option.

The stock option benefit included in employment income must be received as a result of employment from a "qualifying person" that is a corporation or a mutual fund trust. Hence, rights or warrants provided by virtue of shareholdings alone would be excluded from this provision.

ITA: 7(5)
ITA: 7(7)

¶3,270 Rules applicable to stock options for all types of corporations

An employment income inclusion is deemed, for employees of *all* corporations on the exercising of a stock option to be equal to the difference between the fair market value at the date the option is exercised and the option price. However, there is a partial offsetting deduction, in Division C, equal to one-half of the income inclusion, if the option price is equal to or greater than the fair market value of the share at the time the option was granted. In addition, there are certain limitations on the type of shares to be issued and the relationship of the parties before and after the transaction, all of which are discussed in Chapter 10.

ITA: 7(1)

ITA: 110(1)(*d*)

¶3,275 Rules applicable to Canadian-controlled private corporations

An exception to the general rules described above is provided for stock options granted by Canadian-controlled private corporations (CCPC). There is still an employment income inclusion, equal to the excess of the fair market value at the date the option is exercised and the option price. However, the inclusion of that benefit occurs at the time that the shares are disposed of, thereby deferring the inclusion of the benefit.

ITA: 7(1.1)
ITA: 125(7)

Furthermore, there will be a Division C deduction, equal to one-half of the inclusion, if the shares have not been sold or exchanged before the second anniversary date of the day of acquisition. For the purpose of determining the length of the holding period of the shares, shares are deemed to have been disposed of in the order in which they were acquired (i.e., first in, first out). The excess of the actual selling price over the fair market value at the date the option is exercised will result in a capital gain at the appropriate inclusion rate, as discussed in Chapter 7. Note that stock options issued by CCPCs can qualify for a deduction under paragraph 110(1)(*d*) (referred to above) or under paragraph 110(1)(*d*.1), but not both, even if both sets of conditions are met.

ITA: 110(1)(*d*.1)

ITA: 7(1.3)

¶3,280　Rules applicable to public corporations

There is another exception to the general rule that the stock option benefit must be included in income in the year of exercise. For public-company securities, the inclusion of the benefit can be deferred to the earlier of the year in which the shares acquired under the option are disposed of and the year in which the individual dies or becomes a non-resident. To obtain this deferral, the following conditions must be met:　　　　　ITA: 7(8)–(16)

- The securities are acquired after February 27, 2000 by Canadian residents.

- The share is of a class of shares listed on a Canadian or foreign prescribed stock　ITA: 248(1)
exchange, i.e., eligible listed shares.

- The deferral does not apply to options granted by Canadian-controlled private corporations, since a deferral is already available on such options under subsection 7(1.1).

- The deferral is available only if the employee is entitled to a Division C deduction under paragraph 110(1)(*d*), as previously discussed.

- The deferral is not available if the employee was, immediately after the option was granted, a specified shareholder (generally, owning 10% or more of any class of shares) of the employer.

- The deferral is subject to an annual limit of $100,000. The limit is based on the year in which the options vest (i.e., first become exercisable), and on the fair market value of the underlying securities when the options were granted. Thus, for options vesting in a given year, an employee will be able to defer taxation on the acquisition of securities having a total fair market value (determined at the time the options were granted) not exceeding $100,000.

- The deferral is not automatic. It requires that the employee file an election with the employer. The elective nature of the deferral allows an employee who has options in excess of the $100,000 limit vesting in a particular year to choose those options for which the deferral will be claimed.

- The deferral amount is to be reported as a special item on the employee's T4 slip in the year in which the security is acquired. The employee is required to include the deferred amount in computing income from employment when completing the tax return for the year in which the deferral ceases.

For a discussion of the implications on the disposition of shares acquired under a stock option, please refer to Chapter 7.

¶3,285　Valuation of shares

There is usually little difficulty in establishing the value of shares which are traded regularly as would be the case with shares in a public company. However, establishing the value of shares where there is no listing or open market is more difficult. In recent years, comprehensive methods of determining the value of such shares have been used. The CRA's　IC 89-3
approach to valuations of this nature is contained in an Information Circular.

¶3,290 Summary

The following diagram summarizes the rules for income inclusions for stock options.

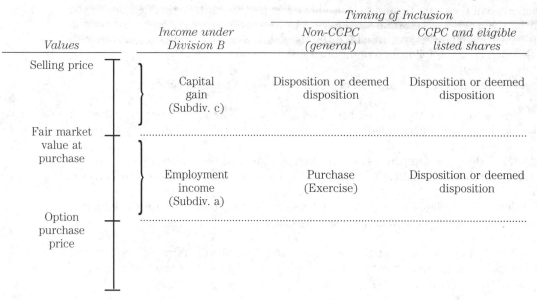

Values	Income under Division B	Timing of Inclusion	
		Non-CCPC (general)	CCPC and eligible listed shares
Selling price	Capital gain (Subdiv. c)	Disposition or deemed disposition	Disposition or deemed disposition
Fair market value at purchase	Employment income (Subdiv. a)	Purchase (Exercise)	Disposition or deemed disposition
Option purchase price			

Example Problem

Mr. Doubletax, who is employed by Public Co. Ltd., was granted an option in year one to purchase up to 5,000 common shares at $10 after completion of his fifth year of employment. The fair market value of the common shares at the time of granting the right was $12. He does not have any other shares.

During Mr. Doubletax's seventh year of employment he decided to exercise part of his right and purchased 1,000 shares with a fair market value of $15 as at that date.

Three years later, Mr. Doubletax sold the shares at $25 per share.

— REQUIRED

(A) Discuss the tax implications of each of the above transactions.

(B) How would your answer differ if the option price was $13 instead of $10?

(C) How would your answer differ if Mr. Doubletax was employed by a Canadian-controlled private corporation?

— SOLUTION

(A) *When option is granted:* There is no tax effect when Mr. Doubletax is granted the right to purchase shares through the stock option plan.

When option is exercised: Mr. Doubletax must take into employment income the difference   ITA: 7(1)
between the fair market value and the option price:

$$1,000 \text{ shares} \times (\$15 - \$10) = \$5,000.$$

The adjusted cost base of the shares, used in the calculation of a capital gain or loss on the disposition of the shares, will be set at the fair market value of the shares at the time of exercising the options (i.e., $15 per share). This amount is equal to the amount paid for the shares with after-tax funds (i.e., $10 per share) plus the amount included in the employee's income and subjected to tax (i.e., $5). Hence, the total adjusted cost base can be considered to be the total tax-paid cost in the shares.

There will be no deduction of one-half, since the option price ($10) is less than the fair   ITA: 110(1)(d)
market value ($12) at the date the option was granted. As a result, one of the conditions necessary to defer the inclusion of the benefit to the year of disposition or deemed disposition is not met.

Note that there has been no disposition at this point; he will have to find the funds to pay the tax from other sources.

When shares are sold: Mr. Doubletax will have a capital gain in the year of disposal calculated on the difference between the proceeds of disposition ($25) and the fair market value as at the date the option was exercised ($15) which is his cost base.[1]

$$1,000 \text{ shares} \times (\$25 - \$15) = \$10,000.$$

The taxable capital gain is ½ of $10,000 and is included in Subdivision c of Division B.

The results can be demonstrated as follows:

Proceeds of Disposition	$25	Capital gain of $10 per share
FMV at Exercise date	$15	
FMV at Grant date	$12	Employment income of $5 per share No Division C deduction is available
Option price	$10	

The fair market value at the grant date is only used to determine whether the Division C deduction is available.

ITA: 110(1)(*d*)

(B) In this part of the question, the option price was changed to $13, which means that he will be eligible for the Division C deduction. In addition, the fair market value of the 5,000 shares at the time the option was granted was $12 per share or $60,000 in total, which is less than $100,000. Therefore, he meets all the conditions for electing to defer reporting the stock option benefit from the year of exercise until the year of sale.

ITA: 110(1)(*d*)

When option is granted: There is no tax effect in the year the option is granted.

When option is exercised: As mentioned above, he can elect to defer the recognition of the benefit until he sells the shares. In this case he will not report any stock option benefit in his income and he will not be able to take the one-half deduction in the seventh year.

If he does not make this election, he will have to take the stock option benefit into income. This will be calculated as follows:

$$1,000 \text{ shares} \times (\$15 - \$13) = \$2,000$$

He will also be entitled to the one-half deduction, since the exercise price was greater than the fair market value at the date the option was granted. It is calculated as follows:

ITA: 110(1)(*d*)

$$\frac{1}{2} \times \$2,000 = (\$1,000)$$

This one-half deduction, effectively, reduces the income inclusion for eligible stock options to the inclusion rate for capital gains.

When the shares are sold: Assuming that he made the election to defer the stock option benefit then in the year of disposal, since nothing was reported in the seventh year, he will report the following:

$$\text{Stock option benefit: } 1,000 \text{ shares} \times (\$15 - \$13) = \$2,000$$

$$\text{Division C deduction: } \frac{1}{2} \times \$2,000 = (\$1,000)$$

$$\text{Capital gain: } 1,000 \text{ shares} \times (\$25 - \$15) = \$10,000$$

The results can be demonstrated as follows:

Proceeds of Disposition	$25	Capital gain of $10 per share
FMV at Exercise date	$15	
Option price	$13	Employment income of $2 per share Division C deduction of $1 per share
FMV at Grant date	$12	

The fair market value at the grant date is only used to determine whether the Division C deduction is available.

ITA: 110(1)(*d*)

(C) *CCPC* — If Mr. Doubletax had been employed by a Canadian-controlled private corporation (CCPC), with which he dealt at arm's length, then he would not have to include any amount in employment income upon exercising his right in the seventh year. Upon disposing of the shares in the tenth year, however, he would have employment income equal to the difference between the fair market value at the time he acquired the shares ($15) and his cost ($10):

ITA: 7(1.1)

$$1,000 \text{ shares} \times (\$15 - \$10) = \$5,000.$$

At the same time, he will also have a capital gain of $10,000:

$$1,000 \text{ shares} \times (\$25 - \$15^{(1)}) = \$10,000.$$

He would be eligible for a deduction of one-half of the employment income inclusion of $5,000, since he had retained the shares for more than two years.

ITA: 110(1)(*d*.1)

Summary of solution	Part A	Part B	Part C
	Public Corporation Option Price < FMV at Grant and Exercise Dates	**Public Corporation Option Price > FMV at Grant and < $100,000 in Total FMV**	**Canadian-controlled Private Corporation**
Year 1: (Option granted)	No tax effects in the year the option is granted.	No tax effects in the year the option is granted.	No tax effects in the year the option is granted.
Year 7: (Option exercised)	Recognize employment income benefit.	No tax effects if election made to defer the recognition of the stock option benefit.	No tax effects until the shares are sold.
Year 10: (Shares sold)	Recognize capital gain only.	Recognize employment income benefit, Division C deduction and capital gain.	Recognize employment income benefit, Division C deduction and capital gain.

Both stock option rules required an employment inclusion of $5,000; the difference was the timing of the inclusion. Where the stock option was offered by a Canadian-controlled private corporation, then the employment inclusion is at the time of disposition of the shares. For stock options from all other corporate employers, the employment inclusion is at the date the option is exercised or when shares are acquired, subject to the proposed $100,000 deferral.

ITA: 7(1), 7(1.1)

The Division C deductions were designed to give the same net effect as a capital gain, at the appropriate net inclusion rate, without permitting these amounts to qualify for the capital gains deduction. Both of these deductions will be discussed in further detail in Chapter 10.

ITA: 110(1)(*d*) or 110(1)(*d*.1)

— *NOTE TO SOLUTION*

[1] His cost is determined as the exercise price ($10) plus an addition to his cost base of the amount per share ($5) included in employment income under section 7. Both of these amounts represent tax-paid dollars which, by their inclusion in the cost base, will not be taxed further on disposition.

¶3,300   DEDUCTIONS FROM EMPLOYMENT INCOME

Subsection 8(1) lists all of the deductions that may be claimed in computing income from an office or employment. The Act specifically limits deductions from employment income to those specified in section 8. To qualify for these deductions, the provisions must be strictly adhered to. Note that the preamble to subsection 8(1) restricts these deductions to expenses which relate in some manner to the earning of employment income.

ITA: 8(2)

At this point, it should also be noted that the Act imposes a general limitation on the deductibility of expenses. To be deductible, the amount of the expenditure must be "reasonable in the circumstances". What is reasonable in the circumstances depends on the particular facts of a situation and may be determined by reference to a standard, such as an industry average or a previously accepted historical average, among others. Another general limitation denies the deduction of an expense incurred to commit an offence under specified sections of the *Criminal Code*.

ITA: 67

ITA: 67.5(1)

¶3,310   Sales/Negotiating Person's Expenses

Expenses incurred for the purpose of earning income from employment for employees who sell property or negotiate contracts may also be deductible. The nature or type of the expenses is not restricted, unlike for other employees, except for expenses of a capital nature.[17] Of course, these expenditures are subject to the general restrictions, just discussed, and a number of specific restrictions and/or exceptions. For example, expenditures in respect of the use of a yacht, camp, lodge, golf course, and membership fees in private clubs are not deductible.

ITA: 8(1)(*f*)

ITA: 8(1)(*f*)(v)

ITA: 8(1)(*f*)(vi), 18(1)(*l*)

Also not deductible are payments to reimburse the employer for the personal use of an employer provided automobile, since these payments reduce the previously-included benefit. The expenses claimed must be substantiated by vouchers or other records.

ITA: 8(1)(*f*)(vii)

ITA: 6(1)(*e*)

The amount of expenses that can be deducted is limited to the amount of the employee's commission income or other amounts, that are fixed by reference to the volume of sales or contracts negotiated.

Note the conditions in the provision that must be met for the expenses to be deductible.

---

[17] In the case of *Gifford v. The Queen*, 2004 DTC 6120 (S.C.C.), the issues were:

   (i) whether the payment made by an employee to a former employee for a client list was a deductible current expense under paragraph 8(1)(*f*) or a non-deductible capital outlay under subparagraph 8(1)(*f*)(v) and

   (ii) whether interest on funds borrowed to buy the list was also deductible under paragraph 8(1)(*f*) or non-deductible under subparagraph 8(1)(*f*)(v).

  Both payments were held to be "on account of capital" and, hence, were prevented by subparagraph 8(1)(*f*)(v) from being deducted.

- The employee must be required to pay his or her own expenses as stipulated in the contract of employment.[18]   ITA: 8(1)(*f*)(i)

- The employee must be ordinarily required to travel away from the employer's place of business.[19]   ITA: 8(1)(*f*)(ii)

- The remuneration must be dependent on volume of sales or contracts.[20]   ITA: 8(1)(*f*)(iii)

- A non-taxable allowance cannot be received, if a deduction under paragraph 8(1)(*f*) is to apply.   ITA: 8(1)(*f*)(iv)

If the allowance is not reasonable, then the sales/negotiating person must include the allowance in income. An unreasonable allowance is one that is less than a reasonable amount, greater than a reasonable amount, or deemed not to be reasonable. He or she may then deduct the expenses, since the employee would not be in receipt of an *excluded* allowance in such circumstances.   ITA: 6(1)(*b*)(v)

ITA: 8(1)(*f*)

The relationship between car allowances and car expenses for sales/negotiating persons and other employees is discussed later in the chapter. Other expenses for sales/negotiating persons will be discussed in more detail in Chapter 4, where comparisons with self-employed salespersons are made.

¶3,320   Any Employee's Travelling Expenses Other Than Motor Vehicle Expenses

¶3,325   Overview

The travelling expenses of employees who are not involved in the selling of property or negotiating of contracts are deductible under one of two provisions:

8(1)(*h*) — Travelling expenses other than motor vehicle expenses

8(1)(*h*.1) — Motor vehicle expenses (discussed later in this chapter)

Two separate provisions are used for reasons which will become apparent after the conditions for these deductions are explored.

Deductible travelling expenses are not restricted as to type of employee or employer. However, three specific conditions must be met to obtain the deduction for an expenditure. Many case situations, discussed below, involve an attempt to deduct expenses for travel between an employee's home and his or her place of work. These are not deductible travelling expenses, but personal or living expenses, unless the travel expenses are incurred between home and work sites away from the employee's usual place of work.[21] The reasonableness of the expenditures and the need for adequate record-keeping to substantiate the deduction were at issue in other court decisions.[22]   ITA: 8(1)(*h*)

---

[18] See two Federal Court of Appeal cases: *The Queen v. Moore*, 90 DTC 6200 (F.C.A.), and *The Queen v. Betz*, 90 DTC 6201 (F.C.A.). In these decisions, the Court expanded the concept of a contractual obligation to include unwritten conditions which would result in an unfavourable performance assessment.

[19] *Healy v. The Queen*, 78 DTC 6239 (F.C.A.).

[20] *Neville v. M.N.R.*, 88 DTC 1546 (T.C.C.). A payment that was made as a percent of an employer's gross profit was held not to be an amount based on volume of sales in *Griesbach v. M.N.R.*, 91 DTC 142 (T.C.C.).

[21] The following cases resulted in a decision for personal or living expenses: *Martyn v. M.N.R.*, 62 DTC 341 (T.A.B.); *Luks v. M.N.R.*, 58 DTC 1194 (Ex. Ct.); *Wilkinson v. M.N.R.*, 66 DTC 344 (T.A.B.); and *Carson v. M.N.R.*, 66 DTC 424 (T.A.B.). On the other hand, in *The Queen v. Merten*, 90 DTC 6600 (F.C.T.D.), the taxpayer was allowed to deduct expenses to travel to work sites away from his usual place of work.

[22] *No. 589 v. M.N.R.*, 59 DTC 41 (T.A.B.), *Niessen v. M.N.R.*, 60 DTC 489 (T.A.B.), and *Winter v. M.N.R.*, 88 DTC 1143 (T.C.C.).

¶3,330 Conditions

The first condition imposed is that the employee must ordinarily be required to carry out his or her duties away from his or her employer's place of business. The CRA's interpretation of the word "ordinarily", in this paragraph only, is habitually or customarily. However, there should be some degree of regularity in the required travelling.[23] ITA: 8(1)(*h*)(i)
IT-522R, par. 32

The second condition requires that the payment of the travelling expenses by the employee must be part of his or her contract. The contract can be either in a written or oral form, but the latter may be harder to prove in a court of law. There have been several court cases involving this issue.[24] ITA: 8(1)(*h*)(ii)

The third condition is that the employee cannot be in receipt of a tax-exempt allowance for travelling expenses, which exclude the allowance if it is reasonable. Therefore, employees who have received an allowance that is greater or less than a reasonable amount can include the allowance in income and can deduct the related expenses, because they would not be in receipt of an excluded (reasonable) allowance in such circumstances. Whether an allowance is reasonable depends upon *all* the facts in a particular circumstance. ITA: 8(1)(*h*)(iii), 6(1)(*b*)(v)–(vii)

Note that the receipt of an excluded allowance for employment use of a motor vehicle precludes the deduction of motor vehicle expenses, but does not preclude the deduction of more general travelling expenses. This is likely the reason for the existence of the two separate deduction provisions. The receipt of an excluded (reasonable) allowance for one type of travelling expense does not preclude the deduction of the other type of travelling expense. ITA: 6(1)(*b*)(vii.1), 8(1)(*h*.1), 8(1)(*h*)

Employees who make deductions under paragraph 8(1)(*f*), (*h*), or (*h*.1) and subparagraph 8(1)(*i*)(ii) or (iii) (office rent and supplies which are discussed in the next section) must file a prescribed form (T2200) signed by their employers certifying that the conditions set out in these provisions were met in the year. However, it appears that the CRA has simplified the administration of the application of some of the conditions in these provisions. For example, an Interpretation Bulletin indicates that, as long as the form T2200 is completed properly by the employer, then the requirement that there must be a contractual arrangement stipulating that the employee must pay for the travelling expenses will be met. Also this Interpretation Bulletin indicates in paragraph 58 that form T2200 should be kept with the taxpayer's records for examination on request. Thus, the form is not required to be filed with the tax return. ITA: 8(10)

IT-522R, par. 33

¶3,335 Limitations

The deduction under paragraphs 8(1)(*f*) and (*h*) of the cost of meals consumed while travelling for an employer is restricted. These costs are deductible only where the meal is consumed when the taxpayer is away, for 12 hours or more, from the municipality or metropolitan area where he or she usually reports for work.[25] ITA: 8(4)

The deduction for the cost of meals consumed and entertainment is limited to 50% of the lesser of the amount paid or payable and a reasonable amount. There are a number of exceptions to these restrictions for meal expenses, as described in some detail in an Interpretation Bulletin entitled "Food, Beverages and Entertainment Expenses": ITA: 67.1

IT-518R

- moving expenses (see Chapter 9); ITA: 62

- child-care expenses (see Chapter 9); ITA: 63

- medical expenses which qualify for non-refundable credit (see Chapter 10); ITA: 118.2

---

[23] The interpretation of the word "ordinarily" was at issue in the cases of *Krieger v. M.N.R.*, 79 DTC 269 (T.R.B.), *The Queen v. Patterson*, 82 DTC 6326 (F.C.T.D.), and *Imray v. The Queen*, 98 DTC 6580 (F.C.T.D.).

[24] *The Queen v. Cival*, 83 DTC 5168 (F.C.A.); *Rozen v. The Queen*, 85 DTC 5611 (F.C.T.D.); and *Hoedel v. The Queen*, 86 DTC 6535 (F.C.A.).

[25] See the case of *Krieger v. M.N.R.*, 79 DTC 269 (T.R.B.).

- the specific products and services of taxpayers who are in the business of providing meals and entertainment;

- meals provided where the primary purpose is for fund-raising for a registered charity;

- reasonable reimbursements to the employer;

- exempted amounts for a special work site;   ITA: 6(6)(*a*)(ii)

- the cost of meals and entertainment at special and remote work sites, subject to some additional restrictions; and   ITA: 6(6)(*a*)(i), 67.1(2)(*e*)

- meals and entertainment, at up to six special events generally available to all employees at the particular place of business.

¶3,340   Receipts by part-time employees for travelling expenses

Personal travelling expenses are not deductible under the normal rules. However, where an individual receives an allowance for or a reimbursement of travelling expenses in respect of the individual's part-time employment, the receipts are treated as income which is exempt from tax found in Subdivision g — "Amounts Not Included in Income". There are several tests which must be met in order to have these travelling expenses qualify for this provision: ITA: 81(3.1)

(a) the part-time employee must have other employment or business income;

(b) the amount received cannot exceed a reasonable amount and the travelling expenses must be in respect of travelling only to and from the part-time employment, not travelling expenses incurred *during* the part-time employment; and

(c) the part-time employment location must be at least 80 kilometres away from both the employee's ordinary place of residence and his or her principal place of business or employment.

Condition (a), above, is waived for individuals who are employed part-time as professors or teachers by designated educational institutions. The purpose of this exception is to facilitate the recruiting of part-time instructors by universities and other educational institutions outside major metropolitan areas.   ITA: 81(3.1)(*a*)(ii)

ITA: 118.6(1)

¶3,350   Other Expenses

¶3,355   Legal expenses

Certain legal expenses incurred by employees are deductible. The expenses are limited to those incurred to collect or establish a right to remuneration owed to the employee by an employer or former employer. [Bill C-33, dated November 22, 2006, proposed to extend this deduction to amounts not owed to the employee directly by the employer, if the amounts, when received, would be taxable as employment income. For example, legal fees incurred by an employee to collect insurance benefits under a sickness or accident insurance policy provided through an employer would be deductible.]   ITA: 8(1)(*b*)

¶3,360   Dues and other expenses[26]

Also deductible are: ITA: 8(1)(*i*)

---

[26] The cases of *Daley v. M.N.R.*, 50 DTC 877 (Ex. Ct.), and *Montgomery, et. al. v. M.N.R.*, 99 DTC 5186 (F.C.A.), deal with professional membership dues; the case of *The Queen v. Thompson*, 89 DTC 5439 (F.C.T.D.), deals with the controversial topic of imputed office rent expense; the case of *Felton v. M.N.R.*, 89 DTC 233 (T.C.C.), deals with deductibility of home office expenses generally; the cases of *Luks v. M.N.R.*, 58 DTC 1194 (Ex. Ct.), and *Thibault v. M.N.R.*, 86 DTC 1538 (T.C.C.), deal with the meaning of "supplies".

- annual professional membership dues paid to maintain standing in a profession recognized by statute;

- office rent paid or salary paid to an assistant;

- the cost of supplies paid; and

- annual union membership dues paid.

One of the requirements that must be met in order for an amount to be deductible is that it must be paid by the employee. However, an amount also qualifies for a deduction if the employer paid the amount and added it to the employee's income as a taxable benefit. [Proposed amendment in Bill C-33, dated November 22, 2006.]

There are a number of restrictions that are placed on these expenses:

ITA: 8(1)(*i*)

(a) First, a limitation is placed on dues which prohibits the deduction of amounts that are not directly attributable to the ordinary operating expenses of the organization which is levying the dues.

ITA: 8(5)

(b) Second, there are the employment contract requirements placed on the amounts deductible for office rent or salary to an assistant and for the cost of supplies.

ITA: 8(1)(*i*)(ii)–(iii)

(c) Finally, remember that the preamble to section 8 restricts deductions to those that are wholly applicable to that source. Hence, a professional accountant who teaches English literature in the secondary school system cannot deduct his or her accounting association dues, but can deduct his or her teaching association dues.

ITA: 8(1)(*i*)(i), 8(1)(*i*)(iv)

As long as form T2200 is completed properly by the employer, it appears that the contractual requirement will be met through this certification procedure. The employer is required to certify by signing form T2200 that the employee was required to maintain an office away from the employer's place of business. Furthermore, an Interpretation Bulletin administratively requires that the deductibility of these expenses, except union dues and professional fees, requires a contract of employment (written or "tacitly understood"), certified by the employer signing form T2200, to permit the deduction of office rent, supplies, or salaries paid by the employee to an assistant or substitute.

ITA: 8(1)(*i*)(ii) (rent and salary paid to an assistant) and 8(1)(*i*)(iii) (supplies)

IT-352R2, par. 13

¶3,365 Tradespersons' tool expenses

A deduction is allowed from employment income earned as a tradesperson in a taxation year to a maximum of $500 for eligible new tools. This deduction is computed as the excess, if any, of the total cost to the individual of one or more eligible tools over $1,000 (indexed after 2007) to a maximum excess of $500. An "eligible tool" is defined to be a tool (including ancillary equipment) that:

ITA: 8(1)(*s*)

ITA: 8(6.1)

- was new and, hence, not used for any purpose whatsoever before it is acquired by the individual;

- is certified by the individual's employer in prescribed form to be required as a condition of, and for use in, the individual's employment as a tradesperson in the year; and

- is, unless the device or equipment can be used only for the purpose of measuring, locating, or calculating, not an electronic communication device or electronic data processing equipment.

The cost of the tools used for computing tax depreciation (i.e., capital cost allowance) or for capital gains purposes is reduced by the amount of this deduction.

ITA: 8(7)

¶3,370 Work space in home

There are restrictions on the deductibility of expenses related to work space in the home for employees. This provision parallels the rules for self-employed individuals as discussed in an Interpretation Bulletin. The provision only applies to individuals who are entitled to deductions for sales expenses or for rent or supplies related to a work space in a home. The effect of the provision is twofold. A deduction is then only permitted if the work space is:
`ITA: 18(13)`
`ITA: 18(12)`
`IT-514`
`ITA: 8(1)(f), 8(1)(i)`

(a) the place where the individual *principally* (more than 50% of the time) performs the employment duties; or
`IT-352R2, par. 2`

(b) (i) used *exclusively* for the purpose of earning employment income during the period, and

(ii) used on a regular and continuous basis for meeting customers or other persons in the ordinary course of performing the employment duties.

As long as more than 50% of the employment duties are performed in the home work space, then test (a) above has been met and test (b) above can be ignored. Where test (a) is not met, then the exclusive condition in test (b)(i) above must be met. The word "exclusively" is not defined in the Act. *Webster's English Dictionary* defines "exclusively" as "to the exclusion of all others" which is a much more onerous test.

Once one of the conditions in (a) or (b) above has been met in the year of the expenditure, then the work space deduction is restricted to employment-source income. However, there is an indefinite carry-forward provision as long as the employee can meet either test (a) or (b) above in the future year of deduction.
`IT-352R2, par. 3`

Supplies related to a work space in the home include expenses paid for the maintenance of the home such as the cost of fuel, electricity, light bulbs, cleaning materials and minor repairs. For an eligible individual, property taxes and insurance paid on a home owned by the individual are deductible. All of these expenses must be allocated between the work space and the personal space of the home on a reasonable basis such as floor space.
`IT-352R2, par. 5`
`ITA: 8(1)(f)`

Note that no provision in section 8 allows the deduction of interest on funds borrowed in any manner for the purchase of a home for any use by the employee.

¶3,375 CPP and EI premiums payable in respect of an assistant

A salary paid by an employee to an assistant or substitute may be deductible if required by the contract of employment of the payer. Such payments may also require the payment of Canada Pension Plan or Employment Insurance premiums that are the responsibility of an employer. Amounts payable by an employee as premiums for CPP and EI in respect of an assistant are deductible.
`ITA: 8(1)(i)(ii)`
`ITA: 8(1)(l.1)`

¶3,380 Registered Pension Plans

¶3,385 Overview

There are two different types of registered pension plans (RPPs): defined benefit and money purchase (defined contribution). Defined benefit plans guarantee a predetermined amount of retirement income based on a flat amount per year of service or a percentage of the employee's earnings over a defined period. The defined benefit RPPs are funded by actuarially-determined contributions by the employee and/or employer. Money-purchase RPPs provide whatever pension income that the contributed funds in the plan can purchase through the acquisition of an annuity. No predetermined amount of pension income is guaranteed under a money-purchase plan. Benefits will depend upon the actual contributions, the investment return of the plan and annuity rates at the date of purchase.

The major objective of pension reform, which became effective for years after 1990, was to eliminate the discrepancies among the various tax-assisted retirement plans by imposing a comprehensive single limit of 18% of employee earnings for all employee and/or employer contributions to registered pension plans (defined benefit and defined contribution), registered retirement savings plans (RRSPs) and deferred profit sharing plans (DPSPs).

Total annual comprehensive dollar limits for money-purchase RPPs for employer and/or employee contributions are set at the following amounts:

2005	2006	2007	2008	2009	2010
$18,000	$19,000	$20,000	$21,000	$22,000	indexed

The dollar limits for 2008 and 2009 will be increased to the greater of the dollar limits shown above and $18,000 indexed with the increase in the average wage for the year after 2006. After 2009, the maximum amount of $22,000 will be indexed with the increase in the average wage for the year. Contribution limits for RRSPs, which are discussed in detail in Chapter 9, will reflect benefits accruing under defined benefit RPPs and contributions to money-purchase RPPs and DPSPs.

Defined benefit plans also have contribution limits for employees and employers; however, the limits that are imposed are set in terms of the maximum pension which can be received on retirement. Contributions to fund the pension are then actuarially determined. Generally speaking, the maximum defined benefit is calculated as 2% of the employee's income, usually an average of the highest income level for 3 to 7 years, times the number of years of service to a maximum of 70%.

Paragraph 8(1)(*m*) provides the statutory authority for an employment deduction in respect of registered pension plans, but only as determined by subsection 147.2(4), which is found under Division G, "Deferred and Other Special Income Arrangements".

A defined benefit RPP must meet the conditions described above and others in order to be "registered". Meeting the conditions implies that the contributions made by an employee, in whatever amount acceptable under the registration conditions, are deductible by the employee. On the other hand, deductible contributions to a money-purchase RPP are restricted annually by the comprehensive dollar limit discussed above.

ITA: 8(1)(*m*)

¶3,400 SPECIFIC PROVISIONS FOR CAR ALLOWANCES AND EXPENSES

This part of the chapter separates and discusses specific provisions pertaining to cars. The focus of this part of the chapter is on cars that are either owned or leased by employees and used for employment purposes. Provisions pertaining to employer-provided cars were discussed previously in this chapter. Provisions pertaining to capital cost allowance restrictions on cars owned by either employees or employers will be discussed in Chapter 5.

Several definitions in respect of cars are briefly *summarized* below:

ITA: 248(1)

(a) Motor vehicle — an automotive vehicle (undefined) designed to be used on highways and streets but not trolley buses or vehicles on rails.

(b) Automobile — a motor vehicle designed to carry up to nine individuals plus baggage, including vans, certain pick-up trucks and station wagons but excluding ambulances, taxis, hearses, vehicle inventory and clearly marked fire department, police [or Emergency Medical Services (EMS)] vehicles.

(c) Passenger vehicle — an automobile acquired or leased after June 17, 1987.

It is important to determine which of the above definitions is being referred to. For example, paragraph 6(1)(*b*) on allowances refers to a motor vehicle, subsection 6(2) on the standby charge refers to an automobile, and section 67.2 on the limitation of deductions (discussed below) refers to a passenger vehicle.

¶3,410 Motor Vehicle Allowances Received from Employers

¶3,415 Overview

As previously discussed, all allowances received by employees are included in income with specified exceptions. Two of these exceptions were explained previously: ITA: 6(1)(*b*)

- *all* allowances pertaining to salespersons and persons who negotiate contracts, and ITA: 6(1)(*b*)(v)

- in respect of allowances, except motor vehicle allowances, for all other employees. ITA: 6(1)(*b*)(vii)

Note that the motor vehicle allowance rules are separate for "ordinary" employees, but included with all allowances for sales/negotiating persons. The reason for the distinction is that ordinary employee allowances for travelling, other than for motor vehicle expenses, have a territorial restriction and are limited to travel away from the municipality and metropolitan area of the employer's establishment. However, the other allowance rules mentioned above, as discussed next, do not have this territorial restriction. ITA: 6(1)(*b*)(vii),
6(1)(*b*)(vii.1)

The following table shows the applicable provisions.

**Exceptions to Employment Income Inclusion
of Travelling Allowances in Paragraph 6(1)(*b*)**

	Sales/Negotiating Persons	*Other Persons*
Allowance other than for motor vehicles	Spar. 6(1)(*b*)(v)	Spar. 6(1)(*b*)(vii)
Allowance for motor vehicles	Spar. 6(1)(*b*)(v)	Spar. 6(1)(*b*)(vii.1)

¶3,420 Allowances for motor vehicles — Other persons

The Act sets out the initial conditions for exempting motor vehicle allowances for employees, other than those who are salespersons or who negotiate contracts. The conditions for exemption are: ITA: 6(1)(*b*)(vii.1)

(a) the allowances must be reasonable in the circumstances (therefore, motor vehicle allowances which are not reasonable, i.e., less than a reasonable amount, greater than a reasonable amount, or deemed not to be reasonable (as discussed below), must be included in income); and

(b) the allowances must be in respect of travelling in the performance of the duties of an office or employment.

An Interpretation Bulletin, "Vehicle and other travelling expenses — Employees", makes some important administrative comments on the application of this provision. First, where an employee receives a set periodic amount (i.e., monthly, weekly, etc.) the amount will be considered to be an excluded advance (prepaid reimbursement) rather than a potentially excludable allowance where: IT-522R, par. 44

(a) there is a beginning-of-the-year agreement between the employee and employer that the employee will receive a stated amount per kilometre for business-related travelling;

(b) there is a year-end accounting for any difference between the advances and the actual business-related kilometres; and

(c) the amounts above are reasonable.

The CRA will, as a general rule, consider the kilometre allowances permitted by regulation as deductions for *employers* as reasonable allowances. These amounts (for 2007), generally, are 50¢ on the first 5,000 kilometres and 44¢ on the remaining kilometres. (See Chapter 4 for further comments on these amounts.) However, at the same time, the CRA acknowledges that reasonableness of an allowance is normally decided based on the particular fact situation.

IT-522R, par. 43; ITR: 7306

¶3,425　Allowance deemed not to be reasonable

Two additional subparagraphs and the preamble thereto modify and restrict the exclusion from income of certain motor vehicle allowances. The preamble deems the allowance received "not to be a reasonable allowance" where:

- the motor vehicle allowance is not based solely on kilometres in respect of use for the employer's business, or

ITA: 6(1)(*b*)(x)

- both an allowance and a reimbursement, in whole or in part for expenses in respect of that use, are received. Excepted is the reimbursement of expenses for supplementary business insurance, toll and ferry charges.

ITA: 6(1)(*b*)(xi)

Whether an allowance is excluded from employment income based on the reasonableness test is critical in determining the deductibility of expenses by the employee. As has been discussed previously in this chapter, the exclusion of a reasonable allowance from employment income results in the prohibition of the deduction of expenses for which the allowance is received.

An allowance is deemed to be unreasonable and, therefore, included in income, if it is received for the use of a motor vehicle and is not based solely on the number of kilometres driven for employment purposes.

ITA: 6(1)(*b*)(x)

The CRA has indicated that, if the employer pays an employee both a flat-rate allowance and a per-kilometre allowance for the same use of the automobile, the whole amount is deemed to be one allowance that is taxable, since it is not based solely on the number of kilometers driven. If an employee received a flat monthly rate for fixed expenses plus a reasonable per-kilometre rate, then the CRA considers the two allowances to be for the same use and combines them as one allowance which is not based solely on kilometres driven. They have indicated that the two allowances can be separated, if the employer pays a reasonable per-kilometre rate for travel outside the employment area and a flat monthly rate for travel inside the employment area. In this case, the two amounts are not for the same use and the per-kilometre allowance, in this case, would not be taxable, but the flat-rate allowance would be.

¶3,430　Expenses

¶3,435　Overview

Motor vehicle expenses are carved out from general travelling expenses for ordinary employees. Motor vehicle expenses for salespersons and negotiating persons (persons who negotiate contracts and who have commission income or income based on volume of sales) still remain deductible. Refer to Exhibit 3-1 which summarizes and compares all employee deductions under paragraphs 8(1)(*f*), (*h*), and (*h*.1).

ITA: 8(1)(*h*), 8(1)(*h*.1)

ITA: 8(1)(*f*)

EXHIBIT 3-1
Comparison of Employee Deduction Provisions

Conditions	Sales/negotiating person's expenses	Travelling Expenses	
	Par. 8(1)(f)	*Par. 8(1)(h)*	*Par. 8(1)(h.1) motor vehicle*
Nature of employment	the taxpayer was employed in the year in connection with the selling of property or the negotiating of contracts for the employer	no restrictions	no restrictions
General type of expenditure	amounts expended by the taxpayer in the year for the purpose of earning income from the employment	amounts expended by the taxpayer in the year for travelling in the course of the taxpayer's employment	amounts expended by the taxpayer in the year in respect of motor vehicle expenses incurred for travelling in the course of employment
Conditions of employment			
Contract*	under the contract of employment was required to pay the taxpayer's own expenses	under the contract of employment was required to pay the travelling expenses incurred by the taxpayer in the performance of the duties of the office or employment	was required under the contract of employment to pay the motor vehicle expenses incurred in the performance of the duties of the office or employment
Duties	was ordinarily required to carry on the duties of employment away from the employer's place of business	was ordinarily required to carry on the duties of the employment away from the employer's place of business or in different places	was ordinarily required to carry on the duties of the employment away from the employer's place of business or in different places
Limits	was remunerated in whole or part by commission or other similar amounts fixed by reference to the volume of the sales made or the contracts negotiated	did not claim a deduction in the year under par. 8(1)(e), (f), or (g)	did not claim a deduction for the year under par. 8(1)(f)
Allowances	was not in receipt of an allowance for travelling expenses in respect of the taxation year that was, by virtue of spar. 6(1)(b)(v), not included in computing his or her income	did not receive an allowance for travelling expenses that was, by reason of spar. 6(1)(b)(v), (vi) or (vii), not included in computing the taxpayer's income for the year	did not receive an allowance for motor vehicle expenses that was, by reason of par. 6(1)(b), not included in computing the taxpayer's income for the year
Restrictions on type of expenditure**			
Capital outlay . . .	not outlays, losses, or replacements of capital or payments on account of capital except interest and capital cost allowances described in par. 8(1)(j)	travelling expenses*** other than motor vehicle expenses and capital expenditures	motor vehicle expenses incurred for travelling other than capital expenditures except interest and capital cost allowances described in par. 8(1)(j)

Conditions	Sales/negotiating person's expenses	Travelling Expenses	
	Par. 8(1)(f)	Par. 8(1)(h)	Par. 8(1)(h.1) motor vehicle
Club dues	not outlays or expenses that would, by virtue of par. 18(1)(l), not be deductible in computing the income for the year if the employment were a business carried on by the taxpayer		
Standby payments	not amounts the payment of which reduced the amount that would otherwise be included in computing the taxpayer's income for the year by reason of par. 6(1)(e)		
Restrictions on amounts of deductible expenditures . . .	not exceeding the commissions or other amounts fixed by reference to the volume of sales made or the contracts negotiated, amounts in respect of the workspace in the home of the individual that meets the conditions set out in spar. 8(13)(a)(i) or (ii) cannot exceed the individual's income for the year from the office or employment computed without reference to any deduction in respect of the workspace	no restrictions	no restrictions

* Subject to the requirements in subsection 8(10) for the filing of form T2200.

** Subsection 8(4) and section 67.1 restrict deductions for meal expenditures.

*** Includes expenses of employee-owned aircraft as well as interest and capital cost allowance on such aircraft as allowed by paragraph 8(1)(j), subject to the limitation in subsection 8(9).

Source: Reproduced with the permission of the Canadian Tax Foundation from, Robert E. Beam and Stanley N. Laiken, "Employee Deductions", Personal Tax Planning Feature (1991), Vol. 39, No. 2 *Canadian Tax Journal*, pp. 338–71, at pp. 340–42, Table 1.

A series of provisions which modify, limit or depend upon paragraphs 8(1)(f), (h) and (h.1) is presented, followed by examples which apply these rules as they pertain to cars.

¶3,440 Motor vehicle and aircraft — Interest and CCA

The deduction of certain expenses which are, in essence, capital in nature; namely, interest on loans and the depreciation for tax purposes (i.e., capital cost allowance) in respect of motor vehicles and aircraft is specifically allowed. A deduction is only available where an employee may deduct expenditures under paragraph 8(1)(f), (h), or (h.1). Hence, it is critical to establish that the employee was not in receipt of a tax-exempt allowance that would preclude a deduction of expenses under these three provisions. In the case of a sales/negotiating person, only a deduction under paragraph 8(1)(f) is limited to the amount of commission income. The interest and CCA deduction is not restricted to the amount of commission income or similar amounts received. These deductions are further restricted as explained below.

ITA: 8(1)(j)

Capital cost allowance will be discussed in some detail in Chapter 5. However, at this stage, all that has to be understood is that accounting depreciation and capital cost allowance (CCA) are quite similar. The major exception is that in respect of depreciable capital properties that are motor vehicles and aircraft the maximum deduction *must* be based on the declining balance method (30% for motor vehicles and 40% for aircraft) and that in the year of acquisition the rates are one-half of the normal rate.

Note that in the case of an aircraft, the use thereof must be *required* for employment purposes. However, a motor vehicle need only be *used* for employment purposes to qualify for a deduction. In addition, the deduction in respect of an aircraft is limited to the amount that is reasonable in the circumstances in relation to the availability of other modes of transportation. ITA: 8(9)

¶3,445 Imputed interest deemed paid

There is an employment income inclusion for a benefit obtained through a low-interest loan to an employee. These benefits are computed, as previously discussed in this chapter. This interest income inclusion in employment income, in respect of interest on funds borrowed to purchase a motor vehicle or aircraft, is *deemed* to be interest *paid*. Hence, this deemed interest payment is eligible for a deduction along with interest actually paid. This rule allows for the deduction of "any interest paid", which would include amounts "deemed to be interest paid". This amount, however, must be prorated for employment kilometres driven or hours flown to arrive at the allowable deduction.

ITA: 6(9)
ITA: 80.4(1), 80.4(3)–(7)
ITA: 80.5
ITA: 8(1)(*j*)
ITA: 8(1)(*j*)(i)

¶3,450 Interest on money borrowed for passenger vehicle

The Act limits the amount deductible in respect of interest on funds borrowed or debt incurred on the acquisition of a passenger vehicle to the lesser of: ITA: 67.2

(a) the actual amount payable (or paid); and IT-522R, par. 28

(b) $300 for each 30-day period that the automobile loan or debt was outstanding in the year. ITR: 7307(2)

Note that there is no rounding of the number of periods to a number of full months as there is in the standby charge rules. The resulting lesser amount is further prorated by the portion of employment use to the total use based on kilometres driven.

¶3,455 Capital cost for passenger vehicle

The Act and Regulations place limits on the capital cost of a passenger vehicle. The limits are set out as follows: ITA: 13(7)(*g*); ITR: 7307(1)

Acquisition date	Maximum capital cost	Reference
After 2000	$30,000 plus PST and GST on the $30,000	Par. 13(7)(*g*) Reg. 7307(1)

Where the passenger vehicle is acquired from a person with whom the purchaser does not deal at arm's length (usually a related person), the capital cost is deemed to be the least of: ITA: 13(7)(*h*), 251

(a) the fair market value;

(b) the undepreciated capital cost of the seller; and

(c) the dollar maximum found in the above summary.

¶3,460 Limitation re cost of leased passenger vehicle

Passenger vehicle leasing costs are limited in a manner equivalent to the $30,000 capital cost restriction as described above. The following formula calculates the deductible portion of the leasing cost. ITA: 67.3 ITR: 7307

Lesser of:

(a) $$\left[\dfrac{A \times B}{30}\right] - C - D - E$$

(b) $$\left[\dfrac{F \times G}{.85H}\right] - D - E$$

where A is a dollar monthly maximum, as prescribed and reflected in the notes below;*

B is the aggregate of the number of days the vehicle was leased for all years to the end of the present year;

C is the aggregate of the lease costs deducted in all preceding years;

D is imputed interest, at the prescribed rate, on refundable amounts (e.g., deposits) over $1,000;

E is total reimbursements receivable in respect of the lease in the year;

F is the total lease charges payable (including PST and GST) for the year;

G is the dollar maximum capital cost prescribed;**

H is the greater of:

(a) a dollar maximum prescribed amount,*** and

(b) the manufacturer's list price.

*Date of lease contract	Maximum monthly deduction	Reference
After 2000	$800 plus PST and GST on the $800	Sec. 67.3 Reg. 7307(3)

** The rules are similar to the capital cost limitations described above. See Reg. 7307(1)(*b*)(iii).

*** Regulation 7307(4) calculates the appropriate number for years after 1997 by multiplying the capital cost maximum amount (see above) by $^{100}/_{85}$, i.e., $^{100}/_{85} \times [\$30,000 \times (1 + .08 + .06)] = \$40,588$, assuming a PST rate of 8% and a GST rate of 6%.

Note that there is no rounding of the 30-day periods in part (a) above as in the rule pertaining to the standby charge.

ITA: 6(2)

Part (a) of the above formula provides a dollar limit, $800 (prescribed for years after 2000) plus PST and GST per month. Recognize, however, that a lease could be devised for almost any car, no matter how expensive, so that the monthly lease payments do not exceed that limit. To discourage this strategy, the further limit in part (b) of the formula was necessary. That part allows a fraction of the total lease charges as a maximum deduction. The fraction is based on the $30,000 maximum capital cost for capital cost allowance purposes for years after 2000, relative to 85% of the manufacturer's list price of the car. The higher the list price in the denominator of the fraction, the lower the value of the fraction and the lower the amount of lease payments that can be deducted.

Leasing a car involves paying for both the capital cost of the car consumed during the leasing period and an interest cost for spreading the payments over time. Therefore, the limit on the deduction of lease payments must provide for a limit equivalent to the limit on capital cost allowance and the limit on interest for a purchased car.

¶3,465 Summary of interplay among deduction provisions

The following diagram illustrates how the deduction provisions discussed above are applied.

ITA: 8(1)(f), 8(1)(h), 8(1)(h.1), 8(1)(i), 8(1)(j)

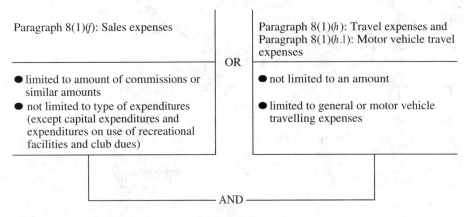

Paragraph 8(1)(*f*): Sales expenses

OR

Paragraph 8(1)(*h*): Travel expenses and
Paragraph 8(1)(*h*.1): Motor vehicle travel
expenses

- limited to amount of commissions or
  similar amounts
- not limited to type of expenditures
  (except capital expenditures and
  expenditures on use of recreational
  facilities and club dues)

- not limited to an amount

- limited to general or motor vehicle
  travelling expenses

AND

Paragraph 8(1)(*i*): Dues and other expenses

Paragraph 8(1)(*j*): Motor vehicle and aircraft costs, as follows:
            (i) interest on funds borrowed
            (ii) capital cost allowance

Where travel expenses, alone, exceed the amount of commissions or similar income, it is advantageous to use the deduction under paragraphs 8(1)(*h*) and (*h*.1), instead of paragraph 8(1)(*f*). Where a deduction is possible for an amount either under paragraph 8(1)(*f*) or paragraph 8(1)(*i*), it is better to deduct under paragraph 8(1)(*i*), which is not limited by commissions or similar income, to preserve deduction room under paragraph 8(1)(*f*).

¶3,470 Application of Rules

The following examples will demonstrate the rules for car allowances and expenses.

Example Problem 1

Mr. Alex Otto Deduckshun acquired an automobile on July 1, 2007, to be used in connection with his duties of employment. Alex is required by contract to use his own car and to pay directly all the expenses. Alex does not have any commission income. The following information, some of which is estimated, relates to the newly acquired car:

Cost of car (including PST and GST)	$38,000
Total kilometres driven in the ownership period	25,000
Total kilometres in respect of his employer's business	15,000
Capital cost allowance rate (½ × 30%)	15%
Interest paid on bank loan in respect of the car	$ 1,950
Gas and oil	1,800
Maintenance	300
Insurance	1,400
Licences	100

Alex lives in a province which has a sales tax of 10% on automobiles; therefore, the effective PST and GST rate would be 16% (10% + 6%).

— REQUIRED

Determine the amount deductible in the taxation year in respect of the car expenditures in the following situations, on the assumption that the above expenses were reasonable: ITA: 8(1)(h.1)

(A) no kilometre allowance was received;

(B) a reasonable allowance of 38¢ per kilometre in respect of employment driving was received;

(C) an unreasonable allowance of 5¢ per kilometre in respect of employment driving was received;

(D) a reasonable allowance of 25¢ per kilometre in respect of employment driving plus a yearly allowance of $2,000 was received;

(E) an unreasonable allowance of $1 per kilometre in respect of employment driving was received.

— SOLUTION

Potentially deductible expenses (before prorating for employment use):

Capital cost allowance limit: ITA: 13(7)(g)

$$(\tfrac{1}{2} \times 30\%) \times (\$30,000 \times 1.16) \ldots\ldots\ldots\ldots\ldots\ldots\ldots \quad \$5,220$$

Interest expense — lesser of:

(a) $1,950 (actual)

(b) $300 \times \dfrac{184}{30} = \$1,840$ 1,840

Gas and oil	1,800
Maintenance	300
Insurance	1,400
Licences	100
	$10,660

Portion relating to employment use:

$$\frac{15,000 \text{ km}}{25,000 \text{ km}} \times \$10,660 = \underline{\$6,396}$$

Alternative Fact Situations:

(A) All of the $6,396 automobile expenses would be deductible, since all the conditions of these provisions have been met as follows: ITA: 8(1)(h.1), 8(1)(j)

(1) the automobile is used in connection with his employment duties;

(2) there is a contractual obligation to use his own car and to pay directly all of the automobile expenses;

(3) a reasonable allowance had not been received; and

(4) he was not eligible for a deduction as a sales/negotiating person in respect of the automobile expenses.   ITA: 8(1)(f)

(B) None of the $6,396 would be deductible, since subparagraph 6(1)(b)(vii.1) exempts reasonable allowances.   ITA: 8(1)(h.1)(iii)

(C) Since the 5¢ per kilometre allowance is not a reasonable amount, Mr. Deduckshun must include the allowance in income and would be permitted the $6,396 deduction.   ITA: 8(1)(h.1), 8(1)(j)

(D) Although the combined package of the two allowances may be reasonable in the circumstances, the Act deems the two allowances not to be a reasonable amount and, hence, taxable, since one of the motor vehicle allowances received was not based solely on kilometres. Since these allowances are taxable, the $6,396 would be deductible.

ITA: 6(1)(*b*)(x)
ITA: 6(1)(*b*)(vii.1)

(E) An unreasonable allowance of $1 per kilometre would be taxable, since the amount is in excess of a reasonable amount. Hence, the restricted expenses of $6,396 would be deductible.

ITA: 6(1)(*b*)(vii.1)

Example Problem 2

Mr. Jonathan is required by his contract of employment to use his own car in the performance of his employment duties and to pay for all expenses. Mr. Jonathan leased a BMW from Expensive Cars Unlimited. The following facts relate to the leased car:

Lease period . . . . Jan. 1, 2007 to Dec. 31, 2008

Lease cost per month including GST and PST . . . . $ 800

Manufacturer's list price, excluding PST and GST $50,000

Mr. Jonathan was not reimbursed for any portion of the lease cost. Mr. Jonathan lives in a province which has a sales tax of 8% and, therefore, would have an effective commodity tax rate of 14% on items subject to both GST and PST.

— *REQUIRED*

Determine the allowable lease cost which qualifies for a deduction under section 67.3 in 2007 before prorating for employment use.

— *SOLUTION*

Lesser of:

(a) $\dfrac{(1.14 \times \$800) \times 365}{30}$ = $\underline{\underline{\$11,096}}$

(b) $\dfrac{(\$800 \times 12) \times (\$30,000 \times 1.14)}{85\% \text{ of the greater of (i)}}$ = $\underline{\underline{\$7,725}}$
$\$40,235^{(1)}$ and (ii) $50,000

Deduction of the lesser amount: $\underline{\underline{\$7,725}}$

— *NOTE TO SOLUTION*

(1) $\dfrac{100}{85} \times (\$30,000 \times 1.14)$ = $40,235

Example Problem 3

Ms. Elana is required by her contract of employment to use her own car in the performance of her employment duties and to pay for all expenses. Ms. Elana leased a Mercedes from Sky's-The-Limit Leasing. The following facts relate to the leased Mercedes:

Lease period . . . . Oct. 1, 2005 to Sept. 30, 2008	
Lease cost per month, including GST and PST	$ 1,600
Manufacturer's list price, excluding PST and GST	$60,000
Total kilometres	30,000
Total employment kilometres	20,000
Gas and oil	$ 1,500
Maintenance	700
Insurance	2,000
Licences	100

— *REQUIRED*

Determine the amount deductible in respect of the car for the year 2007 on the assumption that a total of $13,000 of leasing costs had been deducted *prior to* 2007. Assume a PST rate of 9% for an effective commodity tax rate of 15%.

— *SOLUTION*

Gas and oil	$ 1,500
Maintenance	700
Insurance	2,000
Licences	100

Leasing costs — lesser of:

$$\text{(a)} \quad \frac{(1.15 \times \$800) \times 822 \text{ days}^{(1)}}{30} - \$13,000 = \underline{\underline{\$12,208}}$$

$$\text{(b)} \quad \frac{(12 \times \$1,600) \times (\$30,000 \times 1.15)}{85\% \text{ of the greater of (i) } \$40,588^{(2)}} = \underline{\underline{\$12,988}}$$
$$\text{and (ii) } \$60,000$$

$$\Biggr\} \quad 12,208$$

$$\underline{\underline{\$16,508}}$$

Portion relating to employment use:

$$\frac{20,000 \text{ km}}{30,000 \text{ km}} \times \$16,618 = \underline{\underline{\$11,079}}$$

— *NOTES TO SOLUTION*

[1] 92 days in 2005 + 365 days in 2006 + 365 days in 2007

[2] $(\$30,000 \times 1.15) \times \dfrac{100}{85} = \$40,588$

¶3,500   GST REBATE ON EMPLOYEE DEDUCTIONS

Employees, who are able to deduct GST-paid employment expenses, can obtain a refund of the GST component of these expenses in a similar manner to their employers who are registrants. Although the employee refund mechanism is quite different from the input tax credit system, the effect of this refund is quite similar.

As a general rule, employees do not have GST registration numbers and, hence, are not eligible for input tax credits. However, employees, who have deductible expenses for income tax purposes, may have paid GST on some of those expenses and should be eligible for some sort of refund mechanism. Therefore, in order to refund employees of registrants, other than financial institutions, who have paid GST on non-reimbursed expenses, a GST "rebate" system, as opposed to a GST "input tax credit" system, has been established. The following description is based on a provision of the *Excise Tax Act* (ETA). ETA: 253(1)

The GST rebate system is based on amounts which are deductible from employment income. These deductible amounts will include both the PST and GST components. In the calendar year following the year in which the deduction is made, the employee is eligible to file a rebate application in prescribed form. The employee has four years from the end of the taxation year, in which the expense was claimed for income tax purposes, to apply for the rebate. The amount of GST rebate that is received is then required to be included in income in the year that it is received. This employment inclusion has the effect of offsetting the GST ITA: 6(8)(c) component of the expense deducted in a preceding year. The reason for this effect is that a rebate received in respect of an expense that has been deducted lowers the net cost and, hence, should lower the net deduction.

The goods and services tax rebate is not considered to be a reimbursement received by ITA: 8(11) the taxpayer. As a result, the employee is allowed to deduct, in the year of payment, GST along with the expenses to which it attaches. In view of the required inclusion of the rebate, the rule in subsection 8(11) is needed to allow the deduction of GST which is ultimately offset ITA: 6(8) by the inclusion.

The employee GST rebate is calculated as 6/106 times the amounts deducted for income tax purposes. An employee is not entitled to a GST rebate for expenses in respect of which the employee has received an allowance unless the employer certifies that it did not consider the allowance to be a reasonable allowance and therefore must be included in income. If the allowance was considered to be a reasonable allowance by the employer, it would have ETA: 174 claimed the input tax credit under a provision of the ETA. The certification precludes recovery of the GST by both the employer and the employee.

In the year in which the employee actually receives the rebate, there is an offsetting adjustment under the *Income Tax Act* for the GST component, if any, of the deductible expenses. The Act includes in employment income the GST component of the deductible ITA: 6(8)(c) employment expenses, other than capital cost allowance, for the preceding year. The GST component of the capital cost allowance, which is buried in the cost of the asset, is deemed to ITA: 6(8)(d) be government assistance and, thereby, reduces the capital cost of the respective automobile, ITA: 13(7.1) aircraft or musical instrument.

Example Problem

Ms. G.S. Tax, an employee of Taxable Entity Ltd., which is a registrant for GST purposes, has supplied you with the following information concerning her employment income for 2007.

Ms. Tax uses her own car in the performance of her employment duties away from her employer's place of business and is required by her employment contract to pay for her travel expenses. She is not reimbursed for any of her travel expenses, but she does receive a kilometre allowance. Her employer will certify that it did not consider the allowance to be reasonable at the time it was paid. The example is based on the assumption that her automobile was purchased in early 2007 and was subject to GST.

The following information pertains to Ms. Tax's 2007 employment income as correctly prepared by her accountant. The amount of the expenses indicated reflects all pertinent income tax restrictions (e.g., the limit on capital cost of the automobile, 50% for meals and a proration of employment kilometres to total kilometres). The deductible expenses, where appropriate, include GST and PST, as indicated below.

Employment income

Inclusions:

Salary[1]	$85,000	
Car allowance[1]	3,000	
Premiums paid by Taxable Entity Ltd. for non-group disability insurance[2]	400	
Imputed interest on a car loan[2]	2,160	$ 90,560

Deductions:

Travel expenses:

Transportation, including PST of $240 and GST of $180	$ 3,420	
Accommodation, including PST of $320 and GST of $240	4,560	
Meals, including PST of $200 and GST of $150	2,850	(10,830)

Automobile expenses:

Operating costs, including PST of $120 and GST of $90	$ 1,710	
Interest[2]	3,120	
Insurance and licence[2]	800	
Capital cost allowance[3]	2,000	(7,630)

Professional fees, including GST of $42[4]		(742)
Employment income		$ 71,358

—NOTES

[1] Salary and car allowance are not subject to GST since the definition of property in the ETA excludes money.
ETA: 123(1)

[2] Insurance, licence and interest are exempt supplies.
ETA: Schedule V

[3] Capital cost allowance is not subject to GST or PST. However, there is a GST and PST component in the capital cost allowance claimed.

[4] Membership fees in professional organizations of which an employee must be a member to maintain a professional status recognized by statute, are exempt supplies. However, an election is available to these organizations under this provision to deem these fees to be taxable supplies. This election would normally be made where the majority of the members can obtain a refund under either the input tax credit system or rebate system. In addition, the professional organization will also be able to claim an input tax credit on its acquisition of taxable supplies.
ETA: Schedule V, Part VI, par. 18

—REQUIRED

(A) Calculate the amount of GST rebate which Ms. Tax is entitled to receive in 2008.

(B) Indicate the income tax consequences of the GST rebate.

— SOLUTION

(A) Ms. Tax can apply for a GST rebate in 2008 based on her deductible expenses in 2007. This would normally be done on the filing of her 2007 income tax return. The amount of the rebate would be calculated as: ETA: 253(1)

6/106 of the sum of:

(a) Deductible expenses, including GST and PST

Transportation	$ 3,420
Accommodation	4,560
Meals	2,850
Automobile operating expenses	1,710
Professional fees	742
	$13,282
(b) Capital cost allowance	2,000
	$15,282
(c) Less: any expenses for which a reasonable allowance was received	Nil
	$15,282
6/106 thereof	$ 865

(B) On the assumption that Ms. Tax receives the GST rebate in 2008 she would make the following income tax adjustments in 2008:

Par. 6(8)(*c*) employment income inclusion

$$\frac{\$13{,}282}{\$15{,}282} \times \$865 = \underline{\underline{\$752}}$$

Par. 6(8)(*d*) capital cost reduction

$$\frac{\$2{,}000}{\$15282} \times \$865 = \underline{\underline{\$113}}$$

¶3,600   APPLICATION OF RULES UNDER SUBDIVISION "A"

The following illustration is a comprehensive example of how "employment income" is determined under Subdivision a of Division B. The solution is cross-referenced to the appropriate section in the Act. Read carefully these cross-references and the supporting notes which highlight the key points in each related paragraph. However, note that the assignment problems may contain additional points not covered in this illustration.   ITA: 5, 6, 7, 8

Example Problem

Ms. Employee, who lives and works in Ontario, is employed as an internal auditor by Maxi Mumsales Ltd., a public corporation, for the calendar year 2007. She provides you with the following information concerning her receipts, taxable benefits, and expenditures:

Gross salary		$ 50,000
Income taxes withheld	$16,000	
CPP contributions (max. amount)	1,990	
EI contributions (max. amount)	720	
RPP contributions (money purchase) DEDUCT	3,000	
United Way donation	100	
Reimbursement paid to employer for use of company car and its operating costs	300	(22,110)
Net salary		$ 27,890

Maxi Mumsales Ltd. pays the following amounts on behalf of Ms. Employee:

(A) Premiums for the following medical plans:

    (i) Drug plan — Sun Life .... $ 275

    (ii) Extended health care — Liberty Mutual 350

    (iii) Provincial health insurance plan premiums .... Nil

(B) Maxi Mumsales Ltd. provides Ms. Employee with a car to be used in connection with the duties of her employment. Ms. Employee uses the car 80% for employment and 20% for pleasure based on total kilometres for 2007 of 25,000.

The company paid the following automobile expenses:

    (i) Operating costs (including 8% PST and GST) $3,200

    (ii) Lease costs (including 8% PST of $316 and GST of $237) ... 4,500

(C) Ms. Employee, who must travel regularly away from her employer's place of business, receives a monthly allowance of $400 to cover her accommodation and meals while travelling. She is, however, required by her contract to pay for these expenses directly. Her actual expenses were $3,000, including PST of $210 and GST of $158, for meals and $4,000, including PST of $280 and GST of $211, for accommodation, all of which were reasonable in the circumstances.

Ms. Employee also supplies you with the following selected expenditures:

    (i) Registered retirement savings plan contributions $1,500

    (ii) Legal fees paid in collecting back pay from a former employer (including GST of $11) 200

    (iii) Professional accounting dues (including GST of $17) 300

— *REQUIRED*

(A) Calculate Ms. Employee's employment income for tax purposes for 2007 (as determined by Subdivision a of Division B of the Act).

(B) Compute the GST rebate that should be claimed and the income tax consequences of the rebate to be received in 2008.

— SOLUTION

(A) Employment income:

Reference

Ssec. 5(1)	Salary[1]			$50,000
Par. 6(1)(*a*)	Provincial health insurance plan[2]			Nil
Par. 6(1)(*e*)	Standby charge[3]		$ 750	
Par. 6(1)(*k*)	Operating cost — car[4]	375	$1,125	
	Less: payments to company	300	825	
Spar. 6(1)(*b*)(vii)	Travel allowance[5]			4,800
				$55,625
	Less:			
Par. 8(1)(*b*)	Legal fees[6]		$ 200	
Par. 8(1)(*h*)	Travel expenses[7]		5,500	
Par. 8(1)(*i*)	Professional dues[8]		300	
Par. 8(1)(*m*)	RPP contributions[9]		3,000	(9,000)
	Employment income — Subdivision a[10]			$46,625

(B) GST rebate income tax consequences:

(a) Rebate

6/106 of the sum of:

(i) Deductible expenses, including GST and PST:

Legal fees	$ 200
Travel expenses	5,500
Professional dues	300
	$ 6,000
(ii) Capital cost allowance	Nil
	$ 6,000
(iii) Less any expenses for which a reasonable allowance was received	Nil
	$ 6,000
6/106 thereof	$ 340

(b) Income tax consequences

The GST rebate of $340 must be included in employment income in the year of receipt. Since no capital cost allowance was deducted, there will be no capital cost reduction component of the rebate.

ITA: 6(8)(*c*)

— *NOTES TO SOLUTION*

(1) The Act refers to remuneration *received* in the calendar year only, but this does not mean that the net salary is the amount included in employment income. The Act deems that taxes withheld have been received at the time remuneration etc. was paid.

ITA: 5
ITA: 153(3)

(2) The Act includes all benefits received or enjoyed through employment with certain specific exemptions which do not include public medical plan premiums paid by an employer. However, in Ontario, as in several other provinces, provincial medical plan premiums have been replaced by a health services tax based on total payroll; hence, there is no taxable benefit for individual employees.

ITA: 6(1)(a)

(3) The standby charge will be computed as:

$$\frac{5,000 \text{ km}}{20,004 \text{ km}} \times (\tfrac{2}{3} \times \$4,500) = \$750$$

Ms. Employee is entitled to the standby charge reduction, since she uses the car for business more than 50% of the total kilometres.

(4) Ms. Employee qualifies for the election method of determining a benefit derived from employer-paid automobile operating costs, since her employment-use is in excess of 50% of the total use. The operating costs under this election method would result in a reduced income inclusion of $375 [20% × 25,000 km × $0.22 = $1,100 under the kilometre alternative *versus* (50% × $750) = $375].

ITA: 6(1)(k)(iv)–(v)

(5) Allowances are dealt with in paragraph 6(1)(b), which includes all allowances in income with 10 specific exceptions. One such exception, which is applicable in this situation, applies to most employees, but not salespersons or persons who negotiate contracts, since there is a special provision for them. There are two specific conditions which must be met in order for the allowance not to be taxable. The first condition is that the allowance must be a reasonable amount. The second condition is that the employee must be travelling outside the metropolitan area where his or her employer is located.

ITA: 6(1)(b)(vii)

On the assumption that Ms. Employee's travelling expenses were reasonable in the circumstances, the monthly allowance of $400 ($4,800 annually) was not a reasonable amount since the actual expenses were $7,000. Therefore, the allowance is a taxable allowance and she can claim her actual travel expenses.

ITA: 8(1)(h)

(6) Legal fees are deductible only if they are paid

ITA: 8(1)(b)

● in the year

● to collect, or establish a right to, an amount that, if received, would be included in the employee's employment income.

(7) Ms. Employee can deduct her travelling expenses because she meets all the conditions of the relevant provision. First, she must travel regularly away from her employer's place of business. Second, she is required by contract to pay for these expenses. Finally, she is not in receipt of an exempt allowance since the allowance which she receives is less than a reasonable amount and, as a result, has been included in income.

ITA: 8(1)(h)

ITA: 6(1)(b)(vii)

The deductible expenses are composed of:

Accommodation	$4,000
Meals and entertainment expenses (50% × $3,000)	1,500
	$5,500

Note how the determination of the reasonableness of the allowance was based on the full expenditures which were considered reasonable. The result was that the allowance was not reasonable and, hence, it was included in employment income. However, the meals expenditures were only 50% deductible.

(8) Professional dues are deductible only if the dues are for a profession recognized by statute and if the dues relate to the employment income as per the preamble to section 8.

(9) Registered pension plan: an employee is permitted to deduct, for tax purposes, his or her contributions to a money purchase registered pension plan to a maximum of $20,000 in 2007, but this amount is the maximum amount for the combined employee-employer contributions.

(10) Items excluded from computation:

(a) Employers' contributions to a private health plan, such as the drug and extended health care plans and provincial health service tax levies, are not taxable benefits.   ITA: 6(1)(*a*)

(b) Registered retirement savings plan contributions are deducted under Subdivision e, not Subdivision a.

(c) Income tax is not deductible.   ITA: 8(2)

(d) United Way, a charitable donation, is not deductible under Division B. (A charitable donation made by an individual is eligible for a non-refundable tax credit under Division E.)

(e) CPP contributions and EI premiums are not deductible under Division B, but are eligible for non-refundable tax credits under Division E.

¶3,800   REVIEW QUESTIONS

(1) The best way to calculate employment income is to follow the format used on the personal tax return. Comment on the accuracy of this statement.

(2) It does not matter whether an individual is employed or self-employed since he or she can claim the same expenses under either category as long as the expense was incurred to earn income. Comment on the accuracy of this statement.

(3) If an individual fails any one of the tests which are used to determine employed versus self-employed status then the individual is employed. Comment.

(4) When determining whether a person is employed or self-employed, one of the subtests used in the economic reality or entrepreneur test is the "control test". What does this test involve?

(5) When determining whether a person is employed or self-employed, one of the tests used is the "integration or organization test". What does this test involve?

(6) When determining whether a person is employed or self-employed, one of the tests used is the "specific result test". What does this test involve?

(7) If a bonus cheque is received by an employee, Ms. Defer, on December 15 of this year and she chooses not to cash her cheque until January 5 of next year, then she will be able to defer the tax on the bonus until the next year since individuals are taxed on the cash basis. Comment.

(8) If a bonus is payable to an employee, Mr. Later, on December 15 of this year and he decides that he wants to be taxed on the income in the following year instead of this year, then he can ask his employer to defer the payment of this bonus until next year and accomplish his goal. Comment.

(9) Employees are taxed on income from their employer to the extent that it is a gross payment before withholding tax or a taxable benefit. The employer can deduct, as an expense, the full amount of the gross payments before withholding tax and taxable benefits that are reported on the employee's T4. Comment.

(10) To maximize the after-tax income from a disability insurance policy to a disabled employee, the employer should not pay *any* of the premium for the coverage. Comment.

(11) On June 2 of this year, Opco loaned $10,000 to an employee and did not charge interest. The employee repaid the loan on June 30 of the same year. How many days are included for purposes of determining the deemed interest benefit?

(12) Explain the differences between a reimbursement and an allowance.

(13) Opco bought a new car for its owner-manager that cost the company $40,000 plus $3,200 for PST and $2,400 for GST. How much is the standby charge for this car for a full year assuming it is driven 40% for business purposes?

(14) What are the five conditions that must be met before a sales/negotiating person can deduct expenses?

(15) What are the four conditions that must be met by an employee, who is not a sales/negotiating person, in order to allow him or her to deduct travelling expenses other than car expenses?

(16) Mr. Tax O.N. Wheels is a part-time lecturer at the University of Waterloo. He lives in a location in Toronto which is 105 km away from the university. The rest of the time he has a tax consulting practice which he operates out of his home. The university pays him $0.37 per km to travel to and from the university. He is issued a T4 at the end of the year for his teaching income on the basis that he is a part-time employee. How is the travel allowance of $0.37 per km treated for tax purposes?

(17) Guidelines for the deductibility of expenses related to work space in the home for employees are included in subsection 8(13). Under paragraph (*a*) of this provision the expenses are allowed if one of two conditions are met. In these conditions, the words "principally" and "exclusively" are used. What do these words mean for tax purposes?

(18) Ms. Smith has come to you to ask your tax advice. She has just had a large bonus paid to her on December 31 and wants to defer some of it until next year. She is arguing that since the CRA's portion was not sent to the Receiver General until January 15 she should be able to defer that portion until the next year on the basis that it was not received until January 15 when it was sent to the CRA. What do you think?

¶3,825   MULTIPLE CHOICE QUESTIONS

Question 1

In 2007, Bob's employer provided him with an employer-owned automobile costing $34,500 (including GST and PST) for 12 months. His kilometres for personal use were 15,000 out of a total of 20,000 kilometres. Operating costs paid by his employer during 2007 were $3,300 (including PST and GST). Which one of the following statements is TRUE for 2007?

(A) Bob's minimum standby charge is $8,280.

(B) Bob's minimum operating cost benefit is $2,475.

(C) Bob's minimum operating cost benefit is $3,000.

(D) Bob can elect to use ½ of his standby charge as his operating cost benefit.

Question 2

In 2007, Mary earned a $50,000 annual salary as a computer repair person and received a car allowance of $3,500. The car allowance was paid to her monthly and was not based on the number of kilometres that she drove. Her employment-related expenses (all reasonable) were:

Automobile expenses (gas, parking, CCA)	$3,000
Entertainment	2,000

What is Mary's minimum employment income for 2007?

(A) $53,500

(B) $50,500

(C) $49,500

(D) $49,000

Question 3

Susanne Denholm is employed as a provincial payroll tax auditor and is required by contract to maintain an office in her home. Susanne works at home most of the time and has been provided with a laptop computer and a fireproof audit bag for her files. She has not been provided with any reimbursement or allowance in connection with her home office, which occupies 10% of the square footage of her home. She incurred the following costs to maintain her home in 2007:

Telephone (general line)	$ 600*
House insurance	2,000
Property taxes..	4,000
Heat, hydro & maintenance	5,000
Mortgage interest	24,000

*Susanne estimates that she used her telephone 50% for employment purposes during the year.

What is the maximum amount that Susanne can claim for the costs she has incurred in respect of her home office?

(A) $500

(B) $1,100

(C) $1,400

(D) $3,800

Question 4

On April 1, 2004, E Ltd. made a loan of $100,000 to Mr. Walker, a new employee of the corporation, to assist him in purchasing a residence when he moved from Quebec to commence employment in British Columbia. The loan bears interest at 2%, which is to be paid monthly. The principal of the loan is to be repaid in full on April 1, 2014. The prescribed interest rate on April 1, 2004 was 4%. Assuming that the prescribed interest rate throughout 2007 was 3% and the interest owing on the loan is paid each month, which one of the following amounts represents the increase in Mr. Walker's employment income in 2007 due to the loan.

(A) $1,000

(B) $2,000

(C) $3,000

(D) $4,000

Question 5

Tanya, an employee of a Canadian public company received an option to purchase 1,000 common shares of her employer at $30 per share in March 2006, when the shares were worth $19 per share. In December 2006, when the fair market value was $40 per share, she exercised her options. In January 2007, she sold all the shares for $38 per share. Tanya wants to know what employee benefit she will have to report on her tax return. She wants to pay the lowest amount of taxes possible and wants to elect under the $100,000 stock option rule if she can.

(A) $5,000 in 2006.

(B) $8,000 in 2006.

(C) $8,000 in 2007.

(D) $10,000 in 2007.

Question 6

Tim began employment as a commissioned salesman in July of this year and received a base salary of $60,000 and $5,000 in commissions based on sales for the year. During the year, Tim worked away from the office negotiating sales contracts. Tim is required to pay his own travelling expenses and his employer has signed a T2200 form certifying that requirement and certifying that no reimbursements are paid for any expenses Tim incurs to earn commissions. Tim incurred the following work-related costs from July through December of this year and all expenses are reasonable:

Meals and entertainment for potential customers $14,000

Automobile costs (90% of the following amounts were for employment purposes based on kilometres driven):

Fuel	4,000
Insurance	750
Repairs	2,250
Leasing costs for a car costing $20,000 ($500 per month)	3,000

What is the maximum deduction Tim may claim for employment expenses for the year?

(A) $5,000

(B) $9,000

(C) $14,000

(D) $16,000

¶3,850 EXERCISES

Exercise 1

The appellant is a qualified registered nurse, is entitled to use the traditional letters "R.N." after her name and, in answering the questions contained in her 1966 income tax return, described herself as a "private duty" nurse both in the space provided for employed persons and in the space provided for persons in business or practising a profession. Thus, in trying to answer all the official questions on her return, the appellant indicated, on the one hand, that she was employed "as a private duty nurse" by the Canadian Forces Hospital at Halifax and, on the other hand, that she was in business of practising her profession "as a private duty nurse" in connection with the same hospital. The basic issue to be decided in this appeal is, briefly, what was the taxpayer's correct status vis-à-vis the Canadian Forces Hospital, Halifax in her 1966 taxation year.

The appellant launched the present appeal by Notice of Appeal dated March 7, 1968 in which she alleged (in effect) as follows: that in the relevant 1966 taxation year she was employed by the Canadian Forces Hospital, Halifax, on a day-to-day basis terminable on 24 hours' notice; that the usual so-called fringe benefits made available to and enjoyed by the regular full-time army nursing sisters such as holidays, sick pay, retirement plan, and so on, were not made available to her as a private duty nurse; that the regional surgeon's office in Halifax classified her as a "self-employed R.N."; that in her 1965 return she claimed and was permitted to deduct from her income expenses of a similar type to those disallowed in the 1966 taxation year now under appeal; and that several of her fellow private duty nurses employed at the Canadian Forces Base, Halifax, were employed on the same basis as she was and had claimed expenses of a similar type to those disallowed in this appeal (i.e., the type of expenses one would associate with a private duty nurse). The Minister stated that, in making the assessment now in dispute, he had acted upon the following assumptions of fact — that the appellant is a registered nurse and was employed by the Department of National Defence at the Canadian Forces Hospital and Base, Halifax, during the 1966 taxation year, that in the course of carrying out her engagement as a general duty nurse the appellant was subject to supervision and discipline by the hospital authorities, and that of the expenses allegedly incurred by the appellant only the amount of $25 claimed as "R.N. fees" and the amount of $42.41 being her contribution to the Canada Pension Plan were permitted under the Act.

The appellant testified, in effect, as follows: that she is a registered nurse; that in the relevant 1966 taxation year she was living in Halifax and was employed at the Canadian Forces Hospital (Stadacona Hospital), "not as a staff nurse but more or less as a private duty nurse, though my times were made up ahead of time" (the correct interpretation to be placed on the word "employed" in this appeal appears to be the key to the solution); that private duty nurses are allowed to claim as deductions from income certain expenses such as laundry, uniforms including caps, white shoes and stockings, travelling expenses (in this matter that item amounted to $76.40 made up of 191 days at 40¢ per day) and so on; that the only difference between herself and a private duty nurse is that the hospital deducted her Canada Pension Plan contributions from the per diem amounts payable to her; that she acted as a private duty nurse at Stadacona Hospital in the years 1964, 1965, 1966, 1967 and until April 1968 when she moved from Halifax to Charlottetown and became associated with the Charlottetown Hospital as a relief nurse; that she is presently working under exactly the same conditions under which she carried on at the Canadian Forces Hospital, Halifax, i.e., "If I don't work, I don't get paid, I have no benefits or holidays. I get private duty wages (these amounted to $15 per day in Halifax and now amount to $20 per day). My time is made up. If they get full-time nurses they can let me go"; that she and other private duty nurses were hired by Stadacona Hospital (on a day-to-day basis) to fill in while the hospital "didn't have enough service nurses"; and that in the year 1967 the said hospital "did get a large supply of military nurses in and we were all cut down" (i.e., a number of private duty nurses were simply laid off which was easy to do because they were working on a day-to-day basis). The Hospital supplied all equipment and supplies used by the appellant. The Hospital hired and fired all nursing assistants and other support staff who assisted the appellant in the performance of her duties. The appellant could request the Hospital to hire additional support staff but she personally did not hire them.

During her cross-examination, the appellant also testified, in effect, as follows: that her time sheet in the Canadian Forces Hospital, Halifax, was made out a week in advance; that the said hospital's authority to hire civilian nurses to meet its requirements was only valid while there was a shortage of military nurses; that, as they became available, the civilian nurses were replaced; that the hospital asserted its right to dismiss civilian nurses on 24 hours' notice — "we were told that when we went there to work"; that she, herself, was not replaced by a military nurse in the 1966 taxation year, now under appeal, but later her shifts were cut down and she was eventually replaced in 1968; that she was, of course, obliged to follow hospital regulations with regard to the administration of drugs, medications, and so on, as she would be in any recognized hospital; that, when she was working at the Canadian

Forces Hospital, Halifax, she was told which patients to look after; and that she did not sign any form of contract with the above hospital when she started to work there.

— *REQUIRED*

Is the appellant in this case employed or self-employed? In presenting your answer, discuss the tests that are applied by the courts in this type of situation and consider how the facts relate to these tests.

Exercise 2

ITA: 6(1)(*a*); IT-470R

William Wage-Slave works for an extremely generous employer, Benjamin's Fringe-Benefits Ltd. which paid the following amounts on behalf of William:

(a) Registered pension plan contributions (defined benefit) . . . . NOT $1,000

(b) Provincial medical plan premiums (not a health service levy) . . . . YES 600

(c) Extended health care premiums — Sun Life . . . . YES NO . . . 250

(d) Drug plan premiums — Mutual of Omaha . . . . YES NO . . . 150

(e) Tuition fee for a basket weaving course offered by a local high school . YES 75

(f) Non-cash Christmas gift which the company did expense for tax purposes NO 65

(g) Subsidized lunches at company cafeteria:

  Fair market value 640

  Actual cost 420

  Amount paid by William . . . . PARTLY YES 200

(h) Membership fees in Exclusive Private Club . . . . YES . . . 800

(i) Financial counselling — ABC Investment Counselling Ltd. . . . YES 1,000

— *REQUIRED*

Comment on whether these amounts are taxable.

ITA: 6(1)(*a*); IT-470R

Exercise 3

ITA: 6(1)(*a*); IT-470R

Melanie Manager, a division supervisor for Eli's Ltd., a large department store chain, receives a 35% discount on all merchandise purchased through Eli's Ltd. This discount is available to all executives above assistant department heads. Melanie calculated that the discount saved her $6,000 this year.

— *REQUIRED*

Discuss whether there is a benefit.

ITA: 6(1)(*a*); IT-470R

Exercise 4

ITA: 6(1)(*a*); IT-470R

John Aggressive, an employee of Isaac's Fast Sell Ltd., lives in Burlington and commutes by Go-Train to Toronto where Isaac's Fast Sell Ltd. is located. John, who is bored by reading, decides to move to Toronto in order to cut down his travelling time. Isaac's Fast Sell Ltd. reimburses him for the following amounts:

Moving van costs . . . . $ 500

Reimbursement of actual loss suffered in selling the house   5,000

                                                                                $5,500

— *REQUIRED*

Discuss whether there is a benefit.

ITA: 6(1)(*a*); IT-470R

Exercise 5

ITA: 6(1)(*a*), 6(1)(*f*)

Tanya Taxaware, who is chairperson of her union's negotiating team, has approached you concerning the management's offer in connection with fringe benefits. The company proposes to pay one-half of the premiums of the following plans:

(a) provincial medical plan — not a provincial health levy;

(b) extended health care — a private plan;

(c) dental care — a private plan;

(d) an accident and sickness income protection plan — a private group plan covering up to 50% of the wages.

All of these plans have premiums which are approximately the same. The company at present does not contribute to any of these plans.

— *REQUIRED*

Discuss the tax implications of the company's proposal.

Exercise 6

ITA: 6(9), 8(1)(*j*), 80.4, 80.5

Leonard Loans, an employee of Bertha's Generous Employer Ltd., received the following loans on January 1 of this year from his employer:

6% ..... $15,000 loan to purchase a car to be used primarily for employment purposes,

4% ..... $100,000 loan to purchase a home, and

7% ..... $10,000 loan to consolidate his other debts.

Leonard does not receive a mileage allowance and is specifically required by his contract to pay his car expenses. According to Leonard's travel log, he used the car for employment purposes, for 27,000 kilometres out of a total of 45,000 kilometres.

Assume that the prescribed rates for this year were:

1st Quarter — 7%	3rd Quarter — 8%
2nd Quarter — 6%	4th Quarter — 7%

Leonard paid the interest on these loans on January 15 of the following year.

— *REQUIRED*

Compute the interest benefit and any deduction for interest.

ITA: 6(9), 8(1)(*j*)

Exercise 7

ITA: 7; IT-113R4

Katrina Keyemployee was granted, in year one, an option to purchase 50,000 common shares at $1 per share from her employer, Michael Ltd., a Canadian-controlled private corporation. The shares had an estimated fair market value at this date of $1.50. However, according to the agreement, Katrina could not exercise her option until her fourth employment year. Katrina did exercise her entire option in year five; the fair market value of the shares at that time was $3. Katrina sold all the shares in year six, at $6 per share.

— *REQUIRED*

Discuss the tax implications of the above transactions.

Exercise 8

ITA: 6(1)(*e*), 6(1)(*k*), 6(2)

Ms. Speedster has full use of an employer-owned Mustang GTS purchased for her use in mid-December of last year. It is now January. The original cost to the employer of this classic is $20,000, including PST and GST. Other details of the car for the coming year are as follows:

Capital cost allowance to be claimed by employer	$4,792
Operating costs for the year paid by the employer, including PST, GST, and insurance ($600)	$3,500
Personal-use kilometres	12,000
Number of months available	12
Reimbursement to employer for personal use at 15 cents	$ 400

— REQUIRED

Compute the taxable standby charge and operating cost benefits, if the business-use kilometres are:

ITA: 6(1)(*e*), 6(1)(*k*)

(a) 10,000

(b) 20,000

Exercise 9

Calvin Comptroller, who is employed and lives in Calgary, takes a considerable amount of office work home and, therefore, has built and furnished an office in his fully-paid home. On this year's tax return, he claimed the following expenses in respect of his office which represents approximately ⅛ of the home.

ITA: 8(1)(*i*), 8(13)

Estimated rental value for office space	$1,000
Maintenance — ⅛	250
Taxes — ⅛	200
Insurance — ⅛	80
	$1,530

— REQUIRED

Discuss whether Calvin's course of action was correct.

ITA: 8(1)(*i*), 8(13); IT-352R2

Exercise 10

ITA: 6(1)(*b*), 13(7)(*g*), 67.2; IT-522R

Ms. Internal Auditor, who is employed by Susan's Super Ltd., travels extensively across Canada. According to the terms of her contract, she receives an accommodation allowance of $10,000 per year.

The contract states that she must use her own automobile and pay for all travelling expenses. Ms. Auditor acquired a new car, on January 5, 2007, for $32,000 plus GST and PST at 6%. Her kilometres for business purposes were 15,000 out of a total of 21,000 kilometres.

During the year, Ms. Auditor paid the following amounts, all of which are reasonable in the circumstances and which are supported by receipts:

(a) accommodation, including meals of $4,500 (including PST and GST)	$12,000
(b) total car expenses: gas (including PST and GST)	1,500
maintenance (including PST and GST)	500
insurance	1,200
licences	90
interest on bank loan	4,000

Ms. Auditor calculated her capital cost allowance to be:

$$(½ \times 30\% \times \$32,000) = \$4,800$$

Ms. Auditor also filed the prescribed form (T2200) which her employer had signed. Assume that the employment use of the car is reasonable in the circumstances.

— REQUIRED

Discuss the tax consequences of the allowance and related expenses plus the deductibility of the car expenses.

Exercise 11

ITA: 6(8); ETA: 253(1)

Based on the facts and solution for Exercise 10 determine the potential GST rebate and income tax consequences upon receipt of this amount.

¶3,875   ASSIGNMENT PROBLEMS

Problem 1

Chow Installation and Repair Ltd. ("Chow") is in the business of installing and repairing overhead doors. Chow maintained a list of qualified installers and repair-persons and would contact them as work became available. Chow informed these workers that they would be considered to be running their own business, so no withholding of income tax, EI or CPP was made. Workers were paid by the job and worked mostly on their own. If the person contacted refused the assignment, Chow would call the next person on the list. The person who agreed to the job would go directly to the job site; he or she was not required to report to Chow's work place, except to pick up a door or parts.

Chow supplied the doors and the parts used in the repair or installation. Each worker maintained his or her own truck and tools. Chow, however, owned specialized racks made for transporting the doors and a special drill which could be used on cement. These items were available to any worker who required them.

Chow guaranteed all work for one year. Under the terms of the agreement between Chow and the workers, if a guarantee had to be honoured, the worker would be responsible to fix any defects. If any parts were required to correct the defect, the worker would have to pay for them.

— REQUIRED

Determine whether the workers should be considered employees of Chow or independent contractors. Evaluate this fact situation in detail before arriving at your conclusion. In presenting your answer, discuss the tests that are applied by the courts in this type of situation and consider how the facts relate to these tests.

Problem 2

ITA: 5, 6(1)(*a*), 6(1)(*b*),
80.4; IT-470R

Miriam, the sole tax adviser of a financial planning firm, is contemplating an offer to become Director of Taxation of Neil Manufacturing Limited (NML) of Dundas, Ontario. The offered compensation package would include the following:

- a salary of $132,000 per year, payable monthly;

- a one-time flat allowance of $25,000, payable on acceptance of the position, to help move her and her family to Dundas;

- a company contribution of 6% of her salary to a defined-benefit registered pension plan;

- company payment of the premiums for extended health coverage and a dental plan provided by Star Insurance;

- company payment, valued at $900, for the preparation of her tax return by the company's accountants;

- company payment, valued at $2,500, for her membership in the Dundas Valley Golf and Curling Club;

- a company loan of $200,000 to help finance the purchase of a new home in Dundas. The loan will bear interest at 3.5% per year payable monthly and will be made on May 1, 2007, the closing date on the purchase of the home.

— REQUIRED

Miriam does not deal with many employment-related tax issues and recognizes the need for a corroborating opinion on the tax consequences of this compensation package. She has asked you for your opinion. Comment on the income tax consequences for employment income of each item in the compensation package. Assume that the prescribed rate of interest for employee loans is 7% in the first quarter of the year, 6% in the second quarter, 4% in the third quarter and 7% in the fourth quarter.

Problem 3

ITA: 6(1)(*a*), 6(1)(*e*),
6(1)(*e*.1), 6(1)(*k*), 6(2),
6(2.2)

Your best friend, Mooch, was at a sales conference recently. During one of the breaks, he entered into a conversation with one of the other attendees, Darly, regarding the perks provided by their respective employers. In both cases, the employer provides a car. However, Darly commented on the significant tax advantage available to her since her employer leased the car instead of buying the car. Mooch was able to obtain all of the information from Darly regarding her car.

Mooch has come to you for some "free" tax advice. He has asked you to compare the tax position he is in currently with the employer-owned car to the position that Darly is in with the leased car.

Mooch

Capital cost of the car including PST and GST	$38,772
Capital cost allowance claimed by the employer in 2007	6,375
Operating costs paid by the employer (including PST and GST)	4,250
Kilometres (as calculated from Mooch's log):	
Employment	8,000
Personal	10,000
Amount reimbursed to the company for the personal use at 12 cents per kilometre	$ 1,200

Darly

Lease cost including $1,650 of insurance and PST and GST	$12,450
Operating costs paid by the employer (including PST and GST)	2,975
Kilometres (as calculated from Darly's log):	
Employment	23,000
Personal	9,000
Amount reimbursed to the company for the personal use at 7 cents per kilometre	$ 630

— *REQUIRED*

Calculate the minimum car benefit which would be included in employment income for 2007 for Mooch and Darly.

Problem 4

ITA: 5, 6; IT-470R

Anita Lee, Vice-President of Gary Inc., has asked for your assistance concerning the tax implications of certain amounts and benefits she received from her employer during 2007.

Salary, gross		$ 90,000 — *SECTION 5*
Payroll deductions:		
Income taxes	$36,000	
Canada Pension Plan premiums	1,990 — } *CREDITS*	
Employment Insurance premiums	720 —	
Group accident disability insurance premiums	110	(38,820)
Net pay		$ 51,180

Additional Information

(1) In November 2007, Anita was in a skiing accident and was unable to work for four weeks. During this period she received disability payments totalling $1,600 from Paris Life Insurance Ltd. Half of the disability insurance premiums were paid by Gary Inc. and half by Anita (see payroll deduction above). Anita has paid a total of $350 in disability insurance premiums since she commenced employment at Gary Inc. in 2004.

1,600 − 350 = 1

(2) In 2007, Gary Inc. paid $424 (including GST) for the preparation of Anita's 2006 income tax return and $530 (including GST) for Anita to see a financial planning consultant regarding retirement planning.

(3) Anita is taking courses towards her M.B.A. degree on a part-time basis during the evening. She is taking the courses on her initiative and for her own benefit. During 2007, Gary Inc. paid for the tuition for these M.B.A. courses which amounted to $1,000. Gary Inc. also paid $400 in tuition for Anita to

↳ TAX FREE

attend a two-day computer workshop on company time to learn about the new software system that the company had just installed.

(4) Director's fees of $2,000 were received by Anita from Clint's Hi-Tech Ltd., a company owned by Anita's spouse.

(5) Christmas gift of $200 cash was received and was expensed by Gary Inc.

(6) Anita received an employee loan of $8,000 on January 15, 2007, at 3% interest to purchase a notebook computer for personal use. The interest was payable on each anniversary date of the loan, and Anita paid the interest owing on the loan on the due date in 2008. Assume that the prescribed interest rates applicable to employee loans for 2007 are: first quarter, 7%; second quarter, 6%; third quarter, 8%; fourth quarter, 7%.

(7) For 12 months, Gary Inc. paid Anita a monthly gas allowance of $250 regardless of the number of kilometres she drove. In addition, she was provided with a company-owned automobile costing $38,500 (including PST and GST) at the beginning of January. Anita's kilometres for personal use were 16,000 out of a total of 25,000 kilometres. Operating costs paid (excluding gas) by Gary Inc. during 2007 amounted to $2,920, including insurance of $600 and PST and GST.

(8) Anita and her spouse Clint were provided with Gary Inc.'s condo in the Bahamas for a one-week holiday during the winter. Excluding GST considerations, such accommodation during this peak period would have cost them $500 as opposed to the $100 actually paid by Anita.

(9) Anita used her frequent-flyer points accumulated as a result of her business trips (which had been paid by Gary Inc.) for her holiday in the Bahamas. She saved $800, plus $48 of GST, by using the frequent-flyer points.

(10) Anita bought merchandise from Gary Inc. during the year and saved $180 (excluding GST) using its 30% employee discount, which is available to all employees. Gary Inc.'s mark-up is 100%.

— *REQUIRED*

(A) Calculate Anita Lee's employment income inclusions for 2007 in accordance with the Act and the CRA's administrative position. Assume a PST rate of 10%.   ITA: 5, 6; IT-470R

(B) Explain why you omitted any of the above amounts from your answer in part (A).

(C) If the facts were changed so that Anita had not been provided with a company-owned automo-   ITA: 5, 6
bile and instead used her own car for employment purposes, how would this affect the computation of Anita's employment income in accordance with the Act? Assume that Gary Inc. continues to pay for Anita's car operating costs.

Problem 5   ITA: 5, 6(3)

Chrisa had been an employee of David Hardware, a hardware product distributor, for 15 years. Chrisa sold the David hardware products directly to hardware stores. She was a salesperson and she was paid 100% by commission. Chrisa was personally responsible for all of her business expenses. Expenses, for example, for office supplies, stamps, telephone, parking, entertainment, promotion and samples, were supported by receipts and she deducted them.

During the years that Chrisa was employed by David, she sold products and developed the hardware market in her geographic area. One of the ways in which she developed the market was by "renting" floor space in various stores to display the David products. However, no receipts were received from the various stores, because in many ways the money was considered a "tip" by the managers of the hardware stores. Chrisa did not deduct these expenses. Through this process, Chrisa had significantly increased David's sales in her sales region and she had developed a loyal following in the hardware business.

At the time of Chrisa's departure from David, David paid $15,000 to Chrisa. The conditions of the agreement surrounding the $15,000 payment were as follows:

● David was "buying back" Chrisa's sales territory;

● Chrisa agreed not to enter a similar business to that of David's business, in David's distribution area, for a period of three years; and

● David and Chrisa agreed that the $15,000 would constitute a reimbursement of capital invested by Chrisa (i.e., the amounts she had paid to the stores for the rental of floor space for David products).

— *REQUIRED*

Discuss the income tax implications for Chrisa of the receipt of the $15,000.

Problem 6   ~~EXAM~~

ITA: 5, 6(1), 7, 8(1)

The following information relates to Leonard, a middle-management accountant, not engaged in negotiating contracts, of a public corporation, Peter Productions Ltd. which is located in Ontario.

(A) Salary — gross *TAX*		$ 80,000

Payroll deductions:

Income taxes *AFTER TAX*	$23,500	
Registered pension plan (money purchase; see (B) below) *TAX FREE*	5,500	
Canada Pension Plan contributions *(CREDIT)*	1,990	
Employment Insurance contributions *(CREDIT)*	720	
Charitable donations *(CREDIT)*	350	
Employee's portion of benefit plans (see (B) below) *CLAIM*	800	(32,860)
		$ 47,140

(B) The company paid the following additional matching amounts on behalf of Leonard (an equal amount was withheld from salary as the employee's contribution, as shown in (A) above):

Registered pension plan *FREE*	$5,500
Dental plan — Sun Life Co. *FREE*	175
Group income protection — Royal Insurance Co. *FREE*	225
Extended health care — Liberty Mutual *FREE*	150
Group term life insurance — General Insurance Co. *TAXABLE 6.(4)*	250

6.(1)

The group term life coverage for Leonard was $300,000.

(C) Selected additional information concerning Leonard's receipts, disbursements, and other benefits:

(i) Trip to Europe from one of Peter Productions Ltd.'s clients in appreciation of Leonard's services (including PST and GST) .... $ 6,000   *BENEFIT*

(ii) Periodic payments received from Royal Insurance under the group income protection plan during a three-month illness. This plan had been in existence since 1995 and Leonard's share of the premium since that date was $2,300   12,000

12,000 − 2,300 = TAX-FREE

(iii) Peter Productions Ltd. paid Leonard's annual membership fee in a golf club   2,100

(iv) Early in 2007, Leonard was granted an option to purchase 1,000 of the company's shares for $2.00 per share. At that time the shares were trading on the market at $3.00 per share. Later in the year, Leonard exercised the option and acquired 1,000 shares when they were trading at $4.50 per share. In December of 2007, he needed cash, so he sold the 1,000 shares for $5.00 each.

(4.50−2)×1000= 2,500 S. 7

(v) Leonard paid the following amounts during the year:

Annual membership fee of a professional accounting body (including GST, no PST charged)	800
Registered retirement savings plan	3,500
Legal fees in appealing a tax assessment	1,900

DEDUCTIBLE 8(i)(i)
"DEDUCTIBLE AFTERLOW" 60(i)
" " 60(0)

— *REQUIRED*

(A) Calculate the employment income of Leonard for 2007 in accordance with Subdivision a of Division B.

(B) Indicate why you omitted any of the above amounts.

(C) Compute the GST rebate that should be claimed and the income tax consequences of the rebate to be received in 2008.

Problem 7

ITA: 5, 6, 7, 8, 67.1, 67.2, 67.3; IT-352R2

Robby Beamon has recently been appointed vice-president of sales and marketing for Lori's Unpublished Books Limited, a public company. Robby has come to you for advice regarding the tax implications of his new position. During your meeting you were able to determine the following information:

(A) Remuneration for the year:

Salary — gross		$84,800
Less: Canada Pension Plan contributions	$1,990	
Employment Insurance contributions	720	
Disability insurance premiums	600	3,310
		$81,490
Bonus based on company sales		24,000
Allowances for the year (paid monthly):		
meals, accommodation and air travel		13,000
car		6,300
entertainment		2,000
Moving allowance		15,000

Robby has also been granted an option to acquire 7,500 previously unissued fully-paid shares of Lori's Unpublished Books Limited at $11.50 per share. The fair market value at the time of the grant was $15. One of the conditions was that he must exercise one-third of the option immediately upon it being granted. He did so and acquired 2,500 shares.

(B) Robby has summarized the following expenses related to his employment:

Gas and oil — automobile	$ 3,900
Painting (office only)	100
Licences — automobile	100
Meals (consumed while travelling away for more than 12 hours)	7,000
House insurance	800
Accommodation (while travelling on company business)	10,000
Interest expense — car loan	3,600
General maintenance (house)	300
Car insurance	1,900
Hydro	700
Air travel	4,200
Car maintenance	1,000
Supplies	700
Fuel (house)	1,200
Property taxes	4,500
Mortgage interest	24,000
Salary (to wife, including payroll taxes and employer contributions)	15,000

(C) Lori's Unpublished Books Limited requires Robby to provide an automobile in order to carry out his duties of employment. Robby is responsible for his travelling expenses. On March 17, 2007, he acquired a new car for $46,000, including PST at 10% and GST at 6%, financing part of the acquisition through a bank loan arranged for the same date. The capital cost allowance rate in the first year is effectively 15%. He estimates that he will drive 38,000 kilometres in the course of his employment. He expects his total kilometres to the end of the year to be 45,000. The car and the employment use are reasonable for his position and his work requirements.

(D) Robby's contract also requires that he maintain an office in his home, since no other office is provided. He is responsible for all costs related to the operation of the office. He does not receive an allowance or reimbursement related to any of these costs. Robby has estimated that the office occupies approximately 15% of his home. This estimate is based on square footage. Robby estimates that if he had to rent a comparable amount of space he would have to pay $850 per month plus utilities.

— *REQUIRED*

(A) Calculate Robby's employment income for 2007, assuming that all expenses are reasonable in the circumstances and will be documented. Ignore consideration of the GST rebate.

(B) If the facts in part (A) were changed as follows, what would be the deductible expenses for 2007?   ITA: 8(1)

→ NO INTEREST IN CCA

(i) Lease entered into on March 17, 2007.

(ii) Monthly lease payments are $1,100 including PST at 10% and GST at 6%.

(iii) Employment use accounts for 38,000 km out of a total of 45,000 km for 2007.

(iv) Manufacturer's list price is $46,000 excluding PST and GST.

(C) How would your conclusions in parts (A) and (B) change if Robby was an internal auditor and, therefore, did not receive a bonus based on sales?

Problem 8

ITA: 5, 6, 7, 8, 67.2, 67.3; IT-470R

Anita Flare is a skilled tool and die worker. She has been working for Car Parts Inc., a large manufacturer of parts for the automobile industry for over 10 years. Car Parts Inc. is a Canadian-controlled private corporation. Anita has become their "Jane on the Spot" as far as diagnosing and quickly retooling machinery that breaks down or needs to be updated to run a short order. Anita is single and she rents a home in north Toronto. Because Anita is required to travel for 75% of the year, Car Parts Inc. actually pays the $1,200 monthly rent on Anita's home in Toronto. Anita reimburses the company for 25% of this amount ($300 per month) through payroll deduction as set out below.

The head office of Car Parts Inc. is located in north Toronto. The company, however, has plants that are located throughout Ontario and Quebec, wherever there are large automobile manufacturing operations to be supplied with parts. When a plant requires emergency retooling or repair Anita is sent out to that location to supervise and organize the work. As stated above, this involves about 75% of Anita's total employment hours for any given year. She stays at a particular location for a period of days or weeks depending on the nature of the job involved. She is never at a site for less than 36 hours. For the balance of the year, Anita works at the head office in the research department.

Anita's final 2007 pay stub showed the following totals in respect of the 2007 taxation year.

Gross salary	$115,000
Payroll deductions:	
Income tax withheld	$44,224
Canada Pension Plan contributions	1,990
Employment Insurance premiums paid	720
Contributions to company group RRSP	1,750
RPP contributions on account of current service	5,000
Union dues to Canadian Union of Automobile Workers (GST exempt)	800
Group accident income protection insurance premiums (matched by company)	240
Monthly rent reimbursement (as described above)	3,600

In discussion with Anita you determined that the company also provides the following fringe benefits.

Payment of board and lodging costs at special work sites as required – at cost to company	$18,000
Bonus based on company profits for the year above budgeted targets	12,500
Provision of safety boots and company uniform consisting of 5 shirts and 5 matching pairs of pants; the shirt is embroidered with her name on the front pocket and has the company name on the back	450
Registered pension plan contributions to defined benefit plan	6,750
Monthly allowance of $150 to cover personal phone calls, laundry costs and other incidentals while travelling. (She estimates that she spends $100 per month.)	1,800
Fitness club membership dues to a club with locations across Ontario (including PST and GST); Anita feels that it's important to her productivity to remain in top physical shape as her work can be physically demanding	805

Anita was injured on the job early in the year and received total payments of $11,500 out of the company group income protection plan for 2 months while she was recuperating. She had not previously received any payments under this plan and has paid total premiums of $2,880 into the plan since she began employment 12 years ago (this includes all of the year 2007 premiums paid through December 2007).

Due to her extensive travel, Anita's employer requires her to have an automobile for employment purposes. Anita has provided you with the following details of her automobile expenses.

	Owned car[1]	Leased car
Leasing costs[2]	n/a	$3,680
Gasoline and oil (including PST and GST)	$2,880	1,440
Insurance	1,333	667
Maintenance (including PST and GST)	400	240
Licence	90	30
CCA	1,207	n/a

NOTES:

[1] She owned an automobile until August 31, 2007, at which time she disposed of that vehicle and began leasing a new one. Assume that there are no tax consequences to Anita of the disposition of the automobile other than the fact that she can claim CCA in 2007 on this vehicle, as set out above, since it was a luxury vehicle.

Anita received an automobile loan to purchase the owned automobile. She received the loan on April 1, 2002, for $40,000 but has been making principal repayments annually on April 1 each year. She made the last principal repayment of $8,000 on April 1, 2007. There was no interest payable on the loan. Assume that the prescribed interest rate for employee loans was 6% for all of 2007.

Anita drove the owned car a total of 40,000 km during 2007 of which 35,000 km was employment related.

[2] Anita leased the car as of September 1, 2007, at a cost of $920 a month that includes PST and GST. The lease is for a 3-year period that will expire August 31, 2010. At the time that she leased the car, the manufacturer's list price on the vehicle was $55,000 excluding all taxes.

Anita drove the leased car a total of 20,000 km during 2007 of which 18,000 km was employment related.

— *REQUIRED*

(A) Determine Anita Flare's income from employment under Subdivision a of Division B of the Act for 2007 and cross-reference your answer to the appropriate section of the Act and/or Interpretation Bulletin. Round your answer to the nearest dollar.

¶3,875

(B) Indicate why you did not include any of the above amounts in your answer with the appropriate cross-reference.

(C) Compute the GST rebate that should be claimed and the income tax consequences of the rebate to be received in 2008.

Problem 9

ITA: Subdiv. a of Div. B, 67.1, 67.3; IT-470R

Mr. Ned Negotiator is employed by Snoopy-Snacks Ltd. (a Canadian-controlled private corporation). As of February 15, 2007, Ned was promoted to vice-president sales due to his hard work negotiating puppy snack contracts on behalf of the company. This promotion required Ned to relocate from the Toronto office of Snoopy-Snacks Ltd. to its Victoria, British Columbia office.

Ned has provided you with the following information regarding his 2007 income and expenses. He requests your assistance in determining his 2007 employment income for tax purposes.

Payroll details:

Gross salary		$125,000
Less:		
Income taxes	$45,000	
Canada Pension Plan contributions	1,990	
Employment Insurance contributions	720	
Registered pension plan contributions: defined benefit (post-89 service)	6,750	
Group income protection premiums paid	120	
Group term life insurance premiums paid	180	54,760
		$ 70,240

Employer-paid amounts and fringe benefits paid by Snoopy-Snacks Ltd.:

Dental plan premiums — paid to Star Insurance Company	$ 245
Group term life insurance premiums	90
B.C. provincial health care premiums	640
Group income protection premiums	400
Monthly allowance to cover travel and automobile expenses (based on a flat monthly amount of $400 for travel and $400 for auto)	9,600
Travelling expenses for Ned and his wife to Bermuda for a sales conference. Ned's time was spent attending the conference but his wife was on vacation the entire time. No GST or PST was payable on the trip since it was outside of Canada. One-half of the expenses related to Ned and one-half to his wife.	2,800
A birthday gift (a watch) received while in Ontario (including GST and PST). Snoopy-Snacks Ltd. deducted the cost of this gift as a business expense.	150
Outside financial counselling fees (including GST and no PST). The counselling firm indicated that 80% of its fees relate to counselling for future retirement while the remaining 20% of its fees relate to tax preparation.	2,568

Other Information:

1. Snoopy-Snacks Ltd. provided Ned with some assistance that relates to his move from Toronto to Victoria. The details of that assistance are set out below.

a) Ned purchased a new home in Victoria just prior to his move. However, he could not take possession of that home until April 30, 2007. Snoopy-Snacks Ltd. paid Ned's rent for a Victoria apartment for the months of February through April 2007. The rent paid was $1,200 per month.

½ × (16,500 – 15,000) → ALWAYS
→ 6(20)

b) Ned and Snoopy-Snacks Ltd. agreed that he would receive reimbursement from Snoopy-Snacks Ltd. for one-half of the loss realized by him on the sale of his Toronto home. Ned received $16,500 as a result of this agreement.

c) Ned received an allowance of $15,000 to cover his moving expenses. *→ TAXABLE 6(1)(b)*

In addition to the above, Ned's employer agreed to reimburse him an amount equal to one-quarter of his annual mortgage interest payment for the first five years of his mortgage on his new Victoria home. This was intended to compensate for higher real estate prices in Victoria. For 2007, Ned received $2,000 under the terms of this agreement. *→ 6(1)(b), 6(20)   6(23)*

2. Snoopy-Snacks Ltd. maintains an employee stock purchase plan for certain of its employees. Ned became eligible for this plan after his promotion. During 2007, he was granted an option to purchase 1,000 shares in Snoopy-Snacks Ltd. at an exercise price of $15 per share. At the time this option was granted the fair market value of the shares was $20 per share. On September 15, 2007, Ned exercised the option to purchase 600 of the above shares. The fair market value of the shares was $25 at that time. *→ DEFERRED*

3. Ned had unlimited use of the company's private swimming pool. All management level employees are permitted to utilize this pool. The local private swimming pool charges annual fees of $1,800 per year before GST (no PST). *— NO BENEFIT*

½ DEDUCTIBLE AFTER 2 YRS.

4. Ned had the following expenditures during 2007.

Automobile operating expenditures:

Lease payments for 12 months ($850 a month including PST of 8% and GST of 6%) (lease commenced July 1, 2006 for a period of three years; deducted lease costs for 2006 were $4,585)	$10,200
Gasoline and oil	1,300
Insurance	1,050
Maintenance	180
Licence	120

Travelling expenditures:

12,850 × 22,500/36,000   (8,031)

Meals (consumed while out of metropolitan area for greater than 12 hours)	7,200
Accommodation	12,000

8(1)(h) – 67.1

Ned travelled a total of 36,000 km during 2007 of which 22,500 km were employment-related. The manufacturer's list price on his automobile was $33,000 before GST and PST.

— REQUIRED

(A) Determine Ned's employment income for tax purposes for 2007 and cross-reference your answer to the appropriate sections of the Act and/or Interpretation Bulletins.

(B) Indicate why you did not include any of the above amounts in your answer with the appropriate cross-reference.

(C) Compute the potential GST rebate in 2008, and the income tax consequences upon receipt of the GST rebate.   ITA: 6(8)

[For more problems and solutions thereto, see the CD accompanying this book.]

Chapter 4

Income from Business:
General Concepts and Rules

LEARNING GOALS

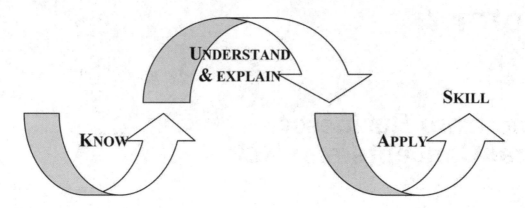

Know

By the end of this chapter you should know the basic provisions of the *Income Tax Act* that relate to the calculation of business income and expenses, and some of the GST implications for business activity. Completing the Review Questions (¶4,800) and Multiple Choice Questions (¶4,825) is a good way to learn the technical provisions.

Understand and Explain

You should understand and be able to explain what business income and expenses are, when to recognize them, and why they are treated the way they are for tax purposes. Completing the Exercises (¶4,850) is a good way to deepen your understanding of the material.

Apply

You should be able to use your knowledge and understanding of business income and expenses to identify and resolve practical problems. Completing the Assignment Problems (¶4,875) and Advisory Case (¶4,880) is an excellent way to develop your ability to apply the material in increasingly complex situations.

OVERVIEW

The focus of this chapter is on Subdivision b of Division B, Part I of the Act. In particular, the provisions dealing with income from business (both inclusions and deductions) will be covered. The final section of the chapter presents the impact of GST legislation on the business activity discussed in the earlier sections of the chapter. The following chart will help to locate in the Act the key provisions discussed in this Chapter.

Part I — Division B
Subdivision b
Business or Property

DIVISION	SUBDIVISION	SECTION
A Liability for tax		
B Computation of income	Basic rules	
	a Office or employment	
C Computation of taxable income	b **Business or property**	9-11 Basic rules
		12-17 Inclusions
D Taxable income earned in Canada by non-residents	c Capital gains and losses	18-21 Deductions
	d Other income	22-25 Ceasing to carry on business
E Computation of tax	e Other deductions	26-37 Special cases
E.1 Minimum tax	f Rules relating to computation of income	
F Special rules		
G Deferred and other special income arrangements	g Amounts not included in income	
	h Cdn corporations and shareholders	
H Exemptions		
I Returns, Assessments, payments, appeals	i Shareholders of non-resident corporations	
	j Partnerships	
J Appeals to the courts	k Trusts	

Subdivision b of Division B of Part I of the Act contains the primary rules for the computation of income from business. Most of what will be covered will be found in sections 9 through 21. Some of the more important provisions are as follows:

Inclusions

> Sec. 9 — A taxpayer's income (loss) for a taxation year from a business is their profit (loss) from that business for the year.

> Sec. 10 — Rules related to inventory

> Sec. 12 — Income inclusions

> Sec. 13 — Rules related to capital cost allowance

> Sec. 14 — Rules related to eligible capital property

Deductions

> Sec. 18 — Limitations on the deductibility of expenses

> Sec. 19 — Limitation on advertising expenses

> Sec. 20 — Deductions permitted

The interaction between section 18 and section 20 is interesting. For example, paragraph 18(1)(*b*) does not allow any deduction that is on account of capital, including depreciation. However, paragraph 20(1)(*a*) allows a deduction for capital cost allowance and paragraph 20(1)(*l*) allows a deduction for doubtful debts. Both of these items are capital in nature.

¶4,000   BASIC RULES

¶4,010   The Concept of Business Income

¶4,015   Income from a business

The word "business" is very broadly defined the Act, although the definition specifically excludes an office or employment. Income from a business for a taxation year is the "profit" therefrom for the year. While the word "profit" is not defined in the Act, Subdivision b contains numerous specific rules regarding amounts to be included in income and amounts which may or may not be deducted for income tax purposes. Furthermore, it must be understood that the word "income" when used in the Act means income after the deduction of expenses currently incurred to produce it.

ITA: 248(1)

ITA: 9(1)

¶4,015.10   *What is profit?*

Profit is the portrayal of income, according to common law, on "sound commercial principles", which may include generally accepted accounting principles (GAAP), unless a particular provision of the Act or principle of common law requires otherwise. This issue was recently explored by the Supreme Court of Canada in the case of *Canderel Ltd. v. The Queen*, and the court provided the following framework for analysis.

98 DTC 6100 (S.C.C.)

(1) The determination of profit is a question of law.

(2) The profit of a business for a taxation year is to be determined by setting against the revenues from the business for that year the expenses incurred in earning that income.[1]

(3) In seeking to determine profit, the goal is to obtain an accurate picture of the taxpayer's profit for the given year.

(4) In calculating profit, the taxpayer is free to use any method which is not inconsistent with:

    (a) the provisions of the *Income Tax Act*;

    (b) established case law principles or "rules of law"; and

    (c) well-accepted business principles.

(5) Well-accepted business principles, which include but are not limited to the formal codification found in GAAP, are not rules of law but interpretive aids. To the extent that they may influence the calculation of income, they will do so only on a case-by-case basis, depending upon the facts of the taxpayer's financial situation.

(6) On reassessment, once the taxpayer has shown that he has provided an accurate picture of income for the year, which is consistent with the Act, the case law, and well-accepted business principles, the onus shifts to the Minister to show either that the figure provided does *not* represent an accurate picture, or that another method of computation would provide a *more* accurate picture.

¶4,015.20   *The role of GAAP*

Specific provisions of the Act can create considerable differences between income for tax purposes and income for accounting purposes. One of the major causes of such differences results from the write-off of capital expenditures over a period of years. However, in recent years, tax treatment in certain areas of the Act, including the valuation of inventory and the deductibility of prepaid expenses, has moved closer to generally accepted accounting principles.

GAAP are often considered to reflect ordinary commercial principles, the legal concept, held by the courts to be a key determinant of profits. Nevertheless, it should be noted that the word "profit" is not required by the legislation to be interpreted in conformity with GAAP, even where the Act is silent on the treatment of a particular transaction.

---

[1] *M.N.R. v. Irwin*, 64 DTC 5227 (S.C.C.); *Associated Investors of Canada Ltd. v. M.N.R.*, [No. 2], 67 DTC 5096 (Ex. Ct.).

¶4,000

While the Canada Revenue Agency (CRA) has often taken the position that profit computed under GAAP most accurately reflects income in these situations, the courts have, on occasion, rejected conformity between income for accounting and tax purposes, particularly in cases where GAAP were at variance with the court's legal concept of ordinary commercial trading and business principles and practices or with a legal concept of income.[2] The case of *The Queen v. Metropolitan Properties Co. Ltd.*, on the measurement of business profit, clearly indicates "the desirability of applying generally accepted commercial and business practice as reflected in the generally accepted accounting principles". Thus, according to the reasoning of the court in the *Metropolitan* case, in the absence of a specific provision, a legal principle, or recognized commercial practice to deal with the tax treatment of a particular transaction, GAAP are applied to meet the objectives of the income tax system.

85 DTC 5128 (F.C.T.D.)

On the other hand, in the case of *Symes v. The Queen*, the Supreme Court of Canada expressed the view that to rely on GAAP for a determination of profit would suggest a degree of control by professional accountants that was inconsistent with a legal test for profit. The Supreme Court suggested the use of "well accepted principles of business (or accounting) practice" or "well accepted principles of commercial trading", but did not suggest how to determine these principles or how to differentiate them from GAAP. As a result, in the absence of a specific provision of the Act or a clearly stated legal principle, reliance on GAAP may provide a reasonable guideline.

94 DTC 6001 (S.C.C.)

Where GAAP envisage more than one method of determining income, the courts have adopted the "truer picture" approach, choosing the method that provides the truer picture of income as in the case of *West Kootenay Power and Light Co. Ltd. v. The Queen*. In this case, considerable emphasis was placed on the matching of expenses to the income that was generated by the expenditure.[3]

92 DTC 6023 (F.C.A.)

¶4,020 Business income versus capital receipt[4]

¶4,020.10 *Overview*

The argument over whether a particular receipt is income in nature or capital in nature has given rise to thousands of court cases over the years. This is primarily due to the taxation treatment of these two items; income receipts are fully taxed and capital receipts are only partially taxed as capital gains. Historically, the inclusion rate for capital gains has ranged from 0% to 75%, with the current inclusion rate being 50%.

The courts have at times applied the analogy of a fruit-bearing tree to cases in which the determination of a capital or income transaction was at issue, in order to focus on how an asset has been used. An investment or capital asset is likened to the tree which produces or can be expected to produce income in the form of fruit. Just as the sale of the tree would be regarded as a capital transaction, the sale of an investment that can produce a form of income from business or property can be regarded as a capital transaction. However, the analogy breaks down under the facts of certain cases.

¶4,020.20 *Objective of the analysis*

At the time of a court hearing, the courts can view in perspective the taxpayer's whole course of conduct for the period before, during and after the transaction in question. To help make the distinction between an income and a capital transaction, the courts attempt to assess the intention of the taxpayer in the transaction. The courts attempt to answer the question: did the taxpayer deliberately seek a profit of an income rather than a capital gain nature? An attempt is made to substantiate this by facts which establish the taxpayer's general course of conduct.

---

[2] There have been many cases in this area, including *M.N.R. v. Publishers Guild of Canada Limited*, 57 DTC 1017 (Ex. Ct.).

[3] For further discussion of the role of GAAP in interpreting profit for tax purposes, see Joanne E. Magee, "The Profit GAAP", *CA Magazine*, April 1995, pp. 32–35.

[4] For a more detailed discussion of this topic, see Robert E. Beam and Stanley N. Laiken, "Adventure or Concern in the Nature of Trade: the Key to Taxpayer Intention", (1996) vol. 44, no. 3 *Canadian Tax Journal*, pp. 888–913.

Secondary intention is a development of more recent years which is established by looking at whether the taxpayer has built into a transaction, at the time of purchase, a profitable alternative in the event that the primary intention is frustrated. For example, if land is acquired for development, but appropriate zoning changes are not approved or other extraneous circumstances frustrate the original intention and subsequently the land is sold at a profit, that profit may be considered to be the result of the alternative business intention and may be regarded as business income.[5]

The concept of secondary intention was clarified in the case of *Racine et al. v. M.N.R.* as follows: 65 DTC 5098 (Ex. Ct.)

> To give a transaction which involves the acquisition of capital the double character of also being at the same time an adventure in the nature of trade, the purchaser must have in his mind, at *the moment of the purchase*, the possibility of reselling *as an operating motivation* for the acquisition; that is to say that he must have had in mind that upon a certain type of circumstances arising he had hopes of being able to resell it at a profit instead of using the thing purchased for purposes of capital. (Italics added.)

In the case of *Armstrong v. The Queen*, the court stated further "that circumstances which force the sale of property or make such a sale attractive do not have the effect of *retroactively converting* a property held to produce income and as a capital property into something of a trading nature". (Italics added.)   85 DTC 5396 (F.C.T.D.)

¶4,020.30   *Observable behavioural factors or "badges of trade"*

While the courts have indicated that taxpayer intention is the objective in a determination of whether a transaction results in a receipt of business income or capital, it should be recognized that intention is a state of mind. Intention must be inferred from an observation of a taxpayer's behaviour or a taxpayer's whole course of conduct. The observable behaviour of a taxpayer may be classified by a set of behavioural factors which may point to the existence of "an adventure or concern in the nature of trade" from which an intention to enter a profit-making scheme can be inferred. The courts have developed a set of indicators, often referred to as "badges of trade" to determine whether an adventure or concern in the nature of trade was present in a transaction and, hence, whether business income resulted.

To determine whether a gain on the disposition of property is business income from an adventure or concern in the nature of trade or a capital gain, it is useful to apply an analytical framework to a fact situation. The objective of applying such a framework is to systematically evaluate the facts to determine whether a transaction or series of transactions bear the "badges of trade". A list of behavioural factors or badges of trade that can be used as a reference might be comprised of the following.

(i) *Relation of the transaction to the taxpayer's business:* A transaction may be regarded as an income transaction if it is very similar to one in which the taxpayer would be involved in his or her normal business or profession. If a taxpayer undertakes a transaction in association with others, then the relationship of the transaction to the normal business or profession of these associates can be considered. This factor is helpful in determining whether a taxpayer had a secondary intention to make a profit on the sale of an asset. If a taxpayer has special knowledge or expertise or had direct access to these, it might be inferred that in a particular transaction a profitable "escape hatch" was known at the time of the purchase.

---

[5] Two good examples of this situation are given by the cases of *Regal Heights Ltd. v. M.N.R.*, 60 DTC 1270 (S.C.C.), and *Fraser v. M.N.R.*, 64 DTC 5224 (S.C.C.).

(ii) *Activity or organization normally associated with trade:* The nature of the activity surrounding a transaction or the level of organization of the transaction may be such that the transaction can be considered "an adventure in the nature of trade" or a transaction which is very similar to one which would be undertaken by a business person normally engaged in such transactions. Two classic cases of this involved British taxpayers one of whom purchased a carload of toilet paper and resold it at a profit[6] and the other of whom purchased a carload of whisky and sold it at a profit[7]. Transacting in such commodities by the carload is an indication of an intention to trade which would result in the gains being assessed as business income. To apply this factor, it is necessary to determine how the transaction in question was organized. If a transaction was handled in the same way as a normal business transaction was handled, in terms of quantities of a commodity purchased, method of promotion and sale, etc., there may be evidence of an adventure in the nature of trade. The Interpretation Bulletin entitled "Adventure or concern in the nature of trade" deals with the concept in more detail, in particular, under the heading "Taxpayer's Conduct". *IT-459, par. 5–8*

(iii) *Nature of the assets involved:* The courts distinguish between fixed assets, which if sold result in a capital transaction, and "circulating" or working capital assets, which if sold result in an income transaction. Hence, the particular use of an asset by a given taxpayer may determine its nature for that taxpayer. Some assets, by their nature, can only be regarded as inventory. For example, whisky or toilet paper cannot produce income in such forms as interest, dividends, rents, etc. Income from these commodities can only be earned when they are sold, as inventory, for a price higher than their cost. The Interpretation Bulletin entitled "Adventure or concern in the nature of trade" deals with this factor under the heading "Nature of the Property". *IT-459, par. 9–11*

(iv) *Number and frequency of transactions by the same taxpayer in a given period of time:* A relatively large number of transactions in a given period of time may indicate that the taxpayer is involved in a business activity which will result in income transactions. Hence, extensive involvement in a particular type of transaction may be indicative of business activity. It should be emphasized, however, that an isolated transaction may still be considered an "adventure in the nature of trade", that is, of a business nature.

(v) *Length of the period of ownership of the asset:* The length of the holding period for an asset may be used to determine whether the asset is being treated as inventory or as a capital asset. The shorter the period of ownership, the more likely is the gain to be regarded as business income from an adventure in the nature of trade.

(vi) *Supplemental work on or in connection with the property disposed of in the transaction:* Work done on a property to enhance its value or to make it more marketable may indicate an adventure in the nature of trade resulting in business income on the disposition. Intensive advertising and promotion of the property for sale would be a similar indicator.

(vii) *Circumstances that caused the disposition:* An unsolicited offer that results in the sale or a sale motivated by an unforeseen need for funds may argue against the existence of an adventure in the nature of trade, because of the evidence of the lack of a plan to turn a profit on a sale.

(viii) *Corporate objects or partnership agreement:* Articles of incorporation may suggest that the corporation was engaged in a business which it had been created to carry on. Some judicial decisions, in the past, have held that a transaction, although unrelated to the taxpayer's usual business, fell within the objects of a corporation as represented by its charter and, as a result, was a transaction of a business nature. This can occur when the objects of a corporation are set out in a very broad manner in its charter to provide for future flexibility. On the other hand, in the case of *Sutton Lumber & Trading Company Ltd. v. M.N.R.*, the Supreme Court of Canada ignored a corporation's objects on the basis that what is relevant is not what a corporation can do under its objects, but what, in fact, it did do. Furthermore, it should be noted that, although some provincial corporation legislation provides for corporations having objects, the *Canada Business Corporations Act* and the *Ontario Business* *53 DTC 1158 (S.C.C.)*

---

[6] *Rutledge v. C.I.R.*, [1929] 14 T.C. 490.
[7] *C.I.R. v. Fraser*, [1942] 24 T.C. 498.

Corporations Act do not provide for stated corporate objects. Thus, the relevance of this factor may be diminished. It should be noted that the stated objectives of a partnership organization, as outlined in a partnership agreement or other document, might be regarded in the same way.

This is not an exhaustive list of behavioural factors that can be observed. The factors used to determine whether a receipt is one of income or capital may depend on the type of property involved. For example, on the sale of real estate, the CRA has developed a list of about 12 factors which the courts have considered and lists them in the Interpretation Bulletin entitled "Profit, capital gains and losses from the sale of real estate". *IT-218R, par. 3*

Factors or badges of trade pertaining specifically to real estate transactions not already indicated in the foregoing list include:

(a) feasibility of the taxpayer's stated intention;

(b) geographical location and zoned use of the real estate;

(c) extent to which stated intention was carried out by the taxpayer;

(d) evidence of a change in stated intention after the purchase;

(e) the extent to which borrowed money was used to finance the acquisition and the terms of the financing; and

(f) factors which motivated the sale.

The Interpretation Bulletin entitled "Transactions in securities" lists some of the factors or badges of trade that are used in distinguishing between a receipt of income and a receipt of capital on the disposition of securities. Some of the factors listed in paragraph 11 of the bulletin and not listed among the factors already discussed include: *IT-479R, par. 11*

(a) knowledge of or experience in securities markets;

(b) time spent studying the securities markets and investigating potential purchases;

(c) financing primarily by margin or other forms of debt; and

(d) advertising or otherwise making it known that the taxpayer is willing to purchase securities.

¶4,020.40 *Summary*

Exhibit 4-1 diagrams the analytical framework developed. Note how an assessment of the existence of badges of trade from the facts is used to infer intention of the taxpayer at the time of the purchase of the property in question. Evidence of the existence of significant badges of trade suggests an intention to engage in a profit-making scheme or an adventure in the nature of trade. The lack of that evidence may suggest an investment intention.

EXHIBIT 4-1

Analytical Framework for Capital versus Income Issue

Evidence of Adventure Based on Behavioural Factors or "Badges of Trade"

- relationship of transaction to taxpayer's business;

- activity or organization associated with trade;

- nature of asset;

- number and frequency of transactions in a given period of time;

- length of period of ownership of asset;

- supplemental work on or in connection with property;

- circumstances that caused disposition;

- if transaction completed by organization, stated objectives of organization as outlined in articles of association or partnership agreement;

- other factors.

inference

Intention of the Taxpayer

Primary:

Did the taxpayer intend to use the asset like an item of inventory or like a capital asset?

Secondary:

If the primary intention to use the asset like a capital asset was frustrated, did the taxpayer have, *at the time of the purchase*, a motivating intention to sell the property at a profit?

determination

Issue for Determination

Is the gain (or loss) from the disposition of property a capital gain (or loss) or business income (or loss)?

Source: Reproduced with the permission of the Canadian Tax Foundation from Robert E. Beam and Stanley N. Laiken, "Adventure or Concern in the Nature of Trade: Badges of Trade as the Key Indicator of Taxpayer Intention", (1996) vol. 44, no. 3 *Canadian Tax Journal*, pp. 888–913.

Example Problem

The taxpayer was the president and general manager of a Canadian company involved in the fabrication of various products of non-ferrous metals, including lead. The company purchased all its lead requirements from a Canadian supplier which was the only producer of lead in Canada. However, the Canadian supplier held the company to a quota and, as a result, the company lost considerable business.

In these circumstances, the Canadian company requested the permission of its U.S. parent to import foreign lead. This meant buying it for future delivery in about three months. The risk of importing lead for future delivery was contrary to the business policy set for the Canadian company by the U.S. parent. However, the taxpayer was granted permission to purchase the lead himself and sell it to the Canadian company, assuming personally whatever risk was involved in the transaction.

The taxpayer made arrangements for the purchase of 1,500 tons of the foreign lead and for its sale to the Canadian company, on its arrival, at the market price of lead on the date of its arrival. He did not, himself, have to put up any money for the purchase of the lead. On the transaction, the taxpayer made a substantial profit.

— *REQUIRED*

Determine whether the profit made by the taxpayer was a capital gain or income from business or property.

— *SOLUTION* [See *M.N.R. v. James A. Taylor*, 56 DTC 1125 (Ex. Ct.).]   56 DTC 1125 (Ex. Ct.)

The taxpayer purchased the lead with the intention of selling it to the Canadian company. His purpose was to alleviate the short supply of lead to which the Canadian company had been held by its Canadian supplier and, hence, to enable the Canadian company to meet the demand for its products. Since the taxpayer, as president and general manager of the Canadian company, was an employee, he was not carrying on a business of his own. Hence, the transaction in question was not related to a business that he was carrying on personally, as might be the case of a commodity dealer.

If the transaction can be considered "an adventure in the nature of trade", then the profit resulting from the transaction would be income from business. An 1896 British case[8] provided the following definition of "trade":

> . . . Trade in its largest sense is the business of selling, with a view to profit, goods which the trader has either manufactured or himself purchased.

A 1904 British case[9] set out a test for determining whether the gain from a transaction was capital or income as follows:

> . . . Is the sum of gain that has been made a mere enhancement of value by realising a security, or is it a gain made in an operation of business in carrying out a scheme for profit-making?

The element of speculation may determine that a transaction is characteristic of what a trader would do. It can be said that the transaction has the "badges of trade". Thus, if the transaction is of the same kind and is carried on in the same way as a transaction of an ordinary trader or dealer in the same kind of property, it may be called an adventure in the nature of trade.

The nature and quantity of the subject matter of the transaction may be such as to exclude the possibility that its sale was the realization of an investment of a capital nature. This would lead to the conclusion that the taxpayer's purchase and sale of 1,500 tons of lead was an adventure in the nature of trade. He could not do anything with the lead except sell it. In fact, he dealt with the lead in the same manner as any dealer in imported lead would have done.

The fact that this was an isolated transaction cannot preclude it from being an adventure in the nature of trade. The word "adventure" implies a single or isolated transaction. Furthermore, it is not essential to a transaction being an adventure in the nature of trade that an organization be set up to carry it into effect. Finally, the fact that a transaction is totally different in nature from any of the other activities of the taxpayer and that he has never entered into a transaction of the kind before or since does not, by itself, preclude it from being an adventure in the nature of trade.

The Exchequer Court of Canada, the predecessor of the Federal Court of Canada, concluded in this case that the taxpayer's transaction was an adventure in the nature of trade and, hence, the profit was taxable as income from business.

---

[8] *Grainger and Son v. Gough*, (1896) 3 R.T.C. 462.

[9] *Californian Copper Syndicate Ltd. v. Harris*, [1904] 5 T.C. 159.

¶4,025 Damages as a receipt of income or capital

¶4,025.10 *Non-performance of business contracts*

Damages received for non-performance of business contracts are usually intended to place the recipient in the same position as he or she would have been had the contract been performed. Since the performance of a business contract usually results in income, damages for non-performance are generally regarded as income.[10]

¶4,025.20 *Cancellation of agency agreements*

While the cancellation of an agency agreement has been held to be income, if such an agreement is of sufficient importance to constitute part of the company's total business structure, the compensation paid on the termination of such a contract may be capital. This was the situation in a United Kingdom decision.[11] In that case an English company entered into an agreement with a competing Dutch company to co-operate in the manufacture and sale of margarine and to share in the resulting profits and losses. The agreement was to last for about 30 years, but it had to be terminated earlier and the Dutch company paid the English company a large sum of money to terminate the agreement. The British House of Lords held that the rights of the English company under the agreement constituted a capital asset and the sum paid for its cancellation was a capital receipt. For a Canadian case in this area see *Parsons-Steiner Limited v. M.N.R.*, which dealt with the cancellation of an agency agreement of 22 years standing accounting for 80% of the appellant's business. In *Pepsi-Cola Canada Ltd. v. The Queen*, a payment made on the termination of a bottling and distributorship agreement was held to be for goodwill and, hence, a capital receipt. On the other hand, compensation for cancelling a contract entered into in the course of the appellant's regular business was held to be taxable as income in *The Great Lakes Paper Company, Limited v. M.N.R.* 62 DTC 1148 (Ex. Ct.) 79 DTC 5388 (F.C.A.) 61 DTC 564 (T.A.B.)

¶4,025.30 *Loss of property*

Damages for loss of property may be regarded as a receipt of capital if the property involved was fixed capital and a receipt of income if the property was working capital such as inventory.[12]

¶4,030 Other receipts or benefits

¶4,030.10 *Profits from an illegal business*

A taxpayer may be carrying on a business of an illegal nature and yet be taxable on the profits. This principle was established in a 1932 United Kingdom case[13] in which the following statement was made:

> . . . The revenue [authorities], representing the state, are merely looking at an accomplished fact. It is not condoning it, or taking part in it. It merely finds profit made from what appears to be a trade, and the revenue laws say that profits made from a trade are to be taxed.

---

[10] The cases of *Sutherland v. M.N.R.*, 60 DTC 13 (T.A.B.), on compensation for losses in construction delays and *Hill v. M.N.R.*, 60 DTC 362 (T.A.B.), on compensation for lease cancellation illustrate this result.

[11] *Van den Berghs, Ltd. v. Clark*, [1935] A.C. 431.

[12] The cases of *Gagnon v. M.N.R.*, 53 DTC 273 (T.A.B.), and *Federal Farms Limited v. M.N.R.*, 59 DTC 1050 (Ex. Ct.), deal with such damages. Whether property was lost or profits were foregone was at issue in *Donald Hart Limited v. M.N.R.*, 59 DTC 1134 (Ex. Ct.), and whether a capital source of income or the income itself was lost was at issue in *Dr. Georges Garneau v. M.N.R.*, 68 DTC 132 (T.A.B.).

[13] *Mann v. Nash*, [1932] 1 K.B. 752.

This was re-established in the Canadian case of *No. 275 v. M.N.R.* Having established this principle, the question of deductions arises in terms of substantiating expenses incurred to produce the profits from an illegal business. This was the situation in *M.N.R. v. Eldridge* involving the operator of a call-girl organization who attempted to claim certain cash expenditures. Substantiated, non-capital expenditures incurred to produce income from an illegal business are normally deductible, under conditions discussed later in this chapter. However, the deduction of specified illegal payments is prohibited. Hence, illegal payments under specified sections of the *Criminal Code* made to government officials in Canada, officials engaged in the administration of justice in Canada, persons under a duty as agents or employees and persons responsible for collecting fares or admission fees are not deductible where the payments are made to induce, or attempt to induce, the recipient to breach his or her duty and the payment is made for doing anything that is an offence under the specified sections of the *Criminal Code*. Refer to the Interpretation Bulletin entitled "Gains from theft, defalcation or embezzlement" for the CRA's position in this area.

55 DTC 439 (T.A.B.)

64 DTC 5338 (Ex. Ct.)

ITA: 67.5

IT-256R

¶4,030.20 *Profits from betting, gambling, and windfalls*

The proceeds of private betting or gambling for mere pleasure have generally been regarded as not taxable as long as the activity is not organized and of a business nature. This will be the case even if the bets, perhaps even made with borrowed funds, are high and the gains substantial. However, someone like a bookmaker will be taxable on his or her profits because he or she will be regarded as carrying on a business. The existence of a system for the minimization or management of risk may indicate a professional gambler. In this case, the winnings would be taxable and, conceivably, the losses would be deductible.[14]

A non-taxable windfall can be distinguished from income if the recipient has no expectation of receiving the payment.[15] Perhaps a more widely recognized form of windfall is a lottery winning, which is not taxable.

¶4,030.30 *Subsidies*

The question of whether a government or any other subsidy is capital or income will depend on the purpose of the subsidy. An income receipt may result from a subsidy to:

- supplement the taxpayer's income or enable him or her to operate at a profit, or
- ensure a reasonable return to the taxpayer on capital invested.

On the other hand, a capital receipt may result from a subsidy to:

- reimburse or assist the taxpayer in respect of a capital outlay, or
- encourage an activity in the public interest such as the prevention of unemployment.

The case of *Saint John Drydock & Shipbuilding Co. Ltd. v. M.N.R.* is a leading Canadian decision on the question of whether a subsidy should be regarded as a receipt of income or capital. The general principles followed by the CRA in making this distinction are set out in the Interpretation Bulletin entitled "Government Assistance — General Comments".

2 DTC 663 (Ex. Ct.)

IT-273R2

¶4,030.40 *Forgiveness of debt rules*

When a taxpayer incurs a debt obligation, the principal amount that is borrowed is not considered to be income. Hence, there is no deduction on the repayment of this debt. Therefore, repayments of principal are made with after-tax funds. As well, when a debt is settled or forgiven by the creditor for less than its principal amount, there should be no tax consequences. However, where interest was paid or payable on the debt amount and was or could be deducted from a source of income, then the debtor has received a tax benefit from the interest expense write-offs. The debt forgiveness rules apply to commercial obligations which are debt obligations incurred for the purpose of earning income from a business or property. Personal debt would normally be excluded from these rules.

---

[14] See the case of *Belawski v. M.N.R.*, 54 DTC 457 (T.A.B.), in this area.

[15] As an example of such an amount see *J.E. Cranswick v. The Queen*, 80 DTC 6057 (F.C.T.D.).

The Act contains complex rules that reduce certain tax-loss carryovers or tax accounts by the amount of debt forgiven, generally where interest charged on the debt was deductible to the debtor. The forgiven amount of the debt is applied to reduce tax values including non-capital loss and net capital loss carryforwards and the capital costs of assets owned by the debtor. The potential effect of these reductions is to increase income through lower tax-free recovery of costs in the future. The balance of debt forgiven that is not otherwise applied to reduce specified tax-loss carryovers or other tax accounts must be included in computing the income of the debtor at an inclusion rate of 50% (or 100% for a partnership). Where the debt was incurred in a business activity, the income inclusion is considered to be income from the business. The effect of this provision is to fully offset the benefit of not having to repay all or part of a debt with after-tax funds. The specific rules on debt forgiveness are beyond the scope of this text.

ITA: 80

ITA: 80(3)–(12)

ITA: 80(13)

ITA: 80

¶4,040   Inventory Valuation

¶4,045   Basis of valuation

¶4,045.10   *Market or lower of cost or market*

The Act permits the valuation of each item in an inventory at the lower of cost or market. A degree of variation is permitted by an income tax regulation which allows all of the items in the inventory to be valued at fair market value. This regulation might be used, where the fair market value of all items is lower than the valuation provided by the lower of cost or market for each item, to maximize cost of goods sold, and, thereby, minimize tax. However, there could be situations where the higher value would be desirable, for example, to reduce a loss that might expire. Again, the choice permitted between the Act and the regulation could be used to provide the higher valuation as necessary, but the effect may be minimal, given the choices permitted. Furthermore, as will be seen from a subsequent discussion, the choice may be permanent, such that the long-term effects of the alternate choice should be considered.

ITA: 10(1)

ITR: 1801

ITA: 10(1)

ITA: 10(1); ITR: 1801

ITA: 10(2.1)

¶4,045.20   *Specific identification*

Where the cost of items in an inventory can be identified, it is the actual laid down cost that must be used. This would include invoice cost plus duties, freight and insurance. In the case of goods in process and finished goods in the inventory of a manufacturing concern, cost will also include the cost of direct labour and in some cases the applicable share of overhead expenses. According to an Interpretation Bulletin, the cost of manufactured goods must include overhead allocated on a direct costing or absorption costing basis. The Act requires the inclusion in cost any non-deductible interest and property taxes on vacant land held as inventory of a business.

IT-473R

ITA: 10(1.1)

¶4,045.30   *First in, first out (FIFO)*

Where individual items cannot be identified for costing, a convention or assumption, usually "first-in first-out" (FIFO), must be applied for the purpose of determining cost of inventory on hand. The use of "last-in first-out" (LIFO) as an assumption about cost has long been fought by the CRA as illustrated by the case of *M.N.R. v. Anaconda American Brass Ltd.* In that case it was held by the Judicial Committee of the Privy Council of the House of Lords of the United Kingdom (to which decisions of the Supreme Court of Canada could be appealed until the mid-1950s), first, that an assumption of any kind in determining inventory value could only be made to the extent that the facts about actual cost were not ascertainable. Furthermore, in the particular case of Anaconda, the LIFO assumption disregarded the actual flow of inventory through the business. This disregard of facts in relation to the flow of goods also made the use of the LIFO assumption objectionable in the case of *Wickett and Craig Ltd. v. M.N.R.* While the use of LIFO conforms to generally accepted accounting principles and increases, relatively, the cost of goods sold to reflect the effects of inflation in periods of rising inventory costs, the Act does not recognize such effects.

55 DTC 1220 (Privy Council)

78 DTC 1382 (T.R.B.)

¶4,045.40 *Meaning of "cost" and "market"*

For the meaning of the word "market" in the valuation of inventory, refer to the C.I.C.A. (Canadian Institute of Chartered Accountants) *Handbook*. Market price may be interpreted to mean:

(a) the current purchase price prevailing for the quantities of goods normally purchased by the taxpayer (useful for raw materials);

(b) realization value, i.e., the selling price which the goods on hand will realize, after deducting the direct cost of making the sale (useful for finished goods); or

(c) replacement value, i.e., the cost of reproducing the article into its present state of completion (useful for semi-finished goods where it is usually not possible to obtain a purchase price and it is not possible to sell the article).

The meaning of the terms "cost" and "market" are further considered in the Interpretation Bulletin entitled "Inventory Valuation". IT-473R

It is interesting to note that the Act specifies that replacement cost must be used for the fair market value of certain property that is advertising or packaging material, parts, supplies or other property of this nature which is considered to be inventory. Note, also, that work in progress of a business that is a profession is considered to be inventory with a fair market value equal to the amount that can reasonably be expected to become receivable after the end of the year. However, for greater certainty, these types of property are considered to be inventory and, hence, subject to the Act's valuation rules for inventory. ITA: 10(4)(*b*)

ITA: 10(1), 10(4)(*a*), 10(5)

The Act requires that the value attributed to the opening inventory be the same as that attributed to the closing inventory of the year before. This ensures that no profits escape tax by a break in the continuity of the inventory figures between the end of one year and the beginning of the next. ITA: 10(2)

A taxpayer must value inventory at the end of a year using the same method as that used at the end of the preceding year. A taxpayer is permitted to change the valuation method used for inventory of a business where permission is obtained from the CRA. The result is to restrict the flexibility in the choice of inventory valuation method from one year to another. However, there may be some flexibility within a particular inventory valuation method. For example, a business that is required to value its inventory at the lower of cost or market at the end of a year because that method was used at the end of the preceding year, may still have a choice in determining cost for the purposes of this valuation method. This provision appears to codify accounting principles requiring that the opening and closing inventories of a given year be valued on the same basis. ITA: 10(2.1)

ITA: 10(2.1)

The CRA can correct the value of opening inventory where it has not been valued as required by the Act. As a result, corrected opening inventory may differ from closing inventory of the preceding year, thereby forcing the effects of the change on the income of the year of the correction only. ITA: 10(1), 10(3)

¶4,045.40

Example Problem

Sam DaBuilder builds houses in various parts of the city. At the end of his fiscal year he has four homes left in his inventory. Sam's records show the following information on each house:

		Actual total cost	Cost to rebuild house	Market list price
1.	Happy Valley Road	$40,000	$50,000	$75,000
2.	Thruway Drive	25,000	20,000	18,000
3.	Low Profit Place	40,000	45,000	42,000
4.	Broken Balloon Lane	25,000	22,000	24,000

From past experience Sam knows that he can sell each house for its market list price less 10% for commissions and bargaining.

— REQUIRED

Using the valuation alternatives available to him, determine the value of Sam's closing inventory. Indicate the basis for each valuation and select the one more advantageous to him, assuming he wants to minimize income for tax purposes. (Assume that the method of valuing inventory could change with permission.)   ITA: 10(2.1)

— SOLUTION

In this case, since the houses are finished, net realizable value would be the appropriate indicator of market value. This would be calculated from the information given by reducing market list price by the 10% direct cost of making the sale. The following would form the basis of the decision:

House	Cost	Market	Lower on each unit
1	$40,000	$ 67,500 (90% of $75,000)	$ 40,000
2	25,000	16,200 (90% of $18,000)	16,200
3	40,000	37,800 (90% of $42,000)	37,800
4	25,000	21,600 (90% of $24,000)	21,600
		$143,100	$115,600

Using the rules in the Act, the inventory could be valued at $115,600 which is the lower of cost or market for each item. The Regulations would permit the use of the market value of all items ($143,100). In this case, if the business is profitable, the more advantageous valuation would be based on the lower of cost or market for each item because it would provide the lower valuation, thereby increasing cost of goods sold and decreasing income subject to tax. On the other hand, if the business is in a loss position for the year, some of the losses can be absorbed by choosing the regulation alternative of market value to decrease cost of goods sold, thereby increasing the gross margin available to offset losses for the year. The choice is limited by the provision of the Act that requires that the method chosen for ending inventory in the current year must be the same as the method used for closing inventory at the end of the previous year unless ministerial permission for a change is granted.

ITA: 10(1)
ITR: 1801

ITR: 1801

ITA: 10(2.1)

¶4,050   Adjustment for depreciation allocation to inventory: an overview of the issue

To the extent that the cost of closing inventory for financial accounting purposes *includes an allocation* by the use of absorption costing of depreciation, obsolescence or depletion write-offs, such an allocation must be added to income for the year. This rule   ITA: 12(1)(*r*) requires the full add-back of depreciation in the reconciliation of income for tax purposes with income for financial accounting purposes. The add-back is required despite the fact that any depreciation included in the cost of closing inventory is not charged as an expense in the year, because the value of closing inventory reduces the cost of goods sold. Since the same allocation for accounting purposes will be included in the cost of opening inventory of the next year, a deduction of the amount of the allocation added in the current year for tax purposes is made in the subsequent year. These adjustments are unnecessary if the taxpayer   ITA: 20(1)(*ii*) has used the direct costing method and, as a result, has not included in the cost of inventory for financial accounting purposes an allowance in respect of depreciation, obsolescence or depletion.

¶4,060   Sole Proprietorship

For fiscal periods that begin after 1994, individuals who report business income, including professional income, generally must report that income on a calendar year basis, according to the definition of "fiscal period". This requirement applies to a sole proprietor-   ITA: 249.1(1) ship and a professional corporation, which is any corporation that carries on the professional practice of an accountant, dentist, lawyer, medical doctor, veterinarian, or chiropractor. The   ITA: 248(1) requirement, also, applies to partnerships in which at least one member is an individual, a professional corporation or another affected partnership.

However, there is a provision for an alternative fiscal period for a business carried on by   ITA: 249.1(4) an individual. A change in the end of a fiscal period can only be made with ministerial   ITA: 249.1(7) concurrence. An off-calendar fiscal year-end for an unincorporated business is possible, if an individual files an election in prescribed form by the date on which the individual must file a tax return for the year. The election can be revoked in a future period, in which case the calendar-year fiscal period must be used.   ITA: 249.1(6)

To prevent a deferral in the reporting of income on an off-calendar fiscal period, addi-   ITA: 249.1(4) tional rules for the reporting of business income must be followed. A formula is provided that   ITA: 34.1 effectively computes income from an unincorporated business with an off-calendar year-end on a calendar year basis by the use of an estimating procedure.

The system applies to, for example, a January 31 business year-end as follows. First, the taxpayer includes income from the unincorporated business for the fiscal period ended, say, January 31, 2007. To this amount, the taxpayer must add an estimate of business income for the "stub period" from February 1, 2007 to December 31, 2007. The estimate is based on a proration of $^{11}/_{12}$ or 11 months of income in the fiscal period ended January 31, 2007. From the sum, the taxpayer can subtract the stub period addition made in the 2006 tax return. However, the alternative method recognizes that there are valid non-tax business reasons for using an off-calendar year-end and allows such a year-end to be maintained.

When an off-calendar year-end reflects less than 12 months of business operations, due   ITA: 34.1(1), 34.1(2) to the commencement of business, the stub-period income addition is adjusted so that an appropriate amount not exceeding 12 months of income is reported in a calendar-year period.

¶4,100 INCLUSIONS

¶4,110 Amounts Received and Receivable

Amounts received for services to be rendered or goods to be delivered are included in income. This represents a divergence from accounting principles which would defer such amounts of income until the year in which they are earned. However, a reasonable reserve for unearned amounts included in income can be taken. The Act's system for reserves will be discussed later in this chapter. The Act would include amounts received such as prepaid rent, payments for the warranty of merchandise and container deposits. A deduction for refunds of amounts previously included in income under this paragraph is provided to offset the fact that a reserve would not be available for a refunded amount.

ITA: 12(1)(*a*)

ITA: 20(1)(*m*)

ITA: 12(1)(*a*)

ITA: 20(1)(*m*.2)

Amounts receivable in respect of services rendered or property sold during the year in the course of business are brought into income. A complementary reserve (limited to three years) is available at least for property sold to recognize the uncertainty of collecting these amounts. An amount will be deemed to have become receivable on the earlier of the day when the account was rendered and the day on which it would have been rendered had there been no undue delay.

ITA: 12(1)(*b*)

ITA: 20(1)(*n*), 20(8)

Amounts included because they are receivable must be legally receivable as a result of the taxpayer's having completed the performance of the service contracted for.[16] Holdbacks, common in the construction industry, are not legally receivable until the year in which the architect's or engineer's final certificate accepting and approving work done is issued. The Act provides that these rules are enacted "for greater certainty" and should not be interpreted to imply that any amount not referred to, such as amounts received and earned in the year, are not to be included in income from business.

ITA: 12(1)(*b*)

ITA: 12(2)

¶4,120 Inducement Payments or Reimbursements

All receipts in the nature of reimbursements or inducements in respect of the acquisition of an asset or the incurring of a deductible expense must be included in income from business or property unless this amount already has reduced the cost of the property or the amount of the expense. The types of receipts contemplated by this provision include inducements, grants, subsidies, reimbursements, etc., and amounts received indirectly from these sources, perhaps, through a not-for-profit entity. An example of such inducements would be receipts by a commercial tenant who was reimbursed by a landlord for part or all of the cost of making leasehold improvements. As an alternative, the recipient may elect to reduce the capital cost or the cost of the related property or the amount of the related expense. The provision brings the tax treatment of such receipts in line with generally accepted commercial principles. This area has been a source of contentious issues which were not fully resolved by the CRA's Interpretation Bulletin, "Premiums and other amounts with respect to leases". Note that this Interpretation Bulletin also deals with the position of the payer which is not specifically dealt with in the legislation.

ITA: 12(1)(*x*)

ITA: 13(7.4), 53(2.1)

IT-359R2

¶4,130 Restrictive Covenants

Payments received for a restrictive covenant must be included in income. To the extent that a taxpayer receives an amount for a restrictive covenant, the amount must be included in income except to the extent that a related person is required to take it into income. For a full discussion on the treatment of payments received for restrictive covenants please refer to Chapter 9, under the heading "Restrictive Covenants".

ITA: 12(1)(*x*)(v.1)

ITA: 56.4(2)

---

[16] The question of when expropriation proceeds are receivable was addressed in the case of *M.N.R. v. Lechter*, 66 DTC 5300 (S.C.C.).

¶4,200 DEDUCTIONS

¶4,210 Deductibility of Expenditures

The first test of deductibility is actually contained in the words of subsection 9(1) which state that:

> subject to this Part, a taxpayer's *income* for a taxation year from a business or property is his *profit* therefrom for the year. (italics added)

As previously indicated, the courts have often relied on ordinary commercial practices (which may also embody generally accepted accounting principles (GAAP)) to provide the basis of profit, unless the Act specifically requires an alternate treatment. Hence, the deductibility of an expenditure under GAAP, subject to ordinary commercial practices, should be considered where the Act is silent on the treatment of the expenditure. The specific provisions of the Act that may require an alternate treatment are contained, generally, in sections 18, 19, 20 and 67.[17]

Sections 18 and 19, in essence, prohibit the deduction of specified expenditures through the use of the words "no deduction shall be made". However, the rules in sections 18 and 19 actually establish general principles or tests of deductibility under the Act. If an expenditure is not prohibited by a rule in section 18 or 19, that is, if an expenditure passes the set of sequential tests in these provisions, the expenditure is deductible. If an expenditure fails one of the tests in section 18 or 19, then subsection 20(1) should be consulted for the existence of a specific exception which would allow the deduction of the expenditure. Some of the more common tests of deductibility pertaining to income from business are discussed here.

¶4,215 General test — To gain or produce income

To pass the general test of deductibility, an expense or outlay must: ITA: 18(1)(*a*)

(a) be made or incurred by the taxpayer for the purpose of gaining, producing or maintaining income; and

(b) be expected to generate income related to the taxpayer's business or property.

The meaning of "for the purpose of gaining or producing income" has been at issue in many cases. While the club dues at issue in *The Royal Trust Company v. M.N.R.* are now   57 DTC 1055 (Ex. Ct.)
specifically not deductible, the case is important in demonstrating the relative remoteness   ITA: 18(1)(*l*)
between the expenditure and its purpose to produce income. That is, while the items listed, including club dues, are not deductible, the principle established in the *Royal Trust* case may   ITA: 18(1)(*l*)
still hold for items not specifically prohibited by that paragraph or others.[18]

Generally, all that need be demonstrated is that the expenditure was expected to generate income, although no income may have been generated. This was the issue in *Booth v.*   79 DTC 595 (T.R.B.)
M.N.R. involving a poet and painter who claimed certain expenses as deductions. Also, *The*   84 DTC 6159 (F.C.T.D.),
Queen v. Lalande and Watelle (affirmed by the Federal Court of Appeal) dealt with the   aff'd 89 DTC 5178 (F.C.A.)
deduction by doctors of legal fees and payments under loan guarantees in situations which could increase their clientele. In the case of *Speck v. M.N.R.*, the Tax Court of Canada held   88 DTC 1518 (T.C.C.)
that a full-time teacher, who incurred losses for three years followed by small profits for two years when he started a part-time business involving the restoration of automobiles, had reasonable expectations of turning a profit and these expectations had been met within the expected five years.

---

[17] This system of testing the deductibility of an expenditure was discussed in the case of *The Queen v. MerBan Capital Corporation Limited*, 89 DTC 5404 (F.C.A.).

[18] Other cases include: *Premium Iron Ores v. M.N.R.*, 66 DTC 5280 (S.C.C.), on legal fees to prepare a U.S. tax appeal; *M.N.R. v. Algoma Central Railways*, 68 DTC 5096 (S.C.C.), on the cost of a geological survey; *Canada Starch Co. Ltd. v. M.N.R.*, 68 DTC 5320 (Ex. Ct.), on the cost of protecting a trademark; and *Bowater Power Co. Ltd. v. M.N.R.*, 71 DTC 5469 (F.C.T.D.), on engineering studies.

¶4,220 Expenditure of a capital nature

An expenditure may pass the test of having been made for the purpose of gaining, producing, or maintaining income, but may still be prohibited as a deduction of an outlay of a capital nature. A capital expenditure has been described in a United Kingdom case[19] by the following statement:

> ... when an expenditure is made, not only once and for all, but with a view to bringing into existence an asset or advantage for the enduring benefit of a trade, ... there is very good reason (in the absence of special circumstances leading to an opposite conclusion) for treating such an expenditure as properly attributable not to revenue but to capital.

ITA: 18(1)(*b*)

¶4,225 Other prohibited deductions

¶4,225.10 *Reserves*

The deduction of a reserve, a contingent liability or a sinking fund is prohibited, except as permitted by the Act. Allowable reserves will be discussed later in this chapter.

ITA: 18(1)(*e*)
ITA: 20(1)

¶4,225.20 *Payments on discounted bonds*

When bonds are issued at a discount, usually because the contractual interest rate is lower than the market interest rate, the cost of the discount is incurred on the repayment of the debt at its face value. A deduction is not permitted for the amount paid or payable in respect of the discount except as specifically computed with deductions that are specifically permitted. This prohibition exists to discourage the issue of debt at a relatively large discount which might provide the holder of the debt with more advantageous capital gains treatment.

ITA: 18(1)(*l*)
ITA: 20(1)(*f*)

¶4,225.30 *Use of recreational facilities and club dues*

Note the prohibition on the deduction of club and other recreational facilities dues, no matter how important they may be to the revenue-producing process. In addition, this provision denies the deduction of expenses incurred for the *use or maintenance* of a yacht, a camp, a lodge or a golf course, unless these facilities are provided to the general public as in the course of the taxpayer's business.[20] Note, also, that the prohibition applies only to expenditures incurred in respect of a yacht, camp, lodge or golf course. Similar expenditures incurred in respect of a restaurant or hotel would not be prohibited. In its decision, the Supreme Court upheld the intention of Parliament to discriminate in this way, based on the very specific words used in the provision. However, the CRA indicated that it had reconsidered its interpretation of the word "facility" in relation to a golf course. The CRA will consider that "facility" as used in that subparagraph should be interpreted in connection with the words "golf course" as to only include recreational amenities provided by a golf club. Accordingly, a "facility" will not include the dining room, banquet halls, conference rooms, beverage rooms or lounges of a golf club and thus the deduction of the cost of meals and beverages incurred at a golf club will not be denied. As a result, the tax treatment of meals and beverages at a golf club will parallel that of meals and beverages consumed at a restaurant.[21]

ITA: 18(1)(*l*)

ITA: 18(1)(*l*)

ITA: 18(1)(*l*)(i)

¶4,225.40 *Political contributions*

There is a specific prohibition against the deduction of political contributions. A limited tax credit is provided.

ITA: 18(1)(*n*), 127(3)

¶4,225.50 *Automobile expenses*

The deduction of an allowance paid or payable to an employee for the employment use of an automobile is limited. However, there is no deduction limit if the amount of the allowance must be included in the employee's income. The ITR prescribes the deductible limit.

ITA: 18(1)(*r*)

ITR: 7306

---

[19] *British Insulated and Helsby Cables Ltd. v. Atherton* [1926], A.C. 205.

[20] In the case of *Sie-Mac Pipeline Contractors Ltd. v. The Queen*, 93 DTC 5158 (S.C.C.), the Supreme Court of Canada held that to use a lodge does not require that it be owned or rented or exclusively controlled.

[21] "Entertainment at golf clubs", TAX WINDOWS FILES, Document number 9803677, February 17, 1998.

According to a Department of Finance News Release,[22] the present rates are, effective for 2007, 50 cents per kilometre for the first 5,000 kilometres driven and 44 cents per kilometre thereafter, with a four-cent per kilometre premium for driving in the Yukon Territory, Northwest Territories or Nunavut.

¶4,225.60   *Payments under the Act*

Any amount paid or payable under the Act is not deductible. This provision would prohibit, for greater certainty, the deduction of federal income taxes, interest and penalties, all of which are imposed under the Act. However, a deduction for interest paid on tax refund that a taxpayer is required to repay because the refund was excessive is allowed.

ITA: 18(1)(*t*)

ITA: 20(1)(*ll*)

¶4,225.70   *Prepaid expenses*

In a move to bring the treatment of certain prepaid expenses for tax purposes in line with the treatment for accounting purposes, the deduction of such expenses in the year of outlay is prohibited. These expenses are deductible only in the taxation year to which the expenses relate. Expenditures treated in this manner are the following: payments for services to be rendered after the end of the year; payments of interest, taxes, rent or royalties in respect of a period after the end of the year and payments for insurance in respect of a period after the end of the year.

ITA: 18(9)

¶4,225.80   *Expenses of investing in sheltered plans*

While interest and certain financing expenses are usually deductible under several provisions in section 20, section 18 prohibits the deduction of these expenses in respect of indebtedness incurred for the purposes listed therein. Note that the items listed pertain to deductible investments in sheltered retirement plans in which income is not taxed as long as it remains in the plan. Also, the deduction of administration fees and investment counselling fees pertaining to certain plans, as discussed in Chapter 9, are prohibited.

ITA: 18(11)

ITA: 18(1)(*u*)

¶4,225.90   *Work space in home*

The deduction of the costs of maintaining a work space in an individual's home (i.e., "a self-contained domestic establishment in which the individual resides"), are prohibited unless the office meets one of the following two tests:

ITA: 18(12)

(a) the work space is the individual's principal place of business; or

(b) it is used on a regular and continuous basis for meeting clients, customers or patients of the individual in earning income from business.

In the case of these exceptions, the costs are deductible only to the extent of income from the business. Thus, these home office expenses cannot be used to create a loss from the business, although a carryforward is available for excess expenses. This carryforward may be indefinite, according to an Interpretation Bulletin, "Work space in home expenses", as long as one of the two tests stated above is met. For the CRA's interpretation of the term "principal place of business" and "regular and continuous basis," see the Interpretation Bulletin. The case of *Jenkins et. al. v. The Queen* addressed the meaning of "principle place of business" for a fisher. The court concluded that the principal place of business is where the "business elements" of the business are engaged in, such as "telephoning customers and suppliers, filling in invoices, doing payroll, maintaining books and records, contacting authorities for licences, preparing tax returns, chasing down receivables, handling complaints, creating business plans, preparing financial statements, talking to accountants and lawyers, etc." The courts stated that "the actual harvesting of fish is the core of a fishing business, but it is not where the business side of fishing occurs."

IT-514, par. 5

2005 DTC 384 (T.C.C.)

---

[22] No. 2006-089, December 27, 2006

¶4,225.100　*Deductibility of provincial capital and payroll taxes*

The federal budget of February 26, 1991, proposed to limit the deduction of provincial capital and payroll taxes. Payroll taxes would include any provincial tax imposed on a taxpayer and set by reference to the salary, wages or other remuneration paid by the taxpayer, except pension and worker's compensation contributions. Provincial health levies are an example of a provincial payroll tax. Capital taxes would include any tax imposed by a province and set by reference to a taxpayer's equity, liabilities or assets, but would exclude real property taxes.

Until a solution to the problems of the deductibility of these taxes is implemented, they are fully deductible. [In the March 19, 2007 federal budget, a temporary financial incentive was announced for provinces to eliminate their general capital taxes and capital taxes on financial institutions, or to change existing capital taxes on financial institutions to minimum taxes. The elimination or restructuring must take effect by January 1, 2011, and the enabling legislation must be enacted on or after March 19, 2007, and before 2011.]

¶4,225.110　*Limitation on accrued expenses*

In normal circumstances a deductible expenditure incurred by one taxpayer is matched, within a reasonable period of time, by the income receipt in the hands of the creditor. However, the Act has provisions to thwart contrived situations between persons not dealing at arm's length or between employers and employees where the debtor uses the accrual method of accounting and the creditor is on the cash method and where actual payment is unduly deferred. ITA: 78

Related persons are deemed not to deal at arm's length with each other. Chapter 6 deals with related individuals and Chapter 12 deals with related corporations and individuals. For the time being, assume that the normal interpretation of "related" applies. In addition, the provision indicates that it is question of fact whether persons not related to each other were, at a particular time, dealing with each other at arm's length. The Interpretation Bulletin entitled "Meaning of Arm's Length" lists the following criteria that could be used in determining whether a transaction has occurred at arm's length: ITA: 251(1)
IT-419R2, par. 23–26

- a common mind directs the bargaining for both parties to the transaction;

- the parties to the transaction were acting in concert without separate interests; and

- one party in fact controls the other party.

In order for an expense (e.g., accrued wages) that remains unpaid at the end of the taxation year to be deductible for tax purposes, it must constitute a genuine liability of the taxpayer. For a genuine liability to exist there must be an enforceable claim by the creditor (e.g., the employee) with a reasonable expectation that the debt in fact will be paid. Where there is not a genuine liability, the amount will be treated as contingent liability or reserve and will be denied.[23] IT-109R2, par. 15(e)
ITA: 18(1)(*e*)

(i) *Unpaid amounts*

Unpaid amounts, in non-arm's length circumstances, are subject to specific rules. Such an unpaid amount must be paid within two years of the end of the taxation year in which it was declared payable or accrued. If an amount remains unpaid after that two-year period, it must be brought back into income on the first day of the third taxation year following that in which the payable was declared. Thus, an unpaid amount declared payable in 2004 must be paid by the end of the 2006 taxation year or be included in income at the beginning of the 2007 taxation year. ITA: 78(1)

---

[23] The question of whether an amount was deductible at all as a real liability or not deductible as a contingent liability was at issue in *The Queen v. V&R Enterprises Limited*, 79 DTC 5399 (F.C.T.D.), and *Toronto Heel Limited v. M.N.R.*, 80 DTC 1250 (T.R.B.).

The two parties can file an election by the date on which the corporation is required to file its tax return for the 2007 taxation year (i.e., by June 30, 2008) that the amount be deemed to have been paid on the first day of the 2007 taxation year and to have been loaned, net of appropriate withholding tax, back to the corporation. Then, the corporation would be liable to remit the amount deemed to have been withheld, by departmental practice, on or before July 15, 2008 in this case, and a repayment of the loan would have no further tax consequences. An Interpretation Bulletin provides further explanation of this provision and a more complete discussion of the interplay of these provisions is contained in Chapter 13, under the heading "Accrued bonuses and other amounts".

ITA: 78(1)(*b*)

IT-109R2

(ii) *Unpaid remuneration and other amounts*

In the case of items of remuneration, the Act requires that salaries, wages, or other remuneration (other than specified exceptions) must be paid within 179 days of the end of the taxation year in which the expense was incurred. If an amount is unpaid after that day, it will be deemed not to have been incurred as an expense and, therefore, will not be deductible until the year in which it is actually paid. However, by administrative practice, the CRA indicates in the Interpretation Bulletin entitled "Unpaid amounts" that a payment made on the 180th day is considered to have been made within the time limit and the rule that denies the accrual will not apply. Other remuneration includes unfunded obligations in respect of pension benefits and retiring allowances. The election for deemed repayment, as described above, is not available for unpaid remuneration. An amount of accrued remuneration must be legally paid.

ITA: 78(4)

IT-109R2, par. 10
ITA: 78(4)

ITA: 78(1)

¶4,230   Reasonable expectation of profit (REOP)

The deduction of personal or living expenses, as defined, in part, as expenses not in connection with a business carried on for profit or with a reasonable expectation of profit, is prohibited. Travel between home and work is one of the expenditures prohibited as personal or living expenses. In this regard, note the difference in treatment between the case of *Mildred Cohen v. M.N.R.*, involving a physically challenged employee who, as a person deriving income from employment, cannot deduct the expenses of travel between home and work, no matter what the hardship may be, and, by contrast, *Cumming v. M.N.R.*, involving a self-employed doctor with an office in his home. Since his base of operations was his home, expenses of travel from that base to the hospital where he rendered services were deductible. The provision would also apply to the deductibility of interest on funds borrowed to purchase personal items such as cars and houses.

ITA: 18(1)(*h*)

ITA: 248(1)

52 DTC 356 (T.A.B.)

67 DTC 5312 (Ex. Ct.)

To be deductible, an expenditure must not only be made or incurred by the taxpayer for the purpose of gaining or producing income, but, as a result of another test and the definition of "personal or living expense", it must be made with "a reasonable expectation of profit". What constitutes a reasonable expectation of profit is dependent on the facts of each particular case. For a long period of time, the CRA, sometimes supported by the Canadian courts, attempted to expand the application of this reasonable expectation of profit, or REOP, test to deny the deduction of losses from business or property sources. Where there was a personal expenditure element to the fact situation, as in the case of a hobby or a partially rented personal residential property, the case for a reasonable expectation of profit was more difficult to make. On the other hand, where the expenditure involved no personal benefit element, that is, it was of a purely commercial nature, the Federal Court of Appeal had suggested in the case of *Tonn et al. v. The Queen*, and confirmed in the case of *Attorney General of Canada v. Mastri et al.*, that the case against a reasonable expectation of profit test is more difficult to make. In the case of *Stewart v. Canada*, the Supreme Court of Canada clarified and limited the application of the REOP test. The Court indicated that the REOP test has no application where there is no personal benefit element to a transaction. Where there is a personal benefit element, the test is only one of a number of factors that can be used to assess the commercial nature of an activity, thereby, undertaken in the pursuit of profit.[24]

ITA: 18(1)(*h*), 248(1)

96 DTC 6001 (F.C.A.)
97 DTC 5420 (F.C.A.)
2002 DTC 6969 (S.C.C.)

---

[24] For a more complete discussion of the *Stewart* case and the jurisprudence that led to that decision, see Rayna F. Laiken and Stanley N. Laiken, "Working with the Source Test, the Supreme Court's Replacement for the Reasonable Expectation of Profit Test", (2002) vol. 50, no. 3, *Canadian Tax Journal*, pp. 1147-1177.

Exhibit 4-2 provides a checklist for planning purposes to provide evidence of a reasonable expectation of profit, where there is a personal benefit in an activity. The checklist may help to assess the commercial nature of an activity and the businesslike behaviour of the taxpayer in that activity. The factors were derived largely from two U.S. studies of jurisprudence on a similar issue in U.S. tax law. Since the factors are based on U.S. jurisprudence, they have no direct precedent value in Canada. However, they are of more general applicability and may provide a basis or a framework for developing arguments for the existence, or lack thereof, of a predominant intention to make a profit from an activity in a Canadian fact situation.

EXHIBIT 4-2
Checklist of General Factors Used to Determine the Existence of a Reasonable Expectation of Profit or of Operating in a Businesslike Manner

---

(1) Manner in which activity is operated:
    (a) activity held out to community as a business
    (b) activity operated in a businesslike manner
    (c) activity operated in manner similar to comparable profitable businesses
    (d) unsuccessful methods discontinued and new ones adopted
    (e) formal books and records maintained
    (f) separate bank account maintained
    (g) record-keeping system provides for the determination of segment profits and relevant costs
    (h) detailed non-financial records maintained
    (i) operating methods changed to improve profitability
    (j) level of advertising or promotion undertaken
    (k) development plan formulated, followed and adjusted
    (l) scale of operations sufficient to be profitable.

(2) Elements of personal pleasure or recreation:
    (a) taxpayer obtains personal pleasure from the activity
    (b) facilities are utilitarian
    (c) conduct of activity involves social or recreational functions (apart from the activity itself)
    (d) long-time interest in activity as a hobby
    (e) operating methods constrained by personal motives
    (f) personal use separately accounted for.

(3) Expertise of the taxpayer or his or her advisers:
    (a) prior experience in the activity
    (b) profit potential determined prior to entry
    (c) pre-entry advice (or prior preparation) sought and followed
    (d) post-entry advice sought and followed
    (e) taxpayer belongs to business-related associations.
    (f) new or superior techniques developed

(4) History of income and loss:
    (a) average ratio of receipts to disbursements
    (b) percentage of years where receipts less than 5% of disbursements
    (c) average magnitude of losses
    (d) trend of losses declining
    (e) number of years activity was operated
    (f) losses due to circumstances beyond taxpayer's control
    (g) percentage of years with profits.
    (h) reasonable start-up period
    (i) trend of gross revenues

(5) Time and effort expended:
   (a) competent and well-informed manager employed
   (b) competent labour employed
   (c) average time spent on activity by taxpayer
   (d) taxpayer withdrew from another business to devote most of his/her time to the activity
   (e) taxpayer did physical labour.

(6) Financial status of taxpayer:
   (a) taxpayer's average income before activity loss
   (b) extent of tax savings from net losses
   (c) average ratio of activity losses to other income
   (d) taxpayer maintains an extravagant standard of living
   (e) majority of taxpayer's other income is from investments
   (f) extent of other net assets of taxpayer.
   (g) amount of capital invested in the operation

(7) Amount of occasional profits:
   (a) ratio of average profit to average loss
   (b) amount of largest profit earned
   (c) ratio of net losses to net assets.

(8) Sale or discontinuance of activity:
   (a) activity sold or discontinued because no chance for profit
   (b) activity sold or discontinued for any reason.

(9) Success of taxpayer in other activities:
   (a) extent of experience in similar successful business
   (b) history of losses in a similar activity.

(10) Expected appreciation of asset value:
   (a) taxpayer expected property to appreciate in value as the major source of investment return.

Sources: Jane O. Burns and S. Michael Groomer, "An Analysis of Tax Court Decisions That Assess the Profit Motive of Farming-Oriented Operations," *The Journal of the American Taxation Association*, Fall 1983, pp. 23-39.

Jack Robison, "Tax Court Classification of Activities Not Engaged in for Profit: Some Empirical Evidence," *The Journal of the American Taxation Association*, Fall 1983, pp. 7-22.

¶4,230.10 *Proposed amendments related to REOP*

On October 31, 2003, the Department of Finance released draft proposals on interest deductibility which also included legislation related to reasonable expectation of profit.

The proposal provides that a taxpayer can deduct a loss from a source that is a business or property only if, in that year, it is reasonable to expect that the taxpayer will realize a cumulative profit from the business or property. Then, a new provision makes it clear that profit, in this context, does not include capital gains or capital losses. [ITA: 3.1(1)] [ITA: 3.1(2)]

While these changes seem straightforward, consider what would happen if a new business began to have financial difficulty and realized losses in excess of previous income. If they determined that they were going to have to close the business, then this proposed rule would deny any losses from that time forward. These future losses from expenditures such as wages, lease payments, severance and other recurring expenses, were previously deductible.

Since their release, there has been significant discussion between tax professionals and the Department on the implications of their proposals. The report of the Joint Committee on Taxation of the Canadian Bar Association and the Canadian Institute of Chartered Accountants states that:

> . . . we are of the view that the Draft Proposals would introduce a fundamental change to the *Income Tax Act* which goes well beyond the case law and administrative practice prior to recent court decisions. We are concerned that the proposals could be used to disallow losses resulting from wholly-legitimate business expenses the deductibility of which would not have been an issue under prior case law or administrative practice. They would create significant issues with respect to the treatment of investments in securities.

In the March 23, 2004 federal budget the following statement was made:

> Assurances were given by the Minister of Finance, Finance officials and the CRA that these releases were not intended to adversely affect the past assessing practices regarding the deductibility of interest on equity investments. The Budget materials acknowledge that significant issues have been raised with them that warrant further consideration.

The Budget Plan 2005, published by the Department of Finance to accompany the February 23, 2005 federal budget, contained the following statement at page 410:

> Many commentators expressed concerns with the proposals' structure, in particular, that the proposals' codification of the "reasonable expectation of profit" test might inadvertently limit the deductibility of a wide variety of ordinary commercial expenses. The Department of Finance has sought to respond by developing a more modest legislative initiative that would respond to those concerns while still achieving the Government's objectives. The Department will, at an early opportunity, release that alternative proposal for comment. This will be combined with a Canada Revenue Agency publication that addresses, in the context of the alternative proposal, certain administrative questions relating to deductibility.

¶4,235 Limitations on amount of deductions for deductible expenditures

Items listed in subsection 18(1) are prohibited from being deducted because of the nature of the expenditure. Another section places a limitation on the amount of an outlay or expense that may be deducted. To be deductible, the amount must be "reasonable in the circumstances." This would suggest a comparison of the amount of an expenditure with the amount of similar expenditures made in similar situations by other taxpayers. The question of a reasonable salary paid to the wife of an owner-manager of a corporation for full-time work as the secretary-treasurer was at issue in *Mulder Bros. Sand & Gravel Ltd. v. M.N.R.* The payment of large bonuses to the wife of the major shareholder of a corporation was at issue in *Doug Burns Excavation Contracting Limited v. M.N.R.* In the case of *Robinson v. M.N.R.*, the Tax Court of Canada indicated that the costs of operating a luxury vehicle for business purposes should be limited in their deduction to a reasonable charge. *(ITA: 67; 67 DTC 475 (T.A.B.); 83 DTC 528 (T.C.C.); 85 DTC 84 (T.C.C.))*

Other expenditures that are limited include:

- food, beverages, and entertainment, *(ITA: 67.1)*
- interest on funds borrowed to purchase a passenger vehicle, and *(ITA: 67.2)*
- costs of leasing a passenger vehicle. *(ITA: 67.3)*

Each of these provisions has been discussed in Chapter 3 and is equally applicable to the computation of deductions from business income, except that GST is not deductible to a registrant where the GST provides an input tax credit. The input tax credit, in effect, eliminates the GST as a cost and, hence, GST should not be deductible in these cases. *(ITA: 248(16))*

Two other limitations are noteworthy:

- illegal payments, and *(ITA: 67.5)*
- fines and penalties. *(ITA: 67.6)*

A deduction is prohibited in respect of an expenditure incurred for the purpose of doing anything that is an offence under section 3 of the *Corruption of Foreign Public Officials Act* involving bribery of a foreign public official to obtain a business advantage or any of the following sections of the *Criminal Code*: *(ITA: 67.5(1))*

- section 119 — bribery of judicial officers, etc.
- section 120 — bribery of officers
- section 121 — frauds on the government
- section 123 — municipal corruption
- section 124 — selling or purchasing office
- section 125 — influencing or negotiating appointments or dealing in offices
- section 393 — fraud in relation to fares, etc.
- section 426 — secret commissions

Deductions are, also, prohibited where the payment is made in a conspiracy to commit an offence under one of the above sections or a conspiracy in Canada to commit a similar offence under the law of another country.

Recent court cases have allowed the deductibility of fines and penalties incurred in the ordinary course of earning income unless the underlying action was so offensive that the fine or penalty could not reasonably be considered to have had an income-earning purpose. To bring certainty to this area of tax law, fines or penalties incurred are not deductible if they are imposed by law — whether by a government, government agency, regulator, court or other tribunal, or any other person with statutory authority to levy fines or penalties. This would include fines and penalties imposed under the laws of a foreign country. This would not include penalties or damages paid under private contracts. Part of this provision includes authority to exempt prescribed fines and penalties from its application, although there are no exemptions at this time.

ITA: 67.6

¶4,240   Deductions specifically permitted

Usually, the general principles and rules (e.g., sections 18, 67, etc.) determining the deductibility of an outlay or expenditure are to be applied first. If a particular outlay or expenditure does not pass the tests of deductibility set out in section 18 or 19, then the lists in section 20 of exceptions to the general principles and rules should be consulted. The wording of subsection 20(1) recognizes that some of the deductions listed in the subsection may be prohibited by a general rule in subsection 18(1), and negates that effect by inserting the words "notwithstanding paragraphs 18(1)(*a*), (*b*) and (*h*), ... there may be deducted. ..." The following are some of the more common deductions provided in section 20.

¶4,240.10   *Write-offs of capital expenditures*

While section 18 prohibits the deduction of a capital nature, section 20 overrides this prohibition and permit the deduction of the capital cost of depreciable capital property and the cost of eligible capital property, respectively, through a system of annual write-offs to be discussed in Chapter 5.

ITA: 18(1)(*b*)
ITA: 20(1)(*a*), 20(1)(*b*)

¶4,240.20   *Interest*

Interest paid or payable on funds borrowed to finance the capital expenditures of a business would be considered as payment on account of capital and, therefore, would be prohibited from deduction. However, the Act specifically provides for the deduction of interest on funds borrowed to earn income, i.e., on the purchase of assets or on indebtedness arising from the acquisition of capital assets. Compound interest is deductible if the base interest is deductible.

ITA: 18(1)(*b*), 20(1)(*c*)

ITA: 20(1)(*c*), 20(1)(*d*)

On October 31, 2003 the Department of Finance released its Draft Proposals on Interest Deductibility. Along with proposed amendments related to REOP (discussed above) was a new Interpretation Bulletin, "Interest deductibility and related issues". This new bulletin is now a prime source for the CRA's administrative position on interest deductibility in that it replaces and cancels five other bulletins and provides commentary on all the key issues and some of the tax planning techniques used to ensure the deductibility of interest. *The Budget Plan 2005*, published by the Department of Finance to accompany the February 23, 2005 federal budget, indicated that an alternative proposal will be released for comment "at an early opportunity".

IT-533

¶4,240.30   *Expenses of issuing shares or borrowing money*

The type of expenses contemplated by paragraph 20(1)(*e*) includes printing and advertising costs, filing fees, legal and accounting fees, registration and transfer fees and commissions or bonuses on the issue or sale of shares. Also, deductible by this provision are similar expenses incurred in the course of becoming indebted on the purchase of capital property acquired to earn income. Similarly, refinancing costs such as rescheduling, restructuring or assumption of debt used for the purpose of earning business income are also deductible under this provision.

Not included in the deduction would be amounts paid or payable on account of the principal amount of the indebtedness. Since the deductible expenditures are still considered to be of a capital nature, the Act requires that the deduction be amortized equally over five years (prorated on a daily basis for short taxation years) to achieve a better matching of expenses and revenues. Any undeducted balance of borrowing costs are deductible for the year in which the debt is fully repaid (otherwise than as a part of a refinancing).[25]

ITA: 20(1)(e)

Annual fees payable as a standby charge, guarantee fee, registrar fee, transfer agent fee, filing fee or any similar fee in respect of borrowing money, incurring indebtedness or rescheduling or restructuring a debt obligation are also deductible.

ITA: 20(1)(e.1)

¶4,240.40 *Premiums on life insurance used as collateral*

A limited deduction is allowed for life insurance premiums where the policy has been assigned as collateral for a loan. The lender must require the assignment of the policy as collateral for the loan. The principal business of the lender must be the lending of money or the purchase of debt obligations. The interest payable on the funds borrowed must be deductible. The deduction is limited to the portion of the premium that represents the net cost of pure insurance.

ITA: 20(1)(e.2)

ITA: 20(1)(c)

¶4,240.50 *Discount on debt obligations*

Subsection 18(1) contains several provisions that would deny the deduction of all or any part of a discount from the face value of a debt obligation like a bond, debenture, note, mortgage, etc. Since the discount would be considered to be of a capital nature, its deduction is prohibited. The amortization of the discount, for financial accounting purposes, over the life of the debt instrument would not be deductible for tax purposes, because the annual amortization would be considered to be in the nature of a prohibited reserve. In addition, the deduction of the *actual cash outlay* on redemption or open market purchase is specifically denied, except to the extent permitted by the Act. The latter provision permits a full deduction of the discount (an actual cash outlay on redemption or maturity) at the earlier of redemption or maturity if:

ITA: 18(1)(b)

ITA: 18(1)(e)
ITA: 20(1)(f)

(i) the debt security is issued at not less than 97% of face value; *and*

(ii) the yield to maturity is not more than $\frac{4}{3}$ of the nominal or coupon interest rate.

If one, or both, of these conditions is not met, then only $\frac{1}{2}$ of the discount is deductible, again at the earlier of redemption or maturity. The $\frac{1}{2}$ fraction is intended to reflect the allowable or deductible portion of a capital loss.

This rule discourages the issue of debt securities at a large discount by agreeing to pay a low rate of interest relative to the market. The concern is that only the lower than normal interest rate would be taxable to the debtholder at full rates and the gain from the discounted issue price to the par value would be a fractionally taxed capital gain to the debtholder. On the other hand, an acceptable discount of 3% is sufficient to account for normal market fluctuations in interest rates between the time of setting the rate and the time of issue of the debt.

¶4,240.60 *The system for reserves under the Act*

The deduction of a reserve is prohibited except for those reserves that are specifically permitted in Part I of the Act. A number of cases have been heard in this area on the question of distinguishing between a reserve that would be prohibited and an amount that represents a real and subsisting liability resulting in a deductible expense.[26]

ITA: 18(1)(e)

The reserves that may be deducted include:

ITA: 20(1)

● reserve for doubtful debts;

ITA: 20(1)(l)

---

[25] Two cases heard under this provision are: *Enterprise Foundry Co. Ltd. v. M.N.R.*, 59 DTC 318 (T.A.B.), on a capital reorganization and *Dominion Electrohome Industries Ltd. v. M.N.R.*, 68 DTC 256 (T.A.B.), on a call premium.

[26] These cases include: *No. 297 v. M.N.R.*, 55 DTC 611 (T.A.B.), on employee bonuses; *Canada Packers Ltd. v. M.N.R.*, 68 DTC 682 (T.A.B.), on an income normalization reserve; *Time Motors Limited v. M.N.R.*, 69 DTC 5149 (S.C.C.), on credit notes; and *Acadia Overseas Freighters Halifax Ltd. v. M.N.R.*, 62 DTC 84 (T.A.B.), on contributions to a mutual insurance fund.

- reserve for goods not delivered and services not rendered or deposits on returnable containers (other than bottles), but limited by another rule;   ITA: 20(1)(*m*), 20(6)

- manufacturer's warranty reserve for amounts paid or payable to an insurer to insure liability under warranty agreement; and   ITA: 20(1)(*m*.1)

- reserve for an amount not due until a later year under an instalment sales contract limited by another rule.   ITA: 20(1)(*n*), 20(8)

Any reserve taken in a given year under one of these provisions must be brought back into income in the following year under one of the following provisions in subsection 12(1):

- reserve for doubtful debts; and   ITA: 12(1)(*d*)

- reserve in respect of certain goods and services, deposits or manufacturer's warranty reserve.   ITA: 12(1)(*e*)

In that following year, a new reserve can be taken based on the taxpayer's circumstances at that time. The inclusion of last year's reserve in income and the deduction of a new reserve this year forces the taxpayer to re-evaluate the circumstances and to establish a new reserve which can be substantiated by these circumstances.

The Interpretation Bulletin entitled "Bad debts and reserves for doubtful debts" describes the method suggested by the CRA for determining an appropriate reserve for doubtful debts.   IT-442R, par. 24

Where a debt has been established by the taxpayer to have become a bad debt, rather than merely a debt of doubtful collectibility, the amount of the bad debt can be written off as an expense. A bad debt written off in this way need not be included in income in the following year. However, if and when a bad debt is recovered, then the amount of recovery is added to income in the year of receipt. It is a question of fact whether a debt has become a bad debt and, hence, uncollectible, rather than simply of doubtful collectibility.   ITA: 20(1)(*p*)   ITA: 12(1)(*i*)

Example Problem 1

The Greyduck Bus Lines Limited issues books of junior student tickets containing 20 transportation passes for $20 per book. The following information relates to books sold and tickets used:

	Year 1	Year 2	Year 3
Number of books sold	2,000	2,500	4,000
Number of tickets used:			
from Year 1 sales	25,000	11,000	expired
from Year 2 sales		31,250	13,750
from Year 3 sales			50,000

— REQUIRED

Compute the effect of these transactions on the net income from business of this company, assuming 10% of the tickets sold in a year are expected to expire at the beginning of the second year from the end of the year of sale.

— SOLUTION

Applicable provisions

Year 1		
Include amount received in income ($20 × 2,000)	$40,000	par. 12(1)(*a*)
Less: reserve for services not provided[1]	11,000	par. 20(1)(*m*)
Income	$29,000	

Year 2		
Include amount received in income ($20 × 2,500)	$50,000	par. 12(1)(*a*)
Add: reserve from previous year	11,000	par. 12(1)(*e*)
	$61,000	
Less: reserve for services not provided[2]	13,750	par. 20(1)(*m*)
Income	$47,250	

Year 3

Include amount received in income ($20 × 4,000)	$80,000	par. 12(1)(*a*)
Add: reserve from previous year	13,750	par. 12(1)(*e*)
	$93,750	
Less: reserve for services not provided[(3)]	22,000	par. 20(1)(*m*)
Income	$71,750	

— *NOTES TO SOLUTION*

[(1)] The reserve is limited to a reasonable amount based on services that it is reasonably expected will have to be provided. In this case, no service will have to be provided for 10% of all tickets sold in the year. Of the 40,000 tickets (20 tickets × 2,000 books) sold in Year 1, 25,000 have been used and 4,000 will expire (10% of 40,000) leaving 11,000 for which service will have to be provided. At $1.00 per ticket ($20.00 ÷ 20) a reasonable reserve would be $11,000 ($1.00 × 11,000). Note that subsection 20(6) limits this reserve to the amount included in income for transportation not provided before the end of the year. In this case transportation has not been provided on 15,000 tickets (40,000 – 25,000) providing a limit at $1 per ticket of $15,000.

[(2)] Using the above process, service will have to be provided for 13,750 tickets since 5,000 (10% of 50,000) will expire and 31,250 have been used. Thus, a reasonable reserve at $1.00 per ticket is $13,750. The limit on this reserve would be on 18,750 tickets (50,000 – 31,250) at $1.00 per ticket or $18,750.

ITA: 20(6)

[(3)] Service will have to be provided for 22,000 tickets since 8,000 (10% of 80,000) will expire and 50,000 have been used. The reserve at $1.00 per ticket would be $22,000 and the subsection 20(6) limit on that reserve would be on 30,000 tickets (80,000 – 50,000) at $1 per ticket or $30,000.

Example Problem 2

On July 1, 2004, Delta Company sold some inventory with a value of $100,000 and a cost of $40,000. A cash down payment of $10,000 was made and the balance was payable in four annual instalments of $20,000 and a final payment of $10,000. The purchaser is at arm's length.

— *REQUIRED*

How much of an inventory sales reserve can the company take in each year covered by the instalment sale? Use a December 31 year-end.

ITA: 20(1)(*n*)

— *SOLUTION*

The Act limits the inventory sales reserve available to a three-year period. A reserve is not deductible for a year-end that is more than 36 months after the sale.

ITA: 20(1)(*n*), 20(8)(*b*)

Calculation of reserve:

	Accounts receivable	*Profit content*
July 1, 2004 — sale price of article	$100,000	$60,000
— cash down payment	10,000	6,000
Dec. 31, 2004 — balance receivable	$ 90,000	
— reserve allowable[(1)]		$54,000
2005 — instalment due	20,000	12,000
Dec. 31, 2005 — balance receivable	$ 70,000	
— reserve allowable[(1)]		$42,000
2006 — instalment due	20,000	12,000
Dec. 31, 2006 — balance receivable	$ 50,000	
— reserve allowable[(1)]		$30,000
2007 — instalment due	20,000	12,000
Dec. 31, 2007 — balance receivable	$ 30,000	$18,000
— reserve allowable (more than 36 months after sale)		Nil

Income effect:

			Net reported income
2004	— Profit on sale [par. 12(1)(b)]	$ 60,000	
	— Reserve [par. 20(1)(n)]	(54,000)	$ 6,000
2005	— Previous year reserve [par. 12(1)(e)]	$ 54,000	
	— Reserve [par. 20(1)(n)]	(42,000)	12,000
2006	— Previous year reserve [par. 12(1)(e)]	$ 42,000	
	— Reserve [par. 20(1)(n)]	(30,000)	12,000
2007	— Previous year reserve [par. 12(1)(e)]	$ 30,000	
	— Reserve [par. 20(1)(n) and ssec. 20(8)]	—	30,000
	Total income reported over four years		$60,000

— *NOTE TO SOLUTION*

$$^{(1)} \text{Reserve} = \frac{\text{gross profit}}{\text{gross selling price}} \times \text{amount receivable}$$

¶4,240.70 *Employer's contribution to registered pension plan*

The deduction of employer contributions to a registered pension plan (RPP) is permitted. Deductible contributions may be made by the employer either in the year to which the deduction is to apply or within 120 days after the end of that taxation year. Contributions made in the 120-day period which are in excess of the deduction limit for the preceding year may be deductible in the year in which they are made if the deduction limit for the year is not exceeded.   ITA: 20(1)(q), 147.2

Two types of RPP are envisaged.

- A defined benefit plan promises a defined retirement benefit which is specified by a formula. In the case of a defined benefit RPP, all contributions are deductible if they are determined by an actuary to be necessary to fund the benefits for which the RPP was registered to provide.

- A money purchase or defined contribution plan specifies a contribution requirement with the retirement benefit dependent on the funds accumulated in the plan at the time of retirement.

In the case of a money purchase RPP, the total of employer and employee contributions are limited to: ITA: 147.1(8)

the lesser of:

(i) 18% of the employee's compensation defined to be employment income inclusions under sections 5 and 6 for the particular year; and   ITA: 147.1(1)

(ii) a specified dollar limit, defined as the money purchase limit.   ITA: 147.1(1)

The limits for money purchase RPPs are as follows:

- for 2005 . . . . $18,000
- for 2006 . . . . $19,000
- for 2007 . . . . $20,000
- for 2008 . . . . $21,000
- for 2009 . . . . $22,000
- for 2010 . . . . indexed

A violation of the limits set for either type of plan can lead to the revocation of the RPP registration status. If this occurs, all amounts in the plan become taxable, having lost their sheltered status.

¶4,240.70

¶4,240.80   *Employer's contribution under a deferred profit sharing plan*

Employer contributions to a deferred profit sharing plan (DPSP) are deductible within limits. An employer may deduct an amount which is paid in the year or within 120 days after the end of the year to a trustee to the extent that the amount was paid in accordance with the terms of the plan and was not deducted by the employer in a previous year.

ITA: 20(1)(*y*)
ITA: 147(8)

A formula is provided to determine the amount of an employer's contribution to a DPSP that is deductible. Generally, where there is no RPP, the employer's contribution limit in respect of an employee for a year is the lesser of:

ITA: 147(5.1)

ITA: 147(5.1)(*a*)

(a) one-half of the money-purchase dollar limit for the year, as discussed above; and

(b) 18% of the employee's compensation (as defined) for the year.

ITA: 147.1(1)

Therefore, to be deductible in a year, contributions should not exceed the lesser amount computed.

Where an employer participates in both a DPSP and an RPP for the benefit of an employee, the employer's total contribution to both plans is limited. It is rare for an employer to provide both a DPSP and an RPP together.

ITA: 147(5.1)(*c*)

¶4,240.90   *Cancellation of lease*

Where the owner of a property is required to pay an amount to a lessee for the cancellation of the lease, the costs of cancelling the lease is treated as a type of prepaid expense, as long as the property continues to be owned by the lessor or by a non-arm's length person. As a result, the costs may be deducted over what would have been the remaining term of the lease, including renewal periods, to a maximum of 40 years. The unamortized balance of these costs (½ of the unamortized balance, in the case of capital property) is deductible if the property is sold. An amount that does not meet the conditions of these two paragraphs is not deductible.

ITA: 20(1)(*z*)

ITA: 20(1)(*z*.1)

ITA: 18(1)(*q*)

¶4,240.100   *Landscaping of grounds*

A deduction of an amount paid in the year for landscaping of grounds around a building that is used to produce income from business is allowed. Were it not for this provision the expenditure would be considered to be of a capital nature.

ITA: 20(1)(*aa*)

¶4,240.110   *Expenses of representation*

The expenses of representation for the purpose of obtaining a licence, permit, franchise or trademark related to the business of a taxpayer are deductible. Given the capital nature of the assets acquired, these expenditures would otherwise be prohibited. Note that the representations must be made to a government body or agency to be deductible.

ITA: 18(1)(*b*), 20(1)(*cc*)

Instead of deducting the full amount allowed, a taxpayer may elect to deduct one-tenth of the full amount in the year of expenditure and the nine immediately following taxation years. The Regulations set out the documents that must be filed to implement the election.

ITA: 20(1)(*cc*)
ITA: 20(9)
ITR: 4100

¶4,240.120   *Investigation of site*

The deduction of an amount paid in the year for investigating the suitability of a site for a building or other structure planned for use in the taxpayer's *existing* business is permitted.

ITA: 20(1)(*dd*)

¶4,240.130   *Utilities service connection*

An amount paid in the year to an arm's length person to make connections for the supply of electricity, gas, telephone service, water or sewers, is deductible. Without this provision no deduction would be permitted, since the expenditure is of a capital nature. Furthermore, no capital cost allowance would be permitted, because the taxpayer normally does not own the service connections.

ITA: 20(1)(*ee*)

¶4,240.140   *Disability-related modifications and equipment*

A deduction, in the payment year, of the full cost of prescribed renovations or alterations to a building used primarily in a business is allowed. The expenditures must be made to enable individuals who have a mobility impairment to gain access to the building or be mobile within it. The building need not be owned by the taxpayer making the expenditure. *ITA: 20(1)(qq)*

The deduction, in the payment year, of the cost of any prescribed disability-specific device or equipment which assists individuals with a sight, hearing, or mobility impairment is allowed. The type of expenditure envisaged includes installation of elevator car position indicators, visible fire alarm indicators, telephone devices, listening devices for group meetings and disability-specific computer software and hardware. *ITA: 20(1)(rr)*

If it were not for these provisions, the expenditures could be considered of a capital nature and could not be expensed. Clearly, the rules provide an incentive to implement social policy.

¶4,240.150   *Convention expenses*

Attendance at a convention may be considered to give rise to expenditures of a capital nature, perhaps, in the form of increased knowledge. However, the Act permits the deduction from a taxpayer's business income of amounts paid in attending up to two conventions per year. Attendance at the convention must be in connection with the business. The location of the convention must be within the territorial scope of the organization holding the convention. Note that an internal business meeting, such as a sales conference within a business, is not considered to be a convention *ITA: 20(10)*

¶4,245   Application of the rules for deduction

To determine the deductibility of an outlay or expenditure after considering the general principles and rules in section 18, the list of deductions under section 20 should be scanned. This can be done quickly by reference to the table of contents for the Act. In addition, commentary under these sections contained in the "Canadian Tax Library" of CCH TAX lists court case decisions for a wide variety of expenditures. This list is based on court decisions made on the question of the deductibility of many types of expenditure for tax purposes. However, it should be noted that because the commentary list is based largely on case law, the deductibility of any particular type of expenditure is heavily dependent on the specific facts of the case and the specific law in force at the time of the case. Care should be taken to determine the facts that resulted in a particular decision and the wording of the Act at the time of the case, since some court decisions may be at variance with current law.

Example Problem

You are the auditor for Corporate Welfare Bum Limited and you have been given an income statement prepared for financial accounting purposes showing a loss for its fiscal year ended December 31, 2007 of $112,000. Your audit uncovers the following:

(a) appraisal expense contains cost of determining asset values for insurance
purposes . . . . $ 4,000

(b) wages expense contains amounts (matched by employees) relating to money-purchase (defined-contribution) registered pension plan contributions, made during the first 120 days of 2008 but allocated by the accountant to 2007, in respect of current services on behalf of the following executives (employment compensation for the year shown in brackets):

President (Mr. C.S. Bum, 100% owner; $150,000)	$ 11,150	
Vice-President ($95,000)	6,000	
Accountant ($80,000)	5,000	
Plant Supervisor ($65,000)	4,000	
Shop Foreman ($48,000)	3,400	
Timekeeper ($27,000)	2,400	31,950

(c) cost of landscaping written off............................... 10,000

(d) legal expenses for

   (i) defence of a suit, brought by a customer, for failure to deliver merchandise on time .... $ 2,500

   (ii) articles of amendment to revise company's articles of incorporation..................................... 3,500

   (iii) cost of disputing income tax 4,000   10,000

(e) revenues included a dividend received from a Canadian subsidiary 80,000

(f) interest expense included amortization of bond discount on bonds maturing in 2008 12,000

(g) opening inventories were valued on the FIFO basis at $184,750 while closing inventories were valued on the LIFO basis rather than the FIFO basis which would have exceeded the LIFO valuation by................... 36,950

(h) miscellaneous expense contained donations for the year to

   (i) duly registered charities .... $ 4,000

   (ii) the NDP political party 7,000   11,000

(i) insurance expense contained whole life insurance premium paid on the life of Mr. C.S. Bum (proceeds payable to the company; not group life) 10,000

(j) salaries expense contained a dividend payable to Mr. Bum 8,000

(k) bad debts expense including $4,000 in respect of a loan to a shareholder of a supplier totalled 10,000

(l) extraordinary maintenance arising from conversion of premises including replacement of heating and air-conditioning systems, plumbing, electrical wiring and concrete foundations in respect of a building was written off to repairs and maintenance in the amount of 150,000

(m) salaries expense included a bonus paid to Mr. Bum 15,000

(n) interest expense included interest in respect of the acquisition of 90% of the shares of another Canadian corporation 115,000

(o) convention expenses over three days of Mr. Bum and his family ($2,000 thereof represents costs relating to Mrs. Bum and the two little Bums, who attended for social purposes only; $500 of the remaining amount relates to the cost of meals consumed by Mr. Bum)........................ 5,000

(p) administration expense contains an embezzlement loss caused by a minor employee of the company 10,000

(q) (i) management bonuses included in wages expense but not paid in 2007   50,000

   (ii) bonuses accrued at the end of 2007 which were not, and will not be, paid in 2008 35,000

(r) property taxes paid in 2007 include an amount paid for the company's fishing lodge 1,000

(s) the company as a lessor agreed to pay and expensed $15,000 on June 30, 2007 to cancel a lease that could have been in force until December 31, 2013 with renewal periods, but in 2007 actually paid only................. 10,000

(t) the company paid damages for failing to deliver goods on time under an action for breach of contract brought by one of its suppliers and the amount was expensed in the financial accounts 12,000

(u) cost of constructing a cement ramp to facilitate wheelchair access to the company's premises, capitalized by the accountant 6,000

— REQUIRED

    Compute the company's income or loss from business or property for tax purposes, but do not compute tax deductions in respect of depreciable capital or eligible capital property. Indicate the applicable sections of the Act or brief reasons to substantiate your answer. Indicate in a separate list the applicable section of the Act or brief reasons for not considering an item in your computations. Make sure all items are accounted for.

— SOLUTION

		Applicable sections
Loss for financial accounting purposes.................	$(112,000)	sec. 9
Add items not deductible for tax purposes:		
Excess allocations to 2007 of RPP contributions[1].....................	$ 2,300	par. 20(1)(q)
Legal expenses for articles revision[2]	3,500	par. 18(1)(b)
Amortization of bond discount[3]	12,000	par. 18(1)(b)
Excess of FIFO over LIFO[4]	36,950	ssec. 10(1)
Donations[5]	11,000	par. 18(1)(a)
Life insurance premium[6]	10,000	par. 18(1)(a)
Dividend payable[7]	8,000	
Bad debt re: loan to shareholder of supplier[8]	4,000	par. 20(1)(p)
Extraordinary maintenance[9]	150,000	par. 18(1)(b)
Convention expenses[10]	2,250	par. 18(1)(h)
Bonuses accrued and not paid[11]	35,000	ssec. 78(4)
Property tax on fishing lodge[12]	1,000	par. 18(1)(l)
Non-deductible prepaid lease cancellation amount[13]........................	13,838 $ 289,838	par. 20(1)(z)
	$ 177,838	
Deduct items deductible for tax purposes:		
Wheelchair access ramp..................	$ 6,000	par. 20(1)(qq)
Income from business or property for tax purposes[14]	$ 171,838	

— NOTES TO SOLUTION

[1] In this case, involving a money-purchase RPP, assuming the employee contributions are matched by the employer corporation and that the employee's contributions are fully deductible, the corporation will have a non-deductible contribution in respect of 2007 computed as follows:

	Pres.	V.P.	Acct.	Super.	Fore.	Time.
Least of:						
(a) Employer plus employee RPP contributions	$22,300	$12,000	$10,000	$ 8,000	$ 6,800	$ 4,800
(b) Money-purchase dollar limit for 2007	$20,000	$20,000	$20,000	$20,000	$20,000	$20,000
(c) 18% of compensation	$27,000	$17,100	$14,400	$11,700	$ 8,640	$ 4,860
Least amount	$20,000	$12,000	$10,000	$ 8,000	$ 6,800	$ 4,800
Less: employer & employee contributions	22,300	12,000	10,000	8,000	6,800	4,800
Employer's non-deductible contributions for 2007	$ 2,300	$ Nil	Nil	Nil	Nil	Nil

Total amount to be added back: $2,300

Since the $2,300 non-deductible amount was contributed in the first 120 days of 2008, it can be a part of the deductible contribution for 2008 without danger of a revocation of the registration status of the RPP, as long as contributions in 2008 do not exceed deduction limits for 2008.

[2] Expenditures on articles of incorporation or articles of amendment are regarded as eligible capital property and are written off over time for tax purposes. This topic will be covered in Chapter 5.

[3] The Act specifically prohibits the amortization of an amount that is capital in nature. The Act prohibits all reserves, except as expressly provided for in the Act. The Act specifically denies the deduction of an actual cash outlay on redemption or open market purchases except to the extent permitted.

ITA: 18(1)(b), 18(1)(e), 18(1)(f), 20(1)(f)

⁽⁴⁾ Departmental practice has disallowed the use of LIFO as an assumption in the costing of inventory when actual cost cannot be identified. This practice is based on the decision in *M.N.R. v. Anaconda American Brass Ltd.*, which established the principle that the facts of inventory flow cannot be disregarded in using an assumption about inventory cost. The same disregard of the facts and substitution of assumptions in relation to the flow of goods made the use of the LIFO method of valuation objectionable in *Wickett and Craig Ltd. v. M.N.R.*   `55 DTC 1220 (J.C.P.C.)` `78 DTC 1382 (T.R.B.)`

⁽⁵⁾ Donations are not deductible in the computation of income if they were not incurred to earn income. However, charitable donations of a corporation are deductible in Division C dealing with the computation of taxable income, and political contributions are eligible for a tax credit in Division E dealing with the computation of tax.   `ITA: 110.1, 127.3`

⁽⁶⁾ Life insurance premiums paid on the lives of officers, employees or shareholders where the policies are payable to the company do not produce income. Hence, the premiums are not deductible unless the policy is required to obtain financing, such as a bank loan. The Act limits the amount of a deductible premium to the net cost of pure insurance, determined by reference to standard mortality assumptions.   `ITA: 20(1)(e.2)`

⁽⁷⁾ Dividends are not paid to produce income; they are a distribution of income after it has been earned.

⁽⁸⁾ The Act requires that an amount be previously included in income if it is to be written off as a bad debt. On this loan, which was not a trade account receivable, no amount would have been included in sales and, hence, in income. However, a further adjustment may be allowed under section 50 which will be discussed in Chapter 8, under the heading "Debts Established to be Bad Debts".   `ITA: 20(1)(p)`

⁽⁹⁾ An expenditure which prolongs the life of an asset is regarded as capital in nature, but an expenditure which restores an asset to its original condition is regarded as an expenditure of an income nature. In this case, the expenditure, as described, appears to be of a capital nature.   `ITA: 18(1)(b)`

⁽¹⁰⁾ Personal or living expenses are specifically prohibited as a deduction, except, for example, an item such as convention expenses specifically allowed. The Act provides that the deductible cost of meals while attending a convention is 50% of the actual cost, on the assumption that the cost is reasonable. Where the fees for a convention do not specify the cost of meals or entertainment included in those fees, the Act will deem the cost to be $50 per day and that amount will be subject to the 50% limitation. In this case, since the cost is specified, 50% of $500, or $250, is not deductible and must be added in the reconciliation.   `ITA: 18(1)(h), 20(10)` `ITA: 67.1(1)` `ITA: 67.1(3)`

⁽¹¹⁾ The bonuses accrued at the end of 2007 are not deductible in 2007, since they were not paid within the time limit. The $35,000 would, therefore, have been added back to 2007 income. These bonuses can only be deducted when they are actually paid.   `ITA: 78(4)`

⁽¹²⁾ The Act arbitrarily disallows certain listed expenditures including one made for the maintenance of a lodge.   `ITA: 18(1)(l)`

⁽¹³⁾ The costs of cancelling a lease are treated as a prepaid expense, as long as the property continues to be owned by the lessor or a person with whom he or she does not deal at arm's length. As such it may be deducted over the remaining term of the cancelled lease, including renewal periods, subject to a maximum limit of 40 years. In this case, the number of days in the remainder of the lease is 184 in 2007 and 6 years of 365 days per year and 2 days for leap years for a total of 2,376 days. Thus, the deduction for 2007 is given by 184/2,376 × $15,000 or $1,162. Therefore, the non-deductible amount of the $15,000 payment is $13,838 (i.e., $15,000 – $1,162). Another rule provides a deduction of the unamortized balance if the property is sold.   `ITA: 20(1)(z)` `ITA: 20(1)(z.1)`

⁽¹⁴⁾ Other items:

(a) The cost of an appraisal made for the purpose of maintaining adequate insurance coverage is regarded as a normal business expense and is deductible.

(b) The Act allows a deduction for an employer contribution to a registered pension plan of the amount calculated in another provision. The amounts calculated in respect of all employees shown other than the President and Vice-President are deductible, as shown in Note (1).   `ITA: 20(1)(q), 147.2(1)`

(c) The deduction of landscaping costs is allowed, even though they might otherwise be considered of a capital nature.

ITA: 20(1)(*aa*)

(d) (i) The cost of defending a suit brought by a customer is regarded as a business expense if it pertains to trading transactions.

   (ii) The cost of disputing an income tax case has been held in the case of *Premium Iron Ores Ltd. v. M.N.R.* to be a business expense. The legal expenses of $4,000 could also be deducted, in which case they should be added back in the computation of income from business.

66 DTC 5280 (S.C.C.)

ITA: 60(*o*)

(e) A dividend received is to be included in income from property.

ITA: 12(1)(*j*)

(f) Bad debt expenses are deductible as long as the account has previously resulted in an inclusion in income. In the normal course of setting up an account receivable a credit would be made to sales, thereby including the amount in income. The treatment of a bad debt expense for tax purposes is identical to the treatment of the expense for financial accounting purposes. In fact, the tax treatment of both the reserve and the expense parallels the accounting treatment. The previous year's reserve is reversed by including it in current income and a new reserve is set up for the current year by taking a deduction. A debt established to be bad is written off and a recovery of such a debt previously written off is included in income.

ITA: 12(1)(*d*), 12(1)(*i*), 20(1)(*l*), 20(1)(*p*)

(g) A bonus expense is a deductible business expense to the extent that it meets the test of being "reasonable in the circumstances." The $50,000 bonus expensed in 2007 is deductible in 2007 as long as it is paid on or before June 28, 2008.

ITA: 18(1)(*a*), 67

(h) The deduction of interest on funds borrowed to buy shares is permitted since dividend income will be earned.

ITA: 20(1)(*c*)

(i) The deduction of Mr. Bum's convention expenses is permitted (except for part of the cost of meals which is limited), as long as the conditions of that provision are met.

ITA: 20(10), 67.1, 67.3

(j) Losses in cash or misappropriation of merchandise sustained by the criminal action of employees or officers will be allowed as deductions from income as being incidental to carrying on of business. However, such a loss attributable to a partner or senior officer is not usually regarded as a normal business risk and is not deductible. In the case of *Cassidy's Limited v. M.N.R.*, the Tax Court of Canada disagreed specifically with the statement in an Interpretation Bulletin in which the CRA stated that, because a theft was committed by a senior employee, the losses resulting from the theft are not deductible by the employer. The Court held that "the amounts lost due to the defalcation were non-capital losses, the deductions of which are deductible in computing profit in accordance with ordinary commercial principles and are not prohibited by the Act" and, hence, allowed the deduction.

IT-185R

89 DTC 686 (T.C.C.)
IT-185R, par. 2(b)

(k) Damages for failure to deliver goods are regarded as normal business expenses.

¶4,250   Sales/Negotiating Person's Expenses Revisited

One of the topics dealt with in the preceding chapter on employment income was the deductibility of the expenses of sales/negotiating persons (i.e., individuals employed in connection with the selling of property or negotiating of contracts). Unlike other employees, sales/negotiating persons can deduct expenses incurred to produce employment income. However, these allowable expenses are limited to the amount of commission income or other similar amounts, fixed by reference to the volume of sales made or the contracts negotiated, received in the year. It is interesting to compare the limited deductions for expenses available to a sales/negotiating person who is an employee with the broader deductions available to a person performing similar functions as an independent business person.

ITA: 8(1)(*f*), 8(1)(*j*)

Provisions introduced in Chapter 3 limit certain deductions allowed to taxpayers, whether they are employed or self-employed or whether they are incorporated or unincorporated.

ITA: 248(1)

¶4,255   Automobiles

The following are some of these common deductions related to automobiles:

• Interest on money borrowed for passenger vehicles,

ITA: 67.2

- Deductible lease payment restriction,
- CCA restriction on passenger vehicles,
- Limit on which CCA may be claimed ($30,000 plus GST and PST for 2007),
- Definition of passenger vehicles.

ITA: 67.3
ITA: 13(7)(*g*), 13(7)(*h*)
ITR: 7307(*b*)
ITA: 248(1)

¶4,260   Automobile allowances

As discussed previously in this chapter, the Act and Regulations limit the deduction by an employer of allowances paid to employees for the use of an automobile in the course of employment or business to a prescribed amount per kilometre, except where the allowance is required to be included in the employee's income under paragraph 6(1)(*b*).

ITA: 18(1)(*r*); ITR: 7306

¶4,265   Office in the home

Also, as previously discussed, the deductibility of the costs relating to a place of business in the residence of a self-employed individual is restricted. A prorated portion of these "home office" expenses, such as rent, capital cost allowance, property taxes, and mortgage interest or operating costs, including heating, electricity, insurance or maintenance may be deducted only if the space is either:

ITA: 18(12)

- the individual's principal place of business; or
- used exclusively by the individual on a regular and continuous basis for meeting clients, customers or patients.

The deduction for home office expenses is further restricted to the income for the year from the business for which the office is used. However, any excess of deduction disallowed in a year may be treated as home office expenses incurred in a following year, according to the Interpretation Bulletin entitled "Work space in home expenses". A parallel provision to restrict the deduction of home office expenses by an employee was presented in Chapter 3.

IT-514, par. 5
ITA: 8(13)

¶4,270   Meals and entertainment

The amount of a deduction by all taxpayers for food, beverage, and entertainment is restricted to the lesser of 50% of the amount paid or payable or a reasonable amount. This limitation applies to all business meals, including food and beverage, as well as to the cost of meals while travelling or attending a seminar, conference, convention or similar function. The restriction also applies to tickets to an entertainment or sporting event, gratuities and cover charges, room rentals to provide entertainment and the cost of private boxes at sports facilities. The limitation applies to the taxpayer incurring the costs in the case where a reimbursement is made. The following are exclusions from the 50% limitation:

ITA: 67.1

(a) the cost to a restaurant, airline or hotel of providing meals to customers in the ordinary course of business,

(b) meals or entertainment expenses relating to an event intended primarily to benefit a registered charity,

(c) the cost of meals or entertainment that is included as a taxable benefit to the employee or where the employer is reimbursed for the cost, and

(d) the cost of meals and recreation provided by an employer for the general benefit of all employees at a particular place of business in respect of occasional events not exceeding six events per year.

The Interpretation Bulletin entitled "Food, Beverages and Entertainment Expenses" presents the CRA's interpretation of this provision.

IT-518R

Example Problem

Ms. Jo Schmaltz is a salesperson who earned a total of $25,000 in 2007, including $4,000 in commissions. She was required to travel in her job and she was required to pay her own expenses, all of which were reasonable in the circumstances and consisted of the following:

(a) entertainment of clients including golf club membership dues of
   $500 (incurred in equal monthly amounts) $3,700

(b) home office expenses (allocated by floor space of office portion of
   home):

mortgage interest	$ 450	
municipal taxes	400	
capital cost allowance	300	
utilities	1,000	
maintenance and repairs	850	3,000

   This is the only office space available for her work.

(c) capital cost allowance on car used 75% for business	3,570
(d) car operating expenses	3,100
(e) convention dues (excluding meals and entertainment)	1,000
(f) travellers' association (a trade union) dues	300
(g) meals while travelling	900

— *REQUIRED*

(A) Compute Jo's minimum employment income for 2007.

(B) Compute Jo's minimum business income, assuming she is an independent business person with $25,000 in sales rather than an employee.

— *SOLUTION*

		Applicable provisions
(A) Employment income		
Salary and commissions	$25,000	sec. 5
Deductions:		
Entertainment[1] (50% of $3,200)	$ 1,600	par. 8(1)(f) par. 18(1)(l) ssec. 67.1(1)
Home office:[2] municipal taxes	400	par. 8(1)(f)
Car operating expenses (75% of $3,100)	2,325	par. 8(1)(f)
Meal expenses (50% of $900)	450	ssec. 67.1(1)
Total	$ 4,775	
Deductions not in excess of commission[3]	$(4,000)	par. 8(1)(f)
	$21,000	
Less: association dues[4]	$ 300	par. 8(1)(i)
CCA on car (75% of $3,570)	2,678	par. 8(1)(j)
Utilities	1,000	par. 8(1)(i)
Maintenance and repairs	850 (4,828)	par. 8(1)(i)
Employment income[5], [6]	$16,172	
(B) Business income		
Sales	$25,000	sec. 9
Deductions:		
Entertainment[7] (50% of $3,200)	$ 1,600	par. 18(1)(a)
CCA on car (75% of $3,570)	2,678	par. 20(1)(a)
Car operating expenses (75% of $3,100)	2,325	par. 18(1)(a)
Convention expenses	1,000	ssec. 20(10)
Meals (50% of $900)	450	par. 18(1)(a)
Association dues	300 (8,353)	par. 18(1)(a)

Income from business[8] (before home office expense)	$16,647	par. 18(1)(*a*)
		par. 20(1)(*a*)
Less: home office expense[9]	(3,000)	par. 20(1)(*c*)
Income from business	$13,647	

Note that the difference between employment income of $16,172 and business income of $13,647 is $2,525. This amount consists of the following expenses that are not deductible from employment income but are deductible from business income:

Interest and CCA on home office ($450 + $300)	$ 750
Non-deductible excess of employment expenses over commissions	775
Convention expenses	1,000
Total	$2,525

— NOTES TO SOLUTION

[1] To be deductible as a salesperson's expenses, an expenditure must be made to earn employment income. However, the relevant provision specifically denies deductions which fall under paragraph 18(1)(*l*), which lists an outlay for the use of a golf course.

ITA: 8(1)(*f*)
ITA: 8(1)(*f*)(vi)

[2] Outlays on account of capital are not deductible except for interest and capital cost allowance on a car used in the course of employment. The interest is on account of the home mortgage and the capital cost allowance is not for a car. Municipal taxes and home insurance are deductible, as confirmed by the decision of the Tax Court of Canada in *Felton v. M.N.R.* In that case, the taxpayer sought to deduct mortgage interest, property taxes, insurance premiums and the cost of utilities for his home as rent. The court held that rent involves only a payment arising out of a landlord and tenant relationship, such that the expenses incurred for an owner-occupied home could not be considered as rent. However, the court did recognize the CRA's assessing practices in respect of maintenance costs and utilities. The Federal Court–Trial Division concurred with the *Felton* decision in *The Queen v. Thompson*.

ITA: 8(1)(*f*)(v), 8(1)(*j*)

IT-352R2, par. 6
89 DTC 233 (T.C.C.)

ITA: 8(1)(*i*)(ii)

89 DTC 5439 (F.C.T.D.)

The Act sets out two tests, one of which must be met, if any amount of home office expense is to be deductible. One requires that the work space be the place where the individual principally performs the duties of the office or employment. The alternative test requires that both of the following conditions be met:

ITA: 8(13)
ITA: 8(13)(*a*)(i)
ITA: 8(13)(*a*)(ii)

(a) the work space is used exclusively for employment during the period in respect of which the deduction relates, and

(b) the work space is used on a regular and continuous basis for meeting customers or other persons in the ordinary course of employment.

If one of the two tests is met, the deductible expenses are limited to the employee's employment income for the year. Therefore, work space deduction cannot create a loss from employment. However, the provision allows for what amounts to an indefinite carryforward. In this case, where all expenses are limited to the amount of commission income, the limitation on home office expenses will have no effect.

ITA: 8(13)(*a*)(i),
8(13)(*a*)(ii)

ITA: 8(13)(*c*)

[3] Note that the salesperson's expense deduction requires that expenses, to be deductible, cannot exceed the commission.

ITA: 8(1)(*f*)

[4] Paragraph 8(1)(*f*) does not restrict the deductions under paragraph 8(1)(*i*) or 8(1)(*j*) (i.e., interest and capital cost allowance on car, utilities and maintenance) to commission income.

[5] Convention expenses may not be deducted from employment income since they are not listed in subsection 8(1).

ITA: 8(2)

(6) Due to the limitation placed on deductible expenses, i.e., expenses cannot exceed commission income, an alternative set of provisions may be preferable. In this case, the employee could make use of the deductions covering travelling expenses and motor vehicle expenses, rather than the salesperson's deduction. Although these rules do not provide for the deduction of entertainment expenses, there is no commission income limitation on the amount of meal expenses deductible (except for the 50% limitation on the cost of meals) or on car operating expenses deductible. Thus, the meal expenses and car operating expenses of $2,775 (i.e., $2,325 + $450) would be deductible as travel and car expenses, and office maintenance and utilities expenses of $1,850 would be deductible; the traveller's association dues would be deductible and capital cost allowance on the car would be deductible. This would result in employment income of $17,397 computed as follows:

ITA: 8(1)(*f*)
ITA: 8(1)(*h*), 8(1)(*h*.1)
ITA: 8(1)(*h*)

ITA: 8(1)(*h*.1)
ITA: 8(1)(*i*)(iii); IT-352R2, par. 6
ITA: 8(1)(*i*)(iv), 8(1)(*j*)(ii)

Salary and commissions			$ 25,000	sec. 5
Deductions:				
Car operating expenses (75% of $3,100)	$2,325			par. 8(1)(*h*.1)
Meal expenses (50% of $900)	450			par. 8(1)(*h*)
Association dues	300			par. 8(1)(*i*)
CCA on car (75% of $3,570)	2,678	(5,753)		par. 8(1)(*j*)
Employment income (before home office expense)			$ 19,247	
Less: home office expense			(1,850)	par. 8(1)(*i*), ssec. 8(13)
Employment income			$ 17,397	

Therefore, in this particular case, using the paragraphs 8(1)(*h*) and (*h*.1) alternative is not better.

(7) Golf club membership dues are not deductible because of the prohibition.

ITA: 18(1)(*l*)

(8) The issue of employment versus self-employment was considered in the previous chapter.

The courts have applied the following three tests as discussed in the previous chapter:

(a) the economic reality or entrepreneur test, i.e., control, ownership of the tools, chance of profit and risk of loss;

(b) integration or organization test, i.e., whether the worker is economically dependent on the organization; and

(c) the specific result test, i.e., a contract envisaging the accomplishment of a specific job or task.

(9) All of the home office expenses, including the interest and capital cost allowance, are deductible to the extent incurred to earn income, if the conditions are met. However, she may not want to claim the capital cost allowance because of the principal residence rules which will be discussed in the chapters on capital gains taxation. The deduction of expenses pertaining to work space in a home are allowed where it is either the individual's principal place of business or used exclusively on a regular and continuous basis for meeting clients, customers or patients of the individual. Deductible expenses cannot exceed the individual's income from business before the deduction of these expenses. However, excess expenses of this nature may be carried forward. As a result of this restriction, home office expenses should be separated from other deductible expenses and deducted last, as shown.

ITA: 18(12)

ITA: 18(12)

ITA: 18(12); IT-514

¶4,280 Ceasing to Carry on Business

¶4,285 Sale of accounts receivable

In order to deduct a reserve for doubtful debts or to write off a bad debt, an amount in respect of the debt must have been included previously in income. This would not be the case, if accounts judged to be doubtful or bad were purchased from someone else. To alleviate the problems that this may cause where:

ITA: 20(1)(*l*), 20(1)(*p*)

• a person has sold all or substantially all of the property used in a business,

- to a purchaser who will continue the business,

the Act provides for a joint election by the vendor and purchaser which permits the purchaser to take the reserve or write-off in respect of accounts receivable.   ITA: 22

To illustrate this election, assume that accounts receivable having a face value of $14,000   ITA: 22
with an existing reserve of $3,000 are sold for their assessed fair market value of $10,000. The
following represents the procedure that must be followed jointly by the buyer and seller to
allow the buyer future reserves and write-offs on the accounts purchased:

	SELLER				BUYER		
Accounts receivable		*Reserve*		*Accounts receivable*		*Reserve*	
$14,000			$3,000	(1) $14,000			NIL
	$10,000(1)						
	4,000(3)	(2) $3,000					
NIL			NIL				

(1) Cash $10,000
     Accounts receivable $10,000

(2) Reserve 3,000
     Income 3,000

(3) Business loss 4,000
     Accounts receivable 4,000

(1) Accounts receivable $14,000
     Cash $10,000
     Income   4,000

NOTE: Buyer could then set up an appropriate reserve for doubtful debts and could write off any of these debts should they prove bad.

Note that the loss to the seller under the election is a business loss. If the election were
not made, the loss of $4,000 would be a capital loss, only ½ allowable as a deduction and only
deductible against taxable capital gains of $2,000.

¶4,290 Sale of inventory

Where a taxpayer disposes of a business or part of a business, any inventory sold is   ITA: 23
deemed to have been sold in the course of carrying on the business. Thus, the proceeds of the
sale result in income for the seller and become the cost of the inventory to the buyer. The
purpose of this provision is to ensure that a lump-sum sale of inventory on the sale of a
business is treated in exactly the same way as the usual sale of inventory in the normal course
of carrying on business.

¶4,300 Professional Business

Amounts receivable in respect of services that have been billed are required to be   ITA: 10(5)(*a*)
included in income from the business of a professional. Work in progress at the end of a year,
representing unbilled services of a business that is a profession, is considered to be inventory.

An election is available to a taxpayer whose business is the professional practice of an   ITA: 34(*a*), 34(*b*)
accountant, dentist, lawyer, medical doctor, veterinarian or chiropractor. The election allows
the taxpayer to exclude from business income any amount in respect of work in progress at
the end of the year. Where the election is made, it must be used in all subsequent taxation
years unless the election is revoked with the permission of the CRA. The CRA's interpretation   IT-457R
of these rules is contained in the Interpretation Bulletin entitled "Election by professionals to
exclude work in progress from income".

¶4,310 Scientific Research and Experimental Development

¶4,315 Meaning of scientific research and experimental development (SR&ED)

"Scientific research and experimental development" is defined to mean the "systematic investigation or search carried out in a field of science or technology by means of experiment or analysis . . . ", including basic research, applied research and experimental development. Activities which result in deductible expenditures in support of the three types of research include engineering or design, operations research, mathematical analysis or computer programming, data collection, testing and psychological research. However, activities which do not result in a deductible expenditure include market research or sales promotion, quality control or routine testing, social sciences or humanities research, natural resource exploration, commercial development of material, products or processes, style changes or routine data collection. The CRA's interpretation of the term "scientific research" is contained in its draft Information Circular entitled "Scientific Research and Experimental Development", which offers some guidelines in the area.[27]

ITA: 248(1)

IC 86-4R4

The term "scientific research and experimental development" recognizes that the bulk of industrial scientific research is concentrated on the experimental development of new products or processes rather than pure or applied research. The inclusion of the words "experimental development" confirms that research does not include projects involving only routine engineering or routine development.

¶4,320 General deduction of expenditures

Generally, research and development expenditures, including most capital expenditures, made in a year are fully deductible. However, any allowable expenditures that are not deducted in a year are placed in a pool and may be deducted in any future year in which the taxpayer carries on business in Canada.

Certain scientific research and experimental development expenditures made in the year can be deducted from income of a business carried on in Canada. The following is a list of expenditures of a current nature:

ITA: 37(1)(a)

(a) for scientific research and experimental development related to the business and directly undertaken by or on behalf of the taxpayer;

(b) to an approved association that undertakes scientific research and experimental development related to the class of business of the taxpayer;

(c) to an approved university, college, research institute or other similar institution to be used for scientific research and experimental development related to the class of business of the taxpayer;

(d) for scientific research and experimental development in Canada to non-profit corporations resident in Canada;

(e) to a corporation resident in Canada for scientific research and experimental development in Canada related to the business of the taxpayer; or

(f) to an approved organization that makes payments to an association, institution or corporation described in (b) to (d) above, for use in scientific research and experimental development related to the class of business of the taxpayer, and where the taxpayer may exploit the results of such research and development.

Expenditures on scientific research and experimental development of a capital nature can be made in Canada by acquiring property (other than land or other non-depreciable property) relating to the business and directly undertaken by or on behalf of the taxpayer.

ITA: 37(1)(b)

The zone in which deductible SR&ED expenditures can be incurred extends to the area that is up to 200 nautical miles from the low-water line along the costs of Canada, as

ITA: 37(1.3)

---

[27] The Tax Court of Canada had occasion to consider the definition of the term in the case of *Sass Manufacturing Limited v. M.N.R.*, 88 DTC 1363.

¶4,310

recognized in the *Oceans Act*. This is known as the exclusive economic zone (EEZ) and includes the airspace above and the subsoil or seabed below that zone.

Expenditures must be related to a business carried on by the person making the expenditure. As indicated, SR&ED expenditures are added to a pool of such costs. They are eligible for a 100% deduction in the year incurred or may be carried forward indefinitely.

ITA: 37(1)(*a*), 37(1)(*b*)

As a further incentive to invest in SR&ED activity, the Act provides for an investment tax credit (ITC, discussed in subsequent chapters) which is a direct reduction of the taxpayer's tax liability. The investment tax credit is calculated as a specified percentage of the SR&ED expenditures made. Since an investment tax credit in respect of SR&ED lowers the cost of the research and development activity, the amount of the investment tax credit reduces the amount of the pool available for deduction in the year following the year of the investment tax credit claim. In addition, any super-allowance benefit amount will reduce the pool. If there is no balance in the pool in that year, because all amounts were previously deducted and no new expenditures were made in the current year, then the investment tax credit is included in income. A reduction of the balance in the pool reduces the future deduction and has the same effect as the income inclusion. The effect of this adjustment for the investment tax credit is to permit a deduction of the net cost of the expenditure after the partial recovery of cost through the investment tax credit. This effect can be illustrated with the following two options:

ITA: 37(1)(*e*)
ITA: 127(9)
ITA: 12(1)(*v*)

	Fully deducted	*Pooled*
Expenditure in year 1	$ 1,000	$1,000
Deducted in year 1	(1,000)	Nil
Available for future deduction	Nil	$1,000
ITC @ 35% of $1,000 claimed in year 1:		
Income inclusion in year 2	$ 350	
Reduction of pool in year 2		(350)
Available for future deduction		$ 650
Net deduction:		
Deduction in year 1 net of inclusion in year 2 (i.e., net deduction over 2 years)	$ 650	
Available for future deduction		$ 650
Net cost:		
Initial expenditure	$ 1,000	$1,000
ITC claimed in year 1	(350)	(350)
Tax saving at, say 20%:		
year 1 — $1,000 × .20	(200)	
later years — $1,000 × .20		(200)
Tax cost: year 2 ($350 × .20)	70	70
Net cost	$ 520	$ 520

Only certain expenditures of a current nature made for scientific research and experimental development carried on outside Canada may be deducted and only in the year that they are incurred. They are not pooled.

ITA: 37(2)

Expenditures on buildings are excluded from the 100% write-off. This includes the capital cost of a building or rent and lease expense incurred in respect of a building. However, expenditures on structures such as a wind tunnel or an experimental wind or hydro energy prototype are not affected and, hence, are eligible for the 100% write-off.

ITA: 37(8)(*d*)

Expenditures eligible for the scientific research and experimental development deduction must be all or substantially all attributable to the prosecution or to the provision of premises, facilities or equipment for the prosecution of such research and development. The Regulations amplify the definition of expenditures that are directly attributable to the prosecution of and to the provision of premises, facilities and equipment for the prosecution of SR&ED in Canada.

ITA: 37(8)(a)

ITR: 2900(2), 2900(3)

Current expenditures that are "directly attributable" to scientific research also qualify. This allows for the prorating of the direct costs of personnel who, while not solely involved with research, do directly perform scientific research part of the time, support scientific research personnel or directly supervise researchers. In the case of capital expenditures, minor or incidental use of equipment for non-research purposes is possible under the "all or substantially all" requirement.

¶4,325 Election method to determine deduction

An election is available as an alternative method for determining which expenditures incurred in Canada will qualify as SR&ED, to be included in the pool. This alternative method, which must be elected in prescribed form each year, is generally simpler for the taxpayer. If the election is used, the Act specifically lists six types of expenditures which will be considered to be for SR&ED carried on in Canada and, therefore, will be included in the taxpayer's SR&ED pool under subsection 37(1). The alternative method is described in more detail in Chapters 11 and 12.

ITA: 37(8)(a)(ii)(B)

This elective method for determining SR&ED expenditures does not account for general overhead expenditures, even if they are directly attributable to the prosecution or the provision of premises for the prosecution of SR&ED in Canada. Such overhead expenditures are treated, under the elective method, as ordinary expenses which are, generally, deductible in the year incurred or eligible for capital cost allowance. However, general overhead expenses are recognized in the method of calculating the investment tax credit discussed in Chapter 12.

¶4,400 THE GST IMPACT ON BUSINESS ACTIVITY

¶4,410 Commercial Activity

As noted in Chapter 2, the issue of whether the person is engaged in a commercial activity is central to the determination of whether a person is required to register and collect GST. Commercial activity means any business that is carried on, an adventure or concern in the nature of trade, or the making of a supply of real property. The meaning of the first two phrases is discussed below, while supplies of real property will be reviewed, in part, in Chapters 5 and 6.

ETA: 123(1)

¶4,415 Carrying on business

To some extent, the concept of carrying on business under the *Income Tax Act* has been adopted for GST purposes. Generally, if an entity is carrying on business for income tax purposes, it is also considered to be carrying on business for GST purposes. However, some entities not considered to be carrying on business for income tax purposes may still be considered to be carrying on business for GST purposes, as the comparable provisions under the ETA are generally broader in scope than those under the *Income Tax Act.*

The term "business" is defined to include a profession, calling, trade, manufacture or undertaking of any kind whatever. However, unlike the definition of carrying on business in the *Income Tax Act*, it is not necessary to establish that the business has a reasonable expectation of profit. Therefore, an entity engaged in activities with continuous, repetitious effort is generally considered to be a business for GST purposes, whether the activity or undertaking is engaged in for profit. The definition specifically excludes an office or employment.

ETA: 123(1)

Because of the absence of the profit test, a number of organizations established on a not-for-profit basis are considered to be carrying on business for GST purposes and, thus, to be engaged in commercial activities. For example, where a hospital operates a parking lot, this is considered to be a commercial activity and the hospital is required to collect GST on that supply. Therefore, even if an activity is considered ancillary to achieving a not-for-profit purpose for income tax purposes, and, therefore, outside the definition of carrying on business for purposes of the *Income Tax Act*, it is still considered to be a business for purposes of the GST.

Another distinction from the *Income Tax Act* is the inclusion of leasing activities in the definition of business. Any activity that is engaged in on a regular and continuous basis that involves the supply of property by way of lease, licence or similar arrangement, is considered to be a business. Thus, rents received from the rental of an automobile, for example, are regarded as being earned from a business for GST purposes, regardless of the effort required by the owner of the automobile to earn the rental income. This can be contrasted with the treatment under the *Income Tax Act*, where the activity may not be considered to be a business, but rather, may be regarded as income from property. This distinction for income tax purposes will be discussed in Chapter 6.

ETA: 123(1)

¶4,420 Adventure or concern in the nature of trade

As noted earlier in this chapter, the definition of business for income tax purposes includes an adventure or concern in the nature of trade. In contrast, this latter phrase is referred to separately in the definition of commercial activity under the ETA. In any event, as the phrase is not defined in the ETA, its meaning under the *Income Tax Act* should offer some insight into its meaning for GST purposes. In this regard, the *Taylor* case referred to earlier in this chapter should be reviewed.

¶4,425 Exclusions from the definition of commercial activity

There are two key activities which are specifically excluded from the definition of commercial activity. As a result, supplies made in the course of these activities will not be considered to be taxable supplies. The supplier of these goods and services is not required to collect GST on these supplies and, in turn, is not entitled to claim input tax credits. They include:

ETA: 123(1)

- that part of a business or adventure or concern in the nature of trade that involves the making of an exempt supply; or

- a business engaged in by an individual, a personal trust or a partnership consisting solely of individuals without a reasonable expectation of profit.

Exempt supplies include, for example, health care services, educational services, and legal aid services. While the making of exempt supplies is excluded from the definition of a commercial activity, the making of zero-rated supplies is not excluded. Thus, any person who sells zero-rated groceries or exports goods in the course of a business or an adventure or concern in the nature of trade, is considered to be engaged in a commercial activity and is entitled to claim input tax credits in respect of GST paid on purchases. Zero-rated supplies are set out in another schedule of the ETA. If a supply is not considered to be made in the course of a commercial activity because it falls within one of these exclusions, or if the supply is not made in the course of a business or an adventure or concern in the nature of trade or is not a supply of real property, the supply will not be a taxable supply and no GST will apply. Although no input tax credit may be claimed for GST paid in respect of these supplies, this GST is deductible for income tax purposes.

ETA: Schedule V

ETA: Schedule VI

¶4,430 Value for tax

GST is imposed on the value of consideration for a supply. Consideration is the price paid for property or services and is, generally, expressed in monetary terms.

ETA: 165(1)

Goods or services are often sold on terms that allow for a discount for prompt payment, or for a penalty in the case of a late payment. The value on which GST is imposed is not affected by the discount or penalty. In either case, GST applies to the amount of consideration shown on the invoice (i.e., the full sale price). If, however, the invoice is for an amount that is net of a cash discount, GST applies on the net amount.

ETA: 161

¶4,435   When GST is payable

GST is generally payable by a recipient of a taxable supply at the time the consideration for the supply is paid to the supplier or the time the consideration becomes due, whichever is earlier. Where partial payments are made in respect of a supply, GST must be paid on each payment. GST generally becomes due when it is invoiced. Specifically, the consideration becomes due on the earliest of:

ETA: 152(1), 168(1), 168(2)

(a) the day on which the invoice for the amount is issued;

(b) the date on the invoice;

(c) the day on which the invoice would have been issued, if not for an undue delay; and

(d) the day on which the amount becomes due under an agreement in writing.

Where property is supplied by way of lease, licence or similar agreement, the consideration is deemed to become due on the day the recipient is required to pay the consideration under the agreement.

ETA: 152(2)

Notwithstanding the general rule, a number of special cases are dealt with in other subsections. For example, where the supply involves goods, liability occurs on the earlier of the date determined under the general rule and the end of the month following the month in which ownership or possession of the goods is transferred to the purchaser. In the case of a deposit, GST is not payable on the deposit until the time the supplier applies the deposit against the consideration for the supply.

ETA: 168(1), 168(3), 168(9)

¶4,440   Automobile operating cost benefits paid by employer

Recall from Chapter 3 that an employer provides a taxable benefit when the employee's operating costs for an employer-provided automobile are paid by the employer. The value of the benefit is determined by one of two methods. The employee may use a per-kilometre method or elect to value the benefit as 50% of the standby charge in respect of the employer-provided car. Likewise, where the employee uses his or her own car but the operating costs are paid by the employer, an operating cost benefit is required to be determined under the *Income Tax Act*. In either case, the registrant employer is required to remit GST equal to a prescribed percentage of 4%[28] of the benefit, however computed. The prescribed percentage is less than 6% to recognize that the benefit includes exempt supplies such as insurance and licence fees.

ITA: 6(1)(*k*), 6(1)(*l*); ETA: l. 173(1)(*d*)(vi)(A)

¶4,450   Input Tax Credits

¶4,455   General rules

Input tax credits are available to registrants for GST paid on goods and services that are purchased for use in a commercial activity. If the use of the input is exclusively in a "commercial activity", which is defined in the ETA to mean "all or substantially all" (and which is interpreted to mean 90% or more), a full credit may be claimed. Conversely, if a business input will not be used at all in respect of a commercial activity, no credit will be allowed. Under this latter rule, if the extent of use in a commercial activity is less than 10%, no credit may be claimed. For example, if an input is to be used 90% or more in the course of making an exempt supply, no credit may be claimed. It is important to note that the test for eligibility is the intended use of the input at the time of purchase. Apart from the change-of-use rules for capital real property discussed in Chapter 8, a registrant is not required to adjust the input

ETA: 169(1)
ETA: 123(1)

---

[28] 10% for purposes of the HST.

tax credit for subsequent changes of use. Registrants are entitled to claim the credit in the reporting period in which the GST is paid or, if earlier, when it becomes payable.

There are circumstances where a purchase will be used in respect of a combination of taxable and exempt supplies. In these cases, except for certain capital goods which are discussed in Chapter 5, registrants are required to apportion the input tax credit between the taxable and exempt activity. For example, if use in a commercial activity represents 70% of the total use, a credit equal to 70% of the GST paid or payable may be claimed.

ETA: 169(1)

The legislation does not prescribe allocation methods to be used in apportioning input tax credits. Provided the allocation basis is reasonable and is used on a consistent basis throughout the fiscal year, the allocation will likely not be challenged by the CRA. The documentation requirements that are necessary to support input tax credit claims are discussed in Chapter 14.

¶4,460 Restrictions

Certain purchases made by a registrant have a personal consumption element or are for goods and services that are available to employees. As a result, there are certain circumstances where input tax credits are not allowed, in full or in part. In many circumstances, the GST restrictions parallel the restrictions contained in the *Income Tax Act* in respect of business deductions. The more significant restrictions include:

¶4,460.10 *Club memberships*

Input tax credits are not allowed in respect of membership fees or dues in any club whose main purpose is to provide dining, recreational or sporting facilities. Common examples of these clubs include business persons' clubs, golf clubs and fitness clubs. However, if meal and entertainment expenses are incurred at the club in respect of a commercial activity, input tax credits are allowed, subject to the recapture rule discussed below.

ETA: 170(1)(a)

¶4,460.20 *Home office expenses*

Input tax credits are not allowed in respect of expenses incurred by an individual in respect of a home office where the office is neither the individual's principal place of business nor a place that is both used exclusively for the purpose of earning income from a business and used on a regular and continuous basis for meeting clients, customers or patients. This provision is consistent with the *Income Tax Act*, which denies a deduction in such circumstances.

ETA: 170(1)(a.1)
ITA: 18(12)

¶4,460.30 *Personal or living expenses*

No input tax credit is allowed where a property or service is purchased exclusively for the personal consumption, use or enjoyment of an officer, employee or related individual. This restriction was referred to in Chapter 3, in the context of employee benefits. An exception to this rule is provided where a registrant acquires property or service exclusively for an employee's personal use; but the input tax credit will be disallowed, unless the property is re-supplied for fair market value consideration to the employee in the reporting period. In these circumstances, as GST will be collected on the resale, an input tax credit is allowed. An additional exception where an input tax credit is allowed is where the property or service would not be a taxable benefit for purposes of the *Income Tax Act*.

ETA: 170(1)(b), 170(1)(c)

For leases in respect of property rented to individuals, no input tax credit is allowed where the property is primarily for personal consumption, use or enjoyment. However, similar to the rule discussed above, an input tax credit is allowed where the property is supplied to the individual and GST is collected on the fair rental value.

¶4,460.40 *Reasonableness*

Another concept is borrowed from the *Income Tax Act*, namely, that of reasonableness. In claiming an input tax credit, the nature or cost of the property or services purchased by

ETA: 170(2)

the registrant must be reasonable in the circumstances, having regard to the nature of the commercial activities of the registrant. In addition, the amount of the input tax credit must be calculated on consideration that is reasonable in the circumstances.

¶4,460.50 *Automobile allowances*

Where an employer has paid an automobile allowance to an employee for travel in respect of the employer's business and the employee is not required to include the allowance in income because the allowance is a reasonable one, the employer is permitted to claim an ITC on that amount.

ETA: 174

¶4,470 Adjustments to Net Tax

The legislation sets out a series of adjustments in computing the net tax to be remitted by a registrant for a particular period. The most common of these adjustments are discussed below.

¶4,475 Excess charges

Where a supplier has charged an amount of GST in excess of what is collectible under the legislation, the supplier may adjust the amount of GST charged if it has not already been collected. If the excess has already been collected, it may be refunded or credited to the customer, provided a credit note is issued to the customer (or a debit note is issued by the recipient of the supply). The supplier is permitted to deduct the excess amount refunded or credited in determining his or her net tax for the reporting period in which the credit or debit note is issued. Conversely, the recipient, if a registrant, is required to add that amount to his or her net tax for that period, or a preceding period, to the extent it was deducted in determining his or her net tax. The refund or credit must be made within four years after the day the GST was charged or collected.

ETA: 232(1), 232(3)

¶4,480 Price reductions

Where a registrant reduces the price in respect of a supply for which GST has been charged but not collected, the registrant may adjust the amount of GST charged. If the GST has already been collected, a refund or credit may be given to the customer, provided a credit note (or debit note) is issued, as described above. The refund or credit must be made within four years of the time the price was reduced.

ETA: 232(2), 232(3)

This rule does not apply where the rules which are discussed earlier in this chapter apply, in respect of cash discounts for prompt payment. The adjustments outlined above may not be made for cash discounts. Registrants are required to collect GST on the full invoice price, regardless of whether a cash discount is subsequently granted for prompt payment. Similarly, registrants who purchase goods that are subject to a cash discount for prompt payment are entitled to claim an input tax credit based on the full invoice price.

ETA: 161, 232(4)

¶4,485 Bad debts

Relief is provided for bad debts. Where GST is remitted but not collected on a debt that is subsequently written off, a registrant is permitted to deduct an amount equal to the tax payable in respect of the supply multiplied by the ratio of the total amount equal to 6/106 (14/114 for HST) of the bad debt written off to the total amount payable for the supply.[29] To be eligible for this relief, the bad debt must be in respect of a supply made to an arm's length party, and the relief must be claimed in the reporting period in which the debt is written off or within four years after the due date of the return for that period. If a bad debt is subsequently recovered after the deduction is made, the ETA requires that the registrant add back to net tax an amount equal to the amount of the bad debt recovered multiplied by the ratio of the tax payable in respect of the supply to the total amount paid or payable on the supply (including GST and applicable provincial taxes).

ETA: 231(1), 231(3)

---

[29] If the amount written off relates to a supply subject to 7% GST or 15% HST, the fractions of 7/107 or 15/115 apply, respectively.

¶4,490   Lease of passenger vehicles

Where a registrant leases a passenger vehicle, to the extent the lease costs exceed the maximum amount deductible under section 67.3 of the *Income Tax Act*, a portion of the input tax credit will be recaptured. This restriction parallels the restriction that limits the maximum input tax credit that can be claimed in respect of the purchase of a passenger vehicle, which is discussed in Chapter 5. The recapture is provided by way of an adjustment to the net tax determination for the appropriate reporting period. For annual filers, the appropriate reporting period is the taxation year. For quarterly and monthly filers, it is the reporting period that begins immediately after the taxation year.

ETA: 235(1), 235(2)

¶4,495   Food, beverages, and entertainment expenses

Section 236 of the ETA contains the rules for food, beverages and entertainment expenses that are subject to section 67.1 of the *Income Tax Act*. Input tax credits for GST paid expenses are allowed in full in the reporting period in which they are incurred. However, at the end of the registrant's fiscal year, there will be a recapture of 50% of the total input tax credits in respect of these expenses. The amount recaptured will be included in the registrant's GST return for the first reporting period in the next fiscal year.

ETA: 236(1.1)

¶4,500   Application of the Rules

Example Problem

Reconsider the facts of the Example Problem involving Corporate Welfare Bum Limited beginning on page 176.

— *REQUIRED*

Outline the proper GST treatment by the corporation of the items presented.

— *SOLUTION*

(1) General

Since the corporation is carrying on business, it is engaged in a commercial activity. Therefore, the corporation is required to register and collect GST on its supplies, i.e., sales of goods or services, which are "taxable supplies." As a registrant, the corporation is entitled to a full input tax credit (ITC) in respect of GST paid or payable on goods and services that it purchases exclusively for use in its commercial activity. If GST collected or collectible on its sales exceeds its ITCs, the corporation must remit the difference. On the other hand, if ITCs exceed GST collected or collectible, a refund of the excess is available.

ETA: 123(1), 169(1)

(2) Items Listed

(a) The appraisal expenses incurred for insurance appraisal purposes are for the provision of an exempt supply of a financial service which does not give rise to an ITC since no GST was payable.

ETA: Schedule V, Part VII

(b) Employer contributions to a registered pension plan involve a payment for an exempt supply on which GST is not charged. As a result, no ITC is available.

ETA: 123(1)

(c) Landscaping costs involve a payment for taxable supplies of goods or services resulting in the availability of an ITC.

(d) Payments for legal services give rise to an ITC since the services are taxable supplies.

(e) Dividends received involve an exempt supply of a financial service on which no GST is collected.

ETA: Schedule V, Part VII

(f) The payment of interest is a financial service which is an exempt supply.

(g) The purchase of inventory involves a taxable supply on which GST is paid. Hence, an ITC is available.

(h) No GST is charged on a donation which involves a transfer of money. As a result, no ITC is available.   ETA: 123(1), 164

(i) Insurance premiums are for an exempt supply of a financial service and no ITC is available since no GST was paid.

(j) The payment of a dividend is an exempt supply of a financial service. No ITC is available.

(k) A loan is a financial instrument which is an exempt supply, on which no GST is charged. Hence, the write-off of this bad debt has no GST effect.

(l) Improvements that are not normal repairs or maintenance are considered to be capital outlays. However, as will be discussed in Chapter 5, there is no amortization of the GST paid on capital outlays. The GST paid provides an ITC at the time of payment.

(m) Amounts paid to employees as remuneration are not supplies, since these amounts are excluded from the definition of services. As a result, remuneration is not subject to GST.   ETA: 123(1)

(n) Interest paid involves an exempt supply of a financial service.

(o) Initially, an ITC is available on the full amount of GST paid in respect of meals and entertainment. However, 50% of the ITC in respect of such expenditures is recaptured in the first reporting period of the next fiscal year.   ETA: 236

(p) Embezzlement losses involve a transfer of money for which there are no GST implications.

(q) Bonuses are employment remuneration excluded from the definition of service and, hence, are not subject to GST.

(r) Property tax involves an exempt supply on which no GST is charged.

(s) A lease cancellation fee paid by a lessor is subject to GST. The payer is deemed to have paid GST equal to 6/106 of the payment and, hence, an ITC is available.

(t) The payer of damages is deemed to have paid or the recipient deemed to have received GST equal to 6/106 of the damages. As a result, the corporation is entitled to an ITC.   ETA: 182

(u) Construction and repair costs involve a payment for taxable supplies for goods or services resulting in the availability of an ITC.

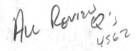

¶4,800   REVIEW QUESTIONS

(1) Mr. Flip is a commissioned real estate client of yours. He has just bought and sold a piece of land in a "quick flip" transaction. What kind of income might this be to him: employment, business, property or capital gain?

(2) Does the Act require that the "profit" from a business be calculated in accordance with generally accepted accounting principles?

(3) Opco Ltd. is in the business of manufacturing equipment under contract for other manufacturers. One of its customers failed to live up to its contract and would not take delivery of or pay for its order. Opco took the customer to court and was awarded the amount of $100,000 as damages. Can this amount be treated as a non-taxable capital receipt by Opco?

(4) Aco Ltd. and Xco Ltd. entered into an agreement to manufacture a new product for the next 20 years. This represented 80% of Aco's business. After 5 years it was decided that the two parties could not work together so Xco paid Aco $500,000 to terminate the agreement. Is the receipt of this amount by Aco considered to be business income?

(5) Donald Corleone owns an illegal gambling house. He has made significant "profits" on this activity, but has not reported the income since he believes it is not taxable. Is he correct?

(6) Opco Ltd. took advantage of a program offered by the government and hired two employees whose wages were partially offset by a government subsidy. The owner felt that since he was really just getting some of his tax dollars back through this subsidy, the amount received would not be taxable. What do you think?

(7) As long as an expenditure was made for the purpose of earning income from a business or property then it is deductible. Is this statement true? Comment.   ITA: 18

(8) One of your clients is having some short-term cash flow problems and cannot pay his year-end tax liability. He decides that he will defer his payment to the Receiver General instead of trying to get another short-term bank loan. He reasons that in either case the interest will be deductible. Comment.

(9) Subsection 18(1) lists those items that are prohibited from being deducted because of the nature of the expenditure. If an expense passes those tests, will it be deductible?

(10) A client had to replace the roof on its factory at a cost of $100,000. The client deducted the cost of the roof on the basis that it was simply replacing the previous roof with a new one of the same quality. Is the cost deductible?

(11) Is the portion of the airline ticket that represents the meal subject to the 50% limitation on meal expenses?

(12) Will a company that offers a warranty with its product be able to deduct a reserve?   ITA: 20(1)(*m*.1)

(13) Under certain circumstances, can capital expenditures be written off in the year?

¶4,825   MULTIPLE CHOICE QUESTIONS

Question 1

Which one of the following items is NOT deductible in computing the income of a corporation under Division B of the Act?

(A) Amounts paid for landscaping business premises.

(B) Interest on money borrowed to finance the purchase of a factory for use in its business.

(C) The premium on a $100,000 term life insurance policy on an employee if the beneficiary of the policy is the employee's family.

(D) Interest and penalties on late income tax payments.

Question 2

Which one of the following amounts is DEDUCTIBLE in computing the income of a corporation under Division B of the Act?

(A) $11,000 of accrued legal fees for a pending law suit. The accrual is an estimate because no work has been done to date by the lawyers.

(B) $4,000 of donations to registered charities made for no business reason.

(C) $15,000 spent on three social events in the taxation year for all employees at a particular location.

(D) $1,500 for golf club membership dues for employees.

Question 3

Which one of the following amounts is DEDUCTIBLE in computing income of a corporation under Division B of the Act?

(A) $5,000 of donations to federal political parties.

(B) $44,000 in accrued bonuses paid 7 months after year-end. The amounts were legal liabilities at year-end.

(C) A $10,000 increase in the financial accounting reserve for warranty expenses.

(D) The $2,000 cost of tickets for meals and entertainment at a gala fund-raising event for a registered charity.

Question 4

XYZ Ltd.'s current financial statement shows a deduction for $20,000 of legal and accounting expenses. This amount consists of the following items:

- $5,000 of legal expenses related to the purchase of an investment in shares;

- $5,000 of legal expenses incurred to dispute a tax assessment;

- $5,000 of legal expenses related to the issuance of debt; and

- $5,000 of accounting fees related to the preparation of a prospectus regarding the issuance of shares.

What amount must be added back to XYZ's financial statement income in the computation of its net income under Division B of the Act?

(A) $13,000

(B) $12,000

(C) $9,000

(D) $5,000

Question 5

Ten years ago, Sam, a real estate agent, purchased a piece of land for $50,000. His intention at that time was to build a rental building on the land and use it to earn rental income, which he did four years ago. In the current year, he sold the land and building for $100,000 and $80,000 respectively after receiving an unsolicited offer.

Based on the facts, which one of the following statements is true?

(A) The CRA may argue that the gain on the sale of the land is a capital gain, because Sam is a real estate agent.

(B) The CRA may argue that the gain on the sale of the land is business income, because of the 10-year holding period of the land.

(C) The CRA may argue that the gain on the sale of the land is business income because of the unsolicited offer for sale.

(D) The gain on the sale of the land will likely be treated as a capital gain for income tax purposes.

Question 6

Which of the following amounts is DEDUCTIBLE in computing the income of a corporation under Division B of the Act?

(A) $13,000 of legal fees to defend a lawsuit brought by a customer.

(B) Accounting losses on the sale of a capital property.

(C) The principal amount of a mortgage on a company's warehouse.

(D) The personal and living expenses of the shareholder who works very hard in the business and is not paid a salary.

¶4,850   EXERCISES

Exercise 1

ITA: 9; IT-218R

The taxpayer corporation, Singh Enterprises Ltd., purchased a property consisting of some eight separate residential apartment buildings. When purchased, the property was ready for profit-producing operation and immediate arrangements were made for such operations.

The principal shareholder of the corporation, Sam Singh, was an individual with a long history of trading in real estate in many different countries. He fully expected that the property would increase in value in the future.

About 11 months after the purchase of the property, circumstances dictated a change in the investments of the corporation and the property was sold for a substantial profit.

— REQUIRED

Determine whether the profit realized by the sale of the property was income from a business or a capital gain.

Exercise 2

ITA: 9

Unloadem Limited had a franchise for the distribution in Saskatchewan of Belchfire automobiles made in Argentina. The business had grown rapidly in its 10 years of existence. However, soon after the expansion of its facilities, Belchfire Motor Industries terminated the distribution agreement and voluntarily agreed to pay Unloadem Limited $225,000.

— REQUIRED

What are the tax implications to Unloadem Limited?

Exercise 3

ITA: 10

Holey Mufflers Limited operates a fast-service repair shop. At the end of its fiscal year its inventory records showed the following:

Item	Number	Actual cost	FIFO cost	Replacement cost	Net realization value
Mufflers	64	$17.50	$16.25	$18.40	$15.50
Tailpipes	157	4.75	4.25	5.00	4.50
Exhaust systems	39	16.25	16.30	17.00	15.50
Shock absorbers	256	19.45	18.85	20.50	19.75
Brackets	932	1.40	1.35	1.50	1.30
Clamps	1,746	.65	.70	.75	.80

— REQUIRED

What values could be used for the total inventory for tax purposes? (Assume that the method of valuing inventory could change with permission.)

ITA: 10(2.1)

Exercise 4

ITA: 18(1)(*l*)

Foistit Limited, a consulting firm in Calgary, owns a small lodge in the Banff area. The lodge is used throughout the year for the purposes of entertaining clients.

— REQUIRED

(A) Comment on the deductibility of maintenance costs in respect of the lodge.

(B) Reconsider the deductibility of these costs if the property is rented during the week to the public and used to entertain clients only on the weekends.

Exercise 5

ITA: 17, 20(1)

Mr. M. Bezzle is the controller with responsibility for tax compliance of International Widget Manufacturing Limited based in Calgary. He has called to ask your advice, as the company's accountant, on various matters pertaining to the company's 2007 tax return. He has asked you the following questions.

(A) On March 1, 2008, the company paid $234,000 for the benefit of 30 employees to a defined benefit registered pension plan. Of the $234,000 paid, $129,000 represents an adjustment required as a result of an actuarial valuation; the remainder was based on a current service contribution equal to 6% of each employee's wages for 2007. What is the total amount that can be deducted for tax purposes in 2007?

(B) The company paid $15,000 representation costs to obtain a special licence from the State of Montana to sell its widgets in the state. This amount was written off in the financial accounts but added back and amortized over a 20-year period in calculating income for tax purposes. How should this item be treated?

(C) The amount of $1,500 spent to connect gas lines on conversion from oil to gas in the Toronto plant was added to the cost of the building for financial accounting purposes and depreciated with the building. How should the amount be treated for tax purposes?

(D) The president's wife is employed full-time as his secretary and paid $7,000 per month. Is this amount deductible and if not, how much is deductible?

— REQUIRED

Provide brief answers to the questions posed by the controller.

Exercise 6

ITA: 20(1)(*f*)

In August 2001, Steel M. Blind Manufacturing Co. Ltd., a venetian blind manufacturer, issued a series of bonds at $891.90 per $1,000 par value. The issue matured in August 2007 and was redeemed at that time at par value. It bears a coupon rate of 9% to yield 12% to maturity.

— REQUIRED

How much of the bond discount can be deducted and in what year can it be deducted?

Exercise 7 62

ITA: 9–12, 18–20

The following information concerning the financial statements of Incredible Incubators Incorporated for its fiscal year ended September 30, 2007 has been presented to you in order to prepare tax returns.

(a) Net income after tax per financial statements	$150,000
(b) Provision for income taxes — current	25,000
— future	130,000
(c) Depreciation expense	40,000
(d) Inventory — on LIFO* basis: opening	125,000
closing	145,000
— on FIFO basis: opening	140,000
closing	155,000
(e) Interest on income taxes paid after due date	2,500
(f) Bond interest expense (including annual discount amortization of $7,500 re bonds issued this year)	39,500
(g) Landscaping costs re factory premises — debited to land account	12,000

* LIFO is used by the company for financial statement purposes.

— REQUIRED

Using the foregoing information, compute income for tax purposes for Incredible Incubators for their fiscal year ended September 30, 2007. [Ignore tax deductions in respect of depreciable capital property.]

Exercise 8

ITA: 9, 12(1)(*e*)(ii), 20(1)(*n*)(ii), 20(8)(*b*)

Quickturn Land Limited bought for cash 25 acres of land at a cost of $107,500 during the year. About two months later the land was sold to a developer for $250,000 consisting of a $110,000 down payment in cash and a note without interest due in one year for the balance. A real estate commission of $12,500 was paid. The company often engages in this type of transaction.

— REQUIRED

Compute the minimum net income for the company in the year of sale and the next year in respect of this transaction.

Exercise 9

ITA: 22

Mr. Flogger has arranged to sell substantially all of the assets of his proprietorship business, including accounts receivable valued at $36,000, to Mr. Sucker who will continue the proprietorship business. At the end of last year, Mr. Flogger had deducted a reserve for doubtful debts of $6,500. The face value of the accounts being sold is $45,000.

— REQUIRED

What are the tax implications to both Mr. Flogger and Mr. Sucker of using section 22 on the sale of accounts receivable?

Exercise 10

ETA: 123(1), 169(1), Schedule V, Part VII

Reconsider the facts of Exercise 7.

— REQUIRED

Outline the proper GST treatment by the corporation of the items presented.

¶4,875　ASSIGNMENT PROBLEMS

Problem 1

ITA: 9; IT-218R

A piece of land was purchased by Yacumflastor Corporation Ltd. for the purpose of constructing a high-rise residential building. Plans were made for the development of the property, surveys were made and the land was stripped and excavated in preparation for construction. Subsequent to this work on the land, it was determined that the location was not suitable for the intended purpose, due to heavy truck traffic in the area. As a result, the property was listed for sale with the realtor who acted in the original purchase. The sale at a substantial profit took place approximately six months from the purchase.

The corporation had been newly formed when the above land was purchased. At about the same time, another piece of land was purchased and was developed into a commercial/industrial plaza which the corporation continues to own as a rental property. The principal shareholder of the corporation, Jake Yacumflastor, owns and operates an electrical contracting business.

The Articles of Incorporation of the corporation contain the following statement of objects:

> . . . to purchase, lease, acquire, hold, manage, develop, operate, pledge and mortgage, either absolutely as owner or by way of collateral security or otherwise, alone or jointly with others and either as principal or agent, property, real or personal, and assets generally of any and every kind of description.

No mention is made of the purchase and sale of land as a business activity.

— REQUIRED

Write a memo for the Yacumflastor Corporation Ltd.'s file evaluating the issue of whether the sale of the land should be treated as a receipt of income or capital gain for tax purposes. Arrive at a conclusion consistent with your analysis of the facts, but indicate the basis for any areas of potential opposition to your conclusion.

Problem 2

ITA: 18(1)(*a*), 18(1)(*h*), 248(1)

The taxpayer, in 1959, purchased 200 acres of property in the Calabogie area of Lanark, as a holiday property for himself and his family. In 1961 it became their principal residence. He worked in Ottawa, both at that time and in the subsequent years; initially he commuted between the Lanark property and his Ottawa job on a daily basis. In the early 1970s he began living in Ottawa during the week and commuting home to the property only on weekends. When the property was first purchased, there was an old brick house on it which was not suitable as a residence for the family. A new house (referred to in the evidence as the D.V.A. house) was built; the family moved into it. It is clear that the family's lifestyle was such as to enjoy the rural location.

In 1974 the taxpayer decided to turn part of the property into a campground; 8 serviced campsites and approximately 12 unserviced sites were created for this purpose. There was as well room for at least 10 other unserviced campsites more or less immediately available and potential for expansion to a much larger number (e.g., 100). Outhouses were built; a trout pond constructed; and the requisite service roads installed. The tax treatment of the expenses incurred with respect to this construction is not part of the dispute in this case.

After these initiatives had been taken, sometime towards the end of 1975 or the beginning of 1976, the taxpayer sought the advice of a consultant with the Ontario Ministry of Tourism, a Mr. Bingham. The advice sought was with respect to the possibility of developing the campground and obtaining a business loan for this purpose. The taxpayer had applied in early 1975 for a loan and was turned down in September of that year.

The taxpayer's consultations with Mr. Bingham in the later half of 1975 and beginning of 1976 led to suggestions for the development of the campsite through the construction of additional facilities: additional serviced sites; proper toilets; laundry facilities; a store on the property; a swimming pool; an activities building which might be used by the campers in bad weather. The taxpayer's accountant, Mr. McCoy, in early 1976 prepared projections as to the proposed profitability of the venture if the proposed development took place. These projections showed losses in the first year (1976–77) but a profit thereafter. The projections were based on information given to Mr. McCoy by the taxpayer and they envisaged the obtaining of a $280,000 loan. The taxpayer applied to the Eastern Ontario Development Corporation, in 1979, for a loan ($45,000, not $280,000). Mr. Bingham was asked to evaluate the loan application from the Department of Tourism's point of view. He was asked to consider: whether the taxpayer had the management capability to effect and operate the proposed development; whether there would be any negative effects on competitors in the area if the development took place; whether the taxpayer's marketing plans looked reasonable. Mr. Bingham's evaluation did not involve any financial analysis of the application. Mr. Bingham recommended that the loan application go forward for the next step, evaluation by the Eastern Ontario Development Corporation. The taxpayer was unable to obtain the loan, because the Eastern Ontario Development Corporation's funds are new money for new projects.

The taxpayer purchased a "pre-fab" house for $40,000 which was constructed across the road from the D.V.A. house. The family moved into that house in January of 1980. The taxpayer contends that he had decided to proceed with the plans for the development of the campsite by turning the D.V.A. house into the general activities building envisaged in the projected development. He states that he planned to add laundry facilities, toilets, etc., thereto. During 1980, the taxpayer rented the D.V.A. house to his daughter for $100 per month. This was not sufficient to cover the mortgage costs of the property. In May of 1980 the taxpayer had a massive heart attack. He was incapacitated until at least September of that year. The taxpayer continued to charge the mortgage expenses of the property as a business expense.

The profit and loss record of the taxpayer's business never showed a profit from the first year of its operation, in 1975 to 1985. The taxpayer has consistently reported losses for the years 1977 to 1983 as follows:

1977	$ 7,985.54
1978	$ 8,676.84
1979	$ 8,383.37
1980	$14,491.57
1981	$24,414.44
1982	$14,350.77
1983	$14,508.35

The gross income for the campground itself for the years 1977 to 1980 was:

1977	$ 86
1978	$134
1979	$258
1980	$520

After 1980, the campground income was reported in a combined fashion with that received from the cottage and farmhouse property; therefore, it cannot be separately identified. The evidence is sketchy with respect to the renting of the cottage, the farmhouse and the D.V.A. house. That which exists does not show a vigorous and concerted effort to run a business. The D.V.A. house, as well as being rented to the taxpayer's daughter for $100 per month in 1980, was rented during a few of the winter months in 1981–82 to some loggers and for approximately six months in 1984 to some miners who were prospecting in the area.

Camp Coupland was listed in a Government of Ontario camping brochure published for the 1981 season and the taxpayer had had some calling cards made with Camp Coupland, the address, a map and rates listed thereon. No expenses for advertising of the Camp were included in his 1975–1985 tax returns.

— *REQUIRED*

Determine whether expenses incurred by the taxpayer during the 1980 and 1981 taxation years are business expenses that are deductible for tax purposes.

Problem 3

ITA: 12(1), 18(1), 20(1); IT-442R

TalkTech Inc. is a manufacturer and wholesaler of cellular communication products. TalkTech Inc's customers are retailers who promote TalkTech Inc.'s products to the general public. TalkTech Inc. has an October 31 year-end. You are conducting a review of TalkTech Inc's year-end accounting records for its 2007 fiscal year and have been provided with the following information.

TalkTech Inc. has the following recorded reserves:

Account	Opening	Additions	Subtractions	Closing
Warranty reserve	$35,000	$10,000	$17,500	$27,500
Allowance for doubtful accounts	32,000	7,500	5,000	34,500

TalkTech Inc. provides a 1-year warranty on most of its products. The warranty is for defects in workmanship or component parts. This warranty is provided as part of the purchase price of TalkTech Inc.'s products. TalkTech Inc. honours its own warranties. The 2007 addition of $10,000 represents a standard percentage of sales made in the 2007 fiscal period. The 2007 subtraction of $17,500 represents an amount actually paid to honour warranties.

The addition of $7,500 to the allowance for doubtful accounts is a result of the application of TalkTech Inc.'s annual year-end aging analysis. In conversation with the controller of TalkTech Inc. you determine that this $7,500 increase in the allowance for doubtful accounts was computed by applying the company's historical collection percentages to the aged accounts receivable balances. Also, during its 2007 fiscal period, TalkTech Inc. wrote off $5,000 (the subtraction noted above) of amounts previously expensed and included in the opening allowance for doubtful accounts. TalkTech Inc. also ended up collecting $1,500 of previously written-off bad debts.

In an attempt to attract a particular retail customer, TalkTech Inc. provided this new customer with an incentive to make a large initial purchase of its products. On April 1, 2007, TalkTech Inc. sold $300,000 worth of cellular phones to CellBlock Limited. TalkTech agreed to the following payment terms in an attempt to entice CellBlock Limited to make the purchase:

- $100,000 due and payable May 1, 2007; and

- $50,000 due and payable January 1 each year starting January 1, 2008 through January 1, 2011.

The cost of the good sold under this contract was $180,000. The delivery date for the cellular phones sold under this contract was May 1, 2007.

One of TalkTech's customers was experiencing financial trouble. As a result, TalkTech Inc. had agreed to make shipments only if payments were received well in advance of the anticipated shipping dates. Under the terms of this agreement, TalkTech Inc. received $40,000 from Phones'N'Things on September 30, 2007. This payment was an advance payment for a shipment of new technology cellular phones which TalkTech Inc. expected to be shipping to customers commencing February 1, 2008. In the event that TalkTech Inc. was unable to honour its contract with Phones'N'Things, a full refund of the $40,000 was payable.

— REQUIRED

(A) Prepare a schedule showing the effect of the above information on income for tax purposes of TalkTech Inc. for the year ended October 31, 2007. From this comparison, determine any adjustments that would be necessary to reconcile accounting income and income for tax purposes for the year.

(B) What would be the tax consequences if the $5,000 subtraction in the allowance for doubtful accounts in 2007 included an account receivable of $800 which was written off only because it has been outstanding for more than 180 days. In fact, it has been outstanding for one year and is part of the opening allowance of $32,000. This $800 could still be collected and there has been no serious attempt to collect it. In fact, the remainder of that customer's account is current and further sales have been made to that customer.

Problem 4

ITA: 18, 19, 20(1), 147.2(1)

You have been assigned to the audit team for B.B. JAMS Ltd., one of your significant clients. Below is the income statement prepared by the company's accountant for the December 31, 2007 year-end.

B.B. JAMS LIMITED
INCOME STATEMENT

FOR THE YEAR ENDED DECEMBER 31, 2007

Sales	$147,840,000
Cost of sales (Note (1))	(119,859,000)
Gross profit	$ 27,981,000
General and administrative expenses (Notes (2)–(7))	(12,374,000)
Selling expenses (Note (8))	(9,311,000)
Income from operations	$ 6,296,000
Other income (Notes (9)–(10))	16,000
Net income before income taxes	$ 6,312,000
Provision for income taxes	(2,528,000)
Net income	$ 3,784,000

Through various discussions with the accountant, you have been able to determine that the following information has been recorded in the financial statements:

(1) JAMS had a number of items of inventory that did not sell well in the current year. For accounting purposes, the accountant has recorded a reserve for inventory obsolescence. The reserve was calculated based on the carrying value of any inventory item that had not had a sale in the last 180 days. The reserve at year-end was $1,285,000.

(2) JAMS provides insurance for employees and paid the following amounts to Nat Insurance Company during the year:

$2,000,000 insurance policy on the life of the president included in insurance expense ($300 per month)	$ 3,600
$1,000,000 insurance policy on the life of the vice-president — marketing included in insurance expense	2,000
Group term life insurance for employees included in salaries and benefits ($37,000 × 12 months)	444,000
Total	$449,600

JAMS is the beneficiary of the policies on the president and vice-president. On June 1, 2007, JAMS renegotiated its bank debt, and due to the ever increasing responsibilities of the president, the bank required the insurance policy on the life of the president as part of the collateral for the loan. The premiums on the policy are equal to the net cost of pure insurance for the policy.

(3) An analysis of the professional fees for 2007 revealed the following expenses:

Legal and accounting fees related to the issuance of shares	$29,300
Legal fees related to amending the articles of incorporation	2,300
Costs incurred regarding the renegotiating of the bank loans	46,100
Costs incurred to defend the company against a wrongful dismissal charge	59,600
Costs related to the structuring of an agreement for the purchase of equipment from a foreign company	38,700
Appraisal costs to determine value of the equipment for the bank	5,100

(4) During the year, there were substantial repairs completed to the outside of the building. After the repairs some of the landscaping had to be redone. The total costs were $139,000. Of this, $23,500 relates to the landscaping costs. The entire $139,000 was included in general and administrative expenses.

¶4,875

(5) A review of the other expense accounts included in general and administrative expenses showed the following:

Depreciation and amortization	$4,560,000
Interest on late payment of municipal taxes	900
Severance payments to four managers*	245,000
Loss from theft by accounting clerk	4,500
Donations to various registered charities	57,000

* All of the amounts were paid in the year.

(6) The salaries and benefits account shows contributions for certain employees to the company's registered pension plan. The contributions were not actually made until March 31, 2008. The pension plan is a defined contribution (money purchase) plan. The company matches the employees' contributions on a dollar for dollar basis.

	Registered pension plan	Employment compensation
President	$13,250	$250,000
Vice-president	10,250	150,000
Accountant	5,400	70,000

(7) In early November 2007, JAMS announced an early retirement package that was made available to employees over the age of 60. In order to provide employees with the time required to assess the offer, the deadline for accepting the package has been set at February 15, 2008. While no formal replies were received as of December 31, 2007, the personnel manager anticipates a high acceptance rate. She expects that the costs associated with the packages will be $672,000. This cost has been accrued in the 2007 financial statements.

(8) The following information was taken from the various selling expense accounts:

Cost of sponsoring presentations at a local theatre company	$15,000
Hockey game tickets given to customers	8,000
Meals and entertainment costs of salespeople	109,500
Staff Christmas party and summer barbecue	43,800
Cost of sponsoring local little league teams	5,000
Memberships for salespeople at local golf courses	12,700

(9) The other income includes a loss on the sale of various fixed assets of $35,900.

(10) During the year, the company had cash on hand for a short period of time due to the timing of certain contract payments. The funds earned interest income of $10,400 while they were held.

Other Information:

(11) The accountant has calculated that JAMS is entitled to claim capital cost allowance and CECA of $5,835,000 in 2007. You have confirmed that this calculation is correct.

(12) In reviewing the income tax assessments, you noted that JAMS had been charged interest of $4,900 on the late payment of instalments. You discussed this with the accountant and determined that the interest was recorded in the income tax expense account.

— *REQUIRED*

Based on the information that you have obtained, calculate the business income for JAMS for December 31, 2007. Show all calculations whether or not they seem relevant to the final answer. Comment on all items omitted from the calculation.

Problem 5

ITA: Subdivisions a and b

Coco Hardy is an apprentice with Sepp, a design house in Toronto. In her spare time, during some evenings and on weekends, she operates a sewing service for clothing manufacturers. She has set aside a spare room in her apartment where she keeps her equipment and materials and performs her services. This room occupies approximately 20% of her apartment. She sews for many of the same companies that deal with her employer, Sepp. The demands of her employment with Sepp will continue to prohibit her from expanding her sewing services. Consequently, she has not advertised for additional sewing work. Her sewing billings average approximately $600 per month.

She and the manufacturers mutually agree upon what type of sewing is to be done in order to meet the manufacturers' production deadlines. Her hourly rates are determined by the type of sewing required for a particular manufacturer. At the end of each month, she will issue a bill to the manufacturers bearing her name, home address, and home telephone number. Her clients pay her the gross amount on the invoice which does not include GST.

Ms. Hardy has incurred some direct sewing expenses and has allocated some of her other costs to her sewing services in respect of the past year as follows:

Direct expenses:

Sewing supplies		$ 2,890
Meals and entertainment for manufacturers		500
Sewing machine repairs		425
Long distance telephone calls to manufacturers		710
Delivery of finished product		1,500
Total direct expenses		$ 6,025

Allocated costs:

Rent ($1,000 per month)	$12,000	
Utilities	2,100	
Insurance	400	
	$14,500	
Allocation to sewing room	× 20%	$ 2,900

Capital cost allowance:

Sewing room furniture	$ 450	
Sewing machine	325	
Automobile for deliveries	1,200	$ 1,975
Total allocated costs		$ 4,875
Total		$10,900

— REQUIRED

(A) Discuss the issues involved in determining whether Ms. Hardy is earning employment income or business income from her sewing service and then reach a conclusion based on the facts.

(B) Compute both income from employment and business, and comment on whether the listed expenses and allocated costs are deductible for income tax purposes under each alternative.

Problem 6

ITA: 8(1)(*f*), 8(1)(*h*), 8(1)(*h*.1), 8(1)(*i*), 8(1)(*j*), 8(3), 18–20

Mr. Peter Rajagopal, who is a salesman in Regina, Saskatchewan, has incurred the following expenses in connection with his employment in 2007. He was not reimbursed and did not receive an allowance in respect of any of these expenses. Peter has a form T2200, signed by his employer, attesting to all of these expenses.

(1) Peter uses one room in his home exclusively as a home office. He uses his home office most days and evenings to do paperwork and make phone calls and his home office computer is connected to his employer's computer system by modem. He visits his office at his employer's premises approximately once a week and spends the remainder of the time on the road, making sales calls throughout Western Canada.

(2) The following expenses relate to Peter's home office which occupies 10% of the square footage of his house:

Utilities	$ 3,100
Mortgage interest	12,000
House insurance	1,150
Municipal taxes	3,050
Maintenance and repairs	2,700
Total	$22,000
10% thereof	$2,200

Capital cost allowance on computer equipment ($6,900 × 15%)	1,035
Rental of photocopier	1,200
Rental of fax machine	200
Office supplies	750
Additional monthly charges for telephone services for family internet connection (12 × $30)	360
Long distance calls	1,000

(3) Peter also has the following promotional expenses:

Meals (with clients in Regina, excluding the cost of his own meals)	$2,100
Theatre tickets	1,200
Promotional gifts	1,300
Country club membership	3,200

(4) Peter paid the following automobile expenses:

Gas & oil	$2,000
Insurance	1,100
Licence	90
Repairs	800
Cellular phone airtime charges (used for employment-related calls only)	700
Parking (employment related)	320

Peter purchased the car that he uses for employment purposes on August 1, 2006 for $50,000 plus $3,000 GST and $5,000 provincial sales tax. Peter did not claim CCA on the car in 2006; therefore, the capital cost allowance rate for the car is 30% in 2007. The car was driven a total of 40,000 km in 2007; 32,000 of the kilometres driven related to Peter's employment use.

(5) Peter also incurred the following travel expenses (while away at least 12 hours):

Airfare	$ 4,520
Meals and accommodation (including $2,400 for meals)	4,960
Registration fees for convention in Vancouver to increase product knowledge	800
Out-of-town entertainment	3,200

(6) Interest on bank loan:

— to buy the computer equipment for the home office in (1) above	$ 320
— to buy the car in (4) above	800

(7) Peter's remuneration from employment is as follows:

Salary	$40,000
Bonus based on company sales	17,000

— REQUIRED

Compute the total deductible amount of expense under each of the following sets of assumptions:

(A) Peter chooses to use the following deductions as an employee:

(i) paragraphs 8(1)(*h*), (*h*.1), (*i*), and (*j*), or

(ii) paragraphs 8(1)(*f*), (*i*) and (*j*).

(B) Peter's situation is changed to that of an independent sole proprietor.

Assume that all the amounts given are accurate, supported by receipts and reasonable in the circumstances. Present your answer in tabular form for ease of comparison of alternatives.

Problem 7

ITA: 37; ITR: 2900(2), 2900(3), 2903

Joe's Widget Manufacturers Inc. (JWMI) is an established manufacturing company with a growing research and development (R&D) department. JWMI is a Canadian-controlled private corporation with no associated companies. The research part of the business is new and the company's accountant has no experience dealing with the tax implications of the expenditures in this area. He has correctly computed the company's net income for tax purposes before specific R&D related adjustments as $615,000 and would like your input on the impact of the transactions described below.

For the year ended December 31, 2007, the following R&D related expenditures were made.

Description	*Amount*
Purchase of lab machinery and lab equipment	$450,000
Purchase of building to house laboratory	120,000
Salaries of lab staff	100,000
Operating costs directly related to the lab	40,000

The lab machinery, equipment and building are used 100% for R&D activities. The lab machinery and equipment have been capitalized for accounting purposes and are being amortized over an eight-year period (net of available investment tax credits as set out below). Thus, amortization expense of $36,562 was recorded for accounting purposes on the lab machinery and equipment. Depreciation expense of $4,800 was recorded on the building.

The company is eligible for investment tax credits at a rate of 35% and has correctly determined that they are eligible for investment tax credits at this rate on all of the above expenditures with the exception of the building. No investment tax credit is allowable on the purchase price of the building. For accounting purposes, the company's accountant has netted the investment tax credits against the related expenditures as follows.

Expenditure	*Gross amount*	*ITC*	*Amount recorded for accounting purposes*
Lab machinery and equipment . . .	$450,000	$157,500	$292,500
Building	120,000	0	120,000
Salaries of lab staff	100,000	35,000	65,000
Operating costs of lab	40,000	14,000	26,000

— REQUIRED

Based on the above information, explain to JWMI's accountant the adjustments necessary in computing income for tax purposes for the years ended December 31, 2007 and 2008.

Problem 8

ITA: 9–12, 18–20, 37, 67.1, 78, 147

The *unaudited* income statement for Lomas & Sons Limited for its year ended December 31, 2007 shows the following:

Sales		$ 795,000
Cost of sales	$350,000	
General and administrative expenses	225,000	
Research and development expenditures	76,700	(651,700)
Operating income		$ 143,300
Other income		20,000
Net income before taxes		$ 163,300
Provision for income taxes:		
— current	$ 27,000	
— future	25,000	(52,000)
Net income after income taxes		$ 111,300

The information in the following notes has already been reflected in the above income statement.

(1) Payment made by company on April 1, 2008, to a defined contribution (money-purchase) registered pension plan for the president of the company in respect of current employment service, allocated to 2007 expenses by the company's accountant; in addition, the president had $7,500 withheld from his compensation of $74,000 for the RPP . . . . $ 7,000

(2) Increase in warranty reserve on company's product (net of expense incurred; based on self-insurance warranty program) 16,000

(3) Depreciation expense recorded in the financial statements 30,000

(4) Landscaping costs re: factory premises 2,500

(5) Interest on bank loan obtained for the purpose of purchasing common shares in Advanco Ltd., a dividend-paying Canadian corporation 6,300

(6) Legal costs of arranging an agreement among shareholders 8,500

(7) Legal and accounting fees related to issue of shares 12,700

(8) Interest on municipal real estate taxes paid late in error 1,000

(9) Golf club membership fees 2,200

(10) Donation to United Way 3,000

(11) Meals and entertainment for clients 4,000

(12) Appraisal fees to determine selling price of fixed assets 6,200

(13) Premium on term insurance on life of president with the corporation as beneficiary; policy was not required to be assigned as collateral for corporate borrowing from the bank 2,800

(14) Management bonuses ($20,000 of the bonuses expensed in 2007, and shown as "Bonus Payable" on the Balance Sheet as at December 31, 2007 has not been paid at the time of filing the corporate tax return on June 30, 2008) 40,000

(15) Amortization of bond discount on bonds issued in 2002 3,400

(16) The company has capitalized and will amortize over five years $90,000 of costs incurred in 2007 related to the purchase of machinery to be used for qualifying research and development. The resultant amortization of the net cost after the investment tax credit was $11,700 and is included in the income statement deduction for research and development expenditures. As well, the company incurred current research and development expenditures of $100,000. These current expenditures will qualify the company for an investment tax credit of $35,000. The $35,000 has been deducted from the expenditure on SR&ED, as shown in the income statement. In the previous year, the company made $95,000 in qualifying SR&ED current expenditures. The company claimed an investment tax credit of $33,250 in respect of these current expenditures.

(17) Interest and penalties on income tax assessments, expensed for accounting purposes 1,250

(18) Items included in the financial accounting statements in arriving at the net profit:

Amount paid by an insurance company on its business interruption insurance to compensate for loss of profits when company was closed down for a month during the year because of a fire 26,800

Dividends received 1,700

Volume rebates and purchase discount 16,000

— *REQUIRED*

Based on the foregoing information, compute the income from business or property for tax purposes, ignoring tax deductions in respect of depreciable capital or eligible capital property for Lomas and Sons Limited in respect of its 2007 fiscal year. In addition, comment on all items not included in your derivation of income from business or property.

Problem 9

ETA: 123(1), 161, 164, 169(1), 170(1)(*a*), 232, 236, Sched. V, Part VII

Reconsider the facts of Problem 8.

— *REQUIRED*

(A) Outline the general GST requirements applicable in this corporate situation.

(B) Indicate which of the items listed in the additional information notes represent costs incurred for:

　　1. taxable supplies, eligible for an ITC, and

　　2. exempt supplies, not eligible for an ITC.

(C) Comment on the appropriate GST treatment of the other items listed in the additional information notes and on the income statement.

[For more problems and solutions thereto, see the CD accompanying this book.]

¶4,880   ADVISORY CASE

London City Electronics Inc.

London City Electronics Inc. has been a client of yours since it started in business five years ago. Dave Birr, the founder, has been very successful with his main product, which is a valve that measures and controls the flow of liquids. It is now the middle of March and you have just started your review engagement field work for the company's December year end when Dave asks you to come into his office to talk to him.

The first thing you do is congratulate him on the good year he had last year. His sales, gross profit, and net income are all up substantially over the previous year. You are surprised when he starts to complain about the poor results so far this year. He indicates that his customers are just now starting to stretch their payments because they are facing increased competition from imports. In fact, one of his customers has given London City Electronics some of its products in exchange for the amount it owed.

To compound this problem, Dave has had some quality control problems in his manufacturing process and he has been receiving a large number of warranty claims. Sometimes he is able to repair the valve before there is significant cost to the customer, but in some cases the customer has had financial losses as a result of the faulty valve.

Dave would like your advice on the tax implications of his situation.

¶4,900   SUPPLEMENTAL NOTES

(This section can be omitted without losing the continuity of the chapter. None of the review questions, multiple choice questions, exercises, or assignment problems utilizes this information.)

¶4,910   Adjustment for Depreciation Allocation in Inventory: An Illustration of the Effect

To illustrate how the legislation deals with the problem of depreciation in inventory, the following example, which expands a similar example used in the Appendix to IT-473R, is presented.

Assumed facts:	Year 1	Year 2
Inventory at beginning of year	Nil	$ 20,000
Cost of goods sold (COGS)	$100,000	200,000
Inventory at end of year	20,000	25,000
Depreciation for year	35,000	80,000
Depreciation included in closing inventory	7,000	10,000
Net income for year per financial statements	50,000	90,000
Amount of depreciation allocated under absorption costing:		
Opening inventory	Nil	$ 7,000
Cost of goods manufactured	$ 35,000	80,000
	$ 35,000	$ 87,000
Closing inventory	(7,000)	(10,000)
Cost of goods sold	$ 28,000	$ 77,000

	Absorption costing — Depreciation allocated to cost of goods sold		Direct costing — Depreciation not allocated to cost of goods sold	
	Year 1	Year 2	Year 1	Year 2
Cost of goods sold:				
Opening inventory	Nil	$ 20,000	Nil	$ 13,000
Cost of goods manufactured	$120,000	205,000	$ 85,000	125,000
	$120,000	$225,000	$ 85,000	$138,000
Closing inventory	(20,000)	(25,000)	(13,000)	(15,000)
Cost of goods sold	$100,000	$200,000	$ 72,000	$123,000
Income for accounting purposes:				
Revenue	$150,000	$290,000	$150,000	$290,000
Cost of goods sold	(100,000)	(200,000)	(72,000)	(123,000)
Unallocated depreciation	Nil	Nil	(35,000)	(80,000)
Net income (accounting)	$ 50,000	$ 90,000	$ 43,000	$ 87,000
Reconciliation to income for tax purposes:				
Net income (accounting)	$ 50,000	$ 90,000	$ 43,000	$ 87,000
Add: depreciation deducted	28,000	77,000	35,000	80,000
Net income before par. 12(1)(r) and par. 20(1)(ii) adjustments	$ 78,000	$167,000	$ 78,000	$167,000
Add: par. 12(1)(r) adjustment	7,000	10,000	Nil	Nil
	$ 85,000	$177,000	$ 78,000	$167,000
Less: par. 20(1)(ii) adjustment	Nil	7,000	Nil	Nil
Net income (tax) before capital cost allowance	$ 85,000	$170,000	$ 78,000	$167,000

Note that the income for tax purposes before capital cost allowance is higher under absorption costing. What is, in total, the full depreciation allocated to the cost of goods manufactured is added back, notwithstanding the fact that the depreciation content in closing inventory was not expensed in the year through the cost of goods sold calculation. While the excess add-back is corrected in the following year by the deduction permitted, it is not clear why those adjustments are necessary. Note that if no adjustments had been made for absorption costing, the net income for tax purposes before capital cost allowance in both years would have been the same as that under direct costing. (See the third line under "Reconciliation to income for tax purposes", above.)

ITA: 12(1)(*r*)

ITA: 20(1)(*ii*)

The amendments introducing these adjustments followed the case of *Quebec North Shore Paper Co. v. The Queen*, in which the Federal Court–Trial Division held that absorption costing which allocates both variable and fixed overheads including depreciation without the adjustments introduced subsequently was the correct method of reconciling net income. It would now appear that direct costing which allocates variable overheads (excluding depreciation) to inventory and which is acceptable to the CRA is preferable because it provides the lower income for tax purposes as illustrated above.

ITA: 12(1)(*r*), 20(1)(*ii*)
78 DTC 6426 (F.C.T.D.)

IT-473R, par. 8

¶4,920 Unregistered Employee Compensation Plans

The type of plan envisaged by the legislation in this area is a benefit arrangement involving an employer contribution to a plan that is not registered under the Act, unlike a registered pension plan or a deferred profit sharing plan. Typical of these unregistered plans is a benefit that is received by the employee at some time after the contribution is made by the employer. The effect of the legislation is to prevent a time lag between the time the employer obtains a deduction for the contribution and the time the employee must include in income an amount received from such a plan.

One type of unregistered plan is termed an "employee benefit plan" which is defined. It is an arrangement under which an employer makes contributions to a "custodian" and under which payments are made for the benefit of employees and certain other persons. The Act denies a deduction of the contributions by the employer at the time they are made. However, the Act permits the deduction by the employer of amounts *paid* under the plan to employees in excess of the income of the plan for the year. At this time, the employee must include in income all amounts received from such a plan unless these amounts are specifically exempted by that paragraph. Tax on income from investments in the plan must be paid each year by the plan itself, by the employer or by the employee if the earnings are distributed.

ITA: 6(1)(*g*), 248(1)

ITA: 18(1)(*o*)
ITA: 32.1

Employee benefit plans became particularly popular in situations where the employer was not taxable either because the employer was in a loss position or because the employer was a non-taxable entity. In these cases, the employer's deduction on contributions was of no consequence. In fact, earnings of the plan could be paid out to such employers and contributed back to the plan with no tax consequences. The result was an indefinite deferral of income for the employee. By including the concept of an employee benefit plan in the definition of a "salary deferral arrangement", the legislation now prevents this deferral of salary without eliminating employee benefit plans involving deferrals that relate to services rendered before July 1986. As discussed in Chapter 3, remuneration deferred by an employee through a "salary deferral arrangement" is taxed on an accrual rather than a cash basis. The deferred remuneration is deductible immediately to the employer. A "salary deferral arrangement" is defined as one that has a main purpose to defer the receipt of remuneration that would otherwise have been paid for services rendered in the year or a preceding year. It excludes a registered pension plan, a profit sharing plan and other statutory plans. It also excludes such arrangements as those governing sabbaticals for teachers and compensation for services as a professional athlete.

ITA: 248(1) "salary deferral arrangement"

Until amendments were made in 1987, the employee benefit plan legislation permitted the deferral of tax on certain pension and retirement arrangements that were not registered plans like RPPs, RRSPs, or DPSPs. To remove the tax benefits from the use of these unregistered plans, rules for retirement compensation arrangements (RCAs) were added to the Act. A "retirement compensation arrangement" is defined at length, with exclusions, to mean, in

ITA: 248(1)

part, a plan or arrangement between an employer and an employee under which contributions are made by the employer to a custodian. The custodian would be required to make payments to the employee on, after or in contemplation of the employee's retirement or loss of an office or employment.

Contributions made by an employer to an RCA are subject to the withholding of a special refundable tax of 50%. The employer receives a deduction for the contribution. Income of the plan, including dividends (without the gross-up) and capital gains, is also subject to the 50% refundable tax. When retirement benefits are paid by the custodian to the employee, the tax is refunded at the rate of $1 of refund for each $2 paid to the employee. Payments received by an employee as benefits from an RCA are included in computing the employee's income. The payment of a 50% refundable tax on contributions to the plan and on income earned in the plan removes any deductibility or deferral advantage between the time the employer receives a deduction for contributions and the time the employee receives an amount to be included in income.

ITA: 207.5
ITA: 20(1)(r)

ITA: 56(1)(x)

Another type of unregistered plan is termed an "employee trust", which is a defined term where certain qualifying conditions are set out for such a plan. Under this type of plan, which is similar to an employees' profit sharing plan, employer contributions and income of the plan are allocated to employees when made or earned respectively. Employer contributions are deductible when made and, at the same time, the employee must include in income all amounts allocated. As a result, the benefits from such a trust are not taxed when received by the employee. The effect is the same as a salary deferral arrangement described above.

ITA: 248(1)
ITA: 6(1)(h)

Chapter 5

Depreciable Property and Eligible Capital Property

LEARNING GOALS

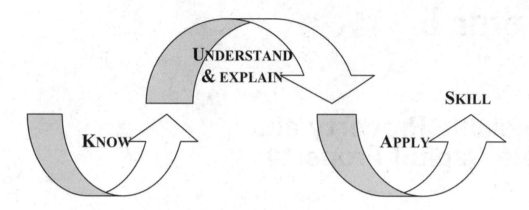

Know

By the end of this chapter you should know the basic provisions of the *Income Tax Act*, and the *Excise Tax Act*, pertaining to the GST, that relate to depreciable and eligible capital property. Completing the Review Questions (¶5,800) and Multiple Choice Questions (¶5,825) is a good way to learn the technical provisions.

Understand and Explain

You should understand and be able to explain how to calculate capital cost allowance and cumulative eligible capital amount, which is the tax equivalent of amortization for capital and intangible property. Completing the Exercises (¶5,850) is a good way to deepen your understanding of the material.

Apply

You should be able to use your knowledge and understanding of depreciable and eligible capital property to advise taxpayers on the tax implications of the purchase of these assets. Completing the Assignment Problems (¶5,875) is an excellent way to develop your ability to apply the material in increasingly complex situations.

OVERVIEW

The system in the Act for amortizing the capital cost of depreciable property and intangibles is fairly straightforward in its concept. Depreciable property write-offs are not encumbered by many of the complicated rules and computations necessary for the financial accounting. However, economic policy incentives to invest in depreciable property are reflected in the rates and methods of write-off of cost.

Although the rules pertaining to depreciable property and eligible capital property (intangibles) have many similarities, the differences require separate discussion in the two major sections of this chapter. The third major section of the chapter discusses the input tax credit system under the GST pertaining to capital property.

The following chart shows that the above rules related to deductions for depreciable and eligible capital property are found in Subdivision b (income or loss from a business or property) of Division B of the Act and in the Regulations.

PART I — DIVISION B
SUBDIVISION b
BUSINESS OR PROPERTY

DIVISION		SUBDIVISION		SECTION	
A	Liability for tax		Basic rules		
B	**Computation of income**	a	Office or employment		
C	Computation of taxable income	**b**	**Business or property**	9-11	Basic rules
D	Taxable income earned in Canada by non-residents	c	Capital gains and losses	12-17	Inclusions
E	Computation of tax	d	Other income	**18-21 20(1)**	**Deductions (incl. CCA/CECA)**
E.1	Minimum tax	e	Other deductions	22-25	Ceasing to carry on business
F	Special rules	f	Rules relating to computation of income	26-37	Special cases
G	Deferred and other special income arrangements	g	Amounts not included in income		
H	Exemptions	h	Cdn corporations and shareholders		
I	Returns, Assessments, payments, appeals	i	Shareholders of non-resident corporations		
J	Appeals to the courts	j	Partnerships		
		k	Trusts		

The major rules related to these deductions are found in the following parts of the Act:

Depreciable capital property

Inclusions:

Ssec. 13(1)	Recaptured CCA
Ssec. 13(2)	Luxury automobiles
Ssec. 13(4)	Replacement property
Ssec. 13(7)	Special rules
Ssec. 13(21)	Definitions
Ssec. 13(21.1)	Loss on certain transfers within affiliated groups
Ssec. 13(26)	Available for use

Deductions:

Par. 18(1)(*b*)	No deduction for depreciation
Par. 20(1)(*a*)	Deduction for capital cost allowance
Ssec. 20(16)	Terminal loss
Reg. 1100	CCA rules
Reg. 7307(1)	CCA limits on automobiles
Reg. Sch. II–VI	Classes of property

Eligible capital property

Inclusions

Ssec. 14(1)	Recaptured CECA
Ssec. 14(3)	Acquisition of eligible capital property
Ssec. 14(5)	Definitions
Ssec. 14(6)	Replacement property
Ssec. 14(12)	Loss on certain transfers within affiliated groups

Deductions

Par. 18(1)(*b*)	No deduction for depreciation
Par. 20(1)(*b*)	Deduction for cumulative eligible capital amount

¶5,000　THE CAPITAL COST ALLOWANCE SYSTEM

¶5,010　Basic Rules

¶5,015　Classes of assets for tangible capital property

¶5,015.10　*Common classes*

An important feature of the capital cost allowance system is the grouping of depreciable property into prescribed classes which are established by the Regulations (Part XI and Schedule II, primarily). When a taxpayer has a number of properties within a particular class, the properties of that class are treated as one unit for the purposes of capital cost allowances. Classes for some of the more common assets are contained in the following list:

ITA: 13(21)

Class 1 (4%)	— most buildings or other structures, including component parts such as electrical wiring and fixtures, plumbing, heating and central air conditioning, acquired after 1987;
[Class MB (10%)	— the March 19, 2007 federal budget proposed to increase the CCA rate from 4% to 10% for buildings used at least 90% (measured by square footage) for manufacturing and processing purposes. This applies to buildings acquired on or after March 19, 2007. Each building added to this class will be put in its own separate class. Since the details at the time of writing were not available, we will refer to this as Class MB to represent Manufacturing Buildings.
Class NRB (6%)	— the March 19, 2007 federal budget proposed to increase the CCA rate from 4% to 6% for non-residential buildings. This applies to buildings acquired on or after March 19, 2007. Each building added to this class will be put in its own separate class. Since the details at the time of writing were not available, we will refer to this as Class NRB to represent Non-Residential Buildings.]
Class 8 (20%)	— miscellaneous tangible capital property, such as furniture, fixtures, and outdoor advertising signs (bought after 1987), and machinery or equipment, such as photocopiers, refrigeration equipment, telephones, and tools costing $200 [$500 proposed by the May 2, 2006 federal budget for tools acquired on or after that date] or more, not included in another class (i.e., general default class for tangible capital property);
Class 9 (25%)	— aircraft, including furniture or equipment attached to the aircraft, and spare parts;
Class 10 (30%)	— automotive equipment, such as automobiles (except taxis and those used in a daily rental business), vans, trucks, tractors, wagons and trailers, and general-purpose electronic data processing equipment with its systems software acquired before March 23, 2004;

Class 10.1 (30%)	— a passenger vehicle with a cost in excess of the prescribed limit (i.e., $30,000 if acquired after 2000);	ITA: 13(7)(g)
Class 12 (100%)	— tools, instruments, and kitchen utensils costing less than $200 [$500 proposed by the May 2, 2006 federal budget for tools acquired on or after that date]; linen, uniforms, dies, jigs, or moulds; rental video cassettes; computer software;	
Class 13	— leasehold interest;	
Class 14	— patent,[1] franchise, concession or licence for a limited period;	
Class 17 (8%)	— roads, parking lots, sidewalks, airplane runways, storage areas, or similar surface construction;	
Class 39 (25%)	— property used in manufacturing or processing acquired after 1987 and before February 26, 1992;	
Class 43 (30%)	— manufacturing and processing machinery and equipment acquired after February 25, 1992;	
[Class ME (50%)	— The March 19, 2007 federal budget proposed to temporarily increase the CCA rate for manufacturing and processing machinery and equipment that would otherwise be included in Class 43 to a 50% straight-line rate. The half-year rule will apply. This applies to property acquired on or after March 19, 2007, and before 2009. Since the details at the time of writing were not available, we will refer to this as Class ME to represent Manufacturing Equipment.]	
Class 44 (25%)[1]	— patents and rights to use patented information acquired after April 26, 1993, for a limited or unlimited period;	
Class 45 (45%)	— general-purpose electronic data processing and ancillary equipment acquired after March 22, 2004 and systems software;	
[Class CE (55%)	— The March 19, 2007 federal budget proposed to increase the CCA rate for computers that currently qualify for Class 45 from 45% to 55%. This applies to property acquired on or after March 19, 2007. Since the details at the time of writing were not available, we will refer to this as Class CE to represent Computer Equipment.]	

A convenient alphabetical list of many depreciable assets can be found in an "Alphabetical List of Assets" in the preface materials and in the Topical Index to the CCH edition of the INCOME TAX ACT, under the heading "capital cost allowance". However, the latter listing contains only property specifically itemized in the class descriptions. Hence, property referred to in more general terms in the class description may not appear in the list.

¶5,015.20   *Basic rules of the system*

The basic rules of the capital cost allowance system are illustrated in Exhibit 5-1 and can be stated for many classes quite simply as follows:

(a) whenever an asset of a particular class is purchased, the full purchase cost (capital cost) is added to the balance known as undepreciated capital cost (UCC) of the class of assets;   ITA: 13(21)

(b) whenever an asset of a particular class is sold under conditions set out in the definition of "disposition of property", the full proceeds of disposition, not in excess of original cost (i.e., the lesser of proceeds and capital cost), is subtracted from the balance in the class of assets (proceeds in excess of capital cost may give rise to a capital gain); and   ITA: 13(21)

(c) at the end of the taxation year,

(i) if the balance in the class of assets (i.e., UCC) is positive and there are still assets in that class,

(A) subtract from the balance in the account ½ of the excess, if any, of purchases minus disposals made in the year (i.e., ½ × (a − b) above),   ITR: 1100(2)

---

[1] Regulation 1103(2h) provides that taxpayers may elect not to use Class 44 for such patents, in which case the property will be classified in Class 14.

(B) deduct up to the maximum capital cost allowance (CCA) at the prescribed rate for the class on the positive balance, and

ITA: 20(1)(*a*)

(C) add back the ½ of the net amount subtracted in (A) above;

(ii) if the balance in the class of assets is negative, take the negative balance into income as recaptured capital cost allowance and set the balance in the class at zero; and

ITA: 13(1)

(iii) if the balance in the class of assets is positive, but all of the assets in the class have been disposed of such that there are no more assets physically in the class, take the positive balance, known as a terminal loss, as a deduction from income and set the balance in the class at zero.

ITA: 20(16)

EXHIBIT 5-1
Basic Rules of the Capital Cost Allowance System
Applied to a Prescribed Class of Assets

Undepreciated capital cost of the class at the beginning of the year	$ xxx	
Add: purchases during the year	xxx	
	$ xxx	
Deduct: dispositions during the year at the lesser of (LOCP):		
(a) capital cost . . . . $ xxx		
(b) proceeds of disposition . . . . $ xxx	(xxx)	
Undepreciated capital cost before adjustment	$ xxx	
Deduct: ½ net amount*	(xxx)	
Undepreciated capital cost before CCA	$ xxx	
Deduct: capital cost allowance in the class for the year	(xxx)	
Add: ½ net amount*	xxx	
Undepreciated capital cost of the class at the beginning of the following year	$ xxx	

---

  * Purchases during the year . . . . $ xxx
     Deduct: lesser of capital cost and proceeds of disposition above . . . . (xxx)
     Net amount (positive amounts only) . . . . $ xxx

Note that the central definition is that of undepreciated capital cost. The capital letters in brackets shown after each item below coincide with the letters in the algebraic formula in the definition. Some of the less mainstream items have been omitted. The definition can be paraphrased, in part, as:

ITA: 13(21)

the sum of:

    (a) the capital cost of depreciable property (A),

    (b) all amounts previously included in income as recapture (B), and

    (c) all amounts of grants and other assistance deemed to be capital cost that were repaid (C)

ITA: 13(7.1)

less the sum of:

    (a) total depreciation previously allowed (E),

ITA: 20(1)(*a*), 20(16)

    (b) for dispositions the lesser of (i) proceeds of disposition net of expenses of disposition and (ii) capital cost (F),

    (c) all amounts of investment tax credit claimed (I), and

ITA: 127(5) or 127(6)

(d) grants and other assistance received or receivable (J).   ITA: 13(7.1)(*f*)

¶5,015.30   *The half-year rule*

The half-year rule, illustrated above, as set out in the Regulations under the heading "Property Acquired in the Year", applies to all classes *except* the following: ITR: 1100(2)

(a) property described in the Regulations pertaining to certified vessels;   ITR: 1100(1)(*v*)

(b) Class 12 paragraphs (*a*) to (*c*), (*e*) to (*i*), (*k*), (*l*), and (*p*) to (*s*) in Schedule II; and

(c) Classes 13, 14, 15, 23, 24, 27, 29, and 34 in Schedule II.

However, despite these exceptions, an adjustment similar in effect to the half-year rule is provided for some classes as follows:

(a) property described as certified vessels in the Regulations;   ITR: 1100(1)(*v*)(iv)

(b) property of Class 13 in Schedule II (leasehold improvements); and   ITR: 1100(1)(*b*)

(c) property of Classes 24, 27, 29, and 34 (some accelerated write-off classes) in Schedule II.   ITR: 1100(1)(*t*), 1100(1)(*ta*)

Thus, it would appear that the only property for which some form of adjustment to reflect the half-year rule is *not* made is the following:

(a) property in Class 12 paragraphs (*a*) to (*c*), (*e*) to (*i*), (*k*), (*l*), (*p*) to (*s*); and

(b) property in Classes 14, 15, and 23.

Exhibit 5-2 lists some common capital property not affected in some manner by the half-year rule. Some of these classes will be discussed further in this chapter.   ITR: 1100(2)

EXHIBIT 5-2
Common Property not Affected by Half-Year Rule

Class	Paragraph	Property
12	(*a*) . . .	a book that is a part of a lending library
	(*b*) . . .	chinaware, cutlery or other tableware
	(*c*) . . .	a kitchen utensil costing less than $200
	(*e*) . . .	a medical or dental instrument costing less than $200
	(*g*) . . .	linen
	(*h*) . . .	a tool costing less than $200 [$500 proposed by the May 2, 2006 federal budget]
	(*i*) . . .	a uniform
	(*k*) . . .	rental apparel or costume, including accessories
14		a patent, franchise, concession or licence for a limited period

---

The half-year rule adjustment was implemented to correct the fact that assets purchased at the end of a taxation year would, otherwise, provide a balance in a class that would be eligible for the maximum capital cost allowance in the year. By effectively reducing the capital cost allowance on purchases (in excess of dispositions) during the year, whenever they are made, the advantage of a late purchase is reduced. Hence, the Act uses a simple, arbitrary adjustment as an alternative to adjusting for the period of ownership during the year of acquisition or disposition.

Notice that no adjustments other than the half-year rule adjustment are made for the length of time in the year that an asset is owned. An asset purchased near the end of the year will normally increase the balance in the asset class resulting in a one-half capital cost allowance claim for the year for that asset net of dispositions. On the other hand, an asset sold near the end of the year will normally reduce the balance in the asset class resulting in a decrease in the amount subject to the capital cost allowance for the year.

¶5,015.40 *Available-for-use rule*

Taxpayers may not start claiming capital cost allowance until the property has become "available for use" by the taxpayer. Very generally, the property is available for use when it is delivered and capable of performing the function for which it was acquired. A building is available for use at the earlier of:

ITA: 13(26)
ITA: 13(27)–(32)
ITA: 13(28)

    (a) when all or substantially all of the building is first used for its intended purpose, and

    (b) the second taxation year after the year of acquisition.

These rules must be consulted for their application to a specific asset under the particular conditions of the asset's purchase.

Since an asset is eligible for a capital cost allowance claim in the year in which it becomes available for use, the half-year rule applies to the asset in that year.

ITR: 1100(2)

A similar rule pertaining to capital expenditures in respect of scientific research and experimental development applies.

ITA: 37(1.2)

¶5,015.50 *CCA as a permissive deduction*

The rate of capital cost allowance applied to each class is specified as a maximum rate. The taxpayer may, therefore, claim any amount of capital cost allowance up to a maximum of the amount given by the capital cost allowance rate multiplied by the balance in the class at the end of the taxation year. Under certain conditions, it may be advantageous for the taxpayer to take less than the maximum amount of capital cost allowance allowed. Only the amount actually taken is deducted from the balance in the class of assets. The remaining balance is carried forward and is available for future capital cost allowance claims. In IC 84-1, the Canada Revenue Agency (CRA) indicates some conditions under which it will accept a request from a taxpayer to reassess a return for a previous year to adjust a permissive deduction such as capital cost allowance.

¶5,020 Taxation year less than 12 months

The statement has been made previously that there is no need to prorate capital cost allowance (other than through the half-year rule adjustment) for the period in a taxation year that an asset was owned by the taxpayer. This applies to full 12-month taxation years. However, in the first or last years of the operation of a business or in a year in which there has been a change in fiscal year, it is possible to have a taxation year of less than a full 12 months. In this case, capital cost allowance must be prorated by the proportion that the number of days in the taxation year is of 365. Hence, the proration pertains only to a short taxation year. It is completely independent of the half-year rule adjustment which must be made, where applicable, irrespective of the length of the taxation year.

ITR: 1100(3)

A common exception to this short-year proration rule is Class 14, which includes limited-life patents, franchises, licences, etc. However, as will be seen later in this chapter, there is a proration of capital cost allowance for assets in Class 14 based on the number of days the asset is owned in a taxation year. Therefore, the effect is quite similar to the short-year proration rule.

ITR: 1100(3)

Note that an employee does not have to prorate the capital cost allowance on his or her automobile in the first year of use of an existing car for employment purposes, although the half-year rule applies to the purchase of a new automobile. Also, where depreciable capital property is used by an individual to produce income from a source that is property (e.g., rental income), rather than business, the full calendar year is considered to be the taxation year of the individual and, therefore, no prorating is necessary.

IT-522R, par. 24

¶5,015.40

¶5,025　Ownership of property

Generally, in order to be eligible for capital cost allowance on depreciable property, the taxpayer must have either title to the asset or all the incidents of title such as possession, use and risk. An exception is Class 13 leasehold improvements that are made by the tenant but the owner of the building has title to the improvements.

In some circumstances, a taxpayer does not always have ownership or a leasehold interest (Class 13) in a capital asset for which he or she has incurred a cost. In this situation the cost incurred does not give rise to a claim for capital cost allowance. Capital cost allowance may not be claimed for such an expenditure. This was the situation in *Saskatoon Community Broadcasting Co. Ltd. v. M.N.R.*, in which the appellant constructed at its cost a new broadcasting gondola in an arena and was given the sole right to use the new gondola, but the facility was the property of the arena company. In this case, the construction costs were held to be a non-deductible capital outlay and the broadcasting company could not take capital cost allowance because it did not own the property and it did not have a leasehold interest in the facility. Under the tax legislation in force since 1972, this type of expenditure would be considered an eligible capital expenditure. This concept will be discussed later in this chapter.

IT-128R, par. 3
58 DTC 491 (T.A.B.)

IT-143R2

¶5,030　Disposition of property

A disposition of property is defined to *include* "any transaction or event entitling a taxpayer to proceeds of disposition of the property". The use of the word "include" in the definition does not necessarily limit the meaning of disposition of property to a situation where there are proceeds of disposition. Thus, the CRA gives examples of events that it considers to be dispositions without any actual proceeds, including cases of property that is stolen, destroyed, confiscated or expropriated without any compensation or property that is lost or abandoned without expectation of recovery. Furthermore, in the case of *The Queen v. Compagnie Immobilière BCN Limitée*, the Supreme Court of Canada indicated that a claim for capital cost allowance could not be made in lieu of a terminal loss deduction when a building no longer existed. Thus, capital cost allowance can only be claimed when property in a class continues to exist. This follows from the operation of the system in which no claim can be made for capital cost allowance on an asset in the year of its disposition.

ITA: 248(1)
ITA: 13(21)

IT-460, par. 3

79 DTC 5068 (S.C.C.)

¶5,035　Automobiles used in employment or business

¶5,035.10　*Class 10.1 automobiles*

Recall that employees who use their own automobiles to earn employment income and who are entitled to a deduction:

- for sales/negotiating person's expenses,

- for travel expenses (other than motor vehicle expenses), or

- for motor vehicle expenses

are entitled to deduct capital cost allowance on the automobiles.

ITA: 8(1)(*f*)

ITA: 8(1)(*h*)

ITA: 8(1)(*h*.1)

ITA: 8(1)(*j*)

Where an automobile is used to earn income from business, capital cost allowance is also deductible. In either case, the capital cost used as the basis for capital cost allowance is limited to $30,000 plus federal sales tax (i.e., GST) and provincial sales tax (PST) (for acquisitions after 2000) for all taxpayers, whether employed or self-employed and whether incorporated or unincorporated. In the case of a registrant, since the input tax credit resulting from a purchase is used immediately to offset the GST paid, there is no effective GST cost to add to capital cost and, therefore, GST is excluded.

ITR: 7307(1)(*b*)
ITA: 13(7)(*g*), 13(7)(*h*)

ITA: 248(16)

Furthermore, the rules relating to recapture of capital cost allowance and terminal losses do not apply to automobiles having a cost in excess of the prescribed limit. For this reason, each automobile, having a cost in excess of $30,000 plus PST and GST, must be placed in a separate Class 10.1 and not pooled.

ITA: 13(2), 20(16.1)

ITR: 1101(1af)

Since the terminal loss rules do not apply to automobiles in Class 10.1, a special capital cost allowance calculation applies in the year of disposition. In the year of disposition of the automobile, one-half of the capital cost allowance that would have been allowed in respect of the automobile, had it not been disposed of, may be deducted. To qualify for this special "half-year rule", the taxpayer must have disposed of an automobile that was included in Class 10.1 and was owned by him or her at the end of the preceding year.

ITR: 1100(2.5)

¶5,035.20 *Class 10 automobiles*

For automobiles that are not included in Class 10.1, but are in Class 10 because they cost less than the prescribed limit, the amount of capital cost allowance claimed is subject to recapture, if the automobile was owned by an employee. A terminal loss on the disposition of the automobile is not allowed as a deduction from employment income. The only deduction in respect of the capital cost of an automobile allowed as an employment income deduction which allows such part of the capital cost "as is allowed by regulation". A terminal loss is not allowed by regulation. Since a terminal loss is not specifically allowed as a deduction from employment income, the Act would prohibit its deduction.

ITA: 13(1), 13(11)

ITA: 8(1)(*j*)(ii)

ITA: 8(1), 8(2)

When an automobile costs less than the prescribed limit and is owned by a taxpayer other than an employee, the usual rules for deducting capital cost allowance, subject to the half-year rule, including recapture, or deducting a terminal loss apply. Hence, these usual rules would apply to an automobile used in a business by and owned by, for example, a proprietor, a partner or a corporation.

¶5,040 Comparison of capital cost allowance and depreciation

¶5,040.10 *Main differences*

Although capital cost allowance for tangible capital assets is the tax equivalent of depreciation there are a number of important differences which give rise to the need for future income tax accounting. While financial accounting uses useful life as the basis of the write-off of a capital expenditure, the tax system might be based on useful life, legal life (as in the case of leasehold improvements or patents) or fiscal policy. While accounting depreciation must adhere to the principles of consistency, the tax system allows for a deduction of any amount up to the maximum permitted for each class. For accounting purposes, differences between book value and proceeds of disposition are considered gains or losses on the sale of an asset. However, the tax system provides for the write-off of the actual decline in value of assets during their holding period. The system requires the inclusion in income of recapture of capital cost allowance where the capital cost allowance deductions have resulted in an undepreciated capital cost that is less than the proceeds of disposition, and the recognition of a terminal loss where capital cost allowance deductions did not fully reflect the decreased value of the asset pool. Under appropriate circumstances, the sale of an asset may also result in a capital gain. However, there can never, under any circumstances, be a capital loss on depreciable capital property. All declines in value are handled through the capital cost allowance deduction and the final adjustment through either recapture or a terminal loss.

¶5,040.20 *Recapture and terminal loss*

The role of the recapture and terminal loss concepts in the capital cost allowance system is to provide for a deduction for tax purposes of the full decline in value of assets over the period of their use. Thus, capital cost allowance will be recaptured when proceeds of disposition exceed undepreciated capital cost, i.e., when assets in a class have been over-depreciated relative to their disposal value as in the following case where there has been no decline in value of the assets:

Capital cost	$10,000	→ Previously claimed as CCA
Proceeds	8,000	Recapture of CCA claimed → reflecting disposition
Undepreciated capital cost	7,000	value in excess of UCC

Similarly, a terminal loss provides for a deduction when proceeds of disposition are less than undepreciated capital cost and there are no assets remaining in the class, i.e., when assets in a class have been under-depreciated relative to their disposal value as in the following case where the decline in value of the assets exceeds the amount of capital cost allowance previously taken:

Capital cost $10,000
Undepreciated capital cost　7,000　⎤→ Terminal loss reflecting additional decline in
Proceeds . . . .　5,000 ⎦→ value over $3,000 of CCA previously claimed

¶5,045 Separate class rule for electronic office equipment

Taxpayers may elect to place one or more specified properties that would ordinarily be classified in Class 8 or Class 10 in a separate class. The specified properties are: ITR: 1101(5p)

(a) general purpose electronic data processing equipment and systems software, normally included in paragraph (*f*) of Class 10;

(b) computer software, presumably systems software for electronic process control or monitor equipment and electronic communications control equipment, normally classified in Class 8 (i.e., not classified in Class 10 or Class 12);

(c) a photocopier, normally included in Class 8; and

(d) electronic communications equipment, such as a facsimile transmission device or telephone equipment, normally included in Class 8.

Property placed in separate classes in this manner must have a capital cost of at least $1,000.

The election allows one or more such properties to be placed in a separate Class 8 or Class 10. The advantage of the separate class would be the availability of a terminal loss deduction when all of the assets in such a class are sold for less than the UCC of that class. If assets of this nature decline in value more rapidly than the CCA rates of 20% for Class 8 and 30% for Class 10 imply, perhaps due to technological obsolescence, then a terminal loss on disposition is likely if these assets are separated from other Class 8 or Class 10 assets.

A special transfer rule allows the transfer of Class 8 and Class 10 assets of a separate class back to their main Class 8 or Class 10 after four taxation years. Hence, if the assets in a separate class have not been disposed of after the four-year period from the end of the taxation year of their acquisition, the potential terminal loss deduction in the separate class will not be available. ITR: 1103(2g)

The separate class election is extended to manufacturing and processing property included in Class 43 costing more than $1,000. The election must be filed with the income tax return for the taxation year in which the property is acquired. After five years, any remaining UCC in each separate class must be transferred into the general Class 43 UCC pool. ITR: 1101(55)
ITR: 1101(59)
ITR: 1103(29)

¶5,050 Computer equipment acquired after March 22, 2004

In recognition of the short useful life for computers, the CCA rate for general-purpose electronic data processing equipment and related systems software, acquired after March 22, 2004, increased to 45% (Class 45) from 30% (Class 10).

The separate class election is not available to computer equipment eligible for the 45% rate. As a transition provision, taxpayers may elect that computer equipment acquired before 2005 be included in Class 10 and, therefore, be eligible for the separate class election.

¶5,055 Computer equipment acquired on or after March 19, 2007

[The March 19, 2007 federal budget proposed to increase the CCA rate for computers that currently qualify for Class 45 from 45% to 55%. This applies to property acquired on or after March 19, 2007. Since the details at the time of writing were not available, we will refer to this as Class CE to represent Computer Equipment.]

Example Problem

Portable Tools Rental Unlimited Limited incorporated and commenced business on April 1, 2002 and has a December 31 year-end. The company rents portable tools for short terms and the following are its transactions:

		Computers Class 10: 30%
2002	100 tools purchased at various times during the year for $950 each	$ 95,000
2003	20 tools purchased in June for $1,000 each	20,000
2005	30 2002 tools (well maintained) sold in November for $1,000 each	30,000
2007	50 2002 tools sold in February for $700 each	35,000

— *REQUIRED*

Prepare a schedule showing the effects of these transactions on Class 10 and on the income of the company for the period of years indicated. (Ignore the leap year effects.)

— *SOLUTION*

		Portable Tools Class 10: 30%
2002	Additions: 100 tools purchased for $950 each	$ 95,000
	UCC at the end of 2002 before adjustment	$ 95,000
	Less: ½ of net amount during the year	(47,500)
	UCC before CCA	$ 47,500
	CCA claimed @ 30%; prorated, because of short first year, for 275 days ($47,500 × .3 × 275/365)	(10,736)
	Add: ½ of net amount during the year	47,500
	UCC at the beginning of 2003	$ 84,264
2003	Additions: 20 tools purchased for $1,000 each	20,000
	UCC at the end of 2003 before adjustment	$104,264
	Less: ½ of net amount during the year	(10,000)
	UCC before CCA	$ 94,264
	CCA claimed @ 30% ($94,264 × .3)	(28,279)
	Add: ½ of net amount during the year	10,000
	UCC at the beginning of 2004	$ 75,985
2004	No additions or dispositions	
	CCA claimed @ 30% ($75,985 × .3)	(22,796)
	UCC at the beginning of 2005	$ 53,189
2005	Disposals: 30 tools sold for $1,000 each (cost: $950 each; $1,500 total capital gain)	(28,500)
	UCC before CCA	$ 24,689
	CCA claimed @ 30% ($24,689 × .3)	(7,407)
	UCC at the beginning of 2006	$ 17,282
2006	No additions or dispositions	
	CCA claimed @ 30% ($17,282 × .3)	(5,185)
	UCC at the beginning of 2007	$ 12,097
2007	Disposals: 50 tools sold for $700 each (cost: $950 each; no capital loss on depreciable property)	(35,000)
	UCC at the end of 2007	$(22,903)
	Recapture of CCA taken into income	22,903
	UCC at the beginning of 2008	Nil

— *NOTE TO SOLUTION*

Had all 90 of the remaining tools in the class been sold for less than $12,097 in 2007 there would have been a positive balance in the class at the end of the taxation year. This would have been written off as a terminal loss under subsection 20(16) against income and the balance in the account would have been set at nil to carry forward.

¶5,060 Exceptions to the Declining Balance Method

¶5,065 Leasehold improvements

Not all classes of assets use a declining balance method of computing capital cost allowance. Special treatment is accorded to a leasehold interest. The capital cost allowance that may be claimed for a leasehold interest (Class 13) after the first year of ownership is the lesser of:

ITR: 1100(1)(*b*), Sch. III

(a) ⅕ of the capital cost of the leasehold interest; and

(b) the capital cost of the leasehold interest divided by the number of 12-month periods from the beginning of the taxation year in which the cost was incurred to the end of the term of the lease plus the first renewal term (i.e., the number of months in the remainder of the lease term plus one renewal option divided by 12). The divisor is not to exceed a total of 40 such 12-month periods.

The first year write-off would be ½ of the above amount to provide the equivalent of the half-year rule.

For example, if a $16,000 leasehold improvement is made on a rented building on which the taxpayer has a lease for five years with two successive options to renew of three years and two years, the capital cost allowance for a year other than the first year would be calculated as follows:

Lesser of: (a) ⅕ of the capital cost (⅕ × $16,000) $3,200

(b) capital cost divided by the number of 12-month periods from the beginning of the taxation year in which the cost was incurred to the end of the term of the lease plus first renewal term not to exceed 40 years

$$\frac{\$16,000}{5+3}$$ $2,000

Thus, $1,000 capital cost allowance would be taken in the first year, $2,000 in each of the next seven years and the remaining $1,000 in the ninth year.

¶5,070 Class 14 limited-life intangibles

Straight-line capital cost allowance is also used for items in Class 14 which generally includes limited-life intangibles such as patents, franchises, concessions or licences. For this class, the capital cost of each property in the class is divided by the remaining legal life, as at the acquisition date, of the property to obtain the amount of capital cost allowance for the year. (Note that the legal life of a patent registered after 1989 is 20 years. If the patent was registered before 1990, its legal life is 17 years.) An Interpretation Bulletin indicates the CRA's view that the capital cost should be prorated over the number of days in the remaining life of the Class 14 asset. Note that this is one of the classes not affected by the half-year rule.

IT-477, par. 4

A taxpayer must classify property that is a patent or a right to use patented information for a limited or unlimited period in Class 44 with a 25% declining balance rate. However, a taxpayer can elect that such property not be included in Class 44. Under this election, patents for a limited period would be classified in Class 14. This election might be used when the

ITR: 1103(2h)

patent is purchased late in its legal life, such that the straight-line capital cost allowance of Class 14 would exceed the 25% declining balance capital cost allowance of Class 44.

¶5,075 Manufacturing and processing machinery and equipment

[The March 19, 2007 federal budget proposed to temporarily increase the CCA rate for manufacturing and processing machinery and equipment that would otherwise be included in Class 43 to a 50% straight-line rate. The half-year rule will apply. This applies to property acquired on or after March 19, 2007, and before 2009. Since the details at the time of writing were not available, we will refer to this as Class ME to represent Manufacturing Equipment.

For example, if an eligible piece of equipment costing $100,000 is purchased, then CCA can be claimed as follows:

Class ME CCA

	Option 1	Option 2	Option 3
Year 1			
Opening balance	$ —	$ —	$ —
Additions	100,000	100,000	100,000
Half-year rule adjustment	(50,000)	(50,000)	(50,000)
	50,000	50,000	50,000
CCA @ 50% SL	(25,000)	—	—
Half-year rule adjustment	50,000	50,000	50,000
Closing balance	75,000	100,000	100,000
Year 2			
Opening balance	75,000	100,000	100,000
CCA @ 50% SL	(50,000)	(50,000)	—
Closing balance	25,000	50,000	100,000
Year 3			
Opening balance	25,000	50,000	100,000
CCA @ 50% SL	(25,000)	(50,000)	(100,000)
Closing balance	$ —	$ —	$ —

Under option 1, CCA is claimed in the first year, so the half-year rule will limit the deduction to one-half of the 50% rate, or effectively 25%. In the second year, the 50% straight-line calculation is made resulting in CCA of $50,000. The remaining balance can be claimed in year 3.

Under option 2, CCA is not claimed in the first year, so it can be claimed at 50% in each of years 2 and 3.

Under option 3, CCA is not claimed in either of years 1 or 2, so the full remaining balance can be claimed in year 3.]

Note that CCA may be claimed on a deduction up to the maximum allowed each year. Hence, the three options shown are not the only options that are possible.

¶5,080 Insurance Proceeds Expended on Damaged Depreciable Property

Any part of insurance proceeds payable for damaged depreciable property that has been expended on repairing the damage within the year or within a reasonable time after the damage must be included in income. The amount included will be offset by the amount that will be deducted as an expense of repairing the property so that there will be no net effect on the taxpayer's income. If any part of the insurance proceeds is not expended in this manner, the unused portion will be treated as proceeds of disposition of depreciable property and will, thus, be treated according to the basic rules for proceeds.

ITA: 12(1)(*f*)

ITA: 13(21) "proceeds of disposition" (*f*)

¶5,090   Involuntary and Voluntary Dispositions

¶5,095   Involuntary dispositions

(Consideration of this segment of the chapter can be deferred, without a loss of continuity, until the material under the heading "Exchanges of Property" is considered in Chapter 8 where the capital gain component of the problem is discussed.)   ITA: 44

Ordinarily any insurance recovery for stolen, lost or destroyed (but not merely damaged) depreciable property or any expropriation proceeds would be considered as "proceeds of disposition" by paragraphs (*b*), (*c*), and (*d*) of the definition of that term. A potential recapture might be offset against the cost of property of the same class acquired later in the year. However, a replacement outlay might not be made in the same year for major assets which take some time to replace even if the taxpayer immediately begins to plan the reconstruction or replacement.[2]   ITA: 13(21)
ITA: 13(1)

The taxpayer may elect in the year of replacement of property stolen, lost, destroyed or expropriated to offset any recapture caused by proceeds for the loss as long as replacement is made by the later of either 24 months after the initial taxation year or by the end of the second taxation year following the year in which proceeds are considered receivable. Proceeds are deemed to have become receivable at the earliest of: ITA: 13(4)

(a) the day the taxpayer has agreed to the full amount of the compensation;

(b) the day the compensation is finally determined by a court or tribunal;

(c) the day that is two years from the day of loss, destruction or taking where a claim or suit has not been taken before the courts;

(d) the day the taxpayer dies or ceases to be a resident of Canada; and

(e) the day immediately before the winding-up of a corporation (other than a Canadian subsidiary owned 90% or more) where the taxpayer is a corporation.

Basically, replacement property is property acquired for the "same or similar use" as the original property and used for gaining or producing income from the "same or similar business" by the taxpayer or related persons. Note that replacement property need not be of the same class of depreciable property as the original property. The CRA's interpretation of the term "same or similar use" and of the term "same or similar business" are set out in an Interpretation Bulletin.   ITA: 44(5)

IT-259R4, par. 16–21

¶5,100   Voluntary dispositions

(Consideration of this segment of the chapter can be deferred, without a loss of continuity, until the material under the heading "Exchanges of Property" is considered in Chapter 8 where the capital gain component of the problem is discussed.)   ITA: 44

The same rules permitting an offset of recapture caused by proceeds of disposition apply on certain voluntary dispositions of depreciable "former business property". However, in this case, replacement must be made by the later of either 12 months after the initial taxation year or by the end of the first taxation year following the year of disposition. The term "former business property" is defined to mean real property (i.e., land and buildings) or an interest therein (i.e., a leasehold interest) that is capital property used primarily for the purpose of earning business income. These rules pertaining to a former business property might be used in a business relocation to avoid recapture on the disposition of buildings.   ITA: 248(1)

Normally, a building is the only depreciable property eligible for the replacement property rules for voluntary dispositions. However, a limited-period franchise, concession or license will also be eligible. The replacement property rules are extended where the transferor and transferee jointly elect to have these rules apply.   Proposed in Bill C-33
Draft Legislation

ITA: 13(4.2), 13(4.3)

---

[2] For an example, see the case of *Korenowsky v. M.N.R.*, 64 DTC 235 (T.A.B.).

Example Problem

Dump's is a department store operating in the area. Its operations are carried on in a building which is owned by the company. The capital cost of the building to Dump's in September 2003 was $400,000. The company has been taking capital cost allowance on the structure on the basis that it is a Class 1 asset with a capital cost allowance rate of 4%. In May 2005, a fire virtually destroyed the building. The only asset which was recovered was an F.A.D. Computer and it was substantially damaged. The computer had been purchased by Dump's in December 2004 at a cost of $75,000 and as a Class 10 asset it had been depreciated at a rate of 30% since 2004.

In August 2005, under an insurance policy with the Risk-Averters Insurance Company, Dump's received $385,000 for the destruction of the building and $25,000 for the damage to the computer. Dump's had the computer repaired to its original condition in 2005 at a cost of $23,000. In 2007, a new building was constructed for $465,000.

— REQUIRED

Trace the effects of these events on the balance of the undepreciated capital cost accounts for each asset from 2003 through to the beginning balance for 2008 in the building account and for 2007 in the computer account. As you trace the effects, indicate all deductions from and inclusions in income from the business for the years indicated. Assume that the appropriate election is made.

ITA: 13(4)

— SOLUTION

(A) Building — Class 1: 4%

2003	Additions: purchase of building	$400,000
	UCC at the end of 2003	$400,000
	CCA claimed @ 4% (($400,000 — ½ × $400,000) × .04)	(8,000)
	UCC at the beginning of 2004	$392,000
2004	No additions or disposals	
	CCA claimed @ 4% ($392,000 × .04)	(15,680)
	UCC at the beginning of 2005	$376,320
2005	Disposals: insurance proceeds	(385,000)
	UCC at the end of 2005	$ (8,680)
	Recaptured CCA taken into income	8,680
	UCC at the beginning of 2006	Nil
2006	No additions or disposals	
	UCC at the beginning of 2007	Nil

ITA: 13(21) "proceeds of disposition" (*c*)

2007	File an amended return for 2005 as follows:		
	UCC at beginning of 2005		$376,320
	Reduction of UCC:[(1)]		
	— normal deduction is lesser of:		
	(i) proceeds	$ 385,000 → $385,000	
	(ii) capital cost	$ 400,000	
	— reduced by lesser of:		
	(i) excess, if any, of $385,000 (as determined above) over UCC of $376,320 at the beginning of 2005 (i.e., recapture)	$ 8,680 → (8,680)	
	(ii) cost of replacement property	$ 465,000	(376,320)
	UCC at the end of 2005		Nil
	Recaptured CCA		Nil
	UCC at the beginning of 2006		Nil

ITA: 13(4)
ITA: 13(4)(*c*)

ITA: 13(4)(*c*)

Building — Class NRB: 6%

2007	Additions: purchase of new building[(2)]	$465,000
	Deemed proceeds of disposition (equal to reduction calculated above)	(8,680)
	UCC at the end of 2007	$456,320
	CCA @ 6% (($456,320 – ½ × $456,320) × .06)	(13,690)
	UCC at beginning of 2008	$442,630

ITA: 13(4)(d)

(B) Computer — Class 10: 35%

2004	Additions: computer	$75,000
	UCC at the end of 2004	$ 75,000
	CCA claimed @ 30% (($75,000 — ½ × $75,000) × .3)	(11,250)
	UCC at the beginning of 2005	$ 63,750
2005[(3)]	Disposals: proceeds of disposition in the amount of unexpended insurance proceeds	(2,000)
	UCC at the end of 2005	$ 61,750
	CCA claimed @ 30% ($61,750 × .3)	(18,525)
	UCC at the beginning of 2006	$ 43,225
2006	No additions or disposals	
	CCA claimed @ 30% ($43,225 × .3)	(12,968)
	UCC at the beginning of 2007	$ 30,257

— NOTES TO SOLUTION

[(1)] To generalize the proceeds reduction rule, it would appear that as long as the cost of the replacement property exceeds the recapture that would otherwise result on the disposition (i.e., the $8,680 above), there will be no actual recaptured capital cost allowance on the disposition. In effect, part of the proceeds of disposition of the former property is transferred from the year in which the disposition occurred to the year in which the replacement property is acquired. This avoids recapture in the year of disposition and reduces the undepreciated capital cost of whichever class of property the replacement property falls into.

ITA: 13(4)(c)

[(2)] The rules allow for a replacement with an asset of another class. The old building was in Class 1; the new building is in Class NRB and still qualifies as replacement property for the rollover.

ITA: 13(4)

[(3)] In 2005, income would be increased by expended proceeds of insurance of $25,000, but this amount would be offset by the deduction of repair expense of $23,000. Thus, the net effect on income is nil which is as it should be. The other $2,000 received is a capital receipt which reduces undepreciated capital cost.

ITA: 12(1)(f)

¶5,110   Change in Use and Part Disposition Rules

Rules are set out for the determination of capital cost and proceeds of disposition in five situations as follows.

ITA: 13(7)

¶5,115   Change from income-producing to other purpose

In this case, property is acquired for producing income, but its use is changed to another purpose. Consider the situation where a taxpayer had a house which he or she rented and later lived in himself or herself. At the time of the change in use, the taxpayer is deemed to have disposed of a depreciable asset at its fair market value. This deemed disposition may result in either recapture or a terminal loss. The deemed reacquisition at fair market value establishes the cost of the asset for personal use. The problem of determining fair market value without a transaction gives rise to cases such as that of *Tripp v. M.N.R.*, in which the value of a house relative to the value of the land on which it was situated was at issue.

ITA: 13(7)(a)

63 DTC 313 (T.A.B.)

¶5,120 Change from non-income-producing to income-producing purpose

In this situation, property is acquired for a non-income producing purpose, but its use is changed to producing income. Consider the case if the first situation were reversed. At the time of the change in use, the taxpayer is deemed to acquire a depreciable asset at its fair market value where that value is less than its cost, representing a decline in value. But where the fair market value of the asset is greater than its cost, representing an increase in value, the capital cost of the asset will, generally,[3] be limited to the lesser of:

ITA: 13(7)(*b*)

(i) the fair market value of the property at the time of the change in use   xxx

(ii) the total of
    (A) cost at the time of the change in use   xxx
    (B) the fair market value of the property at the time of the change
        in use   xxx
        less: cost at the time of change in use   xxx

        excess, if any   xxx

        ½ of excess   xxx   xxx

As a result of this latter rule, the capital cost of the asset for the purposes of computing capital cost allowance is limited to the sum of two components. That sum consists of the actual cost of the asset before the change in use plus the amount, if any, of taxable capital gain resulting from the deemed disposition on the change in use. Therefore, there can be no step-up in the capital cost to fair market value, because the step-up in capital cost is limited to ½ of the gain from actual cost up to fair market value.[4]

The capital cost of the asset after the change in use and the application of the limited step-up will reflect an amount that has been fully tax paid by the owner. Since the taxpayer will pay tax on only ½ of the capital gain, only ½ of the gain may be added to the original cost. The rationale for this limitation is that the stepped-up capital cost will provide the base for future CCA which is fully deductible from business or property income. A taxpayer should only expect to fully deduct a cost that was fully tax paid.

The half-year rule to reduce first-year capital cost allowance would appear to apply because the conditions which provide exceptions to this rule for property of a class in Schedule II are not met. In particular, the condition that the property, subject to the change in use to income-producing purposes, would not have been *depreciable* property at the time of the change in use if its previous use was non-income-producing is not met. It makes some sense to impose the half-year rule at the change in use to income-producing purposes, because the half-year rule would usually not have been applied on acquisition for the previous non-income-producing purpose. Note that a change in use from income-producing purpose to non-income-producing purpose should not be affected by the half-year rule, because the property would not be depreciable property if its purpose is not income-producing.

ITR: 1100(2.2)
ITR: 1100(2.2)(*f*)

¶5,125 Property acquired for multiple purposes

In this case, property is acquired both for producing income and for another purpose. For example, consider the situation where a taxpayer buys a duplex and lives in one half, renting the other half. At the time of the purchase, ½ of the cost of the building is allocated to depreciable assets of the taxpayer. On the sale of the property, ½ of the proceeds is regarded as proceeds of the depreciable asset by the same paragraph.

ITA: 13(7)(*c*)

---

[3] The actual formula in paragraph 13(7)(*b*) provides for an adjustment in respect of the capital gains deduction. Such a deduction is only available for qualified farm property which might be subject to a change in use. As a result, the adjustment will not be common.

[4] For a more detailed discussion of paragraphs 13(7)(*b*), (*d*) and (*e*), see Robert E. Beam and Stanley N. Laiken, "Changes in Use and Non-Arm's Length Transfer of Depreciable Property", *Canadian Tax Journal*, Vol. 35, No. 2, March-April 1987, pp. 453.

¶5,130   Change in proportion of use for producing income and other purposes

Here, a change occurs in the relation between the use of property for producing income *ITA: 13(7)(d)* and its use for another purpose. This might be the case where one room out of eight in a house is used for business and at a particular time a second room is converted to business use. Any such increase in the use of the property for income-producing purposes is deemed to be an acquisition of property. The capital cost would be deemed to be equal to the proportion (in this case $\frac{1}{8}$) of the fair market value where that value is less than the proportion of its cost of the total property, at the time, representing the increase in use. Where the fair market value of the property is greater than its cost, the capital cost of the additional part of the property used for income-producing purposes is limited to capital cost plus the taxable capital *ITA: 13(7)(b)* gain as described above.

The calculation of the capital cost of the part of the property converted to income-producing purposes can be computed, generally,[5] as follows:

The aggregate of:
   (A) the fraction of the property converted to income-
        producing purposes times the lesser of:
        (I) the fair market value of the full property at the time of the
            increase in income-producing use xxx

        (II) the cost of the full property at the time of the increase in
             income-producing use xxx

        fraction above times the lesser amount of (I) and (II) xxx

   (B)(I) the fraction (used above) of the fair market value of the full
          property at the time of the increase in income-producing use xxx
          less:
        (II) the fraction (used above) of the cost of the full property at the
             time of the increase in income-producing use................. xxx
        excess, if any xxx

     ½ of excess xxx
   Capital cost: (A) + (B) xxx

The effect of this calculation is similar to that discussed above. *ITA: 13(7)(b)*

Any decrease in the proportion of income-producing use is treated as a disposition at the proportion of the fair market value of the total property, at the time of the decrease in use. Technically, when an automobile is being used by an employee or in business partially to earn income and the proportion of income-producing use changes from one year to another, there *ITA: 13(7)(d)* has been a change in the relative use of the asset to which these rules would apply. This would result in the need to make a fair market valuation each year and to apply the rules accordingly in the computation of capital cost allowance. In practice, capital cost allowance can be computed first on the full undepreciated capital cost of the automobile and then reduced by an adjustment for the proportion of personal use of the automobile based on personal mileage to total mileage for the year. The net result is the amount of capital cost allowance that can be considered attributable to the income-producing use.

Example Problem

Mr. Greenjeans purchased a brick building suitable for the relocation of his retail store including storage and office space on March 1, 2005, at a cost of $60,000 (exclusive of land). On September 15, 2006, when the fair market value of the building was $80,000, he converted one-quarter of the building to residential facilities and began to use that area as his personal residence. He continued to use the remainder of the building for his retail operation. On October 31, 2007, when the fair market value of the building was $96,000, he moved out of the residential facilities and converted them back to business use.

---

[5] The adjustment for the effects of the capital gains deduction, which would only apply to qualified farm property, has been omitted from the formula.

— *REQUIRED*

Assuming that Mr. Greenjeans claims maximum capital cost allowance, prepare a schedule showing the effects of these events for 2005, 2006, and 2007.

— *SOLUTION*

		Building Class 1: 4%
2005	Addition: purchase building...............................	$60,000
	UCC, December 31, 2005.................................	$60,000
	CCA claimed @ 4% (($60,000 — ½ × $60,000) × .04)...........	(1,200)
	UCC, January 1, 2006..................................	$58,800
2006	Disposal: conversion of ¼ of building to personal use resulting in deemed disposition (¼ × $60,000).................	(15,000)[1]
	UCC, December 31, 2006................................	$43,800
	CCA claimed @ 4% ($43,800 × .04)......................	(1,752)
	UCC, January 1, 2007..................................	$42,048
2007	Addition: conversion of ¼ of building to business use resulting in deemed acquisition................................	22,000[2]
	UCC, December 31, 2007................................	$64,048
	CCA claimed @ 4% (($64,048 — ½ × $22,000) × .04)...........	(2,122)[3]
	UCC, January 1, 2008..................................	$61,926

ITA: 13(7)(*d*)

— *NOTES TO SOLUTION*

[1] ¼ of the building originally cost $15,000 (¼ × $60,000) and now has a fair market value of $20,000 (¼ × $80,000). The balance in the class is never reduced by more than the equivalent of original cost on a disposition or deemed disposition, that is, the balance in the class is reduced by ¼ of the lesser of capital cost ($60,000) and proceeds of disposition ($80,000). The remaining excess of actual or deemed proceeds over original cost may result in a capital gain. An Interpretation Bulletin provides further examples involving partial disposition of depreciable property.

ITA: 13(7)(*d*)(ii)

IT-418

[2] The cost of ¼ of the building used for residential facilities is equal to its fair market value at the time of the change in use (i.e., ¼ × $80,000 = $20,000). Since the fair market value of ¼ of the building (¼ × $96,000 = $24,000) is greater than ¼ of its cost (¼ × $80,000 = $20,000), the capital cost of ¼ of the building will be limited (applicable to a fractional change in use) to the aggregate of:

ITA: 13(7)(*d*)(i)

(a)	25% of the lesser of:		
	(i) fair market value at the time of the increase in income-producing use...................................	$96,000	
	(ii) cost at the time of the increase in income-producing use ...	$80,000	
	25% of $80,000..		$20,000
(b)	proceeds of disposition deemed to result (25% of $96,000).....	$24,000	
	less: cost at the time of the increase in income-producing use (25% of $80,000)............................	(20,000)	
	excess, if any......................................	$ 4,000	
	½ of excess..		$ 2,000
	capital cost addition on change in use...................		$22,000

[3] Note that the half-year rule would appear to apply on this change in use, because the condition in the Regulations would not be met. Since the previous use of the property was not income-producing, it would not have been depreciable capital property. As a result, the half-year rule would not have been applied to this property in its previous use.

ITR: 1100(2.2)(*f*)

Note, also, that capital cost allowance is not prorated for a short year, in these cases, because the business existed in a year before the year of the change in use or the original acquisition for business use.

¶5,135   Non-arm's length transfer of depreciable property

These rules are discussed in more detail in Chapter 8, under the heading "Consideration in Non-Arm's Length Transfers", and in Chapter 16, under the heading "Depreciable capital property". They apply where depreciable property is transferred between persons not dealing at arm's length, which is also discussed in Chapter 6, under the heading "Related persons". These rules prevent the realization of benefits from a transfer motivated by the fact that the increase in value over cost is taxable to the transferor as a capital gain (i.e., ½ taxable), but would be fully depreciable from fair market value at the time of the transfer to the transferee if it were not for these rules. The adjustment to the capital cost of property transferred to the non-arm's length transferee is similar to the calculation presented for a change in use of property, where only cost plus the taxable capital gain to the transferor can be depreciated by the transferee. ITA: 13(7)(*e*)
ITA: 251
ITA: 13(7)(*e*)
ITA: 13(7)(*b*)

¶5,140   Capital cost reduction for cost assistance

When a grant, subsidy, forgivable loan, deduction from tax, investment allowance or other assistance is received on the acquisition of property, the amount of such assistance received reduces the capital cost of depreciable property, so that CCA is claimed only on the net cost of the asset. ITA: 13(7.1)

¶5,150   Franchises and Similar Property

It should be noted that Class 14 includes certain property that is a patent, franchise concession or licence for a limited period. The cost of such property is expensed under the capital cost allowance system by taking straight-line capital cost allowance over the remaining legal life of the property as indicated earlier. Note in particular that this property must have a limited life. The amounts that can be considered as the capital cost of a patent were at issue in *Weinberger v. M.N.R.* The court held that not only the amount paid to have the invention patented but also the costs to produce and perfect the invention to the point where the patent can be obtained are considered to be the capital cost of the patent. 64 DTC 5060 (Ex. Ct.)

If the cost of a patent is added to Class 14, because the taxpayer has elected that the property not be included in Class 44, it will be eligible for capital cost allowance on a straight-line basis over its remaining legal life (17 years if registered before 1990 and 20 years if registered after 1989), as discussed previously. However, the CRA suggests that expenditures incurred in making any representation for the purpose of obtaining a franchise or a patent (among others) to a government or public body relating to a business of the taxpayer would be deductible immediately. In lieu of an immediate deduction, the taxpayer may elect in prescribed manner to deduct one-tenth of the amount otherwise eligible for deduction in each of the 10 consecutive years beginning with the year in which the expenditure is made. Thus, three possibilities for dealing with expenses of representation, in this situation, may be available: ITR: 1103(2h)
IT-99R5, par. 11
ITA: 20(1)(*cc*)
ITA: 20(9)

(a) an immediate deduction of the cost; ITA: 20(1)(*cc*)

(b) a deduction of the cost over a 10-year period; and ITA: 20(9))

(c) capitalization of the cost in the appropriate CCA class (14 or 44) or in the eligible capital property pool (see below).

Any amount deducted immediately or over 10 years is subject to recapture. ITA: 13(12)

Certain property, such as franchises, may have an indefinite life in contrast to a limited life (Class 14). If this is the case, the property is likely an eligible capital property subject to amortization through the cumulative eligible capital account which will be discussed in the next section of this chapter. It will be seen that eligible capital property excludes intangible property that is depreciable property. A franchise of any kind may be considered as intangible property, but because a franchise for a limited period is listed in Class 14 it is depreciable property and, therefore, cannot be eligible capital property.

¶5,200   ELIGIBLE CAPITAL PROPERTY

¶5,210   Basic Rules

Under the pre-1972 Act, certain items of intangible property were known as "nothings" because they were capital in nature, and, hence, not deductible as a business expense, but not tangible assets and, hence, not depreciable. Such "nothings" included the cost of purchased goodwill,[6] the cost of a franchise for an indefinite life and incorporation costs among others. When these assets were sold, proceeds were treated by the vendor as a capital receipt with no tax consequences and by the purchaser as a non-deductible, non-depreciable expenditure.

Under the present Act, most of these items, and others discussed in the Interpretation Bulletin entitled "Meaning of Eligible Capital Expenditure", are defined as "eligible capital expenditures". This definition includes capital outlays that are not otherwise specifically allowed or disallowed as deductions under the Act and made after 1971 for the purpose of earning income (other than exempt income) from business. (See the Interpretation Bulletin entitled "Separate Businesses" for an indication of the concept of a "business".) Note that the definition of "eligible capital expenditures" specifically excludes certain expenditures. Also, note that expenditures made prior to 1972 are not now deductible.   `IT-143R3` `ITA: 14(5)`

In general, three-quarters of each eligible capital expenditure is added to the "cumulative eligible capital" (CEC) account.   `ITA: 14(5)`

The change to a $\frac{1}{2}$ capital gains inclusion rate for dispositions after October 17, 2000 does not affect the $\frac{3}{4}$ fraction used to calculate additions to the CEC account or disposals of eligible capital property (ECP). Instead, a special "$\frac{2}{3}$" adjustment is applied when calculating the income inclusion for a negative balance in the CEC pool for taxation years ended after October 17, 2000. The $\frac{2}{3}$ adjustment converts a $\frac{3}{4}$ amount in the CEC pool to a $\frac{1}{2}$ amount (i.e., $\frac{2}{3} \times \frac{3}{4} = \frac{1}{2}$).

The November 22, 2006 Technical Amendments contained in Bill C-33 propose to make an adjustment to the amount added to the cumulative eligible capital account on a non-arm's length purchase. The adjustment is similar in effect to the adjustment on the purchase of depreciable property. The usual addition of $\frac{3}{4}$ of the purchase purchaser's cost must be reduced by $\frac{1}{2}$ of the non-arm's length seller's business income inclusion from the gain on the sale of eligible capital property (item A in the definition of "cumulative eligible capital").   `ITA: 13(7)(e)` `ITA: 14(1)(b)` `ITA: 14(5)`

The balance in the CEC account is amortized on a declining balance basis using a maximum rate of 7% (for fiscal periods commencing after the change dates defined as "adjustment time", indicated above, and 10% for fiscal periods commencing before the change dates above). The amount of annual amortization is referred to as the "cumulative eligible capital amount" (CECA). The Interpretation Bulletin entitled "Transactions Involving Eligible Capital Property" discusses the effects of transactions involving eligible capital property on the balance in the CEC account and provides an extended numerical example in Schedule B.   `ITA: 20(1)(b)` `IT-123R6`

¶5,220   Similarities with Capital Cost Allowance System

The system for taking deductions on eligible capital expenditures is very similar to that for depreciable capital property. The major differences, based on the rules in effect after the adjustment time, are:

(a) there is only one account or pool that is used to record purchases and dispositions of eligible capital expenditures (ECE) for a particular business. This account is called the "cumulative eligible capital" (CEC) account, as indicated above, and is amortized on a declining balance basis to a maximum of 7% of the balance in the account. (The definition of the cumulative eligible capital account appears somewhat more complex because it accumulates all adjustments to the account since 1971. Note that the ECE definition parallels directly the definition of undepreciated capital cost);   `IT-206R` `ITA: 20(1)(b)` `ITA: 14(5)` `ITA: 14(5)` `ITA: 13(21)`

---

[6] The meaning of "goodwill" was considered in *Losey v. M.N.R.*, 57 DTC 1098 (Ex. Ct.).

(b) expenditures made prior to 1972 are completely ignored (but dispositions of property whenever purchased are considered);

(c) only $\frac{3}{4}$ of eligible capital expenditures (ECE) (which is equivalent to capital cost in the capital cost allowance system) and $\frac{3}{4}$ of proceeds called an "eligible capital amount" (ECA) affect the account;[7] and

(d) there is no half-year rule.

Similar to the capital cost allowance system, it is the balance of cumulative eligible capital (CEC) which is equivalent to undepreciated capital cost at the end of the taxation year or on termination of the business that is important. At that time:

(a) if the balance of CEC is positive and the business is to continue, take amortization as a deduction at a maximum of 7% (after the adjustment time) of the balance of CEC and subtract that amount from the balance to be carried forward to the next year;

(b) if the balance of CEC is negative, for any taxation year ending after October 17, 2000, take into business income:

   (i) the lesser of:

      (A) the negative balance, and

      (B) all cumulative eligible capital amounts claimed in prior years

         less

         deductions previously recaptured in prior year business income inclusions

   PLUS

   (ii) $\frac{2}{3}$ of the negative CEC balance less (i) above (i.e., $\frac{2}{3}$ of the excess, if any, of (A) minus (B) above).

   The business income is effectively a recapture of previous deductions plus $\frac{1}{2}$ of the absolute gain on the disposal. The $\frac{2}{3}$ adjustment factor effectively converts from a $\frac{3}{4}$ rate to a $\frac{1}{2}$ [$\frac{2}{3} \times \frac{3}{4} = \frac{1}{2}$].

(c) if the balance of cumulative eligible capital is positive, but the business has been terminated, take the positive balance as a deduction which is the equivalent of a terminal loss from income;   ITA: 24

(d) the provision related to non-arm's length transactions operates in much the same way as for capital cost allowance purposes. The ECP system restricts the eligible capital expenditure of a non-arm's length purchaser of eligible capital property where the vendor has claimed a capital gains deduction[8] in respect of the disposition of the eligible capital property; and   ITA: 14(3) / ITA: 13(7)(*e*) / ITA: 110.6

(e) replacement property rules defer recognition of recaptured cumulative eligible capital amounts on the disposition of eligible capital property where the property is replaced within one year of the end of the year of disposition, in the same manner as the CCA system.   ITA: 14(6), 14(7) / ITA: 13(4)

---

[7] The eligible capital amount (ECA) is determined in item E of the definition of "cumulative eligible capital" in subsection 14(5) and referred to in subsection 14(1).

[8] Available to an individual who has disposed of qualified farm property, such as a farm marketing quota.

¶5,230   Illustration of the Rules

¶5,235   Common aspects

The more common aspects of these rules are illustrated in Exhibit 5-3.

EXHIBIT 5-3
Cumulative Eligible Capital Account
[Sec. 14]

Facts

Assume a corporation commencing business purchases a store in year one and pays $5,000 for goodwill. In year one and in year two the full 7% deduction is claimed. In year three the store is sold and $6,500 is received for goodwill.

In year three, assume that the corporation purchases another store and pays $4,450 for goodwill. In year three the full 7% deduction is claimed. In year four, the corporation ceases to carry on the business and sells the business to a person other than a corporation controlled by it. No part of the proceeds can be attributed to goodwill.

Application of Rules and Definitions

Year	Ssec. 14(5) Cumulative eligible capital item A	Ssec. 14(5) Cumulative eligible capital item E	Par. 20(1)(b) Cumulative eligible capital amount 7% deduction	Ssec. 14(5) Cumulative eligible capital
1 Purchase	$3/4 \times \$5,000$ $= \$3,750$			$ 3,750
1 CECA			$263 $(7\% \times \$3,750)$	$ 3,487
2 CECA			$244 $(7\% \times \$3,487)$	$ 3,243
3 Disposal		$(3/4 \times \$6,500$ $= \$4,875)$		($1,632)*
3 Purchase	$3/4 \times \$4,450 =$ $\$3,338$			$ 1,706
3 CECA			$119 $(7\% \times \$1,706)$	$ 1,587
4 Business Closed			$1,587 (sec. 24)	Nil

* $263 + $244 + $3/4 ($6,500 − $5,000) = $1,632 (equal to the negative balance for post-adjustment time purchases). If the goodwill of $4,450 is not purchased in Year 3, then there would be a business income inclusion as follows:

    a) the lesser of:
       i) $1,632
         and
      ii) $263 + $244 = $507
         lesser amount $507
    PLUS
    b) $2/3 \times$ ($1,632 − $507)   750
                                                 $1,257

The $1,257 can also be calculated by adding the recaptured CECA of $507 to ½ of the gain ($6,500 − $5,000).

¶5,240   Non-arm's length transactions

The following examples illustrate the effects of a non-arm's length transaction in eligible capital property, assuming a sale for $100,000.

If the seller has no balance in the cumulative eligible capital account, the following would occur:

(a) sale of eligible capital property:

cumulative eligible capital balance			Nil
disposal: ¾ of $100,000			$ (75,000)
balance			(75,000)
inclusion in income — lesser of:			
• (i) negative balance above	$75,000		
(ii) amortization previously deducted	Nil		
lesser amount		Nil	
• plus ⅔ ($75,000 – Nil)		$50,000	50,000
untaxed amount			25,000
balance			Nil

Note that the $50,000 inclusion in income is one-half of the economic gain on the disposition of the property, i.e., $50,000 = ½ ($100,000 proceeds – Nil cost).

(b) purchase of eligible capital property by non-arm's length person:

purchase: ¾ × $100,000	$75,000
less adjustment: ½ of seller's gain inclusion (½ × $50,000)	(25,000)
cumulative eligible capital balance	$50,000

Note how the non-arm's length purchaser will be allowed to amortize only $50,000, which is the amount of the seller's gain that was subject to tax.

If the seller has a balance in the cumulative eligible capital account of, say, $20,000 and the seller has claimed amortization, previously, of $13,000 on property with a full cost of $44,000, the following would occur:

(a) sale of eligible capital property:

cumulative eligible capital balance			$20,000
disposal: ¾ of $100,000			(75,000)
balance			(55,000)
inclusion in income – lesser of:			
• (i) negative balance above	$55,000		
(ii) amortization previously deducted	$13,000		
lesser amount		$13,000	
• plus ⅔ ($55,000 – $13,000)		28,000	41,000
untaxed amount			14,000
balance			Nil

Note that the $41,000 inclusion in income is one-half of the seller's economic gain on the disposition of the property (i.e., $28,000 = ½ ($100,000 proceeds – $44,000 cost)) plus the "recapture" of amortization previously deducted (i.e., $13,000).

(b) purchase of eligible capital property by non-arm's length person:

purchase: ¾ × $100,000	$75,000
less adjustment: ½ of seller's gain inclusion (½ × $28,000)	(14,000)
cumulative eligible capital balance	$61,000

Note how the non-arm's length purchaser will be allowed to amortize only $61,000, which is equal to the seller's:

(i) cumulative eligible capital balance before the disposition	$20,000
(ii) "recapture" of previously deducted amortization	13,000
(iii) ½ of the economic gain of $56,000 (i.e., $100,000 − $44,000))	28,000
total	$61,000

The $20,000 represents a tax-paid cost that the seller had a right to recover through amortization and the other two amounts were subject to tax and, hence, became tax-paid. The total tax-paid cost of $61,000 can be recovered through amortization deducted by the purchaser in the future.

¶5,250   Election re: Capital Gain

Although the capital gains inclusion rate of ½ is reflected in the income amount on the disposal of CEC, the additions and reductions to the cumulative eligible capital pool are still done at a rate of ¾. There may be instances where a taxpayer would prefer to recognize an economic gain on eligible capital property as a capital gain rather than as a reduction to the available cumulative eligible capital pool. An example of such an instance would be if the taxpayer has available capital losses, either currently or carried over from another taxation year. ITA: 14(1)

An election is available that allows a taxpayer to treat a gain on the disposition of eligible capital property as a capital gain. The following conditions are necessary to take advantage of this provision. ITA: 14(1.01)

(i) The property disposed must be eligible capital property of a business, but not goodwill.

(ii) The cost of the property to the taxpayer must be determinable.

(iii) The proceeds of disposition of the property must exceed the cost.

(iv) The taxpayer's exempt gains balance in respect of the business must be NIL.

(v) The taxpayer must elect in the taxpayer's return of income for the year. ITA: 14(1.01)

If the above conditions are met, then the proceeds of disposition of the property are deemed to be equal to the cost of that property. Then, the taxpayer is deemed to dispose of a capital property with proceeds equal to the actual proceeds and an adjusted cost base equal to the cost of the eligible capital property. If the property disposed is an eligible capital property that is a qualified farm property, then the capital property deemed to be disposed is deemed to be a qualified farm property. ITA: 110.6(1)

> ### Example Problem
>
> Ms. Chalupshka has operated an accounting practice with a December 31 year-end since 2004. She paid $16,000 for a client list when she started the practice in 2004. On August 27, 2007, she sold the practice, including her client list which was allocated $28,000 of the proceeds. The balance in the CEC account on January 1, 2007 was $8,976.
>
> — *REQUIRED*
>
> Compute Ms. Chalupshka's business income from the sale of the client list in 2007.

— SOLUTION

	CEC a/c
Cumulative eligible capital, January 1, 2007	$ 8,976
2007 Disposal: deemed proceeds = cost of client list (¾ × $16,000)	(12,000)
Cumulative eligible capital, December 31, 2007	$ (3,024)
Inclusion in business income	3,024[(1)]
Cumulative eligible capital on cessation of business	Nil
Deemed disposal of capital property	
Deemed proceeds	$ 28,000
Deemed ACB	(16,000)
Capital gain	$ 12,000
Taxable capital gain (½)	$ 6,000
Income inclusion	
Business income	$ 3,024
Taxable capital gain	6,000
Total	$ 9,024

ITA: 14(1.01)

— NOTE TO SOLUTION

[(1)] The inclusion is computed as follows:

(a) lesser of:
    (i) Negative balance . . . . $ 3,024
    (ii) Total CECA claimed [(¾ × $16,000) – $8,976] $ 3,024

    lesser amount $3,024
(b) ⅔ ($3,024 – $3,024) . . . . nil

Inclusion in business income $3,024

¶5,300   CAPITAL PERSONAL PROPERTY AND THE INPUT TAX CREDIT SYSTEM UNDER GST

¶5,310   Basic Rules

An integral part of the GST system is the ability to claim input tax credits (ITCs) on business inputs and thus avoid the cascading or compounding of tax through the production and distribution chain. In order to qualify for an ITC, the property or service must have been purchased for use in a *commercial activity*. In determining the net remittance for a reporting period, the total ITC for the period is deducted from the tax collected or collectible for that period. Where the total ITC for the period exceeds the tax collected or collectible, the registrant will be entitled to a refund.

An important feature of the ITC mechanism is that purchases and sales need not be matched in order to claim an ITC. The credit can be claimed for the period in which the tax is paid or becomes payable. Similarly, for purchases of capital property, there is no requirement for amortization. Under the general input tax credit rules, a registrant may claim an ITC for the tax paid on the purchase of property or a service which was acquired for use in commercial activities. However, special rules have been developed for capital property, due to the fact that the useful life of capital property generally often extends for several years and the use of the property may change over that period. Under the *Excise Tax Act* (ETA), capital property is divided into two main groups — capital personal property and capital real property, and different rules apply to each group.

For GST purposes, capital property is defined to include any property that is capital property for income tax purposes, other than property included in Class 12 (for example, small tools or utensils costing less than $200, video tape, computer software, etc.) or Class 14 (for example, patents, franchises, concessions or licences for a limited period, etc.) of the capital cost allowance classes. This definition for GST purposes applies regardless of whether the registrant is a taxpayer under the *Income Tax Act*.

ETA: 123(1)

Separate rules apply to passenger vehicles and aircraft that are acquired by an individual or a partnership, and certain input tax credit restrictions apply to all passenger vehicles. These topics are discussed below.

The rules for capital real property are discussed in Chapter 8.

¶5,320 Passenger Vehicles and Aircraft

Restrictions on claiming ITCs apply to passenger vehicles owned by all registrants, with special additional rules applying to passenger vehicles owned by registrants that are individuals or partnerships. Many of these rules are based on the rules for passenger vehicles under the *Income Tax Act*. For example, the definition of passenger vehicle under the ETA has the meaning assigned under the *Income Tax Act*.

ITA: 248(1)

¶5,325 Passenger vehicles owned by registrants other than individuals and partnerships

Following the rules for deductibility under the *Income Tax Act*, the ETA refers to specific paragraphs of the *Income Tax Act*. As a result, no input tax credit may be claimed on the portion of the cost of a vehicle that exceeds $30,000 for years after 2000 excluding GST and provincial sales tax. Similarly, an input tax credit may not be claimed in respect of an improvement to the extent the accumulated cost of the vehicle, including the improvement, exceeds $30,000.

ETA: 201
ITA: 13(7)(*g*), 13(7)(*h*)
ETA: 202(1)

As with other capital personal property (i.e., capital property other than capital real property), a full input tax credit may be claimed for the first $30,000 of the cost of passenger vehicles where the primary-use test is met. If the use in a commercial activity is 50% or less, no input tax credit may be claimed.

On the actual disposition of a passenger vehicle, the sale is subject to GST only where the vehicle was used primarily in a commercial activity prior to that time. In addition, a registrant may be entitled to claim an input tax credit on all or a portion of the cost of the vehicle that exceeded the prescribed threshold, e.g., $30,000 for years after 2000, which was previously denied.

ETA: 203(1)

¶5,330 Passenger vehicles and aircraft owned by registrants who are individuals or partnerships

Registrants who are individuals (e.g., sole proprietorships) or partnerships are entitled to claim a full input tax credit in respect of the acquisition of a passenger vehicle only if the vehicle is used exclusively (i.e., 90% or more) in a commercial activity. Similarly, a full input tax credit may be claimed in respect of any improvement only if the vehicle was used exclusively in a commercial activity since its acquisition and will continue to be so used immediately after the improvement. As with other registrants, no input tax credit may be claimed on the portion of the cost of a vehicle (or improvements thereto) that exceeds $30,000, exclusive of provincial sales tax and GST.

ETA: 202(2)
ETA: 202(3)

If the vehicle or aircraft is used less than exclusively in a commercial activity, a full input tax credit may not be claimed in respect of the acquisition or improvement. However, the

ETA: 202(4)

individual or partnership is entitled to claim an input tax credit equal to 6/106 of the capital cost allowance claimed for income tax purposes, to the extent the vehicle or aircraft is used in a commercial activity. For example, if an individual purchases a car for $16,000 (including GST) for use 60% in a commercial activity, the individual would be able to claim an input tax credit equal to $82 (i.e., $\frac{1}{2} \times 30\%$ of $16,000 \times 60\% \times 6/106$) in the first year. An input tax credit may also be claimed in subsequent years based on capital cost allowance claims.

On the actual disposition of a passenger vehicle or aircraft, GST applies only if the vehicle or aircraft was used exclusively in a commercial activity since its acquisition.

ETA: 203(3)

Where an individual or partnership sells a passenger vehicle that immediately before that time was used exclusively in a commercial activity the following applies. The individual or partnership is entitled to claim an input tax credit in the same manner as other registrants (as discussed above) on all or a portion of the cost on acquisition and any improvements, that exceeded $30,000 and that was previously denied.

ETA: 203(1)

¶5,800 **REVIEW QUESTIONS**

(1) In the year of acquisition only one-half of the capital cost of an asset is added to the CCA class. Comment.

(2) If an asset is sold for less than the UCC balance in the class then there will be a terminal loss. Comment.

(3) The "cost amount" of depreciable property is the original cost of the asset. Comment.

(4) The "capital cost" of depreciable property is the original cost of the asset before any CCA is claimed. Comment.

(5) The half-year rule applies to all property acquired in all CCA classes. Comment.

(6) The half-year rule is designed to take into account the period of ownership during the year and the fact that not all assets are purchased at the beginning of the year. Comment.

(7) CCA can be claimed in the year that title and the incidence of ownership are acquired by the taxpayer. Comment.

(8) Once a CCA claim has been made a taxpayer cannot go back and change the amount of the prior year's claim. Comment.

(9) When the fiscal period of a business is less than 365 days then the CCA must be prorated for the number of days in the fiscal year. Comment.

(10) Once an asset has been disposed of, then no CCA can be claimed on that asset. Comment.

(11) A client just bought a new piece of equipment that cost her $50,000. Because of the nature of the asset she has received a government grant of $15,000 to help pay for it. She thinks she can only depreciate $35,000. Comment.

(12) It has just cost a client $20,000 in legal fees to obtain a patent on some new equipment. Given his profitability, he is unhappy that he can only depreciate these costs as a Class 14 asset over the 20-year life of the patent but his controller says that he does not have any choice. Comment.

(13) Mrs. Smith has just incorporated her company to carry on a retail business. As part of the start-up costs she has paid $800 to have the company incorporated and $10,000 to obtain the indefinite-life franchise that she wanted. Each of these expenditures are eligible capital expenditures and since they are different they each go into their own CEC pool. Comment.

(14) Mr. Finis has just come to tell you that he has decided to wind up his business and retire. He is in the process of selling all of his assets but he cannot find one buyer who will continue the business and pay him something for goodwill. He is disappointed since he has a balance of $15,000 in his CEC account that cannot be used. Comment.

Au M/6
62

¶5,825   MULTIPLE CHOICE QUESTIONS

Question 1

X Ltd. purchased a $50,000 passenger vehicle in 2007. What is the maximum amount that X Ltd. may claim as capital cost allowance for the vehicle in 2007, ignoring provincial sales taxes and the goods and services tax?

(A) $7,500

(B) $9,000

(C) $4,500

(D) $4,050

Question 2

R Ltd. owns a restaurant business which it carries on in rented premises. R Ltd. redecorated and renovated and made $80,000 of leasehold improvements. The lease expires on December 31, 2012 (5 years) and has two successive renewal options of 3 years each. Assuming that R Ltd. has a December 31 year-end, what is the maximum CCA that R Ltd. can claim in 2007 in respect of these improvements?

(A) $5,000

(B) $8,000

(C) $10,000

(D) $16,000

Question 3

In the year, ABC Ltd. purchased goodwill relating to a business for $100,000. Assuming ABC Limited has no other depreciable or eligible capital property, what is the maximum write-off that ABC Ltd. can claim for this goodwill in the year?

(A) $2,500

(B) $3,500

(C) $7,000

(D) $5,250

Question 4

On January 1, 2005, ABC Ltd. signed a 5-year lease for retail space for a store. The lease expires on December 31, 2009, and has two successive renewal options for three years each, In 2007, ABC Ltd. made $60,000 of leasehold improvements to this space. Assuming that ABC Ltd. has a December 31 year-end, what is the maximum capital cost allowance claim that ABC Ltd. can make in 2007 in respect of these improvements?

(A) $3,750

(B) $5,000

(C) $6,000

(D) $7,500

Question 5

During the year, Swiss Restaurants purchased the following assets for its restaurant and catering business:

Moulds for fancy chocolate items ($300 each)	$ 1,200
An accounting program (computer software)	600
Linens for tables in the restaurants	400
Cutlery, dishes and kitchen utensils costing less than $500 each	15,000

What is the maximum CCA claim for these assets?

(A) $8,600

(B) $16,300

(C) $16,900

(D) $17,200

Question 6

The new controller of a pharmaceutical company has asked you how the legal costs to obtain a patent on a new drug are treated for tax purposes. Which one of the following options is not available?

(A) include in Class 14,

(B) include in Class 44,

(C) deduct in the year incurred, or

(D) treat as an eligible capital expenditure.

¶5,850 EXERCISES

Exercise 1

ITA: 14(5), 20(1)(a);
ITR: 1100

Businesses in two plazas operating on either side of a very busy city street decided to pool their promotional efforts. They also decided to build an overpass so that customers could avoid crossing the street when shopping at the plazas. The overpass was constructed at a cost of $150,000 after appropriate arrangements were made with the city because the footings to the overpass had to be placed on city property. These arrangements did not include a leasehold interest in the city property.

— *REQUIRED*

In what class of assets can the overpass be placed for capital cost allowance?

Exercise 2

ITA: 20(16.1), 21(1);
ITR: 1100(2.5), 1100(6)

Slick Sales is a commission salesman who has been claiming capital cost allowance on his automobile under paragraph 8(1)(j). The automobile was purchased for $38,000 (including PST of 8% and GST of 7%) in October 2005. The undepreciated capital cost of his automobile at January 1, 2007, was $18,475. In 2007, he sold the automobile for $12,000. Slick does 75% of his driving for employment purposes out of 16,000 kilometres of total driving.

— *REQUIRED*

(A) What are the tax consequences in 2007 to Slick on the sale of the old car?

(B) What are the tax consequences in 2007 if Slick buys a new car in October 2007 for $36,000 including PST (8%) and GST (6%)? His net commission income after deducting cash expenses for 2007 is $3,000.

Exercise 3 62

ITA: 20(1)(a); ITR: 1100;
Sched. II, III

The following balances were found in the various classes of depreciable assets on the books of Wasting Assets Ltd., as at January 1, 2007:

Class 1 (see (1) below)	$120,000
Class 8	75,000
Class 10 (truck for transportation of goods)	40,000
Class 13 (see (2) below)	42,000
Class 14 (see (3) below)	54,400

Additional information and transactions during 2006:

(1) The Class 1 undepreciated capital cost represents two buildings costing $100,000 each. One building was sold for $150,000 during 2007.

(2) The Class 13 balance relates to a long-term lease on a warehouse for 30 years with an option to renew for a further 20 years. The original cost of the leasehold improvements in 1991 was $50,000.

(3) Class 14 consists of a patent for 20 years costing $68,000 on January 1, 2003. (Ignore the effects of the leap years in the period).

(4) Purchases during the year:

Manufacturing equipment	$50,000
Office equipment	10,000

— *REQUIRED*

Prepare a schedule showing the maximum capital cost allowance deductions for tax purposes in 2007.

Exercise 4

ITA: 13(4)

(If consideration of the topics of involuntary and voluntary dispositions has been deferred to Chapter 8, this exercise should also be deferred.)

Windswept Storage Ltd. had a brick warehouse that was completely destroyed by a tornado early in its 2006 fiscal year ended December 31. The building had cost $300,000 and its Class 3 undepreciated capital cost at the time of its destruction was $221,000. Agreement was reached on the insurance claim later in 2006 when the company received only $295,000. A new brick building was fully constructed by August 2007 for $400,000.

— REQUIRED

Trace the effects of these events on the balance of the undepreciated capital cost from 2006 through to the beginning balance for 2008, assuming that the proper election is made.

ITA: 13(4)

Exercise 5

ITA: 13(7)(*d*)

Smilely Service purchased a car in 2005 for $14,600. His business use of the car during 250 days each year based on mileage of 16,000 kilometres in total and the fair market values of the car in each of the years to the present were as follows:

	Business use	Fair market value
2005	85%	$14,600
2006	80%	12,200
2007	90%	9,800

— REQUIRED

Compute the maximum capital cost allowance that can be claimed.

Exercise 6

ITA: 14(1), 20(1)(*b*)

Ms. Glutton sold her unincorporated grocery business in 2007 and received $45,000 for goodwill. The business had a December 31 year-end.

— REQUIRED

If the grocery store had been purchased on January 2, 1995 with a payment of $10,800 for goodwill at that time, compute the effect of the 2007 sale on Ms. Glutton's income. Assume that maximum deductions for amortization have been made in previous years, except in the years 1997 to 2005 inclusive when no amount was claimed since the business only had losses.

ITA: 20(1)(*b*)

Exercise 7 62

ITA: 14(1), 20(1)(*b*)

Buylo Ltd., which has been in the same business, except as noted below, since 1999, made the following purchases and sales throughout the period 1999 to 2007.

Jan. 1, 1999	Purchased goodwill at $40,000.
June 1, 2001	Purchased a government licence with an indefinite life for $50,000.
Mar. 1, 2003	Purchased a trademark for $20,000.
Nov. 1, 2004	Purchased goodwill for $50,000.
Sept. 7, 2005	Sold 1998 goodwill for $100,000.
Aug. 3, 2007	Sold all of the remaining assets of the business to a competitor for $500,000 of which $150,000 could be attributed to the licence and $200,000 to the trademark.

— REQUIRED

Calculate the income for the 2005 and 2007 taxation years, assuming the company always took the maximum tax amortization deductions each year for its fiscal years ending December 31. Calculate the amount of cumulative eligible capital as at January 1, 2008.

ITA: 14(1), 20(1)(*b*)

¶5,850

¶5,875   ASSIGNMENT PROBLEMS

Problem 1

ITA: 13(1), 13(2), 20(1)(a), 20(16.1); ITR: 1100(1), 1100(2.5), 1101(5p), 1103(2h), 7307(1)(b); Sch. II, III

On March 1, 2006, Jennifer Lobo began operating as a sole proprietorship and purchased the licence to manufacture the computer software version of the latest trivia game, "Tax is a Microcosm of Life on CD". During the remainder of 2006, she acquired the following assets:

Manufacturing equipment	$20,000
Tools (each costing under $500)	16,000
Dies and moulds	8,000
Computer equipment and systems software	12,000
Photocopier	6,000
Office furnishings	15,000
Customer lists (expected to be used indefinitely)	4,000
Delivery van	30,000
T.V. commercial video tape	22,000
Chairs and tables (for the employee eating area)	2,500
Cutlery and dishes (for the employee eating area)	2,000
Table linens (for the employee eating area)	1,200
Automobile (for use by sales personnel visiting clients)	38,000
Licence to manufacture, based on patented information, "Tax is a Microcosm of Life on CD" for 3 years ending February 29, 2009	30,000
Made improvements on the building that she leased on March 1, 2006; the lease was for 3 years with two successive options to renew of 3 years and 4 years	9,000

During 2007, she made the following additional purchases and disposals:

Bought a brick building and land in May to be used 95% for manufacturing; an appraisal indicated that the building represented 45% of the total cost of the property	$200,000
Sold the photocopier	(4,000)
Sold the automobile	(23,000)
Sold the T.V. commercial video tape	(18,000)
Sold some of the tools (costing less than $500 each)	(5,000)

—*REQUIRED*

Prepare a schedule to show the maximum capital cost allowance for the fiscal years ended December 31, 2006 and December 31, 2007, ignoring GST and PST considerations. Where choices are available, state the reasons for your decision. Ignore the effects, if any, of the leap year.

Problem 2

ITA: 13(4)

(If consideration of the topics of involuntary and voluntary dispositions has been deferred to Chapter 8, this problem should also be deferred.)

Elaine Barblaik owns an apartment building which she holds for rental income. In November 2006, Elaine settled with municipal authorities on expropriation proceeds for the property including the building. The agreed expropriation proceeds for the building and the separate sale proceeds for the appliances and fixtures are indicated in the following data:

	Expropriated building Cl.3	*Sold appliances & fixtures*
Cost	$406,000	$26,000
UCC January 1, 2006	188,500	7,250
Proceeds	362,500	2,600

Since negotiations had been prolonged, Elaine was able to anticipate the approximate date of settlement and, as a result, she was able to replace in 2007 the assets expropriated.

Replacement cost for the building and the cost of new appliances and fixtures were as follows:

Building $1,276,000
Appliances and fixtures   46,400

— REQUIRED

Trace the effects of these events on the undepreciated capital cost for both assets through to the opening balance on January 1, 2008 assuming no further additions are made to either class of assets.

Problem 3

ITA: 13(7)

On January 20, 2006, a personal residence which originally cost $280,000 was converted into a rental property. At this time the property had a fair market value of $320,000. On June 1, 2008, the property was converted back to a personal residence. At that time the property had a fair market value of $305,000.

— REQUIRED

If the building is the only asset in Class 1, which has a 4% capital cost allowance rate, how much capital cost allowance may be deducted for the years 2006 through 2008, inclusive? [Note that where an individual has income from property, the taxation year for that income is the full calendar year, i.e., there cannot be a short taxation year for that income.]

Problem 4

ITA: 14, 20(1)(*b*)

Sharp is a musician who paid $500 in 1997 for an indefinite-life licence to perform in the subway walkway areas. In 2002, Sharp decided to try a different approach to developing a following. He purchased the name of a popular local band that stopped performing earlier that year. The cost of the name was $16,128 and the appropriate amount was included in the January 1, 2003 balance below. In 2003, he purchased an indefinite-life licence from the city for $5,000 which allowed him to perform on a street-corner on Saturday afternoons. In 2004, Sharp found that he wanted to spend more time in the studio, so he sold the street-corner licence for $6,000. In 2007, Sharp decided to break up his band and pursue a career as an accountant. He sold the band name for $20,000.

Sharp has not yet filed his tax return for 2007. The year-end of the business is December 31. The following information is available with respect to the cumulative eligible capital account:

(a) the balance in the cumulative eligible capital account, on January 1, 2003, was $11,492, and

(b) the total cumulative eligible capital amount claimed prior to 2003 was $979.

— REQUIRED

Prepare a schedule calculating the balance of the cumulative eligible capital account on January 1, 2008, and calculating the impact on income for 2007.

Problem 5

ITA: 14, 20(1)(*b*),
20(1)(*cc*); IT-206R

Con-Glo Corporation has been involved in various food services businesses since its incorporation in 1993. Con-Glo has a December 31 year-end. You have been asked by the controller to examine the transactions involving various intangible assets due to an impending sale of the business. The controller wants to ensure that he understands the implications on the sale. You have been provided with the following information.

Shortly after the business was incorporated, Con-Glo purchased its first family restaurant. The purchase price included $43,000 for goodwill. After operating this business for a number of years and ensuring that it was profitable, another restaurant was purchased in 2000. The purchase again included goodwill in the amount of $68,000. The second restaurant had more of a roadhouse atmosphere. The business had obtained a liquor licence. The value of the licence at the time of the purchase was $21,133, and this amount was allocated to the licence in the purchase agreement.

Con-Glo operated the two restaurants until 2002 when it purchased a fast food franchise. The franchise was for an undefined number of years and cost $103,000.

The fast food restaurant, while successful, was too much of a drain on the time of the owners of Con-Glo and was sold in 2004. The value of the franchise agreement was determined to be $110,000.

In 2005, it was determined that the original family restaurant would be more successful if it obtained a liquor licence. In order to obtain the licence a presentation had to be made to the liquor licensing board. Con-Glo paid $29,000 in legal fees related to the presentation to the board.

In 2006, the second restaurant was sold. Con-Glo received $80,000 for the goodwill and $60,000 for the liquor licence.

Due to health problems of the owner's wife, Con-Glo is also considering a sale of the balance of their restaurants in 2007. The selling price will include $250,000 for goodwill.

— *REQUIRED*

Prepare a schedule calculating the balance of the cumulative eligible capital account as of January 1, 2008, and determine the impact of the above transactions on income for 2000 through 2007. Assume that the opening balance on January 1, 2000, was $20,865, the 1994 to 1999 CECA deductions were a total of $11,385, and that the company took the maximum tax write-offs that it was entitled to in each of the years 2000 to 2005. (Hint: consider paragraph 20(1)(*cc*).) Assume also that Con-Glo was deemed to be in the same business in respect of its restaurant and catering business as per IT-206R.

Problem 6

ITA: 13, 14, 20(1)(*a*), 20(1)(*b*); ITR: 1100; Sched. II, III

Jon's Auto Parts Ltd., which manufactures small equipment, was incorporated in 1980 and had the following balances in its records concerning its capital assets as at January 1, 2007.

	Depreciation		CCA	
Type of asset	*Straight-line*	*Book value*	*Class*	*UCC*
Land	Nil	$102,000		Nil
Building	40 years	272,000	3	$153,000
Equipment.	5 years	163,000	8	39,000
Rolling stock — trucks etc. (for transportation of goods)	3 years	306,000	10	170,000
Leasehold improvements (see note (1) below)	life of lease	113,000	13	165,000
Licences	5 years	70,000	14	87,393

Additional Information

(1) The Class 13 assets consist of:

— Improvements to a leased warehouse costing $100,000 in 2006. The remaining length of the lease in 2006 was 6 years with two successive options of 4 years.

— Improvements to a leased office space for head office downtown, costing $81,600 in 2005. The remaining length of the lease was five years with an option to renew for an additional one year.

(2) The licences were purchased to start on April 22, 2005, at a cost of $110,500 and had a life of five years.

(3) During 2007, the company had the following capital transactions:

Additions:
— Purchased, in June, a new concrete manufacturing building costing $1,625,000, including $325,000 for land.
— Additional expenditures re the building:
Paved parking lot for employees . . . . $ 97,000
Erected a steel fence around an outside storage area 65,000
— Further renovations to leased office space, costing 51,000
— Purchased equipment:
Office equipment . . . . $ 47,000
Manufacturing equipment (August). 255,000
Radio communication equipment 60,000
— Purchased a distributing licence on March 1, 2007, for 5 years from a foreign manufacturing company of a related product line, cost: $240,000.
— Paid $34,500 in legal fees in reorganizing the capital structure.

Disposals:

	Cost	Book value	Proceeds
Equipment — office	$ 16,250	$ 4,225	$ 1,950
Brick building in Cl. 3 (excluding land)	390,000	272,000	568,000

— *REQUIRED*

Prepare a schedule for tax purposes to reflect the above transactions and calculate the maximum write-off for tax purposes. (Ignore the effects of the replacement property rules in subsection 13(4) and the effects of leap years.)

Problem 7

ITA: 13, 14, 18–20;
ITR: 1100; Sched. II, III

The controller of Choleva Products Limited has provided you with the following draft income statement as well as some notes that she made during the preparation of this statement.

Choleva Products Limited

STATEMENT OF INCOME
For the year ended December 31, 2007

Sales		$8,300,000
Cost of goods sold (Note (1))		6,800,000)
Gross profit		$1,500,000
Commission income		70,000
		$1,570,000
Administrative and marketing expenses (Note (2))	$500,000	
Depreciation and amortization (Note (3))	80,000	
Interest on long-term debt (Note (4))	70,000	
Interest on bank indebtedness	120,000	(770,000)
		$ 800,000
Gain on disposal of property, plant and equipment (Note (3))		40,000
Net income before income taxes		$ 840,000
Provision for income taxes		(400,000)
Net income after income taxes		$ 440,000

Notes Prepared by Controller:

(1) The cost of goods sold expense includes the following amounts:

(a) A $9,000 loss from a theft by a warehouse employee;

(b) A $15,000 reserve for future decline in the value of inventory because of new products expected to be introduced by the competitor. There was no such reserve in 2006.

(2) Administration and marketing expenses include:

(a) An $11,000 increase in the reserve for warranty expenses;

(b) $4,000 of donations to registered charities;

(c) $1,500 for golf club membership dues for the Vice-President of Sales and $2,000 for meals and entertainment expenses at the golf club. The Vice-President of Sales uses the club to generate sales;

(d) $85,000 in accrued bonuses, including $62,000 paid to employees on May 31, 2008, and $23,000 paid to employees on June 30, 2008;

(e) A $15,000 year-end party for all employees;

(f) $8,000 of financing fees incurred in connection with the mortgage of the corporation's new plant, including legal fees of $6,000 and an appraisal fee of $2,000;

(g) $5,000 of legal fees in connection with the purchase of shares of another company; and

(h) $300 for an upgrade of word-processing software.

(3) The fixed asset section of the controller's working papers indicate the following:

(a) The undepreciated capital cost balances at December 31, 2006 were as follows:

Class 3	$200,000
Class 8	60,000
Class 10	80,000
Class 13	37,500
CEC	5,000

(b) Gain on disposal of property of plant and equipment consists of the profit on the sale of the corporation's only Class 3 asset (proceeds: $180,000; original cost in 1992: $300,000). The land on which the building was situated was also sold for its fair market value which was equal to its cost in 1992.

(c) During 2007, the corporation made the following purchases:

- A new office building was purchased in October for $700,000. The cost of the related land was $400,000. It cost $20,000 to pave part of the land for use as a parking lot and $30,000 to erect fencing;

- New office furniture was purchased for $25,000. This purchase replaced office furniture which was sold for its $4,000 net book value (original cost: $10,000);

- An unlimited life franchise was purchased for $100,000;

- A 10-year licence to use patented information (expiring June 30, 2017) was purchased on July 1 for $20,000; and

- Improvements on its leased head office premises which were rented in 2005 for 4 years with two successive options to renew for 5 years and 5 years. Improvements had originally been made in 2005 in the amount of $45,000. Additional improvements were made in 2007 at a cost of $28,000.

(d) During the year, the corporation sold some small tools (each costing less than $500) for their net book value of $500.

(4) Interest on long-term debt includes:

(a) Bond discount amortization in the amount of $2,000;

(b) $18,000 of interest on bonds issued to buy shares in another company; and

(c) $50,000 of interest on the mortgage on the new plant.

— *REQUIRED*

Calculate the corporation's minimum income from business or property for the year ended December 31, 2007, under the provisions of the Act. Assume all expenses are reasonable in the circumstances. Support your treatment of each item listed above with a reason or a section reference. Ignore the effects of leap years.

[For more problems and solutions thereto, see the CD accompanying this book.]

¶5,880 ADVISORY CASES

Case 1: Dundas Printing Inc.

Dundas Printing Inc. has been in business for the past 20 years. It has only been in the past three years that Bill Peach has taken over the operations from his father (who founded the company and is now retired). As a result of his new-found management freedom and changes in the marketplace, Bill has decided to expand his operations.

One of the printing presses he needed to buy would have been too expensive if he had bought it new, so he found a used press at half the price. The drawback is that it will take some time to get the press into production, since it needs some repairs to put it into workable condition. However, Bill feels that this is still a good buy since it will meet his needs for the next five years, by which time new technology will probably make it obsolete and he will be forced to buy a new machine.

Before his retirement, Bill's father drove a car that the company had purchased for his use at a cost of $45,000. The car was given to Bill for his use on his father's retirement. Bill has now decided that he is going to trade in this car for a car that he always wanted — a sports car that is going to cost $65,000 less the trade-in value of $25,000 for the old car. Bill promises to take you for a ride when it is delivered.

In order to increase his market share, Bill bought all of the assets of one of his competitors. This not only gave him access to some important customers, it also allowed him to acquire some specialized equipment and skilled operators. The vendor had wanted to sell Bill the shares of his company, but Bill had convinced the vendor to sell him the assets, instead, including goodwill of $40,000.

Bill would like your advice on the tax implications of his plans.

Case 2: Kingston Carpets Inc.

Kingston Carpets Inc. ("Kingston") has been operating a retail carpet business out of the same location for the past 18 years. It has been very successful in gaining business from the local developers, who use Kingston almost exclusively to provide their flooring. In addition, Kingston is used extensively by the area insurance adjusters for carpet replaced due to fire and other damages. This business did not come to Kingston overnight. The owners, Andy and Sue Greene, have always spent much of their time promoting their business to these markets.

Both Andy and Sue are avid golfers. They each belong to a different golf club, in order to be members at the clubs where most of their customers play. They find that golf is an activity that has paid off, since they have conducted a significant amount of business through their contacts at the golf clubs. They will often use these clubs for lunch and dinner meetings with customers, as well as for the company's seasonal holiday party.

Last year, the company bought a building across the street from its original retail store. The previous owner had been leasing out the building and had not spent much money on repairs over the last five years. As a result, while Kingston Carpets paid a relatively low price for the property, it has had to spend a considerable amount on repairs over the past year. Prior to this purchase, Kingston had been leasing its space.

To maintain their image of success, Sue and Andy both drive expensive cars and often entertain customers at their cottage or on their boat. This approach seems to work, and their customers are always asking when the next outing will be.

Besides treating their customers well, Sue and Andy also treat their employees well. All employees belong to the group benefit plan that provides extended health care, dental, life insurance, and disability coverage. Because of the low coverage from the company's group life and disability insurance, Andy and Sue have had the company take out individual policies on both of them. The beneficiary on the life insurance policies is the company, and on the disability policies the beneficiaries are Andy and Sue.

One of their valued employees was recently divorced and during the divorce her family home was sold. In order to keep her concentrating on business, Andy and Sue had the company loan her enough to buy a house. The loan was secured by the house and no interest was charged. At that time, the company did not have enough cash to make this loan so it had to borrow the funds at prime plus ½%.

In addition to all of this, Andy and Sue have been actively involved in a number of charitable and political activities and have made donations to both. Even these activities have turned into business opportunities. Last year, they gave a donation to a local charity and shortly thereafter they received an order for the new carpet that was to go in the charity's offices.

Advise Sue and Andy on the tax implications of their situation and that of Kingston Carpets.

¶5,900   SUPPLEMENTAL NOTES

(This section can be omitted without losing continuity of the chapter. None of the review questions, multiple choice questions, exercises or assignment problems utilizes this information.)

¶5,910   Lease-Option Arrangements

As has been shown, the capital cost allowance system allows for the write-off of the decline in value of a pool of assets over the period of their ownership. When the decline in value has not been as great as the capital cost allowance deducted, as evidenced by proceeds of disposition in excess of the undepreciated capital cost of a class of assets, provision is made to recapture the excess capital cost allowance previously deducted. Recapture is included in income, when it arises, to offset the capital cost allowance previously deducted that exceeded the decline in value of the pool of assets.

A similar problem arises on a lease-option arrangement. An asset may be leased for a period of time and at the end of that period an option to purchase the asset may be exercised. If the lease arrangement is regarded as a true rental agreement and not as a purchase, the lease payments would be deducted in full during the years of the lease arrangement. On the purchase of the asset by the exercise of the option, the capital cost of the asset would ordinarily be established at the purchase price under the option. If the asset is sold for more than that capital cost, a capital gain which is partially taxable would ordinarily result. However, the gain in value from the purchase price under the option should be regarded as a recapture of some of the lease payments previously deducted from income in full.

The rules provide for the calculation of that recapture. These rules are invoked when the lease arrangement is not regarded as a financing arrangement for the purchase of an asset (i.e., a "capital" lease), but as a rental arrangement (i.e., an "operating" lease). The CRA indicated[*] that whether a lease is a capital lease or an operating lease "will depend on the legal relationship created by the terms of the agreement".   ITA: 13(5.2), 13(5.3)

It may be instructive to consider the conditions for a capital lease set out in the CICA *Handbook* at section 3065.06. (Refer, also, to the issue raised by the Emerging Issues Committee in EIC-30.) The CRA formerly used the following conditions under which a transaction would be considered to be a sale rather than a lease:

(a) the lessee automatically acquires title to the asset after the payment of a specified amount in rentals;

(b) the lessee is required to buy the asset by the termination of the lease;

(c) the lessee has the right to buy the asset, by the end of the lease, at a price which is substantially less than the estimate, at the beginning of the lease, of the fair market value of the property at the time of acquisition; or

(d) the lessee has the right to buy the asset, by the end of the lease, at a price which, at the beginning of the lease, is such that no reasonable person would not buy the asset.

One rule applies where a taxpayer has acquired, on the exercise of a purchase option, depreciable capital property or real property (i.e., land and buildings) from a lessor to whom the taxpayer has paid rent under an operating lease for the use of the property at a capital cost or cost less than the fair market value. This situation would usually be regarded as an operating lease, if the option price represented an estimate, at the time the rental arrangement was made, of the fair market value of the asset. However, as a result of market conditions that arise during the rental period, the actual fair market value at the time of the exercise of the purchase option was higher. The taxpayer is deemed to acquire the property, at the time of the exercise of the option, for an amount equal to the lesser of: ITA: 13(5.2)

(a) the fair market value of the property at the time of the exercise of the option, and

---

[*] "Income Tax Technical News No. 21", June 14, 2001.

(b) (i) the actual cost of the property at the time of the exercise of the option, *plus*

(ii) all previous payments of rent for the use of the property.

The excess, if any, of the deemed cost, determined above, over the actual cost under the option is considered to be capital cost allowance taken by the taxpayer. As a result, any proceeds of disposition from the ultimate sale of the property up to the deemed cost of the property will reduce the undepreciated capital cost balance of the asset class to which the property belongs, thereby creating either potential or actual recapture. This recapture will offset, to some extent, the benefit derived from the previous deduction of rental payments for the property.

When the property, that is leased and then purchased under an option, is non-depreciable real property (e.g., land), the property is deemed to be depreciable property of a separate class as prescribed by the Regulations. Class 36 is prescribed for this purpose and is used only to determine the recapture of previous rental payments on the ultimate sale of the non-depreciable real property acquired under a purchase option. The balance in this class is not eligible for capital cost allowance.

ITR: 1101(5g)

Another rule applies where a taxpayer disposes of the option to purchase depreciable capital property or real property that has previously been rented, rather than exercising the option. In this case, the excess of the proceeds of disposition for the option over the cost of the option is included in income as recapture.

ITA: 13(5.3)

ITA: 13(1)

Example Problem

Mr. Britelite leased a car for the exclusive use of his business for three years at a cost of $500 per month. The lease agreement with the arm's length lessor provided Mr. Britelite with an option to buy the car at the end of the three years for $6,500 which was estimated, at the time of signing the lease, to be the fair market value of the car at the end of the three years. However, at the time the option was exercised, at the end of the third year, the fair market value of the car was actually $8,000 and the car was sold in the following year for $7,500. The car was the only asset in Class 10 of the business and no capital cost allowance was claimed in the class before the car was sold.

— *REQUIRED*

What are the tax implications of these transactions?

— *SOLUTION*

The terms of the lease do not appear to classify it as a capital lease. None of the conditions specified by the CRA appears to apply. Ownership of the car by Mr. Britelite at the end of the lease is not assured, given the terms of the lease, including the option purchase price.

IT-233R, par. 7

During the three years that the lease was in force, the lease payments of $500 per month were fully deductible if the car was used exclusively for business purposes.

When the car was purchased for $6,500, at the end of the third year, the Act would deem the capital cost to be the lesser of:

ITA: 13(5.2)(a)

(a) the fair market value of the car at the time of its purchase under the option .... $ 8,000

(b) (i) the actual cost of the car at the time of its purchase under the option .... $ 6,500
plus
(ii) all previous lease payments for the use of the car ($500 × 12 × 3) 18,000 $24,500

Mr. Britelite's business will be deemed to have deducted capital cost allowance in respect of the car equal to the excess of the deemed cost of $8,000, as computed above, over the $6,500 actual cost. As a result, the net addition to the undepreciated capital cost of Class 10 will be $6,500 and Mr. Britelite will be potentially liable for a recapture on proceeds up to the $8,000 of deemed capital cost.

ITA: 13(5.2)(b)

When the car was sold in the fourth year for $7,500, a recapture of $1,000 (i.e., $7,500 – 6,500) would result. Conceptually, this recapture represents an excess of deduction for the lease payments relative to the actual decline in the value of the car. The lease payments were originally computed based on an estimated decline in value of the car to $6,500 but the actual decline in value was only to $7,500 by the time of its sale. This $1,000 of recapture represents lease payments that were fully deducted in excess of the real decline in value of the car.

The effects of the above example on Class 10 can be traced as follows:

	Car Class 10: 30%	
Addition of deemed capital cost	$ 8,000	ITA: 13(5.2)(a)
Less: deemed capital cost allowance	1,500	ITA: 13(5.2)(b)
UCC	$ 6,500	
Less: CCA claimed	Nil	
UCC	$ 6,500	

Disposition — Lesser of:		
(a) proceeds of disposition	$7,500	
(b) capital cost	$8,000	
lesser amount		(7,500)
Recapture		$(1,000)

Had CCA been claimed on the $6,500 of UCC, the amount of recapture would be higher, reflecting the recovery on the disposition of that CCA claimed, as well as some of the past lease payments deducted.

¶5,920 Leasing Property

The provisions of section 16.1 are designed to curtail the advantages of leasing in certain situations. Accelerated capital cost allowance is of little or no advantage to an owner of depreciable capital property, if the owner is in a loss position or is otherwise not taxable. In those cases, it becomes advantageous to lease property from a lessor who can benefit from the accelerated capital cost allowance. In return, the lessee can, perhaps, obtain lease-payment terms that are relatively more favourable, because of the tax advantage to the lessor.

By virtue of the Regulations designed to remove this advantage, a limit is placed on the capital cost allowance that a lessor can claim on certain leasing property. An assumption is made that the lease is, in effect, a loan with interest at a rate prescribed by the Regulations. ITR: 4302 The payments received by the lessor are considered to be blended payments of interest and principal. The amount of capital cost allowance that can be claimed by the lessor is, then, limited to the lesser of the principal component of the blended payment and the capital cost allowance (without the application of the half-year rule) that would otherwise be computed by the lessor on the leased property.

This limitation on a lessor applies only to taxpayers whose principal business is leasing. The limitation applies only to "specified leasing property" which is defined to include depre- ITR: 1100(1.11) ciable property with a fair market value in excess of $25,000, leased to an arm's length lessee for a term of more than one year.

Certain property is exempt from the limitation on capital cost allowance. "Exempt ITR: 1100(1.13)(a) property" is defined to include:

(i) certain general purpose office furniture or office equipment included in Class 8 or certain general purpose electronic data processing equipment included in Class 10;

(ii) furniture, appliances and other similar properties designed for residential use;

(iii) passenger vehicles, vans or pick-up trucks;

(iv) highway trucks or tractors with a "gross vehicle weight rating" of under 11,778 kilo-grams;

(v) trailers designed to be hauled by a truck or tractor described in (iv) above; and

(vi) a building, or part of a building, including component parts.

Property that appears to be subject to the restrictions might be characterized very generally as high-cost, heavy equipment. However, the specifics of these definitions must be consulted in a particular case. Exempt property might generally be characterized as property for which capital cost allowance rates fairly closely approximate physical or economic depreciation rates, rather than investment incentive rates.

Lessees are, generally, not affected by the restrictions on capital cost allowance claimed by lessors. As a result, lessees may deduct the full amount of lease payments made. However, a special election is available for property (other than prescribed property, defined a regulation) leased from certain arm's length lessors for more than one year. If the election is filed jointly by the lessee and the lessor, the lessee will be treated as if he or she had borrowed an amount equal to the fair market value of the leased property at the rate prescribed by the Regulations. The lessee can deduct capital cost allowance and the assumed interest payment in each rental payment. The lessor's tax position is not affected by the election, although the lessor's capital cost allowance deduction may be limited by the rules applicable to lessors, as discussed above.

ITA: 16.1(1)

ITR: 8200

ITR: 4302

ITR: 1100(1.1)

¶5,930   Capital Personal Property for GST Purposes

A full input tax credit will be allowed where capital personal property is purchased for use primarily in a commercial activity. If the primary-use test is not satisfied, no part of the tax will be creditable. "Primarily" is interpreted by the CRA to mean greater than 50%.

ETA: 199(2)

It should be noted that any subsequent change in the proportion of commercial use over the life of the capital property may trigger adjustments in the GST.

There may be cases where improvements are made to capital personal property. A registrant is allowed to claim an ITC for GST paid or payable on an improvement that has been made to capital personal property. For this rule to apply, the property must be used primarily in a commercial activity at the time the tax is paid or payable on the improvement.

ETA: 199(4)

The term "improvement" is defined to include any consideration paid or payable in respect of capital property that would be included in determining the adjusted cost base (capital cost) of the property for the purposes of the *Income Tax Act*.

ETA: 123(1)

The sale of capital personal property is subject to GST where the property is being used primarily in commercial activities prior to sale. If the primary-use test is not met, the sale is not subject to GST.

ETA: 200(3)

Modified rules apply to capital personal property acquired and used by financial institutions.

ETA: 204

Chapter 6

Income from Property

LEARNING GOALS

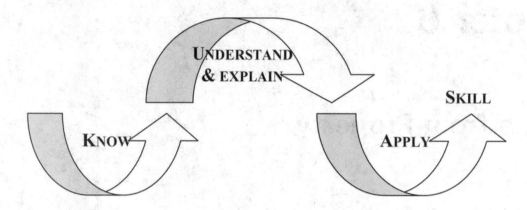

Know

By the end of this chapter you should know the basic provisions of the *Income Tax Act* that relate to property income and the income attribution rules that are uniquely applicable to property income. It is important to know the distinction between property income and business income, since they are two separate sources of income on which different income tax rules may apply. You should also know a little about how the GST affects some property income issues. Completing the Review Questions (¶6,800) and Multiple Choice Questions (¶6,825) is a good way to learn the technical provisions.

Understand and Explain

You should understand and be able to explain the tax treatment of specific types of property income and expenses, including the basic questions of who will pay the tax, and when and how much tax will be paid. You should also understand some basic tax planning strategies that can be utilized in real life to maximize the after-tax return on investment.

Apply

You should be able to apply your knowledge and understanding of property income to real life situations. Completing the Assignment Problems (¶6,875) and Advisory Cases (¶6,880) is an excellent way to develop your ability to identify tax issues and to apply the material in increasingly complex situations.

OVERVIEW

Income for tax purposes (Division B income) is calculated by determining income from each source separately. We have already dealt with two sources of income before this chapter: employment income and business income. Both business income and property income are determined by Subdivision b of Division B in Part I of the *Income Tax Act* (the Act). Although most of the rules dealing with these two sources of income are similar, it is important to notice that there are significant differences. Since some sources of income are treated more generously than the others for tax purposes, such as partial inclusion in income (even exemptions from income) for tax purposes, generous deductions, or lower tax rates, taxpayers will naturally try to characterize their income to a source which will give better tax treatments. Various anti-avoidance rules are introduced to prevent abusive planning. {ITA: 3}

The characterization of property income and business income is a question of fact. In general, investors earn income from property with a relatively passive approach. For example, when an individual invests in bonds, he or she can earn interest income without doing much work. This gives rise to property income. On the other hand, if an individual actively trades bonds in the capital market, the interest income may be classified as business income. In general, business income requires more activities in a process that combines time, effort, and capital investment.

Note that income or loss from property does not include capital gains or capital losses. This exclusion is important when considering the deductibility of an expenditure that depends on producing income from property.[1]

ITA: 9(3)

The GST implication of several of the topics introduced in the discussion of the Act are presented in this chapter.

The following chart provides an overview of the location of most of these provisions.

PART I — DIVISION B
SUBDIVISION b
BUSINESS OR PROPERTY

DIVISION		SUBDIVISION		SECTION	
A	Liability for tax		Basic rules		
B	**Computation of income**	a	Office or employment		
C	Computation of taxable income	**b**	**Business or property**	9-11	Basic rules
		c	Capital gains and losses	12-17	Inclusions
D	Taxable income earned in Canada by non-residents	d	Other income	18-21	Deductions
		e	Other deductions	22-25	Ceasing to carry on business
E	Computation of tax	**f**	**Rules relating to computation of income**	26-37	Special cases
E.1	Minimum tax				
F	Special rules			67	General limitation
G	Deferred and other special income arrangements	g	Amounts not included in income	67.1	Meals and entertainment
		h	Cdn corporations and shareholders	67.2-67.4	Automobiles
H	Exemptions	i	Shareholders of non-resident corporations	67.5	Illegal payments
I	Returns, assessments, payments, and appeals			68	Allocation of price
				69	Inadequate consideration
J	Appeals to the courts	j	Partnerships	70-72	Death
		k	Trusts	**73-75.1**	**Attribution**
				76	Security in satisfaction of income debt
				77	Bond conversion
				78	Unpaid amounts
				79-79.1	Foreclosure
				80-80.04	Settlement of debt
				80.1	Expropriation re foreign property
				80.2	Reimbursement re Crown resource property
				80.3	Drought-induced sale of livestock
				80.4-80.5	**Deemed interest**

---

[1] The case of *The Queen v. Young*, 89 DTC 5234 (F.C.A.), illustrates this issue of deductibility.

Subdivision b of Division B of Part I of the Act contains the primary rules for the computation of income from property. Like the rules for business income discussed in Chapter 4, most of what will be covered will be found in sections 9 through 21.

Some of the more important provisions are as follows:

Inclusions

Sec. 9 Income (loss) for a taxation year from a property is the profit (loss) from that property for the year.

Sec. 12 Income inclusions

Sec. 13 Rules related to capital cost allowance

Sec. 15 Rules for shareholder benefits (discussed in Chapter 13)

Deductions

Sec. 18 Limitations on the deductibility of expenses

Sec. 20 Deductions permitted

In addition, Subdivision f of Division B also provides some rules that are relevant to the computation of property income. For example, the attribution rules determine who is to report the property income received by a particular person. As well, there is a deemed interest benefit to be reported by an individual who received a loan by virtue of their shareholding (discussed in Chapter 13).

ITA: 74.1–74.5

ITA: 15, 80.4

¶6,000   INCLUSIONS

¶6,010   Interest Income

¶6,015   The meaning of interest

The term "interest" is not defined in the Act. The Supreme Court of Canada has defined interest to be "the return or consideration or compensation for the use or retention by one person of a sum of money, belonging to, in a colloquial sense, or owed to, another." This definition has been adopted by the Canada Revenue Agency (CRA). It is unclear in many situations whether an amount paid or payable is in the nature of interest or, as in the case of a discount on a bond, is something else. Partly in order to clarify the issue and to forestall taxpayers from converting amounts from interest to capital, provisions have been legislated in the Act and the Regulations deeming amounts to be interest and requiring them to be brought into income at specified intervals.

IT-396R, par. 12

¶6,020   Method of reporting income

In effect, the primary method for computing interest on a "debt obligation" is the annual accrual method. The Act requires the use this method for corporations, partnerships, certain trusts, and individuals. The term "debt obligation" is not defined in the Act, although the term is used in the definition of an "investment contract". The CRA indicates that "the term 'debt obligation' is considered to include, for example, bank accounts, term deposits, guaranteed investment certificates, Canada Savings Bonds, mortgages, corporate bonds and loans". Thus, the annual accrual method would appear to be required for most common sources of interest income. However, when interest is received, it must be included in income to the extent that the interest has not been included previously by the accrual method. As a result, it is not possible to defer the recognition of, for example, compounding interest by using the cash method to report that interest only when it is received. Therefore, there may be a disadvantage to a compounding-interest debt security, because interest must be accrued and reported annually such that tax is levied in a year when no payment of interest is actually made.

ITA: 12(3)
ITA: 12(11)(*a*)
ITA: 12(4)
IT-396R, par. 19

ITA: 12(1)(*c*)

¶6,025 Accrual rules for individuals

The Act requires that individuals holding an interest in an investment contract include in income, on every anniversary of that contract, any interest accrued to that day, to the extent that it has not previously been included in income. An "investment contract" is defined as any debt obligation other than a salary deferral arrangement, various types of income-based debt, certain government-sponsored debt for small businesses, or prescribed contracts (of which there are none at the present). "Anniversary day" is defined as the day that is one year after the day before the date of issue and every successive one year interval, unless the contract is disposed of before such a day.

ITA: 12(4), 12(11)(*b*)

ITA: 12(11)(*a*)

Example Problem

Ms. N. Vestor purchased a $1,000 face value bond on January 2, 2007, for $1,000. The bond was issued on the same date, January 2, 2007. Interest is payable at 8% compounded semi-annually on uncashed coupons on each of June 30 and December 31 at the investor's option.

— *REQUIRED*

(A) If Ms. Vestor does not exercise her option to receive interest, when would she first have to include an amount in income?

(B) What would be the result if she exercised her option on December 31 for interest payable on both June 30 and December 31, 2007?

— *SOLUTION*

(A) The first "anniversary day" would be January 1, 2008, which is the day that is one year after the day before (January 1, 2007) the date of issue (January 2, 2007). As a result, $81.61 would be required to be included in income in 2008. The inclusion was computed as follows:

ITA: 12(4), 12(11)

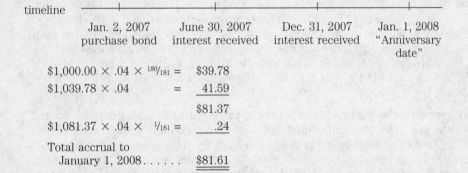

timeline

| Jan. 2, 2007 purchase bond | June 30, 2007 interest received | Dec. 31, 2007 interest received | Jan. 1, 2008 "Anniversary date" |

$$\$1,000.00 \times .04 \times {}^{180}/_{181} = \$39.78$$
$$\$1,039.78 \times .04 = 41.59$$
$$\$81.37$$
$$\$1,081.37 \times .04 \times {}^{1}/_{181} = .24$$

Total accrual to
January 1, 2008 . . . . . . $81.61

(B) The $81.37, received on December 31, 2007, would be included in income to the extent it had not previously been included in income. Thus, only $0.24 (i.e., $81.61 − $81.37) would be included in income in 2008. Interest is included to the extent that it was not otherwise included in computing the taxpayer's income for the taxation year or any previous taxation year.

ITA: 12(1)(*c*)

ITA: 12(4)

¶6,030 Other interest income provisions

Interest that is accrued to the date of transfer on bonds sold or otherwise transferred is brought into the income of the transferor. For example, a bond earning 9% interest per annum paid annually is purchased for face value of $1,000 and sold for $1,045 mid-way through the year. The excess of $45 over cost reflects interest for a half year and must be included in full. It is not a capital gain. Note that the Act allows the recipient (transferee) of the bonds to deduct an amount equal to that included in the income of the transferor.

ITA: 20(14)(*a*)

ITA: 20(14)(*b*)

Interest and principal may be blended by making a loan at a discount but redeemable at par, or made at par but repayable at a premium. The question is whether the discount or premium is interest income or capital gain. A number of factors must be considered. These factors include the amount determined by the terms of the loan agreement and the price at which the property is sold.

For example, government treasury bills do not bear interest, but are issued at a discount from their face value. The discount rate is determined by the prevailing interest rate. The value of repayment is a blend of interest and principal payments. The portion received by the investor in excess of cost is included as interest income which is fully taxable. ITA: 12(1)(c), 16(4)

There is not necessarily an interest component in all payments of this nature. A taxpayer need not charge interest in such a transaction. If the property is sold at fair market value, no interest component in the payments will be assumed. On the other hand, an interest inclusion provision will apply to the sale of property if the contractual price, in total, exceeds the fair market value of the property.[2] ITA: 16(1)

Interest on a scholarship trust fund is not taxable to a parent or grandparent who establishes the fund under the registered education savings plan (RESP) legislation.[3] This provision, which is discussed in more detail in Chapter 9, shelters the accumulated interest such that no tax is paid on it until it is paid out for the benefit of the child. At that time, if it arises, the interest is considered to be the income of the recipient child. ITA: 146.1

¶6,040 Payments Based on Production or Use

¶6,045 Concept of the provision

Any amount received that is dependent on the use of or production from property is taxed as income. Despite the clarity of the provision, it has been the subject of many appeals because ordinary instalment payments of principal which are not taxed as income may not be substantially different from payments based on production or use which are taxed.[4] Also, the distinction between a receipt of income or a receipt of capital has some bearing in this area. Payments that may be expressed as instalments of the sale price of property, but are actually payments depending on the use of or production from that property are taxed, although they may appear to be capital in nature. In certain circumstances, therefore, payments that would otherwise be considered capital and given capital gains treatment are brought into income and fully taxed. Furthermore, property is broadly defined as including not only real and personal property, but also intangible property such as patents, franchises and rights of all kinds. ITA: 12(1)(g) ITA: 248(1)

When selling a property, the buyer and the seller can determine the sales price in various ways. For example, the price can be a lump-sum amount of money payable upon closing of the agreement, or, in the case of an instalment sale, the sales price can be payable over a period of time. Alternatively, the price may be determined by reference to a formula which is dependent on the use of, or production from, the property. The example problem below gives more description of such a transaction and its tax treatments.

---

[2] This was the situation in the case of *Groulx v. M.N.R.*, 67 DTC 5284 (S.C.C.).

[3] Interest on scholarship trust funds has had an interesting history. The CRA, initially, took the position in an Interpretation Bulletin that such interest credited to a taxpayer's account with the trust would be considered annual interest income of the contributing taxpayer. However, in some of these trusts the interest cannot be withdrawn, but is used to provide scholarships for the taxpayer's children if they qualify under the terms of the trust. If the children do not qualify, the interest is used to provide scholarships for other people's children and the original capital contributed is returned. This position was appealed by the taxpayer in the case of *The Queen v. Quinn*, 73 DTC 5215 (F.C.T.D.). The court held that no taxpayer should be required to pay tax on money he had not received beneficially or had not the right to receive and might never, in fact, receive. This situation illustrates the fact that a departmental position, even if it is published as an Interpretation Bulletin, can be successfully challenged by the taxpayer, notwithstanding the weight that might be given to such administrative policy and interpretation by the courts as reiterated by the Federal Court of Appeal in *The Queen v. Royal Trust Corporation of Canada*, 83 DTC 5172, at 5177.

[4] Cases under this provision can be classified by the type of property sold. Oil and gas rights were an issue in the case of *Ross v. M.N.R.*, 50 DTC 775 (Ex. Ct.). Timber was the subject of the cases of *Mouat v. M.N.R.*, 58 DTC 694 (T.A.B.); *Hoffman v. M.N.R.*, 65 DTC 617 (T.A.B.), and *The Queen v. Mel-Bar Ranches Ltd.*, 89 DTC 5189 (F.C.T.D.). Gravel and rock were sold in the cases of *Pallet v. M.N.R.*, 59 DTC 230 (T.A.B.), and *M.N.R. v. Lamon*, 63 DTC 1039 (Ex. Ct.). The rights to books and manuals were at issue in *Gingras v. M.N.R.*, 63 DTC 1142 (Ex. Ct.), and *LaRue v. M.N.R.*, 67 DTC 553 (T.A.B.), and the sale of equipment was considered in *R. C. Huffman Construction Co. Ltd. v. M.N.R.*, 65 DTC 597 (T.A.B.). A payment for the use of patents was considered in *Porta-Test Systems Ltd. v. The Queen*, 80 DTC 6046 (F.C.T.D.). Finally, the sale of a franchise was the subject of *M.N.R. v. Waintown Gas and Oil Co. Ltd.*, 52 DTC 1138 (S.C.C.). The exception for sales of agricultural land in paragraph 12(1)(g) does not apply to mineral and oil rights on the land. This was the situation in the case of *Ade v. M.N.R.*, 67 DTC 23 (T.A.B.).

The Act provides that any amount received based on production or use of property disposed must be included as property income. The purpose of this rule is to prevent taxpayers from characterizing property income as capital gains (a topic discussed in Chapters 7 and 8), which will attract lower tax rate through partial inclusion of income for tax purposes.

ITA: 12(1)(g)

Example Problem

The appellant, a farmer, entered into an agreement with the Department of Highways of Alberta under which she granted the Department the right to enter upon her land for the purpose of taking clay for use in the construction of a highway. Employees of the Department removed the crop growing on the land designated in the agreement, removed the topsoil from the area, removed the quantity of clay subsoil required for highway construction, replaced the topsoil and levelled off the area. Pursuant to the agreement, the appellant received compensation of $2,271 in full settlement of "general damages, loss of crop, cost of restoring areas and reduction of yields." The Minister added the $2,271 to the appellant's declared income. The appellant objected.

ITA: 9(1), 12(1)(g)

— REQUIRED

Decide this case on the basis of whether the receipt of $2,271 can be considered business or property income under either or both of the sections cited by the Minister.

— SOLUTION [see *Randle v. M.N.R.*, 65 DTC 507 (T.A.B.).]

Consider first whether the receipt was one of business or property income. At best the situation involved an adventure in the nature of trade which is part of the definition of the word business, thereby making the receipt part of business income. The receipt was not like normal income from property in the nature of dividends, interest, rents or royalties and there is little to connect the payment to business activity. There was no intention either of a primary or secondary nature to make a profit from a business operation in this situation. The receipt was more like a reimbursement for a capital item. The relation of the transaction to farming is fairly remote except for the compensation for current crops. The nature of the asset involved is more like fixed capital in land than working capital in inventory except, again, for the current crop. Furthermore, it is unlikely that this was a frequent transaction, indicating a non-business income receipt. Finally, damages for loss of earnings capacity, as this seemed to be, are not income, but are generally regarded as a capital receipt which will be taxed more favourably with partial income inclusion.

ITA: 9(1)
ITA: 248(1)

Next, consider whether the payment was dependent on production or use. No relation between the amount received and the amount of clay taken is indicated. There was no continuing activity in the sale of clay which might indicate more clearly a payment dependent on production or use. Finally, the agreement indicated that the appellant did not sell the clay or the land, but received money in compensation for damages sustained.

ITA: 12(1)(g)

It might be concluded, therefore, that most of the money was compensation for the loss of a portion of a capital asset and for restoring it to its former state of production. However, the amount paid for the current crop in the designated area as part of the appellant's inventory should be included in income.

¶6,050   Dividends from Corporations Resident in Canada

¶6,055   The issue

In Chapter 2, we discussed the question of who is liable for tax in Canada. We learned that an individual is liable for tax and so is a corporation. Therefore, generally, most corporate income is taxed twice: first at the corporate level as income and then in the hands of shareholders, as dividends. Without any adjustments in the tax rules, taxpayers would be penalized by double taxation, if they earn the same amount of income through corporations as opposed to earning income directly.

The Act contains a number of special rules designed to provide relief from double taxation of income earned through a corporation. In the following section, we will discuss one of the mechanisms introduced in the Canadian tax system to address the double taxation problem.

¶6,060   Overview of the Canadian dividend tax system

There are different ways to mitigate the double taxation problem. The basic objective is that the same total amount of tax should be paid if a corporation earns an amount (then pays dividends to the shareholders from its after-tax earnings), or if the individual earns that same amount personally. The following is the tool used in the Act to achieve this objective in theory:

- the individual shareholder must include in income the full pre-tax income earned by the corporation by grossing up the amount of the dividend received and calculating tax on that base, and

- the individual should receive a dividend tax credit for all the income tax paid by the corporation.

¶6,060.10   *Difference between a tax deduction and a tax credit*

You will see more examples of income reductions and tax credits in Chapters 9 and 10. In general, a tax credit reduces the tax otherwise payable and is a dollar-for-dollar reduction of a tax liability. The dividend tax credit that we will discuss in this section is a tax credit that will reduce the taxpayer's tax otherwise payable. On the other hand, an income reduction reduces taxable income. The tax savings from the income reduction is dependant on the person's marginal tax rate.

¶6,060.20   *The current dividend gross-up and dividend tax credit system*

The Act uses two calculations, with different rates, of the gross-up and the dividend tax credit. The use of which type depends on the type of corporation that issued the dividends and the type of income from which the dividends are issued. Note that different types of corporations (e.g., public versus private) with different types of income (e.g., active business income versus investment income) will be taxed at different tax rates.

(i) Dividends from the active business income of a Canadian-controlled private corporation (CCPC) that is taxed at the low corporate rate or from the investment income of a CCPC (as discussed in Chapter 12)

In this situation, the dividends received plus a 25% gross-up will be included in the individual's income. Thus, the individual shareholder's income would include the grossed-up dividend. Recall from the earlier discussion that the gross-up, when added to the actual dividends received, is to place the individual shareholder in approximately the same income position that the corporation was in before it paid corporate tax on its income.

ITA: 82(1)
ITA: 12(1)(*j*)

This dividend income (125% of the amount received) will be subject to tax in full at the individual's tax rate which is dependent on his or her income level. We will outline more about the progressive tax rate system in Chapter 10. As discussed above, to mitigate the problem of double taxation, the Act allows for a dividend tax credit which will reduce the tax on dividends paid to the individual.

ITA: 121

The federal dividend tax credit rate is as follows (same amount but different calculations):

- 16.67% of the dividends paid,

- $\frac{2}{3} \times 25\%$ (gross-up) = 16.67% of dividends paid, or

- $13\frac{1}{3}\% \times 125\%$ (grossed-up dividend) = 16.67% of dividends paid.

Each province offers dividend tax credits which will reduce an individual's provincial tax payable. The federal tax credit together with the provincial dividend tax credit is intended to approximate the tax paid by the corporation on the individual shareholder's behalf. Note that the calculation may not work out to the exact amount of the tax paid on the dividends. We will discuss this issue of imperfections in more detail in Chapter 12.

(ii) Dividends from a public corporation resident in Canada taxed at the general corporate rate and a CCPC resident in Canada distributed from business income taxed at the general corporate rate (not the low corporate tax rate)

In this situation, the gross-up rate will be 45% and the dividend tax credit will be as follows (same amount but different calculations):

- 27.5% of the dividends paid,

- $^{11}/_{18} \times 45\%$ (gross-up) = 27.5% of the dividends paid, or

- 19% (rounded) $\times$ 145% (grossed-up dividends) = 27.5% of the dividends paid.

¶6,060.30 *Conditions*

Note that the dividend gross-up and tax credit procedure applies where:

- individual shareholders receive the dividend (corporate shareholders are discussed in Chapter 11); and

- dividends are received from Canadian resident corporations (dividends received by individuals from non-resident corporations are fully taxed).

¶6,060.40 *Illustration*

As an example of the effect of the dividend treatment for individuals, consider two individuals, one paying federal tax at a marginal rate of 15.5% and the other paying federal tax at the top marginal rate of 29%. Assume that both individuals live in a province with a tax on income rate of 10% and 17%, respectively. Also assume that the combined federal and provincial dividend tax credit is equal to the gross-up. Each shareholder receives a dividend of $300 from:

(a) the active business income of a CCPC taxed at the low corporate rate, and

(b) the income of a public corporation resident in Canada.

The following computations would be made:

(a) Dividends from the active business income of a CCPC taxed at the low corporate rate

		25.5%	46%
Taxpayer's marginal tax rate (federal and provincial)		25.5%	46%
Dividend . . . . (A)		$300.00	$300.00
Add: gross-up of 25% of dividend		75.00	75.00
Grossed-up dividend subject to tax		$375.00	$375.00
Tax on grossed-up dividend at marginal tax rate		$ 95.63	$172.50
Less: federal and provincial dividend tax credit (equal to the gross-up)		(75.00)	(75.00)
Net tax payable . . . . (B)		$ 20.63	$ 97.50
After-tax dividend [(A) − (B)]		$279.37	$202.50

(b) Dividends from the income of a public corporation resident in Canada

		25.5%	46%
Taxpayer's marginal tax rate (federal and provincial)		25.5%	46%
Dividend	(A)	$300.00	$300.00
Add: gross-up of 45% of dividend		135.00	135.00
Grossed-up dividend subject to tax		$435.00	$435.00
Tax on grossed-up dividend at marginal tax rate		$110.93	$200.10
Less: federal and provincial dividend tax credit (equal to the gross-up)		(135.00)*	(135.00)
Net tax payable	(B)	Nil**	$ 65.10
After-tax dividend [(A) – (B)]		$300.00	$234.90

---

* The dividend tax credit is not affected by the individual's marginal tax rate.

** The excess dividend tax credit of $24.07 ($110.93 – $135.00) is available to deduct from federal tax on other income.

Example Problem

I.M.A. Plunger faces a 12% provincial tax on income and a federal tax rate of 22% at the margin. On an investment of $5,000 in the shares of a Canadian-resident public corporation, he receives $362.50 of taxable dividends for a yield of 7.25%. He is considering the alternative of investing his funds in a bond paying 9%. Assume that the combined federal and provincial dividend tax credit is equal to the gross-up.

— *REQUIRED*

Compute the after-tax return from the alternative investments to compare their desirability.

— *SOLUTION*

(A) Dividend

Dividend	$362.50
Add: gross-up of 45% of dividend	163.13
Grossed-up dividend subject to tax	$525.63
Tax on grossed-up dividend @ 34% (i.e., 22% + 12%)	$178.72
Less: dividend tax credit (federal and provincial)	(163.13)
Net tax payable	$ 15.59
After-tax dividend ($362.50 – $15.59)	$346.91

(B) Interest

Interest income (9% of $5,000)	$450.00
Tax payable @ 34%	$153.00
After-tax interest ($450.00 – $153.00)	$297.00

— *NOTE TO SOLUTION*

Although the pre-tax dividend yield of 7.25% is lower than the pre-tax interest yield of 9%, the after-tax return from the dividend of $346.91 or 6.94% of the investment is greater than the after-tax return from the interest of $297.00 or 5.94% of the $5,000 invested. Furthermore, it should be remembered that there may be a greater potential for a return from capital gains on the shares compared to the bond. This would influence the decision when the after-tax dividend yield is lower than the after-tax interest yield. Note that investment in shares will normally be riskier than investment in bonds.

¶6,070   Income Attribution

¶6,075   The reason for attribution rules

Under the Canadian income tax system, an individual is a taxpayer who is liable for tax on his or her taxable income. An individual's taxable income is subject to a progressive tax structure. Under such a structure, if an individual earns more income, his or her tax rate increases. For example, if Dad earns $100,000, he will pay more tax than if Mom and Dad each earn $50,000. Thus, the high income taxpayer will have an incentive to reduce tax by splitting income with family members who earn less income and pay tax at a lower rate. For example, if the high income taxpayer, Mr. A, has some bonds which earn interest income, Mr. A pays tax on the interest income earned on the bonds at the top marginal tax rate. Mr. A can transfer the bonds to his five-year-old daughter who has no other source of income. His daughter will not have to pay tax on the interest income (due to personal tax credits) or will pay tax at a much lower rate.

In order to protect the integrity of the progressive tax system, the Act has introduced various attribution rules to prevent certain forms of income splitting among the immediate family members.

ITA: 74.1–74.5,
56(4.1)–(5)

"Income attribution" is a process of allocating income earned on the property that was transferred to a non-arm's length individual back to the original owner. In the case discussed earlier, although the five-year-old daughter owns the bonds after the transfer, for tax purposes, the interest income earned on the bonds will be attributed back to Mr. A and taxed in his hands.

The word "transfer" has been used frequently throughout the various attribution rules. It includes a sale, whether or not the proceeds are at fair market value. Financing the sale by a loan does not change the concept of a transfer in this context. Gifting is also a form of transfer.

¶6,080   Definition of related persons

As indicated above, the attribution rules apply to certain non-arm's length individuals. The Act deems related persons not to deal at arm's length with each other. Exhibit 6-1 attempts to present schematically all of the provisions defining related individuals, as well as the CRA's interpretations. Related individuals are diagrammed in relation to a taxpayer (i.e., "you"). On the horizontal axis, do not attempt to make the individuals at the extreme outer limits (i.e., the second bullet) related to each other. They are only related to "you" in respect of this chart. Note that where the word "spouse" is used, it is intended to include the concept of a common-law partner, including a same-sex partner.

ITA: 251(1)(a)

ITA: 251, 252; IT-419R2

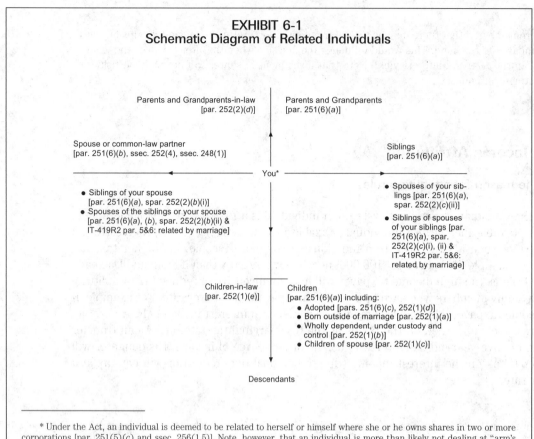

EXHIBIT 6-1
Schematic Diagram of Related Individuals

Parents and Grandparents-in-law
[par. 252(2)(*d*)]

Parents and Grandparents
[par. 251(6)(*a*)]

Spouse or common-law partner
[par. 251(6)(*b*), ssec. 252(4), ssec. 248(1)]

Siblings
[par. 251(6)(*a*)]

You*

- Siblings of your spouse
  [par. 251(6)(*a*), spar. 252(2)(*b*)(i)]
- Spouses of the siblings or your spouse
  [par. 251(6)(*a*), (*b*), spar. 252(2)(*b*)(ii) &
  IT-419R2 par. 5&6: related by marriage]

- Spouses of your sib-
  lings [par. 251(6)(*a*),
  spar. 252(2)(*c*)(ii)]
- Siblings of spouses
  of your siblings [par.
  251(6)(*a*), spar.
  252(2)(*c*)(i), (ii) &
  IT-419R2 par. 5&6:
  related by marriage]

Children-in-law
[par. 252(1)(*e*)]

Children
[par. 251(6)(*a*)] including:
- Adopted [pars. 251(6)(*c*), 252(1)(*d*)]
- Born outside of marriage [par. 252(1)(*a*)]
- Wholly dependent, under custody and
  control [par. 252(1)(*b*)]
- Children of spouse [par. 252(1)(*c*)]

Descendants

* Under the Act, an individual is deemed to be related to herself or himself where she or he owns shares in two or more corporations [par. 251(5)(*c*) and ssec. 256(1.5)]. Note, however, that an individual is more than likely not dealing at "arm's length" with herself or himself by virtue of the definition of this term [par. 251(1)(*b*)] which bases this type of relationship on the facts of the particular situation at a particular moment in time. Therefore, be careful which term is being used — "related" or "arm's length."

¶6,085 Transactions subject to income attribution

¶6,085.10 *An individual transfers or loans property to a spouse or common-law partner or to a person who becomes his or her spouse or common-law partner*

Income or loss incurred on the transferred property as well as capital gains and losses from the final sale (as discussed in Chapter 8) of the property to a third party may be subject to attribution. The attribution rules apply when an individual transfers or loans property to a spouse or common-law partner including a person who becomes his or her spouse or common-law partner. **ITA: 74.1(1)**

"Common-law partner" is defined as a person who cohabits at that time in a conjugal relationship with the taxpayer and either **ITA: 248(1)**

(a) has so cohabited with the taxpayer for a continuous period of at least one year, or

(b) would be the parent of a child of whom the taxpayer is a parent.

Where at any time the taxpayer and the person cohabit in a conjugal relationship, they are deemed to be cohabiting in a conjugal relationship unless they were not cohabiting at the particular time for a period of at least 90 days because of a breakdown of their conjugal relationship. This definition covers both common-law spouses and same-sex partners.

Attribution of income or loss from property, but usually not capital gains or losses, will, also, occur on a transfer or loan to a minor (i.e., under the age of 18) who is a non-arm's length person (plus a niece or nephew) as interpreted in a CRA Interpretation Bulletin. **ITA: 74.1(2), 74.3, 251, 252**
IT-419R2

Attribution continues until that person attains the age of 18. Both subsections pertain to direct or *indirect* transfers or loans to or *for the benefit of* the person. Thus, a transfer or loan to a trust in which the spouse or common-law partner or minor is a beneficiary will result in attribution, as discussed in more detail in Chapter 18. Attribution means that the income or loss earned by the spouse or common-law partner or minor is considered to be the income or loss of the transferor during his or her lifetime as long as he or she is resident in Canada.

We will use examples to demonstrate the various tax consequences of the following transactions:

Example 1

- Mr. A is taxed in the top bracket (highest personal tax rate) and he owns a bond which is worth $50,000. Mr. A paid $50,000 for the bond. It earns $5,000 of interest income (one type of property income).

- Mrs. A (Mr. A's spouse) has no income.

- Mr. A gave the bond to Mrs. A.

The tax consequences are as follows: when Mr. A gives the bond to Mrs. A, there will be no gain or loss (fair market value equals cost). After the bond has been given to Mrs. A, the $5,000 annual interest income will be subject to the attribution rule, since the transfer of the bond was not at fair market value when it was given to Mrs. A. Note that all gifts of income-earning property are subject to the attribution rules as well as any transfers of property not at fair market value. The $5,000 interest income will be included in Mr. A's income instead of Mrs. A's income. If Mrs. A sells the bond to a third party, any gains or losses from selling the bond will also be attributed back to Mr. A (as discussed in Chapter 8). *[ITA: 73(1)]* *[ITA: 74.1(1), 74.5(1)]* *[ITA: 74.2]*

Now, change the above transaction to have Mr. A sell the bond to Mrs. A at its fair market value of $50,000 for cash and they jointly elect out of the automatic rollover. The tax consequences will change. The attribution rule will not apply to the $5,000 of interest income because Mrs. A paid fair market value for the bond and they elected out of the rollover. The $5,000 interest income will be included in Mrs. A's income. *[ITA: 73(1)]* *[ITA: 74.5(1)]*

Example 2

Example 2 is similar to Example 1, except that Mr. A makes a loan of $50,000 to Mrs. A instead of giving the bond to her or taking cash from her. Mr. A charges Mrs. A interest on the loan at a rate which is lower than the prescribed interest rate. The tax consequences are that the $5,000 annual interest income will be included in Mr. A's income and taxed at his marginal tax rate.

If Mr. A charges interest at the lesser of the prescribed rate or an arm's length commercial rate, the $5,000 annual property income will be included in Mrs. A's income. The interest charged by Mr. A must be paid by Mrs. A within 30 days of the end of each year in which the loan is outstanding. The attribution rule will not apply, due to the fair market value consideration paid by Mrs. A in this situation. However, Mrs. A will be able to deduct the interest she pays from her interest income on the bond, leaving little, if any, income to be taxed at her lower rate. *[ITA: 74.5(2)]*

¶6,085.20 *An individual transfers or loans property to a minor (i.e., under the age of 18) who is a non-arm's length person or a niece or nephew*

Attribution of income or loss from property, but not capital gains or losses, may occur on a transfer of property or a loan to a minor.

Example 1

- Mr. A is taxed in the top bracket and he owns a bond worth $50,000. The original cost to Mr. A is $50,000. The bond produces $5,000 of interest income.

- Junior is Mr. A's son. He is 15 years old and he has no income.

- Mr. A gives the property to Junior.

The tax consequences are similar to the ones between Mr. A and his spouse. However, when Junior sells the property to a third party, the capital gains or losses will not be subject to the attribution rules (as discussed in Chapter 8). Junior will include the capital gains or losses in his income.

If Mr. A sells the property to Junior and takes back a loan, the attribution rule will apply unless the loan is for the $50,000 fair market value and Mr. A charges interest at the lesser of the prescribed rate or an arm's length commercial rate. Junior must pay interest to Mr. A within 30 days of the end of each year in which the loan is outstanding. Junior will be able to deduct the interest paid, minimizing the income-splitting benefit.

¶6,090 Avoiding income attributions

An exception to the application of these attribution rules is provided by the legislation. This provision requires a number of very specific conditions to be fulfilled before the taxpayer will be exempted from the attribution rules. First, if the fair market value of the property transferred does not exceed the fair market value of the consideration received in return, that is, if the property is sold for its fair market value, then these attribution rules will not apply. Therefore, all gifts of income-earning property are subject to the attribution rules as are transfers for consideration which is less than the fair market value of the property transferred. Second, if the transferor takes back a debt, then interest that is at least equal to the lesser of the prescribed rate or an arm's length rate (to be referred to here as a "commercial" rate) must be charged. In addition, the interest must be paid within 30 days of the end of each and every year in which the debt was outstanding, or attribution will occur. If funds are loaned directly, then interest at a commercial rate, as determined above, must be charged and paid on the loan, or attribution will occur. *ITA: 74.5*

Note that where a transfer or loan takes place at fair market value, the benefits of income splitting are reduced or eliminated. Where one person buys an income-producing property for, say, cash, the purchaser acquires the income-producing property and may claim the income, but the seller receives the cash which might be invested in other income-producing property. The fair market value consideration will help to avoid attribution of income from property and, often more importantly, capital gains on a transfer to a spouse or a common-law partner. Avoiding the attribution of capital gains may provide a significant benefit. Similarly, a loan at a commercial rate creates income to the lender, thereby reducing or eliminating any splitting advantage on income from property, but places the borrower in a position to earn a capital gain that will not be attributed to the lender.

Third, an additional restriction is placed on all spousal transfers of property. Normally, accrued income on depreciable capital property and other capital property is automatically deferred on the transfer of such property to a spouse or a common-law partner. However, to avoid attribution, the deferral must be waived by the transferor spouse. Hence, a disposition will occur at the fair market value, triggering a capital gain or loss. However, if the property is qualified small business corporation shares or qualified farm property, the capital gains deduction could be used to offset all or part of the income inclusion. *ITA: 73(1)*

For example, consider the case of Spouse A, whose income is taxed in the top bracket and who owns a property worth $50,000 that produces $5,000 of income. If that property is sold for cash to Spouse B who has no other source of income and Spouse A elects to transfer the property at its fair market value, Spouse B will have the $5,000 of income from property. However, Spouse A will have the $50,000 in cash proceeds on the sale of the property. If that $50,000 is reinvested in Spouse A's hands, the income will attract tax at the top rate and the benefits of income splitting would be negated, unless the original property generated a large capital gain on its ultimate disposition by Spouse B. At that time, the capital gain would not be subject to attribution because the original transfer of the property took place for fair market value consideration. *ITA: 73(1)*

Fourth, there is an exception to the attribution rules which applies where spouses live separate and apart by reason of a breakdown of their marriage. Any income or loss that relates to the period of separation is excepted from attribution. *ITA: 74.5(3)*

> ### Summary
> ### Avoiding Income Attribution On Transferred Property
>
> *Subsection 74.5(1)*
>
> 1. Fair market value consideration must be received by the vendor.
> 2. If part of the consideration is debt, then interest must be charged at the prescribed rate and always paid by January 30th.
> 3. If it is a transfer to a spouse or common-law partner, then they must elect out of the rollover in subsection 73(1).
>
> *Subsection 74.5(3)*
>
> 4. If the spouses or common-law partners are living separate and apart by reason of the breakdown of their relationship. (This exception applies to property income, but not capital gains, unless an election has been made.)

¶6,095　Anti-avoidance rules relating to attribution

A number of anti-avoidance rules are contained in these attribution provisions. One rule prevents the refinancing of an old loan by the substitution of a commercial rate loan for a loan that would result in attribution under the rules. This rule applies to attribute income from property financed with the original loan or property substituted therefor.

ITA: 74.1(3)
ITA: 74.1(1), 74.1(2)

An anti-avoidance rule is provided to prevent circumventing the attribution rules by the use of "back-to-back" loans and transfers. The rule envisages a situation where property is deposited with a financial institution paying no interest with an agreement that the same amount as that deposited be loaned to the depositor's spouse at a nominal rate of interest, say, 2%. In this case, the use of the intermediary would be disregarded. The attribution rules will apply to include, in the income of the original transferor, the income earned by the property owned by the ultimate transferee. Of course, if such a back-to-back loan is made at a commercial rate or a back-to-back transfer is made for fair market value consideration, then no attribution will take place.

ITA: 74.5(6)

The avoidance of the attribution rules by the use of loan guarantees is prevented. For example, instead of Spouse A lending income-producing property to Spouse B, Spouse A could guarantee a loan made by another person or a financial institution to Spouse B who would use the proceeds of the loan to buy income-producing property. Unless a commercial rate of interest is charged and paid on the loan to Spouse B, Spouse A will have to include the income from the property.

ITA: 74.5(7)

A general anti-avoidance rule is provided to prevent "artificial transactions" which would benefit from the application of the attribution rules. In the past, taxpayers have devised transactions or a series of transactions known as "reverse attribution plans" to have income attributed to a low-income taxpayer. Therefore, if one of the main reasons for a loan or transfer is to reduce the amount of tax that would be paid, the attribution rules discussed will not apply in cases where such reverse attribution is attempted. Another example of such artificial attribution is given in a CRA Interpretation Bulletin.

ITA: 74.5(11)

IT-511R, par. 26

Two Interpretation Bulletins indicate that an individual can remunerate a spouse or a related minor for services provided in a business carried on by the payer as long as certain conditions in the Act are met. These conditions require that the amount paid must be deductible in determining the payer's business income (according to the general rules of deductibility discussed in Chapter 4) and included in the recipient's income. Payments under the child tax benefits program are excepted from the income attribution rule applicable on transfers or loans to minors. As a result, the income attribution rules do not apply to income arising from child tax benefits transferred or loaned to the child.

IT-510, par. 18; IT-511, par. 25
ITA: 74.5(12)(*b*)

ITA: 74.1(2)

Finally, anti-avoidance rules generally prevent income splitting through the use of a corporation. This provision is discussed at greater length in Chapter 13.

ITA: 74.4

¶6,100 More types of income subject to attribution

Note that the income attribution rules apply only to the transfer of property that results in income or loss from property rather than income or loss from business. This distinction was at issue in the case of *Lackie v. The Queen*, in which the taxpayer transferred a farm to his wife from which she sold gravel at an agreed price per ton. The amounts received were taxable as income. The CRA argued that this income was from property transferred by the taxpayer to his spouse and, therefore, was subject to the attribution rules and taxable as income in the hands of the taxpayer. On the other hand, the taxpayer contended that attribution was improper because the income was from business rather than property. The court held that the income was from property because the taxpayer's wife did not sell gravel as a business but granted a licence to work a gravel pit on her land. It was clear to the court that the amounts received were dependent on the use of property.

79 DTC 5309 (F.C.A.)

ITA: 12(1)(*g*)

The term "property" is defined in the Act. It includes substituted property, but does not include income earned on attributed income, often referred to as "second-generation" income. For example, if a $10,000 bond, bearing interest at 10% annually, is given to a spouse, the $1,000 of interest income received by the recipient of the bond is attributed to the transferor spouse. If the $1,000 is reinvested by the recipient spouse at, say, 10%, the $100 of interest earned on the reinvested interest is not attributed to the transferor spouse. The $100 is income earned on income, i.e., the $1,000, that has been attributed. Hence, the $100 is referred to as second-generation income.

ITA: 248(5)

¶6,105 Loans or transfers to non-arm's length individuals who are 18 years of age or older

The attribution rules do not apply to loans or transfers to non-arm's length persons who are 18 years of age or older. However, anti-avoidance rules prevent the avoidance of tax on *loans* between non-arm's length individuals. Income from property resulting from a low-interest or a no-interest loan by an individual to another non-arm's length individual will be attributed back to the lender. The key condition for the attribution rule to apply is that one of the main reasons for the loan is to reduce or avoid tax on income from the property or substituted property. Therefore, loans between non-arm's length individuals, both of whom are taxed at the same rate, would appear not to be caught by these provisions. Similarly, if the loaned funds are spent on non-income-producing property (e.g., personal-use property, living expenses, etc.), then the "one of the main reasons" test would not be met. Note that the attribution rules apply only to loans, but not to sales or gifts.

ITA: 74.1–74.5
ITA: 56(4.1)–(4.3)

ITA: 74.1
ITA: 56(4.1)

ITA: 56(4.1)

Loans that bear a commercial or arm's length rate of interest are exempt from the attribution rule. The interest must, in fact, be paid within 30 days of the end of the year in respect of which it was charged for the exemption to apply. Refinancing a loan subject to the above attribution rule with another loan will not circumvent the attribution rule.

ITA: 56(4.1), 56(4.2),
56(4.3)

¶6,110 Summary of income attribution rules

Exhibit 6-2 attempts to summarize the major rules pertaining to the attribution of income from property.

EXHIBIT 6-2
Attribution of Income* from Property**
Conceptual Summary

Recipient	Transaction		
	Transfer by gift	*Transfer by sale*	*Transaction involving loan*
Spouse or common-law partner*** [ssec. 74.1(1)]	• *Income or loss from property attributed to transferor*	• *If no fair market value considera-tion received: Income or loss from property attributed to transferor* • *If fair market value considera-tion received:**** No attribution*	• *If no interest at a commercial rate paid: Income or loss from property attributed to transferor* • *If interest at a com-mercial rate paid:**** No attribution*
Minors who are not at arm's length [secs. 251 and 252] or who are nieces and nephews [ssec. 74.1(2)]	• *Income or loss from property attributed to transferor*	• *Same as for trans-fer by gift (depen-dent on whether fair market value consideration received)*	• *Same as for transfer by gift (dependent on whether fair market value consideration received)*
Other non-arm's length individuals not subject to section 74.1 [ssec. 56(4.1)]	• *No attribution*	• *No attribution*	• *Income only from property attributed to transferor, if one of the main reasons for the loan was to reduce or avoid tax and mar-ket rate of interest not paid*

* Excluding second-generation income.

** Including substituted property as defined in subsection 248(5). Income from business is not attributed in any of these transactions. Attribution of capital gains or losses is discussed in Chapter 8.

*** Attribution of capital gains and losses on transfers or loans to a spouse is discussed in Chapter 8.

**** To avoid attribution, the taxpayer must elect to waive the deferral of accrued income under subsec-tion 73(1) (discussed in Chapter 8) and must transfer for fair market value consideration. Where a loan is involved, interest at a commercial rate must be paid within 30 days of the end of every year in which the loan is outstanding.

¶6,115 Tax on split income earned by persons under 18 years of age (the "Kiddie Tax")

¶6,115.10 *Overview*

Note that the income attribution rules, discussed above, do not apply to income from a business, such as a proprietorship or a partnership, transferred to a minor. As will be seen in a subsequent chapter, the corporate attribution rules do not apply to dividends from certain private corporations that carry on an active business in Canada. To address this exclusion from attribution rules, a specific anti-avoidance rule has been introduced. In general, the kiddie tax rules apply to dividends from a private Canadian or foreign corporation. The tax rate on these dividends is the top marginal tax rate of an individual, and the amount of tax payable is net of the dividend tax credit and the foreign tax credit. This tax eliminates the incentive to income split through distributions of dividends from private corporations to minor children.

¶6,115.20   *Split income*

The special tax on split income applies to the following types of income that are earned by persons under 18 years of age:

- taxable dividends from shares that are not listed on a prescribed Canadian or foreign stock exchange (i.e., essentially, shares of a private corporation) and that are received directly or indirectly through a trust or partnership;

- shareholder benefits included in the minor's income under section 15;

- partnership or trust income derived from the provision of goods and services to a business that is carried on by

  (i) a person related to the minor,

  (ii) a corporation which has a "specified shareholder" who is related to the minor, or   ITA: 248(1)

  (iii) a professional corporation which has a shareholder who is related to the minor.

¶6,115.30   *Tax treatment of split income*

The split income is:

- subject to tax at the top marginal rate, including applicable surtax, instead of the graduated rates;

- not eligible for any deductions or credits, except for the dividend tax credit and foreign tax credits; and

- eligible for an offsetting deduction from taxable income equal to the specified income, so that this amount would not be taxed again normally under Part I of the Act.

Note that the tax on split income applies to the minor, at the top marginal tax rate, and not to   ITA: 56(5), 74.5(13)
the transferor of the property, on income that would not otherwise be subject to the attributions rules.

¶6,115.40   *Exceptions to tax on split income*

The special income splitting tax does not apply to:

- income paid to individuals over 18 years of age;

- taxable dividends from shares listed on prescribed Canadian or foreign stock exchanges;

- reasonable remuneration to minors;

- capital gains on the disposition of the shares of private Canadian or foreign corporation;

- income from property inherited from a parent;

- minors who have no parent who is resident in Canada at any time in the year; or

- income from property inherited from someone other than a parent, if the minor is in full-time attendance at a post-secondary institution or is eligible for the disability tax credit.

¶6,120   What else can be income split?

In general, income splitting is still permissible under certain situations. For example, the spousal RRSP contribution is allowed. The March 19, 2007 federal budget proposed to allow income splitting on pension income. We will discuss this topic more in later chapters.

¶6,200 DEDUCTIONS

¶6,210 Carrying Charges on Land

¶6,215 Limitation on deduction — Vacant land

Carrying charges, such as interest and property taxes, on vacant land are only deductible to the extent of the taxpayer's net income from the land. If the property is a capital property, the carrying charges that are not deducted will be added to the cost base of the land. A deduction of the cost base of the land is only available when the land is sold, thereby, reducing the capital gain of the property. This topic is covered in Chapter 7.

ITA: 18(2), 18(3)
ITA: 53(1)(*h*)

These rules apply to property developers whose business is the sale or development of land, or to land that is held, but not used, in a business. This restriction discourages speculation in real estate (no intention to use the real estate for business purpose but to hold the piece of property for capital gains). Land which is used or held primarily for an income-producing purpose is exempted from the above limitation. In a special case where the land is vacant for part of the year and used for business for the remainder, the carrying charges would be deductible, as the Act does not specify a time period in the year. However, the costs during construction on the land would not be deductible. (See ¶6,220.)

ITA: 18(2)(*d*)

ITA: 18(2)

The limitation extends to land held primarily for resale or development and vacant land held by a business but not used in the course of the business. However, corporations whose principal business is the leasing, rental or sale, and the development for lease, rental or sale of real property are permitted to deduct carrying charges on vacant land, in excess of net income before deducting carrying charges. The limit of this deduction is the corporation's "base level deduction". That limit is interest computed at the prescribed rate (as previously discussed in this Chapter in respect of shareholder loans) on a loan of $1,000,000 outstanding throughout the year.

ITA: 18(2), 18(3)
ITA: 18(2)(*f*)

ITA: 18(2.2)

Example Problem

In 2005, Mr. Walkovia acquired a vacant lot in a downtown area of the city, intending to build an office complex. By late 2007, he decided to abandon the project. The property was disposed of just before the end of the year. It was not considered to have been held for speculation because of the unforeseen problems encountered in the development.

While the property was owned by Mr. Walkovia, it had been used as a city parking lot with the following results:

	2005	2006	2007
Net income (loss) before interest and property taxes*	$11,000	$ 6,000	$ (3,000)
Interest and property taxes	9,500	10,000	10,500

* This amount is equal to gross revenue in excess of all other expenses

— REQUIRED

(A) Consider the effect of these data on the income of Mr. Walkovia for tax purposes.

(B) If the land had been owned by a corporation whose principal business was the development and sale of land, what would be the effects of these data? Assume a prescribed rate of interest of 8% throughout the period in question.

— SOLUTION

(A) Since the land, held for development in this case, is not excluded from the limitation, interest and property taxes will be deductible only to the extent of gross revenues in excess of all other expenses, i.e., net income before interest and property taxes. As a result, the following amount would be reported as income for the years indicated:

ITA: 18(2)

	2005	2006	2007
Gross revenue less expenses other than interest and property taxes	$11,000	$ 6,000	$(3,000)
Less: Interest and property taxes	9,500	6,000	Nil
Income (loss) for the year	$ 1,500	Nil	$(3,000)
Non-deductible interest and property taxes added to adjusted cost base of land	Nil	$ 4,000	$10,500

(B) In this case, a loss created by the deduction of interest and property tax is permitted. However, the excess of interest and property tax that is deductible is limited to an amount of interest computed at the 8% prescribed rate, assumed in this case, on a notional principal amount of $1,000,000. The $80,000 limit in this case is referred to as the base level deduction. The following losses would be reported by a corporation: — ITA: 18(2)(*f*)

	2005	2006	2007
Gross revenue less expenses other than interest and property taxes	$ 11,000	$ 6,000	$ (3,000)
Less lesser of:			
(a) interest and property taxes	$ 9,500	$10,000	$10,500
(b) base level deduction	$80,000	$80,000	$80,000
lesser amount	(9,500)	(10,000)	(10,500)
Income (loss) for the year	$ 1,500	$(4,000)	$(13,500)

Note that the losses are of value to a corporation if it generates sufficient income from other sources to be shielded by the deduction of the losses. That is, the value of losses is inherent in the ability to shield income from tax.

¶6,220 "Soft Costs" Relating To Construction of Buildings or Ownership of Land

"Soft costs" include interest expenses, legal and accounting fees, mortgage fees, insurance, and property taxes. Soft costs incurred, during the period of construction, renovation, or alternation of a building, are not deductible as current expenses, and must be added to the cost of the building. Similarly, such costs in respect of the ownership of the land on which the building is under construction must also be capitalized.

Note that the restriction on the deduction of these expenses only applies to expenses incurred before completion of construction, renovation, or alternation of the building. The Act provides for the determination of the date on which the work is completed. It is also worth noting that the Act specifies that capitalization is required for the costs "attributable" to, and not merely incurred in, the period of construction. For example, a company must capitalize the interest on the bank loan it took out to construct a building for the time during which construction took place. If the company chose to prepay some of the interest before construction commenced, it still would not be able to deduct the interest in the current year. — ITA: 18(3.3) — ITA: 18(3.1)

Costs such as capital cost allowance on the building, the landscaping expenses, and disability-related modifications to buildings are exempted from the above rules. The Act also permits a taxpayer to deduct soft costs incurred in the year up to the taxpayer's income earned on the building under construction, renovation, or alternation.

Issuance costs, such as accounting fees and underwriter fees, are one-time costs to acquire financing for the project of acquiring long term capital assets. While some portion of such costs is inevitably attributable to the period of construction, it is difficult to determine how much. Therefore, the general tax treatment is to amortize these costs over five years instead of through the CCA schedule of the underlying asset.

ITA: 20(1)(*e*)

¶6,230 Rental Properties

¶6,235 Separate classes — Rental property costing over $50,000

Recall that, in general, capital cost allowances are computed on the balance at the end of the year in a pool or class of similar assets. Dispositions throughout the year reduce the balance in a class and may even cause the balance to be negative. However, such a negative balance, to the extent that it is offset by a purchase of more assets for the class during the year, will not result in recapture. Thus, the ability to offset a negative balance in a class of assets with purchases of similar assets during the year reduces or eliminates the need to pay tax on income from recapture of capital cost allowances.

Each rental property purchased that costs $50,000 or more must be placed in a separate capital cost allowance (CCA) class. This will result in recapture when a building is sold for proceeds in excess of the undepreciated capital cost in the class (i.e., when the UCC balance becomes negative at the end of the taxation year). The purpose of the rule is to prevent taxpayers from avoiding recapture of CCA when selling a rental property by buying another rental property of the same class. If rental properties are allowed to be grouped together, a taxpayer can buy a new rental property by the end of the taxation year to offset a negative balance. The separate class rule intends to force recognition of recapture each time the pool has a negative balance, as a result of a sale.

¶6,240 Losses from rental property

The Act further restricts the deduction of CCA on rental properties to the extent that it does not create or increase a net loss from all rental properties combined. By this rule, a taxpayer cannot use CCA on rental properties to create a loss or increase a loss from this type of assets to shelter other sources of income.

As an exception to this rule, losses created by capital cost allowances on rental property will not be deductible from non-rental income. However, rental property is narrowly defined to mean the rental building, thereby excluding furniture and fixtures from this treatment. As a result, the regulations dealing with leasing properties were added to prohibit the deduction of losses from non-rental income created by capital cost allowance on furniture and fixtures leased in a building except for corporations in the business of leasing property. Thus, a taxpayer cannot shelter other sources of income by offsetting a loss created by capital cost allowances on a rental building or leasing properties against those other sources of income, unless the taxpayer is a corporation or a partnership of corporations whose principal business was the property rental or leasing business.

ITR: 1100(11)–(14);
IT-195R4

ITR: 1100(15)–(20)

Example Problem

Auntie Inflation owns six rental buildings with the following information pertaining to each:

	Building					
	1	*2*	*3*	*4*	*5*	*6*
Cost	$30,000	$132,000	$71,000	$49,000	$350,000	$47,000
UCC, January 1, 2007	22,000	90,000	49,000	40,000	238,000	38,000
Rental revenue in 2007	1,600	17,000	8,000	3,800	45,000	6,000
Cash expenses:						
Interest	Nil	$ 1,200	$1,700	Nil	$ 3,200	$1,400
Property taxes	$400	3,000	1,500	$ 800	8,000	1,200
Other expenses	800	11,000	7,500	1,600	29,000	5,800

Late in 2007, buildings 1 and 2 were sold for proceeds of $40,000 and $91,000 respectively. Building 5 was purchased in 1981. All other buildings were purchased after 1987.

— REQUIRED

Prepare a schedule showing the maximum capital cost allowance which may be claimed for tax purposes assuming she owns no other rental properties. Assume all buildings are of brick construction.

— SOLUTION

	Class 1: 4%			Class 3: 5%
	Under $50,000	Build- ing 2	Build- ing 3	Building 5
UCC, January 1, 2007	$100,000	$90,000	$49,000	$238,000
Dispositions during the year	30,000[(1)]	91,000	—	—
UCC, December 31, 2007	$ 70,000	$(1,000)	$49,000	$238,000
CCA for 2007 (max.: $4,300 below)	2,800[(2)]	—	1,500[(2)]	Nil[(2)]
Recapture	—	1,000	—	—
UCC, January 1, 2008	$ 67,200	Nil	$47,500	$238,000

Total rental revenue in 2007	$ 81,400
Add: recapture [ssecs. 13(1)–(3)]	1,000
Less: total cash expenses	(78,100)
Net before CCA	$ 4,300
CCA — Amount deductible re: limitation[(2)]	(4,300)
Loss on rental properties	Nil

— NOTES TO SOLUTION

[(1)] The balance is never reduced by more than the original cost on the disposition of an asset; capital gain of $10,000 (i.e., $40,000 – $30,000).

[(2)] CCA potentially available in 2007:

Buildings with cost under $50,000 (4% of $70,000)	$ 2,800
Building 3 (4% of $49,000)	1,960
Building 5 (5% of $238,000)	11,900
Total	$16,660

Where deducting the maximum allowable CCA is not possible, as in this case, or not desirable, it is usually advisable to take CCA in lower-rate classes first. This preserves a higher balance in the higher-rate classes for the future when it may be possible to deduct relatively higher amounts of CCA in the higher-rate classes.

¶6,250　Depreciation-Based or Similar Tax Shelters[5]

Depreciation-based or similar tax shelters such as residential buildings, films, yachts, hotels, recreational vehicles and nursing homes have been available in the past. They have been used as a tool of fiscal policy to encourage investment in certain areas by providing a

---

[5] For a discussion of the general tax and investment implications of tax shelters which provide for an immediate or a rapid write-off of costs, see Lawrence I. Gould and Stanley N. Laiken, "Depreciation-Based Tax Shelters: Are They Worth the Risks?" *CA Magazine*, April 1983, pp. 38–41.

fast write-off. For example, a high CCA rate, or a large absolute dollar write-off of an amount invested will reduce the after-tax cash outflow of the initial investment. As extensive use of these shelters is perceived as abuse of the system by the Department of Finance, the ability to shelter other income with losses created by capital cost allowances has been either eliminated or reduced in effect. This was the case for residential buildings, films, yachts, hotels, nursing homes, recreational vehicles, computer software and other similar properties. The federal government imposed restrictive measures with the stated objective to "improve the fairness of the tax system and prevent abuses through aggressive tax shelter promotion." However, from time to time, other assets become the subject of depreciation-based tax shelters and, therefore, it is important to understand, conceptually, how they are used.

Consider the following typical example of a simple tax shelter, based on a hypothetical Class 10 asset. An investor could purchase a percentage of the asset through a partnership. The investor could be required to pay as little as 5% of the full investment in cash and he or she typically would sign an unconditional note for the balance which is usually payable in two to seven years. As long as the full investment amount is at risk by the investor, he or she could take Class 10 declining balance capital cost allowance of 30%, subject to the half-year rule, of the full amount of the investment in the year in which the investment was made. This principle was supported by the case of *Mandel v. The Queen*, and the Act codifies these "at risk" rules under specified conditions where a limited partnership is used. In the case of *Signum Communications Inc. v. The Queen*, based on facts which pre-dated subsection 96(2.2), the Federal Court — Trial Division held that in the absence of a statutory at-risk rule, there was no reason to limit losses to the amount of capital invested in a partnership, despite the decision in the *Mandel* case.

78 DTC 6518 (F.C.A.)

ITA: 96(2.2)

88 DTC 6427 (F.C.T.D.)

Assets sold as tax shelters have been very high risk investments, with probably only a small chance that the investment would be profitable. The main advantage of an investment in a sheltered asset has been a tax deferral which was most valuable to those in the higher tax brackets. For example, an investor purchasing a $100,000 interest in an asset may have had to pay only $5,000 in the first year, but was entitled to a $15,000 tax deduction of capital cost allowance at the 30% rate for Class 10, subject to the half-year rule. However, the $95,000 balance will have to be paid, and the investor may be confronted by cash flow problems if he or she receives no income from the asset. These investments are also usually very illiquid.

It should be realized that *all* investments shelter the cost of the investment from taxation. For example, it will be demonstrated in the next two Chapters how the cost of an investment in stock is "written off" against the proceeds of disposition when the stock is sold. It can be shown that the advantage of the faster write-off of a tax shelter cannot provide a profit for an investment that does not return both its cost and its after-tax carrying charges. Thus, an investment decision should be made primarily on its value as an investment without regard to any accelerated tax write-off that may be available and should not be based solely on the advantage of an early or large write-off of the investment. There is little advantage to making a $100,000 investment that turns out to be almost worthless, in order to write off the $100,000 and save about $50,000 in taxes!

¶6,260 Interest Deduction

¶6,265 Proposed legislation

On October 31, 2003, the Department of Finance released, for public comment, draft proposals, regarding the deductibility of interest, which deal with the issue of reasonable expectation of profit. These proposals, along with an Interpretation Bulletin on interest deductibility and related issues, released on October 31, 2003 by the CRA, form the current government position on the deductibility of interest. However, actual legislation has not been passed at the time of writing (July 2007).

IT-533

"Interest" is not a defined term in the Act. The determination of what is interest is a question of law. The definition of interest has been addressed in several court decisions, including *Shell Canada Limited v. The Queen* and *Miller v. The Queen*. As in *Miller*, interest for tax purposes is generally accepted to mean an amount that has met three criteria. These criteria are:

99 DTC 5669 (S.C.C.)
85 DTC 5354 (F.C.T.D.)

- the amount must be calculated on a day-to-day accrual basis,

- the amount must be calculated on a principal sum (or a right to a principal sum), and

- the amount must be compensation for the use of the principal sum (or the right to the principal sum).

In general, interest represents payment for the use of debt capital. The Act allows a taxpayer to deduct interest on money borrowed to earn income from business or property.

ITA: 20(1)(*c*)

A taxpayer can deduct interest if it:

- is paid or payable in the year,

- arises from a legal obligation,

- is payable on borrowed money that is used for the purpose of earning income (other than exempt income) from a business or property, and

- is reasonable in amount.

There are some statutory limits on the deduction of interest. We have discussed some of them in Chapter 4. The followings are a few examples:

- the deduction of interest imposed under the Act is denied;

ITA: 18(1)(*t*)

- the deduction of interest on funds borrowed to buy vacant land is limited;

ITA: 18(2)

- interest that is part of "soft costs" must be capitalized;

ITA: 18(3.1)

- the deduction of interest paid to certain non-residents is limited;

ITA: 18(4)–(8)

- the deduction for interest on borrowed fund to make a contribution to tax sheltered retirement savings fund, such as RRSPs, is denied.

ITA: 18(11)

Note that the interest on interest is called compound interest. Compound interest is deductible if the original amount borrowed meets the test of interest deductibility. However, a compound interest is only deductible when it is paid and not when it is payable.

¶6,270   Loss of the source of income

From the above section, we know that the general principle of interest deductibility is that the borrowed money must be used for the purpose of earning income from a business or property. However, a problem can arise if an investment financed with debt declines in value and is sold at a loss. The investor reinvests the proceeds but does not pay off the loan. Should interest still be deductible when the source of income is lost?

¶6,270.10   *Example*

A taxpayer borrows $10,000 to acquire an income-producing property. During the holding period of that property, the interest has been deducted from income for tax purposes. When the property declines in value to $6,000, the property is sold and the taxpayer invests the $6,000 of proceeds in another income-producing property. The original loan has not been repaid.

¶6,270.20 *Analysis*

If we use the general principle of interest deductibility, the interest on the remaining debt would no longer be deductible as it is not currently used for the purpose of earning income from a business or property. The Act addresses this issue. A rule applies to deem the $4,000 of borrowed money to continue to be used for the purpose of earning income from the property, as long as the original property was capital property (other than real estate or depreciable property). This allows the interest on the $4,000 to qualify for the deduction.

ITA: 20.1

¶6,275 Capitalization of interest

At the taxpayer's election, the Act permits certain borrowing costs and interest to be treated as non-deductible expenses and added to the cost of depreciable property in respect of which the expenses were incurred. This election might be made, for example, if the deduction of such costs would create a loss that could not be absorbed in the loss carry-over period which will be discussed in a later Chapter. The costs eligible for such deferment are amounts otherwise deductible as interest and other expenses of borrowing money. This is particularly advantageous if the interest is in respect of assets in fast write-off classes such as Class 12.

ITA: 21

ITA: 20(1)(*c*), 20(1)(*d*), 20(1)(*e*)

¶6,290 **Personal Loan Planning and Interest Deductibility**

¶6,295 Deductibility of interest expenses

In general, as indicated above, expenditures made or incurred for the purpose of gaining or producing income from property are deductible from that income. The amounts of such expenditures must be reasonable in the circumstances. Under the current concept of interest deductibility, there need only be a reasonable expectation of earning income. No income need actually be earned in a year, in order to deduct interest paid or payable in that year. In the case of *Fallis v. M.N.R.*, the taxpayer was not allowed to deduct interest when he could never hope to receive as much interest as he paid. In the case of preferred shares held by an individual, the CRA will allow an interest expense deduction to the extent of the grossed-up dividend income. On the other hand, if the preferred shares can be freely converted into common shares, interest expense on funds borrowed to buy the preferred shares will be fully deductible irrespective of the dividend rate on those shares. Also, interest at a reasonable rate on funds borrowed to buy common shares will be fully deductible irrespective of the dividend yield, which may even be zero, because of the reasonable expectation of an increase in the dividend rate on common shares.

ITA: 20(1)(*c*)

66 DTC 233 (T.A.B.)

IT-533, par. 31

The deductibility of interest is determined by the use of the borrowed funds. Thus, interest paid on a mortgage, the proceeds of which are used to invest in certain securities, is deductible because the interest is paid in respect of funds used to produce income. On the other hand, interest on funds borrowed to purchase personal property is not deductible because it is not used to produce income. Also, interest on funds borrowed to invest in commodities as a capital investment was held by the Tax Court of Canada not to be deductible in *Hastings v. M.N.R.* The Court agreed with the Crown's position that the ordinary rules relating to expenses being deducted in the income-earning process do not apply to the capital gains sections of the Act.

88 DTC 1391 (T.C.C.)

Loan planning would suggest that the taxpayer borrow funds which will be used to produce income, thereby making the interest tax deductible. This permits the taxpayer to allocate his or her savings to purchases such as assets used for personal purposes including the family home or a car not used for business which do not produce income.

Great care must be taken in maintaining the connection between the interest paid and the use of the funds borrowed. In one case, a taxpayer received a loan from his employer and used the proceeds to finance the purchase of securities. He secured the loan with a mortgage on his house. In this situation, the interest on the loan was deductible. However, when the taxpayer was transferred and he sold his house, he had to pay off the loan from the proceeds of sale. He then purchased another house in his new work location and financed the purchase with a mortgage. He deducted mortgage interest on the new house against his investment income on the same basis as before, but the CRA disallowed that interest deduction. It was argued that the money was not used to produce income, but to acquire the new house. In this case, the taxpayer did not maintain the connection between the loan and the use of the funds. Had he not paid off the employer's loan but secured the loan with a new mortgage on the new home, he would have maintained that connection.

IT-533, par. 9–14

This position, taken by the CRA, was confirmed in the case of *The Queen v. Bronfman Trust*, when the Supreme Court of Canada held that what was important was the use of the borrowed funds. In this case, the Supreme Court, in its examination, was not able to trace the funds borrowed directly to an income-earning source (eligible use source) and, hence, denied the deduction of the related interest. It would appear that in these cases, the decision in the *Bronfman Trust* case would stand. Therefore, in order for interest on borrowed funds to be deductible, the taxpayer must still trace the funds borrowed to an income-producing purpose.

87 DTC 5097 (S.C.C.)

IT-533, par. 13

¶6,300   Commentary on two Supreme Court decisions on interest deductibility — Singleton and Ludco

¶6,300.10 *Singleton*

2001 DTC 5533 (S.C.C.)

(i) Facts

Singleton, involved a lawyer who had a capital account in his law firm with a balance of at least $300,000. Mr. Singleton's firm paid him his $300,000 capital and he used the funds to purchase a new house. On the same day, he borrowed $300,000 and contributed it to his firm as a capital contribution, where it was used by the firm as working capital in its business. The loan was secured on the house. Although the house was purchased in his wife's name, Mr. Singleton was legally obligated to make the mortgage payments, thereby fulfilling the requirement that the interest be paid pursuant to a "legal obligation".

(ii) Issue

The issue of *Singleton* is whether the borrowed money was used for the purpose of earning income from a business.

(iii) The Supreme Court of Canada Decision

The Supreme Court of Canada held that the interest payments were deductible under the *Income Tax Act*. The court concluded that, given the effect of the legal relationships, the taxpayer borrowed money and used that money to refinance the capital account in the law firm. This was a direct and eligible use of funds within the meaning of the provision which allows the deduction of interest on borrowed funds.

ITA: 20(1)(c)

¶6,300.20 *Ludco*

2001 DTC 5505 (S.C.C.)

(i) Facts

In *Ludco*, the taxpayer used approximately $7.5 million of borrowed money to purchase shares in two offshore corporations in the Bahamas (known as a tax haven). During the period in which it held the shares, Ludco deducted approximately $6 million of interest and included $600,000 of dividends in its incomes. When the shares were disposed of, it reported a gain of $9,200,000. The Minister disallowed the deduction of the $6 million interest expense on the grounds that the shares were acquired to earn a capital gain (partially included in income for tax purposes as a different source) instead of for the purpose of earning income from property.

(ii) Issue

The issue in the *Ludco* case is whether the $7.5 million borrowed funds was used by the taxpayers for the purpose of earning income from property when the investment earned only $600,000 of dividend income.

(iii) The Supreme Court of Canada Decision

In its decision, the Supreme Court of Canada held that the word "income" in the provision of the Act which allows deduction of interest on borrowed funds meant gross and not net income. Therefore, the taxpayer only needs to have a reasonable expectation of earning some income to support his interest deduction.

¶6,305 Tax Planning

¶6,305.10 *Overview*

Tax is an important factor affecting investment decisions. The objective of this section is to provide a brief discussion that is useful for thinking about how taxes affect investment decisions.

When an investor has multiple investment opportunities, but limited funds, the rule of thumb is to compare the after-tax return on available funds. If the investor has to borrow to invest, the investment decision may depend on that financing. On the other hand, the interest deductibility depends on the type of investment undertaking. In general, if the funds are borrowed to acquire property that is used to generate property income, then interest paid on the loan is deducible for tax purposes. Interest on a loan used to buy a personal asset such as a home is, generally, not deductible. The following examples illustrate the differences in after-tax returns on investments.

¶6,305.20 *Illustration*

(i) Facts

Ms. Prudent has always considered investing her savings to be a high priority. This year she has saved $5,000; however, she has just discovered that she will need to purchase a new car which will cost an additional $5,000 with her trade-in. She can borrow the funds for the car from the dealer at a very favourable rate of 5.9%, while funds borrowed from a stockbroker to invest in corporate shares will cost 7%. She is in a 25.5% (combined federal and provincial) tax bracket. How could Ms. Prudent accomplish her goals at a minimum cost in this situation?

(ii) Analysis

Ms. Prudent should buy the car with her accumulated savings of $5,000 and borrow $5,000 from the stockbroker for her investments. While the pre-tax cost of the investment loan will be higher than a car loan, the 7% will be deductible resulting in an after-tax cost of 5.2% (i.e., 7% (1-0.255)) compared with the 5.9% car loan which is not tax deductible. The result is a saving of 0.7% which, on a loan of $5,000, would amount to about $35 in the first year.

¶6,305.30 *Conclusion*

From the above analysis, we can see that the general strategy is that you should buy personal assets with your own funds (since interest is not deductible on borrowed funds used to purchase personal assets) and then use these assets as collateral to borrow to invest in assets that will earn property income (since interest is deductible in that situation).

If you already have a mortgage on the personal asset, and it can be prepaid without penalty, you should pay it down using your own cash. However, if the mortgage is not open for such payments in full or in part, it may be worthwhile setting aside savings for the purpose of paying down the mortgage when it is due for renewal. Paying down an old, low-interest mortgage may not be the best investment, but certainly paying down one at a higher interest rate is worth considering.

¶6,400   DIFFERENCES BETWEEN BUSINESS AND PROPERTY INCOME

At this point, it would be worthwhile comparing some of the provisions which have been examined so far and which distinguish between business and property income.

¶6,410   Applicable To Business Income Only

- write-off of eligible capital property;   ITA: 20(1)(*b*)

- reserves;   ITA: 20(1)(*m*), 20(1)(*m*.1), 20(1)(*m*.2), 20(1)(*n*)

- certain specific expenses:

  — expenses of representation;   ITA: 20(1)(*cc*)

  — site investigation;   ITA: 20(1)(*dd*)

  — utilities services connection;   ITA: 20(1)(*ee*)

- convention expenses;   ITA: 20(10)

- short-year proration for capital cost allowance.   ITR: 1100(3)

¶6,420   Applicable To Property Income Only

- restriction on capital cost allowance for rental properties;   ITR: 1100(15)

- attribution rules;   ITA: 74.1

- foreign taxes on property income in excess of 15% deductible.   ITA: 20(11)

¶6,500   GST AND PROPERTY INCOME

¶6,510   Interest and Dividends

Interest and dividends are exempt from GST. A number of provisions and definitions in the *Excise Tax Act* (ETA) must be reviewed to explain the basis for this exemption. First, financial services rendered to residents in Canada are exempt from GST. A "financial service" is defined to include a broad range of transactions and services. For example, the payment or receipt of interest, dividends, or any other amount in respect of a "financial instrument" is included in the definition of financial service. A "financial instrument" is defined to include a debt security, an equity security, an insurance policy, etc. A "debt security" is defined in the same subsection to mean a right to be paid money and includes a deposit of money. An "equity security" is defined to mean a share of the capital stock of a corporation or any interest in or right to such a share. Consequently, payments of interest and dividends in respect of financial instruments are exempt from GST. It is important to note that the definition of financial service contains several exclusions. For example, paragraph (*r*) of the definition excludes the provision of a professional service by an accountant, actuary, lawyer or notary in the course of a professional practice. Consequently, these services are subject to GST in the normal manner.

ETA: Part VII of Sch. V
ETA: 123(1)

ETA: 123(1)

¶6,520   "Soft Costs"

GST applies to sales and rentals of real property unless the supply is specifically exempt under Part I of Schedule V (such as sales of *used* residential housing and long-term residential rents). The GST affects real estate developers and builders in the same manner that it affects other businesses that make taxable supplies. To the extent property and services are purchased for use in commercial activities, input tax credits in respect of the GST paid on those purchases may be claimed. For example, when a builder incurs GST in respect of legal and accounting fees during the period of construction, renovation or alteration of a building or in respect of the ownership of the related land, the tax may be recovered as an input tax credit.

Certain other soft costs incurred by builders are classified as exempt supplies under the ETA, and hence, not subject to GST. These would include, for example, interest, insurance, and property taxes. As discussed above, interest is exempt as a financial service. Similarly, insurance premiums are exempt as financial services. Property taxes are exempt.

ETA: Part VII, Sch. V
ETA: sec. 21, Part VI, Sch. V

Since sales of *used* residential properties are exempt from GST, special rules have been incorporated into the ETA to deal with "substantial renovations" of used residential properties. These rules are intended to ensure that persons in the business of renovating homes for resale are treated in the same manner as builders of new homes. The term "substantial renovation" is defined to mean:

ETA: 123(1)

> ... the renovation or alteration of a building to such extent that all or substantially all of the building that existed immediately before the renovation or alteration was begun, other than the foundation, external walls, interior supporting walls, floors, roof and staircases, has been removed or replaced where, after completion of the renovation or alteration, the building is, or forms part of, a residential complex.

Since the sale of a substantially renovated home is treated as the sale of new residential property, GST is charged on the sale and the builder is able to claim input tax credits on purchases of property and services. Consequently, any GST paid on soft costs would be recoverable.

Where a residential property is renovated and the renovation is not considered to be substantial, the sale of the property is exempt as a sale of used residential property. However, the renovator is required to pay GST on certain costs incurred in renovating the property. The GST is calculated by reference to all costs of completing the renovation or alteration that would be included in determining the adjusted cost base of the property for income tax purposes, other than:

ETA: Part I, Sch. V
ETA: 192

- the costs of acquiring the property;

- interest and the cost of other financial services; and

- the cost of other purchases on which the renovator previously paid GST.

¶6,800 REVIEW QUESTIONS

(1) Billy Hilly has come to you to tell you that he has found a great way of generating income of which only one-half is taxable as a capital gain. He buys a bond that pays interest annually and he holds it until just before the payment date and then he sells it, including the accrued interest, at a gain. Comment.

(2) One of your clients does not want to buy the compounding series Canada Savings Bonds any more since the new interest accrual rules cause the interest earned to be taxable annually rather than at maturity. Comment.

(3) Mr. Saleprop owns an unincorporated business. In recognition of his wife's considerable contribution of her time and skills to the business he gives her a one-half share of the business income. Comment.

(4) Mr. Smith has just guaranteed a bank loan that his wife has taken out to buy shares in a corporation carrying on a business that she is starting. He is concerned about the attribution rules. Comment.

(5) Opco Inc. recently borrowed $300,000 to buy 30 acres of industrial land. The corporation has constructed a building, shipping and receiving areas and parking for employees on this property using up 20 acres. The remaining 10 acres is available for future needs. Is all of the interest on the $300,000 loan deductible?

(6) Rent Co. Ltd. is a corporation in the residential rental business. Because of some recent purchases, its financing costs are high and it is operating at a break-even before CCA this year. However, in the prior three years it made a profit. Can the corporation claim CCA to create a loss this year to carry back to the prior years, using the carryover rules in Division C, to offset income in those years?

(7) Ms. Cautious has just bought some gold as a protection against inflation. However, she did not have the cash to make the purchase so she borrowed from the bank to buy the gold. This is the first time that she has done this and she plans to hold the gold for some time. She is repaying the loan over three years. Will she be able to deduct all or some of her interest expense? Explain.

(8) You have been told of a court case where a taxpayer borrowed money initially to purchase a home, because some of the funds that he was to receive from Iran had not arrived when expected. When the funds at last arrived, interest rates had risen above that rate he was paying on his house mortgage. He then chose to invest his money at these higher interest rates instead of paying off the mortgage. He deducted the interest portion of his mortgage payments on his tax return. Comment.

(9) A client is in the process of selling his house and buying a bigger one. However, the real estate market has slowed down and in order to sell his existing house he is going to have to take back a mortgage for $100,000 at 8% for a five-year term. Since he does not have any extra cash, he is going to have to borrow that $100,000 from you in order to buy his new house. Is the interest going to be deductible on his mortgage? If not, how might he restructure the transaction to make it deductible?

(10) You have just interviewed a new client and have discovered that she borrowed to buy shares in a private corporation five years ago. The loan is still outstanding but the corporation has since gone bankrupt. Is the interest she is paying on the loan still deductible?

¶6,825   MULTIPLE CHOICE QUESTIONS

Question 1

Max is planning to invest in preferred shares of a friend's Canadian-controlled private corporation, which are paying a $12,000 dividend per year from income taxable at the low corporate rate. Assuming that Max is in the top federal tax bracket (29%) and that the provincial tax on income rate in his province is 17%, how much income tax will Max pay on this income? Also assume that the combined federal and provincial dividend tax credit is equal to the dividend gross-up.

(A) $1,350

(B) $3,900

(C) $6,900

(D) $5,520

Question 2

Wendy Jang owns three rental buildings. All of the buildings were purchased after 1987 and are of brick construction:

	Property		
	1	2	3
Original cost	$120,000	$ 80,000	$150,000
UCC at Jan. 1	100,000	75,000	150,000
Rental revenue for the year	58,000	22,000	20,000
Expenses for the year:			
Interest	20,000	10,000	8,000
Property taxes	13,000	6,000	11,000
Other	17,000	4,000	1,000

What is the maximum CCA that Wendy Jang can claim on the rental properties for the year?

(A) $13,000

(B) $10,000

(C) $7,000

(D) $6,500

Question 3

In the year, Mr. P made the following loans and gifts to family members to split income with his family members. Which one of the loans and/or gifts will result in income being attributed to Mr. P?

(A) A gift of $100,000 to his son, Peter, age 21. Peter invested the money in a term deposit and earned $3,000 of interest income.

(B) An interest-free loan of $100,000 to his mother-in-law, Mabel, age 81. Mabel invested the money in mutual funds and earned $12,000 of dividend income.

(C) An interest-free loan of $100,000 to his daughter, Daphne, age 28. Daphne bought a cottage and used it for personal use.

(D) A gift of $100,000 to his wife, Debbie. Debbie put the money in her non-interest bearing chequing account and paid all the family's household expenses from the account. She then used $100,000 of her own money to invest in the stock market and earned $10,000 of dividend income.

Question 4

Which of the following items is DEDUCTIBLE by Canadian taxpayers in the computation of income from business or property in Subdivision b of Division B of the Act?

(A) Commissions paid on the purchase of an investment in common shares. ~~Not correct~~

(B) The premium paid on a $100,000 term life insurance policy on the taxpayer's life which is required as <u>collateral</u> for a $100,000 bank loan used to purchase a $100,000 investment in common shares. *Deductible 20(1)(e.2)*

(C) Interest expenses on a loan to invest in a registered retirement savings plan. *18(11) No*

(D) Commissions paid on the sale of an investment in common shares.

Question 5

During 2007, Mike received two cheques, one in the amount of C$20,000, the other in the amount of C$8,500. The $20,000 cheque was a dividend from business income taxed at the low corporate rate of a Canadian-controlled private corporation. The $8,500 cheque was a dividend from a foreign corporation, net of the $1,500 of foreign tax withheld by the foreign country from the dividend payment. Which of the following amounts must Mike include in his income for Canadian income tax purposes in respect of these two dividend cheques?

(A) $20,000   *20,000*

(B) $28,500

(C) $30,000

(D) $35,000

Question 6

Ron Bordessa is 18 years of age. He inherited shares of Royal Roads Ltd., a private corporation, on his grandfather's death three years ago. Which of the following statements is true?

(A) Any dividend that Ron receives on these shares will be subject to the tax on split income.

(B) The tax on split income does not apply to any dividends on these shares because they were inherited. *Not*

(C) Any capital gains that Ron received on these will be subject to the tax on split income. *No 15(2)*

(D) The tax on split income does not apply to any dividend on these shares because Ron has reached the age of 18.

¶6,850 EXERCISES

Exercise 1

ITA: 12(1)(*c*), 12(4), 12(11)

What would be the *first* year in which the taxpayer would have to include interest in income in each of the following cases and to which years would that interest relate?

(A) A corporation with a June 30 year-end buys a bond that pays interest semi-annually on March 31 and September 30 from its previous owner on January 1, 2007.

(B) An individual buys a compounding GIC on November 1, 2007.

(C) An individual buys a zero coupon bond, issued on January 1, 2007, in 2007.

(D) An individual buys a compound Canada Savings Bond issued November 1, 2007.

(E) On June 1, 2007, an individual buys a $1,000 bond paying $40 interest by cheque each May 31 and November 30. The bond was issued on December 1, 2006.

Exercise 2

ITA: 74.1, 74.5

(A) A husband wants his wife to have a $1,000 Canada Savings Bond that he owns paying interest at 7%. What are the consequences to the couple during the year if:

(i) he gives the bond to her without receiving any financial consideration from her in return?

(ii) he sells the bond to her for $1,000 plus accrued interest to the date of sale in return for cash?

(iii) he sells the bond to her for $1,000 plus accrued interest to the date of sale in return for a demand note which she signs payable to him without interest?

(iv) he cashes the bond lending the proceeds to her in return for a promissory note which she signs payable to him without interest but with a definite repayment period and she uses the funds from the loan to buy a similar bond?

(B) Would any of the above answers change for the current year if he undertook the same transactions with a trust set up in favour of a child aged 15 instead of his wife?

(C) Would any of the above answers change if he undertook the same transactions with a child aged 20?

Exercise 3

ITA: 18(2)

A downtown hotel bought a vacant lot adjacent to the hotel building. Comment on the deductibility of property taxes and interest paid on funds borrowed to buy the property if:

(i) the property is used as a parking lot for hotel guests;

(ii) the property was bought for potential gains on future sale but in the meantime it is being used as a public parking lot generating net revenues before the taxes and interest of 75% of the expenditures for taxes and interest;

(iii) the property was bought for future expansion of the hotel and in the meantime is being used under the same condition as in (ii) above.

Exercise 4

ITR: 1100

Mr. Provident is a salaried employee who invests in small rental properties. He bought one such property last year and at the beginning of this year the undepreciated capital cost balances for that property were as follows:

Class 1 — brick building	$148,000
Class 8 — furniture and fixtures	25,000

This year he bought another property for $150,000 including land valued at $12,500. The net income before capital cost allowance for each property this year was:

property 1	$ 9,270
property 2	3,750

— *REQUIRED*

Compute the maximum capital cost allowance on these rental properties for the current year.

Exercise 5

ITA: 20(1)(a); ITR: 1100, 1101(1ac)

Ms. Alimeag owns two rental properties. One produced rental revenue of $13,500 and had allowable expenses (excluding capital cost allowance) of $11,250. The other had rental revenue of $22,500 and expenses of $18,750. Data on the two Class 3 buildings are as follows:

	Property A	Property B
Capital cost	$360,000	$600,000
UCC, January 1	$330,000	$480,000

During the year, Property A was sold for net proceeds of $336,000.

— *REQUIRED*

(A) What is the effect of the above information on the income of Ms. Alimeag for the year?

(B) Can an election be made under subsection 13(4) if Property A is replaced by the end of the next year?

¶6,875   ASSIGNMENT PROBLEMS

Problem 1

ITA: 12(1)(*g*); IT-462

The Country Pie is a highly recognized baker of quality pies in Beamsville, Ontario. The current proprietor, Rudolph Strudel, started the business about 20 years ago with an initial purchase of equipment of $150,000 and built up the name of the company by closely supervising the pie production process. Many have said that it is this attention and his recipes that have made the business a success. Rudolph has decided to sell his business and move to the coast to get away from the pressures of running a business. An offer has been made for the assets of The Country Pie by Big Food Corporation Ltd. ("BFC"). There was a meeting of the minds as to the value of the fixed assets of The Country Pie. However, there was considerable dispute as to the value of The Country Pie name in generating pie sales after a purchase by BFC. Consequently, it is proposed that the full proceeds be determined in part by future sales.

The BFC offer is for $50,000 cash; $60,000 to be paid on the basis of sales over the next three years with any balance of the $60,000 remaining at the end of the third year payable at that time; and 25% of gross sales in the next five years. As part of the agreement, Rudolph would provide consulting services to BFC as needed during the next three years.

— REQUIRED

Discuss the income tax implications to Rudolph of the proposal from BFC.

Problem 2

ITA: 12(1)(*c*), 12(1)(*j*), 74.1, 74.5, 82(1); IT-510, IT-511R

Mr. Wiser is contemplating investing in two different mutual funds. His investment options are set out below.

Amount	Mutual Fund	Distribution
$2,000	International Income Fund	Annual interest of 8.0%
$2,000	Canadian Dividend Fund	Annual dividend of 6.0%

Mr. Wiser contemplates holding both mutual funds for the same period of time — from purchase to December 31, 2011. Mr. Wiser is in the top federal income tax bracket (29%). Mr. Wiser's provincial tax on income rate is 17%. Assume that the combined federal and provincial dividend tax credit is equal to the dividend gross-up. Assume that the Canadian Dividend Fund receives and distributes dividends from Canadian-resident public corporations.

— REQUIRED

(A) Based on the above information, which mutual fund should Mr. Wiser prefer?

(B) Can Mr. Wiser achieve any advantage by purchasing the above mutual fund in the name of his 8 year old daughter who has no other source of income?

(C) Mr. Wiser's spouse is currently attending university on a full-time basis and has no source of income. Can Mr. Wiser achieve any advantage by lending $2,000 to his spouse and having her purchase the above mutual fund? The $2,000 loan would be evidenced by a promissory note repayable in 4 equal annual installments on each of December 31, 2007 to 2010 and bearing interest at a commercial rate.

Problem 3

ITA: 18(2)–(3)

Furniture Focus Limited provides competitive prices to consumers by using a no-frills approach to displaying its product in large stores surrounded by ample parking. Furniture Focus Limited has excess land that is not currently used in its business. This vacant land is rented to the adjacent automobile dealer who stores new cars on it.

For the year ended December 31, 2007, Furniture Focus Limited had the following operating expenses:

Sales	$35,000,000
Cost of goods sold	(20,000,000)
Gross profit	$15,000,000
Selling expenses	(5,000,000)
General and administrative expenses	(2,000,000)
	$ 8,000,000
Other income	50,000
Net income	$ 8,050,000

The general and administrative expenses include $30,000 of interest and $5,000 of property taxes on the vacant land rented to the automobile dealer. There are no other expenses connected with this land. Other income includes $10,000 of rental income paid by the automobile dealer.

— *REQUIRED*

Determine the income tax consequences of the various payments related to the vacant land.

Problem 4

ITA: 20(1)(*a*); ITR: 1100(11), 1101(1ac); Sched. II

Sara Shimizu is the owner of two rental properties, 509 Brunswick Avenue and 356 Spadina Road. These properties were purchased six years ago for $525,000 and $600,000, respectively. In 2007, 509 Brunswick Avenue was sold for $550,000. A reasonable allocation of this amount is considered to be 75% to the building and 25% to the land. The following income and expenses were incurred in renting out the two properties in 2007:

Rental	$ 60,000
Interest on mortgage	(40,000)
Operating costs	(15,000)
Promotion costs for sale of property	(5,000)
Net income	0

There are no meal or entertainment expenses included in the $5,000 of sales promotion costs. At December 31, 2006, the undepreciated capital cost of 509 Brunswick Avenue was $383,500 and that of 356 Spadina Road was $400,000.

— *REQUIRED*

Determine the income from property for income tax purposes assuming Sara wishes to report the least amount possible for tax purposes in 2007.

Problem 5

ITA: 18, 20

It is early January 2007 and the president of BDC Distributing Limited, a client of your firm, called recently to discuss the tax implications regarding the construction of a new building. BDC has been growing rapidly and needs new warehouse space. They have been unable to locate any suitable space in the existing buildings in town and, therefore, have decided that their only option is to build their own building. They have identified the site and have estimated the costs of the project. These projected costs (and dates of completion) are as follows:

The land that has been identified will be purchased on February 15, 2007, for $405,000. There is no significant site preparation required so construction of the building can commence immediately. The cost of the building is estimated to be $1,348,000 plus the costs noted below. It is anticipated that BDC will be able to occupy the building on October 31, 2007.

BDC currently has an architect finalizing the drawings for the building. The architect fees, which will all be paid in 2007, will amount to $7,200. There will also be fees of $2,100 for an engineer to examine the drawings.

BDC has arranged for the financing required for the project. The project will be financed with a mortgage of $875,000 and $1,000,000 of preferred shares issued on January 15, 2007. Interest on the mortgage is payable semi-annually on July 15 and January 15 at a rate of 8% per annum. The preferred shares pay dividends of 5% per annum, payable semi-annually on July 15 and January 15. There will be a number of costs incurred in order to issue the debt and shares. These costs are legal and accounting fees of $18,450, commissions of $58,300 and registration fees of $1,800 for amending the articles of incorporation to allow the issuance of the preferred shares.

The balance of the costs related to the building are summarized below:

Building insurance from April 15, 2007 @ $450 per month	$ 3,825
Property taxes from February 15, 2007 @ $770 per month	8,085
Soil testing to determine location of footings for building	1,825
Relocation expenses	34,100
Utilities service connections estimated to be completed on May 20, 2007	3,800
Mortgage insurance premium from March 1, 2007 of $325 per month	3,250
Maintenance from October 31, 2007	2,500
Utilities from October 31, 2007	6,300
Landscaping	15,500

— *REQUIRED*

Advise the corporation of the impact of the proposed transactions on their December 31, 2007 income tax return.

Problem 6

ETA: 123(1), Sch. V, Parts VI, VII

Reconsider the facts of Problem 5. Assume that GST was paid, where applicable, in addition to the amounts shown.

— *REQUIRED*

Calculate the GST consequences of the transactions presented.

Problem 7

ITA: Subdivision b

John Investor has provided you with the following information related to his various investment holdings as of December 31, 2007.

Interest earned on joint bank account with his spouse (spouse contributes equally)	$ 2,000
Interest earned on his investment account (not joint) with his investment broker	800
Interest earned on 2006 personal income tax assessment	450
Interest on short-term investments:	
$20,000 term deposit taken out November 30, 2007 (interest at maturity in six months)	
Accrued interest from December 1 — December 31, 2007	85
$200,000 GIC purchased November 1, 2006 (interest payable at maturity on October 31, 2009)	
Accrued interest from November 1, 2006 — October 31, 2007	16,000
Accrued interest from January 1, 2007 — December 31, 2007	16,214
Government of Canada Treasury Bills purchased for $9,009 on January 1, 2007	
Amount received on maturity on December 31, 2007	10,000
Cash dividends received from investment in common shares of Canadian resident public corporations	24,000
Cash dividends received from common shares in US corporations (net of $3,000 of foreign withholding taxes; all in $CDN)	17,000

Rental details from operation of two separate rental properties:

	Property 1	Property 2
Gross rental revenue	$ 30,000	$ 46,000
Utilities	5,000	8,000
Property taxes	2,400	3,500
Repairs	1,500	4,800
Mortgage interest	20,000	32,000
Opening UCC	$368,209	$520,225

[handwritten: ⊃EXP]

[handwritten: (1,200) LOSS   1,100   (2,300)]

[handwritten: CAN'T USE, CCA $0, COMBINE]
[handwritten: INCOME < 0]

Interest expenses paid during 2007:

Interest on bank line of credit used for investing in shares described above ..... $50,000 *[handwritten: NET 20(1)(c)]*

Interest on loan to acquire an automobile for his daughter for her 18th birthday .... 3,200 *[handwritten: 18(2) CAN'T]*

Interest on a parcel of vacant land (purchased in 2002, the land does not generate any income) .... 10,000 *[handwritten: CAN'T]*

— *REQUIRED*

Prepare a calculation of John's property income. Comment on the income tax implications of items not included in your calculations.

Problem 8

ITA: 18(1), 20(1)(c);
IT-533

Funds are borrowed by an individual from a financial institution at an 11% per annum interest rate to purchase the following unrelated investments:

(a) gold coins on which gains or losses will be treated as capital gains or losses;

(b) an RRSP portfolio of investments yielding 12.5% in interest;

(c) a five-year GIC paying interest at 8% per annum;

(d) common shares of a Canadian-resident public corporation paying no dividends;

(e) preferred shares of a Canadian-resident public corporation paying 7% dividends;

(f) preferred shares of a U.S. corporation paying 9% dividends;

(g) $100,000 of assets used in an unincorporated business which generated net income of $9,750 before drawings of $18,000 for the year;

(h) lottery tickets which yielded $75,000 in winnings which were reinvested in short-term securities yielding 13%; and

(i) common shares of a Canadian-resident public corporation paying dividends of 6%; later in the year the shares were sold at a small gain to repay a 14% second mortgage on a principal residence.

— *REQUIRED*

Determine the deductibility of the interest expense in each of the unrelated cases.

[For more problems and solutions thereto, see the CD accompanying this book.]

¶6,880   ADVISORY CASE

Kitchener Medical Inc.

Joe McMillan and Bill McDonald were finally able to hold the grand opening for their medical supply import business. It had been an expensive party, but both Joe and Bill felt that their suppliers, customers, and new employees had appreciated it.

It seemed like a long time ago that they got the idea and started to develop their plans. In fact, the idea had been introduced to them 12 months ago during a trip they took to California to look for business opportunities. Once they returned, they began to do their own research. They had one of the local universities do some market research for them to see whether their idea was viable. The research supported their idea of importing medical supplies from a large U.S. supplier to compete against other importers for the Canadian market.

Six months ago, the U.S. supplier put them in touch with their local importer, Beam Inc., whose owner wanted to retire. Since that time, they have been busy negotiating with Mr. Beam and the supplier, finding their own leased warehouse space (Beam Inc.'s space was too small), visiting customers, setting up the office and modern control systems and assessing the employees of Beam Inc. Even before the opening, they had spent $25,000 of their own money on expenses such as:

- their initial travel costs to California (July, last year);

- market research (September, last year);

- negotiating the operating line of credit (May, this year);

- leasehold improvements, equipment (May, this year);

- travel and entertainment expenses (January to June, this year); and

- legal and accounting costs for the incorporation (June, this year).

But now it is all coming together. Joe is going to provide the initial capital, including the personal guarantee to the supplier and the bank, and Bill is going to manage the business. They have bought the inventory, customer lists, accounts receivable, and equipment from Beam Inc. Their initial lease is for five years with two, five-year renewal options.

Advise Joe and Bill on the tax implications of the issues raised by this situation. Assume that they incorporated a company in June, but they have not used it in any way yet, and that it is now July when they are asking for your advice.

¶6,900   SUPPLEMENTAL NOTES

(This section can be omitted without losing the continuity of the Chapter. None of the review questions, multiple choice questions, exercises, or assignment problems utilizes this information.)

¶6,910   Prescribed Debt Obligations

Regulations define specific methods of determining the interest deemed to accrue for debt obligations that have a variety of interest payment terms, including variable and contingent interest obligations. These regulations apply for purposes of determining the accrued interest under other provisions. There are four prescribed debt obligations.

ITR: 7000

ITA: 12(9)

ITA: 12(3), 12(4), 12(11), 20(14), 20(21)

A Type I debt obligation is one that does not have an interest payment that is stipulated to be payable in respect of a principal amount; for example, a zero coupon bond. The accrued interest is determined by multiplying the principal amount by the interest rate equal to the yield that equates the cost of the debt obligation with the present value of all future payments.

ITR: 7000(1)(*a*)

ITR: 7000(2)(*a*)

A Type II debt obligation has disproportional rights to principal and interest such as a stripped bond where the coupons and residue are sold separately. The accrued interest will be determined in the same manner as Type I if there is a single future payment. Where there is more than one payment, the method used to calculate the interest income is the same as Type III, which is described below.

ITR: 7000(1)(*b*)

ITR: 7000(2)(*b*)

A Type III debt obligation is one, other than a Type I or Type II debt obligation, that has a stated interest rate (including any bonus) that increases at some point in time — for example, a guaranteed investment certificate (GIC) that has a higher interest rate after the first two years. The accrued interest is prescribed to be the greater of (1) the maximum interest stipulated for the year and (2) the accrued interest based on the yield that equates the principal amount of the debt to the present value of all maximum future payments.

ITR: 7000(1)(*c*), 7000(3)

ITR: 7000(2)(*c*)

The Regulations expand a debt obligation that can be classified as Type III. The interest payable on this type of obligation is fixed at the date of issue and the rate of interest never decreases. An example would be a GIC which pays interest at stipulated rates per year which increase by one percentage point per year from the year of issue through its five-year term. In this case, the accrued interest would be determined on a yield to maturity basis. The actual interest payable would not be relevant in determining accrued interest for this type of obligation.

ITR: 7000(2)(*c*.1)

A Type IV debt obligation does not qualify as any of the first three types and has an interest rate that is contingent upon a subsequent event, such as an interest rate that increases if the debt is held to maturity. Another example would be a GIC that has a return which is tied to a stock market index. The accrued interest is determined to be the maximum interest rate potentially payable.

ITR: 7000(1)(*d*)

ITR: 7000(2)(*d*)

Example Problem 1

A zero coupon bond (one paying no interest) is issued on July 1, 2007, for $659. It matures on June 30, 2011 for $1,000.

— *REQUIRED*

(A) If Tacks E. Nuff purchased the bond on the issue date and held it to maturity, when and how much interest would he be required to include in income each year?

(B) How would your answer differ if the purchaser was a corporation with a December 31 taxation year-end?

— *SOLUTION*

(A) A zero coupon bond is a prescribed debt obligation. The amount of interest deemed to accrue is determined as follows:

ITR: 7000(1)(a), 7000(2)(a)

Step 1

Compute the yield (i) on the bond: $659 = \dfrac{\$1,000}{(1 + i)^4}$

    i = approximately 11%

Step 2

Compute the annual accrued interest on the accrued value of the bond:

An individual taxpayer would recognize the following accrued income, beginning in the year of the first anniversary day on June 30, 2008:

Year	Accrued income of an individual for tax purposes	Total accrual on bond
2007	Nil	
2008	$659 × .11 = $ 72	$659 + $72 = $ 731
2009	731 × .11 = 80	731 + 80 = 811
2010	811 × .11 = 89	811 + 89 = 900
2011	900 × .11 = 99	900 + 99 = 999
	$340	

(B) A corporation would include the accrued interest in income on an annual basis (e.g., $36 in 2007, assuming the corporation had a fiscal year ending December 31). Since the "anniversary day" definition applies only to an "investment contract" and the term "investment contract" does not apply to a corporation subject to the accrual rule, a normal annual accrual method must be used by a corporate taxpayer.

ITA: 12(3)

Year ended December 31	Accrued interest	Amount owing on bond
2007	$659 × 0.054* = $36	$659 + $36 = $ 695
2008	695 × 0.11 = 76	695 + 76 = 771
2009	771 × 0.11 = 85	771 + 85 = 856
2010	856 × 0.11 = 94	856 + 94 = 950
2011	950 × 0.054 = 51	950 + 51 = 1,001
	$342**	

---

* Approximate six-month rate resulting in annual 11 per cent effective rate.

** Difference in total from (A), above, due to rounding.

Example Problem 2

Mr. Lot Stu Learn acquired a non-transferable $5,000 five-year compound-interest GIC in 2007. The GIC pays 9% annual interest; however, the interest is reduced to 7% per annum if the GIC is cashed early.

— *REQUIRED*

(A) At what rate must interest be included in the taxpayer's income each year?

(B) What are the tax consequences of cashing the GIC early?

— *SOLUTION*

(A) This GIC is a prescribed debt obligation because the interest payable depends on a contingency (holding period) existing after the year. The CRA uses this example, although it considers the GIC to be a debt in which the interest in a year is less than interest in a subsequent year. Regardless, the Regulations would deem interest income to accrue at 9% per year.

(B) If the certificate is disposed of before maturity, any over-accrued interest already recognized for tax purposes would be deductible in the year of disposition. Note, however, that the taxpayer may have been forced to prepay tax on interest that he ultimately does not receive.

ITR: 7000(1)(*d*)

IT-396R, par. 23

ITR: 7000(1)(*c*)

ITR: 7000(2)

ITA: 20(21)

¶6,920 Proposed Amendments to Interest Deductibility and REOP

On October 31, 2003, the Department of Finance released draft proposals on interest deductibility which also included legislation related to reasonable expectation of profit.

A proposal provides that a taxpayer can deduct a loss from a source that is a business or property only if, in that year, it is reasonable to expect that the taxpayer will realize a cumulative profit from the business or property. Then, another provision makes it clear that profit, in this context does not include capital gains or capital losses.

ITA: 3.1(1)

ITA: 3.1(2)

While these changes seem straightforward, consider what would happen if a new business, began to have financial difficulty and realized losses in excess of previous income. If they determined that they were going to have to close the business, then this proposed rule would deny any losses from that time forward. These future losses from expenditures such as wages, lease payments, severance and other recurring expenses, were previously deductible.

Since their release, there has been significant discussion between tax professionals and the Department on the implications of their proposals. The report of the Joint Committee on Taxation of the Canadian Bar Association and the Canadian Institute of Chartered Accountants states that:

> we are of the view that the Draft Proposals would introduce a fundamental change to the *Income Tax Act* which goes well beyond the case law and administrative practice prior to recent court decisions. We are concerned that the proposals could be used to disallow losses resulting from wholly-legitimate business expenses the deductibility of which would not have been an issue under prior case law or administrative practice. They would create significant issues with respect to the treatment of investments in securities.

In the March 23, 2004 federal budget, the following statement was made:

> Assurances were given by the Minister of Finance, Finance officials and the CRA that these releases were not intended to adversely affect the past assessing practices regarding the deductibility of interest on equity investments. The Budget materials acknowledge that significant issues have been raised with them that warrant further consideration.

The Budget Plan 2005, published by the Department of Finance to accompany the February 23, 2005 federal budget, contained the following statement at page 410:

> Many commentators expressed concerns with the proposals' structure, in particular, that the proposals' codification of the "reasonable expectation of profit" test might inadvertently limit the deductibility of a wide variety of ordinary commercial expenses. The Department of Finance has sought to respond by developing a more modest legislative initiative that would respond to those concerns while still achieving the Government's objectives. The Department will, at an early opportunity, release that alternative proposal for comment. This will be combined with a Canada Revenue Agency publication that addresses, in the context of the alternative proposal, certain administrative questions relating to deductibility.

Example Problem

A parent with two children is preparing a will. One child is active in the parent's business and the other is not. The parent is considering the following two options with respect to the business:

(a) leave the business to the child who will be active in the business on the condition that the child give the other child an amount equal to the 50% of the fair market value of the business on the parent's death, and

(b) leave 50% of the business to each of the two children on the condition that the child who will be active in the business buy the 50% left to the other child.

In either case, the active child will have to borrow the funds to pay the other child.

— REQUIRED

Advise the parent on the better alternative for the child who will be active in the business.

— SOLUTION

Based on the use of the borrowed funds, the interest incurred under the second alternative will be deductible, because the funds will be used to buy shares which will produce income. Interest incurred under the first alternative will not be deductible, because the use of the borrowed funds will not produce income.

¶6,930   GST and Property Income

¶6,935   Payments based on production or use

The definition of supply provides, among other things, that supply means the provision of property or a service in any manner, including licence, rental or lease. Consequently, most rents, royalties and similar payments that are dependent on the use of or production from property are subject to GST, provided that they do not relate to exempt or zero-rated supplies. For example, where the author of a book receives royalty payments that are based on the number of books sold in Canada, the payments will be subject to GST. Under the place of supply rules (discussed in Chapter 2), a supply of rights to intangible personal property (such as intellectual property) that may be used in whole or in part in Canada will be deemed to be made in Canada. For example, if the worldwide rights to use a patent or copyright are granted, the supply is deemed to be made in Canada, even if the Canadian rights are never exercised. Conversely, a supply is deemed to be made outside Canada if the property cannot be used in Canada. For example, the supply of a copyright that does not include Canadian rights is deemed to be made outside Canada. *ETA: 123(1)* *ETA: 142(1)* *ETA: 142(2)*

The supply of most rights to explore for or exploit natural resources is deemed not to be a supply and, hence, any consideration paid in respect of such a right is not subject to GST. This includes any right to an amount computed by reference to the production (including profit) from, or to the value of production from, any mineral deposit or peat bog or deposit of peat, or any forestry, water or fishery resources. However, this provision does not apply to the supply of a natural resource property right to consumers, or to non-registrants who acquire the right in the course of making resales to consumers. As a result, these fees are subject to GST. *ETA: 162*

¶6,940   Rental properties

Long-term leases of residential real property are exempt from GST. For this exemption to apply, the tenant must occupy the particular residential complex (such as a house) or unit (such as an apartment) for a period of at least one month. This exemption does not apply to hotels, motels, etc., where all or substantially all of the units are rented out for periods of less than 60 days. However, an exemption is available for short-term stays in rooming and boarding houses. While residential landlords need not collect GST on rents, input tax credits may not be claimed in respect of GST paid by these landlords on purchases of property and services. The net GST remitted by the landlord may be added to the adjusted cost base for *ETA: sec. 6, Part I, Sch. V* capital property, and to other deductible expenses for income tax purposes. However, a residential rental property rebate is available for landlords, equal to 36 per cent of the tax imposed (or 2.5 percentage points of tax), for newly-constructed, substantially-renovated or converted residential rental accommodation used for long-term rental accommodation. The rebate also applies to the construction of additions to residential rental property and to the leasing of land that is used for residential purposes. The full rebate is available for units valued up to $350,000 (and is equal to $7,560 (36% × $350,000 × 6% GST). The rebate is phased out for residential units valued between $350,000 and $450,000, and is eliminated for units valued at $450,000 or more.

On leases of commercial property, landlords are required to charge GST and are eligible to claim input tax credits in the normal manner for tax paid on purchases of property and services.

Chapter 7

Capital Gains: An Introduction

LEARNING GOALS

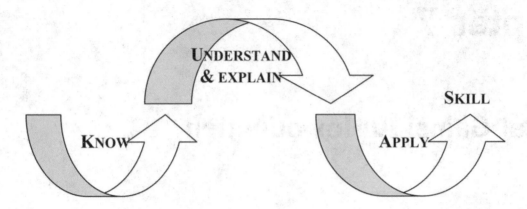

Know

By the end of this chapter you should know the basic provisions of the *Income Tax Act* that relate to capital gains and losses. Completing the Review Questions (¶7,800) and Multiple Choice Questions (¶7,825) is a good way to learn the technical provisions.

Understand and Explain

You should understand and be able to explain

● how to calculate proceeds of disposition and the adjusted cost base to determine the capital gain or loss;

● how capital gains and losses are taxed;

● the special rules for principal residences, personal-use property, and listed personal property;

● the special case of an allowable business investment loss; and

● how capital gains and losses fit in to the calculation of income for tax purposes.

Completing the Exercises (¶7,850) is a good way to deepen your understanding of the material in this chapter.

Apply

You should be able to apply your knowledge and understanding of the rules pertaining to capital gains and losses in a way that accomplishes a client's goals. Completing the Assignment Problems (¶7,875) is an excellent way to develop your ability to apply the material in increasingly complex situations.

OVERVIEW

Subdivision c of Division B of Part I of the Act contains the primary rules for the computation of taxable capital gains and allowable capital losses.

The following chart will help to locate these provisions in the Act.

PART I — DIVISION B
SUBDIVISION c
CAPITAL GAINS & LOSSES

DIVISION		SUBDIVISION		SECTION	
A	Liability for tax		Basic rules		
B	**Computation of income**	a	Office or employment		
C	Computation of taxable income	b	Business or property		
D	Taxable income earned in Canada by non-residents	**c**	**Capital gains and losses**	38	TCG/ACL
		d	Other income	39	CG/CL
		e	Other deductions	39.1	Exempt CG balance
E	Computation of tax	f	Rules relating to computation of income	40	General rules
E.1	Minimum tax			41	LPP
F	Special rules			42	Warranty
				43	Part disposition
G	Deferred and other special income arrangements	g	Amounts not included in income	43.1	Life estates
				44	Replacement property
H	Exemptions	h	Cdn corporations and shareholders	44.1	Small business share rollover
I	Returns, assessments, payments, and appeals	i	Shareholders of non-resident corporations	45	Change in use
				46	Personal-use property
				47	Identical property
J	Appeals to the courts	j	Partnerships	48.1	SBC goes public
		k	Trusts	49	Options granted
				50	Loss on debt/shares
				51	Convertible property
				52	Cost of certain property
				53	ACB adjustments
				54	Definitions
				54.1	Exception: principal residence
				54.2	Shares and capital property
				55	Deemed capital gain

Some of the more important provisions are as follows:

Sec. 39 Meaning of capital gain, capital loss and business investment loss

Sec. 40 General rules including principal residence exemption

Sec. 41 Listed personal property

Sec. 44 Replacement property rules

Sec. 45 Change in use

Sec. 46 Personal-use property

Sec. 47 Identical properties

Sec. 52 Cost

Sec. 53 Adjustments to cost base

Sec. 54 Definitions

In addition, Subdivision f of Division B provides some rules that are relevant to the inclusion of capital gains income. For example, the attribution rules determine whether the capital gains or losses received by a particular person should be attributed to someone else.

ITA: 74.2, 74.3

This Chapter introduces the concepts needed and the following Chapter discusses them in further detail.

¶7,000 OVERVIEW OF THE TAXATION OF CAPITAL GAINS

¶7,010 History

Prior to 1972, capital gains were not taxed under the Act. Canada was one of the few western nations which had never levied a tax on the disposition of capital property. With our government's concern for equity among taxpayers, a complete set of rules for the taxation of capital gains was introduced to the legislation. These rules have become an additional source of confusion for tax practitioners, the Canada Revenue Agency (CRA) and taxpayers. Slowly since 1972, the government has been revising the rules in this particular subdivision, although these revisions have introduced more complexity during this time.

One of the most significant changes is to the inclusion rate for capital gains. The inclusion rate is the percentage that is applied to the capital gain with the result being included in income as a taxable capital gain. Since tax on capital gains was introduced in 1972 this inclusion rate has changed four times as shown below:

Time Period	Inclusion Rate
1972 to 1987	50%
1988 and 1989	66⅔%
1990 to February 27, 2000	75%
February 28 to October 17, 2000	66⅔%
After October 17, 2000	50%

¶7,020 Capital Receipt Versus Income Receipt Revisited

The Act does not define a capital gain. The provisions merely set out the technical computations to be made once it has been determined whether a transaction is an income receipt or a capital receipt. Hence, taxpayers and their advisers must turn to the guidelines which have been laid down by the courts through past judicial decisions. Even then, there is no clear-cut set of rules which will apply in all situations. The result has been one of the most confusing and controversial areas of taxation giving rise to thousands of court cases since the advent of federal income taxation in Canada.

A set of behavioural factors, which were introduced in Chapter 4, were developed by the courts to help in determining whether the transaction may fall into the capital category or the income category. However, each situation must be judged in relation to facts surrounding the particular transaction and in many cases may warrant professional advice. In determining the facts, the taxpayer's whole course of conduct before, during and after the transaction in question should be reviewed.

¶7,025 Primary intention

The objective of most decisions is to determine the intention of the taxpayer. First, there may be an indicator in the taxpayer's behaviour of *primary intention*, that is, did the taxpayer intend to make a business or trading profit on the transaction? If the answer to this question, as determined by observing the facts of the taxpayer's behaviour, is affirmative, then the transaction is likely income.

¶7,030 Secondary intention

The courts may, also, examine the evidence of the taxpayer's behaviour to establish whether the taxpayer had any *secondary intention*, especially in respect of, but not limited to, real estate transactions. Secondary intention may be thought of as an alternative or secondary objective in the mind of the taxpayer at the time of the purchase which motivated the purchase and which would come into operation later if the primary objective is thwarted. For example, a developer purchases a piece of property for an apartment complex which he or she plans to operate as an investment property by collecting rent. However, zoning bylaws cannot be altered to accommodate the proposed project and the developer subsequently sells the property at a profit. The courts would likely view this as an income transaction by way of the taxpayer's secondary intention, on the assumption that the taxpayer, as a developer, would know at the time of purchase that he or she could remove himself or herself from the situation at a profit when the primary objective could not be achieved.[1]

¶7,035 Badges of trade or behavioural factors

The factors, often referred to as "badges of trade", used to establish intention to engage in an adventure or concern in the nature of trade and previously discussed in Chapter 4, include but are not limited to:

(a) the relationship of the transaction to the taxpayer's business;[2]

(b) the nature of the activity or organization associated with trade (recall the British cases of the large quantities of toilet paper and whiskey referred to in Chapter 4 and refer to the CRA's Interpretation Bulletin entitled "Adventure or concern in the nature   IT-459 of trade", also discussed in Chapter 4);

(c) the nature of the assets involved in the transaction;[3]

(d) the number and frequency of transactions within a given period of time;

(e) the length of the period of ownership of the asset;

(f) any supplemental work on or in connection with the property; and

(g) if the transaction was completed by an organization, the stated objectives of the organization, as outlined in articles of association or incorporation or a partnership agreement.[4]

---

[1] The cases of *Rosenblatt v. M.N.R.*, 55 DTC 1205 (Ex. Ct.), *Stekl v. M.N.R.*, 59 DTC 1262 (Ex. Ct.), and *Regina Shoppers Mall Ltd. v. The Queen*, 89 DTC 5482 (F.C.A.), illustrate the focus on intention by the courts.

[2] This factor is illustrated by the cases of *Atlantic Sugar Refineries v. M.N.R.*, 49 DTC 602 (S.C.C.), and *Gairdner Securities v. M.N.R.*, 54 DTC 1015 (S.C.C.).

[3] This factor is illustrated by the case of *Great West Exploration Ltd. v. M.N.R.*, 57 DTC 444 (T.A.B.).

[4] This factor is illustrated by the cases of *Sutton Lumber & Trading Co. Ltd. v. M.N.R.*, 53 DTC 1158 (S.C.C.), *Laverne Asmussen Ltd. v. M.N.R.*, 61 DTC 440 (T.A.B.), and *Western Leaseholds v. M.N.R.*, 59 DTC 1316 (S.C.C.).

The more complete description of these factors presented in Chapter 4 should be reviewed. Reference should also be made to an Interpretation Bulletin where the CRA lists about 12 factors pertaining to real estate transactions. Where a disposition of securities is at issue, the CRA lists some relevant factors to consider in its Interpretation Bulletin entitled "Transactions in securities".

IT-218R, par. 3

IT-479R, par. 11

¶7,040 Terminology

Before attempting to read the pertinent sections in Subdivision c, it is necessary to become acquainted with the basic terminology and abbreviations illustrated below.

Accounting terminology				*Income tax terminology*	
Selling price		$xx	....	Proceeds of disposition (P of D)	Sec. 54
Cost	$xx		....	Adjusted cost base (ACB)	Sec. 54
Selling costs	xx	(xx)	....	Expenses of disposition (SC)	Ssec. 40(1)
Profit (Loss)		$xx	....	Gain (Loss)	
		(xx)	....	Exemption or reserve, if any	Sec. 40
		$xx	....	Capital gain (CG) or Capital loss (CL)	Sec. 39
		$xx	....	Taxable capital gain (TCG) or Allowable capital loss (ACL)	Sec. 38

Capital gains treatment requires a disposition. The Act contains the definition of "disposition" of property. Generally, a disposition includes any transaction entitling a taxpayer to proceeds of disposition. This definition, then, specifies situations that are considered to be dispositions. In some cases, transfers of property, which do not give rise to actual proceeds, will be deemed to be dispositions for tax purposes. These will include deemed dispositions:

ITA: 248(1)

- on the change in use of property;

ITA: 45(1)

- on the death of a taxpayer;

ITA: 70(5)

- by way of gift during the lifetime of a taxpayer; and

ITA: 69(1)

- when a taxpayer ceases to be a resident of Canada.

ITA: 128.1(1)

"Proceeds of disposition" defined in the definitions section for capital gains is a much broader term than "selling price" because it includes deemed proceeds.

ITA: 54

"Adjusted cost base" defined in the definitions section for capital gains also encompasses more than the traditional accounting "laid-down cost". There are over 40 specific adjustments to the accounting actual cost. Selling costs are not included in the adjusted cost base and, hence, may in themselves give rise to a capital loss.

ITA: 54
ITA: 53

"Exemptions" are deducted from the "gain" in order to arrive at the capital gain. There are two major exemptions: one pertains to a principal residence (a permanent exemption from tax) and the other provides a reserve for amounts not due in the year (a tax deferral). These are discussed in detail later in this Chapter.

A taxable capital gain (allowable capital loss) is the portion of the capital gain (capital loss) taken into income. The inclusion rate is currently ½.

Business investment losses (BILs), as defined, are capital losses which occur on the disposition of either shares or debt of a small business corporation. The term "small business corporation" is defined in the Act and discussed in more detail in a subsequent Chapter. Generally, a small business corporation is a Canadian-controlled private corporation. All or substantially all of its fair market value of its assets are:

ITA: 39(1)(c)

ITA: 248(1)

(a) used to carry on an active business primarily in Canada;

(b) shares or debt of connected (as discussed in a subsequent Chapter) small business corporations; or

(c) a combination of (a) and (b).

While these BILs are still capital losses, only fractionally deductible, they are given special treatment as an incentive for investment. The fractional amount deductible, which uses the same inclusion rate as capital losses (i.e., ½ currently), is called an allowable business investment loss (ABIL). The use of ABILs will be discussed later in this Chapter.

Another way of looking at the terminology is to compare the description before (100%) and after (50%) the inclusion rate has been applied. For example,

100%	50%
Capital gain	Taxable capital gain
Capital loss	Allowable capital loss
Business investment loss	Allowable business investment loss
Capital gains exemption	Capital gains deduction

¶7,050 Capital Gains Deduction

From 1985 until February 22, 1994, there was a lifetime exemption for capital gains of $100,000 for individuals, other than trusts. This deduction was eliminated for taxable capital gains realized after February 22, 1994, but individuals were given an opportunity to elect to realize taxable capital gains accrued to February 22, 1994, which could be offset by the deduction in their 1994 tax return. The benefit of the election was to gain an increase in the adjusted cost base of the property on which the election was made or to create a notional account balance of elected gains. The increase in ACB reduces future capital gains exposed to tax. The notional account balance for eligible capital property or mutual funds can be used to reduce future gains on these properties. There continues to be a capital gains exemption of up to $500,000 [$750,000 under a proposal of the March 19, 2007 federal budget] of capital gains on qualifying shares of a small business corporation and certain farming and fishing property. The application of these rules will be discussed in some detail in Chapter 13 which deals with planning for the corporate owner-manager. — ITA: 110.6

¶7,060 Election re: Disposition of Canadian Securities

A taxpayer can elect (on form T123) that the disposition of "Canadian securities" *only* will always be a capital receipt, despite the aforementioned common law guidelines. Until the introduction of these rules, the CRA had not consistently assessed taxpayers on trading transactions in which there was an obvious intention to make a quick profit rather than to hold the shares as an income-producing investment. The dilemma is resolved with this election. It should be noted, however, that once this election is made, it will remain in force forever unless the taxpayer, at the time of a disposition, is one of the prescribed taxpayers listed in the provision who are not permitted this election. One of the exclusions is a "dealer in securities" and, of course, it will be a matter of fact whether an individual will be considered to be a "dealer" because of his or her past and present trading activities. The general rules used by the CRA to determine whether securities transactions will be afforded capital or income treatment are outlined in an Interpretation Bulletin. — ITA: 39(4)–(6) — ITA: 39(5) — IT-479R

The CRA's administrative position in respect of commodity transactions, including futures, is quite similar to the statutory provisions in respect of Canadian securities discussed above. The guidelines which must be adhered to are set out in the Interpretation Bulletin entitled "Commodity futures and certain commodities". — IT-346R

¶7,070   Avoidance   *SKIP*

Prior to Tax Reform in 1987, there was a very broad anti-avoidance provision in respect of capital gains in Subdivision c. Many tax advisers were of the opinion that the provision was too wide in scope and could not be enforced. The provision was replaced by the general anti-avoidance rule (GAAR), which will be described in some detail in Chapter 13. However, there are a number of aspects concerning the GAAR to be aware of even at this stage.

ITA: 245(2)

(1) According to the CRA, the GAAR is a provision of last resort and all other avenues (i.e., specific statutory anti-avoidance provisions) must be exhausted before the GAAR will be applied.

(2) The CRA has prepared an extensive Information Circular on the GAAR, including numerous examples as to when the GAAR would or would not apply in the opinion of the Department.

IC 88-2; ITA: 245

(3) The GAAR will not apply to a transaction(s) which is primarily motivated by a non-tax purpose, e.g., estate planning.

Specific anti-avoidance provisions exist to prevent a corporation from converting a capital gain into a dividend which would normally avoid income tax when the parties involved are corporations. These rules will be covered in more detail in Chapter 16.

ITA: 55(2)

¶7,100   GENERAL RULES

¶7,110   Computation of Capital Gains and Capital Losses

A gain on the disposition of property is determined as:

ITA: 40(1)(*a*)(i), 54

(a) proceeds of disposition

   minus

(b) the aggregate of:

   (i) adjusted cost base, and

   (ii) expenses of the disposition.

A loss is generally a negative amount resulting from the application of the above, that is, adjusted cost base and expenses of disposition minus proceeds of disposition. However, there can be no such loss on depreciable capital property, since the total decline in value should have been accounted for through the capital cost allowance system.

ITA: 39(1)(*b*)(i)

¶7,115   Proceeds of disposition

In most cases, proceeds of disposition will be the value of the consideration received or receivable. Where a deemed disposition occurs, the proceeds usually will be deemed to be the fair market value of the property at the time of the disposition.

The definitions of terms for purposes of capital gains and losses are provided in a definition section within Subdivision c. The definition of "proceeds of disposition" found in this section provides some very specific inclusions and exclusions that go beyond our normal idea of proceeds. In addition, the following is a list of Interpretation Bulletins that give further guidance:

ITA: 54

IT-185R	Losses from theft, defalcation or embezzlement
IT-220R2	Capital cost allowance — proceeds of disposition of depreciable property
IT-259R4	Exchanges of property
IT-460	Dispositions — absence of consideration

One of the components of the proceeds of disposition of shares, a partnership interest or business assets might be an agreement not to compete with the purchaser. This is known as a restrictive covenant. This topic is covered by a comprehensive package of provisions related to payments received by individuals for covenants. For a full discussion on the treatment of payments received for covenants, please refer to Chapter 9.

¶7,120 Adjusted cost base and capital cost

The "adjusted cost base" of most capital property, as defined, is usually its cost plus or minus legislated adjustments. Cost is not defined for taxation purposes. The usual starting point is *cost* for accounting purposes which comprises laid-down cost, including the invoice cost, relevant provincial sales, excise, and customs taxes, insurance, freight and, perhaps, some start-up costs. Where the person is a GST registrant and is eligible for an input tax credit, the GST should be excluded from adjusted cost base, because the GST is not a cost if it is recovered by an input tax credit.

ITA: 54
ITA: 53

Cost for accounting purposes is then modified. A provision establishes the cost base as amounts in respect of the value of the property which have been included in the taxpayer's income. For example, the cost of property received as a dividend in kind is the fair market value of the property received. Similarly, the cost of certain stock dividends is established as a defined amount depending upon the time frame in which the stock dividends were issued. Note that a stock option benefit, as determined for employment income, is excluded from the application of the general rule that establishes cost because the amount of the stock option benefit determined on the acquisition of shares is added to the actual cost of the shares purchased as discussed in Chapter 3.

ITA: 52
ITA: 52(2)
ITA: 52(3)
ITA: 7
ITA: 52(1)
ITA: 53(1)(*j*)

There is an important exception to the above general rules in respect of depreciable property. In order to preserve the integrity of the capital cost allowance system, the adjusted cost base of depreciable property cannot be allowed to fluctuate as a result of the previously-mentioned adjustments. Hence, the "adjusted cost base" of depreciable property is defined to be its capital cost, which in turn takes us back to *cost* for accounting purposes without adjustments. The next Chapter shows that some of these adjustments are done to proceeds of disposition rather than capital cost.

ITA: 52 or 53

ITA: 54

From the gain, certain exemptions, such as the exempt portion relating to a principal residence and reserves relating to amounts not yet due, could be deducted in order to arrive at the capital gain.

¶7,125 Reserves

A capital gains reserve for dispositions, where all or part of the proceeds are payable after the end of the year, is the lesser of a reasonable amount and an amount that brings 20% of the gain into income in the year of disposition and each of the immediately following four years. As a result, the usual maximum period over which the gain can be spread for inclusion in income is five years, including the year of disposition. A reasonable reserve is not defined in the Act. The CRA has taken the position that a reasonable reserve is based on prorated uncollected proceeds times the gain. The following examples are based on the CRA's interpretation of a reasonable reserve. The formula for the reserve is:

IT-236R4 (archived and no longer in force), par. 4
ITA: 40(1)(*a*)(iii)

$$\text{Lesser of (a) } \frac{\text{proceeds not yet due}}{\text{total proceeds}} \times \text{gain} = \begin{array}{l}\text{reasonable reserve (i.e., the fraction of} \\ \text{the gain represented by the portion of} \\ \text{total proceeds not due at the end of} \\ \text{the year)}\end{array}$$

(b) ($\frac{1}{5}$ of gain) $\times$ (4 – number of preceding taxation years ending after disposition)

The CRA's interpretation of the applicability of the reserve provision has indicated that the reserve is based on amounts that are payable to the taxpayer after the end of the year. Where a demand note is accepted on a disposition, eligibility for a reserve can be perfected by adding a condition that the note be payable, say, 10 days after demand. A demand made at the end of the year does not require payment until 10 days later with this condition.

IT-236R4 (archived and no longer in force), par. 2

A claim is available for a similar reserve with a maximum 10-year period (rather than five years) on the transfer of certain farm property, shares in a family farm corporation, an interest in a family farm partnership and shares of a small business corporation to a child.

ITA: 40(1.1)

Consistent with the general scheme of the Act for the deduction of reserves, in the year following the deduction of a reserve, the preceding year's reserve will be taken into income, and a new reserve will be deducted in accordance with the above rules.

ITA: 40(1)(a)(ii)

Example Problem

Ms. Gamma sold a capital property for $200,000 on December 31, 2007. Of that price, $180,000 was not due until December 2008. The adjusted cost base of the property was $130,000 and the selling costs were $20,000.

— *REQUIRED*

Determine the taxable capital gain for 2007 and 2008 using the capital gains reserve provision.

ITA: 40(1)(a)

— *SOLUTION*

		2007
Proceeds of disposition		$200,000
Adjusted cost base	$130,000	
Expenses of disposition	20,000	(150,000)
Gain		$ 50,000
Less reserve — lesser of:		
(a) $\frac{\$180,000}{\$200,000} \times \$50,000 =$	$ 45,000	
(b) $(\frac{1}{5} \times \$50,000) \times (4 - 0) =$	$ 40,000	(40,000)
Capital gain		$ 10,000
Taxable capital gain ($\frac{1}{2}$ of capital gain)		$ 5,000

		2008
Inclusion in income of 2007 reserve		$ 40,000
Less 2008 reserve — lesser of:		
(a) $\frac{\text{Nil}}{\$200,000} \times \$50,000 =$	Nil	
(b) $(\frac{1}{5} \times \$50,000) \times (4 - 1) =$	$ 30,000	Nil
Capital gain		$ 40,000
Taxable capital gain ($\frac{1}{2}$ of capital gain)		$ 20,000

Note that the $50,000 of original capital gain is included in income over the two years in which proceeds were collected. The reserve simply allows the original gain to be spread over a maximum of 5 or 10 years, or the period of collection if that period is shorter.

Since a reserve is a permissive or optional deduction, it may not always be wise to take the reserve. For example, if the gain was triggered in a year in which the taxpayer's income and tax rate were lower than other years, deferral of the gain through a reserve would be pointless. However, a time-value of money advantage may be gained by a deferral to a future year, even if income will be taxed at a higher rate in that year. Similarly where the taxpayer wishes to use up the capital gains exemption for qualified small business corporation shares or qualified farm property immediately, the reserve should not be claimed.

¶7,130   Adjustments to the Cost Base

As previously noted, the laid-down cost of capital assets may be subjected to certain adjustments which are not recognized for accounting purposes. These adjustments describe a variety of specific additions to and deductions from adjusted cost base. These adjustments reflect amounts that would otherwise be treated as capital gains or losses or amounts of ordinary income, but have instead been deferred. The result of the adjustments is to reduce or increase the cost base of the property for purposes of measuring a future capital gain or loss. For example, non-deductible interest and property taxes on unproductive land can be added to the adjusted cost base of the land, as discussed in Chapter 6. A benefit under a stock option plan included in employment income can be added to the cost base of the shares acquired, on the basis that the amount of the benefit represents a tax-paid cost of the shares. On the other hand, grants, subsidies and other types of government assistance of this nature must be deducted from the cost base of the non-depreciable capital property acquired, on the basis that the cost of the asset has been reduced by the amount of assistance.

ITA: 53

ITA: 18(2)
ITA: 53(1)(*h*)
ITA: 7
ITA: 53(1)(*j*)

ITA: 53(2)(*k*)

A negative adjusted cost base could result at any time if the sum of the amounts deducted is greater than the cost of the property plus the sum of amounts added to it. With the exception of a partnership interest in a general (but not a limited) partnership, such a negative amount is deemed to be an immediate capital gain at the time that an adjustment causes the adjusted cost base to become negative. At the same time, the adjusted cost base is brought to zero and future adjustments are made from that zero base.

ITA: 40(3)

ITA: 53(1)(*a*)

¶7,200   SPECIFIC PROVISIONS FOR THE TAXATION OF CAPITAL GAINS

¶7,210   Principal Residence Exemption

This Chapter demonstrates the basic concepts in the rules for principal residences. The next Chapter will expand upon these basic concepts and look at some important exceptions.

Generalizing that there are no capital gains subject to tax on principal residences may be inaccurate. In fact, there may be a gain but it can be exempted, wholly or partially, by designating the home as the taxpayer's principal residence for certain *specific* years. Note that the CRA states that a taxpayer may designate any residence as his or her principal residence as long as he or she ordinarily inhabits the home, even for a short period. This may be the case when the residence was disposed of early in the year or acquired late in the year. Also, a seasonal residence can be considered to be ordinarily inhabited.

IT-120R6, par. 5

A "principal residence" defined as virtually any housing unit or right to such a unit owned by the taxpayer either by himself or herself or jointly and ordinarily inhabited by the taxpayer, the taxpayer's spouse or former spouse, or the taxpayer's child at any time in the year. To be a principal residence, the property must be designated as such in the year of disposal. The exemption applies not only to the building but also up to one-half hectare of subjacent and adjacent land. If all of the land exceeds one-half hectare, the additional land must be shown to be necessary to the taxpayer's use and enjoyment to be eligible for this exemption. There have been a number of court cases dealing with this issue of necessity to use and enjoyment.[5]

ITA: 54

A taxpayer owning more than one residence can designate only one of his or her residences for a given year as the principal residence for years after 1981. This is done at the time when an actual or deemed disposition is reported. Although the regulations require that a designation form (T2091) be filed with the tax return in the year of the disposition, the CRA does not require this form to be filed unless there is a taxable capital gain after applying the exempt portion according to the designation rules.

IT-120R6, par. 7

---

[5] See *The Queen v. Yates*, 83 DTC 5158 (F.C.T.D.), affirmed by 86 DTC 6296 (F.C.A.), *Haber v. The Queen*, 83 DTC 5004 (F.C.T.D.), *Augart v. The Queen*, 93 DTC 5205 (F.C.A.), and *Carlile v. The Queen*, 95 DTC 5483 (F.C.A.).

The exempt portion of a gain on the disposition or deemed disposition of a principal residence is calculated by the following *oversimplified* formula: ITA: 40(2)(*b*)

$$\frac{1 + \text{number of years designated}}{\text{number of years owned}} \times \text{gain}$$

In using this formula the following points should be noted:

(a) only one housing unit can be designated as a principal residence, after December 31, 1981, per family unit which is defined in the definition of "principal residence" to include spouses and their unmarried minor children;   ITA: 54

(b) the years referred to in the numerator and denominator refer to those years after 1971;

(c) deemed dispositions and the resultant modification to the formula will be discussed in the next Chapter;

(d) the taxpayer must be resident in Canada for tax purposes; and

(e) the actual formula contains a factor that reduces the gain by an amount based on an election made in 1994 to utilize the general capital gains deduction of $100,000 which was eliminated on February 22, 1994.

Since a family can only designate one housing unit as a principal residence for any particular year, the 1 + in the numerator of the fraction was intended to protect one housing unit in a situation where a family sells one house and buys another in the same year. In that situation, the family owns two houses in the year, but can only designate one as the principal residence for that year. In the following examples, the 1 + rule will be used in other situations involving the ownership of more than one housing unit by a family in a particular year.

Note that to be in the position to use the 1 + in the numerator, the taxpayer must be willing to designate the housing unit as a principal residence for at least one year. That is, the numerator can never be 1 + 0. The exemption formula containing the 1 + is not applicable at all if the taxpayer does not designate the housing unit as the principal residence for any year. Therefore, the minimum numerator will be 1 + 1.

Example Problem

Mr. Taxobservant is in the process of retiring and moving to another city. He decides to sell his two residences and provides you with the following information as at September 30, 2007, the date of sale.

Residence	Date of purchase	Selling price	Cost
City home	1998	$170,000	$100,000
Cottage	2003	90,000	40,000

— *REQUIRED*

Calculate the minimum total taxable capital gain on the disposition of the two residences.

— *SOLUTION*

In the five taxation years 1998 to 2002, Mr. Taxobservant owned only one residence — the city home. Therefore, there is no option in these years but to designate the city home as his principal residence.

The remaining problem is to find the allocation of the five "option" years 2003–2007 which will minimize the total capital gain on the two residences. To find this allocation, note two facts:

(1) Mr. Taxobservant can designate only one residence as his principal residence in any year.

(2) From the formula for the exempt portion of the capital gain, it can be seen that designating a particular residence as a principal residence for an additional year generally will decrease the capital gain on that residence by its gain per year of ownership.

Therefore, a first guess, as to the best allocation of the option years, is to use all of these years to designate, as a principal residence, the residence with the higher gain per year of ownership.

The city home has been owned during 10 years (1998–2007, inclusive) while the cottage has been owned during 5 years (2003–2007, inclusive). The gains per year are $7,000 for the city home and $10,000 for the cottage:

	City home	Cottage
P of D	$170,000	$90,000
ACB	(100,000)	(40,000)
Gain	$ 70,000	$50,000
Gain per year	$\dfrac{\$70,000}{10 \text{ years}} = \$7,000$	$\dfrac{\$50,000}{5 \text{ years}} = \$10,000$

Thus, a first guess would be to designate the cottage for all of the option years 2003–2007 (and to designate the city home for the no-option years 1998–2002). This produces a total capital gain on the two residences of $28,000, all of which is on the city home:

	City home	Cottage
Gain	$70,000	$50,000
Exemption	$\dfrac{1+5}{10} \times \$70,000 =$ (42,000)	$\dfrac{1+5}{5} \times \$50,000 =$ (50,000)*
Capital gain	$28,000	Nil

---

* The exemption cannot exceed the gain.

This first guess can be improved upon. Note that because of the "one plus" in the formula for the exempt portion of the capital gain, it is wasteful to designate the cottage for all of its years of ownership. The cottage would still have a zero capital gain if it was designated as a principal residence for 4 years instead of 5 years. This reduces the total capital gain to the minimum possible amount of $21,000:

	City home	Cottage
Gain	$70,000	$50,000
Exemption	$\dfrac{1+6}{10} \times \$70,000 =$ (49,000)	$\dfrac{1+4}{5} \times \$50,000 =$ (50,000)
Capital gain	$21,000	Nil
Taxable capital gain (½ × $21,000)	$10,500	Nil

**Principal Residence Exemption
Steps to Follow**

1. Calculate the capital gain per year for each principal residence.
2. Determine if any of the years of ownership have been allocated to previous principal residences.
3. Allocate the years available to each residence to optimize the exemption. More years are initially allocated to the residence with the highest gain per year. Change that allocation if you can increase the exemption.

¶7,220   Personal-Use Property

While gains on "personal-use property" (PUP), defined as property used primarily for personal use or enjoyment, are subject to tax, losses on such property may not be deducted. The loss on any particular item is considered to be a personal or living expense. Personal-use property will typically generate losses on disposal because such property often declines in value over time through use.

ITA: 54

ITA: 40(2)(g)(iii)

For the purpose of calculating the capital gain or loss on any disposal of PUP, the taxpayer's cost is deemed to be the greater of the adjusted cost base of the property and $1,000. Similarly, the taxpayer's proceeds of disposition are deemed to be the greater of actual proceeds and $1,000.

ITA: 46(1)

If a taxpayer disposes of any part of a personal-use property, for the purposes of computing the capital gain or loss on the disposal, the $1,000 minimum cost and the $1,000 minimum proceeds must be apportioned on the basis of the proportion of the PUP attributable to the part disposed of. These "part disposition" rules also apply to a disposition of part of a personal-use property that would ordinarily be disposed of as a set. Thus, several dispositions of pieces of the set would be considered to be parts of a single PUP disposition. If all of the pieces of a set are acquired by one person or by a group consisting of persons who are not dealing at arm's length, the taxpayer is deemed to have made a single disposition.

ITA: 46(2)

ITA: 46(3)

Example Problem

Consider the sale of the following personal-use properties:

	PUP #1	PUP #2
ACB	$ 800	$1,300
P of D	1,200	700

— *REQUIRED*

Compute the capital gain or capital loss in the two above situations.

— *SOLUTION*

PUP #1		PUP #2	
P of D	$1,200	Deemed P of D	$1,000
Deemed ACB	(1,000)	ACB	(1,300)
CG	$ 200	CL	Nil

Losses arising from debts, which are personal-use property and are uncollectible, will be recognized to the extent that the gain was previously recognized on the disposition of personal-use property in return for the debt.

ITA: 50(2)

¶7,230   Listed Personal Property

"Listed personal property" (LPP), which is a specifically defined term, is a special subset of personal-use property. Hence, all of the personal-use property rules previously described also apply to listed personal property, except that capital losses arising on the disposition of LPP can be utilized, but only to the extent of LPP capital gains. In addition, there are carryover provisions so that unused LPP capital losses can be carried back three years and forward seven years but once again to be applied only against LPP gains. Unlike all other loss carryover provisions which are found in Division C, these carryovers are applied in Division B, using the capital loss amount rather than the allowable capital loss amount, i.e., 100% of the loss instead of ½. This result is achieved through a special term "net gain", which is defined as listed personal property capital gains minus:

ITA: 54

ITA: 41(2)

(a) listed personal property capital losses in the year; and

(b) listed personal property capital losses arising from the seven preceding years or the three years immediately following.

As a result of the specification of the carryover amounts in this way, there need be no concern for differing capital gains inclusion rates in the carryover period for LPPs. Furthermore, these losses can be deducted at the option of the taxpayer, except that the earliest losses must be deducted before any losses of a subsequent year.

Examine carefully the very restrictive list of capital property, which qualifies for the listed personal property rules found in the definition of the term. The list is limited to a taxpayer's personal-use property that is a: ITA: 54

(a) print, etching, drawing, painting, sculpture, or other similar work of art,

(b) jewellery,

(c) rare folio, rare manuscript, or rare book,

(d) stamp, or

(e) coin.

If an item cannot be found in that list, it is not LPP and, therefore, capital losses cannot be applied against capital gains.

¶7,240   Pooling of Identical Assets Purchased After 1971

There are many and varied methods of arriving at a cost base for identical assets for accounting purposes. However, for tax purposes, there is only one method, namely, the "*floating weighted-average method*".

For stock transactions, the floating weighted-average cost is calculated by dividing the aggregate of the costs of the identical properties by the number of such identical properties.

For bonds, debentures, notes, etc., the floating weighted-average cost is calculated by dividing the aggregate of the cost of the identical properties by the quotient obtained when the principal amounts of all the identical properties are divided by the principal amount of the property disposed of. For example, assume that an individual purchased three $1,000 bonds of a corporation for $2,880. Later, a $500 bond of the same series of bonds of the corporation was purchased for $490. The weighted-average cost of one of the $1,000 bonds is:

$$\frac{\$2,880 + \$490}{((3 \times \$1,000) + \$500)/\$1,000} = \$963$$

Similarly, the weighted-average cost of the $500 bond is:

$$\frac{\$2,880 + \$490}{((3 \times \$1,000) + \$500)/\$500} = \$481 \text{ (or one-half the cost of a \$1,000 bond)}$$

Many investors purchase shares or units of mutual funds to hold outside of RRSP investments. Mutual funds allocate their income to their investors, such that the income is taxable to the investors and not to the mutual fund. As a result, investors must include in their income for tax purposes the amount of net investment income, such as interest and dividends, and net taxable capital gains paid or payable to them in the year. Often income so allocated to the investor is reinvested in additional units in the fund. Since reinvested income amounts would have been taxed in the hands of the investor, whether or not actually distributed, these amounts can be added to the adjusted cost base of the investor's units in the fund. However, the adjusted amount for capital gains would be the full capital gain rather than the taxable capital gain. For dividends, the adjusted amount would be the actual dividend, not the grossed-up dividend. After the reinvestment, the ACB of each unit owned in the mutual fund must be averaged by dividing the total ACB of all units in the mutual fund owned by the investor by the total number of units owned.

When an investor redeems or disposes of units in a mutual fund, a capital gain (or loss) is realized. The calculation of the capital gain (or loss) follows the normal formula of proceeds of disposition minus the sum of the investor's ACB and selling costs. This capital gain (or loss) is separate and distinct from the taxable capital gains allocated from the income of the fund which are made annually and taxed as paid or declared payable.

Example Problem

Consider the following transactions in the shares of Dachshund Airways Ltd:

Date	Type of transaction	Number of shares	Cost per share (selling price)	Total cost (selling price)
April 1995	Purchase	100	$1	$ 100
March 1997	Purchase	150	2	300
Aug. 1999	Sale	(200)	(3)	(600)
June 2003	Purchase	100	4	400
July 2005	Purchase	300	5	1,500
Oct. 2007	Sale	(250)	(6)	(1,500)

— REQUIRED

Compute the taxable capital gains, if any, on the 1999 and the 2007 sales.

— SOLUTION

August 1999 sale:

P of D (200 shares @ $3)	$ 600
ACB (200 shares @ $1.60[1])	(320)
CG	$ 280
TCG (¾ × $280)	$ 210

October 2007 sale:

P of D (250 shares @ $6)	$1,500
ACB (250 shares @ $4.40[2])	(1,100)
CG	$ 400
TCG (½ × $400)	$ 200

There are 200 shares with a weighted average cost of $4.40 on hand after the 2007 sale.

— NOTES TO SOLUTION

[1]
100 shares @ $1 =	$100
150 shares @ $2 =	300
250	$400

$400 ÷ 250 = $1.60 per share

[2]
50 shares @ $1.60 =	$ 80
100 shares @ $4.00 =	400
300 shares @ $5.00 =	1,500
450	$1,980

$1,980 ÷ 450 = $4.40 per share

¶7,250 Disposition of Shares Acquired Under a Stock Option

¶7,255 Disposition of newly-acquired securities

Under the stock option benefit rules there is a special provision which applies when a taxpayer disposes of a security that is identical to other securities owned by the taxpayer. The provision deems a particular security, as designated by the taxpayer, to be the security that is the subject of the disposition. In order for this subsection to apply, certain conditions, as set out in the technical notes to this subsection, must be met. | ITA: 7(1.31)

- The particular security must have been acquired under an employee stock option agreement, as described in the Act. | ITA: 7(1)

- The disposition must occur no later than 30 days after the taxpayer acquires the particular security.

- There must be no other acquisitions or dispositions of identical securities in the intervening period; that is, after the acquisition of the particular security and before the disposition in respect of which the designation is being made. It should be noted, however, that this does not preclude the taxpayer from acquiring other identical securities at the same time as the disposition in respect of which the designation is being made.

- The taxpayer must make the designation in the return of income that is filed for the year in which the disposition occurs. It is expected that the CRA will accept, as the form of designation, the calculation of the capital gain or loss in respect of the disposition on the basis that it is the particular security that is the subject of the disposition.

- The taxpayer must not have designated the particular security in connection with the disposition of any other security.

Consider the following facts. On May 1, 2006, Joseph acquires 750 shares of his corporate employer on the open market. On May 1, 2007, he acquires another 750 shares on the open market. On May 1, 2008, he acquires an additional 1,000 shares under employee stock options. Immediately thereafter, he sells 1,500 shares. In his return of income for 2008, he designates the 1,000 stock option shares as constituting part of the shares that were sold. The 1,500 shares being sold by Joseph are deemed to be comprised of the 1,000 stock option shares and 500 of the 750 shares that Joseph acquired on the open market. | ITA: 7(1.3), 7(1.31)

It should be noted that the Act accommodates the practice of specific identification. The significance of specific identification is that it allows a taxpayer to deduct a portion of the employment benefit that the taxpayer is deemed to have received in respect of the taxpayer's acquisition of a qualifying employee option security, if the taxpayer disposes of the security by donating it to a qualifying charity within 30 days after its acquisition. | ITA: 7(1.31)
ITA: 110(1)(*d*.01)
ITA: 7(1)

It should also be noted that securities to which this provision applies are deemed, for the purpose of the cost-averaging rule, not to be identical to any other securities owned by the taxpayer. Consequently, the adjusted cost base (ACB) of each such security and, thus, the capital gain or loss on the disposition of the security, is determined without regard to the ACB of any other securities owned by the taxpayer. | ITA: 47(3)
ITA: 7(1)
ITA: 47(1)

¶7,260   Adjusted cost base of shares

The Act provides for an addition to the ACB of a share acquired by a taxpayer under an employee option agreement. The amount that is added to the ACB is the amount of the employment benefit that the taxpayer (or a non-arm's length person) is deemed to have received in connection with the acquisition of the security. The amount is generally equal to the excess of the fair market value of the security at the time it is acquired over the amount paid to acquire the security under the option. The amount is added to the ACB in the year in which the benefit is deemed to have been received, which is generally the year in which the taxpayer acquires the security. However, in the case of an option granted by a Canadian-controlled private corporation (CCPC) to an arm's length person, a rule applies to defer recognition of the benefit to the year in which the taxpayer disposes of the security. *ITA: 53(1)(j)* *ITA: 7(1)* *ITA: 7(1.1)*

For all employee option securities acquired after February 27, 2000, the employment benefit is included in the ACB of the security from the time of acquisition, even if recognition of the employment benefit is deferred, for tax purposes, until the taxpayer disposes of the security. This will be primarily relevant where securities for which a deferral is provided are exchanged for new securities, but in circumstances in which there is no rollover available, in respect of the disposition of the old securities, for capital gains purposes. The immediate inclusion in the ACB of the old securities ensures that the determination of the capital gain or loss on the disposition of those securities is not distorted by the exclusion of the deferred employment benefit associated with the acquisition of those securities. *ITA: 53(1)(j)* *ITA: 7(1.1), 7(8)* *ITA: 7(1.5)*

¶7,265   Identical properties

The Act requires that the cost of identical properties acquired by a taxpayer be averaged over all such properties. Generally, this results in each of the properties having the same adjusted cost base (ACB), thus, ensuring that the capital gain or loss on the disposition of any one of the properties can be determined without having to identify a particular property as the property that has been disposed of. *ITA: 47(1)*

Certain securities acquired after February 27, 2000, are exempt from the cost-averaging rule by deeming such securities not to be identical to any other securities acquired by the taxpayer for the purposes of this cost-averaging rule. The specific securities to which this exemption applies are as follows: *ITA: 47(1), 47(3)*

- Securities (i.e., shares of a corporation and units of a mutual fund trust) acquired under an employee option agreement for which a deferral is provided and securities acquired in exchange for such securities under specified circumstances. *ITA: 7(1.1), 7(8)* *ITA: 7(1.1)*

- Securities acquired under an employee option agreement where the securities are designated by the taxpayer and deemed by the Act to be the securities that are the subject of a disposition of identical securities occurring within 30 days after the acquisition. *ITA: 7(1.31)*

- Employer shares received by an employee as part of a lump sum payment on withdrawing from a deferred profit sharing plan (DPSP), where the employee filed an election in respect of those shares. Such an election allows the taxpayer to defer taxation on the growth of the shares while they were held by the plan until such time as the employee disposes of the shares. *ITA: 147(10.1)*

The effect of a security being exempted from the cost-averaging rule is that the ACB of the security and, thus, the capital gain or loss on its disposition, is determined without regard to the ACB of any other securities owned by the taxpayer. In other words, each security to which the exemption applies has its own unique ACB. *ITA: 47(1), 47(3)*

It should be noted that it is possible to determine when each security which is exempted from the cost averaging rule is disposed of by the taxpayer. As noted above, the Act deals with situations in which there is an acquisition of an employee option security and a disposition of an identical security within 30 days. Another provision of the Act deals with securities *ITA: 7(1.3), 7(1.31)* *ITA: 47(3)* *ITA: 7(1.31)* *ITA: 7(1.1) or 7(8)* for which a deferral is provided (referred to as "deferral securities"). In general terms, the Act deems a taxpayer to dispose of deferral securities only after having disposed of non-deferral securities, and then to dispose of deferral securities in the order in which they were acquired. Since it is possible to determine exactly when a particular security is disposed of, the fact that the security has its own unique ACB is not problematic.

ITA: 147(10.1)
ITA: 7(1.3)
ITA: 47(3)

It should also be noted that, where an employee acquires a deferred security after February 27, 2000, the deferred employment benefit is added to the ACB of the security at the time it is acquired even though the benefit is not subject to taxation until the security is disposed of.

ITA: 7(1.1), 7(8)
ITA: 53(1)(*j*)

The following example problem illustrates the effect of the cost-averaging exemption, in conjunction with the rules for determining the order of disposition of identical securities and the ACB rule for employee option securities.

ITA: 47(3)
ITA: 7(1.3), 7(1.31)
ITA: 53(1)(*j*)

Example Problem

Year	
2005	Simon acquired 500 shares of Pubco Inc. (a public company) on the open market at a cost of $20 each.
2006	Simon exercised an employee stock option and acquired 700 more shares of Pubco Inc. at a cost of $15 each. The fair market value of the shares at exercise was $25 per share and the fair market value of the shares at the time the option was granted was $13 per share.
	Simon elected to defer the recognition of the employment benefit associated with this option.
2007	Simon sold 400 shares of Pubco Inc. for $30 per share.

— REQUIRED

Compute the income effect of the sale of the shares, the remaining deferral of employment benefit and the adjusted cost base of the remaining shares.

— SOLUTION

Because of the election to defer the recognition of the employment benefit associated with the stock option the shares acquired under the option are in a separate pool for ACB purposes. Therefore the ACBs of the two pools of Publco Inc. shares are:

ITA: 7(8), 47(3)

Open market:	Cost	500 shares × $20	$10,000
Stock option:	Cost	700 shares × $15	$10,500
	Benefit	700 shares × $10	7,000
	Total ACB		$17,500

The ACB of the shares acquired under the option is the actual cost ($15) plus the deferred employment benefit ($25 − $15 = $10).

ITA: 53(1)(*j*)

Employment income deferral:	700 shares × $10	$7,000

The 400 shares that are sold are deemed to have come out of the open market pool first. As a result, the only income to report is a taxable capital gain, which is calculated as follows:

ITA: 7(1.3)

Proceeds	400 shares × $30	$12,000
ACB	400 shares × $20	(8,000)
Capital gain		$ 4,000
Taxable capital gain		$ 2,000

The employment income deferral of $7,000 continues until the stock option shares are sold.

The ACB of the 100 open market shares remaining is $20 per share.

The ACB of the 700 stock option shares remains at $25 per share.

¶7,270 Cost of Certain Properties

The cost of property is usually incurred by the acquisition of the property with after-tax funds. Thus, when a capital property is acquired for $100, the funds used in the purchase have usually been subjected to income tax. That is why, on the disposition of the property for, say, $150, the $100 of cost is not taxed; only the $50 of gain above cost is taxed. Thus, cost is recovered tax free on a disposition, because it represents an amount on which tax was already paid.

Normally the cost of capital property or the capital cost of depreciable capital property is the laid-down cost for accounting purposes. However, a number of provisions deem the *cost* to be an amount other than laid-down cost. Where a taxpayer has acquired property and an amount in respect of the value of the property is included in the taxpayer's income, that amount is added to the cost of the property. For example, if a shareholder had a benefit in kind (i.e., in property) which was included in his or her income, then the income inclusion would be added to the cost of the property so received. Since the income inclusion in respect of the benefit would be taxed, the amount of the benefit can be considered as a tax-paid cost of the property, according to the concept of cost discussed above. There is one notable exception to this rule, namely, an employment income inclusion arising from a stock option benefit, which is discussed in the next part of the Chapter.

ITA: 52

ITA: 52(1)
ITA: 15(1)

ITA: 52(1)
ITA: 7

The cost of property in respect of dividends in kind (non-cash dividends) and lottery prizes is the fair market value. Note that the prize itself is not subject to an income inclusion.

ITA: 40(2)(f), 52(2), 52(4)

The cost of stock dividends which has had varying tax treatments over the years. Prior to April 1, 1977, a stock dividend was treated in the same manner as any other dividend for purposes of determining income. Its cost base, however, was deemed to be equal to its paid-up capital which is generally the stated capital[6] on the accounting balance sheet. This treatment is also applied to all stock dividends after May 22, 1985. For the period after March 31, 1977 to May 22, 1985, stock dividends, for public companies only, were deemed not to be dividends. Hence, there was no income inclusion, and the cost base of the stock received as dividend was deemed to be nil. This treatment resulted in a larger eventual capital gain. Therefore, public companies could offer to their shareholders different classes of shares paying either ordinary dividends subject to the gross-up and tax credit rules or stock dividends which resulted in future capital gains treatment. With the introduction of the capital gains exemption in 1985, this latter option was removed.

ITA: 52(3)

TAXATION OF STOCK DIVIDENDS

Time Period	Taxation of Dividend	ACB Adjustment
Prior to April 1/77	Taxed on increase in PUC	ACB increased by PUC increase
April 1/77 to May 22/85	Not taxed (public companies)	No ACB adjustment
After May 22/85	Taxed on increase in PUC	ACB increased by PUC increase

Example Problem

Mr. Adjusted-Shares purchased 1,000 shares of Sure-Fire Limited, a public corporation, at $50 per share in 1983. Mr. Adjusted-Shares received the following dividends subsequent to that time:

1984	A stock dividend of 10% which resulted in an increase in the paid-up capital of $10 for each share issued.
1996	A stock dividend of 10% which resulted in an increase in the paid-up capital of $10 for each share issued.
1998	Cash dividend of $5 per share.
2004	A stock dividend of 10% which resulted in an increase in the paid-up capital of $10 for each share issued.

---

[6] In some provinces, this amount may be the par value.

— REQUIRED

Compute the taxable capital gain or allowable capital loss if Mr. Adjusted Shares sold 100 of the above shares in 2007 for $45 per share plus brokerage of $100.

— SOLUTION

2007	P of D (100 shares @ $45)		$4,500
	ACB (100 shares @ $39.23[(1)])	$3,923	
	Selling cost	100	(4,023)
	Capital gain		$ 477
	Taxable capital gain (½ × $477)		$ 239

— NOTE TO SOLUTION

[(1)] 1983	1,000	shares — purchased @ $50 each	$50,000
1984	100	shares — stock dividend of 10%	Nil
	1,100		
1996	110	shares — stock dividend of 10% @ $10 each	1,100
	1,210		
2004	121	shares — stock dividend of 10% @ $10 each	1,210
	1,331		$52,310

$52,310 ÷ 1,331 = $39.30

¶7,280 Adjustments to the cost base

As previously noted, the term "adjusted cost base" is defined in the definitions section of Subdivision c. This provision states that the adjusted cost base of depreciable property is its capital cost and for all other capital property the cost of the property adjusted. The definition then further restricts this adjusted cost to a positive amount.

ITA: 54

ITA: 53

Subsection 53(1) (additions) and subsection 53(2) (reductions) set out a number of adjustments some of which we have already examined.

- The cost base of land is increased by interest and property taxes denied.

ITA: 18(2), 53(1)(*h*)

- The employment income inclusion arising from the acquisition of shares through a stock option is added to the cost of the share.

ITA: 7, 53(1)(*j*)

- Reasonable costs of surveying or valuing property in respect of its acquisition or disposition which are denied are added to the cost of the property.

ITA: 18(1)(*b*), 53(1)(*n*)

- The cost of property is reduced by government assistance for capital property.

ITA: 53(2)(*k*)

- The cost base of a bond is reduced by the amount of accrued interest paid for on the purchase of a bond and deducted from interest earned during the holding period of the bond.

ITA: 20(14), 53(2)(*l*)

There are also a number of adjustments in respect of shares of a corporation, many of which will be described in more detail in later Chapters. But a conceptual understanding of these adjustments is necessary in determining the adjusted cost base of a particular class of shares.

- The cost base of shares is increased by deemed dividends that arise in transactions (with some exceptions) where the paid-up capital of the corporation is increased by more than the increase in the fair market value of the net assets of the corporation.

ITA: 53(1)(*b*), 54(1)

(Paid-up capital of shares is generally (but not always) the stated or par value for accounting purposes and is discussed in more detail in Chapter 15.)

- The cost base of shares received as consideration for any transfer of property to a corporation is increased by the amount of any capital loss denied by reason of a "stop-loss" rule applied on the transfer.

ITA: 53(1)(*f*.2)
ITA: 40(3.6)(*b*)

¶7,290 Superficial losses

A "superficial loss", as defined in the Act is usually, but not necessarily, associated with the trading of securities. A taxpayer might own securities with an accrued capital loss at the end of the year. The securities are sold to trigger the loss which is used to offset a capital gain previously realized in the year. Then the taxpayer repurchases the same or identical securities, almost immediately, because of their long-term potential. In this case, the taxpayer has converted a "paper" loss into a realized loss, but after the repurchase continues to own essentially the same securities. This is the essence of a superficial loss in which the taxpayer is denied the loss at the time of the disposition but is permitted to add the superficial loss to the adjusted cost base of the substituted property. This adjustment has the effect of delaying the triggering of the loss. There are three conditions necessary in order to establish a superficial loss:

ITA: 54

ITA: 53(1)(*f*)

- the taxpayer or an "affiliated person", in essence, the taxpayer's spouse or a corporation controlled by either the taxpayer or the taxpayer's spouse, must dispose of the property;

ITA: 251.1(1)

- the taxpayer or an affiliated person acquires or re-acquires the same or identical property during the period beginning 30 days before the disposition and ending 30 days after the disposition; and

- the taxpayer or an affiliated person, at the end of the period referred to in point (b), still owns at least some of the property.

Example Problem 1

Mr. Sureloss buys 1,000 shares of Nogain Ltd. at $10 per share on October 1, 2006. On December 15, 2006, Mr. Sureloss sells 1,000 shares at $5. On January 3, 2007, he buys 1,000 shares at $6. On November 15, 2007, he sells 1,000 shares at $10.

— *REQUIRED*

Compute the taxable capital gain or allowable capital loss on each of the above transactions.

— *SOLUTION*

Dec. 15, 2006	P of D (1,000 shares @ $5)	$ 5,000
	ACB (1,000 shares @ $10)	(10,000)
	Capital loss	Nil

There is a superficial loss of $5,000, since he purchased the shares within the 30-day time limit and still owns the shares at the end of the period which is 30 days after December 15. In essence, the purchase on January 3, 2007 allows him to maintain his ownership position in the shares after the sale.

Nov. 15, 2007	P of D (1,000 shares @ $10)	$10,000
	ACB (1,000 shares[(1)])	(11,000)
	Capital loss	(1,000)

Since Mr. Sureloss has no shares on hand 30 days after the sale on November 15, 2007, there cannot be a superficial loss.

— NOTE TO SOLUTION

(1) 1,000 shares @ $6 = $ 6,000
       Dec. 15 Sup. loss =   5,000
                              $11,000

Example Problem 2

Ms. Taxconfused is considering selling all of her remaining shares of Overrated Mining Ltd., a public corporation. She is uncertain of the adjusted cost base of the shares. The following is the historical data concerning her holdings in Overrated Mining Ltd.

June 1, 1982	Purchased 500 shares @ $2 per share.
Jan. 15, 1984	Received a stock dividend of 10%. The paid-up capital of the corporation was credited with one dollar for each share issued.
July 1, 1991	Purchased additional 1,000 shares @ $5 per share.
April 15, 1999	Received a stock dividend of 10%. The paid-up capital of the corporation was credited with $6 for each additional share.
June 19, 2007	Purchased an additional 1,000 shares @ $9.
Aug. 1, 2007	Sold 500 shares @ $5 plus commission of $150.

— REQUIRED

Determine the adjusted cost base of Ms. Taxconfused's shares in Overrated Mining Ltd.

— SOLUTION

Adjusted cost base

June 1, 1982	500 shares @ $2 — purchase		$ 1,000
Jan. 15, 1984	50 shares — 10% stock dividend		Nil
July 1, 1991	1,000 shares @ $5 — purchase		5,000
	1,550		
April 15, 1999	155 shares — 10% stock dividend @ $6		930
June 19, 2007	1,000 shares at $9		9,000
	2,705		$15,930
Aug. 1, 2007	(500) P of D 500 shares @ $5	$2,500	
	ACB (500 shares × $\frac{\$15,930}{2,705}$)	(2,945)	(2,945)
		$ (445)	
	SC	(150)	
	Capital loss	$ 595	
2,205	shares @ $5.89		$12,985

¶7,300 COMPUTATIONAL RULES

¶7,310 Section 3 Revisited

In Chapter 1, a cursory examination was made of section 3 in the process of section identification. Now that several technical components have been examined, the carryover rules contained in section 3 will be highlighted.

Paragraph 3(*a*) includes the aggregate of all income from each non-capital source: property, business, office and employment, plus the other non-capital sources of income found in Subdivision d of Division B which is examined in Chapter 9. The amount determined for each source must be a positive amount (i.e., losses or an excess of deductions over inclusions from a particular source are not considered here).

Paragraph 3(*b*) deals with taxable capital gains and allowable capital losses, and is composed of the excess of:

(1) all taxable capital gains, excluding those from LPPs

plus

(2) listed personal property taxable net gains as computed in subsection 41(2) and discussed previously

minus

(3) allowable capital losses, except for

(i) LPP losses, and

(ii) allowable business investment losses (ABILs).

Paragraph 3(*c*) adds together paragraphs 3(*a*) and (*b*) and subtracts Subdivision e deductions such as moving expenses, alimony, RRSPs, etc. All of these topics will be covered in Chapter 9.

Paragraph 3(*d*) subtracts various types of losses from any excess amount calculated in paragraph 3(*c*). The losses deducted are from the following sources:

(1) office, employment, business and property (i.e., losses from non-capital sources), and

(2) ABILs.

Note the special treatment accorded to ABILs. Normally, allowable capital losses can only be claimed against taxable capital gains. However, ABILs have no such restriction and, hence, are deducted along with other losses from non-capital sources (e.g., losses from business and property). Deducting ABILs, effectively, against all sources of income, rather than only against net taxable capital gains may result in a more rapid deduction of ABILs, which is the intent of the ABIL investment incentive. As a capital loss, however, ABILs are still only ½ deductible.   ITA: 3(*b*) ITA: 3(*d*)

¶7,320 Allowable Business Investment Losses

The definition of a "business investment loss" includes capital losses arising from the disposition of shares and debts of a small business corporation (SBC). An SBC is generally defined to be a Canadian-controlled private corporation, where all or substantially all of the fair market value of the assets were, at that time, used principally in an active business carried on primarily in Canada. Assets would include the shares of SBCs which were connected to the holding corporation. (The concept of a "connected" corporation is discussed in Chapter 12.) For the purposes of a business investment loss only, an SBC which ceases to meet the conditions in the definition of an SBC will still be considered as an SBC if at any time in the 12 months preceding the disposition it met the conditions in the definition of an SBC.   ITA: 39(1)(*c*) ITA: 248(1) ITA: 186(4) ITA: 39(1)(*c*)

Since business investment losses (BILs) are really only a subset of capital losses, allowable business investment losses (ABILs) for a particular year are determined by the same inclusion rates as allowable capital losses as follows:

Time Period	Inclusion Rate
Prior to 1988	50%
1988 and 1989	66⅔%
1990 to February 27, 2000	75%
February 28 to October 17, 2000	66⅔%
After October 17, 2000	50%

A portion of a BIL, equal to an amount of capital gains that has previously benefited from a capital gains deduction, is disallowed. The capital gains deduction referred to is either a past claim for the general capital gains deduction that was eliminated or the continuing capital gains deduction for shares of a qualified small business corporation or qualified farm property. This disallowed portion reduces the BIL and resultant ABIL, for purposes of the deduction under paragraph 3(*d*). In effect, an individual cannot obtain a benefit of the capital gains deduction on capital gains that are not offset by capital losses in the form of BILs, at the same time as he or she obtains a benefit from ABILs which offset non-capital sources of income under paragraph 3(*d*). A fraction (see above chart) of the disallowed BIL reverts to an allowable capital loss for the year realized. This allowable capital loss will possibly offset taxable capital gains which will not be available for the capital gains deduction, as a result. `ITA: 39(9)`

Any portion of the ABIL (i.e., an amount that has not been disallowed), which is not deducted under paragraph 3(*d*), is added to the non-capital losses for the year subject to the non-capital loss carryover rules, discussed in Chapter 10 for individuals and Chapter 11 for corporations. However, if the ABIL, which was treated as a non-capital loss, is not used by the end of the 10th carryforward year, it becomes a net capital loss, in essence, reverting to its original character as an allowable capital loss, restricted by the net capital loss carryover rules.

The portion of a BIL that is disallowed is computed as the lesser of: `ITA: 39(9)`

(a) the BIL for the year (before deducting the disallowed portion) . . . . $xxxx

(b) the cumulative capital gains deduction claimed in previous years × a factor (the factor is 2 for years prior to 1988, ³⁄₂ for 1988 and 1989, ⁴⁄₃ for 1990 to February 27, 2000, ³⁄₂ for February 28, 2000 to October 17, 2000 and 2 after October 17, 2000 to adjust the capital gains deduction to a full capital gain amount which is parallel with the full BIL amount) . . . . $xxxx
minus: the cumulative disallowed portion of BILs in preceding years . . . . . (xxxx)

$xxxx

Note that part (a) above uses the full business investment loss (not the fractional allowable business investment loss). However, the capital gains *deduction* is a fractional amount. Therefore, to make parts (a) and (b) comparable, the capital gains deduction must be adjusted to convert the deduction to a full amount of gain that has been exempted. Hence, multiplying a 1999 capital gains deduction, for example, by ⁴⁄₃ adjusts the ³⁄₄ fractional amount to the required full amount (i.e., ⁴⁄₃ × ³⁄₄ = 1).

Exhibit 7-1 attempts to map the treatment of BILs under the provisions described above.

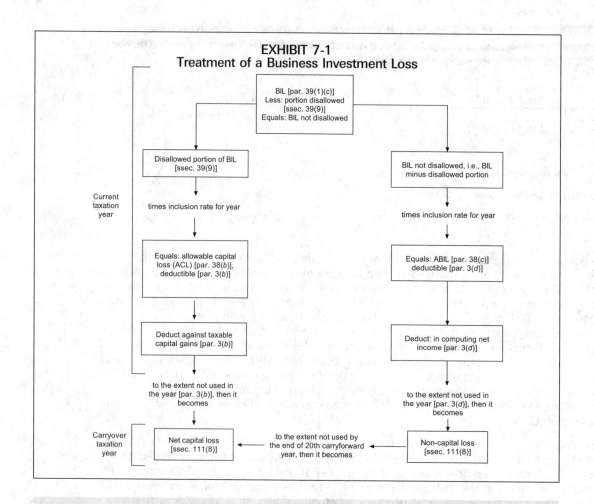

EXHIBIT 7-1
Treatment of a Business Investment Loss

Example Problem

	2005	*2006*	*2007*
Employment income	$10,000	$12,000	$15,000
Business income (loss)	(25,000)	6,000	10,000
Property income (loss)	3,000	(2,000)	1,000
Capital gains (capital losses)			
LPP	2,000	(5,000)	7,000
PUP	(4,000)	8,000	2,000
Other	10,000	(17,000)*	4,000

———————
* Includes a business investment loss of $2,000.

— REQUIRED

Determine the income under Division B according to section 3, after filing any necessary amended returns for each of the years indicated above. (For the purposes of this type of problem, dealing with each item, line-by-line, across the years, will help keep track of carryovers more easily than dealing with income one year at a time.)

— SOLUTION

	2005	2006	2007
Par. 3(*a*) — Sum of income from non-capital sources (non-negative):			
Employment	$ 10,000	$12,000	$15,000
Business (no losses)	—	6,000	10,000
Property (no losses)	3,000	—	1,000
	$ 13,000	$18,000	$26,000
Par. 3(*b*) — Sum of net taxable capital gains (non-negative):			
LPP	Nil[1]	Nil	$ 2,000[2]
PUP	Nil[3]	$ 4,000[4]	1,000[5]
Other	$ 5,000[6]	(4,000)[7]	2,000[8]
	$ 5,000	Nil	$ 5,000
Sum of par. 3(*a*) and par. 3(*b*)	$ 18,000	$18,000	$31,000
Par. 3(*d*) — Sum of losses from non-capital sources:			
Business loss	(18,000)[9]	—	—
Property loss	—	(2,000)	—
ABIL	—	(1,000)[10]	—
Income under Division B	Nil	$15,000	$31,000

—NOTES TO SOLUTION

[1] The $2,000 listed personal property capital gain in 2005 was offset and removed by amending the 2005 return for the 2006 loss, carried back to 2005. Note how LPP losses are carried over in their full amount, not their fractional allowable amount. Therefore, no consideration need be given to changing capital gains inclusion rates, if applicable, in the carryover period for LPPs.

[2] There was still $3,000 of the listed personal property capital loss in 2006 to be applied against the listed personal property gain in 2007, of $7,000 (($7,000 − $3,000) × ½ = $2,000).

[3] No losses are allowed on the personal-use property assets.

[4] ½ × $8,000.

[5] ½ × $2,000.

[6] ½ × $10,000.

[7] Only $4,000 of the allowable capital loss of $7,500 [½ ($17,000 − $2,000)] was applied to reduce paragraph 3(*b*) amount to nil. The remaining $3,500 will be applied to another year but under Division C, not Division B.

[8] ½ × $4,000.

[9] Only $18,000 of the business loss of $25,000 was applied to bring the income under Division B to nil. The remainder ($7,000) may be carried back three years and forward seven, but these losses are deductible in the carryover year in Division C, not Division B.

[10] The *allowable* business investment loss is $1,000 (½ × $2,000).

¶7,800   REVIEW QUESTIONS

(1) Tom, Dick and Harry formed a partnership in order to invest in a tract of land just outside a large urban area. Five years later, the partnership sold the property making a large profit. According to the partnership agreement, profits from this venture were to be split equally. Discuss whether this is an income or a capital receipt.

(2) Rachel Real-Estate-Salesperson invests her spare cash in "good land buys" which she occasionally finds. This year Rachel sold one of these properties and realized a large profit. Is this an income or a capital receipt?

(3) Winston Windfall, an accountant, uses his spare time and cash to trade in low-cost mining shares listed on a Canadian stock exchange. Winston made a large profit this year on his stock market transactions. Is this profit income or capital gain?

(4) Diana Developer purchased some land to erect a shopping centre which she intended to sell. However, zoning bylaws could not be changed and Diana sold the property at a large profit. Is this profit income or a capital gain?

(5) Doug Daily-Double spends his Saturday afternoons at the race track. This year Doug was extremely fortunate and his net winnings were $15,000. How will these winnings be taxed?

(6) A client invested in a rental property some years ago and paid $10,000 as a down payment and $150,000 was in the form of a mortgage. Recently, the vacancy rate has climbed and the value of the property has fallen. She thinks that she will just walk away from the property and let the mortgage company take over the property. What will her proceeds of disposition be?

(7) As a result of a reorganization in a company in which Mr. Smith is a shareholder, he has just had a return of some of the corporation's capital. As a result, the adjusted cost base of his shares has become negative. This does not bother him since he has been told that as long as he continues to own the shares he will not have to recognize this built-in capital gain. Comment.

(8) Mr. Confused has come to you with a problem. He owns the family cottage and his wife owns the house in town. Both housing units were purchased after 1981. They are thinking of selling both of these properties and moving to another province. He thought they could each claim the principal residence exemption to avoid any tax but someone has told him that they can only claim one of the residences. In general terms can you explain the rules to him?

(9) Ms. Spill bought a cottage property on a lake that has since become polluted. As a result, the value of the property has declined and she has sold it, since no one wants to go there anymore. She realized a loss on the sale and wants to claim the loss on her personal return. Can she do it?

(10) What is the "$1,000 rule" as it relates to personal-use property? Does the same rule apply to listed personal property?

(11) Mr. Div has come to you to have his personal tax return done. He sold some shares of a public corporation that he has owned for some years and wants help in minimizing his tax on the transaction. One point that is confusing him is the stock dividend that he received this year. He does not know how to treat the dividend for tax purposes. Please help him.

(12) Under Divisions B and C, what happens when the capital losses exceed the capital gains in any one year?

(13) If you were to win a Mazda Miata in a lottery, what would the cost base be to you given that you might want to sell it to buy a car more fitting (boring) for an accountant?

(14) Ms. Devious has had her company buy her a car and register it in her name. The CRA   ITA: 15(1)
discovered this and has assessed her with a shareholder benefit for $35,000, the value of the car. Ms. Devious is going to have to sell the car to pay the tax liability. What will her cost base be on the car?

¶7,825 MULTIPLE CHOICE QUESTIONS

Question 1

On April 1, 2007, X Ltd., with a December 31 year-end, sold a parcel of land, a capital property with an adjusted cost base of $100,000, for $600,000. The $600,000 proceeds were payable in the form of a mortgage, with principal payments of $90,000 due every six months, starting on October 1, 2007. What is the minimum taxable capital gain that X Ltd. must report in 2007?

(A) $100,000

(B) $50,000

(C) $75,000

(D) $37,500

Question 2

During the year, Mina sold the following personal assets, all of which she had acquired after 1971:

	Cost	Proceeds	
Automobile	$20,000	$18,000 ×	
Boat	600	1,500 ×	5υ6
Painting	600	1,300 ✓	3υ6
Jewellery	1,400	200 ✓	(4υ6)

Her capital gain for the year from these dispositions is:

(A) $900

(B) $800

(C) $500

(D) $400

Question 3

Mike purchased 100 shares of Pubco (a taxable Canadian corporation and public company) in 2004 for $3.11 per share plus $39 in commissions. In 2005, Mike purchased another 100 shares of Pubco for $4 per share plus a brokerage commission of $50. On March 1, 2007, when the shares were worth $6 per share, Mike gifted half the Pubco shares to his eight-year-old son and half to his wife (no special elections were filed). What is the amount of the taxable capital gain that Mike must report in 2007?

(A) $100

(B) $122

(C) $200

(D) $400

Question 4

Amanda sold her cottage for $130,000 in May 2007. The cottage cost her $50,000 in 2000 and qualifies as a principal residence. The only other principal residence that Amanda has owned during her lifetime was her Toronto home, which she owned from 1998 to 2006. Even though she sold it for $200,000 more than it cost, she did not report the gain on her 2006 tax return because it was her principal residence. What is the minimum taxable capital gain that Amanda must report on her 2007 tax return in respect of the sale of the cottage?

(A) $80,000

(B) $25,000

(C) $30,000

(D) $50,000

Question 5

A Canadian resident individual received a stock dividend from a public corporation of one share. The dividend is a taxable dividend. The stock dividend resulted in an increase in the paid-up capital of $4 for each share issued but the fair market value of each share is $10. Which of the following statements is correct about the stock dividend received?

(A) The cost of the stock is deemed to be $4 and the individual's net income increases by $4.

(B) The cost of the stock is deemed to be $4 and the individual's net income increases by $5.80.

(C) The cost of the stock is deemed to be $10 and the individual's net income increases by $10.

(D) The cost of the stock is deemed to be $10 and the individual's net income is deemed to be $14.50.

Question 6

Donna Jailal has provided you with the following information in connection with her income tax return for the year:

Capital Gains:

Shares	$1,600
Personal-use property	700
Listed personal property	500

Capital Losses:

Shares	$ 820
Personal-use property	1,000
Listed personal property	140

Listed personal property losses from the previous year 100

What is the minimum net taxable capital gain that she must report as Division B income for the year?

(A) $370

(B) $740

(C) $870

(D) $920

¶7,850 EXERCISES

Exercise 1

ITA: 40(2)(*b*)

Peter Principal-Residence has only two residences which he wishes to dispose of in 2007. The following facts relate to those residences:

	Date pur- chased	Cost	Real estate commis- sion	Estimated selling price
City home	1992	$180,000	$12,000	$247,000
Cottage	1997	90,000	6,000	164,000

— REQUIRED

Determine how Peter must designate residences in order to achieve the minimum capital gain.

Exercise 2

ITA: 41, 54

Karl Kapitalgains disposed of the following assets in 2007, all of which were bought subsequent to 1971:

	Sale price	Cost	Selling cost
Painting	$2,000	$ 300	$100
Antique clock	1,200	250	20
Outboard motor	750	500	15
Gold coin	600	1,000	10

— REQUIRED

Determine Karl's net taxable capital gain for the year.

Exercise 3

ITA: 53(1)(*f*), 54

Ivan Investor purchased the following shares of Solid Investments Ltd.:

March 1, 2006	100 shares @ $30 including brokerage
June 1, 2007	150 shares @ $35 including brokerage
January 10, 2008	200 shares @ $26 including brokerage

On December 15, 2007, Ivan sold 200 shares @ $25 less brokerage of $75.

— REQUIRED

(A) Determine Ivan's taxable capital gain or allowable capital loss on his December 15, 2007 disposition.

(B) Compute the adjusted cost base of the shares on hand on January 10, 2008.

Exercise 4

ITA: 53(2)

Miriam Marketwise decided to purchase shares in Strippit Limited, a public company, listed on the Canadian Venture Exchange. Miriam purchased 1,000 shares at $35 per share plus brokerage of $500 on December 10, 1983.

Miriam received the following dividends during the intervening years:

February 1, 1984	A stock dividend of 5% with a paid-up capital of $10 per share.
April 10, 1990	A stock dividend of 10% with a paid-up capital of $10 per share.
August 1, 2004	A stock dividend of 20% with a paid-up capital of $10 per share.

— *REQUIRED*

Determine the adjusted cost base of Miriam's shares as at December 31, 2007.

Exercise 5

ITA: 53

Imanin Vestor invested $2,000 on April 1, 2006, in Suckers Mutual Fund sold by a major financial institution. Her investment purchased 72.788 units of the fund. On December 31, 2006, the fund allocated $96.37 of capital gains to her account. As a result, the $96.37 was reinvested in the fund to purchase 3.774 units at the market value of $25.535 per unit.

On June 30, 2007, she sold 25 of her units for a total of $718.

— *REQUIRED*

Compute the effects of these events on income for tax purposes in 2006 and 2007.

Exercise 6

ITA: 3, 39, 41

Simple Simon has the following sources of income and losses for tax purposes:

	2006	2007
Employment income	$25,000	$30,000
Property income	10,000	(4,000)
Business income — other	8,000	(9,000)
Capital gains (capital losses):		
— Listed personal property (Note 1)	4,000	(1,500)
— Personal-use property	8,000	(1,000)
— Shares — Canadian-controlled private corporation (Note 2)	(6,000)	(2,000)
— Public corporation	(12,000)	9,000

Additional Information

(1) Simon has a capital loss from listed personal property of $1,000 carried forward from 2003.

(2) These losses qualify as business investment losses. No capital gains deduction has ever been claimed.

— *REQUIRED*

Determine Simple Simon's Division B income according to the ordering rules in section 3 for 2006 and 2007. (Deal with each item line-by-line across the years, rather than computing income one year at a time.)

¶7,875   ASSIGNMENT PROBLEMS

Problem 1

Jean-Luc, the taxpayer in this case, was experienced in retail real estate, having originally been employed by a fast-food chain of restaurants. His duties were to locate, acquire and open restaurants on behalf of his employer. He acquired extensive knowledge in packaging sites for retail operations.

Two years ago, Jean-Luc began to work as an employee for Jorge, a successful builder of homes and condominiums, real estate developer for investment of rental apartments and retail plazas, and trust company owner. Jean-Luc was employed on a salary and bonus basis. At the time, Jean-Luc was also a licensed real estate broker and owned a brokerage firm.

Jean-Luc's first project for Jorge involved developing a retail complex in Toronto. He was instrumental in obtaining two anchor tenants as well as two others. This was a successful venture.

His second venture involved a strip plaza in London, Ontario. By the time Jean-Luc and Jorge were prepared to purchase the property, most of the pre-development work had been completed and two nationally recognized restaurant chains had signed letters of intent and/or offers to lease. These two tenants represented 60% of the rentable area of the plaza. With those tenants in place, other tenants were prepared to rent because of the traffic which would be generated by the presence of the two popular fast-food restaurants. As a result, financing the project would not be a problem.

All of the leases which were negotiated were of the "net-net" type — the landlord being responsible only for its financing costs. The tenants were responsible for all other costs and expenses involved with the plaza, in addition to their own businesses.

A partnership of Jorge (74%), Jean-Luc (24%) and Shloimie (2%), the long-time accountant for Jorge, was established to own the plaza. Neither Jean-Luc nor Shloimie paid for his respective interest in the partnership. Jean-Luc considered this to be a long-term project that would provide income for his children's future. Jorge and Shloimie regarded the project as an opportunity to acquire and own an income-producing property with very little investment, since most of the funds were provided by debt financing.

City planning and zoning for the plaza was approved and most of the financing was in place. Last year, about a year after the purchase by the partnership, the building was completed to the point where the tenants took possession. Shortly thereafter, the tenants completed their respective areas and were in operation and paying rent. Temporary financing was in place and permanent financing was being negotiated pending a drop in interest rates at the time.

This year, Jorge began to have financial difficulties and his assets were liquidated by his creditors. Since his creditors did not have security on the plaza project, Jorge was in a position to sell that asset in an orderly manner. Although Jorge controlled the partnership, he received Jean-Luc's consent to sell the property. Jean-Luc's share of the gain on the sale was about $157,000.

Jean-Luc filed his tax return for this year showing the gain as a capital gain.

— REQUIRED

A CRA assessor has just called to indicate that she is considering a reassessment of the income in question as income from a business, an adventure in the nature of trade, or from a profit-making undertaking or concern.

As Jean-Luc's tax adviser, evaluate the fact situation and recommend a course of action.

Problem 2

hold

ITA: 20(1)(*n*), 20(8), 40; IT-152R3

— CAPITAL GAIN

Loof Lirpa bought a parcel of land in 1988. It was his intention that he would build a family home on the land some day. However, the city continued to delay issuing permits to landowners in the area and eventually Loof purchased another home. He held onto the land for a number of years but has now decided that he needs the cash and will sell the property. The details related to his purchase of the land are set out below.

Purchase Price: $4,000; Purchase Date: May 21, 1988

Loof has received an offer from an acquaintance to purchase the land. The payment terms are set out below and are considered to represent fair market value.

Purchase Price: $160,000; Purchase Date: October 1, 2007

Payment terms: $40,000 down payment on purchase date; $20,000 payable on January 1 each year for the period January 1, 2008 through January 1, 2013 inclusive. Interest: Interest is payable at 6% annually on the unpaid balance.

Loof is uncertain as to whether the disposition is on account of capital or income.

— *REQUIRED*

Compare the income tax consequences to Loof of this sale if the sale is on account of capital and, alternatively, if it is on account of income. Do not calculate the interest income. Ignore the consequences and calculation of the interest income.

Problem 3   ITA: 40(2)(*b*), 54

Mr. Doug Hart, who lives in Ontario, is contemplating moving to Switzerland. He came to you to discuss the tax consequences of disposing of his residences, as indicated below, in April 2007. He is single and ordinarily inhabits each of the residences for several months each year. He has never used his principal residence exemption since purchasing these properties.

The following information relates to the proposed 2007 dispositions.

Residence	Date of purchase	Cost	Selling price
Toronto home	2000	$160,000	$240,000
Farm in Quebec	2002	100,000	148,000
Condominium in Florida	2005	150,000	186,000

— *REQUIRED*

Compute the minimum amount of taxable capital gains that Mr. Hart will have to report in 2007.

Problem 4   ITA: 40(2)(*b*), 54

Ms. Twoholmes has come to you for advice on the tax consequences of the disposition of the following two residences in 2007:

Residence	Date of purchase	Cost	Selling price
Regina home	1996	$400,000	$517,500
Cottage	2001	250,000	375,000

— *REQUIRED*

Compute the minimum amount of taxable capital gains.

Problem 5   *Section 41(b)*   ITA: 41, 46

Mr. Ar Fl sold the following assets in 2007, all of which were purchased in the 1990s:

	Cost	Proceeds	Gain/(Loss)
Oil painting	$2,500	$ 500 *1000*	*(1,500)*
Canoe *p.u.p*	700 *1000*	500 *1000* *2,200*	*0*
Rare coin	1,300	500 *1000*	*(300)*
Bible produced in 1635	800 *1000*	5,000	*4000*
Antique car	15,000	10,000	*0*
Antique chair	300 *1000*	1,200	*200*
Antique table	1,500	2,000	*500*

Mr. Ar Fl has an unclaimed capital loss on listed personal property of $1,200 arising in 2004.

— REQUIRED

What is the amount of Mr. Ar Fl's net taxable capital gain for 2007?

Problem 6

ITA: 47, 53

Sherman Stockwatcher likes to invest in the stock market for the long term. While some of his investments have been failures, some have been very successful. Generally, he has been very fortunate in buying certain stocks at a relatively low price and selling them at their peak. One such stock is Headed For the Sky Corporation, a public corporation. Sherman has provided the following trade information related to this investment:

Nov. 8, 1981	Purchased 1,000 shares at initial offering price of $5.
Apr. 15, 1982	Purchased 2,000 shares at price of $3.50.
June 6, 1983	Sold 500 shares at $2.75, incurred brokerage commission of $50.
July 2, 1983	Purchased 2,000 shares at $4.
Apr. 30, 1984	Received a stock dividend of 10% of shares held; stock dividend increased corporation's paid-up capital by $.50/share.
June 20, 1992	Two-for-one stock split.
Nov. 8, 2000	Purchased 2,000 shares at $6.
Jan. 12, 2004	Received a stock dividend of 10% of shares held; stock dividend increased corporation's paid-up capital by $1/share.
Nov. 5, 2007	Sold 10,000 shares for $7.50/share, incurred brokerage commission of $650.

— REQUIRED

Calculate the taxable capital gain or allowable capital loss on the above transactions.

Problem 7

ITA: 3, 41

Dave Stieb reported the following information for tax purposes:

	2005	2006	2007
Business income	$ 60,000	$ 65,000	$70,000
Property income	2,000	3,000	(1,000)
Capital gains:*			
Listed personal property	5,000	(7,000)	3,000
Personal-use property	(2,000)	5,000	4,000
Other	(8,000)**	6,000	(16,000)

* Brackets indicate capital loss.
** Includes a $4,000 business investment loss.

— REQUIRED

Compute the income under Division B for each year *after* making the necessary amendments to the returns of other years. (Deal with each item line-by-line across the years, rather than computing income one year at a time.) Assume that no capital gains deduction was ever claimed.

Problem 8

ITA: Division B, Subdivisions a, b, c

Mr. Rich, a new client, has invested in rental properties, principal residences and other capital property with inheritance monies and other liquid cash. He provides you with the following information with respect to his 2007 taxation year.

Mr. Rich is employed by Wealth Inc., a Canadian-controlled private corporation, and received the following income and benefits:

(1) Salary (net)			$50,490
Payroll deduction:			
Income taxes		$15,100	
CPP		1,990	
EI		720	
Registered pension plan (defined benefit: current service)		3,700	21,510
			$72,000

(2) Mr. Rich paid professional fees of $500 to the Professional Engineers of Ontario.

(3) Mr. Rich, who is engaged in negotiating contracts for his employer, received for the entire year a monthly allowance for travelling and car expenses of $550 and $650, respectively.

In September of 2007, Mr. Rich sold his car for $12,500 and purchased a new car costing $35,000, including PST of 8% and GST of 6%. Mr. Rich purchased his previous car in January 2004 for $30,000 plus PST and GST. The UCC at January 1, 2007 was $10,000. CCA has been taken each year on a prorated basis to reflect the use for employment purposes. Mr. Rich's kilometres for personal use were 6,250 out of a total kilometres of 25,000.

Mr. Rich's employment contract requires him to use his own car and pay all of his expenses.

Travelling expenses:

Meals	$ 3,500
Accommodation	4,500
Gas and oil	2,100
Insurance	800
Maintenance	500
Licence	130
	$11,530

(4) Mr. Rich sold two lots of his stock options. He provides you with the following:

1st lot — 450 shares sold on March 15, 2007, for $26.50 per share. These shares were purchased in February 2000 for $8 at which time the shares were valued at $10.50.

2nd lot — 600 shares sold on December 5, 2007, for $25 per share. These shares were purchased on April 12, 2007, for $15 at which time the shares were valued at $21. The fair market value at the date of grant was $17.

(5) Mr. Rich received an interest-free loan of $9,000 on March 12, 2007, to enable him to purchase shares of Wealth Inc. The loan was outstanding until the shares were sold on December 5, at which time the loan was repaid. Assume that the prescribed rate throughout the year was 7%.

In addition, during 2007, Mr. Rich received the following income from various sources including certain capital dispositions.

(A) Mr. Rich sold the following assets:

	Cost	Proceeds
Antique foot stool	$1,100	$ 900
Painting	950	1,500
Stamp collection	250	850

(B) During 2007, Mr. Rich sold his two residences, in order to purchase a larger home in an expensive suburb. The following facts relate to these two residences:

	Date purchased	Cost	Commission	Proceeds
City home	1998	$95,000	$21,000	$350,000
Cottage	1993	15,500	12,000	200,000

(C) In addition to his residences, Mr. Rich owns two rental properties. The following information pertains to these two properties:

	Wealthier St.	Richmount St.
Cost of land	$70,000	$100,000
Cost of building	$55,000	$ 80,000
UCC — January 1, 2007, Class 1	$39,000	$ 65,000

	Wealthier St.	Richmount St.
Rental revenue in 2007	$18,000	$ 7,600
Expenses:		
Taxes (property)	$ 2,100	$ 1,800
Other expenses	4,300	6,100
Mortgage interest	3,600	Nil
	$10,000	$ 7,900

The Richmount St. rental property was sold in November for $250,000, including $140,000 for the land, before a commission of $9,000. Mr. Rich took back a $100,000 first mortgage on the property for 5 years. Mr. Rich will receive a capital repayment each year, excluding the first year, of $20,000.

Mr. Rich purchased the Wealthier St. rental property by placing a mortgage on his home. His monthly payments are $450 per month, of which $300 per month represents interest.

(D) Mr. Rich gifted his wife $10,000 in June 2007 to allow her to invest in the stock market. Mrs. Rich decided to be a cautious investor for the first while; as a result, she invested the $10,000 in Treasury Bills which earned $600 from June to December of 2007.

(E) In addition, Mr. Rich decided to provide his younger brother, who is 22, with a non-interest bearing loan of $5,000 to allow him to complete his Masters in Marine Biology. Mr. Rich's brother paid his tuition fees with the funds.

(F) Mr. Rich gifted $8,500 to each of his twin children, Dolly and Camp, aged 15. Both children placed their monies in high interest-bearing savings accounts each receiving interest of $1,050 in 2007.

(G) Mr. Rich received dividends from the following investments:

Foreign Co. — a foreign corporation (net of $88 withholding tax)	$500
Wealth Inc. — a Canadian-controlled private corporation (from income taxed at the low corporate rate)	800

(H) Mr. Rich owns two mutual funds, Dumark Mutual Fund and Paget Mutual Fund. He received a T3 slip from Dumark Mutual Fund indicating the following income amounts allocated to his account and reinvested in 2007:

Capital gains	$1,200
Actual amount of dividends	345
Taxable amount of dividends	500

Mr. Rich had invested $20,000 in the Dumark Fund in 2006. This resulted in the purchase of 1,640.824 units of the fund. In 2006, income of $46.31 was allocated to his account and reinvested. The reinvestment resulted in the purchase of 3.845 units at the market value of $12.044 per unit. The 2007 income allocation resulted, on reinvestment of the $1,545, in the purchase of 119.358 units at the market value of $12.944 per unit. Late in 2007, after the income allocation, Mr. Rich sold 1,000 units for a total of $12,881.

He also received a T5 slip from Paget Mutual Fund indicating that he had received a $280 capital gains dividend during 2007.

(I) Mr. Rich sold a $100,000 Government of Canada bond for $115,327. This bond paid interest semi-annually at an interest rate which was much higher than current interest rates. The proceeds received of $115,327 included accrued interest of $5,327. Mr. Rich had purchased the bonds when they were originally issued for $98,000.

(J) In 2004, Mr. Rich loaned $120,000 to his brother-in-law's company which was a small business corporation. The loan paid interest at commercial rates, but no interest was received in 2007 because the company went into receivership. As an unsecured creditor, Mr. Rich received 10 cents on the dollar ($12,000) in 2007 in full payment of this loan.

(K) Mr. Rich has a listed personal property loss, carried forward from 2001, of $500.

— REQUIRED

Determine Mr. Rich's Division B income according to the ordering rules in section 3 for 2007. Assume that Mr. Rich claimed $60,000 of his capital gains exemption in prior years.

Problem 9

ITA: 52; 53

Ms. Plummet decided to purchase shares in Schvantz Ltd., a public company. She purchased 800 shares at $25 per share plus brokerage of $690 on May 24, 1989.

The following additional transactions took place:

June 30, 1990	— Purchased 500 shares of Shtupp Metals Ltd., a public company, at $35 plus brokerage of $600.
Aug. 20, 1990	— Purchased 1,100 additional shares of Schvantz Ltd. at $30 plus brokerage of $940.
Aug. 27, 1992	— Sold 900 shares of Schvantz Ltd. at $24.50 per share plus brokerage fee of $760.
Sept. 20, 1992	— Purchased 600 additional shares of Schvantz Ltd. at $19.50 plus brokerage of $400.
Oct. 31, 1992	— Sold 200 shares of Shtupp Metals Ltd. at $32 per share plus brokerage fee of $220.
June 9, 1995	— Sold 250 shares of Schvantz Ltd. at $32 per share plus brokerage fee of $275.
May 24, 1999	— Received a 10% stock dividend from Shtupp Metals Ltd. (i.e., 30 shares) of which $20 per share issued was credited to paid-up capital.
June 30, 2002	— Sold 150 shares of Shtupp Metals Ltd. at $36.50 per share plus brokerage fee of $165.
Aug. 20, 2004	— Received 10% stock dividend from Schvantz Ltd. of which $20 per share issued was credited to paid-up capital.
Dec. 28, 2007	— Sold 350 shares of Schvantz Ltd. at $29 per share plus brokerage fee of $355, settlement date January 4, 2008.

— REQUIRED

Calculate the taxable capital gain or allowable capital loss for Ms. Plummet from each of the above sales.

[For more problems and solutions thereto, see the CD accompanying this book.]

¶7,900 SUPPLEMENTAL NOTES

(This section can be omitted without losing the continuity of the Chapter. None of the review questions, multiple choice questions, exercises or assignment problems utilizes this information.)

¶7,910 Cost of Assets Owned on December 31, 1971

Since the government did not want to tax capital gains which had accrued up to December 31, 1971, certain special transition rules, called the Income Tax Application Rules, 1971 (ITAR), were developed to eliminate these gains from taxation under this subdivision when property purchased prior to 1972 was disposed of after 1971.

The median rule or tax-free zone method applies automatically to all taxpayers. The rule establishes the cost of non-depreciable capital property owned on December 31, 1971 for the beginning of the new system which taxes capital gains, as follows: `ITAR: 26(3)`

ACB = The middle figure of:

(a) Proceeds of disposition
(b) Valuation-day value
(c) Cost

if any two of these are equal they become the initial ACB

The Valuation-day (V-day) value rule is an election which applies only to individuals. As an alternative to the median rule, this V-day rule establishes the cost of capital property owned on December 31, 1971, for the beginning of the new system, as follows: `ITAR: 26(7)`

ACB = Valuation-day value

Two Valuation days were designated to establish cost at the beginning of the new system under this rule. December 22, 1971 was chosen for publicly-traded securities and December 31, 1971 was chosen for all other capital property. `ITAR: 24`

It is presumed by law that a taxpayer will use the median rule unless he or she elects the V-day value rule. The CRA has taken the position that when the capital gain is the same under both methods, then the taxpayer has the right to defer making the election until there is a difference between the two methods. From then on the taxpayer must adhere to the method chosen for all property owned prior to 1972. `ITAR: 26(7)`

The following six cases illustrate the application of the median rule (alternatively referred to as the tax-free zone method) and the V-day rule. Note how the rule used establishes a base against which gains or losses under the new system of taxation of capital gains are measured. The objective is to prevent pre-1972 gains or losses from being taxable or allowable.

| | Facts | | | Capital gain | | | |
| | | | | Under median rule | | Under V-day rule | |
Case	Actual cost	V-day value	P of D	Adjusted cost base	Capital gain (loss)	Adjusted cost base	Capital gain (loss)
1	$2,000	$3,000	$5,000	$3,000	$2,000	$3,000	$2,000
2	5,000	3,000	2,000	3,000	(1,000)	3,000	(1,000)
3	3,000	2,000	5,000	3,000	2,000	2,000	3,000
4	3,000	5,000	2,000	3,000	(1,000)	5,000	(3,000)
5	2,000	5,000	3,000	3,000	Nil	5,000	(2,000)
6	5,000	2,000	3,000	3,000	Nil	2,000	1,000

Note how the adjusted cost base is established at the same value under both rules in Cases 1 and 2. Note, also, how in Case 1, the $1,000 (i.e., $3,000 – $2,000) gain that accrued before 1972 is not included in the capital gain. Similarly, in Case 2, the $2,000 (i.e., $3,000 – $5,000) of loss that accrued prior to 1972 is not considered part of the capital loss. Note that when the median rule is used and the proceeds of disposition amount is the middle number, there is no gain or loss. That is because proceeds fall in the "tax-free zone" between cost and V-day.

¶7,920 Additional Rules for a Residence Owned On and After December 31, 1981

Amendments made effective for 1982 and subsequent years introduced rules to prevent certain perceived abuses of the principal residence rules. For years prior to 1982, it was possible for both spouses to each designate a residence as his or her principal residence as long as each residence was inhabited by the owner-spouse sometime during the year. For example, one spouse could designate the city home as a principal residence while the other spouse could designate a recreational residence. Hence, both residences could be fully protected from tax on capital gains by the maximum use of the designation rules. The following changes were made to eliminate the above situation.

(1) Paragraph (*c*) in the definition of "principal residence" was modified for taxation years after 1981 such that the principal residence designation is limited to one per family unit, which generally includes the spouses and their single children under 18. A trust of which a spouse is the beneficiary (i.e., a spousal trust) can benefit from the principal residence exemption. Certain personal trusts that are not spousal trusts, i.e., not established for the benefit of a spouse, may also qualify for the principal residence exemption. ITA: 54

(2) For residences owned on December 31, 1981, there is a transitional rule which modifies the exemption rules to provide for the calculation of a gain equal to the lesser of: ITA: 40(6)

(a) an amount determined under the rules in paragraph 40(2)(*b*), as discussed above, applied to the gain for the total period of ownership to the date of sale, including the one-plus rule but with the family unit restriction for years after 1981; and

(b) the sum of:

(i) an amount determined under the rules in paragraph 40(2)(*b*) (see (a) above) applied to the gain to December 31, 1981, and ITA: 40(6)(*a*)

(ii) an amount determined under the rules in paragraph 40(2)(*b*) applied to the gain from December 31, 1981 to the date of sale, including the family unit restriction but no one plus in the numerator of the exemption fraction ITA: 40(6)(*b*)

minus

(iii) the excess of the fair market value as at December 31, 1981 over the actual proceeds. ITA: 40(6)(*c*)

Part (b) of the above calculation applicable on an eventual disposition after 1981 assumes that there was a disposition on December 31, 1981, at the fair market value at the time and a reacquisition at the same value on January 1, 1982. The purpose of the above rules is to provide for residences owned on December 31, 1981, the same measure of protection, as formerly allowed, before the change in legislation. There is no one plus provided in the numerator of the exemption fraction in part (b)(ii) above, because it is not needed for the intended purpose discussed previously. As a result of the assumed disposition on December 31, 1981, and reacquisition on January 1, 1982, an individual would not be assumed to sell the house and repurchase it in the same year. Hence, there is no need for the intended protection of the one-plus rule in this situation.

The following schematic diagram summarizes the applicability of the appropriate rules outlined above:

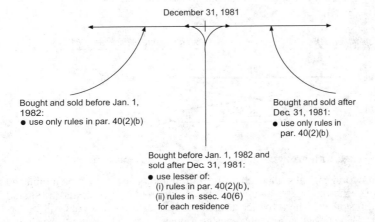

December 31, 1981

Bought and sold before Jan. 1, 1982:
● use only rules in par. 40(2)(b)

Bought and sold after Dec. 31, 1981:
● use only rules in par. 40(2)(b)

Bought before Jan. 1, 1982 and sold after Dec. 31, 1981:
● use lesser of:
(i) rules in par. 40(2)(b),
(ii) rules in ssec. 40(6) for each residence

Example Problem 1

ITAR: 26(7)

Ms. Observanttax decides to sell the two residences listed below in 1999. She has not elected to use V-day value to establish cost at the beginning of 1972; that is, the median rule must be used.

Residence	Date of purchase	Cost	Dec. 31/71 V-day value	December 31, 1981 — FMV	Selling price
City home	1968	$60,000	$100,000	$180,000	$322,500
Cottage	1978	40,000	—	100,000	152,500

— *REQUIRED*

Calculate the minimum total capital gain on the disposition of the two residences.

— *SOLUTION*

(Note that the following analysis only applies to homes owned on December 31, 1981.)

Determine options to calculate.

By subsection 40(6), the capital gain on a residence is the lesser of the paragraph 40(2)(*b*) gain on that residence and the subsection 40(6) gain on that residence. This is true for each residence separately. Therefore, by simple arithmetic, the total capital gain on the two residences must be the least of the following four amounts:

(a) the paragraph 40(2)(*b*) gain on the city home plus the paragraph 40(2)(*b*) gain on the cottage;

(b) the subsection 40(6) gain on the city home plus the subsection 40(6) gain on the cottage;

(c) the paragraph 40(2)(*b*) gain on the city home plus the subsection 40(6) gain on the cottage;

(d) the subsection 40(6) gain on the city home plus the paragraph 40(2)(*b*) gain on the cottage.

The following schematic diagram outlines the four alternatives described above:

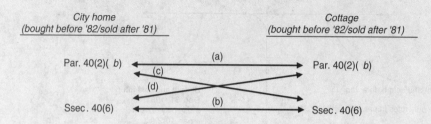

The four options are joined with arrows and lettered according to the description above.

To obtain the minimum total capital gain, each of the four amounts above must be minimized separately by appropriately choosing, for each year, the residence Ms. Observanttax should designate as her principal residence. Then, the least of the four minimized amounts will be the minimum total capital gain.[7] The principal residence designations filed with her tax return should be chosen accordingly.

The first step is to calculate the gains per year of ownership on the two residences. For gains determined under paragraph 40(2)(*b*), this should be the gain per year of ownership over the total post-1971 period as computed above. However, for gains determined under subsection 40(6), the gains per year should be computed separately for the period after 1971 and before 1982 (the pre-1982 gain) and the period after 1981 (the post-1981 gain).

Step 1 — Determine gain per year of ownership

	City home		Cottage	
Total period gain				
P of D	$322,500		$152,500	
ACB	(100,000)		(40,000)	
Gain	$222,500		$112,500	
Gain per year	$\dfrac{\$222,500}{28 \text{ years}}$	= $ 7,946	$\dfrac{\$112,500}{22 \text{ years}}$	= $ 5,114
Pre-82 gain				
P of D — deemed	$180,000		$100,000	
ACB	(100,000)		(40,000)	
Gain	$ 80,000		$ 60,000	
Gain per year	$\dfrac{\$ 80,000}{10 \text{ years}}$	= $ 8,000	$\dfrac{\$ 60,000}{4 \text{ years}}$	= $15,000
Post-81 gain				
P of D	$322,500		$152,500	
ACB — deemed	(180,000)		(100,000)	
Gain	$142,500		$ 52,500	
Gain per year	$\dfrac{\$142,500}{18 \text{ years}}$	= $7,917	$\dfrac{\$ 52,500}{18 \text{ years}}$	= $ 2,917

ITA: 40(2)(*b*)

ITA: 40(6)(*a*)

ITA: 40(6)(*b*)

Step 2 — Assignment of no-option years

The years 1972–77 should be used to designate the city home, which was the only residence owned in those years.

The option years 1978–1999 are allocated below in steps 3 to 7.

---

[7] This procedure follows Alan Macnaughton, "Minimizing Tax on Capital Gains on Principal Residences", a paper presented at the 1986 annual meeting of the Canadian Academic Accounting Association.

Step 3 — Gains determined under par. 40(2)(*b*) for both dwellings

From Step 1, the gains per year of ownership over the total period (28 years) are $7,946 for the city home versus $5,114 for the cottage. Hence a first guess is to allocate all of the 22 option years 1978–1999 to the city home. However, as before, this results in one year being wasted because of the one-plus rule. This is corrected by designating the cottage as the taxpayer's principal residence for one year and allocating the remaining 21 option years to the city home.

	City home	Cottage	
Total period gain			ITA: 40(2)(*b*)
Gain	$222,500	$112,500	
Exemption	(222,500)[1]	(10,227)[2]	
Capital gain	Nil	$102,273	

Step 4 — Gains determined under ssec. 40(6) for both dwellings

From Step 1, the cottage has the higher pre-1982 gain per year ($15,000 versus $8,000) while the city home has the higher post-1981 gain per year ($7,917 versus $2,917). Therefore, as a first guess, all pre-1982 option years should be allocated to the cottage while all post-1981 years should be allocated to the city home.

As before, the one-plus rule causes us to move one year in the pre-1982 period to the city home. This leaves the cottage's pre-1982 gain at zero while decreasing the pre-1982 gain of the city home. Thus, the cottage should be designated as a principal residence for all but one of the four pre-1982 option years (1978–81). The city home should be designated for one of the pre-1982 option years as well as the six no-option years (1972–77).

Under subsection 40(6), the one-plus rule is used only in computing the pre-1982 gain and is not used in calculating the post-1981 gain. Therefore, there is no reason to change the allocation of all post-1981 years to the city home.

	City home	Cottage	
Sum of:			
(a) Pre-82 gain			ITA: 40(6)(*a*)
Gain	$ 80,000	$ 60,000	
Exemption	(64,000)[3]	(60,000)[4]	
Capital gain	$ 16,000	Nil	
and			
(b) Post-81 gain			ITA: 40(6)(*b*)
Gain	$142,500	$ 52,500	
Exemption	(142,500)[5]	Nil[6]	
Capital gain	Nil	$ 52,500	
Total capital gain	$ 16,000	$ 52,500	ITA: 40(6)

Step 5 — Gains determined under par. 40(2)(*b*) for city home and ssec. 40(6) for cottage

Since the city home's gain is computed under paragraph 40(2)(*b*), its gain per year from Step 1 is $7,946. This should be compared to the subsection 40(6) gains per year for the cottage of $15,000 for the pre-1982 period and $2,916 for the post-1981 period. Therefore, our first guess is to assign all pre-1982 option years to the cottage and all post-1981 years to the city home.

Again, because of the one-plus rule, our first guess should be changed by moving one pre-1982 option year to the city home. This leaves the cottage's pre-1982 gain at zero while reducing the paragraph 40(2)(*b*) gain of the city home. Thus, the city home should be designated for the 1972–77 no-option years, one pre-1982 option year, and all of the years 1982–99. The cottage should be designated for just four years (the remaining pre-1982 option years).

	City home	Cottage	
Total period gain			ITA: 40(2)(*b*)
Gain	$222,500		
Exemption	(206,607)[7]		
Capital gain	$ 15,893		

	City home	Cottage
Sum of:		
(a) Pre-82 gain			ITA: 40(6)(a)
Gain		$ 60,000
Exemption		(60,000)[8]
Capital gain		Nil
and		
(b) Post-81 gain			ITA: 40(6)(b)
Gain		$ 52,500
Exemption		Nil[9]
Capital gain		$ 52,500
Total capital gain		$ 52,500	ITA: 40(6)

ITA: 40(6)(a) appears beside the Pre-82 gain block; *ITA: 40(6)(b)* beside the Post-81 gain block; *ITA: 40(6)* beside Total capital gain.

Step 6 — Gains determined under ssec. 40(6) for city home and par. 40(2)(b) for cottage

The gain per year of $5,114 over the total period for the cottage should be compared to the gains per year on the city home of $8,000 in the pre-1982 period and $7,917 in the post-1981 period. The first guess is to allocate all option years to the city home. Because of the one-plus rule, this allocation can be improved by moving one pre-1982 option year to the cottage.

	City home	Cottage
Total period gain			ITA: 40(2)(b)
Gain.......................................		$112,500
Exemption		(10,227)[10]
Capital gain		$102,273
Sum of:		
(a) Pre-82 gain			ITA: 40(6)(a)
Gain.......................................	$ 80,000	
Exemption	(80,000)[11]	
Capital gain	Nil	
and		
(b) Post-81 gain			ITA: 40(6)(b)
Gain.......................................	$142,500	
Exemption	(142,500)[12]	
Capital gain	Nil	
Total capital gain	Nil		ITA: 40(6)

Step 7 — Comparison of total gains on the two dwellings under Steps 3 to 6

```
Step 3:       0 + $102,273 = $102,273
Step 4: $16,000 +   52,500 =   68,500
Step 5:  15,893 +   52,500 =   68,393
Step 6:       0 +  102,273 =  102,273
```

The conclusion is that the minimum capital gain is produced under Step 5 and, therefore, the principal residence designations should be made as recommended in that step. Thus, Ms. Observanttax could designate the cottage as her principal residence for the years 1979 to 1981 and designate the city home as her principal residence for the years 1972 to 1978 and 1982 to 1999. This will produce a total capital gain on the two residences of $68,393 with a taxable capital gain of $51,295 (at the ¾ inclusion rate).

— NOTES TO SOLUTION

(1) $\dfrac{1 + 27}{28}$ × \$222,500 = \$222,500; years designated — 1972–76 and any 21 years from 1978–99

(2) $\dfrac{1 + 1}{22}$ × \$112,500 = \$10,227; year designated — any one of 1978–99 not designated in (1) above

(3) $\dfrac{1 + 7}{10}$ × \$80,000 = \$64,000; years designated — 1972–77 and any one of 1978–81

(4) $\dfrac{1 + 3}{4}$ × \$60,000 = \$60,000; years designated — any three of 1978–81 not designated in (3) above

(5) $\dfrac{18}{18}$ × \$142,500 = \$142,500; years designated — 1982–99

(6) $\dfrac{0}{18}$ × \$52,500 = 0; years designated — none

(7) $\dfrac{1 + 25}{28}$ × \$222,500 = \$206,607; years designated — 1972–77, 1982–99 and any one of 1978–81

(8) $\dfrac{1 + 3}{4}$ × \$60,000 = \$60,000; years designated — any 3 of 1978–81 not designated in (7) above

(9) $\dfrac{0}{18}$ × \$52,500 = 0; years designated — none

(10) $\dfrac{1 + 1}{22}$ × \$112,500 = \$10,227; years designated — any one of 1978–81

(11) $\dfrac{1 + 9}{10}$ × \$80,000 = \$80,000; years designated — 1972–77 and any three of 1978–81 not designated in (10) above

(12) $\dfrac{18}{18}$ × \$142,500 =\$142,500; years designated — 1982–99

Example Problem 2

Mr. Dwellings owns two residences in British Columbia: a cottage and a Vancouver home, both of which were purchased prior to 1982. He anticipates disposing of his Vancouver home in 1999 and would like some advice on how to minimize the taxable capital gain on this disposition and yet provide maximum protection to the cottage (purchased in 1970), which has a smaller capital gain. The following facts relate to the Vancouver home:

Cost — 1965	\$250,000
FMV — 1971	300,000
FMV — 1981	510,000
FMV — 1999	450,000

— REQUIRED

Calculate the minimum capital gain on the anticipated sale of the Vancouver home while saving the maximum number of designations for the cottage.

— SOLUTION

The Vancouver home has actually declined in value from the December 31, 1981 value (\$510,000 to \$450,000). Since paragraph 40(6)(*c*) permits a reduction of the gain under the sum of the preceding two paragraphs, the optimum solution should take this fact into account.

Step 1 — Determine gain per year of ownership

Total period gain   ITA: 40(2)(*b*)

P of D	$450,000
ACB	(300,000)
Gain	$150,000

$$\text{Gain per year of ownership} \quad \frac{\$150,000}{28 \text{ years}} = \$\ 5,357$$

Pre-1982 gain   ITA: 40(6)(*a*)

P of D — deemed	$510,000
ACB	(300,000)
Gain	$210,000

$$\text{Gain per year of ownership} \quad \frac{\$210,000}{10 \text{ years}} = \$\ 21,000$$

Therefore, assume that the capital gain will be determined by subsection 40(6) and designate the Vancouver home for enough years to remove all of the gain.

Step 2 — Determine the number of years of designation to remove all the gain

Gain (pre-1982)		$210,000
less: reduction		
FMV — December 31, 1981	$510,000	
less actual P of D	(450,000)	(60,000)
		$150,000

ITA: 40(6)(*c*)

$$\frac{\$150,000}{\$21,000} = 7.14 \text{ years required to remove entire gain}$$

Therefore, designate only six years to the Vancouver home in the pre-1982 period using the one-plus rule for the other year.

Step 3 — Calculate minimum capital gain

Lesser of:

(a) Total period gains   ITA: 40(2)(*b*)

Gain as per Step 1	$150,000	
Exemption: $\dfrac{1+6}{28} \times \$150,000$	(37,500)	$112,500

(b) Pre-1982 gain   ITA: 40(6)(*a*)

Gain as per Step 1	$210,000	
Exemption: $\dfrac{1+6}{10} \times \$210,000$	(147,000)	$\ 63,000
plus: Post-1981 gain		Nil
less: excess		
FMV — December 31, 1981	$510,000	
Actual P of D	(450,000)	(60,000)
Net gain		$\ 3,000

ITA: 40(6)(*b*)
ITA: 40(6)(*c*)

ITA: 40(6)

Therefore, the minimum capital gain is $3,000 and 22 years of designations remain to be assigned to the cottage as follows:

Pre-1982 — 4 years

Post-1981 — 18 years to 1999

¶7,930 Principal Residence on Farm Land

The gain on the disposition of land used in a farming business that included a principal residence may be computed in one of two ways. The gain on the housing unit plus up to one-half hectare of land may be reduced by an amount computed by the general formula. Alternatively, the farmer may elect to compute an exemption of $1,000 plus $1,000 for every year after the later of 1971 and the last acquisition date that the property was designated as a principal residence and during which he or she was resident in Canada. The CRA's interpretation of these provisions can be found in an Interpretation Bulletin.

ITA: 40(2)(*b*)

ITA: 40(2)(*c*)

IT-120R6, par. 20-24

¶7,940 GST Rules for Dispositions of Residential Property and Used Goods

The disposition of capital personal property for GST purposes was discussed in Chapter 5 while the rules relating to dispositions and changes in use of capital real property will be discussed in Chapter 8. The sale of shares, which is discussed in Chapter 15, is an exempt supply under the GST and, hence, there are no GST consequences. This part of the Chapter will address the GST rules relating to dispositions of used residential or personal-use property and dispositions of used goods.

¶7,945 Sales of used residential or personal-use real property

GST applies to all sales of real property unless a specific exemption is provided. For example, sales of new residential housing are subject to GST. Sales of used residential complexes, or interests therein, are exempt from GST. Unlike the principal residence exemption under the *Income Tax Act*, the exemption for GST purposes is not limited to a single property.

ETA: Sch. V, Part I, s. 2

The term "residential complex" is defined to include a detached house, semi-detached house, rowhouse unit, multi-unit residential condominium or apartment complex, together with any common areas and land that are reasonably necessary for the use and enjoyment of the residential unit. A residential complex does not include a hotel, a motel, an inn, a boarding or lodging house, or other similar property that provides all, or substantially all, accommodation for periods of less than 60 days. A building generally constitutes a residential complex only in respect of the part that includes residential units. Thus, if an apartment building contains one floor of commercial space and 10 floors of residential units, only the latter 10 floors will constitute a residential complex.

ETA: 123(1)

A residential complex includes a single family dwelling in which a business is carried on, provided the dwelling is used primarily (i.e., more than 50%) as a residence for individuals. If the "primarily test" (i.e., the more than 50% test) is not met, a supply of real property that includes a residential complex and other real property that is not part of the residential complex is deemed to be two separate supplies. Accordingly, the supply of the residential portion will be exempt if it qualifies as a used residential complex, and the other part of the property will be subject to the general rules. This rule will apply, for example, where an accountant uses a house primarily for his or her practice and not primarily as a residence.

ETA: 136(2)

Although the sale of the residential complex may be exempt, various fees related to the sale are subject to GST. These include, for example, real estate commissions, legal fees, appraisal fees, survey fees, and home inspection fees. No GST is payable in respect of exempt financial services, such as mortgage brokerage or mortgage insurance fees.

Sales of real property by an individual or a personal trust are exempted, other than: ETA: Sch. V, Part I, s. 9

- real property that is capital property used primarily

  — in a business carried on by the individual or trust with a reasonable expectation of profit, or

  — if the individual or trust is a registrant

    - in making taxable supplies of the real property by way of lease, licence, or similar arrangement, or

    - in any combination of the uses described above;

- real property sold

  — in the course of a business of the individual or trust, or

  — where the individual or trust has filed an election with the Minister in prescribed form and manner and containing prescribed information, in the course of an adventure or concern in the nature of trade of the individual or trust;

- a parcel of land that was subdivided or severed by the individual, trust or settlor of the trust (subject to certain exemptions);

- certain deemed supplies;

- a residential complex or an interest in a residential complex; or

- where an individual or personal trust has bought taxable real property and pursuant to a joint election, subsequently sells it back to the vendor within one year, pursuant to a right or obligation under the original purchase and sale agreement between the parties.

A "personal trust" is defined as a testamentary trust, or an *inter vivos* trust that is a   ITA: 248(1)
personal trust (within the meaning assigned by the *Income Tax Act*) all the beneficiaries
(other than contingent beneficiaries) of which are individuals, and all the contingent beneficiaries of which, if any, are individuals, charities, or public institutions.

Under this provision, most sales of country properties kept for personal use, non-commercial hobby farms and other non-business land are exempt from GST. Sales of residential
complexes are excluded from this exemption because they are covered in another provision,
as discussed above. Where real property is sold in the course of an adventure or concern in
the nature of trade, an election may be made to treat the sale as taxable. Such an election may
be made, for example, by an individual or trust who acquires real property for resale purposes
and not for personal use. If such an election is made, the individual or trust, if a registrant,
would be entitled to recover any GST paid on the acquisition of the property (for example, if it
was not purchased from another individual who held the property as personal-use real
property) and on any subsequent improvements. As discussed in Chapter 6, sales of substantially renovated used housing in the course of a business are treated as sales of new housing
and, therefore, are subject to GST.

The rules relating to exempt sales of real property by public sector bodies will not be
discussed in this Chapter.

The conversion of a commercial property to a residential complex, and *vice versa,* will be
discussed in Chapter 8.

¶7,950   Sales of used goods and acceptance of trade-ins

Under the general GST rules, the sale by a registrant of a used good is subject to GST. If a
used good sold by a registrant is purchased by another registrant for use in a commercial
activity, the normal input tax credit rules apply. The sale of a used good by a non-registrant is
not subject to GST.

Where a registrant accepts a used good (or a leasehold interest therein) as full or partial consideration for another good, the supplier has to collect GST only on the net amount if the trade-in is for consumption, use or supply by the supplier in the course of commercial activities and the person trading in the property is not required to collect GST (i.e., is not a registrant). For example, this rule would apply to an automobile dealer who accepts a trade-in from a consumer. The dealer would charge tax on the difference between the value of the new car and the value of the trade-in.

ETA: 153(4)

There are certain exceptions to this rule. For example, it does not apply to any supply of a trade-in that is a zero-rated supply (e.g., a supply of zero-rated farming equipment), or to a supply made outside Canada (e.g., a trade-in delivered outside Canada to the supplier of the new good).

If the used good is traded in by a registrant, the purchase of the new good and the trade-in are treated as two separate transactions, both of which are subject to GST.

Chapter 8

Capital Gains: The Finer Points

LEARNING GOALS

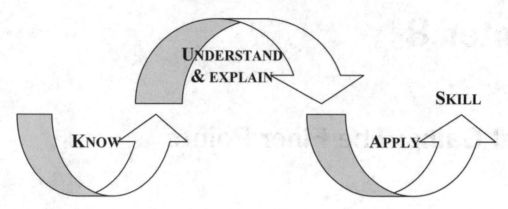

Know

By the end of this chapter you should know some more advanced provisions of the *Income Tax Act* that relate to capital gains and losses. Completing the Review Questions (¶8,800) and Multiple Choice Questions (¶8,825) is a good way to learn the technical provisions.

Understand and Explain

You should understand and be able to explain

● Some of the finer points related to capital gains.

● Bad debts on capital property.

● Non-arm's length transfers and the attribution rules.

● Death of a taxpayer issues for capital property.

Completing the Exercises (¶8,850) is a good way to deepen your understanding of the material.

Apply

You should be able to apply your knowledge and understanding of the rules pertaining to capital gains and losses in a way that accomplishes a client's goals. Completing the Assignment Problems (¶8,875) is an excellent way to develop your ability to apply the material in increasingly complex situations.

OVERVIEW

This chapter will re-examine some of the topics introduced in the preceding chapter and enlarge upon some of the technical refinements involved in the application of these rules. Additional areas of the capital gains system will also be explored.

As mentioned in chapter 7, Subdivision c of Division B of Part I of the Act contains the primary rules for the computation of taxable capital gains and allowable capital losses. Some of the more important provisions were reviewed at the beginning of the last chapter.

In addition, Subdivision f of Division B provides some rules that are relevant to the computation of property income. For example, in this chapter we will look at the rules related to the deemed disposition of capital property on the death of an individual as well as the attribution rules and non-arm's length transfers.

ITA: 70, 73, 74.2

In Division F the rules dealing with the treatment of capital property when an individual ceases to be or becomes a resident of Canada will be reviewed.

The following chart will help to locate in the Act, the major provisions dealt with in this chapter.

Part I — Division B
Subdivision c
Capital Gains & Losses

DIVISION		SUBDIVISION		SECTION	
A	Liability for tax				
B	**Computation of income**		Basic rules		
		a	Office or employment		
C	Computation of taxable income	b	Business or property		
D	Taxable income earned in Canada by non-residents	c	Capital gains and losses	38	TCG/ACL
				39	CG/CL
		d	Other income	39.1	Exempt CG balance
E	Computation of tax	e	Other deductions	40	General rules
E.1	Minimum tax	f	Rules relating to computation of income	41	LPP
F	Special rules			42	Warranty
G	Deferred and other special income arrangements			43	Part disposition
		g	Amounts not included in income	43.1	Life estates
				44	Replacement property
H	Exemptions	h	Cdn corporations and shareholders	44.1	Small business share rollover
I	Returns, Assessments, payments, appeals	i	Shareholders of non-resident corporations	45	Change in use
				46	Personal-use property
J	Appeals to the courts	j	Partnerships	47	Identical property
		k	Trusts	48.1	SBC goes public
				49	Options granted
				50	Loss on debt/shares
				51	Convertible property
				52	Cost of certain property
				53	ACB adjustments
				54	Definitions
				54.1	Exception: principal residence
				54.2	Shares and capital property
				55	Deemed capital gain

¶8,000 VARIOUS CAPITAL GAINS PROVISIONS

¶8,010 Foreign Exchange Gains and Losses

Taxpayers must first determine whether the foreign exchange gain or loss arose from an income or a capital receipt, using the common law rules discussed in Chapters 4 and 7. For income receipts, the full gain or loss will be included in arriving at business or property income under Subdivision b. For capital receipts, the net capital gain or loss is determined in the normal manner. However, for individuals the net capital gain or loss is reduced by a maximum of $200.

ITA: 39(2)

Example Problem

Mr. Fast-Dollar made the following capital transactions which resulted in currency gains and losses during the following years:

	2005	2006	2007
Total currency gains	$800	$180	$250
Total currency losses	300	40	400

— *REQUIRED*

Compute the capital gains (losses) on foreign currency for each of the years shown.

— *SOLUTION*

	2005	2006	2007
Net capital gain (loss)	$500	$140	$(150)
Exempt portion of excess	200	140	(150)
Capital gain (loss)	$300	Nil	Nil

It should be noted that a currency gain or loss must be distinct and separate from another transaction that may have given rise to the currency transaction. For example, the sale of an article must be computed in Canadian dollars valued at the time of the sale in order to arrive at a gain or loss on that disposition. A subsequent conversion of foreign funds received would give rise to the currency gain or loss.

¶8,020 Part Disposition

If a taxpayer makes a partial disposition of a capital property, he or she must allocate a reasonable portion of the total adjusted cost base of the capital property to the proceeds of partial disposition to determine the capital gain or loss. The portion of this cost allocated to the part sold should be in the ratio of the value of the part sold to the total value of the capital property. A valuation problem is very likely to arise, particularly if the value of the part sold is not, in fact, proportional to total value. This might be the case, for example, where a taxpayer owns land with lake frontage and the half of the property fronting on the lake is sold leaving the other half without such lake access.

ITA: 43

¶8,030 Exchanges of Property

¶8,035 The basic deferral

This particular provision permits the deferral of some or all of the capital gain on property which is disposed of and which is subsequently replaced. There are two basic types of disposition which qualify for this deferral (often referred to in practice as a "rollover"):

¶8,000

(a) an involuntary disposition of property which has been lost, stolen, destroyed or taken by order of statutory authority (e.g., expropriation, bankruptcy); and

(b) a voluntary dispositions of real property referred to as "former business property" that usually occur on the relocation of a business.

The deferral for a voluntary disposition is limited to former business property. "Former business property" as used in this provision is defined as real or immovable property which has a common law definition of "land and buildings" and limited-period franchises, concessions or licences on which an election has been made [proposed in Bill C-33, introduced on November 22, 2006]. ITA: 44(1)(*b*), 248(1)

ITA: 13(4.2)

This topic has been partly covered in Chapter 5 in connection with the deferral of recapture realized on depreciable property. That material should be reviewed as preparation for the following discussion of the deferral of a capital gain in these situations. An election to defer either recapture or a capital gain is, also, deemed to be an election to defer the other. ITA: 13(4), 44(4) ITA: 13(4), 44(1)

In the year of the disposition, a taxpayer may choose to:

(a) recognize the usual capital gain (i.e., P of D minus ACB and selling costs), or

(b) elect to report the capital gain as the lesser of:

(i) the actual capital gain in (a) above, and

(ii) the excess, if any, of proceeds for the old property over the cost of replacement (i.e., the amount of the proceeds not spent on the new property),

if he or she has replaced the property,

(a) in the case of a voluntary disposition, by the later of the end of the first taxation year after the year of disposition and 12 months after the end of the year of disposition, or

(b) in the case of an involuntary disposition, by the later of the end of the second taxation year after the year of disposition and 24 months after the end of the year of disposition.

The disposition of the old property is deemed to have occurred only when the proceeds are "receivable". In the case of involuntary dispositions, the rules for determining when proceeds are receivable can be summarized (for situations excluding the death of a taxpayer or the winding-up of a corporation) as the earliest of: ITA: 44(2)

(a) the day the taxpayer has agreed to the full amount of the compensation;

(b) the day the compensation is finally determined by a court or tribunal; and

(c) the day that is two years from the day of loss, destruction or taking where a claim or suit has not been taken before the courts.

The election does not apply immediately where the taxpayer does not purchase the replacement property in the same year the proceeds of disposition become receivable. In the year in which proceeds of disposition become receivable, the disposition is handled in the normal manner by reporting the gain. If the replacement property is acquired within the allowed time, an amended return would be filed for the year in which the proceeds became receivable to implement the rollover.

The adjusted cost base for the replacement property under the election above will be reduced by the deferred capital gain. This is the essence of a rollover or deferral which, in this case, is accomplished by the reduction of the adjusted cost base of the new property. By reducing the adjusted cost base, a future capital gain (or reduced capital loss) in the amount of the deferred gain will arise on the ultimate disposition of the new property. ITA: 44(1)(*f*)

Replacement property is defined as property acquired for the same or a similar use as the original property and for gaining or producing income from the same or a similar business. The CRA's current interpretation of "same or similar use" and "same or similar business" is contained in an Interpretation Bulletin. ITA: 44(5)

IT-259R4, par. 16-17, 18-21

Net capital gains reserves may arise from exchanges of property situations. For example, proceeds may become receivable in a year, but they are not due until a subsequent year, such that a capital gains reserve is available. When the reserve is included in income in the year after the reserve is deducted, the included reserve would normally qualify for this election.

Example Problem 1

Quick Growth Stores Ltd. has decided to change the present location of its retail store, now in a suburban mall, to the Yonge Street strip in downtown Toronto. The following facts relate to the disposition of the original property in March 2006.

	Land	Cl.3 Building	Cl.8 Equipment
Cost	$30,000	$50,000	$5,000
UCC	—	30,000	1,500
Proceeds	70,000	100,000	500

Quick Growth Ltd. purchased its Yonge Street property in August 2007 for the following amounts:

Land	$100,000
Building — brick	150,000
Equipment	20,000

The company wishes to elect to defer both the capital gain and the recapture.

ITA: 13(4), 44(1)

— REQUIRED

Indicate the tax consequences if Quick Growth Stores Ltd. elects, assuming that its fiscal year-end is December 31.

— SOLUTION

This situation involves the voluntary disposition of a former business property in respect of the land and building. As a result, the taxpayer corporation must replace the land and building within the later of one taxation year or 12 months from the end of the December 31, 2006 taxation year (i.e., the taxation year of the disposition), in order to obtain the benefits of the rollover. It is often helpful to use a time line to graph the qualifying period of replacement as follows:

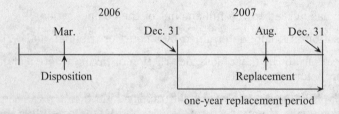

(A) Effect of election to defer capital gains — Filed on an amended return for 2006

ITA: 44

Gain to be recognized in year of disposal — 2006

ITA: 44(1)(e)

			Land	Building
(i)	Capital gain, computed as:			
	Lesser of: (I)	P of D	$ 70,000	$100,000
		ACB	(30,000)	(50,000)
		Capital gain	$ 40,000	$ 50,000
	(II)	P of D	$ 70,000	$100,000
		Replacement cost	(100,000)	(150,000)
		Excess, if any	Nil	Nil

The lesser of the actual capital gain and the proceeds not spent on the replacement property is nil in both cases. Therefore, the full amount of the gain can be deferred by reducing the adjusted cost base of the replacement land and building.

Adjusted cost base of replacement land is

$100,000 – $40,000 = $60,000   ITA: 44(1)(*f*)

Adjusted cost base of replacement building is

$150,000 – $50,000 = $100,000   ITA: 44(1)(*f*)

(ii) Equipment — Nil

Equipment does not qualify as "former business property". In any case there is a loss which is not allowed as a capital loss.   ITA: 39(1)(*b*)(i)

Comments:

(1) In the above situation, the entire capital gain is deferred through the reduction of the adjusted cost base of the replacement property, since the amount actually spent on the replacement property was greater than the proceeds of disposition for the old property. The intent of the provision is to allow a deferral of all or some part of the actual capital gain and, hence, the tax on that gain, where the proceeds have been spent to acquire a new property. Conceptually, if the proceeds have been spent in this manner, there would be no funds from the disposition of the old property to pay the taxes, so the taxes are deferred. Note how the reduction in the adjusted cost base of the replacement property implements the deferral. Consider the replacement land which was acquired at a cost of $100,000. Its cost base is $60,000 after the adjustment for the deferred gain. If that land were sold immediately for its indicated value of $100,000 (it was just purchased for that amount), a capital gain of $40,000 (i.e., $100,000 – $60,000) would be realized. That capital gain is exactly the gain on the old land that was deferred.

(2) Since the replacement property was acquired after the filing of the 2006 corporate tax   IT-259R4, par. 3
returns (June 30, 2007), the resultant capital gain and any recapture must be reported in the year of disposition. A request for an amended return must be made in the year of acquisition. Acceptable security may be provided in lieu of the payment of outstanding taxes.

(B) Effect of election to defer recapture, re building — Filed on an amended return for 2006.

2006

	Cl.3: 5%
UCC immediately before disposal	$30,000
Less: deemed disposal reducing UCC	
— normal deduction: lesser of:	
(i) cost ($50,000)	
(ii) P of D ($100,000) $50,000	
— reduced by the lesser of:	
(i) amount determined above ($50,000) less UCC above ($30,000) 20,000	
(ii) cost of replacement ($150,000)	30,000
UCC, December 31, 2006.	Nil

ITA: 13(4)(*c*)

Comment:

As long as the cost of replacement ($150,000) is greater than the amount of the recapture ($20,000) that would otherwise result on the disposition, there will be full deferral of the recapture.

2007		*Cl. NRB:* * 6%	
Add: Capital cost of replacement property			ITA: 13(4)(*d*)
Cost of replacement	$150,000		
Less: reduction for deferred gain	50,000		ITA: 44(1)(*f*)
Deemed capital cost	$100,000		
Less: reduction for deferred recapture	20,000	$80,000	ITA: 13(4)(*d*)
UCC, December 31, 2007		$80,000	
CCA, 2007 (6% of ½ × $80,000)		2,400	
UCC, January 1, 2008		$77,600	

* [Proposed new class for non-residential buildings, unnumbered at the time of writing (July 2007).]

Comment:

Normally, when depreciable property of a class is sold and replaced with property of the same class in the year of disposition, all or some part of the potential recapture on the disposition is offset by the purchase before the end of the year. For example, if the new building had been purchased for $100,000 in 2006 and if it could have been added to the *same* class as the old building, the following UCC balance would have resulted:

UCC immediately before disposal		$ 30,000
Less lesser of:		
(i) cost of building disposed of	$ 50,000	
(ii) proceeds of disposition	$100,000	
lesser amount		(50,000)
Add: capital cost of replacement building		100,000
UCC, December 31, 2006		$ 80,000

Note that this is the same amount as the UCC balance at December 31, 2007 after the rollover is implemented.

ITA: 13(4)

In deferring the recapture, the election provides two additional benefits:

ITA: 13(4)

(i) it allows for a replacement to take place in a subsequent year, and

(ii) it allows for a replacement with a property in a different class.

Example Problem 2

Reconsider the facts in Example Problem 1. In this example, Quick Growth Ltd. purchased less expensive land in 2007.

Land...	$ 45,000
Building — brick (same as Example Problem 1)	150,000
Equipment (same as Example Problem 1)	20,000

— *REQUIRED*

Indicate the tax consequences for the land only, if Quick Growth Ltd. elects under section 44 (assuming that its fiscal year-end is December 31).

— SOLUTION

The gain on the land to be recognized in year of disposal (2006) is now $25,000, computed as:

Lesser of: (A) P of D	....	$70,000
	ACB	(30,000)
	CG	$40,000
(B) P of D	....	$70,000
	Replacement cost	(45,000)
	Excess, if any	$25,000

Adjusted cost base in 2007 of replacement property is:

Replacement cost	....	$ 45,000
Deferred gain [$40,000 – $25,000]	....	(15,000)
ACB of replacement property	....	$ 30,000	ITA: 44(1)(*f*)

¶8,040 Election for additional deferral

ITA: 44(6)

This particular election permits the proceeds on the dispositions of former business property (land and buildings) to be reallocated between the two components so that less capital gain or recapture would be triggered. This election appears to recognize the fact that when a property consisting of land and building is sold, it is usually sold for proceeds which represent the fair market value of the total property. In this situation, the land and building are not priced separately. Therefore, the original allocation of proceeds between land and building may have been fairly arbitrary.

Example Problem

Reconsider the facts in Example Problems 1 and 2 above.

— REQUIRED

Indicate tax consequences of electing an additional deferral in respect of the building, based on the facts in Example Problem 1, and the land, based on the facts in Example Problem 2.

ITA: 44(6)

— SOLUTION

Re-examining the facts of Example Problem 2 above, it would be possible to elect to transfer $25,000 of the land proceeds to the building proceeds, thereby eliminating the capital gain. Note that the trade-off is a reduced capital cost of the building and, hence, a lower capital cost allowance base. Therefore, the cost of deferring tax on $25,000 of capital gain now is less capital cost allowance over the holding period of the building in the future.

(A) Effect of election

ITA: 44(6)

Gain to be recognized in year of disposal (2006)

ITA: 44(1)(*e*)

(i) Capital gain, computed as:		Land	Building
Lesser of: (I)	Actual P of D	$ 70,000	$100,000
	Election	(25,000)	25,000
	Deemed P of D	$ 45,000	$125,000
	ACB	(30,000)	(50,000)
	CG	$ 15,000	$ 75,000

ITA: 44(6)

(II) Deemed P of D above	$ 45,000	$125,000
Replacement cost	(45,000)	(150,000)
Excess, if any	Nil	Nil

Adjusted cost base of replacement land is:

$45,000 – ($15,000 – Nil) = $30,000   ITA: 44(1)(*f*)

Adjusted cost base of replacement building is:

$150,000 – ($75,000 – Nil) = $75,000   ITA: 44(1)(*f*)

Comment:

Note that the key to a reallocation of proceeds that will successfully defer more of the capital gain is a replacement cost of one of the assets (i.e., either land or building) that is sufficiently in excess of original proceeds of disposition to allow for an increase in proceeds on that asset without triggering a gain. In this case, the replacement cost of the building, at $150,000, exceeds the original proceeds of the old building of $100,000. Therefore, up to $50,000 can be added to the proceeds and still leave the excess of proceeds over replacement cost of nil. In this case, only $25,000 needs to be removed from the proceeds of the land to allow all of the gain to be deferred.

(B) Effect of election to defer recapture on building — Filed on an amended return for 2006.

2006

			Cl.3:5%	
UCC immediately before disposal			$30,000	
Less: deemed disposal reducing UCC				ITA: 13(4)(*c*)
— normal deduction: lesser of:				
(i) cost ($50,000)				
(ii) P of D ($100,000)[1]	$ 50,000			
— reduced by the lesser of:				ITA: 13(4)(*c*)
(i) amount determined above ($50,000) less UCC above ($30,000)		20,000		
(ii) cost of replacement ($150,000)		30,000		
UCC after disposal			Nil	

2007

			Cl. NRB: 6%	
Add: Capital cost of replacement property				ITA: 13(4)(*d*)
Cost of replacement.	$150,000			
Less: reduction for deferred gain	75,000			ITA: 44(1)(*f*)
Deemed capital cost	$ 75,000			
Less: reduction for deferred recapture	20,000	$55,000		ITA: 13(4)(*d*)
UCC, December 31, 2007			$55,000	
CCA, 2007 (6% of ½ × $55,000)			1,650	
UCC, January 1, 2008			$53,350	

Comment:

The results of using the election for additional deferral can be compared with the original application of the deferral as follows:

ITA: 44(6)

	Without election	With election	Difference
Capital gains recognized:			
land	$ 25,000	Nil	$25,000
building	Nil	Nil	Nil
ACB of replacement property:			
land	30,000	$30,000	Nil
building	100,000	75,000	25,000
UCC (before CCA) of replacement building	80,000	55,000	25,000

The above shows that $25,000 less capital gain on the land has to be recognized as a result of the election. This is reflected in the adjusted cost base of the building which is $25,000 lower. This lower ACB will potentially result in a higher capital gain on the ultimate disposition of the building, if it is sold for a capital gain. Also, the UCC of the building is $25,000 lower, resulting in less annual CCA. To evaluate the trade-off the following should be compared:

ITA: 44(6)

(i) the tax that would be paid now on a capital gain of $25,000 or a taxable capital gain of $12,500 (i.e., ½ × $25,000), and

(ii) the present value of the CCA tax shield[2] from $25,000 of capital cost in Class NRB.

— NOTES TO SOLUTION

[1] Note that the deemed proceeds arising from the election are not applicable for the purpose of a deferral of recapture, since the election is only applicable to Subdivision c which deals with taxable capital gains and allowable capital losses.

ITA: 44(6)
ITA: 13, 44(6)

[2] The present value of the CCA tax shield, including the effect of the half-year rule, can be computed from the following:

$$PV = \frac{C \times R \times T}{R + I} \times \frac{1 + I/2}{1 + I}$$

where PV = present value of the CCA tax shield,
     C = capital cost of the asset,
     R = rate of CCA for the class,
     I = after-tax discount rate,
     T = tax rate.

Replacement Property

Deferral of Capital Gain
Summary

Key Question: Did you spend at least the proceeds on the replacement property?

If you spend at least the proceeds from the sale of the former property to buy the replacement property, then the full amount of the gain will be deferred. The deferral is built into the reduction of the cost base of the replacement property.

If you sell both land and building then this concept applies to the combined proceeds and the combined replacement cost.

Deferral of Recapture
Summary

Key Question: Did you spend at least the amount of the recapture on the replacement property?

If you spend at least an amount equal to the potential recapture from the sale of the former property to buy the replacement property, then the full amount of the recapture will be deferred. The deferral is built into the reduction of the undepreciated capital cost of the replacement property.

¶8,050 Proceeds on Disposition of Building

An interesting situation arose in the case of *The Queen v. Malloney's Studio Limited*, in which the taxpayer agreed to sell land clear of buildings and, therefore, had to demolish an existing building before disposing of the land. The Minister allocated part of the proceeds of disposition for the property to the demolished building resulting in recapture. The taxpayer argued that all of the price related to the land. The Supreme Court of Canada held that the price related only to the land because the building was not part of the sale. No part of the price was for property "damaged, destroyed, taken or injuriously affected" because the purchase did not cause the damage as envisaged by the definition of "proceeds of disposition". Since none of the proceeds for the property had to be allocated to the building, the taxpayer could deduct a terminal loss on the building and, at the same time, all of the proceeds created a capital gain which was only fractionally taxable.

78 DTC 6278 (S.C.C.)

ITA: 13(21)

Perhaps as a reaction to the result of the above case, a provision was added to the Act to provide rules to allocate proceeds of disposition between land and buildings on their sale. Where a building is sold for proceeds that are less than its proportionate share of the undepreciated capital cost of its class, this provision will apply. In the situation where the land is sold in the same taxation year as the building, the amount which is treated as proceeds of disposition of the building may be greater than the fair market value of the building, thereby reducing or eliminating the potential terminal loss. At the same time, the capital gain on the sale of the land will be reduced by the amount of the terminal loss eliminated on the building. As a result, the potential terminal loss on the building will be used to offset the gain on the land. The result is to convert what might have been a terminal loss fully deductible into a reduction of a capital gain, in essence, three-quarters deductible.

ITA: 13(21.1)

Where the land is not disposed of in the same year, one-half of the apparent terminal loss on the building will be deductible, resulting in what is, in effect, an allowable capital loss on the sale of the building instead of an ordinary loss. However, the deductible amount of the loss will technically be considered a business loss.

Example Problem

Trash-it Limited owned a real property which it sold during the current taxation year for a total of $200,000. The land had a fair market value of $150,000 and an adjusted cost base of $100,000. The building had a fair market value of $50,000. It was the only building in the class which had an undepreciated capital cost of $75,000 and a capital cost of $90,000.

— REQUIRED

(A) Determine the tax consequences of the sale of the building in this transaction.

(B) If the purchaser wanted to buy only the building for $50,000 and remove it at his or her own expense to another location, what would be the tax consequences of the sale of the building?

— SOLUTION

(A) If proceeds of disposition of the building are considered to be equal to its fair market value of $50,000 which is less than the undepreciated capital cost of the class and the capital cost, the proceeds of disposition of the building will be deemed to be the following:

ITA: 13(21.1)(*a*)

P of D of building = lesser of:

(i)   (I) FMV of land and building $200,000

     minus

     (II) lesser of:

        — ACB of land .... $100,000 ⎫

        — FMV of land .... $150,000 ⎬   100,000

                                    $100,000

(ii) greater of:

     (I) FMV of building .... $50,000 ⎫

     (II) lesser of capital cost and UCC of

          building .... $75,000 ⎬ $75,000

= $75,000

Since proceeds of disposition are deemed to be equal to the undepreciated capital cost of the class, there is no terminal loss and no recapture. Note that proceeds of disposition of the land will be deemed to be:

(i) P of D of land and building.................. $200,000

minus

(ii) deemed P of D of building (above)............   75,000 $125,000

This will result in a capital gain of $25,000 on the land (i.e., $125,000 – $100,000).

If it were not for the rule being illustrated, there would have been a capital gain on the land of $50,000 (i.e., $150,000 – $100,000) and a terminal loss on the building of $25,000 (i.e., $50,000 – $75,000). The effect of the rule can be seen from the following comparison:

ITA: 13(21.1)(*a*)

Income effect	*Without* *par. 13(21.1)(a)*	*With* *par. 13(21.1)(a)*
Taxable capital gain on land:		
½ × $50,000	$ 25,000	
½ × $25,000		$12,500
Terminal loss on building...............	(25,000)	(Nil)
Effect on net income	NIL	$12,500

The rule has converted the terminal loss on the building, which is normally fully deductible, into an amount that is, in effect, only ½ deductible by reducing the gain on the land (which is only ½ taxable). Note that this conversion of a terminal loss only occurs if there is a capital gain on the land.

ITA: 13(21.1)(*a*)

(B) In this case, proceeds of disposition of the building will be deemed to be the following: ITA: 13(21.1)(*b*)

P of D of building = (i) P of D of building (without ssec. 13(21.1)) $ 50,000

    plus

    (ii) greater of:

        (I) UCC of building
            (Class 3) $75,000
                                                            } $75,000
        (II) FMV
            of building $50,000

        minus P of D of building in
            (i) above $50,000

        excess × ½ .... $25,000 × ½ $ 12,500

                                                            $ 62,500

    UCC of class...   75,000

    Terminal loss .... $(12,500)

Note how the decline in value of $25,000 from undepreciated capital cost to fair market value of the building has been rendered, essentially one-half deductible in this situation. This effect parallels that illustrated in part (A) above.

Disposal of Land and Building

Ssec. 13(21.1)

Summary

Key Question: Was there a capital gain on the land and a terminal loss on the building?

If so, an amount equal to the terminal loss (but not greater than the capital gain) will reduce the proceeds on the land and increase the proceeds on the building. This will reduce the capital gain and the terminal loss will be eliminated.

¶8,060   Election on Change in Use

When a taxpayer changes the use of property, he or she is deemed to have sold that property at the fair market value and to have reacquired the same property immediately thereafter at the fair market value which becomes his or her new adjusted cost base. Where property has a dual use, its cost must be apportioned between the uses on a percentage basis and that basis will be used on the disposition of the property. If the percentage for a particular use is changed either up or down, there will be a proportionate deemed disposition and reacquisition at the fair market value at that time.[1] Note that these rules are similar in concept to the rules pertaining to depreciable property with respect to changes of use and the capital cost allowance system.   ITA: 45(1)(*a*), 45(1)(*b*), 45(1)(*c*)

        ITA: 13(7)

The CRA indicates that a change in use does not include a transfer of property from one income-producing use to another such use by the same taxpayer. As examples, the CRA suggests that the change-in-use rules do not apply when real estate used to produce income from a business or property is converted to inventory, because holding the property as inventory is still an income-producing use. Similarly, the rules do not apply where inventory is converted to capital property which is used to produce income from a business or property. The Interpretation Bulletin provides numerical examples of how to handle these conversions   IT-218R, par. 11

        IT-218R, par. 15

---

[1] The case of *Woods v. M.N.R.*, 78 DTC 1576 (T.R.B.), illustrates the application of subsection 45(1) and the consequences of a deemed disposition.

to separate income gains from capital gains by the use of a "notional disposition". It is only on an actual disposition that income gains alone may be realized in these situations.

For personal-use property *only*, a taxpayer may elect to defer the capital gain until such time as he or she:

- decides to dispose of the asset;

- is deemed to dispose of the asset; or

- decides to rescind the election.

This election applies only when the property was used originally for personal use and remains in force until one of the above conditions occurs. For example, a taxpayer may have a yacht which is used for personal use. Later, the taxpayer decides to rent out his or her yacht. He or she may elect to defer the potential gain on the change in use. This election will remain in force even when he or she changes its use back to personal use unless, of course, he or she rescinds the election. However, this election is not available in a situation where the property was first used to produce income and then is changed to personal use.

ITA: 45(2)

Example Problem

A taxpayer purchased a yacht in 1999 at a cost of $24,000. In 2002, the taxpayer changed the use and rented the yacht for the next two years. The fair market value at the time the property became an income-producing asset was $30,000. During 2004, he converted the yacht back to exclusive personal use. The fair market value at this time was $33,000. In 2007, the taxpayer sold the yacht for $60,000.

— REQUIRED

Compare the taxable capital gain arising with and without the election to be deemed not to have changed the use.

ITA: 45(2)

— SOLUTION

	No election made by taxpayer	Ssec. 45(2) election made by taxpayer
2002		
Deemed proceeds of disposition	$30,000	
Less: adjusted cost base	24,000	
Capital gain	$ 6,000	
Taxable capital gain (½ × $6,000)	$ 3,000	Nil
2004		
Deemed proceeds of disposition	$33,000	
Less: adjusted cost base	30,000	
Capital gain	$ 3,000	
Taxable capital gain (½ × $3,000)	$ 1,500	Nil
2007		
Proceeds of sale	$60,000	$60,000
Less: adjusted cost base	33,000	24,000
Capital gain	$27,000	$36,000
Taxable capital gain (1/2)	$13,500	$18,000

Notes to Example Problem

Theoretically, there should be no difference in the total taxable capital gain between the two options available, only a timing difference in the payment of the tax. Where the inclusion

ITA: 45(2)

rate is constant, the election would normally be the preferred treatment, since the change in use has not generated any cash. Hence, there are a number of other factors to be considered:

(a) Does the taxpayer have any capital losses which he or she may wish to trigger?

(b) Will the taxpayer move to a higher tax bracket in the future?

(c) Conversely, does the taxpayer anticipate a decrease in income at some time in the future?

If the facts in the example problem had been reversed and the taxpayer had acquired the yacht for rental purposes and subsequently converted the yacht to personal use, this election would not be available. However, if the property was a rental building which was converted to personal use and was designated as a principal residence in a subsequent disposition, a rollover or deferral would be provided, as discussed subsequently. ITA: 45(3)

If an election is made not to have a change in use, then there will be no need to determine the UCC of the yacht, since it is deemed to still be personal-use property. If an election is not made, then a UCC must be determined and these rules, as explained in Chapter 5, will result in a UCC in 2002 of $27,000 (cost of $24,000 plus the TCG at 50% of $6,000). On the deemed disposition in 2004, there may be recapture to the extent that any CCA was claimed on the yacht. ITA: 45(2)
ITA: 13(7)

¶8,070   Principal Residence Revisited

¶8,075   Application of the change-in-use elections ITA: 45(2), 45(3)

The change-in-use election can also be used in connection with a principal residence where the initial change of use is from personal use to income-producing use. Paragraph (*d*) of the definition of a "principal residence" permits a taxpayer, who changes the use of his or her home, to choose to designate this home as his or her principal residence for up to four years, as long as he or she has elected not to have changed the use under subsection 45(2). You should note that the election and the designation as a principal residence are two separate and distinct acts. The CRA normally permits a taxpayer to file a retroactive election in connection with a principal residence *only*. A further consequence of the election is that the taxpayer cannot claim capital cost allowance against any income from that property. ITA: 45(2)

ITA: 54

ITA: 45(2)

IT-120R6

ITR: 1102(1)(*c*)

The definition of a "principal residence", together with another rule, provides for a similar four-year maximum designation in situations where the property was converted from an initial income-producing purpose to personal use and is designated as a principal residence. This election must be made on the earlier of 90 days after a ministerial demand or the normal filing due date (see Chapter 14) for the year of the disposition of the property. Note that this provision is not applicable in respect of recapture and this election will be revoked if any capital cost allowance is claimed. The combination of the two change-in-use elections cannot exceed four years. ITA: 45(3), 54

ITA: 45(4)
ITA: 45(2), 45(3)

The exemption formula discussed in the last chapter must now be modified to take into account a possible change in use as follows: ITA: 40(2)(*b*)

$$\frac{1 + \text{the number of years for which the property is designated after the later of December 31, 1971 and the date on which it was last acquired}}{\text{Number of years during which the property was owned after the later of December 31, 1971 and the date on which it was last acquired}} \times \text{gain realized}$$

"The date on which it was last acquired" can, if applicable, refer to a deemed reacquisition for personal use after a change in use.

Example Problem

Mr. On-the-Move owned a home in Calgary which he purchased in 1996. During 1999, he decided to relocate because of business reasons and moved to Vancouver. He rented an apartment in Vancouver and rented out his Calgary home. In 2005, he returned to Calgary to live in his original home. He anticipates selling the Calgary home in 2007 and retiring. The following data relates to his home:

Calgary home:	Cost	1996	$140,000
	FMV	1999	200,000
	FMV	2005	320,000
	Proceeds	2007 (estimated)	415,000

— *REQUIRED*

(A) Compute the minimum capital gain, based on the above information. Assume Mr. On-the-Move makes an election on a late-filed basis when he files his 2005 tax return.

ITA: 45(2); IT-120R6, par. 28

(B) Re-do Part (A) on the assumption that Mr. On-the-Move does not elect.

— *SOLUTION*

Part (A) — Election to be deemed not to have changed the use

ITA: 45(2)

When Mr. On-the-Move moves out of the Calgary home and begins to rent it out, there is a deemed disposition on the change in use. However, if he makes an election, then the result is that there is no change in use and the property remains a personal-use property. In addition, paragraph (d) of the definition of a "principal residence" provides that it is possible for this property to be designated as his principal residence for up to four additional years even though he is not living there. This would allow him to designate the property as his principal residence for the years 1996-1999 and 2005-2007 based on the years he lived there and for the years 2000-2003 based on the four additional years. The only year missing is 2004 and it is protected with the "1+" rule.

ITA: 45(2)
ITA: 54

	Calgary home
Gain	$ 275,000
Exempt portion	(275,000)[1]
Capital gain	Nil
Taxable capital gain	Nil

Since an election is made to deem there not to be a change in use of the Calgary home, then there is no need to determine UCC.

ITA: 13(7), 45(2)

Part (B) — No election

ITA: 45(2)

In 1999, when Mr. On-the-Move moves out of his Calgary home and begins to rent it to earn income, there is a deemed disposition on the change in use. Since he has been living in the house since he bought it in 1996, he can claim the principal residence exemption on the gain that results from the deemed disposition. By designating the years 1996 to 1998 he can eliminate the full gain as shown below.

ITA: 45(1)

	Calgary home
2000	
P of D, deemed	$ 200,000
ACB	(140,000)
Gain	$ 60,000
Exempt portion	(60,000)[2]
Capital gain	Nil

Since no election was made on the Calgary home, then the UCC in 1998 will be deemed to be $185,000 (cost of $140,000 plus the TCG at 75% of $60,000). On the deemed disposition of the Calgary home in 2005, there will be recapture to the extent that any CCA was claimed on the home between 1999 and 2005.

ITA: 13(7)

In 2005, when he returns to Calgary and moves back into the house, there is another change in use and a resulting deemed disposition. In this case the principal residence exemption can be claimed for the years 1999 and 2005, since the house was his principal residence at some point during each of those years.

	Calgary home
P of D — actual	$ 320,000
ACB — deemed	(200,000)
Gain	$ 120,000
Exempt portion	(51,429)[3]
Capital gain	$ 68,571
Taxable capital gain (½)	$ 34,286

Finally, when the Calgary home is sold in 2007, there would be no capital gain as shown below.

	Calgary home
P of D — estimated	$ 415,000
ACB — deemed	(320,000)
Gain	$ 95,000
Exempt portion	(95,000)[4]
Capital gain	Nil

In summary, by making no elections, he will report a capital gain of $34,286 in 2005 along with any recaptured CCA that also has to be reported.

If he had made the election in 2005 when the house was changed from income-producing to personal-use property, then the capital gain could be deferred and would not have to be reported until the actual disposition in 2007.

ITA: 45(3)

— NOTES TO SOLUTION

(1) $\dfrac{1 + 11}{12} \times \$275{,}000 = \$275{,}000$; 1996–1999 — owner-occupied

2000–2003 — paragraph (*d*) of the definition of "principal residence", maximum 4 years

2005–2007 — owner-occupied.

ITA: 54

(2) $\dfrac{1 + 3}{4} \times \$60{,}000 = \$60{,}000$; 1996–1998.

(3) $\dfrac{1 + 2}{7} \times \$120{,}000 = \$51{,}428$; 1999, 2005 — owner-occupied.

(4) $\dfrac{1 + 2}{3} \times \$95{,}000 = \$95{,}000$; 2006–2007.

¶8,080 Interpretation Bulletin IT-120R6 — Principal residence

The Interpretation Bulletin is an excellent example of how administrative practice differs from the actual law. For example, the term "ordinarily inhabited" has been interpreted by the CRA, for purposes of this section only, to mean "a short period of time in the year". However the facts of each particular case must be considered. Therefore, a taxpayer who abuses the application of this CRA interpretation could conceivably be reassessed and potentially taken to court on this issue.

IT-120R6, par. 5

One should note the difference between partial changes in use where there are no structural changes and partial changes where there are structural changes. In cases where the change in use is "ancillary" or secondary to the main purpose of the residence, the CRA's view is that no change has taken place for the purpose of this section. Therefore, the taxpayer may still designate the residence as a principal residence as long as he or she does not claim any capital cost allowance. Where the change is more substantial, then this option does not exist. In this case, the residence will have more than one use and each must be treated differently for tax purposes.

IT-120R6, par. 30, 31

¶8,085 Section 54.1 — Extended designation

This relieving provision was added to aid taxpayers and their spouses who are transferred by their employers to another location. In such an event, paragraph (*b*) of the definition of a "principal residence" applies, without the four-year limitation, as long as the taxpayer complies with the specific conditions of this subsection. Since nothing is said to the contrary, the aforementioned interpretation of the word "ordinarily" should stand.

ITA: 54

¶8,090 Subsection 40(4) — Transfer between spouses

¶8,090.10 *Single-ownership situations*

This provision enables the transfer of a wholly owned principal residence from one spouse to another with complete or partial relief from the taxation of the capital gain depending upon the principal residence designation circumstances. This rule does not apply to the interspousal transfer of a home which was previously *jointly-owned* (discussed later in this part of the chapter). The provision does apply where one spouse owns a residence solely and transfers this residence to the other spouse.

ITA: 73(1), 70(6)

ITA: 40(4)

A provision determines the period of ownership for the transferee spouse for purposes of the principal-residence exempting formula . The result is that the transferee spouse is deemed to have owned the property since the time the transferor spouse originally acquired it. Thus, the recipient spouse will be able to designate the home as a principal residence for the same years that it would have qualified for the transferor spouse.

ITA: 40(2)(*b*), 40(4)(*a*)

The years of designation by the transferee spouse for the period of ownership by the transferor spouse are those years which were actually designated by the transferor spouse, plus those years after the transfer for which the transferee spouse ordinarily resided in the transferred residence. This automatic interspousal rollover or deferral rule must be applicable (i.e., no election out of this rollover), so no gain would be recognized on the transfer.

ITA: 40(4)(*b*)

ITA: 73(1)
ITA: 40(4)(*b*)(ii)

It is recommended that a designation form be completed by the transferor spouse, even if it is not filed, so that the recipient spouse can determine the appropriate designation on the ultimate disposition of the property. This would fully protect the capital gain on the residence, if it had been the only one owned by the family unit.

If the transfer to the recipient spouse takes place as a result of the death of the transferor spouse, the actual designation requirement by the transferor spouse is removed, but the residence must have been ordinarily inhabited by the transferor spouse for the years before death that the recipient spouse chooses to designate the home.

ITA: 70(6)

ITA: 40(4)(*b*)(i)

Where two residences are owned by one spouse, the transfer of one of the residences to the other only offers partial relief because of the limitation of one principal residence per family unit for years after 1981. In this situation, the transferee spouse will be deemed to have owned the property since the time the transferor spouse originally acquired the property. However, the years of designation will be limited to those years in which the transferor actually designates the transferred residence as his or her principal residence plus those years in which the transferee spouse "ordinarily inhabited" the transferred residence.[2] Therefore, one of the two properties will be left unsheltered at least, in part, by the designation rules in paragraph (*c*) of the definition of a "principal residence". A disposition by, or the death of the spouse who owns the two properties would trigger a taxable capital gain on the less-designated property minus an exemption based on the ever-present extra year of designation (one-plus rule) and the number of years owned.

ITA: 54

Example Problem

Spouse A owns two residences:

	Residence 1	Residence 2
FMV	$100,000	$200,000
ACB	50,000	100,000
Year of acquisition	1995	1995

Both spouses have resided in the home since 1996. In 2002, Spouse A transferred Residence 2 to Spouse B as a gift. Spouse B sold the transferred residence in 2007 for $300,000. Spouse A has not designated, at any time, Residence 2 as his principal residence.

— REQUIRED

(A) Compute the effect of the above transaction as if subsection 40(4) did not exist.

(B) Apply subsection 40(4) to the transaction.

(C) Apply subsection 40(4) to the transaction on the assumption that spouse A had previously designated Residence 2 for two years.

---

[2] See the CRA technical interpretation document 9502557, February 9, 1995.

— SOLUTION

(A) As if subsection 40(4) did not exist

2002 —Transfer of residence to Spouse B (rollover automatically applies since the facts do not indicate that Spouse A elected not to have the rollover apply; refer to the discussion of the attribution rules later in this chapter for a more detailed explanation of this provision)   ITA: 73

P of D (deemed)	$100,000
ACB	(100,000)
Gain	Nil

ITA: 73

Note that no principal residence designation was required to reduce the gain to nil.

2007 —Spouse B sells home

P of D	$300,000
ACB (deemed)	(100,000)
Gain	$200,000

ITA: 73

Exemption . . . . . $\dfrac{1 + 5 \text{ years designated by B}}{6 \text{ years owned by B}} \times \$200,000 =$ (200,000)

Capital gain	Nil

Years of designation: any five of 2002 to 2007.

The gain of $200,000 was completely eliminated by Spouse B designating Residence 2 for five years under the principal residence rules, because:

- Spouse B owned the residence for six years (2002 to 2007, inclusive), and

- Spouse B ordinarily inhabited the residence for those years.

Hence, the entire gain is eliminated and Spouse A has saved the designation of years 1996 to 2001, plus one year of 2002 to 2007.

Note that there is no attribution since the capital gain is nil. However, depending upon the use of the $300,000 proceeds by Spouse B, there is potential attribution under the substituted property rule, discussed later in this chapter.

(B) With subsection 40(4)

2007 —Spouse B sells home

P of D	$ 300,000
ACB (deemed)	(100,000)
Gain	$ 200,000

ITA: 73

Exemption . . . . $\dfrac{1 + 10^{(1)}}{11^{(2)}} \times \$200,000 =$ (200,000)

Capital gain[3]	Nil

The application of subsection 40(4) results in the same nil capital gain, but has eliminated all the principal residence designation years for Spouse A for Residence 1, except for one year.

(C) The answer would be the same as Part (B). The years designated would be the two years designated by Spouse A, plus eight years by Spouse B for a total of 10 years, thereby, eliminating the entire gain.

— NOTES TO SOLUTION

(1) Spouse B can designate the transferred residence for the actual years or deemed years that he or she owned and ordinarily inhabited the residence (10 years) plus any other years for which Spouse A made a designation (in this case nil).

(2) The number of years owned includes the ownership years of Spouse A.   ITA: 40(4)(*a*)

(3) The taxable capital gain, if any, will be attributed back to Spouse A, if realized during his or her lifetime.

Additional Notes:

● If this transfer had been as a consequence of Spouse A's death, the years of designation available would be expanded to include the potential designations available to Spouse A (or his or her legal representative). Hence, the entire gain would be exempt, but Residence 1 could not be designated for the years used to designate Residence 2.

● This example was designed to demonstrate how subsection 40(4) is applied and no tax planning was taken into account. Some of the factors which should be considered would be:

　　● the relative size of the future gain on the two homes;

　　● the tax rates of the respective spouses who own the homes; and

　　● the potential application of the attribution rules to the ultimate non-exempt capital gains on the homes.

¶8,090.20 *Joint-ownership situations*

Where two residences are each jointly owned by spouses, subsection 40(4) does not have   ITA: 54
any effect, since the definition of a "principal residence" governs years of joint ownership. Hence, each spouse enjoys an unrestricted right to designate either residence as his or her principal residence under the exemption formula. A transfer of ownership so that one resi-   ITA: 40(2)(*b*)
dence is wholly owned by one spouse and the other residence is wholly owned by the other spouse will maximize the potential principal residence designation for years owned before 1982. Therefore, there will be no tax consequences, since both spouses have owned, although only partially, the residence for the entire period. The transferee spouse can designate the entire residence as his or her principal residence.

As previously mentioned in Chapter 7, after 1981 the legislation permits only one principal residence exemption per family which would include spouses and single children under 18.

¶8,100 Leaving and Entering Canada

Tax rules for taxpayers who become or cease to be resident in Canada are provided by   ITA: 128.1
the Act. When a taxpayer ceases to be a resident of Canada, all of that person's capital   ITA: 128.1(4)
property is deemed to have been disposed of at its fair market value. Such capital property would consist of shares, including shares of private corporations, bonds, real estate outside Canada, boats, recreational vehicles and automobiles, among others. Where the taxpayer is an individual, the following properties, generally, those that would be subject to Canadian tax in the hands of a non-resident, are exempted from the deemed disposition:

(a) Property that can be described, conceptually, as:

　　● Canadian property that is not very movable, such as real property or capital property used in a business carried on through a permanent establishment in Canada, or

　　● Canadian property that is not very liquid or marketable, such as employment-related stock options.

The taxpayer will continue to be liable for tax on the disposition of such property, but as a non-resident. However, the taxpayer may elect not to have this exemption apply so that capital gains (losses) are triggered to offset other capital losses (gains).   ITA: 2(3)

(b) Property of a business carried on by the individual in Canada. Income from such property, including capital property, eligible capital property and property described in the inventory of the business, will be taxable as business income earned by a non-resident.   ITA: 2(3)

(c) The right to receive certain payments such as pension payments and other retirement benefits, including rights under RRSPs, RPPs and DPSPs, or a right under a registered education savings plan on which the taxpayer will be liable for withholding tax.

A taxpayer is prevented from triggering only allowable capital losses while protecting potential taxable capital gains through the available elections previously described. In this situation, losses, except listed personal property losses, are restricted to the taxable capital gains actually triggered by the deemed disposition.   ITA: 128.1(4)

The Act provides an exception in the case of a short-term resident of Canada. The tax on departure does not apply to capital property which an individual owned on last becoming a resident of Canada, if he or she resided in Canada for 60 months or less during the 10 years preceding his or her departure. Under these conditions, he or she will be exempt from the deemed disposition on any property, which he or she brought with him or her and took away again. Also exempt is property acquired by inheritance or bequest after the individual last became resident in Canada. However, the taxpayer will still be subject to the rules of this section on other property he or she acquired while he or she was resident in Canada.   ITA: 128.1(4)

To set the cost of property for a person entering Canada such that the taxpayer is taxed only on gains subsequent to his or her entry, the Act provides that where a taxpayer becomes a Canadian resident, he or she is deemed to have acquired all of his or her property other than taxable Canadian property and inventory or eligible capital property of a business carried on in Canada at its fair market value at the time.   ITA: 128.1(1)

¶8,110 Options   IGNORE

There are two basic types of option: an option to buy property (known as a call option) and an option to sell property (known as a put option). As a general rule, when an option is granted, there is a disposition of a property with an adjusted cost base of nil by the grantor or issuer. The result is a capital gain to the grantor in the amount of the proceeds for the option. The grantee or holder of the option has acquired a capital property with an adjusted cost base equal to the amount paid for the option. If the option expires, the grantor's or issuer's tax position remains unchanged and the grantee has a capital loss in the year of expiration.   ITA: 49(1)

There are two exceptions to the general rule noted above.

- When an option in respect of a principal residence is granted, there is no disposition. As a result, if an option on a principal residence expires, there would have been no inclusion for the grantor and, therefore, no tax effect. The grantee would be denied a loss on expiration, because the option on a principal residence would be regarded as a personal-use property.   ITA: 49(1)(a), 40(2)(g)(iii), 54

- The other exception is for an option granted by a corporation to another person to buy securities to be issued by the corporation. In this case, the corporation has no disposition at the time the option is granted. However, if the option expires, the corporation is deemed to have disposed of a capital property with an adjusted cost base of nil. The proceeds are deemed to be equal to the amount, if any, received for granting the option. As a result, when this type of option expires, a capital gain is realized.   ITA: 49(2)

If an option to acquire property (i.e., a call option) is exercised, then the granting of the   ITA: 49(3)
option and its exercise are deemed not to be a disposition. Also, note that when the option is
exercised, there is a disposition of the property underlying the option and the grantor or
issuer becomes a vendor and the grantee or holder becomes a purchaser. On the exercise of
the option, the vendor of the optioned property must include the consideration, received for
the option, in proceeds of disposition of the property sold in the year in which the option is
exercised. The vendor, who was the grantor of the option, can file an amended return for the
year, in which the amount received for the option was included in income, to remove the
amount received for the option from income for that year. This amended return must be filed   ITA: 49(4)
by the time the return for the year, in which the option was exercised, must be filed. The
purchaser of the property must add the cost of the option held to the cost of the property.

If an option to sell property (i.e., a put option) is exercised, the rules are similar to those   ITA: 49(3), 49(3.1)
for the exercise of a call option. Note, however, that the grantor of a put option is the
purchaser of the property on exercise of the option and will have been paid an amount by the
vendor of the underlying property. The granting of the option and its exercise are deemed not
to be a disposition of property. The vendor of the optioned property, who paid for the right to
"put" or sell the property to the purchaser of the optional property, must deduct the amount
paid for the option from proceeds of disposition of the property sold. The purchaser of the
optioned property must deduct the amount received for the put option from the cost of the
property acquired. The grantor of the option (i.e., the purchaser of the property in this case)
can file an amended return for the year in which the amount received for the option was
included in income and to exclude the amount received for the option from income in the   ITA: 49(4)
year of the grant.

The basic rules for the taxation of options as capital property are summarized in
Exhibit 8-1.

EXHIBIT 8-1
Basic Rules for Taxation of Options as Capital Property

Event	Option to buy property (Call)		Option to sell property (Put)	
	Grantor (Seller)	**Grantee (Buyer)**	**Grantor (Buyer)**	**Grantee (Seller)**
Option granted	• Amount received for option included as capital gain	• Amount paid for option is ACB of option	• Amount received for option included as capital gain	• Amount paid for option is ACB of option
Option exercised	• Amount received for option added to proceeds of underlying property sold	• Amount paid for option added to ACB of underlying property purchased	• Amount received for option deducted from cost of underlying property purchased	• Amount paid for option deducted from proceeds of underlying property sold
	• File amended return (if necessary) for year option granted to remove capital gain from income		• File amended return (if necessary) for year option granted to remove capital gain from income	
Option expired	• No change in tax position	• Amount paid for option realized as a capital loss	• No change in tax position	• Amount paid for option realized as a capital loss

Example Problem

Ms. Smart owned a capital property that had an adjusted cost base of $100,000. In 2005, she granted Mr. Shnook an option to buy the property from her by the end of 2007 at an option price of $160,000. Mr. Shnook paid $16,000 to Ms. Smart for the option.

— *REQUIRED*

(A) What are the income tax implications to Ms. Smart and Mr. Shnook in 2005?

(B) What are the income tax implications to Ms. Smart and Mr. Shnook in 2007 if:

(i) the call option expires?

(ii) the call option is exercised?

— *SOLUTION*

(A) In 2005, Ms. Smart has granted a call option with an adjusted cost base of nil and proceeds of disposition of $16,000. On this disposition, in 2005 she must report a capital gain of $16,000. Mr. Shnook has acquired a capital property in the option with an adjusted cost base of $16,000.

(B)(i) If the option expires at the end of 2007, because Mr. Shnook chooses not to exercise it and acquire the capital property, then there are no further tax implications to Ms. Smart. She has already included the capital gain in 2005 on granting the option and she retains the capital property with an adjusted cost base of $100,000. In 2007, Mr. Shnook has a capital loss of $16,000, since the option held at that cost has become worthless on expiration. Of course, that capital loss can only be applied to a capital gain in the current year, 2007, the three preceding years, 2004, 2005, and 2006, or any year subsequent to 2007.

(ii) If the call option is exercised in 2007 and Mr. Shnook acquires the property for $160,000, then Ms. Smart can file an amended return for 2005 to remove the $16,000 capital gain from her income in that year. However, her proceeds of disposition on the sale in 2006 will amount to the $160,000 received as the agreed price under the option plus the $16,000 received for the option in 2005. Thus, she will report in 2007 a capital gain of $76,000 (i.e., $160,000 + $16,000 − $100,000). Mr. Shnook will have acquired the property which will have an adjusted cost base of $176,000 (i.e., $160,000 + $16,000).

¶8,120 Debts Established to be Bad Debts

Where a debt taken back from the purchaser of a capital property is established to have become a bad debt, the seller can elect to have disposed of the debt and to have reacquired it immediately at a cost equal to nil. The deemed disposition results in a capital loss to offset any part of the gain on disposition of the property represented in the debt. The deemed reacquisition at a nil cost may result in a further capital gain if any part of the debt is ultimately collected.

ITA: 50(1)

A deemed disposition of the shares of an insolvent corporation occurs to realize the capital loss if:

ITA: 50(1)(b)(iii)

- neither the corporation nor a corporation controlled by it carries on business in the year;

- the fair market value of the shares is nil;

- it is reasonable to expect that the corporation will be dissolved or wound up and will not start to carry on business; and

- the taxpayer elects to have this provision apply.

There will be another deemed disposition for proceeds of disposition equal to the ACB of the shares before the subsection 50(1) deemed disposition if:

ITA: 50(1.1)

- the taxpayer elects a deemed disposition; and

ITA: 50(1)(b)(iii)

- within 24 months of the disposition the corporation or a corporation controlled by it carries on business and the taxpayer or a non-arm's length person owns the shares.

This deemed disposition will result in the realization of a capital gain equal to the capital loss realized by the election. The shares are deemed to be reacquired at the adjusted cost base immediately before the disposition.

ITA: 50(1)(*b*)(iii)
ITA: 50(1.1)

Note that there is no provision for an "allowance for doubtful debts" in computing capital gains. At best, a reserve is provided for the uncollected gain portion of the proceeds, payable after the end of the year. This, of course, does not help the taxpayer when the amount of the debt is payable in the year but not collectible, because the debt has become bad. Also, the treatment of a bad debt resulting from the disposition of personal-use property is different. In that case, the Act allows a capital loss, only to the extent of the capital gains on the original disposition.

ITA: 50(2)

¶8,130   Convertible Properties

Where a taxpayer acquires shares from a corporation on the conversion of a convertible security, referred to as a convertible property, the exchange is deemed not to have been a disposition of property. The cost to the taxpayer of the shares received is deemed to be the adjusted cost base to him or her of the convertible property immediately before the exchange. There is a further condition in this rollover provision that the taxpayer must not have received any consideration (such as cash) other than shares in exchange for his or her convertible property.

ITA: 51

Consider, as an example, a convertible debenture acquired at face value of $100. The conversion privilege entitles the holder to five common shares. If the privilege is exercised, the taxpayer is deemed to have acquired the new shares at $20 each ($100/5). If the fair market value of the shares is $30 each, the taxpayer has effectively deferred recognition of a $50 per bond or a $10 per share capital gain.

¶8,140   Capital Gains Deferral   *Ignore*

An individual is permitted to defer the recognition of a capital gain in respect of certain small business investments. To obtain the deferral, the proceeds from the sale of the small business investment must be used to acquire other small business investments. The deferred gain on the old investments will reduce the ACB of the new investments, which is similar to the treatment of replacement property discussed earlier.

ITA: 44.1(2)

The following are some of the considerations:

- The individual can establish a permitted deferral less than the maximum amount available by designating a lesser amount of replacement shares.

- The permitted deferral is the amount of a capital gain from the disposition that can be deferred. It reduces the gain of the individual for the disposition.

- A "permitted deferral" of an individual is calculated using the formula

  $(G/H) \times I$ where

  G   is the lesser of the individual's proceeds of disposition from the old small business investment and the cost to the individual of a replacement share;

  H   is the individual's proceeds of disposition from the old small business investment; and

  I   is the individual's capital gain from the old small business investment.

- A qualifying disposition of an individual is a disposition of common shares of the capital stock of a corporation owned by the individual where each such share was:

  - an eligible small business corporation share of the individual,

- a common share of the capital stock of an active business corporation throughout the time it was owned by the individual, and

- owned by the individual throughout the 185-day period that ended immediately before the disposition.

- The active business of the corporation has to be carried on primarily in Canada at all times in the period that began when the individual last acquired the share and ended when the disposition occurred (the "ownership period"), if that period is less than 730 days. In any other case that active business has to be carried on primarily in Canada for at least 730 days during the ownership period.

ITA: 44.1(9)

- The term "eligible small business corporation" is relevant for the purposes of the term "eligible small business corporation share". An eligible small business corporation, at a particular time, means a Canadian-controlled private corporation all or substantially all of the fair market value of the assets of which is, at that time, attributable to assets of the corporation that are

  - assets used principally in an active business carried on primarily in Canada by the corporation or an eligible small business corporation related to it,

  - shares of or debt issued by other eligible small business corporations related to the corporation, or

  - a combination of those two types of assets.

An asset of the corporation that is a share or a debt issued by a related corporation is deemed to have a carrying value of nil.

An eligible small business corporation share of an individual is a common share issued by a corporation to the individual where:

- at the time the share is issued, the corporation was an eligible small business corporation and immediately before, and

- after that time the total carrying value of its assets and the assets of corporations related to it does not exceed $50 million.

Example Problem

Jennifer S. Lee disposes of shares of corporation A with an adjusted cost base of $3,000,000 for proceeds of disposition of $4,500,000. Jennifer immediately purchases replacement shares in corporations B with a cost of $2,200,000 and in corporation C with a cost of $2,300,000. All shares are eligible small business corporation shares.

— *REQUIRED*

Compute the capital gain, after the deferral, on the disposition of the shares of corporation A and the ACB of the replacement shares in corporations B and C.

— *SOLUTION*

Jennifer's capital gain without the deferral would be calculated as:

Capital gain otherwise determined:

Proceeds	$4,500,000
ACB	3,000,000
Capital gain	$1,500,000

Permitted deferral:

G/H × I = $4,500,000/$4,500,000 × $1,500,000 =	$1,500,000

G = lesser of:

    1. Proceeds of disposition = $4,500,000

    2. Cost of replacement shares = $4,500,000

H = Proceeds of disposition = $4,500,000

I = Capital gain = $1,500,000

Jennifer's capital gain that will be reported is calculated as follows:

Capital gain otherwise determined	$1,500,000
Less: Permitted deferral	1,500,000
Capital gain	$ Nil

The ACB reduction is determined by the formula D × (E/F) found in the definition of the reduction, and is applied as follows::   *ITA: 44.1(1)*

Corporation B: $1,500,000 × ($2,200,000/$4,500,000) = $ 733,333

Corporation C: $1,500,000 × ($2,300,000/$4,500,000) = $ 766,667

Note that the sum of the ACB reductions is $1,500,000, which is equal to the total capital gain deferred.

The adjusted cost base of the replacement shares is, therefore:

Corporation B: $2,2000,000 – $733,333 = $1,466,667

Corporation C: $2,300,000 – $766,667 = $1,533,333

Note that the sum of these ACBs is $3,000,000, which is actual cost net of the permitted deferral.

¶8,150   Certain Shares Deemed to be Capital Property

Where a person disposes of all or substantially all of the assets used in an active business to a corporation, the shares received in consideration are capital property of that person. This provision allows a person to transfer business assets to a corporation in exchange for shares, then sell the shares and have the gain or loss treated as a capital gain or loss. It should be noted that the definition of "business" for purposes of this provision does not include an adventure or concern in the nature of trade. As a result, it must be an ongoing business that is transferred, not just a trading asset.   *ITA: 248(1) "business"*   *ITA: 54.2*

¶8,200   NON-ARM'S LENGTH TRANSFERS AND THE ATTRIBUTION RULES REVISITED

¶8,210   Non-Arm's Length Transfers

¶8,215   Who does not deal at arm's length?

The non-arm's length transfer rules are designed to prevent tax avoidance in certain transactions between persons not dealing at arm's length. The term "arm's length" is defined by providing that related persons are deemed not to deal with each other at arm's length. A taxpayer (or anyone not dealing at arm's length with the taxpayer) and an *inter vivos* or testamentary trust cannot deal at arm's length, if the taxpayer is an income or capital beneficiary of the trust.   *ITA: 69(1)*   *ITA: 251(1)(a)*   *ITA: 251(1)(b)*

It is a question of fact whether persons not related to each other are dealing with each other at arm's length. The CRA sets out in an Interpretation Bulletin the following criteria, which have generally been used by the courts to determine whether a transaction has occurred at "arm's length": ITA: 251(1)(*c*)
IT-419R2

- was there a common mind which directs the bargaining for both parties to a transaction?;

- were the parties to a transaction acting in concert without separate interests?; and

- was there "de facto" control?

Refer to paragraphs 24 and 25 of the bulletin for more details on these points. These conditions may arise in dealings between business partners or close friends.[3]

Summary
Who Does Not Deal at Arm's Length
Subsection 251(1)

1. Related persons.
2. A beneficiary, or anyone not dealing at arm's length
with the beneficiary, and the *inter vivos* or testamentary trust.
3. It is a question of fact.

Related persons are further defined in terms of individuals and corporations. Related individuals are those connected by blood, marriage or adoption and these connections are further specified. A schematic diagram of related individuals under the Act was presented in Chapter 6 as Exhibit 6-2. Non-arm's length relationships between persons and corporations require control, either by one person or a group of related persons. Control in this situation means control of more than 50% of the voting shares. The concept of control is expanded in situations involving related groups and in the case of a person holding certain options. The subsection also indicates that a person is deemed to be related to himself or herself in cases where the person owns shares in two or more corporations. Remember that the word "person" is defined to include a corporation such that two corporations can be related. Furthermore, two corporations are related if they meet one of the six conditions set out in the Act. ITA: 251(2), 251(2)(*b*),
251(6); IT-419R2, par. 11

ITA: 251(5)

ITA: 248(1)
ITA: 251(2)(*c*)

¶8,220 Transactions with non-arm's length individuals

¶8,220.10 *Overview*

Normally, the market forces of demand and supply will place the value of a transaction at fair market value. However, non-arm's length transactions may not reflect a normal transaction driven by the market forces. For that reason, the Act deems related persons not to deal at arm's length with each other. In addition, it is a question of fact whether unrelated persons deal with each other at arm's length. ITA: 251(1)(*a*)

ITA: 251(1)(*c*)

When a taxpayer enters into a transaction with a related party (non-arm's length person) or with an unrelated party in which the transaction is considered not to be at arm's length, special rules apply to prevent the elimination or reduction of tax by selling at a price other than the fair market value. ITA: 69

¶8,220.20 *Conceptual Illustration*

Assume that Mr. A owns a property with a fair market value of $10,000 and that he originally paid $5,000 for that property. He decides to sell the property to his daughter, who is under 18, for $8,000. Note that this price is lower than the fair market value (FMV).

---

[3] In the case of *Grant et al. v. M.N.R.*, 87 DTC 16, the Tax Court of Canada describes in some detail the factors to be taken into account in determining whether unrelated persons are not dealing at arm's length.

Tax consequence to Mr. A:

	Sale at $8,000	*Sale at $10,000*
Deemed proceeds of sales (FMV)	$10,000	$10,000
Cost base (original payment)	(5,000)	(5,000)
Gain	$5,000	$5,000

If Mr. A's daughter sells the property immediately at $10,000 (FMV), she will have to recognize a gain of:

	Sale at $8,000	*Sale at $10,000*
Proceeds of sales	$10,000	$10,000
Cost base (amount she paid)	(8,000)	(10,000)
Gain	$2,000	Nil

Total gain from the transaction:

	Sale at $8,000	*Sale at $10,000*
Mr. A	$5,000	$5,000
Daughter	2,000	Nil
Total	$7,000	$5,000

If Mr. A sold the property to his daughter at fair market value, the total gain will be $5,000. Since the related party did not use fair market value as consideration, a total gain of $7,000 is subject to tax which means that the $2,000 gain is taxed twice. These special anti-avoidance rules in the Act penalize taxpayers who enter into transactions which are not at fair market value.

ITA: 69

A penalty similar to the above also occurs when the selling price is higher than the fair market value.

¶8,220.30   *The technical rules*

Generally, in situations involving the non-arm's length transfer of anything, including both tangible and intangible property, the transferor is deemed to receive proceeds equal to its fair market value at the time of the transfer, if the actual transfer price is less than fair market value. This rule would include gifts for no proceeds. Note, however, that no downward adjustment is made to the actual price received if it is more than fair market value. On the other side, the transferee is deemed to have acquired property at a cost equal to its fair market value at the time of the transfer if he or she paid more than fair market value or if he or she received it as a gift, bequest or inheritance, but not if he or she paid less than fair market value. In the case of a payment of less than fair market value, no adjustment is made to the actual price paid. There are exceptions to these rules on the transfer of such property to a spouse under certain conditions.

As mentioned previously, non-arm's length transfers, for a price either greater than or less than fair market value, can involve a one-sided adjustment to the transfer price. This can be more easily seen in Exhibit 8-2. Where the amount is in excess of fair market value only the purchaser is deemed to have transacted at fair market value with the seller having received proceeds at the higher price. Thus, the seller may have income or a capital gain on the transaction and the purchaser may ultimately have to include a similar amount of income or capital gain on disposition. Where the amount is less than fair market value, but the transfer is not a gift, the seller is deemed to have received proceeds equal to fair market value while there is no adjustment made to the actual price paid by the purchaser. Again, the seller may have income or a capital gain on the transaction and the purchaser may ultimately have to include a similar amount of income or capital gain on disposition. In this case, a gift would be better since both the transferor and the transferee are deemed to have made the transfer at fair market value and no double-counting will result.

These rules have implications for the operation of the capital cost allowance system in these cases. Deeming proceeds of disposition and cost of acquisition to be the fair market value will affect potential recapture of capital cost allowance on disposition and the base on which capital cost allowance is computed on acquisition.

EXHIBIT 8-2
Consideration in Gifts and Non-arm's Length Transfers

Non-arm's length transfer	*Seller or transferor*	*Purchaser or transferee*
Proceeds greater than fair market value	no adjustment to actual proceeds received	deemed acquisition at fair market value [par. 69(1)(*a*)]
Proceeds less than fair market value	deemed proceeds at fair market value [par. 69(1)(*b*)]	no adjustment to actual amount paid
Gift, bequest or inheritance	deemed proceeds at fair market value [par. 69(1)(*b*)*]	deemed acquisition at fair market value [par. 69(1)(*c*)*]

* Note that these fair market value rules apply to gifts even at arm's length.

Where the property being transferred between non-arm's length parties is depreciable property, there are special rules to determine what the undepreciated capital cost (UCC) of the property is to the acquirer. The results depend on whether an election is made under the interspousal rollover not to have the automatic rollover apply and whether there is an accrued gain on the property at the time of transfer.

ITA: 13(7)(*e*)

ITA: 73(1)

If no election is made on the interspousal transfer, then the property will automatically roll over at UCC. If an election is made, then the property will be disposed of at fair market value and the UCC of the property to the acquirer will be deemed to be equal to:

ITA: 73(1)
ITA: 13(7)(*e*)

Cost of the property to the transferor immediately before the transfer

plus: the taxable capital gain realized on the transfer

The addition of only the taxable capital gain restricts the UCC of the property to the transferee to the amount on which the transferor has paid tax.

¶8,230 Attribution Rules

¶8,235 Capital gains on spousal transfers or loans

In Chapter 6, the attribution rules, relating to income from property only, were discussed for transfers and loans. Capital gains and losses are also similarly attributed back, but only to the transferor spouse or common-law partner for all transfers (i.e., gifts and sales) or for loans. Capital gains and losses arising from transfers and loans to related and deemed related minors do not result in attribution to the transferor (except for *inter vivos* transfers of farming property which is tax-deferred by a rollover and beyond the scope of this text). A series of anti-avoidance provisions apply attribution to transactions such as:

ITA: 74.2(1)

ITA: 75.1

- back-to-back loans and transfers to third parties,

ITA: 74.5(6)

- repayment of loan through additional transfers and loans,

ITA: 74.1(3)

- loan guarantees for all or part of the principal and/or interest, or

ITA: 74.5(7)

- artificial transactions which use the attribution rules to the taxpayer's advantage.

ITA: 74.5(11)

"Common-law partner" is defined as "a person who cohabits ... in a conjugal relation- ITA: 248(1)
ship with the taxpayer ... for a continuous period of at least one year".

The justification for the attribution of capital gains on property transferred between ITA: 73
spouses or common-law partners is found in the interspousal rollover rule, which has the
effect of deferring any accrued gains on transfers between spouses or common-law partners.
The deferral occurs because the transferor is automatically deemed to have transferred the
property at proceeds exactly equal to his or her adjusted cost base immediately prior to the
transfer. Note here that the transfer is an actual transaction which must be reported, even
though the gain is nil. The transferee spouse, or common-law partner, will have an adjusted
cost base exactly equal to the deemed proceeds of disposition at the time of transfer (the
transferor spouse's, or common-law partner's, adjusted cost base). When the transferee
spouse, or common-law partner, disposes of the property, the gain or loss will be attributed
back to the transferor spouse, or common-law partner, as long as they are married or in a
common-law relationship.

The provision which pertains to the attribution of capital gains, continues to apply to ITA: 74.5(3)(b)
spouses, or common-law partners, living apart by reason of a breakdown of their marriage or
common-law relationship. In this situation, however, when both spouses or common-law ITA: 74.5(3)(b)
partners have jointly elected, capital gains attribution does not apply. The election must be
filed with the tax return of the transferor spouse or common-law partner in any year ending IT-511R, par. 20
after the separation occurs. Note that this provision is much harsher than the attribution
relieving provision for income from property which does not require that an election be filed. ITA: 74.5(3)(a)

Alternatively, the transferor spouse or common-law partner can elect not to have inter- ITA: 73(1)
spousal rollover apply and the normal non-arm's length rules apply under section 69 as
previously discussed. Hence, the property will be deemed to have been disposed of at the fair
market value at the date of transfer. There would be no capital gains attribution on subsequent dispositions of transferred property, as long as consideration equal to the fair market
value of the property transferred was received by the transferor and the taxpayer elected not
to use the interspousal rollover. If the consideration included a loan, then the interest rate
must be on a commercial basis (the lesser of the prescribed rate at the time the loan was ITA: 74.5(1)(a),
made and the non-arm's length rate as determined by the marketplace) and the accrued 74.5(1)(c)
interest must be actually paid no later than 30 days after each and every December 31 that
the loan is outstanding. ITA: 74.5(1)(b)

If the property is sold to a spouse or common-law partner at less than the fair market
value and the taxpayer elects not to use the interspousal rollover, there would be a double
penalty.

- First, the attribution rules would apply to both income and capital gains, since the fair ITA: 74.5(1)(a)
  market value of the property transferred and the consideration received are not equal.

- Second, the adjusted cost base of transferred property would be the actual price paid
  by the acquiring spouse and not the deemed proceeds of disposition of the transferor
  spouse since the adjustment to fair market value is one-sided. Hence, the avoided ITA: 69(1)(c)
  capital gain would be taxed twice.

If, however, the transfer had been a gift, then both the proceeds and the adjusted cost ITA: 69(1)(b)(ii), 69(1)(c)
base would be bumped to the fair market value. Again, the attribution of future income and
capital gain would not have been avoided, however, since no consideration was received.

¶8,240 Recapture

In order to prevent the avoidance of recapture on the transfer of depreciable property ITA: 73(2)
between spouses, the following additional rules apply. When the undepreciated capital cost is
less than the capital cost to the transferor, then for purposes of capital cost allowance
computations:

(a) the capital cost to the transferee is deemed to be the capital cost to the transferor;
    and

(b) the difference between the capital cost and the deemed capital cost to the spouse
    will be treated as a capital cost allowance taken by the transferee.

¶8,245   Summary of provisions

**Summary
Avoiding Income Attribution
On Transferred Property**

Subsection 74.5(1) — Fair Market Value Transfer
1. Fair market value consideration must be received by the vendor.
2. If part of the consideration is debt then interest must be charged at the prescribed rate and always paid by January 30 of the following year.
3. If it is a transfer to a spouse or common-law partner, then they must elect out of the interspousal rollover.

Subsection 74.5(3) — Relationship Breakdown
4. The spouses or common-law partners are living separate and apart by reason of the breakdown of their relationship.

Exhibit 8-3 expands the exhibit on property income attribution rules introduced in Chapter 6 to include the application of the capital gains attribution rules discussed in this chapter. Exhibit 8-4 summarizes the rules pertaining to minors and other non-arm's length persons.

**EXHIBIT 8-3
Transfers or Loans of Property to Spouse or Common-law Partner
Conceptual Summary**

(A) Proceeds and Cost on Transfer

Transaction	*Transferor's proceeds*	*Transferee's cost*
(1) gift ● no election out of inter-spousal rollover*	Transferor's ACB/UCC	Transferor's ACB/UCC
● elect not to have rollover	FMV [par. 69(1)(*b*)]	FMV [par. 69(1)(*c*)]
(2) sale ● no election out of inter-spousal rollover	Transferor's ACB/UCC	Transferor's ACB/UCC
● elect not to have rollover	greater of: ● actual proceeds ● FMV [ssec. 69(1)]	Lesser of: ● actual cost ● FMV [ssec. 69(1)]

(B) Attribution of Income and Capital Gains

	Business income	*Property income***	*Capital gains****
On transferred or loaned property and substituted property****	n/a	Attributed [ssec. 74.1(1)]	Attributed [sec. 74.2]

However, neither property income nor capital gains are attributed if the following two conditions are met:
 (1) fair market consideration is received,***** and
 (2) the election out of the interspousal rollover is used.

---

* The interspousal rollover applies *automatically* on a transfer of property between spouses or common-law partners at the ACB of the property; that is, the transferor spouse or common-law partner is deemed to have received proceeds of disposition equal to ACB and the transferee spouse or common-law partner is deemed to have acquired the property at the same ACB. However, the provision contains an election that allows the spouses or common-law partners not to have the rollover apply, in which case the normal non-arm's length rules apply to the transaction which will be considered to have taken place at fair market value.

** Including losses but excluding second-generation income from property.

*** Including capital losses and including second-generation capital gains (losses) after December 31, 1987.

**** Substituted property is defined in subsection 248(5).

***** To avoid attribution, the taxpayer must elect to waive the deferral of accrued income afforded by the interspousal rollover and must transfer for fair market value consideration. Where a loan is involved, interest must be paid within 30 days of the end of every year in which the loan is outstanding.

EXHIBIT 8-4
Transfers or Loans of Property to Minors and Other
Non-arm's Length Individuals
Conceptual Summary

(A) Proceeds and Cost on Transfer

	Transferor's proceeds	*Transferee's cost*
(1) gift	FMV [par. 69(1)(*b*)]	FMV [par. 69(1)(*c*)]
(2) sale	greater of: ● actual proceeds ● FMV [ssec. 69(1)]	Lesser of: ● actual cost ● FMV [ssec. 69(1)]

(B) Attribution of Income and Capital Gains

	Business income	*Property income**	*Capital gains*
Minors** who are not at arm's length (generally, related) or who are nieces and nephews . . . ● on transferred*** or loaned property and substituted property****	n/a	Attributed [ssec. 74.1(2)]	n/a
Other non-arm's length individuals not subject to section 74.1 ● only on loaned property if one of the main reasons for the loan was to reduce or avoid tax	n/a	Attributed [ssec. 56(4.1)]	n/a

---

* Including losses but excluding second-generation income from property.

** An income-splitting tax applies at the top marginal tax rate on dividends or shareholder benefits received by minors from private corporations and certain income from a partnership or trust. (See Chapter 6 for a discussion of this provision.) Income that is subject to the income-splitting tax is not be subject to the attribution rules.

*** To avoid attribution the taxpayer must transfer for fair market value consideration. Where a loan is involved, interest must be paid within 30 days of the end of the year in which the loan is outstanding.

**** Substituted property is defined in subsection 248(5).

¶8,300   DEATH OF A TAXPAYER

¶8,310   Deemed Disposition on Death

Capital gains may be triggered upon the death of a taxpayer depending on the status of the beneficiaries and the type of assets transferred. Death is the final opportunity to tax unrealized gains that have accrued to the taxpayer. Generally, the taxpayer is deemed to have disposed of all his or her capital assets at their fair market value as at the date of his or her death.

ITA: 70(5)(*a*)

In respect of non-depreciable capital assets transferred on death to a spouse, the basic rules are similar to those on transfer between living spouses. The deceased is deemed to have disposed of the assets at his or her adjusted cost base and the surviving spouse or common-law partner assumes that cost base. Hence, no capital gain or recapture will be triggered unless the estate so elects not to have the interspousal rollover on death apply, or until the surviving spouse or common-law partner disposes of the assets. ITA: 70(6), 73

ITA: 70(6.2)
IT-305R4

Depreciable property received by a beneficiary, other than a spouse or common-law partner, is also deemed to be disposed of at fair market value at the date of death. Any resulting capital gain or recapture would be included on the deceased's final return. The beneficiary's deemed cost would be the fair market value of the property received. However, if the fair market value was less than the original cost, then the beneficiary's cost would be the deceased's cost and the excess of cost over fair market value would be deemed to have been taken as CCA. As a result, the beneficiary's UCC is the fair market value. Where a spouse or common-law partner is the beneficiary of depreciable property and where no election out of the rollover has been filed, the proceeds of disposition are deemed to be the undepreciated capital cost prorated on a capital cost basis. ITA: 70(5)(a)

ITA: 70(6.2)

Chapter 14 discusses, in some detail, the various filing alternatives available upon death of a taxpayer.

¶8,400   INCOME RECONCILIATION REVISITED *SKIP*

One of the major adjustments to accounting income in its conversion to income for tax purposes is the exclusion of book gains and losses on the disposition of capital property and the inclusion of taxable capital gains and allowable capital losses.

Example Problem

Capital Transactions Ltd. has disposed of the following capital assets during 2007:

	Proceeds of disposition	Cost	Book value	Undepreciated capital cost
Securities	$ 500	$ 5,000	n/a	n/a
Land	52,500	30,000	n/a	n/a
Building*	76,250	20,000	$ 3,000	$4,500
Equipment**	500	10,000	1,000	1,500

* Ignore section 44 considerations.
** Only asset in class.

— *REQUIRED*

Indicate the adjustments to be made in the reconciliation of accounting income to income for tax purposes.

— *SOLUTION*

Reference	ADDITIONS	
Sec. 3	Securities — book loss: ($500 – $5,000)	$ 4,500
Sec. 38	Land — taxable capital gain: ($52,500 – $30,000) × ½	11,250
Sec. 38	Building — taxable capital gain: ($76,250 – $20,000) × ½	28,125
Sec. 13	Building — recapture: ($4,500 – $20,000)	15,500
Sec. 3	Equipment — book loss: ($500 – $1,000)	500
		$ 59,875

Reference	DEDUCTIONS		
Sec. 38	Securities — allowable capital loss: ($500 – $5,000) × ½	$	2,250*
Sec. 3	Land — book gain: ($52,500 – $30,000)		22,500
Sec. 3	Building — book gain: ($76,250 – $3,000)		73,250
Par. 39(1)(*b*)	Equipment — capital loss		Nil
Ssec. 20(16)	— terminal loss ($1,500 – $500)		1,000
		$	99,000

* Can only be deducted to the extent that there are taxable capital gains.

¶8,800   REVIEW QUESTIONS

(1) Mrs. Snowbird has been going south for many years and usually keeps some U.S. currency handy in case she needs it. This year, because of some unusual fluctuations in the Canadian dollar, she realized an exchange loss on her U.S. dollar transactions of $2,500. How will this be taxed?

(2) Mr. Cottage bought six acres of lake-front property 15 years ago for $24,000. This year, he sold the three acres that are not on the lake to a neighbour who wanted the woodlot. His proceeds on the three acres sold are $30,000. Discuss what the cost base of the three acres sold would be.

(3) Mr. Farmer had 20 acres of his farm expropriated by the city for industrial land in 2006. Because he disputed their value, the proceeds were not finally decided until 2007 How soon does he have to replace the land in order to defer the tax on the capital gain realized on the sale of the land?

(4) Opco Ltd. had a large piece of equipment destroyed by fire with the insurance proceeds being paid and the machine replaced in the same year. Can the replacement property rules be applied?

(5) Mrs. Smith owns 100% of Holdco Inc. which in turn owns 100% of Opco Inc. Holdco owns the building which is used by Opco in its active business and rents it to Opco under a 5-year lease. Mrs. Smith wants to sell the building and buy a bigger one for the same purpose, but she has been told that the building is considered to be a rental property and, therefore, does not qualify for the replacement property rules since it is not a "former business property". She has asked for your comments.   ITA: 248(1)

(6) Mr. Carr bought and operated a parking lot for the past 10 years. He has now decided that it is time to do something different. However, instead of selling the parking lot he wants to rezone the property and develop and sell condominium apartments. On July 1 of last year, he applied for rezoning and on December 1 of last year, he received the zoning change and a building permit. By October 31 of this year, he had completed construction and sold the units. What kind of income would he have to report and when?

(7) On July 1 of this year, John Smith died leaving his wife and four children in financial difficulty. In order to earn extra income Mrs. Smith painted the basement, put carpet down, and then rented it to students. Comment on the tax issues.

(8) On July 1 nine years ago, Ms. Mover was transferred with her family to Victoria from Toronto by her employer, a large public company. She was sure that the value of her Toronto house would go up significantly so she kept it and rented a house in Victoria. It was this year that the same employer moved Ms. Mover and her family back to Toronto, at which time they moved back into their house. However, they found that the neighbourhood had changed significantly so they decided to sell the house and buy in another location. Discuss how much of the principal residence exemption she can claim on the sale of the Toronto home.

(9) Last year Ms. Madeit inherited $5 million from her uncle's estate and is now appalled by the amount of tax that she has to pay on her interest income. She has always liked the Cayman Islands and has decided to move there permanently in order to avoid Canadian tax. Her only assets are $5 million of term deposits but she has heard that there is a lot of tax to pay on leaving the country. What do you think?

(10) Mr. State was transferred to Canada by his employer four years ago and is now being transferred back to the U.S. At the time he entered Canada he held shares in his U.S. employer which are listed on the TSX Stock Exchange. He still owns all these shares and is unhappy about all the tax he is going to have to pay on the deemed disposition. Advise him.   ITA: 128.1(4)

(11) Ms. Green has been told that a good way to create a capital gain is to buy shares on the stock market and then sell someone an option to buy the shares at a price slightly higher than the current market price. Her understanding is that the proceeds on the sale of the option is a capital gain. What advice can you give her?

(12) Mr. Oats is a farmer who is fortunate enough to have farm land close to the city. Because of the prime location he has been approached to sell the land, but he is reluctant to do so since he wants to farm for the next five years. However, he is willing to sell someone an option to buy the land in five years at what he thinks is a generous price. He is to receive $50,000 for granting this option. He thinks he can defer the gain on granting the option until the year of sale by reducing the ACB of his land by $50,000. What do you think?

(13) Last year Ms. Sorry sold some land that was capital property and realized a capital gain of $150,000. As part of the proceeds she took back a note for $100,000 at 12% which unfortunately was unsecured. This year she realized that the note will become a bad debt, but since she has not disposed of

the note she does not think that it can be used for tax purposes. What is your advice to her? What would be the result if the land that was sold was personal-use property?

(14) Mr. Roller bought a convertible debenture two years ago for $10,000 and is now in the process of converting it into common shares of the company. The debenture is convertible into 1,000 common shares. At the time of the conversion the common shares are worth $20 each. What are the tax effects of the disposition of the debenture and the acquisition of the shares?

(15) Mrs. Generous owns 20 acres of land that have an appraised value of $100,000. She is considering selling the land to a friend for $50,000 in order to have the friend living closer to her. The two individuals are not related. What tax issues would you discuss with her?

(16) Scott was 25 years old when his father Bill gave him shares in Bell Canada as a gift. Bill had paid $1,000 for them 10 years ago and they were worth $5,000 at the time of the gift. Scott has come to you to find out how much tax he will have to pay. Discuss the tax implications to Scott and Bill of the gift.

¶8,825 MULTIPLE CHOICE QUESTIONS

Question 1

Mega Ltd., which has a May 31 year-end, had its land and building expropriated on June 30, 2007, and received $1 million of compensation from the government for the expropriation. Which one of the following is the deadline for Mega Ltd. to replace the property with another property costing at least $1 million in order to defer the entire recapture and capital gain on the disposition of the expropriated property?

(A) On or before May 31, 2009.

(B) On or before June 30, 2009.

(C) On or before December 31, 2009.

(D) On or before May 31, 2010.

Question 2

On December 31 of this year, Ms. Y gave her six-year-old child some common shares of a public corporation with an adjusted cost base of $900,000 and a fair market value of $1,000,000. Which one of the following statements is TRUE?

(A) The attribution rule will apply to attribute to Ms. Y any future dividends received by her child on the shares. This attribution will continue until the year in which the child becomes 18 years old.

(B) The attribution rule will apply to attribute to Ms. Y any future dividends received by her child on the shares as well as any capital gains or losses if her child sells the shares. This attribution will continue until the year in which the child turns 18 years of age.

(C) Ms. Y will report no gain or loss on the transfer of property this year because it is a gift.

(D) Ms. Y will report a $100,000 taxable capital gain on the gift this year.

Question 3

Ms. Y sells a stock (adjusted cost base $900,000) to her husband for $800,000 cash (the fair market value of the stock) and elects out of the interspousal rollover. Which one of the following statements is TRUE?   ITA: 73(1)

(A) Ms. Y will report an allowable capital loss of $50,000 which she can only deduct against taxable capital gains.

(B) Ms. Y does not have a capital loss because transfers to a spouse are made for proceeds equal to adjusted cost base.

(C) Ms. Y does not have a capital loss because of the superficial loss rules.

(D) The attribution rule will apply to attribute to Ms. Y any future dividends received by her husband on the shares as well as any capital gains or losses if her husband sells the shares.

Question 4

Mr. T ceased to be a resident of Canada on September 1, 2007. At that date, he owned the following assets:

	Year acquired	Cost	Fair market value Sept. 1, 2007
Rental real estate in Canada.	1992	$50,000	$100,000
Registered retirement savings plan	2000	60,000	80,000
Painting.	2003	6,000	10,000
Shares of a public corporation (listed) resident in Canada (owns less than 1%)	2004	10,000	40,000

Which one of the following amounts represents Mr. T's minimum taxable capital gain on the above assets for 2007?

(A) $15,000

(B) $17,000

(C) $27,000

(D) $42,000

Question 5

Mr. Smith died on June 30 of this year and left his entire estate to his son, Mark. His executor has provided you with a list of assets and their fair market value at the date of death.

List of Assets	Cost	Fair Market Value
Toronto home (sole principal residence since 1990)	$100,000	$240,000
Rental property in London, Ontario		
— Land	50,000	100,000
— Building (UCC: $2,000)	25,000	35,000
Mutual fund units	12,000	60,000
Shares of a public companies	90,000	100,000

What is the amount that must be included in Mr. Smith's Division B income for the year of death?

(A) $59,000

(B) $70,500

(C) $82,000

(D) $152,000

Question 6

Gary Chin purchased his first and only principal residence in 1990 for $50,000. The residence was in Toronto, and when he was transferred to Windsor because of a promotion to managing partner in 2001, he rented the residence. The residence was worth $150,000 in 2001 and he elected to be deemed not to have changed the use of the residence. Gary rented an apartment in Windsor with the expectation of moving back into his Toronto residence on retirement. On January 1, 2007, Gary received an unsolicited offer of $250,000 for the Toronto residence and sold it. Which of the following is a true statement?

ITA: 45(2)

(A) There is no taxable capital gain to report in 2001 or 2007 in respect of the principal residence.

(B) There is no capital gain to report in 2001 in respect of the principal residence. The taxable capital gain is $5,556 in 2007 in respect of the principal residence.

(C) The taxable capital gain is $50,000 in 2001 and $50,000 in 2007 in respect of the principal residence.

(D) The taxable capital gain is $100,000 in 2007 in respect of the principal residence.

¶8,850 EXERCISES

Exercise 1

ITA: 39(2)

When he was vacationing in Florida this year, Joe Retired sold, for US$10,000, his antique car which he purchased four years ago for C$4,000. Joe was paid in U.S. dollars. The Canadian currency was valued at 87¢ U.S. at the time of the sale. When Joe returned, he converted the U.S. currency to Canadian dollars and received $11,765 Canadian dollars.

— REQUIRED

Compute the taxable capital gain or allowable capital loss, if any, arising on the above transactions.

Exercise 2

ITA: 13(4), 44

Tax Processing Ltd.'s computer was completely destroyed in a fire in 2005. The insurance company has been disputing the claim. In the meantime, the company is renting computer time until the claim is settled. The following facts relate to the destroyed computer:

Capital cost	$50,000
UCC immediately before the fire — Class 10	17,150

During 2006, the insurance company paid $60,000 in respect of the claim. The company continued to rent computer time for another 24 months when it then purchased a new-generation computer for $70,000.

— REQUIRED

Indicate the tax consequences for Tax Processing Ltd. for the above years.

Exercise 3

ITA: 40(2)(b), 45, 54, 54.1

Howard Homeowner, who presently lives in Vancouver, is considering moving to Montreal. Although Howard intends to purchase a home in Montreal, he does not want to sell his fully-paid Vancouver home in case he decides to return some time in the future. Howard would rent his Vancouver home which cost him $50,000 in 1993 and now has a fair market value of $350,000.

— REQUIRED

Discuss the tax implications concerning Howard's Vancouver home if:

(A) Howard is self-employed; or

(B) Howard is employed.

Exercise 4

ITA: 128.1(4), 115

Mr. Emigrant, a United States citizen, entered Canada on June 1, 2002, and became resident in Canada for tax purposes. Mr. Emigrant had a capital asset A which he brought with him upon his entry to Canada. The cost of the asset was $2,000 and the fair market value was $5,000 at the time of entry. In 2003, Mr. Emigrant purchased another capital property B for $10,000. Mr. Emigrant is considering returning to the United States on a permanent basis in 2007. He estimates that the two properties will have fair market values of $12,000 for A and $20,000 for B.

— REQUIRED

Discuss the tax consequences of Mr. Emigrant's pending departure from Canada.

Exercise 5

ITA: 49

Doctor Quick, a general practitioner, has decided to move into a larger office/residence. On July 1, 2006, he paid $5,000 to Devalued Properties Ltd., a developer, for a one-year option to purchase a residential building which he would use 50% for business and 50% as his principal residence. On February 1, 2007, Dr. Quick assigned his option to another medical practitioner, Dr. Slow, for $2,000. On May 1, 2007, Dr. Slow exercised the option and paid $100,000 for the building.

— *REQUIRED*

Discuss the tax implications in the above situation for Doctors Quick and Slow and for Devalued Properties Ltd.

Exercise 6

ITA: 251

Which of the following individuals are not at arm's length with Ms. Gamma:

(A) her brother's wife?

(B) her niece?

(C) her husband from whom she is legally separated?

(D) an unrelated person?

Exercise 7

James Meadows is not at arm's length with his son Hayden. James wants Hayden to have a painting that cost him $1,200 and now has a fair market value of $1,500. What are the consequences under the non-arm's length transfer rules to James and Hayden if:

ITA: 69(1)

(A) he sells the painting to him for $2,000?

(B) he sells the painting to him for $1,200?

(C) he gives the painting to him without any financial consideration?

Exercise 8

ITA: 73, 74.1, 74.2, 74.5; IT-511R

Alice Attribution is considering the following courses of action in transferring assets to her spouse this year:

(A) gifting to her husband shares with a fair market value of $15,000 and an adjusted cost base of $12,000;

(B) selling to her husband shares with a fair market value of $15,000 and an adjusted cost base of $12,000 for cash of $15,000. An election out of the interspousal rollover was made;

ITA: 73(1)

(C) selling to her husband shares with a fair market value of $15,000 and an adjusted cost base of $12,000 for a $15,000 non-interest bearing promissory note with a definite repayment period;

(D) gifting to her husband $15,000 such that he purchases the shares on the open market; and

(E) lending her husband $15,000 evidenced by a non-interest bearing promissory note with a definite repayment period such that he purchases the shares on the open market.

— *REQUIRED*

Discuss the tax implications arising from the above transactions and any subsequent disposition by the spouse.

Exercise 9

ITA: 20(1)(*l*), 20(1)(*p*), 22, 38, 39, 50

Reconsider Exercise 9 of Chapter 4 and explain the tax implications if Mr. Flogger and Mr. Sucker do not use the section 22 election on the sale of the accounts receivable.

¶8,875 ASSIGNMENT PROBLEMS

Problem 1

ITA: 13(4), 44

During its year ended December 31, 2007, Power Boat Corporation Ltd. sold its facilities in downtown Toronto. As the sale occurred in December, business activity was at a low. New facilities were purchased in February 2008 in Parry Sound on the shores of Georgian Bay. The corporation sold its Toronto land and building for $300,000 and $200,000, respectively. This land and building had a cost in 1991 of $50,000 and $100,000, respectively. At the end of 2006, the building had an undepreciated capital cost of $55,000 for income tax purposes. In Parry Sound, the corporation purchased land and building for $75,000 and $350,000, respectively.

— REQUIRED

(A) Prepare two calculations of the income tax consequences of the above move, one without an election for additional deferral and one with this election. ITA: 44(6)

(B) If the property disposed of by the corporation in 2007 had been an apartment building held for rental purposes:

(i) what would the tax consequences of a sale of the property have been after a replacement of the property with another apartment complex in 2008?

(ii) what would the tax consequences on an expropriation have been after a replacement of the property with another apartment complex in 2008?

Problem 2

ITA: 13(4), 44

On March 1, 2007, Raymond Fan, a sole proprietor, sold his garden supply store in downtown Toronto to a competitor because of declining sales caused by competition from large suburban hardware and grocery stores. The following information relates to the sale of the business:

	Proceeds	Cost	UCC/ CEC Jan. 1, 2007
Accounts receivable	$ 6,000	$10,000	—
Land	120,000	65,000	—
Building — Class 3	170,000	62,000	$28,000
Equipment — Class 8	3,000	1,200	300
— Class 10	4,000	12,000	800
Inventory	5,200	7,000	—
Goodwill	52,000	—	—

Raymond's business year-end coincided with the calendar year. Raymond has been in the same business since 1989. As of December 31, 2006, there was a balance in the allowance for doubtful accounts for tax purposes of $1,300.

Subsequent to the sale of the business, Raymond worked for his brother, Kevin, who owned a shoe store. However, Raymond became bored and when a garden supply store on a busy highway north of Toronto came on the market in late November 2008, he immediately bought it. The following information relates to his purchase of assets of the new business:

Land	$105,000
Building	220,000
Equipment — Class 8	9,000
— Class 10	11,000
Goodwill	Nil

— REQUIRED

(A) Compute the minimum amount Raymond must include on his 2007 tax return in respect of the sale of the business, before any election is made to defer capital gains and recapture. ITA: 13(4), 44

(B) Show the effect on Raymond's 2007 (amended) and 2008 tax returns if he elects to defer capital gains and recapture after purchasing the new business, but does not elect for additional deferral.

ITA: 13(4), 44
ITA: 44(6)

(C) Discuss whether Raymond should have elected for additional deferral.

(D) If the above situation had been an involuntary disposition instead of a voluntary disposition, how would your answer under part (B) differ?

Problem 3

ITA: 13(21.1)

Johnny Derelict had purchased a dilapidated apartment block, The Eyesore, 20 years ago for $220,000. At the time, the purchase price had been allocated $80,000 to the land and $140,000 to the building. The Eyesore is the only building Johnny owns and is considered a Class 3 asset for CCA purposes. To date, Johnny has claimed CCA of $37,000.

HighBrow Towers has acquired all the lots in the same block as Johnny's building, except for The Eyesore. Johnny realized that as the last hold-out he was in an enviable negotiating position with HighBrow. HighBrow was desperate to gain ownership of The Eyesore and tear it down. After receiving ever-escalating offers, Johnny agreed to accept HighBrow's offer of $1,000,000.

— *REQUIRED*

Advise Johnny regarding the allocation of the purchase price between the land and building.

Problem 4

ITA: 40(2)(*b*), 45(2), 54

Ms. Andrews purchased a home in Waterloo in 1997 at a cost of $86,000. She lived in the home until January 29, 2000, at which time she moved to Vancouver and rented a home in Vancouver. At the time of the move, Ms. Andrew's Waterloo residence had risen in value to $230,000. Expecting that real estate prices would continue to rise, Ms. Andrews chose to retain ownership of her Waterloo home and rented it to a third party.

In June 2006, Ms. Andrews decided she missed living in Waterloo and chose to return. She returned to Waterloo where she took up residence in her Waterloo home. At the time, the Waterloo residence had a fair market value of $294,000. In March 2007, Ms. Andrews decided she was tired of living in the city. She sold her Waterloo home for $284,000 and moved to the countryside.

Prior to filing her 2007 personal tax return, Ms. Andrews has requested your advice in minimizing the capital gains she must report on the sale of her home.

— *REQUIRED*

Calculate the minimum capital gain for Ms. Andrews on the sale of her home under the following circumstances:

(A) assuming that Ms. Andrews elects to be deemed not to have changed the use, and

ITA: 45(2)

(B) assuming that the election is not made.

Problem 5

ITA: 7, 69, 73, 74.1, 74.2,
74.5, 56(4.1), 110(1)(*d*)

During 2006, Madame Moneybucks exercised a stock option that she held in her employer (a CCPC). It is now November 2007. She is currently contemplating a number of scenarios in terms of the shares she received under the 2006 stock option exercise. She has asked you to explain the tax consequences of her actual and contemplated transactions.

The details of the stock option exercised during 2006 are as follows.

Number of shares purchased	Exercise price	Fair market value of shares at exercise date	Fair market value of shares at grant date
6,000	$20	$35	$20

The current fair market value of a share is $42.

Madame Moneybucks is married and has two children (ages 21 and 15). She is expecting large dividends to be paid on the above shares in December 2007 and each December on an ongoing basis. She also expects that the shares will increase in value quite considerably over the near future. As a result, she is looking for a means of splitting income with her immediate family. She is proposing the following scenarios in terms of distributing these shares amongst her immediate family:

(1) gift the shares to her spouse and children (⅓ to her spouse and ⅓ to each child);

¶8,875

[handwritten: DEEMED AT FMV]

[handwritten: ↗74.5 ↗120.4]

(2) sell the shares to her spouse and children (⅓ to her spouse and ⅓ to each child) for cash proceeds of $20 per share; or

[handwritten: 69(1)(b)]

(3) sell the shares to her spouse and children (⅓ to her spouse and ⅓ to each child) in exchange for a note payable of $42 per share. *[handwritten: CAPITAL GAIN] ADJUSTED COST BASE EQUAL TO THE SALE]*

The note payable described in (3) above will be payable over five years with no interest. Since the note pays no interest and is repayable over future years, the estimated present value of the note is $25 per share.

— REQUIRED

Prepare a memorandum to Madame Moneybucks explaining the income tax consequences of her completed and proposed transactions.

Problem 6

ITA: Subdivisions b and c; ETA: 123(1), 169(1), 170(1)(a), 174, 231, 236

PITA Co. Ltd. is a nutritional consulting firm that advises manufacturers and distributors on consumers' dietary needs and preferences. For its year ended December 31, 2007, it reported net income before taxes of $900,000 for financial statement purposes. This amount included a gain on the disposition of land held as capital property of $50,000 and of a building (not the only one in the class) of $95,000. The corporation also realized an accounting loss of $20,000 on securities and of $10,000 on a trademark. These assets were acquired for the following amounts:

> land . . . . $120,000 in 1996
>
> building . . . . . 100,000 in 1996 (UCC of the class is $125,000)
>
> securities . . . . 50,000 in 2005
>
> trademark . . . . 80,000 in 2004

The proceeds of disposition of these assets were as follows:

> land $150,000
>
> building 120,000
>
> securities 30,000
>
> trademark 70,000

The corporation has reported accounting depreciation of $80,000 and wishes to claim the maximum available capital cost allowance of $100,000. During 2007, the corporation also made payments in respect of interest on unpaid income taxes ($1,500), charitable donations ($10,000), and an annual employee dinner-dance in December 2007 ($14,000). During 2007, the corporation established that an unsecured $5,000 note receivable in respect of the sale (as capital property) of a parcel of land in the prior year had become a bad debt. This was not reflected in the financial statements.

— REQUIRED

(A) Prepare a reconciliation between net income for financial statement purposes and net income for income tax purposes for the year ended December 31, 2007. Support your reconciliation with references to the *Income Tax Act*.

(B) Discuss in general terms the treatment of these items by the corporation for purposes of the GST.

Problem 7

ITA: 13(7)(e), 70(5)(a), 70(5)(b), 70(5)(c), 70(6)(d), 70(6)(e); ITR: 1100(2)(h), 1102(14)(d)

On July 31, 2007, Mary McArthur passed away after a lengthy illness. Mary was survived by her husband and one adult child, Margaret. Both her husband and daughter are residents of Canada. Information related to Mary's assets as at July 31, 2007, is set out below.

[handwritten: NO ATTRIBUTION FOR OLDER CHILD OF DIVIDENDS OR CAPITAL GAINS]

Description	Cost	UCC	Fair market value	Beneficiary
Rental property — Toronto, Ontario				
Land	$40,000	n/a	$ 100,000	Spouse
Building (Class 3)	55,000	$15,000	145,000	Spouse
Rental property — Stratford, Ontario				
Land	25,000	n/a	45,000	Daughter
Building (Class 1)	65,000	42,000	93,000	Daughter
CBS shares (see Note below)	nil	n/a	1,000,000	Spouse
Bell Canada shares (see Note below)	nil	n/a	150,000	Daughter

Note:

Mary inherited these shares from her father upon his death in 2005. Her father had an adjusted cost base of $250,000 in the CBS shares. The fair market value of the CBS shares on the date of his death was $500,000. Her father had an adjusted cost base of $150,000 in the Bell Canada shares. The fair market value of the Bell Canada shares on the date of his death was $180,000.

— REQUIRED

(A) Compute the minimum income and/or taxable capital gains to be reported by Mary McArthur for 2007 in respect of the above noted assets. Ignore any available elections.

(B) Determine the cost amounts of the above assets to the respective beneficiaries.

[For more problems and solutions thereto, see the CD accompanying this book.]

¶8,880   ADVISORY CASES

Case 1: Belleville Furniture Inc.

Belleville Furniture Inc. ("Belleville") is a manufacturer of high-quality dining room furniture. This is the second generation of the Parker family that has owned the company, and the founder's son, Dave Parker, is having some problems since foreign imports are being brought into Ontario and sold at a price lower than Belleville's cost. Dave is certainly concerned about the short term, but feels that within the next eight to twelve months Belleville can adjust its sourcing of raw materials and the manufacturing process in order to reduce its costs to the point where its can be competitive, not only in the local market, but also in the North-Eastern United States.

Dave's immediate problem is that when he asked the bank to increase Belleville's operating line of credit enough to cover Belleville's operational problems for the next eight to twelve months, the bank became concerned since its sole security for the operating loan is the inventory and the under 90-day accounts receivables. To maintain the existing line of credit, and to even consider the increase, the bank wants personal guarantees from both of Dave and his wife, Nancy, as well as a collateral mortgage on the company's building. As a result, Dave has you working on cash flow projections to support the loan, his lawyer is preparing the collateral mortgage, and an appraiser is preparing a valuation of the property. Dave feels that his chances of being approved are good.

Dave has agreed that he will sell the 20% interest that he personally owns in a company that operates a lumber mill that supplies Belleville. Dave bought the shares from the company on incorporation five years ago for $50,000 to help the arm's length supplier start the lumber mill. The other 75% of the company is owned by the supplier who has agreed to have his holding company buy the shares from Dave for $40,000 in cash. Dave had borrowed all the money for this investment through an interest-only demand loan with the bank. The bank has agreed to leave the full amount of the loan outstanding as long as Dave contributes the full $40,000 of proceeds into Belleville.

To prepare for its entry into the U.S. market, Belleville will set up a U.S. dollar bank account at its local bank for deposits from U.S. customers.

Dave would like your advice on the tax implications of his situation.

Case 2: Sudbury Processing Inc.

Sudbury Processing Inc. has had some tough times. In December 2005, just before its December 31st year end, there was a fire in its processing plant which destroyed the building and most of the contents. Tom Haskett, the owner, had to move fast to get back in operation before he lost customers to the competition.

Tom owns all the shares of Sud Holdings Inc. ("Holdings"). Holdings owns all the shares of Sudbury Processing Inc. ("Processing"), which is the operating company. Holdings also owns the land, building, and equipment used by Processing (the ones destroyed by fire).

In order to get back into business, Tom had Processing lease a new building until he could make arrangements for a new permanent home. He had some delay in making any new arrangements, because he and the insurance company had a difference of opinion on the replacement value of the building and equipment that were destroyed. They eventually agreed in March 2007, and Holdings received the cheque shortly thereafter for the building, equipment, and some repairs. However, the delay meant Tom had to make alternate arrangements for acquiring new equipment, so Processing entered into an equipment lease with an option to buy it at the end of the five-year term. Luckily, Processing had business interruption insurance, which paid it $10,000 per month for four months until it was up and running again.

In July 2007, Tom made the final decision on a new factory. He decided not to build at the old location. Instead, that land is being sold and new property is being bought with the intention of constructing a new building in the next couple of years. On the sale of the existing land, the purchaser wants a warranty that there are no environmental problems as a result of the fire. Holdings and the purchaser agreed that if there were any problems, then Holdings would pay $20,000 of the purchase price back. Rather than purchase the new parcel of land at this time, Tom has had Holdings buy an option to acquire the land at any time in the next two years for an agreed-upon price.

Advise Tom on the tax implications of Sudbury's situation.

¶8,900   SUPPLEMENTAL NOTES

(This section can be omitted without losing the continuity of the chapter. None of the review questions, multiple choice questions, exercises or assignment problems utilizes this information.)

¶8,910   Pre-1972 Assets Revisited

¶8,915   Non-depreciable capital property

In the preceding chapter, several adjustments to the cost base were demonstrated for assets purchased *subsequent* to December 31, 1971. However, with non-depreciable assets held on this date, the median rule is one of the two methods used to establish adjusted cost base at the beginning of 1972. The effect of this rule is to adjust proceeds of disposition, as used in the median rule, by reversing any section 53 adjustments that are made to adjusted cost base after 1971. Note that despite the length of time elapsed since 1971, long-term fixed assets, such as land, may be still disposed of currently.

ITA: 53

ITAR: 26(3)
ITAR: 26(3)(c)

There are three distinct steps in arriving at the adjusted cost base of non-depreciable assets owned on December 31, 1971.

Step 1. Calculate the "adjusted proceeds" by taking the actual proceeds and reversing the ACB adjustments, that is, by adding to proceeds of disposition reductions to the cost base and deducting from proceeds of disposition additions to the cost base.

ITA: 53

Step 2. Use the adjusted proceeds in Step 1, in arriving at the median figure or "deemed cost," that is, in comparing the three relevant amounts in the median rule, to establish adjusted cost base at January 1, 1972.

Step 3. Calculate the adjusted cost base at the time of the disposition by adding or subtracting the actual section 53 adjustments, as required, to the "deemed cost".

Step 4. Calculate the capital gain or loss in the normal manner.

Example Problem

The following information relates to the sale of land which is capital property purchased in 1968:

	Situation (a)	Situation (b)	Situation (c)
	(Expressed in thousands (000s))		
Cost (1968)	$ 80	$ 80	$ 80
Valuation-day value	120	120	120
Proceeds of disposition in 1999	150	100	50
Ssec. 18(2) denial of interest and property taxes	10	10	10

— REQUIRED

Determine the taxable capital gain on the 1999 disposition using the median rule.

ITAR: 26(3)

— SOLUTION

The denial of the deduction for interest and property taxes results in an addition to the cost base.

ITA: 18(2), 53(1)(*h*)

Situation (a)

Step 1: Adjusted proceeds ($150 – $10) $140

Step 2: Deemed cost = median of:
  (a) Cost . . . . $ 80 ⎤
  (b) Valuation-day value . . . . . .   120 ⎬ $120
  (c) Adjusted proceeds . . . .   140 ⎦

Step 3: ACB ($120 + $10) $130

Step 4: P of D (actual) $150
  ACB . . . .   (130)
  CG . . . . $ 20
  TCG (¾ × $20) . . . . $ 15

Situation (b)

Step 1: Adjusted proceeds ($100 – $10) . . . . $ 90

Step 2: Deemed cost = median of:
  (a) Cost . . . . $ 80 ⎤
  (b) Valuation-day value . . . . . .   120 ⎬ . . . . $ 90
  (c) Adjusted proceeds . . . .   90 ⎦

Step 3: ACB ($90 + $10) $100

Step 4: P of D (actual) $100
  ACB . . . .   (100)
  CG . . . .   Nil
  TCG (¾ × Nil) . . . .   Nil

Situation (c)

Step 1: Adjusted proceeds ($50 – $10) . . . . $ 40

Step 2: Deemed cost = median of:
  (a) Cost . . . . $ 80 ⎤
  (b) Valuation-day value . . . . . .   120 ⎬ . . . . $ 80
  (c) Adjusted proceeds . . . .   40 ⎦

Step 3: ACB ($80 + $10) . . . . $ 90

Step 4: P of D (actual) . . . . $ 50
  ACB . . . .   (90)
  CL . . . . $(40)
  ACL (¾ × $40) . . . . $(30)

¶8,920   Depreciable property

One of the important exceptions to the use of the median rule is "depreciable property". Paragraph (*a*) of the definition of "adjusted cost base" in the Act defines the adjusted cost base of depreciable property as being its capital cost. Hence, for depreciable property, the median and fair market value rules which determine the adjusted cost base at the beginning of 1972 for capital assets owned on December 31, 1971, cannot apply. However, in order to avoid taxing the accrued gain until Valuation day, a special rule applies, to adjust proceeds of disposition rather than adjusted cost base. The adjustment is necessary only when the capital cost is less than both:

ITAR: 20(1)(*a*), 26(3), 26(7); ITA: 54

(a) Valuation-day value, and

(b) proceeds of disposition.

Where the capital cost is greater than either of the above amounts, then the capital cost is the adjusted cost base. It should be emphasized that there can be no capital loss on the disposition of depreciable property. Any such decline in value is handled through the capital cost allowance system.

ITAR: 20(1)(*a*)

Assume, for example, that proceeds of disposition are $10,000; V-day value is $7,000; and capital cost is $5,000. In this case, the capital gain would be computed in the following manner:

Capital cost		$5,000
Plus the excess, if any		
Proceeds of disposition	$10,000	
Less: V-day value	7,000	3,000
Deemed proceeds		$8,000
Less: capital cost		5,000
Capital gain		$3,000

Note that the effect of the ITAR is to adjust actual proceeds so that the difference between the adjusted or deemed proceeds and capital cost is equal to the capital gain since V-day. In the example, this amount is $3,000 (i.e., $10,000– $7,000). The definition of adjusted cost base for depreciable property is the original capital cost with no adjustment. Therefore, were it not for the ITAR, the capital gain would be computed as proceeds minus capital cost. In the example, this amount is $5,000 (i.e., $10,000 – $5,000), not V-day value of $7,000. Consequently, the effect of the ITAR is to obtain protection from being taxed on gains accrued up to Valuation day, because capital cost cannot be adjusted according to the definition of adjusted cost base for that property.

ITAR: 20(1)(*a*); ITA: 54 "adjusted cost base" (*a*)

¶8,930   Exempt Capital Gains Balance and Exempt Gains Balance

Where an individual made an election on an investment in a flow-through entity held on February 22, 1994, an exempt capital gains balance was created. A flow-through entity includes a mutual fund and a partnership. These entities flow their income out to their investors to be taxed in the hands of the investors. The individual investor would have made an election in his or her 1994 tax return to trigger all or some of the accrued capital gains on the investment in order to use up the expiring general capital gains deduction. Instead of increasing the ACB of the investment to the individual, the elected gain was added to this special account, called the exempt capital gains balance, of the individual in respect of the particular entity. An election would have been made separately on each flow-through entity held by the investor to the extent necessary to absorb the capital gains deduction. Hence, the individual would have an exempt capital gains balance for each separate entity for which an election was made.

ITA: 39.1(1)

The exempt capital gains balance can be used to shelter either a capital gain of the entity that is flowed out to the individual or a capital gain realized on the disposal of the interest in the entity itself. However, the balance must have been used before January 1, 2005. At that time, any unused balance expired. However, a provision allows an addition of, in essence, the exempt gains balance at the end of the year 2004 to the ACB of the investment in the flow-through entity. The balance for a particular entity will also expire when the individual disposes of all of the interest in the entity and the realized gains have not been large enough to use up the remainder of the exempt capital gains balance.

ITA: 53(1)(*p*)

A similar election was available for a component of the gain on eligible capital property. If a taxpayer owned eligible capital property on February 22, 1994, and had not used all of the general capital gains deduction available, a special election on a component of the accrued gain was possible. The effect of the election was to trigger as much of the accrued taxable capital gain component of eligible capital property as could be offset by available capital gains deduction. Since the elected taxable capital gain was offset by an equal amount of capital gains deduction, no incremental taxable income resulted from the election.

The benefit of the election results from the addition of the elected taxable capital gain on eligible capital property to the "exempt gains balance". That balance can be used to reduce a negative balance in the CEC account on a disposition after February 22, 1994. The election had no effect on the balance in the CEC account used for the purposes of the amortization deduction. Therefore, the election had no immediate effect on the annual deduction, but only a future effect on a disposition.

ITA: 14(5)

ITA: 20(1)(*b*)

¶8,940 Warranties

The traditional method of accounting for warranties through a reserve, in respect of items sold as inventory, is not permitted for tax purposes. Such a reserve is denied, since there is no specific provision for the deduction of this type of reserve. Only the actual expenditures incurred on servicing inventory sold under warranty may be deducted for tax purposes as ordinary business expenses.

ITA: 18(1)(*e*)

In respect of *capital property*, like land used as a fixed asset in a business, proceeds of disposition must include all amounts received or receivable as consideration for warranties. Then, a reduction of proceeds is recognized, if a cost is incurred before the filing-due date for the year of sale or a capital loss is recognized for a cost incurred subsequently, to the extent that the cost incurred was laid out to fulfil the legal obligation under the warranty. In effect, either adjustment to income at the time the warranty cost is incurred is intended to offset the amount included in proceeds of the disposition which may have resulted in a capital gain at the time of disposition. Recall that capital losses can only be applied to capital gains realized in the year of loss, in the preceding three years or in any subsequent year.

ITA: 42

The type of situation in which this adjustment might be used would be, for example, the sale of land held as a capital asset subject to a warranty that it is environmentally clean. Proceeds of disposition would include all amounts received or receivable in respect of the sale, including any amount received or receivable in respect of the warranty. If it is discovered later that the land is polluted in some manner, any expenditure made to clean the land under the warranty obligation will be considered to be a reduction of proceeds or a capital loss, depending on when the cost is incurred.

¶8,950 Attribution and the CRA Policy on Substituted Property

Prior to May 22, 1985, the CRA took the position that there would be no further attribution on capital gains which had been included in the transferor's income even though these subsequent transactions were technically caught by the substituted property rules. However, a subsequent Interpretation Bulletin reversed this policy. An analysis of the example presented in this Bulletin appears to indicate that only capital property transferred to a spouse after December 31, 1987, is subject to the new interpretation of including, in income, all capital gains on substituted property. Therefore, pre-1988 capital property acquisitions will only have an income inclusion to the extent the capital gain realized has not

ITA: 248(5); IT-258R2

IT-511R (Feb. 21, 1994), par. 27

been previously attributed. However, proceeds on the sale of pre-1988 capital property acquisitions invested in substituted capital property after 1987 will be subject to full attribution.

Example of Capital Gains Attribution between Spouses

IT-511R, par. 27

1978	*Facts*	One spouse (transferor) gifted property with the following attributes to the other spouse (transferee):

        ACB .... $ 50,000
        FMV $100,000

ITA: 73(1)

     Results Proceeds of disposition are automatically deemed to be the adjusted cost base of the transferred property ($50,000) under the inter-spousal rollover; hence, there is no capital gain in the year of transfer. (Note 1)

              The transferee has an ACB of $50,000.

1982   *Facts* The transferee sold the transferred property for $120,000 and acquired substituted property for the same amount.

     Results A capital gain of $70,000 ($120,000 – $50,000) is attributed back to the transferor.

ITA: 74.2

              The transferee's ACB of the substituted property is $120,000.

1988   *Facts* The transferee sold the substituted property for $200,000 and reinvested all of the proceeds in new substituted property.

     Results A portion of the capital gain ($66,667) is attributed back to the transferor, since the acquisition of the property occurred in the pre-1988 period.

              A capital gain of $80,000 ($200,000 – $120,000) is realized.

              The attributed portion of the $80,000 capital gain is computed as:

$$\frac{\text{FMV at the date of original transfer}}{\text{Proceeds of disposition of the previous sale (1978)}} \times \begin{array}{c}\text{Capital gain on} \\ \text{present sale}\end{array}$$

$$\frac{\$100,000}{\$120,000} \times \$80,000 = \$66,667$$

              The transferee's ACB of the second substituted property is $200,000.

1999   *Facts* The transferee sold the second substituted property acquired in 1988 for $250,000.

     Results All of the resultant capital gain of $50,000 ($250,000 – $200,000) is attributed back to the transferor since the acquisition was post-1987. Any future capital gain arising from the investment of the $250,000 will be fully attributable to the transferor.

Note 1: If the transferor had elected in 1978 not to have section 73 apply, then proceeds of disposition would have been FMV of $100,000, triggering a capital gain of $50,000 in the hands of the transferor. The transferee's ACB would have been $100,000. The overall numerical result would not change because of the election, except that $50,000 of capital gain would be recognized earlier.

Note 2: Any income from property earned on the transferred property and property substituted therefor would also be subject to attribution under section 74.1.

¶8,960 GST and Capital Real Property

¶8,965 Input tax credits on acquisitions of capital real property

This part of the chapter will focus on the input tax credit rules for capital real property. These rules apply to real property that is capital property of a registrant; they do not apply to real property that is held as inventory. As noted in Chapter 5, capital property is defined in the *Excise Tax Act* (ETA) to include any property that is capital property for income tax purposes, other than property included in Class 12 or Class 14 of the capital cost allowance classes. This definition for GST purposes applies regardless of whether the registrant is a taxpayer under the *Income Tax Act*.

ETA: 123(1)

The term "real property" is defined in the ETA to include:

ETA: 123(1)

(a) in respect of real property in the Province of Quebec, immovable property and every lease thereof,

(b) in respect of property in any other place in Canada, buildings and adjacent land, land and tenements of every nature and description, and every estate or interest in real property, whether legal or equitable, and

(c) a mobile home, a floating home and any leasehold or proprietary interest therein.

Separate sets of rules relating to input tax credits for capital real property are applicable, depending on whether the registrant is an individual (i.e., a sole proprietorship), or any other type of business. The rules for individuals are designed to account for any personal use of capital property. The special rules that apply to public sector bodies and financial institutions will not be discussed in this chapter.

The ETA contains the rules for capital real property owned by a registrant that is not an individual. Unlike acquisitions of capital personal property, acquisitions of capital real property generate proportional input tax credits based on the extent of use in a commercial activity (i.e., the same as the rules for the acquisition of goods and services in general). As an example, if capital real property is acquired for use 30% in a commercial activity, an input tax credit equal to 30% of the GST paid or payable on acquisition may be claimed. This may occur, for example, where a portion of a residential apartment building is rented to retailers. Since residential rents are exempt supplies, only the portion of the building used by the retailers will generate input tax credits. The apportionment may be done on the basis of floor space or rental income.

ETA: 206

No input tax credit is available, however, where the extent of commercial use is less than 10% of total use. On the other hand, a full input tax credit may be claimed where use in a commercial activity is exclusive, i.e., 90% or more. (In the case of financial institutions, exclusive use is interpreted as 100%.)

A provision of the ETA applies where a registrant who was previously unable to claim an input tax credit, for example, when the capital real property was used exclusively in non-commercial activities, begins to use the property in a commercial activity. In these circumstances, a proportional input tax credit may be claimed at that time. For example, if a medical practice acquires a building to be used exclusively for the provision of exempt health services, no input tax credit may be claimed. If, at some later date, 40% of the building is rented to other businesses, a proportional input tax credit may be claimed at that time.

ETA: 206(2)

The ETA deals with acquisitions of, and improvements to, capital real property by a registrant who is an individual. No input tax credit may be claimed on the acquisition or subsequent improvement of the property, respectively, if the use of the property is primarily (i.e., more than 50%) personal. For example, if an accountant acquires a building to be used 40% for his or her practice and 60% for his or her residence, no input tax credit can be claimed. If the property is used primarily in a commercial activity, an input tax credit in proportion to the commercial use is allowed.

ETA: 208
ETA: 208(1), 208(4)

Acquisitions of Capital Real Property

Registrants	Proportion of use	Amount of credit
Entities other than individuals	Commercial use≤10%	No input tax credit
	10%<Commercial use<90%	Input tax credit based on proportion of commercial use
	Commercial use≥90%	Full input tax credit
Individuals	Personal use>50%	No input tax credit
	Personal use≤50%	Input tax credit based on proportion of commercial use

¶8,970 Change-of-use rules for capital real property

Capital real property may undergo several changes in use over its useful life. The change-of-use rules for capital real property require registrants to carefully monitor the use of such property and to keep records of any GST paid in respect of the property. There is also the need to track the cost of subsequent improvements to the property, since these may impact the amount of the input tax credit claimed on a change in use. An improvement in respect of property is defined in the ETA to mean any property or service that is supplied for the purpose of improving the property, to the extent that the cost would be included in determining the adjusted cost base of the property for purposes of the *Income Tax Act*.

ETA: 123(1)

A specific rule deals with minor changes in use. If the change in use is less than 10% of the total use of the property, the use of the property will be deemed not to have changed.

ETA: 197

¶8,975 Dispositions of capital real property

Where a registrant other than an individual sells capital real property, the sale is generally subject to GST. The definition of commercial activity includes the making of a supply of real property. However, where the property was used as a residential apartment building, the sale is exempt and no GST need be collected. If, on the other hand, the vendor previously claimed an input tax credit, for example, for the use of the building by retailers, the sale would be taxable, as discussed below.

ETA: 123(1)

Where the property was used partially in commercial activities prior to sale, the registrant must account for GST based on the full sale price. However, the registrant is entitled to claim an input tax credit equal to the "basic tax content" of the property. This term means, generally, the amount of GST that the person was required to pay on the property at the time of acquisition and on improvements thereto, after deducting any amounts (other than input tax credits) the person was entitled to recover by way of a rebate, remission, or otherwise, and after taking into account any depreciation in the value of the property. Thus, any GST paid on the original acquisition that was not previously claimed as an input tax credit may be recovered, provided the value of the property has not declined.

ETA: 193(1)

Where an individual who is a registrant sells real property, the GST status of the sale depends on the use of the property before the sale. Where the property was used primarily for personal purposes, the sale is exempt. Where the property was used in commercial activities and not primarily for personal purposes, the sale is subject to GST and the individual is entitled to an input tax credit, as described above.

ETA: 193(1)

Special rules are contained in the ETA to provide rebates to non-registrants on taxable sales of capital real property. Since non-registrants are not entitled to claim input tax credits, the rebate mechanism was established to prevent double taxation. For example, where a doctor sells a building used exclusively in supplying exempt medical services, GST must be charged but no input tax credit may be claimed. The doctor is able to claim a rebate equal to the basic tax content of the property. The application must be filed within two years after the day the consideration for the sale became due or was paid without becoming due.

ETA: 257

ETA: 257

Chapter 9

Other Sources of Income and Deductions in Computing Income

LEARNING GOALS

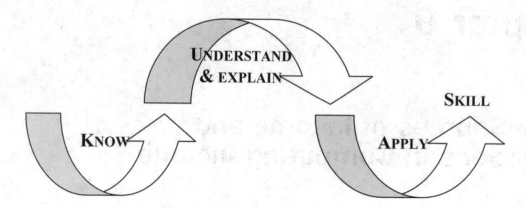

Know

By the end of this chapter you should know the basic provisions of the *Income Tax Act* that relate to other income and other deductions. Completing the Review Questions (¶9,800) and Multiple Choice Questions (¶9,825) is a good way to learn the technical provisions.

Understand and Explain

You should understand and be able to explain:

• The nature of income such as pensions, retiring allowances, support payments, and scholarships and bursaries.

• The nature of other deductions such as RRSPs, moving expenses, child care expenses, and the disability support deduction.

Completing the Exercises (¶9,850) is a good way to deepen your understanding of the material.

Apply

You should be able to apply your knowledge and understanding of these forms of income and deductions in a way that accomplishes a client's goals. Completing the Assignment Problems (¶9,875) is an excellent way to develop your ability to apply the material in increasingly complex situations.

OVERVIEW

This chapter will highlight the following:

Division B — Computation of Income

Subdivision d — Other sources of income

Subdivision e — Deduction in computing income

Subdivision g — Amounts not included in income

Division G — Deferred and Other Special Income Arrangements

The sectional list for these subdivisions of the Act, located at the front of the CCH edition of the CANADIAN INCOME TAX ACT, should be used to find quickly specific inclusions and deductions in doing the problem material in this and subsequent chapters.

PART I — DIVISION B
SUBDIVISION d
OTHER INCOME

DIVISION		SUBDIVISION		SECTION	
A	Liability for tax				
B	**Computation of income**		Basic rules	56	General
C	Computation of taxable income	a	Office or employment	56.1	Support
D	Taxable income earned in Canada by non-residents	b	Business or property	56.2-56.3	Debt forgiveness
E	Computation of tax	c	Capital gains and losses	56.4	Restrictive Covenants
E.1	Minimum tax	d	**Other income**	57	Certain pensions
F	Special rules	e	**Other deductions**	58	Gov't annuities
G	**Deferred and other special income arrangements**	f	Rules relating to computation of income	59-59.1	Resource property
H	Exemptions	g	**Amounts not included in income**	60	Other deductions
I	Returns, assessments, payments, appeals	h	Cdn corporations and shareholders	60.1	Support
J	Appeals to the courts	i	Shareholders of non-resident corporations	60.2	Refund of AVC's
		j	Partnerships	61-61.1	IAAC's
		k	Trusts	61.2-61.4	Debt forgiveness
				62	Moving expenses
				63	Child care expenses
				64	Attendant care
				64.1	Individual absent from Canada
				65-66.8	Resource
				81	Amounts not included in income
				146	RRSP
				146.01	Home Buyers' Plan
				146.02	Lifelong Learning Plan
				146.1	RESP
				146.3	RRIF
				147	DPSP
				147.1-147.4	RPP
				148	Life insurance policies
				148.1	Eligible funeral arrangements

¶9,000   OTHER SOURCES OF INCOME

Section 56 presents a list of miscellaneous types of income from a non-capital source, other than employment in Subdivision a and business or property in Subdivision b. Section 56.1 extends the rules pertaining to marital breakdown situations. Sections 57 to 59.1, which will not be discussed in this text, deal with certain pension plans, government annuities and resource properties in more detail.

¶9,010   Benefits in the Nature of Pensions

This provision includes in income superannuation or pension benefits including those received under the *Old Age Security Act* and the Canada Pension Plan. An Interpretation Bulletin discusses the inclusion of these benefits. "Retiring allowances" are included, as discussed further below. "Death benefits" are also defined very precisely for the purposes of the Act and are included. Note the exemption of a maximum of $10,000 of death benefit contained in the definition of the term. Any benefits received under the *Employment Insurance Act* are taxable.

ITA: 56(1)(a)(i)–(iv),
248(1) "retiring
allowances"; IT-499R

248(1) "death benefits"

¶9,015   Income splitting — Canada Pension Plan

Spouses or common-law partners, who meet certain conditions, can split equally their Canada Pension Plan income. The term "spouse or common-law partner" is defined as two persons, regardless of sex, who co-habit in a conjugal relationship and have done so for a continuous period of at least 12 months. The amount which can be shared is 50% of the combined CPP benefits received but prorated by the length of the time the individuals have been living together in relation to the contributory period. This income sharing arrangement would be most useful where the individuals have different tax rates and amounts of income. Where one individual was a contributor and the other individual was not, then the non-contributor must be at least 60 years of age at the time of this election. Applications are available from the Income Security Programs Department of Human Resources Development Canada.

ITA: 248(1) "common-law
partner"

¶9,020   Income splitting — Pension income

As a result of legislation enacted on June 22, 2007, and effective for 2007, targeted assistance is provided to pensioners and seniors by allowing an individual resident in Canada to allocate to the individual's resident spouse or common-law partner up to one-half of the individual's pension income (eligible pension income) that qualifies for the pension income tax credit.

ITA: 118(3)

For individuals aged 65 years and over, eligible pension income includes annuity payments under a registered pension plan, a registered retirement savings plan, or a deferred profit sharing plan or payments out of a registered retirement income fund. For individuals less than 65 years of age, eligible pension income includes annuity payments under a registered pension plan and certain other payments received as a result of the death of the individual's spouse or common-law partner.

ITA: 60.03(1), 118(7)

Since this will reduce one person's income, and probably cause another to pay tax, there is a requirement that both parties agree to the splitting of the income.

ITA: 60.03(2)

¶9,030   Retiring Allowances and Other Payments on Termination of Employment

In the absence of any express terms as to termination in a contract of employment, which is covered in Chapter 3, the general principle is that all other payments on the termination of employment are taxable as a retiring allowance. The provision excepts amounts out of an employee benefit plan, a retirement compensation arrangement, or a salary deferral arrangement. All three of these are plans specifically defined and are not particularly common.

ITA: 6(3), 56(1)(a)(ii),
248(1) "employee benefit
plan", "retirement
compensation
arrangement", "salary
deferral arrangement"

The definition of a retiring allowance excludes pension income and death benefits, but specifically includes payments in respect of:

ITA: 248(1) "retiring allowance"

(a) retirement from an office or employment in recognition of long service; or

(b) loss of office including court-awarded damages received by the taxpayer, or as a bequest, by a dependant or relation of the taxpayer or his or her legal representative.

In the case of *Schwartz v. The Queen*, the Supreme Court of Canada had an opportunity to determine that a lump sum payment was not a retiring allowance on the facts of the case. The taxpayer had entered into a written agreement for employment, but before the employment had commenced, the taxpayer was informed that his services were not required. He received the lump sum payment as damages for the termination of the employment contract. The Canada Revenue Agency (CRA) argued that the lump sum was a retiring allowance. However, the Supreme Court of Canada concluded that the argument was inconsistent with the requirement in the definition of "retiring allowance" of retirement from employment. Since the employment was only intended and not actual, there was no "employment" according to the definition of that term.

96 DTC 6103 (S.C.C.)

ITA: 56(1)(*a*)(ii)
ITA: 248(1) "employment", "retiring allowance"

¶9,040 Support Receipts and Payments

¶9,045 Overview

The spousal or child support income inclusions and deductions are mirror images of each other. If the amount paid is not deductible then the receipt is usually not income to the recipient. The following discussion is applicable to both the receipts and payments.

ITA: 56(1)(*b*), 60(*b*)

In the case of *Thibaudeau v. The Queen*, the Federal Court of Appeal ruled that a separated custodial parent did not have to include child support payments as part of her income. However, the court did not rule on the deductibility of the husband's payments in this case. The court's decision was based on a finding of instances of discrimination against separated custodial parents in the Act. As an example of such discrimination, the court indicated that a non-separated custodial parent is not required to include support payments from a spouse in income. (Of course, the payer spouse does not get a deduction in that case.) If this situation had been allowed to stand, such support payments, deductible to the payer but not includable by the recipient, would escape tax altogether.

94 DTC 6230 (F.C.A.)

In the decision of the Supreme Court of Canada on the appeal of the case of *The Queen v. Thibaudeau*, the Court ruled that the custodial parent was required to include the child support payments in her income. The majority opinion concluded that the fact that the tax saving resulting from the inclusion/deduction system does not benefit both parents equally does not infringe the equality rights protected by the Canadian Charter of Rights and Freedoms.

95 DTC 5273 (S.C.C.)

As a result of the *Thibaudeau* case, the inclusion–deduction system related to child support only was changed, as discussed below. These changes are applied to agreements or orders made or changed after April 30, 1997.

¶9,050 Spousal support

¶9,050.10 *Conditions*

The CRA is very strict on its interpretation of support receipts and deductions. All aspects of these rules must be adhered to. Support amounts, except amounts that relate to child support, are deductible if the following five tests are met:

ITA: 56(1)(*b*), 56.1(4), 60(*b*)

- the payments are made as allowances on a periodic basis, as discussed below;

- the payments are made for the maintenance of the recipient;

- the recipient has discretionary use of the amounts;

- the payments are made to a spouse or common-law partner or former spouse or common-law partner who is living apart from the payer because of the breakdown of their marriage or common-law partnership, or paid by a natural parent of a child of the recipient; and

- the payments are made pursuant to an order of a competent tribunal or a written agreement.

¶9,050.20 *Definitions*

A spouse or common-law partner is described as an individual of either sex who cohabited with the recipient in a conjugal relationship or is the parent of the child of the recipient. ITA: 248(1) "common-law partner"

The definition of an allowance for purposes of the above paragraphs is embodied in the definition of the term "support amount". The provision does not completely define an allowance, but does limit an allowance to an amount over which the recipient has discretion as to how the funds will be spent. ITA: 56.1(4) "support amount"

In the case of *Gagnon v. The Queen*, the Supreme Court of Canada considered the meaning of allowance. Three conditions must be met for an amount to be regarded as an allowance in the Court's view: 86 DTC 6179 (S.C.C.)

- the amount must be limited and predetermined;

- the amount must be paid to enable the recipient to discharge a certain type of expense; and

- the recipient must be able to dispose of the amount completely.

The Court elaborated on the last condition. As long as the recipient benefits from the amount, it is not relevant that he or she has to account for it or that he or she cannot apply it to certain types of expense at his or her complete discretion.

As noted previously, all of these provisions require that the payments be made on a periodic basis. The Federal Court of Appeal decision in *The Queen v. McKimmon* listed some of the criteria which should be used in determining whether a payment is made on a periodic basis and whether in fact the payment is a deductible allowance or an instalment of a lump or capital sum which is not deductible. 90 DTC 6088 (F.C.A.)

¶9,050.30 *Payments to third parties*

Certain payments to third parties made under an order or agreement or any variation of either are deductible as spousal support payments by the payer and deemed received and, hence, included by the person who benefits from the payment. Payments envisaged include medical bills, mortgage payments or tuition fees. ITA: 56.1, 60.1

Third-party payments, whether or not they are made on a periodic basis, will be deemed to be an allowance for the discretionary use of the recipient and, hence, deducted by the payer and included by the person who benefits, if they meet the following criteria: ITA: 56.1(2), 60.1(2)

- the payments are made in the year or preceding year under an order of a competent tribunal or written agreement;

- the expense was incurred for the maintenance of a spouse or common-law partner or former spouse or common-law partner; and

- the court order or written agreement alludes specifically to subsections 56.1(2) and 60.1(2).

Note that the use of this provision requires the agreement of both parties. If they do not agree to include the effects of these provisions in their documentation, the third-party amounts will not be deemed to be an allowance. These payments exclude the acquisition of tangible property, unless it involves an expenditure on medical expenses or educational expenses. The acquisition, improvement or maintenance of a self-contained domestic establishment, as defined, also qualify as payments that are deemed to be an allowance. Note that interest and principal payments are limited to 20% of the original principal amount of the debt. ITA: 248(1) "self-contained domestic establishment"

¶9,050.20

Amounts that are received/paid in respect of support before a court order or written agreement is made, are considered to have been received/paid under the order or agreement. However, the subsequent order or agreement must be made before the end of the year following the receipt/payment. In addition, the subsequent order or agreement must provide for the prior support to be deemed to have been received/paid under the order or agreement.   ITA: 56.1(3)

¶9,055   Child support

Amounts paid in respect of support or maintenance of a child are not deductible by the payer and are not included in the income of the recipient. Any amount not identified in the agreement or order as being solely for the support of the recipient spouse or former spouse will be considered to be an amount payable for child support.

For this purpose, the term "child support amount" is defined. These rules apply to new written agreements or court orders made or to existing written agreements or court orders changed after April 30, 1997.   ITA: 56.1(4) "child support amount"

¶9,060   Legal fees in connection with support payments

Under current common law, it appears that legal fees incurred to enforce pre-existing rights to support payments are deductible.[1] The CRA suggested that legal and accounting fees incurred to enforce pre-existing rights to support are deductible.[2] Subsequently, the CRA announced[3] that it had reconsidered its position that legal costs incurred to establish rights to support are considered to be non-deductible capital outlays or personal or living expenses. The CRA now considers legal costs incurred to obtain spousal support under the *Divorce Act*, or under the applicable provincial legislation, in a separation agreement to have been incurred to enforce a pre-existing right to support. This position is based on the case of *Gallien v. The Queen*. The CRA further indicated that it now accepts that legal costs of seeking to obtain an increase in support or to make child support non-taxable are also deductible.   IT-99R5, par. 18   IT-99R5, par. 17   2000 DTC 2514 (T.C.C.)

¶9,070   Annuity Payments

An "annuity" is defined in the Act. The full amount of an annuity payment is included in income unless it is required to be included under another provision of the Act or unless it is subject to income accrual rules. If the full amount of the annuity payment is included in income, then the capital portion of the annuity, if any, is deducted.   ITA: 12.2(1), 248(1)   ITA: 56(1)(d), 60(a)

The full amount of an annuity payment that resulted from certain registered retirement savings plan contributions that were deductible by the taxpayer is included in income.   ITA: 56(1)(d.2)

¶9,080   Amounts Received from Deferred Income Plans

¶9,085   Inclusion provisions

The following paragraphs take into income amounts received by the taxpayer through the deferred income plans indicated:

Paragraph 56(1)(h)	Registered retirement savings plan (RRSP)
Paragraph 56(1)(h.1)	Home buyer's plan (HBP)
Paragraph 56(1)(h.2)	Lifelong learning plan (LLP)
Paragraph 56(1)(i)	Deferred profit sharing plan (DPSP)
Paragraph 56(1)(q)	Registered education savings plan (RESP)
Paragraph 56(1)(t)	Registered retirement income fund (RRIF)

---

[1] See the *McColl* case, (T.C.C.) 2000 DTC 2148, which cites for support the cases of *Burgess*, (F.C.T.D.) 81 DTC 5192, *Evans*, (S.C.C.) 60 DTC 1047, and *Wakeman* (T.C.C. — Informal Procedure) 96 DTC 3220.

[2] Paragraph 18 of IT-99R5 also refers to the *Sembinelli* case (F.C.A.), 94 DTC 6636.

[3] *Income Tax Technical News*, No. 24, October 10, 2002.

The detailed rules governing these plans are found in Division G "Deferred and Other Special Income Arrangements". RRSPs and RRIFs will be discussed in more detail later in this chapter.

¶9,090   Registered education savings plans (RESPs)

¶9,090.10   *Concept and limits*

RESPs, as defined, allow individuals to contribute, without an annual limit, to a plan to fund post-secondary education of a qualified beneficiary. The lifetime contribution limit in respect of a beneficiary is $50,000 over a maximum of 21 years. The maximum number of years is 25 for a single beneficiary RESP under which the beneficiary is an individual who is entitled to a disability tax credit. Contributions are not deductible when contributed to the plan and, hence, they are not taxable when the plan allows their withdrawal. Neither the trust holding the property of a plan nor the contributor or subscriber is taxable on the income earned by that property, so the investment income of the plan is sheltered.

ITA: 146.1(1)
ITA: 204.9(1)

ITA: 146.1(5), 146.1(6)

The accumulated investment income is taxable to a beneficiary as he or she receives the funds to pay for education expenses while enrolled as a full-time student in a post-secondary educational institution, called "educational assistance payments". Educational assistance payments can be made in connection with occupational skills programs at educational institutions certified by the Minister of Human Resources and Skills Development.

ITA: 56(1)(*q*), 146.1(1)

Eligibility for education assistance payments from an RESP is extended to part-time studies. Students 16 years of age or older may receive up to $2,500 of education assistance payments for each 13-week semester of part-time study. A greater amount may be approved by the Minister of Human Resources and Social development on a case-by-case basis.

A family plan RESP can be established for a number of beneficiaries related by blood or adoption. The income from such an RESP can be paid to any one or more of the beneficiaries who pursue higher education. However, the RESP cannot allow an individual to become a beneficiary after he or she turns 21.

¶9,090.20   *Canada Education Savings Grant (CESG)*

To increase the attractiveness of saving for education through an RESP, the government provides a CESG of 20% of the first $2,500 of annual contributions to an RESP for the benefit of children up to age 18.[4] This amounts to a maximum grant of $500 per year per child. The CESG is paid directly to the RESP. The maximum CESG that can be *paid* to an RESP in respect of a particular beneficiary is $7,200. In the case of a family plan RESP involving more than one beneficiary, the maximum CESG that can be *received* by a particular beneficiary as educational assistance payments is $7,200. CESG contribution room of $2,500 per year is accumulated for each child under 18 years old. Thus, where less than a $2,500 contribution is made in a year, the 20% grant will be paid in a subsequent year when RESP contributions are made. If a child does not pursue higher education to qualify for educational assistance payments, the CESG must be repaid to the government by the RESP.

The CESG matching rate for contributions made to an RESP by low and middle-income families on or after January 1, 2005 is determined as follows. Where a child is the beneficiary of the RESP and under the age of 18 throughout the year, the first $500 contributed in the year will attract:

- a 40% CESG matching rate, if the qualifying net income of the child's family is $35,000 or less and

- a 30% CESG matching rate if the qualifying net income of the child's family is between $35,000 and $70,000.

There is no carry-forward of the enhanced rate to future years and the income thresholds are indexed to inflation for 2005 and subsequent taxation years.

---

[4] Part III.1 of the *Department of Human Resources Development Act.*

¶9,090.30   *Canada Learning Bond (CLB)*

In addition, a CLB provides a source of education savings for children of low-income families. Each child born on or after January 1, 2004 is eligible for an initial CLB of $500 and subsequent annual CLB's of $100 in each year up to and including the year the child turns 15, provided that the child's family is entitled to the National Child Benefit (NCB) supplement in the year (Chapter 10). The total amount of the CLB payments cannot exceed $2,000 per child and can be transferred to an RESP at any time before the child reaches 18. While no separate application is required, eligibility is linked to entitlement for the National Child Benefit supplement. The CLB is payable into an RESP of which the child is a beneficiary.

¶9,090.40   *Distribution from an RESP*

An RESP is permitted to distribute any part of its accumulated income to the subscriber after 1997, under certain conditions, as follows:

- the subscriber is alive;

- each beneficiary of the RESP is either:

    (i) over 21 years of age and not eligible to receive educational assistance payments, or

    (ii) has died;

    and

- the RESP has been in existence for at least 10 years.

ITA: 146.1(2)(*d*.1)

These distributions are included in the subscriber's income. The Minister may waive the "over 21 years of age" and the "at least 10 years" restrictions where a beneficiary under an RESP is mentally impaired. The distributions may be rolled over to the subscriber's (or his or her spouse's) RRSP, to the extent that the subscriber has contribution room. The limit on this rollover is $50,000. A 20% tax is imposed on the amount of the RESP distribution received in excess of the limited amount transferred to RRSPs.

ITA: 146.1(2.2), 204.94

¶9,095   Registered disability savings plan (RDSP)

To help parents and others save for the long-term financial security of a child with a severe disability, the March 19, 2007 federal budget proposed to introduce a new registered disability savings plan (RDSP) with a Canada Disability Savings Grant (CDSG) program and Canada Disability Savings Bond (CDSB) program. The RDSP will be based generally on the existing RESP design.

¶9,095.10   *Eligibility*

Generally, any person eligible for the disability tax credit (DTC) and resident in Canada, or the parent or other legal representative of such a person, will be eligible to establish an RDSP. The DTC-eligible individual will be the plan beneficiary.

¶9,095.20   *Tax treatment*

Contributions to an RDSP will not be deductible, but the investment income will accrue tax-free. Contributions will not be included in income when paid out, but the investment income will be included in income when it is paid out.

¶9,095.30   *Contributions*

Contributions to an RDSP will be limited to a lifetime maximum of $200,000 in respect of the beneficiary, with no annual limit. There will be no restriction on who can contribute to the plan. Contributions will be permitted until the end of the year in which the beneficiary attains 59 years of age.

¶9,095.40   *Canada Disability Savings Grants (CDSGs)*

To provide additional direct government assistance to help ensure the future financial security of a child with a severe disability, RDSP contributions made in the year will qualify for CDSGs at matching rates of 100%, 200%, or 300%, depending on family net income and the amount contributed.

Family net income	up to $74,357	over $74,357
CDSG	300% on first $500	100% on first $1,000
	200% on next $1,000	

The family net income threshold will be indexed to inflation for 2008.

There will be a lifetime limit of $70,000 on CDSGs paid in respect of an RDSP beneficiary. An RDSP will be eligible to receive CDSGs until the end of the year in which the beneficiary attains 49 years of age.

¶9,095.50   *Canada Disability Savings Bonds (CDSBs)*

To ensure that RDSPs help promote the future financial security of children with a severe disability in lower-income families, CDSBs of up to $1,000 will be paid annually to the RDSPs of low and modest-income beneficiaries and families. CDSBs will not be contingent on contributions to an RDSP.

The maximum $1,000 CDSB will be paid to an RDSP where family net income does not exceed $20,883. The CDSB will be phased out gradually for those with family net income between $20,883 and $37,178.

There will be a lifetime limit of $20,000 on CDSBs paid in respect of an RDSP beneficiary. An RDSP will be eligible to receive CDSBs until the end of the year in which the beneficiary attains 49 years of age.

¶9,095.60   *Payments*

Payments from an RDSP will be required to commence by the end of the year in which the beneficiary attains 60 years of age. Payments will be subject to a maximum annual limit determined by reference to the life expectancy of the beneficiary and the fair market value of the property in the plan. The beneficiary or their legal representative will be permitted to encroach on the capital and income of the plan.

¶9,095.70   *Death or cessation of disability*

Where the beneficiary of an RDSP either ceases to be eligible for the DTC or dies, the funds in the RDSP will be required to be paid to the beneficiary or pass to his or her estate. That amount will be included in the beneficiary's income

¶9,100   Education Assistance Payments

These provisions include in income:

(a) scholarships, fellowships, bursaries or prizes for achievement in a field of endeavour of the taxpayer in excess of the taxpayer's scholarship exemption for a taxation year, and project grants, received by artists, net of the related, contractual project expenses; and

ITA: 56(1)(*n*), 56(3)(*c*)

(b) research grants in excess of expenses which are unreimbursed, non-personal or living expenses, except for *bona fide* travelling expenses, incurred in carrying on the research.

ITA: 56(1)(*o*)

The scholarship exemption is generally $500. However, there is a full exemption for scholarships, fellowships, and bursaries received by a taxpayer in connection with the taxpayer's enrolment in a program in respect of which the taxpayer may claim the education tax credit, that is, a designated educational institution.

ITA: 56(3)(*a*)

ITA: 56(3)(*b*)

[The March 19, 2007 federal budget proposed to extend the full exemption of scholarships and bursaries to those received for elementary and secondary schools. This is effective for 2007 and subsequent years.]

There are certain restrictions on the amounts which qualify as scholarships, bursaries, prizes, etc. Amounts received from a registered education savings plan, amounts received in the course of a business and amounts received in respect of employment are excluded. Note that the grant portion of provincial or federal education assistance payments is considered to be income under this paragraph. Certain prescribed prizes are excluded from income completely. Generally, these prizes may be described as recognition by the general public for meritorious achievement in the arts, sciences or public service; thus these amounts do not represent a payment in respect of a contract of service.

ITA: 56(1)(*n*)

ITR: 7700

¶9,110 Other Inclusions

Included in income are amounts received as legal costs awarded by a court on an appeal from an assessment of any tax, interest or penalties, as well as any reimbursement of costs received as a result of decisions under the *Employment Insurance Act* or Canada Pension Plan. These receipts are included if the expenses incurred are deducted or deductible.

ITA: 56(1)(*l*), 60(*o*)

A taxpayer must include amounts received as an award or reimbursement of legal expenses paid to collect or establish a right to a retiring allowance or benefits under a pension plan. Excluded are legal expenses relating to a division or settlement of property arising from a marriage or other conjugal relationship.

ITA: 56(1)(*l*.1)

Social assistance payments are included in income and, if the recipient is married, the amount received must be included by the spouse with the higher income. Finally, Workers' Compensation is included.

ITA: 56(1)(*u*), 56(1)(*v*)

¶9,120 Indirect Payments   NOT COVERED - DON'T READ

¶9,125 Overview

These anti-avoidance provisions invoke the principle of constructive or effective receipt by imputing to the taxpayer:

- income diverted at his or her direction to someone else either for the taxpayer's benefit or to satisfy the desire of the taxpayer to benefit the other person;[5]

ITA: 56(2)

- any rights to income transferred by the taxpayer, while resident in Canada, to someone with whom he or she was not dealing at arm's length; and

ITA: 56(4)

- income earned on non-arm's length loans which do not yield a commercial rate of interest (see Chapter 6).

ITA: 56(4.1), 56(4.2), 56(4.3)

¶9,130 Conditions

The provision pertaining to indirect payments specifies the following four conditions:

ITA: 56(2)

- there must be a payment or transfer of property to a person other than the taxpayer;

- the payment or transfer must be made pursuant to the direction or with the concurrence of the taxpayer;

- the payment or transfer must be for the benefit of the taxpayer, or a benefit that the taxpayer desired to confer on the other person; and

---

[5] For a more detailed analysis of this provision, see Robert E. Beam and Stanley N. Laiken, "Recent Developments on Subsection 56(2): Indirect Payments", Personal Tax Planning Feature (1995), vol. 43, no. 2, *Canadian Tax Journal*, pp. 447–469.

- the payment or transfer would have been included in the taxpayer's income if it had been made to the taxpayer.

If all of these conditions are met, the payment or transfer is included in the taxpayer's income to the extent that it would be if the payment or transfer had been made directly to the taxpayer.

The CRA has attacked certain family income splitting schemes by applying these indirect payments provisions. In the case of *Champ v. The Queen*, part of the dividends payable on shares owned by the taxpayer's wife was included in the taxpayer's income. It was found that the taxpayer had directed the payment of dividends on his wife's shares without the payment of dividends on his shares which were essentially the same. On the other hand, in the case of *The Queen v. McClurg*, subsection 56(2) was held not to be applicable in facts very similar to *Champ* but where there were contractual restrictions upon the payment of dividends. The case of *The Queen v. Neuman*, involved facts that were slightly different from those in the *McClurg* case. The decision to apply subsection 56(2) in the *Neuman* case was based on the power of the taxpayer to ratify the dividends paid to his wife and the distinction with the *McClurg* case on the wife's lack of contribution to the corporation.

In its decision on the case of *Neuman v. The Queen*, the Supreme Court of Canada held that subsection 56(2) does not apply to the dividend income received by Neuman's wife. This decision established that there is no requirement for the shareholder to make a business contribution to the corporation in order to earn the dividend. Dividends are paid to shareholders simply as a return on their investment in the corporation, not as compensation for work done for the corporation. This conclusion clarifies the uncertainty left by the *McClurg* case on the issue.

83 DTC 5029 (F.C.T.D.)

91 DTC 5001 (S.C.C.)

96 DTC 6464 (F.C.A.)

98 DTC 6297 (S.C.C.)

¶9,140 Restrictive Covenants   NOT COVERED - DON'T READ

¶9,145 Inclusion

The provision on restrictive covenants [proposed in Bill C-33, dated November 22, 2006] sets out rules with respect to amounts that are received or receivable after October 7, 2003 in respect of a restrictive covenant.

ITA: 56.4

The term "restrictive covenant" is defined to mean an arrangement, an undertaking or a waiver of a right or advantage that affects, in any way, the acquisition or provision of property or services by the taxpayer or someone not dealing at arm's length with the taxpayer.

ITA: 56.4(1)

The starting point is to include in income the total of all amounts received or receivable by the taxpayer, or non-arm's length person, in respect of a restrictive covenant.

ITA: 56.4(2)

A deduction is provided for a bad debt if the amount was previously included in income as a payment for a restrictive covenant. Section 68 addresses the allocation of amounts between restrictive covenants and the other property being disposed of.

ITA: 56.4, 60(f)

¶9,150 Exclusion

The amounts to which the income inclusion for restrictive covenants do not apply are set out in the Act. Basically, the exceptions are for those amounts that are included in income somewhere else. The result is that payments for restrictive covenants will be taxable in some manner. The following are the three items that are not taxed as restrictive covenants because they are taxed elsewhere.

ITA: 56.4(2), 56.4(3)

¶9,150.10 *Employment income*

The restrictive covenant inclusion rule will not apply if the amount is included in employment income or will be included when received. This might be the case where an employee leaves and is paid an amount not to work for a competitor. In this case there may not be any shares or assets sold that might cause part of the payments to be allocated in a different way. While employment income is normally taxed on the received basis, if the employee agreed to the covenant more than 36 months before the end of the taxation year, then the payments for

ITA: 56.4(2)

ITA: 6(3.1)

the restrictive covenant may be included in employment income even though it is not actually received.

¶9,150.20 *Eligible capital property*

The restrictive covenant inclusion rule will not apply to an amount if the payment received is required by the description of item E in the definition of "cumulative eligible capital", which requires that ¾ of the payment be credited to the CEC pool. The purchaser and the taxpayer must jointly elect for this exception to apply. This might apply, for example, where a partnership sells its business and the restrictive covenant proceeds are included in with the proceeds for the goodwill.

ITA: 56.4(2)
ITA: 14(5)

¶9,150.30 *Proceeds of disposition*

The restrictive covenant inclusion rule will not apply to the extent that the amount is added to the proceeds of disposition of an "eligible interest". An "eligible interest" is capital property that is a partnership interest or a share of a corporation where the partnership or the corporation is carrying on a business. This might occur where the share or the partnership interest is disposed of and the shareholder or partner enters into a restrictive covenant. For this to be the case, the following conditions must be met:

ITA: 56.4(2)

- the amount must directly relate to the taxpayer's disposition of an "eligible interest";

ITA: 56.4(1)

- the disposition of the "eligible interest" must be to the purchaser of the restrictive covenant;

- the amount received or receivable must be consideration for an undertaking not to compete with the purchaser;

- the amount cannot exceed the amount determined by a formula;

- the amount is included in the proceeds of disposition of the "eligible interest"; and

- the taxpayer and the purchaser of the restrictive covenant have elected to apply this exception.

¶9,155 Schematic of the system for restrictive covenants

The following diagram illustrates how section 56.4 fits into the taxation of restrictive covenant payments:

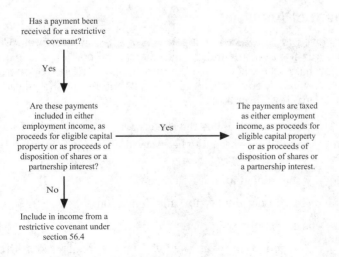

¶9,200 AMOUNTS NOT INCLUDED IN COMPUTING INCOME

The Act lists a number of specific types of income that would ordinarily have to be included in income subject to tax, but are excluded from the computation of income. Note the very limited scope of these exclusions each of which meets a specific problem area.

ITA: 81

¶9,210 Specific Examples

The more common components of this section are summarized below:

- amounts exempted by other federal statutes or foreign tax agreements;

  ITA: 81(1)(*a*)

- certain pension or other payments related to war services;

  ITA: 81(1)(*d*)

- war service pensions of a country which has reciprocal arrangements with Canada;

  ITA: 81(1)(*e*)

- compensation by the Federal Republic of Germany, for war victims;

  ITA: 81(1)(*g*)

- income and capital gains from personal injury award property for individuals under 21 years of age;

  ITA: 81(1)(*g*.1), 81(1)(*g*.2)

- social assistance payments based on a needs test;

  ITA: 81(1)(*h*)

- payments out of a profit sharing plan;

  ITA: 81(1)(*k*)

- expense allowances of elected municipal officers and members of provincial legislature; and

  ITA: 81(2), 81(3)

- allowance for or reimbursement of part-time employment travel expenses. (See Chapter 3 for a detailed discussion of this provision.)

  ITA: 81(3.1)

¶9,300 DEDUCTIONS IN COMPUTING INCOME

Subdivision e deals with deductions which are permitted by law but which are not attributed to a particular source of income like employment, business, property, or capital gains. This concept of a source is important because most deductions under Division B must be for expenditures incurred in order to earn specific types of income. However, this set of deductions, although deductible from certain types of income, applies to items which do not necessarily earn income themselves, such as tuition fees, alimony, etc.

ITA: 4(2)

¶9,310 Capital Element of Annuity

All annuity payments received are included in income as previously indicated. Certain annuities are purchased out of tax-paid dollars and, hence, the capital portion of the annuity payment, representing this purchase price, is removed under this paragraph. The method of computing the capital element of a contractual annuity is set out in the Regulations. In essence, the capital element is given by the ratio:

ITA: 56(1)(*d*), 56(1)(*d*.2)

ITR: 300

$$\frac{\text{the capital outlay to buy the annuity}}{\text{the total payments to be received or expected to be received under the contract}}$$

This ratio would be multiplied by the annual annuity payment.

The following annuity payments do not qualify for this deduction:

(a) a superannuation or pension benefit;

(b) a payment under a registered retirement savings plan or registered retirement income fund; or

(c) a payment resulting from a deferred profit sharing plan.

2007 → 20,000

These types of annuities are excluded because they are paid out of income which has not been subjected to tax; that is, the cost of these annuities has been allowed as a deduction in computing income.

¶9,320   Registered Retirement Savings Plans

The rules regarding the tax treatment of registered retirement savings plans (RRSPs) reflect a comprehensive overhaul of the taxation of retirement savings, referred to as pension reform. Pension reform received Royal Assent on June 27, 1990, after six years of government task forces, studies, green papers, press releases and draft legislation. The scope and impact of the pension legislation on Canadians is pervasive and, as a result, it is complex. Many of the Regulations relating to the legislation are very technical in nature and will not be dealt with in this text.

¶9,325   Objectives of pension reform

The objectives of pension reform were:

- to provide equal access to tax assistance regardless of the type of plan with which an individual funds his or her retirement;

- to provide flexibility in the pension system; and

- to tighten up the system to close both actual and perceived loopholes.

These objectives have been accomplished through the integration of limits for various types of pension plans with the limits for RRSPs.

In order to provide the same amount of tax assistance to an individual for retirement savings, regardless of whether the retirement is funded through a registered pension plan (RPP), a deferred profit sharing plan (DPSP) or an RRSP, under pension reform a comprehensive annual limit for tax-assisted retirement savings — 18% of earned income up to a maximum phased-in dollar limit. The fairly generous contribution limits give individuals an incentive to provide for their retirement years.

¶9,330   Types of tax-assisted retirement plans

There are several basic types of pension plans, and the pension legislation attempts to equalize the tax assistance provided to an individual whether he or she earns retirement income through a defined-benefit registered pension plan (DBP), a money-purchase registered pension plan (MPP), a DPSP, or an RRSP.

¶9,330.10   *Defined-benefit registered pension plans*

Under a DBP, *the benefit that is to be paid* to each employee *is defined* usually in regard to a certain percentage of an employee's earnings in the last few years of employment, regardless of the cost to the employer or the earnings experience of the plan. The benefit that is tax-assisted is limited to a maximum. The employer contributions are deductible, provided that they are certified by an actuary to be necessary to fund the accruing benefits of the plan as registered with the CRA. The employee contributions are deductible, subject to a maximum.

The maximum tax-assisted benefit that may be provided to an individual under a defined-benefit registered pension plan is 2% per year of the individual's average best 3 years of remuneration times the number of years of pensionable service, with a phased-in dollar limit. For example, if an individual has pre-retirement earnings of $111,111 in 2007, it would provide for a maximum tax-assisted pension of $77,770, or 70% of the individual's pre-retirement earnings. Assuming that the individual has 35 years of pensionable service, $111,111 × 2% = $2,222 per year, which buys a pension of $77,770, if expended annually over an effective period of 35 years.

The following table summarizes the scheduled increases.

Year	Money Purchase Limit	Maximum Pension Per year of Service	Maximum Pension (35 yrs)	Employment Income Needed
2007	$20,000	$2,222	$77,770	$111,111
2008	$21,000	$2,333	$81,665	$116,667
2009	$22,000	$2,444	$85,540	$122,222
2010	indexed	indexed	indexed	indexed

¶9,330.20   *Money-purchase registered pension plans*

Under an MPP, which is sometimes called a defined contribution plan, *the contribution*, that is required by the employer and the employee, *is defined* rather than the benefit. The retirement benefit for the individual is acquired through the purchase of an annuity on the open market with the contributions made to the plan plus the earnings generated from those contributions while they are held in the plan. The tax-assisted contributions of both employees and employers are limited to a maximum each year as indicated in ~~Exhibit 9~~=1.

 CHART ABOVE

¶9,330.30   *Deferred profit sharing plans*

Under this type of arrangement, only an employer may contribute a limited amount to a plan for the employee, which is based on the performance or the profits of the business. The funds must vest irrevocably in the employee after two years of employment, and the plan may invest in equity shares of the employer if they qualify.

¶9,330.40   *Registered retirement savings plans*

Basically, an RRSP is a tax shelter provided under the Act to give an individual an incentive to save money for his or her retirement years. Within certain limits, the individual can claim tax deductions for contributions to his or her own RRSP, or a spousal RRSP. Since income can accumulate in the plan on a pre-tax basis, RRSPs can play an important part in an individual's overall retirement and tax planning.

If funds are withdrawn from an RRSP prior to maturity, the proceeds are subject to tax when received. If an RRSP is held until maturity, the accumulated RRSP funds may be received as a lump sum, in which case the funds are included in the individual's income and taxed at his or her marginal rate in the year received. Alternatively, the funds may be used to purchase a retirement annuity or may be transferred to a registered retirement income fund (RRIF). Both of these options would defer the receipt of the funds and, consequently, would defer tax on these funds until received in the form of retirement income. Tax savings will be realized if the funds are received and taxed in years when the individual's marginal tax rate is lower than in his or her pre-retirement years. The effect of the deferral of tax on income accumulating within the shelter can even offset the effect of a higher marginal tax rate on retirement income, making the RRSP shelter very attractive to most investors.

Technically, an RRSP is a contract, accepted for registration by the Minister of National Revenue, between an individual (the annuitant) and an entity that is authorized to carry on the business of selling such contracts (the carrier). RRSPs are available from banks, trust companies, life insurance companies, credit unions, caisses populaires, mutual funds and stockbrokerage firms.

¶9,335   Types of RRSPs

In general, the RRSPs available may be categorized into three types, all of which are of a money-purchase nature:

- life insurance company plans;

- other financial institution plans; and

- self-administered plans.

¶9,335.10   *Life insurance company plans*

Life insurance companies are currently the only kind of financial institution permitted to offer deferred life annuities. Deferred annuities accumulate funds on behalf of the policy owner until maturity, at which time the annuity is converted into income.

Some deferred annuities have guaranteed rates of interest for specified terms and others are invested in segregated funds or mutual funds which are professionally managed by the insurance company. Some companies also offer RRSPs with a life insurance component, in which case only the RRSP or savings portion of the total premium is tax deductible. In certain provinces and in specified circumstances, insurance company RRSPs are protected against creditors.

¶9,335.20   *Other financial institution plans*

Other financial institutions, such as banks, trust companies or credit unions, sponsor plans which are invested in savings deposits, term deposits and guaranteed investment certificates (GICs). They also offer plans which are invested in mutual funds or pooled fund trusts. These funds may be invested in mortgages, bonds, equities, money market instruments or a combination thereof. Some specialized funds are invested in high-risk investments providing venture capital. Others are invested in specific segments of the economy. Although one can select the type of fund for one's RRSP, the underlying investments are selected by the fund manager. Typically, investment management charges are levied against the underlying investment funds rather than the RRSP. However, sales or redemption charges may be applied against the RRSP on purchases or sales of units in the fund.

¶9,335.30   *Self-administered plans*

A self-administered RRSP can be set up with most financial institutions or a stock broker. A trustee will hold and administer the RRSP investments, but the individual can select investments or, if desired, an investment adviser can do it.

A self-administered RRSP can be invested in a wide variety of qualified investments, including publicly-traded debt and equity securities, as well as publicly-traded warrants or rights to acquire qualified investments. It can also be invested in certain mutual funds, mortgages, Canada Savings Bonds, treasury bills, and strip coupon bonds and certificates.

Often, administration fees are paid by a taxpayer in respect of a self-administered RRSP (or RRIF, as discussed subsequently). Investment counselling fees may, also, be paid in respect of property in these retirement shelters. However, no amount is deductible by a taxpayer in respect of payments made for services pertaining to these sheltered plans.   ITA: 18(1)(*u*)

¶9,340   Integration of limits

In order to provide the same amount of tax assistance to an individual for retirement savings, regardless of whether it is funded through an RPP, a DPSP, an RRSP or a combination thereof, a comprehensive annual limit for tax-assisted retirement savings is being phased in.

This comprehensive annual limit is determined using certain key assumptions with respect to retirement savings.

First, the maximum amount of tax-assisted retirement savings that the government is willing to fund through tax assistance for each individual is $77,770 in 2007. That amount was derived as a multiple of the average wage. Second, it is assumed actuarially that $9 of contributions buys $1 of annual pension income.

Under a DBP, an individual generally must have a combined pension contribution of $2,222 a year over the equivalent of 35 years to pay out the 2007 maximum pension of $77,770, and so at the maximum it will be possible to make combined employer/employee contributions equal to the lesser of 18% of the individual's compensation from the employer for the year, or $20,000 (= $2,222 × 9) a year.

Under an MPP, tax-assisted contributions at the maximum may equal the lesser of 18% (9 × 2%) of earnings or $20,000 per year (total contributions made by the employer and employee) and should result in an accumulation of funds in the plan of up to $77,770 of 2007 pension income, generally, after the equivalent of 35 years. The cap of $20,000 for 2007 limits the amount of pensionable earnings that may receive tax assistance to $111,111 (18% of $111,111 is $20,000).

Under a DPSP, the maximum contribution limit is the lesser of 18% of earnings and 50% of $20,000 for 2007, since only the employer may make contributions. This lower limit will leave more contribution room for the individual to make a deductible RRSP contribution.

To integrate the tax assistance provided to individuals who fund their retirement savings with a combination of RRSPs, pension plans and deferred profit-sharing plans, the RRSP contribution limit is 18% of earned income for the *prior* year to a 2007 maximum of $20,000, plus or minus any adjustments for benefits provided to the individual under an RPP or a DPSP in the *prior* year.

¶9,345   Contribution limits for RRSPs

Using these assumptions, a system has been put in place to determine an individual's RRSP deduction limit and RRSP dollar limit. These limits are defined in subsection 146(1) and are described in Exhibit 9-1.

Employers are to report the Pension Adjustment (PA) (a measure of the pension benefits an employee is entitled to under an RPP and/or a DPSP) on an employee's T4 slip on or before February 28 of the year following the year in which the benefits accrued. From February to August of that year, the CRA will use the PA reported by the employer plus the prior year's earned income as calculated from the individual's personal tax return to create a pension account for each individual. The CRA will then provide an RRSP contribution limit statement with the taxpayer's Notice of Assessment for the tax return filed. For example, the Notice of Assessment for a taxpayer's 2006 tax return filed by April 30, 2007 will contain a calculation of the RRSP contribution limit for 2007.

An individual may contribute to an RRSP at any time up to and including 60 days after the year-end, or, for example, until February 29, 2008 in order to claim an RRSP deduction on his or her 2007 tax return. The CRA will check the deduction against its pension file to determine if the RRSP contribution is deductible.   ITA: 146(5)

An added advantage of the system is that if an individual is not able to contribute the maximum amount to an RRSP, he or she is allowed to "carry forward" any unused deduction limit. There is no time restriction on the carryforward of an individual's unused RRSP deduction room. This feature is discussed in more detail subsequently.

If funds are borrowed to make contributions to an RRSP (or an RPP or DPSP), interest on the borrowed funds is not deductible. The reason for this denial of an interest deduction is probably that the income from the investments in the sheltered retirement plans is not taxed as long as it remains in the plan.   ITA: 18(11)

The annual deduction limits for 2006 to 2011 are outlined in Exhibit 9-1. Exhibit 9-2 shows the earned income needed for the maximum RRSP deductible contribution at 18%.

EXHIBIT 9-1
2006–2011 Annual RRSP Deduction and Dollar Limits
[ssec. 146(1)]

If the individual is:	*The annual contribution limit for 2006–2011 is:*
• a member of an RPP or a DPSP,	(A) the individual's unused RRSP deduction room carried forward from the previous year*
	plus
	(B) the lesser of:
	(i) the RRSP dollar limit
	— for 2006, $18,000
	— for 2007, $19,000
	— for 2008, $20,000
	— for 2009, $21,000
	— for 2010, $22,000
	— for 2011, indexed
	and
	(ii) 18% of earned income for the prior year
	minus
	(C) the pension adjustment for the prior year reported to the CRA by the individual's employer and any past service pension adjustment reported by his or her employer during that particular year.
• a self-employed individual or an individual not described above,	(A) the individual's unused RRSP deduction room carried forward from the previous year
	plus
	(B) the lesser of:
	(i) the RRSP dollar limit
	— for 2006, $18,000
	— for 2007, $19,000
	— for 2008, $20,000
	— for 2009, $21,000
	— for 2010, $22,000
	— for 2011, indexed
	and
	(ii) 18% of earned income for the prior year.

EXHIBIT 9-2
RRSP Limits

	2006	2007	2008	2009	2010	2011
RRSP						
RRSP Dollar Limit	$18,000	$ 19,000	$ 20,000	$ 21,000	$ 22,000	indexed
Earned income needed	$00,000	$105,550	$111,111	$116,667	$122,222	indexed

¶9,350   Definition of earned income for RRSPs

If an individual was a resident of Canada throughout the year, earned income, as defined,   ITA: 146(1)
will include the individual's income for a period in the year throughout which the individual
was a resident in Canada from:

- an office or employment, generally including all taxable benefits, less all employment-related deductions, but not including any deduction for RPP contributions, employee contributions to a retirement compensation arrangement (RCA) or a clergyman's residence;

- a business carried on by the individual either alone, or as a partner actively engaged in the business;

- property, when derived from the rental of real property or from royalties in respect of a work or invention of which the individual was the author or inventor;

- support payments included in computing the individual's income;

- an amount included in income from supplementary unemployment benefit plans, net research grants, and support receipts in computing the individual's income; and

- the amount of disability pension received after 1990 by an individual under the Canada or Quebec Pension Plan;

less the total of the individual's loss or deduction for a period in the year throughout which
the individual was resident in Canada from:

- a business carried on by the individual either alone, or as a partner actively engaged in the business;

- property, where the loss is sustained from the rental of real property; and

- support payments deductible in computing the individual's income.

For the purposes of determining the earned income of such an individual, the income or
loss of the individual for any period in a taxation year is the individual's income or loss
computed as though that period were the whole taxation year.

Note that earned income does not include superannuation or pension benefits (including
CPP/QPP and OAS benefits), retiring allowances, Employment Insurance benefits, death
benefits, amounts received from an RRSP or taxable benefits from a DPSP or a revoked plan.
It also does not include investment income, taxable capital gains, or scholarships and bursaries.

Also note that it is the earned income of the preceding year which is relevant for
purposes of calculating the maximum deductible RRSP contribution.

¶9,355   Calculation of the pension adjustment (PA)

Since a pension adjustment is reported to the individual by his or her employer on a T4
slip, in most cases it will not be necessary for the individual to calculate his or her PA. To do
some advance tax planning for an individual, it may be necessary to get a rough idea of what
the individual's PA will be for future years. Conceptually, the PA represents the value of tax-assisted or sheltered benefits accruing to the taxpayer in a year. Hence, it reflects the amount
of the dollar limit that has been used by employer and employee contributions to an RPP
and/or DPSP, leaving the balance of the dollar limit available for a deductible RRSP contribution.

For example, if an individual's earned income is \$72,000 and PA is \$11,960, that individual's RRSP contribution would be limited to:

18% of earned income (18% of $72,000)	$12,960
Less: PA	11,960
Net limit for RRSP	$ 1,000

The following provides a non-technical indication of how the PA is determined.

(1) *PA for DBP:* The PA for a DBP is based on a formula which reflects the actuarial assumptions made about contributions providing pension income. The objective of the formula is to quantify the contribution room used by contributions to an RPP. The formula is beyond the scope of this text.

(2) *PA for MPP:* The PA for an MPP is equal to the total of the employer's and the employee's contributions in the year.

(3) *PA for DPSP:* The PA for a DPSP is equal to the employer's contributions in the year.

¶9,360   RRSP contribution room carried forward

An advantage of the system is that if an individual is not able to contribute the maximum amount, he or she is allowed to "carry forward" the unused deduction limit. There is no time restriction on this carryforward. The "unused RRSP deduction room" is defined in subsection 146(1). For example, if an individual's maximum annual RRSP contribution limit in 1998 is $10,000, but he or she made a contribution of only $7,000, he or she will be permitted to make an additional deductible RRSP contribution of $3,000 at any time in the future. However, even if he or she makes up the contribution in, for example, 2007, remember that he or she will lose the tax-sheltering on the income that would have been earned on the $3,000 from 1998 until 2007, and on any future income earned on this amount for the balance of his or her career. Therefore, it is important to contribute the maximum to an RRSP as soon as possible.

¶9,365   Excess contribution

¶9,365.10   *Penalties for excess contributions*

The penalty provisions for RRSP overcontributions are fairly severe. There is a 1% per month penalty until the "excess" for the year is removed from the plan.   ITA: 204.1(2.1)

In determining whether there is an excess, the individual includes all amounts contributed by the individual to the plan (other than specified transfers) and all gifts made to the plan, other than gifts made by the individual's spouse. Overcontributions of premiums in the 60-day grace period after the end of the year usually are not considered to be part of the "excess", since the individual can claim them in the year or in the following year.

In order to avoid the 1% per month penalty, the excess amount may be withdrawn from the plan, but it will be included in the individual's income in the year of receipt. This income   ITA: 146(8)
can be reduced by an offsetting deduction if it is withdrawn in the year in which the excess was contributed or in the following year. The withdrawal of contributions on a tax-free basis   ITA: 146(8.2)
is allowed only where the taxpayer is not deliberately making excess contributions.

If the excess is not withdrawn in those particular years, but is instead left in the plan, then the individual will include in income this excess contribution when it is eventually withdrawn and there will be no offsetting deduction, resulting in double taxation. It is, therefore, not advisable to leave an excess contribution in an RRSP, as benefits of tax-free compounding in the plan are unlikely to offset the combination of the 1% per month penalty and the double taxation on withdrawal.

¶9,365.20   *Additional contribution*

There is a threshold amount for an excess contribution, which has been set at a cumula-   ITA: 204.2(1.1)
tive amount of $2,000. This means that at any point in time[6] an individual may contribute up to $2,000 in excess of his or her deductible contribution limit without incurring a penalty. The

---

[6] After February 26, 1995.

purpose of this excess allowance is to provide a margin of error for inadvertent excess contributions and for the operation of group RRSP arrangements. In a family context, both spouses or common-law partners may contribute an additional $2,000, so that in total $4,000 may be sheltered without penalty. Children who did not attain the age of 18 in the previous year may not make this additional contribution. Individuals who contribute to both their own RRSP and a spousal RRSP may not make an additional contribution of more than $2,000 in total.

Even though the individual will not be able to deduct the excess $2,000 contribution for tax purposes as would be the case if it was a regular RRSP contribution, a sum of money could be accumulated using the benefits of tax-free compounding. If, however, the individual makes a maximum deductible contribution every year, when the excess is eventually withdrawn the individual may be subject to double tax, as the funds were not deductible when the contribution was made, but they are taxable when the individual withdraws them. This double tax may be avoided, since the rules provide for an indefinite carryforward of undeducted contributions. If the individual simply reduces the contribution that he or she would otherwise make in a later year (prior to the withdrawal) and claims the additional $2,000 contribution as a deduction under the carryforward provisions, no double tax will result, because all contributions will have been fully deducted.

Even if the individual was not certain that he or she would use the carryforward rules to eliminate double taxation, it may still be advantageous to make additional contribution. Assuming a 10% rate of return and a 50% personal tax rate, if the individual leaves the $2,000 in the RRSP for 15 years or longer, the benefits of tax-free compounding will outweigh the cost of the taxes that must be paid when the funds are withdrawn.

All or part of an individual's additional $2,000 contribution can be made by the individual to a spousal RRSP, but care must be taken so that the spousal attribution rules (see below) and the regular attribution rules do not apply.   ITA: 74.5(12)

¶9,370   Contributions of property

In addition to cash contributions, an individual may be able to contribute certain types of property, such as shares, units of a mutual fund, or Canada Savings Bonds, to an RRSP. The individual will generally need to have a self-administered RRSP if he or she wishes to make a non-cash contribution. If an individual contributes property, he or she is entitled to a deduction equal to the fair market value of the property at the time of the contribution, but keep in mind that the individual is still subject to the normal contribution limits and that the Act restricts the type of property that may be held in an RRSP.

The individual will be considered to have sold the property at its fair market value at the date of contribution. Although any resulting capital gain is subject to tax in the individual's hands, the individual cannot claim any capital loss that arises.   ITA: 40(2)(g)(iv)

¶9,375   Application

Example Problem

Mr. Confused reported the following income for tax purposes in 2006:

Employment income — Subdivision a	$81,000
Dividend received from taxable Canadian corporation (grossed up)	1,200
Rental loss	(2,500)
Total	$79,700

Included in the employment income computation was a deduction for a current contribution to a registered pension plan of $3,200. His employer reported a Pension Adjustment (PA) on his T4 for 2006 of $10,000. Mr. Confused made $5,000 of tax-deductible support payments to his former spouse in 2006.

— REQUIRED

Calculate the maximum RRSP contribution that Mr. Confused can deduct as an annual contribution in 2007, as determined under the definition of "RRSP deduction limit", and advise Mr. Confused as to when he can make his contribution. Is there any other advice that you might want to give Mr. Confused in 2007 regarding his contributions?

— SOLUTION

Mr. Confused's earned income for 2006 is calculated as follows:

ITA: 146(1)

Employment income — Subdivision a	$81,000
Add back RPP contribution	3,200
Deduct: Support payment made	(5,000)
Rental loss	(2,500)
Total earned income for 2006	$76,700

In respect of 2007, Mr. Confused is able to deduct the following:

Lesser of:

(a) 18% of 2006 earned income of $76,700 = $13,806, and

(b) the dollar limit for 2007 of $19,000

less PA for 2006 of $10,000 reported by his employer in respect of the year.

Mr. Confused is able to contribute $3,806 (i.e., $13,806 – $10,000) to his RRSP in respect of 2007. The contribution may be made at any time in 2007 and within the first 60 days of 2008, which is by February 29, 2008. However, Mr. Confused will probably have to wait until the end of February 2007 to make an early 2007 contribution, since he will not know his PA for 2006 until he receives his T4. If Mr. Confused was really cautious, he might want to wait until he receives his Notice of Assessment for his 2006 tax return in which the CRA will issue him a 2007 RRSP contribution limit statement. However, he will have lost the benefit of tax-free compounding on his contribution from March until he receives his Notice of Assessment and makes his contribution. You should inform him that if he has the information at hand respecting the pension benefits that he accrued in the year, you could assist him by calculating his PA and he could make his contribution on the first day of January in 2007.

You should also advise Mr. Confused that because of the way the penalties for an overcontribution work, he may make a one-time additional contribution of up to $2,000 in 2007 and the funds may be left to accumulate tax-free in his RRSP. Although this contribution is not taxdeductible, a sum of money can be built up over the life of his RRSP. This will be preferable to Mr. Confused investing in debt instruments or stocks outside of his RRSP, since the income will not be taxed. In order to avoid tax when Mr. Confused withdraws the $2,000 from his plan, he may be able to use the carryforward rules to his advantage by making a contribution that is $2,000 less than his allowable contribution in a year just prior to the withdrawal of the $2,000 from the plan. Then, he will have room to deduct the $2,000. Even if Mr. Confused is not able to use the carryforward rules to eliminate the tax when he withdraws the funds from the plan, if Mr. Confused is able to leave the additional $2,000 in the plan for a period of about 15 years, assuming that his rate of return on the funds was 10%, he would still be better off making the additional contribution.

¶9,380 Contributions to spousal (or common-law partner) RRSP

A "spousal (or common-law partner) plan", which is a defined term, is a plan under which an individual makes contributions to an RRSP but his or her spouse (or common-law partner) is the annuitant. An individual's contributions to both his or her plan and a spousal (or common-law partner) RRSP are restricted in total to the individual's own contribution limit. Therefore, a contribution made by an individual to a spousal (or common-law partner) RRSP does not affect the spouse's or common-law partner's personal RRSP contribution limit for the year.

ITA: 146(1), 146(5.1)

A spousal RRSP could be set up for a common-law partner. Two individuals of either sex are considered to be common-law partners of each other when they are cohabiting in a conjugal relationship and either (a) they have so cohabited throughout the preceding 12 months, or (b) they are parents of the same child.

ITA: 248(1) "common-law partner"

A spousal (or common-law partner) RRSP can be used to achieve income splitting on retirement. Tax savings will be realized if the retirement income from the RRSP will be taxed at lower marginal tax rates in the spouse's or partner's hands. For example, assuming an individual intends to retire in 20 years and his or her RRSP earns a 10% annual rate of return, the individual could contribute $5,000 to a spousal (or common-law partner) RRSP for the next three years. At retirement, this would give the individual's spouse or partner a 15-year annuity of about $12,000 per year. If the spouse or partner will pay tax on this income at a marginal tax rate of about 26%, compared to about 46% in the individual's hands, the individual will realize annual tax savings of about $2,400 on this retirement income. To the extent that the contributions to a spousal (or common-law partner) RRSP exceed the individual's deductible limit, the income on withdrawal will be attributed back to the individual and will be subject to tax in his or her hands, because the non-deductible contribution would not meet the exception to the attribution rules.

ITA: 74.5(12)(a)

Provided an individual has earned income, contributions can be made to a spousal (or common-law partner) RRSP until the end of the year in which the spouse attains 71 years of age. These deductible contributions can be made even if the contributor is over 71.

There are other factors that an individual should consider when deciding whether to contribute to a spousal (or common-law partner) RRSP. The individual should be aware that amounts contributed to a spousal plan become the property of his or her spouse. This should be considered in view of any provincial laws governing the division of assets in the event of a marital breakdown.

¶9,385   Attribution on spousal (or common-law partner) RRSPs

An individual may contribute to a spousal (or common-law partner) RRSP to gain some benefit from income-splitting. However, special rules apply to curtail such income-splitting if the RRSP is used for short-term income splitting.

Attribution applies to include in the contributing individual's income all premiums paid to any spousal (or common-law partner) RRSP in a three-year period, even if the premiums are not deducted or deductible in the three years. As a consequence, attribution will apply on withdrawal of the funds by the spouse if:

ITA: 146(8.3)

- the individual paid a premium to *any* spousal (or common-law partner) plan in the current year or the preceding two years; and

- the premium is required to be included in computing the income of the individual's spouse or common-law partner.

ITA: 146(8)

If such withdrawals are included in the spouse's or partner's income, the amount withdrawn, up to the amount of the premiums paid by the individual in the three-year period, will also be included in the individual's income. In order to eliminate double counting, if the income is attributed to the individual who made the contribution, an offsetting deduction is allowed to the spouse or common-law partner.

ITA: 146(8.6)

Similar rules apply where the individual's spouse or common-law partner receives an amount in excess of the minimum amount from a RRIF and the RRIF received property from an RRSP to which the individual paid a premium in the three-year period. The amount received by the individual's spouse or common-law partner in excess of the minimum amount will be included in the individual's income rather than the spouse's or partner's.

ITA: 146.3(5.1)

¶9,390   Withdrawals before retirement

An RRSP may generally be terminated at any time prior to maturity (generally retirement) and the proceeds distributed to the individual. However, the gross amount received must be included in his or her income. Of course, the benefit of a tax-free accumulation of funds will be lost. An individual may make partial withdrawals from an RRSP without terminating the plan.

The trustee of the RRSP must withhold tax from the amount withdrawn by the individual. The tax withheld may be claimed as a credit on the individual's income tax return as income taxes paid in the year. The withholding tax rate is based on the amount withdrawn — 10% of the amount if it is $5,000 or less; 20% of the amount if it is between $5,000 and $15,000; and 30% of the amount if it exceeds $15,000, except in Quebec.

ITR: 103(4), 103(6)

Tax withheld at source from RRSP withdrawals may be minimized by making sure that each withdrawal is for $5,000 or less. Any tax liability related to the withdrawal in excess of the amount withheld must be paid when the individual files his or her tax return for the year.

¶9,395 Home Buyers' Plan (HBP) JUST READ NOTE)

Under the Home Buyers' Plan, individuals may withdraw up to an aggregate of $20,000 from any of their RRSPs to buy an owner-occupied home without having to pay tax on the withdrawal. Form T1036 must be used to report the withdrawal and to get the exclusion from income. These withdrawals must be repaid in annual instalments over a maximum period of 15 years. The repayment period begins in the second calendar year following the calendar year in which the withdrawal is made. However, the individual may elect to have a repayment made in the first 60 days of a year treated as having been made in the preceding year. Hence, if $20,000 is withdrawn in 2007, the minimum annual repayment of $1,333 (i.e., $20,000/15) must be made on or before March 1, 2010, being 60 days after 2009 which is the second calendar year after the 2007 year of withdrawal.

ITA: 146.01

A qualifying home must generally be acquired before October 1 of the calendar year following the year of the withdrawal. Under specified conditions, this acquisition deadline can be extended. Only a first-time home buyer may make use of this plan. An individual will be considered to be a first-time home buyer, if neither the individual nor the individual's spouse or common-law partner owned a home and lived in it as the "principal place of residence" in any of the five calendar years beginning before the time of withdrawal. An individual is excepted from this five-year requirement on the termination of the marriage or common-law relationship.

An individual is allowed to participate in an HBP more than once in his or her lifetime. However, the individual must have repaid all amounts previously withdrawn under the HBP before the beginning of the year in which he or she participates in a new HBP.

The first-time home buyer condition need not be met, also, under specific circumstances. The conditions are that:

(a) the individual is entitled to claim the disability tax credit; and

ITA: 118.3(1) (as discussed in Chapter 10)

(b) the HBP withdrawal by the disabled individual or a related individual is to enable the disabled individual to acquire and live in a dwelling that is more accessible by the individual or that is better suited for the personal needs and care of the individual.

Ordinary contributions made to an RRSP within 90 days before a withdrawal will not be allowed as a deduction, except to the extent that the RRSP balance after the withdrawal is more than the amount of the contribution. Hence, an amount that is both contributed and withdrawn within the 90-day period will not be deductible as an RRSP contribution.

Any amount scheduled for repayment, but not repaid in the appropriate year will be included in the individual's income for the year. For example, if the minimum annual repayment is $1,333 and the individual only repays $1,000, the $333 will be included in income and subjected to tax. On the other hand, an individual may repay more than the minimum scheduled repayment for a year. In this case, there will be less to repay over the remainder of the 15-year period and the minimum annual repayments can, but need not, be reduced for subsequent years.

¶9,400   Tax-free RRSP withdrawals for lifelong learning plan (LLP) ~~Same as 3395~~

Individuals are allowed to make tax-free withdrawals from their RRSPs for lifelong learning. The objective is to give taxpayers greater access to funds for retraining. Similar to the Home Buyers' Plan, individuals must repay the amount they withdraw over a fixed period of time.

ITA: 146.02

A maximum of $10,000 per year can be withdrawn from an RRSP by an individual who is enrolled at a designated educational institution in full-time training or higher education requiring not less than 10 hours per week on courses or work in the program for at least three consecutive months during the year. Students with disabilities qualify if engaged in part-time studies. Further withdrawals can be made for a period of up to four years, but total withdrawals cannot exceed $20,000. Also, contributions made within 90 days of a withdrawal are not eligible for tax-free withdrawal.

ITA: 118.6(1)

Amounts withdrawn are repayable in 10 equal annual instalments. The first repayment must be made at the earlier of:

(a) the year following the last year that the student was enrolled on a full-time basis, that is, where the student is not entitled to annual full-time education tax credits for at least three months in two consecutive years; or

(b) 60 days following the fifth year after the first withdrawal.

Repayments simply replenish, without interest, amounts withdrawn from the RRSP. Hence, these repayments are not deductible. If an amount is not repaid on time, it is included in the individual's income in that year.

Individuals may participate in this withdrawal program any number of times during their lifetime. However, no new withdrawals are permitted until all repayments from a previously started program have been made. Of course, while the funds are not in the RRSP, they are not earning sheltered income and there is no opportunity to replenish that income.

¶9,405   Retirement options

¶9,405.10   *Overview*   ~~Same as 9,400~~

Although an RRSP must mature by the end of the year in which the individual reaches the age of 71, the individual does not have to wait until then to obtain retirement income from the RRSP. An RRSP can be matured at any time before the end of the year in which an individual reaches the age of 71. As an alternative, the individual can make withdrawals from the plan. This allows an individual the flexibility to take an early retirement should he or she so desire.

At maturity, the accumulated funds may be withdrawn from an RRSP. Tax must be paid at the individual's marginal tax rate on these funds. As an alternative, he or she may purchase one or a combination of available maturity options. These options provide an individual with retirement income in varying amounts over different periods of time. Tax is deferred until he or she actually receives retirement income.

Retirement options which are currently available are:

Fixed-term annuities	• provide benefits up to age 90, or if the spouse or common-law spouse is younger than the individual, and he or she so elects, until the spouse or common-law partner reaches age 90.
	• may provide fixed or fluctuating income.
Life annuities	• provide benefits during the individual's life, or during the lives of the individual and his or her spouse or common-law partner.

Registered retirement income funds . . .

- may have a guaranteed pay-out option.
- may provide fixed or fluctuating income.
- are essentially a continuation of an RRSP.
- provide the individual with retirement income from the investment of the funds accumulated in a matured RRSP for the individual's life.

Under federal and provincial pension legislation, the proceeds of locked-in RRSPs that arise on the transfer of a lump-sum payment of vested benefits from an RPP must be used to purchase a life annuity or RRIF at retirement.

¶9,405.20   *Considerations when choosing an option*

A number of factors should be considered when deciding which option or combination of options to choose upon maturity of an RRSP:

- the rate of return;
- current and future income needs;
- the tax that would be payable currently if an annuity or RRIF were not purchased to defer tax;
- the income stream that would result from a particular annuity or RRIF;
- the present age of the individual and that of his or her spouse or common-law partner;
- the extent to which the individual wants to personally manage his or her retirement income; and
- the size of the estate the individual wishes to leave to his or her beneficiaries.

¶9,405.30   *Fixed-term and life annuities*

With a fixed-term annuity, all of the funds accumulated in an RRSP will be paid out over the term of the annuity. The monthly retirement income the individual receives will vary, depending on the interest rate the issuer anticipates earning on the funds. However, with a life annuity, the retirement income will also depend on the sex and age of the individual and the options he or she chooses to attach to the annuity. Retirement income is highest for a straight life annuity (i.e., payments cease upon death, even if this occurs shortly after purchasing the annuity). Retirement income is lower if a guaranteed pay-out or guaranteed term option is added. These options guarantee that a certain amount of funds will be paid out, or that funds will be paid for a specified number of years, regardless of when the individual dies.

When an annuity is purchased, the retirement income will be determined for the term of the annuity. Once the annuity is in place, no further involvement with regard to investment decisions is required on the individual's part. In addition, no adjustments in income occur if interest rates subsequently rise or fall.

¶9,410   RRIFs

Generally the following rules apply.

ITA: 146.3

- A RRIF may be established at any time before the end of the year in which the individual reaches the age of 71. Early retirement can therefore be accommodated by a RRIF.
- It is possible to have more than one RRIF at a time. As a result, several different RRIFs can be set up in order to diversify a RRIF portfolio.
- Although a minimum amount must be withdrawn each year, an individual may withdraw any amount in excess of this minimum.

The fact that an individual is able to withdraw any amount in excess of the minimum allows him or her to match cash needs in any given year. The minimum required withdrawal for ages under 79 is calculated as the value of the RRIF at the beginning of each year, divided by the factor $(90 - X)$ where X is the age of the individual at the beginning of the year. Thus, in the first year of the RRIF, no amount need be withdrawn unless he or she so desires. In the second year, if the individual was 65 years old when the RRIF was established, he or she must withdraw at least $\frac{1}{25}$ of the value of the fund at the beginning of the year. The amount withdrawn in the year may be received in one lump-sum payment or periodically throughout the year (e.g., monthly), depending upon the terms of the RRIF. For ages after 78, the minimum amount is derived by multiplying the value of the RRIF at the beginning of the year by a prescribed factor for the age of the annuitant or the annuitant's spouse or common-law partner, if elected.

ITR: 7308(3)

ITR: 7308

Amounts withdrawn from a RRIF in excess of the minimum amount, however, will be subject to withholding tax at the same rates that are applicable to RRSP lump-sum withdrawals.

If an individual so elects at the commencement of the RRIF and his or her spouse or common-law partner is younger, the individual may have the minimum payment out of the RRIF based on the age of the spouse or common-law partner. This election does not automatically make the spouse or common-law partner the annuitant under the RRIF after the individual's death.

Generally, RRIF funds may be invested in the same types of investments as RRSPs. The RRIF may be self-administered. That is, an individual may personally determine, along with the trustees of the RRIF, what investments are made by it. As with an RRSP, a RRIF is not taxed on its earnings. Thus, income accumulates on a tax-free basis in the RRIF.

When choosing which investments to hold in a RRIF, an individual should consider the same factors that he or she would have considered in choosing investments for an RRSP. Liquidity is a particularly important factor when choosing investments to be held in a RRIF, since a portion of the funds must be withdrawn each year to provide retirement income.

¶9,415 Treatment of RRSPs and RRIFs on death

¶9,415.10 *Spouse or common-law partner as beneficiary*

If the individual has a RRIF at the time of death, his or her spouse or common-law partner may continue to receive the income from the RRIF (become the annuitant under the RRIF) or receive a lump sum under the RRIF (become the beneficiary under the RRIF), provided that the individual specified that this was his or her intention, either in the RRIF contract or under the terms of his or her will.

If the spouse or common-law partner becomes the annuitant under the RRIF, payments may continue to be made to the spouse or partner, or to the estate for the benefit of the spouse or partner. If the spouse or partner becomes the beneficiary under the RRIF, the lump sum may be paid directly to him or her, or to an estate for the benefit of the spouse or partner. In the situation where the spouse or partner does not become the annuitant or the beneficiary under the RRIF, the RRIF must be collapsed and the value of the RRIF must be paid to any other named beneficiary or the individual's estate.

Amounts paid to a spouse or common-law partner as a named beneficiary from an RRSP (whether lump-sum or otherwise), or as an annuitant or beneficiary under a RRIF, will be taxable to the spouse or partner when received. Amounts paid from an RRSP to the individual's estate for the benefit of his or her spouse or partner will also be taxable to that spouse or partner, provided that the spouse or partner and the legal representatives of the estate file a joint tax election to this effect. If this election is not filed, the fair market value of all of the property of the RRSP fund at the time of his or her death will be included in the deceased's income for the year of death. If the individual intends to have his or her spouse or partner as beneficiary, it will generally be preferable for the individual to name the spouse or partner as beneficiary under the RRSP, rather than to file the election after death, in order to minimize probate fees. The election is made by filing T2019 (RRSP refunds of premiums designation — Spouse).

In the CRA's view, a similar election may not be available where an amount out of a RRIF is paid to an individual's estate for the benefit of his or her spouse or common-law partner. If the individual intends to have his or her spouse or partner as an annuitant or a beneficiary under the RRIF, the individual should name the spouse or partner as an annuitant or as a beneficiary under the contract or under the terms of the will, so that the RRIF amounts will not be included in the individual's income for the year of death.

Where amounts received out of an unmatured RRSP are taxed in the spouse's or partner's hands, he or she may defer tax on all or any portion of the amount by making either a direct or indirect transfer of the funds to an RRSP (if the spouse or partner is under the age of 71, a RRIF, or by purchasing a fixed-term or life annuity within 60 days after the taxation year of receipt.

ITA: 60(*l*)

¶9,415.20   *Financially dependent child or grandchild as beneficiary*

Where the spouse or common-law partner is not the beneficiary, or the beneficiary or annuitant in the case of a RRIF, the proceeds from a RRIF, an unmatured RRSP or the commuted value of an RRSP annuity must be included in the individual's income for the year of death. An exception occurs in certain circumstances where the beneficiary is a financially dependent child or grandchild even if the deceased individual had a surviving spouse or partner when he or she died, if the proceeds are considered to be a "refund of premiums" as defined.

ITA: 146(1)

A child or grandchild is not considered financially dependent, if his or her income for the year preceding the year in which the annuitant died exceeded the basic personal credit amount ($8,929 in 2007) for that preceding year. This amount is increased by $6,890 to $15,819 if that child or grandchild is infirm.

In these circumstances, it is possible to have, or to elect to have such proceeds taxed in the hands of the child or grandchild. In the case where a dependent child or grandchild is mentally or physically infirm, tax may be deferred on such proceeds if either a direct or indirect transfer is made by the child or grandchild, or his or her representative, to an RRSP (if under the age of 71), a RRIF or an annuity within 60 days after the taxation year of receipt.

ITA: 146(8.1), 146.3(6.1)

ITA: 60(*l*), 60.011

In the case where the child or grandchild is not physically or mentally infirm, tax may be deferred on such proceeds if they are used to acquire an annuity with a term not exceeding 18 minus the age of the child or grandchild at the time the annuity is acquired. The annuity must be acquired in the year the proceeds are included in the child or grandchild's income. In these cases, it will generally be preferable for the individual to name the child or grandchild as the beneficiary under the terms of the will.

¶9,415.30   *Other beneficiaries*

If the individual names a person other than his or her spouse or common-law partner (or, in limited circumstances, a child or grandchild) as a beneficiary under the RRSP or as beneficiary or annuitant under the RRIF, the estate will be faced with paying any tax liability resulting from the individual's death, even though it may not have sufficient funds to do so because the proceeds have been paid to the named beneficiary.

¶9,415.40   *Contributions for year of death*

If, at the time of death, the individual has not made an RRSP contribution for the year of death, his or her legal representative may make a spousal or common-law partner RRSP contribution under the normal rules. Such a contribution will be deductible in the year of death, provided the contribution is made within 60 days of the end of the year of death.

ITA: 146(5.1)

¶9,420 Transfers of Retirement Income and Sheltered Amounts

In general, lump-sum amounts of retirement income can be transferred on a tax-free   ITA: 147.3
basis, but only where the amounts are transferred directly from one plan to another. When
amounts are transferred directly, they generally are not included in income and consequently
it is not necessary to claim an offsetting deduction.

The rollover of periodic pension income out of an RPP, DPSP, Old Age Security (OAS)
and Canada Pension/Quebec Pension Plan (CPP/QPP) is generally prohibited. Restrictions are
also placed on the amounts that may be transferred from defined benefit RPPs to money
purchase RPPs and RRSPs. The result is to restrict the opportunity for individuals to obtain
further tax deferral on receipts of periodic pension income.

¶9,425 Direct transfer

Lump-sum RPP and DPSP amounts are transferable on a tax-free basis, but *only through
a direct transfer* for:

- lump-sum amounts out of RPPs (other than lump-sum amounts that relate to an   ITA: 147.3
  actuarial surplus) to another RPP or to an RRSP under which the individual is an
  annuitant;

- lump-sum amounts of DPSPs to an RPP, an RRSP or to certain DPSPs; and   ITA: 147(19), 147(20)

- property from an unmatured RRSP to an RPP, to another RRSP or to a RRIF.   ITA: 146(16)

When such direct transfers are made, the amount transferred is not included in income,
and does not give rise to a deduction. If, however, the individual receives the funds personally, the amount will be included in his or her income for tax purposes in the year it is
received and the individual will not be able to contribute the funds (i.e., transfer them
indirectly) to his or her RRSP to avoid the income inclusion.

Unlimited lump-sum transfers may be made directly from one MPP to another, from an
MPP to a DBP, from a DBP to another DBP, but transfers from a DBP to an MPP or RRSP are
limited to prescribed amounts.

¶9,430 Retiring allowances

Retiring allowances may be transferred tax-free, within certain dollar and time limits, to   ITA: 6(1)(*a*)(iv), 248(1)
an RRSP or an RPP. A retiring allowance is defined to be an amount received (other than a   "retiring allowance"
superannuation or pension benefit, an amount received as a consequence of the death of an
employee or employment benefits derived from certain specified counselling services):

(a) upon or after retirement of an individual from an office or employment in recognition
of his or her long service, or

(b) in respect of a loss of an office or employment of an individual, whether or not
received as, on account or in lieu of payment of damages or pursuant to an order or
judgment of a competent tribunal

by the individual or, after his or her death, by a dependant or relation of the individual or by
the legal representative of the individual.

The rollover of a retiring allowance to an RRSP or an RPP may be made within the   ITA: 60(*j*.1)
following limits:

- $2,000 for each year or part thereof during which the individual was employed by the
  employer or related employer with respect to service before 1996;

plus

- $1,500 for each year or part year of service counted for the $2,000 limit prior to 1989
  for which the employer RPP and DPSP contribution did not vest at the time of
  retirement.

The $1,500 limit is technically computed as the number of pre-1989 years or part years of employment in excess of the equivalent number of pre-1989 years in respect of which employer contributions had vested. The use of the term "equivalent number of years" allows for a fractional number of years to be used, when, to use the example presented in explanatory notes, an employee has worked seven pre-89 years and 60% of the employer's contributions have vested. In that case, the non-vested years would be counted as 2.8 years (i.e., 7 years – 60% of 7 years) and, hence, at $1,500 per non-vested years, $4,200 (i.e., 2.8 × $1,500) could be deducted on a transfer of a retiring allowance.

The amount that may be deducted may not exceed the total of the amounts paid by the individual in the year or in the 60 days after the end of the year as a contribution to an RPP. Excluded from that limit are amounts deductible: (1) for employee contributions to an RPP, and (2) as a premium to an RRSP under which he or she is the annuitant, other than the portion that has been designated as a transfer of a refund of premiums to a spouse or child as a consequence of death or for certain direct transfers of amounts out of a RRIF or an RRSP.

ITA: 8(1)(*m*)

ITA: 60(*l*)

The following is a *simplified* formula for the deductible amount of a retiring allowance transferred to an RRSP. The deductible transfer cannot exceed the least of:

(a) the sum of:

   (i) $2,000 × the number of pre-'96 years during which the individual was employed (as described above) XXX

   (ii) $1,500 × the equivalent number of non-vested pre-89 years (as described above) XXX

                                                                   XXX

(b)* total RRSP premium contributions XXX

(c) the amount of the retiring allowance XXX

---

   * Item (b), in the actual legislation, consists of total RRSP contributions and non-deductible RPP contributions made by the employee. However, it would be unusual for an employee to have made a non-deductible RPP contribution under the current legislation (unless past service contributions were made) and, as a result, that part of the rule has been omitted for simplicity.

The limit in part (b) above reflects the fact that an individual cannot deduct more than the amount actually transferred or contributed into a sheltered plan.

Example Problem

   Consider the following facts:

Retiring allowance received by I. Wasfired in 2007	$30,000
Earned income in 2006	66,000
PA reported by employer in 2006	10,880
Number of pre-'96 years during which he was employed since November of 1984	12
Percentage of vesting for pre-1989 years of service	60%

— REQUIRED

   Determine the amount that I. Wasfired is able to deduct if he transfers the maximum he can to his RRSP.

ITA: 60(*j*.1)

— SOLUTION

   I. Wasfired is only able to contribute $27,000 to his RRSP without overcontributing to the plan in 2007, determined as:

ITA: 60(*j*.1)

Sum of $2,000 \times 12^{(1)}$ = ...	$24,000
$1,500 \times 2^{(2)}$ = ...	3,000
Total..	$27,000

I. Wasfired may deduct a $27,000 transfer in respect of his $30,000 retiring allowance to an RRSP, plus his annual contribution for 2007.

— *NOTES TO SOLUTION*

$^{(1)}$ Since the legislation only refers to years, not full years, it is reasonable to assume part years would qualify.

$^{(2)}$ In the five pre-1989 years (i.e., 1984 to 1988, inclusive) during which the taxpayer was employed, 60% of the employer's contributions vested. Therefore, the equivalent non-vested years would be counted as two years (i.e., 5 years – 60% of 5 years) and, hence, an additional $1,500 may be deducted in respect of each of those two equivalent non-vested years.

¶9,440   Overpayments and Other Deductions

¶9,445   Overpayments included in income

The Act permits the deduction of certain overpayments of receipts which have already been included in income, but to which the taxpayer was not entitled, and, hence, must repay (e.g., pension benefits, unemployment insurance and education assistance payments). ITA: 60(*n*), 60(*q*), 60(*v*.1)

¶9,450   Objections and appeals

Also, deductible are amounts paid in the year in respect of fees or expenses incurred in an objection or appeal under the Act and other specified legislation. The expenditures that are deductible could include accounting fees incurred in the preparation of an objection or appeal as well as legal costs. ITA: 60(*o*)

¶9,455   Legal fees to establish a right

Legal expenses paid by the taxpayer to collect or establish a right to a retiring allowance or pension benefits are deductible. The deduction of legal expenses is limited to the amount of retiring allowance or pension benefits at issue, net of any transfers of a retiring allowance to an RRSP or RPP. Excess legal expenses can be carried forward seven years to be deducted against related retiring allowance or pension benefits in those years. ITA: 60(*o*.1)

ITA: 60(*j*.1)

¶9,460   OAS clawback

A deduction is permitted for the amount of Old Age Security (OAS) benefits that a taxpayer must repay under the clawback provision of the Act. Where an individual's income under Division B, before deducting the clawback, exceeds $63,511 in 2007, all or some part of the Old Age Security benefits are taxed back. The amount of repayment is computed as: ITA: 60(*w*), 180.2

The lesser of:

(a) OAS benefits		$xxx
(b) income under Division B without par. 60(*w*) deduction	$ xxx	
Less:	63,511	
Excess, if any	$ xxx	
15% of excess, if any		$xxx

OAS benefits are currently about $5,900 per year. Therefore, a Division B income of $70,000 (before the clawback deduction) would result in a clawback of $973 (i.e., 15% of ($70,000 – $63,511)). Since $973 of the benefits must be repaid as a special tax, the clawback is allowed as a deduction. In essence, the deduction equates net income effects with cash effects as follows:

ITA: 60(*w*)

ITA: Part I.2, 180.2

	Income effect	Cash effect	
Receipt	$ 5,900	$ 5,900	ITA: 56(1)(*a*)
Clawback	(973)	(973) (Part I.2 tax)	ITA: 60(*w*)
Net effect	$ 4,927	$ 4,927	

¶9,470 Moving Expenses

¶9,475 Deductible expenditures

Taxpayers are permitted to deduct the moving expenses in respect of an eligible relocation under certain prescribed limitations imposed by the Act.

ITA: 62(3), 248(1)
"moving expenses"

These deductible expenses include:

(a) reasonable travelling costs in moving the family members to the new residence;

(b) transporting or storing household effects;

(c) the cost of meals and accommodation near the old residence or an acquired new residence for a period not exceeding 15 days;

(d) lease cancellation costs in respect of the old residence;

(e) selling costs of the old residence;

(f) the cost of legal services, transfer taxes or registration taxes, but not goods and services tax, in respect of the new residence but only where the old residence is being sold;

(g) mortgage interest, property taxes, insurance premiums and costs associated with maintaining heat and power, to a maximum of $5,000, payable in respect of a vacant "old residence" for a period during which reasonable efforts are being made to sell the "old residence"; and

(h) the cost of revising legal documents to reflect the taxpayer's new address, replacing driving licences and automobile permits and obtaining utility connections and disconnections.

Note that selling costs of the old residence may be deducted as moving costs or as selling costs for capital gains purposes.

¶9,480 Flat-rate deductions by administrative practice

By administrative CRA practice, taxpayers may choose a simplified method to calculate certain travel expenses for moving. Instead of substantiating actual expenses by receipts, the taxpayer may use various pre-established flat rates. Individuals may claim a flat rate of $17 a meal, to a maximum of $51 per day, per person, without receipts. An individual may determine the deduction for vehicle expenses by multiplying the number of kilometres driven by the flat rate in the following list for the province or territory from which travel begins:

Province or Territory	2006 Cents/km*
Alberta	47.5
British Columbia	47.5

Province or Territory	2006 Cents/km*
Manitoba	45.5
New Brunswick	47.5
Newfoundland and Labrador	50.5
Northwest Territories	54.5
Nova Scotia	47.5
Nunavut	54.5
Ontario	48.5
Prince Edward Island	47.5
Quebec	51.5
Saskatchewan	44.5
Yukon	57.0

*www.cra.gc.ca/travelcosts — 2007 rates will be available on the CRA Web site in 2008.

Vehicle expenses covered by the flat rate include operating and ownership expenses as follows:

- operating expenses: fuel, oil, tires, licence fees, insurance, maintenance and repairs

- ownership expenses: depreciation, provincial tax and finance charges

¶9,485 Eligible relocation

There are two distinct categories of taxpayers contained in the definition of "eligible relocation": ITA: 248(1) "eligible relocation"

(a) taxpayers who move to a new business or employment location in Canada may deduct their moving expenses from their income in that new work location; or

(b) students who move to attend a post-secondary institution on a full-time basis either in or out of Canada may deduct their moving expenses from student income. ITA: 62(2)

There are a number of specific limitations imposed upon the above two groups of taxpayers. The following are the most important:

(a) the taxpayer must move 40 kilometres (measured by the shortest normal route available to the travelling public)[7] closer (as discussed in Chapter 3, under the heading "Housing loss and housing cost benefits") to his or her new work location or post-secondary institution;

(b) moving expenses, which exceed the income from the new work location in the year of move, can be deducted, but only in the following year, against income from that new work location; and

(c) the taxpayer cannot be reimbursed by or be in receipt of an allowance from his or her employer for the moving expenses he or she is claiming, unless the reimbursement or allowance is included in income.

The income limitation on moving expenses may not be clear in its application to the situation of an individual who fits both categories of taxpayer recognized in paragraph (a) of the definition of "eligible relocation". For example, a full-time student who moves to a university over 40 kilometres away may have both income from a research grant and part-time employment income from outside of the educational institution in the new location. The provision limits the *aggregate* of moving expenses, ITA: 62(1)(c), 248(1) "eligible relocation"

ITA: 62(1)(c)

---

[7] The case of *Giannakopoulos v. The Queen*, 95 DTC 5477 (F.C.A.), appears to have established this method of measurement of the 40 kilometres.

(a) in the case of an employee or self-employed individual, to income from employment or business in the new location, *and*

(b) in the case of a full-time student, to income from a research grant.

The use of the word "and" between cases (a) and (b) above may allow a deduction of moving expenses from the sum of both categories of income in the case of the student, as presented. The relevant Interpretation Bulletin does not address the issue directly, but deals with the two cases separately, without commenting on a situation involving a combination of the two categories of income for a student. The authorized form T1-M and the accompanying information are not entirely clear either. Note that, with the full exemption for scholarship income, the exclusion from a student's income of scholarships means that they provide no base for a moving expense deduction.

IT-178R3, par. 2(d), 10(e)

Also it appears that the actual move does not have to be accomplished in the same year as the change in the work location.[8]

¶9,490 Child Care Expenses

¶9,495 Eligibility

Child care expenses are permitted to be deducted in the same year that the taxpayer incurs these expenses in the process of earning income. Note that these provisions restrict the deduction to the parent or supporting individual with the lower income, except during a period where that individual is:

- a student in full-time or part-time attendance at a designated educational institution or a secondary school in Canada;

ITA: 63(2)(b) (clause (i)(A) of factor C)

- infirm and incapable of caring for children for at least two weeks;

ITA: 63(2)(b) (clause (i)(B) of factor C)

- confined to prison for at least two weeks; or

ITA: 63(2)(b) (clause (i)(C) of factor C)

- living apart from the higher-income taxpayer throughout a period of at least 90 days commencing in the year due to a marital or common-law relationship breakdown.

ITA: 63(2)(b) (clause (i)(D) of factor C)

Income for this purpose is determined to be the income before the child care expense deduction and the deduction for the clawback of certain social assistance payments like OAS. Where the incomes of two taxpayers are equal, the individuals must agree to treat the income of one of them as higher.

ITA: 63(2), 63(2.1)
ITA: 60(w)

The case of *Fiset v. M.N.R.*, challenged successfully the above interpretation. In this particular situation, the Tax Court of Canada determined that since one spouse had no income and since nil is not an amount (of income), the provision could not be applied. However, section 3 was amended subsequently so that no income is zero amount, not nil. Therefore, a taxpayer with no income will have a zero "amount".

88 DTC 1226 (T.C.C.)

Another interesting judicial development involving child care expenses is the case of *Symes v. The Queen et al.* In this case, the self-employed taxpayer claimed the expenses as a business expense rather than a child care expense. The CRA had denied the expenses as personal living expenses. The taxpayer also argued that there was a violation of rights under subsection 15(1) of the *Charter of Rights and Freedoms*. The Supreme Court of Canada held that the language of the child care expense deduction provision specifically encompasses the purpose for which the taxpayer had incurred her nanny expenses. As a result, the business expense deduction provisions could not be interpreted to permit her a child care business expense deduction. Furthermore, the taxpayer failed to show that women disproportionately pay child care expenses, to prove that the child care expense deduction provision violates subsection 15(1) of the Charter. The taxpayer's evidence showed only that women disproportionately bear the responsibility for caring for children in society.

ITA: 18(1)(h)
94 DTC 6001 (S.C.C.)
ITA: 9(1), 18(1)(a), 63
ITA: 18(1)(h)

ITA: 62
ITA: 9, 18(1)(a), 18(1)(h)

---

[8] See *Beyette v. M.N.R.*, 89 DTC 701 (T.C.C.), for a decision on this issue.

¶9,500 Limitations

There are several additional restrictions which should be noted:

- an eligible child includes a child who turned 16 years of age during the year, since he or she was "during the year" under 16 years of age;   ITA: 63(3)

- the payments cannot be made to certain individuals listed under paragraph (*b*) of the definition of "child care expense", including persons under 18 years of age who are related to the taxpayer by blood, marriage or adoption and a person claimed as a dependant;   ITA: 63(3), 118, 251(6)

- the maximum amount claimable for a child's attendance at a boarding school or camp is $175 (i.e., $1/40$ of $7,000) per week for each child under the age of seven at the end of the year or for a child who has a severe and prolonged mental or physical impairment and $100 (i.e., $1/40$ of $4,000) per week for any other eligible child. These rules are set out in paragraph (*c*) of the definition of "child care expense" and the definition of "periodic child care expense";   ITA: 63(3)

- earned income, which is one of the limiting factors in determining the child care deduction, is defined very specifically (note the difference between this definition and the "earned income" definition for a registered retirement savings plan). Specifically, the definition of "salary or wages" does not apply to section 63. This definition of earned income reflects the original purpose of the child care expense deduction provision which was to encourage individuals who had to care for young children to enter the workforce as employees, to carry on a business, to carry on research under a grant, or attend an educational institution to upgrade work skills and knowledge; and   ITA: 63(3), 248(1) "salary or wages" ITA: 146(1)

- expenses must be substantiated by receipts bearing the social insurance number of the person performing the service.   ITA: 63(1)

¶9,505 Deduction calculation

The following formulae reflect the maximum child care deduction.

(a) The lower income spouse is restricted to a deduction of the least of: ITA: 63(1)

   (i) generally an amount paid in the year by the taxpayer or supporting person;[9]   ITA: 63(1)(*a*), 63(2)(*b*)(vi)

   (ii) $4,000 for each eligible child seven years of age or older, $7,000 for each eligible child under age seven at the end of the year and $10,000 for each child who has a severe and prolonged mental or physical impairment; and   ITA: 63(3) "annual child care expense amount"

   (iii) $2/3$ of the earned income of the taxpayer as defined   ITA: 63(2.3)(*e*), 63(3)

   minus the amount deducted by the higher-income spouse under part (b) below.   ITA: 63(1)(*f*)

(b) The higher income spouse, where the lower income taxpayer is a person described in clauses (i)(A) to (D) and subparagraph (ii) of the definition of factor C in the formula for the deduction allowed by the higher-income spouse, is restricted to a deduction of the lesser of: ITA: 63(2)(*b*)

(i) the least of (i)[10], (ii) and (iii) described in (a) above and computed using the earned income of the higher income supporting person; and

(ii) the sum of:

   (A) $250 (i.e., $1/40$ of $10,000) times the number of children who have a severe and prolonged mental or physical impairment,

---

[9] A "supporting person" is defined in subsection 63(3). However, where the taxpayer is the higher-income spouse, the payments made by a supporting person and deductible by the taxpayer are restricted to those payments made by a person living separate and apart from the taxpayer for a period of at least 90 days due to marital or common-law relationship breakdown.

[10] Paragraph 63(1)(*c*) excludes, from part (a)(i) above, amounts used in computing a child care deduction of another individual.

¶9,500

(B) $175 (i.e., $\frac{1}{40}$ of $7,000) times the number of children under seven years of age at the end of the year, and

(C) $100 (i.e., $\frac{1}{40}$ of $4,000) times the number of other eligible children,

times the number of weeks the lower income spouse was a person described in clauses (i)(A) to (D) and subparagraph (ii) of the definition of factor C in the formula applicable to the deduction by the higher-income spouse.

ITA: 63(2)(*b*)

Clause (i)(A) of the definition of factor C in the formula applicable to the deduction by the higher-income spouse describes a full-time student, that is, one who is enrolled in a program of not less than three consecutive weeks duration that requires not less than 10 hours per week on courses or work. The dollar limit on the deduction that may be claimed by the working spouse when the other spouse is a part-time student, described in subparagraph (ii) of the definition of factor C, is, also, $175 (i.e., $\frac{1}{40}$ of $7,000) per child under age 7 and $100 (i.e., $\frac{1}{40}$ of $4,000) per child age 7 to 16. However in the case of a part-time student, the limit is computed for each month of studies. Months are counted where the part-time student is enrolled at an educational institution in Canada in an eligible program lasting at least three consecutive weeks and involving a minimum of 12 hours spent on courses each month.

ITA: 63(2)(*b*)

¶9,510 Encouragement for parent to attend school

The legislation provides a child care expense deduction to single parents in full-time or part-time attendance at either a designated educational institution or a secondary school in Canada and to two-parent families when both parents are in full-time attendance in school at the same time. Full-time attendance is defined, for that purpose, as enrolment in a program of at least three consecutive weeks duration that requires the individual to spend at least 10 hours per week on courses or work in the program. Part-time attendance is defined as enrolment in a program of at least three consecutive weeks duration that requires the individual to spend not less than 12 hours per month on courses in the program. The limits of the deduction are the amounts paid in respect of child care to a maximum of $250 (i.e., $\frac{1}{40} \times$ $10,000) per week of attendance per child who has a severe and prolonged mental or physical infirmity, $175 (i.e., $\frac{1}{40}$ of $7,000) per week of attendance per child under 7 at the end of the year and $100 (i.e., $\frac{1}{40}$ of $4,000) per week of attendance per child over age 6 and under age 16 at any time during the year. The income limit for this deduction is based on all amounts included in computing the individual's Division B income for the year, not just earned income.

ITA: 63(2.2), 63(2.3)

ITA: 63(2.2)(*a*)(i)

ITA: 63(2.2)(*a*)(ii)

ITA: 63(2.3)(*b*)

¶9,515 Application

Example Problem

Efficacious and Useful Xiao are married. The cost of child care expenses for three eligible children (ages 4, 5 and 9) was $175 per week for 52 weeks.

Efficacious' earned income	$45,000
Useful's earned income	12,000

Useful was determined to be physically infirm by a qualified medical practitioner and he was confined to bed for a period of 10 weeks.

— *REQUIRED*

Compute the child care expense deduction under section 63 for 2007.

— *SOLUTION*

Since the lower-income spouse (Useful) is infirm and incapable of caring for children for at least two weeks in the year, it is possible for the higher-income spouse (Efficacious) to claim a deduction for part of the child care expenses as demonstrated below.

Efficacious' child care deduction is the lesser of:

(a) the least of:

    (i) an amount paid in the year ($175 × 52) .... $ 9,100

    (ii) $7,000 × 2 children = $14,000

        $4,000 × 1 child = ...   4,000 $18,000   ....$9,100

    (iii) ⅔ × $45,000 = ... $30,000

(b) the sum of:

    (i) $175 × 2 children = ... $350

    (ii) $100 × 1 child = ...   100 $450 × 10 weeks = $4,500

   Lesser amount: $4,500

Useful's child care deduction is the least of:

    (i) ($175 × 52 weeks) = ... $ 9,100

    (ii) ($7,000 × 2 children) + ($4,000 × 1 child) = ... $18,000 $8,000

    (iii) (⅔ × $12,000) = ... $ 8,000

   minus the amount deducted by Spouse A   4,500

                                     $3,500

Therefore, the sum of both spouses' claim ($4,500 + $3,500) is limited, in this case, to the $8,000 amount which is ⅔ of the lower income spouse's earned income. The computational format used above is similar to that found in form T778. The format simplifies the effect on the calculation, which might otherwise require that the amount used in part (a)(i) of Efficacious' deduction calculation be determined as the minimum amount after all other parts of the calculation, so that only the $4,500 amount actually deductible by Efficacious is shown in part (a)(i). This follows from a possible strict interpretation of the rule, which would not permit Useful to deduct an amount that is "included in computing the amount deductible" by Efficacious, in this case. Technically, the full $9,100 used in part (a)(i) of Efficacious's calculation was included in computing the amount deductible by Useful. The simplified calculation used in the example problem, above, arrives at the correct distribution between Efficacious and Useful and is apparently acceptable, as evidenced by the computational format used in the authorized form, T778.

ITA: 63(1)(c)

ITA: 63(1)(c)

¶9,520 Disability Support Deduction

Disability support expenses incurred to enable a taxpayer to work or to attend a secondary school or a designated educational institution are fully deductible from the disabled person's income. The deduction is subject to a dollar deduction limit. The following services or equipment, among others, used by disabled persons qualify for the deduction: sign-language interpretation services, real-time captioning services, teletypewriters, optical scanners and electronic speech synthesizers.

ITA: 64

In addition, the refundable medical expense supplement (RMES) provided in the calculation of an individual's tax includes 25% of the total of the allowable expenses claimed under the non-refundable medical expense tax credit and the new disability supports deduction. For details on this supplement, please refer to Chapter 10.

ITA: 122.51

¶9,520

An individual, who has a specified impairment in physical or mental function, such as speech, hearing, eyesight or learning or who has a severe and prolonged mental or physical impairment and who qualifies for the impairment credit, may deduct expenses paid to an unrelated attendant, who is at least 18 years of age, to enable the individual to work as an employee, carry on a business, carry on research, or attend a designated educational institution or a secondary school at which the individual is enrolled in an educational program. The deduction for disability support is limited to the lesser of: ITA: 118.3

ITA: 64

(a) the amount paid in the year to the attendant net of any reimbursement; and

(b) the sum of:

  (i) the total of:

    (A) employment income inclusions or the taxable portion, if any, of scholarships and bursaries or net research grants, or

    (B) income from business, and

  (ii) where the taxpayer is a student, the least of:

    (A) $15,000,

    (B) $375 times the number of weeks in the year during which the individual attends the institution or school, and

    (C) the amount by which the individual's total income exceeds the individual's income, that is income aggregated in (b)(i), above.

¶9,530   Expenses of Residents Absent from Canada

The Act extends the deductibility of child care expenses and disability support expenses to an individual who is absent from, but still resident in, Canada. Such an individual, who is physically absent from Canada throughout all or some part of a taxation year, would otherwise be precluded from these deductions for expenditures made outside of Canada by the wording contained in the child care and disability support deduction provisions. This provision in section 64.1, to extend deductibility, is an apparent reaction to the strict interpretation of the child care expense and disability support deduction provisions taken by the courts in cases involving members of the Canadian Armed Forces. The provision appears to be directed to individuals who are physically absent from Canada for most of a year, but are deemed to be resident. However, the wording of the provision would also appear to apply to individuals who are considered to be resident by the common law principle of continuing ties to Canada. ITA: 63, 64, 64.1, 250(1)

ITA: 63, 64
ITA: 63, 63

¶9,800 REVIEW QUESTIONS

(1) Ms. Tired had been working for the same employer for the past 10 years and was tired of her job. She decided to quit and travel to Australia for a year. On leaving, her employer paid her a lump-sum amount of $15,000, since Ms. Tired had been a good employee of theirs and they were hoping she might come back to work for them when she returned to Canada. Ms. Tired had no intention of working for them again but was grateful for the payment. Comment on how this payment should be taxed.

(2) Mr. Early has worked for the provincial government for the past 35 years and was now eligible for early retirement. As part of his retirement package he is entitled to a lump-sum payment for unused sick days in the amount of $20,000 and unused vacation days of $25,000. On retirement, he is going to receive a cheque for $45,000 as payment for the above amounts. How will this amount be taxed?

(3) Charles and Dee Vorce have decided to end their 12-year marriage. As part of their written separation agreement, they agree that Charles will pay Dee $3,000 per month for her personal support and maintenance, including $1,200 per month for the mortgage on the house that Dee will be living in. The original principal amount of the mortgage is $120,000. What limitations, if any, will Charles encounter when deciding the deductibility of the payments related to the mortgage?

(4) Mark and Ann have agreed to a separation agreement that requires Ann to pay $2,000 per month to Mark as an allowance for his maintenance. Initially, this payment will consist of $1,500 paid to Mark directly and $500 paid to the financial institution that holds the mortgage on his condominium. Mark may change this arrangement at any time to have the full $2,000 paid to him directly. Comment on the deductibility of these payments.

(5) Sam Student reached an agreement with his employer to pay for his education and living expenses while he returned to university. The agreement was that, if he returned to work for his employer when he graduated, there would be no repayment of the amounts he received. If he did not return to work for his employer, the payments he received would have to be repaid in full. How would this be treated for tax purposes?

(6) Mrs. Smith, a 75 year-old widow, has applied for and received the Old Age Security Supplement. This payment is based on the fact that her income is below a certain threshold amount. She has asked you to tell her how this is treated for tax purposes.

(7) Mr. Slippery, a consultant, did some work for ACME Corporation with the agreed-upon fee being $15,000. When the time came for the billing to be done, Mr. Slippery sent an invoice to ACME with instructions that the cheque be made payable to his wife. What would your comments be to Mr. Slippery and his wife on this arrangement?

(8) How do you determine how much of the employer's contributions to a defined benefit pension plan are deductible?

(9) What is the maximum tax-assisted benefit that may be provided to an individual under a defined benefit plan?

(10) What is the major difference between a defined benefit pension plan and a money purchase pension plan?

(11) One of the RRSP contribution limits is 18% of the prior year's earned income. How was the "18%" arrived at?

(12) In 2007, one of the RRSP contribution limits is $19,000. How was this "$19,000" arrived at?

(13) Joe is confused. He is trying to understand the pension rules and he cannot understand why the limit on a money purchase pension plan is based on 18% of this year's income while the limit for an RRSP is based on last year's income. Explain this difference to him.

(14) It has been said that if an individual makes a $2,000 overcontribution (i.e., under the penalty limit) to an RRSP, and as long as the money is left in the RRSP for 15 years or longer at a 10% return and a 46% personal tax rate, then the benefits of compounding will outweigh the cost of the taxes that might be paid when the funds are withdrawn, even if the $2,000 is never deductible. Can you show how this calculation was arrived at? If the rate of return was only 8%, how long would the funds have to be left in the RRSP?

(15) Jennifer wanted to withdraw $20,000 from her RRSP in January in order to buy a new car. She had spent a long time accumulating this amount, but felt that it was more important to buy a car now than accumulate for retirement later. How can she minimize the tax that is withheld on the $20,000 taken out of the plan?

(16) Mr. Mort, a widower, has died and now his executor has come in to administer the will. His only assets on his death were an RRSP worth $150,000 and his house and other personal assets worth $150,000. Both of his children were grown up so he thought that his was a simple estate. He left the RRSPs to his daughter, Kim, and the residue to his son, Jim. Is there likely to be any conflict between the beneficiaries?

(17) Joan had worked for the same employer for 20 pre-'96 years. Two years ago she was fired. She took legal action against her former employer on the basis that it was wrongful dismissal. This year she won her case and was awarded $40,000. She then paid her legal fees of $8,000 and contributed $35,000 to her RRSP as a retiring allowance. She is glad the case has been settled since she has not worked since her dismissal. What would you show on her personal tax return for the year based on this information?

ITA: 60(*j*.1)

¶9,825   MULTIPLE CHOICE QUESTIONS

Question 1

Max retired in 2007 and received a $100,000 retiring allowance. Max worked for his employer from April 1975 to January 2007. He never belonged to a registered pension plan or a deferred profit sharing plan during any of those years. What is the maximum amount of retiring allowance that Max can shelter from tax by transferring it to his RRSP?

(A) $42,000

(B) $63,000

(C) $66,500

(D) $88,500

Question 2

Ms. Assad wants to know the maximum RRSP contribution she can make in 2007 or in the first 60 days of 2008 that will be fully deductible on her 2007 tax return. The following information was taken from Ms. Assad's 2006 tax return:

Income from employment	$44,000
RPP contributions	1,000
Moving expenses	300
Support received	3,600
Pension income	6,000
Real estate rental income	1,400
Interest income	

The pension adjustment reported by Ms. Assad's employer for 2006 was $4,000. Ms. Assad also has a $1,000 unused RRSP deduction limit room which has carried forward from 2006.

What is the maximum RRSP contribution that Ms. Assad can make in 2007 or in the first 60 days of 2008 and deduct fully on her 2007 tax return?

(A) $4,920

(B) $5,000

(C) $6,000

(D) $16,000

Question 3

Meg and James Rashev were both employed full-time during the year. The Rashevs have 4 children: Joanne (age 17), Susie (age 14), Sarah and Kelly (4 year old twins). The Rashevs employed a nanny to look after their children and paid her $15,000 for the year. In addition, during July, the 14-year old went to overnight camp for two weeks at a cost of $250 per week. The Rashevs' family income is summarized below:

	Meg	James
Salary & taxable benefits	$ 46,000	
Employment expenses [sec. 8]	(2,800)	
Business income:		
Revenues		$ 50,000
Expenses deductible for tax purposes		(32,000)
Interest income	800	1,500

Which one of the following represents the maximum child care deduction that can be claimed by the Rashevs in the year?

(A) James can claim a deduction of $12,000.

(B) Meg can claim a deduction of $13,000.

(C) James can claim a deduction of $18,000.

(D) James can claim a deduction of $15,200.

Question 4

Ms. Chiu moved from Toronto to Vancouver to start a new job. She earned $40,000 from her Toronto job and $50,000 from her Vancouver job in the year of the move. Ms. Chiu incurred the following costs of moving all of which can be substantiated by receipts:

Moving van to transport household effects	$ 5,000
Travelling costs — self, spouse and two children	3,000
Legal fees — Vancouver house	900
Legal fees — Toronto house	1,100
Loss on sale of Toronto house	25,000
Hotel costs while waiting for Vancouver house — $100 per day for 30 days	3,000
House hunting trip (prior to Vancouver move)	800

Travelling costs consist of three meals a day for four persons over five full days, gas and other car costs, and hotel for five nights at $100 per night. The distance moved between Toronto and Vancouver was 4,430 kilometres.

Which one of the following amounts represents the maximum amount that Ms. Chiu can deduct as moving expenses on her personal income tax return for the year of the move?

(A) $9,500

(B) $12,169

(C) $13,669

(D) $13,800

Question 5

Sahar's income for tax purposes for 2006 and 2007 is as follows:

	2006	2007
Salary	$100,000	$110,000
Taxable benefits under sections 6 and 7	8,000	8,000
Travel expenses under section 8	(3,000)	(2,000)
Registered pension plan contributions under s. 8	(4,200)	(4,200)
Business losses	(1,000)	(1,200)
Rental income (net of expenses and CCA)	3,200	3,600
Spousal support paid	(12,600)	(12,000)
Net income under Division B	$ 90,400	$102,200

Which of the following statements is correct?

(A) The earned income that should be used to calculate her child care expense deduction for 2007 is $110,000.

(B) The earned income that should be used to calculate her RRSP deduction for 2007 is $106,400.

(C) The earned income that should be used to calculate her child care expense deduction for 2007 is $102,200.

(D) The earned income that should be used to calculate her RRSP deduction for 2007 is $94,600.

Question 6

Natalie Doak moved 1,000 km from Winnipeg, on March 1, 2007, to a new job and earned $40,000 in her new work location. Her employer reimbursed the costs of selling her old residence and purchasing her new residence. She did not receive any allowance or reimbursement in respect of the following expenses, all of which she paid in 2007:

Moving van	$ 2,600
Travelling costs to move Natalie and family (4 persons in all)	900
Cost of cleaning house in new work location	100
Cost of painting and installing new carpets and windows	10,000
Cost of maintaining vacant former residence for 3 months until it was sold (mortgage interest and property taxes of $3,000 per month)	9,000
Cost of changing address on legal documents	100
House hunting trips for new residence	3,000
	$25,700

Travelling costs consist of three meals a day for four persons over three full days, gas and other car costs, and hotel for two nights at $100 per night.

What amount can Natalie claim for moving expenses in 2007?

(A) $25,700

(B) $15,967

(C) $12,600

(D) $8,967

¶9,850 EXERCISES

Exercise 1

ITA: 56(1)(*b*), 56.1, 60(*b*), 60.1

Uriah and Ursalla Unhappy decided to terminate their marriage of 10 years. On June 1 Uriah moved out. From the period of June 1 to October 31, Uriah paid Ursalla $900 per month, made up of $200 for the support of herself and $700 for their two children. On November 1, 2007, Uriah and Ursalla signed a written separation agreement which confirmed the $900 a month payment. In addition the agreement provided that Uriah would pay the monthly mortgage payment of $400 on the home which is in Ursalla's name and all medical expenses for the children. During November and December Uriah made the appropriate payments as per the written agreement and paid $100 of dental bills in respect of the children.

— REQUIRED

Discuss the tax implications of the above facts for both Uriah and Ursalla.

Exercise 2

ITA: 60(*i*), 146(1), 146(5)

Don Deplanner contributed $5,000 to a spousal RRSP on February 15, 2008. Don's income for tax purposes for 2006 is as follows:

Salary	$70,000
Taxable benefits	1,200
	$71,200
Less: Registered pension plan contributions — defined contribution	(2,800)
Employment income — Subdivision a	$68,400
Rental loss	(5,000)
Dividend income from taxable Canadian corporations grossed up	800
Interest income — Canada Savings Bonds	400
Division B income	$64,600

Don's employer reported a PA of $6,084 in respect of 2006.

— REQUIRED

Determine the maximum amount Don can deduct on his 2007 tax return in respect of his 2008 contribution to his spouse's RRSP and the amount, if any, that he can deduct in respect of his own RRSP.

Exercise 3

ITA: 60(*i*), 60(*j*.1)

I.M. Retired received the following amounts for 2007, the year of his retirement:

Employment income (see (1) below)	$ 7,000
Pension income:	
Lump-sum RPP payment from a defined benefit plan	100,000
Superannuation payments (eight monthly pension payments of $3,000)	24,000
Old Age Security pension	5,800
Canada Pension Plan	11,900
Retiring allowance	50,000
Interest income	8,000
	$206,700

Additional Information

(1) I.M. Retired resigned his position on April 1, 2007. The employment income for tax purposes above includes a $300 contribution to his employer's registered pension plan.

(2) On April 1, 2007, Mr. Retired had his employer transfer directly the lump-sum payment from the RPP to his RRSP. In addition, Mr. Retired transferred all but $10,000 of his retiring allowance directly to his RRSP.

(3) Mr. Retired has been employed by the same employer for 22 pre-'96 years beginning in October 1974 and all of the employer pension contributions have vested.

(4) Mr. Retired was 65 on October 31, 2006.

(5) Mr. Retired's employer reported a PA for him of $700 in respect of 2006. Mr. Retired's earned income for 2006 was $120,000.

— *REQUIRED*

Determine the tax consequences of the above transactions for 2007, supported by your computations.

Exercise 4

ITA: 62

Edwin Employee was transferred from Vancouver to Montreal by his employer on October 1, 2007. The following expenses were incurred by Edwin:

Air fare for family	$ 1,300
Moving cost of furniture	1,000
Cost of disposing of Vancouver home	
— legal fees	500
— real estate commission	10,000
Cost of purchasing Montreal home	
— prepaid realty taxes	500
— legal fees	1,000
— Quebec transfer tax	300

Edwin's employment income for tax purposes earned in Montreal during 2007 was $7,000. Edwin's employer reimbursed Edwin for $5,000 of the moving expenses.

— *REQUIRED*

Calculate the amount that Edwin can deduct as moving expenses.

ITA: 62

Exercise 5

ITA: 63

Charles Childcare was a university student in full-time attendance for 30 weeks and worked as a salesman for the balance of the year. His wife, Cathy, was also employed. The Childcares have four children: Sharon 17, Shawn 14, Sally 6 and Stephen 4. Child care expenses for the year amounted to $200 per week for 52 weeks. Charles' and Cathy's receipts and withholdings are summarized below:

	Charles	*Cathy*
Gross salary	$23,000	$47,000
Taxable fringe benefits	850	4,000
Interest income	200	—
Scholarship	3,600	—
Student loan	2,500	—

Deductions from Charles' and Cathy's employment income were:

	Charles	*Cathy*
Income taxes withheld	$ 3,800	$13,700
RPP contributions	2,000	3,700

— *REQUIRED*

Calculate the child care expenses deduction allowed to Charles and Cathy Childcare for 2007.

¶9,875   ASSIGNMENT PROBLEMS

Problem 1

ITA: 60(*i*), 60(*j*.1), 146(5), 146(5.1), 146(8.2), 146(8.3), 147.3(4), 147.3(9)

Mr. Rui retired from his job with Wise and Foresighted Consulting Ltd. on February 28, 2007. He had been employed continuously by the same employer since December 1980. Mr. Rui expects that his 2007 income for tax purposes will be as follows:

Employment income	$ 7,000
Pension income:	
Monthly superannuation (10 months of $3,450)	34,500
Old Age Security	5,900
Canadian Pension Plan	10,300
Retiring allowance	55,000
Farming income	20,000
Income from rental of apartment	10,800
Royalty income from books written by Mr. Rui	14,200
Interest income	12,000
Total income	$169,700

Additional Information

(1) Mr. Rui's 2007 employment income is net of an RPP contribution of $300. His PA for 2007 is expected to be $600.

(2) Mr. Rui has been a member of his employer's pension plan since he commenced working there in 1980. The employer's contributions have vested in Mr. Rui for each year he has been a member of the plan.

(3) Mr. Rui will be 71 in February 2008. His wife is now 67.

(4) In 2007, Mrs. Rui withdrew $6,000 from her RRSP. Mr. Rui had made the following contributions to Mrs. Rui's RRSP: January 2007 — $2,000; April 2006 — $1,000; February 2005 — $1,000; December 2004 — $3,000. Mr. Rui did not deduct the January 2007 contribution in 2006.

(5) Mr. Rui's employer reported a PA for him of $7,000 in 2006. His earned income in 2006 was $66,000.

(6) Mr. Rui's employer paid the retiring allowance to Mr. Rui in 2007, and Mr. Rui contributed his entire $55,000 retiring allowance to his RRSP in January 2008.

(7) Mr. Rui has unused RRSP deduction room from prior years of $5,000.

— *REQUIRED*

(A) Determine the tax implications of Mrs. Rui's $6,000 RRSP withdrawal.

(B) Determine Mr. Rui's maximum tax deductible RRSP contribution for 2007. What additional RRSP contribution should Mr. Rui make for 2007?

(C) It is now February 2008. What are the tax implications to Mr. Rui of the $55,000 transfer of his retiring allowance to his RRSP?

(D) What additional planning steps would you advise Mr Rui to take in connection with his RRSP in 2008?

Problem 2

ITA: 5, 6, 8, 12, 20, 39, 40(2), 56, 60, 75, 146

Ms. Sui is an executive of a large public retail corporation, Clothes to You Ltd., situated in Dundas, Ontario. Ms. Sui is not married. However, she has two adopted children, ages 8 and 10, who reside with her.

Ms. Sui has provided you with the following information for 2007:

Clothes To You Ltd.:

Gross salary	$150,000
Commission income	30,000
Canada Pension Plan contributions	(1,990)
Employment Insurance premiums	(720)
Registered pension plan contributions (money purchase)	(6,000)
Income taxes deducted	(55,000)

(1) Clothes To You Ltd. provides Ms. Sui with an automobile. The annual lease cost of the car, including PST and GST, is $18,400. Ms. Sui is reimbursed for her operating expenses when using the car for business. Clothes To You Ltd. also pays for any insurance, licence fees and repairs and maintenance related to the operation of the automobile. The operating expenses for the year totalled $6,200, including PST and GST. She used the car 10,000 km for pleasure and 30,000 km for business. She is charged $200/month for the use of the car and operating costs.

(2) Ms. Sui received stock options in the year. She has the option to purchase 20,000 shares at $3.50/share. The value of the shares at the date of the issue of the option was $3.50/share. Ms. Sui has not yet exercised any of her options.

(3) Ms. Sui received a piece of artwork worth $750, including PST and GST, from the company at Christmas time.

(4) Clothes To You Ltd. paid $1,300, including GST, for her membership in a fitness club. The corporation also paid Private Health Insurance premiums of $350.

Investment Receipts:

Interest income	$1,100
Dividends received from Canadian-resident public corporations	7,500
Dividends from U.S. corporation — net of 15% withholding tax (in Cdn. $)	680

Other Items:

(1) Annuity payments under contract from Profound Life Assurance Co. The capital portion of the annuity was $650 .... $2,000

(2) Net proceeds on the sale of her house on March 15, 2007 — net of real estate commission of $12,000 .... $188,000

The house cost $90,000 in 1994. She had previously sold her pre-1971 cottage in 1996, giving the cottage the maximum designation as a principal residence in order to have a nil taxable capital gain.

(3) At Christmas 2006, Ms. Sui gave each of her children a 6%, $2,000 five-year bond.

(4) Ms. Sui received a termination payment of $28,000 from her previous employer. She contributed all of this amount to her RRSP. Ms. Sui worked for her previous employer from February 15, 1986 to January 10, 2007. In that period, 80% of that employer's contribution had vested.

Expenditures/Losses:

(1) Investment counsellor's fees .... $ 1,100

(2) Interest on bank loan to purchase shares 850

(3) Registered retirement savings plan contribution 6,500

Ms. Sui's earned income in 2006 was $170,000. The PA on her 2006 T4 was $6,000.

(4) Ms. Sui incurred meals and entertainment expenses........................ 8,300

(5) Rental loss (before CCA) 3,500

(6) Ms. Sui invested in a limited partnership tax shelter in 2007. The loss per form T5013 is $3,200. She invested $5,000 in the partnership units in early 2007.

— *REQUIRED*

Calculate Ms. Sui's income under Division B for 2007, using the ordering rules in section 3.

Problem 3

ITA: 62; IT-178R3

Sue and George Shaker lived in Halifax, Nova Scotia, while George completed his combined law and MBA degree at Dalhousie University. The Shakers purchased a home in Halifax when they first moved to Nova Scotia. Due to contracting mononucleosis in his second year of the program, George completed his degree in December of 2007 rather than in the spring of 2007.

George excelled in the program and had numerous job offers. He finally accepted a job with NorthAm Co. in Toronto. In order to convince George to accept the job, NorthAm Co. offered to pay the Shakers an amount equal to any loss that they incurred on the sale of their Halifax home and provide them with a $10,000 moving allowance.

Sue has been working for an insurance company in Halifax while George has been attending school. Sue intends to find work in Toronto, but will be unable to continue working for the same insurance company.

George accepted the job with NorthAm Co. in September 2007. During October 2007, George and Sue flew to Toronto to look for a home. They spent a week in Toronto and on the fifth day managed to find and purchase a home with the purchase contract closing on December 15, 2007. The remaining two days were spent arranging for painting and cleaning of the new home. Their expenditures on that trip were:

Two Air Canada tickets (return Halifax to Toronto)	$ 1,200
Motel room, 7 days @ $75 per day	525
Meals, 7 days @ $50 per day	350
Car rental	350

George and Sue managed to sell their Halifax home. That sale closed on December 15, 2007. The statement of account from the lawyer (dated January 15, 2008) revealed the following expenses:

Real estate commission	$7,000
Legal fees, old home	2,000
Legal fees, new home	2,500
Land transfer tax, new home	1,000

The house in Halifax was sold for $140,000. The Shakers had originally paid $160,000 for the house. NorthAm Co. provided a cheque for $27,000 in February 2008 to reimburse them for the loss and the real estate commission. (NorthAm Co. did not include the legal costs when calculating the loss eligible for reimbursement.)

Subsequent to finalizing the sale of their Halifax home and George's completion of his exams, Sue and George packed up their car and drove to Toronto. The trip took 7 days due to a leisurely pace and some bad weather delays, and since their home was not ready when they arrived, they stayed in a nearby motel for 11 days.

The cost of trip and stay in motel was as follows:

Meals, 18 days @ $100 (substantiated by receipts)	$1,800
Motel room, 18 days @ $80	1,440
Gasoline (2000 kilometres driven)	250

In late December, the Shakers paid a moving bill consisting of $5,000 for the actual move and $250 for storage. George received the $10,000 allowance for moving expenses in December 2007. He commenced work for NorthAm Co. in January 2008 at a salary of $80,000 per year. Sue commenced work for Toronto Insurance Co. in September 2008 at a salary of $85,000 per year.

— REQUIRED

Calculate the allowable moving expenses for the Shakers for both 2007 and 2008. Discuss the tax treatment of the loss reimbursement. Assume that all expenditures made were reasonable and can be substantiated by receipts.

Problem 4

ITA: 63

Nina Diamond and Len Dirkfeld are married and have five children: Lindsay age 18, Trevor age 15, James age 7, Ben age 5, and Rebecca age 3. During 2007, they paid a nanny $250 per week for 50 weeks to look after their children while they worked. During July, they paid $3,000 ($1,500 each) for Trevor and James to go to an overnight summer camp for four weeks. In addition, they paid their child Lindsay $300 to babysit the other children at various times when they worked late.

Len is a doctor and has his own practice. Nina worked full-time as a computer consultant during the first eight months of the year. In September, she went back to university on a full-time basis for 13 weeks. On December 11, her courses were finished and she went back to work.

Nina and Len's incomes are summarized below:

	Nina	Len
Salary	$50,000	
Taxable benefits	3,000	
Employment expenses	(800)	
Employment income	$52,200	
Business income		$120,000
Interest income	2,000	3,000
Rental income		6,000
RRSP contribution	(5,000)	(10,000)
Net income under Division B	$49,200	$119,000

— REQUIRED

(A) Compute the maximum 2007 child care deductions for Nina Diamond and Dr. Len Dirkfeld. Show all calculations.

(B) How would your answer to (A) change if Nina went back to university for 13 weeks on a part-time basis rather than a full-time basis. Assume Nina took a minimum of 12 hours of courses each month, but do not redo all the calculations.

Problem 5

ITA: 56(1)(a), 60(b), 60(i), 60(j.1), 60(o), 60.1, 62, 63, 146(1), 146(5), 146(8.2), 147.3

In early July 2007, Dr. Elaine Matthews separated from her husband of some years. She maintained full custody of the couple's only child, a six-year-old girl. Since May 1, 1985, Dr. Matthews had been working as a public health consultant for the Oshawa region. Just prior to her separation she had chosen to take advantage of a severance package from the Oshawa region. She accepted a staff position at Joseph Brant Memorial Hospital in Burlington, Ontario and moved directly from Oshawa to Burlington on September 1, 2007. She sold the former family home in Oshawa on September 15, 2007. Her husband had rented an apartment in Oshawa in late July 2007.

Dr. Matthews has some experience preparing her own tax returns but she has been particularly busy in recent months. She started her 2007 return but quickly decided she simply did not have time to finish it. She requested your assistance in completing her return.

You met with Dr. Matthews to go over her tax information related to 2007 and determined that she had correctly calculated her income under Subdivisions a, b, and c of Division B to total $158,488. Included in this correct computation were the following items:

¶9,875

Salary (from former employer)	$ 96,000
Salary (from Joseph Brant Memorial Hospital)	60,000
Taxable benefits under section 6 of the *Income Tax Act*	1,743
Registered pension plan contributions (defined benefit plan)	(6,750)
Consulting income (reported as business income)	8,000
Interest income from investments	540
Taxable dividends from investments	1,250
Share of rental loss from childhood home inherited from her parents	(1,495)
Net taxable capital gains	4,800
Interest paid on investment loans	(2,400)
Loss from limited partnership investment (rental property)	(3,200)
	$158,488

She provided you with the following *additional details* relating to 2007:

Miscellaneous income

Severance from former employer	$ 41,538

Transfer of RPP accrued from former employer

Her former employer made a direct transfer of her accumulated RPP benefits (within prescribed limits) to her RRSP; her former employer had made vested contributions for the years 1987 through 2007	$210,000

Spousal support

Under the terms of her separation agreement signed in September 2007, Dr. Matthews paid the following amounts for support of her husband:

Support ($500 a month for September — December)	$ 2,000
Rent on his new Oshawa apartment ($750 a month for September — December)	3,000

Moving Expenses from Oshawa to Burlington

Gas for house-hunting trips (4 trips made during late August 2007)	$ 40

Selling costs of former Oshawa home (owned 100% by her; sold September 15, 2007):

Real estate commissions	$ 12,000
Legal fees	1,050

Costs of purchasing new Burlington home:

Legal fees	$ 850
Land transfer tax	3,250

Costs of moving herself and her household effects:

Moving van to transport belongings	$ 600
Gas to drive herself and her daughter (120 kms driven)	15
Hotel (2 nights while new home was being painted and cleaned; 2 × $100)	200
Meals (same two days as above 2 × $55)	110

You have determined that the distance from her new home to Joseph Brant Hospital is 3.5 km. The distance from Joseph Brant Hospital to her former home was 115 km.

Care of her daughter

Part-time nanny employed January 1–August 31	$ 8,976
YMCA summer camp for two weeks in July while nanny was on vacation ($200 a week)	400
Fall term (September–December) tuition fees for private school (excluding before and after school daycare)	4,000
Before and after school daycare for September–December (provided on premises of private school)	720
Fall term (September–December) transportation to private school	1,200

Registered retirement savings plan contributions

Transfer of severance pay from former employer . . . . $ 30,000
Personal contributions through employment (March–December 2007)   8,000
Personal contributions through employment (January–February 2008) . . .   1,000

Her 2006 earned income for RRSP purposes was $120,000; her employer had reported a pension adjustment on her 2006 T4 of $8,500; she had no unused RRSP contribution room at the start of 2007 and no undeducted balance of RRSP contributions

Legal fees paid

Legal representation during separation proceedings to establish require-
ments to make support payments . . . . $ 1,600
Appeal of her 2005 income tax assessment (which she won)   1,200

— *REQUIRED*

Complete the calculation of income under Division B. Show all calculations whether or not they are necessary to the final answer. Explain briefly any items not used in your calculations.

Problem 6

ITA: Division B

Ms. King had a busy year in 2007. During the year, she formally separated from her husband and retained custody of her five year-old daughter, Kelly. She also decided that she needed a fresh start in another city, so she quit her job in Belleville, Ontario, and got a new job in Windsor. Ms. King and her daughter moved to Windsor, Ontario, in November 2007. She has asked you to help her estimate her 2007 personal income tax liability. In order to help you, she has prepared the following list of all the transactions which she thinks might be of interest to you.

(1) Her employment income from her employer in Belleville for the first 11 months of 2007 was $55,000. Her deductions at source included CPP/EI of $2,710 and income tax of $20,000.

Her Belleville employer paid her a retiring allowance of $15,000 to compensate her for the fact that she was not a member of a pension plan and to reward her for years of service to the company (from 1980 to 2007).

Before she left the Belleville employer, a public company, she exercised a stock option that she had for 800 shares. When this option had originally been granted, the share price was $15. The exercise price of the option was $17. At the time she exercised the option, the market price was $25. She immediately sold these shares on the open market for $25.

(2) Her new employer in Windsor agreed to pay some of her moving expenses, but in order to simplify things, they were going to give her an allowance of $8,000. She was responsible, then, for her own expenses.

Her moving costs were as follows:

Moving company charges $5,500
Gas for trip to Windsor at the time of the move (600 kms driven)   50
Motel in Belleville for one night on the day of the move   75
Meals during the day of the move and during the trip to Windsor   100
Lease cancellation charge in Belleville   200
                                                                                  $5,925

She had made a trip to Windsor to look for an apartment for her and Kelly and she had incurred the following expenses:

Gas for trip to Windsor . . . . $ 50
Motel costs in Windsor   150
Meals   75
                                                                                   $275

¶9,875

(3) Her income from her new employer in Windsor during the month of December was $5,000.

(4) During the year she incurred the following expenses for the care of Kelly:

Food and clothing	$6,000
Babysitter costs while she was at work	3,000

(5) Ms. King incurred legal fees of $3,200 to establish her right to support payments in connection with the finalization of the separation agreement. She feels that this was well spent, since her lawyer was successful in getting her husband to pay child support to her for Kelly in the amount of $800 per month, starting in February 2007. So far, her husband has been making these payments on time.

She also had trouble with her 2005 tax return and had to pay her previous accountant $400 to deal with the CRA. It turns out that the CRA has correctly assessed her return.

(6) She is totally confused by the RRSP rules, so she wants you to tell her what the maximum amount is that she can contribute to her RRSP for 2007. She wants you to assume that she will make these payments within the time deadlines when you calculate her tax liability.

(7) Five years ago, Ms. King inherited some shares in a Canadian-resident public company, Facai Ltd., from her mother. She believed that the shares were capable of making money for her. She sold the shares in 2007, in order to put money into a mutual fund that a friend recommended. Her mother had paid $5,000 for these shares in 1981 and at the time of her mother's death, the shares were worth $60,000. Ms. King sold them for $180,000.

Ms. King received cash dividends from these shares during the year in the amount of $8,621.

(8) One of her good friends had been a battered wife, so Ms. King had donated $2,000 to the local registered charity which protects battered women.

(9) Ms. King gave you a copy of her 2006 tax return and it showed employment income of $55,000, child care expenses of $2,000 and taxable dividends of $10,000. She made the maximum RRSP contribution for 2006.

— *REQUIRED*

Calculate Ms. King's income under Division B for 2007. Explain why you omitted any amounts from your calculations. Show all calculations.

[For more problems and solutions thereto, see the CD accompanying this book.]

Chapter 10

Computation of Taxable Income and Taxes Payable for Individuals

LEARNING GOALS

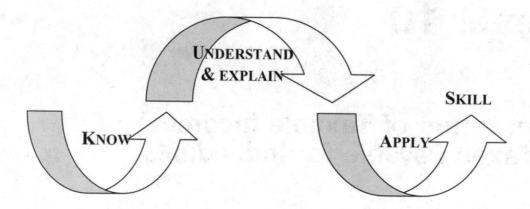

Know

By the end of this chapter you should know the basic provisions of the *Income Tax Act* that relate to the calculation of taxable income and taxes payable for individuals. Completing the Review Questions (¶10,800) and Multiple Choice Questions (¶10,825) is a good way to learn the technical provisions.

Understand and Explain

You should understand and be able to explain how taxable income is computed. With this base you should then understand and be able to explain how federal tax is calculated and how the many refundable and non-refundable tax credits are determined. Completing the Exercises (¶10,850) is a good way to deepen your understanding of the material.

Apply

You should be able to apply your knowledge and understanding of the determination of taxable income and tax liability in a way that accomplishes a client's goals. Completing the Assignment Problems (¶10,875) is an excellent way to develop your ability to apply the material in increasingly complex situations.

OVERVIEW

This chapter is divided into two major parts. The first major segment deals with a discussion of the provisions used to compute taxable income. The Act simply defines taxable income as income plus or minus amounts permitted under Division C. This chapter will cover a list of miscellaneous items in Division C which specifically pertain to individuals. The capital gains deduction will be introduced briefly in this chapter and discussed more fully in Chapter 13. This chapter will deal with the carryover of losses incurred in another year from the perspective of an individual taxpayer.

ITA: 2(2)

ITA: 110.6

The second major segment of this chapter discusses the computation of tax for individuals, including coverage of tax rates, tax credits and minimum tax. This discussion follows a long list of tax credits for such things as marital status, dependants, age, pension income, charitable donations, medical expenses and disability, among others, and for transfers of certain of these credits to another taxpayer. Many of the tax credits in Division E are dependent in some way on Division B income. Therefore, it is necessary first to calculate Division B income and, then, to determine if a Division E tax credit is deductible to the limit of tax on Division C taxable income. If the Division C deductions result in a negative taxable income, taxable income becomes zero.

The following chart will help locate the major provisions of the Act considered in this chapter.

PART I — DIVISIONS C, E & E.1
COMPUTATION OF TAXABLE INCOME
COMPUTATION OF TAX

DIVISION	SUBDIVISION	SECTION	

DIVISION

A	Liability for tax
B	Computation of income
C	Computation of taxable income
D	Taxable income earned in Canada by non-residents
E	Computation of tax
E.1	Minimum tax
F	Special rules
G	Deferred and other income arrangements
H	Exemptions
I	Returns, assessments, payments, appeals
J	Appeals to the courts

SUBDIVISION

a	Individuals
a.1	Child tax benefit
b	Corporations
c	All taxpayers

SECTION

110	Deductions
110.2	Lump-sum payments
110.6	CG exemption
110.7	Prescribed zone
111	Losses
111.1	Ordering
114-114.2	Part-year resident

117-117.1	Tax rates
118-118.95	Personal credits
120	Income from o/s prov
120.2	Min tax c/over
120.4	Tax on split income
121	Dividend tax credit
122	Tax on trust
122.3	Empl o/s Canada
122.5	GST credit
122.51	Refundable medical expense supplement

122.6-122.64	Child tax benefit
126	Foreign tax credit
126.1-127.41	Other tax credits

127.5	Obligation
127.51	Minimum amount
127.52	Adjusted Taxable Inc
127.53	Basic exemption
127.531	Basic credit
127.54	Definitions
127.55	Application of 127.5

¶10,000   COMPUTATION OF TAXABLE INCOME FOR AN INDIVIDUAL

¶10,010   Miscellaneous Division C Deductions and Additions

¶10,015   Employee stock options

¶10,015.10   *Granted by corporations other than Canadian-controlled private corporations*

Employees, who acquire shares from a corporation other than a Canadian-controlled private corporation under a stock option agreement, are required to include in their employment income a benefit. The benefit is computed as the amount by which the fair market value of the shares at the time the shares were acquired exceeds the price actually paid (i.e., the exercise price). The employment benefit is then added to the adjusted cost base of the shares, so that any resultant capital gain reflects the increase in value since the acquisition date. Also, the adjusted cost base reflects the sum of amounts that have been previously taxed, that is, amounts that have been tax-paid.

ITA: 7(1)

ITA: 53(1)(*j*)

There is a deduction of ½ of the employment benefit referred to as a "stock option deduction" available in Division C in the computation of taxable income. The stock option deduction can be claimed if the exercise price was not less than the value of the share at the time the option was granted. In addition, there are certain limitations on the type of shares issued (i.e., prescribed shares which are described as, in essence, common shares. Also, an arm's length relationship of the parties must exist before and after the exercising of the option. Note there are no tax consequences upon the granting of an option.

ITA: 110(1)(*d*)
ITR: 6204

¶10,015.20   *Decline in value of shares*

In some instances where employees have been granted stock options the value of the shares has subsequently declined to the point where the fair market value is less than the exercise price. As a result of this decline, employers may want to reduce the exercise price to the current fair market value. This, however, will disqualify the option for the Division C deduction, since the exercise price may be less than the fair market value at the time the option was granted. In recognition of this, a proposed amendment in Bill C-33, tabled November 2006, allows employers to reduce the exercise price without jeopardizing the employee's Division C deduction, as long as the following conditions are met:

ITA: 110(1)(*d*)
ITA: 110(1.7), 110(1.8)
ITA: 110(1)(*d*)

- the exercise price is reduced at a time when the fair market value of the securities is less than the old exercise price,

- the old exercise price was not less than the fair market value of the securities when the option was granted, and

- the new exercise price was not less than the fair market value of the securities at the time of the price reduction.

For example, assume that the original option was granted when the fair market value of the shares was $20 and the option had an exercise price of $22. This option would have qualified for the Division C deduction. If the share value drops to $10 and the company reduces the option price to $12 then these proposed amendments allow this security to continue to qualify for the deduction.

ITA: 110(1)(*d*)

¶10,015.30   *Deferral of benefit*

One exception to the requirement to include the benefit in the year of exercise of the option is provided for stock options on publicly-listed shares where certain conditions are met. These conditions were listed in Chapter 3, under the heading "Rules applicable to public corporations". Where the employment income benefit is deferred on the first $100,000 worth of shares acquired under option, the stock option deduction is also deferred to the year of disposition of the shares.

¶10,015.40   *Granted by a Canadian-controlled private corporation*

Another exception to the requirement to include the benefit in the year of exercise of the option is provided for stock options granted by a Canadian-controlled private corporation (CCPC). There is an employment inclusion of the same amount, but the income is deferred until the year the shares are disposed of. Furthermore, the stock option deduction can be claimed if the shares have not been sold or exchanged before the second anniversary date of the day of acquisition.

ITA: 7(1.1), 110(1)(*d*.1)

Note that for stock options granted by a CCPC, there are two possibilities for a stock option deduction.

(1) The shares acquired under the option are held for the two-year period and, thus, qualify for the CCPC deduction, or

ITA: 110(1)(*d*.1)

(2) the exercise price is not less than the value of the shares at the date the option was granted and, thus, qualify for the general deduction.

ITA: 110(1)(*d*)

However, only one of the two possibilities can apply.

¶10,015.50   *Summary of stock option rules*

Where the stock option deduction is claimed, effectively, only ½ of the difference between the exercise price and the value at the date of exercise is taxable, similar to a capital gain. While the net numerical result is a ½ inclusion, the net amount is not a taxable capital gain and, therefore, not eligible for the capital gains deduction on qualified small business corporation shares (QSBCS).

The schematic diagram on stock options introduced in Chapter 3 can be expanded now to include the effects of the stock option deduction.

| | | Division C deduction = 50% of benefit | | Timing of inclusion and deduction | |
| | Income under Division B | Non-CCPC | CCPC | Non-CCPC (general) | CCPC and eligible listed shares* |
Values					
Selling price	Capital gain ½ taxable (Subdiv. c)			Disposition or deemed disposition	Disposition or deemed disposition
Fair market value at purchase	Employment income (Subdiv. b)	if: FMV at date option granted ≤ exercise price	if: FMV at date option granted ≤ exercise price or shares held ≥ 2 years from date of purchase (except for deemed disposition at death)	Purchase	Disposition or deemed disposition
Option exercise price					

* The inclusion of the stock benefit and, hence, the deduction in Division C is deferred in the case of publicly-listed shares on the first $100,000 of optioned shares, valued at the grant date, in any one year. Other conditions for the deferral are outlined in Chapter 3.

Note that the fair market value of the shares at the date that the option is granted is relevant only for the condition that allows the ½ stock option deduction.

Example Problem

Malenkov Mfg. Ltd. granted Ms. Yampolsky, its Vice-president, an option to purchase 10,000 shares for $5 per share. On March 10, 2007, she acquired the 10,000 shares under the option. The following pertains to the shares:

	Date	FMV
Option granted	March 10, 2001	$10
Option exercised	March 10, 2007	20
Shares sold	March 10, 2010	30

— REQUIRED

(A) Determine the tax consequences on the above dates if Malenkov Mfg. Ltd. was:

(i) a public company, or

(ii) a Canadian-controlled private corporation.

(B) Redo Part (A) assuming the exercise price had been set at $10 per share.

— SOLUTION

(A) (i) March 10, 2001 — No tax consequences
    March 10, 2007 — Employment income of $150,000 (10,000 shares × ($20 – $5)) ITA: 7(1)
      — No stock option deduction and no $100,000 deferral since the exercise price ($5) was less than the value on the grant date ($10) ITA: 7(9)(b), 110(1)(d)
      — Adjusted cost base of each share increased by $15 per share to $20, so that the $15 per share benefit is not taxed again on disposition ITA: 53(1)(j)
    March 10, 2010 — Taxable capital gain of $50,000 (½ ($30 – $20) × 10,000 shares)

(ii) March 10, 2001 — No tax consequences

    March 10, 2007 — No tax consequences

    March 10, 2010 — Employment inclusion of $150,000 (10,000 shares × ($20 – $5)) ITA: 7(1.1)
      — Adjusted cost base of each share increased by $15 per-share to $20 ITA: 53(1)(j)
      — Stock option deduction of $75,000 (½ × $150,000), since the shares were held over two years ITA: 110(1)(d.1)
      — Taxable capital gain of $50,000 (½ ($30 – $20) × 10,000 shares); may qualify for the qualified small business corporation share capital gains deduction

(B) If the exercise price had been $10, equal to the fair market value of the shares at the date of grant, the two results would have been as follows:

	(B)(i)	(B)(ii)
Employment income (10,000 shares × ($20 – $10))	$100,000	$100,000
Division C deduction (½ × $100,000)	(50,000)	(50,000)
	$ 50,000	$ 50,000
Taxable capital gain	50,000	50,000
	$100,000	$100,000

ITA: 110(1)(d) or (d.1)

In addition, the public company shares would have qualified for the $100,000 deferral by being eligible for the Division C deduction. ITA: 7(8), 110(1)(d)

¶10,015.50

The primary difference between (A) and (B) is that the stock option deduction is available to the non-CCPC, since the exercise price is not less than the fair market value at the time the option was granted. Also, for the CCPC option, the benefit does not have to be reported until the year of disposal.

ITA: 110(1)(*d*)

The effect of these provisions is to give a treatment equivalent to capital gains for stock option benefits accruing up to the date of acquisition and included in employment income, without providing eligibility for the QSBC share capital gains deduction where applicable.

¶10,020   Deduction for certain receipts

A number of refundable and non-refundable tax credits provided to an individual taxpayer are reduced by the individual's Division B income. Certain social assistance payments received by individuals are included in their Division B income and may affect these tax credits. However, there is no intention to tax these payments in the hands of the recipient. As a result, a deduction is provided in Division C, in the computation of taxable income, to offset the inclusion of the payments in Division B. The sources of income which qualify for this treatment are:

ITA: 110(1)(*f*)

- the Guaranteed Income Supplement,

- social assistance payments,

- workers' compensation, and

- amounts that are exempt income by virtue of a tax treaty.

¶10,025   Home relocation loan

A special deduction is available to partially offset an imputed interest income inclusion in situations where an employee has obtained a "home relocation loan" as a result of an employment relocation. A home relocation loan is defined as, in essence, a loan used to acquire a home which is at least 40 kilometres closer to an employee's new work location than his or her old residence. The intention of this special deduction is that an employee could receive the equivalent of a $25,000 interest-free loan without including a deemed interest benefit in taxable income. The maximum deduction is the imputed interest benefit and the duration of the deduction is the lesser of five years or the life of the home relocation loan. A loan received by a taxpayer that is used to repay a home relocation loan is deemed to be the same loan as the home relocation loan and to have been made on the same day. In addition, the same "lesser of" benefit is provided for a home relocation loan as is provided for a home purchase loan (refer to Chapter 6). Hence, the low-interest benefit can be computed on the principal amount of the loan outstanding in the year at a rate which is the lesser of

ITA: 80.4

ITA: 110(1)(*j*)
ITA: 248(1) "home relocation"

ITA: 80.4

ITA: 110(1.4)

ITA: 80.4(4)
ITA: 80.4

(a) the prescribed rate at the time the loan was made, and

(b) the changing prescribed rates during the year the loan was outstanding.

The deduction is computed as the least of three amounts:

ITA: 110(1)(*j*)

(a) interest on the whole home relocation loan as computed using the "lesser of" rule *minus* interest paid during that year and 30 days thereafter (i.e., the net imputed interest benefit on the home relocation loan itself);

ITA: 80.4(1)(*a*), 80.4(4)

(b) interest on a $25,000 home relocation loan using the "lesser of" rule, but restricted to a maximum of five years (i.e., interest at the appropriate prescribed rate computed on a principal amount of $25,000); and

ITA: 80.4(1)(*a*), 80.4(4)

(c) total benefits from all low-interest or no-interest loans.

ITA: 80.4

Example Problem

Ms. Kishke joined May Kostcha Ltd. on February 1, 2007 as chief corporate tax officer. On that date she received an interest-free loan of $100,000 to assist her in the financing of a new home, since she was moving from Kingston in eastern Ontario, to Dundas in southern Ontario, to take the position. In addition, she was given a loan of $20,000 bearing interest at 3% payable on December 31 of each year that the loan is outstanding. This loan was to assist her with other costs associated with her move. The interest was paid when due.

— *REQUIRED*

Determine the effects of these loans on Ms. Kishke's taxable income in 2007. Assume prescribed rates for 2007 as follows: 4% for the first quarter, 5% for the second quarter, 4% for the third and fourth quarters.

— *SOLUTION*

The imputed interest benefit would be computed on these loans with the "lesser of" rule for a home relocation loan as follows. *ITA: 80.4(1), 80.4(4)*

Loan to purchase house: *ITA: 80.4(1)(a), 80.4(4)*

The "lesser of rule" can be applied in each quarter of the year during the year that the loan is outstanding. Since the 4% rate applicable in the first quarter of the loan is less than or equal to the prescribed rate in each of the other three quarters, the 4% rate will be applicable for all of the year, computed as follows:

4% of $100,000 × $^{334}/_{365}$ =		$3,660
Loan for general purposes:			*ITA: 80.4(1)(a)*
4% of $20,000 × $^{59}/_{365}$ =	$ 129	
5% of $20,000 × $^{91}/_{365}$ =	249	
4% of $20,000 × $^{92}/_{365}$ =	202	
4% of $20,000 × $^{92}/_{365}$ =	202	782
		$4,442
Interest paid (3% of $20,000 × $^{334}/_{365}$)		(549)	*ITA: 80.4(1)(c)*
Benefit		$3,893	*ITA: 80.4*

Since the $100,000 loan is a home relocation loan, the following deduction may be taken in the calculation of taxable income: *ITA: 110(1)(j)*

Least of:

Benefit computed on $100,000 home relocation loan net of reduction for interest paid (interest-free loan)	$3,660
Interest computed on a $25,000 loan 4% of $25,000 × $^{334}/_{365}$)	$ 915
Total benefit net of interest paid for year	$3,893

ITA: 80.4, 110(1)(j)(i)

ITA: 80.4(1)(a), 110(1)(j)(ii)

ITA: 80.4, 110(1)(j)(iii)

Therefore, the Division C deduction would be $915 in 2007. *ITA: 110(1)(j)*

It may be rare to see a case where the deduction is equal to the total benefit for the year. *ITA: 80.4, 110(1)(j)*

¶10,030 Loss Carryovers   ~~READ NOTES~~

Commentary in previous chapters has alluded to the fact that losses which cannot be applied in the year in which they occur because of a restriction in Division B may be deducted in Division C by carrying the losses back three years through amended returns and/or applying the balance of the losses to future years, subject to any further restrictions as indicated below.

¶10,030

¶10,035 Non-capital loss carryovers

ITA: 111(1)(*a*)

A "non-capital loss" (non-CL) available for carryover is a defined term. For individuals, the definition can be summarized in computational form as follows:

ITA: 111(8)

Aggregate of:

Amounts computed as losses from non-capital sources:		
Loss from an office or employment	$xxx	
Loss from business	xxx	
Loss from property	xxx	
Allowable business investment loss	xxx	
Amount deducted as capital gains deduction	xxx	
Amount deducted as net capital losses	xxx	
Amount deductible as:		
Stock options	$xxx	
Social assistance and other payments	xxx	
Home relocation loan	xxx	xxx
		$xxx
Less: aggregate of net incomes:		
Income from office or employment	$xxx	
Income from business	xxx	
Income from property	xxx	
Income from other sources	xxx	
Taxable capital gains (other than from listed personal property)	$xxx	
Taxable net capital gain from listed personal property	xxx	
	$xxx	
Less: allowable capital losses (other than from listed personal property and allowable business investment losses)	xxx	xxx*
		$xxx
Less: other deductions	xxx	xxx*
		$xxx*
Less: farm loss (included in loss from business above)		xxx
Non-capital loss carryover		$xxx*

ITA: 3(*d*)

ITA: 110.6

ITA: 111(1)(*b*)

ITA: 110(1)(*d*), (*d*.1), (*d*.2), (*d*.3)

ITA: 110(1)(*f*)

ITA: 110(1)(*j*)

ITA: 3(*c*)

ITA: 56–59

ITA: 60–66

---

* Cannot be negative [sec. 257].

Note that in order to become a carryover non-capital loss, a current year's loss from non-capital sources must, in essence, exceed income from all other sources in the current year. Non-capital losses may be carried over as follows, with the earliest losses being applied first:

	Carry back	*Carry forward*
For taxation years ending before March 23, 2004	3	7
For taxation years ending after March 23, 2004 and before 2006	3	10
For taxation years ending in 2006 and later	3	20

Note that the portion of an allowable business investment loss, which is discussed in some detail in Chapters 7 and 13, not used in the year of loss, becomes a non-capital loss and is available for carryover in the manner just described.

¶10,040 Net capital loss carryovers

ITA: 111(1)(*b*)

A "net capital loss" (net CL) for a particular taxation year available for carryover to another year is defined to be the excess of allowable capital losses over taxable capital gains for that particular year plus allowable business investment losses not absorbed in the seven-year carryforward period as a non-capital loss, as discussed above. Net capital losses may be carried back three years and forward indefinitely. It is important to note that net capital

ITA: 111(8) "net capital loss"

losses for a particular year are calculated using the inclusion rate of that year. The following are the historical inclusion rates.

Capital Gains Inclusion Rate:

Years	Inclusion Rate
1972–1987	$\frac{1}{2}$
1988, 1989	$\frac{2}{3}$
1990–February 27, 2000	$\frac{3}{4}$
February 28, 2000 – October 17, 2000	$\frac{2}{3}$
After October 17, 2000	$\frac{1}{2}$

Since net capital losses may arise in years with different capital gains inclusion rates to be deducted against other net taxable capital gains computed by other inclusion rates, it is necessary to convert net capital losses to the capital gains inclusion rate appropriate to the carryover year in which the net capital loss is deducted. Net capital losses realized in a year with a lower inclusion rate must be increased when carried forward to a year with a higher inclusion rate. Net capital losses realized in a year with a higher inclusion rate must be decreased when carried back to a year with a lower inclusion rate.

The amount of the net capital loss to be deducted in the year, taking into account any differences in the rates of inclusion, is computed using the following formula:

ITA: 111(1.1)

the lesser of:

(a) net taxable capital gains for the year; and

ITA: 3(*b*)

(b) the total of each amount for different years of net capital losses determined by the formula

$$A \times \frac{B}{C}$$

where A is the amount of the net capital loss arising from a particular "loss year" and claimed in Division C in the current year;

ITA: 111(1)(*b*)

   B is the inclusion rate for the year in which the net capital loss is to be deducted; and

   C is the inclusion rate for the year in which the loss was realized.

For example, a net capital loss of $9,000 realized in 1999 with its $\frac{3}{4}$ inclusion rate would be converted to $6,000 in 2007 with its $\frac{1}{2}$ inclusion rate (i.e., $9,000 $\times$ $\frac{1}{2}$/$\frac{3}{4}$ = $6,000). Conceptually, the $9,000 net capital loss in 1999 resulted from a $12,000 capital loss (i.e., $9,000 $\times$ $\frac{4}{3}$). The same $12,000 capital loss in 2007 would result in a net capital loss of $6,000 (i.e., $12,000 $\times$ $\frac{1}{2}$).

Note that both the words "deducted" and "claimed" are used in reference to net capital losses. The word "claimed" appears to refer to net capital losses in their original, unadjusted amount as computed in the "loss year" at the inclusion rate for that year. The word "deducted" appears to refer to the net capital losses after they have been adjusted by the formula to the inclusion rate appropriate for the year in which they will offset taxable capital gains.

ITA: 111(1.1)
ITA: 111(1.1)(*b*)(iii)(A) to (B)

Example Problem

Larry Loser had net capital losses of $10,000 in the taxation year ending December 31, 1987 and $2,000 in each of the taxation years ending December 31, 1989 and 1994. He had capital gains of $5,000 in 1998, $4,000 in 1999, and $3,000 in 2007. He has had no other capital gains or losses.

¶10,040

— REQUIRED

Determine the maximum amount to be deducted in the taxation years 1998, 1999, and 2007.

ITA: 111(1)(*b*), 111(1.1)

— SOLUTION

	1998	1999	2007
Net taxable capital gain:			
Capital gains realized	$ 5,000	$ 4,000	$ 3,000
Taxable capital gain	$ 3,750	$ 3,000	$ 1,500

ITA: 3(*b*)

Adjusted deduction —			
Lesser of:			
(i) TCG above	$ 3,750	$ 3,000	$ 1,500
(ii) total of adjusted net capital losses of loss years (see carry-over below)	$19,250	$15,500	$ 8,333
Lesser amount	$3,750	$ 3,000	$ 1,500

ITA: 111(1.1)(*a*)
ITA: 3(*b*)

Net capital loss carryovers: Year loss incurred	1987	1989	1994	Total
Unadjusted net CL	$10,000	$2,000	$2,000	
Adjusted to 1998 inclusion rate at ¾	$15,000[1]	$2,250[1]	$2,000	$19,250
Utilized in 1998 (see above)	(3,750)	Nil	Nil	(3,750)
Available in 1999	$11,250	$2,250	$2,000	$15,500
Utilized in 1999 (see above)	(3,000)	Nil	Nil	(3,000)
Available in 2007	$ 8,250	$2,250	$2,000	$12,500
Adjusted to 2007 inclusion rate	$ 5,500[2]	$1,500[2]	$1,333[2]	$ 8,333
Utilized in 2007	(1,500)	Nil	Nil	(1,500)
Available in 2008	$ 4,000	$1,500	$1,333	$ 6,833

—NOTE TO SOLUTION

[1] The $10,000 of 1987 net capital loss is a fractional amount computed at a ½ inclusion rate. This amount is adjusted to the 1998 inclusion rate of ¾ as follows:

$$\$10,000 \times \sqrt[3]{4}/\frac{1}{2} = \$15,000$$

The $2,000 of 1989 net capital loss is a fractional amount computed at a ⅔ inclusion rate. This amount is adjusted to the 1998 inclusion rate of ¾ as follows:

$$\$2,000 \times \sqrt[3]{4}/\frac{2}{3} = \$2,250$$

The $2,000 of 1994 net capital loss is a fractional amount computed at a ¾ inclusion rate. Therefore, it need not be adjusted for use before February 28, 2000.

[2] The losses are adjusted from the ¾ inclusion rate (as adjusted above) to the ½ inclusion rate as follows:

1987: $8,250 × ½/¾ = $5,500

1989: $2,250 × ½/¾ = $1,500

1994: $2,000 × ½/¾ = $1,333

These adjustment factors do nothing more than convert the fractional loss of a particular year into a full loss by dividing by ½, ⅔ or ¾ in the denominator (i.e., item C in the formula) and then computing the net capital loss at the inclusion rate for the year of the deduction by multiplying by ¾, ⅔, or ½ in the numerator (i.e., item B in the formula). Hence, $10,000 divided by ½ is $20,000 which was the full capital loss in 1987 before the ½ inclusion rate was applied.

Then $20,000 multiplied by ¾ produces $15,000 which is the net capital loss stated in terms of a ¾ inclusion rate used before February 28, 2000.

Note that the losses carried forward from the "loss year" are those from the earliest loss year. This is illustrated in the net capital loss carryover calculation presented above. Note, also, how net capital losses deducted in a particular year, as modified by the adjustments for different inclusion rates, are limited to net taxable capital gains of that year.

ITA: 111(3)

ITA: 111(1)(*b*)
ITA: 111(1.1)(*a*)

¶10,045 Restricted farm loss carryovers

ITA: 111(1)(*c*)

Restricted farm losses (RFL) available for carryover (i.e., losses not deductible in the current year under section 31 because they exceed the limit of losses up to $2,500 plus one-half of losses in excess of $2,500 to a maximum of another $6,250) may be carried back three years and forward 20 years. They may be deducted only to the extent of income from a farming business.

¶10,050 Farm loss carryovers

ITA: 111(1)(*d*)

Farm losses are business losses, but are given a separate carryforward of 20 years. A farm loss is defined in the Act and is separated from other business losses in the definition of non-capital loss carryovers, to accommodate a previous difference in the carryforward period that existed for losses incurred in taxation years ending before March 23, 2004. The three-year carryback is also available.

ITA: 111(8)

¶10,060 Capital Gains Deduction — Historical Overview

Individuals can shelter up to $500,000 [$750,000 proposed in the March 19, 2007 federal budget] of capital gains on qualified small business corporation shares, qualified farm property, or qualified fishing property used in a family fishing business by claiming a capital gains deduction in the computation of taxable income.

The capital gains deduction originated in 1985. The 1985 federal budget introduced a lifetime cumulative deduction for net taxable capital gains (net TCGs) for individuals (other than trusts) resident in Canada. The announced purpose of this deduction was to provide an incentive for investment. Until the February 25, 1992 federal budget, the deduction was virtually unrestricted as to type of capital gains on a disposition. The February 25, 1992 federal budget imposed a restriction on the capital gains deduction resulting from the disposition, after February 1992, of most real property (i.e., land and buildings), described as non-qualifying real property. Since the whole thrust of the present Act is to tax a fraction of capital gains, the introduction of this provision created considerable complexity in the legislation, to accommodate this exception.

The February 22, 1994 federal budget eliminated the $100,000 lifetime general capital gains deduction for gains realized on dispositions of property occurring after the budget date. However, the budget did not eliminate the $500,000 lifetime capital gains exemption for shares of a qualified small business corporation or for qualified farm property. This exemption uses the same rules and calculations as the exemption that was eliminated, so much of the complexity remains.

The budget which eliminated the $100,000 lifetime general capital gains exemption contained a provision which would allow an individual to recognize all or any part of the gains on the taxpayer's capital property accrued to February 22, 1994. Generally, the individual had to file an election with his or her 1994 tax return to recognize an amount of accrued gain that could be offset by the available capital gains exemption. The gain that was recognized by this election will reduce future capital gains by either increasing the cost of the property elected on or creating a special account which can be drawn down by future capital gains on those assets. These special accounts are called "exempt gains balance" for eligible capital property and "exempt capital gains balance" for mutual funds.

For example, consider the case of an individual who owns capital property, such as shares of a public corporation, which cost $10,000 and had a fair market value of $40,000 on February 22, 1994. The individual had $15,000 of the lifetime general capital gains exemption left in 1994. On filing the 1994 tax return, the individual could elect to have received proceeds of disposition on the shares of $25,000, resulting in a capital gain of $15,000 which would be offset by the exemption. The adjusted cost base of the shares could then be increased to the elected proceeds of $25,000.

Since the general capital gains exemption has been eliminated, it will not be discussed further. The capital gains deduction available on qualified small business corporation shares will be discussed in Chapter 13.

¶10,070 Ordering of Division C Deductions   DON'T READ

¶10,075 General ordering rules for Division C

Section 111.1 provides the following order of relevant deductions under Division C:

Sec. 110	Other deductions
Sec. 110.2	Lump-sum payments
Sec. 111	Loss carryovers
Sec. 110.6	Capital gains deduction
Sec. 110.7	Residing in prescribed zone.

¶10,080 Ordering of section 111 loss carryovers

Loss carryovers can be applied in any order within section 111, subject to the general ordering rules for Division C, except that the oldest losses are always applied first. Therefore, careful consideration should be given as to which type of losses are used first. Generally speaking, the most restricted types of loss carryovers should be applied first. For example, since net capital losses can only be applied against net taxable capital gains, then net capital losses should be applied in years in which net taxable capital gains arise, unless it is expected that these gains will arise regularly in the future. Losses which have a carryback provision should be used immediately, if possible, so that taxes are refunded as soon as possible.

ITA: 111.1, 111(3)(*b*)

Example Problem 1

The following information has been provided by your client, Karl Konfused:

DON'T NEED TO KNOW

	2005	2006	2007
Capital gains (CG)	—	$84,000	$44,000
Capital losses (CL) (excluding BIL)	$ 6,000	—	—
Business investment loss (BIL) before adjustment	18,000	—	30,000

ITA: 39(9)

Additional Information

(1) Karl had a $10,000 net capital loss which arose in 1998, and has not been deducted previously.

(2) Karl had no capital gains prior to 2005 and he did not claim any net capital losses in any preceding years.

(3) In 2007, Karl had a rental property loss of $1,000 and had no property income in 2005 or 2006.

— *REQUIRED*

(A) Determine Karl's income from the sources indicated for 2005 to 2007 according to the ordering rules in section 3.

(B) Determine Karl's taxable income from the sources indicated for 2005 to 2007 according to the ordering rules in Division C after amending the returns.

— *SOLUTION*

(A)

	2005	2006	2007	
Income from non-capital sources (≥0)	Nil	Nil	Nil	ITA: 3(*a*)
Net taxable capital gains (≥0):				ITA: 3(*b*)
taxable capital gains	Nil	$ 42,000	$ 22,000	
allowable capital losses	$ (3,000)	—	—	
	Nil	$ 42,000	$ 22,000	
Sum of non-capital and capital sources	Nil	$ 42,000	$ 22,000	ITA: 3(*c*)
Losses from non-capital sources and ABILs:				ITA: 3(*d*)
rental property loss	—	—	(1,000)	
ABIL	$ (9,000)	—	(15,000)	
Division B income	0	$ 42,000	$ 6,000	ITA: 3(*e*)

(B)

	2005	2006	2007	
Division B income from (A)	0	$ 42,000	$ 6,000	
Less: net capital losses	Nil	(9,667)[1]	Nil	ITA: 111(1)(*b*)
non-capital losses (2005 ABIL carried forward to 2006)	Nil	(9,000)	Nil	ITA: 111(1)(*a*)
Taxable income (Division C)	Nil	$ 23,333	$ 6,000	

The foregoing solution illustrates how the various components fit into the full calculation of Division B income and taxable income.

— *NOTE TO SOLUTION*

[1] Loss continuity schedule	1998	2004	Total
Unadjusted net CL	$ 10,000	$ 3,000	
Adjusted to 2006 inclusion rate ($10,000 × ½ / ¾)	$ 6,667	$ 3,000	$ 9,667
Utilized in 2006	(6,667)	(3,000)	(9,667)
Available in 2007	Nil	Nil	Nil

Example Problem 2

Larry Loss-Carryover provides you with the following income (losses) for tax purposes for the years 2005 to 2007:

	2005	2006	2007
Employment income	$25,000	$ 32,000	$40,000
Business income:	20,000	(36,000)	40,000
Property income from Canadian interest	3,000	4,000	5,000
Capital gains (capital losses):			
Listed personal property	6,000	(10,000)	12,000
Other	15,000	(14,000)	2,250

Larry also provides the following additional information:

(1) Loss carryovers:

Listed personal property loss arising in 1998	$ 2,000
Non-capital loss arising in 1999 from a business	35,000
Net capital loss arising in 1999	18,000

(2) Larry did not claim a capital gains deduction or net capital losses in the years 1985 to 2004.

— *REQUIRED*

Dealing with each item line-by-line across the years, rather than one year at a time:

(A) determine Larry's income for 2005 to 2007 according to the ordering rules in section 3, and

(B) determine Larry's taxable income for 2005 to 2007 according to the ordering rules in Division C after amending the returns.

— *SOLUTION*

(A)

	2005	2006	2007	
Income from non-capital sources (≥0):				ITA: 3(*a*)
Employment	$25,000	$ 32,000	$ 40,000	
Business income	20,000	Nil	40,000	
Property from Canadian interest	3,000	4,000	5,000	
	$48,000	$ 36,000	$ 85,000	
Net taxable capital gains (≥0):				ITA: 3(*b*)
Listed personal property[1]	Nil	Nil	$ 3,000	
Other	$ 7,500	(7,000)	1,125	
	$ 7,500	Nil	$ 4,125	
Sum of non-capital and capital sources	$55,500	$ 36,000	$ 89,125	ITA: 3(*c*)
Losses from non-capital sources		(36,000)		ITA: 3(*d*)
Income — Division B	$55,500	Nil	$ 89,125	ITA: 3(*e*)

(B)

	2005		2007	
Income — Division B	$55,500		$ 89,125	
Net capital loss[2]	(7,500)		(4,125)	ITA: 111(1)(*b*)
Non-capital loss[3]	(35,000)		Nil	ITA: 111(1)(*a*)
Taxable income (Division C)	$13,000		$ 85,000	

— *NOTES TO SOLUTION*

[1] The listed personal property loss from 1998 is applied against the 2005 listed personal property gain of $6,000 leaving $4,000 which will be offset by the listed personal property capital loss of 2006 carried back. The remaining 2006 listed personal property capital loss of $6,000 will be carried forward and applied against the 2007 listed personal property capital gain of $12,000 leaving a net capital gain of $6,000 of which ½ will be taken into income. Note that listed personal property losses are carried over in their full capital loss amounts.

(2) (A) Net capital losses

ITA: 111(1)(b),
111(1.1)(a), 111(8)

	2005	2006	2007
Lesser of:			
(i) net TCGs for the year	$ 7,500	N/A	$ 4,125
(ii) total of adjusted net capital losses of loss years	$12,000	N/A	$11,500
Lesser amount	$ 7,500		$ 4,125

(B) Net capital loss continuity schedule

	1999	2006	Total
Unadjusted net CL	$18,000	$7,000	
Adjusted to 2005 inclusion rate	$12,000	N/A	$12,000
Utilized in 2005	(7,500)	N/A	(7,500)
Available in 2006	$ 4,500	—	$ 4,500
Realized in 2006	—	$7,000	7,000
Utilized in 2006	Nil	Nil	Nil
Available in 2007	$ 4,500	$7,000	$11,500
Utilized in 2007	(4,125)	Nil	(4,125)
Available in 2008	$ 375	$7,000	$ 7,375

(3) Non-capital loss continuity schedule

Non-capital loss — 1999	$35,000
2005 application	(35,000)
Balance of 1999 non-capital loss	Nil
Non-capital loss — 2006	
Business loss	$36,000
less: sum of income sources for the year .... (36,000)	Nil
Balance	Nil

ITA: 3(c)

Since individuals are eligible for non-refundable tax credits, it is advantageous to have at least $8,648 of taxable income in 2005. This amount increases to $8,839 in 2006 and $8,929 in 2007, as discussed later in this chapter.

¶10,090 Taxable Income of Non-Residents

In the discussion of residence in Chapter 2, it was established that a part-time resident of Canada is taxed on worldwide income for the part of the year that the individual is resident in Canada. The taxable income for the period of part-time residence of an individual is calculated under Division D. A non-resident individual is subject to Part I tax on income from employment in Canada, from carrying on business in Canada and from the disposition of taxable Canadian property. In addition, a non-resident is subject to Canadian withholding tax on Canadian-source income such as interest, dividends, alimony and pension receipts.

ITA: 114
ITA: 115
ITA: 212

¶10,090

Consider the case of an individual who is an international business consultant who decided to move the base of operations of the business to another country and to continue to provide service to Canadian clients from that base. Assume the individual ceases to be a resident on May 15 of the year, but continues to carry on the unincorporated business of providing consulting services in Canada periodically after that date. This individual would be taxed in Canada on worldwide income for the period to May 15 and only on Canadian-source business income after that date for the rest of the year. If the individual remains a non-resident in the following year, then only Canadian-source business income would be taxed in that year. *ITA: 114(a), 114(b)*

Income for the period of part-time residence is computed in the normal manner, including the deduction of most amounts allowed in Division B. The Division C deductions reasonably applicable to the period of part-time residence are also deductible. The taxable income of a non-resident with Canadian-source income is computed under Division D. Certain Division C deductions may be claimed in respect of that income earned in Canada.

Non-residents are required to pay tax on their "taxable income earned in Canada" for the year. "Taxable income earned in Canada" is the income that would be determined under section 3 with some adjustments to confine the calculation to Canadian-sources of the non-resident. In particular, the term "taxable Canadian property" necessary for the determination of income from its disposition is defined. Then, Division C deductions as appropriate to the Canadian-source income may be claimed. These deductions include those in respect of stock options exercised, charitable donations, and loss carryovers reasonably applicable to Canadian-source income. The Canada Revenue Agency's (CRA) interpretation of these provisions is contained in their Interpretation Bulletin entitled "Non-residents — Income earned in Canada". *ITA: 2(3), 110.1(1), 111*
ITA: 2(3)(c)
ITA: 115(1)(b)
ITA: 115(1)(d)–(f)
ITA: 110(1)(d),
110(1)(d.1)
ITA: 110.1(1), 111;
IT-420R3

¶10,100   COMPUTATION OF TAX FOR INDIVIDUALS

¶10,110   Basic Computation of Tax

¶10,115   Tax rates

A provision sets out the rates of tax applicable to individuals. These amounts, which have been indexed for 2007, are presented in Exhibit 10-1. *ITA: 117(2)*

EXHIBIT 10-1
2007 Federal Income Tax Brackets

Taxable income	*Tax*
$37,178 or less	15.5%
In excess of $37,178	$5,763* + 22% on next $37,179
In excess of $74,357	$13,942** + 26% on next $46,530
In excess of $120,887	$26,040*** + 29% on remainder

* Computed as 15.5% of $37,178 = $5,763 (rounded)

** Computed as $5,763 + 22% of $37,179 = $13,942 (rounded)

*** Computed as $13,942 + 26% of $46,530 = $26,040 (rounded)

¶10,120   Annual indexing adjustment

The Act provides for the annual indexing of certain dollar amounts used in the calculation of tax or tax credits. *ITA: 117.1*

The indexing formula is based on the annual increase in the Consumer Price Index for the 12-month period ending September 30 of the year before the year in which the indexing is to apply.

¶10,125   Overview of tax credit and tax calculation system

Exhibit 10-2 summarizes the key items in the calculation of tax credits and income tax payable. The first line in Exhibit 10-2 results from applying the tax table in Exhibit 10-1 to the taxpayer's taxable income for the year. Total federal income tax is reduced by two basic types of credits, non-refundable and refundable, which are deducted at one of three different stages of the calculation.

EXHIBIT 10-2
Summary of Income Tax Calculation

Total federal income tax on taxable income [ssec. 117(2) and sec. 117.1]		$xxx
Subtract: Total non-refundable tax credits (see Exhibit 10-3)	$xxx	
Federal dividend tax credit [sec. 121]	xxx	xxx
Basic Federal Tax		$xxx
Subtract: Federal foreign tax credits [sec. 126]		xxx
Federal tax		$xxx
Subtract: Federal political contributions tax credit [ssec. 127(3)]	$xxx	
Other federal tax credits	xxx	xxx
Net federal tax		$xxx
Add: Tax on Old Age Security benefits [sec. 180.2]		xxx
Total federal tax		$xxx
Add: Provincial tax	$xxx	
Provincial surtax	xxx	xxx
Total payable		$xxx
Subtract: Total income tax deducted at source	$xxx	
Federal refundable tax credits (e.g., employee and partner GST rebate)	xxx	
Tax paid by instalments	xxx	
Provincial refundable tax credits	xxx	xxx
Balance payable or refundable		$xxx

Non-refundable tax credits like the marital status tax credit or the dividend tax credit are subtracted from federal tax. To the extent that these credits exceed federal tax, the excess is not refundable and, therefore, is of no value to the taxpayer. Some non-refundable tax credits are referred to as "above-the-line tax credits", because they are subtracted from federal tax to arrive at Basic Federal Tax. Exhibit 10-3 lists these non-refundable tax credits. Some non-refundable tax credits like federal foreign tax credits and federal political contributions tax credits can be termed "below-the-line tax credits", because they are subtracted after the calculation of Basic Federal Tax. These "below-the-line tax credits" are not magnified by the territorial or non-resident tax effects, discussed below.

EXHIBIT 10-3
Types of Non-refundable Tax Credits

- Basic personal amount
- Spousal amount
- Equivalent-to-spouse amount
- Amounts for dependent children (if ≥18 years and infirm)
- Child amount
- Additional personal amounts
- Caregiver amount

- Age amount
- Canada employment amount
- Adoption expense amount
- Public transit tax credit
- Children's fitness amount
- Canada or Quebec Pension Plan contributions
- Employment Insurance premiums
- Pension income amount
- Disability amount
- Disability amount transferred from a dependant other than spouse
- Tuition and education [and textbook] amounts
- Tuition and education [and textbook] amounts transferred from a child
- Amounts transferred from spouse
- Medical expenses
- Donations and gifts
- Interest paid on student loans
- Dividend tax credit

Some tax credits are refundable and, hence, are subtracted last. To the extent that these tax credits, such as the federal credit for employment outside Canada or certain provincial tax credits, exceed total tax payable, the excess is refunded, along with excess tax withholdings from payroll or excess tax instalments on income not subject to withholdings. Other tax credits like the GST credit and the child tax benefit involve a calculation of an amount that is deemed to be tax-paid and, hence, result in a "refund" of the deemed tax.

It is important to understand the difference between a tax credit and a tax deduction. A tax deduction reduces a taxpayer's income subject to tax at a particular marginal tax rate. Therefore, a deduction from income or taxable income saves the taxpayer an amount that increases with the taxpayer's level of income and, hence, tax rate. For some taxpayers, it may take $4 of deduction to save $1 in tax (i.e., at a 25% tax rate), while for other taxpayers, only $2 of deduction will save the $1 in tax (i.e., at a 50% tax rate). A tax credit is a direct reduction of the taxpayer's tax bill at a specified rate. A "below-the-line" credit of $1 results in a tax reduction of $1. An "above-the-line" credit of $1 results in a tax reduction of $1 plus the savings in non-resident tax, discussed below. The objective of the tax credit system is to provide all taxpayers with the same level of tax reduction regardless of their marginal tax rate.

¶10,130 Provincial and Territorial Tax

ITA: 120

The significance of Basic Federal Tax is that it is the base for additional tax on non-residents. Therefore, any tax credit subtracted before Basic Federal Tax reduces this non-resident tax which is based on a "tax on tax" structure. As a result, a 15.5% federal tax credit for, say, marital status, has a magnified effect in reducing total tax by 22.9% where the non-resident tax rate is 48% of Basic Federal Tax (i.e., .155 × (1 + .48) = .229). These tax credits are non-refundable tax credits.

All of the provinces and territories use a "tax on income" (TONI) structure for computing provincial tax. In such a structure, provinces may adopt the federal calculation of taxable income or make adjustments to it. Provinces may use the federal brackets or change them. Provincial rates are specified for income in these brackets. Provinces specify their own non-refundable credit amounts. For provincial tax rates, tax brackets and tax credit amounts, see the preface material in a current edition of the CCH CANADIAN INCOME TAX ACT. For the purposes of this book, where provincial tax is calculated for individuals, the following table, using the federal brackets, will be used. In addition, the provincial rate for the non-refundable credits will be assumed to be 10% of the federal base. For example, the provincial basic personal amount will be 10% of $8,929 or $893.

Taxable income	Tax
$37,178 or less	10%
In excess of $37,178	$3,718* + 12% on next $37,179
In excess of $74,357	$8,179** + 15% on next $46,530
In excess of $120,887	$15,159*** + 17% on remainder

* Computed as 10% of $37,178 = $3,718 (rounded)

** Computed as $3,718 + 12% of $37,179 = $8,179 (rounded)

*** Computed as $8,179 + 15% of $46,530 = $15,159 (rounded)

¶10,140   Section 118 Tax Credits

The provision for personal tax credits begins by presenting the following general formula for computing non-refundable personal tax credits: ITA: 118(1)

$$A \times B$$

where A is the appropriate percentage for the year, defined to mean the lowest percentage rate of individual tax (i.e., 15.5% for 2007),   ITA: 117(2), 248(1)

B is the aggregate of the following tax credit bases:

(a) married or common-law partnership status,

(b) wholly dependent person (i.e., equivalent-to-married status),

(b.1) child amount,

(c) single status,

(c.1) in-home care of relative,

(d) dependants, and

(e) additional amount.

Therefore, the personal tax credits are computed as 15.5% of a dollar amount indexed for 2007. The personal tax credit for individuals, other than the taxpayer, are limited by the Division B income of the dependant. However, dependants are allowed to earn a certain amount of Division B income before the tax credit is reduced.

For the purposes of this chapter, the amount of Division B income of a dependant before the tax credit is reduced will be called the "threshold income".

¶10,145   Married status credit   ITA: 118(1)(*a*)

The tax credit base for married or common-law partner (referred to as spouses) status is computed as the sum of the following two amounts: ITA: 118(1)(*a*)

Basic personal tax credit base in 2007		$8,929
Spouse's tax credit base in 2007	$8,929	
Less: spouse's Division B income in 2007	xxx	
Net amount (non-negative)		xxx
Total tax credit base		$ xxx
Tax credit (15.5% of total)		$ xxx

ITA: 257

The total tax credit is a maximum of $2,768 (i.e., 15.5% of $8,929 + 15.5% of $8,929). This tax credit is available if an individual supports his or her spouse. Note, however, that the spouse's tax credit base is reduced by the Division B income of the dependent spouse for the whole year, even if the marriage occurred in the year.

On the other hand, if the individual was living apart from his or her spouse at the end of the year because of a marriage breakdown, only the spouse's income for the year, while married and not separated, is considered.

The base for an individual's basic personal tax credit is scheduled to increase to $10,000 in 2009. The increase is being phased-in beginning in 2007.

ITA: 118(3.1)

The CRA's position has been that in the year of marriage both spouses cannot claim each other even if the quantum limitations have been adhered to since they both cannot have supported each other.[1]

A common-law partner is treated like a spouse. The term "common-law partner" is defined as two persons, regardless of sex, who co-habit in a conjugal relationship and have done so for a continuous period of at least one year or who is the parent of a child of whom the taxpayer is also a parent.

ITA: 248(1) "common-law partner"

Hence, the married status tax credit is allowed in a common-law relationship if the conditions in the extended meaning are met and the conditions in paragraph 118(1)(a) are met.

¶10,150   Equivalent-to-married status for wholly dependent person credit

ITA: 118(1)(b)

A tax credit base equal to the tax credit base for married status is provided in respect of a wholly dependent person where the taxpayer is not entitled to a married credit (i.e., an individual who is not married or living in a common-law relationship). This provision might apply to an individual who, at any time in the year, was single, divorced, separated, widowed and who supported a relative. The calculation of the credit is the same as that shown for the married credit, with the Division B income of the wholly dependent person in excess of the threshold reducing the credit.

ITA: 118(1)(b)

ITA: 118(1)(a)

A number of additional conditions must apply for the tax credit to be available.

- The dependent person must live, at some time in the year, in the same self-contained domestic establishment as the taxpayer claiming the tax credit. The dependant must be wholly dependent for support on that taxpayer and/or other persons. The taxpayer need not own the residence. A rental unit qualifies.

  ITA: 248(1) "self-contained domestic establishment"
  IT-513R, par. 11–22

- The dependant must be related to the taxpayer by blood, marriage or adoption. As a result, nieces, nephews, aunts, uncles and cousins would not qualify as a marital equivalent under this provision (unless they fit the definition of child which is very broad and should be examined).

  ITA: 251(6)
  ITA: 252(1)

- Unless the dependant is a child of the taxpayer, the dependant must be resident in Canada.[2]

- Unless the dependant is the parent or grandparent of the taxpayer or is dependent by reason of physical or mental infirmity, the dependant must be under 18 years of age at any time in the year. In the case of *The Queen v. Mercier*, the taxpayer argued that the age requirement for children discriminates against single parents with children 18 years of age or older who, in the opinion of the taxpayer, should qualify for the credit and, hence, violates the Charter of Rights and Freedoms. The Court held that the provision does not violate the equality guarantee of the Charter.

  97 DTC 5081 (F.C.T.D.)

- Only one equivalent-to-married tax credit is available to a taxpayer.

  ITA: 118(1)(b), 118(4)(a)

- The dependant cannot be claimed under this tax credit if the dependant has been claimed under the married status credit by another taxpayer.

  ITA: 118(4)(a.1)

---

[1] This position has been confirmed by a decision by the Federal Court–Trial Division in *The Queen v. Robichaud*, 83 DTC 5265.

[2] Refer to *Ruzicka v. The Queen*, 95 DTC 365 (T.C.C.), for a discussion of the rules related to non-residents.

- Where two taxpayers are eligible for the equivalent-to-married tax credit in respect of the same person or the same domestic establishment, only one person is permitted the tax credit and only one equivalent-to-married tax credit can be claimed for a given domestic establishment. If the taxpayers cannot agree as to who should have the tax credit, then neither can have the tax credit. For example, Tom and Donna, who are both single, support their mother in the same domestic establishment. Either Tom or Donna can have the tax credit, but not both. If they cannot agree, then neither can have the tax credit.

ITA: 118(1)(*b*)

ITA: 118(4)(*b*)

- Where a taxpayer has claimed a dependant under this paragraph, neither the taxpayer nor any other taxpayer can claim that dependant for the 18 years of age or older and infirm credit or the caregiver credit. For example, if a married couple with one infirm child, 20 years of age, separates during the year and the spouse who supports the child claims the child under the equivalent-to-married credit, then that spouse cannot make an additional claim as a dependent child 18 years of age or older and infirm. The other spouse also cannot make a claim for that child even if he or she did, in fact, wholly support the child during part of the year.

ITA: 118(4)(*c*)

ITA: 118(1)(*b*)
ITA: 118(1)(*d*)

- Where an individual is required under the terms of a written agreement or court order to make payments in the year in respect of the support of a child, the individual is not entitled to claim any personal tax credit in respect of the child.

ITA: 118(5)

It might be noted that the interpretation of the phrase "at any time in the year is an unmarried person" appears to have the effect of enabling a person who presently qualifies for an equivalent-to-married tax credit and marries during the year to still qualify for this tax credit in the year of marriage, but not subsequently. Of course, the person claiming a dependant would not be allowed a claim for marital status.

ITA: 118(1)(*b*); IT-513R, par. 11–17
ITA: 118(1)(*b*)
ITA: 118(1)(*a*)

¶10,155 Child amount

ITA: 118(1)(*b*.1)

The child amount is a non-refundable child tax credit for parents based on an amount of $2,000 × 15.5% = $310 for each child under the age of 18 at the end of the year.

Where the child resides together with the child's parents throughout the year, either of those parents may claim the credit. In other cases, the credit is claimable in respect of a child by the parent who is eligible to claim the wholly dependent person credit for the year in respect of a child (or who would be eligible if that child were the parent's only child).

For the year of the birth, adoption or death of a child, the full amount of the credit is also claimable.

Any unused portion of the credit is transferable to the parent's spouse or common-law partner.

¶10,160 Single status — Basic personal tax credit

ITA: 118(1)(*c*)

The base of the basic personal tax credit is set at $8,929 in 2007 and, when multiplied by 15.5%, provides a tax credit of $1,384 (rounded) for 2007.

ITA: 118(1)(*c*)

¶10,165 Caregiver credit for in-home care of relative

ITA: 118(1)(*c*.1)

Individuals are entitled to a credit of up to $623 (i.e., 15.5% of $4,019) for residing with and providing in-home care for an adult relative. For this purpose, the relatives include the individual's child or grandchild or the individual's or spouse's common-law partner's parent, grandparent, brother, sister, aunt, uncle, nephew or niece. A parent or grandparent must either have attained the age of 65 years or be dependent because of physical or mental infirmity. All other dependent relatives must have attained the age of 18 and be dependent because of mental or physical infirmity.

The base amount of $4,019 is reduced by the dependant's income in excess of $13,726. The credit is not available if the dependant's income exceeds $17,745.

Where an individual is entitled to an equivalent-to-married credit for a dependent, no one can claim the caregiver credit or the credit for infirm dependants age 18 or older in respect of that dependant.

ITA: 118(1)(*b*), 118(4)(*c*), 118(4)(*d*)

¶10,170   Dependants credit

ITA: 118(1)(*d*)

A dependant is defined to include, for this purpose, a child, grandchild, parent, grand-parent, brother, sister, uncle, aunt, niece or nephew of the taxpayer or the taxpayer's spouse or common-law partner. However, the dependants must have attained the age of 18 before the end of the year in order to qualify for the tax credit. Also, the individual must be dependent on the taxpayer because of mental or physical infirmity.

ITA: 118(1)(*d*)

ITA: 118(6)

The tax credit is computed for 2007 as:

Dependant's tax credit base		$4,019
Less: dependant's Division B income	$ xxx	
threshold amount	5,702	
Net amount (non-negative)		xxx
Net tax credit base (non-negative)		$ xxx
Dependant's tax credit (15.5% of net) (maximum of $623 — rounded)		$ xxx

The CRA indicates that mental or physical infirmity in respect of the dependent person should require the infirm person to be dependent during a considerable period of time and not just temporarily.[3]

IT-513R, Appendix A

Note that the maximum amount of the dependant credit is the same as that of the caregiver credit, but the income threshold is much lower for the dependant credit. Thus, the dependant credit can be eliminated more quickly, making the caregiver credit more attractive, numerically. However, the caregiver credit has the more restrictive condition that the dependant must ordinarily reside in the same self-contained domestic establishment as the taxpayer claiming the credit.

The tax credit available for a dependent person must be shared by all individuals who are entitled to a tax credit in respect of the same dependant. Where these supporting individuals cannot agree on an allocation of the tax credit, the Minister may make the allocation. Furthermore, a taxpayer who is entitled to a deduction for support payments for a spouse is not entitled to claim a tax credit for the spouse. However, the CRA does permit a tax credit claim in the year of separation or divorce. Where an individual is required under the terms of a written agreement or court order to make payments in the year in respect of the support of a child, the individual is not entitled to claim any personal tax credit in respect of the child. This provision is necessary to parallel the non-deductibility of child support payments as discussed in Chapter 9. The subsection ensures that, since the child support payments are not deductible, the supporting parent would not be able to claim this deduction.

ITA: 118(4)(*e*)

ITA: 60(*b*)
ITA: 118(5)
IT-513R, par. 27

ITA: 118

¶10,175   Additional amount

ITA: 118(1)(*e*)

Where a taxpayer is entitled to claim a dependant for the equivalent-to-married (ETM) credit, the dependant cannot be claimed under the caregiver credit or the credit for infirm dependants age 18 or older.

ITA: 118(4)(*e*)

Where the caregiver credit or the credit for an infirm dependant age 18 or older would have been larger than the ETM credit, the difference can be claimed under this provision as an additional credit. The effect is to allow the equivalent of the caregiver credit for a person in respect of whom the ETM credit is claimed.

¶10,180   Age credit

ITA: 118(2)

The non-refundable age tax credit is computed on a base of $5,177 for 2007. Since the appropriate percentage for the year is 15.5%, the tax credit for 2007 is $802 (rounded). It is available to an individual who has attained the age of 65 years before the end of the year.

ITA: 118(2)

---

[3] A court case dealing with this issue is *The Queen v. Diaz*, 81 DTC 5112 (F.C.T.D.).

However, this age tax credit is reduced by 15% of the excess of the individual's Division B income over $30,936 and is, thus, completely eliminated when the net income exceeds $65,449.

For example, if an individual's Division B income is $55,000, the age tax credit would be computed as:

Age tax credit base				$5,177
Less: base reduction of lesser of:				
(a) Credit base				$5,177
(b) Division B income		$55,000		
Less: threshold		30,936		
Excess, if any		$24,064	× .15 =	$3,610
Lesser amount				3,610
Net base				$1,567
Age tax credit: 15.5% of $1,567				$ 243

¶10,185   Pension income amount   ITA: 118(3)

This non-refundable pension tax credit is determined as follows:

Age 65 and Older

The pension credit is equal to 15.5% of the lesser of:

1. $2,000, and

2. the "pension income"

Pension income includes, but is not limited to: ITA: 118(7)

(a) a payment in respect of a life annuity arising from a superannuation pension fund or plan;

(b) an annuity payment under a registered retirement savings plan or a payment under a registered retirement income fund;

(c) an annuity payment under a deferred profit sharing plan; and

(d) the income portion of other annuity payments.

Under Age 65

The pension credit is equal to 15.5% of the lesser of:

1. $2,000, and

2. the "qualified pension income"

The only difference is to change the definition of pension income to qualified pension   ITA: 118(7)
income. Qualified pension income includes:

(a) a payment in respect of a life annuity arising from a superannuation pension fund or plan; or

(b) certain annuities or payments received by the individual as a consequence of the death of the individual's spouse.

Certain amounts are not included in pension income or qualified pension income. These   ITA: 118(8)
excluded amounts are:

(a) the Old Age Pension or Supplement;

(b) the Canada Pension Plan (or provincial plan) pension;

(c) a death benefit;

ITA: 248(1) "death benefit"

(d) the amount of any payment which is included in income and then deducted under another provision such as lump-sum payments from withdrawing from a pension fund, an RRSP or a DPSP, retiring allowances, or pension benefits or DPSP benefits transferred into a spousal RRSP; and

(e) a payment out of or under a salary deferral arrangement, a retirement compensation arrangement, an employee benefit plan, an employee trust or a prescribed provincial pension plan.

¶10,190 Canada employment credit

This non-refundable credit is computed as 15.5% times the lesser of:

ITA: 118(10)

• The individual's employment income for the year, and

• $1,000.

This $1,000 amount will be indexed after 2007.

¶10,195 Summary of personal tax credits

Exhibit 10-4 provides a summary of the numerical components of the most common personal tax credits.

ITA: 118, 118.3

EXHIBIT 10-4
Section 118 Tax Credits (rounded)

	Maximum tax credit	Tax credit base	Division B income threshold
Par. 118(1)(a), (b), or (b.1):			
Basic personal	$1,384	$8,929	N/A
Spouse or equivalent	1,384	8,929	N/A
Child amount	310	2,000	N/A
Par. 118(1)(c): Single person	1,384	8,929	N/A
Par. 118(1)(c.1): Caregiver	623	4,019	13,726
Par. 118(1)(d): Dependants, age 18 and infirm	623	4,019	5,702
Ssec. 118(2): Age	802	5,177	30,936
Ssec. 118(3): Pension	310	2,000	N/A
Sec. 118.3: Disability amount	1,068	6,890	N/A

For the purposes of this book, where provincial tax credits are calculated for individuals, a rate of 10% (equal to the lowest provincial rate used in this book) will be applied to the above federal tax credit base, net of any applicable reduction for income in excess of the federal Division B income threshold.

Example Problem

George, age 50, has the following dependants, each of whom has Division B income as indicated for 2007:

Dependant	Age at year-end	Division B income
Spouse	45	$3,500
Son (residing with George and his spouse)	14	2,725

Son (residing with George and his spouse)....................	16	2,800	
Daughter (physically infirm, but not living at home)	18	5,000	
Mother (age 65 and residing with George and his spouse)	70	10,000	

— *REQUIRED*

Determine the personal tax credits available under section 118 for each of George's dependants for 2007. All of the dependants live with George.

— *SOLUTION*

	Wife [118(1)(a)]	Children × 2 (< 18)	Daughter (18 and infirm) [118(1)(d)]	Mother (age 65) [118(1)(c.1)]
Division B income	$3,500		$5,000	$10,000
Threshold income	N/A	N/A	(5,702)	(13,726)
Excess income	$3,500		$ 0	$ 0
Tax credit base.............	$8,929		$4,019	$ 4,019
Excess income	(3,500)		0	0
Net tax credit base	$5,429	$4,000	$4,019	$ 4,019
Tax credit @ 15.5% (rounded)	$ 841	$ 620	$ 623	$ 623

Note that neither of the sons provides a dependant tax credit. They are covered under the Child Tax Benefit system, discussed later in this chapter.

ITA: 118(1)(*d*)

¶10,200 Adoption Expense Tax Credit

ITA: 118.01

The Act provides a non-refundable tax credit of up to $10,445 in the year in which an adoption is completed for eligible adoption expenses incurred during the adoption period. Details of the credit are as follows:

- eligible adoption expenses include:

    (i) fees paid to an adoption agency licensed by a provincial or territorial government,

    (ii) court costs, legal and administrative expenses,

    (iii) reasonable travel and living expenses of the child and the adoptive parents,

    (iv) document translation fees,

    (v) mandatory fees paid to a foreign institution, and

    (vi) any other reasonable expenses required by a provincial or territorial government or an adoption agency licensed by a provincial or territorial government,

- the adoption period is the period that:

    (a) begins at the earlier of the time that the child's adoption file is opened with a provincial or territorial ministry responsible for adoption (or with an adoption agency licensed by a provincial or territorial government) and the time, if any, that an application related to the adoption is made to a Canadian court, and

    (b) ends at the time of the adoption.

- an eligible child is one who has not reached the age of 18 years at the time that the adoption is completed.

¶10,210   Public Transit Passes Credit

This non-refundable tax credit is based on the total of all amounts paid in the year in respect of eligible public transit passes. The amounts paid for passes for the use of the individual taxpayer, the individual's spouse or common-law partner, or a child of the individual, who has not reached the age of 19 before the end of the year. An eligible public transit pass is a public transit pass that is valid for a period of at least one month of public transit. Public transit includes transit by local bus, streetcar, subway, commuter train, commuter bus, and local ferry. Receipts for passes must be retained for verification purposes. ITA: 118.02

[The March 19, 2007 federal budget proposed to extend the eligibility for this credit to accommodate:

- electronic payment cards for costs related to the use of public transit for at least 32 one-way trips during an uninterrupted period not exceeding 31 days, and

- weekly passes where an individual purchases at least four consecutive weekly passes.

Both of these proposals apply to transactions after 2006.]

¶10,220   Children's Fitness Credit

This non-refundable tax credit is based on up to $500 of eligible fees for enrolment of a child under the age of 16 in an eligible program of physical activity. The credit can be claimed by either parent, for the 2007 taxation year and subsequent taxation years. It must be supported by a tax receipt that contains sufficient information for the CRA to monitor compliance. ITA: 118.03

Eligible expenses include those for the operation and administration of the program, instructors, renting facilities, equipment used in common (e.g., team jerseys provided for the season), referees and judges, and incidental supplies (e.g., trophies). Expenses that are not eligible include the purchase or rental of equipment for exclusive personal use, travel, meals, and accommodation.

On December 19, 2006, it was announced that an eligible program of prescribed physical activity is defined as:

> An ongoing, supervised program, suitable for children, in which substantially all of the activities undertaken include a significant amount of physical activity that contribute to cardio-respiratory endurance, plus one or more of muscular strength, muscular endurance, flexibility and balance.

To recognize the particular challenges that children with disabilities face, the age limit for them to qualify is 18 years instead of 16 years. In addition, a separate $500 non-refundable tax credit for disabled children who spend a minimum of $100 on registration fees for eligible programs is provided. The extra $400 recognizes the extra costs that children with disabilities encounter when involved in programs such as these.

¶10,230   Charitable Gifts Credit ITA: 118.1

¶10,235   Basic rules

The non-refundable charitable donation tax credit is calculated by the following formula: ITA: 118.1(3)

$$(A \times B) + C (D - B)$$

where A is 15.5% (i.e., the appropriate percentage for the year);

B is the first $200 of total gifts; ITA: 118.1(1) "total gifts"

C is 29% (i.e., the highest federal marginal tax rate for the year); and

D is the individual's total gifts (if over $200) for the year.

In essence, the tax credit amounts to 15.5% of total gifts up to $200 and 29% for total gifts in excess of $200. For the purposes of this book, where provincial tax credits are calculated for individuals, a rate of 10% will be applied to total gifts up to $200 and 17% (equal to the highest provincial tax rate used in this book) for total gifts in excess of $200.

The definition of total gifts indicates the following four components:

(a) total charitable gifts, including gifts to:

- Canadian registered charities (including Canadian universities),

- registered Canadian amateur athletic associations,

- prescribed universities outside Canada,

- certain tax-free housing organizations in Canada,

- Canadian municipalities,

- the United Nations or its agencies, and

- charities outside Canada to which the Government of Canada has made a donation in the year or the preceding year;

(b) total Crown gifts;

(c) total cultural gifts; and

(d) total ecological gifts.

¶10,240   Income limit and carryforward

If the eligible donations in a year exceed the maximum of 75% of Division B income, the excess amount should be carried forward and claimed first, before the current year gifts, in the next five years. Donations may only be carried forward five years subject to the 75% limitation in that year. The income limitation is found in the definition of "total gifts". This carryforward is permitted to the extent that the donations are not claimed in the current year, even though they may not exceed 75% of Division B income in the current year. The annual Division B income limitation of 75% of the donor's net income for the year is increased by 25% of:

ITA: 118.1(1)
ITA: 118.1(2.1)

ITA: 118(1) "total gifts"

- recapture of CCA arising on a gift of depreciable capital property; and

- taxable capital gains arising on the donation of a capital property.

A limit of 100% of Division B net income applies for gifts:

- made in the year of death; or

ITA: 118.1(4)

- of ecologically sensitive land.

ITA: 118.1(1)

The 75% of Division B income limit should not be expected to apply in most cases. However, the limit would become an effective limit, if gifts are made in an unusual year of relatively low income or a loss year.

¶10,245   Total charitable gifts

Gifts made to certain types of organizations listed under the definition of "total charitable gifts" may be eligible for the tax credit to a maximum tax credit base of 75% of Division B income. Only the gifts to these specified organizations are eligible and they must be supported by proper receipts.

ITA: 118.1(1)

ITA: 118.1(2)

¶10,240

Where gifts of capital property and works of art, which are inventory to the donor, have a fair market value greater than adjusted cost base or cost amount, and the gift is not cultural property, the taxpayer may make a designation of a transfer price. The taxpayer can designate a transfer price between fair market value[4] and adjusted cost base or cost amount as proceeds of disposition and the value of the gift. Capital gains or income could, thus, be avoided by selecting the adjusted cost base or cost amount; but the value of the gift and the resultant tax credit under these paragraphs would be lower.

ITA: 118.1(1)
ITA: 118.1(6)
ITA: 118.1(7)

If personal-use property is acquired as part of an arrangement under which the property is gifted to a charity, then the $1,000 rule will not apply. This rule is designed to prevent abuses connected with the donation of art and other personal-use property.

ITA: 46

¶10,250 Gifts of publicly traded securities

The income inclusion rate for capital gains from gifts of publicly traded securities (unless donated to private charitable foundations) is reduced to zero for this purpose, instead of the usual 50%. Securities eligible for this treatment include shares listed on a prescribed stock exchange.

ITA: 38(*a*.1); ITR: 3200, 3201

¶10,255 Total cultural gifts

Where an artist makes a cultural gift that is a work of art created by the individual and that is property in the artist's inventory, the artist is deemed to have received proceeds of disposition equal to the cost to the artist of the work of art. A cultural gift is included in the definition of "total cultural gifts" and means objects that the Cultural Property Export Review Board has determined meets certain conditions. The result of this provision is that the artist is entitled to a credit based on the full fair market value of the art donated, but has no income to report as a result of the donation and its consequent disposition of the art from inventory. There is no net income limitation and there is a five-year carryforward.

ITA: 118.1(7.1)
ITA: 118.1(1)

¶10,260 Tickets to events

Where a charitable organization issues receipts for the price of tickets to fund-raising events involving an element of entertainment or other benefit for the donor, only the excess of the amount paid over the fair market value of the benefit received is allowed to be considered part of the charitable gift.

¶10,265 Total Crown gifts

Gifts made to the Government of Canada or to the government of a province are considered to be gifts made to Her Majesty and are defined as Crown gifts. There is a 75% of net income limitation to equal the limitation on other charitable gifts. Again, there is a five-year carryforward on these gifts.

ITA: 118.1(1)

¶10,270 Total ecological gifts

A net income limitation of 100% applies to donations of certain ecologically sensitive land. This provision is meant to encourage the conservation and protection of Canada's environmental heritage and applies to qualified donations of land including qualified donations of covenants, servitudes and easements. As a further incentive, for ecological gifts made on or after May 2, 2006, any capital gain realized on the donation (other than gifts to a private foundation) are subject to a zero capital gains inclusion rate.

ITA: 38(*a*.2)

¶10,280 Medical Expense Credit

¶10,285 Calculation of the credit

Not all medical and health care costs are fully covered by a provincial health insurance plan or by a private health services plan. Expenses that must be borne by the taxpayer may

---

[4] An interesting court case on the issue of fair market valuation in this context is *Friedberg v. The Queen*, 89 DTC 5115 (F.C.T.D.), affirmed by the Federal Court of Appeal (92 DTC 6031).

qualify for the non-refundable medical expense credit. For example, certain cosmetic or elective procedures and a fraction of dental services may not be covered.

The medical expense tax credit is calculated as: ITA: 118.2(1)

$$A [(B - C) + D]$$

where

A   is 15.5% (i.e., the appropriate percentage for the year)

B   is medical expenses listed in the legislation for the individual, spouse or common-law partner and children not reaching 18 before the end of the year   ITA: 118.2(2), 118.2(3)

C   is the lesser of:
- $1,926 (indexed for 2007), and
- 3% of the individual's net income

D   is the lesser of:
- $10,000 and
- E – F

where

E   is the total of all medical expenses incurred by the taxpayer on behalf of any other dependant, and   ITA: 118(6)

F   is the lesser of:
- $1,926 (indexed for 2007)
- 3% of the other dependant's net income

In essence, the federal tax credit is 15.5% (10% used for provincial tax credit) of medical expenses in excess of the $1,926 for 2007 or 3% of the Division B income threshold. The medical expenses must be proven by filing receipts and must be paid within any 12-month period ending in the year unless the individual dies in the year. Where the individual dies in the year, the medical expenses must be paid by the claimant for the deceased person within any period of 24 months that includes the date of death.

¶10,290   Medical expenses

The legislation includes over 30 detailed paragraphs outlining the very technical rules and conditions defining medical expenses. A brief description of these paragraphs is provided below; however, a careful examination of these provisions and an Interpretation Bulletin must be made in order to determine the eligibility of each item[5]   ITA: 118.2(2)

                   IT-519R2

(a) — This paragraph includes in the tax credit base general medical expenses (illness, hospitalization, etc.) paid to dentists, nurses and medical practitioners (a wider term than medical doctors for the taxpayer, his or her spouse and dependants of the individual. Hence, either spouse may qualify for a tax credit for the expenses of each other. For other dependants, the definition includes most individuals related to the taxpayer and dependent on the taxpayer for support.   ITA: 118(6), 118.4(2); IT-519R2, par. 3

(b), (b.1), (b.2), (c) and (d) — These five provisions deal with full-time or part-time attendants or attendants for the care of an individual eligible for the impairment credit and/or full-time care in a nursing home, group home or otherwise. Each provision has its own unique conditions. The amount eligible for the credit in respect of attendant care for an individual eligible for the impairment credit is limited to $10,000 ($20,000   ITA: 118.3

---

[5] For cases dealing with a variety of medical expense claims, see: *Demont v. The Queen*, 2002 DTC 3924 (T.C.C. — Informal Procedure), dealing with health care services and transportation expenses; *Weeks v. The Queen*, 2001 DTC 5035 (F.C.A.), dealing with the cost of devices, equipment or other chattels purchased for in-home care of a disabled person; *Pagnotto v. The Queen*, 2001 DTC 3797 (T.C.C. — Informal Procedure), dealing with medical services and drugs; *Donahue v. The Queen* (T.C.C. — Informal Procedure), dealing with medical services and devices; *Klywak v. The Queen* 2004 DTC 3143 (T.C.C. — Informal Procedure), dealing with medical devices; *Motkowski v. The Queen*, 2003 DTC 3968 (T.C.C. — Informal Procedure), dealing with home alterations; and *Seely v. The Queen*, 2002 DTC 4009, dealing with home alterations.

in the year of death). More than $10,000 can be claimed in respect of an individual, but no impairment credit or attendant care deduction can be claimed in respect of that individual.

(*e*) — This category of expense, for care and training for the mentally or physically handicapped, is not completely medical in nature.

(*f*), (*g*) and (*h*) — These provisions deal with the transportation of taxpayers to medical centres. Note that for travel expenses envisaged in paragraph (*h*), individuals may choose a detailed or simplified method to calculate certain travel expenses. The detailed method would use actual costs, substantiated by receipts. The simplified method applies to meals and vehicle expenses which can be based on flat rates. The flat rate for meals is $15 per meal to a maximum of $45 per day, per person. The flat rate for vehicle expenses is based on the province or territory in which the individual travels and varies by province or territory. (See Chapter 9, under moving expenses, for a detailed list of rates for vehicle expenses.)

(*i*), (*i*.1) — These provisions deal with certain specific medical equipment or products.

(*j*) — These paragraph allows for the expenses of eyeglasses, etc. for the taxpayer, his or her spouse or a dependant.

(*k*) — The cost of specialized equipment dealing with oxygen and of insulin and of other specified substances is allowable by virtue of this paragraph.

(*l*) — This paragraph permits certain specific expenses related to the care of a trained dog who assists the blind or deaf and the cost of an animal trained to assist an individual who has a severe and prolonged physical impairment.

(*l*.1) — This paragraph allows a reasonable cost for arranging a bone marrow transplant or organ transplant.

(*l*.2), (*l*.21) — These paragraphs allow expenses for modifying a home if an individual is confined to a wheelchair for a long period of time, lacks normal physical development, or has a severe and prolonged mobility impairment.

(*l*.3) — This paragraph allows expenses for rehabilitative therapy to adjust for speech or hearing loss, including training in lip reading and sign language.

(*l*.4) — Amount paid on behalf of an individual with a speech or hearing impairment for sign language interpretation or real-time captioning services if the payment is made to a person who is in the business of providing such services.

(*l*.41) — Amount paid on behalf of an individual with a mental or physical impairment for note-taking services if the payment is made to a person who is in the business of providing such services and the individual has been certified as requiring those services.

(*l*.42) — The cost of voice recognition software used by an individual with a physical impairment if the individual has been certified as requiring that software.

(*l*.43) — This paragraph allows expenses for reading services used by an individual who is blind or who has a severe learning disability, if the need for the service is certified in writing by a medical practitioner and paid to persons engaged in the business of providing such services;

(*l*.44) — This paragraph allows expenses for deaf-blind intervening services used by an individual who is both blind and profoundly deaf (if paid to persons engaged in the business of providing such services);

(*l*.5) — This paragraph allows a maximum of $2,000 incurred to move an individual to housing that is more accessible or in which the individual is more mobile or functional.

(*l*.6) — This paragraph allows reasonable expenses relating to alterations to a home driveway to facilitate access to a bus by an individual with a severe and prolonged mobility impairment.

(*l*.7) — This paragraph allows the lesser of $5,000 and 20% of the cost of a van adapted within six months of its purchase for use by an individual using a wheelchair.

(*l*.8) — This paragraph allows reasonable expenses incurred to train an individual to care for a relative having a mental or physical infirmity. The relative must be either a member of the taxpayer's household or dependent on the taxpayer for support.

(*l*.9) — This paragraph allows expenses for remuneration for therapy provided to the patient because of the patient's severe and prolonged impairment.

(*l*.91) — This paragraph allows expenses for remuneration for tutoring services that are rendered to, and are supplementary to the primary education of, the patient who has a learning disability or mental impairment.

(*m*) — This paragraph provides the statutory authority for a regulation which supplements the equipment listed in paragraphs (*i*) and (*k*) noted above and may stipulate a dollar limit for claims in respect of a particular device or equipment.

ITA: 5700

(*n*) — Drugs and prescriptions, etc., as prescribed by a medical practitioner and administered by a pharmacist, are allowed by virtue of this paragraph.

(*o*) — This provision allows certain diagnostic services such as x-rays, laboratory tests, etc.

(*p*) — The cost of dentures made in a province by an authorized person is allowed by this provision.

(*q*) — This paragraph allows a premium for a private health services plan. To the extent that the premium has been deducted in computing the individuals business income, it is not deductible as a medical expense.

(*r*) — The incremental cost, to an individual who suffers from celiac disease, of acquiring gluten-free products if the individual has been certified as requiring a gluten-free diet.

(*s*), (*t*) — These paragraphs allow expenses for drugs or medical devices obtained under Health Canada's Special Access Programme;

(*u*) — This paragraph allows expenses:

- for the purchase of medical marihuana or marihuana seeds, from Health Canada, for use by a patient who is authorized to possess marihuana for medical purposes under the Marihuana Medical Access Regulations (MMAR) or who holds an Exemption for possession under Section 56 of the *Controlled Drugs and Substances Act* (CDSA); and

- for the purchase of medical marihuana, for use by a patient who is authorized to possess marihuana for medical purposes under the MMAR or who holds an Exemption for possession under Section 56 of the CDSA, from an individual who possesses a Designated-person Production Licence under the MMAR to cultivate or produce marihuana for medical purposes on behalf of that patient or who holds a designated person Exemption for cultivation or production under Section 56 of the CDSA to cultivate or produce marihuana for medical purposes on behalf of that patient.

Example Problem

Mr. Taxpayer has income under Division B of $25,000 and $30,000 for 2006 and 2007, respectively. His wife and children have no income in these years. He incurs the following receipted medical expenses on behalf of himself, his wife, and three dependent children.

2006 — None prior to August

August	Dental bills for children	$ 325
September	Hospital bill and drugs	200*
November	Prescription drugs	65
December	Prescription drugs	125
	Total medical expenses	$ 715 (B)

Less the lesser of:
- (a) $1,926
- (b) 3% of Division B income (3% of $25,000) .... 750 (C)

Net base for tax credit (B – C) .... Nil

2007 — January	Eyeglasses for himself and wife	$ 225
February	Eyeglasses for 3 children	340
March	Orthodontic work for children	1,500
July	Chiropractor for Mr. Taxpayer	400*
	Total medical expenses	$2,465

* Excess over amount paid by a provincial medicare program.

— REQUIRED

Determine the maximum amount Mr. Taxpayer can claim as a medical expense tax credit in 2007.

ITA: 118.2(1)

— SOLUTION

Since the only restriction on the 12-month period is that it must end in the particular taxation year, Mr. Taxpayer should choose the 12 months ending in July 2007.

The medical expense tax credit is computed by the following formula:

$$A ((B – C) + D)$$

where A = .155

B = total medical expenses (as computed below)

C = lesser of:
- (a) $1,926
- (b) 3% of Division B income (as computed below)

D = nil in this case

2006 — August to December: total medical expenses	$ 715
2007 — January to July: total medical expenses	2,465
Total	$3,180 (B)

Less the lesser of:
- (a) $1,926
- (b) 3% of Division B income (3% of $30,000) .... 900 (C)

Net base for medical expense tax credit (B – C) $2,280

Medical expense tax credit: A (B – C) = .155 × $2,280 = $ 353

Note that had Mr. Taxpayer's wife had some income that would attract tax in excess of her other tax credits, but less than her husband's, there may be a greater benefit to the family if she claimed the medical expense tax credit because the 3% threshold would be lower.

Note, also, that the CRA has indicated that prepaid medical expenses only qualify as valid medical expenses when they are made in the same 12-month period during which the medical services are rendered.[6]

¶10,295   Notch provision for dependants

As discussed above, a taxpayer may claim a medical expense tax credit for the medical expenses of the taxpayer, the taxpayer's spouse or any dependent individual. Where a person, other than the taxpayer's spouse, qualifies as a dependant, the taxpayer may include the medical expenses of that person when computing the medical expense tax credit.

ITA: 118(6)

ITA: 118.2(1)

Specifically, medical expense claims made on behalf of minor children are pooled in item B of the medical expense tax credit formula with those of the taxpayer and his or her spouse or common-law partner, subject to the taxpayer's minimum expense threshold (the lesser of 3% of net income and $1,926) without regard to the income of the minor child.

For medical expenses, to a maximum of $10,000, paid on behalf of other dependent relatives (e.g., child who has reached the age of 18, parent, grandparent, niece, nephew, etc.) taxpayers can claim qualifying medical expenses paid on behalf of such a dependant that exceed the lesser of 3% of the dependant's net income and $1,926. This reduction is embedded in item D of the medical expense tax credit formula.

Example Problem

Mr. Taxpayer's father is a dependant. His father's Division B income is only $8,500 for 2007. During the year, Mr. Taxpayer paid medical expenses of $1,000 on behalf of his father and $2,500 for himself. Mr. Taxpayer's Division B income is $100,000 for 2007.

ITA: 118(6)

— REQUIRED

Determine the maximum amount that Mr. Taxpayer can claim as a medical expense tax credit in 2007.

ITA: 118.2(1)

— SOLUTION

The medical expense tax credit is computed by the following formula

$$A\,[(B - C) + D]$$

If Mr. Taxpayer claims his father's medical expenses:

A =   .155

B =   total medical expenses, i.e., $2,500 for taxpayer

C =   lesser of $1,926 and 3% of $100,000, i.e., taxpayer's Division B income = $1,926

D   is the lesser of:
- $10,000 and
- E – F

where

E =   the total of all medical expenses incurred by the taxpayer on behalf of the father, i.e., $1,000, and

F =   lesser of:
- $1,926 and
- 3% of the father's net income, i.e., 3% of $8,500 = $255

15.5% × [($2,500 – $1,926) + ($1,000 – $255)] = $204

---

[6] See Tax Windows Files, Document number 2005-13326117.

¶10,295

¶10,300   Credit for Mental or Physical Impairment (Disability Tax Credit)

¶10,305   Amount of and conditions for impairment credit

The Act provides the formula for calculating the non-refundable tax credit for an individual with a mental or physical impairment and the conditions for entitlement to the credit. The tax credit for 2007 is $1,068 (i.e., 15.5% of $6,890). This tax credit is available to taxpayers who have "one or more severe and prolonged impairments in physical or mental functions" that has been certified by a medical doctor. A health professional, other than a medical doctor, may be eligible to certify the impairment. An optometrist may certify the existence of an impairment of sight. An audiologist may certify an impairment of hearing. An occupational therapist may certify the existence of an impairment with respect to an individual's ability to walk or to feed or to dress himself or herself. A psychologist may certify to the existence of an impairment with respect to an individual's ability to perceive, think and remember. A speech-language pathologist may certify a severe and prolonged speech impairment. A physical therapist may certify a marked restriction in walking. Cumulative effects of multiple restrictions must usually be certified by a medical doctor.   ITA: 118.3(1)

The impairment, or the cumulative effect of multiple restrictions, must have caused the individual to be markedly restricted all or almost all of the time in his or her basic activities of daily living. The impairment must have lasted or be expected to last for a continuous period of at least 12 months. Such impairment would include blindness, deafness and other listed impairments. It would also occur where, even with the use of appropriate devices, medication or therapy, the individual is generally unable (or requires an inordinate amount of time) to feed or to dress himself or herself or perform specified fundamental functions.[7]   ITA: 118.4(1)

No claim can be made under this subsection if a claim has been made for a full-time attendant or care in a nursing home. However, a claim for expenses of an attendant costing less than $10,000 in computing the medical expense tax credit will not deny this impairment tax credit.   ITA: 118.2(1) ITA: 118.2(2)(*b*.1)

A supplement amount of $4,019 for 2007 is available for each disabled child under the age of 18 years at the end of the year. The supplement amount is reduced by the excess of the total of child care and attendant care expenses paid in the year and deducted in respect of the child, over $2,354 (for 2007).

¶10,310   Transfer of impairment credit

A transfer of this credit is available to a taxpayer, if the dependants themselves cannot use all or some part of this credit. The impaired dependant must use as much of the credit as necessary to reduce his or her federal income tax to zero, before the remainder can be transferred. The transfer of the unused part of the impairment credit is available to a taxpayer if: ITA: 118(1)(*c*.1), 118.3(2)

- the taxpayer claimed an equivalent-to-married credit for the dependant;   ITA: 118(1)(*b*)

- the dependant was the taxpayer's child, grandchild, parent, grandparent (including in-laws), brother, sister, aunt, uncle, nephew or niece, and the taxpayer could have claimed an equivalent-to-married credit for that dependant if the taxpayer did not have a spouse or common-law partner and if the dependant did not have any income;   ITA: 118(1)(*d*)

- the dependant was the taxpayer's child or grandchild and the taxpayer claimed them as a dependant or for the caregiver credit;   ITA: 118(1)(*d*) ITA: 118(1)(*c*.1)

- the dependant was the taxpayer's child or grandchild and the taxpayer could have claimed them as a dependant or for the caregiver credit if they had no income; or   ITA: 118(1)(*c*.1), 118(1)(*d*)

---

[7] For cases on various impairments, see *The Queen v. Hamilton*, 2002 DTC 6836 (F.C.A.), dealing with celiac disease; *Johnston v. The Queen* (F.C.A.), 98 DTC 6169, dealing with arthritis; *Overdyk v. M.N.R.*, 83 DTC 307 (T.R.B.), dealing with partial paralysis; *Tanguay v. The Queen*, 97 DTC 3309 (T.C.C.), dealing with an individual who could not dress himself due to a hip problem; and *Radage v. The Queen*, 96 DTC 1615 (T.C.C. — Informal Procedure), dealing with intellectual limitations or perceiving, thinking and remembering.

- the dependant was the taxpayer's parent or grandparent (including in-laws) and the taxpayer could have claimed them as a dependant of for the caregiver credit if they had no income.

The net result of these rules is that if a parent supports two or more disabled children, the parent is entitled to the transfer of the unused portion of the impairment tax credit of those children, even though only one child may be claimed as an equivalent-to-married tax credit.[8] The spousal transfer of this credit is discussed later.

ITA: 118.8

The legislation deals with the allocation of the impairment tax credit where more than one individual is entitled to the credit for the same dependant. A definition of impairment is contained in the provision and applies not only to the disability credit, but also to the medical expenses credit. A definition of the term used to describe a medical practitioner is also contained in the provision and appears to codify the description in an Interpretation Bulletin.

ITA: 118.3(3)

ITA: 118.2, 118.3, 118.4
ITA: 118.4(2)
IT-519R2, par. 3

¶10,320 Tuition, Education, and Textbook Credits

¶10,325 Tuition fees

The federal tuition fee tax credit is equal to 15.5% (10% used for provincial tax credit) of eligible tuition fees paid in respect of that year. The Act provides for a tax credit in respect of tuition fees paid to an educational institution in Canada. The fees must be paid to a university, college or other educational institution in respect of courses at a post-secondary school level, or an institution certified by the Minister of Human Resources Development providing courses that furnish a person, who is at least 16 years of age at the end of the year, with skills for an occupation. The total of fees paid to a qualified institution in a year must exceed $100.[9]

ITA: 118.5
ITA: 118.5(1)(a)

Tuition fees for full-time and part-time students include items such as library and laboratory charges. Also, eligible for the credit are mandatory ancillary fees, other than student association fees, required to be paid by all full-time and part-time students for courses at the post-secondary school level. Eligible fees include those charged for health services and athletics. In addition to student association fees, the following are excluded: charges for property to be acquired by students, services not ordinarily provided at post-secondary educational institutions in Canada and tax exempt financial assistance to students. Also, mandatory charges paid for the construction, renovation or maintenance of a building or facility, generally, do not qualify for the credit. A fee that would be eligible, but for the fact that it is not required from all students, may be claimed to a limit of $250.

The tax credit for tuition paid in the year to a university outside Canada is more restricted. The student must be in full-time attendance at a university in a course leading to a degree. The course must be of at least 13 consecutive weeks' duration. A tax credit for fees paid by a Canadian resident who commuted to an educational institution providing courses at the post-secondary level in the United States is allowed. Again, the amount of the fees paid in the year to a particular institution must exceed $100.

ITA: 118.5(1)(b)

ITA: 118.5(1)(c)

¶10,330 Education credit

This federal credit is calculated by a formula which multiplies 15.5% (10% used for provincial tax credit) of $400 by the number of months in the year during which the individual was enrolled in a qualifying educational program as a full-time student at a designated educational institution. Part-time students at a qualifying post-secondary educational institution who are eligible for the disability tax credit or who, by reason of their certified mental or physical impairment, cannot be enrolled on a full-time basis are treated like full-time students. The enrolment must be proven by filing a certificate issued by the educational institution. Where the student is enrolled at an institution certified by the Minister of Human Resources Development, the purpose of the enrolment must be to obtain or improve skills for an occupation. The terms "designated educational institution" and "qualifying educational program" are defined.

ITA: 118.6(1), 118.6(2), 118.6(3)

---

[8] See *Blais v. M.N.R.*, 85 DTC 61 (T.C.C.).

[9] See *Dumas v. M.N.R.*, 79 DTC 726 (T.R.B.), which was decided when the threshold was $25.

Part-time students (other than students eligible for the impairment tax credit) may claim a federal credit of 15.5% (10% used for provincial tax credit) of $120 per month during which he or she was enrolled at a designated educational institution and specified educational program. The program must require the student to spend not less than 12 hours in the month on courses in the program.

Post-secondary students enrolled in distance education programs or correspondence courses may meet the full-time or part-time requirements if the courses meet the required standards.

Two Interpretation Bulletins discuss the detailed rules governing the education tax credit and tuition fee tax credit, respectively. These bulletins provide some very important interpretation of the technical terms relating to these credits and should be examined carefully. In particular, note the difference between the interpretation of "full-time attendance" in the two bulletins.

IT-515R2, IT-516R2

IT-516R2, par. 9–12, IT-515R2, par. 9–11

¶10,335 Textbook credit

A non-refundable textbook tax credit is available in addition to the education tax credit. The credit base is:

ITA: 118.6(2.1)

- $65 for each month for which the student qualifies for the full-time education tax credit amount, and

- $20 for each month that the student qualifies for the part-time education tax credit amount.

¶10,340 Carryforward

The unused portion of a student's tuition fee, education, and textbook tax credits can be claimed by the student in a subsequent taxation year. This allows an indefinite carryforward of these credits by the student to the extent that they are not transferred in the year earned to a spouse or supporting individual. Students are permitted to transfer part of the unused credits and carry forward the remainder.

ITA: 118.61

¶10,345 Transfer of tuition, education, and textbook credits to spouse and parent and grandparent

The tuition fee, education, and textbook credits may be transferred to a spouse or to a parent or grandparent of the student. To qualify, the student must designate, in writing, an amount transferred to a spouse or to a parent or grandparent. The formula for calculating the amount that may be claimed as a tax credit by the spouse or by the parent or grandparent is the lesser of:

ITA: 118.8, 118.81, 118.9

(a) the amount determined by the formula A – B

where A is the lesser of:

    (a) $775 (i.e., 15.5% of $5,000), and

ITA: 118.01, 118.02, 118.03

    (b) the student's tuition credit and education credit for the year (excluding unused amounts carried forward).

    B is the amount of the student's Part I tax payable after deducting credits for personal, age, pension, and employment, public transit passes, children's fitness, mental or physical impairment, EI and CPP, and unused tuition and education, and

ITA: 118, 118.3, 118.7

(b) the amount designated by the student in writing for the transfer to a spouse or to a parent or grandparent.)

In effect, this formula allows the transfer of the excess of up to $775 of a student's tuition, education, and textbook credits over those credits required by the student to reduce federal tax to nil.

Example Problem

Debbie, who is not dependent upon any person, was enrolled as a full-time student at the University of Toronto for eight months during 2007. Debbie provides you with the following information for 2007:

Scholarship income	$12,000
Summer employment	9,000
Interest income — Canadian	1,000
Qualified tuition fees paid in 2007 (8 months)	4,500

— REQUIRED

(A) Determine the amount of Debbie's federal tuition and education credits which can be deducted by her parent.

(B) Determine the amount of Debbie's unused federal tuition and education tax credits at the end of 2007.

— SOLUTION

(A) Scholarship income [not taxable]		$ Nil
Employment income		9,000
Interest		1,000
Division B and taxable income		$10,000
Federal tax @ 15.5%		$ 1,550
Basic personal tax credit ($8,929 × 15.5%)		(1,384)
Canada employment credit ($1,000 × 15.5%)		(155)
Federal tax payable		$ 11

Tuition fee, education, and textbook tax credit:

Tuition fee tax credit (15.5% of $4,500)	$	698
Education tax credit (15.5% of $400 × 8)		496
Textbook tax credit (15.5% of $65 × 8)		81
Total tax credit	$	1,275

Tuition fee and education tax credit transfer to parent:

Lesser of:		
(a) $775		
(b) Student's tuition fee and education tax credit: $1,275	$	775
Less: amount of student's Part I tax net of secs. 118, 118.02, 118.03, 118.3, 118.61, and 118.7 credits		11
Net amount available for transfer	$	764

(B) Unused tuition, education, and textbook tax credits at Dec. 31, 2006		Nil
Plus: 2007 tuition, education, and textbook credits	$1,275	
Less: Debbie's tax payable before deducting the current year's tuition, education, and textbook credits	(11)	$1,264
Minus: Unused tuition, education, and textbook credits deducted in 2007		(Nil)
Tuition, education, and textbook credits transferred		(764)
Unused tuition, education, and textbook tax credits at Dec. 31, 2007		$ 500

¶10,350   Credit for interest on student loans

A student may deduct a federal tax credit of 15.5% (10% used for provincial tax credit) of interest on a federal or provincial student loan payable in respect of the year or in any of the five preceding taxation years. Qualifying loans are those made under the *Canada Student Loans Act* or a similar provincial statute.

ITA: 118.62

¶10,360   Credit for Employment Insurance Premiums and CPP Contributions

The federal tax credit is equal to 15.5% (10% used for provincial tax credit) of:

ITA: 118.7

(a) all amounts payable by the individual in respect of an employee's premiums for Employment Insurance;

(b) all amounts payable by the individual as an employee's contributions under the Canada (or Quebec) Pension Plan; and

(c) all amounts payable by the individual as a contribution for self-employed earnings under the Canada (or Quebec) Pension Plan.

For 2007, the Employment Insurance premium rate for the employee is 1.8% of earnings to a maximum annual earnings amount of $40,000. At this level of earnings the maximum level of premium of $720.00 is reached. (Employers must pay a premium of 2.52% (i.e., 1.4 times the employee payment), for a total maximum of $1,008.00.)

The rate of contribution to the Canada Pension Plan for 2007 is 4.95% of pensionable earnings. The maximum pensionable earnings is $43,700 with a basic exemption of $3,500. Thus, the maximum contribution is calculated as follows:

$$4.95\% \text{ of } (\$43,700 - \$3,500) = \$1,989.90$$

For a self-employed individual, the maximum is twice the above amount or $3,979.80.

¶10,370   Transfer of Unused Credits to Spouse or Common-law Partner

Certain unused tax credits may be transferred to a spouse or common-law partner. These tax credits are:

ITA: 118.8

(a) the tuition, education, and textbook credits (to a maximum of $775);

ITA: 118.5, 118.6

(b) the age amount;

ITA: 118(2)

(c) the pension income amount;

ITA: 118(3)

(d) the mental or physical impairment credit; and

ITA: 118.3(1)

(e) the child amount.

The amount that may be transferred is calculated by the following formula:

$$A + B - C$$

where A is the lesser of:
- $775, and
- the spouse's tuition fee, education, and textbook tax credits;

B is the sum of the following tax credits available to the spouse:
- the age amount,
- the pension income amount,
- the mental or physical impairment credit, and
- the child amount; and

C is the amount, if any, by which
(a) the spouse's Part I tax payable after deducting:

- the basic single personal credit,   ITA: 118(1)(c)
- unused tuition, education, and textbook credits, and   ITA: 118.61
- the EI and CPP credits   ITA: 118.7

exceeds

(b) the lesser of:

 (i) the tuition, education, and textbook credit deductible by the spouse; and

 (ii) the spouse's Part I tax payable after deducting:

- the basic personal credit,
- the adoption expense credit,
- the Canada employment credit,
- the public transit passes credit,
- the children's fitness credit,
- the impairment credit,
- the unused tuition, education, and textbook credits, and
- the EI and CPP credit.

Example Problem

Mrs. Aged, age 75, received the following income in 2007:

Registered pension plan payments	$ 700
Old Age Security pension	5,900
Canada Pension Plan payments	600
Interest from Canadian corporations	400
Division B income	$7,600

Mrs. Aged has been confined to a wheelchair for several years but is quite active and is registered as a full-time student at a post-secondary institution for eight months, paying tuition of $2,000 at the senior citizens' rate.

— REQUIRED

Calculate the amount of federal tax credit transfer available to her husband for 2007.   ITA: 118.8

— SOLUTION

Transfer of credits to Mr. Aged in accordance with the formula:
A + B – C   ITA: 118.81

(A) Tuition, education, and textbook credits transferred
  Lesser of: (a) dollar limit .... $ 775

    (b) tuition, education, and textbook tax credits
    [15.5% of ($2,000 + ($400 + 65) × 8)] .... $ 887

    lesser amount .... $ 775

(B) Age credit .... $ 802
  Pension credit[1] 109
  Impairment credit 1,068   1,979
                        $2,754

(C) Mrs. Aged's Part I tax ($1,178 = 15.5% of $7,600) net of the
  basic personal tax credit ($1,384), unused tuition, education,
  and textbook credits (nil), and CPP and EI credits (nil) ...... $ Nil
  Minus lesser of:
  (i) tuition, education, and textbook tax credits deductible by Mrs. Aged .... Nil

> (ii) Mrs. Aged's Part I tax ($1,178) net of the basic personal tax credit ($1,384), the impairment credit ($1,068), Canada employment (nil), adoption (nil), public transit passes (nil), children's fitness (nil), the unused tuition, education, and textbook credits (nil), and CPP and EI credits (nil) . . . .   Nil
>
> lesser amount . . . .   Nil   (Nil)
>
> $2,754

— NOTE TO SOLUTION

(1) The Old Age Security pension and CPP payments do not qualify for the pension tax credit. The pension credit is calculated as 15.5% of the lesser of:

   (a) $2,000; and

   (b) pension income of $700.

ITA: 118(8)

¶10,380   Dividend Tax Credit and Subsection 82(3) Election

¶10,385   Dividend tax credit

The federal dividend tax credit available to an individual is a non-refundable tax credit. There are two rates of dividend tax credit depending on the source of the dividends:

ITA: 121

- a rate of $\frac{2}{3}$ of the gross-up applies to dividends paid by a Canadian-controlled private corporation (CCPC) from income subject to tax at the low rate applicable to active business income (ABI), and

ITA: 82(1)(*b*)(i)

- a rate of $\frac{11}{18}$ of the gross-up applies to dividends paid by

ITA: 82(1)(*b*)(ii)

   (i) a public corporation resident in Canada (and any other non-CCPC resident in Canada) from income subject to tax at the general corporate tax rate, and

   (ii) a CCPC resident in Canada to the extent that its income (other than investment income) is taxed at the general corporate rate.

Since the gross-up is a fraction of the dividend, the dividend tax credit can be calculated in three different ways depending on the information available:

Source of dividend	CCPC, on income taxed at the low rate on ABI	Canadian-resident public corporation or other corporation on income taxed at the general rate
Fraction of gross-up	$\frac{2}{3}$	$\frac{11}{19}$
Dividend paid	$16\frac{2}{3}$%	27.5%
Grossed up dividend	$13\frac{1}{3}$%	18.97 (rounded to 19% in this text)

For the purposes of this book, unless otherwise stated, where provincial tax credits are calculated for individuals, a theoretical dividend tax credit rate will be applied to the grossed up dividend as follows:

- a provincial rate of $6\frac{2}{3}$% where the 25% gross-up apples, and

- a provincial rate of 12% where the 45% gross-up applies.

Theoretically, the combined federal and provincial dividend tax credit should equal the gross-up of 25% or 45% of the dividend or 20% or 31% of the grossed-up dividend. This will be explored in Chapter 12. This would imply a provincial dividend tax credit rate applied to the grossed-up dividend of:

- 6⅔%, i.e., 13⅓% federal + 6⅔% provincial for a total of 20% of the grossed-up dividend, and

- 12%, i.e., 19% federal + 12% provincial for a total of 31% of the grossed-up dividend.

However, provinces, in their use of the tax-on-income (TONI) structure, may specify their own rate of dividend tax credit.

¶10,390   Election to transfer dividends to spouse

An election is available to deem taxable dividends from taxable Canadian corporations received by one spouse or common-law partner, who cannot use the dividend tax credit because of low income, to be received by the other spouse or common-law partner. However, this election can only be used if the married personal tax credit claimed by the higher income spouse for the dependent spouse or common-law partner is increased or created by transferring the dividend income in this way. If the election can be made, the taxpayer must include the grossed up dividends transferred from the spouse or common-law partner, but may deduct the dividend tax credit available on the dividends.   ITA: 82(3)

Consider the following situations where the low-income spouse has $300 of grossed up dividends from Canadian-resident public corporations plus some other source of income.

Calculation of taxpayer's married tax credit	Case 1	Case 2	Case 3
Spouse's Division B income before election	$9,000	$6,500	$2,000
Married credit:			
Spouse base	$8,929	$8,929	$8,929
Spouse's Division B income	(9,000)	(6,500)	(2,000)
Net credit base	Nil	$2,429	$6,929
Credit @ 15.5% of net credit base	Nil	$ 376	$1,074
Spouse's Division B income after election	$8,700	$6,200	$1,700
Married credit:			
Spouse tax credit base	$8,929	$8,929	$8,929
Spouse's Division B income	(8,700)	(6,200)	(1,700)
Net credit base	$229	$2,729	$7,229
Credit @ 15.5% of net credit base (rounded)	$36	$ 423	$1,121

In Case 1, an election is available, since after the election, a credit for the spouse has been created. In Case 2, the spousal credit has increased from $376 to $423 by the transfer of the dividends and, hence, the election is available. In Case 3, the election is available, since the spousal credit has increased from $1,074 to $1,121.

¶10,400   Credits for Part-Time and Non-Residents

Generally, for the period of residence in Canada of a part-time resident, the individual can deduct specified tax credits prorated by the number of days that the individual is resident in the year divided by the number of days in the calendar year: ITA: 118.91

- basic personal amount, married amount, equivalent-to-married amount, dependant amount and caregiver amount;   ITA: 118(1)

- age amount;   ITA: 118(2)

- impairment amount either for the taxpayer or transferred from a dependant; ITA: 118.3

- unused credits transferred from a spouse; and ITA: 118.8

- unused tuition and education amounts transferred from a child or grandchild. ITA: 118.9

All other personal amounts may fully be claimed if they relate to the period of residence. These include:

- the pension credit; ITA: 118(3)

- Canada employment credit; ITA: 118(10)

- the adoption expense credit; ITA: 118.01

- public transit passes credit; ITA: 118.02

- children's fitness credit; ITA: 118.03

- charitable gifts; ITA: 118.1

- medical expenses; ITA: 118.2

- tuition, education, and textbook credits; ITA: 118.5, 118.6

- credit for interest on student loan; and ITA: 118.62

- EI and CPP credits. ITA: 118.7

A non-resident individual (i.e., an individual who at no time in the year is resident in Canada) may deduct tax credits for the following amounts: ITA: 118.94

- charitable donations, including Crown gifts and cultural gifts; ITA: 118.1

- impairment amount for the taxpayer, but not for a dependant; ITA: 118.3(1)

- tuition credit; and ITA: 118.5

- EI, CPP (or QPP) credits. ITA: 118.7

Credits for all other personal amounts may be deducted if all or substantially all of the individual's worldwide income for the calendar year is included on the return.

¶10,410 Ordering of Credits

Section 118.92 provides an ordering rule for computing basic federal tax payable by an individual under Part I of the Act. The tax credits discussed, all of which are above-the-line non-refundable tax credits, must be applied in the following order:

Ssec. 118(1)	— married, equivalent-to-married, child, single, dependant, and caregiver tax credits;
Ssec. 118(2)	— age credit;
Sec. 118.7	— Employment Insurance and Canada (or Quebec) Pension Plan credits;
Ssec. 118(3)	— pension credit;
Ssec. 118(10)	— Canada employment credit;
Sec. 118.01	— adoption expense credit;
Sec. 118.02	— public transit passes credit;
Sec. 118.03	— children's fitness credit;
Sec. 118.3	— mental or physical impairment credit (including dependant's unused credit);
Sec. 118.61	— unused tuition, education, and textbook tax credits carryforward;
Sec. 118.5	— tuition fee credit;
Sec. 118.6	— education credit;
Sec. 118.9	— transfer of tuition fee, education, and textbook credits;
Sec. 118.8	— transfer of unused spouse's credits;
Sec. 118.2	— medical expense credit;
Sec. 118.1	— charitable gifts credit;

Sec. 118.62   — credit for interest on student loan;

Sec. 121   — dividend tax credit.

¶10,420   Income Not Earned in a Province

This provision imposes a surtax of 48% on federal tax of an individual applicable proportionally to income for the year not earned in a province. A definition of the term "income earned in the year in a province" is provided.

ITA: 120(1)
ITA: 120(4); ITR: 2600

The purpose of this provision is to achieve a tax rate on income earned outside of Canada and taxable in Canada which approximates the total federal and provincial income tax on income earned in Canada.

¶10,430   Credit for Employment Outside Canada

Some relief is provided for an employee who is employed outside Canada on a temporary basis. Since, in most cases, the employee will not have made a clean break from Canada, he or she will still be resident in Canada for tax purposes. In order to provide a standard of living equivalent to that in Canada, employers have had to offer increased salaries or living allowances which resulted in a higher tax burden with no increase in disposable income to the employee. This section was enacted to help the competitive position of Canadian corporations in bidding for export contracts.

ITA: 122.3

This section applies to employees of specified employers who perform specified duties outside of Canada for more than six consecutive months. The tax credit is based on the proportion of tax otherwise payable. The fraction is the lesser of:

(a) $80,000, prorated on a daily basis; and

(b) 80% of the employment income which can reasonably be attributed to those specified duties, to his or her total income;

reduced by:

(c) certain deductions provided in Division C.

This credit is not available where employment is by an employer that is, in essence, an "incorporated employee" (as discussed in Chapter 12).

¶10,440   Refundable Goods and Services Tax Credit (GSTC)

A refundable goods and services tax credit (GSTC) is provided. This credit is designed to offset all or part of the GST for families and individuals with lower incomes. Application for the credit is made with the taxpayer's income tax return, but the credit is received separately in quarterly instalments. The payments based on the taxpayer's 2007 income tax return are made in July and October 2008 and in January and April 2009. Eligibility for the credit and the amount paid in each quarter reflects changes in family circumstances that occurred before the end of the preceding quarter. Thus, for example, the birth of a child during the year can increase the GSTC in the next quarter, rather than only in the next year. For 2007, the amount is the sum of:

ITA: 122.5, 122.5(3)

ITA: 122.5

(a) $237 for an eligible individual, other than a trust, who is, at the end of the year resident in Canada and married, a parent or over 18 years of age;

ITA: 122.5(1), 122.5(2)

(b) $237 for a qualified relation (as discussed below) or for a qualified dependant (as discussed below) in respect of whom the individual is entitled to deduct an amount under equivalent-to-married status;

ITA: 118(1)(b)

(c) $125 for each other qualified dependant of the individual; and

(d) where the individual has no qualified relation for the year:

(i) $125 if the individual has one or more qualified dependants for the year,

(ii) if the individual has no qualified dependants for the year, the lesser of:

(A) $125 and

(B) 2% of the excess, if any, of the individual's Division B income for the year over the base (i.e., $7,705 in 2007).

A qualified relation is a cohabiting spouse or common-law partner. However, the credit cannot be double counted (i.e., the individual or the spouse or common-law partner may make the claim but not both). A qualified dependant is also defined as, in essence, a person who is claimed as a dependant or a child of the individual who resides with the individual at the end of the year. Two credits cannot be claimed in respect of the same person as an eligible individual and as a qualified dependant.

ITA: 122.5(1), 122.5(2), 122.6

ITA: 118

The credit is reduced by 5% of combined incomes, as set out in the definition of "adjusted income" over a $30,936 threshold for 2007. The refundability feature arises from the wording in the provision, which deems the amount of the credit to have been paid as tax like the refundable child tax credit.

ITA: 122.5(1)

ITA: 122.5(3)

Example Problem

Woody Carver is divorced and has custody of his two children, ages 8 and 13. Woody had net income of $35,000 for 2007.

— *REQUIRED*

Compute the refundable goods and services tax credit, beginning in July 2008, assuming no changes in his family situation.

— *SOLUTION*

Credit ($237 + $237 + $125 × 1)	$599
Add the GSTC supplement for single parents	125
	$724

Deduct: Income	$ 35,000	
Threshold	(30,936)	
Excess	$ 4,064	
5% of the excess		(203)
GST credit		$ 521

This credit will be paid in four instalments of $130.25 in July and October 2008 and January and April 2009.

¶10,450 Refundable Medical Expense Supplement

A refundable medical expense supplement (RMES) is provided for eligible individuals. An eligible individual is an individual who is resident in Canada throughout the year and 18 years of age or older at the end of the year. The individual's total business and employment income (excluding disability benefits) for the year must be at least $2,984 for 2007. The individual's adjusted income for a taxation year is defined as being the total of the income of the individual and of the individual's cohabiting spouse.

ITA: 122.51, 122.51(1)

The supplement is calculated as follows:

    lesser of:
        (a) $1,022, and
        (b) the total of
            (i) 25/15.5 of the medical expense tax credit claimed by the eligible individual for
                the year, and   *ITA: 118.2*
            (ii) 25% of the amount deductible for disability support   *ITA: 64*
    less: 5% of the amount, if any, by which
        (a) the individual's adjusted income
    exceeds
        (b) $22,627 for 2007.

Since this is a refundable federal tax credit, it does not affect provincial tax. However, an adjustment for the effect of provincial tax is contained in the 25/15.5 fraction used in the above calculation.

This supplement is completely eroded by the 5% reduction, when adjusted income is $43,067 (i.e., ($1,022/.05) + $22,627).

The supplement is deemed to be tax paid as part of the individual's tax liability for the year, like income tax withheld. Thus, it is available for refund if total tax paid or deemed paid exceeds tax payable for the year. *ITA: 122.51(1)*

The addition of 25% of the disability support deduction to the RMES ensures that disabled persons do not see their refundable medical expense credit reduced if they claim their cost of disability support as a deduction instead of a credit. The purpose of the RMES is to provide an incentive for Canadians with disabilities to work. The RMES is intended to offset the loss of coverage for medical and disability-related expenses when individuals move from social assistance to work.

¶10,460 Refundable Canada Child Tax Benefit

The Canada Child Tax Benefit (CCTB) is the main federal instrument for the provision of financial assistance to families with children. The CCTB has the following components: *ITA: 122.6–122.64*

- the base benefit, which is targeted to low and middle-income families, and

- two supplements:

  - the National Child Benefit (NCB) supplement, which provides additional assistance to low-income families, and

  - in recognition of the special needs of low and modest-income families with a disabled child, a $2,351 (for 2007) Child Disability Benefit (CDB) paid for children who meet the eligibility criteria for the disability tax credit.

The CCTB is paid monthly. The amount of the payments is based on family income and child care expenses of the base taxation year, as defined. The payments are not taxable and not subject to clawback. *ITA: 122.6*

An eligible individual is entitled to a CCTB calculated in respect of qualified dependants who are generally children who have not attained the age of 18 years. *ITA: 122.6, 122.61(1)*

The following is a table of the maximum benefits available under the CCTB.

	July 2006	July 2007
Base Benefit		
Basic amount per child	$ 1,255	$ 1,283
Additional benefit for 3rd and subsequent children	88	90
Additional benefit for children under 7 years	249	Nil

	July 2006	July 2007
NCB Supplement		
First child	1,945	1,988
Second child	1,720	1,758
Third and subsequent child	1,637	1,673
Total CCTB Benefit — 7 and older		
First child	3,200	3,271
Second child	2,975	3,041
Third and subsequent child	2,980	3,046
Total CCTB Benefit — under 7		
First child	3,449	3,271
Second child	3,224	3,041
Third and subsequent child	3,229	3,046
Child Disability Benefit		
Each child	2,300	2,351
Phase-Out Thresholds		
Base benefit phase-out starts at	36,378	37,178
Supplement phase-out ends at	36,378	37,178
Disability benefit phase-out starts at	36,378	37,178

To target the increase in the NCB supplement to lower-income families, the income threshold at which the NCB supplement begins to be phased out will be adjusted.

Since tax preparation software manages the calculations, the point to remember is who qualifies for this benefit.

The child must be a "qualified dependent" which means a person, who:

1. has not attained the age of 18 years,

2. is not a person who has been claimed for the equivalent to married credit, and

3. is not a person in respect of whom a special allowance under the *Children's Special Allowances Act* is payable.

The person receiving the benefit must be an "eligible individual" which means a person, who:

1. resides with the child,

2. is the parent of the child who primarily fulfils the responsibility for care and upbringing,

3. is resident in Canada,

4. is not an employee of a country other than Canada, and

5. is, or whose cohabiting spouse or common-law partner is, a Canadian citizen or a person who is a permanent resident, a temporary resident or a protected person. Each of these terms is defined under federal legislation.

The Universal Child Care Benefit (UCCB) was introduced to provide families with $1,200 per year for each child under the age of six years. Amounts received under the UCCB are taxable to the lower-income spouse or common-law partner, but are not included in the calculation of income-tested benefits delivered through the income tax system. The UCCB does not reduce the Old Age Security or Employment Insurance benefits and does not reduce the child care expense deduction.

With the introduction of the UCCB, the CCTB enhancement for children under the age of seven years is eliminated.

¶10,470   Working Income Tax Benefit (WITB)

¶10,475   Overview

[For many low-income Canadians, taking a job can mean being financially worse off. To improve their incentives and lower their barriers to employment, the WITB was introduced in the March 19, 2007 federal budget, effective for 2007.]

The WITB will provide a refundable tax credit equal to 20% of each dollar of earned income in excess of $3,000 to a maximum credit of $500 for single individuals without dependants (single individuals) and $1,000 for families (couples and single parents). Earned income for purposes of the WITB means the total amount of an individual's or family's income for the year from employment and business and is determined without reference to any losses arising or claimed in that year.

To target assistance to those with low income, the credit will be reduced by 15% of net family income in excess of $9,500 for single individuals and $14,500 for families. Hence, no WITB is available when a single individual's earned income reaches $12,833 (i.e., $500/.15 + $9,500) or a family's earned income reaches $21,167 (i.e., $1,000/.15 + $14,500). Net income will be calculated on the same basis as is currently used for the Canada Child Tax Benefit and the GST credit.

An individual will be eligible for the WITB if resident in Canada throughout the year and 19 years of age at the end of the year. In addition, a single parent must be the primary caregiver to the dependent child in Canada.

Students, as defined for the education tax credit, with no dependent children, who are enrolled as full-time students for more than three months in the year will not be eligible for the WITB.

¶10,480   WITB supplement for persons with disabilities

Persons with disabilities face significant barriers to their participation in the labour force. The WITB will provide an additional supplement for each individual, other than a dependant, who is eligible for the disability tax credit and who has at least $1,750 of earned income and who meets the other eligibility requirements for the WITB. For each dollar in excess of $1,750, the individual will be supplemented at a rate of 20% up to a maximum credit of $250. This supplement will be reduced by 15% of net family income in excess of $12,833 for single individuals and $21,167 for families.

¶10,485   WITB prepayment

To maximize the effectiveness of the WITB, it is proposed that a prepayment mechanism be put in place beginning in 2008. Individuals and families who are eligible for the GST credit, and who will be eligible for the WITB, will be eligible to apply to the CRA for a prepayment of one-half of their estimated WITB.

¶10,490   Foreign Tax Credits

Since a resident of Canada is subject to tax on worldwide income, any income earned   ITA: 126(1), 126(2)
from a foreign source must be included in total income being taxed in Canada. However, the foreign income may also have been taxed in the country in which it was earned. In the absence of a tax treaty which removes the income from the tax base of either Canada or the other country, the income would be taxed twice. The Act provides tax credits deductible from   ITA: 126
tax payable in Canada for income tax paid in another country. Residents of Canada may claim a tax credit for non-business income tax paid (such as tax on investment income) in another country and a tax credit for business income tax paid in another country. Both credits are limited to a proportion of tax payable in Canada that can be considered to be attributed to the income from the foreign source. This limit is computed by formula.

For individuals, the foreign non-business tax credit is computed as the lesser of: ITA: 126(1)

(a) non-business income tax paid to a foreign country, and

(b) $\dfrac{\text{net non-business foreign income included under Division B}}{\text{total income included under Division B net of certain adjustments}} \times$ tax for the year otherwise payable under Part I

Note that part (b) attempts to estimate the Canadian tax paid on the foreign income. As a result, the credit against Canadian tax cannot exceed the estimated Canadian tax paid on the foreign income.

The definition of "non-business income tax" excludes an amount that was deductible from property income in respect of foreign taxes in excess of 15% on income from property and an amount that was deducted in respect of foreign non-business income tax paid. ITA: 20(11), 20(12), 126(7)

The denominator of the fraction, which uses total income under Division B as the base, is reduced by amounts that are attributable to specific types of income which are offset by Division C deductions and, hence, do not generate tax. These amounts include:

(a) amounts deducted as net capital losses; or ITA: 111(1)(b)

(b) amounts deductible in respect of:

(i) shares, ITA: 110(1)(d), (d.1), (d.2), or (d.3)

(ii) a deduction for workers' compensation or social assistance, or ITA: 110(1)(f)

(iii) a home relocation loan. ITA: 110(1)(j)

The term "tax for the year otherwise payable under this Part" is defined for the purposes of the foreign non-business income tax credit. As it applies generally to individuals, it is the tax payable under Part I of the Act before specified deductions from tax, including the deduction of the dividend tax credit and the credit for employment outside Canada. ITA: 126(7) "tax for the year otherwise payable under this Part" (a)

The foreign business income tax credit, also, applies to individual taxpayers and is similar in its calculation. The major difference is that any business income tax paid but not deducted is available as an "unused foreign tax credit" to be carried back three years and forward 10 years. This foreign tax credit will be dealt with in more detail, as it applies to corporations, in the next chapter. ITA: 126(7)

Where either non-business or business income taxes paid are not deductible as a credit, all or part of the excess may be eligible for a deduction from an individual's liability for surtax. Furthermore, a non-deductible excess of non-business income tax paid may be eligible for a provincial foreign tax credit. ITA: 126, 180.1(1.1)

¶10,500 Federal Political Contribution Tax Credit

A tax credit is available for contributions to a registered federal political party or a candidate for election to the House of Commons. Receipts signed by the registered agent of the party or the official agent of the candidate are required to substantiate the credit claimed. The maximum credit is $650 which is reached with a contribution of $1,275 or more on the following sliding scale: ITA: 127(3)

Contribution	Credit
$400 or less	75% of the contribution
More than $400, but not more than $750 . . .	$300 + 50% of the contribution over $400
More than $750, but not more than $1,275	$475 + 33⅓% of the contribution over $750
More than $1,275	$650

¶10,510   Tax on Old Age Security Benefits

The Part I.2 tax results in the repayment of federal Old Age Security benefits included in computing the taxpayer's income, to the extent that the taxpayer's income is in excess of an indexed threshold ($63,511 for 2007). The repayment is computed as:

ITA: 60(*w*), 180.2

the lesser of:

(a) Old Age Security benefits		$xxx
(b) income under Division B without par. 60(*w*) deduction	$ xxx	
less	63,511	
excess, if any	$ xxx	
15% of excess, if any		$xxx

Note that the amount of this tax is deductible from income; however, offsetting the Part I.2 tax in part (b) above through the deduction removes the potential double tax on this amount, as discussed in Chapter 9.

ITA: 60(*w*)

Example Problem

Jimena Buck, a widow, received the Old Age Security benefit of $5,900 in 2007. Her Division B income, excluding the deduction for the Part I.2 tax, is $65,000.

ITA: 60(*w*)

— *REQUIRED*

Outline all of the tax implications of receiving the Old Age Security benefit in this case.

— *SOLUTION*

(a) The amount of the Old Age Security benefit received must be included in Jimena's income.

ITA: 56(1)(*a*)

(b) The following repayment of the Old Age Security payment is required:

ITA: 180.2

the lesser of:

(i) Old Age Security benefit		$ 5,900
(ii) Division B income (excluding clawback deduction)	$65,000	
less	63,511	
excess, if any	$ 1,489	
15% of excess		$ 223

ITA: 60(*w*)

(c) The $223 repayment is deductible.

ITA: 60(*w*)

(d) The net effect is as follows:

(i) inclusion of Old Age Security benefit	$ 5,900	
(ii) deduction of repayment	(223)	$ 5,677
(iii) cash received	$ 5,900	
(iv) repayment of Old Age Security benefit (paid special Part I.2 tax)	(233)	$ 5,677

¶10,520   Tax Reduction on Retroactive Lump-Sum Payments

When an individual receives a lump-sum payment in a year that relates to prior years, the graduated tax rate schedule, when applied to the lump sum, may result in more income tax payable in the year of receipt than in the prior years had the lump sum been spread over those previous years. The legislation provides for a reduction of tax on the following lump sums:

ITA: 110.2, 120.31

- income from an office or employment or income received because of the termination of an office or employment, received under the terms of a court judgment, arbitration award or in settlement of a lawsuit;

- superannuation or pension benefits, other than non-periodic benefits;

- spouse or child support payments; and

- employment insurance and other benefits that may be prescribed by regulations.

The right to receive the lump sum must have existed in a prior year. For the tax reduction to apply, the lump sum received in the year must be at least $3,000.

The amount of income that is eligible for this special treatment is deducted in arriving at taxable income and then subject to notional tax. The notional tax is calculated as if the lump-sum payment had actually been received in the year to which it related. Interest, calculated at a prescribed rate, is added to the tax to reflect the fact that the notional tax was not actually paid in a previous year.

ITA: 110.2, 120.31

This calculation will not affect any income-based benefits or deductions in those prior years.

¶10,530 Application of Rules for Computation of Tax and Credits

Example Problem

The following 2007 correct computation of taxable income for John Q. Citizen has been prepared for your analysis:

Income — Division B		
Employment income for tax purposes		$51,550
Business and property income, composed of:		
Dividends from Canadian-resident public corporations (grossed up)	$ 4,500	
Dividends — Foreign ($150 of tax withheld)	1,000	5,500
Pension income (including OAS benefit of $5,900)		15,000
Taxable capital gain		2,500
		$74,550
Less: Subdivision e deductions:		
RRSP contributions	$ 1,000	
Old Age Security benefit clawback	1,348	
Moving expenses	1,050	(3,398)
Division B income		$71,152
Less: net capital losses		(1,000)
Taxable income		$70,152

Additional Information

(1) John, age 67, and his wife Jill, age 64, are both resident in your province. Jill has no income and is blind.

(2) John has made the following selected payments in 2007:

Donations:	
Federal political party (registered)	$ 500
Provincial political party (registered)	400
United Appeal (registered)	500

(3) John's employer correctly withheld the following amounts:

Employment Insurance	$ 720
Canada Pension Plan	1,990

(4) John filed his return on April 30, 2008.

— *REQUIRED*

Compute the total amount of federal taxes payable for the year.

— *SOLUTION*

Sec. 117	Federal tax on first　$37,178　.		$ 5,763
	Tax on balance　　32,974　@ 22%		7,254
	$70,152		
	Total		$13,017
	Less: federal non-refundable tax credits:		
Ssec. 118(1)	Basic personal credit base	$ 8,929	
	Married credit base	8,929	
Ssec. 118(10)	Canada employment credit base	1,000	
Ssec. 118(2)	Age credit base[1]	—	
Sec. 118.7	Employment Insurance credit base	720	
	Canada Pension Plan credit base	1,990	
Ssec. 118(3)	Pension credit base	2,000	
Sec. 118.8	Transfer of spouse's impairment credit base	6,890	
		$30,458	
	15.5% thereof		(4,721)
			$ 8,296
Sec. 118.1	Charitable donations tax credit		
	First　　$200 @ 15.5%	$　31	
	Excess　$300 @ 29%	87	(118)
	$500		
Sec. 121	Federal dividend tax credit (19% × $4,500)		(855)
	Basic federal tax		$ 7,323
	Less: other federal tax credits:		
Sec. 126	Federal foreign tax credit[2]		
	Lesser of:		
	(a) $150		
	(b) $\dfrac{\$1,000}{\$71,152 - \$1,000} \times (\$7,323 + \$855) = \underline{\underline{\$117}}$		$　(117)
	Federal tax		$ 7,206
Ssec. 127(3)	Federal political donations[3]		(350)
	Net federal Part I tax payable		$ 6,856
Sec. 180.2	Old Age Security benefit clawback[4]		1,348
	Net federal tax payable		$ 8,204

— *NOTES TO SOLUTION*

[1]　The age credit is not available since Division B income is too high.

Age tax credit base	$5,177

Less: base reduction of lesser of:

(a) Amount of credit base $5,177

(b) Division B income $71,152
    Less: threshold   30,936
                                 $40,216 $\times$ .15 = $6,032

    Lesser amount 5,177

Net base . . . . Nil

$^{(2)}$ In this case, the foreign non-business tax credit is computed as the lesser of:

(a) the foreign non-business tax paid, and

(b) $\dfrac{\text{the foreign non-business income included under Division B}}{\text{Division B income less net capital losses claimed}} \times$ basic federal tax plus dividend tax credit

$^{(3)}$ The Act permits the deduction of a contribution to a federal registered party or person nominated as a candidate to serve in the House of Commons. The formula is: **ITA: 127(3)**

75% of first $400 . . . . $300
50% of next $350 ($500 – $400 in this situation) 50
33⅓% on next $525 (none in this situation) . . . . Nil
                                       $350

The maximum credit is $650 on $1,275 of contributions.

$^{(4)}$ Lesser of:

(a) Old Age Security benefit . . . . $5,900 **ITA: 60(w)**

(b) income under Division B (excluding clawback deduction) $72,500
    less   63,511
    excess, if any . . . . $ 8,989

    15% of excess $1,348

¶10,540 Minimum Tax   *[handwritten: NOT RESPONSIBLE FOR / AND APPENDIXES]*

The minimum tax addresses a government concern about the ability of some high-income individuals to take advantage of tax incentives and shelter virtually all of their income. Thus, a signal that minimum tax might apply in a particular case would be large deductions of CCA on tax shelters or large resource property deductions. **ITA: 120.2, 127.5**

¶10,545 Minimum amount

An individual's minimum tax is calculated by the following formula: **ITA: 127.51**

$$A (B - C) - D$$

where A is 15.5% (i.e., the appropriate percentage for the year),

    B is adjusted taxable income, **ITA: 127.52**

    C is the basic exemption, and **ITA: 127.53**

    D is the basic minimum tax credit. **ITA: 127.531**

This "minimum amount" minus a special foreign tax credit is then compared to regular Part I tax, net of all non-refundable tax credits (generally, before adding the 48% surtax for income not earned in a province). The greater amount becomes the basis of federal Part I tax for the year. The special foreign tax credit, which is basically equal to the greater of the foreign tax credit determined under normal rules or 15.5% of foreign income is the only credit available to a taxpayer subject to minimum tax.

ITA: 127.54(2)

All other tax credits, such as dividend tax credits and political donation credits will not be deductible from the minimum amount. In addition, even where the minimum amount is less than Part I tax, the restricted tax credits will be available only to the extent that Part I tax payable for the year does not go below the minimum amount.

¶10,550 Adjusted taxable income

The provision sets out the rules for computing adjusted taxable income, being a recalculation of taxable income using certain assumptions set out in the section. The CRA's form T691, for simplicity, starts with regular taxable income and adds back or subtracts amounts to arrive at adjusted taxable income. The amounts added back include:

ITA: 127.52

- the portion of the loss (including a share of a partnership loss) from certified film or videotape properties that relates to CCA or carrying charges such as interest and financing charges;

- losses on resource properties as a result of certain incentive deductions such as Canadian exploration expense, Canadian development expense, depletion allowance, or Canadian oil and gas property expense;

- 30% of the excess of capital gains over capital losses for the year;

- $^3/_5$ of the employee stock option deductions and the other share deductions;

ITA: 110(1)(d), 110(1)(d.1), 110(1)(d.2), 110(1)(d.3)

- the home relocation loan deduction; and

ITA: 110(1)(j)

- losses of investments required to be identified under the tax shelter identification rules.

Deducted in computing adjusted taxable income are:

- the gross-up of Canadian dividends; and

- the non-deductible fraction of allowable business investment losses claimed in the year.

¶10,555 Basic exemption

In the case of an individual, other than a trust, the basic exemption is $40,000. Therefore, it is only adjusted taxable income in excess of $40,000 that is subject to minimum tax.

ITA: 127.53(1)

¶10,560 Basic minimum tax credit

An individual's basic minimum tax credit is the sum of the following tax credits that may be deducted in computing tax payable under Part I of the Act:

ITA: 127.531

Ssec. 118(1)	— Personal credits for married status, equivalent-to-married status, child, single, dependants, and caregiver;
Ssec. 118(2)	— Age credit;
Ssec. 118(10)	— Canada employment credit;
Ssec. 118.01(2)	— Adoption expense credit;
Ssec. 118.02(2)	— Public transit pass credit;
Ssec. 118.03(2)	— Children's fitness credit;
Sec. 118.1	— Charitable gifts credit;
Sec. 118.2	— Medical expense credit;
Ssec. 118.3(1)	— Mental or physical impairment credit;
Sec. 118.5	— Tuition credit;
Sec. 118.6	— Education credit;

Sec. 118.61   — Unused tuition and education tax credits;

Sec. 118.62   — Credit for interest on student loan; and

Sec. 118.7   — Credit for Employment Insurance premium and CPP contribution.

¶10,565   Minimum tax carryforward

To recognize that a taxpayer who is not normally subject to minimum tax may, through unusual circumstances, be subject to minimum tax in a given year, the Act contains a carryforward provision. A taxpayer may carry forward for seven years the excess of the minimum tax over regular Part I tax for a particular year. The amount of the carryforward deductible in a subsequent year is restricted to the excess of regular Part I tax over the minimum tax in that subsequent year. As a result, in a carryforward year in which Part I tax exceeds the minimum tax, all or some part of the minimum tax paid in the previous year is recoverable as, in essence, a tax credit against Part I tax payable.

ITA: 120.2

¶10,570   Impact of the minimum tax

The minimum tax directly affects only a small minority of Canadian taxpayers. The $40,000 basic exemption generally protects most non-top bracket taxpayers from minimum tax. Most top bracket taxpayers who do not invest in tax shelters are also unlikely to be affected by the minimum tax. However, it is necessary for taxpayers who could potentially be affected to do minimum tax calculations as a part of their tax planning each year. Thus, the tax adds a significant additional degree of complexity to the tax system.

Example Problem 1

Determine the federal tax payable in 2007 by Scoop, an unmarried taxpayer, with the following sources of income and deductions and a $400 federal political donation tax credit.

Employment income for tax purposes	$ 90,000
Interest income	15,000
Cash dividend from Canadian-resident public corporation	12,800
Gross-up on dividend @ 45%	5,760
Taxable capital gain ($\frac{1}{2} \times$ $112,500)	56,250
RRSP contribution	(7,500)
Support of former spouse	(20,000)
Tax shelter loss due to film CCA	(25,000)
Net income for tax purposes	$127,310
QSBC share capital gains deduction	(50,000)
Taxable income	$ 77,310

Maximum Employment Insurance of $720 and CPP of $1,990 were withheld from salary.

— *SOLUTION*

Regular Part I tax

on first	$74,357			$ 13,942
on balance of	2,953	@ 26%		768
	$77,310			$ 14,710

Less tax credits:

Basic personal (15.5% of $8,929)	$1,384	
Employment Insurance (15.5% of $720)	112	
CPP (15.5% of $1,990)	308	
Employment (15.5% of $1,000)	155	
Dividend tax credit (19% of $18,560)	3,526	$ (5,485)
Basic federal tax under regular rules		$ 9,225(A)
Less: political donation tax credit (75% of $400)		(300)
Federal tax under regular rules		$ 8,925(B)

Adjusted taxable income:

Taxable income		$ 77,310
Add back: 30% of capital gain		33,750
CCA loss		25,000
Less: dividend gross-up		(5,760)
Adjusted taxable income		$130,300
Less: basic exemption		(40,000)
Net		$ 90,300

Minimum tax before minimum tax credit (15.5% of $90,300)		$ 13,997

Less basic minimum tax credit:

Basic personal	$1,384	
Employment Insurance premium	112	
CPP	308	
Employment	155	(1,959)
Minimum amount		$ 12,038(C)
Federal tax — greater of (B) and (C)		$ 12,038

Therefore, minimum tax is incurred in this situation.

¶10,800　REVIEW QUESTIONS

(1) Ms. Gnu, a new client of yours, has brought in her tax information and is confused. In prior years, she has had some financial difficulties and has lost money in a number of her business ventures. As a result, she has some net capital and some non-capital losses. This year, she earned some income, but she does not know how to decide which losses to apply against this income. What advice do you have for her?

(2) Mr. Izzy Dumorwhat earns over $130,000 of employment income and has come to you to talk about his investment income. He earns $10,000 of dividend income from a Canadian-resident public corporation in the year. He wants you to tell him what his marginal tax rate is on this dividend income.

(3) Mr. Phil D. Ayer earns over $130,000 of employment income and has come to you to talk about his investment income. He earns $10,000 of interest income in the year. He wants you to tell him what his marginal tax rate is on this interest income.

(4) Ms. Borscht earns over $130,000 of employment income and has come to you to talk about her investment income. She realized a $10,000 capital gain in the year and wants you to tell her what her marginal tax rate is on this capital gain.

(5) Ms. Aarts is a painter who specializes in watercolours. In the artistic tradition, she does not make a great deal of money. In fact, she has never made over $20,000 of taxable income in any year. This year is no exception. She expects to have taxable income of $20,000 but she is also planning to donate one of her watercolours to a local charity to be used in one of their fundraising events. The value of the painting is $8,000 and her cost of the painting is $200. She has heard that there are special rules for artists making charitable donations of their work but she does not know if these rules will help her. She does not make any other donations. What is your advice?

(6) During the year Ms. Hurry had full-time employment income from employer A of $45,000 and from employer B of $50,000. In addition, she had income from an unincorporated business of $30,000. Both employer A and employer B each deducted $1,990 from her salary for CPP. What impact will the CPP contributions for her employment and business income have on her personal tax return?

(7) ABC Contracting Inc., a taxable Canadian corporation, has a construction contract in Kuwait. Mr. Jones has been asked to move from Canada to Kuwait to help with the supervision. He will be there for a period of 15 months, after which time he will move back to Canada to take up his duties with the company. Due to the short-term nature of the work he will not move his family with him. He will move to Kuwait on January 1, 2007, and will not come back to Canada until April 1, 2008. His income for 2007 while in Kuwait will be $120,000. Comment on the tax issues in 2007.

¶10,825 MULTIPLE CHOICE QUESTIONS

Question 1

Banbury Ltd. (BL) is a Canadian-controlled private corporation. Brad King is one of BL's employees and deals at arm's length with BL. On April 30, 2004, Brad was granted an option to purchase 1,000 BL shares at $2 per share. Brad exercised the stock option on June 30, 2005, when the market price was $5 per share. In December 2007, Brad sold the shares for $7 each. The fair market value of the shares on April 30, 2004, was $2.50.

Which one of the following amounts represents the increase in Brad's taxable income resulting from the above transactions?

(A) $3,000 in 2005 and $1,000 in 2007

(B) $2,250 in 2005 and $1,000 in 2007

(C) $2,500 in 2007

(D) $4,000 in 2007

Question 2

Bob, a widower who is 65 years old, has correctly calculated his taxable income for 2007 as follows:

Employment income under Subdivision a	$10,000
Pension income (registered pension plan)	20,000
Old Age Security and Canada Pension Plans	10,000
Dividends from Canadian-resident public corporations (grossed up)	2,500
Interest income	5,000
	$47,500

What is the maximum amount (rounded to the nearest dollar) of federal income tax credits that Bob can claim on his 2007 tax return?

(A) $2,266

(B) $2,276

(C) $2,741

(D) $3,126

Question 3

In 2007, Shabir Hassam attended McGill University on a full-time basis for eight months, paying tuition fees of $3,900 for that period. In April 2007, Shabir moved back to Toronto to stay with his family and worked as a waiter. Shabir earned $8,500 in wages and $500 in tips during the summer. His moving costs were $200 to Toronto in April 2007 and $500 to Montreal in September 2007. Shabir also received a $1,100 scholarship from McGill in September 2007.

What is the maximum amount of federal personal income tax credits that Shabir can transfer to a parent in respect of his university education in 2007?

(A) $605

(B) $702

(C) $775

(D) $1,181

Question 4

Kyle, who is employed by a Canadian-controlled private corporation, had the following sources of income for the year:

Salary	$ 60,000
Dividends from Canadian-resident public corporation (amount received)	20,000
Employee stock option benefit	200,000
Capital gain	200,000

The stock option benefit relates to 50,000 shares that Kyle acquired under an employee stock option plan in January 2007 when the fair market value of the shares was $10 per share. Kyle paid $6 per share for the stock, which was the fair market value of each share at the time that the employee stock options were granted to him. He sold the stock when it was worth $14 per share.

Kyle is married and his wife works full-time. Their three children attend university. Each child has transferred the $5,000 maximum amount of education, tuition, and textbook credits to Kyle.

Based on this information, what is Kyle's federal Part I tax for the year under the regular rules, ignoring the minimum tax rules?

(A) $65,419
(B) $68,319
(C) $70,929
(D) $94,419

Question 5

Based on the information in Question 4, above, what is Kyle's minimum amount of federal tax for the year under minimum tax, after deducting minimum tax credits?   ITA: 127.53

(A) $54,261
(B) $51,936
(C) $44,961
(D) $35,661

¶10,850 EXERCISES

Exercise 1

ITA: 3, 111

The following information has been provided by your client, Ms. C.G. Investor.

	2005	2006	2007
Capital gains (CG)	$37,500	$50,000	$11,250
Capital losses (CL) (excluding BIL)	15,000	—	22,500
Business investment loss (BIL)	—	30,000	—

Additional Information

(1) The above capital gains do not include capital gains from qualified farm property or qualified small business corporation shares.

(2) Ms. Investor had a $7,500 net capital loss which was realized in 2003.

(3) Ms. Investor has never had a taxable capital gain prior to 2005 and did not claim any net capital losses in 1985 to 2004.

(4) Ms. Investor had a property loss of $7,000 in 2006 and property income of $1,000 and $2,000 for 2005 and 2007, respectively.

— REQUIRED

(A) Determine Ms. Investor's income from the sources indicated for 2005 to 2007 according to the ordering rules in section 3.

(B) Determine Ms. Investor's taxable income from the sources indicated for 2005 to 2007 according to the ordering rules in Division C after amending the returns.

Exercise 2

ITA: 118, 122.6, 122.61; IT-513R

Dan Dependant, age 50, supported the following persons during 2007:

	Net income for tax purposes
Wife, Dolly, age 45	$3,000
Son, Don, age 24	3,800
Son, Dave, age 18, infirm	3,200
Daughter, Doris, age 17	2,800
Son, Dan Jr., age 14	Nil
Mother, infirm, age 83	6,000

Don is attending university; Dave has been unemployed most of the year; and Doris and Dan Jr. attend high school. Ages are given as of the end of 2007.

— REQUIRED

Determine Dan's total federal personal tax credits under section 118 for 2007.

Exercise 3

ITA: 118; IT-513R

Jack and Jill were married on December 1, 2007. Jill and her two children of a previous marriage moved into Jack's home. Jill's children are 14 and 16 years of age and have no income.

Jack and Jill have the following income for tax purposes for 2007:

	Prior to the marriage	Subsequent to the marriage
Jack	$33,000	$3,000
Jill	8,800	800

— REQUIRED

(A) Determine the optimum personal tax credits under section 118 for both Jack and Jill for 2007.

¶10,850

(B) How would your answer change in 2008 if the income levels remain the same?

Exercise 4

ITA: 8(1)(*m*), 56(1)(*a*), 118(3)

Sluggo Transient was employed for a little under two years at the Banff Springs Hotel as a bellboy. When Sluggo resigned his position, he withdrew his total contributions of $800 from his employer's pension plan. Sluggo's contribution to this plan for his last year was $300.

— *REQUIRED*

Determine the tax consequences of the above situation.

Exercise 5

ITA: 118.6, 118.8, 118.9

Sammy Student, who was a resident of Canada and who attended the University of Alberta on a full-time basis for eight months during 2007, has employment income for tax purposes of $5,000. He paid tuition fees of $1,800 in 2007. Withheld from his income were $94 in Employment Insurance premiums and $74 in CPP contributions.

— *REQUIRED*

(A) Determine the amount Sammy can transfer under section 118.8 or 118.9 to another qualified person.

(B) List the potential persons to whom Sammy can transfer his tuition and education tax credits.

Exercise 6

ITA: 118.8

Tina Transfer, age 72, has income for tax purposes from the following sources in 2007:

Pension income:		
Old Age Security pension	$5,900	
Canada Pension Plan	2,755	
Registered pension plan	350	$ 9,005
Investment income:		
Canadian bank interest		100
Total Division B income		$ 9,105

— *REQUIRED*

Determine the amount Tina can transfer to her husband Tom in 2007.

Exercise 7

ITA: 82(3)

Mr. Eighty-Two-Three, a resident of your province, cannot decide whether it would be advisable to elect to include in his income, his wife's dividends of $900 received from Canadian-resident public corporations. This is her only income for 2007.

— *REQUIRED*

Determine whether Mr. Eighty-Two-Three should elect under subsection 82(3) for 2007 assuming his federal tax rate is 29%.

Exercise 8

ITA: 126(1)

The following selected information has been taken from the 2007 tax return of Adam Amazing, who is a bachelor:

Income — Division B	$156,800
Taxable income	150,800
Basic federal tax	34,715

Included in the Division B income was foreign interest of $1,500. Withholding tax of $225 had been deducted by the foreign government. This income is not subject to an international tax agreement.

Also included in the computation of Division B income were $300 of dividends received from Canadian-resident public corporations. Included in the computation of taxable income were deductions for net capital losses carried forward of $6,000.

ITA: 111(1)(*b*)

— REQUIRED

Determine the amount of the federal foreign tax credit that can be claimed.

Exercise 9   ITA: Division E, E.1

Compute the federal tax at the top bracket, under minimum tax and regular Part I tax for 2007 on $100 of:

(A) interest;

(B) cash dividends from Canadian-resident public corporation;

(C) capital gains.

Exercise 10   ITA: Division E, E.1

The following is a correct calculation (ignoring surtaxes) of Betty Bucks' Division E tax payable for 2007:

Employment income		$160,000
Dividends from Canadian-resident public corporation		30,000
Gross-up @ 45%		13,500
Loss created by resource property shelter		(103,500)
Net income for tax purposes and taxable income		$100,000

Tax on first	$ 74,357	. . . .	$ 13,942
on next	25,643	@ 26%	6,667
	$100,000		$ 20,609

Less tax credits:		
Basic personal (15.5% × $8,929)	$1,384	
Employment Insurance premiums (max.)		
(15.5% × $720)	112	
CPP contributions (max.) (15.5% × $1,990)	308	
Dividend tax credit (19% of $43,500)	8,265	
Employment (15.5% of $1,000)	155	(10,224)
Division E tax		$ 10,385

— REQUIRED

Determine if Betty Bucks is subject to minimum tax in 2007.

¶10,875   ASSIGNMENT PROBLEMS

Problem 1

ITA: Division B, C

The following tax information is extracted from Mrs. Hawkins' books and records:

Employment income per T4s (excluding effects of items below)	$72,000
Interest income	5,000
Capital gains (on securities)	9,900
Deductible carrying charges	1,000

The following balances are losses carried forward from December 31, 2006:

Non-capital loss arising — 2001	$24,000
— 2002	26,000
— 2005	28,000
Total non-capital losses	$78,000
Net capital loss arising in 2006	$12,000

During the latter part of 2007, Mrs. Hawkins moved from Montreal to Toronto to commence working for Leaves Co. Ltd. She received a $100,000 housing loan from Leaves Co. Ltd., which she used to help purchase a house in Toronto. Mrs. Hawkins received the interest-free loan on October 1, 2007.

Mrs. Hawkins previously worked for Les Habitants Co. Ltée (a public company). Prior to leaving Les Habitants Co. Ltée, Mrs. Hawkins exercised the stock option that she held in Les Habitants Co. Ltée. Mrs. Hawkins was able to purchase 2,000 listed common shares of Les Habitants Co. Ltée for $4 per share (the fair market value of the shares at the time the option was granted). The shares were trading at $10 per share at the time she exercised her option to purchase the shares.

Assume that the prescribed interest rate for the last quarter of 2007 is 7%.

— REQUIRED

Calculate Mrs. Hawkins' income and taxable income in 2007, in accordance with the ordering rules of Divisions B and C.

Problem 2

ITA: 3, 111

The following information has been provided by your client, Mr. Stanley Norman:

	2005	*2006*	*2007*
Employment income	$75,000	$80,000	$ 90,000
Property income (loss)	(4,000)	3,000	(6,000)
Capital gains (CG)	144,000	—	160,000
Capital losses (CL) (excluding BIL)	18,000	22,500	80,000
Business investment loss (BIL)	36,000	54,000	—

Additional Information

(1) The above capital gains do not include capital gains from qualified farm property or qualified small business corporation shares.

(2) Mr. Norman had a $21,000 net capital loss which was realized in 2003.

(3) Mr. Norman has not had a capital gain prior to 2005 and did not claim a net capital loss in the period 1985 to 2004.

— REQUIRED

Dealing with each item line-by-line across the years, rather than one year at a time:

(A) determine Mr. Norman's income from the sources indicated for 2005 to 2007 according to the ordering rules in section 3, and

(B) determine Mr. Norman's taxable income from the sources indicated from 2005 to 2007 according to the ordering rules in Division C after amending the returns.

Problem 3

ITA: 3, 111, 111.1

The following selected tax information has been taken from the books and records of your client, Mr. Taxloss.

	2006	2007
Employment income	$ 30,000	$ 38,000
Other business income (loss)	(15,000)	(23,000)
Property income:		
Canadian interest	7,000	15,000
Rental income from real property (loss)	3,000	(5,000)
Other income — pension	7,000	7,000
Capital gains (capital losses)*:		
Listed personal property	6,000	20,250
Other personal-use property	2,000	(4,000)
Other capital property	6,000	(45,000)
Other deductions:		
RRSP	1,000	3,000
Support of former spouse	7,000	7,000

---

* The 2007 other capital property loss includes a business investment loss of $24,000.

The following balances are losses carried forward from December 31, 2005:

Non-capital loss arising in 2003	$33,000
Net capital loss arising in 2004	25,000
Listed personal property loss arising in 2003	5,000

Mr. Taxloss was not a member of a registered pension plan and, hence, his pension adjustment for the relevant years was nil. His earned income for 2005 was $33,250.

— REQUIRED

Prepare a schedule for the calculation of income and taxable income for 2006 and 2007, in accordance with the ordering rules under Divisions B and C, after applying any loss carryforward and loss carryback provisions through an amended return. (Deal with each item line-by-line across the years, rather than computing income one year at a time.)

Problem 4

ITA: 56(1)(*u*), 56(1)(*v*), 74.1(1), 110(1)(*f*), 118, 118.3, 118.6, 118.9, 122.6, 122.61

Mrs. Plant, age 47, is married and has three children: Amanda, age 24, Joan, age 17, and Courtney, age 16. Her own income for tax purposes of $60,000 includes employment income of $52,000.

Amanda has been certified as impaired by a medical doctor. Her only income is $6,000 from social assistance payments relating to her disability. She took a university course on a part-time basis for four months. Mrs. Plant paid her tuition fees of $300.

Joan attended a university on a full-time basis in another city for eight months, had employment income for tax purposes of $4,200 from a summer job while living at home and received a $2,500 scholarship. Mrs. Plant paid Joan's tuition fees of $3,000 and Joan paid her own moving costs to and from the university which were $150 each way.

Courtney, who is attending high school, had employment income for tax purposes of $2,800 from summer employment and a part-time job.

Mr. Plant, age 50, has the following sources of income:

Worker's Compensation payment	$5,000
Cash dividends from shares of Canadian-resident public corporations purchased with Mrs. Plant's savings	4,000
Bank account interest earned from reinvestment of dividend income	100

¶10,875

— *REQUIRED*

(A) Calculate the non-refundable tax credits available to Mrs. Plant for 2007. Compute Joan's taxable income to determine if any of her tuition, education, and textbook tax credits will be available to Mrs. Plant. Prepare detailed calculations supporting your claim. All ages are given as of the end of 2007.

(B) Determine whether Mrs. Plant is entitled to claim the Canada Child Tax Benefit.

Problem 5

ITA: 118, 118.2–118.9;
IT-513R

Mrs. Hopeful, age 66, separated from her husband on October 17, 2007. She started receiving support payments from Mr. Hopeful of $2,500 per month in November 2007. All of the support payments made commencing in November 2007 are considered to be pursuant to the divorce settlement. Of the $2,500 monthly payment, $1,000 is for the support of their daughter, Rachel. (In 2007, Mr. Hopeful earned a salary of $100,000 per year and also earned other investment income.) Mrs. Hopeful has income of $26,200.

Their eldest daughter Rachel is 40 and infirm and lives with Mrs. Hopeful since she is severely mentally handicapped. She has been certified as impaired by a medical doctor. A part-time attendant helps care for Rachel at a cost of $12,000 per year. Rachel has no income.

— *REQUIRED*

Discuss the tax credits related to her daughter Rachel that are available to Mrs. Hopeful.

Problem 6

ITA: 118.2

Mr. Unfortunate provides you with the following medical expenses and additional information for himself and members of his family who live with him, when he asks you to prepare his 2007 tax return.

Assume that you have correctly computed the incomes under Division B for 2007 as follows:

Mr. Unfortunate	$55,000
Mrs. Unfortunate	Nil
Son, age 19	8,000
Son, age 15	2,000
Daughter, age 14	1,800

Medical expenses for 2007:

February	Prescription drugs for daughter	$ 20
May	Doctor's bill paid for son, 16	15*
June	Chiropractor's bill for the past year	1150*
July	Glasses for Mr. and Mrs. Unfortunate	300
		$1,485

Medical expenses to March 31, 2008:

February	Orthodontist fee for daughter		$2,550
March	Expenses relating to older son's car accident:		
	Hospital	$1,500	
	Surgery	1,000	
	Drugs	200	2,700*

Additional expenses anticipated by May 31, 2008:

(a) Additional medical bills from son's accident	$ 750*
(b) Eyeglasses for his younger son and daughter ($225 each)	450
(c) Dental bills (⅔ for Mr. & Mrs. Unfortunate)	375
(d) Chiropractor's bill for the past year	1,050

_____

* Excess over provincial plan payments.

— *REQUIRED*

Discuss the tax implications of Mr. Unfortunate claiming the above medical expenses for each of 2007 and 2008. Assume that all income amounts for 2008 will be the same as those for 2007.

Problem 7

ITA: 82, 118, 118.8

Mr. and Mrs. Realestate, ages 55 and 50, received the following income during 2007:

Mr. Realestate:

Employment income (commission)	$15,000
Employment expenses	(13,000)
Investment income:	
Canadian interest	2,000
Dividends received (in Cdn. $):	
Canadian-resident public corporations	950
U.S. corporations (net of 15% withholding tax)	680
Mrs. Realestate:	
Employment income	54,000
Investment income:	
Canadian interest	1,000
Dividends received from Canadian-resident public corporations	2,000

— *REQUIRED*

Calculate Mrs. Realestate's federal tax (ignoring the foreign tax credit) under the following situations:

(A) No election to include spousal dividends.

ITA: 82(3)

(B) With an election to include spousal dividends.

ITA: 82(3)

Problem 8

ITA: 118.5; IT-516R2

Stuart Student presents to you the following information concerning tuition fees paid for 2005, 2006, and 2007.

2005	Harvard University, Masters in Business Administration, fall term	$15,000
2006	Harvard University, Masters in Business Administration, winter and fall terms	30,000
2007	Harvard University, Masters in Business Administration, winter term	15,000
	Re-read fee for failed course	300
	Make-up course at Harvard for failed course, July–August	3,000
	Income tax course at University of Toronto, fall term; the tuition fee of $500 was waived, since Stuart's father was a member of the faculty	Nil
	Fitness course taken at a local secondary school in Ontario	35

— *REQUIRED*

Discuss the tax implications of the above tuition fee payments.

Problem 9 ✓

ITA: 117, 118, 121, 122.2, 122.5, 122.6–122.64, 180.1

Patty Parent, a single parent of two children (ages 4 and 2) works part-time as a clerk in a law office. She has provided you with the following information for 2007:

Income:	
Workers' Compensation payments	$ 9,000
Employment income (Subdivision a)	25,000
Cash dividend from Canadian-resident public corporations	480
University scholarship received	600
Expenses:	
Canada Pension Plan contributions	1,064
Employment Insurance contributions	450
Cost of subsidized day care for the children (3 days a week)	2,400
University tuition paid for a 3-month evening course	600

Patty receives the Workers' Compensation payment because of the accidental death of her husband two years ago. Her two minor children have no income.

Patty had $700 of tax withheld from her employment income and has paid no income tax instalments.

— *REQUIRED*

(A) Based on the information above, compute Patty's total federal and provincial tax for 2007 and her tax refund or balance due.

(B) Determine if Patty is eligible for the refundable goods and service tax credit and Canada Child Tax Benefit. Explain.

Problem 10

ITA: Division B, C, E

Hymie and Alan, both age 70, married, and retired successful businessmen, love to argue. The one fact that they agree upon is that they pay too much income tax. They both receive $5,900 of Old Age Security payments each year. Hymie has $52,000 of income from a registered pension plan. Alan receives $52,000 in dividends from the active business income taxed at the low rate in his incorporated business, a Canadian-controlled private corporation, which is now managed by his son. The spouses of both Hymie and Alan have no income for tax purposes and are under 65 years of age.

— *REQUIRED*

Determine which one of the two pays the most federal income tax for 2007. Ignore the possible transfer of dividends to a spouse.

ITA: 82(3)

Problem 11

ITA: Division E, E.1

Mrs. Entrepreneur, a client of yours, generally has employment income from her company and some investment income. In early 2007, you arranged Mrs. Entrepreneur's affairs such that she would crystallize her $500,000 capital gains exemption on qualified small business corporation shares. For 2007, her income is estimated as follows:

Employment income (CPP $1,990)	$ 42,500
Interest	12,000
Dividends from Canadian-resident public corporations	20,000
Gross-up @ 45%	9,000
Taxable capital gains	250,000
Interest expense	(10,000)
RRSP contribution	(14,500)
Capital gains deduction	(250,000)
Taxable income	$ 59,000

— *REQUIRED*

Calculate what effect, if any, minimum tax will have on Mrs. Entrepreneur's 2007 federal tax payable.

[For more problems and solutions thereto, see the CD accompanying this book.]

Chapter 11

Computation of Taxable Income and Tax After General Reductions for Corporations

LEARNING GOALS

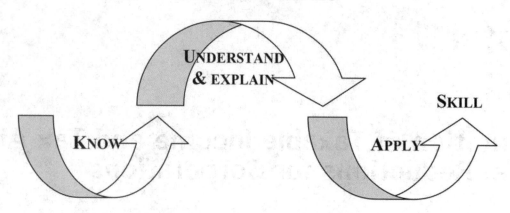

Know

By the end of this chapter you should know the key provisions used in the calculation of the taxable income and the basic tax, net of some general tax credits, for a corporation. Completing the Review Questions (¶11,800) and Multiple Choice Questions (¶11,825) is a good way to learn the technical provisions

Understand and Explain

You should understand and be able to explain:

- why most Canadian-source inter-corporate dividends are deducted in the calculation of taxable income, after having been included in Division B income for tax purposes;
- how loss carryovers are restricted — particularly, after an acquisition of control;
- how federal corporate taxes are computed with an abatement for provincial taxes; and
- how and why certain tax credits are provided to corporations to reduce basic federal tax.

Completing the Exercises (¶11,850) is a good way to deepen your understanding of the material.

Apply

You should be able to apply your knowledge and understanding of the key provisions pertaining to the calculation of:

- taxable income for a corporation to evaluate the consequences of an acquisition of control and to decide on the best strategy for dealing with losses in that situation, and
- tax for a corporation to do a basic calculation of corporate tax.

Completing the Assignment Problems (¶11,875) is an excellent way to develop your ability to apply the material in increasingly complex situations.

OVERVIEW

In the computation of the taxable income of a corporation, several deductions may be taken from the net income for tax purposes determined in Division B of Part I of the Act. Three of these, namely, charitable donations, loss carryovers and intercompany dividends, are covered in the example problem material of this chapter. The computation of tax for a corporation is made under the provisions of Part I, Division E, Subdivisions b (which applies only to corporations) and c (which applies to all taxpayers). This chapter introduces the basic computation of tax for corporations. Next, several tax credits are introduced. The manufacturing and processing profits deduction, which is available only for qualifying corporations, is alluded to. Then two tax credits that are available to all taxpayers, including corporations and individuals, are presented with a focus on their applicability to corporations: the foreign tax deduction and the investment tax credit.

The following chart will help to position in the Act some of the major provisions dealt with in this Chapter.

PART I — DIVISIONS C
TAXABLE INCOME — CORPORATE

DIVISION	SUBDIVISION	SECTION

DIVISION			**SUBDIVISION**		**SECTION**	
A	Liability for tax					
B	Computation of income					
C	**Computation of taxable income**				110.1	Donations
					110.5	Foreign tax addition
D	Taxable income earned in Canada by non-residents				111	Loss carryovers
					112	Dividends–Canadian
					113	Dividends–foreign
E	**Computation of tax**		a	Individuals		
			a.1	Child tax benefit		
E.1	Minimum tax		**b**	**Corporations**		
F	Special rules		**c**	**All taxpayers**	123-123.3	Tax rates and surtax
G	Deferred and other special income arrangements				123.4	Tax reductions
					124	Prov abatement
					125	Small Business ded'n
H	Exemptions				125.1	Mfg and Proc credit
I	Returns, Assessments, payments, appeals				125.4 - 125.5	Cdn film/video credit
J	Appeals to the courts					
					126	Foreign tax credit
					127 - 127.41	Other tax credits

¶11,000　COMPUTATION OF TAXABLE INCOME FOR A CORPORATION

¶11,010　Overview

Recall that taxable income results from the deduction of certain amounts listed in Division C of Part I from net income for tax purposes computed under Division B of Part I. The following is the calculation of taxable income showing the different components of Division B income and the deduction of Division C deductions.

ITA: 110.1, 111, 112

Sources of Income:	
Employment	$xxx
Business & property	xxx
Capital gains & losses	xxx
Other income	xxx
Other deductions	xxx
Division B Income	$xxx
Division C Deductions	(xxx)
Taxable Income	$xxx

A corporation cannot earn employment income. Very few items of "other income" or "other deductions" pertain to most corporations.

Exhibit 11-1 lists the common Division C deductions and indicates which of these are available to corporations.

EXHIBIT 11-1
Selected Division C Deductions

Provisions	Deduction	Individuals	Corporations
Par. 110(1)(d), (d.1)	Employee stock options	X	
Par. 110(1)(f)	Deductions for certain social assistance payments	X	
Par. 110(1)(j)	Home relocation loan	X	
Par. 110.1(1)(a)	Charitable gifts*		X
Par. 110.1(1)(b)	Gifts to Her Majesty*		X
Par. 110.1(1)(c)	Gifts of cultural property to institutions*		X
Par. 110.1(1)(d)	Ecological gifts*		X
Sec. 110.2	Lump-sum payments	X	
Sec. 110.6	Capital gains deduction	X	
Par. 111(1)(a)	Carryover of non-capital losses	X	X
Par. 111(1)(b)	Carryover of net capital losses	X	X
Par. 111(1)(c)	Carryover of restricted farm losses	X	X
Par. 111(1)(d)	Carryover of farm losses	X	X
Par. 111(1)(e)	Carryover of limited partnership losses	X	X
Sec. 112	Dividends from Canadian corporations		X
Sec. 113	Dividends from foreign affiliates		X

* Non-refundable tax credits available in subsection 118.1(3) for an individual.

¶11,020   Deduction of Taxable Dividends

Certain dividends received by a corporation are deductible in the calculation of its taxable income. This deduction offsets the inclusion of the dividend under Subdivision b of Division B, so that qualifying dividends have no effect on the taxable income of the corporation. The dividends that qualify for the deduction are from: `ITA: 112(1)`

(a) taxable Canadian corporations;   `ITA: 112(1)(a)`

(b) taxable subsidiary corporations resident in Canada;   `ITA: 112(1)(b)`

(c) non-resident corporations carrying on business in Canada and, hence, taxable in Canada; and   `ITA: 112(2)`

(d) foreign affiliates which have been appropriately taxed in a foreign jurisdiction which has a treaty with Canada.   `ITA: 113`

¶11,025   Purpose

The purpose of the deduction is to prevent the double taxation of corporate income. When dividends are paid, the source of the dividends is usually after-tax retained earnings of the payer corporation. If a recipient corporation were to pay tax on the dividends it receives, the income that gave rise to the dividends would effectively be taxed twice. A provision prevents that second imposition of tax at the level of the recipient corporation. In fact, retained earnings can, in many cases, be flowed through any number of shareholder corporations in the form of taxable dividends without attracting tax under Part I. When the retained earnings are ultimately paid as dividends to an individual shareholder, the dividend gross-up and tax-credit mechanism will operate to reduce, at the individual taxpayer level, the potential double taxation of income generated by a corporation.   `ITA: 112(1)`

¶11,025.10   *Concept of integration of individual and corporate tax on income*

The dividend deduction for corporate shareholders is the second building block of the theory of integration. The first building block, the dividend gross-up and tax credit for individual shareholders, was previously discussed in Chapters 6 and 10. The function of the dividend deduction for a corporation is to remove some of the potential multiple taxation of dividend income as the income moves through a series or chain of corporations.

Simply stated, the integration concept, discussed in more detail in Chapter 12, requires that a tax system should be designed so that a taxpayer is indifferent (i.e., pays the same amount of tax), no matter what type of entity or person earns the income. In the context of corporations and their shareholders under a perfectly integrated tax system, the total tax burden should be identical whether the individual receives the income directly or indirectly, as a shareholder, from dividends through the corporate structure.

The Canadian income tax system is not perfectly integrated. Near perfect integration occurs numerically where the combined corporate rate of tax (federal and provincial) is equal to:

- 20% for Canadian-controlled private corporations on their business income eligible for a low rate of tax, and

- about 31% for Canadian-resident corporations on their business income subject to the higher general rate of tax.

However, even at these rates there are flaws in the system. For example, the dividend tax credit should represent the underlying tax paid by the corporation. However, under our present income tax system, even when the corporation has not paid any tax due to losses, for example, shareholders still receive a dividend tax credit.

¶11,025.20   *Application of the concept of integration*

To illustrate the corporate dividend deduction aspect of integration, assume that there is a chain of three taxable Canadian corporations: A Ltd., a Canadian-resident public corporation, owns 100% of B Ltd., which in turn owns 100% of C Ltd. Also, assume that each of the corporations is taxed at a combined rate of 35%, and the individual shareholders of A Ltd. are all taxed at a combined rate of 40%; all of the after-tax income is passed up to the next level in the form of eligible dividends, i.e., eligible for the 45% gross-up and tax credit in the hands of an individual shareholder. In the absence of a corporate deduction for dividends received from another corporation the following would result.

Person	Income	Tax	Divi-dend
C Ltd.	$1,000	$350	$650
B Ltd.	650	228	422
A Ltd.	422	148	274
Shareholders of A Ltd.	397*	36**	238***
		$762	

* $274 × 1.45 (i.e., the grossed-up dividend)
** ($397 × .40) − ((.19 + .12) × $397) = $36 where .12 reflects the provincial dividend tax credit.
*** Cash received (i.e., $274 − $36).

The result of this example is that on the $1,000 of income initially earned by C Ltd., the ultimate tax burden is $762. The dividend deduction, as discussed above, eliminates the corporate tax in both B Ltd. and C Ltd. The tax burden remaining would be composed of the $350 on the income earned initially by C Ltd. and the tax of $85 on the $943 grossed-up dividend received by the individual shareholders calculated as follows:

Dividend received by shareholders of A Ltd.	$ 650
Gross-up (1.45 × $650)	293
Grossed-up dividend	$ 943
Tax @ 40%	$ 377
Dividend tax credit @ (19% federal + 12% provincial) of $943	(292)
Net tax on shareholders of A Ltd.	$ 85

The total income tax is now $435 compared to $762. However, as can be seen, there is still some degree of double taxation even with the dividend tax credit when the corporate tax rate is at this level (i.e., $435 versus $400 under perfect integration).

¶11,025.30 *Conclusion*

From the above example, one can conclude that where dividend income flows through a series of corporations there will be only two incidents of income tax. Initially, the corporation that earns the business or property income will pay income tax and eventually the individual shareholder who receives the income in the form of a dividend will also pay some income tax. In the next chapter, the topic of integration will be expanded even further with different corporate rates and other factors.

¶11,030 Dividends paid from untaxed income

Over the years, the intercorporate dividend deduction has created problems which the government has attempted to rectify. For example, a corporation may pay a dividend from income that was not taxed in the payer corporation. This might occur when income for accounting purposes is higher than income for tax purposes, due to a more rapid write-off of assets for tax purposes. The utilization of carried-over losses may also offset income, so that some amounts that are distributed as dividends may not be taxed fully in the corporation that pays the dividend. This is usually due to timing differences between the payment of the dividend and the offset of losses. In these cases, there is a breakdown of the assumption that underlies the intercorporate dividend deduction, namely, that the dividend deduction prevents double taxation because the income that gave rise to the dividends *was* taxed in the payer corporation. This problem is compounded when individual shareholders gross up the dividends and deduct a dividend tax credit, on the assumption that the payer corporation or a predecessor corporation paid tax on the income it distributed as dividends. The purpose and effect of the dividend gross-up and tax-credit mechanism will be discussed more fully in the next chapter.

¶11,035 "After-tax financing"

Another problem that is linked with the intercorporate dividend deduction occurs when what has become known as "after-tax financing" is undertaken. A corporation that has generated losses in the past may not find debt financing attractive. This is because the deduction for interest expense provides no immediate tax relief where the corporation does not have to pay tax currently. Instead, the interest expense deduction merely increases the corporation's non-capital losses which may be deductible in the future or may expire. Alternatively, a corporation with unused losses could issue preferred shares to another corporation, such as a financial institution, to obtain the necessary financing. The result is that the corporation that issues the preferred shares will, obviously, not receive a deduction for dividends paid on the preferred shares. However, the financing corporation, because of the intercorporate dividend deduction, will not ordinarily pay tax on the dividends it receives. Consequently, because interest income is taxable and dividends are ordinarily not, the financing corporation may be prepared to lend funds at a rate lower than the market rate of interest. Rules are designed to eliminate the benefits of after-tax financing on "term preferred shares", "short-term preferred shares" and collateralized preferred shares.

ITA: 248(1)

ITA: 112(2.1)–(2.9)

¶11,040 Dividends paid on shares subsequently sold for a loss

The intercorporate dividend deduction is also linked to a potential problem when dividends are received on shares held by a corporation for a short period and subsequently sold at a loss. Such dividends would ordinarily be deductible in computing taxable income, or in the case of certain dividends (e.g., capital dividends), would be tax exempt. On the other hand, the loss on the disposition of the shares would be deductible as an allowable capital loss (if the shares were held as a capital property), or as a business loss (if the shares were held as inventory). It may be argued that, to some extent, the loss on disposition may have been caused by the payment of the dividend; for example, witness the normal decline in the value of shares after the ex-dividend date.

Consequently, there are rules that, when certain conditions are present, will reduce the corporation's capital loss or inventory loss by an amount equal to the aggregate of certain types of dividends received on such shares prior to the disposition. The loss reductions will occur if one of the following conditions is present:

ITA: 112(3), 112(3.01), 112(4)

(a) the corporation owned the shares for less than 365 continuous days immediately prior to the disposition date, or

(b) the corporation owned more than 5% of the issued shares of any class of the capital stock on which the dividends were received.

The type of dividends that will reduce such capital losses are essentially taxable dividends (deductible in computing the corporation's taxable income), and tax-exempt capital dividends received on the shares during the period of ownership. Similarly, inventory losses are reduced by deductible taxable dividends received by any taxpayer-shareholder plus non-taxable dividends received.

ITA: 112(3), 112(4)

¶11,050 Charitable Donations

While individuals are provided with a non-refundable tax credit for various donations, as discussed in Chapter 10, corporations are permitted a deduction in Division C. The types of donation that provide a corporation with this deduction are the same as the types of donation that provide an individual with a tax credit. Also, a corporation's deduction for gifts is, generally, limited to 75% of the corporation's net income for tax purposes under Division B.

ITA: 110.1(1)

However, the deduction is limited to 100% of the amount of a taxable capital gain in respect of gifts of appreciated capital property. As well, the deduction limit is 100% of any CCA recapture arising on the gift of depreciable capital property.

Any unused donations for a given year can be carried forward five years to be deducted in a carryforward year. The total claim for donations carried forward to a year and current donations made in that year cannot exceed the Division B income limit. The maximum donation need not be deducted in a given year, such that undeducted amounts are available within the carryforward period. To be deducted, a donation must be proven, if necessary, by a receipt that contains prescribed information.

ITA: 110.1(2)

¶11,060 Loss Carryovers

¶11,065 Non-capital loss

A non-capital loss for a particular year, as it affects a corporation (for the purposes of this text), is generally defined to include:

ITA: 111(8)

Aggregate of:

losses from business	$ xxx
losses from property	xxx
allowable business investment losses	xxx
net capital losses deducted in the year	xxx
dividends deductible under sec. 112 (and certain other dividends)	xxx
	$ xxx (E)

Less aggregate of the amounts determined under par. 3(c):

income from business	$ xxx	
income from property (including dividends deductible under sec. 112)	xxx	
income from other sources [secs. 56–59]	xxx	
taxable capital gains (other than from listed personal property)	$ xxx	
taxable net gains from listed personal property	xxx	
	$ xxx	
less: allowable capital losses (other than from listed personal property) in excess of allowable business invest-ment losses that are included in allowable capital losses	(xxx)*	xxx *
		$ xxx
less: other deductions [secs. 60–66]	(xxx)	$ (xxx)* (F)
		$ xxx *
Less: farm loss (included in losses from business above)		(xxx) (D)
Non-capital loss		$ xxx *

---

* Cannot be negative.

This definition is designed to offset the current year's losses from various sources (items (E) and (D)) against the current year's income from other sources (item (F)). Then the balance or the unabsorbed excess loss can be carried over and deducted in another year. Non-capital losses and farming and fishing losses may be carried back three taxation years and forward 20 taxation years. To carry losses back to a taxation year for which a return has been filed, the corporation need only file one form (Schedule 4) and not a full, amended tax return.

ITA: 111(1)(*d*), 111(8)

ITA: 111(1)(*a*), 111(1)(*d*), 111(8)

Although a 20-year carryforward period is quite long, it is possible for carried-over losses to expire. Planning should be undertaken to ensure that the losses are utilized within the carryover period. Income can be increased to absorb non-capital losses by omitting optional or permissive deductions such as capital cost allowances, cumulative eligible capital amounts, scientific research and experimental development expenditures or reserves. The deduction of these amounts can be deferred to future years when there is offsetting income. The Canada Revenue Agency (CRA) usually permits the revision of a permissive deduction for a prior year. An Information Circular indicates that a letter to the director of the taxpayer's district taxation office that outlines the requested revisions will be sufficient if other conditions set out in paragraphs 9 and 10 are met. In addition, the corporation should consider the sale of unnecessary or redundant assets to generate income which could be used to absorb losses. The CRA may also allow the substitution of one type of loss for another, as long as the year in which the substitution is made is still open to assessment (as discussed in Chapter 14). For example, a non-capital loss may have been carried back to a year in which there was a net taxable capital gain. Subsequently, an allowable capital loss may arise. The resultant net capital loss may be carried back and substituted for the non-capital loss, leaving the freed non-capital loss available for carryforward.

IC 84-1, par. 11

Example Problem

The operations of Bigloss Ltd. generated the following data for its December 31, 2007 taxation year:

Business losses	$(60,000)
Dividends received and deducted under sec. 112	10,000
Bond interest	5,000
Allowable business investment loss	(3,000)
Taxable capital gains	15,000
Allowable capital losses	(7,000)
	$(40,000)

In its 2006 taxation year, its first profitable year in several, Bigloss Ltd. had taxable income under Division C of $40,000.

— REQUIRED

Compute the non-capital loss for Bigloss Ltd. in 2007 and determine the amount of that loss that can be carried back to 2006.

— SOLUTION

Before calculating the non-capital loss for 2007, a review of the construction of section 3 income would be useful in understanding the basic concept. The following calculation reorganizes the above information using the ordering and application rules in section 3.

Par. 3(*a*)	Income — business	Nil	
	— property: dividends	$10,000	
	interest	5,000	$15,000

Par. 3(*b*)	Net taxable capital gains:			
	Taxable capital gains	$15,000		
	Allowable capital losses	(7,000)	8,000	
Par. 3(*c*)	(No Subdivision e deductions taken)		$23,000	
Par. 3(*d*)	Business loss	$60,000		
	Allowable business investment loss	3,000	(63,000)	
Net income from Division B			Nil	

Non-capital loss arising in 2007:			
Business loss		$ 60,000	
Allowable business investment loss		3,000	
Dividends		10,000	
		$ 73,000	

Less:	Par. 3(*c*) income (as shown above):				ITA: 3(*a*)
	Income from property				
	Bond interest	$ 5,000			
	Dividends (see commentary below)	10,000	$15,000		
	Net taxable capital gains				ITA: 3(*b*)
	Taxable capital gains	$15,000			
	Allowable capital loss	(7,000)	8,000	(23,000)	

Non-capital loss for 2007		$ 50,000

Carryback of non-capital loss to 2006:		
Lesser of:		
(a) Non-capital loss (as calculated above)		$ 50,000
(b) Taxable income for 2006		$ 40,000

Thus, $40,000 of the 2007 non-capital loss could be carried back to 2006 leaving $10,000 to carry forward to 2008 through 2027.

Dividend income deductible in the calculation of a corporation's taxable income (i.e., $10,000), when added to the business loss and the allowable business investment loss, has the effect of offsetting the dividend income included in the paragraph 3(*c*) income under paragraph 3(*a*). As a result, this dividend income has no effect on the amount of losses available for carryover. As previously discussed, dividends are deductible to offset the dividend income inclusion and, therefore, have no effect on the taxable income of a corporation. Therefore, a similar adjustment is necessary to the non-capital loss calculation to remove the effect of the inclusion of these dividends in property income, as shown above. If the addition of taxable dividends to the business loss had not been made, the 2006 non-capital loss available for carryover would have been only $40,000 (i.e., $60,000 + $3,000 − $23,000), not $50,000 as shown above.

ITA: 12(1)(*j*), 112

¶11,070   Treatment of allowable business investment loss

A "business investment loss" is a capital loss that arises from the disposition of shares or debt of a "small business corporation". The concept of a small business corporation (SBC) is discussed in some detail in Chapter 13. A business investment loss (BIL) must arise from either an arm's length disposition of the shares and/or debt, establishing a debt to be bad, or a bankruptcy action.

ITA: 39(1)(*c*), 248(1) "small business corporation"
ITA: 50(1)

An "allowable business investment loss" (ABIL) is defined as ½ of a business investment loss. Unlike an allowable capital loss, an allowable business investment loss may, in the year in which it is realized, be deducted against any source of income. Hence, the deductibility of an allowable business investment loss is less restricted than an allowable capital loss. To the extent that it cannot be absorbed against these other sources of income in the year in which it is incurred, it becomes part of the aggregate of non-capital losses to be carried over in the manner discussed above. Furthermore, any amount of allowable business investment loss that cannot be utilized within the carryover period of a non-capital loss can be added to net capital losses which can be carried forward indefinitely as discussed next. See Exhibit 7-1 for a flowchart summary of these rules.

ITA: 3(d), 38(c)

Example Problem

The operations of Biggerloss Limited generated the following data for the year ended December 31, 2007:

Business investment loss on sale of shares	$116,000
Capital gains	4,000
Other capital losses	10,000
Other Division B income	30,000

— REQUIRED

Compute the taxable income of the corporation for 2007 and indicate the loss carryovers available for other years.

— SOLUTION

Par. 3(a)	Other Division B income		$30,000
Par. 3(b)	Taxable capital gains (½ × $4,000)	$ 2,000	
	Allowable capital losses (½ × $10,000)	(5,000)	Nil
Par. 3(c)	Income		$30,000
Par. 3(d)	Allowable business investment loss deductible (max: ½ × $116,000 = $58,000)		(30,000)
	Income and taxable income		Nil
	Net capital loss available for carryover		$ 3,000[(1)]
	Non-capital loss available for carryover		$28,000[(2)]

— NOTES TO SOLUTION

[(1)] (½ × $10,000 capital loss incurred in the year) *less* ($2,000 claimed in the year as an allowable capital loss) = $3,000.

[(2)] (½ × $116,000 business investment loss incurred in the year) *less* ($30,000 claimed in the year as an ABIL) = $28,000.

¶11,075 Net capital losses

¶11,075.10 *Definition*

For corporations, a "net capital loss" (net CL) is, essentially, the excess of allowable capital losses, excluding losses on listed personal property and allowable business investment losses, over taxable capital gains, including taxable net gains from listed personal property.

ITA: 111(8)

This is given by the following computational format:

Allowable capital losses excluding losses on listed personal property and allowable business investment losses	(A)	$xxx
Less: taxable capital gains including taxable net gains from listed personal property	(B)	(xxx)
	(A – B)	$xxx
Add: allowable business investment loss unutilized in the tenth year of its carryforward as a non-capital loss (see comment in previous section)		xxx
Net capital loss		$xxx

The exclusion of allowable capital losses on listed personal property results from the fact that listed personal property losses are carried forward and back under Division B, not Division C, as are all other allowable capital losses. (See Chapter 7 for a more complete discussion.) The term "net gain" from listed personal property refers to the amount of taxable capital gain net of the application of any listed personal property current losses and loss carryovers.

¶11,075.20   *Adjustment for years with different inclusion rates*

Net capital losses can be carried back three taxation years and forward indefinitely. However, they can only be deducted to the extent of the excess, if any, of taxable capital gains over allowable capital losses in the carryover years. Rules which determine the amount that a person may deduct in respect of net capital losses are the result of the differing inclusion rates for capital gains and capital losses discussed in Chapter 10. ITA: 111(1.1)

The historical inclusion rates are as follows:

Prior to 1988	$\frac{1}{2}$
1988 and 1989	$\frac{2}{3}$
1990 to February 27, 2000	$\frac{3}{4}$
February 28 to October 17, 2000	$\frac{2}{3}$
After October 17, 2000	$\frac{1}{2}$

The purpose of the rules is to ensure that the amount of net capital losses, carried forward or carried back from a taxation year with a particular inclusion rate, is converted to the inclusion rate of the taxation year in which the net capital losses are deducted. This is done by means of a formula as illustrated below.

Assume the following facts for a corporation which has $45,000 of net capital losses (representing $\frac{3}{4}$ of a $60,000 capital loss) realized in 1997 and available for carryforward:

	2000	2001
Capital gains realized.................................	$60,000	$10,000
Capital losses realized	(10,000)	(4,000)
Net capital gains	$50,000	$ 6,000
Inclusion rate for the year	$\frac{2}{3}$*	$\frac{1}{2}$

---

* After February 27, 2000 and before October 18, 2000.

The following net capital losses could be deducted under par. 111(1)(*b*):

	2000	2001
Net taxable capital gain for the year	$33,333	$ 3,000
Net capital loss deduction under par. 111(1)(*b*) per ssec. 111(1.1) as computed below	(33,333)	(3,000)
Effect on taxable income	Nil	Nil

The limit on the net capital loss deduction is given by:

ITA: 111(1.1)

	2000	2001
Lesser of:		
(a) Net taxable capital gain for the year	$33,333	$ 3,000

ITA: 3(*b*)

(b) $A \times \dfrac{B}{C}$

Where A = net capital loss from a loss year available for deduction in the particular year (see below)	$45,000	$ 7,500
B = inclusion rate in particular year of deduction	$\frac{2}{3}$	$\frac{1}{2}$
C = inclusion rate in loss year	$\frac{3}{4}$	$\frac{3}{4}$
$45,000 × $\frac{2}{3}$ / $\frac{3}{4}$	$40,000	
$7,500 × $\frac{1}{2}$ / $\frac{3}{4}$		$ 5,000
Net capital loss deduction (lesser amount)	$33,333	$ 3,000

Note that the denominator C in the fraction B/C, in effect, divides the net capital loss A by the inclusion rate of the loss year. Thus, when the 1997 net capital loss of $45,000, which is a $\frac{3}{4}$ amount, is divided by $\frac{3}{4}$, the result is $60,000, which was the full capital loss in 1997. Then, B, which is the inclusion rate for the year in which the loss is being deducted, is multiplied by the full loss, the result is $\frac{2}{3}$ of $60,000, or $40,000, which is the net capital loss for 2000.

To deal with the carryover of these losses conceptually, it may be easier to carry full amounts of capital losses realized either back or forward against full gains in the carryover year. Then the appropriate inclusion rate could be applied to the net full gains in the carryover year. Unfortunately, as discussed below, the definition of net capital loss (i.e., the amount available for carryover) is given in terms of the fractional allowable capital losses.

The amount of net capital loss realized in 1997 and deducted in 2000 and 2001 and, hence, the amount of net capital loss available for carryforward after 2001 can be reconciled as follows:

	Capital loss (gross amount)	Net capital loss at 1997 inclusion rate of $\frac{3}{4}$	Adjustment factor B/C	Adjusted net capital loss deducted
Loss realized in 1997	$60,000	$45,000		
Loss deducted in 2000 limited to net gains realized in the year	(50,000)	(37,500)	$\frac{2}{3}$ / $\frac{3}{4}$	$33,333
Loss available in 2001	$10,000	$ 7,500		
Loss deducted in 2001 limited to net gains realized in the year	(6,000)	(4,500)	$\frac{1}{2}$ / $\frac{3}{4}$	$ 3,000
Loss available after 2001	$ 4,000	$ 3,000	$\frac{1}{2}$ / $\frac{3}{4}$	$ 2,000

¶11,080 Restrictions and ordering of deductions

A taxpayer can choose how much, if any, of its previously unclaimed carried-over losses ITA: 111(3) to deduct in a particular year and in which order to deduct such losses and other Division C deductions. However, the taxpayer must deduct a loss of a particular type (that is, non-capital loss, net capital loss, restricted farm loss or farm loss) in the chronological order in which the loss was incurred. Logic would suggest that those deductions in Division C, which are more restricted in their deductibility, be claimed as soon as possible and before those deductions which are less restricted.

There are two basic types of restriction on losses available for carryover.

(1) The first is a restriction on the type of income against which the loss carryover can be deducted. This type of restriction is often referred to as "streaming".

(2) The other is a restriction on the number of years a loss can be carried over.

For example, a net capital loss can only be applied against net taxable capital gains, but is unrestricted as to carryforward time. A non-capital loss can be applied against any source of income, but is time-restricted. A restricted farm loss is restricted both as to the type of income against which it can be applied and to time. Therefore, restricted farm losses should usually be deducted first. Between net capital losses and non-capital losses, the decision depends on whether taxable capital gains are anticipated. If there are current taxable capital gains and an examination of the corporation's balance sheet indicates no accrued or prospective capital gains, then net capital losses should probably be deducted before non-capital losses.

EXHIBIT 11-2
Summary for Carryover Rules for Division C Deductions

Type of deduction	Type of income applied against	Carryover Back	Carryover Forward
Dividends	Any type	*	*
Donations	Any type	0	5
Net capital losses	Net taxable capital gains	3	Indefinitely
Non-capital losses	Any type	3	7/10/20**
Restricted farm losses	Farm income	3	10/20***
Farm losses	Any type	3	10/20***

Application of Division C deductions
Consider: (1) Type of income the deduction can be applied against.
        (2) Number of years available in the carryover period.
        (3) The likelihood that the type of income needed will arise in the carryover period.
Generally apply most restrictive first.

---

    * Technically, no carryover rule applies specifically to dividends, although they have an impact on the non-capital loss carryover balance.

    ** 10 for taxation years ending after March 22, 2004, and 20 for taxation years ending after 2005.

    *** 20 for taxation years ending after 2005.

¶11,085 Choice to deduct net capital losses to preserve non-capital losses

Item E in the definition of non-capital loss enables taxpayers, at their option, to deduct ITA: 111(8) net capital losses to preserve non-capital losses. The purpose of this choice is to correct a long-standing anomaly in the legislation which inadvertently penalized taxpayers in certain specific situations, as shown in the example below. Whether a taxpayer decides to utilize this option depends upon whether the corporation is expected to generate, in the near future, adequate business income or taxable capital gains.

The non-capital loss can be increased by the amount of any net capital loss actually deducted for that year. The only restriction on the deduction of a net capital loss is that there is a net taxable capital gain in the year that is at least equal to the net capital loss being deducted. For example, assume that a corporation (or an individual) has in 2007 a business loss of $100,000, a net taxable capital gain of $40,000 and an adjusted net capital loss of $60,000 carry forward. The tax consequences are as follows:

Par. 3(*a*): Income from business	Nil
Par. 3(*b*): Net taxable capital gain	$ 40,000
	$ 40,000
Less: Subdivision e deductions	Nil
Par. 3(*c*):	$ 40,000
Par. 3(*d*): Business loss	(100,000)
Par. 3(*f*): Division B income	Nil

If the definition of non-capital loss did not contain the addition for net capital losses deducted, a corporation could deduct $40,000 of the net capital loss of $60,000 (equal to the net taxable capital gain) but would not do so because such a deduction would have no impact upon the taxable income which would still be zero. In addition, if the $40,000 was deducted, the taxpayer would no longer have a potential use of the $40,000 net capital loss in the future when the taxpayer is in a taxable position.

ITA: 3(*b*), 111(8)

The non-capital loss for the 2007 taxation year without the addition would be:

Par. 3(*d*): Business loss	$ 100,000
Par. 3(*c*): — see above calculation	(40,000)
Non-capital loss	$ 60,000

The result is that the net taxable capital gain has been used to offset the business loss resulting in a lower non-capital loss (i.e., $60,000 versus $100,000). The taxpayer may or may not be happy with this result depending upon the taxpayer's expected future income sources. Since net capital losses can only be applied to net taxable capital gains (i.e., $40,000) a potential net capital loss deduction has been blocked by the current business loss of $100,000.

The addition of deducted net capital losses to the non-capital loss balance provides a positive tax consequence to claiming a net capital loss deduction, even though the deduction has no impact upon the taxable income as shown below.

Division B income — see previous sec. 3 computation	Nil
Division C — net capital loss deduction limited to par. 3(*b*) amount	$ (40,000)
Taxable income	Nil

ITA: 111(1)(*b*)

However, as a result of the deduction of net capital losses, the non-capital loss is increased by a net capital loss deducted:

Par. 3(*d*): Business loss	$100,000
Add: Net capital loss deducted in the year	40,000
	$140,000
Less: Par. 3(*c*) balance — see above	40,000
	$100,000

The result is that $40,000 of the net capital loss carryover has been deducted under Division C to offset the $40,000 of net taxable capital gain under paragraph 3(*b*). This preserves the full $100,000 of business loss to be carried over as a non-capital loss, which can be deducted from any source of income in a carryover year.

Example Problem

The following data summarize the operations of Parliamentary Fertilizers Limited, a Canadian-controlled private corporation, for the years 2005 to 2008 ended December 31.

	2005	2006	2007	2008
Income (loss): fertilizer business	$ 62,500	$(187,500)	$75,000	$100,000
Dividend income — taxable Cdn. corporation	37,500	62,500	12,500	—
Capital gains (losses)	25,000	(50,000)	7,500	12,000
Charitable donations made	(18,750)	(10,000)	(12,500)	(6,000)
Income (loss): other business	7,500	(20,000)	2,500	5,000
Income (loss) per financial accounting statements	$113,750	$(205,000)	$85,000	$111,000

The corporation has a net capital loss balance of $18,750 which arose in 1997.

— REQUIRED

Calculate the taxable income of the company for each of the years indicated, on the assumption that future other business income and taxable capital gains are uncertain, and tabulate the losses available for carryover at the end of 2008. (For the purposes of this type of problem, dealing with each item, line-by-line, across the years, will help keep track of carryovers more easily than dealing with income one year at a time.)

— SOLUTION

		2005	2006	2007	2008
Par. 3(a)	Income from business				
	— fertilizer	$ 62,500	—[1]	$75,000	$100,000
	— other	7,500	—[1]	2,500	5,000
	Income from property	37,500	$ 62,500	12,500	—
		$107,500	$ 62,500	$90,000	$105,000
Par. 3(b)	Taxable capital gain	12,500	—	3,750	6,000
	Allowable capital loss	—	—[2]	—	—
Par. 3(c)	Total	$120,000	$ 62,500	$93,750	$111,000
Par. 3(d)	Loss from business				
	— fertilizer	—	(187,500)[3]	—	—
	— other	—	(20,000)	—	—
	Income for the year[4]	$120,000	Nil[3]	$93,750	$111,000
Sec. 112	Dividends from taxable Canadian corporations	(37,500)[5]	—[6]	(12,500)[5]	—
		$ 82,500	Nil	$81,250	$111,000
Sec. 110.1	Donations made				
	— carryover	—	—	(10,000)	—
	— current	(18,750)	—	(12,500)[7]	(6,000)
		$ 63,750	Nil	$58,750	$105,000
Par. 111(1)(b)	Net capital losses	(12,500)[8]	—	(3,750)[8]	(6,000)[8]
		$ 51,250	Nil	$55,000	$ 99,000
Par. 111(1)(a)	Non-capital losses	(51,250)[9]	—	(55,000)[9]	(99,000)[9]
	Taxable income	Nil	Nil	Nil	Nil

— NOTES TO SOLUTION

[1] Items aggregated from the various non-capital sources under paragraph 3(*a*) cannot be negative. Losses from these sources are deducted under paragraph 3(*d*).

[2] Allowable capital losses are only deductible to the extent of taxable capital gains under paragraph 3(*b*). The remainder is available for carryover to another year.

[3] Losses from the various non-capital sources and from allowable business investment losses are only deductible under paragraph 3(*d*). However, the net income amounts after the deductions in paragraph 3(*d*) cannot be negative. Note that the excess of the deductions in paragraph 3(*d*) over the aggregate income in paragraph 3(*c*) is only one component of the addition to the non-capital loss carryover balance computed below.

[4] Income for the year cannot be negative. There is no statutory order in which Division C deductions must be taken. However, the time and source restrictions of loss carryovers, as previously discussed, should be taken into account. In addition, where the income under Division B is not large enough to cover all potential Division C deductions, then the dividend deduction under section 112 should always be taken first. Dividends from taxable Canadian corporations are the only Division C deduction for corporations which do not have a carryover clause.

[5] Dividends from taxable Canadian corporations should be deducted first in case there is not enough income for any further Division C deductions. Undeducted dividends cannot be carried over.

[6] A deduction in the computation of taxable income should not be taken if it reduces the balance to a negative number, since normally negative taxable income has no meaning. The one exception to this rule is in respect of net capital losses which can be added to the non-capital loss balance if they are deducted in a particular year.

[7] The deduction of charitable donations is limited to 75% of Division B income for the year. Donations not deducted in the year they are made, can be carried forward to the next five taxation years. However, the Division B income limitation applies to the sum of donations carried forward and current donations. Since the unused donations of a particular taxation year have a time restriction of 5 years, it would be advisable to claim them prior to claiming current year donations.

[8] Deductions for net capital loss carryovers are restricted to the extent of the net taxable capital gains included in paragraph 3(*b*) for the carryover year.

Subsection 111(1.1) adjusts the 2005 net capital loss deduction by a formula which corrects for the fact that in the loss year (1997) the inclusion rate for capital gains was three-quarters, while in the year that the loss is being claimed (i.e., 2005) the inclusion rate is one-half.

Lesser of (a) amount under par. 3(*b*) in 2005	$12,500
(b) $A \times \dfrac{B}{C} = \$18,750 \times \frac{1}{2} / \frac{3}{4} = $	$12,500

where: A is the amount of the net capital loss available (i.e., $18,750) from 1997 (the loss year),

B is the ½ inclusion rate for the deduction year (i.e., 2005), and

C is the ¾ inclusion rate for the loss year (i.e., 1997).

Since the inclusion rate is the same for 2006 and 2007, no adjustment is necessary for the 2006 capital loss:

Net capital loss for 2006 (½ × $50,000)	$25,000
Loss deductible to the extent of net capital gains under par. 3(*b*):	
2007 — limited to TCG	(3,750)
	$21,250
2008 — limited to TCG	(6,000)
Remaining carryforward	$15,250

(9) "Non-capital loss" is computed for carryforward in:

ITA: 111(8)

	2005	2006	2007	2008
Sum of:				
(a) loss from business or property	Nil	$207,500	Nil	Nil
(b) ABIL	Nil	Nil	Nil	Nil
(c) dividends deductible under sec. 112	$ 37,500	62,500	$ 12,500	Nil
(d) net capital loss deducted	12,500	Nil	3,750	$ 6,000
	$ 50,000	$270,000	$ 16,250	$ 6,000
Less:				
(e) par. 3(c) total	(120,000)	(62,500)	(93,750)	(111,000)
Non-capital loss for the year	Nil	$207,500	Nil	Nil
Non-capital loss carryforward balance:				
Non-capital loss carryforward to the year	Nil	Nil	$156,250	$101,250
Added in the year	Nil	$207,500	Nil	Nil
Applied	Nil	(51,250)*	(55,000)	(99,000)
Non-capital loss carryforward balance	Nil	$156,250	$101,250	$ 2,250

* Carried back to 2005.

¶11,090 Acquisition of Control of a Corporation and Its Effect on Losses

¶11,095 Conceptual overview

When control of the corporation is acquired by another person or another group of persons, a corporation's ability to carry forward or carry back non-capital losses or farm losses is severely restricted. In addition, net capital losses, losses from property and allowable business investment losses (ABILs) that are unutilized at the time of the acquisition of control may not be carried forward — they simply expire.

ITA: 111(4), 111(5), 111(5.1), 111(5.2), 111(5.3)

As mentioned previously, the loss utilization restrictions become operative when control of a corporation is acquired by another person or another group of persons. The acquisition of control is considered to occur when control over the voting rights (i.e., *de jure* control that exists where more than 50% of the votes necessary to elect the Board of Directors is held) of the corporation is acquired by a person or group of persons. While it is clear that control refers to voting control, some uncertainty exists as to how the CRA will interpret the phrase "group of persons" for the purposes of these rules. The CRA has indicated that it will look for evidence of a group's intention to "act in concert" to control a corporation.

IT-302R3, pars. 3–6

Corporations are often unable to generate appropriate or sufficient income to utilize losses and, hence, are unable to recover taxes previously paid or reduce taxes payable. Consequently, such loss corporations become attractive targets for acquisition by profitable corporations which, through a variety of strategies, could shelter their income from tax by utilizing the losses of the acquired corporation. Because such strategies ultimately result in reduced tax revenues, the government, understandably, does not view such transactions with favour. As a result, over the years the government has introduced increasingly restrictive legislation to curb such transactions which are sometimes referred to as "tax-loss trading".

Two of the more common loss utilization strategies are outlined as follows:

(1) In the first, after control of the loss corporation is acquired, the operations of the income-earning acquirer corporation and the loss corporation are restructured so that income is generated in the latter corporation. For example, the assets of a profitable business or division in the income-generating corporation are transferred to the loss corporation. Usually the transfer will be accomplished by means of a tax-free rollover by

ITA: 85(1)

moving profit-generating assets to the loss corporation (discussed in Chapter 16). The income that is so generated is used to absorb the losses of the loss corporation.

(2) The second strategy involves implementing intercompany transactions which produce expense deductions to the income-generating corporation while generating income for the loss corporation. Interest on loans, rental contracts and commission contracts are examples of such intercompany transactions.

The legislative restrictions which are aimed at curtailing the utilization of tax losses, are based on certain transactions and events which are deemed to occur when there has been an acquisition of control. These transactions and events, as well as other rules that comprise the restrictions, are discussed below.

¶11,100 Deemed year-end

The corporation is deemed to have a taxation year-end immediately before the time of the acquisition of control of the corporation (referred to hereinafter as the "deemed taxation year-end"). The result is that various adjustments that are normally made at a year-end, are required to be made before the acquisition of control. For example, the requirement that inventory be valued at the lower of cost or market at a taxation year-end will cause any accrued losses in inventory to be realized. This adjustment will increase the corporation's pre-acquisition non-capital losses or farm losses. As will be explained later, such pre-acquisition losses are available for carryforward, but only after certain restrictive conditions are satisfied. The advent of the deemed year-end causes other adjustments (discussed below) to increase the corporation's pre-acquisition of control non-capital losses and farm losses.

ITA: 249(4)

ITA: 10; ITR: 1801

As a result of the deemed year-end, the corporation is required to satisfy the normal compliance requirements of filing tax returns, reviewing unpaid amounts, determining the status of charitable donations and loss carryovers and their carryforward period, etc.

ITA: 78(1), 78(4)

However, a short taxation year that may result from an acquisition of control will not advance the replacement period required to benefit from the rollovers available for an involuntary or voluntary disposition. These rollovers allow a full 24 months and 12 months after an involuntary and voluntary disposition, respectively, from the end of the short taxation year in which such a disposition occurs.

ITA: 13(4), 44(1)

Unless the deemed year-end coincides with the corporation's normal year-end, the corporation may have two taxation years lasting less than 24 months in total. To illustrate this, assume that a corporation whose normal taxation year-end is December 31, experiences an acquisition of control on April 1, 2007. The corporation will have a deemed year-end of March 31, 2007. If the corporation chooses to return to its original taxation year-end of December 31, the corporation will have two taxation years ending in the 12-month period ending December 31, 2007. The first taxation year will be 3 months long, the second 9 months long. If the corporation chose a date for its subsequent taxation years to be, say, March 31, as permitted, it would then have two taxation years lasting a total of only 15 months — namely, the deemed taxation year ending on March 31, 2007 will be 3 months long and the taxation year ending March 31, 2008 will be 12 months long. The foregoing example can be illustrated with the following diagram:

ITA: 249(4), 249(4)(*d*)

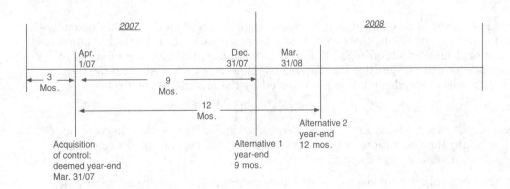

The upshot of this is that the normal 276-month (3 years back plus 20 years forward) carryover period for non-capital losses is reduced. This, in itself, represents a constraint in that the corporation has a shorter period over which to generate income to utilize the losses. A short taxation year will also cause any capital cost allowance or small business deduction (discussed in Chapter 12) to be proportionately reduced.

¶11,105 Accrued or unrealized losses on inventory

A taxpayer is required to value its inventory at the end of each taxation year. The Act requires that each item of inventory be valued at the lower of cost and market (LCM), while the Regulations permit valuation at the fair market value of the entire inventory. Either way, the result is that any accrued or unrealized inventory losses are realized in the deemed taxation year, thus, decreasing the taxpayer's income or increasing its non-capital losses or farm losses in the pre-acquisition period.

ITA: 10(1)

ITR: 1801

¶11,110 Accrued or unrealized losses on accounts receivable

The restrictions and their consequences that apply to accrued inventory losses are parallelled in the provisions that relate to accrued losses on accounts receivable. The largest amount that a corporation could deduct as a reserve for doubtful accounts for each separate trade receivable, must be claimed as an actual bad debt in the deemed taxation year. That is, where there has been an acquisition of control, the normal method of computing a reserve by aging the accounts and applying a fixed percentage to each age category is not permitted. Instead, each debt must be considered individually as to its collectibility and, if collection is doubtful, the debt must be written off as a bad debt. The amount deducted is deemed to be a separate debt and any amount or amounts subsequently received in respect of the separate debt must be included in income.

ITA: 20(1)(*l*), 20(1)(*p*)
ITA: 111(5.3)

IT-442R, par. 24

ITA: 12(1)(*i*)

As is the case in accrued inventory losses, accrued losses on accounts receivable become part of time-limited non-capital or farm losses, which are deductible only if certain restrictive conditions are satisfied.

¶11,115 Accrued or unrealized losses on depreciable capital property

Accrued or unrealized losses on depreciable capital property are measured as the amount by which:

(a) the undepreciated capital cost (UCC), at the deemed year-end, in a prescribed class

exceeds the aggregate of:

(b) the fair market value of all the property in the class at the deemed year-end, plus

(c) any capital cost allowance (CCA) and any terminal losses deducted in that class in the deemed taxation year.

ITA: 111(5.1)

The excess is deemed to be claimed as a capital cost allowance deduction from income for the deemed taxation year. Thus, the corporation's income/loss for the deemed taxation year is increased or decreased accordingly. Where there is a loss, the ultimate effect is to increase the corporation's pre-acquisition non-capital losses or farm losses. At the same time, the balance of the undepreciated capital cost is reduced by the amount of the excess.

ITA: 20(1)(*a*), 111(5.1)

The restrictive aspects of the rule are, therefore, as follows:

- first, an accrued loss (i.e., unclaimed capital cost allowance) that would otherwise not be subject to any time limitation, as far as its deductibility is concerned, becomes part of a time-limited non-capital loss or farm loss;

- second, the corporation commences the first post-acquisition of control taxation year with a reduced undepreciated capital cost balance in the particular class.

¶11,120   Accrued or unrealized losses on eligible capital property

Rules that deem accrued or unrealized losses on eligible capital property to be realized apply in much the same way as the rules, discussed above, that apply to depreciable capital property. The accrued or unrealized losses on eligible capital property are measured as the amount by which:

ITA: 111(5.2)

    (a) the cumulative eligible capital (CEC) balance of a particular business at the deemed year-end

exceeds the aggregate of:

    (b) three-quarters[1] of the fair market value, at the deemed year-end, of the eligible capital property of the business, plus

    (c) any amount deducted, in respect of that business (cumulative eligible capital amount) in the deemed taxation year.

ITA: 20(1)(*b*)

The consequences of these rules that apply to eligible capital property are similar to those that apply to depreciable property with respect to the time restrictions that affect non-capital losses and farm losses, as well as the impact that the adjustment has on the cumulative eligible capital balance of the corporation in the first taxation year after the acquisition of control.

¶11,125   Accrued or unrealized losses on non-depreciable capital property

Accrued or unrealized capital losses on non-depreciable capital property are deemed to have been realized at the deemed taxation year-end. The accrued losses are measured as the excess of:

ITA: 111(4)(*c*), 111(4)(*d*)

    (a) the adjusted cost base (ACB)

over

    (b) the fair market value,

at the deemed year-end, of each non-depreciable capital property (e.g., marketable securities, land used in the business) of the corporation. These rules result in the following:

- first, the capital losses that are so triggered, offset any capital gains produced in the deemed taxation year or increase any existing net capital losses of the corporation;

- second, the adjusted cost base of each affected capital property is reduced by the amount of the applicable excess.

Therefore, any deemed realized allowable capital losses that cannot be utilized against taxable capital gains realized in the deemed taxation year become part of the corporation's net capital losses immediately before the acquisition of control. If nothing further is done, these allowable capital losses, now embedded in the net capital loss balance, will expire. However, there are two possible remedies to this situation. First, the net capital losses can be deducted in arriving at taxable income for the deemed taxation year to the extent of net taxable capital gains in that year. As previously discussed, these deducted net capital losses will increase the non-capital loss balance. However, a further set of restrictions (discussed later in the chapter) is imposed on the utilization of non-capital losses on an acquisition of control. The second alternative is to create elective taxable capital gains to offset the deemed allowable capital losses as described in the next section.

¶11,130   Elective capital gains and recapture

¶11,130.10   *Election range*

A corporation is permitted to elect to have a deemed disposition for any depreciable or non-depreciable capital property on which capital gains or recapture have accrued. The

ITA: 111(4)(*e*)

---

[1] The three-quarters fraction is used in order to place components (a) and (b) of the formula on a common basis, since the CEC balance is a ¾ amount, based on original cost that has been amortized.

objective of the elective provision is to permit the corporation to trigger capital gains or recapture, which is income from business, to reduce the amount of net capital losses or non-capital losses that would otherwise expire on account of the acquisition of control. Upon making the election, the corporation must also choose (i.e., designate) an amount to represent the deemed proceeds of disposition. The designated amount or deemed proceeds must be equal to the lesser of:

(a) the fair market value of the property; and

(b) the greater of:

    (i) the adjusted cost base of the property, and

    (ii) an amount designated (or chosen) by the corporation.

The effect of the above rule is that the corporation can choose proceeds of disposition (amount designated) at any point between fair market value and the adjusted cost base of the particular capital property. This rule also prevents the designated amount from being greater than the fair market value of the property. In addition, the designated amount (proceeds of disposition) cannot be less than the adjusted cost base (capital cost in respect of depreciable property). Note that the election is not available where an accrued terminal loss exists since that loss is deemed to be realized automatically. However, the above formula does allow a corporation to elect proceeds of disposition which would trigger recapture on depreciable capital property.

ITA: 111(5.1)

¶11,130.20   *Optional election*

In determining the optimal or minimum amount which should be designated where there are losses about to expire, the following formula should be used to trigger a taxable capital gain. This taxable capital gain should be sufficient to offset expiring losses. The elected proceeds will be:

ITA: 111(4)(e)

the sum of:

(a) 2 (based on a ½ inclusion rate) times the sum of:

    (i) any allowable capital loss arising in the deemed taxation year about to expire,

    (ii) the net capital losses about to expire, and

    (iii) the sum of the property losses and ABILs about to expire; and

(b) the adjusted cost bases of the properties chosen to be elected upon.

The taxable capital gain, using the above deemed proceeds of disposition, should result in the utilization of all of the losses about to expire upon the acquisition of control.

This procedure of creating only enough taxable capital gains to offset the property losses and capital losses about to expire also optimizes the step-up in the cost base of an asset elected upon as discussed below. In addition, this minimum elected amount preserves the business losses which can be utilized after the acquisition of control.

In summary, the deemed proceeds on the asset(s) chosen to be elected upon can be determined as follows:

$$\begin{array}{c}\text{Deemed proceeds}\\\text{of disposition}\end{array} = \begin{array}{c}2 \times ((\text{i}) + (\text{ii}) + (\text{iii}))\\\text{(as described above)}\end{array} + \begin{array}{c}\text{the ACB(s) of properties}\\\text{chosen to be elected upon}\end{array}$$

¶11,130.30   *Consequences of the election*

The properties and amounts elected upon must be designated in the corporation's tax return for the deemed taxation year. While a corporation will focus mainly on the capital gain implications of an election, an election made in respect of a depreciable capital property may, also, give rise to recaptured capital cost allowance which may affect the non-capital losses of

ITA: 111(4)(e)

the corporation. Consequently, both the capital gain and recaptured capital cost allowance implications must be carefully considered when an election is contemplated.

The rules also provide for a deemed reacquisition of the depreciable or non-depreciable capital properties that are elected upon. A non-depreciable capital property is deemed to be reacquired at a cost equal to the amount of the deemed proceeds of disposition. For the purpose of computing future capital gains or losses, a depreciable capital property is deemed to be reacquired at a cost equal to the amount of the deemed proceeds of disposition. On the other hand, for the purpose of determining future capital cost allowance and recapture amounts, a depreciable capital property is deemed to be reacquired at a cost equal to the amount that is the capital cost plus the realized taxable capital gain (i.e., ½ of the capital gain elected). Thus, the increase in the base for capital cost allowance is limited to the amount of the gain that has been included in income, i.e., the taxable capital gain plus recapture.

ITA: 111(4)(*e*)

ITA: 13(7)(*f*)

Where the deemed proceeds give rise to recapture, but no capital gain is triggered at the same time, the capital cost is deemed to be that amount immediately before the disposition (original capital cost). Capital cost allowance is deemed to have been taken equal to the excess of the original capital cost over the deemed proceeds calculated according to the formula described above. The result of this provision is to retain the original capital cost for purposes of future recapture calculations and to prevent double counting of the recapture recognized on the exercise of the election.

ITA: 111(4)(*e*)(iii), 111(4)(*e*)(iv)

For example, Multi-losses Inc. needs to trigger enough income to offset the expiry of $10,000 of property losses just prior to an acquisition of control. Multi-losses Inc. has already elected and designated an amount equal to the accrued capital gain on all the other capital and depreciable assets. The only asset remaining is a depreciable one that has a capital cost of $70,000, an undepreciated capital cost of $35,000 and fair market value of $60,000.

Obviously, there is no accrued capital gain on the depreciable asset. In fact, there has been a decline in value. Capital losses are denied on depreciable assets, because a decline in value is handled through the CCA system. There is, however, potential recapture to a current maximum amount of $25,000 (i.e., $35,000 – $60,000), depending upon the designated amount or proceeds of disposition. Therefore, Multi-losses Inc. may attempt to designate, in this fact situation, an amount of $45,000 as the proceeds of disposition so that a desired $10,000 of recapture will be triggered.

ITA: 39(1)(*b*)(i)

In this case, however, the elected amount or deemed proceeds must be equal to the lesser of:

> (a) the fair market value of the asset $60,000
>
> (b) the greater of:
>
> > (i) the ACB of the asset $70,000
> >
> > (ii) the amount designated $45,000

$70,000

$60,000

As a result of the formula, the full $25,000 of recapture must be included in income, calculated as:

ITA: 111(4)(*e*)

UCC		$35,000
Less: the lower of:		
(a) capital cost	$70,000	
(b) proceeds	60,000	60,000
Recapture		$25,000

Therefore, in some cases, it may not be worthwhile to elect, because all of the unrealized recapture will be triggered.

From the perspective of the Multi-losses Inc., the capital cost is deemed to be the original capital cost of the acquired corporation, i.e., $70,000. In addition, Multi-losses Inc. is deemed to have taken capital cost allowance equal to the difference between the capital cost of $70,000 and the proceeds of $60,000. The effect of these two deeming provisions is to make Multi-losses Inc. assume responsibility for the remaining potential recapture of $10,000. The undepreciated capital cost, on which future capital cost allowance may be computed, is now set at $60,000.

¶11,135 Allowable business investment losses and losses from property

As a general rule, non-capital losses include allowable business investment losses (ABILs) and losses from property. However, when there has been an acquisition of control of a corporation, the rules restrict the carryover of non-capital losses or farm losses to those losses which can reasonably be attributed to the carrying on of a business. As a result, unutilized allowable business investment losses and losses from property expire after the deemed taxation year and must be removed from the non-capital loss balance. Even ABILs and property losses created in years prior to the acquisition of control are removed from the non-capital loss balance.

ITA: 111(5)

¶11,140 Unused charitable contributions

A corporation's unused charitable contributions cease to be deductible after the deemed year-end resulting from an acquisition of control. Furthermore, the deduction of a gift of property made after an acquisition of control is denied if the property was owned at the time of the acquisition of control and it was expected that a gift of the property would be made after the acquisition of control. The purpose of these provisions is to discourage charitable deduction trading transactions.

ITA: 110.1 (1.2)

¶11,145 Deductibility of non-capital losses after an acquisition of control

¶11,145.10 *Requirement that the loss business be carried on with a reasonable expectation of profit*

Non-capital losses and farm losses carried forward to taxation years beyond the deemed taxation year are deductible only if the following conditions are satisfied:

ITA: 111(5)(*a*)(i)

(i) the business that generated the losses must be carried on throughout the year in which the corporation seeks to make a deduction for non-capital losses or farm losses; and

ITA: 111(1)(*a*), 111(1)(*d*)

(ii) the particular business must be carried on for profit or with a reasonable expectation of profit.

An important feature of this rule is that the legislation identifies the non-capital losses and farm losses with a particular business. Note that the word "business" is not synonymous with the word "corporation"; that is, a corporation can carry on more than one business.

With regard to the condition (b) above, there are no guidelines in the Act dealing with the "expectation of profit" test in this context. Accordingly, there is some uncertainty as to how the CRA will apply this test. One court case on the issue is *Garage Montplaisir Ltée v. M.N.R.*, where the court discovered that the acquisition of the loss corporation was for the purpose of eliminating a competitor, not for the purpose of earning income from the loss business. On appeal to the Federal Court–Trial Division, it was found that there was no evidence that the taxpayer had continued to carry on any significant part of the loss business "for profit or with a reasonable expectation of profit". The latter decision was affirmed by the Federal Court of Appeal.

92 DTC 2317 (T.C.C.)

96 DTC 6557 (F.C.T.D.)

2001 DTC 5366 (F.C.A.)

¶11,145.20 *Requirement that non-capital losses must be applied only against income from the same or similar products or services*

The principle of identifying non-capital losses and farm losses with a particular business is only the first step in determining the deductibility of these losses. As a second step in the

ITA: 111(5)(*a*)(ii);
IT-302R3, par. 13

determination, non-capital losses and farm losses that are carried forward beyond the deemed taxation year are deductible only against income generated by the particular business and by any other business substantially all of whose income is derived from the sale, leasing, rental or development of similar properties or the rendering of similar services.

This other business is often referred to, generally, as a "similar" business, but the wording of the Act may be more restrictive in specifying "similar properties" or "similar services". The CRA's opinion of the meaning of the word "similar" in this context is interpreted as "of the same general nature or character". IT-302R3, par. 14; IT-206R; IT-259R4

Note that, in addition to the more obvious horizontally integrated business, a vertically integrated business is also considered a similar business. It is not clear whether products or services from various stages of a vertically integrated business are considered to be similar for the purposes of this provision. The case of *Manac Inc. Corp. v. The Queen* presents facts to address this issue. Although the decision in this case was based on the "substantially all" condition in the provision, the court made the following comments on the vertical integration and the "similar properties" issue: "we do not see how property which loses its identity when incorporated into an end product can be described as property similar to the end product". 98 DTC 6605 (F.C.A.)

In any case, only income from a business can be offset by losses that are carried over. The wording of the Act, therefore, precludes income from property, for example, from being offset by these carryover losses.

The principle of matching the losses of a particular business against income from that business or the income of similar products and services is sometimes referred to as "streaming". Because the stream of income against which the losses can be applied is limited, there is an increased possibility that losses will not be deductible in the appropriate carryover period. Hence the principle of streaming is inherently restrictive as far as the utilization of losses is concerned.

¶11,150 Loss carryback rules

The preceding commentary focuses on the carryforward of non-capital losses and farm losses. In general, the restrictions that were described above apply with equal effect in situations where post-acquisition of control losses are carried back to a taxation year preceding the acquisition of control. Again, only income from a business can be offset by these carryover non-capital losses. ITA: 111(5)(*b*)

¶11,155 Summary and application

The effects of the restrictive legislation on loss utilization, following an acquisition of control, may be summarized as follows:

(a) net capital losses, allowable business investment losses, property losses and unused charitable contributions expire and are not carried forward beyond the deemed taxation year;

(b) accrued losses of various kinds are deemed to be realized and, thus, increase the amount of non-capital losses and farm losses of a corporation; as non-capital losses or farm losses, they are subject to time restrictions as to their deductibility; and

(c) the principle of streaming, which matches losses from a particular business against income from the particular business and a similar business, increases the likelihood that non-capital losses and farm losses will not be deductible within their carryforward periods.

Example Problem 1

Wonder Inc.'s tax return for its year ended December 31, 2007, showed the following balances in its loss accounts:

Type of Loss	Balance	Year Incurred
Net capital loss	$ 8,000	2005
Non-capital loss	$10,000	2006

During the period January to December 2008, Wonder Inc. earned business income of $1,000 per month, computed in accordance with the *Income Tax Act*. On April 1, 2008, an unrelated person acquired 51% of the voting shares of Wonder Inc.

— *REQUIRED*

Discuss the tax implications of the above information.

— *SOLUTION*

Legal control (greater than 50% of the voting shares) of Wonder Inc. has been acquired by an unrelated person. This has the following tax implications for Wonder Inc.:

ITA: 256(7)(*a*)

(1) The taxation year of Wonder Inc. is deemed to have ended on March 31, 2008, being immediately before the acquisition of control.

ITA: 249(4)(*a*)

(2) A new taxation year is deemed to begin April 1, 2008.

ITA: 249(4)(*b*)

(3) Wonder Inc. can choose any date up to 53 weeks in the future as its new taxation year end.

ITA: 249(4)(*d*)

(4) The net capital loss expires on March 31, 2008, and can never be deducted by Wonder Inc. after that date.

ITA: 111(4)(*a*)

(5) The non-capital loss, to the extent that it is a loss from carrying on business (not a loss from a property source), can be deducted in future taxation years, provided the following tests are met:

(i) the business in which the loss was incurred is carried on at a profit or with a reasonable expectation of profit throughout the taxation year the loss is claimed, and

ITA: 111(5)(*a*)(i)

(ii) the non-capital loss is deducted against income from the business that generated the non-capital loss and/or income from a business selling similar products or providing similar services.

ITA: 111(5)(*a*)(ii)

Thus, Wonder Inc. will claim $3,000 of its non-capital loss to offset its taxable income (i.e., three months × $1,000) for the three-month deemed taxation year ended March 31, 2008. As to whether the remaining $7,000 will ever be deducted depends on point (5) above.

The net capital loss cannot be deducted in the deemed year ended March 31, 2008, as there are no capital gains to deduct it against. Since it expires on March 31, 2008, it will never be used.

Example Problem 2

On May 1, 2007, an unrelated person acquired 60% of the voting shares of Novell Inc. The values of the assets owned by Novell Inc. at May 1, 2007, were as follows:

Assets	Cost	UCC/CEC	FMV
Inventory	$10,000	N/A	$ 8,000
Accounts receivable	20,000	N/A	15,000
Equipment	30,000	$28,000	12,000
Marketable securities	40,000	N/A	10,000
Eligible capital property	50,000	36,000	42,000

In determining the value of the receivables, the collectibility of each debt was considered individually.

— *REQUIRED*

Which of the accrued (unrealized) losses in the above assets must be recognized by Novell Inc. in determining its income for tax purposes for the deemed year ended April 30, 2007?

— *SOLUTION*

The accrued loss in the inventory must be recognized. Inventory is valued at the lower of cost or market	$ 2,000	ITA: 10(1); ITR: 1801
The largest amount that Novell Inc. could deduct as a reserve for doubtful accounts for each trade receivable, must be claimed as a bad debt	5,000	ITA: 20(1)(*l*), 20(1)(*p*), 111(5.3)
The UCC of the equipment is reduced to $12,000. The reduction is deducted as CCA in the deemed year-end	16,000	ITA: 111(5.1)
The ACB of the marketable securities is reduced to $10,000. The reduction is deemed to be a capital loss in the deemed year-end. The allowable capital loss is $30,000 × ½ = $15,000 and is deductible only to the extent there are taxable capital gains in the deemed year ended April 30, 2007, or in any of the three preceding years. No such gains are evident in this case.		ITA: 111(4)(*c*), 111(4)(*d*)
The CEC for the eligible capital property is reduced to $31,500, being ¾ × FMV ($42,000). The reduction is deducted as CECA in the deemed year-end	4,500	ITA: 111(5.2)
Total reduction to the business income of Novell Inc. for its deemed year ended April 30, 2007	$27,500	

Example Problem 3

Universal Ltd.'s tax return for its year ended December 31, 2006, showed the following balances in its loss accounts:

Type of Loss	Balance	Year Incurred
Net capital loss	$12,000*	1999
Non-capital loss	$10,000	2006

*In 1999 the capital gain inclusion rate was 75% so the adjusted net capital loss is $12,000 × ½ / ¾ = $8,000, which is available for carry-forward to 2007.

On June 1, 2007, an unrelated person acquired 75% of the voting shares of Universal Ltd. The accountant has calculated the business loss for the deemed year ended May 31, 2007, to be $25,000, including the accrued losses required to be recognized on the acquisition of control. The capital assets owned by Universal Ltd. at June 1, 2007, had the following values:

Capital Assets	Cost	UCC/CEC	FMV
Land	$ 40,000	N/A	$ 70,000
Building	60,000	$45,000	90,000
	$100,000		$160,000

The accountant is projecting income of $100,000 for Universal Ltd. over the next 12 months. The projected income is from the business that incurred the losses.

— *REQUIRED*

Universal Ltd. is considering making an election. Recommend the asset(s) that should be designated and the amount(s) which should be designated in the election.

ITA: 111(4)(*e*)

— *SOLUTION*

Universal Ltd. should elect to recognize a taxable capital gain of $8,000 in order to utilize the $8,000 adjusted net capital loss expiring May 31, 2007. The election should be made on the land and not on the building as recapture would be incurred on the building. Such recapture would reduce the current (deemed) year's business loss and, thus, would be disadvantageous, because there would be $15,000 (i.e., $60,000 − $45,000 = $15,000 recapture) less in non-capital losses to carry forward to the next 20 years.

To trigger a $8,000 taxable capital gain on the land, proceed of $56,000 should be designated. (Current ACB of the land ($40,000) + desired taxable capital gain grossed up to the full capital gain ($8,000 × 2) = $56,000). The resulting income under section 3 and taxable income for the year would be calculated as follows:

par. 3(*a*) income from business, property		$ Nil
par. 3(*b*) taxable capital gains ($56,000 – $40,000) × ½ . . .	$ 8,000	
allowable capital loss	0	8,000
par. 3(*c*)		$ 8,000
par. 3(*d*) loss from business	$(25,000)	
loss from property	0	(25,000)
Division B net income (technically cannot be negative)		$(17,000)
Division C deductions:		
Net capital losses (only restricted by par. 3(*b*) amount)		(8,000)
Non-capital losses		0
Non-capital loss for the deemed year ended May 31, 2007		$(25,000)

Universal has non-capital losses of $10,000 + $25,000 = $35,000 at May 31, 2007. This amount can be used to offset the prospective $100,000 of income from the business that generated the loss, if at least $35,000 of the income is actually earned. This is the same with or without the election. The advantage of the election is that the ACB of the land is bumped up to $56,000. The higher ACB of the land will reduce a future capital gain on a disposition.

ITA: 111(4)(*e*)

Example Problem 4

Chandra Inc. is a ladies' shoe retailer with a December 31 year-end. During its first fiscal year in 2006, the corporation incurred non-capital losses of $37,500 and capital losses of $4,000. On December 1, 2007, the voting shares of Chandra Inc. were sold to Maysha Ltd., a retailer of ladies' handbags, belts and costume jewellery. Maysha Ltd. is a well-established business that operates a number of profitable retail outlets.

Accounting and income tax data relating to Chandra Inc.'s operations from January 1 to November 30, 2007, were assembled for the purpose of the share-sale transaction. The data contained the following information:

(1) Loss from retail operations $12,500

(2) Long-term debt from Farrford Inc. written off (Farrford Inc., a small
business corporation and manufacturer of ladies' shoes, was declared
bankrupt on March 1, 2007)   12,000

(3) Values of various assets at November 30, 2007:

Assets	Cost	UCC	FMV
Inventory	$24,000	—	$22,000
Store fixtures and equipment	36,000	$35,000	30,000
Marketable securities	9,000	—	5,000
Land	86,000	—	126,000
Building	110,000	104,000	118,000

During the short year ended December 31, 2007, Chandra Inc. produced net income for tax purposes of $3,500. No other income or losses were incurred. Chandra Inc. chose to return to its December 31 year-end for business reasons.

During its 2008 taxation year, the financing and marketing operations of Chandra Inc. were revamped and integrated with those of Maysha Ltd. As well, Chandra Inc.'s inventory was expanded to include merchandise carried in the Maysha Ltd. stores.

Chandra Inc.'s operations during the year ended December 31, 2008, produced the following income (losses):

Retailing operations — ladies' shoes	$(5,000)
— handbags, belts, jewellery	12,000
Taxable capital gain on marketable securities	8,000

— *REQUIRED*

(A) Discuss the income tax implications of the acquisition of control of Chandra Inc. on December 1, 2007, ignoring all possible elections/options.

(B) Determine the income tax consequences of the acquisition of control of Chandra Inc. under the assumption that:

(i) the maximum amount of elections/options is utilized, and

(ii) the partial amount of all elections/options is utilized so that only enough income is generated to offset the losses which would otherwise expire in the acquisition of control.

For each of the above alternatives, determine the appropriate cost, undepreciated capital cost or adjusted cost base value for each of inventory, shop fixtures, marketable securities and paintings at December 1, 2007.

— *SOLUTION*

First, it is necessary to determine the losses and potential elections available at the deemed year-end as follows:

Non-capital losses carried forward from 2006	$37,500

Current-year losses from non-capital sources and ABIL:	
Retail operations	$12,500
ABIL (Farrford Inc. loan: ½ × $12,000)	6,000
Inventory loss ($22,000 – $24,000)	2,000
Deemed CCA on store fixtures ($30,000 – $35,000)	5,000
	$25,500

ITA: 38(1)(*c*), 39(1)(*c*), 50(1)

ITA: 10(1); ITR: 1801

ITA: 111(5.1)

Potential election of recapture on building ($110,000 – $104,000)	$ 6,000

ITA: 111(4)(*e*)

Net capital losses carried forward from 2006 ($4,000 × ½)	$ 2,000

ITA: 111(1)(*b*), 111(8)

Current-year allowable capital losses:	
Securities (½ × ($5,000 – $9,000))	$ 2,000

ITA: 111(5.1)

ITA: 111(4)(*e*)

Potential election of taxable capital gain:	
Land (½ × ($126,000 – $86,000))	$20,000

Building (½ × ($118,000 – $110,000))	$ 4,000

The preceding data can be summarized as follows:

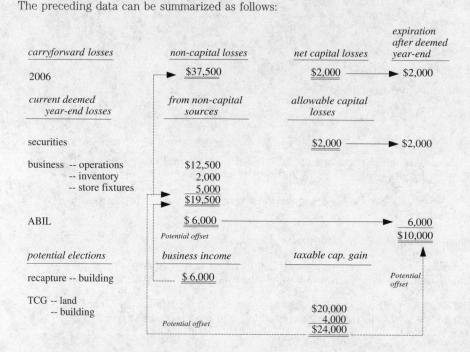

The following statements will become evident from an understanding of how the system computes income for tax purposes and taxable income. With that understanding, the consequences of the acquisition of control can be determined from the above summary of the data.

General conclusion

(a) No election

If no election is made, there is no income to offset the current business loss of $19,500 or the non-capital loss carryforward of $37,500. Therefore the non-capital loss available to carry forward from November 30, 2007, is $57,000 (i.e., $19,500 + $37,500).

(b) Maximum election

If the maximum election is made, the $6,000 of recapture offsets or reduces the business loss, leaving $13,500 (i.e., $19,500 – $6,000) of net business loss. The $24,000 of taxable capital gain offsets the $10,000 of expiring losses, leaving $14,000 (i.e., $24,000 – $10,000) to offset the remaining $13,500 of business loss. There is still $500 (i.e., $14,000 – $13,500) of taxable capital gain which offsets some of the $37,500 non-capital loss carryforward. As a result, the non-capital loss available for carry forward from November 30, 2007, is $37,000.

(c) Partial election

If only a partial election is made to offset the $10,000 of expiring losses, the current business loss of $19,500 is not offset and, hence, is available to carry forward, along with the $37,500 of non-capital losses, from November 30, 2007, for a total of $57,000.

Specific analysis

(A) Compute the Division B income of Chandra Inc. for its taxation year deemed to end on November 30, 2007 as a result of the acquisition of control on December 1, 2007. Division B income is calculated, using the ordering rules in section 3, as follows:

ITA: 249(4)

	No election
Par. 3(a): Income from non-capital sources (≧ 0)	Nil

Par. 3(b): Net taxable capital gains (≧ 0):

Deemed taxable capital gain (elective):		
land.............................	Nil	
building	Nil	
Accrued allowable capital loss (automatic):		
securities	$ (2,000)	Nil

Par. 3(c): par. 3(a) + par. 3(b)	Nil

	No election

Par. 3(d): Losses from non-capital sources and ABILs:

Loss from retail operation	$(12,500)	
Deemed recapture (elective) on building	Nil	
ABIL — Farrford Inc. loan	(6,000)	
Accrued losses — Inventory (automatic)	(2,000)	
Deemed CCA — Store fixtures (automatic)	(5,000)	$(25,500)

Division B income	Nil
Optional net capital loss deducted	Nil
Non-capital loss deducted................................	Nil
Taxable income	Nil

Determine the relevant tax balances, at November 30, 2007, as follows:

		No election
Non-Capital Losses Available for Carryforward at Deemed Taxation Year Ended Nov. 30, 2007:		
Balance from Dec. 31, 2006		$ 37,500
Non-capital loss — Nov. 30, 2007:		
Par. 3(d) losses — see above	$ 25,500	
Add: net capital losses deducted	Nil	
	$ 25,500	
Less: par. 3(c) income — see above	Nil	25,500
		$ 63,000
Less: losses utilized at Nov. 30, 2007...........	Nil	
losses not utilized but expired: ABIL	$ 6,000	6,000
Available for carryforward from Nov. 30, 2007		$ 57,000
Net Capital Losses Available for Carryforward		Nil
Other Tax Balances:		
Inventory[1]		$ 22,000
Store fixtures[2] — UCC		$ 30,000
Marketable securities[3] — ACB		$ 5,000
Land[4] — ACB		$ 86,000
Building[5] — UCC		$ 104,000
ACB		$ 110,000

In the one-month taxation year ended December 31, 2007, Division B income is $3,500. This would allow a deduction of $3,500 from the non-capital loss balance carried forward from November 30, 2007, leaving a non-capital loss balance to carry forward from December 31, 2007, of $53,500 (i.e., $57,000 – $3,500). The $3,500 is deductible because the ladies' shoe retail business ("the particular business") was carried on throughout the year ending December 31, 2007, for profit. The non-capital loss is applied against income from the particular business.

ITA: 111(1)(a)

¶11,155

Division B income for the full year ended December 31, 2008, is calculated, using the ordering rules in section 3, as follows:

Par. 3(*a*): Income from handbags, etc. retailing	$12,000
Par. 3(*b*): Taxable capital gains — securities	8,000
Par. 3(*c*): par. 3(*a*) + par. 3(*b*)	$20,000
Par. 3(*d*): Loss from shoes retailing	(5,000)
Division B income	$15,000

Non-capital losses available for carryforward from December 31, 2008, are computed under two possible assumptions as follows:

Assumption 1: The retailing of handbags, belts, jewellery is the sale of "similar" products.

Balance from Dec. 31, 2007 (see above)	$ 53,500
Less: Non-capital losses claimed against "streamed" income included in net income in the year	12,000[6]
Balance at Dec. 31, 2008	$ 41,500[7]

Assumption 2: The retailing of handbags, belts, jewellery is not the sale of "similar" products.

Balance from Dec. 31, 2007	$ 53,500
Less: Non-capital losses claimed against "streamed" income included in net income in the year	Nil[8]
Balance at Dec. 31, 2008	$ 53,500[9]

(B)(i) The analysis, in (A) above, of Division B income, non-capital losses available for carryforward from November 30, 2007, and the other tax balances is repeated under the assumption that all possible elections/options are utilized. The "no election" results, as determined above, are presented for comparative purposes.

		No election		Maximum election	
Par. 3(*a*):	Income from non-capital sources (≧ 0)		Nil		Nil
Par. 3(*b*):	Net taxable capital gains (≧ 0):				
	Deemed taxable capital gains (elective):				
	land	Nil		$ 20,000	
	building	Nil		4,000	
	Accrued allowable capital loss (automatic):				
	securities	$ (2,000)	Nil	(2,000)	$ 22,000
Par. 3(*c*):	Par. 3(*a*) + par. 3(*b*)		Nil		$ 22,000
Par. 3(*d*):	Losses from non-capital sources and ABILs:				
	Loss from retail operations	$(12,500)		$(12,500)	
	Deemed recapture (elective): building ...	Nil		6,000	
	ABIL — Farrford Inc. loan	(6,000)		(6,000)	
	Accrued losses (automatic): inventory ...	(2,000)		(2,000)	
	Deemed CCA (automatic): store fixtures	(5,000)	$(25,500)	(5,000)	(19,500)
Division B income			Nil		$ 2,500
Optional net capital loss deducted			Nil		(2,000)[10]
Non-capital loss deducted			Nil		(500)
Taxable income			Nil		Nil

Determine the relevant tax balances, at November 30, 2007, as follows:

Non-Capital Losses Available for Carryforward at Deemed Taxation Year Ended Nov. 30, 2007:

	No election	Maximum election
Balance from Dec. 31, 2006	$ 37,500	$ 37,500
Non-capital loss — Nov. 30, 2007:		
Par. 3(*d*) losses — see above	$ 25,500	$ 19,500
Add: net capital losses deducted	Nil	2,000
	$ 25,500	$ 21,500

Less: par. 3(*c*) income — see above	Nil	25,500	22,000	Nil
		$ 63,000		$ 37,500
Less: losses utilized at Nov. 30, 2007	Nil		$ 500	
losses not utilized but expired: ABIL	$ 6,000	6,000	Nil	500
Available for carryforward from Nov. 30, 2007		$ 57,000		$ 37,000

	No election	*Maximum election*
Net Capital Losses Available for Carryforward	Nil	Nil
Other Tax Balances:		
Inventory	$ 22,000	$ 22,000
Store fixtures — UCC	$ 30,000	$ 30,000
Marketable securities — ACB	$ 5,000	$ 5,000
Land — ACB	$ 86,000	$126,000[11]
Building — UCC	$104,000	$114,000[12]
— ACB	$110,000	$118,000[12]

Note how under the "no election" alternative, the non-capital loss balance is larger than in the "maximum election" alternative. However, under the latter alternative, the ACBs of the land and building and the UCC of the building are larger. Non-capital losses must be recovered by offsetting them against income in what remains of their 20-year carryforward. The ACBs of the land and building will be recovered on their sale. The UCC will be recovered through CCA at the Class 1 rate of 4% declining balance, if the building was purchased in 2006. The better alternative depends on how optimistic the new owners are about generating enough income within the next 20 years to offset the non-capital losses. If they are optimistic, then the "no election" alternative is better, because the non-capital losses will shield income from tax more quickly than the CCA tax shield and the ACB. shield of capital gains on a disposition. Also, the 20-year carry-forward period gives the corporation a long time to become profitable. If it cannot generate profits of at least $57,000 in that time period, it may not stay in business sustaining continual losses.

(B)(ii) The amount of the partial election should be sufficient to offset the ABIL of $6,000, the allowable capital loss of $2,000 and the net capital loss of $2,000 that will expire if not used in the deemed taxation year. This requires income, therefore, of $10,000. Since creating recapture only serves to reduce the loss in paragraph 3(*d*) and a taxable capital gain is needed to offset the expiring allowable capital loss and net capital losses, a taxable capital gain of $10,000 should be created. This will require a capital gain of $20,000 (i.e., 2 × $10,000). If an election is made on the land to be deemed to have disposed of it at $106,000 (i.e., $86,000 + $20,000), a deemed taxable capital gain of $10,000 will result. None of the capital gain on the building should be elected, because, if the election is made, recapture will result, in addition to the capital gain, when an election is made for deemed proceeds above capital cost.

Under the assumption that a partial election of a capital gain of $20,000 is made on the land, the analysis, in (B)(i) above, of Division B income, non-capital losses available for carryforward from November 30, 2007 and the other tax balances is repeated. The "no election" and the "maximum election" results, as determined above, are presented for comparative purposes.

		No election	*Maximum election*		*Partial election*	
Par. 3(*a*):	Income from non-capital sources (≧ 0)	Nil	Nil		Nil	
Par. 3(*b*):	Net taxable capital gains (≧ 0):					
	Deemed taxable capital gains (elective):					
	land	Nil	$ 20,000		$ 10,000	
	building	Nil	4,000		Nil	
	Accrued allowable capital loss (automatic):					
	securities	$ (2,000)	Nil	(2,000)	$22,000	(2,000)	$ 8,000

		No election	Maximum election	Partial election
Par. 3(c):	Par. 3(a) + par. 3(b)	Nil	$22,000	$ 8,000
Par. 3(d):	Losses from non-capital sources and ABILs:			
	Loss from retail operations	$(12,500)	$(12,500)	$(12,500)
	Deemed recapture (elective): building	Nil	6,000	Nil
	ABIL — Farrford Inc. loan	(6,000)	(6,000)	(6,000)
	Accrued losses (automatic): inventory	(2,000)	(2,000)	(2,000)
	Deemed CCA (automatic):			
	store fixtures	(5,000) $(25,500)	(5,000) (19,500)	(5,000) (25,500)
Division B income		Nil	$ 2,500	Nil
Optional net capital loss deducted		Nil	(2,000)[10]	$(2,000)[10]
Non-capital loss deducted		Nil	(500)	Nil
Taxable income		Nil	Nil	Nil

Determine the relevant tax balances, at November 30, 2007, as follows:

Non-Capital Losses Available for Carryforward at Deemed Taxation Year Ended Nov. 30, 2007:

	No election		Maximum election		Partial election	
Balance from Dec. 31, 2006		$ 37,500		$ 37,500		$ 37,500
Non-capital loss — Nov. 30, 2007:						
Par. 3(d) losses — see above	$25,500		$19,500		$25,500	
Add: net capital losses deducted	Nil		2,000		2,000	
	$25,500		$21,500		$27,500	
Less: par. 3(c) income — see above	Nil	25,500	22,000	Nil	8,000	19,500[13]
		$ 63,000		$ 37,500		$ 57,000
Less: losses utilized at Nov. 30, 2007	Nil		$ 500		Nil	
losses not utilized but expired:						
ABIL	$ 6,000	6,000	Nil	500	Nil	Nil
Available for carryforward from						
Nov. 30, 2007		$ 57,000		$ 37,000		$ 57,000
Net Capital Losses Available for Carryforward		Nil		Nil		Nil
Other Tax Balances:						
Inventory		$ 22,000		$ 22,000		$ 22,000
Store fixtures — UCC		$ 30,000		$ 30,000		$ 30,000
Marketable securities — ACB		$ 5,000		$ 5,000		$ 5,000
Land — ACB		$ 86,000		$126,000		$106,000
Building — UCC		$104,000		$114,000		$104,000
ACB		$110,000		$118,000		$110,000

Note that the amount of non-capital losses available for carryforward of $57,000 under the "partial election" alternative is the same as the amount under the "no election" alternative. In the list of other tax balances, the only difference between the "partial election" and the "no election" alternatives is the ACB of the land which is higher for the "partial election" alternative. Therefore, the "partial election" alternative is better than the "no election" alternative.

Comparing the "maximum election" alternative with the "partial election" alternative, the amount of the non-capital losses available for carryforward under the "partial election" alternative is higher than the amount under the "maximum election" alternative, because some of the business losses of the deemed year-end were offset by income elected under the maximum election option. However, the tax balances for the land and building are higher for the "maximum election" alternative. Only the increased UCC balance under the "maximum election" alternative shields income from tax immediately after the deemed year-end through increased CCA. The maximum present value of the CCA shield from the increased UCC in Class 1 of $10,000 (i.e., $114,000 − $104,000) can be calculated by formula to be about $571, assuming a 20% corporate tax rate and a 10% rate of return (i.e., $C(d/(d + r))t = \$10,000 \times (.04/(.04 + .10)) \times .20 = \$571$). However, the increased non-capital loss balance is available to shield income from tax in the next 20 years. The better alternative depends on how optimistic the new owners of the corporation are in generating at least the additional $20,000 (i.e., $57,000 − $37,000) of income against which the additional non-capital losses available for carryforward can be offset in the next 20 years. Again, if they are not optimistic about turning the business profitable in the next 20 years, they may not be in business very long.

— NOTES TO SOLUTION

[1] The tax cost at December 1, 2007 is $22,000, being either the value based on LCM or FMV.
ITA: 10(1); ITR: 1801

[2] The undepreciated capital cost balance at December 1, 2007 is $30,000, being the previous $35,000 undepreciated capital cost balance less the $5,000 excess that was deemed to be a deduction of capital cost allowance claimed in the year ending November 30, 2007. Capital cost allowance claimed for the short taxation years ended November 30, 2007, and December 31, 2007, must be prorated for the number of days in each of those taxation years.
ITA: 20(1)(a), 111(5.1)

[3] The adjusted cost base balance at December 1, 2007, is $5,000, being the previous $9,000 adjusted cost base less the $4,000 excess which was deemed to be a capital loss in the year ending November 30, 2007.

[4] The adjusted cost base balance at December 1, 2007, remains at $86,000, since no election was made.
ITA: 111(4)(e)

[5] The adjusted cost base at December 1, 2007, remains at $110,000 and the UCC remains at $104,000, since no election was made.
ITA: 111(4)(e)

[6] The corporation's income for tax purposes for the year ending December 31, 2008, is $15,000 as computed by section 3. The corporation may apply the losses of the ladies' shoe retail business against the total of the corporation's *income* from that business and from the sale of similar products. The result of the aggregation is, therefore, $12,000, being nil from the ladies' shoe retail business plus $12,000 from the sale of similar products with the $8,000 taxable capital gain being excluded. Thus, the maximum deduction is $12,000.
ITA: 111(5)(a)(ii)

[7] This amount is available for carryforward as follows:

2006 Dec. 31 non-capital loss balance:			
2006 non-capital loss	$37,500		
Less: Dec. 31, 2007 deduction	$ 3,500		
Dec. 31, 2008 deduction	12,000	15,500	$22,000
2007 Nov. 30 non-capital loss:			
Loss from retail operation	$12,500		
Deemed CCA — store fixtures	5,000		
Inventory loss	2,000	19,500	
			$41,500

The 2006 loss expires on December 31, 2025, i.e., in 20 taxation years, including the deemed taxation year at November 30, 2007, and the one-month taxation year at December 31, 2007. The November 2007 loss expires on December 31, 2026, i.e., in 20 taxation years.

[8] The corporation's income for tax purposes for the year ending December 31, 2008, is $15,000. However, the corporation may make a deduction to the extent of nil under this assumption because the ladies' shoe retail business generated no income in the year and there was no income from the sale of similar products or services by the assumption made in this alternative.
ITA: 111(5)(a)(ii)

[9] This amount is available for carryforward as follows, assuming a December 31 taxation year-end is chosen:

— $34,000   (being the 2006 loss of $37,500 – $3,500 claimed in the December 31, 2007 year) expires on December 31, 2024;

— $19,500   (see note (7)) expires on December 31, 2026, i.e., 20 taxation years.

[10] On the assumption that the optional net capital loss deduction is taken in order to increase the non-capital losses for the deemed taxation year.

[11] The adjusted cost base balance at December 1, 2007 is $126,000, being the deemed proceeds of disposition in the deemed disposition elected upon.
ITA: 111(4)(e)

[12] The adjusted cost base balance (i.e., capital cost, in the case of depreciable property) at December 1, 2007, for future capital gains purposes, is $118,000, being deemed proceeds of disposition in the deemed disposition elected upon. The UCC $114,000 at the same date is increased by all of the recapture of $6,000, but only ½ of the capital gain of $8,000 elected as deemed proceeds on the deemed disposition, (i.e., $104,000 + $6,000 + ½ × $8,000).
ITA: 13(7)(f), 111(4)(e)

[13] The addition of $19,500 to the non-capital loss balance is logical, since the $19,500 represents the loss from business sources for the deemed year-end.

¶11,160   Taxable Income of a Corporation in General

Recall that the starting point for the calculation of a corporation's taxable income is its net income for tax purpose computed under Division B. Where financial statements have been prepared using generally accepted accounting principles, it may be necessary to adjust income for financial accounting purposes to income for tax purposes as determined by Division B. This usually involves a reconciliation process, introduced in previous chapters. Generally, expenditures deducted for financial accounting purposes but not deductible for tax purposes, must be added to financial accounting income, and expenditures not deducted for financial accounting purposes but deductible for tax purposes may be deducted in the reconciliation. To perform this reconciliation in the preparation of a corporate tax return, Schedule 1 is completed.

ITA: 110–112

Example Problem

Frenzied Taxpayers Limited reported a net loss for financial accounting purposes of $53,000 for 2006 and a net income of $126,000 for 2007. It showed a provision for income taxes of $113,000 for 2007 only. Expenses deducted for financial accounting purposes in both years included: charitable donations of $15,000 per year, depreciation of $105,000 per year and bond discount amortization of $5,000 per year. The corporation included in financial accounting income, in both years, dividends from taxable Canadian corporations of $23,000 and dividends of $15,300 net of a 15% withholding tax from foreign corporations which were not foreign affiliates. The corporation had no capital gains in either year.

In 2006, capital cost allowance of $14,800 (i.e., less than the maximum of $14,844) had been taken on a brick building (Class 1) leaving an undepreciated capital cost balance of $356,250 on January 1, 2007, the beginning of the 2007 taxation year. In addition, $44,800 in capital cost allowance had been taken on equipment leaving an undepreciated capital cost balance of $179,200 on January 1, 2007. In 2007, no additions or disposals were made to these classes of assets.

The corporation had non-capital losses of $18,000 available for carryover until 2009 and a 1999 net capital loss of $5,000 available for carryover.

— REQUIRED

Calculate the taxable income of the corporation for the years indicated.

— SOLUTION

		2006		2007
Net income (loss) per financial statements		$(53,000)		$126,000
Add items not deductible for tax purposes:				
Provision for income taxes[1]		—		$113,000
Withholding tax on foreign dividends[2]	$ 2,700		2,700	
Charitable donations[3]	15,000		15,000	
Depreciation	105,000		105,000	
Amortized bond discount[4]	5,000	127,700	5,000	240,700
Deduct items tax deductible:				
Capital cost allowances[5]		(59,600)		(50,090)
Income for tax purposes		$ 15,100		$316,610

	2006	2007	
Deductions in computation of taxable income:			
Inter-company dividends	$ 23,000[6]	$ 23,000	ITA: 112
Charitable donations			ITA: 110(1)(*a*)
— carried over	—	15,000[7]	
— current	Nil[7]	15,000[7]	
Non-capital loss carryover[8]	—	18,000	ITA: 111(1)(*a*)
Net capital loss carryover[9]	— (23,000)	— (71,000)	ITA: 111(1)(*b*)
Taxable income	Nil	$245,610	

— *NOTES TO SOLUTION*

[1] Income tax is not an expenditure made to produce income. It is an appropriation of profits after they have been earned.

[2] This is not an expenditure made to produce income for tax purposes, but an appropriation of profits after they have been earned. However, a foreign tax credit may be available in the computation of tax.

[3] Donations, normally, are not deductible in the computation of income, but are deductible in the computation of taxable income of a corporation.

[4] Bond discount amortizations are prohibited, but payments reflecting bond discounts are deductible at the earlier of redemption or maturity. ITA: 18(1)(*f*), 20(1)(*f*)

[5] Capital cost allowances for 2007 were computed as follows:

	Building Class 1: 4%	Equipment Class 8: 20%
2007: UCC, January 1, 2007	$356,250	$179,200
CCA for 2007 (expense $50,090)	(14,250)	(35,840)
2008: UCC, January 1, 2008	$342,000	$143,360

[6] Even though $23,000 was deducted, only $15,100 of the dividends deducted have any effect since there is no loss carryover for dividends not deducted. Even where there is a loss from business and property, the addition to the non-capital losses of dividends deducted under section 112 is offset by the paragraph 3(*c*) income which in fact includes the dividends in question. The dividend deduction only neutralizes the paragraph 3(*c*) inclusion, as can be seen by a substitution of these numbers in the definition of non-capital loss. ITA: 111(8)

[7] The amount of charitable donations that may be deducted in a year is limited to 75% of income as computed in Division B of Part I. However, charitable donations not deducted in the current year can be carried forward five years. ITA: 110.1(1)(*a*)

[8] Non-capital losses would not be deducted in 2006, because after the dividends have been deducted, there is no income against which to absorb them in that year.

[9] Net capital loss carryovers cannot be deducted in 2006 and 2007 because there were no taxable capital gains against which to absorb them in these years. However, if there are net taxable capital gains available under paragraph 3(*b*) in the future or in the 3 years before 2006 (to the extent the taxable capital gains have not been offset by allowable capital losses), there is a potential increase in the non-capital losses at the taxpayer's discretion. The decision to utilize this option will depend upon which source of income will be generated first, business income or net taxable capital gains.

¶11,200   BASIC COMPUTATION OF TAX FOR ALL CORPORATIONS

¶11,210   Objectives of Provisions Affecting Taxation of Corporations

Although a corporation is regarded as a separate entity, in an economic sense the separation of a corporation and its shareholders may be artificial. However, the flexibility provided by corporations, often involving tax planning, has resulted in considerable complexity of the legislation pertaining to the taxation of corporations. This legislation appears to have three main objectives.

The first objective is the alleviation of the multiple taxation of corporate income by taxing income at the level of the corporation and, then, at the level of the shareholder on dividends received from after-tax corporate earnings. The Act attempts to integrate these two taxes primarily by way of the dividend gross-up and tax credit mechanism. If the system of integration were perfect, it would completely eliminate the double taxation of corporate income, as previously discussed at the beginning of this chapter and demonstrated in Chapter 12. The Canadian system of integration is not perfect in this sense, but it does remove much of the effect of double taxation on investment income and some types of business income. The examination of this aspect will be continued in detail in the next chapter.

The second objective of these provisions is to prevent the avoidance of tax through the use of a corporation. In prior years, there was a considerable incentive to convert amounts that would normally be distributed to *individual* shareholders as dividends into amounts that resulted in capital gains. This was known as "dividend stripping" and many provisions were put in place to stop this practice. The incentive to convert dividends into capital gains was renewed with the introduction of the capital gains deduction which continues for shares of qualified small business corporations. Major anti-avoidance provisions are found in the Act. However, in making distributions to *corporate* shareholders, there has been an incentive to convert what might be taxed as a capital gain into a non-taxable intercorporate dividend. Hence, provisions to prevent such "capital gains stripping" have been implemented.

ITA: 55(2)

ITA: 110.6, 245, 246

The third objective of these provisions is to provide tax incentives to certain types of corporations. The small business deduction, which will be discussed in the next chapter, is probably the most important of these. The small business deduction will be shown to substantially reduce tax for a Canadian-controlled private corporation. The manufacturing and processing profits deduction will be alluded to. Investment tax credits, including the credit for scientific research expenditures, will be discussed.

¶11,220   General Rates for Corporations

¶11,225   Overview of rates and credits

The general federal rate of tax to be paid on the taxable income of all corporations under Part I of the Act is 38%. However, the basic federal rate of 38% is subject to modification, depending on the type of corporation. The Act levies a surtax, the rates for which have fluctuated over the years, on a defined base of federal tax payable. This surtax will be eliminated, effective, January 1, 2008. The Act provides for a tax rate reduction for corporations. Another provision reduces the federal tax payable, in recognition of provincial income taxes, by an amount equal to 10% of the corporation's taxable income earned in a province or territory of Canada. Two other provisions reduce federal tax payable, for certain corporations, by means of the small business deduction and manufacturing and processing profits deduction, respectively. Foreign tax credits are available to reduce federal tax payable. Another provision exists for a number of tax credits, including the political contribution tax credit, the investment tax credit, and the apprenticeship job creation tax credit, which reduce the amount of federal tax payable.

ITA: 123
ITA: 123.2–127

ITA: 123.2
ITA: 123.4
ITA: 124

ITA: 125, 125.1

ITA: 126
ITA: 127

¶11,230 Corporate surtax

Federal corporate surtax, which will continue to apply until December 31, 2007, is computed, generally, as follows:

Base amount of Part I tax	38.00%
Deduct: 10% of taxable income	10.00
Net amount	28.00%
Corporate surtax @4% of net amount	1.12%

The base amount of Part I tax is 38% of taxable income. The surtax, generally, is 1.12% (i.e., 4% of (38% − 10%)) of taxable income.

¶11,235 Effect of provincial corporate tax rates

In addition to the federal taxes imposed, each province levies an additional income tax on a corporation's taxable income. Furthermore, the taxable income calculation may vary from province to province because of provincial taxing statutes. The provincial rate varies from province to province, but on the whole lies between 9.9% and 17%.

¶11,240 Effect of corporation type

As mentioned previously, the type and status of the corporation has a bearing on how its income is taxed. There are three major classifications of corporations to be concerned with. These are described as follows:

(a) a "public corporation" is one which is resident in Canada and has a class of shares listed on a prescribed Canadian stock exchange or meets certain conditions prescribed in Part XLVIII of the Regulations and either elects to be a public corporation or is so designated by the Minister; ITA: 89(1); ITR: 3200, 4800

(b) a "private corporation" is a Canadian resident company which is not a public corporation and is not controlled by one or more public corporations or prescribed federal Crown corporations; and ITA: 89(1)

(c) a "Canadian-controlled private corporation" is a private corporation not controlled directly or indirectly by non-residents, public corporations or any combination of the two. ITA: 89(1)

As a result of the combined federal and provincial rate and several of the modifications to that rate, the rates of tax applicable to Canadian corporations will vary from a low of about 15.6% to a high of about 38.1%, depending on the classification of the corporation and the type of income earned.

¶11,245 General rate reduction

The Act provides a corporation with a deduction from tax, computed by multiplying the corporation's "general rate reduction percentage" by its "full-rate taxable income". The "general rate reduction percentage" is currently 7%. The "full-rate taxable income" of a corporation, generally, is a corporation's taxable income that has not benefited from special rate reductions, such as the manufacturing and processing profits deduction (alluded to later in this chapter and discussed in the Supplemental Notes at the end of the chapter) and the small business deduction (discussed in Chapter 12), among others. The amount of the rate reduction is dependent on the nature of the corporation. Paragraph (a) of the definition of "full-rate taxable income" applies to corporations other than Canadian-controlled private corporations (CCPCs). For the purposes of this chapter, full-rate taxable income is the amount of the corporation's taxable income minus income, if any, eligible for the manufacturing and processing profits deduction. Examples of this calculation are presented later in this Chapter. ITA: 123.4(2)
ITA: 123.4(1)

The general rate reduction will increase by one-half a percentage point for 2008, one percentage point for 2009 and two percentage points for the 2010 and 2.5 percentage points for 2011 and later calendar years. This would mean that by 2011 the general rate reduction would be 9.5%.

The following table shows the future federal corporate tax rates as currently proposed.

	2006	**2007**	**2008**	**2009**	**2010**	**2011**
Basic	38.00	38.00	38.00	38.00	38.00	38.00
Abatement	(10.00)	(10.00)	(10.00)	(10.00)	(10.00)	(10.00)
General rate reduction	(7.00)	(7.00)	(7.50)	(8.00)	(9.00)	(9.50)
	21.00	21.00	20.50	20.00	19.00	18.50
Surtax	1.12	1.12	—	—	—	—
	22.12	22.12	20.50	20.00	19.00	18.50

¶11,250 Abatement from Federal Tax for Income Earned in a Province

¶11,255 Purpose of the provision

A federal abatement of 10% of a corporation's taxable income earned in Canada is deducted from income tax otherwise calculated. This abatement is based on taxable income earned in a Canadian province or territory; that is, the reduction allows for the imposition of such a provincial tax. All of the provinces and the territories impose an income tax on corporations at basic rates which vary from 9.9% to 16%. In all but Alberta and Quebec, this tax is filed with and collected by the federal government together with the federal tax. Alberta and Quebec have their own rules for the taxation of corporations. All of these tax rates are set out in the "Current Tax Rates and Credits" section at the beginning of the CCH edition of the CANADIAN INCOME TAX ACT. — ITA: 124(1)

Exhibit 11-3 shows a hypothetical calculation, applicable to most corporations, of effective total tax on taxable income eligible for the abatement. Note that the provincial tax is calculated separately on a tax base which may or may not equal taxable income under the federal Act depending on the particular province levying the tax. For illustrative purposes only, Exhibit 11-3 *assumes* that the tax base for income earned in a hypothetical province is equal to taxable income for federal corporate income tax. The exhibit also assumes that the provincial corporate rate of tax is 13% of the taxable income earned in that province.

EXHIBIT 11-3
Hypothetical Tax Rates applicable to
Taxable Income eligible for Abatement

Basic federal tax rate [ssec. 123(1)]	38.00%
Federal abatement for provincial tax [ssec. 124(1)]	(10.00)
Net federal tax	28.00%
Federal surtax @ 4% of net federal tax of 28.00% [sec. 123.2]	1.12
Total	29.12%
Federal tax reduction for 2007	(7.00)
Net federal tax	22.12%
Provincial tax (assumed)	13.00
Effective total tax	35.12%

¶11,260 Applicable income tax regulations

Part IV of the Regulations provides the prescribed method to determine the taxable income earned in a province by a corporation. The term "taxable income earned in the year in — ITR: 400(1), 402 a province" by a corporation is defined as being the aggregate of the taxable incomes of the corporation earned in the year in each of the provinces. The Regulations also set out the method of calculating the taxable income earned in a particular province during the year. The taxable income earned in a particular province is that taxable income which is attributable to a *permanent establishment* that the corporation has in the province. If a company has no permanent establishment in a province, it will not have earned any taxable income in that province for the purposes of the abatement.

The term "permanent establishment" is defined as a fixed place of business of the corporation, including an office, a branch, a mine or oil well, a farm, a timber land, a factory, a workshop or a warehouse. Where the corporation does not have a fixed place of business, its permanent establishment is the principal place in which the corporation's business is carried out. A corporation is deemed to have a permanent establishment in a place, if the corporation carries on business through an employee or agent, established in a particular place:

ITR: 400(2), 400(2)(*b*)

(a) who has general authority to contract for his or her employer or principal; or

(b) who has a stock of merchandise owned by his or her employer or principal from which he or she regularly fills orders which he or she receives.

However, the fact that a corporation has business dealings through a commission agent, broker or other independent agent, or maintains an office solely for the purchase of merchandise, does not of itself mean that the corporation has a permanent establishment. The use of substantial machinery or equipment in a particular place at any time in a taxation year constitutes a permanent establishment in that place as does the ownership of land in a province by a corporation that, otherwise, has a permanent establishment in Canada. The CRA indicates that the application of the criteria for a permanent establishment set out in the Regulations will often involve questions of fact which must be answered by the circumstances of each case.

ITR: 400(2)(*d*), 400(2)(*e*), 400(2)(*f*)

IT-177R2
ITR: 400(2)

¶11,265   Cases on the meaning of permanent establishment

The case of *M.N.R. v. Panther Oil and Grease Manufacturing Co. of Canada Ltd.* presents a specific fact situation. Here the taxpayer had a factory in Ontario, but maintained a sizable sales force throughout Canada under the direction of district sales managers. These sales managers were under the direction of division managers, one of whom lived in Quebec. He had an office, not listed as the company's, in his home. The division and district managers kept a small quantity of the company's goods on hand for small orders when quick delivery was requested. However, most orders were filled from Ontario.

61 DTC 1222 (Ex. Ct.)

It was held that the extensive sales organization in Quebec, itself, constituted a branch in that province and district managers constituted "agencies" of the company. It was also found that the stock of merchandise from which small orders were filled qualified as a permanent establishment.

In the case of *Enterprise Foundry (N.B.) Ltd. v. M.N.R.*, the appellant was incorporated in New Brunswick, but all of its sales were made to customers in Quebec. About 40% of its orders were filled from a stock of merchandise maintained in a public warehouse in Montreal. The taxpayer's key employee had the authority to deliver goods from the stock of merchandise and also had general authority to contract for his employer. It was held that there was a permanent establishment in Quebec.

64 DTC 660 (T.A.B.)

Example Problem

The taxpayer corporation, whose head office was in Ontario, manufactured electrical appliances which it sold exclusively to wholesalers throughout the country. The company employed a sales representative and junior salesmen in the Province of Quebec. Orders received by the sales representative, who had no authority to accept them, were forwarded to head office and, if accepted there, the goods were shipped directly to the purchaser. During the years in question, the Quebec representative maintained an office in his home at his own expense. There was no agreement with the company to set up the office, but he found it convenient to do so. The company supplied him with company stationery and literature, price sheets, catalogues, sales promotional material and inter-office memoranda. He was also supplied with substantial quantities of samples of the company's products the value of which varied from $4,700 to $11,000 to be used in demonstrations and in promoting sales. The telephone directory did not list the representative's residence as the company's place of business and there was no business sign of any type on the premises. The office was used for taking orders and for training junior salesmen.

During six months of one year, the company maintained a stock of appliances valued at about $120,000 in rented warehouse space in Montreal and filled Quebec orders from this stock. The company had no employees at that warehouse; the handling of goods there was carried out by the warehouse personnel. The company had no control over any part of the warehouse and the public had no knowledge of the company's goods being stored there.

— *REQUIRED*

Determine whether or not the company has a "permanent establishment" in the Province of Quebec by reference to Regulation 400(2).

— *SOLUTION*

[Reference: *M.N.R. v. Sunbeam Corporation (Canada) Ltd.*, 61 DTC 1063 (Ex. Ct.).]

The definition of "permanent establishment" begins with a general statement and then lists seven situations which describe specific permanent establishments. Consider the potentially applicable specific provisions first.

ITR: 400(2)

(1) A corporation must carry on business through an employee or agent who has general authority to contract or who has a stock of merchandise owned by the employer from which he regularly fills orders. In this case, the sales representative had no authority to accept orders. Furthermore, orders were filled from head office in Ontario. Therefore, the conditions for a permanent establishment are not met.

ITR: 400(2)(*b*)

(2) Did the company meet the condition of the Regulations that refers to the use of substantial machinery and equipment? The use of the company's sample appliances for demonstration purposes was not "the use of substantial machinery or equipment" in Quebec. The provision was probably intended to refer to the use of heavy or large machinery or equipment by such persons as contractors or builders who may move such equipment from one province to another in carrying out their normal operations.

ITR: 400(2)(*e*)

If none of the specific conditions in the Regulations are met, the analysis should turn to the more general definition of "permanent establishment". The following questions can be posed.

ITR: 400(2)

(1) Did the company have a fixed place of business including an office, a branch or a factory? The office of the Quebec sales representative was not an office of the company. This office was maintained by the sales representative in his home for his own convenience and at his own expense. There was no business sign of any sort on the premises and the telephone directory did not list the residence as the company's place of business.

(2) Did the company have a warehouse in the Province of Quebec? The company merely used the facilities of another company's warehouse for the storing of goods. The company had no control over the warehouse. As a result, the warehouse cannot be considered a fixed place of business of the company.

On the basis of this analysis, it was held that the company did not have a permanent establishment in Quebec.

¶11,270 Taxable income earned in a province or territory

Once it is determined that a corporation has a permanent establishment in a province or territory, a portion of the company's taxable income is attributed to that jurisdiction. To determine the attribution, a formula must be used. The formula is based on the proportion of gross revenues earned through a permanent establishment in a province or territory and the

ITR: 402

proportion of salaries and wages expense paid through the same permanent establishment in that jurisdiction, relative to total gross revenues and salaries and wages expense, respectively, of the corporation. The total taxable income allocated to all provinces and territories provides the basis for the 10% abatement. The allocations to individual jurisdictions, other than Alberta and Quebec, provide the basis for provincial or territorial corporate income tax.

A taxpayer must first determine the gross revenue for the year which is reasonably attributable to each permanent establishment. Rules are provided for determining the permanent establishment to which gross revenue is attributable where merchandise is shipped by a corporation to its customers outside of Canada.

ITR: 402(3)(*a*), 402(4)

Where the gross revenue reasonably attributable to a permanent establishment in a province has been determined, this amount will be divided by the corporation's total gross revenue for the year and the resulting fraction will be multiplied by its taxable income for the year. Certain types of investment income including interest on securities, dividends and rentals or royalties from properties not used in the main business of the corporation are excluded from gross revenue.

ITR: 401, 402(5)

It will also be necessary to determine the aggregate of the salaries and wages paid in the year by the corporation to employees of a permanent establishment in each particular jurisdiction. This will then be divided by the aggregate of all salaries and wages paid in the year by the corporation and the resulting fraction will be multiplied by its taxable income for the year.

ITR: 401, 402(3)(*b*)

Example Problem

Barry and the Wild Bunch Limited, with its head office in Ottawa, Ontario and other permanent establishments in the provinces of New Brunswick and Quebec, and in the United States, has taxable income of $325,000.

Assume that the corporation's gross revenue and salaries and wages are attributable to its permanent establishments as follows:

ITR: 402

	Gross revenue	Salaries and wages
Ontario	$ 780,000	$ 130,000
New Brunswick	2,340,000	520,000
Quebec	2,600,000	585,000
U.S.	390,000	65,000
Total	$6,110,000	$1,300,000
Dividends not attributable [Reg. 402(5)]	130,000	—
	$6,240,000	$1,300,000

— REQUIRED

Compute the amount of the company's taxable income attributable to each province and determine the amount of the company's abatement.

ITA: 124(1)

— SOLUTION

The proportion of taxable income attributable to each province would be computed as follows:

ITR: 402

	Gross revenue		Salaries & wages		
	Amount	%	Amount	%	Average %
Ontario	$ 780,000	12.8%	$ 130,000	10.0%	½ (12.8% + 10.0%) = 11.4%
New Brunswick	2,340,000	38.3	520,000	40.0	½ (38.3% + 40.0%) = 39.2%
Quebec	2,600,000	42.6	585,000	45.0	½ (42.6% + 45.0%) = 43.8%
Subtotal	$5,720,000	93.7%	$1,235,000	95.0%	½ (93.7% + 95.0%) = 94.4%
U.S.	390,000	6.3	65,000	5.0	
Total	$6,110,000	100.0%	$1,300,000	100.0%	

Allocation of taxable income to each province:

Ontario	11.4% of $325,000 =	$ 37,050
New Brunswick	39.2% of $325,000 =	127,400
Quebec	43.8% of $325,000 =	142,350
Total taxable income earned in a province or territory		$306,800

ITA: 124(1)

The amount deductible from the corporation tax otherwise payable would be computed as follows:

10% of $306,800 .... $30,680

ITA: 123.2

Note, however, that, in this case, the surtax is applied to federal tax otherwise payable after a deduction of 10% of the full taxable income of $325,000.

¶11,300   TAX DEDUCTIONS/CREDITS

¶11,310   Manufacturing and Processing Profits Deduction

ITA: 125.1

The Act provides a deduction from corporate tax, in essence a tax credit, for manufacturing and processing (M&P) profits taxable in Canada. The amount of this tax deduction or credit is the same as the general rate reduction on other business income taxable in Canada. As a result, there is no difference in the net federal tax rate applied to M&P profits or the rate applied to profits from other types of business, such as retailing, wholesaling, service, etc.

Apparently, the main reason for the continued existence of the M&P profits deduction legislation in the federal Act is to accommodate provinces that offer an M&P profits deduction from provincial tax based on the federal calculation of M&P profits. For that reason, the technical details of the federal M&P legislation are discussed in the Supplemental Notes at the end of this chapter.

¶11,320   Foreign Tax Deduction

¶11,325   Purpose and approach

ITA: 126

Residents of Canada, including corporations, are taxable on their world income even though part of this income may have been subject to tax in a foreign country. Foreign tax deductions are designed to mitigate the effects on a Canadian individual or corporate taxpayer of double taxation on income arising from a source outside Canada. Relief is granted by means of a deduction, from the Canadian tax otherwise payable, of all or part of the foreign tax.

The theory underlying this arrangement for a tax deduction is that the country where the income is earned has the first right to tax the income. If the country of the taxpayer's residence levies a higher rate of tax on the income, the taxpayer will pay tax at the higher rate, but part of that tax is paid to the country where the income was earned while the remainder will be paid to the country of the taxpayer's residence.

Since the foreign tax deduction is meant to reduce Canadian tax on foreign income that has been taxed elsewhere, there is no foreign tax deduction available on foreign income that is not taxed in Canada. If a source of income is exempt from tax in Canada, there is no Canadian tax to reduce with a foreign tax deduction. For example, certain dividends received by corporations resident in Canada from corporations, such as foreign subsidiaries, resident in another country are not taxable in Canada. Such dividends are, effectively, not taxable in Canada because, although they are included in Division B income, they are deductible in the calculation of taxable income in Division C. This provision is similar to the provision which

ITA: 113

ITA: 112

provides a deduction for dividends received from taxable Canadian corporations. These dividends, from foreign affiliates, that are deductible under section 113 are not eligible for the foreign tax credit, since any tax "that may reasonably be regarded as having been paid by the taxpayer in respect of income from a share of the capital stock of a foreign affiliate of the taxpayer" is excluded from foreign tax which is eligible for the credit. A foreign affiliate is defined, basically, as a corporation in which the taxpayer has at least 10% equity ownership.

On the other hand, types of foreign income that are included in Canadian income and, hence, are eligible for a foreign tax deduction include: income from an unincorporated foreign branch, dividend income that is not eligible for deduction in the calculation of taxable income (e.g., dividends from a country with which Canada does not have a tax treaty, such as the Cayman Islands), or dividends income from a corporation which is not a foreign affiliate.

The Act takes three separate approaches to the foreign tax deduction. The first two, on which this chapter will focus, apply to residents of Canada. One refers to "non-business-income tax". The other refers to "business-income tax". The third applies to non-residents of Canada referring to tax on certain capital gains on "taxable Canadian property". Where the taxpayer is eligible for a foreign tax deduction for "non-business-income tax" or on "business-income tax" paid to more than one foreign country, the taxpayer is required to compute separate deductions for each country. It should be emphasized that with few exceptions, the same rules apply to both individuals and corporations. However, the following discussion will focus on the foreign tax deduction rules as they apply to corporations.

¶11,330 Non-business income tax deduction

¶11,330.10 *Calculation*

Where a taxpayer has non-business income (e.g., interest income) from another country and has paid foreign income or profits taxes to the government of that country or to the government of a state, province or other political subdivision of that country, the taxpayer may take a deduction from Canadian tax equal to the lesser of:

(i) the foreign non-business-income tax paid in respect of that foreign income; and

(ii) $$\frac{\text{foreign non-business income (Div. B)}}{\begin{array}{c}\text{Income (Div. B) for the year}\\ \text{(from all sources) plus or}\\ \text{minus certain amounts}\end{array}} \times \text{tax otherwise payable [ssec. 126(7)]}$$

Note that part (ii) attempts to estimate the Canadian tax paid on the foreign income. As a result, the credit against Canadian tax cannot exceed the estimated Canadian tax paid on the foreign income.

Both the numerator and denominator of the fraction in part (ii) above are limited to the amounts of income (excluding income from a foreign affiliate) attributable to the period in the year during which the taxpayer was resident in Canada.

The amounts to be subtracted from the Division B income of a corporation in the denominator of the fraction are:

(i) the claims for net capital losses carried over because they directly offset taxable capital gains, with the result that they are not taxed; and

(ii) the amount of taxable dividends received and deductible and the amount of dividends received from a foreign affiliate and deductible, because they are not taxed under Part I.

Marginal references (right margin):
126(1)(*a*)
ITA: 95(1)
ITA: 113
ITA: 126(1), 126(2)–(2.2), 126(6)
ITA: 126(1), 126(7)
ITA: 111(1)(*b*)
ITA: 112, 113

¶11,330.20   *Definition of "tax otherwise payable"*

The term "tax otherwise payable" is defined. For purposes of the non-business income tax deduction, "tax otherwise payable" is defined in paragraph (a) of the definition of the term. For corporations, it is the tax for the year after deducting the 10% abatement and the tax rate reduction before deducting the manufacturing and processing profits deduction, the foreign tax deduction, and some other deductions from tax. The surtax is included in tax otherwise payable. The net result is to determine an amount of tax that would include the Canadian tax on foreign non-business income. That amount would be net of the abatement and the general reduction for a corporation, other than a Canadian-controlled private corporation. Note that if a Canadian resident corporation's only source of income is from a foreign non-business asset that is not real property, i.e., real estate,[2] all of its taxable income would be considered to be earned in a province and the corporation would receive a tax abatement of 10% of its full taxable income. Therefore, the Canadian tax otherwise payable on that income would be after the 10% reduction.

ITA: 126(7)

ITA: 124
ITA: 123.4, 125, 125.1, 126
ITA: 127, 127.2–127.4

¶11,330.30   *Interpretation of terms*

The following should be noted about the term "non-business income tax paid" as it applies to a corporation:

ITA: 126(1), 127(7)

(a) the foreign tax must be paid, not merely payable and the conversion of the foreign tax into its Canadian-dollar equivalent must be made at the rate of exchange prevailing at the time payment is made;

(b) the foreign tax must generally be in the nature of an income or profits tax;

(c) the term includes such income tax paid to the government of another country or to the government of a state, province or other political subdivision of that country;

(d) the term excludes "business income tax" paid in the other country; and

(e) foreign non-business income tax deducted as an expense in Division B must be excluded. Unlike a foreign "business" income deduction, described below, an unused foreign non-business income deduction cannot be carried forward. Therefore, consideration should be given to using the deduction from income for these amounts. Since a deduction from tax (i.e., a tax credit) is preferable to a deduction from income, eligibility for a foreign tax credit should be determined first, with any unused balance of foreign taxes paid being taken as a deduction. This may result in a circular calculation because of the credit's dependence on net income after the deduction. An algebraic approach may be necessary to solve this problem.

ITA: 20(12)

¶11,335   Business income tax deduction

Where a resident of Canada carries on business in a foreign country, the foreign tax deduction rules allow for a three-year carryback and a 10-year carryforward of unabsorbed foreign business income tax paid in a taxation year. Thus, foreign business income tax paid in a taxation year but not deducted may be carried over and treated as if it were paid in a carryover taxation year.

In the case of a corporation resident in Canada, it would be considered to carry on business in a foreign country if the corporation had an *unincorporated* branch in that foreign country. If the Canadian resident corporation established a subsidiary in the foreign country, the business income of the subsidiary would be taxed by the foreign country as a separate entity and no business foreign tax credit would be available to the parent. Where the corporation operates in foreign countries through unincorporated branches, a business foreign tax credit will arise.

The deduction, as it applies to a corporation, is computed as the least of:

ITA: 126(2)

---

[2] Where the non-business income-producing asset is real property located in a foreign jurisdiction, the presence of real property would normally result in a permanent establishment in that country and, hence, the corporation would not be eligible for the federal abatement.

(a) the total of the "business-income tax paid" for the year in respect of all businesses carried on through an unincorporated branch by the taxpayer in a particular country, plus any "unused foreign tax credit" from other years in respect of the same country as the taxpayer may wish to claim;

ITA: 126(7) "business-income tax paid"

(b) $\dfrac{\text{foreign business income}}{\substack{\text{income (Div. B) for the year} \\ \text{(from all sources) plus or} \\ \text{minus certain amounts}^{(1)}}} \times$ tax otherwise payable[2]

(c) the tax otherwise payable[3] for the year after deducting any non-business income tax deduction under subsection 126(1).

---

[1] The amounts to be added to and subtracted from Division B income are the same as those that were identified for the non-business income tax deduction.

[2] The "tax for the year otherwise payable", in this case, is defined in paragraph (c) of the definition of the term. It is the tax before any deduction for the federal tax abatement and other corporate tax credits, but after the addition of the surtax. Note that, if foreign business income were a Canadian resident corporation's only source of income, none of its taxable income would likely be considered to be earned in a province and the corporation would receive no tax abatement. Therefore, the Canadian tax otherwise payable on that income would be before the 10% abatement.

ITA: 126(7)
ITA: 124, 123.2
ITA: 125–127.41

[3] The "tax for the year otherwise payable", in this case, is defined in paragraph (b) of the definition of the term. It is the same amount as that described in note (2), above, from paragraph (c) of the definition.

ITA: 127(7)

Example Problem 1

You have audited the books of International Moneygrubbers Limited, a public corporation, and have determined that the income for tax purposes of $472,000 for the year ended December 31, 2007, has been calculated correctly. The following additional data are available:

Interest received from:	
a U.S. company (net of $3,000 tax withheld)	$17,000
a British company (net of $1,500 tax withheld)	8,500
Business income (net of $9,800 tax paid) earned from an unincorporated	
branch in Turkey	18,200
Donations	20,000
Dividend received from a taxable Canadian corporation	52,000
Taxable income earned in a province (computed by Reg.)	375,000

— *REQUIRED*

Compute the maximum foreign tax credit available to the corporation for 2007.

— *SOLUTION*

(a) Calculation of taxable income:

Income for tax purposes		$472,000
Less: donations	$20,000	
dividends	52,000	72,000
Taxable income		$400,000

ITA: 110(1)(a)
ITA: 112

(b) Calculation of tax otherwise payable:
(i) For foreign non-business income tax credit:

Tax otherwise payable (38% of $400,000)	(A)	$152,000
Less: 10% of $375,000		37,500
Net		$114,500
Surtax (1.12% of $400,000))		4,480
Tax rate reduction @ 7% of $400,000		(28,000)
Tax otherwise payable	(B)	$ 90,980

(ii) For foreign business income tax credit:[1]

Tax otherwise payable, per (A) above	$152,000
Add: surtax	4,480
Less: tax rate reduction	(28,000)
Tax otherwise payable .... (C)	$128,480

(c) Calculation of foreign tax deduction:[2]

ITA: 126(1)

(i) Foreign non-business income:

Interest from U.S. company
lesser of:

(I) tax paid .... $3,000 → $3,000

(II) $\dfrac{\text{income from U.S.}}{\text{income less dividends}} \times \begin{array}{l}\text{tax otherwise}\\ \text{payable (B)}\end{array}$

$= \dfrac{\$20,000}{\$472,000 - 52,000} \times \$90,980$ $4,332

Interest from British company
lesser of:

(I) tax paid .... $1,500 → $1,500

(II) $\dfrac{\text{income from Britain}}{\text{income less dividends}} \times \begin{array}{l}\text{tax otherwise}\\ \text{payable (B)}\end{array}$

$= \dfrac{\$10,000}{\$472,000 - 52,000} \times \$90,980$ $2,166

(ii) Foreign business income:
least of:

ITA: 126(2)

(I) tax paid .... $ 9,800

(II) $\dfrac{\text{income from Turkey}}{\text{income less dividends}} \times \begin{array}{l}\text{tax otherwise}\\ \text{payable (C)}\end{array}$

$= \dfrac{\$28,000}{\$472,000 - 52,000} \times \$128,480$ .... $ 8,565 → $8,565

(III) tax otherwise payable (C) less
non-business income tax deduction
($128,480 − ($3,000 + 1,500)) $123,980

(d) Total foreign tax deduction:

Foreign non-business income

U.S. source	$ 3,000	
British source	1,500	$ 4,500
Foreign business income		8,565
Total deduction from tax		$13,065

—*NOTES TO SOLUTION*

[1] If the Canadian income tax effects on foreign investment income could be isolated, as in the case where the corporation's only source of income was foreign non-business income (other than from real property), such as interest income, it would be considered to be earned in the province of which the taxpayer is a resident and, therefore, would be eligible for the federal tax abatement. As a result, it is the tax otherwise payable (B) after the abatement on which the non-business income tax deduction is based. On the other hand, foreign business income is assumed to be earned in a permanent establishment in the foreign country and, therefore, is not eligible for the federal tax abatement. Thus, the tax otherwise payable (C) before the abatement is the relevant base for the business income tax deduction.

[2] Note how these credits against Canadian tax do not exceed foreign tax paid on the foreign income. These reductions of Canadian tax are also restricted to the estimated amount of Canadian tax paid on the foreign income.

Example Problem 2

Reconsider the facts in Example Problem 1 with the additional information that income for tax purposes of $472,000 includes manufacturing and processing profits (MP, as determined by the Regulations) that will earn a tax deduction of $25,200. Assume that the foreign tax credits remain the same.

ITR: 5200

— REQUIRED

Calculate total tax payable under Part I using a 11% provincial rate of tax applied to federal taxable income earned in a province.

— SOLUTION

Taxable income (as computed in Example Problem 1)		$400,000
Part I tax on taxable income:		
Tax @ 38% on $400,000		$152,000
Deduct: Federal tax abatement (10% of $375,000)		37,500
Net amount		$114,500
Add: Corporate surtax (1.12% of $400,000)		4,480
		$118,980
Deduct: M&P deduction	$25,200	
Tax rate reduction[1]	2,800	
Non-business foreign tax credit[2]	4,500	
Business foreign tax credit[3]	10,245	42,745
Total federal tax		$ 76,235
Provincial tax @ 11% of $375,000		41,250
Total taxes payable		$117,485

— NOTES TO SOLUTION

[1] Tax rate reduction

Taxable income:		$400,000
Less: M&P profits deduction ÷ .07 ($25,200 ÷ .07)		360,000
Net		$ 40,000
7% of $40,000		$ 2,800

[2] Foreign non-business tax deduction — See part (c) of Example Problem 1.

[3] Foreign business tax deduction — The tax otherwise payable in this case will differ from that computed in part (b)(ii) of Example Problem 1, because the tax rate reduction is only $2,800, in this case, and the M&P profits deduction is ignored in the definition. As a result, tax otherwise payable is computed as:

Basic federal tax	$152,000
Add: surtax	4,480
Less: tax rate reduction	(2,800)
Tax otherwise payable	$153,680

In this case, the foreign business income tax credit becomes:
least of:

(a) tax paid	$ 9,800

(b) $\dfrac{\text{income from Turkey}}{\text{income less dividend}} \times$ tax otherwise payable

$\dfrac{\$28,000}{\$472,000 - \$52,000} \times \$153,680 =$	$10,245

(c) tax otherwise payable less non-business income tax deduction ($153,680 − ($3,000 + $1,500))	$149,180

¶11,340   Investment Tax Credit

¶11,345   Overview

¶11,345.10   *Purpose*

The investment tax credit (ITC) was introduced in 1975 as a temporary extra incentive to stimulate new investment in Canada in certain specific business sectors and regional locations. Since that time, the original credit has been pared back to apply regionally only to the Gaspé and the Atlantic provinces for certain specific capital expenditures. However, three credits apply to all of Canada: scientific research and experimental development (SR&ED) expenditures, apprenticeship job creation tax credit, and child care spaces tax credit [proposed in the March 19, 2007 federal budget].

Conceptually, the available investment tax credit is simply calculated by applying a "specified percentage" or other limit for one of the categories described above to the capital cost of the asset acquired or the expenditure incurred. The actual amount of the ITC claimed by the taxpayer is deducted in the following taxation year from the capital cost of the asset acquired or the SR&ED pool. In addition, there is a carryover mechanism for available investment tax credits not claimed in a particular year.

The purpose of this section is to introduce, conceptually, the ramifications of this extremely important tax credit and to provide some simple examples of its application.

¶11,345.20   *Computation of investment tax credit*

One provision defines the basis for the computation of the available investment tax credit: the category of the asset or expenditure that is eligible for a credit, the "specified percentage" or the expenditure limit applicable to that category and the carryover rules.

ITA: 127(9)

The cost of the capital asset to which the "specified percentage" is applied must be reduced by all government assistance (e.g., grants, subsidies, loans, etc.) and non-arm's length third-party assistance including certain specified contract payments for goods and services.

ITA: 127(11.6)–(11.8), 127(16)–(21)

The amount of the *available* investment tax credit which can be applied in a year is limited only by the Part I tax remaining after the deduction of any of the other corporate tax credits. Those available ITCs that are not applied in the year of acquisition or expenditure can be carried back three taxation years and forward 20 taxation years. Because of the generous carryforward time-frame, it is reasonable that ITCs should be deducted last.

Exhibit 11-7 lists the investment tax credit rates which apply to the most common types of properties and expenditures, incurred by taxpayers other than Canadian-controlled private corporations (which are discussed in Chapter 12), which give rise to such credits. The specified percentages listed in the Exhibit vary, depending on the geographic location and nature of the property or expenditure.

All of the terms describing property will be discussed in more detail following the Exhibit.

EXHIBIT 11-4
Rates of Investment Tax Credits
(Non-Canadian-controlled private corporations only)
[ssec. 127(9)]

	Atlantic provinces and Gaspé	*Balance of Canada*
Qualified property	10%	0%
Qualified SR&ED*	20	20
Apprenticeship expenditure**	10	10
[Child care spaces***	25	25]

* SR&ED refers to scientific research and experimental development as discussed in Chapter 4.
** Limited to $2,000 per eligible apprentice.
*** Limited to $10,000 per eligible space.

¶11,350   Qualified property

¶11,350.10   *Time of acquisition*

"Qualified property" is property that is a prescribed building, grain elevator or machinery and equipment. Generally, a taxpayer is considered to have acquired depreciable property when title passes or when the taxpayer obtains all the incidents of title including possession, use and risk. Property is deemed not to have been acquired and, hence, not eligible for ITC until the property is "available for use", as discussed in Chapter 5.

ITR: 4600; ITA: 127(9)

ITA: 127(11.2)

¶11,350.20   *Type of property*

To be "qualified property" the property must be new property which has not been used for any purpose prior to its acquisition. It must also meet certain other conditions prescribed by a regulation which lists prescribed buildings and prescribed machinery and equipment.

ITR: 4900

¶11,350.30   *Use of the property*

To qualify for the credit, the prescribed building or machinery and equipment must be used primarily in one of a broad range of activities. There is no minimum use period and no provision for recapture of the credit in the event of a change to a non-qualifying use or the sale of the asset. Uses of qualified property are listed in paragraphs (*c*) and (*d*) of the definition of "qualified property". In the case of *Mother's Pizza Parlour (London) Limited et al. v. The Queen*, the Federal Court–Trial Division (affirmed by the Federal Court of Appeal) held that buildings from which dining room, take-out and delivery service was provided were not used for processing goods for sale, but for selling finished goods, since all ingredients for the pizza, including the dough, were purchased from independent suppliers. Hence, the building was not "qualified property" eligible for an investment tax credit at the time. In the case of a building, which is used primarily for eligible activities and partly for functions such as administration or warehousing, the entire cost would be recognized, providing the principal use of the building is an eligible activity.

ITA: 127(9)
85 DTC 5271 (F.C.T.D.), aff'd 88 DTC 6397 (F.C.A.)

¶11,350.40   *Capital cost reduction*

In the taxation year following the year in which the investment tax credit is claimed, the capital cost of the depreciable asset is reduced by the amount of the credit claimed. In situations where the asset no longer exists (i.e., the property has been disposed of), there would be an income inclusion as a substitute for the capital cost reduction of the capital asset.

ITA: 12(1)(*t*), 13(7.1)(*e*)

Example Problem

In 2007, Investit Limited has acquired $100,000 of Class 8 (20%) assets eligible as "qualified property" for the 10% investment tax credit in the Gaspé area. The corporation's federal income tax rate after the abatement and the general rate reduction is 22.12%. Its taxable income before capital cost allowance on the eligible property is $30,000.

The corporation is not eligible for any other tax credits and paid no tax in the preceding three years.

— *REQUIRED*

(A) What is the maximum investment tax credit available?

(B) Compute the net federal Part I tax payable after the investment tax credit.

(C) What is the amount of the investment tax credit available for carryover?

(D) Compute the UCC balance in Class 8 at the end of the following year, assuming the new assets are the only assets in the class.

— *SOLUTION*

(A) The maximum investment tax credit available will be $10,000 (i.e., 10% of $100,000).

(B)

Taxable income before capital cost allowance on qualified property	$30,000
Less: capital cost allowance on qualified property:	
½ × 20% of $100,000	(10,000)
Taxable income	$20,000
Net federal tax @ 22.12%	$ 4,424
Less: investment tax credit	(4,424)
Net federal tax payable under Part I	Nil

(C) The remaining investment tax credit of $5,576 (i.e., $10,000 – $4,424) may be carried back three and forward 20 years.

(D)

UCC in Class 8 before CCA in first year	$100,000
Less: CCA claimed in first year	(10,000)
UCC at beginning of second year	$ 90,000
Less: ITC claimed in first year	(4,424)
UCC before CCA in second year	$ 85,576
Less: CCA claimed in second year	(17,115)
UCC balance after CCA	$ 68,461

Note that any investment tax credit for depreciable property carried over to another year and used to reduce tax in that year will reduce the undepreciated capital cost balance in the year following the year of use or the year following the purchase, whichever is later. This will occur until the remaining investment tax credit is fully utilized or expires. The undepreciated capital cost balance will not be reduced by expired investment tax credits. Under certain conditions, it may be worthwhile to deduct no capital cost allowance in order to be able to claim more investment tax credit that would otherwise expire. However, the facts of each case must be analyzed carefully.

¶11,355 Qualified scientific research expenditure

¶11,355.10 *Overview*

Scientific research and experimental development expenditures are very generously treated by Canadian tax legislation. Not only is there a potential 100% write-off of qualifying expenditures and equipment, but there is also a 20% investment tax credit available. In addition, many of the provincial governments provide additional incentives for SR&ED expenditures. In the next chapter it will be shown that certain qualifying Canadian-controlled private corporations benefit from an even greater "specified percentage" and a potential refund for unclaimed ITCs.

ITA: 37

¶11,355.20 *Qualified SR&ED expenditure*

"Qualified expenditure" is defined to include scientific research and experimental development expenditures on new property and described in the Act as current expenditures and capital expenditures. Excluded are prescribed expenditures listed in the Regulations. Note that the Act excludes any capital expenditure made in respect of a building, including a leasehold interest (other than a prescribed special purpose building). The definition also excludes any rental expense incurred for a building (other than a prescribed special purpose building). The provision further excludes payments made to others to enable the recipient to acquire a building or a leasehold interest in a building.

ITA: 127(9); ITR: 2903
ITA: 37(1)(*a*), 37(1)(*b*)
ITR: 2902
ITA: 37(8)(*d*)

¶11,355.30   *Application*

In the taxation year following the year in which an ITC deduction is made, the amount of the ITC claimed is deducted from the pool of unclaimed SR&ED expenditures. Remember that both current and capital expenditures that are eligible SR&ED expenditures are either written off in the year of the expenditure or placed in a pool of unclaimed expenditures. Therefore, for capital expenditures that are eligible SR&ED expenditures there is no capital cost from which the ITC could be deducted; hence, the deduction reduces the unclaimed SR&ED expenditure pool. Where this pool is nil, then there would be an income inclusion.   ITA: 12(1)(*t*)

Example Problem

In 2007, Developit Limited incurred $100,000 of qualified scientific research and experimental development expenditures eligible for the 20% investment tax credit. The corporation's federal income tax rate after the abatement and the general rate reduction is 22.12%. Its taxable income before the deduction of the SR&ED expenditures under section 37 is $150,000.

The corporation is not eligible for any other tax credits and paid no tax in the preceding three years.

— *REQUIRED*

(A) What is the maximum investment tax credit available?

(B) Compute the net federal Part I tax payable after the investment tax credit.

(C) What is the amount, if any, of the investment tax credit carryover?

(D) Compute the corporation's deduction or income included in the following year if no further SR&ED expenditures are made.

— *SOLUTION*

(A) The maximum investment tax credit is:
20% of $100,000 = $20,000

(B) Taxable income before sec. 37 deduction	$150,000
Sec. 37 deduction	(100,000)
Taxable income	$ 50,000
Net tax @ 22.12%	$ 11,060
Investment tax credit (maximum)	(11,060)
Net federal tax payable under Part I	Nil

(C) The remaining investment tax credit of $8,940 (i.e., $20,000 –$11,060) may be carried back three years and forward 10 years. In this particular case, the corporation paid no tax in the preceding three years, so it must carry the balance of ITC forward.

(D) Sec. 37 SR&ED expenditures in 2007	$100,000
Sec. 37 SR&ED deduction in 2007	(100,000)
Balance at the beginning of 2008	Nil
ITC claimed in 2007	(11,060)
Recapture in 2008	11,060
Balance of ITC claimed in 2007	Nil

ITA: 12(1)(*t*)

As the remaining ITC of $8,940 is claimed in a carryforward year, the amount claimed must be brought into income, as recapture, in the year following the year of claim.

Had there been a balance of the $100,000 that was not deducted under section 37, the balance would form a pool of SR&ED expenditures which could be deducted in a future year. Where a balance in the SR&ED pool exists, the amount claimed as ITC in a year is deducted from the balance in the SR&ED pool in the following year.

¶11,355.40   *Prescribed proxy amount*

Where business overhead expenses can be allocated to scientific research and experimental development costs, such overhead expenses will be included in the base on which the 20% investment tax credit for SR&ED expenditures is calculated. In a situation where a business is unable to allocate overhead expenses to SR&ED, the investment tax credit base would be relatively lower, resulting in a lower investment tax credit. As an alternative to allocating overhead expenses, for the purposes of computing the investment tax credit, use of a prescribed proxy amount (PPA) is permitted. The PPA is computed by a formula, provided in the Regulations, which is based on salaries paid to employees directly engaged in SR&ED in Canada. Use of the PPA method to account for overhead expenses in the calculation of the SR&ED investment tax credit must be elected annually. A more elaborate discussion of the PPA method and an example in which the calculation is demonstrated is presented in Chapter 12, where the application of the SR&ED investment tax credit to Canadian-controlled private corporations is discussed. However, it should be recognized that the PPA election is available to all taxpayers eligible for a SR&ED investment tax credit.

ITA: 127(9) "qualified expenditure" (b)
ITR: 2900(4), 2900(5)

ITA: 127(5)

¶11,360   ITC for Apprenticeship Expenditures

The apprenticeship expenditure ITC is provided to encourage employers to hire new apprentices in eligible trades. Employers receive a non-refundable tax credit equal to 10% of the salaries and wages paid to "eligible apprentices". "Eligible salary and wages" are defined to include the amounts paid to an eligible apprentice in respect of the first 24 months of the apprenticeship. Excluded from the definition is remuneration that is based on profits, bonuses, fringe benefits, and stock options. The maximum credit is $2,000 per apprentice per year. Unused credits may be carried back 3 years and forward 20 years to reduce federal income taxes otherwise payable.

ITA: 127(11.1)
ITA: 127(9) "eligible apprentice"

Special rules apply where an apprentice works for two or more related employers to limit the credit to $2,000. In essence, one corporation in a related group must be designated as the employer of an eligible apprentice who is employed by more than one corporation in the group.

ITA: 127(11.4)

An eligible apprentice is one who is working in a qualifying trade in the first two years of his or her provincially registered apprenticeship contract with an eligible employer. The qualifying trades are prescribed in the Regulations and include the 45 trades currently included in the Red Seal trades, which allow a journey person to engage in his or her trade in any province or territory in Canada where the trade is recognized.

¶11,370   [ITC for Child Care Spaces]

[The March 19, 2007 federal budget proposed to implement an ITC for taxpayers, other than taxpayers in the business of providing child care services, who create child care spaces for their employees and for the surrounding community. The amount of the ITC is equal to:

the lesser of:

(a) $10,000, and

(b) 25% of the taxpayer's eligible expenditures in respect of the child care space.

An "eligible expenditure" will be defined to be an expenditure incurred for the sole purpose of the creation of a new child care space in a licensed child care facility operated for the benefit of children of the employees of the taxpayer and other children. Specifically, eligible expenditures will include:

- the cost of depreciable property, other than a motor vehicle or property attached to a residence of certain individuals who are owners or employees of the taxpayer's business, and

- a "specified child care start-up cost", including:
  — landscaping to create an outdoor play area for children,

— initial fees for licensing, regulatory, and building permits,
— architectural fees for designing the child care facility, and
— children's educational material.

A provision will recapture the ITC claimed on an eligible expenditure if there is a disposition of the property included in an eligible expenditure or if the child care space ceases to be available within five calendar years after the creation of the space.]

¶11,800   REVIEW QUESTIONS

(1) Mr. Confused has been trying to prepare the corporate tax returns for his company and cannot seem to get the treatment of charitable donations sorted out. He cannot find the place to put the tax credit for the donations and he is not sure what the limits are. Can you help him?

(2) If a company finds that it has non-capital loss carryovers that are going to expire in the next few years, what tax planning steps can be taken to use up some of these losses without selling the company or buying another company?

(3) Mr. Jones has just bought all of the shares of a company that has some net capital losses being carried forward as well as accrued capital losses on some of its assets. What happens to them? Is there any relief?

(4) There are two basic types of restrictions on losses available for carryover. What are these restrictions and how do they affect the application of losses?

(5) Mr. Magoo bought all the shares of Profitco Ltd. on July 1 of this year, and is expecting to combine the profitable operations of Profitco with the loss operations of his current corporation. However, for Profitco's deemed year-end of June 30, he hopes to offset the six months of profitable operations with a full year of CCA in order to minimize the tax liability. Profitco's normal year-end was December 31. Comment on his plan.

(6) What are the three main objectives of tax provisions affecting the taxation of corporations?

(7) MultiCo Inc. has permanent establishments in Ontario and Alberta. The Alberta operation normally accounted for 20% of the allocation of taxable income. However, in the current year, a salesman in Ontario sold a large order to a customer in Alberta and the goods were shipped directly from Ontario. How does this special sale impact the allocation to Alberta?

(8) Since residents of Canada are taxable on their world income, why does Canada give a foreign tax credit for taxes paid to another country?

(9) In the calculation of non-business foreign tax credit the "tax otherwise payable" calculation is reduced by the 10% federal abatement. Why?

(10) Lossco Inc. has a loss from operations for the year while at the same time earning interest of $5,000 from the U.S. on which $750 of tax was withheld. How can Lossco treat the $750 of foreign tax paid on its tax return?

¶11,825   MULTIPLE CHOICE QUESTIONS

Question 1

Helen acquired all of the voting shares of Lossco from a non-related individual on February 1, 2007. Lossco has always had a December 31 year-end since its incorporation. Which one of the following statements is TRUE?

(A) Lossco had a deemed year-end February 1, 2007.

(B) Lossco may select any date, within the 53-week period commencing February 1, 2007, as its new year-end.

(C) Lossco must continue to have a December 31 year-end unless the CRA grants permission for a change.

(D) Lossco had a deemed year-end on January 31, 2007 and is required to keep January 31 as its year-end for the future.

Question 2

Jim acquired control of Smart Ltd. from an unrelated person on May 15, 2007. The following information relates to the inventory and capital assets owned by Smart Ltd. at that time.

	Cost	FMV
Inventory	$120,000	$100,000
Land	200,000	140,000
Building	100,000	75,000
Marketable securities	20,000	30,000

For its taxation year ended on May 14, 2007, Smart Ltd. is required to recognize a capital loss of:

(A) $85,000

(B) $80,000

(C) $60,000

(D) $50,000

Question 3

On April 1, 2007, Calm Corp purchased 72% of the voting shares of X Ltd. from an unrelated person. The tax position of the fixed assets of X Ltd. at that time is summarized below.

	Cost	UCC	FMV
Automobiles (Class 10)	$100,000	$ 42,000	$45,000
Computer equipment (Class 45)	64,000	38,000	33,000
Computer software (Class 12)	30,000	Nil	5,000
Office furniture & equipment (Class 8)	80,000	58,000	48,000

The business loss of X Ltd. for the year ended March 31, 2007, will be increased by deemed CCA of:

(A) $7,000

(B) $10,800

(C) $15,000

(D) $23,000

Question 4

For its year ended December 31, 2006, its first year-end since its incorporation, Lossco reported the following income (losses) for tax purposes.

| Business loss (retailer of widgets) .... | $ (20,000) |
| Capital loss .... | (6,000) |

On January 1, 2007, Profitco acquired control of Lossco from an unrelated person and transferred its profitable gadget retailing business to Lossco. For its year ending December 31, 2007, Lossco is expected to have the following income/losses.

Business loss (widgets)	$(3,000)
Business income (gadgets)	15,000
Taxable capital gain on sale of capital asset in March 2006	
(capital asset was owned since March 2005)	6,000

Assuming widgets and gadgets are similar products, which one of the following statements is TRUE?

(A) For its year ending December 31, 2007, Lossco will be able to deduct net capital losses of $3,000, provided the widget retailing business is carried on throughout the taxation year ended December 31, 2007 with a reasonable expectation of profit.

(B) For its year ending December 31, 2007, Lossco will be able to deduct non-capital losses of $18,000 (maximum), provided the widget retailing business is carried on throughout the taxation year ended December 31, 2007, with a reasonable expectation of profit.

(C) For its year ending December 31, 2007, Lossco will be able to deduct non-capital losses of $12,000 (maximum), provided the widget retailing business is carried on throughout the taxation year ended December 31, 2007, with a reasonable expectation of profit.

(D) For its year ending December 31, 2007, Lossco will be able to deduct non-capital losses of $15,000 (maximum), provided the widget retailing business is carried on throughout the taxation year ended December 31, 2007, with a reasonable expectation of profit.

Question 5

During 2007, Curran Ltd, a public corporation, has net income for tax purposes of $600,000, including $100,000 of dividends from taxable Canadian corporations and $250,000 of manufacturing and processing profits all of which is eligible for the M&P deduction. It made $200,000 of charitable donations during the year. Income earned in a province was 90%.

What is Curran Ltd's taxable income for the year?

(A) $600,000

(B) $500,000

(C) $400,000

(D) $300,000

Question 6

Refer to the facts given in Question 5 above. What is Curran Ltd.'s federal tax payable for the year?

(A) $51,860

(B) $68,520

(C) $69,360

(D) $72,860

¶11,825

¶11,850 EXERCISES

Exercise 1

ITA: 110.1, 111

Generous Limited has income (loss) under Division B of $(7,350) in 2006, $22,050 in 2007, and $14,700 in 2008. During this period it made donations to registered charities of $2,625 in 2006, $4,700 in 2007, and $12,000 in 2008. It also made a donation of ecologically sensitive land valued at $19,700 to the Government of Canada in 2007. The company began operations in 2006.

— *REQUIRED*

Compute the corporation's taxable income for the years indicated.

Exercise 2

ITA: 110.1, 111

Determined Limited predicts, with reasonable accuracy, its income under Division B before capital cost allowances will be: $100,000 in 2005, $115,000 in 2006, and $132,250 in 2007. Capital cost allowances available are expected to be $200,000 in 2005, $170,000 in 2006, and $150,000 in 2007. It made charitable donations of $10,000 in 2001 and $11,500 in 2002, which it could not absorb before 2005.

— *REQUIRED*

How can the company maximize its charitable donation deduction while minimizing the taxes it pays in the period shown? (Hint: Take advantage of the loss carryover rules.)

Exercise 3

ITA: 111(8)

Losses Unlimited Limited has computed the following income (loss) for the year ended December 31, 2007:

Loss from business	$(129,000)
Income from property including dividends of $10,750 received from taxable Canadian corporations	32,250
Capital gains	46,400
Capital losses	(12,000)
Business investment loss	(16,000)

The corporation has a net capital loss of $27,000 arising from 2001.

— *REQUIRED*

Compute the corporation's non-capital loss for the year.

Exercise 4

ITA: 111(8)

Capital Losses Limited had a large allowable capital loss of $51,750 on one transaction during its taxation year ended December 31, 2007. In addition, the following information pertains to its situation for the year:

Income from business	$155,250
Income from property	17,000
Taxable capital gain	4,700
Allowable business investment loss (not included in above allowable capital loss)	(8,300)

— *REQUIRED*

Compute the corporation's net capital loss for the year.

Exercise 5

ITA: 111(1), 111(1.1)

Given income from business of $55,500 and a taxable capital gain of $37,000 in 2007, how much of the following losses will be available for carryforward after this year:

Non-capital losses (expiring beyond 2007)	$82,500?
Net capital losses (1999)	$60,000?

Exercise 6

ITA: 111(4), 111(5),
111(5.1), 111(5.2)

All of the voting shares of Loser Limited, a manufacturer of widgets, have been acquired by Holdco Ltd., an investment holding company. At the time of the acquisition on March 10, 2007, Loser Limited had non-capital business losses of $600,000 generated in 2006. Loser Limited also had $30,000 of net capital losses carried forward from 1999. As well, at the time of the acquisition, it was discovered that the balance of undepreciated capital cost in its Class 8 was $70,000 while the fair market value of the assets in that class was only $40,000. The balance in its cumulative eligible capital account (being from the acquisition on August 31, 2006, of an exclusive customer list) was $50,000 while the fair market value of the customer list was $68,000. The corporation's inventory had a cost of $630,000, while its market value was $680,000. The book value of the corporation's receivables was $240,000, while its realizable value was estimated at $225,000. The corporation's only non-depreciable capital property, land, had accrued gains of $56,000 over its cost of $200,000. Loser Limited has a December 31 year-end.

The corporation had business losses of $3,000 from January 1 to March 9, 2007.

The holding company will inject added capital and augment the management of Loser Limited in an attempt to turn Loser's widget manufacturing business around.

— *REQUIRED*

(A) What are the tax implications of the acquisition of the shares of Loser Limited by Holdco Ltd., assuming the maximum election under paragraph 111(4)(*e*) is made?

(B) Determine the minimum amount of elected proceeds under paragraph 111(4)(*e*) to offset expiring losses, if the accrued gains on the land were $100,000 instead of the $56,000 and Loser Limited had an additional loss arising from property of $10,000.

Exercise 7

ITA: 3, 110.1–112

Reconsider the example problem of Frenzied Taxpayers Limited in this chapter at page 578. If $7,900 less capital cost allowance had been taken in 2006, all $23,000 of the inter-company dividends could have been deducted, pursuant to section 112, in 2006.

— *REQUIRED*

Re-calculate the taxable income of the corporation for the years indicated after taking $7,900 less in capital cost allowance for Class 8 in 2006. Comment on whether the corporation is in a better tax position at the end of 2007 with respect to capital cost allowance and taxable income under this alternative.

Exercise 8

ITA: 110.1, 111, 112

Puttingitall Together Limited, a Canadian corporation, had its net income under Division B computed as follows for the year ending December 31:

Par. 3(*a*)	Income from non-capital sources:	
	Income from business operations	$ 66,625
	Income from foreign property	7,175
	Dividends from taxable Canadian	
	corporations	12,300
Par. 3(*b*)	Net taxable capital gains	30,750
Income under Division B		$116,850

During the year the corporation made charitable donations of $80,000. Its carryforward position from the previous year was as follows:

Charitable donations	$10,250
Non-capital losses	61,500
Net capital losses (realized in 1999)	41,000

— *REQUIRED*

Compute the corporation's taxable income for the current year.

Exercise 9

ITA: 126

Exporter Limited is a Canadian public company carrying on a part of its business through an unincorporated branch in Japan. Its income from that business in Japan for the current taxation year

ended December 31 was 77,575,723 yen. The corporation paid income tax insta·
during the year of 31,006,289 yen. During the year the exchange rate was i
dollars.

During its current taxation year ended December 31, Exporter's income u
$2,500,000 excluding the income from Japan. During the year, the corporation re
$100,000 from taxable Canadian corporations. This amount was included in the co.
sion B income. The corporation was also able to deduct $25,000 of its net capital losses u
There was no foreign investment income during the year.

— REQUIRED

Compute the corporation's foreign business tax credit for the year.

Exercise 10

Maxprof Limited is a Canadian public company with the following income under Division B for its
taxation year ended December 31, 2007:

Manufacturing profits (all eligible for M&P profits deduction)	$1,495,000
Foreign business profits (before $36,800 in taxes paid)	115,000
Dividends from taxable Canadian corporations	517,500
Dividends from foreign investments (before $25,875 in taxes withheld)	172,500
Canadian interest income (investment income)	345,000
Income under Division B	$2,645,000

During the year the company made donations of $69,000 to registered charities and $5,750 to
federal political parties. It was carrying forward non-capital losses of $127,600. It is considered to earn
86% of its taxable income in Canada, as computed by the Regulation.

— REQUIRED

Compute the federal Part I tax payable for the year.

Exercise 11

ITA: 127

Consider the following data:

Cost of qualified property eligible for investment tax credit in Nova Scotia	$900,000
Capital cost allowance class (rate)	Class 1 (4%)
Taxable income before capital cost allowance on above	$300,000
Federal tax rate after abatement, surtax and reduction	22.12%
Federal political contributions tax credit	$500

— REQUIRED

Compute the amount of the investment tax credit that will be deductible for the year and the net
federal Part I tax payable after the investment tax credit.

Exercise 12

ITA: 110–112, 123, 125.1, 126, 127, 127.1

Reconsider the data in Exercise 10. Assume that "qualified property" for Class 43 has been
purchased in the Atlantic provinces for $3,500,000 in the year. Also, assume that manufacturing profits
given as $1,495,000 in Exercise 10 will be reduced by capital cost allowance on this new property to
equal the amount eligible for the M&P profits deduction.

— REQUIRED

Compute the maximum investment tax credit deduction for the year.

¶11,875 ASSIGNMENT PROBLEMS

ablem 1

ITA: 3, 110.1–112

The following data summarize the operations of Red Pocket Limited for the years of 2004 to 2007 ded September 30.

	2004	2005	2006	2007
Income (loss) from business	$54,000	$32,000	$(75,000)	$62,500
Dividend income — Taxable Canadian corporations	42,500	22,500	18,000	10,500
Taxable capital gains	11,000	2,500	5,000	9,000
Allowable capital losses	2,000	4,500	3,500	—
Allowable business investment loss	3,750	—	—	—
Charitable donations	23,000	9,000	3,000	13,000

The corporation has a net capital loss balance of $13,500 which arose in 1999.

—REQUIRED

Compute the taxable income for Red Pocket Limited for the years indicated and show the amounts that are available for carryforward to 2008. (Deal with each item line-by-line across the years, rather than computing income one year at a time.)

Problem 2

ITA: 111(4), 111(5), 111(5.1), 249(4)

On November 1, 2007, Chris purchased all the issued shares of Transtek Inc. from an acquaintance, Tom. Transtek carries on a transmission repair business and has done so since its incorporation on January 1, 2006. In addition to the transmission repair business, Transtek rents out a small building it owns. Neither the transmission repair business nor the rental endeavour has been successful.

When Chris purchased Transtek, his financial projections indicated that Transtek would have significant income within two years. Chris credited Transtek's failure to Tom's brash personality and laziness. Chris, on the other hand, has a strong work ethic and has many contacts in the automotive industry to refer work to him.

The values of the capital assets owned by Transtek at the time of purchase by Chris are as follows:

	Repair shop		Rental property	
	Land	Building	Land	Building
FMV	$140,000	$230,000	$70,000	$120,000
Cost/ACB	80,000	150,000	90,000	120,000
UCC	—	147,000	—	120,000

Chris selected June 30, 2008, as the first fiscal year-end for Transtek after his purchase. The following is a schedule of Transtek's income (and losses) from its inception, January 1, 2006, through June 30, 2009.

Period	Transmission repair business	Rental income (loss)	Capital Loss
Jan. 1/2006–Dec. 31/2006	$(40,000)	$(2,000)	$(10,000)
Jan. 1/2007–Oct. 31/2007	(60,000)	(5,000)	—
Nov. 1/2007–June 30/2008	(25,000)	6,000	—
July 1/2008–June 30/2009	54,000	11,000	—

—REQUIRED

(A) Discuss the tax implications of the acquisition of Transtek Inc. on November 1, 2007, ignoring all possible elections/options.

(B) Determine the tax consequences of the acquisition of Transtek Inc. under the assumption that:

(i) the maximum amount of all elections/options is utilized; and

(ii) the partial amount of all elections/options is utilized so that only enough income is generated to offset most or all of the losses which would otherwise expire on the acquisition of control.

Problem 3

ITA: 111(4), 111(5), 111(5.1), 249(4)

In 2006, a chain of bakeries, called Buscat Ltd., commenced operation. The industry is highly competitive and because of Mr. Buscat's lack of marketing skills, the corporation incurred losses in the first three taxation years of operations as follows:

Taxation year-end	Non-capital losses	Capital losses
Dec. 31, 2006	$60,000	$12,000
Dec. 31, 2007	45,000	8,000
Dec. 31, 2008	25,000	4,000

On July 1, 2009, Mr. Buscat decided to sell 75% of his common shares to Mr. Bran, owner of Buns Plus Ltd. Mr. Bran has been in the business of supplying bread dough, pastry dough and bun bags for 10 years and has been very successful. Buns Plus Ltd. has two divisions: a bakery and a coffee shop, which it intends to transfer to Buscat Ltd.

The following income tax data relates to Buscat Limited's operations from January 1, 2009 to June 30, 2009:

(a) Business loss (before inventory valuation) $10,000
(b) Allowable capital loss 2,000
(c) Property loss 5,500
(d) Assets at June 30, 2009:

	Cost/ACB	UCC	FMV
Inventory	$ 85,000	—	$ 65,000
Land	155,000	—	195,000
Building (Class 1)	65,000	$45,000	75,000
Bakery equipment	100,000	86,000	70,000

During the later part of the 2009 calendar year, the bakery/coffee shop of Buns Plus Ltd. was transferred to Buscat Ltd. For the six-month period ending on December 31, 2009, Buscat Limited had net income of $90,000 from all its businesses.

The net income earned was as follows:

Buscat bakery	$(55,000)
Buns Plus bakery	130,000
Coffee shop	15,000
	$ 90,000

In the 2010 taxation year, Buscat Ltd. expects to earn $250,000, of which $65,000 will be from the original Buscat bakery business and $20,000 from the coffee shop business.

— *REQUIRED*

Prepare an analysis of the income tax implications of the acquisition of shares. In your analysis, consider the two election options from which an election choice is most likely to be made.

Problem 4

ITA: 9–20, 38–55, 110.1–112

The controller of Video Madness Inc. has prepared the accounting income statement for the year ended April 30, 2007:

VIDEO MADNESS INC.

INCOME STATEMENT

FOR THE YEAR ENDED APRIL 30, 2007

Sales		$995,000
Cost of sales	$523,000	
Administrative expenses	185,000	708,000
Operating income		$287,000
Other income and expenses		55,000
		$342,000
Provision for income taxes		102,000
Net income		$240,000

Other Information

(1) Included in the calculation of "Administrative expenses":
   (a) Interest on late income tax payments .... $ 435
   (b) Depreciation and amortization (maximum capital cost
       allowance of $149,500) 104,900
   (c) Club dues for the local Country Club 1,750
   (d) Federal political contributions 2,500
   (e) Donations to registered charities 22,500
   (f) Property tax with respect to vacant land not being used
       in the course of the business 3,000
   (g) Life insurance premium with respect to the president
       (the company is the beneficiary; not required for financing) 1,950

(2) Included in the calculation of "Other income and expenses":
   (a) Landscaping of ground around new premise 4,800
   (b) Fees paid with respect to the investigation of a suitable site for the
       company's manufacturing plant 5,500
   (c) Dividends received from taxable Canadian corporation of $42,800 and
       foreign corporation dividends received (not from a foreign affiliate) of
       C$5,500 48,300
   (d) Gain from the sale of another piece of land, used in the business, sold
       for $200,000 in March (purchased for $73,800) 126,200
   (e) Loss on sale of investments held as capital property purchased for
       $85,000 and sold for $75,000 10,000

(3) Loss carryforwards from 2006 are:
   (a) Non-capital losses 73,800
   (b) Net capital losses (realized in 1999) 75,000

— *REQUIRED*

Prepare a schedule reconciling the accounting net income to income for tax purposes and taxable income. Indicate the appropriate statutory reference for your inclusions or exclusions.

Problem 5

ITA: 124; ITR: 400

The taxpayer, whose head office was in Manitoba, manufactured and sold various fans. Local sales agencies were maintained in Ontario and in Quebec. At the Ontario agency, two qualified representatives handled business under the company name. They were authorized to sign quotations. Contracts could be made, terms of payment arranged and credit given without reference to the head office in Winnipeg. The company name was displayed for public visibility, was used on calling cards, and was listed in the telephone directory. The Ontario agency, occupying one-half of a building with warehouse facilities, maintained an inventory worth about $6,000. Orders for standard-sized fans were filled from stock-in-trade. Orders for large fans were filled from the head office in Winnipeg. The Quebec agency was substantially similar to that in Ontario.

— *REQUIRED*

Determine whether or not the company has a "permanent establishment" in the provinces of Ontario and Quebec. In reaching a conclusion, compare this situation with the case of *M.N.R. v.* *Sunbeam* discussed in this chapter.

61 DTC 1063 (Ex. Ct.)

Problem 6

ITA: 123, 124, 126

Barltrop Limited is a Canadian public company involved in the software consulting business. Its controller provided you with the following information related to its 2007 taxation year ended December 31:

Income under Division B from consulting business including $100,000 earned in U.S. operations (before deducting $16,000 U.S. tax paid)	$264,000
Canadian investment royalty income	10,000
U.K. non-foreign affiliate income (before $3,000 tax withheld)	20,000
Taxable dividend received from non-connected Canadian corporations	5,000
Taxable capital gains...	6,000
Charitable donations	100,000
Unused foreign tax credit in respect of U.S........................	3,000
Net capital losses carried forward arising in 1999	12,000

Barltrop Limited has permanent establishments in the U.S., B.C. and Alberta. Its gross revenues and salaries and wages data have been allocated as follows:

	British Columbia	*Alberta*	*U.S.*
Gross revenues...............	$3,000,000	$3,000,000	$4,000,000
Salaries and wages..............	500,000	300,000	200,000

Assume that the British Columbia corporation tax rate is 12% and the Alberta rate is 10%. Also, assume that taxable income for Alberta is computed on the same basis as federal taxable income.

Gross revenues exclude income from property not used in connection with the principal business operation of the corporation.

— REQUIRED

Compute the total tax payable by the company for the 2007 taxation year, including provincial tax. Show all calculations.

Problem 7

ITA: 12(1)(*t*), 37, 127(5)–(11); ITR: 2900

Infotech is a public company in its first year of business in the information technology industry. It operates out of a plant in Ottawa, Ontario. In 2007, it incurred $2,200,000 of scientific research and experimental development expenditures (SR&ED) which qualify for deduction under subsection 37(1) of the Act. The breakdown of these expenses is as follows:

Current SR&ED expenditures			$1,700,000
Capital SR&ED expenditures			
• new equipment		$300,000	
• used equipment		200,000	500,000
Total SR&ED expenditures			$2,200,000

ITA: 37(1)(*a*)
ITA: 37(1)(*b*)

Infotech's federal income tax rate after abatement is 22.12%. Its taxable income before deducting the $2,200,000 claim under section 37 is $3,200,000.

— REQUIRED

(A) Compute the maximum investment tax credit available to Infotech in 2007.

(B) Compute the company's net federal Part I tax payable after the investment tax credit, assuming a maximum section 37 deduction is claimed.

(C) What is the amount, if any, of the investment tax credit carryover?

(D) Compute the company's deduction or income inclusion in the following year if no further SR&ED expenditures are made.

Problem 8

ITA: 123, 124, 125.1, 126, 127(5)

Up, Up and Away Limited is a public corporation that manufactures hot air balloons in the province of New Brunswick. For the year ended September 30, 2007, its accounting income statement was as follows:

Sales	$1,225,000
Cost of sales and other expenses including CCA	(725,000)
Operating profit..	$ 500,000
Other net income	198,500
Net income before taxes	$ 698,500
Provision for taxes	(200,725)
Net income	$ 497,775

Selected Additional Information

(1) Other income includes:

Dividends from taxable Canadian corporation	$ 85,000
Canadian interest income	52,500
Foreign interest income, net of withholding taxes of $10,000	61,000

(2) Up, Up and Away Limited has a non-capital loss carryforward of $255,545.

(3) Up, Up and Away Limited purchased qualified equipment costing $250,000 which is eligible for the investment tax credit.

(4) The M&P profits tax reduction has been correctly computed as $25,757.

(5) Donations to registered charities were $9,755 (deducted from accounting income).

— *REQUIRED*

Calculate the total taxes payable for 2007 using a 13% provincial rate of tax.

Problem 9

ITA: 123, 124, 125.1, 126, 127(5)

Tecniquip Limited is a public corporation whose head office is located in Toronto, Ontario. The activities of the corporation are carried on through permanent establishments in the provinces of Ontario and Alberta, and in the United States.

The following is an allocation of selected items for the fiscal year ended December 31, 2007.

	Ontario ($ '000)	Alberta ($ '000)	U.S. ($ '000)	Total ($ '000)
Sales	$ 6,000	$ 400	$ 4,600	$11,000
Salaries	$ 2,540	$ 960	$ 2,360	$ 5,860

For the year ended December 31, 2007, Tecniquip Limited obtained the following results:

Income from manufacturing operations in Ontario	$1,000,000
Income from manufacturing operations in Alberta	240,000
Income from manufacturing operations in the United States (before C$200,000 of US taxes paid)	800,000
	$2,040,000
Canadian-source interest income (investment)	12,000
Foreign-source investment income (before $3,000 in foreign tax withheld)	20,000
Taxable capital gain	10,000
Taxable dividends from taxable Canadian corporations	15,000
Net income under Division B	$2,097,000

In computing income from manufacturing, the corporation claimed a deduction of $150,000 under subsection 37(1) of the Act for scientific research and experimental development (SR&ED). $100,000 of the deduction related to expenditures of a current nature and $50,000 was the cost of equipment purchased during the year for use by it in scientific research and experimental development carried on in Canada. No SR&ED expenditures are expected to be made in 2008.

During the year, the corporation made charitable donations totalling $50,000 and claimed non-capital losses of $60,000 and the net capital losses carried forward from 1999 of $9,000.

The M&P profits tax deduction has been correctly computed as $67,529.

— *REQUIRED*

Compute the federal Part I tax payable and provincial tax at 12% for Ontario and 10% for Alberta, assuming that taxable income allocated to those provinces is the appropriate provincial tax base. Show all calculations, whether or not necessary to your final answer.

[For more problems and solutions thereto, see the CD accompanying this book.]

¶11,880   ADVISORY CASE

King Enterprises Inc.

Ian King has operated a successful office supply wholesaling business, King Enterprises Inc., for many years. Last week, he called to tell you that he is interested in putting an offer in on the shares of a company that is in some financial difficulty, Royal Forms Inc. ("Royal").

Royal is in the business of producing custom, as well as standard, forms for business use. In fact, Royal is a supplier of King Enterprises. This company has been in business for the past eight years, but has been losing money for the past six years. Last year they sold the land and building they used in their operations in a depressed real estate market, in order to get some cash. Their big problem seems to be that they are undercapitalized.

Ian sees this purchase as a real opportunity for him to pick up a company at a bargain price, turn it around to profitability and, at the same time, reduce King Enterprises' tax liability with the losses. He would like you to prepare a report for him on the tax issues before he decides whether to make an offer.

¶11,900 SUPPLEMENTAL NOTES

(This section of the text can be omitted without losing the continuity of the chapter. None of review questions, multiple choice questions, exercises, or assignment problems utilizes this information.)

¶11,910 Manufacturing and Processing Profits Deduction

¶11,915 Introduction

This deduction from tax (i.e., a tax credit) is a tax incentive to all incorporated Canadian manufacturing and processing businesses taxable in Canada. The provision operates to reduce the net rate of federal tax, after the federal abatement, on manufacturing and processing (M&P) income to 21% (without the effect of surtax in 2007). In general, the reduced rate of tax applies to the lesser of the corporation's Canadian manufacturing and processing profits (a specifically defined term) and the portion of the corporation's taxable income considered to be derived from eligible manufacturing and processing activities. The base for this deduction excludes manufacturing and processing profits eligible for the small business deduction, discussed in the next chapter. Exhibit 11-4 summarizes the provisions as they would apply to a corporation that is not a Canadian-controlled private corporation.

ITA: 125.1(1)(*a*)

ITA: 125.1(1)

EXHIBIT 11-5
Manufacturing and Processing Profits Deduction
for Public Corporations

7% (i.e., the rate equal to the general rate reduction for 2007) of lesser of:

(a) manufacturing and processing profits, and

(b) taxable income, less 3* times the foreign business tax deduction [ssec. 126(2)] (computed without reference to the general rate reduction).

---

* [Proposed in Bill C-33, tabled on November 22, 2006.]

Exhibit 11-6 illustrates how the manufacturing and processing profit deduction affects the calculation of effective total corporate tax introduced in Exhibit 11-3.

EXHIBIT 11-6
Hypothetical Tax Rates applicable to Taxable Income
eligible for Provincial Manufacturing and Processing Profits Deduction

---

Federal tax rate [ssec. 123(1)]	38.00%
Abatement for provincial tax [ssec. 124(1)]	(10.00)
Net federal tax after abatement	28.00%
Federal surtax @ 4% of above net federal tax of 28% [sec. 123.2]	1.12
M&P deduction [par. 125.1(1)(*a*)]	(7.00)
Net federal tax	22.12%
Provincial tax (assumed)*	11.00
Effective total tax	33.12%

---

* Some provinces have a reduced tax rate for M&P profits.

Note that the net federal tax at 22.12% is the same as that shown in Exhibit 11-3 after the general rate reduction in 2007. The only difference in rates results from a lower provincial rate where a province provides for an M&P deduction.

¶11,920 Eligibility

Corporations with income from a manufacturing or processing business qualify if gross revenues from Canadian manufacturing and processing exceed 10% of gross revenue from all Canadian active businesses. The term "manufacturing and processing" is not defined in the Act. Thus, the general meaning of the term as modified by case law applies. The term "manufacture" has been interpreted to mean the application of physical labour or mechanical power. The CRA indicates that the manufacture of goods normally involves "the creation of something or the shaping, stamping or forming of an object from something".

ITA: 125.1(3) "manufacturing or processing" par. (l)

IT-145R

"Processing" implies the use of some raw material to begin with. The ordinary meaning of the word (from a dictionary) would appear to include most food service establishments in terms of food preparation (but not serving) and packaging. The CRA views packaging and wrapping activities as "processing" provided that they are carried on in conjunction with other manufacturing and processing activities. Breaking bulk and repackaging are generally considered processing. Thus, processing appears to include all of those operations which render a product more usable, that is, more marketable.

IT-145R

The following are some examples of cases in which the meaning of the term "manufacturing or processing" has been addressed. In *Nova Scotia Sand and Gravel Ltd. v. M.N.R.*, the Federal Court of Appeal held that excavating and extracting gravel for sale constituted manufacturing and processing. Intercepting and distributing a television signal was held not to be processing of goods in *London Cable TV v. M.N.R.* However, packaging of potatoes and carrots after various preparatory steps was held to be processing in *Federal Farms Ltd. v. M.N.R.*, and slitting, levelling, and shearing of steel was held to be processing in *Admiral Steel Products Ltd. v. M.N.R.* In *Mother's Pizza Parlour et al. v. The Queen*, the Federal Court of Appeal held that a restaurant building was not used primarily for the preparation of food and, hence, was not used in a processing activity.

80 DTC 6298 (F.C.A.)

76 DTC 1328 (T.R.B.)
66 DTC 5068 (Ex. Ct.)
66 DTC 174 (T.R.B.)
88 DTC 6397 (F.C.A.)

The Act specifically lists in the definition of "manufacturing or processing" 12 activities that are not considered to be "manufacturing or processing". Note how an exception to the negative definition of manufacturing or processing can be used such that, for example, processing of iron ore beyond the pellet stage is considered to be manufacturing or processing. Furthermore, the CRA has published its view on the excluded activities of construction, farming, and fishing.

ITA: 125.1(3), "manufacturing or processing" par. (g)

IT-145R

Once manufacturing or processing activities have been identified, it is necessary to determine Canadian-source manufacturing and processing profits. The Regulations prescribe the rules referred to in the definition of "Canadian manufacturing or processing profits" for determining manufacturing or processing profits. The Regulations set out a formula presented in Exhibit 11-7 for the computation of that portion of a corporation's profits that can be attributed to manufacturing and processing profits. Certain activities are considered to result in manufacturing and processing profits while other activities do not. "Qualified activities" are listed in the Regulations along with a list of activities that are not included in the term "qualified activities". It is essential to become thoroughly familiar with the specific wording of all of the definitions in these Regulations.

ITA: 125.1(3)
ITR: 5200

ITR: 5202

EXHIBIT 11-7
Manufacturing and Processing Profits Formula for Most Corporations

$$MP = \frac{ML + MC}{L + C} \times ADJUBI$$

MP — Canadian manufacturing and processing profits eligible for the reduced rate of income tax.

ML — Cost of manufacturing and processing labour, i.e., $^{100}/_{75}$ of direct manufacturing and processing labour, to a maximum of L, below.

L — Cost of labour, i.e., total labour related to income earned in Canada.

MC — Cost of manufacturing and processing capital, i.e., $^{100}/_{85}$ of direct manufacturing and processing fixed annual capital cost (i.e., 10% of gross cost), to a maximum of C, below.

C — Cost of capital, i.e., total fixed annual capital cost (i.e., 10% of gross cost) related to active business income earned in Canada.

ADJUBI — Adjusted business income, i.e., net active business income earned in Canada (other than resource profits).

¶11,925   Elements of the Formula for Determining Manufacturing and Processing Profits

¶11,925.10   *Adjusted business income*

This is the base of income from which a portion is segregated for special treatment as manufacturing and processing profits by applying the low rate of tax. That base is essentially all active business income from Canadian sources including the activities listed in the definition of "manufacturing or processing". Net resource income which reduces adjusted business income is, in general terms, income on which a depletion allowance is permitted plus any income that arises from the sale of resource properties. For the purposes of this Regulation, the definition of "active business" should be used. In the case of *Canadian Marconi Company v. The Queen*, the Supreme Court of Canada held that income from short-term investments was income from an active business and that it could be included in "adjusted business income". Perhaps, that is why the definition of the M&P base removes only Canadian and foreign investment income of Canadian-controlled private corporations, from taxable income in determining the base for the manufacturing and processing profit deduction. For such a corporation, investment income is treated separately for purposes that will be discussed fully in Chapter 12.

[Margin references: ITR: 5202, 5203(1); ITA: 125.1(3); ITA: 65; ITR: 5203(1); ITA: 248(1); 86 DTC 6526 (S.C.C.); ITA: 125.1(1)(b)(iii)]

¶11,925.20   *Cost of capital and cost of manufacturing and processing capital*

The definitions of these terms are contained in the Regulations. "Cost of capital" includes virtually all depreciable property of the corporation other than such assets used in foreign business operations and those used to earn income other than active business income. The "gross cost" of an asset means its capital cost with some adjustments such as:

[Margin reference: ITR: 5202]

(a) add back grants, subsidies, investment tax credits, etc. that were subtracted from capital cost;

[Margin reference: ITA: 13(7.1)]

(b) eliminate capitalized interest added; and

[Margin reference: ITA: 21]

(c) add back amounts deducted due to debt forgiveness.

[Margin reference: ITA: 80]

Note that the definition uses only 10% of the gross cost of property to, in a sense, annualize the cost of capital property and put such property on a parallel basis with the cost of labour which is an annual cost.

¶11,925

"Rental cost" means the rents incurred under a lease, whether a "net" lease or a "gross" lease, for the use of a property.   ITR: 5202

To determine the "cost of manufacturing and processing capital", it is necessary to identify depreciable assets which are used directly in "qualified activities" and to determine the extent of such use. For certain assets such as buildings, material handling equipment, etc., it is necessary to make an allocation of cost on some reasonable basis. The definition of "qualified activities" begins with a list of nine specific activities. The definition, then, adds all other activities that are performed in Canada directly in connection with manufacturing or processing and scientific research and experimental development as defined in the Regulations. Then, it concludes with a list of six activities that are not to be considered qualified activities. Note how receiving and storing of raw materials are considered to be qualified activities but purchasing of raw materials is not and storing of finished goods is not. The 100/85 gross-up applied to the cost so determined is to allow for costs which, while not directly related to manufacturing and processing, are ancillary to that activity. Note that the grossed-up cost cannot exceed the "cost of capital".   ITR: 5202   ITR: 2900

¶11,925.30 *Cost of labour and cost of manufacturing and processing labour*

The definitions of these terms are included in the Regulations. "Salaries and wages" is defined to mean salaries, wages and commissions, but does not include remuneration in the form of pension benefits, living allowances, stock option benefits, automobile standby charges, etc. Fringe benefits need not be excluded if insignificant. Also, included in the cost of labour are fees paid or payable to non-employees for functions relating to management or administration, scientific research and services normally performed by an employee.   ITR: 5202

To determine the "cost of manufacturing and processing labour", it is necessary to calculate that portion of the cost of labour that reflects the extent to which salaries and wages and fees were paid or payable in connection with qualified activities as discussed above. Similarly, a 100/75 gross-up allows for ancillary costs. However, the grossed-up cost of manufacturing and processing labour cannot exceed the "cost of labour".

¶11,930 Application of the Rules

Example Problem

The following data pertain to Effluent Processing Company Limited, a public corporation, for its taxation year ended December 31, 2007:

Processing revenues in Canada		$2,500,000
Processing expenses:		
direct labour	$1,427,500	
allocated portion of administration, material and plant overhead expenses	947,500	$2,375,000
Wholesale sales of fertilizer in Canada		$1,350,000
Wholesale expenses:		
direct labour	$ 322,500	
allocated portion of administration, material and plant overhead expenses	865,000	$1,187,500

The company's processing and wholesaling capacity is provided by owned fixed assets having a capital cost of $3,125,000 and leased fixed assets having an annual lease cost of $62,500. Seventy per cent of the owned fixed assets and 85% of the leased assets are used in processing.

In addition to the revenues noted above, the company received dividends in the amount of $25,000 from a Canadian subsidiary and interest income (i.e., investment income) of $40,000 from long-term government bonds which will be held to maturity in 2010. Administration and overhead expenses include $125,000 paid in salaries and wages to people not engaged in qualified manufacturing and processing activities.

— REQUIRED

(A) Calculate Canadian manufacturing and processing profits for the company in 2007.

(B) Calculate the manufacturing and processing profits deduction for 2007 assuming that the company is not eligible for a small business deduction.   ITA: 125.1(1)(*a*)

(C) Calculate Part I taxes payable for 2007, assuming that all taxable income is earned in a province which uses federal taxable income as its base for a 11% provincial tax rate.

— SOLUTION

(A)   (i)   Calculation of "adjusted business income":

Processing sales	$2,500,000	
Less: processing expenses	2,375,000	$ 125,000
Wholesaling sales	$1,350,000	
Less: wholesaling expenses	1,187,500	162,500
Total (ADJUBI)		$ 287,500

Note that dividend and interest income is not income from an active business and, therefore, it is not included in adjusted business income.

(ii)   Calculation of "cost of capital":

10% of gross capital cost of owned assets (10% of $3,125,000)	$ 312,500
Rental cost of assets	62,500
Cost of capital (C)	$ 375,000(I)

(iii)   Calculation of "cost of manufacturing and processing capital":

Portion of cost of capital used in qualified M&P activities

70% of $312,500	$ 218,750
85% of $62,500	53,125
Total	$ 271,875
100/85 of total (100/85 × $271,875) (MC)	$ 319,853(II)
Lesser of (I) and (II)	$ 319,853

(iv)   Calculation of "cost of labour":

Salaries and wages (direct labour)

Processing	$1,427,500
Wholesaling	322,500
Administration and overhead	125,000
Total (L)	$1,875,000(III)

(v)   Calculation of "cost of manufacturing and processing labour":

Portion of cost of labour used in qualified M&P activities	
Direct processing labour	$1,427,500
100/75 of labour (100/75 × $1,427,500)	$1,903,333(IV)
Lesser of (III) and (IV)	$1,875,000

(vi)   Calculation of "manufacturing and processing profits":

$$MP = \frac{MC + ML}{C + L} \times ADJUBI$$

$$= \frac{\$319,853 + \$1,875,000}{\$375,000 + \$1,875,000} \times \$287,500$$

$$= \underline{\$280,453}$$

(B) Calculation of manufacturing and processing profits deduction from tax:

7% of the lesser of:

     (i) Canadian manufacturing and processing profits $280,453

(ii) Taxable income:

Income from all sources			
Business income (see (A)(i) above) . . .	$287,500		
Dividend income	25,000		
Interest income	40,000	$352,500	
Less: inter-company dividends		25,000	$327,500

7% of $280,453 = (19,632)

(C) Calculation of Part I taxes payable:

Taxable income	$327,500
Basic federal tax (.38 × $327,500)	$124,450
Deduct: federal tax abatement (10% of $327,500)	32,750
Net amount	$ 91,700
Add: corporate surtax (4% of ($124,450 − 10% of $327,500))	3,668
	$ 95,368
Deduct: manufacturing and processing profits deduction	(19,632)

tax reduction

taxable income $327,500	
less: M&P profits deduction ÷ .07 ($19,632 ÷ .07)	
(should be equal to M&P profits eligible for	
M&P deduction) 280,457	
net . . . . $ 47,043	
7% of $47,043	(3,293)
Part I tax payable (federal)	$ 72,443
Provincial tax (11% of $327,500)	36,025
Total tax payable	$108,648

ITA: 123.2

ITA: 123.4(2)

¶11,940   Branch Tax

A branch tax is imposed on non-Canadian corporations carrying on business in Canada through a branch that is not a separate entity incorporated in Canada. A Canadian corporation is defined as a corporation which is presently resident in Canada and was incorporated in Canada or has been resident in Canada continuously since 1971. This tax is charged in addition to any Part I tax and is computed as 25% (unless reduced by a tax treaty) of after-tax Canadian-source income, after a number of technical adjustments such as an allowance for investment in property in Canada which is defined by Regulation. The branch tax is intended to put the branch in the same position as a Canadian subsidiary which must withhold tax on dividends paid to the foreign parent. The branch tax, in essence, is paid on Canadian-source income of the branch that is not retained and reinvested in Canada, just as a withholding tax is levied on dividends which represent income that is not retained and reinvested in Canada.

ITA: 219

ITA: 89(1)

ITR: 808

The branch tax applies only to non-resident corporations. The base of the tax is taxable income earned in Canada, with adjustments to that base outlined in subsection 219(1). Details of the calculation are provided in an Interpretation Bulletin.

ITA: 219

IT-137R3

This tax is subject to any overriding provisions within any of the income tax treaties. For example, the rate under the Canada–U.S. Tax Treaty is 5%. The Interpretation Bulletin discusses the effect of the tax treaties on branch tax. The comprehensive treaties exempt corporations resident in the other country from Canadian tax unless there is a permanent establishment in Canada.

IT-137R3

Example Problem

International Links Inc. is a telecommunications company incorporated in the U.S. with a December 31 year-end. It began operating one small pilot project office in Toronto in fiscal 2006 in addition to its 52 U.S. offices. The corporation is not resident in Canada; however, the Canadian office is considered a permanent establishment. The corporation's taxable income from Canadian operations was $280,000 in 2007. It received $60,000 in dividends from investments in other Canadian-controlled private corporations and realized a $20,000 capital gain on land used in the Canadian business. The corporation has $50,000 of qualified investment property in Canada. At the end of fiscal 2006, it had $20,000 of qualified investment property.

— *REQUIRED*

Compute the corporation's branch tax liability on the assumption that the Ontario provincial corporate tax rate is 14%. (Ignore surtaxes.)

— *SOLUTION*

5%[1] of:

Taxable income earned in Canada	$280,000	ITA: 219(1)(*a*)
Add: Amounts deducted under par. 115(1)(*d*.1)	60,000	ITA: 219(1)(*b*)
Non-taxable portion of capital gain on a taxable Canadian property (land) used in Canadian business	10,000	ITA: 219(1)(*d*)
Amount claimed in previous year as investment allowance	20,000	ITA: 219(1)(*g*)
Deduct: Tax payable under Part I less tax attributable to net taxable capital gain on non-business property	(78,400)[2]	ITA: 219(1)(*h*), 219(1.1)
Tax payable to a province less tax attributable to net taxable capital gain on non-business property	(39,200)[3]	ITA: 219(1)(*h*.1), 219(1.1)
Allowance in respect of qualified investment property in Canada	(50,000)[4]	ITA: 219(1)(*j*)
	$202,400	
Branch tax (5% × $202,400)	$ 10,120	

— *NOTES TO SOLUTION*

[1] The Protocol to the Canada–U.S. Tax Treaty now limits the rate of branch tax to 5%.

[2] $280,000 × (38% – 10%). This tax rate is the basic federal rate net of the federal abatement. Note that the taxable capital gain realized was on business property. Hence the tax on the gain is not removed from federal Part I tax.

[3] $280,000 × 14%. This tax rate reflects a provincial rate of tax on Canadian business income. Note that the taxable capital gain realized was on business property. Hence the tax on the gain is not removed from provincial tax.

[4] Regulation 808(2) lists the specific components of qualified investment property in Canada. Although the regulation is quite detailed with numerous exceptions, it is clearly written. Reference to this regulation will be necessary when determining qualified investment property.

Chapter 12

Integration for Business and Investment Income of the Private Corporation

LEARNING GOALS

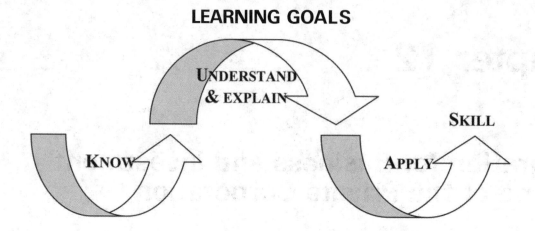

Know

By the end of this chapter you should know how the income tax system works to integrate the tax on individual shareholders with the tax on private corporations for business and investment income. Completing the Review Questions (¶12,800) and Multiple Choice Questions (¶12,825) is a good way to learn the technical provisions.

Understand and Explain

You should understand and be able to explain:

- the concept of integration;

- how the small business deduction from tax is computed and how it helps to achieve integration of business income;

- the rules for the association of corporations and why they exist;

- the base on which the additional investment tax credit for a Canadian-controlled private corporation is computed and how it is limited for scientific research and experimental development expenditures;

- what investment income of a private corporation is and how it is taxed to achieve integration; and

- the advantages and disadvantages of incorporating sources of business income and sources of investment income.

Completing the Exercises (¶12,850) is a good way to deepen your understanding of the material.

Apply

You should be able to apply your knowledge and understanding of the key provisions pertaining to:

- associated corporations, where that term is used in the legislation;

- the calculation of:

— the small business deduction,

— the additional investment tax credit for scientific research and experimental development expenditures,

— the income taxes on investment income of a private corporation, including refundable tax, and

- the complete calculation of taxes payable by a private corporation with income from business and investment sources.

Completing the Assignment Problems (¶12,875) is an excellent way to develop your ability to apply the material in increasingly complex situations.

OVERVIEW

This chapter deals with the provisions of the Act which attempt to integrate the taxation of private corporations with the taxation of the shareholders of those corporations. Following an introduction to the concept of integration, this chapter will consider both the integration of business income and investment income. While the word "integration" is not used in the Act, a series of provisions attempts to implement a system of integration which is designed to achieve certain objectives.

One of the most important reductions of tax available to corporations is the small business deduction which applies to Canadian-controlled private corporations as defined in subsection 125(7). This chapter will discuss the rules for computing the small business deduction. It will also deal with the rules for computing the additional investment tax credit where a corporation is eligible for the small business deduction. Then the chapter considers the integration of investment income, including the refundable tax system. This chapter presents the remaining rules that must be followed to make a complete calculation of the tax payable by a corporation.

The following chart will help to position in the Act some of the major provisions dealt with in this Chapter.

PART I — DIVISIONS E AND F

COMPUTATION OF TAX - CORPORATE

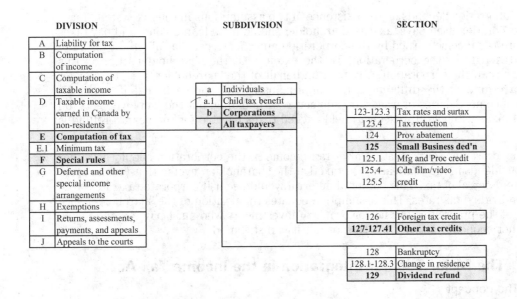

DIVISION		SUBDIVISION		SECTION	
A	Liability for tax				
B	Computation of income				
C	Computation of taxable income				
D	Taxable income earned in Canada by non-residents	a	Individuals		
		a.1	Child tax benefit		
		b	**Corporations**	123-123.3	Tax rates and surtax
		c	**All taxpayers**	123.4	Tax reduction
E	**Computation of tax**			124	Prov abatement
E.1	Minimum tax			**125**	**Small Business ded'n**
F	**Special rules**			125.1	Mfg and Proc credit
G	Deferred and other special income arrangements			125.4-125.5	Cdn film/video credit
H	Exemptions				
I	Returns, assessments, payments, and appeals			126	Foreign tax credit
				127-127.41	**Other tax credits**
J	Appeals to the courts			128	Bankruptcy
				128.1-128.3	Change in residence
				129	**Dividend refund**

¶12,000   THE CONCEPT OF INTEGRATION

¶12,010   Problems Addressed by Integration

From a legal perspective, a corporation is an entity separate from its shareholders. In economics, however, there is no more separation between a corporation and its shareholders than between a proprietorship and its proprietor, a partnership and its partners or an investment portfolio and its owner.

As a taxpayer, a corporation is a person which is taxed separately from the natural persons (individuals) who are its shareholders. Hence, this could give rise to double taxation, with the same income being taxed, first, at the corporate level and then, again, at the individual shareholder level. Conceptually, a corporation should really be treated as a non-taxable conduit through which income flows to the individual shareholders, in the same way that a proprietorship business or a partnership business is a conduit through which income flows to the individual proprietor or partners. However, as subsequent comments in this chapter will illustrate, if only individuals and not corporations are subject to tax, problems of an economic or political nature may arise.

¶12,020   Objectives of Integration

Ideally, integration should cause the total tax paid by a corporation and its shareholders to be equal to the total tax paid by an individual who carries on the same economic activity directly and not through the corporation. By integrating the corporate and personal tax systems, the double taxation of corporate income can be avoided. This would make the tax system neutral with respect to the form of organization, used to carry on an economic activity, because there would be no tax advantage or disadvantage to one form of organization over another. Integration would also make the system equitable by ensuring that the tax imposed on income passed through a corporation to an individual is equal in amount to the tax that is imposed on the same amount and type of income earned directly by an individual. Stated differently, the total tax levied on the corporation and the individual in the former situation should be equal in amount to the tax imposed on the individual in the latter situation.

Perfect integration depends on the existence of two assumptions in the tax system. First, where the corporation itself pays tax, the shareholder should include in income and pay taxes on the full pre-tax income earned by the corporation and then receive a full credit for all of the income tax paid by the corporation. To the extent that the shareholder's tax on this income is less than the corporation's tax paid on behalf of the shareholder, the shareholder should get a refund of the difference. This approximates the approach that is taken for employment income. Salaries or wages are subject to withholding, but the employee gets full credit for all taxes withheld. If taxes withheld exceed taxes payable for the year, a refund is due.

The second assumption is that all after-tax income of the corporation should be either paid out as dividends in the year earned or taxed at the shareholder level in that year to avoid the indefinite deferral of tax. This potential deferral would occur if corporate tax rates were lower than individual tax rates. This assumption equates the position of the shareholder with the position of the proprietor, partner or owner of investments who must pay tax on income from his or her economic activity whether or not it is distributed.

¶12,030   The Major Tool for Integration in the Income Tax Act

¶12,035   The concept

The mainstay of the integration system as it applies to individual shareholders of all taxable Canadian corporations is the gross-up and tax credit procedure which is illustrated in Exhibit 12-1. The gross-up is intended to add to the dividend received by the individual shareholder an amount equal to the total income tax (including provincial tax) paid by the corporation on the income that gave rise to the dividend. Thus, the grossed-up dividend is intended to represent the corporation's pre-tax income. The shareholder will pay tax on the grossed-up dividend at his or her personal rate. The combined federal and provincial tax credit is intended to give the shareholder credit for the total tax paid by the corporation on the shareholder's behalf. This procedure is intended to equalize the tax paid on the income that is flowed through the corporation to its shareholders, with the tax paid on the same income that is earned directly. The potential double taxation of corporate income is thereby avoided.

¶12,040 Application of the concept in theory

Historically, integration has worked where the corporate tax rate was 20%. As shown in column A of Exhibit 12-1, $1,000 of corporate income attracts tax of $200. The resulting $800 is paid as a dividend to an individual who then grosses this up by 25%, or $200, resulting in taxable income of $1,000, which was equal to the pre-tax corporate income. The individual then pays personal tax on the dividend at, for example, 34%, or $340, and receives a dividend tax credit equal to the underlying corporate tax of $200. The end result is that the corporation and individual together pay the same amount of tax ($340) as if the individual earned the income directly. This is an example of perfect integration.

To address issues that arose from the imperfections in the integration system where the corporate tax rate was considerably higher than 20%, a different gross-up and tax credit for "eligible dividends" paid out of the general rate income pool (GRIP) was introduced. Column B of Exhibit 12-1, assumes an underlying corporate tax rate of 31%. Then, the gross-up is 45% to return the personal income to the pre-tax corporate level. Again, the dividend tax credit is equal to the underlying corporate tax and gross-up to result in the shareholder being indifferent between earning the $1,000 personally or through a corporation.

"Eligible dividends" are, generally, dividends paid by:

(i) public corporations resident in Canada and subject to the general corporate tax rate, and

(ii) CCPCs resident in Canada to the extent that their income, other than investment income, is subject to tax at the general corporate tax rate; that is, the corporation has a balance in its "general rate income pool" (GRIP).

The GRIP, in general concept, includes:

the sum of:

- the corporation's GRIP at the end of the preceding taxation year (can be negative or nil),

- the after-tax business income of the corporation taxed at the high rate, assuming a combined federal and provincial general corporate tax rate of 32% (note that the 45% gross-up and tax credit works perfectly with a 31% combined corporate tax rate, but the GRIP definition assumes a 32% rate; also, business losses reduce the GRIP), and

- eligible dividends received from other corporations

less:

- eligible dividends paid in the preceding taxation year.

There are also special rules:

- to allow a CCPC that receives an "eligible dividend" to pay an "eligible dividend", and

- to require a corporation that can normally pay an "eligible dividend" but has received an "ineligible dividend" to pay the "ineligible dividend" first, or be subject to a penalty.

EXHIBIT 12-1
Theoretical Taxation of Dividends to Individuals
That Demonstrates Perfect Integration

	A	B
Corporation		
Corporate income	$1,000	$1,000
Corporate tax, including provincial tax (*theoretical* rate, i.e., 20% and 31%)	(200)	(310)
After-tax earnings available for dividends	$ 800	$ 690
Individual Shareholder		
Dividend	$ 800	$ 690
Gross-up (*theoretically* equal to corporate tax or 25% and 45% of the dividend)	200	310
Taxable income (*theoretically* equal to pre-tax corporation income)	$1,000	$1,000
Personal tax, including provincial tax (assumed rate of 34%)	$ 340	$ 340
Dividend tax credit, including effect of provincial tax (*theoretically* equal to corporate tax/gross-up)	(200)	(310)
Net tax	$ 140	$ 30
Total Taxes Paid		
Corporation	$ 200	$ 310
Shareholder	140	30
Total	$ 340	$ 340
Earned Directly by Individual (tax @ 34%)	$ 340	$ 340

Under perfect integration, the corporate tax is like a withholding tax on the shareholder's income which the corporation earns on behalf of the shareholder. In a sense, it is similar to the withholding of tax on the salary or wages of an employee. Thus, the corporate tax prevents the tax on income earned by a corporation from being deferred until a dividend is paid and is then taxed in the hands of the shareholder. When the shareholder receives a dividend, the full pre-tax income earned by the corporation is reported by the shareholder, through the gross-up mechanism, just as an employee reports gross salary or wages. Then, tax is computed at the shareholder's personal rate. In the same way that taxes withheld from salary or wages are used to reduce the employee's final tax payable, so the dividend tax credit (representing the tax paid by the corporation) reduces the shareholder's tax payable on the dividend income.

¶12,045 Basis for the calculation of the dividend tax credit

A major assumption in Exhibit 12-1 is that the dividend tax credit is equal to the underlying corporate tax and the gross-up. Using the facts in Exhibit 12-1, this can be illustrated as follows:

¶12,045

	A	B
Calculation based on gross-up		
Dividend gross-up from Exhibit 12-1	$ 200	$ 310
Federal dividend tax credit		
⅔ of the gross-up	$ 133	
¹¹/₁₈ of the gross-up		$ 189
Provincial dividend tax credit		
⅓ of the gross-up	67	
⁷/₁₈ of the gross-up		121
	$ 200	310

	A	B
Calculation based on grossed-up dividend		
Grossed-up dividend from Exhibit 12-1	$1,000	$1,000
Federal dividend tax credit		
13⅓% of the grossed-up dividend	$ 133	
19% of the grossed-up dividend		$ 190
Provincial dividend tax credit		
6⅔% of the grossed-up dividend	67	
12% of the grossed-up dividend		120
	$ 200	$ 310

As you can see, the total dividend tax credit is equal to the assumed corporate tax rate. In column A, the total is 20% (13⅓% + 6⅔%) and in column B the total is 31% (19% + 12%).

The federal dividend tax credit provides for the credit to be equal to two-thirds of the gross-up on taxable dividends, other than eligible dividends, from a corporation resident in Canada, and ¹¹/₁₈ of the gross-up on eligible dividends received. The 13⅓ and 19 percentages that are used in the above computation are determined as follows: ITA: 82(1)(*b*), 121

	A	B
Cash amount of dividend received	$ 1,000	$ 1,000
Gross-up [par. 82(1)(*b*)]: 25%/45%	250	450
Grossed-up taxable amount of dividend	$ 1,250	$ 1,450
Federal dividend tax credit [sec. 121]: ⅔ or ¹¹/₁₈ of gross-up	$ 167	$ 275
Federal dividend tax credit as a percentage of grossed-up taxable amount of dividend:	13⅓%	18.97%

Dividends eligible for the 25% gross-up are:

- dividends from the active business income of CCPCs that is eligible for the small business deduction
- dividends from the investment income of CCPCs

Dividends eligible for the 45% gross-up are:

- dividends from the active business income of CCPCs that is **not** eligible for the small business deduction
- dividends from Canadian public companies, and other corporations that are not CCPCs, that are resident in Canada and subject to the general corporate income tax rate

Where the combined federal and provincial corporate rate of tax is anything other than 20% or 31%, the system of integration breaks down. The imperfections in the integration system will be considered in more detail in this chapter. The chapter will also consider some tools of integration that help to bring the corporate rate of tax close to the perfect 20% on the first $400,000 of active business income and on all of the investment income earned by a Canadian-controlled private corporation.

¶12,100   INCOME FROM AN ACTIVE BUSINESS OF A CCPC

¶12,110   Introduction to the Small Business Deduction

The small business deduction represents a credit against the tax otherwise payable on income "from an active business carried on in Canada" and is designed only for small "Canadian-controlled private corporations" in order to assist them to retain capital to expand their businesses. Note, however, that the corporation does not have to be "small" in order to qualify for the credit.

The benefits of the small business deduction are phased out for very large Canadian-controlled private corporations. The rules that implement this phase-out are presented in the next segment of this topic.

Exhibit 12-2 illustrates how the small business deduction affects the calculation of the effective total corporate tax introduced in Exhibit 11-3.

EXHIBIT 12-2
Tax Rates Applicable to Taxable Income Eligible for Small Business Deduction

Federal tax rate [ssec. 123(1)]	38.00%
Federal abatement for provincial tax [ssec. 124(1)]	(10.00)
Net federal tax after federal abatement.	28.00%
Federal surtax @ 4% of above net federal tax	1.12
Small business deduction [ssec. 125(1)]	(16.00)
Total federal tax	13.12%
Provincial tax (hypothetical) on income qualifying for small business deduction	5.00
Effective total tax	18.12%

Note that the effective total tax rate is close to the 20% total corporate tax rate that results in perfect integration.

The federal small business deduction is scheduled to increase in 2008 (16.5%) and again in 2009, when it will reach 17%. The effective federal tax rate on income eligible for the small business deduction is set out in the following table.

	2006	2007	2008	2009	2010	2011
Annual business limit	$300,000	$400,000	$400,000	$400,000	$400,000	$400,000
Effective federal tax rate	13.12%	13.12%	11.5%	11.0%	11.0%	11.0%

The hypothetical provincial tax rate of 5% used in Exhibit 12-2 above reflects an average provincial equivalent of the federal small business deduction. Remember that in Chapter 11, Exhibit 11-3 used an assumed provincial rate of 13% because most provincial basic tax rates lie between 9.9% and 16%. Most provinces also give an equivalent small business tax credit, giving an effective provincial rate of approximately 5% on the first $400,000 (and more in some provinces) of active business income.

The prime qualification that a corporation must meet to get the benefit of the small business deduction is that it be, throughout the taxation year, a "Canadian controlled private corporation" (CCPC). This term is discussed by the CRA in an Interpretation Bulletin. A CCPC is distinguished, on the basis of control, from a "private corporation". A "private corporation" is further distinguished from a "public corporation", primarily on the basis of whether any of the corporation's shares are listed on a prescribed Canadian or foreign stock exchange.

ITA: 89(1), 125(7)

IT-458R2

¶12,120 Mechanics of Calculation of Small Business Deduction

¶12,125 The basic limits

¶12,125.10 *Eligibility*

A Canadian-controlled private corporation calculates its tax liability by first applying the standard corporate rate to its total taxable income. After this basic tax amount is determined, the corporation makes various additions (e.g., surtax) and deductions (e.g., M&P profits deduction, investment tax credit, etc.) to determine the final taxes payable. One such deduction is the small business deduction.

A corporation must be a Canadian-controlled private corporation *throughout* the year to qualify for the small business deduction which is a credit deducted from the tax otherwise payable. For such a corporation, the deduction is calculated by the following formula:

ITA: 125(1)

¶12,125.20 *The formula*

Small business deduction = 16% (i.e., the "small business deduction rate" for the year) of the least of:

ITA: 125(1), 125(1.1)

(a) net Canadian active business income (i.e., income minus losses);

(b) taxable income earned in Canada achieved by removing from the total taxable income, foreign-source income estimated as the sum of:

(i) foreign-source investment income, estimated as $10/3^1$ times the foreign tax credit on foreign non-business income, determined without reference to the additional refundable tax on investment income,

ITA: 126(1)

(ii) foreign-source business income, estimated as 3^1 times the foreign tax credit on foreign business income, and

ITA: 126(2)

(iii) taxable income exempt from Part I tax by reason of an enactment of Parliament; and

(c) the business limit, i.e., $400,000 *less* any portion allocated to associated corporations (to be discussed later in this chapter).

ITA: 125(2), 125(3)

¶12,125.30 *Interpretation of the formula*

Items (b)(i) and (ii) ensure that foreign income not taxed in Canada, because of a foreign tax credit, is removed from the base amount on which the small business deduction is calculated. This is necessary since Canada should not allow the small business deduction on income on which the corporation does not pay tax as a result of a foreign tax credit or base a tax credit on income that is not Canadian-source active business income.

[1] [Bill C-33, tabled on November 22, 2006, proposed to change the factor applied to the business foreign tax credit from 10/4 for the 2003 and subsequent taxation years.]

Conceptually, the adjustment in item (b)(i), above, removes from taxable income an estimate of foreign investment income by multiplying by $^{10}/_3$ the tax credit which is assumed to be 30% of the foreign investment income. The 30% rate is based on an assumed corporate rate of 40% reduced by the 10% federal abatement for income earned in a province or territory. Investment income is subject to that abatement, because it is thought to be earned in a province or territory where the corporation is established, as explained in the previous chapter in the discussion of the foreign tax credit calculation.

Conceptually, the adjustment in item (b)(ii), above, removes from taxable income an estimate of foreign business income by multiplying by 3 the tax credit which is assumed to be $33^1/_3$% of the foreign business income. The $33^1/_3$% rate is intended to approximate corporate income tax rates on this type of income (i.e., 38% + 1.12% − 7% (general rate reduction) = 32.12%, say, 33.33%).

Similarly, item (b)(iii) removes from the base for the small business deduction an amount that is not subject to tax. This removal follows from the concept that an amount that is not taxed in Canada should not be in the base for a tax credit which reduces taxes payable in Canada.

¶12,130   Elimination of small business deduction for large CCPCs

Large Canadian-controlled private corporations are not fully eligible for the small business deduction. The amount of the small business deduction is phased out or "clawed back" with a formula based on the amount of taxable capital employed in Canada for the preceding taxation year. The phase-out range is taxable capital employed in Canada between $10 and $15 million. The business limit of $400,000 for purposes of the small business deduction is reduced by $1 for every $12.50 (i.e., ($15,000,000 − $10,000,000) ÷ $400,000) of taxable capital employed in Canada in excess of $10 million. To offset the effect of short taxation years on this reduction of a CCPC's business limit, the large corporations tax base is grossed up to reflect a full taxation year. Reductions in the business limit for short taxation years are based on a daily proration. *ITA: 125(5.1), Part I.3*

The above limitation also applies to a group of associated corporations. Therefore, the associated corporations' total taxable capital employed in Canada in excess of $10 million serves as the basis for the corporate group's business limit reduction.

"Taxable capital employed in Canada" is a term that is defined in the Act. A computational format is provided for a non-financial corporation in the Supplemental Notes at the end of this chapter. *ITA: 181.2*

This reduction in the small business deduction is implemented through the formula: *ITA: 125(5.1)*

$$A \times \frac{B}{\$11,250}$$

where,

A   is the corporation's business limit for the year, and

B   is 0.225% × (D − E).

where,

D   is the corporation's total taxable capital employed in Canada for its preceding taxation year,

E   is $10,000,000.

While the reduction is theoretically based on taxable capital employed in Canada, the formula uses the large corporations tax, which is no longer applicable. The $11,250 in the formula represents the former Part I.3 tax rate of 0.225% on $15 million of taxable capital employed in Canada (0.225% × ($15 million − $10 million) = $11,250). Note that when taxable capital reaches $15,000,000, the business limit is fully clawed back.

¶12,130

Example Problem

Little-Big Inc., a Canadian-controlled private corporation, has a fiscal year-end of December 31. Little-Big Inc. is not associated with any other corporation and all of its income is earned in Canada. The following selected tax information has been provided for 2007:

Active business income	$ 350,000
Taxable income	500,000
Taxable capital employed in Canada in 2006	13,000,000

— REQUIRED

Determine Little-Big Inc.'s small business deduction for the 2007 taxation year.

— SOLUTION

Business limit:

Before reduction	$ 400,000

Reduction:

$$\$400,000 \times \frac{.00225 \times (\$13,000,000 - \$10,000,000)}{\$11,250} = \qquad (240,000)$$

Business limit	$ 160,000

Small business deduction for 2007:

16% of least of:

(a) active business income	$350,000
(b) taxable income	$500,000
(c) business limit	$160,000
Least amount	$ 160,000
16% of $160,000	$ 25,600

¶12,140   Definition of "Active Business"

¶12,145   The "default" definition

As will be discussed in more detail later in this chapter, one of the major problems with the implementation of the small business deduction in 1972 was the lack of a statutory definition of "active business". An Interpretation Bulletin outlined the CRA's opinion of the meaning of the term, but it was often successfully challenged in the courts. A definition of "active business" was subsequently added to the legislation.   IT-73R6

The current definition of the term reads as follows: ITA: 125(7)

"active business carried on by a corporation" means any business carried on by the corporation other than a specified investment business or a personal services business and includes an adventure or concern in the nature of trade.[2]

Note how this definition is a "default" definition, since the income must be determined not to be from a specified investment business or a personal services business.

---

[2] Note that this definition is used only for the purpose of section 125. A definition of "active business" can be found in subsection 248(1) which is to be used whenever the term is used elsewhere in the Act. The phrase, "an adventure or concern in the nature of trade", is not included in the definition of "active business" in subsection 248(1). However, the phrase is part of the definition of "business" in subsection 248(1).

¶12,150 Specified investment business

A "specified investment business" (SIB), which is excluded from that definition of "active business", is defined to mean: ITA: 125(7)

- a business (other than the business of a credit union or of leasing property other than real property)

- the principal purpose of which is to derive income from property (including interest, dividends, rents and royalties),

- *unless* the corporation employs in the business throughout the year *more than* five full-time employees.

In the unusual case of *The Queen v. Hughes & Co. Holdings Ltd.*, the court first   94 DTC 6511 (F.C.T.D.)
considered, in detail, the meaning of full-time employee. The court then held that the condition of "more than five full-time employees" means "more full-time employees than five (full-time employees)", that is, at least six full-time employees. Therefore, the taxpayer could not combine five full-time employees with several part-time employees to meet this condition. The CRA adopts the court's interpretation on this point and interprets this condition to mean   IT-73R6, par. 15
six or more full-time employees.

In paragraph (*b*) of the definition "specified investment business", the Act goes on to allow an exception where a corporation would have employed more than five full-time employees but does not because another corporation associated with it provides the services that would otherwise have been performed by its own employees.

A specified investment business is restricted to a business which generates property income, including dividends, interest, rent (leasing) and royalties. Note that by virtue of the exception contained in the brackets in the definition, the business of leasing movable property (i.e., not real property) is an active business. The taxation of investment income, including income from a specified investment business, will be discussed later in the chapter.

¶12,155 Personal services business

A "personal services business" (PSB) is also excluded from the definition of the term   ITA: 125(7)
"active business". A "personal services business" is defined to mean:

- a business of providing services where

  (i) an individual who performs services on behalf of the corporation ("incorporated employee"), or

  (ii) any person related to the incorporated employee

  is a specified shareholder defined to mean, in part, an owner, directly or indirectly, of   ITA: 248(1) "specified shareholder"
  10% or more of the shares of the corporation;

- the incorporated employee would reasonably be regarded as an officer or employee of the entity to which services are provided;

- *unless*

  (iii) the corporation employs throughout the year more than five full-time employees, or

  (iv) services are provided to an associated corporation (to be discussed subsequently).

To determine whether "the incorporated employee would reasonably be regarded as an officer or employee of the entity to which services are provided", it may be necessary to perform an employee versus self-employed analysis, as presented in Chapter 3. The package of common law tests should be applied to the facts pertaining to the relationship between the incorporated employee and the entity to which services are provided. This was done in the case of *Criterion Capital Corporation v. The Queen*. Criterion was held not to be carrying   2001 DTC 921 (T.C.C.)
on a PSB and, hence, was eligible for the small business deduction, in part, on the application of the "control" and "ownership of tools" tests.

A corporation carrying on such a personal services business is not eligible for a small business deduction in respect of its PSB income. Furthermore, such a corporation is denied any deductions from the income of the personal services business of the corporation, other than salary, wages and other benefits provided to the individual who performed the services in respect of the personal services business. In addition, the corporation may deduct amounts, in respect of the PSB, that would have been deductible by an employee as costs incurred in selling property or negotiating contracts or legal expenses incurred in collecting amounts owing for services. As indicated in Chapter 11, the credit for employment outside Canada is not available to a corporation carrying on a PSB.

ITA: 18(1)(p)

¶12,160   Income incidental to an active business

"Income of the corporation for the year from an active business" includes any income for the year from an "active business", including any income for the year pertaining to or incident to that business; income from a property held for investment in Canada is specifically excluded.

ITA: 125(7)

Ancillary income incidental to the carrying on of an active business will, therefore, be considered as income from an active business in addition to income directly from an active business. Examples of such ancillary income include interest from short-term investment of surplus cash, recaptured capital cost allowance on assets used in the active business, interest on accounts receivable and bad debt recoveries, among others. IT-73R6, paragraph 5 indicates the CRA's interpretation of the concept of ancillary income.

It is important to note that a corporation may have income from more than one source. Therefore, it is necessary to analyze the corporate income (Division B) and break it down into its components.

¶12,170   Associated Companies

¶12,175   Overview

When two or more Canadian-controlled private corporations are associated for tax purposes, the business limit of $400,000, or the reduced amount, must be allocated annually, in any manner, among the associated companies for the purpose of determining the small business deduction in each company. A number of other provisions of the Act, also, rely on the concept of association. These include the definitions of the terms "specified investment business" and "personal services business" which were introduced previously in this chapter. The concept of association is, also, used to determine certain limits and rates for the investment tax credit, as discussed later in this chapter.

ITA: 125(3), 127(10.1), 127.1

ITA: 125(7)

ITA: 125(10.1), 127.1

The deeming rule, which will be discussed subsequently in this chapter, pertaining to certain intercorporate payments, depends on association between corporations.

ITA: 129(6)

¶12,180   Related persons

The term "associated corporations" may depend on the definition of "related persons". Related persons include relationships between individuals, between individuals and corporations and between corporations.

ITA: 251, 256

¶12,180.10   *Related individuals*

The key to the definition of relationships is found in relationships between individuals who are connected by blood relationship, marriage or adoption. Exhibit 12-3 (which was introduced in Chapter 6 as Exhibit 6-2) attempts to diagram these relationships (i.e., individuals who are related to a taxpayer (i.e., "you")) schematically. On the horizontal axis, do not attempt to relate individuals at the extreme outer limits (i.e., the second bullet) to each other. They are related to "you".

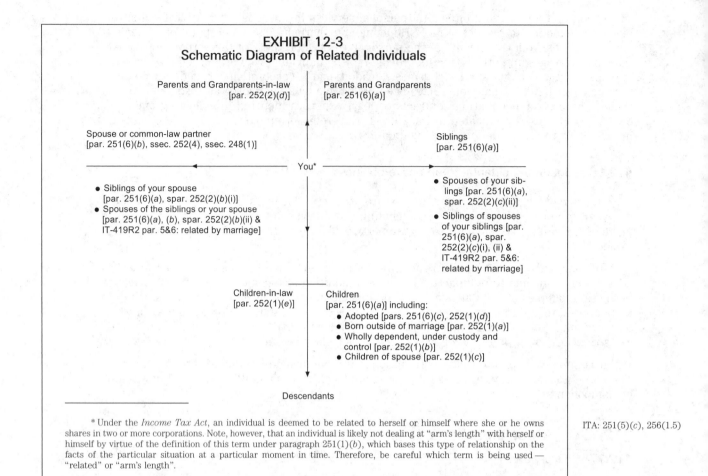

EXHIBIT 12-3
Schematic Diagram of Related Individuals

Parents and Grandparents-in-law [par. 252(2)(*d*)]

Parents and Grandparents [par. 251(6)(*a*)]

Spouse or common-law partner [par. 251(6)(*b*), ssec. 252(4), ssec. 248(1)]

Siblings [par. 251(6)(*a*)]

You*

- Siblings of your spouse [par. 251(6)(*a*), spar. 252(2)(*b*)(i)]
- Spouses of the siblings or your spouse [par. 251(6)(*a*), (*b*), spar. 252(2)(*b*)(ii) & IT-419R2 par. 5&6: related by marriage]

- Spouses of your siblings [par. 251(6)(*a*), spar. 252(2)(*c*)(ii)]
- Siblings of spouses of your siblings [par. 251(6)(*a*), spar. 252(2)(*c*)(i), (ii) & IT-419R2 par. 5&6: related by marriage]

Children-in-law [par. 252(1)(*e*)]

Children [par. 251(6)(*a*)] including:
- Adopted [pars. 251(6)(*c*), 252(1)(*d*)]
- Born outside of marriage [par. 252(1)(*a*)]
- Wholly dependent, under custody and control [par. 252(1)(*b*)]
- Children of spouse [par. 252(1)(*c*)]

Descendants

* Under the *Income Tax Act*, an individual is deemed to be related to herself or himself where she or he owns shares in two or more corporations. Note, however, that an individual is likely not dealing at "arm's length" with herself or himself by virtue of the definition of this term under paragraph 251(1)(*b*), which bases this type of relationship on the facts of the particular situation at a particular moment in time. Therefore, be careful which term is being used — "related" or "arm's length".

ITA: 251(5)(*c*), 256(1.5)

Certain individuals who would normally be regarded as related to other individuals are not considered to be related for tax purposes. These individuals, who do not appear in Exhibit 12-3, include: aunts, uncles, nieces, nephews and cousins.

Note that where the word "spouse" is used, the provision extends to a "common-law partner". This term is defined as two persons, regardless of sex, who co-habit in a conjugal relationship and have done so for a continuous period of at least 12 months.

ITA: 248(1) "common-law partner"

¶12,180.20 *Relationships involving corporations*

Corporations can be related to individuals and other corporations. The key to understanding corporate relationships is the concept of control. In this context, control refers to legal (*de jure*) control which is generally understood to mean the right of control that rests in the ownership of such number of shares of the corporation as to give a majority of the voting power in the corporation. Control can either be direct or indirect. The latter, for example, could be accomplished through an intermediary corporation.

An example of indirect control would be where A, an individual, owns 80% of the voting shares of A Ltd. which in turn owns 60% of the voting shares of B Ltd. A has more than 50% of the votes of A Ltd. and in turn controls 60% of the votes of B Ltd. through his or her control of A Ltd.

The rules that govern corporate relationships are based on control by individuals or corporations, or groups of either or both. Conceptually, a person (an individual or corporation) is related to a corporation if that person controls the corporation. Similarly, if a person is a member of a related group that controls the corporation, then the person and the corporation are related. A related group is a group of persons each of whom is related to each

ITA: 251(2)(*b*)(i)

member of the group. In addition, persons, who are themselves related to the controlling person(s), are deemed to be related to the controlled corporation.

A relationship rule expands these concepts to include control by related and unrelated groups, and is summarized below.   ITA: 251(2)(*c*), 251(4)

Two corporations are related where:

(a) both corporations are controlled by the same person(s) which could be referred to as a common group;

(b) one corporation is controlled by one person, who is related to a person or any member of a related group that controls the other corporation;

(c) one corporation is controlled by one person or a related group and that person or one member of the related group is related to each member of an unrelated group which controls the other corporation; and

(d) two corporations are controlled by unrelated groups and at least one member of one of the groups is related to each member of the other group.

Example Problem

Consider the following two groups, each of which controls a corporation with a 50/50 ownership of the shares:

Group One Ltd.   Mom and Dad
Group Two Ltd.   Child of Mom and Dad and Mom's brother

— REQUIRED

Determine whether Group One Ltd. and Group Two Ltd. are related.

— SOLUTION

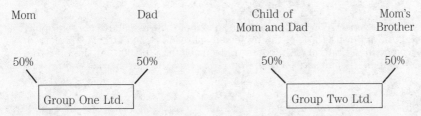

Group Two Ltd. is controlled by an unrelated group since it is composed of an uncle and a niece/nephew. Group One Ltd. is controlled by a related group, because Mom and Dad are related through marriage. In this situation, each member of the related group that controls Group One Ltd. is related to each member of the unrelated group that controls Group Two Ltd.

Therefore, the corporations are related.   ITA: 251(2)(*c*)(v)

¶12,185   Basic association rules

Conceptually, two companies are associated for tax purposes, when one company controls the other, or both companies are controlled by the same person or group of persons. However, the definition of associated corporations goes on to list other conditions for association. Therefore, the definition must be consulted to properly evaluate a particular set of facts. The first two general rules each require that only one straightforward condition be met in order to apply.   ITA: 256, 256(1)(*a*), 256(1)(*b*)

The last three general rules each contain three conditions, all joined by the word "and", which means that all three conditions must be satisfied for the rule to apply.   ITA: 256(1)(*c*), 256(1)(*d*), 256(1)(*e*)

¶12,185.10　*Paragraph 256(1)(c)*

The three conditions that must be met for this rule to apply are:

(i) each of the corporations must be controlled, directly or indirectly in any manner whatever, by a person (which includes an individual or another corporation) (hereinafter referred to as the "control test");

(ii) the person who controls one of the corporations must be related to the person who controls the other corporation (hereinafter referred to as the "related test"); and

(iii) either of the two persons owns not less than 25% of the issued shares of any class, other than a specified class (as defined below), of the capital stock of each corporation (hereinafter referred to as the "cross-ownership test").

Shares of a "specified class" are excluded from the cross-ownership conditions. The term "specified class" is defined to mean a class of shares where: ITA: 256(1.1)

(a) the shares are neither convertible nor exchangeable;

(b) the shares are non-voting;

(c) dividends payable on the shares are fixed in amount or rate;

(d) the annual rate of dividend on the shares, expressed as a percentage of the fair market value of the consideration for which the shares were issued, does not exceed the prescribed rate of interest at the time the shares were issued; and

(e) the amount that a holder of the shares is entitled to receive on their redemption, cancellation or acquisition by the corporation (or by a person not at arm's length with the corporation) cannot exceed the fair market value of the consideration for which the shares were issued (usually, their paid-up capital) plus any unpaid dividends.

The exclusion of a specified class of shares and the 25% cross-ownership test allow a person to invest funds in a corporation controlled by a related person without subjecting his or her own corporation to the consequences of association.

Example Problem

Dad and Son (age 25) both own 100% of the common shares of their respective corporations: Dadco Ltd. and Sonco Ltd. Dad owns 100% of the preferred shares of Sonco Ltd. The preferred shares are voting, bear a dividend rate of 8%, and are redeemable at $100,000. At the time the preferred shares were issued, the prescribed rate was 10% and the fair market value was $100,000.

— *REQUIRED*

Determine whether Dadco Ltd. and Sonco Ltd. are associated under subsection 256(1). Substantiate your conclusions by reference to the related provisions of the Act and the conditions contained therein.

— *SOLUTION*

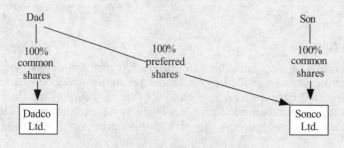

Dadco Ltd. and Sonco Ltd. are associated because: ITA: 256(1)(c)

(a) the corporations are controlled directly by either Dad or Son;

(b) Dad and Son are related by blood (i.e., parent–child);   ITA: 251(1)(a), 251(6)

(c) one of the persons (Dad) owns not less than 25% of issued shares of any class of both corporations, other than specified shares (i.e., 100% of the common shares of Dadco Ltd. and 100% of the preferred shares of Sonco Ltd.); and

(d) the preferred and common shares are not specified shares since both classes have voting rights.   ITA: 256(1.1)

¶12,185.20   *Paragraph 256(1)(d)*

Whereas the preceding rule applies to two corporations each controlled by a single person, this rule applies to a situation in which one corporation is controlled by a single person and the other corporation is controlled by a group of persons. The three conditions (involving a control test, a related test and a cross-ownership test) that must be met are:

(i) one of the corporations must be controlled, directly or indirectly in any manner whatever, by one person (control test);

(ii) that person must be related to each member of a group of persons (not necessarily a related group) that controls the other corporation (related test); and

(iii) that person must own not less than 25% of the issued shares of any class, other than specified shares, of the capital stock of the other corporation (cross-ownership test).

Example Problem

Mom owns 100% of the common shares of Momco Ltd. Her adult daughters, No. 1 and No. 2, each own 35% of the common shares of Sibco Ltd. Mom owns the remaining 30% of the outstanding common shares of Sibco Ltd.

— REQUIRED

Determine whether Momco Ltd. and Sibco Ltd. are associated. Substantiate your conclusions by reference to the related provisions of the Act and the conditions contained therein.

— SOLUTION

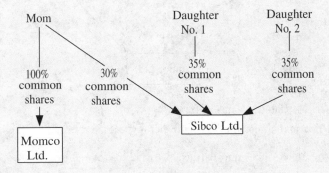

Momco Ltd. and Sibco Ltd. are associated because: ITA: 256(1)(d)

(a) one person (Mom) controls one corporation (Momco Ltd.);

(b) that person (Mom) was related to each person (daughters No. 1 and No. 2) in the group that controls the other corporation (Sibco Ltd.) because of the parent–child relationship. Note that the condition would also be met if the controlling group was either Mom and Daughter No. 1 or Mom and Daughter No. 2, since Mom is deemed to be related to herself as a shareholder of both corporations;   ITA: 251(1)(a), 251(5)(c), 251(6)(a)

(c) that person (Mom) owns not less than 25% of non-specified shares in the other corporation (30% of the common shares of Sibco Ltd.); and

(d) the common shares of Sibco Ltd. are not specified shares since these shares have voting rights and no restriction on the amount of dividends.

¶12,185.30   *Paragraph 256(1)(e)*

Finally, this rule applies to two group-controlled corporations if the following three conditions (involving a control test, a related test and a cross-ownership test) are met:

(i) each of the corporations must be controlled, directly or indirectly in any manner whatever, by a related group (control test);

(ii) each member of one of the related groups must be related to all of the members of the other related group (related test); and

(iii) one or more members of both related groups must own, either alone or together, not less than 25% of the issued shares of any class, other than a specified class, of shares of the capital stock of the other corporation (cross-ownership test).

Example Problem

Alpha and Beta, who are married, each own 50% of the common shares of AB Ltd. Their son, Alpha Jr., age 30, and his wife own 40% and 30%, respectively, of the common shares of Junior Ltd. Beta owns the other 30% of the common shares of Junior Ltd.

— *REQUIRED*

Determine whether AB Ltd. and Junior Ltd. are associated. Substantiate your conclusions by the related provisions of the Act and the conditions contained therein.

— *SOLUTION*

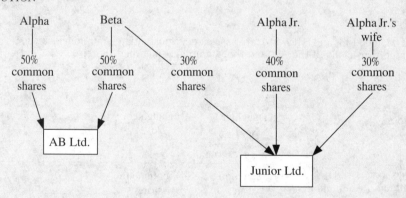

AB Ltd. and Junior Ltd. are associated because: ITA: 256(1)(*e*)

(a) each corporation (AB Ltd. and Junior Ltd.) is controlled by a related group:

- AB Ltd. is controlled by Alpha (50%) and Beta (50%) who are related by marriage,   ITA: 251(1)(*a*), 251(6)(*b*)

- Junior Ltd. is controlled by any of:

  (i) Alpha Jr. (40%) and his wife (30%) who are related by marriage,   ITA: 251(1)(*a*), 251(6)(*b*)

  (ii) Beta (30%) and Alpha Jr. (40%) who are related by blood,   ITA: 251(1)(*a*), 251(6)(*a*)

  (iii) Beta (30%) and Alpha Jr.'s wife (30%) who are related through the extended   ITA: 252(1)(*e*)
  definition of child,

  (iv) Alpha Jr. (40%), Alpha Jr.'s wife (30%) and Beta (30%), all of whom are related;

(b) each member of one related group (Alpha and Beta) is related to all members of the other related group. Note that in cases (ii), (iii), and (iv) above, Beta is related to herself as a shareholder of both corporations;   ITA: 251(5)(*c*)

(c) one (or more) member of *both* related groups (Beta) must own not less than 25% (Beta owns 30% in Junior Ltd.) of the issued shares of any class other than specified shares of the other corporation; and

(d) common shares are not specified shares.   ITA: 256(1.1)

The following is a list of the key words used in each of the paragraphs of subsection 256(1).

Par. (*a*)	controlled
Par. (*b*)	controlled, person, group of persons
Par. (*c*)	controlled, person, related, owned not less than 25%, specified class
Par. (*d*)	controlled, person, group of persons, related, owned not less than 25%, specified class
Par. (*e*)	controlled, related group, owned not less than 25%, specified class

¶12,190   Concept of control

¶12,190.10   *Legal control*

As a first approximation to the interpretation of the concept of control, the common law definition of legal or *de jure* control can be applied. Legal control means ownership of more than 50% of the voting shares or, more precisely, "ownership of such a number of shares as carries with it the right to a majority of the votes in the election of the Board of Directors".[3] Indirect control applies to the situation where there are multi-tiered corporations but is still based on legal control of more than 50% of the voting shares. For example, assume there is a chain of corporations whereby each parent corporation has 60% of all the voting shares of its subsidiary:

A Ltd. —60%→ B Ltd. —60%→ C Ltd. —60%→ D Ltd.

In each situation, the parent corporation controls its subsidiary. A Ltd. directly controls B Ltd. and indirectly controls C Ltd. and D Ltd. B Ltd. directly controls C Ltd. and indirectly controls D Ltd. Note that control is not multiplicative. Since A Ltd. controls B Ltd., A Ltd. can cause B Ltd. to vote all of B Ltd.'s shares in C Ltd. according to A Ltd.'s wishes. Therefore, A Ltd. controls, indirectly, C Ltd.[4] Furthermore, the Interpretation Bulletin should be consulted for   IT-64R4
the CRA's view of these rules.[5]

¶12,190.20   *Factual control*

A broadening of the concept of legal control may occur in fact situations to which the concept of "control in fact" applies. Using factual control to determine association further restricts the multiplication of the small business deduction by extending the circumstances under which corporations are considered to be associated. As indicated, the concept of control has been interpreted to mean legal or *de jure* control that vests in the ownership of more than 50% of the voting shares, as set out in the *Buckerfield's* case.[6] The expression "controlled, directly or indirectly in any manner whatever" when used throughout the Act,   ITA: 256(5.1)
extends the concept of control to actual or *de facto* control which might exist by virtue of a person having any direct or indirect influence. The Technical Notes which accompanied the

---

[3] Stated in the case of *Buckerfield's Limited et al. v M.N.R.*, (Ex. Ct.) 64 DTC 5301.

[4] For a case on indirect holdings resulting in control see *Vineland Quarries and Crushed Stone Ltd. v. M.N.R.*, 66 DTC 5092 (Ex. Ct.).

[5] As examples of the application of these rules to a fact situation see the cases of *Radio CFUN Limited* and *Wellport Broadcasting Limited v. M.N.R.*, 69 DTC 420 (T.A.B.); *Southside Car Market Ltd. et al. v. The Queen*, 82 DTC 6179 (F.C.T.D.); *Wynndel Logging Co. Ltd. v. M.N.R.*, 80 DTC 1125 (T.R.B.); *Roclar Leasing Ltd. et al. v. M.N.R.*, 81 DTC 544 (T.R.B.); and *B.B. Fast & Sons Distributors Ltd. v. The Queen*, 84 DTC 6554 (F.C.T.D.), affirmed by the Federal Court of Appeal (86 DTC 6106).

[6] See also the case of *The Queen v. Imperial General Properties*, 85 DTC 5500 (S.C.C.).

introduction of the legislation provided the following example of actual control: "where a person held 49% of the voting control of a corporation and the balance was widely dispersed among many employees of the corporation or held by persons who could reasonably be considered to act in respect of the corporation in accordance with his wishes". The Note stated further that "whether a person can be said to be in actual control of a corporation, notwithstanding that he does not legally control more than 50% of its voting shares, will depend in each case on all of the circumstances".

¶12,195   Extended meaning of control

The concept of control is further broadened by another provision. In determining whether a corporation was controlled by a group of persons, a group means any two or more persons each of whom owned shares of the same corporation. A corporation can be considered to be controlled at the same time by several persons or groups of persons. This concept is shown in the preceding example problem dealing with paragraph 256(1)(*e*). Note how four different groups control Junior Ltd.

ITA: 256(1.2)(a), 256(1.2)(b)

A person or group of persons will be deemed to control a corporation when the person or group owns:

ITA: 256(1.2)(c)

(i) shares representing more than 50% of the fair market value of all issued and outstanding shares of the corporation, or

(ii) common shares representing more than 50% of the fair market value of all issued and outstanding common shares of the corporation.

Note how this rule ignores the voting rights of the shares and looks at the underlying value of the shares in question. For example, assume that a corporation is capitalized with $1,000,000 of non-voting retractable shares owned by Individual A and $1,000 of common shares owned by Individual B. Both A and B control the corporation — Individual B through his or her voting rights and Individual A through the preferred shares which represent more than 50% of the total fair market value of the share capital of $1,001,000.

Since the value of a share can be affected by voting rights and certain other special features, these features are to be disregarded for the purposes of determining the fair market value of a share in this context. Likewise, "term preferred shares" and shares included in a "specified class" should be disregarded for purposes of making the fair market valuation.

ITA: 256(1.2)(g)

ITA: 248(1)

ITA: 256(1.1), 256(1.2), 256(1.6)

¶12,200   Ownership of shares

¶12,200.10   *Look-through rules*

The association rules use both of the words "controlled" and "owned". As previously demonstrated, indirect control of a corporation can flow through a chain of corporations through *de jure* control. However, the courts have held that ownership, including indirect ownership, cannot be traced through a chain of corporations. Therefore, provisions were enacted to provide a series of indirect ownership rules which are referred to as the "look-through" rules. These rules apply where shares of a corporation are held by another corporation, a partnership or a trust. A shareholder of a corporation, a member of a partnership or a beneficiary of a trust that holds shares in a corporation would be deemed to own a number of the shares of the corporation as is proportionate to his or her economic interest in the corporation, partnership or trust that actually owns the shares.

ITA: 256(1.2)(d), 256(1.2)(e), 256(1.2)(f)

¶12,200.20   *Example of control and ownership through a corporation*

Consider the facts in the following diagram:

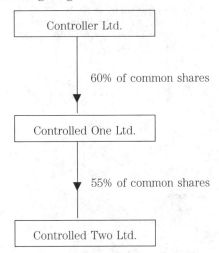

With its 60% ownership of the common shares of Controlled One Ltd., Controller Ltd. controls Controlled One Ltd. Since Controller Ltd. controls Controlled One Ltd., it can cause Controlled One Ltd. to vote the latter's 55% controlling interest in Controlled Two Ltd. in the interest of Controller Ltd. Therefore, Controller Ltd. controls Controlled Two Ltd. through Controlled One Ltd. Controller Ltd. does not own any shares directly in Controlled Two Ltd. through its ownership of shares in Controlled One Ltd. However, paragraph 256(1.2)(*d*) deems Controller Ltd. to *own* 33% (i.e., 60% of 55%) of Controlled Two Ltd.

¶12,200.30   *Shares owned by a minor*

Another such rule deems that shares of a corporation owned by a minor child are owned by each parent of the child. Even if the shares are deemed to be owned by the minor child by another provision of section 256, the shares will be deemed to be owned by each parent. However, an exception is provided if it may reasonably be considered that the child manages the business and affairs of the corporation and does so without a significant degree of influence by the parent. This exception is intended to accommodate young entrepreneurs.

ITA: 256(1.3)

¶12,200.40   *Two other deeming rules*

One of these rules pertains to rights to acquire shares (e.g., options) or rights to cause a corporation to redeem shares of other shareholders. The holder of such rights is deemed to be in the same position as if the rights were exercised. The other rule deems a person to be related to himself or herself in his or her capacity as shareholder of two or more corporations.

ITA: 256(1.4)

ITA: 256(1.5)

¶12,205   Association with third corporation

Where two corporations, that would not otherwise be associated, are both associated with a third corporation, the two corporations are normally deemed to be associated with each other. However, relief from this deeming rule is available, for the purposes of the small business deduction only, if the third corporation is not a Canadian-controlled private corporation or if the third corporation elects not to be associated with either of the other two corporations. For this election to apply, the two corporations associated through a third corporation cannot be associated by any other rule. Note that the election is an annual one. The result of the election is that the business limit of the third corporation is deemed to be nil.

ITA: 256(2)

ITA: 125

Example Problem

H and W, a married couple, have incorporated their separate businesses, H Ltd. and W Ltd., both of which are CCPCs. In order to avoid duplication of administrative costs, H and W incorporated a management corporation, M Ltd., to provide support services for H Ltd. and W Ltd. H and W each own 50% of the common shares of M Ltd.

— REQUIRED

Determine whether H Ltd., W Ltd. and M Ltd. are associated.

— SOLUTION

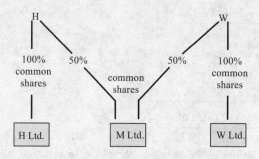

H Ltd., W Ltd. and M Ltd. are all associated with each other.

H Ltd. and M Ltd. are associated: *ITA: 256(1)(d)*

- H controls (100% of common shares) H Ltd.;

- H and W control M Ltd. (50% of common shares each);

- H is related to:

    (a) W through marriage; and   *ITA: 252(1)(a), 252(6)(b)*

    (b) H through the deemed related rule for a shareholder; and   *ITA: 256(1.5)*

- H owns not less than 25% of non-specified shares of the other corporation (100% of H Ltd. and 50% of M Ltd.).

W Ltd. and M Ltd. are associated also, using the same logic.   *ITA: 256(1)(d)*

Therefore, H Ltd. and W Ltd. are associated through a common third corporation, M Ltd.. Note that without M Ltd., H Ltd. and W Ltd. would not be associated.   *ITA: 256(2)*

However, if M Ltd. elects, in prescribed form and on a year-by-year basis, not to be associated with either of the other two corporations, then H Ltd. and W Ltd. are deemed not to be associated for that particular year for purposes of the small business deduction. The business limit of M Ltd. is deemed to be nil for the taxation year, so that M Ltd. cannot, itself, benefit from the small business deduction. No election is needed if M Ltd. is not a Canadian-controlled private corporation.

¶12,210 Deemed association

Where one of the main reasons for the separate existence of two corporations that are otherwise not associated is tax considerations, the two corporations may be deemed to be associated. The provision also contains a reasonableness test.[7] The decisions in the *Jutan Importers* and *Leggat Leasing* cases (see footnote 7) suggested that if the taxpayer can show a valid, non-tax reason for the separate existence of a corporation, the presence of a tax reason should not result in the application of the deemed association rule.   *ITA: 256(2.1)*

---

[7] For examples of fact situations in which the predecessor to subsection 256(2.1) (i.e., subsection 247(2)) was at issue, see the cases of *Doris Trucking Company Limited v. M.N.R.*, 68 DTC 5204 (Ex. Ct.); *Jordans Rugs Ltd. et al. v. M.N.R.*, (Ex. Ct.) 69 DTC 5290; *Griffin Head Farms Limited v. M.N.R.*, 72 DTC 1225 (T.R.B.); *C.P. Loewen Enterprises Ltd. v. M.N.R.*, 72 DTC 6298 (F.C.T.D.); *Jutan Importers Ltd. v. M.N.R.*, 76 DTC 1289 (T.R.B.); *Leggat Leasing (Halton) Limited v. M.N.R.*, 78 DTC 1035 (T.R.B.); *Lenco Fibre Canada Corp. v. The Queen*, 79 DTC 5292 (F.C.T.D.); *Covertite Limited v. M.N.R.*, 79 DTC 136 (T.R.B.); and *Alpha Forming Corp. Ltd. et al. v. The Queen*, 83 DTC 5021 (F.C.T.D.). A more recent Tax Court of Canada case on this issue, where the decision was in favour of the taxpayer, is *LJP Sales Agency Inc. v. Her Majesty the Queen*, 2004 DTC 2007 (T.C.C.).

¶12,220   Corporate Partnerships

The associated corporations rules were designed to prevent the splitting of a business into numerous corporations each of which could qualify for the maximum small business deduction. Thus, corporations within an associated group must share that maximum small business deduction. To prevent the splitting of a business into numerous non-associated corporations operating as partners and each qualifying for the maximum small business deduction, further rules were designed to require that the maximum annual small business deduction limit of $400,000 be shared by corporate partners or groups of corporate partners. These rules are necessary because partnerships are not taxed as separate entities as will be discussed in Chapter 18.

ITA: 125(6)

¶12,230   Manufacturing and Processing Profits and the Small Business Deduction

In the previous chapter, the manufacturing and processing profits deduction was alluded to without reference to the effect of the small business deduction on the manufacturing and processing profits deduction. Essentially, there is no manufacturing and processing profits deduction on that portion of Canadian manufacturing and processing profits eligible for the small business deduction. The amount of manufacturing and processing profits deduction for a CCPC is derived conceptually as the excess of manufacturing and processing profits over the amount of income eligible for the small business deduction. Hence, income eligible for the small business deduction will not be eligible for the M&P profits deduction as well.

ITA: 125.1(1)

Exhibit 12-1 and Exhibit 12-2 are equally applicable in determining the effective total corporate tax rate for income from manufacturing and processing activity that is eligible for the small business deduction.

Example Problem

During its first taxation year (of 365 days) which ended December 31, 2007, Touchee-Feelee Ltd., a Canadian-controlled private corporation, reported the following incomes:

Manufacturing and processing profits	$ 80,000
Total active business income earned in Canada (including M&P)	105,000
Foreign active business income (foreign tax paid $1,125)	5,000
Taxable income	75,000
Division B income	110,000
Taxable dividends paid in the year	40,000

The corporation carries on business in Canada and is not associated with any other Canadian-controlled private corporation. All foreign tax paid is recovered as a foreign tax credit under subsection 126(2). According to the formula in Regulation 402, 96% of the corporation's taxable income is earned in a province in Canada.

— *REQUIRED*

Compute the tax payable for 2007 by the corporation under Part I of the Act, assuming a 5% provincial rate of tax.

— SOLUTION

Taxable income		$ 75,000
Basic federal tax (38% of $75,000)		$ 28,500
Federal abatement (10% of 96% of $75,000)		(7,200)
Federal surtax (1.12% of $75,000)		840
Foreign business tax credit		(1,125)

Small business deduction:
  16% of least of:

    (a) Income from active business carried on in
        Canada $105,000

    (b) Taxable income $75,000
        Less: 3 × foreign business income tax credit (see
            above: 3 × $1,125) . . . . (3,375) $ 71,625

    (c) Business limit $300,000

    16% of $71,625 . . . . (11,460)

Manufacturing and processing profits deduction (all of this income is eligible
for the small business deduction) . . . .   Nil

Federal Part I tax payable		$ 9,555
Provincial tax @ 5% of 96% of $75,000		3,600
Total tax payable		$ 13,155

¶12,240   Investment Tax Credit Revisited

¶12,245   Overview

The investment tax credit (ITC), as described in Chapter 11, is also available for Canadian-controlled private corporations. However, additional incentives are provided for CCPCs. These incentives are obtained by adhering to a strict set of limitations many of which are similar to the restrictions for the small business deduction. This section will describe the advantages and limitations imposed by the legislation.

¶12,250   The ITC rate for CCPCs

¶12,250.10   *Basic rates*

Investment tax credits are presently restricted to qualifying scientific research and experimental development (SR&ED) expenditures for all jurisdictions within Canada. The one very limited exception is the credit for qualifying property expenditures for the Atlantic provinces and the Gaspé at a rate of 10% as described in Chapter 11. The basic SR&ED rate is   ITA: 127(9) 20% for all taxpayers including individuals, trusts and corporations. This basic ITC rate of 20% has no dollar limit, except that all of the qualifying expenditures must meet the rules set out in section 37, as described in Chapter 4.

¶12,250.20   *Additional rate of ITC for SR&ED expenditures*

An additional ITC incentive of 15% is provided where the taxpayer is a CCPC throughout   ITA: 127(10.1) the taxation year in which the expenditure is made. This additional rate results in a combined tax credit rate of 35%. However, the 15% additional credit bears additional restrictions as described below.

¶12,240

The additional 15% credit is restricted in total to $2,000,000 of qualifying expenditures, referred to as the SR&ED expenditure limit, but only where the preceding year's taxable income of the corporation and all associated corporations does not exceed the small business deduction limit for the year (i.e., $400,000). Where the preceding year's taxable income of the corporation and all associated corporations exceeds $400,000, the SR&ED expenditure limit of $2,000,000 is reduced by $10 for every dollar of excess. Once the corporate group's taxable income reaches $600,000 the SR&ED expenditure is reduced to zero. The actual calculation of the expenditure limit in the provision is, generally, $6,000,000 minus 10 times the greater of $400,000 and the taxable income of the associated group for the immediately preceding taxation year.

ITA: 127(10.2)

¶12,255 Refundable investment tax credit

Since many small Canadian businesses may not be in a position to pay taxes because of a weak profit position or losses incurred, the investment tax credit is not a strong incentive to invest. Therefore, cash refunds are available to certain taxpayers, in respect of available investment tax credits which cannot be used to offset taxes payable in a particular year. The extent to which a refund is available is a function of the status of the taxpayer, the nature of the expenditure that gave rise to the credit and when the expenditure was made. Investment tax credits that are available for deduction in a taxation year and which cannot be offset against taxes payable or converted into a cash refund, are available for carryover back three taxation years and forward 10 taxation years. However, any ITC that is deducted or refunded in the year must be included in income for the following year in respect of current SR&ED expenditures or deducted from the capital cost of qualifying depreciable capital property acquisitions.

ITA: 12(1)(t), 13(7.1)
ITA: 127.1

ITA: 12(1)(r), 13(7.1)

The refundable investment tax credit rates available to a qualifying CCPC are:

(a) 100% cash refund of the available 35% ITC based on qualifying SR&ED current expenditures not in excess of the expenditure limit for the year;

(b) 40% cash refund of the available 35% ITC based on qualifying SR&ED capital expenditures; and

(c) 40% cash refund of the available 20% ITC on qualifying SR&ED current expenditures in excess of the expenditure limit.

Note that the available ITC refers to the ITC as determined by the rules described in the previous section of this chapter.

Example Problem

Small Limited, a CCPC with a December 31 year-end, spent $2,000,000 in current SR&ED expenditures in 2008. Small Limited is not associated with any other corporation and may be eligible for an ITC of 35%.

— *REQUIRED*

Determine the amount of ITCs and refundable ITCs for 2008 on the assumption that its taxable income for the preceding year was:

(a) $400,000,

(b) $500,000, and

(c) $600,000.

— *SOLUTION*

Taxable income of preceding year	Expenditure limit	Refundable ITC	Non-refundable ITC
(a) $400,000	$2,000,000	$700,000[1]	Nil
(b) 500,000	1,000,000[2]	430,000[3]	$120,000[4]
(c) 600,000	Nil[5]	160,000[6]	240,000[7]

— *NOTES TO SOLUTION*

(1) 35% × $2,000,000

(2) $6,000,000 – ($500,000 × 10)

(3) ($1,000,000 × 35%) + ($1,000,000 × 20%) × 40%

(4) ($2,000,000 – $1,000,000) × 20% × 60%

(5) $6,000,000 – ($600,000 × 10)

(6) $2,000,000 × 20% × 40%

(7) $2,000,000 × 20% × 60%

¶12,260　Prescribed proxy amount

As indicated in Chapter 11, an elective alternative for the treatment of SR&ED overhead expenditures eligible for the investment tax credit was introduced to reduce the amount of record-keeping required. Under this annual election, referred to as a prescribed proxy amount (PPA), a prescribed amount rather than the actual overhead expenditure is eligible for ITC. Under the PPA election, the actual overhead expenditures are deductible from business income as ordinary expenditures rather than as SR&ED expenditures, which are credited to the SR&ED expenditure pool and written off as required. For a more detailed explanation of the treatment of SR&ED expenditures, see Chapter 4. The major difference in the write-off treatment of the two methods is the 20-year limited period of carryforward for ordinary business expenses, as compared to the indefinite carryover for the SR&ED expenditure pool. `ITA: 37`

The PPA is only used in respect of the determination of ITCs related to SR&ED expenditures, not the deduction of overhead expenditures. The statutory reference to a PPA is found in the definition of the ITC base, a qualified expenditure. The PPA itself is defined in and computed by the Regulations. `ITA: 127(9)` `ITR: 2900(4), 2900(5)`

The PPA is basically a substitute for an item-by-item accounting for and allocating of overhead expenditures *directly* attributable to SR&ED in Canada. The PPA (i.e., the amount eligible for the ITC) is 65% of the salary base which is the portion of the salaries of employees directly engaged in SR&ED in Canada. The "portion", referred to above, is determined on a reasonable time allocation basis for each employee engaged in SR&ED, including direct technical management activities. For employees who spend all or substantially all (i.e., 90%) of their time on qualifying SR&ED activities, the whole amount of their salaries is included in the salary base. `ITR: 2900(4)`

A modification to this rule relates to "specified employees". A specified employee is one who is a specified shareholder of the corporate employer or who does not deal at arm's length with the employer-entity. A specified shareholder is defined as a person who owns, together with the shares of related persons, 10% or more of any class of shares of the corporation. The salary base for specified employees is limited to the lesser of three-quarters of their full salary and 2.5 times the year's maximum pensionable earnings for CPP purposes (i.e., $43,700 for 2007). `ITA: 248(1) "specified employees", "specified shareholder"` `ITR: 2900(7)`

Where a PPA election is used, eligible expenditures for SR&ED and the related ITC are restricted to the following non-overhead expenditures: `ITA: 37`

(a) wages and benefits of employees *directly* engaged in SR&ED activities;

(b) leasing expenses of equipment, other than general-purpose office equipment or furniture, used *all or substantially all* in SR&ED activities;

(c) qualifying third-party payments for subcontracted SR&ED activities;

(d) costs of materials used directly in SR&ED activities;

¶12,260

(e) qualified SR&ED capital expenditures used *all or substantially all* (i.e., at least 90%) in SR&ED activities but excluding general purpose office equipment or furniture — see the next topic below; and

(f) capital cost allowance on 50% of the cost of leased equipment, other than general-purpose office equipment or furniture used *primarily* (i.e., more than 50%, but less than 90% (see (b) above)), for SR&ED activities. (See the next topic heading for an expansion of this topic.)

A restriction prevents the PPA from being greater than the total amount, with some adjustments, that would otherwise be deductible as business expenses.

ITR: 2900(6)

As a consequence of this election, the definition of a qualified expenditure has been expanded to include PPAs. Therefore, ITCs in respect of a PPA are treated in the same manner as all ITCs in respect of SR&ED and reduce the SR&ED expenditure pool. ITCs in respect of PPAs are also eligible for refundable investment tax credit treatment as previously discussed.

¶12,265 Capital expenditures

Under the normal SR&ED rules, a qualifying capital expenditure must be intended to be used *all or substantially all* (i.e., 90%) in SR&ED activities. This rule is a particularly harsh one since equipment, which is used less than 90% for SR&ED purposes and, therefore, is *shared* with other business activities, does not qualify for an ITC unless it can meet the 90% test.

ITA: 37

Therefore, ITC rules exist for equipment which is *shared* between SR&ED activities and other business activities, referred to as *shared-use-equipment*. The ITC rate on shared-use-equipment is one-half the normal rate and is earned on a usage basis over two time-periods (one-quarter for each time-period). These shared-use-equipment capital expenditures are not deductible as SR&ED, but must be deducted under the normal CCA rules.

ITA: 37(1)(*b*)

The first time-period starts with the initial usage of the shared-use-equipment until the end of the next taxation year which must be at least 12 months after the initial use. The second time-period again begins with the initial use but ends at the second following taxation year that is at least 24 months after the initial usage. Furthermore, the equipment can only qualify for the second time-period ITC if it qualified initially for the first time-period ITC.

Example Problem

Mr. A owns all the common shares of ABC Limited, a Canadian-controlled private corporation. ABC Limited incurred certain costs in the development of a new process that qualifies for SR&ED expenditures treatment.

Direct material	$250,000
Direct labour	200,000
Indirect material and labour costs	150,000

Of the indirect costs, Mr. A believes that approximately 20% is applicable to the development of the new process, but the corporation's accounting system is not sophisticated enough to identify the direct overhead costs.

Included in the direct labour costs is a salary of $50,000 paid to Mr. A's daughter, a professional engineer who spent 90% of her time on SR&ED activities.

ABC Limited has not had any SR&ED expenditures in the past and had taxable income for the preceding year of $135,000. ABC Limited is not associated with any other corporation. The corporation does not anticipate that it will have any taxable income for this taxation year.

— REQUIRED

Describe the tax treatment of the direct and indirect development costs of the new process on the assumption that the new process meets the requirements as SR&ED expenditures for the taxation year ending December 31, 2008.

— SOLUTION

All of the direct material and direct labour costs, for a total of $450,000, are deductible as current SR&ED expenditures since they are directly attributable to the development of the new process. Any amount of these expenses that are not deductible this year will qualify for the SR&ED expenditure pool and can be deducted in any future year. Any ITC deducted or refunded in this year or in future years is deducted from the expenditure pool.

ITA: 37

In addition, all of the direct material and direct labour costs qualify for an ITC of 35% since ABC Limited's taxable income in the preceding year was under the small business deduction limit (i.e., $400,000 for the calendar year 2007) and the total of these direct costs was less than the expenditure limit of $2,000,000. The ITC would be $157,500, i.e., 35% of $450,000.

Since the indirect material and labour costs cannot be traced directly to the development of the new process, they are not deductible under section 37 but are expensed in the normal manner under section 9. An ITC can also be claimed on the indirect material and labour costs of $150,000 by electing the proxy amount method for the current taxation year. The amount of the ITC is calculated below:

Direct labour costs	$200,000
Less: Daughter's salary (a specified employee)	50,000
	$150,000

Plus: Eligible portion of the daughter's salary — Lesser[1] of:

(a) 75% of $50,000 = $ 37,500	
(b) 2.5 × $43,700 = $109,250	$ 37,500
	$187,500
Amount eligible for the proxy amount (65% of $187,500)	$121,875
ITC 35% thereof	$ 42,656

Note that these labour costs are used as the basis of the proxy amount for overhead. The deduction of labour expenses and other overhead expenses as business expenses is not affected by this proxy amount calculation.

Mr. A's daughter is considered to be a specified shareholder since she is *deemed* to own all of her father's shares and, therefore, owns not less than 10% of the issued shares (i.e., 100% in this situation).

ITA: 248(1) "specified shareholder" (*a*)

Since ABC Limited does not expect to have any taxable income this year it can apply for a 100% cash refund of the total ITCs of $200,156 ($157,500 + $42,656). Alternatively, ABC Limited can apply these ITCs against taxes payable in the three preceding years or against future taxes in the next 20 years.

In the following taxation year, ABC Limited will have to include in income the amount of the ITC deducted or refunded of $200,156.

ITA: 12(1)(*t*)

— NOTE TO SOLUTION

[1] Limited by Regulation 2900(7) for a specified employee, but cannot exceed the portion of actual salary allocated to SR&ED (i.e., 90% of $50,000 or $45,000, in this case).

¶12,270 Incorporated Business Income and Integration

¶12,275 Corporate tax rate incentives to incorporate in general

Now that the complete system for the taxation of business income has been presented, an analysis can be done to determine whether there is a tax advantage to incorporating business income. The answer to the question is affected largely by the corporate tax rate applicable to the business income. Generally, business income not eligible for the small business deduction at the corporate level will attract higher tax costs when earned through a corporation than when earned directly by an individual even with the 45% gross-up and tax credit. Exhibit 12-4 illustrates this point, using the corporate tax rates developed in Exhibit 11-3.

EXHIBIT 12-4

Taxation of Active Business Income Not Eligible for Small Business Deduction

Corporation		
Income	$1,000	
Corporate tax — 35.12%		
(38% – 10% + 1.12% – 7% + 13%) .... (A)	(351)	
Available for dividend	$ 649	
Individual		
Dividend	$ 649	
Add: gross-up (45%)	292	
Income subject to tax	$ 941	
Combined federal and provincial tax rate	*25%*	*46%*
Tax on dividend before credit	$ 235	$ 433
Total dividend tax credit (($^{11}/_{18}$ + $^{7}/_{18}$) of $292)	(292)	(292)
Net tax	$ (57)	$ 141
Add: tax paid by corporation .... (A)	351	351
Total tax .... (B)	$ 294	$ 492
Tax on income if unincorporated .... (C)	$ 250	$ 460
Tax cost of incorporating on $1,000 of income .... (B) – (C)	$ 44	$ 32
Deferral (prepayment) of tax through a corporation .... (C) – (A)	$ (101)	$ 109

However, there may be the possibility of a tax deferral to the extent that dividends from the business income earned are not paid out immediately. This deferral possibility exists when the personal taxes which must be paid immediately on directly-earned business income exceed the corporate taxes, on the same business income. For example, in Exhibit 12-4, for the top tax bracket, the combined federal and provincial personal tax rate is 46%. Hence, item (C) is $460 and (C) – (A) in the last line of the exhibit reflects a deferral of $109. If the time value of money is considered, this deferral advantage may outweigh the added tax cost of incorporating this business income in a province with relatively high personal tax rates. Of course, there are other, non-tax reasons for incorporating such business income.

On active business income eligible for the small business deduction, a small tax saving results from the incorporation of such income compared to receiving it directly if the total corporate tax rate is lower than the theoretical 20% where integration is perfect, using the 25% gross-up and tax credit on low-rate business income. There is, however, the possibility of deferring tax on dividends ultimately distributed to the shareholders by delaying that distribution. Exhibit 12-5 illustrates these effects which result in a small tax saving using the theoretical corporate tax rates developed in Exhibit 12-2. Remember that, although most provincial corporate rates lie between 9.9% and 16%, the equivalent of the federal small business deduction is also given by most provinces to give an approximate effective rate of 5%.

EXHIBIT 12-5
Taxation of Active Business Income Eligible for Small Business Deduction

Corporation			
Income	$1,000		
Corporate tax — 18.12% (38% − 10% + 1.12% − 16% + 5%) . . . . (A)	(181)		
Available for dividend	$ 819		
Individual			
Dividend	$ 819		
Add: gross-up (25%)	205		
Income subject to tax	$1,024		
Combined federal and provincial tax rate		*25%*	*46%*
Tax on dividend before credit		$ 256	$ 471
Total dividend tax credit (($\frac{2}{3}$ + $\frac{1}{3}$) of $205)		(205)	(205)
Net tax		$ 51	$ 266
Add: tax paid by corporation . . . . (A)		181	181
Total tax . . . . (B)		$ 232	$ 447
Tax on income if unincorporated . . . . (C)		$ 250	$ 460
Tax cost (saving) of incorporation on $1,000 of income . . . (B) - - (C)		$ (18)	$ (13)
Deferral of tax equivalent through a corporation . . . . (C) − (A)		$ 69	$ 279

The foregoing calculations can be summarized by Exhibit 12-6, which averages the tax cost and deferral or prepayment between the two personal tax rates.

It will take a provincial rate of tax below 6.88% (20% − (38% − 10% + 1.12% − 16%)) to provide tax savings from the incorporation of income eligible for the small business deduction. For all higher provincial income tax rates, the total corporate tax rate will be above the 20% rate necessary for perfect integration of the tax on low-rate income and, as a result, there will be a tax cost to incorporation.

¶12,280 Specific tax savings (cost) and deferral (prepayment) possibilities

The concept of a "tax cost" is based on the excess of the total tax liability when the income is flowed through a corporation as compared to income earned through an unincorporated business. Under the tax cost concept it is assumed that all of the after-tax cash of the corporation will be paid out in dividends. In Exhibit 12-4, the tax cost at an individual's lowest rate of tax (25%) is $44 whereas the tax cost at the highest tax rate (46%) is only $32. The difference between the two is $12 which is due largely to the difference in the tax rates of 21% (46% − 25%) times the $59 difference between the individual's unincorporated business income of $1,000 and the grossed-up dividend income of $941. Therefore, as an individual's tax increases, the tax cost of using a corporation decreases.

¶12,280

A tax prepayment or deferral is based on a similar concept except for the assumption that none of the corporate after-tax cash is paid out immediately but is retained in the corporation. The ultimate benefits of a deferral are twofold: the present value of the deferred tax payment and after-tax financing costs avoided by the use of its retained earnings. In Exhibit 12-4, at the lowest rate of an individual's tax (25%) there was a prepayment of taxes of $101 because of the difference between the individual's low rate (25%) and the corporate rate of 35.12% or 10.12% on the business income of $1,000. At the highest rate of individual tax (46%), there was a small tax deferral of $109 (rounded) (i.e., 46% − 35.12% = 10.88%; 10.88% × $1,000 = $108.80 of business income) because of the lower corporate tax rate. The higher the individual tax rate relative to the corporate tax rate, the greater the potential deferral.

EXHIBIT 12-6
Summary of Tax Cost and Deferral from Incorporating Business Income

Type of active business income	*Average tax cost (saving)**	*Average tax deferral (prepayment)**
Not eligible for small business deduction (Exhibit 12-4)	3.8%	4.0%
Eligible for small business deduction (Exhibit 12-5)	(1.6)	17.4

* Average of highest and lowest tax rates.

Note from Exhibits 12-4 and 12-5 that tax costs decrease as personal tax rates increase and the deferral advantage increases as personal tax rates increase. The above averages show that tax cost decreases as corporate tax rates decrease and the deferral advantage increases as corporate tax rates decrease.

¶12,285   Summary of advantages and disadvantages of incorporating active business income

From the foregoing analysis, it should be possible to draw some conclusions of both a tax and non-tax nature regarding the incorporating of business operations.

¶12,285.10   *Advantages of incorporation*

The advantages of incorporation appear to include the following:

- limited liability, although it should be recognized that to the extent creditors of an incorporated business demand personal guarantees from shareholders, limited liability is negated;

- tax savings if the combined corporate tax rate is under 20%;

- tax deferral at higher personal income levels on business income not eligible for the small business deduction and at all personal income levels on business income eligible for the small business deduction;

- income splitting potential in carefully planned and very restrictive situations (as discussed previously with respect to the attribution rules and tax on split income) with family members as employees or shareholders;

- estate planning advantages on the transfer of future growth in the corporation's shares to children (as discussed in a subsequent chapter);

- availability of registered pension plans, including defined-benefit plans, to the owner as an employee of a corporation is not possible in the unincorporated form;

- separation of business and personal activities;

- stabilization of income of the individual through salary payments or greater flexibility in the timing of the receipt of income subject to personal tax;

- continuity of the separate legal entity;

- deferral of accrued capital gains on transfer of shares to a spouse (as discussed in a subsequent chapter);

- potentially easier access to financing;

- availability of the capital gains exemption for qualified small business corporation shares or business investment loss treatment for securities of a small business corporation; and

- availability of the deferral of capital gains on the sale of eligible small business corporation shares, if replacement shares are acquired.

ITA: 44.1(1)

¶12,285.20 *Disadvantages of incorporation*

The disadvantages of incorporating business operations appear to include:

- a tax cost if the combined corporate tax rate is over 20%;

- a prepayment of tax at lower levels of personal income on business income not eligible for the small business deduction;

- the additional costs of maintaining a corporation including payment of provincial capital and payroll taxes; and

- a loss of the availability of business and capital losses to offset personal income. While this disadvantage may be offset, to some extent, by the availability of allowable business investment loss treatment for shares of a small business corporation, the loss is only one-half deductible and it is deductible only on sale of the shares or bankruptcy of the corporation.

Often the tax saving, if any, or deferral will, in many cases, outweigh the disadvantages of incorporating such income, at least for rates of corporate tax in existence at less than 20%. This is particularly so where business income eligible for the small business deduction is earned through a corporation.

¶12,300 INCOME FROM INVESTMENTS OF A CCPC

¶12,310 Overview of Integration for Income from Investments of a CCPC

¶12,315 Purpose

¶12,315.10 *Investment income*

(i) The theory

The tax system provides special rules for private corporations which are meant to eliminate some of the tax biases between income earned by an individual and income earned by a corporation. One bias arises from the potential double taxation of investment income. For the moment, think of investment income as property income (i.e., interest, rents, etc., but not dividends). Later on, a more precise definition will be given. Without special rules, investment income would be taxed once in the corporation and again at the shareholder level when dividends are paid. To eliminate this bias, the concept of a refundable tax was developed, whereby a portion of the initial corporate tax on such income is refunded when dividends are paid. The tax on investment income was intended to be reduced to an approximate rate of tax of 20%. The dividend tax credit then would allow the shareholder credit for that 20% tax paid by the company and complete integration of corporate and personal taxes would be achieved. Thus, a Canadian who transfers his or her investments to a private corporation and flows the income through the corporation, would, theoretically, retain the same amount of after-tax investment income as he or she would if the investments were held personally and had received the income from the investments directly.

When investment income is flowed through a corporation, an indefinite deferral of tax is possible if the initial corporate tax rate is relatively low and if the investment income is left in the corporation and not distributed by way of dividends to the shareholders. In contrast, an individual Canadian who holds his or her investments personally, is required to pay tax on the income as it is received or accrued. The tax system attempts to eliminate this bias by ensuring that investment income earned in a corporation is taxed initially at a high corporate rate. Then the corporate tax is partially refunded when the investment income is distributed, by way of taxable dividends, to the corporation's shareholders who then pay tax on the income at their personal rate.

The system of integration was intended to bring the effective corporate rate of tax on investment income down to 20%. This rate is the same rate that was intended to apply on up to $400,000 of active business income. As mentioned previously, at a corporate rate of 20% the objective of theoretically perfect integration is achieved. However, the specific rules applied to each type of income achieve the objective in opposite ways. On the one hand, the rules applied to active business income provide for a low initial rate of corporate tax, after the small business deduction, to allow for greater retention of income for reinvestment in the business. On the other hand, the rules applied to investment income provide for a high initial rate of corporate tax to prevent the use of a corporation as a means of deferring tax on investment income. When retained earnings are distributed as dividends, the dividend refund was intended to bring the total effective corporate tax rate on that investment income down to 20%.

The provisions which increase the dividend gross-up and tax credit on eligible dividends do not apply to investment income earned in a Canadian-controlled private corporation. As a result, for dividends from investment income, the gross-up is 25% and the federal dividend tax credit is ⅔ of the gross-up or 13⅓% of the grossed-up dividend.

Exhibit 12-7 shows the tax rates on which the refundable system for investment income was based theoretically to achieve perfect integration.

EXHIBIT 12-7
Theoretical Corporate Tax Rates for Perfect Integration on Investment Income Eligible for a Dividend Refund and the First $400,000 of Active Business Income of a Canadian-Controlled Private Corporation

	Investment income	Active business income
Federal tax rate (theoretical)	40%	40%
Abatement for provincial tax	(10)	(10)
Net federal tax	30%	30%
Small business deduction	—	(16)
Refund of tax paid on investment income on the payment of dividends	(20)	—
Net federal tax after dividend refund and small business deduction	10%	14%
Provincial tax (theoretical)	10%	6%
Effective total tax	20%	20%

(ii) The reality: Imperfection

The theoretical model in Exhibit 12-7, in reality, does not operate perfectly for a number of reasons. First, the basic federal tax rate is 38%, not 40%. Second, the theoretical model ignores surtaxes. Finally, provincial taxes are generally greater than the theoretical model, e.g., 10% to 16% for investment income and up to 8% for the first $400,000 of active business income.

Even with these imperfections, it would be possible to defer tax on investment income through the use of a corporation, because the total tax at the corporate level would be less than the top personal tax rate in most provinces. In order to remove the deferral of tax on investment income, an additional refundable tax of 6⅔% is levied.

ITA: 123.3

Exhibit 12-8 shows the effective tax rate on investment income, including the additional refundable tax of 6⅔%.

EXHIBIT 12-8
Effective Tax Rate on Investment Income*

Federal tax rate	38.00%
Abatement for provincial tax	(10.00)
Net federal tax.	28.00%
Federal surtax: 4%	1.12
Additional refundable tax	6.67
Refund on the payment of dividends	(26.67)
Net federal tax after dividend refund	9.12%
Provincial tax** (hypothetical)	14.50
Effective total rate	23.62%

* Investment income includes all types of property income such as interest, royalties and rent, but does not include dividends from taxable Canadian corporations.

** A provincial corporate tax rate of 10.88% on investment income would result in an effective total tax rate of 20% which would result in perfect integration. However, provincial taxes vary between 10% and 16%.

Exhibit 12-9 shows a calculation of effective total tax applicable to taxable investment income of a Canadian-controlled private corporation eligible for a refund on the payment of dividends, referred to as a dividend refund, using a hypothetical provincial rate and including the 6⅔% additional refundable tax on investment income.

EXHIBIT 12-9
Comparison of Tax Rates Applicable to Investment Income Eligible for a Dividend Refund and on the First $400,000 Active Business Income of a Canadian-controlled Private Corporation

	Investment income[1]	Active business income[2]
Federal tax rate [par. 123(1)(a)]	38.00%	38.00%
Abatement for provincial tax [ssec. 124(1)]	(10.00)	(10.00)
Net federal tax	28.00%	28.00%
Federal surtax @ 4% of above net	1.12	1.12
Additional refundable tax on investment income	6.67	Nil
Small business deduction	—	(16.00)
Refund on payment of dividends from investment income [ssec. 129(1)]	(26.67)	—
Net federal tax after dividend refund	9.12%	13.12%
Provincial tax (theoretical)	14.50[3]	5.00[4]
Effective total tax	23.62%	18.12%

[1] Investment income includes all types of property income except dividends from taxable Canadian corporations.

[2] This column of the table reflects the tax on the first $400,000 of active business income. Over $400,000, there is no small business deduction, but there is a 7% general rate reduction; therefore, the effective tax rate would be 36.62%, assuming a full hypothetical provincial tax rate of 14.5%.

[3] A provincial corporate tax rate of 10.88% on investment income would result in an effective total tax of 20% (excluding surtaxes) which would allow for perfect integration. However, provincial tax rates average around 13%.

[4] Several provinces also give a small business deduction on the first $400,000 (or more) of active business income. In this example, a 5% provincial small business deduction was assumed.

Exhibit 12-9 clearly demonstrates that effective tax rates for investment income and active business income, at or below $400,000, are approximately the same and close to perfect integration. However, where the $400,000 active business income has been exceeded, there is a significant difference in the effective tax rates on these two types of income (i.e., 36.62% for business income versus 23.62% for investment income.) This difference may encourage some taxpayers to attempt to re-characterize some of their active business income (over $400,000) as investment income so as to attract the investment income net rate (23.62%) which has no cap (like the $400,000 business limit). Remember, however, that one important downside of investment income is that the initial corporate tax rate before the dividend refund is at the high 43.62% rate (i.e., no general rate reduction) plus a $6\frac{2}{3}$% additional refundable tax and that dividends must be paid in order to trigger the refund of Part I tax of $26\frac{2}{3}$%. While the corporate rate after the refund is low at 23.62% (i.e., 43.62% + 6.67% − 26.67%), the shareholders receive a dividend which is taxable to complete the integration process.

Remember too that the higher 45% dividend gross-up and tax credit apply to business income taxed at the high rate. On high-rate income the theoretical rate for integration is 31%. As a result, the discrepancy is not as great, and the incentive to re-characterize high-rate business income as investment income is greatly reduced.

¶12,315.20 *Portfolio dividends*

Another bias arises because intercorporate dividends are deductible in order to arrive at taxable income and, therefore, not subject to tax under Part I of the Act. By placing dividend-yielding investments in a corporation, an individual, particularly one in a high tax bracket, could defer tax on dividend income indefinitely. A $33\frac{1}{3}$% Part IV refundable tax that certain corporations pay on such dividends is intended to eliminate this bias.

ITA: 186

If it were not for the Part IV tax on what are referred to as "portfolio dividends", it would be extremely attractive for an individual to make portfolio investments in dividend-producing shares through an investment holding corporation. No tax would be paid under Part I on the dividends received by the holding corporation. By contrast, an individual who owned the portfolio investments directly, would pay tax under Part I at his or her personal rate on any dividends received. Thus, the Part IV tax of $33\frac{1}{3}$% levied on the recipient corporation is an initial tax roughly equivalent to the tax that would be paid by the individual in the top federal tax bracket receiving a dividend from a taxable Canadian corporation. The Part IV tax is fully refundable when the recipient corporation itself pays a dividend to its shareholders. Thus, after the refund, the corporation is effectively not taxed on the dividend that it received from another corporation and passed on to its shareholders. This preserves the integration system by preventing double taxation of the income that gave rise to the original dividend from the originating corporation to the holding corporation.

¶12,320 Conceptual illustration of integration

Exhibit 12-10 illustrates conceptually how investment income, such as interest income, capital gains and portfolio dividends are integrated through a private corporation that qualifies for refundable tax treatment. Recall that one of the objectives of the integration system is to ensure that income from investments, which flows through a qualifying private corporation to its shareholders, bears the same total tax burden (at the combined corporate and individual level) that would be borne on that income if it were earned directly by an individual. For simplicity of illustration, and to demonstrate total integration, the corporate tax is assumed to be 40% plus the additional refundable tax of $6\frac{2}{3}$% and the dividend tax credit, including the provincial tax effect, is assumed to be equal to the $\frac{1}{4}$ gross-up, except for portfolio dividends from Canadian-resident public corporations eligible for the 45% gross-up. Remember that CCPCs that receive "eligible dividends" can flow those dividends out to the shareholders as dividends eligible for the 45% gross-up. The combined federal and provincial tax rates for individuals is assumed to be 34% for this illustration, although *any individual's combined federal and provincial marginal tax rate* could have been used to show perfect integration. Under these assumptions, this objective of integration is met perfectly.

EXHIBIT 12-10
Conceptual Illustration of Integration

	$100 Interest income	$200 Capital gain		$100 Portfolio dividend	
		Taxable	Non-taxable	25% gross-up	45% gross-up
Corporation					
Income	$100	$100	$100*	$100	$100
Tax: @ 40% on investment income [Part I]	(40)(A)	(40)(A)		—	—
@ 33⅓% on portfolio dividend [Part IV]	—	—		(33)(A)	(33)(A)
Additional refundable tax @ 6⅔%	(7)(B)	(7)(B)		—	—
	$ 53	$ 53		$ 67	$ 67
Refund on payment of dividend (see amounts below)					
26⅔% of investment income	27(C)	27(C)		—	—
33⅓% of portfolio dividends	—	—		33(C)	33(C)
Available for payment of dividend	$ 80	$ 80		$100	$100
Shareholder (34% hypothetical combined marginal tax rate)					
Dividend received	$ 80	$ 80		$100	$100
Gross-up (25%/45%)	20	20		25	45
Income for taxes	$100	$100		$125	$145
Tax @ 34% (assumed)	$ 34	$ 34		$ 43	$ 62
Less: dividend tax credit, including provincial (approx.) ...	(20)	(20)		(25)	(45)
Net tax paid	$ 14	$ 14		$ 18(D)	$ 17(D)
Summary of tax paid					
Corporation (net of refund) (A) + (B) – (C)	$ 20	$ 20		Nil	Nil
Shareholder	14	14		$ 18	$ 17
Total	$ 34	$ 34		$ 18	$ 17
Tax paid on equivalent amount of income if received directly by investor	$ 34	$ 34		$ 18**	$ 17**

    * This amount can be paid as a capital dividend which is received by the shareholder tax free (as discussed in a subsequent chapter).

    ** The calculation would be identical to that resulting in amount (D).

¶12,330　Special Refundable Taxes in Respect of Income from Investments of a CCPC

¶12,335　Aggregate investment income

Aggregate investment income is broadly defined to include income from property, plus net taxable capital gains, less certain adjustments. Property income, for the purposes of this definition, includes net income from all property, other than (a) exempt income and (b) dividends which are deductible in computing taxable income. The meaning of the term "income from property" is amplified by the definition "income" or "loss" which includes income from a specified investment business *carried on in Canada*, but excludes income from the following sources:

ITA: 129(4)

(a) from any property that is incident to or pertains to an active business carried on by a corporation, or

(b) from any property used or held primarily for the purpose of earning income from an active business carried on by the corporation.

Net losses from property are deducted from the foregoing amounts of property income.

Foreign investment income is calculated as aggregate investment income from foreign sources. Hence, aggregate investment income includes that income from both Canadian and foreign sources.   ITA: 129(4)

As part of the system of integration, one-half of the capital gains and capital losses that is not included in income, is included in the corporation's capital dividend account (discussed in a subsequent chapter). The Act permits the corporation to pay a dividend out of the capital dividend account. The capital dividend is received free of tax by the shareholder. This completes the full integration of capital gains through a private corporation or Canadian-controlled private corporation and, with respect to the tax-free portion of the capital gains, places the shareholder in the same position as if he or she received the gain directly.   ITA: 89(1) ITA: 83(2)

¶12,340 Additional refundable tax (ART)

¶12,340.10 *Basic rules*

For Canadian-controlled private corporations, a refundable tax is imposed on "aggregate investment income". This tax can be summarized as follows: ITA: 123.3

$6\frac{2}{3}\%$ × the lesser of:

(a) aggregate investment income, and   ITA: 129(4)

(b) taxable income minus the amount on which the small business deduction is based.

Aggregate investment income (AII) can be summarized as follows: ITA: 129(4)

- Net taxable capital gains for the year,
- Less: net capital losses deducted under Division C,
- Plus: income from property (Canadian and foreign)*,
- Less: dividends deducted under Division C,
- Less: losses from property (Canadian and foreign).

---

* Includes interest, royalties, rents and dividends.

¶12,340.20 *Avoiding the potential circular calculation with ART*

The calculation of the ART has been complicated by the fact that a number of the components of the corporate tax calculation are interrelated. For example:

- the small business deduction must be calculated in order to complete the ART;
- the foreign tax credit (FTC) calculations are needed to calculate the small business deduction; and
- the "tax for the year otherwise payable under this Part", which normally would include the ART, is needed to calculate the FTCs.   ITA: 126(7)

As a result, there could have been a circular calculation if the following provisions were not introduced:

- the "tax for the year otherwise payable under this Part" for the business FTC excludes ART; and   ITA: 126(7)

- the small business deduction calculation that grosses up the non-business FTC ($^{10}/_3$ × non-business FTC) must be calculated on the assumption that the non-business FTC calculation does not include the ART. ITA: 125(1)(b)(i)

To minimize confusion, Exhibit 12-11 sets out the steps that should be taken when calculating the ART when foreign tax credits are involved. Of course, where computer tax software is being used, this circularity issue does not have to be addressed, as it does in a manual calculation.

EXHIBIT 12-11
Steps to be taken to Calculate ART when FTCs are Involved

---

(1) Calculate the non-business FTC excluding ART from the "tax for the year otherwise payable under this Part" [spar. 125(1)(b)(i), ssec. 126(1)].

(2) Calculate the business FTC (by definition, this excludes ART from "tax for the year otherwise payable under this Part" [ssec. 126(2)].

(3) Calculate the small business deduction using the above numbers.

(4) Calculate the ART.

(5) Recalculate the final non-business FTC and include ART in the "tax for the year otherwise payable under this Part".

(6) Recalculate the business FTC with the final non-business FTC (normally, no change will result).

¶12,345 "Refundable dividend tax on hand" (RDTOH)

¶12,345.10 _The concept_

"Refundable dividend tax on hand" (RDTOH) may be viewed as an account which accumulates all of the tax paid by a private company on its portfolio dividend income (i.e., Part IV tax at $33^1/_3$%) and a portion of the Part I tax paid by a Canadian-controlled private corporation on other investment income. The principal components of the account are as follows:

- the refundable portion of Part I tax (including the ART) that is paid on investment income; ITA: 129(3)(a)

- the amount of Part IV tax that is paid on taxable dividends (the Part IV tax is discussed in more detail below); and ITA: 129(3)(b), 186

- the RDTOH balance at the end of the previous year, less "dividend refunds" (explained below) of the previous year that arise when the corporation pays taxable dividends. ITA: 129(3)(c), 129(3)(d)

The taxes that are accumulated in the RDTOH account are refundable to the company at the rate of $1 of refund for every $3 of taxable dividends paid. These refunds are commonly referred to as "dividend refunds", which reduce the balance in the refundable dividend tax on hand account. ITA: 129(1)(a)(i) ITA: 129(3)(d)

The following diagram of a "gravity bin" or "water tank" illustrates these rules conceptually:

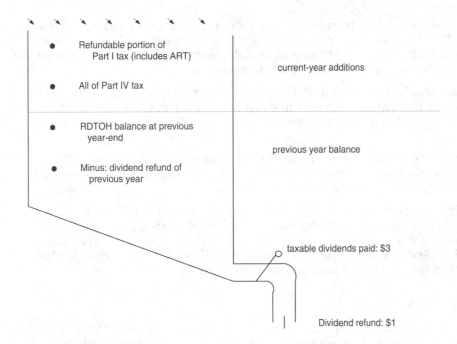

- Refundable portion of Part I tax (includes ART)
- All of Part IV tax

current-year additions

- RDTOH balance at previous year-end
- Minus: dividend refund of previous year

previous year balance

taxable dividends paid: $3

Dividend refund: $1

¶12,345.20   *Interpretation of the law*

"Refundable dividend tax on hand" (RDTOH) is illustrated, in part, in Exhibit 12-12. The basic purpose of the calculation is to aggregate the two types of refundable taxes (i.e., refundable portion of Part I tax for investment income (shown in the Exhibit) and Part IV tax for portfolio dividends), net of the amount of refundable taxes actually received. ITA: 129(3)

EXHIBIT 12-12
Refundable Portion of Part I Tax [par. 129(3)(*a*)]

The amount added to RDTOH in a taxation year in respect of Part I tax is the total of:

  (a) where the corporation was a CCPC throughout the year, the least of:

     (i) $26\frac{2}{3}\%$ × aggregate investment income

        less the net of: non-business foreign tax credit

              minus: $9\frac{1}{3}$* × foreign investment income

    (ii) $26\frac{2}{3}\%$ × (taxable income less the total of:

        • the amount eligible for the small business deduction

        • $\frac{25}{9}$** × non-business foreign tax credit

        • 3*** × business foreign tax credit)

    (iii) Part I tax minus surtax.

---

   * The notional federal tax rate for non-business income is 36% (i.e., 38% – 10% + 1.12% + 6.67% = 35.7%). $9\frac{1}{3}\%$ is the notional 36% rate less $26\frac{2}{3}\%$.

  ** $\frac{25}{9}$ is the equivalent of $\frac{100}{36}$, based on the notional 36% rate.

  *** $33\frac{1}{3}\%$ is the notional federal tax rate for foreign business income (38% + 1.12% – 7% (general reduction) = 32.12%, say, 33.33%)). [Proposed in Bill C-33, tabled November 22, 2006.]

The refundable portion of the Part I tax is designed to produce a refundable tax equal to $26\frac{2}{3}\%$ of investment income (excluding most dividends). The provisions establish aggregate investment income, net of expenses, from which net capital losses deducted in the year and losses for the year from property sources are subtracted. The justification for deducting the net capital losses is that since investment income is computed at the net income level, it is possible that taxable capital gains included in income could be offset by net capital losses ITA: 129(4)
ITA: 111(1)(*b*) which are deducted at the taxable income level after the computation of income for tax purposes. Since no Part I tax would be payable on such taxable capital gains, no refund of unpaid tax should apply to such gains. Hence, net capital losses claimed are deducted from aggregate investment income eligible for refundable treatment.

The calculations ensure that no refundable tax is calculated on foreign investment income which gives rise to a foreign tax credit in the year. Such foreign income will, therefore, not result in a refund of Canadian taxes that have not been paid as a result of the foreign tax credit.

The adjustments to taxable income are made to restrict the amount of the refund where other items (i.e., the small business deduction and foreign-source income) have reduced the taxable income below the investment income subject to tax.

Finally, the refundable portion of Part I tax is limited by the amount of tax payable under Part I, because there should not be a potential refund of a portion of Part I tax that has not been paid. Such non-payment of Part I tax may be due to the carryover of losses, deductions such as the small business deduction and the M&P profit deduction, or credits such as foreign tax credits, investment tax credits and political donations credits.

¶12,350 "Deeming rules"

What are known in practice as "deeming rules" are provided as an anti-avoidance provision that converts what would be property income (e.g., rent and interest) into active business income. However, this deeming provision only applies in situations where the income was derived from an associated corporation that had deducted the same amount in determining its active business income.

ITA: 129(6)

Were it not for these deeming rules, it would be possible for a corporation that was approaching the $400,000 business limit for its small business deduction to transfer certain of its assets to a new associated corporation which would rent the assets back to the original corporation. The rental expense incurred by the original corporation would be deductible, thereby reducing its active business income and preventing income in excess of $400,000 from being taxed at full corporate rates. The rental income to the new corporation would be considered income from property or income from a specified investment business and would, therefore, be eligible for refundable treatment. However, as a result of the deeming rules, the amounts received are deemed to be active business income of the recipient.

As a result, the combined active business income of the original corporation and of the new corporation, which receives rent deemed to be active business income is the same as it would have been if the new corporation had not been set up; that is, the fact that the two corporations must share the $400,000 business limit has no effect on the total active business income of the group. Thus, any active business income in excess of $400,000 within the associated group will be taxed at full corporate rates as it would have been without the new corporation. These deeming rules are summarized in Exhibit 12-13.

EXHIBIT 12-13
"Deeming Rules" [ssec. 129(6)]

Conditions	(1) Amount that would be income of the recipient corporation from property.	(2) Amount deductible in computing income from an active business of an *associated* payer corporation.
Effect	(1) Amount not included in income from property.	(2) Amount deemed to be income of the recipient from an active business [spar. 129(6)(*b*)(i)].
Application of small business deduction	Eligible for the small business deduction to the extent that the associated group of corporations has not exceeded the $400,000 business limit [ssec. 125(1)].	

As indicated previously, the incentive to re-characterize business income, that would be taxed at the high corporate rate, as investment income is greatly reduced with the higher 45% gross-up and tax credit on eligible dividends. However, combined federal and provincial corporate tax rates may exist that make the imperfection of the taxation of high-rate business income a greater tax cost than the imperfection of the taxation of investment income. As a result, the incentive to re-characterize income in this context may continue.

¶12,355   Part IV tax on portfolio and other dividends

Normally, when a private corporation (or a "subject corporation", which is discussed below) receives a taxable dividend from another Canadian company (or an exempt dividend from a foreign affiliate), the dividend is deductible, in Division C, in computing taxable income. However, a 33⅓% tax must be paid on some of these dividends. A calculation of the Part IV tax is made in the T2 corporate tax return to meet the filing requirements for this tax. Late-filed payments of this tax are subject to interest at the prescribed rate. This special Part IV tax is fully refundable to the corporation when the dividend income is passed on to its shareholders as previously discussed. ITA: 186(1)(*a*)
ITA: 187(1), 187(2)
ITA: 129(1)(*b*)

Part IV tax is a temporary tax of 33⅓% levied on "assessable dividends" received by a "private corporation" or a "subject corporation" with an exception for dividends received from "connected corporations".

¶12,355.10   *Assessable dividends*

Dividends subject to Part IV tax have often been referred to as "portfolio dividends" even though the Act does not use this term. The term "assessable dividend" is defined to include dividends that are deductible under Division C. ITA: 186(3)

¶12,355.20   *Private corporation*

A private corporation is a corporation that is resident in Canada and that is neither a public corporation nor controlled by a public corporation. ITA: 89(1)

¶12,355.30   *Subject corporation*

A "subject corporation" a corporation resident in Canada (other than a private corporation). A subject corporation is controlled (in the common law sense of ownership of shares with more than 50% of the votes), whether because of a beneficial interest in one or more trusts or otherwise, by or for the benefit of an individual or related group of individuals. An example is a Canadian public corporation that is controlled in the manner described above. This part of the Part IV tax provision was directed to investment holding corporations which were, essentially, private corporations, but which could otherwise avoid Part IV tax by listing a class of their shares on a prescribed exchange to meet the definition of a public corporation. The result of being a "subject corporation" is to be treated as a private corporation with respect to Part IV tax and its refund only (i.e., the refundable Part I tax provisions do not apply). Rules provide for a subject corporation to keep track of its RDTOH. ITA: 186(3)

ITA: 186(5)

¶12,355.40   *Connected corporation*

A corporation is connected with another corporation where: ITA: 186(4)

(a) the corporation is controlled by the other corporation (where control represents ownership of more than 50% of the voting shares by any combination of the other corporation and persons with whom it does not deal at arm's length); or

(b) the corporation's shares are held by the other corporation and these shares represent more than 10% of the voting shares and more than 10% of the fair market value of all the issued shares in the corporation.

The definition of control is expanded for the purposes of the concept of connected corporation. The provision requires that in determining "control", shares owned by non-arm's length persons must be included in that determination. For example, this provision allows ITA: 186(2) avoidance of the Part IV tax where the share ownership is split in lots of 10% among family members.

This concept of a "connected corporation" is illustrated in Exhibit 12-14.

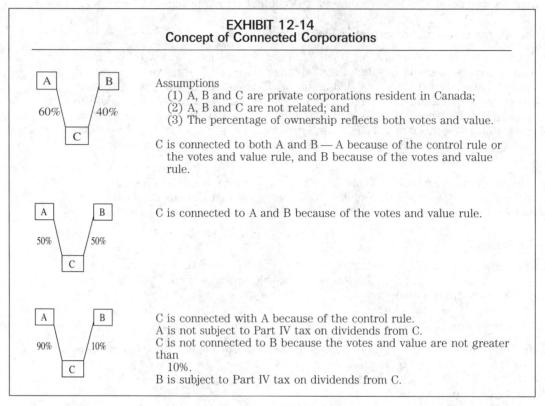

EXHIBIT 12-14
Concept of Connected Corporations

Assumptions
  (1) A, B and C are private corporations resident in Canada;
  (2) A, B and C are not related; and
  (3) The percentage of ownership reflects both votes and value.

C is connected to both A and B — A because of the control rule or the votes and value rule, and B because of the votes and value rule.

C is connected to A and B because of the votes and value rule.

C is connected with A because of the control rule.
A is not subject to Part IV tax on dividends from C.
C is not connected to B because the votes and value are not greater than
   10%.
B is subject to Part IV tax on dividends from C.

Note that the "connected" concept flows from C to A and B. Therefore, C may be connected to A and B, but A and B are not connected to C.

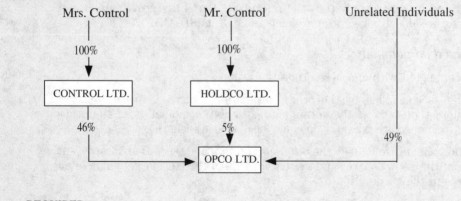

Example Problem

Mr. and Mrs. Control hold common shares in two private corporations resident in Canada, as shown in the chart below. These corporations in turn hold common shares in another private corporation, Opco Ltd. The balance of the common shares are held by unrelated individuals. Assume that the share-ownership percentage also reflects their underlying value.

— *REQUIRED*

Determine whether Opco Ltd. is connected to Holdco Ltd. and Control Ltd.

¶12,355.40

Opco Ltd. is not connected to Holdco Ltd. through the votes and value rule since Holdco Ltd. holds less than 10% of the common shares (i.e., 5%). However, Opco Ltd. is connected to Holdco Ltd. by virtue of the control rule as modified by the extended meaning of control. This latter provision extends the meaning of control by including shares belonging to non-arm's length persons, including other corporations and persons who do not deal at arm's length with the other corporations. In this situation, Control Ltd. and Holdco Ltd. are not dealing at arm's length since both corporations are related because Mr. and Mrs. Control are related through marriage. Therefore, for purposes of determining control, Holdco Ltd. is deemed to own the shares held by Control Ltd. (i.e., 46%) plus the shares owned directly (i.e., 5%) giving Holdco Ltd. effective voting control of Opco Ltd.

ITA: 186(4)
ITA: 186(4)(a), 186(2)

ITA: 251(2)(a), 251(2)(b), 251(2)(c)(ii)

Opco Ltd. is connected to Control Ltd. through both the votes and value rule and the extended meaning of control rule as described above.

ITA: 186(4)(a), 186(4)(b), 186(2)

¶12,360 Dividend refund

The private corporation will obtain a dividend refund each year equal to the lesser of:

ITA: 129(1)(a)

(a) ⅓ of all taxable dividends paid in the year, and

(b) the corporation's RDTOH at the end of the year.

A dividend refund is only available to a private corporation if it has that status at the time that it pays the taxable dividend. Thus, where plans exist for control of a private corporation to be acquired by a public corporation, consideration should be given to paying taxable dividends to shareholders prior to the time when control changes in order to maximize the dividend refund to the corporation.

¶12,365 Anti-avoidance rule

The Part IV tax is generally not payable on dividends received from companies with which the private corporation (or a "subject corporation") is "connected", i.e., where the recipient corporation has more than merely a portfolio interest in the shares of the payer corporation. However, where a connected private corporation has been entitled to a refund of tax in the year, the receiving corporation will pay a refundable Part IV tax. The amount of the tax represents its share of any tax refunded to the payer corporation as a result of the dividend. This prevents corporations in a connected group from escaping the Part IV tax by the payment of dividends from a corporation in the group, receiving portfolio dividends, to another corporation in the group.

ITA: 186(1)(b)

For example, assume A Ltd. owns 100% of B Ltd. and B Ltd. received a $100 portfolio dividend from some other corporation. B Ltd. would pay the 33⅓% Part IV tax of $33 on the dividend it received. If B Ltd. then paid A Ltd. a dividend of $100, B Ltd. would receive its dividend refund of $33. The $100 dividend would not be a portfolio dividend to A Ltd. because A Ltd. controls B Ltd. and, therefore, is "connected" (as discussed above) with B Ltd. If it were not for this anti-avoidance rule, A Ltd. would thus not be taxable on the dividend from B Ltd. This would defeat the purpose of the Part IV tax which is to avoid indefinite deferrals of tax on dividends of this nature. Thus, the anti-avoidance rule prevents such an escape from the Part IV tax by taxing A Ltd. under Part IV on the $33 dividend refund received by B Ltd. on the payment of the $100 dividend. Had A Ltd. owned only 51% of B Ltd., A Ltd. would have paid the Part IV tax only on its share of the dividend refund to B Ltd., i.e., on 51% of $33 for a tax of $16.83. Thus, A Ltd. pays Part IV tax on its proportionate share of the B Ltd. dividend refund triggered by the dividend paid by B Ltd.

ITA: 186(1)(b)

¶12,370 Summary of conditions for Part IV tax

Exhibit 12-15 summarizes the conditions under which the Part IV tax is paid on dividends received based on the percentage ownership of a recipient corporation in a payer corporation.

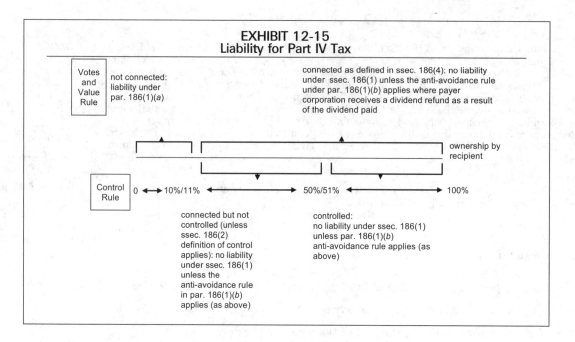

EXHIBIT 12-15
Liability for Part IV Tax

¶12,375   Application of non-capital losses

The recipient private corporation may *choose* to reduce the amount subject to the Part IV tax by applying otherwise available non-capital losses of the year or of a carryover year. These losses *cannot* be deducted subsequently from other income under Division C. Either the non-capital losses can be deducted, in effect, from dividend income subject to Part IV tax or they can be deducted in the calculation of taxable income subject to Part I tax. The same non-capital losses *cannot* be deducted under both provisions. It is, therefore, usually preferable to use the losses against income taxed at normal corporate rates, under Part I if that is possible, since the tax savings are usually greater and the Part IV tax otherwise payable is potentially refundable to the corporation.

ITA: 186(1)(*c*), 186(1)(*d*)

¶12,380   Actual Application of the Scheme

The following two examples demonstrate the interaction of Part I tax and the refundable taxes. The first example problem deals with Canadian investment income and active business income. The second example adds the element of portfolio dividends subject to Part IV tax and then demonstrates the interaction of the two refundable taxes on Refundable Dividend Tax on Hand and the Dividend Refund.

Example Problem 1

Microtax Corporation Limited, a Canadian-controlled private corporation with a December 31, 2007 year-end, has made the following calculation of its taxable income.

Canadian investment income	$1,000
U.S. investment income ($150 withheld at source)	1,000
Canadian active business income	1,000
	$3,000
Donations	500
Taxable income	$2,500

— *REQUIRED*

Compute the refundable portion of the corporation's Part I tax for 2007. Assume a 10% provincial tax rate and that the foreign tax credit is equal to the amount of foreign tax withheld.

— SOLUTION

Part I tax on taxable income:

Tax @ 38% on $2,500		$ 950
Deduct: Federal tax abatement (10% of $2,500)		250
Net amount		$ 700
Add: Corporate surtax @ 1.12% of $2,500		28
Additional refundable tax ($6^{2/3}\%$ × $1,500^{(1)}$)		100
		$ 828
Deduct: Non-business foreign tax credit (assumed equal to tax		
paid)	$ 150	
Small business deduction (16% of $1,000)	160	
Tax reduction$^{(2)}$	Nil	310
Total federal tax under Part I		$ 518
Provincial tax @ 10% of $2,500		250
Total tax		$ 768

Refundable portion of Part I tax:

Least of:

(a)	$26^{2/3}\%$ × aggregate investment income (AII) ($26^{2/3}\%$ × $2,000)		$ 533	
	Less: non-business foreign tax credit	$ 150		
	minus: $9^{1/3}\%$ × foreign investment income ($9^{1/3}\%$ × $1,000)	(93)	(57)	$476
(b)	Taxable income	$ 2,500		
	Less: Amount eligible for the SBD	(1,000)		
	$^{25}/_9$ × non-business FTC	(417)		
	3 × business FTC	—		
	$26^{2/3}\%$ × $ 1,083 =			$289
(c)	Part I tax – surtax ($518 – $28)			$490
	Least amount			$289

— NOTES TO SOLUTION

$^{(1)}$ $6^{2/3}\%$ × lesser of:

Aggregate investment income (AII)	$2,000
Taxable income (TI) – income eligible for SBD ($2,500 – $1,000)	$1,500

$^{(2)}$ There is no tax reduction in this case since all active business income is eligible for the small business deduction and any other income of this CCPC is aggregate investment income.

Example Problem 2

Lifetax Limited is a Canadian-controlled private corporation with its first fiscal year ended December 31, 2007. The following data resulted in the indicated computation of taxable income and Part I tax payable:

Taxable dividends paid during the year	$ 30,000
Active business income (assume equal to income eligible for the small business deduction)	$148,560

Investment income:

Taxable capital gains less allowable capital losses . . . . $ 3,000

Net income from property:

Canadian-source rental income   2,000

Foreign-source (before foreign tax of $375) interest income   2,500

Total Canadian and foreign investment income   7,500

Dividends (eligible for deduction under sec. 112 from non-connected Canadian-resident public corporations)   13,000

Total net income $169,060

Deduct: dividends   13,000   ITA: 112

net capital losses   700

Taxable income $155,360

Part I tax on taxable income:

Tax @ 38% on $155,360 . . . . $ 59,037

Deduct: Federal tax abatement (10% of $155,360)   15,536

Net amount . . . . $ 43,501

Add: Corporate surtax @ 1.12% of $155,360   1,740

Additional refundable tax (6⅔% × $6,800*)   453

$ 45,694

Deduct: Non-business foreign tax credit (assumed equal to tax
paid) . . . . $ 375

Small business deduction (16% of $148,560)   23,770

Tax reduction** . . . .   Nil   24,145

Total federal tax under Part I . . . . $ 21,549

Provincial tax (assumed) @ 10% of $155,360   15,536

Total tax . . . . $ 37,085

*6⅔% × lesser of:

(a) AII ($3,000 + $2,000 + $2,500 – $700) = $6,800

(b) TI – SBD amount ($155,360 – $148,560) = $6,800

**There is no tax reduction in this case, since all active business income is eligible for the small business deduction and any other income of this CCPC is aggregate investment income.

— REQUIRED

Compute the refundable dividend tax on hand at the end of the 2007 taxation year and the dividend refund for the 2007 taxation year.

— SOLUTION

Part IV tax on taxable dividends received:

Taxable dividends subject to Part IV tax $13,000

Part IV tax payable: 33⅓% of $13,000 . . . . $ 4,333[1]

Refundable dividend tax on hand:

Refundable portion of Part I tax:

Least of:

(a)   26⅔% × aggregate investment income (AII)
(26⅔% × $6,800) . . . . $ 1,813

Less: non-business foreign tax credit . . . . . . $ 375

minus: 9⅓% × foreign investment
income (9⅓% × $2,500) . . . .   (233)   (142) $ 1,671

(b) Taxable income	$ 155,360	
Less: Amount eligible for SBD	(148,560)	
$^{25}/_9$ × non-business FTC ($375)	(1,042)	
3 × business FTC	—	
26⅔% ×	$ 5,758	= $ 1,535

(c) Part I tax – surtax ($21,549 – $1,740)	$19,809
Refundable portion of Part I tax	$ 1,535
Part IV tax payable	4,333
Refundable dividend tax on hand	$ 5,868

Dividend refund:

Taxable dividends paid: $30,000 × ⅓	$ 10,000(F)	
Refundable dividend tax on hand at year end	$ 5,868(G)	
Dividend refund: lesser of (F) and (G)		$ 5,868

Summary of taxes payable:

Part I tax (including assumed provincial tax)	$37,085
Part IV tax	4,333
	$41,418
Less: dividend refund	5,868
Net taxes payable	$35,550

—NOTE TO SOLUTION

[1] Had any of the dividends deductible under section 112 been received from a connected corporation, such dividends would not have been subject to the Part IV tax, unless those dividends gave rise to a dividend refund to the connected corporation.

¶12,390   Imperfections in the Integration System for Income from Investments of a CCPC

¶12,395   Tax deferral at higher tax rates on personal income

When investment income or portfolio dividends are received by a corporation and ultimately distributed to shareholders as a dividend, the corporation pays tax when the income is earned and the shareholder pays tax when the dividend is received. There may be a time lag between the time the income is earned by the corporation and the time the corporation pays a dividend from that income. However, when such income is earned directly by an individual, tax must be paid on the income when received. If a taxpayer pays taxes at personal rates higher than the effective corporation rate on such income, there may be a tax deferral benefit of incorporating the income if the corporation does not pay dividends in the same year as it earns the income. Exhibits 12-16 through 12-19 illustrate the flow-through of portfolio dividends subject to the Part IV tax, dividends not subject to the Part IV tax, capital gains and interest, respectively. The effects of different rates of personal tax on the shareholder receiving dividends from the after-tax earnings of the corporation are being illustrated in these exhibits. Note that in all but one of these cases, there is a tax deferral when the shareholder is taxed at personal rates in excess of the 46⅔% theoretical corporate tax rate (combined provincial and federal rates) which is possible in the top tax bracket in provinces that have a personal tax rate in excess of 17⅔%. In the case of the flow-through of dividends not subject to Part IV tax (Exhibit 12-17) there is a tax deferral at all personal rates for shareholders.

Remember that CCPCs that receive "eligible dividends" can flow those dividends out to the shareholders as dividends eligible for the 45% gross-up.

EXHIBIT 12-16
Theoretical Flow-through of Portfolio Dividends
Subject to Part IV Tax

Corporation

Taxable dividend included in net income		$1,000
Deduction for taxable dividend [sec. 112]		(1,000)
Taxable income		Nil
Part IV tax paid currently at 33⅓% . . . . (A)		$ 333
Income remaining after tax.		$ 667
Dividend refund [ssec. 129(1)] . . . . (B)		333
Total available for dividends		$1,000

	25% Gross-up		*45% Gross-up*	
Shareholder (combined federal plus provincial tax rate)	*25%*	*46%*	*25%*	*46%*
Taxable dividend received	$1,000	$1,000	$1,000	$1,000
Gross-up	250	250	450	450
Taxable income	$1,250	$1,250	$1,450	$1,450
Total combined tax	$ 313	$ 575	$ 363	$ 667
Dividend tax credit (theoretically equal to gross-up)	(250)	(250)	(450)	(450)
Net tax . . . . (C)	$ 63	$ 325	$ (87)	$ 217
Total tax paid: (A) – (B) + (C).	$ 63	$ 325	$ (87)	$ 217
Tax payable by shareholder if $1,000 dividend earned directly	$ 63	$ 325	$ (87)	$ 217

NOTE: Some tax on this income can be deferred by shareholders whose total personal rates of tax exceed 46⅔% for dividends grossed up by 25% (i.e., (46⅔ of $1,250) – $250 = $333) or 54% for dividends grossed up by 45% (i.e., (54% of $1,450) – $450 = $333) if the corporation does not immediately distribute dividends from income received.

EXHIBIT 12-17
Theoretical Flow-through of Dividends Not Subject to Part IV Tax

Corporation

Taxable dividend included in net income		$1,000
Deduction for taxable dividend [sec. 112]		(1,000)
Taxable income . . . . (A)		Nil
Total available for dividends.		$1,000

[*Exhibit 12-17 — continued*]

	25% Gross-up		45% Gross-up	
Shareholder (theoretical federal plus provincial tax rate)	*25%*	*46%*	*25%*	*46%*
Taxable dividend received	$1,000	$1,000	$1,000	$1,000
Gross-up	250	250	450	450
Taxable income	$1,250	$1,250	$1,450	$1,450
Total combined tax	$ 313	$ 575	$ 363	$ 667
Dividend tax credit (theoretically equal to gross-up)	(250)	(250)	(450)	(450)
Net tax .... (B)	$ 63	$ 325	$ (87)	$ 217
Total tax paid: (A) + (B)	$ 63	$ 325	$ (87)	$ 217
Tax payable by shareholder if $1,000 dividend earned directly	$ 63	$ 325	$ (87)	$ 217

NOTE: All tax on this income can be deferred by all shareholders regardless of their personal rates of tax if the corporation does not immediately distribute dividends from income received.

EXHIBIT 12-18
Theoretical Flow-through of Capital Gains Eligible for Refundable Tax

Corporation		
Actual capital gain	$1,000	
Taxable capital gain ($\frac{1}{2} \times$ $1,000)	$ 500*	
Part I		
Tax on taxable capital gain (theoretical — 40%)	$ 200	
Additional refundable tax at $6\frac{2}{3}$% of $500	33	
(A)	$ 233	
Income remaining after tax ($500 – ($200 + $33))	$ 267	
Potentially refundable tax ($26\frac{2}{3}$% of $500) .... (B)	133	
Total available for dividend on taxable capital gain	$ 400	
Shareholder (theoretical federal plus provincial tax rate)	*25%*	*46%*
Taxable dividend received	$ 400	$ 400
Gross-up	100	100
Taxable income	$ 500	$ 500
Total combined tax	$ 125	$ 230
Dividend tax credit (theoretically equal to gross-up)	(100)	(100)
Net tax .... (C)	$ 25	$ 125
Total tax paid: (A) – (B) + (C)	$ 125	$ 230
Tax payable by shareholder if $500 taxable capital gain in excess of capital gains deduction earned directly	$ 125	$ 230

* The other $500 can be distributed tax free as a capital dividend.

NOTES: (1) Some tax on capital gains eligible for refundable tax can be deferred by shareholders whose total personal rate of tax exceeds $46\frac{2}{3}$% if the corporation does not immediately distribute dividends from income received.

(2) If the capital gains had not been generated by a CCPC and, therefore, had not been eligible for refundable tax, the total tax paid through the corporation would have been higher than that paid by an individual generating the capital gain directly.

EXHIBIT 12-19
Theoretical Flow-through of Interest Eligible for Refundable Tax

Corporation

Interest income	$1,000	

Part I

Tax in corporation (theoretical — 40%)	$ 400	
Additional refundable tax at 6⅔%	67	
(A)	$ 467	
Income remaining after tax ($1,000 − $400 − $67)	$ 533	
Potentially refundable tax (26⅔% of $1,000) .... (B)	267	
Total available for dividends	$ 800	

Shareholder (theoretical federal plus provincial tax rate)	*25%*	*46%*
Taxable dividend received	$ 800	$ 800
Gross-up	200	200
Taxable income	$1,000	$1,000
Total combined tax	$ 250	$ 460
Dividend tax credit (theoretically equal to gross-up)	(200)	(200)
Net tax .... (C)	$ 50	$ 260
Total tax paid: (A) − (B) + (C)	$ 250	$ 460
Tax payable by shareholder if $1,000 interest income earned directly	$ 250	$ 460

NOTES: (1) Some tax on interest eligible for refundable tax can be deferred by shareholders whose total personal rate of tax exceeds 46⅔% if the corporation does not immediately distribute dividends from income received.

(2) If the interest had not been earned by a CCPC and, therefore, had not been eligible for refundable tax, the total tax paid through the corporation would have been higher than that paid by an individual earning the interest directly.

¶12,400 Permanent tax savings or costs

¶12,400.10 *Dividend tax credit*

Recall the following about the dividend gross-up and tax credit procedure:

(i) the gross-up is intended to place the shareholder in an income position equivalent to that of the corporation before it paid corporate taxes; and

(ii) the tax credit is intended to give the shareholder credit against his or her taxes for the taxes paid by the corporation on the income from which the dividend was paid.

Theoretically, the tax credit (including the effect on provincial tax) for the shareholder should equal the gross-up because the gross-up represents taxes paid by the corporation for which the shareholder gets a tax credit. In practice, however, the tax credit may be either less than or greater than the gross-up.

The following calculations illustrate the situation of a shareholder in a province with a hypothetical provincial dividend tax credit rate of 6% when the dividends are from the active business income of a CCPC subject to the low rate of tax or investment income of a CCPC subject to refundable tax.

¶12,400

Gross-up	25.0%

Tax credit:

Federal ($\frac{2}{3} \times 25\% = 13\frac{1}{3}\%$ of 125%)	16.7%
Provincial tax credit (6% of 125%)	7.5
Total tax credit	24.2%
Total cost of imperfection in dividend tax credit (24.2% − 25.0%)	0.8%

The total or combined tax credit, which includes the provincial dividend tax credit, is often used in illustrations where a combined federal and provincial tax rate is also used. Provincial dividend tax credits for dividends subject to the 25% gross-up range from 3.7% to 7.7% of the grossed-up dividend. At 3.7%, there is a 4.6% tax cost of imperfect integration. At 7.7%, there is a 6% tax cost. Perfect integration requires a provincial dividend tax credit rate of 6.64%.

The following calculations illustrate the situation of a shareholder in a province with a hypothetical provincial dividend tax credit rate of 9%, when the dividends are from the high-rate business income of a Canadian-resident corporation.

Gross-up	45.0%

Tax credit:

Federal tax credit ($\frac{11}{18} \times 45\% = 10\%$ of 145%)	27.7%
Provincial tax credit (9% of 145%)	13.1
Total tax credit	40.6%
Tax cost of imperfection in dividend tax credit (40.6% − 45.0%)	4.4%

The provincial dividend tax credit rates for dividends eligible for the 45% gross-up range from 6.2% to 12% of the grossed-up dividend. At 6.2% there is an 8.5% tax cost of imperfect integration. At 12%, there is a 0.1% tax cost. Perfect integration of these dividends requires a provincial dividend tax credit rate of 12.1%.

¶12,400.20   *Other causes of imperfection*

Either a tax saving or a tax cost will result from changes in the federal corporate tax rate. Exhibit 12-20 shows the effects of a range of such federal rates, including the additional refundable tax of $6\frac{2}{3}\%$, between 40% and 50% while other factors are held constant. The Exhibit shows that, below the $46\frac{2}{3}\%$ corporate rate, there is an advantage to incorporating investment income. Hence, the 38% federal rate will provide for such an advantage. Where the corporate rate is above $46\frac{2}{3}\%$, there is a tax cost to incorporating investment income. Exhibit 12-21 shows a reduction in the tax advantage of incorporating investment income with all other factors held constant, when provincial corporate rates are in excess of 12%. This type of analysis is important and should be understood in order to react to future rate changes.

EXHIBIT 12-20

Tax Saving or Cost Resulting from Changes in the Federal Corporate Tax Rate Generated by Incorporating Investment Income other than Dividends

Federal corporate rate before provincial abatement (theoretical)	*40%*	*50%*
Income (assume interest eligible for refundable tax)	$300	$300
Corporate tax including additional refundable tax @ 6⅔%	(120)	(150)
Net before tax refund potentially available	$180	$150
Add: refundable tax (26⅔% of $300)	80	80
Available for dividend	$260	$230
Add: gross-up	65	58
Taxable income of shareholder	$325	$288
Tax on shareholder @ 40% overall (assumed)	$130	$115
Less: dividend tax credit (assumed equal to gross-up)	(65)	(58)
Net tax on shareholder	$ 65	$ 57
Add: tax paid by corporation (net of refund)	40	70
Total tax paid	$105	$127
Tax if income earned directly and taxed @ 40%	$120	$120
Tax saving (cost)	$ 15	$ (7)

EXHIBIT 12-21

Tax Cost Resulting from Provincial Corporate Rate greater than 10% Generated by Incorporating Investment Income other than Dividends (assuming a 38% federal rate and a 10% federal abatement)

Provincial rate (corporate)	*12%*	*17%*
Combined federal and provincial rate (corporate)	*47%*	*52%*
Income (assume interest eligible for refundable tax)	$300	$300
Corporate tax (38% + 6⅔% − 10% + provincial rate)	(141)	(156)
Net before tax refund potentially available	$159	$144
Add: refundable tax (26⅔% of $300)	80	80
Available for dividend	$239	$224
Add: gross-up	60	56
Taxable income of shareholder	$299	$280
Tax on shareholder @ 40%	$120	$112
Less: dividend tax credit (assumed equal to gross-up)	60	56
Net tax on shareholder	$ 60	$ 56
Add: tax paid by corporation (net of refund)	61	76
Total tax paid	$121	$132
Tax if income earned directly and taxed @ 40%	$120	$120
Tax cost	$ 1	$ 12

¶12,405 Summary of advantages and disadvantages of incorporating investment income eligible for refundable tax

¶12,405.10 *Advantages*

The advantages of incorporating investment income eligible for refundable tax would appear to include the following:

- a tax deferral if the shareholder's combined marginal tax rate is greater than the theoretical combined corporate rate of $46\frac{2}{3}$%;

- a negligible absolute tax saving as a result of the operation of the dividend tax credit in some provinces and a small tax saving where the combined federal and provincial corporate tax rate is less than the theoretical $46\frac{2}{3}$%;

- greater flexibility in the timing of the receipt of income subject to personal tax;

- estate planning advantages on the transfer of property and the transfer of future growth to children (as discussed in a subsequent chapter);

- possible family income splitting in carefully planned and very restrictive situations (to be discussed subsequently with respect to the corporate attribution rules) through family members as shareholders and, perhaps, employees; and

- possible avoidance of foreign estate taxes by placing foreign property in a Canadian corporation.

¶12,405.20 *Disadvantages*

On the other hand the disadvantages of incorporating investment income would appear to include the following:

- a prepayment (as opposed to a deferral) of tax if the shareholder's combined marginal tax rate is less than the corporate tax rate plus the additional refundable tax;

- an additional tax cost if the combined federal and provincial corporate tax rate is ever raised to a rate in excess of the theoretical $46\frac{2}{3}$%;

- an additional cost of maintaining a corporation in the form of administrative, accounting and legal costs as well as provincial capital taxes; and

- a loss of the availability to the individual of investment and capital losses.

Given the relatively small tax savings resulting from the incorporation of investment income in many cases, these disadvantages may outweigh the advantages. However, the beneficial effects of estate planning and income splitting must be analyzed.

¶12,500 COMPREHENSIVE SUMMARY OF TYPES OF CORPORATE INCOME AND FEDERAL CORPORATE INCOME TAX RATES

Exhibit 12-22 presents a comprehensive summary of types of corporate income that can be earned by a Canadian corporation and the federal marginal income tax rates applicable to each type of income.

EXHIBIT 12-22
Summary of Corporate Income Types and Federal Marginal Tax Rates

	ABI			Investment		Cdn. dividends	
	Cdn.	For'n.	PSB	Cdn.	For'n.	Conn.	Port.
Business & property:							
Business	X						
Interest, rent				X	X		
Foreign branch		X					
Dividends						X	X
Employment			X				
Taxable capital gains				X	X		
Net Income for Tax							
	%	%	%	%	%	%	%
Federal Part I tax rates:							
Basic	38.00	38.00	38.00	38.00	38.00		
Abatement	(10.00)		(10.00)	(10.00)	(10.00)		
	28.00	38.00	28.00	28.00	28.00		
Surtax (4% × 28%)	1.12	1.12	1.12	1.12	1.12		
	29.12	39.12	29.12	29.12	29.12		
Eligible for:							
SBD	16.00						
M&P > SBD	7.00						
RDTOH				26.67	26.67	33.33	33.33
FTC		Yes			Yes		
General rate reduction	7.00	7.00	7.00				
Additional refundable tax				6.67	6.67		
Part IV tax:							
3 × dividend refund						33.33	
Portfolio dividend							33.33

Example Problem

James Fish Processors Inc. (JFPI) is a Canadian-controlled private corporation located in Burnaby, British Columbia. The company's income for tax purposes for its December 31, 2007 taxation year-end was calculated correctly as follows:

Processing income[1]	$ 145,000
Wholesaling income	195,000
Maintenance service contract loss	(65,000)
Patent income[2]	45,000
Rental income[3]	35,000
Taxable capital gains net of losses[4]	55,000
Recapture of CCA[4]	15,000
Interest income on outstanding account receivable on wholesaling income	10,000
Interest income from loan to wholly owned subsidiary[5]	20,000
Interest income from a sinking fund trust for replacement of a building	50,000
Foreign business income (gross amount — $Cdn.)[6]	40,000
Foreign non-business income (gross amount — $Cdn.)[7]	25,000

Dividends from CCPCs (non-connected)		12,500
Dividends from the wholly owned subsidiary which received a $1,500 dividend refund as a result of paying this dividend		17,500
Profit on sale of excess land[8]		90,000
Net income for tax purposes — Division B		$ 690,000

---

[1] Processing income was correctly computed according to the provisions of Regulation 5200.

[2] The patent income has been determined to be property income.

[3] The rental income was derived from leasing the entire space on a 5-year lease in an unused warehouse in a small town in the northern part of the province.

[4] The net taxable capital gain and the recapture concerned the disposition of certain specialized maintenance service equipment.

[5] The funds were used to buy equipment for its active business.

[6] Foreign income tax in the amount of $10,000 ($Cdn.) was paid on the foreign business income.

[7] Withholding tax on the non-business income was $4,000 ($Cdn.).

[8] The land had been held for approximately 5 years. It was purchased with the intent of realizing a profit on sale.

Additional Information:

(1) JFPI made the following selected payments during the year:

Political donations	$ 7,500
Charitable donations	22,500
Dividends paid on July 15, 2007	37,500

(1) The balances in the tax accounts on January 1, 2007 were:

Charitable donation carryforward	$ 2,500
Unused business foreign tax credit	3,500
Non-capital losses	42,500
Net capital losses (arising in 1999)	13,500
RDTOH balance	Nil

(3) Taxable income earned in British Columbia, which is the only Canadian jurisdiction in which JFPI operates, is approximately 85% of the total.

(4) The business limit is all allocated to JFPI.

— *REQUIRED*

(A) Calculate the federal tax and provincial tax at an assumed net rate of 10% on federal taxable income payable by the company for 2007.

(B) Compute the refundable dividend tax on hand balance as at December 31, 2007, and compute the dividend refund for 2007.

— *SOLUTION*

Analysis of Division B Income

	ABI			Investment		Dividend		
Source	Cdn.	For'n.	PSB	Cdn.	For'n.	Conn.	Port.	Total
Processing	$145,000							$145,000
Wholesaling	195,000							195,000
Maintenance service	(65,000)							(65,000)
Patent				$ 45,000				45,000
Rental				35,000				35,000
Net taxable capital gains				55,000				55,000
Recapture	15,000							15,000

Interest — A/R	10,000						10,000
loan	20,000[1]						20,000
sinking fund			50,000				50,000
Foreign		$40,000		$25,000			65,000
Dividend					$17,500	$12,500	30,000
Profit	90,000						90,000
Division B income	$410,000	$40,000	Nil	$185,000	$25,000	$17,500	$12,500	$690,000

(A) Tax Payable

Division B income		$ 690,000
Division C deductions:		
Charitable donations ($22,500 + $2,500) — max. 75% of $690,000	$25,000	
Dividends from taxable Canadian corporations ($17,500 + $12,500)	30,000	
Non-capital losses	42,500	
Net capital losses ($13,500 × ½ / ¾)	9,000	(106,500)
Taxable income		$ 583,500
Tax @38% of $583,500		$ 221,730
Deduct: Federal abatement (10% of 85% of $583,500)		49,598
Net amount		$ 172,132
Add: Corporate surtax (1.12% of $583,500)		6,535
Additional refundable tax (Schedule 1)		12,233
		$ 190,900
Deduct: Non-business foreign tax credit (Schedule 2)	$ 4,000	
Business foreign tax credit (Schedule 3)	13,500	
Small business deduction (Schedule 4)	64,000	
M&P profits deduction (M&P profits less than income eligible for the SBD)	Nil	
Tax reduction (Schedule 5)	Nil	
Federal political contributions tax credit — max.	650	(82,150)
Part I tax payable		$ 108,750
Provincial tax @ 10% of 85% of $583,500		49,598
Part IV tax payable ((33⅓% of $12,500) + $1,500)		5,667
Total tax		164,015
Less: dividend refund		(12,500)
Net tax		$ 151,515

Schedule 1: Additional refundable tax

6⅔% of lesser of:

(a) AII ($185,000 + $25,000 + $17,500 + $12,500 − $9,000 − $30,000)	$ 201,000
(b) Taxable income − SBD amount[2] ($583,500 − $400,000)	$ 183,500

6⅔% of $183,500 = $12,233

Schedule 2: Non-business foreign tax credit

Lesser of:

(a) Amount paid . . . . $ 4,000

(b) $\dfrac{\text{Foreign non-business income}}{\text{Div. B} - (\text{Divs.} + \text{Net CL})}$ $\times$ tax after abatement + surtax + ART

$\dfrac{\$25,000}{\$690,000 - (\$30,000 + \$9,000)} \times \$190,900$ . . . . $ 7,331

Lesser amount = $4,000

Schedule 3: Business foreign tax credit

Least of:

(a) Amount paid + unused amount ($10,000 + $3,500) . . . . $ 13,500

(b) $\dfrac{\text{Foreign business income}}{\text{Div. B} - (\text{Divs.} + \text{Net CL})}$ $\times$ tax before abatement + surtax – general rate reduction

$\dfrac{\$40,000}{\$690,000 - (\$30,000 + \$9,000)} \times (\$221,730 + \$6,535 - \text{Nil})$ $ 14,025

(c) Tax otherwise payable – non-business FTC:
  ($221,730 + $6,535 – Nil) – $4,000 = ... $224,265

Least amount = $13,500

Schedule 4: Small business deduction

16% of least of:

(a) Active business income (Canadian-source) $410,000

(b) Taxable income. $583,500

Less: $^{10}/_3 \times$ NBFTC ($^{10}/_3 \times \$4,000$) $13,333

3 $\times$ BFTC (3 $\times$ $13,500)   40,500   53,833 $529,667

(c) Business limit (all allocated to JFPI) $400,000

16% of $400,000 = $64,000

Schedule 5: General tax reductions

taxable income. $583,500

less: M&P profits deduction ÷ .07 . . . . $ Nil

$^{100}/_{16}$ of the small business deduction   400,000

AII   201,000   (601,000)

net. . . . . $ Nil

7% of Nil . . . . $ Nil

(B) *Refundable Portion of Part I Tax*

Least of:

(a) 26⅔% of AII (26⅔% of $201,000). . . . . $ 53,600

Less: non-business foreign tax credit . . . . . $ 4,000

minus: 9⅓% of foreign investment
income (9⅓% of $25,000)   2,333   1,667 $ 51,933

(b) Taxable income $583,500

   Less: Amount eligible for SBD $400,000

        $^{25}/_9$ × NBFTC ($^{25}/_9$ × $4,000) 11,111

        3 × BFTC (3 × $13,500) 40,500   451,611

   26⅔% of .... $131,889 $ 35,170

(c) Part I tax – surtax ($108,750 – $6,535) $102,515

Least amount = $35,170

RDTOH

   Balance, January 1, 2007 .... Nil

   Add: Refundable portion of Part I tax .... $ 35,170

        Part IV tax 5,667

   Balance, December 31, 2007 .... $ 40,837

Dividend refund

   Lesser of:

   (a) Taxable dividends paid × ⅓ ($37,500/3) .... $ 12,500

   (b) RDTOH balance, December 31, 2007 .... $ 40,837

   Lesser amount = $12,500

— *NOTE TO SOLUTION*

   [1] The interest on the loan to the subsidiary is deemed to be active business income. JFPI   ITA: 129(6)
and the subsidiary are associated. The interest is ordinarily income from property, but is deducted
from the ABI of the associated payer.

   [2] Initially, the SBD amount is assumed to be $400,000, since Canadian-source ABI is
$410,000 and taxable income (before adjustment for foreign tax credits) is $583,500. This assumption, which is verified later in Schedule 4, allows for a calculation of ART.

¶12,800   REVIEW QUESTIONS

(1) Explain the purpose behind the concept of integration.

(2) It has been said that "ideal integration depends on the existence of two factors in the tax system". Briefly explain what they are.

(3) The dividend gross-up and tax credit has been described as the major tool of integration in the Act. Give a brief explanation of how it works in theory.

(4) What is the purpose of the small business deduction?

(5) On July 15th of this year, Mr. Smith bought all the shares of a company which was the Canadian subsidiary of a U.S. parent. There are no losses or ITCs being carried forward by the company. What advice would you have for Mr. Smith with regard to his choice of year-end for the acquired corporation?

(6) Give an example of when paragraph 125(1)(*b*) will give a lower limit for the small business deduction than paragraph 125(1)(*a*).

(7) What is the purpose of subparagraphs 125(1)(*b*)(i) and (ii)? Explain the overall concept and why they use the fractions they do in each of them.

(8) List some tax and non-tax advantages of incorporation.

(9) List some tax and non-tax disadvantages of incorporation.

(10) Mr. Mould has just started up a manufacturing operation to supply parts to the auto industry. Given his need for start-up capital, he is happy that his tax rate is reduced by both the small business deduction of 16% and the M&P profits deduction of 7%. Comment.

(11) Are there any tax rules that prevent an individual from deferring tax on portfolio dividends by flowing them through a corporation?

(12) What are five tools that are used in the tax laws to integrate the taxation of investment income earned through a corporation?

(13) Theoretically, what does the 25% or 45% gross-up on dividends from taxable Canadian corporations represent?

(14) Theoretically, what does the dividend tax credit represent?

(15) Explain how integration theoretically works if a $1,000 capital gain is realized in a CCPC.

(16) Mr. Owner owns all the shares of Holdco which in turn owns all of the shares of Opco, a CCPC carrying on an active business in Canada. In recent years, Opco has done very well and its income is well in excess of the business limit. Last year Mr. Owner paid a dividend of $150,000 from Opco to Holdco. However, since he needed the cash in Opco to expand, he loaned the money back to Opco and charged 10% interest. The interest charged to Opco amounted to $15,000 in the year. How will this interest income be taxed in Holdco?

(17) A number of years ago a reorganization was undertaken so that now A Ltd. owns voting preferred shares in B Ltd. These preferred shares have only 7% of the votes and are now only worth 7% of the value. The other shares of B Ltd. are owned by the son of the only shareholder of A Ltd. Are A Ltd. and B Ltd. connected?

(18) Under paragraphs 186(1)(*c*) and (*d*), the recipient private corporation may choose to reduce the amount subject to the Part IV tax by applying otherwise available non-capital losses of the year or of a carryover year. Either the non-capital losses can be deducted from dividend income subject to Part IV tax or they can be deducted in the calculation of taxable income subject to Part I tax. What factors should be considered in deciding which option to choose?

¶12,825   MULTIPLE CHOICE QUESTIONS

Question 1

Concept Corp, a CCPC, <u>correctly</u> calculated its taxable income for its year ended December 31, 2007 as follows:

Income from retailing business carried on in Canada	$ 120,000
Loss from retailing business carried on in United States	(20,000)
Interest income from long-term bonds	30,000
Taxable capital gain from sale of a capital asset	5,000
Net income	$ 135,000
Non-capital losses	(3,000)
Taxable income	$ 132,000

Concept Corp and X Ltd. are associated corporations. X Ltd. claimed a 16% small business deduction on $285,000 for 2007. The taxable capital of Concept Corp and X Ltd. is significantly less than $10,000,000. Which one of the following amounts is the maximum 16% small business deduction for Concept Corp for 2007?

(A) $16,000

(B) $18,400

(C) $19,200

(D) $21,120

Question 2

M Ltd. provides management advisory services to ACC Ltd. and is not involved in any other business. Mr. Mud is the sole shareholder and only employee of M Ltd. Mr. Mud and his son each own 50% of the issued shares of ACC Ltd. Which one of the following statements is TRUE?

(A) If Mr. Mud would reasonably be regarded as an employee of ACC Ltd., but for the existence of M Ltd., then M Ltd. is carrying on a "personal services business".

(B) M Ltd. is carrying on a "personal services business", unless it employs in the business more than five full-time employees throughout the year, which it does not.

(C) M Ltd. is carrying on a "specified investment business".

(D) M Ltd. is carrying on an "active business".

Question 3

B Ltd. is a Canadian-controlled private corporation which manufactures plastic bottles. The following information relates to its year ended June 30, 2007.

Active business income earned in Canada	$420,000
Canadian manufacturing and processing profits	395,000
Net income, Division B	420,000
Taxable income	420,000

B Ltd. is not associated with any other corporation. B Ltd. did not earn any foreign business income nor any investment income. B Ltd.'s taxable capital is well below $10,000,000. Which of the following amounts is the maximum manufacturing and processing profits deduction for the June 30, 2007 year:

(A) Nil

(B) $1,400

(C) $23,170

(D) $27,650

Question 4

A Ltd., a private corporation, received dividends from B Ltd. and C Ltd. during its year ended December 31, 2007.

	B Ltd.	C Ltd.
Amount of dividend received by A Ltd.	$120,000	$120,000
Percentage of shares owned by A Ltd. (votes and value)	70%	8%
Dividend refund received by the payer of the dividend	$ 40,000	$400,000

A Ltd. and C Ltd. are not related. All three are taxable Canadian corporations. Which one of the following amounts is the Part IV tax payable by A Ltd.?

(A) $60,000

(B) $64,000

(C) $68,000

(D) $80,000

Question 5

Joanne owns 55% of the common shares of J Co. and Doug (her spouse) owns 55% of the common shares of D Co. Which of the following would make J Co. and D Co. associated?

(A) If Joanne owned 25% of the common shares of D Co.

(B) If Doug owned 25% of the common shares of J Co.

(C) If a trust for their twin two year-old daughters controls T Co. and no special elections were made.

(D) All of the above.

Question 6

In which of the following situations are X Ltd. and Y Ltd. NOT associated?

(A) Rod owns 10% of voting shares of X Ltd. and 50% of the voting shares Y Ltd. and Patrick owns 60% of the voting shares of X Ltd. and 10% of the voting shares of Y Ltd. Rod and Patrick are not related.

(B) The adult son of the controlling shareholder of X Ltd. controls Y Ltd. and owns 25% of the voting shares of X Ltd.

(C) A mother controls Company X. Her two adult daughters each own 30% of the voting shares of Y Ltd. Her adult son owns 25% of the voting shares of Y Ltd.

(D) Both (A) and (C).

¶12,850 EXERCISES

Exercise 1

ITA: 125(7)

The taxpayer company carried on the business on a comparatively small scale of lending money on mortgages. The company was operated by two individuals who also owned and managed a number of other companies. All the companies operated out of the same office premises and used more or less the same office staff and equipment. The taxpayer company had no full-time employees. It was listed in the telephone directory but did no direct advertising. No attempt was made to keep track of the amount of time spent by the office staff on the work of each company and no specific charge was made for office space, use of telephones and equipment or staff.

The company made loans to potential borrowers referred to it by independent agents. Its clientele came mainly from those who found it difficult to obtain loans through the normal commercial channels. The agents had a general idea of the sort of loans which might be acceptable, but because those were relatively high-risk loans, the company had to examine them very carefully. Occasionally, an outside appraisal was made, but normally someone from the company would visit the property to examine it. Often considerable negotiations as to terms were involved. Post-dated cheques for five years would be obtained from borrowers and turned over to the bank as collateral for the company's line of credit.

For the year in question, the company held three mortgages involving $11,084. The sale of a small property, interest and other income resulted in total income of $4,609. Net income before taxes was shown as $3,479. The mortgages outstanding and net income of the company increased continuously from the year in question to the present time. During the year in question, the company's line of credit at the bank was estimated at $7,500 to $15,000, but it is now $25,000.

— REQUIRED

From the facts provided in the case, determine the type of business that is carried on by the company under the current legislation.

Exercise 2

ITA: 251

(A) By reference to provisions of the *Income Tax Act*, determine which of the following individuals or groups of individuals are not at arm's length with Alpha Corporation Limited:

(i) Mr. Beta, who owns 25% of the shares of Alpha and is not related to any other shareholders.

(ii) Mr. Beta and his brother, who together own 55% of the shares of Alpha and they are not related to any other shareholder.

(iii) Mr. Delta, who has an option to purchase all of the shares held by Mr. Beta and his brother anytime during the next three years.

(iv) Mr. Epsilon, who has an option to purchase all of the shares held by Mr. Beta and his brother from their estates within five years of their death.

(B) By reference to provisions of the *Income Tax Act*, determine under which of the following conditions Tau Corporation Limited and Lambda Corporation Limited do not deal with each other at arm's length:

(i) Tau is controlled by two brothers, A and B, and Lambda is controlled by A.

(ii) Three unrelated individuals together control Tau and one of these individuals controls Lambda.

(iii) Tau is related to Sigma Corporation Limited and Sigma is related to Lambda.

Exercise 3

ITA: 251, 256

Consider each of the following unrelated cases:

(A) Janna owns 55% of the shares of Jay-one Ltd. and 70% of the shares of Jay-two Ltd. Jay-one Ltd. owns 60% of the shares of Jay-three Ltd. The remaining shares in all three corporations are owned by persons unrelated to Janna.

(B) Rayna owns 30% of the common shares of Benco Ltd. and all of the shares of Rayco Ltd. The other 70% of the common shares of Benco Ltd. are owned by Rayna's cousin. However, Rayna's mother owns all of the voting preferred shares of Benco Ltd. and has sufficient votes to elect more than 50% of the Board of Directors of Benco Ltd.

(C) Adam owns 100% of the shares of Adamco Ltd. and 25% of the shares of Kidco Ltd. His daughter and son-in-law each own 20% of the shares of Kidco Ltd. and the remainder of the shares are owned by persons unrelated to all three.

(D) Sister One and Sister Two each own 50% of Sisco Ltd. and 25% of Cousco Ltd. Each sister has a daughter over the age of 18 who owns 25% of Cousco Ltd.

— *REQUIRED*

In each unrelated case, determine whether the corporations named are associated. Substantiate your answer by reference to specific provisions of subsection 256(1).

Exercise 4

ITA: 125(1), 256(1), 256(2.1)

Alpha and Beta are two sisters living in Halifax. While Alpha controls Taxit Ltd., Beta owns 25% of the shares of the corporation. Beta also owns 100% of the shares of Sibling Ltd. The active business income for Taxit during the current taxation year was $465,000 and for Sibling was $560,000. The taxation years for both corporations end December 31.

— *REQUIRED*

How much should each company claim as a small business deduction on their active business income for the taxation year?   *HAVE TO SHARE, MIGHT HAVE TAXIT OWN LESS THAN 25% OF BETA*

Exercise 5

ITA: 251, 252, 256

The common shares of Chutzpah Enterprises Limited were owned by the three Chutzpah brothers as follows:

Aleph Chutzpah	40%
Bett Chutzpah	40%
Gimbel Chutzpah	20%

The common shares of Schlock Sales Limited were owned by the following:

Bett Chutzpah	45%
Dallied Chutzpah	45%
Unrelated person	10%

Aleph Chutzpah is married to Dallied Chutzpah.

— *REQUIRED*

Determine whether the two corporations are associated. Substantiate your answer by reference to specific provisions of subsection 256(1).   *OWNS MORE THAN 25%*

256(1)(c)

Exercise 6

ITA: 123–126

The following data pertains to Moosonee Company Limited, a Canadian-controlled private corporation for its fiscal year ended December 31, 2007:

Canadian-source business income including $84,000 of manufacturing and processing profits	$110,000
Foreign investment income ($1,050 in tax withheld)	7,000
Income under Division B	117,000
Taxable income all of which is earned in Canada	79,700

— *REQUIRED*

Compute the federal Part I tax payable plus provincial tax at a 5.5% rate for 2007 if all of the business income is considered to be active. Assume that the foreign non-business tax credit is equal to the foreign tax paid through withholding.

Exercise 7

ITA: 186

Ex Ltd., a Canadian-controlled private corporation, received a taxable dividend of $90,000 from its Canadian subsidiary Little Ex Ltd. The subsidiary had paid a total dividend of $120,000 and had received a dividend refund of $18,000.

— REQUIRED

Compute the Part IV tax payable by Ex Ltd.

Exercise 8

ITA: 123–127, 129, 186

Why Limited is a Canadian-controlled private corporation operating solely in Newfoundland and Labrador. For its taxation year ended December 31, 2007, the company reported the following income under Division B:

Active business income	$ 85,000
Taxable capital gain	37,500
Canadian-source interest income	45,000
Taxable portfolio dividends from Canadian-resident public corporations	18,750
Income under Division B	$186,250

The corporation is carrying forward the following amounts:

Non-capital losses	$ 37,500
Net capital losses (arising in 1999)	68,750

The balance in the refundable dividend tax on hand account at December 31, 2006 was nil. On November 30, 2007, the company paid $112,500 in taxable dividends to its shareholders all of whom are individuals. The taxable portfolio dividends of $18,750 were received on November 1, 2007.

— REQUIRED   ⌐⟶ NOT CONNECTED

(A) Compute the federal Part I tax and provincial tax at an 8% rate payable by the company for 2007.

(B) Compute the refundable dividend tax on hand balance as at December 31, 2007 and compute the dividend refund for 2007.

Exercise 9

ITA: 123–127, 129, 186

Ay Ltd. is a Canadian-controlled private corporation with a December 31, 2007 fiscal year-end. The company operates primarily in Alberta, but has a very small business operation in the U.S. where 5% of its total taxable income as calculated by Regulation 402(3) is generated. Taxable income for the year is calculated as follows:

Canadian-source business income		$ 90,000
Dividends from CCPCs:		
Non-connected corporations		30,000
Wholly owned corporation which received a dividend refund of $4,000 as a result of paying the dividend		20,000
Canadian-source investment income		50,000
Foreign-source non-business income (foreign tax credit will be $4,000)		30,000
Foreign-source business income (foreign tax credit will be $1,000)		20,000
Canadian-source taxable capital gains		20,000
Income under Division B		$260,000
Less: donations	$ 40,000	
taxable dividends from CCPCs	50,000	
non-capital losses	20,000	
net capital losses	20,000	130,000
Taxable income		$130,000

The refundable dividend tax on hand account had a nil balance at the end of the previous year. No dividends were paid in the preceding year. Dividends of $70,000 had been paid during the year to the only shareholder, an associated corporation which has only income from investments.

— REQUIRED

(A) Compute the federal Part I tax and provincial tax at a 7% rate (using federal taxable income as the tax base) payable by the company for the 2007 taxation year.

(B) Compute the refundable dividend tax on hand balance at the end of the year and the dividend refund for the taxation year.

Exercise 10

ITA: 125, 129, 186, 256(1)

Splitinc Limited is owned 50% by Husband Ltd. and 50% by Wife Ltd. The two holding companies are 100% owned by Mr. Split and Mrs. Split, respectively. Splitinc Limited derives all of its income from active business carried on in Canada. It rents facilities from Husband Ltd. to which it pays $120,000 in annual rent, deducting this amount as a business expense. Splitinc also pays dividends to the two holding companies which is the only other income of those corporations.

— REQUIRED

(A) What is the nature of the rental income to Husband Ltd.?

(B) Is there a Part IV tax liability for the two holding companies on the dividends received from Splitinc Limited?

Exercise 11

ITA: 125, 129, 256

Janna Management Limited owns a building most of which it rents to Rayna Consulting Services Limited which carries on an active business. Janna and Rayna each own 50% of both corporations. Janna Management Limited also provides managerial, administrative and maintenance services to the unincorporated professional practice of Dr. Adam. The result of these transactions is that Janna Management Limited receives 60% of its income from rent and 40% from providing services and has available an excess business limit for the purposes of the small business deduction.

— REQUIRED

Determine the nature of its income and the deductions from tax available to Janna Management Limited.

Exercise 12

ITA: Part I, IV

Dane Tee lives in a province with a 15.5% corporate tax rate and owns an investment portfolio that generated the following Canadian-source income during the year:

Interest	$ 7,000
Portfolio dividends from CCPCs.....................................	15,000
Capital gains...	6,000

Her cash needs require that $15,000 of the corporation's after-tax profits be distributed as a dividend. The corporation will retain and reinvest the remainder. She already has taxable income of $20,000 from other sources. She has federal personal tax credits of $1,400 and provincial tax credits of $900.

— REQUIRED

Compare the total tax on the income from the portfolio with the total tax if a corporation owned the securities.

¶12,875 ASSIGNMENT PROBLEMS

Problem 1

ITA: 125(7)

The taxpayer company, a private corporation, owned and operated a small shopping centre from which it received rental income. There were seven separate tenants, only one of them being what is sometimes referred to as a "Triple A" tenant, namely, a Canadian bank. The corporation, through its principal officer, negotiated all the leases, took care of all the complaints from the tenants and arranged for the maintenance of the shopping centre. It required some activity by the company almost daily. The rental income of the company was mainly for use of the property, but also, to a much lesser extent, for services and other things supplied by the company such as heat, repairs, etc.

— *REQUIRED*

From the facts provided in the case, determine the type of income that the corporation derives from the business that it carries on under the current legislation.

Problem 2

ITA: 256

Consider each of the following unrelated cases, involving the ownership of the common shares of Canadian-controlled private corporations, for taxation years of all corporations ending on December 31:

(A) Leah Ltd. owns 55% of the shares of Elaine Ltd.

(B) Ms. Miriam owns 51% of the shares of Miri Ltd. and 60% of the shares of Ethan Jay Ltd.

(C) Ms. Irene and Mr. Mordechai each own 50% of the shares of IL Ltd. In addition, they each own 50% of the shares of Philip Ltd. Ms. Irene and Mr. Mordechai are not related.

(D) Mrs. Lyn owns 60% of the shares of LBD Ltd. and Mrs. Sarah owns the other 40%. Mrs. Lyn and Mrs. Sarah each own 50% of the shares of Alex Ltd. Mrs. Lyn and Mrs. Sarah are not related.

(E) Janna Ltd., Rayna Ltd. and Adam Ltd. each own ⅓ of the shares of Stan Ltd. Janna Ltd. and Rayna Ltd. each own 50% of the shares of Jonathan Ltd.

(F) Ms. Ruth owns all of the shares of Rick Ltd. Ms. Ruth owns 25% of the shares of Daniel Ltd. and Ms. Ruth's daughter, Elana, who is over 18 years old owns the other 75%.

(G) Mr. Joshua owns 100% of the shares of Gord Ltd. and Ms. Dahlia owns 100% of the shares of Rosalyn Ltd. Mr. Joshua and Ms. Dahlia each own 30% of the shares of Rebecca Ltd. The other 40% of the shares of Rebecca Ltd. are owned by strangers. Mr. Joshua is the brother of Ms. Dahlia's husband.

(H) Mrs. Yael owns 60% of the shares of Benjamin Ltd. and 30% of the shares of Livi Ltd. Another 25% of the shares of Livi Ltd. are owned by Benjamin Ltd. and the remaining 45% of the shares of Livi Ltd. are owned by strangers.

(I) Ms. Daniella owns 60% of the shares of Veggie Ltd. and 25% of the shares of Beef Ltd. Mr. Adam, who is not related to Ms. Daniella, owns the other 75% of the shares of Beef Ltd. Ms. Daniella holds an option to buy all of the shares owned by Mr. Adam at any time in the next 10 years.

(J) Mr. and Mrs. Jonathan each own 50% of Ethan Ltd. Mr. Jonathan and his two brothers and one sister each own 25% of Maya Ltd.

— *REQUIRED*

In each of the above *unrelated* cases determine whether the corporations are associated. Substantiate your answer by reference to the specific conditions in the provisions of section 256, and consider all possible alternatives.

Problem 3

ITA: 256

Consider each of the following unrelated cases, involving the ownership of shares of Canadian-controlled private corporations. Assume all of the issued shares are common shares unless specifically stated otherwise.

(A) Rachel and Monica, friends, each own 50% of the issued shares of A Ltd. In addition, Rachel owns 80% and Monica owns 20% of the issued shares of B Ltd.

(B) Charlie and Claudia are siblings. Charlie owns 80% of A Ltd. which in turn owns 40% of B Ltd. Claudia owns 60% of B Ltd.

(C) Bob, Bill and Bert are three brothers who share equally the income of a professional partnership. The partnership owns 100% of the shares of A Ltd. Bert owns 100% of the shares of B Ltd.

(D) Anne and Barbara are sisters. They each own 100% of their respective corporations, A Ltd. and B Ltd. A Ltd. and B Ltd. each own 40% of the shares of C Ltd.

(E) Valerie, Brandon, and Claire are strangers. They each own ⅓ of the shares of A Ltd. Brandon owns 40% of the shares of B Ltd. The remaining 60% are owned by Claire. Claire also owns 100% of the shares of C Ltd.

(F) Valerie and her two nieces each own 25% of the shares of A Ltd. Valerie's husband, Dilon, and his nephew each own 50% of the shares of B Ltd. Dilon also owns the remaining 25% of the shares of A Ltd.

(G) Father owns 100% of the shares of F Ltd. His son, Sean, age 17, owns 100% of the common shares of S Ltd. F Ltd. owns 30% of the issued preferred shares of S Ltd. The preferred shares have the following characteristics:

- non-voting,

- dividend rate fixed at 6%,

- redeemable at $1,000 per share, and

- issue price $1,000 per share.

The prescribed rate of interest was 8% at the time the preferred shares were issued.

— REQUIRED

Determine which of the corporations are associated and substantiate your answer by reference to specific provisions of the Act.

Problem 4

ITA: 256

Both corporations in this case were incorporated for the purpose of buying and selling anti-freeze products. Warren Packaging Limited sold its product ("Dual Duty") to wholesalers who serviced and supplied garages and service stations ultimately for the consumers. Its sole shareholder and president was Mr. Warren. Bradford-Penn Oil Inc. sold its product ("Viceroy") to retailers who sold it on a cash and carry basis to its clients. Mr. Warren's wife was the sole shareholder and president of the latter company.

In essence, both companies were directed by the same person in the same premises. They both had the same year-end. The product came in bulk from the same supplier and was packed in smaller quantities with the different brand names.

Management of the companies felt that it was too risky to have the same company distribute the anti-freeze product to both the wholesalers and the retailers. There was only one supplier of bulk anti-freeze available to the two corporations and that supplier marketed its own brand and, as a result, was also in competition with Warren Packaging and Bradford-Penn Oil. Maintaining the source of supply at a competitive price made the business risky.

Management also felt that it was necessary to have two companies with two different brand names to cover the wholesale market and the retail market. Experience had shown that if the same brand were supplied to both the wholesalers and the retailers, one or the other of the markets would be lost. Even if the same company name appeared on the package of the two different brands, it would be difficult to maintain both markets because of price differentials from the different outlets to the ultimate consumers.

In his testimony, Mr. Warren testified that he did not remember his counsellor discussing taxation with him when he decided to separately incorporate the two companies. He also testified that he had given a personal guarantee to the bank to obtain a loan for Warren Packaging Limited and he felt it was necessary to have a limited liability in that corporation. He believed that limited liability was accomplished by his wife's sole ownership of the shares of Bradford-Penn Oil Inc.

— REQUIRED

(A) Would subsection 256(5.1) apply in this case and, if so, what would be the effect of that application?

(B) Assuming that subsection 256(5.1) does not apply, determine whether Warren Packaging Limited and Bradford-Penn Oil Inc. are associated. Provide reasons for your determination by reference to the legislation and to the facts of the case.

Problem 5

ITA: 123–126

The accountant, Ryan Mailling, of Double-D Retailing Ltd. (DRL), a Canadian-controlled private corporation, has requested your assistance with respect to the calculation of the company's Part I tax payable.

Ryan has provided you with the following information.

(1) DRL is not associated with any other corporation.

(2) For DRL's December 31 taxation year-end, the corporation reported:

Active business income	$320,000
Investment income	
Canadian	5,000
Foreign	12,000
Charitable donations	9,000
Net capital loss deducted	2,000
Non-capital loss deducted	10,000
Taxable income	316,000

(3) Withholding tax on the foreign investment income was $1,800.

(4) Taxable capital employed in Canada in 2006 was $11,900,000.

— REQUIRED

Calculate the federal Part I tax payable for the taxation year ended December 31, 2007. Assume that the foreign non-business tax credit is equal to the foreign tax paid through withholding. Show all calculations whether or not relevant to the final answer.

Problem 6

ITA: 37, 127(5)–(11), 127.1

Natalia, a resident of Canada, owns 100% of the shares of New Age Limited (NAL). NAL carries on scientific research and experimental development (SR&ED) activities with respect to finding the ingredients for a cream which will reduce fat and tone muscles when massaged into the skin.

During its fiscal year ended December 31, 2007, NAL incurred the following costs related to its SR&ED activities:

Salaries for research technicians and assistants	$600,000
Materials consumed	200,000
Supplies consumed	40,000
Small equipment purchased for the laboratory	80,000
A special machine purchased to mix the ingredients in a temperature controlled environment	100,000

The machine and the lab equipment will have no value when the research project is completed.

Additional overhead costs were incurred in 2007 because of the SR&ED project. The accounting system was not sophisticated enough to properly allocate these expenses. Overhead expenses for the year totalled $500,000.

NAL paid Natalia a bonus of $40,000 in 2007 in addition to her salary of $80,000. Natalia spent 25% of her time on the SR&ED project in 2007.

NAL does not expect to have any taxable income for 2007. It had taxable income of $100,000 in 2005. Its taxable capital does not exceed $10,000,000. It is not associated with any other corporation.

— REQUIRED

(A) Which of the above costs incurred by NAL in 2007 qualify for deduction under subsection 37(1) as qualifying SR&ED expenditures?

(B) Determine the amount of ITCs and refundable ITCs for 2007.

Problem 7

ITA: 110.1–112, 123–126, 127(3)

Neville Ltd. is a Canadian-controlled private corporation which was incorporated in 1986 with a December 31 year-end. In 2007, Neville Ltd. earned net income of $250,000 before taxes for accounting purposes. Included in the calculation of that amount were the following items:

Canadian active business income:	
— manufacturing profits	$ 74,000
— other Canadian active business income	85,000
Dividends from taxable Canadian subsidiary corporations	8,000
Other Canadian investment income:	
— rental income	$ 4,000
— interest income	15,000
— royalty income	1,000
— taxable capital gain	9,000
U.S. interest income ($2,000 withheld)	15,000
U.S. business income ($20,000 tax paid)	96,000
Income under Division B	$307,000
Donations to registered charities	$ 60,000

The company also has the following balances at January 1, 2007:

1999 Non-capital loss	$ 20,000
1999 Net capital loss	15,000
Charitable donations carried forward from 2006	10,000

The company retails its products in Canada and the U.S. Its total proportion of taxable income earned in Canada, as per Regulation 402, is 75%. Assume that the provincial tax rates on taxable income are 12% and that Neville Ltd.'s foreign tax credits are equal to the U.S. tax withheld on the income.

Neville Ltd.'s 100% owned subsidiary has used $250,000 of the business limit for the small business deduction in 2007. Together, Neville Ltd. and its subsidiary have $8 million of taxable capital in Canada.

— REQUIRED

Compute the federal Part I tax and provincial tax payable by Neville Ltd. for 2007. Show *all* calculations.

Problem 8

ITA: 123–127, 129, 186

The following selected information has been taken from the records of Sharp Ltd., a Canadian-controlled private corporation, for its fiscal year ended December 31, 2007.

(1) Income for tax purposes:

Active business income (retailing)	$100,000
Foreign business income (retailing)	60,000
Canadian bond interest	20,000
Foreign bond interest	10,000
Taxable dividends received from taxable Canadian corporations	40,000
Taxable capital gains	30,000
Net income under Division B	$260,000

(2) Division C deductions claimed:

Donations	(2,000)
Net capital losses	(5,000)
Non-capital losses	(13,000)
Taxable dividends received from taxable Canadian corporations	(40,000)

(3) Taxable income **$200,000**

(4) Part I tax payable is $23,657 including surtax of $2,240 and additional refundable tax of $3,667. In computing Part I tax, the following deductions were made:

Small business deduction	$16,000
Foreign non-business tax deduction	1,500
Foreign business tax deduction	18,000

(5) Summary of taxable dividends received from taxable Canadian corporations:

Date received	Payer	% of voting shares owned	Amount of dividend received	Dividend refund received by payer corp.
Aug. 1, 2007	A Ltd.	6%	$20,000	$30,000
Oct. 1, 2007	B Ltd.	80%	20,000	5,000
			$40,000	

(6) Summary of dividends paid by Sharp Ltd.:

Type of dividend	Amount	Date declared	Date paid
Taxable dividend	$60,000	July 15, 2007	Aug. 15, 2007
Tax-free ssec. 83(2) dividend	20,000	Oct. 15, 2007	Nov. 15, 2007
Taxable dividend	24,000	Dec. 15, 2007	Jan. 15, 2008

(7) The refundable dividend tax on hand balance at December 31, 2006 was $12,000. The dividend refund for 2006 was $4,000.

— *REQUIRED*

(A) Compute the dividend refund for 2007.

(B) What would change if Sharp Ltd. was a private corporation, and not a CCPC? Explain.

Problem 9

ITA: 123–127; 129, 186

Multi Enterprises Ltd. is a Canadian-controlled private corporation whose fiscal period coincides with the calendar year. For the year 2007, the company's taxable income was calculated as follows:

Income from manufacturing net of CCA		$191,000
Dividends from taxable corporations:		
(a) connected corporation, dividend payment triggering a dividend refund of $2,750 to the wholly owned subsidiary		11,000
(b) non-connected corporation (portfolio dividends)		20,000
Taxable capital gain	$29,000	
Allowable capital losses	12,000	17,000

Royalties		9,000
Recapture of CCA on disposal of sales equipment		4,000
Income from rental of an apartment building (no full-time employees and tenants provide virtually all of their own services)		14,000
Foreign non-business income (i.e., interest income) (foreign tax credit of $3,450 equal to foreign tax withheld)		23,000
Foreign business income (foreign tax credit of $1,800 equal to foreign tax paid)		6,000
Interest charged on accounts receivable		5,000
Net income for tax purposes		$300,000
Less: net capital losses carried over	$ 7,000	
non-capital losses carried over	10,000	
donations	26,000	
dividends from taxable Canadian corporations	31,000	74,000
Taxable income		$226,000

At December 31, 2006, there was a nil balance in the refundable dividend tax on hand account. The company paid $72,000 in dividends during 2007 to individual shareholders.

It has been agreed that $250,000 of the business limit for small business deduction will be claimed by the parent, Multi Enterprises Ltd., leaving the remainder for the subsidiary.

The company has a permanent establishment in New Brunswick and in the United States. Its gross revenue, net of dividends and net of rentals, and its salaries and wages are attributed to its permanent establishments as follows:

	Gross revenue	Salaries & wages
New Brunswick	$1,776,000	$238,000
United States	220,000	16,000
Totals	$1,996,000	$254,000

In the United States a salesman worked out of his home in which he kept a small stock of merchandise from which he filled orders.

During the year the company purchased machinery and equipment (Class 43) in the amount of $32,000 for use in its southern New Brunswick manufacturing facilities. Capital cost allowance for the year has been adjusted for this purchase.

— *REQUIRED*

(A) Compute the federal Part I tax and assumed provincial tax at a 10% rate on federal taxable income payable by the company for 2007. Show in detail the calculation of all deductions in the computation, using a separate schedule for each special deduction. In calculating the small business deduction list all ineligible items of income, if any, and indicate the amount of the business limit available for the subsidiary.

(B) Compute the refundable dividend tax on hand balance as at December 31, 2007, showing, in detail, your calculations and compute the dividend refund for 2007.

Problem 10

ITA: 110.1–112, 123–127

The controller of Tek Enterprises Ltd. provided the Accountant with the following information.

Tek Enterprises Ltd.

Income

For the fiscal year ended December 31, 2007

Canadian wholesaling income		$251,500
Canadian retail business income		50,000
Foreign retail business income (before foreign tax paid of $15,000)		40,000
Taxable capital gains		4,500
Interest income:		
Canadian long-term bonds	$20,000	
Interest on accounts receivable outstanding for more than 30 days in the Canadian retail business	5,000	25,000
Dividend income:		
From taxable Canadian corporations	$ 9,000	
From foreign corporations (before foreign tax of $1,800) (Tek Enterprises Ltd. owns less than 5% of the shares)	12,000	21,000
Net income		$392,000

Notes:

(1) Tek Enterprises Limited is a CCPC. It is not associated with any corporations. It paid federal Part I tax of $35,000 in 2006.

(2) The following items were deducted in the computation of income above:

SR&ED expenditures (current in nature)	$50,000
Charitable donations	75,000
Federal political contributions	1,000

(3) The taxable capital gain was calculated as follows:

	Marketable securities	Equipment	Total
Proceeds	$15,000	$ 200	$15,200
Cost	3,000	3,200	6,200
Gain (Loss)	$12,000	$ (3,000)	$ 9,000
			× ½
			$ 4,500

(4) The corporation has net capital losses (incurred in 1999) of $13,000. It has unused foreign business tax credits (from 2006) of $100.

The Accountant assigned a junior staff member to calculate the federal Part I tax payable for Tek Enterprises Ltd. The following is his calculation.

Net income	$392,000
Dividends	(21,000)
Donations	(75,000)
Net capital losses	(13,000)
Taxable income	$283,000

Basic federal tax (40% × $283,000)			$113,200
Abatement: Taxable income	$283,000		
Foreign business income	(40,000)		
	$243,000 × 10%	24,300	
			$137,500
Surtax (1.12% × $137,500)		1,540	
			$139,040

Foreign tax credit:

Lesser of: (a) Foreign tax paid ($15,000 + $1,800) = $16,800

(b) $\dfrac{\text{Foreign income } \$52,000}{\$283,000 + \$21,000 + \$13,000} \times \$143,000 = \$23,457$ (16,800)

Small business deduction:

16% × the least of: (a) Active business income:

Wholesaling business	$251,500	
Cdn. retail business	50,000	
Foreign retail business	40,000	
	$341,500	
(b) $283,000 – 4 × $16,800 =	$215,800	
(c) Business limit:	$300,000	(34,528)

Political contribution tax credit	(650)
General rate reduction (7% × $283,000)	19,810
Federal Part I tax payable	$ 67,252

— *REQUIRED*

Write a memo in point-form explaining to the junior staff member the errors in his calculation. Do not redo the calculations. Only describe his incorrect procedures in arriving at Part I tax so that the calculation may be redone correctly.

Problem 11

ITA: 123–127, 129, 186

Rob's Shameless Self-Promotion Sales (RSS-PS) Inc. is a Canadian-controlled private corporation located in London, Ontario. For its fiscal year ended December 31, 2007, the corporation had correctly calculated its income for tax purposes under Division B as follows:

Canadian source:	
Consulting income	$160,000
Advertising agency loss	(30,000)
Rental income from warehouse fully rented on a 5-year lease	20,000
Retailing income	75,000
Interest on outstanding accounts receivable in retailing business	25,000
Recapture of CCA from sale of fixtures used in retailing business	25,000
Interest income from 5-year bonds	75,000
Taxable capital gain	70,000
Dividends from non-connected taxable Canadian corporations	12,000
Foreign sources:	
Interest earned on Bermuda bank account (no withholding tax)	20,000
U.S. business income (foreign tax credit of $7,581 equal to foreign tax paid)	23,000
Division B net income for tax purposes	$475,000

Additional information:

RSS-PS Inc. made the following selected payments during the year:

Scientific research and experimental development (current expenses and new equipment)	$100,000
Charitable donations	14,000
Taxable dividends	120,000

The balance in the tax accounts on December 31, 2006 were:

Charitable donations from 2004	$ 1,000
Non-capital losses from 2003	56,000
Net capital losses from 1999	18,000
Refundable dividend tax on hand	20,000
Dividend refund for 2006	9,000

Taxable income earned in Canada is considered to be 90% of the total earned by RSS-PS Inc. RSS-PS Inc. allocated $270,000 of its $400,000 business limit to other associated corporations. The only scientific research and experimental development expenditures of the associated group were made by RSS-PS Inc.

— *REQUIRED*

(A) Compute the federal Part I tax and provincial tax at a 11.5% rate on federal taxable income for the 2007 taxation year.

(B) Compute the dividend refund for 2007 and the amount of any Refundable Dividend Tax on Hand to be carried forward.

Problem 12

ITA: 125, 129, 186, 256

Carl owns 100% of the issued shares of Compunet. He incorporated Compunet earlier this year to provide computer consulting services to Vitamins Inc., a retailer of energy-producing vitamins. Prior to the incorporation of Compunet, Carl headed the computer service division of Vitamins Inc. One hundred per cent of the issued shares of Vitamins Inc. are owned by Carl's cousin, Vince.

Carl's daughter, Sulee, received a degree in computer science from the University of Toronto in April and has been employed by Compunet as a computer consultant since then. Sulee and Carl work well together. They are the only employees of Compunet.

Compunet owns a warehouse. One-half of the warehouse is rented to Vitamins Inc. and the remainder is rented to Mindblasters, a wholly owned subsidiary of Compunet. Mindblasters is a successful retailer of computer games.

During the current year, Compunet received taxable dividends from Mindblasters and paid taxable dividends to Carl.

— *REQUIRED*

Determine the type(s) of income being earned by Compunet, the rate of tax for each type and any refunds available.

Problem 13

ITA: 125, 129, 256

Lemon Ltd. provides management services for Toys-4-U Limited (Toys), a manufacturer of educational toys, and for certain other corporations described below. Les Lemon is the sole shareholder and only employee of Lemon Ltd. Prior to this year, Les had been employed by Toys as vice-president of financial and administrative services.

Les owns all of the common shares of Slum Landlord Ltd. (Slum), which is in the business of renting commercial properties. Slum has no employees, except for Les, and subcontracts all maintenance and administrative services. Slum's income for tax purposes can be broken down as follows:

Lemon Ltd.	10%
Cheap Leasing Ltd. (see below)	25%
Arm's length parties	65%
	100%

Les is also involved with Cheap Leasing Limited (Cheap), which is in the business of leasing educational equipment. The ownership of the common shares of Cheap is as follow:

Les Lemon	25 shares
Lucy Lemon, Les' wife	20 shares
Lemon Ltd.	30 shares
Larry Lemon, Les' uncle	10 shares
Arm's length parties	15 shares

Cheap derives approximately 80% of its income from the educational equipment leasing business. The balance of its income is interest from a loan to Toys. Cheap has four employees in addition to Les.

All of the above corporations are Canadian-controlled private corporations and have December 31 year-ends.

— *REQUIRED*

Identify the various sources of income for the above corporations indicating the reasoning behind your conclusions. Also indicate the *federal* tax rate and any refundable taxes applicable to each income source.

Problem 14

ITA: Part I, IV

Mr. Horseshoes, a resident of a province with a 41% effective corporate tax rate (before the additional refundable tax), has just won a lottery prize of $750,000. He is considering the following investment of these funds: $200,000 of bonds yielding 8% and $550,000 of common shares of Growth Unlimited Limited (a CCPC earning active business income less than the business limit), which pay a dividend to yield 5%. Having taken a course in security analysis, Mr. Horseshoes can predict with great confidence that he will realize a 10.5% capital gain on the shares within the year. Mr. Horseshoes currently has taxable income of $30,000. He has federal personal tax credits of $2,000.

— *REQUIRED*

(A) Advise Mr. Horseshoes on whether he should use an investment corporation with a permanent establishment in the province of which he is a resident to hold the securities he proposes to purchase. Include in your analysis the realization of the predicted capital gain. Use 2007 personal tax rates. Also, consider any non-quantitative factors that may be relevant to the decision.

(B) Do the above analysis again, using a 40% effective corporate tax rate before the additional refundable tax.

[For more problems and solutions thereto, see the CD accompanying this book.]

¶12,880 ADVISORY CASE

Waterloo Group

Mickey and Nicki Waterloo are husband and wife entrepreneurs. Most of the time, when they start a business, they will do so with another person, in order to let that person handle the day-to-day business matters and, also, to provide a potential buyer at some point in the future. Usually this other person will have a shareholding in the operating company, but Mickey and/or Nicki will maintain control. It is, also, usual for each company to have a shareholder agreement with a buy/sell provision that calls for a corporate repurchase on death, disability, bankruptcy, or retirement. Maximizing the use of the small business deduction is also a goal.

At this time, Mickey and Nicki have the following interests, which are all held through a holding company (Holdco) owned 100% by Mickey.

(1) Holdco owns 20% of a company called Sales Co. Inc. The other 80% is owned by Joe Sales, who runs the company. In order to finance the operations, Holdco has invested $100,000 in non-voting preference shares with a redemption value of $100,000 and a dividend rate of 8%.

(2) Holdco and Fred Smith have shared ownership of two companies. Holdco owns 90% of Retail One Inc. and 10% of Retail Two Inc., while Fred owns the other 10% of Retail One Inc. and 90% of Retail Two Inc.

Mickey and Nicki share ownership in two companies. Mickey owns 40% of Ours Inc., Nicki owns 100% of Mine Inc., and Mine Inc. own 60% of Ours Inc. Both Mickey and Nicki are actively involved in these businesses.

On the advice of their lawyer, they set up a discretionary trust for their two children, Dick, who is 12 years old, and Jane, who is 10 years old. This trust borrowed money from the bank (with personal guarantees from Mickey and Nicki) and bought treasury shares from a newly incorporated company, Kids Are Fun Inc. This company sells games through a retail store. It was capitalized with a loan from Nicki.

Advise Mickey and Nicki of the tax implications of the share ownerships outlined above on the small business deduction.

¶12,900   SUPPLEMENTAL NOTES

(This section of the text can be omitted without losing the continuity of the chapter. None of review questions, multiple choice questions, exercises, or assignment problems utilizes this information.)

¶12,910   Common Law Background to Current Legislation on Definition of "Active Business"

As long as Canadian tax legislation has provided for a low rate of tax on relatively low amounts of corporate income, there has been an incentive for taxpayers to incorporate their operations. Certainly, non-tax advantages, as discussed later in the chapter, are present in the incorporated form. However, the small business deduction overshadowed the other benefits of incorporation and many businesses were incorporated to qualify for that deduction.

To provide some perspective on the rules that currently exist in this area, some common law history is important. Many of the rules that are in force resulted from court decisions that are presented in this discussion.

Over the years, the CRA has looked very carefully at corporations which appeared to have been formed solely for the reduction of taxes. It has used a number of types of arguments against such corporations. In a relatively early case, *Kindree v. M.N.R.*, the incorporated practice of a medical doctor was challenged on the grounds that a corporation cannot practise medicine under the particular provincial law governing such practice. This precedent-setting decision still stands today where provincial corporate legislation does not allow for the incorporation of "personal corporations" as are allowed, for example, in Alberta. `64 DTC 5248 (Ex. Ct.)`

Another approach taken by the CRA was to argue that a corporation was a sham creating an appearance that was not justified in substance. A corporation found to be such a sham could be disregarded for tax purposes. This type of argument was not successful[8] and this line of argument has not been used by the CRA for a number of years.

As a refinement of the sham arguments, the CRA used the approach that for a corporation to avoid being considered a sham it had to have a valid business purpose other than the purpose of reducing taxes. The arrangements in the case of *M.N.R. v. Leon et al.* were judged not to have such a legitimate business purpose and, further, to be for the sole purpose of reducing taxes. However, the majority of subsequent cases did not support this extended definition of a sham (i.e., no business purpose).[9] In the case of *The Queen v. Daly*, the court indicated that the "business purpose" test was unnecessary and, in fact, that the saving of tax is a good reason for entering a transaction. This conclusion was confirmed by the Supreme Court of Canada in *Stubart Investments Limited v. The Queen*, which indicated that the conclusion in the *Leon* case could be disregarded in many situations. The decision in *The Queen v. Vivian*, on the issue of a management services corporation being a sham, followed the *Stubart* reasoning. `76 DTC 6299 (F.C.A.)` `81 DTC 5197 (F.C.A.)` `84 DTC 6305 (S.C.C.)` `84 DTC 6452 (F.C.A.)`

If a corporation could not be challenged by the foregoing arguments, then the question arose as to whether or not it could qualify for the very favourable small business deduction. The small business deduction, which was introduced in 1972, was computed on the corporation's Canadian-source active business income. However, as previously indicated, there was no statutory definition of the term "active business". (In general terms, "active business", as a defined term for use in computing the small business deduction, was applicable to taxation years commencing after 1979.) While the applicability of the term to many situations was obvious, it was not necessarily clear in a large number of situations which gave rise to a number of key appeals.

---

[8] *Sazio v. M.N.R.*, 69 DTC 5001 (Ex. Ct.), and *M.N.R. v. Cameron*, 72 DTC 6325 (S.C.C.).

[9] Other cases heard on the question of the business purpose included: *The Queen v. Burns*, 73 DTC 5219 (F.C.T.D.); *Petritz v. M.N.R.*, 73 DTC 5243 (F.C.T.D.); *Holmes et al. v. the Queen*, 74 DTC 6143 (F.C.T.D.); *Connor v. M.N.R.*, 75 DTC 85 (T.R.B.); *Fotheringham v. M.N.R.*, 77 DTC 275 (T.R.B.); *Handa v. M.N.R.*, 78 DTC 1191 (T.R.B.); and *Mendels v. M.N.R.*, 78 DTC 6267 (F.C.T.D.).

The appeals that were heard in this area can be categorized by the type of corporation that argued that its income should be considered to be derived from an active business. One such type of corporation was the small investment corporation which was formed to hold income-producing property such as real estate, shares, bonds or mortgages. In such cases, the issue was whether the income of the corporation came from property or from business.[10] A case involving the rental of buildings became a leading case in this area. In that case, *The Queen v. Cadboro Bay Holdings*, a very liberal interpretation of "active business" was used. It would appear that the issues addressed in this category of cases have now been resolved by the statutory definition of a "specified investment business". If a corporation carries on such a business, the income from that business is treated as investment income and, therefore, is not eligible for the small business deduction. However, if the corporation's business does not fit that definition, the income might be considered active. `ITA: 125(7)` `77 DTC 5115 (F.C.T.D.)`

A second category of corporation can be termed the personal service corporation and is sometimes referred to as an incorporated employee. The *Sazio* and *Cameron* cases provide good examples of such corporations while the *Leon* case shows an unsuccessful attempt to establish such a corporation. These situations often involve a contract of employment being replaced by a contract between the former employer and a corporation owned by the former employee whereby the corporation would provide the services of the former employee. The new corporation hires the former employee to perform those services. Typically, the corporation would have one major client (i.e., the former employer) and few, if any, employees other than the owner of the new corporation. This type of business activity became a particularly troublesome area. As a result, to limit the potential benefits of incorporation where corporations provided personal services, such as that in the *Daly* case, further rules were introduced which excluded a "personal services business" from the definition of "active business". The first reported case on the definition of a "personal services business" was *Hushi v. M.N.R.*, in which the court applied the tests for determining whether an individual was employed or self-employed (as discussed in Chapter 3).[11] `ITA: 125(7)` `89 DTC 30 (T.C.C.)`

A third category of corporation can be called a management corporation. This type of corporation was formed to provide management services to an unincorporated professional practice that could not itself be incorporated because of the laws governing the particular profession. The unincorporated professional practice would hire the corporation at a fee usually equal to cost plus 15% to provide administrative, management and other services as well as facilities and equipment. The professional or that person's spouse would own the corporation.[12] Such arrangements now seem to be included in the definition of "active business" unless they fall into the definition of a "personal services business". Even if the operations of the management corporation are considered an "active business", the CRA will attempt to minimize the advantage of the small business deduction by challenging the 15% mark-up on certain services and items provided to the professional practice. Since it is the 15% mark-up that is taxed at a potentially low rate in the corporation, the advantage of the corporation can be reduced by this assessment practice.[13]

¶12,920   Taxable Capital Employed in Canada

Taxable capital employed in Canada is computed (on Schedule 33) for non-financial corporations, generally, as follows: `ITA: 181.2(2)–(5)`

---

[10] Cases heard to determine whether the lending of money on mortgages could be considered to result in income from an active business included *MRT Investments Ltd. et al. v. The Queen*, 75 DTC 5224 (F.C.T.D.), and *The Queen v. Rockmore Investments*, 76 DTC 6156 (F.C.A.).

[11] For another case on this topic, see *Toushan v. M.N.R.*, 89 DTC 568 (T.C.C.).

[12] The case of *DBSK Management Ltd. v. M.N.R.*, (T.R.B.) 75 DTC 219 involves a good example of such a corporation.

[13] See the court decision in *R.L. Smith v. M.N.R.*, 87 DTC 132 (T.C.C.), for a case in this area.

Share capital		$xxx
Add: contributed surplus	$xxx	
retained earnings and other surpluses	xxx	
reserve funds (except amounts deducted under Part I)	xxx	
loans and advances	xxx	
indebtedness represented by bonds, debentures, notes, mortgages, etc.	xxx	
other indebtedness outstanding for more than 365 days before the year-end	xxx	
dividends payable	xxx	xxx
Capital [ssec. 181.2(3)]		$xxx
Less: allowance for investments in other corporations [ssec. 181.2(4)]		xxx
Taxable capital		$xxx
Percentage of capital employed in Canada		× x%
Taxable capital employed in Canada		$xxx

The investment allowance is calculated, generally, as follows:

ITA: 181.2(4)

Add the carrying values at the end of the year of the following assets:	
shares of another corporation	$xxx
loans or advances to another corporation	xxx
dividends receivable	xxx
investment allowance	$xxx

The amounts added to the investment allowance of a particular corporation represent amounts that would be in the taxable capital of another corporation and, hence, will be taxed in that other corporation.

Taxable capital is calculated using the unconsolidated balance sheet accounts of a corporation determined in accordance with generally accepted accounting principles for the current taxation year. While current accounts payable, including current income taxes payable, are excluded from this base, deferred income tax reserves and other non-tax-deductible reserves are included in the tax base. Taxable capital employed in Canada is then determined by applying the federal abatement percentage of taxable income earned in a province as discussed in the previous chapter.

ITA: 181(3)

Example Problem

Mammoth Corporation, a public corporation in the retailing business, had the following year-end balance sheet:

	($ 000s)
Current assets	20,000
Investment in Little Corp.	10,000
Loan receivable from Cash Poor Limited	15,000
Fixed assets, net of $260,000,000 of accumulated depreciation	300,000
Goodwill, net of $30,000,000 of amortization	55,000
Total assets	400,000

	($ 000s)
Accounts payable	25,000
Income taxes payable	5,000
Dividends payable	10,000
Mortgages payable	160,000
Future income taxes	40,000
Contingent liability (re: lawsuit)	10,000
Common shares	100,000
Retained earnings	50,000
Total liabilities and equity	400,000

The investment in Little Corp. represents 100% of its common shares and is accounted for at cost.

Mammoth's taxable income for its taxation year was $40,000,000 and 88% of its taxable income was earned in a province.

— *REQUIRED*

Determine Mammoth's taxable capital employed in Canada.

— *SOLUTION*

Capital
Capital stock [par. 181.2(3)(a)]	$100,000,000
Retained earnings [par. 181.2(3)(a)]	50,000,000
Mortgages payable [par. 181.2(3)(d)]	160,000,000
Dividends payable [par. 181.2(3)(e)]	10,000,000
Future income taxes [par. 181.2(3)(b)]	40,000,000
Contingency [par. 181.2(3)(b)]	10,000,000
Total capital	$370,000,000

Investment allowance [ssec. 181.2(4)]
Investment in Little Corp.	$ 10,000,000
Loan receivable from Cash Poor Limited	15,000,000
Total investment allowance	$ 25,000,000

Taxable capital ($370,000,000 – $25,000,000) $345,000,000

Taxable capital employed in Canada
(88% of $345,000,000) $303,600,000

Chapter 13

Planning the Use of a Corporation and Shareholder–Manager Remuneration

LEARNING GOALS

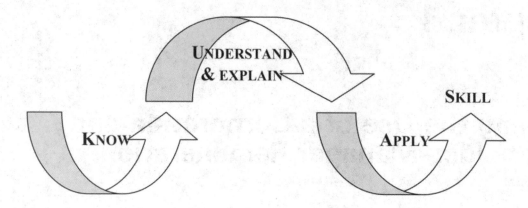

Know

By the end of this chapter, you should know the basic provisions of the *Income Tax Act* that relate to the compensation of a corporation's owner-manager and that relate to the general anti-avoidance rule. Completing the Review Questions (¶13,800) and Multiple Choice Questions (¶13,825) is a good way to learn the technical provisions.

Understand and Explain

You should understand and be able to explain:

- the more common elements in the remuneration of a shareholder-manager, including salary, bonus, dividend, and loan and the considerations needed to make a choice;

- the salary versus dividend trade-off, including the amount of dividends that can be distributed tax free;

- the reasons for the use of a holding corporation, the benefits of the capital gains deduction, and rules that inhibit family income splitting through a corporation; and

- why the general anti-avoidance rule exists and how it has been interpreted and used.

Completing the Exercises (¶13,850) is a good way to deepen your understanding of the material.

Apply

You should be able to apply your knowledge and understanding of the key elements of compensation to:

- choose the optimal compensation components to minimize remuneration costs in a particular owner-manager situation;

- maintain the eligibility of shares for the capital gains exemption;

- avoid the adverse income tax effects of using a corporation to split family income; and

- generally determine whether the general anti-avoidance rule might apply in a particular planning situation.

Completing the Assignment Problems (¶13,875) is an excellent way to develop your ability to apply the material in increasingly complex situations.

OVERVIEW

The previous chapter demonstrated that the integration system, when applied to business income earned by a corporation, can result in tax savings in certain cases where the combined federal and provincial rate of tax on corporations is less than the 20% or the 31% rate on which the gross-up and tax credit rates are based. Further tax savings and flexibility through the use of a corporation for business income are possible, if proper planning is undertaken. This chapter discusses planning considerations by beginning with the planning of employment remuneration for the shareholder-manager. It then examines the question of whether to pay salaries and similar income or to pay dividends. While much of the discussion is set out in terms pertaining to an individual owner of a business, the principles can be applied, with appropriate modification, to a group of owners controlling the business. Some other planning aspects of using corporations pertaining to holding companies, the qualified small business corporation share (QSBCS) capital gains exemption and attribution are discussed next. The final section of the chapter discuss the general anti-avoidance rule (GAAR) of the *Income Tax Act*, which may limit more aggressive planning and, hence, must be considered.

ITA: 74.4, 110.6

ITA: 245

For the purposes of computing the total income tax of an individual, the following table will be used in this chapter. Provincial rates of tax are hypothetical. Actual provincial rates vary. In addition, provincial tax brackets may vary, due to the use of a provincial Consumer Price Index and the impact of provincial surtaxes. Provinces may also establish a different number of tax brackets.

Combined Federal and Provincial Tax Rates

		Federal		Provincial		Total	
Taxable Income		Tax on lower limit	Tax rate on excess	Tax on lower limit	Tax rate on excess	Tax on lower limit	Tax rate on excess
—	$ 37,178	—	15.5%	—	10%	—	25.5%
$ 37,179	74,357	$ 5,763	22%	$ 3,718	12%	$ 9,480	34%
74,358	120,887	13,942	26%	8,179	15%	21,121	41%
120,888	and over	26,040	29%	15,159	17%	41,199	46%

¶13,000　EMPLOYMENT REMUNERATION

¶13,010　Considerations in Choosing Elements of Shareholder-Manager Remuneration

¶13,015　Cash needs

The prime consideration in deciding on remuneration for the shareholder-manager is his or her cash requirements, both immediately and in the future on retirement. The objective of the decision is to find the optimum method of providing the shareholder-manager with the necessary cash, while at the same time leaving the corporation with maximum cash for reinvestment. This process might involve paying out more than necessary in salaries and bonuses, as long as this is reasonable. The purpose of such payments would be to be taxable at the corporate level only on income eligible for the small business deduction or to qualify for Canada Pension Plan, registered retirement savings plan, deferred profit sharing plan or registered pension plan contributions. Any after-tax salary paid to the shareholder-manager in excess of his or her cash requirements can be loaned back to the corporation for reinvestment.

¶13,020 Individual's tax bracket

Also important to the remuneration decision are the other sources of income that the shareholder-manager may have. If he or she is already in a high tax bracket, it might be wise to freeze salaries and bonuses to take advantage of a tax deferral on the income left in the corporation, even though the ultimate total tax may be higher. The time value of money may make the saving now greater than the added cost at some time in the future.

For example, consider the case of a corporation taxable at a net 36% rate, including provincial tax. This corporation faces the choice of whether to pay a bonus of $100 now or a dividend of $100 at some time in the future. Exhibit 13-1 shows the comparative calculation that might be made assuming that the individual tax rate (federal plus provincial) is approximately 46%. The "dividend later" column is broken down into two options. Column A shows the results if the dividend gross-up and tax credit is 25%. Column B assumes that active business income not eligible for the small business deduction would qualify for the enhanced gross-up and credit of 45% on eligible dividends.

EXHIBIT 13-1
Comparison of $100 Paid as a Bonus Now or as a Dividend in the Future

	Bonus now	Dividend later A	Dividend later B
Corporation			
Corporate income	$1,000	$1,000	$1,000
Bonus	1,000	—	—
Corporate taxable income	Nil	$1,000	$1,000
Corporate tax @ 36% (rounded)	—	(360)	(360)
Funds available for dividend	Nil	$ 640	$ 640
Shareholder			
Income	$1,000	$ 640	$ 640
Dividend gross-up 25%/45%	—	160	288
Taxable income	$1,000	$ 800	$ 928
Combined federal and provincial tax @ 46% (rounded)	$ 460	$ 370	$ 427
Dividend tax credit @ 25%/45% of actual dividend (combined federal and provincial effect)	—	(160)	(288)
Net tax	$ 460	$ 210	$ 139
Cash available	$ 540	$ 430	$ 501
Tax deferral ($460 – $360)		$100	$100
Tax cost ($460 – ($360 + $210)) and ($460 – ($360 + $139))		$110	$ 39

¶13,025 25% dividend gross-up and credit

Where the gross-up is 25%, there is a tax deferral of $100 (i.e., $460 – $360) because the initial tax on the corporation for the dividend alternative is $360 while the tax on the individual for the bonus alternative is $460, but when the dividend is paid, personal tax of $210 must be paid on the dividend. Thus, paying a dividend in the future will result in a lower tax now by $100 and a higher tax later by $110.

The number of years that the dividend must be deferred for the tax deferral advantage to exceed the tax cost can be determined using the following analysis involving the time value of money. Assume that the pre-tax time value of money is 10% for both the owner-manager and the corporation. This is reasonable if the owner-manager can reinvest a bonus in the corporation by lending the after-tax bonus amount to the corporation at a pre-tax 10% interest rate. A $1,000 bonus will attract tax at an assumed 46% rate in the hands of the owner-manager who can reinvest the $540 (i.e., $1,000 (1 – .46)) at a pre-tax 10% rate or an after-tax rate of 5.4% (i.e., 10% (1 – .46)) for n years. Income earned by the corporation on the reinvested bonus will be offset by the tax deductible interest paid by the corporation on the loan from the owner-manager.

On the other hand, if the corporation does not pay the bonus, it will pay tax at the assumed 36% total rate, leaving it with $640 (i.e., $1,000 (1 – .36) after tax. That $640 can be reinvested by the corporation at a pre-tax 10% or an after-tax 6.4% (i.e., 10% (1 – .36)) for n years. However, in n years, the accumulated amount will be paid as a dividend and taxed at a net combined federal and provincial rate, after the dividend gross-up and tax credit in the top bracket, of about 33% after the 25% gross-up, or about 22% after the 45% gross-up.

In the case of a dividend grossed up by 25%, the number of years, n, for the accumulated after-tax bonus to equal the accumulated after-tax dividend in the hands of the owner-manager is about 22 years.[1] After about 22 years, the deferral advantage from the dividend alternative is higher than the tax cost of not paying the bonus immediately. The lower the discount rate used, the higher is the breakeven number of years, n. Also, the higher the corporate tax rate used, the higher is the breakeven number of years. This analysis assumes a constant time value of money and constant personal and corporate tax rates over the period.

¶13,030   Proposed 45% dividend gross-up and credit

Column B in Exhibit 13-1 shows the effect of the 45% gross-up on eligible dividends, i.e., dividends paid from active business income not eligible for the small business deduction. In this case, the tax deferral of $100 does not change from Column A; the corporate tax on the income of $1,000 is still lower than the personal tax on the bonus of $1,000. However, the tax cost on the payment of a dividend is reduced significantly from $110 to $39 as a result of the reduction in the marginal tax rate on dividends from about 33% to about 22%. As a result, the number of years that the income must be left in the corporation for the deferral to offset the cost is reduced from approximately 22 years to approximately 8 years. This can be calculated by substituting the 22% effective tax rate on these dividends into the formula used previously.

¶13,035   Availability of tax deferral

A tax deferral of this nature will be possible wherever the initial corporate rate of tax is less than the individual's personal rate of tax. In cases of lower corporate tax rates, it can be shown with an analysis similar to the above that a tax deferral is possible with negligible additional tax on the ultimate dividend. Therefore, the deferral advantage can be much greater than that shown, particularly for a corporation eligible for the small business deduction.

¶13,040   Avoid exceeding the business limit for the small business deduction

As shown in the previous chapter, the availability of the small business deduction is essential to certain tax deferrals and possible savings on business income. Thus, the remuneration policy should be designed to maintain corporate income below the business limit of $400,000 to prevent Canadian business income from being taxed at full corporate rates and,

---

[1] This result was achieved by solving the following equation for n:

$$\$1,000 \, (1 - .46)(1 + .10 \, (1 - .46))^n = \$1,000 \, (1 - .36)(1 + .10 \, (1 - .36))^n(1 - .33)$$

$$n \approx 22 \text{ years.}$$

The formula can be generalized as follows:

$$\$1,000 \, (1 - t_p)(1 + r \, (1 - t_p))^n = \$1,000 \, (1 - t_c)(1 + r \, (1 - t_c))^n(1 - t_{pd}).$$

The number of years, n, can be solved using logarithms.

hence, to be double-taxed when integration is not perfect.[2] Yet, such a policy must recognize that added salary or bonuses necessary to its implementation, taxed at a high personal rate of a shareholder-manager, may have adverse tax consequences not considered in the above breakeven analysis. Salary may increase a payroll tax such as the health levy, used in several provinces to finance health care. The interim measure limiting the deductibility of payroll taxes to November 1994 levels (i.e., any increases by way of rate increases or new taxes will not be deductible) will have further planning implications for the payment of salary.

The payment of interest or dividends is favoured, if it is desirable to reduce the cumulative net investment loss (CNIL) account, as will be discussed later in this chapter, to preserve access to the QSBCS capital gains deduction. Note that interest paid on shareholder debt has the same effect as salary in reducing corporate income to the business limit of $400,000 and attracts the same tax as salary in the hands of the individual. However, interest income reduces the cumulative net investment loss and salary does not.

Other considerations would include the company's need for funds to be used in the business, as indicated above. They would also include the effects of the remuneration decision on the value of the company's shares which may be important if a sale of the business is contemplated. Finally, changes in tax rates and tax law in general must be monitored constantly in terms of their effect on the remuneration decision.

¶13,050   Salaries, Bonuses, and Other Payments to the Shareholder-Manager

¶13,055   General guidelines

A primary guideline to follow is to ensure that various basic deductions and personal tax credits available to employees and individuals, in general, are fully utilized by the payment of salaries and bonuses or other similar amounts of employment income. These basic deductions and credits would include items listed in section 8 of the Act and Division C and personal tax credits listed in Division E.

As already indicated, another guideline would involve the payment of salaries and bonuses, perhaps to reduce active business income to as low a level approaching the business limit of $400,000 business limit, as would be considered reasonable to avoid double taxation on income taxed at a corporate rate in excess of 20%. This can also be accomplished by having a shareholder, who cannot be paid a salary, hold some of his or her investment in the corporation in the form of debt such that the corporation can make interest payments which will reduce corporate income. Again, payments of this nature, which are not needed immediately by the shareholder, can be loaned back to the corporation. When needed, the funds can then be withdrawn as a repayment of debt with no further tax consequences.

¶13,060   Salaries and bonuses

In order to be deductible by the corporation, salaries and bonuses paid, must be reasonable in the circumstances. There are no concrete guidelines as to what is meant by the word "reasonable". Where the employee is at arm's length with the corporation, generally any salary and/or bonus would qualify as "reasonable". However, this is not the case in the situation of a controlling shareholder-manager. In such a case, the value of his or her services may be assessed. The Canada Revenue Agency (CRA) could look at what executives in other corporations are being paid. The gross revenue and profitability of the corporation are probably the major factors to consider when justifying a large salary or bonus to a key person.[3]

On the other hand, there may be no incentive for the CRA to use section 67 to challenge the amount of salary paid to a controlling shareholder-manager. While the salary may be

ITA: 67

---

[2] Even with the 45% gross-up and tax credit, there is some double tax if combined federal and provincial corporate tax rates exceed 31%.

[3] For a case on the issue of the reasonableness of bonuses, see *La Compagnie Ideal Body Inc. v. The Queen*, 89 DTC 5450 (F.C.T.D.). See also "Shareholder/Manager Remuneration" in *Income Tax Technical News No. 22*, Canada Customs and Revenue Agency, January 11, 2002.

deductible to the corporation, it is included in the income of the recipient shareholder-manager. At high salary levels, the tax on the income in the hands of the shareholder-manager will generally be higher than the tax saving from the deduction of salary by the corporation.

In the case of *Totem Disposal Co. Ltd. v. M.N.R.*, the Tax Review Board held that the company's policy of limiting its net income to below the small business deduction limit by the accrual of management salary was for the purpose of tax reduction and not for the purpose of gaining or producing income. Therefore, the accrued salary expense was not allowed. This decision would not necessarily preclude the actual payment, as opposed to accrual, of a reasonable salary or bonus to achieve the same objective. In contrast to the *Totem Disposal* case, the Tax Court of Canada, in rejecting the argument that accruals were not made to produce income, set out the following criteria[4] for deductibility:

81 DTC 493 (T.R.B.)

- reasonableness of the bonus in relation to profit and services rendered;

- payment for real and identifiable service;

- some justification for expecting a bonus over regular salary (e.g., a company policy);

- reasonableness of the time between determining profit and establishing the bonus; and

- a legal obligation to pay the accrued bonus.

Where a director's resolution authorizing payment of management bonuses contained uncertainties regarding the actual payment, the Tax Court of Canada, in *Samuel F. Investments Limited v. M.N.R.*, held that the liability was contingent in nature and, therefore, not deductible.

88 DTC 1106 (T.C.C.)

The CRA's position on the issue of reasonableness of salaries or bonuses is that the reasonableness of salaries or bonuses paid to employee-shareholders is to be determined based on the facts of the case. However, they will generally not challenge the reasonableness of salaries or bonuses to shareholder-managers if profits are usually distributed by way of bonuses to the shareholder-managers or the company has a policy of paying bonuses to compensate them for their special knowledge or skills.[5]

¶13,065   Accrued bonuses and other amounts

¶13,065.10   *Unpaid remuneration*

Where an amount in respect of employee remuneration (including salaries, wages, pension benefits, and retiring allowances) is unpaid 180 days after the end of the employer's fiscal period, the amount is deductible only in the employer's fiscal period in which the amount is actually paid. (By administrative practice, the CRA allows payment on the 180th day, despite the clarity of the legislation on this point.) Thus, the accrual method is denied to the employer on amounts unpaid after the 179-day period. Note that a shareholder-manager has far greater flexibility when the corporation's fiscal year ends during the last 179 days of the calendar year. Since a bonus can be paid at any time during the following 179 days from the year-end of the accrual, income can be triggered in the current calendar year by a payment to the owner-manager. Alternatively, income can be deferred to the following year by an accrual in the fiscal period and a payment in the following year, if this is more beneficial. Of course, the benefit from deferring the payment of the bonus to the employee is reduced considerably by the requirement by the employer to withhold tax at the time of paying the bonus. With a fiscal year-end in the first half of the calendar year, the accrued bonus must be paid in the same calendar year, as it is accrued, thereby reducing the deferral flexibility.

ITA: 78(4)

IT-109R2, par. 10

---

[4] These criteria were quoted in the case of *Earlscourt Sheet Metal Mechanical Limited v. M.N.R.*, 88 DTC 1029 (T.C.C.).

[5] Question 42 of the "CRA Round Table" in the *1981 Conference Report* of the Canadian Tax Foundation.

¶13,065.20   *Non-arm's length accruals other than remuneration*

Where an amount, other than remuneration, is deductible by a taxpayer, like a corpora- ITA: 78(1)
tion, and owed to a non-arm's length person, like a majority shareholder. Another limited
accrual rule applies to the unpaid amount. As an example of the application of these rules,
consider a situation where *property* owned by a majority shareholder personally is transferred to a corporation in return for certain income payments, such as, a royalty payment.
The royalties can be accrued by the corporation as an expense in one year and paid up to two
years after the taxation year of the corporation in which the amount was accrued. This gives
the company an immediate expense deduction, but the shareholder, if using the cash basis,
has no income until the amount is paid. The amount must be paid prior to the end of the
second taxation year after the year in which it is expensed where the shareholder is not at
arm's length with the corporation. If it is not paid by the end of the second taxation year ITA: 78(1)(*a*)
following the year of accrual, the amount must be added back to the income of the corporation in the third taxation year of the corporation following the year of accrual. This could
result in double taxation, unless the shareholder forgives the amount payable, because on
ultimate payment the corporation would not get a deduction, while the shareholder would
have to report the income. On the forgiveness of a debt of this nature, the forgiven amount
would be included in income. However, if section 78 applies, the amount payable is consid- ITA: 80(1)
ered "an excluded obligation" and the debt forgiveness rules will not apply.

To avoid this problem, the corporation and the shareholder-manager must file an agree- ITA: 78(1)(*b*)
ment on or before the date on which the corporation must file its tax return for the third
taxation year following the year of accrual. This agreement deems the amount to have been
paid by the corporation and received by the shareholder-manager on the first day of the third
taxation year following the year of accrual. In addition, the amount deducted is deemed to
have been lent back to the corporation by the shareholder-manager.

¶13,065.30   *Example of non-arm's length accrual effects*

For example, assume a corporation's year-end is June 30. Royalties accrued on June 30,
2005 must be paid by June 30, 2007 or added back to the corporation's income for the year
ended June 30, 2008 unless an election is filed on or before December 31, 2008. In that case, ITA: 78(1)(*b*)
the royalties are deemed to have been received by the non-arm's length shareholder-manager
and loaned back to the corporation on July 1, 2007. The effect of the election is to put the
shareholder in the same position as he or she would have been had the royalties actually been
paid. When the corporation ultimately repays the loan resulting from the unpaid royalties,
there are no further tax consequences because the royalties were already taxed on their
deemed receipt under the election.

The election can be filed late, that is, after the filing deadline. However, if the election is ITA: 78(3)
filed late, 25% of the unpaid amount is added back in the third year to the corporation's ITA: 78(1)(*a*)
income. This will not affect the treatment of the full unpaid amount. Thus, in the above
example, 25% of the unpaid amount would be added back to the corporation's income in the
2008 taxation year, but under the election the entire amount of unpaid royalties would be
deemed to have been paid by the corporation and received by the shareholder-manager and
to have been loaned back on July 1, 2007. When the corporation ultimately pays back the loan,
there will be no further tax consequences. The corporation will have deducted the entire
amount of royalties in its 2005 taxation year, but will have added back 25% in its 2008
taxation year. Thus, the 25% amount will, in effect, not have been deducted, thereby creating
a penalty for a late-filed election.

The foregoing non-arm's length accrual rules and their effects, which apply if the accrual
is not actually paid within two years, can be diagrammed as follows, assuming a $10,000
royalty accrual:

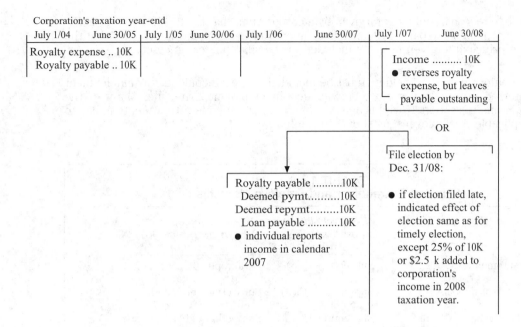

¶13,065.40 *Genuine, not contingent liability*

There are other potential problems with the accrual of amounts. In order to be deductible in the year accrued, there must be a legal obligation to pay the amount. If the legal obligation is not established, then a deduction would be allowed only in the year of payment and not in the year of accrual. Thus, the liability should be established by recording the amount in the minutes of the directors' meeting prior to the year-end and by attempting to establish, in the case of a bonus, some formula for computing the bonus representing objective standards. The payment should not be made contingent on some event which might take place after the year-end. Having established a real liability in this manner, if the amount is not paid on time and if the election is not filed, the shareholder may decide to forgive the amount so that the corporation need not pay it, subject to the double taxation previously mentioned.

An Interpretation Bulletin suggests that if an unpaid amount does not constitute a genuine liability, no deduction will be allowed. The Interpretation Bulletin states that "for genuine liability to exist, there must be an enforceable claim by the creditor with a reasonable expectation that the debt will in fact be paid by the debtor." ITA: 18(1)(*e*); IT-109R2, par. 12(e)

¶13,070 Shareholder Benefits and Loans

¶13,075 Shareholder benefits

There are provisions that are designed to prevent the distribution of part of the accumulated surplus of a corporation (other than by way of taxable dividends) to shareholders while the corporation is a going concern. There are exceptions to the broad application of these rules for particular situations that are dealt with elsewhere in the Act, notably in the provision dealing with the taxation of dividends and options. In all other cases, the Act requires an amount to be included in income, but the amount is not deemed to be a dividend and, therefore, is not eligible for the dividend tax credit. This provision was applied in the case of *No. 403 v. M.N.R.*, in which a controlling shareholder purchased a house from his company at $38,000 when it had been purchased a year earlier by the company for $45,000. The $7,000 benefit to the shareholder was included in his income from property. In this situation, the corporation will be considered to have received proceeds equal to its fair market value at the time of the sale to the shareholder. If this sale triggers any income, it must be included by the corporation. In this particular case, if the corporation's cost was $45,000, there would have been no income with proceeds of $45,000. ITA: 15(1)

57 DTC 120 (T.A.B.)

ITA: 69(4)

Where a loan to a shareholder is forgiven by a corporation, that is, the shareholder is not required to repay all or some part of the principal amount of the loan, a rule provides that the amount of the principal forgiven must be included in the shareholder's income.

ITA: 15(1.2)

ITA: 15(1)

Benefits conferred on shareholders must be included in their income just as employment benefits conferred on employees must be included in employment income. Many of the related subsections in section 15, applicable to shareholders, provide a treatment similar to section 6, applicable to employees, as shown in Exhibit 13-2.

ITA: 15(1); 6(1)(*a*)

EXHIBIT 13-2
Selected Shareholder and Employee Benefits

	Shareholder subsection 15(1) and	*Employee paragraph 6(1)(a) and/or*
Automobile	Subsection 15(5)*	Paragraphs 6(1)(*e*), (*k*) and subsection 6(2)
Interest on loans . . .	Subsections 15(9) and 80.4(2)	Subsections 6(9) and 80.4(1)
Forgiveness of loans	Subsection 15(1.2)	Subsection 6(15)

* Refers to subparagraph 6(1)(*e*)(i) and subsections 6(1.1) and (2).

The question often arises, when dealing with a shareholder-manager, as to which provision is applicable — section 6 dealing with employees or section 15 dealing with shareholders. The capacity (often referred to by the Latin word *qua*) in which the person is operating and which, in turn, depends upon the specifics of the particular relationship, will determine which provision will apply. A good rule of thumb is that a person operates in his or her capacity as shareholder (that is, *qua* shareholder) if he or she receives a benefit which he or she would not have received if he or she was an ordinary employee.[6]

The word "benefit" is another of those key words that is undefined and yet sprinkled liberally throughout the Act. The standard test to determine whether a benefit has been conferred on a shareholder is the "*bona fide* transaction" test as set out in *M.N.R. v. Pillsbury Holdings Ltd.* The court made the distinction between a *bona fide* transaction and transactions that are devices and arrangements for conferring benefits or advantages on a shareholder. A *bona fide* transaction might occur where a shareholder deals with the corporation in the same manner or capacity as a customer (i.e., *qua* customer) or as a supplier (i.e., *qua* supplier).

64 DTC 5184 (Ex. Ct.)

Once it has been established that a benefit has been conferred, then the next step is to determine its value, if any. In *Youngman v. The Queen*, the Federal Court of Appeal determined that the value of a benefit of a house provided to its shareholders was not based on the equivalent rental fair market value, but instead was based on the value of the house itself.

90 DTC 6322 (F.C.A.)

Example Problem 1

Smartmoney Manufacturing Ltd. built a 21-room house for its principal shareholder-officer on a country property owned by him. The company expensed the costs as promotion expenses on the basis that he would use the property to entertain distributors of the company's products to ensure continuing outlets for the company's products.

— *REQUIRED*

Consider the tax consequences to the individual and the company in this case.

---

[6] For a more detailed discussion of this topic see Robert E. Beam and Stanley N. Laiken, "The 'Capacity' Issue in Corporate Transactions with Shareholders", Personal Tax Planning Feature (1992), Vol. 40, No. 2, *Canadian Tax Journal*, pp. 412–439.

— SOLUTION

The value of the house plus the GST, if any, on that value must be included in the income of the shareholder since it represents a benefit conferred on the shareholder. Since the company does not own the property on which the house was built and it has expensed the cost on its books, it appears clear that the shareholder has received a taxable benefit.

ITA: 15(1)

The company would ordinarily be allowed to deduct an expenditure made or incurred to produce income. In this case, the house would be a capital asset subject to the capital cost allowance system to the extent that some part of the house was used for business purposes. However, if the house is considered to be a lodge, in any way, the Act would prohibit the corporation from deducting any expense or outlay considered for the use or maintenance of that property.

ITA: 18(1)(*l*)(i)

Example Problem 2

Mr. Edwards owns all of the outstanding shares of Edwards Inc., a large property management company, which manages over 20 large apartment buildings. One spring Mr. Edwards had the repair crew spend five days at his cottage making extensive repairs to the building. The value of these repairs was $8,500 (excluding GST). Because of his busy schedule, Mr. Edwards apparently forgot to tell his controller to send him a bill for the work done.

— REQUIRED

If the CRA were to discover this transaction during their audit, how would they reassess?

— SOLUTION

The CRA would begin by assessing Mr. Edwards a shareholder benefit in the amount of $8,500 plus GST of $595 (i.e., 7% of $8,500), since funds of the corporation were directed to the benefit of a shareholder. This amount would be treated as income from property in the calendar year that the repairs were made.

ITA: 15(1)

The company, Edwards Inc., would probably also be reassessed to deny the deduction for the cost to the company of the repairs on the basis that the expenses were not incurred to earn income since no billing was ever sent, or on the basis that the expense was a personal or living expense.

ITA: 18(1)(*a*), 18(1)(*h*)

As a result, there is double taxation. Mr. Edwards includes an amount in income for which the company does not receive a deduction.

¶13,080   Shareholder loans

¶13,080.10   *Principal*

Normally, when funds are borrowed, the principal amount of the debt, that is, the amount borrowed, is not considered to be income and the amount of the debt repaid is not deductible. Incurring and repaying the debt is a capital transaction. However, in the case of a shareholder, particularly a significant shareholder who can influence the decisions of the corporation, it would be easy to escape tax on the distribution of corporate surplus, if it were not for the shareholder loan. In the absence of these rules, a shareholder could borrow funds from the corporation, instead of receiving taxable salary, interest or dividends from the corporation, and never repay these funds. However, certain circumstances are recognized as exceptions.

ITA: 15(2)

ITA: 15(2.2)–(2.6)

Loans and other forms of indebtedness to shareholders (other than corporate shareholders) or to persons not at arm's length with the shareholder (i.e., connected with a shareholder) are required to be included in income of the borrower for the year in which the loan was made. In the case of *The Queen v. Silden*, the Federal Court of Appeal confirmed that subsection 15(2) must be applied where a loan is made to a shareholder. The capacity in which the individual receives the loan, i.e., as a shareholder or as an employee, is not relevant to the application of that rule, but maybe relevant for certain specific exceptions. Related persons, discussed in a previous chapter, do not deal with each other at arm's length.

ITA: 15(2.1)

93 DTC 5362 (F.C.A.)

ITA: 251, 252

¶13,080.20   *Exceptions*

There are two general exceptions to the application of the shareholder loan inclusion rule. The first excepts indebtedness between non-resident persons. The second excepts debt that arises in the ordinary course of the lender's business, as long as *bona fide* arrangements are made at the time the loan is made for repayment within a reasonable time. This exception protects a borrower who happens to be a shareholder of, for example, a bank at which he or she borrowed.

ITA: 15(2.2)
ITA: 15(2.3)

Another provision allows specific exceptions for four types of loans, for which the principal amount can be excluded from a shareholder's income if received:

ITA: 15(2.4)

    (a) a loan made by the corporation to a shareholder who is, also, an employee, but not a specified employee (defined, very generally, as an employee who, together with non-arm's length persons, owns at least 10% of the shares of any class of a corporation or who does not deal at arm's length with the corporation); or

ITA: 248(1) "specified employee"

    (b) a loan made by the corporation to a shareholder who is, also, an employee to assist him or her to acquire:

        (i) a home for his or her own occupation (even if the loan is made to the employee's spouse),

ITA: 15(2.4)(b)

        (ii) previously unissued, fully paid shares of the corporation purchased directly from the corporation, or

ITA: 15(2.4)(c)

        (iii) a motor vehicle (as defined) to be used in the performance of his or her duties of employment.

ITA: 15(2.4)(d), 248(1)

For the principal amount of the loan to be excluded, there are two additional conditions. The first condition requires that the loan arise because of the employee's employment (often referred to, using the Latin, *qua* employee) and not because of his or her shareholdings (*qua* shareholder). The second condition requires that *bona fide* arrangements be made at the time of the loan for repayment within a reasonable period of time. An Interpretation Bulletin suggests that normal commercial practice is used as the basis for *bona fide* arrangements. For example, a 25-year amortization period would be appropriate for a housing loan and the security of a mortgage on the property should be taken for large loans.

ITA: 15(2.4)(e)

ITA: 15(2.4)(f)
IT-119R4, par. 12

Thus, for the shareholder loan inclusion rule, the recipient of the loan must be a shareholder. Note that all four of the exceptions in subsection 15(2.4) require that the recipient also be an employee. Therefore, to exclude the principal amount of the loan under all four of the exceptions, the recipient must be an employee. An employee-capacity condition is imposed on these exceptions, which results in exclusion of the principal, if the other conditions are met. That is, the loan must be received by the employee in his or her capacity as an employee, in addition to meeting the other conditions, for the loan to be excluded.

ITA: 15(2)

ITA: 15(2.4)(e)

A loan that is fully repaid within one year of the end of the taxation year of the lender in which it was made is excluded if the repayment is not part of a series of loans and repayments.

ITA: 15(2.6)

Consider the following facts. Sally owns all the outstanding shares of Sally Inc. On July 15, 2006, Sally Inc. loans Bob, Sally's brother, $10,000 to buy a sailboat. Sally Inc. has a December 31 year-end. On January 1, 2008, the loan is still outstanding. In this case, Bob received a loan from Sally Inc. and Bob is connected to his sister Sally, the shareholder, because they are related. Since the loan was not repaid before January 1, 2008, Bob will have to take the principal amount of the loan, $10,000, into income in the year the loan was received which was 2006.

¶13,080.30 *Deduction of repayment*

Where an amount has been included in income for a preceding year, the taxpayer is permitted to deduct any repayment of the loan from his or her income in the year of repayment provided the repayment was not part of a series of loans and repayments. While the CRA states in an Interpretation Bulletin that whether a repayment is part of such a series is a question of fact, it also states that a shareholder's loan account with several loan and repayment transactions will give rise to a series unless there is clear evidence otherwise.

ITA: 15(2), 20(1)(j)

IT-119R4, par. 29

The CRA also states in the same Interpretation Bulletin that, notwithstanding that there is a series of loans and repayments, they will administratively allow a deduction for a decrease in the loan account, unless the decrease is temporary. A numerical example of the application of the CRA's policy on how the net decrease should be calculated is provided, based on a FIFO allocation of repayments of the loan balance. However, the calculation of both the inclusion in income and the deduction are based on administrative practice only. However, since this is a particularly tricky area in practice, the Bulletin should be studied carefully.

ITA: 20(1)(j)

IT-119R4, par. 36

The CRA's practice is to consider that dividends, salaries or bonuses paid or credited to the shareholder loan account (i.e., amounts owing to the shareholder by the corporation) to repay the balance at the end of the previous year are not part of a "series of loans or other transactions and repayments" for purposes of these two provisions. Income Tax Technical News, No. 3, dated January 30, 1995 and the Interpretation Bulletin, indicate that the Agency has based its position on two Tax Court of Canada cases.[7]

IT-119R4, par. 29

Note that not all charges to a shareholder loan account are necessarily *bona fide* loans. Some charges might be construed as salary, dividends or an appropriation. Therefore, it is necessary to properly document loans. If the corporation incurs interest charges, it should in turn charge interest to the shareholder or some of the interest it pays may be disallowed as not for the purpose of earning income. This applies even if the loan falls under the exception rules discussed above. [Draft legislation on interest deductibility, released on December 20, 1991, but not introduced into Parliament, addressed the issue of deducting interest paid to a third party to provide funds for employee and shareholder loans. A proposal would permit the deduction of reasonable interest paid by an employer on funds borrowed to make a loan to an employee or a prospective employee. Similarly, another proposal would allow the deduction of interest paid by a corporation on funds borrowed to make a loan to a shareholder. However, the deduction in this case is limited to the amount of the shareholder's imputed interest benefit discussed below.] An Interpretation Bulletin comments on the deductibility of interest on borrowed money used to make interest-free loans to employees and shareholders. The CRA's position is similar to that proposed in the 1991 Draft Legislation for loans to employees. However, the CRA makes the statement that "interest on money borrowed to make interest-free loans to individuals in their capacity as shareholders would not generally qualify."

[ITA: 20(1)(c)(v) proposed]

[ITA: 20(1)(c)(vi) proposed]

ITA: 80.4

IT-533, par. 26

¶13,080.40 *Imputed interest benefit*

Where the principal amount of the loan is not included in income because it meets one of the exclusion conditions discussed above, a provision dealing with imputed interest on loans may apply. The Act requires any person who received a loan or otherwise incurred a debt by virtue of:

ITA: 80.4

- an individual's employment or intended employment (as discussed in Chapter 3),

- shareholdings in a corporation, or

- a shareholding of a person who does not deal at arm's length with a shareholder,

to include in his or her income an amount in respect of interest on low-interest or interest-free loans. The *qua* or capacity issue is very relevant for purposes of the imputed interest benefit rules. It is always a question of fact whether a person will receive a benefit under this section by virtue of his or her employment or by virtue of his or her shareholdings.

ITA: 6(9), 15(9)

---

[7] *Joel Attis v. M.N.R.*, 92 DTC 1128, and *Uphill Holdings Ltd. et al. v. M.N.R.*, 93 DTC 148.

An interest benefit is imputed by one rule as a consequence of a previous, a current or an intended office or employment. Another rule imputes an interest benefit by virtue of the taxpayer's shareholdings in the lending corporation or a related corporation. A taxpayer may fall into either category, depending on the facts under which the loan was granted. Therefore, a decision will have to be made as to the source of this benefit based on the facts of the situation.

ITA: 80.4(1)
ITA: 80.4(2)

If the loan is a "home purchase loan" or a "home relocation loan", the definitions of which are applicable only to loans by virtue of employment, the imputed interest benefit is calculated for each quarter[8] as the lesser of:

ITA: 80.4(4), 80.4(7)(*a*), 248(1)

(a) the prescribed rate in effect at the time the loan was received; and

(b) the prescribed rate (changed on a quarterly basis) in effect during that quarter.

However, a new loan will be deemed to have been received every five years on longer-term home purchase or relocation loans. This deemed disposition will have the effect of changing the rate of imputed interest at least every five years. Finally, the interest benefit is the amount of imputed interest in excess of the interest actually paid in the year or within 30 days after the end of the taxation year on the loan.

ITA: 80.4(6)

Note that a home relocation loan is eligible for a deduction of the imputed interest benefit on the first $25,000 of the loan under certain specific rules in Division C, which was explained more fully in Chapter 10.

ITA: 110(1)(*j*)

An interest benefit is imputed to a person who receives a loan by virtue of shareholdings rather than as a consequence of employment. The recipient of the loan may include a shareholder or a person not at arm's length with a shareholder of a corporation who receives a loan from, or incurs a debt to, the corporation or a related corporation. Since the special provisions for a home purchase loan or a home relocation loan refer only to a loan received by virtue of an office or employment, these provisions cannot apply where the loan is received by virtue of shareholdings. In this case, the individual must include in income the amount by which interest on the loan computed at the prescribed rate tied to the treasury bill rate exceeds the interest actually paid in the year or within 30 days after the end of the taxation year on such a loan.

ITA: 80.4(2)

ITA: 80.4(4)

ITR: 4300(7)

Two additional exceptions to the application of the imputed interest rules are provided. First, a benefit will not arise where the rate of interest payable is equal to or greater than the rate of interest that would have been agreed upon in an arm's length transaction at the time the obligation was incurred. Second, where the principal amount of the loan has already been included in the income of a person, the loan is from imputed interest, whether the loan is received by virtue of employment or shareholdings.

ITA: 80.4(3)
ITA: 80.4(3)(*a*)

ITA: 80.4(3)(*b*)

Receiving a loan by virtue of shareholding and receiving a deemed interest benefit is not as common as receiving a loan by virtue of employment and receiving a deemed interest benefit. This is the case since receiving a loan by virtue of shareholding may result in the loan principal being included in income. However if an individual receives a loan by virtue of shareholding and repays it within the time period required to avoid including the principal in income, then there will be a deemed interest benefit by virtue of shareholdings included in income.

The Act deems the interest benefit to be interest paid or payable in the year pursuant to a legal obligation for purposes of interest deduction provisions, as long as the conditions of these two interest deduction provisions are met. Thus, an offsetting deduction may be available for interest deemed to have been paid, depending on the use of the borrowed funds.

ITA: 80.5
ITA: 8(1)(*j*), 20(1)(*c*)

¶13,080.50   *Application of shareholder loan rules*

Exhibit 13-3 provides a flow chart of the shareholder loan rules in sections 15 and 80.4 and the consequences of their application.

---

[8] The quarter-by-quarter method is used by the CRA for the "lesser of" calculation and may result in a slightly smaller income inclusion than the traditional annual calculation.

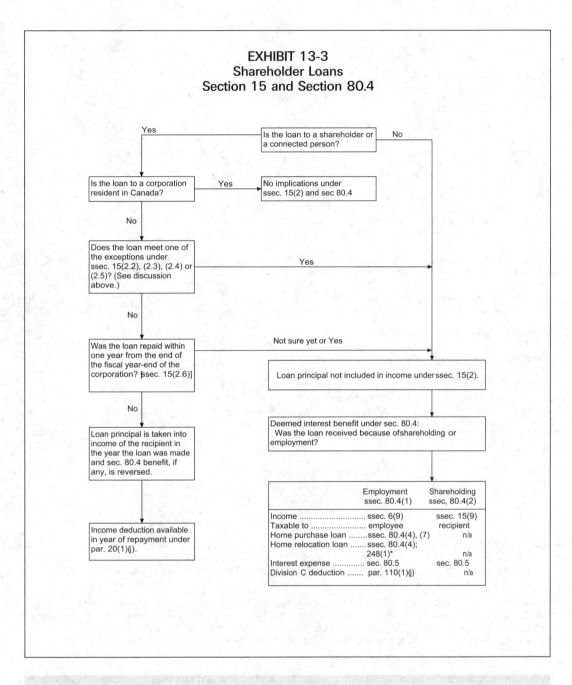

EXHIBIT 13-3
Shareholder Loans
Section 15 and Section 80.4

Example Problem

Mr. I.M. Portly owns all the outstanding shares of Run for Your Life Limited, a health and fitness club. He is the company president. On July 1, 2007, the company made a loan to Mr. Portly of $19,500 which he used to acquire an automobile at fair market value. All of the other six employees of the corporation are eligible to receive this type of loan on the same terms and four have, in fact, taken advantage of the opportunity. He requires the automobile to carry out his business duties for the company. (He drives behind members of the club in case of an emergency while they are jogging.) The loan is repayable in two equal annual instalments starting July 2008 without interest.

— REQUIRED

(A) Does Mr. Portly receive a taxable benefit in 2007? Substantiate your answer.

(B) Can the company's income position be affected either positively or negatively by this loan? Again, substantiate your answer.

Assume a prescribed rate of 4% throughout the relevant period in this problem. For a table of actual prescribed rates set out in Regulation 4301(1), see Chapter 14, or the table of Prescribed Quarterly Interest Rates in the Tables of Rates and Credits section in the preface materials of the CCH Edition of the CANADIAN INCOME TAX ACT.

— SOLUTION

(A) The general rule applies to Mr. Portly since he is a shareholder, but an exception rule permits the loan described to be exempted from inclusion in income because:　　　　ITA: 15(2), 15(2.4)

(i) the loan was to assist a shareholder/employee to purchase a motor vehicle to be used by him in the performance of the duties of his office;　　　　ITA: 15(2.4)(*d*)

(ii) the loan was received because of his employment and not because of his shareholdings, since all employees were eligible for this type of loan and four have received one;　　　　ITA: 15(2.4)(*e*)

(iii) *bona fide* repayment arrangements were made; and

(iv) repayment was scheduled within a reasonable time.　　　　ITA: 15(2.4)(*f*)

However, the fact that this was an interest-free loan results in the application of the interest benefit rule. Since Mr. Portly is probably acting in his capacity as an employee, he will be deemed to have received a benefit equal to the unpaid interest on the loan calculated at the prescribed rate in effect during the period in the year that the loan was outstanding. The prescribed rate, for this purpose, is given as 4% for all relevant quarters. Therefore, the amount of the benefit would be calculated as follows:　　　　ITA: 80.4(1)

$$
\begin{array}{ll}
4\% \text{ of } \$19,500 \times {}^{92}\!/_{365} = & \$\ \ 196.60 \\
4\% \text{ of } \ \ 19,500 \times {}^{92}\!/_{365} = & \underline{\ \ \ \ 196.60} \\
& \underline{\$\ \ 393.20}
\end{array}
$$

The $393.20 will be considered interest paid on a car loan for purposes of determining Mr. Portly's deduction of interest paid from employment income. This will allow him to deduct the business-use portion of the interest deemed to have been paid within the limits for the deduction of interest.　　　　ITA: 80.5, 8(1)(*j*)
ITA: 67.2

(B) From the company's position, the foregone interest on the loan is not an allowable deduction. In fact, if the loan had been for more than the fair market value of the car and the car was bought from the company, interest income could be imputed to the company. However, there is no need to charge interest in a *bona fide* loan and no interest will be imputed in a fair market value transaction.　　　　ITA: 16(1)

If the company borrowed the funds which it loaned to Mr. Portly, it would be able to deduct the interest it paid provided it was part of reasonable total remuneration to Mr. Portly as an employee.　　　　IT-533, par. 26

¶13,090   Other Planning Considerations for Shareholder-Manager Remuneration

¶13,095   Income splitting

It is possible to pay a spouse or other family members a tax-deductible salary. Of course, the salary must be reasonable in the circumstances and based on the value of the actual services performed for the business, as discussed previously. Such payments will split the income of a business so that it is subject to tax at lower personal tax rates. The trade-off for this benefit is the possible loss of a marital status tax credit for the spouse.

Unlike the case of remunerating a controlling shareholder-manager with salary, there may be an incentive for the CRA to challenge, on the basis of reasonableness, the deduction of the amount of salary paid to relatives, because they may be in a lower tax bracket than the corporation after the payment of salary. The case of *Gabco Limited v. M.N.R.* presents an interesting situation of this nature. Late in 1962, Jules, the president of a construction company, hired Robert, his brother aged 19, with the intention of making him the number two man. Robert immediately became an energetic and innovative driving force in the company and, according to his brother Jules, gave better service than anyone in the company, including the superintendent who was Robert's immediate superior. The company deducted the following sums from its income as expenses for Robert's remuneration: $20,371 for three months in 1962 consisting of $851 in salary and $19,520 in bonus and $35,673 in 1963 consisting of $5,280 in salary and $30,393 in bonus. These bonuses were paid in accordance with the company's practice of paying its permanent employees mainly by way of a yearly bonus proportionate to each employee's shareholdings which were based on service.

The CRA took the position that only $1,800 in 1962 and $7,200 in 1963 was a reasonable deduction for remuneration in the circumstances. This position was based on Robert's youth, his record of academic failures and the fact that his earnings for the three months in 1962 were greater than the superintendent's salary for that year. An expert appearing for the company testified that Robert was, in fact, the number two man in the company and that, as such, he would normally receive 70% of the most senior man's salary. Jules' salary was $48,000 in 1962 and $57,000 in 1963.

The company's position was upheld on the basis that Robert's remuneration was reasonable in the circumstances. The question to be answered was: would a reasonable business person have paid the remuneration in the circumstances? It was found that the bonus arrangement was a legitimate way of remunerating the company employees. Having regard to Robert's contemplated status in the company, which was subsequently fulfilled, and to the legitimate consideration of future benefits to be derived from his employment, the court found that his remuneration for the three-month period in 1962 was not unreasonable but in proportion to the value of his services to the company. The court also found, on the basis of the evidence that 70% of the most senior person's salary was a normal salary for his second in command, that Robert's remuneration for 1963 was reasonable.

¶13,100 Fringe benefits

The remuneration package for a shareholder-manager may include a number of fringe benefits such as private health insurance and group sickness or accident insurance, among others. It might include retirement benefits from an employer's contribution to a registered pension plan. Since only employees are eligible, the owner of an unincorporated business, who is not considered to be an employee, cannot participate in such a pension plan. However, a personal contribution to a registered retirement savings plan could still be made. There are criteria which must be met by a registered pension plan for a shareholder-manager.

Sometimes the life and disability insurance coverage provided in the group insurance package is not adequate to meet the needs of the shareholder-manager. If the company were to pay for additional life insurance premiums on an individual policy owned by the shareholder-manager (in his or her capacity as a shareholder), then the full premium would be a shareholder benefit. Similarly, if the company were to pay the premiums on a disability insurance policy owned by the shareholder-manager, and if the benefit was received in his or her capacity as shareholder, then the full amount of the premium would be a shareholder benefit.

A retiring allowance could also be paid by the company which would receive a tax deduction. The tax on that income could be deferred by the shareholder-manager by rolling the allowance into a registered retirement savings plan or a registered pension plan. Note, however, that the Act will restrict the amount that can be rolled in this manner. A limit, for years of service prior to 1989, of $3,500 will apply for each year that the taxpayer was not a member of a registered pension plan, or was a member of a plan whose benefits for those years did not vest, and $2,000 for each year that the taxpayer was a member of such a plan

Margin references: ITA: 67; 68 DTC 5210 (Ex. Ct.); IT-470R; ITA: 147.1; ITA: 15(1); ITA: 60(j.1)

whose benefits did vest. For years of service after 1988 and before 1996, there is a single limit of $2,000 for each year of service. Therefore, no amount in respect of years of service after 1995 can be rolled into an RRSP.

Finally, a company car can be provided as a fringe benefit. Exhibit 13-4 presents an example which shows the possible advantage of the company providing a car subject to the standby charge in comparison with the individual providing himself or herself with the same car. The decision in this comparison will depend on the specific facts of each case. However, the calculation at the bottom of Exhibit 13-4 would suggest a benefit to a company car when the actual cost of the personal use of the company car exceeds the amount of the benefit that must be added to the shareholder-manager's employment income for the particular car in question. It should be noted that if the car is used primarily for personal purposes as a perquisite there may be a difference in favour of the company providing the car as illustrated in the example. Note that the example neutralizes the company's position by assuming that lease costs and operating costs would be added to the salary of the shareholder-manager where he or she assumed these expenses. Exhibit 13-4 is a relatively simple example. The analysis can be much more complex (e.g., luxury cars with a cost or lease payments over $30,000 or $800, respectively).

EXHIBIT 13-4
Company Car as a Fringe Benefit

Assumptions:

Annual car lease cost (added to salary if leased by
  shareholder-manager), including PST (8%) and GST (6%) . . . . $ 6,000
Annual operating costs of car (added to salary if leased by
  shareholder-manager) . . . . $ 2,880
Shareholder-manager has taxable income before car benefit of:
  if car leased by company $154,000
  if car leased personally ($154,000 + $6,000 + $2,880) $162,880
Business use of car (4,800/24,000 km) 20%

Shareholder-Manager Pays Tax on Benefit	*Shareholder-Manager Leases Car Personally*	
Benefit from use of car:	Incremental taxable income	$ 8,880
— value of operating costs of personal use [par. 6(1)(k)] (22¢ × 19,200 km) 4,224	Less: deduction for business use of car (20% of ($2,880 + $6,000))	(1,776)
— standby charge* [par. (1)(e)] (⅔ × $6,000) 4,000		$ 7,104
$ 8,224	GST rebate (6/106 × $1,776)	$ 101
	Tax @ 46% on income	$ 3,268
Tax @ 46% . . . . $ 3,783	Tax @ 46% on GST rebate	$ 46
	Net tax ($3,268 – $101 + $46) . . .	$ 3,213

Difference: $570

Conclusion: If considering only net cash in shareholder-manager's hands he or she would choose to lease the car personally.

Reason: Cost of personal use of car ($8,880 — $1,776)+GST rebate
  included in the year of receipt ($101) $7,205
    Less: benefit added to income under ssec. 6(1) ($4,224 + $4,000)   8,224

Net income difference $1,019

Tax on net saving @ 46% . . . . $ 469
GST rebate received   101

Total cash difference . . . . $ 570

Note that present value considerations on the rebate which is received and taxed in the following year have been ignored, although the tax on the rebate inclusion is considered by the inclusion of the rebate in income. Also, ignored is the effect of the input tax credit (ITC) received by the corporation if it incurs the annual lease and operating costs. If the corporation pays additional salary equal to its net costs for these items after ITC and, hence, if the shareholder-manager must pay the GST from other sources, it can be shown that the shareholder-manager's after-tax retention is reduced by the after-tax equivalent of the GST costs.

---

* Since business travel does not comprise the primary (usually more than 50%) purpose of the distance travelled, the reduction factor in subsection 6(2) does not apply (i.e., A/B = 1 in the formula). Lease costs in this calculation include PST @ 8% and GST @ 6%.

¶13,200 SALARY VERSUS DIVIDENDS

¶13,210 The Basic Trade-Off

On the one hand, salaries which are deductible by the corporation are subjected to personal tax. On the other hand, dividends which are not deductible by the corporation must be generated from income that is subjected to corporate tax; in turn, such dividends are subjected to personal tax which is reduced by the dividend tax credit.

Exhibit 12-1 demonstrated that integration of personal and corporate income tax works perfectly if the combined corporate tax rate is 20% where the 25% gross-up applies and 31% where the 45% gross-up applies. Since the federal tax rate on income eligible for the small business deduction is 13.12%, a provincial corporate tax rate of 6.88% (20.00% – 13.12%) on this type of income would provide perfect integration. If the provincial tax rate is less than 6.88% then there is an advantage from incorporating income eligible for the small business deduction and receiving dividends, since the dividend tax credit claimed on the personal tax return will be greater than the underlying corporate tax. If the provincial corporate tax rate is higher than 6.88%, then there will be a disadvantage from incorporating this type of income since the dividend tax credit will be less than the underlying corporate tax. In this case, salary, and not dividends, will generally be preferred. Since the federal tax rate on business income subject to the higher corporate tax rate is 22.12%, the breakeven provincial corporate tax rate on that income must be 8.88% (31% – 22.12%).

Further, salaries can reduce income to maintain corporate income at or below the $400,000 business limit for the small business deduction, whereas dividends will not. On the other hand, dividends reduce the cumulative net investment loss balance, to help preserve access to the capital gains deduction and may generate a dividend refund, but salaries do not.

¶13,220 Amounts of Taxable Dividends that Can Be Distributed Tax-Free

Exhibit 13-5 demonstrates that it is possible to distribute a considerable amount of dividends which will be received tax-free by the shareholder, if he or she has no other sources of income. This fact might be advantageous in family income splitting where various members of a family hold different classes of shares. However, in the case of *Champ v. The Queen*, the court rejected such an arrangement where the two classes of common shares were identical, but dividends were only paid on one class. The court treated the two share classes as one and assigned a proportional share of the dividends to each class. The basis for this decision was the corporate common law rule that dividends must be shared *pro rata*. 83 DTC 5029 (F.C.T.D.)

The case of *The Queen v. McClurg*, presents a different set of facts resolved in favour of the taxpayer because the Articles of Incorporation allowed the "sprinkling" of dividends among various classes of shares at the discretion of the directors. However, it must be remembered that in order for the company to pay the dividends indicated it must generate income which will be subjected to corporate taxes. 91 DTC 5001 (S.C.C.)

Dividends distributed out of low-rate income (small business deduction) are subject to the 25% gross-up, while dividends distributed out of high-rate active business income are subject to the 45% gross-up. Exhibit 13-5 shows the possibility of receiving a significant dividend without any personal tax.

EXHIBIT 13-5

Amounts of Taxable Dividends That Can Be Distributed Almost Tax-Free in 2007

	25% Gross-up	45% Gross-up
Taxable dividend[1], [2]	$30,632	$ 73,121
Gross-up (25%/45%)	7,658	32,904
Taxable income	$38,290	$106,025
Federal and provincial tax	$ 9,858	$ 35,105
Less: assumed personal tax credits	(2,200)	(2,200)
dividend tax credit	(7,658)	(32,905)
Total tax[3]	$ —	$ —
Net cash retained	$30,632	$ 73,121

NOTES: [1] Amounts will change with indexing of tax brackets. The increase in dividends will be approximately equal to the increase in the indexing factor for the year.

[2] None of these amounts will be affected by the minimum tax.

[3] Federal tax cannot be negative, since the tax credits are non-refundable. Therefore, the dividend was calculated to arrive at a basic federal tax of nil. As a result, some provincial tax must be paid, but the provincial tax rate is lower than the federal tax rate.

¶13,230 Distribution Out of Income Taxed at Small Business Rate

Exhibit 13-6 shows the tax saving resulting from the payment of a dividend rather than salary from income eligible for the small business deduction in a province with a 5% corporate tax rate. Generally, dividends from the active business income of a CCPC taxed at the low rate are preferred to salary at all personal rates when total corporate rates are less than 20%. This is because the dividend tax credit is larger than the tax paid by the corporation, resulting in what is known as "over-integration" which produces a tax savings from the use of a corporation. Corporate rates will be less than 20% where a corporation is eligible for the federal small business deduction and where the provincial corporate tax rate is about 7% or less.

However, there is a range which will vary annually with indexing within which a combination of salaries and dividends will provide the lowest tax cost. Below the lower limit of the range, which is approximately equal to the level of the individual's total personal credit base (i.e., the level of income at which tax is offset by personal tax credits), salaries alone result in the lowest tax cost because they are deductible by the corporation and in the hands of the individual are offset by personal credits and, therefore, not taxable. Above the upper limit of the range, dividends alone result in the lowest tax cost. The latter case is demonstrated in Exhibit 13-7 using a $120,000 level of pre-tax corporate income. In that case, the payment of the salary is not fully integrated, because it is deductible by the corporation at a relatively low tax rate, assumed to be 18.12%, and taxable to the individual at a relatively high rate, including provincial tax, at a 46% rate. On the other hand, the dividend benefits from "over-integration" because the total corporate rate of tax is less than 20%.

An appropriate range can be computed for situations where the corporate income accrues to a single owner-manager or for more than one owner-manager. When corporate tax rates total 20% or more, salaries alone will result in the lowest tax cost.

EXHIBIT 13-6
Income eligible for Small Business Deduction

		Individual	
		Combined federal and provincial tax bracket	
		26.0% *(up to $37.2K)*	*46%* *(120.9K +)*
Tax on $1,000 of salary	(A)	$ 260	$460
Tax on $1,000 corporate income distributed as a dividend after corporate tax:			
Corporate tax @ 18.12% (i.e., 38% – 10% + 1.12% – 16% + 5% (assumed prov.))	(B)	$ 181	$181
Combined federal and provincial personal tax* on remainder distributed as a dividend (tax on $1,000 – $181 = $819 dividend)		61	266
	(C)	$ 242	$447
Tax saving on dividend alternative (A) – (C)		$ 18	$ 13
Tax deferred while funds left in corporation (A) – (B)		$ 79	$279

* Includes the effect of the combined federal and provincial rates on the grossed-up dividend and dividend tax credit — e.g., at the lower personal rate: [26% of ($\frac{5}{4}$ × $819) – 20% of ($\frac{5}{4}$ × $819)] and at the higher personal rate: [46% of ($\frac{5}{4}$ × $819) – 20% of ($\frac{5}{4}$ × $819)].

EXHIBIT 13-7
Salary Versus Dividends

A. Data

Company earns $120,000 of active business income eligible for small business deduction.

Shareholder has no other income and has federal personal tax credits of $2,000 and provincial personal tax credits of $1,290 that are allowable for both regular Part I tax and minimum tax.

B. Comparison*	*Salary*	*Dividend*
Pre-tax corporate income	$ 120,000	$ 120,000
Salary.	(120,000)	—
Taxable income of corporation	—	$ 120,000
Corporate tax @ 18.12% (i.e., 38% – 10% + 1.12% – 16% + 5%)	—	(21,744)
Available for payment of dividend	—	$ 98,256
Personal tax on salary or dividend	$ 37,545	$ 14,234**
Add: corporate tax	—	21,744
Total tax paid	$ 37,545	$ 35,978
Difference. $1,567		
Savings as a percentage of $120,000 . . . . 1.3%		
Savings as a percentage of tax on salary 4.2%		

* Includes the corporate surtax.
** Federal minimum tax would not apply to the dividend, as shown by the following calculation of federal tax:

Greater of:

(a) regular basic federal tax under Part I on dividend of $98,256.	$ 8,327	
(b) minimum tax [15.5% of ($98,256 – $40,000) – $2,000]	$ 7,030	} $ 8,327

Example Problem 1

Ethan Corporation Limited, a Canadian-controlled private corporation carrying on business in a province with a 5% corporate tax rate on its income (i.e., a total corporate tax rate of 18.12%), has earned $36,000 in its taxation year ended December 31 before a salary has been paid to the shareholder-manager. The shareholder-manager has federal personal tax credits of $2,500 and provincial personal tax credits of $1,613.

— *REQUIRED*

(A) If the full $36,000 is to be distributed either by way of salary or dividends, which should be chosen?

(B) Is there a combination of salary and dividends that is better?

— *SOLUTION*

	Part A		Part B
Corporation:	*Salary*	*Dividend*	*Combination*
Income before salary .... (I)	$36,000	$36,000	$36,000
Salary	(36,000)	—	(12,808)
Taxable income	Nil	$36,000	$23,192
Corporate tax @ 18.12% (i.e., 38% – 10%			
+ 1.12% – 16% + 5%) .... (II)	Nil	(6,523)	(4,202)
Available for dividend	Nil	$29,477	$18,990
Shareholder:			
Income from salary and/or dividend*	$36,000	$29,477	$31,798
Gross-up	—	7,369	4,747
Taxable income	$36,000	$36,846	$36,545
Federal tax	$ 5,580	$ 5,711	$ 5,664
Personal tax credits	(2,500)	(2,500)	(2,500)
Dividend tax credit	—	(4,913)	(3,165)
Basic federal tax (B.F.T.)**	$ 3,080	Nil	Nil
Provincial tax	3,600	3,685	3,655
Provincial personal tax credits	(1,613)	(1,613)	(1,613)
Provincial dividend tax credit	Nil	(2,456)	(1,582)
Total tax .... (III)	$ 5,067	Nil	$ 460
Cash retained (I – (II + III))	$30,933	$29,477	$31,338

* A dividend of these amounts would not be affected by the minimum tax.

** Cannot be negative.

Note that in Part A, when the dividend is paid, there is an excess of $1,702 in federal non-refundable dividend tax credit and personal tax credits that cannot be used to offset tax on other income. Suppose salary were increased by $100. At the corporate level the following would occur since all of the income is distributed:

Increase in salary expense	$ 100.00
Decrease in corporate tax ($100 × .1812)	(18.12)
Decrease in amount available for dividend	$ 81.88

At the shareholder-manager level the following would occur since all of the income is distributed:

Increase in salary	$ 100.00
Decrease in dividend	(81.88)
Decrease in gross-up	(20.47)
Decrease in taxable income	$ (2.35)
Decrease in federal tax @ 15.5% of $2.35	$ (.36)
Decrease in federal dividend tax credit (13⅓% of ⁵⁄₄ × $81.88) ...	13.65
Increase in basic federal tax	$ 13.29

Thus, every $100 increase in salary within the 15.5% federal marginal tax bracket will result in an increase in federal tax of $13.29 where all the income is distributed. To eliminate $1,702 (i.e., $5,711 – 2,500 – 4,913) in excess federal dividend tax credit with additional salary, a salary of $12,808 (i.e., $1,702/.1329) should be paid.

Note that this mix of salary and dividend in Part B is better than the all-salary alternative by $405 (i.e., $31,338 – $30,933). Note also that a tax saving of $405 is the difference between the tax of $4,202 at the corporate level plus $460 at the provincial personal level resulting from a salary of only $12,808 and the tax of $5,067 at the shareholder level resulting from a salary of $36,000. Thus, where the all-dividend remuneration is not taxed in the hands of the shareholder-manager due to excess federal dividend tax credit, it is better to pay a combination of some dividends and some salary to reduce the tax at the corporate level and offset any excess federal dividend tax credit at the shareholder level. Note that the difference between the cash retained of $29,477 from the all-dividend alternative of Part A and the cash retained of $31,338 from the combination alternative of Part B is $1,861. This is exactly the difference in corporate tax plus provincial personal tax paid between the two alternatives (i.e., $6,523 – ($4,202 + $460) = $1,861).

Note that a salary was found to bring basic federal tax to nil since the federal tax rate is higher than the provincial rate.

Example Problem 2

Bryan Hill owns all of the issued shares of Hill & Associates Inc., a consulting firm he started five years ago. Bryan's only source of income is from the corporation and he has federal personal, non-refundable tax credits of $2,500 and provincial tax credits of $1,613. The corporation has a tax rate of 18.12% on its income eligible for the small business deduction.

— REQUIRED

Determine the best combination of salary and/or dividend that Bryan should take in order to minimize the total corporate and personal tax for the year, assuming that the corporation earned net income of $100,000 before owner compensation and income tax. Bryan needs a pre-tax amount of $36,000 in cash to meet his personal expenses.

— SOLUTION

		Salary	Dividend	Combination[1]
Corporation				
Income before salary	(I)	$100,000	$100,000	$100,000
Salary		(36,000)	—	(9,096)
Taxable income		$ 64,000	$100,000	$ 90,904
Corporate tax @ 18.12% (i.e., 38% – 10% + 1.12% – 16% + 5%)	(II)	(11,597)	(18,120)	(16,472)
Available for dividend		$ 52,403	$ 81,880	$ 74,432
Paid as dividend		—	(36,000)	(26,904)
Retained by corporation		$ 52,403	$ 45,880	$ 47,528
Shareholder				
Income from salary		$ 36,000	—	$ 9,096
Income from dividend		—	$ 36,000	26,904
Gross-up		—	9,000	6,726
Taxable income		$ 36,000	$ 45,000	$ 42,726
Federal tax		$ 5,580	$ 7,484	$ 6,984
Personal tax credits		(2,500)	(2,500)	(2,500)
Dividend tax credit (13⅓% of ⁵⁄₄ × dividend)		—	(6,000)	(4,484)

Basic federal tax	$ 3,080	Nil	Nil
Provincial tax	3,600	4,657	4,384
Provincial personal tax credits	(1,613)	(1,613)	(1,613)
Provincial dividend tax credit	Nil	(3,000)	(2,242)
Total tax . . . . (III)	$ 5,067	$ 44	$ 529
Net cash retained initially (I – (II + III))	$ 83,336	$ 81,836	$ 82,999
Ultimate tax on dividend[2]	(9,171)	(8,029)	(8,317)
Net retained ultimately after tax	$ 74,165	$ 73,807	$ 74,682

— *NOTES TO SOLUTION*

[1] Note that, when the remuneration is paid as a dividend, there is an excess of $1,016 in federal non-refundable dividend tax credit and personal tax credits that cannot be used to offset tax on other income.

In this case, the marginal analysis to use up the excess tax credits is a little different, because only part of the corporate income is being distributed. Suppose salary were increased by $100. At the corporate level, the following would occur:

Increase in salary expense	$ 100.00
Decrease in corporate tax ($100 × .1812)	(18.12)
Decrease in amount available for dividend	$ 81.88

This only affects the amount retained by the corporation. At the shareholder-manager level, the following would occur when $100 of dividend is traded for $100 of salary:

Increase in salary	$ 100.00
Decrease in dividend	(100.00)
Decrease in gross-up	(25.00)
Decrease in taxable income	$ (25.00)
Decrease in federal tax @ 22% of $25.00	$ (5.50)
Decrease in federal dividend tax credit (13⅓% of ⁵⁄₄ × $100.00)	16.67
Increase in federal tax	$ 11.17

Thus, every $100 increase in salary within the 22% federal marginal tax bracket will result in an increase in tax of $11.17. To eliminate $1,016 in excess federal dividend tax credit with additional salary, a salary of $9,096 (i.e., $1,016/.1117) should be paid as part of the combination of salary and dividends of $26,904 to total the pre-tax $36,000 in cash needed.

[2] When the amount retained by the corporation is paid out as a dividend, it will attract personal tax at that time. The combined federal and provincial tax can be estimated at a rate of 17.5% (i.e., (34% – 20%) of 1.25 × dividend) of the cash dividend paid. When this amount is deducted from the net cash retained initially, the ultimate net after-tax retention is computed. Of course, the tax on the dividend paid from corporate retention has not been reduced by the time value of money, which depends on when the dividend is ultimately paid.

This situation shows that it would be best to pay a combination of salary and dividends since it results in $518 (i.e., $74,682 – $74,164) of additional after-tax cash. This result is largely due to the fact that the combined federal and provincial corporate tax rate is slightly less than 20%.

¶13,240 Distributions Out of Income Not Eligible for the Small Business Deduction

To this point the analysis has focused on the question of salaries versus dividends as remuneration from income eligible for the small business deduction. Exhibit 13-8 presents the comparison for income *not* eligible for the small business deduction. Note that salaries will generally be preferable. However, where income is taxed at the high corporate rate on business income, the dividend alternative produces a tax deferral advantage for individuals in the higher tax brackets. Recognize that the amount of tax deferred can be reinvested in the corporation to, perhaps, make up the added tax cost. Thus, the added tax cost of not paying a salary may be offset by the deferral advantage of dividends if there is no immediate need for the funds. In making this comparison, it is important to consider the amount of this deferral advantage and the length of time the added tax can be deferred by delaying the payment of dividends.

Exhibit 13-8 uses the 45% dividend gross-up and related tax credit on dividends paid out of high tax rate active business income. In this case, we are assuming that the income under consideration is above the small business deduction business limit of $400,000 and is, therefore, eligible for this new treatment.

Under the 26% tax column, the personal tax on the dividend is actually negative. This is as a result of the fact that the enhanced dividend tax credit is greater than the tax and, therefore, available to offset tax on other income.

The result is that the tax cost on the dividend alternative is not significant, and the tax deferral at the 46% personal tax rate can provide an advantage to leaving the money in the corporation and paying a dividend at a later date.

EXHIBIT 13-8
Canadian Business Income not eligible for Small Business Deduction

		Individual	
		Combined federal and provincial tax bracket	
		26% (up to $37.2K)	*46%* ($120.9K +)
Tax on $1,000 of salary	(A)	$ 260	$460
Tax on $1,000 corporate income distributed as a dividend after corporate tax: Corporate tax @ 33.12% (i.e., 38% – 10% + 1.12% – 7% + 13.5%)	(B)	$ 356	$356
Personal tax* on remainder distributed as a dividend (tax on $1,000 – $356 = $644)		(47)	140
	(C)	$ 309	$496
Tax cost on dividend alternative (C) – (A)		$ 49	$ 36
Tax deferral (prepayment) while funds left in corporation (A) – (B)		$ (96)	$104

* Includes the effect of the combined federal and provincial rates on the grossed-up dividend and dividend tax credit — e.g., at the lower personal rate, $26\% \times (\text{Dividend} \times 1.45) - (.45 \times \text{Dividend}) = -0.073 \times \text{Dividend}$, and at the higher personal rate, $46\% \times (\text{Dividend} \times 1.45) - (.45 \times \text{Dividend}) = 0.217 \times \text{Dividend}$.

¶13,250 Summary of the Salary Versus Dividends Issue

The factors affecting a decision on whether to remunerate the shareholder-manager of a corporation by salary or by dividends include the following:

- the corporate tax rate, including both federal and provincial components with surtaxes, applicable to the type of income of the corporation;

- the personal tax rate, including both federal and provincial components with surtaxes, applicable to the shareholder as a result of income other than that from the business;

- whether the dividends are eligible for the 45% dividend gross-up and tax credit;

- the amount of the shareholder's personal tax credits and deductions; and

- the shareholder's participation in the Canada Pension Plan, registered pension plans and registered retirement savings plans which require income in the nature of salary rather than dividends.

The number of variables involved in a specific set of circumstances make it necessary to do a set of calculations similar to those presented in this chapter to determine the best mix of salaries and/or dividends in the particular case.

The ranking found in these computations will not be the same in all circumstances. At much lower levels of pre-tax corporate income the payment of dividends will be better. At much higher levels of pre-tax corporate income the payment of salary may be better. Generally, an optimal mixture of salary and dividends can be found where the total corporate tax rate is less than 20% as is the case, for example, where income is eligible for the small business deduction and a provincial corporate tax rate is about 7% or less.

Where the corporate rate is above 20%, it may be preferable to distribute all of the owner-manager's remuneration in the form of salary, unless the dividend is eligible for the 45% dividend gross-up and tax credit and dividends are expected to be deferred.

Recognize that if no salary is paid, the owner-manager does not have income that will qualify him or her to make deductible Canada Pension Plan or registered retirement savings plan contributions. Each of these provides for an initial tax deduction, the sheltering of income and the deferral of the ultimate payment of tax until the receipt of benefits. Similar benefits can be achieved when funds are left in the corporation after dividends have been paid to provide the shareholder-manager with the same disposable income as a required amount of salary.

One variable that has not been analyzed in detail is the effect of a provincial payroll tax when salary is paid to the owner-manager. Several provinces use a health levy, based on a percentage of salary or wages paid by an employer, to finance health care. [This additional tax cost of paying a salary would increase under the February 26, 1991 federal budget proposal which would place a $10,000 annual cap on the amount of provincial payroll and capital taxes that may be deducted in computing income under Division B. The proposed additional deduction from taxable income in Division C, at 6% of taxable income, may not fully compensate for the non-deductible provincial tax in excess of the $10,000 deduction ceiling, depending on the circumstances. Implementation of this proposal has been deferred until further notice.]

¶13,300   OTHER PLANNING ASPECTS OF USING CORPORATIONS

¶13,310   Use of Holding Companies

¶13,315   An extension of integration

Inserting a holding company between a shareholder and another company requires an extension of the concept of integration, discussed in the previous chapter, to allow income ultimately to flow through the holding company to the shareholder to be taxed in his or her hands. To put this into effect, dividends must not be taxed at the corporate shareholder's level. This occurs under Part I since intercorporate dividends between Canadian companies are deductible under Division C leaving the taxable income of the recipient unaffected. However, there is the possibility of a tax under Part IV of the Act on such dividends received by a private corporation. This tax is refundable when the recipient corporation pays a taxable dividend to its shareholders such that the recipient corporation itself is not ultimately taxable on the dividends that pass through to the individual shareholder.

¶13,320   Compensation

Where there are two or more owner-managers of an operating company, the use of holding companies may give more flexibility in the salary–dividend mix decision. Where there is only one corporation, the payment of dividends must be done, under corporate law, *pro rata* according to the shareholdings. Therefore, one shareholder-manager cannot normally receive all dividends and the other shareholder-manager cannot receive all salary. By inserting a management-holding company between each of the shareholders and an operating company, the operating company can pay only dividends to the holding companies. Then each holding corporation can determine what dividends are appropriate for its shareholder(s).

For example, assume Jim and Bob each own 50% of Jimbo Inc. and each have different cash flow needs. Bob is nearing retirement and wants to defer his income while Jim has a young family and needs cash. If dividends are paid, then both Jim and Bob will receive the dividends *pro rata* even if Bob does not want them. They will each then be liable for personal income tax on these dividends. In this case, each of Jim and Bob could set up holding companies to own their shares of Jimbo Inc. as follows:

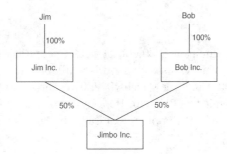

As dividends are paid from Jimbo Inc. they will be received by the holding companies without either Part I or Part IV tax. Bob can then defer his personal tax liability by leaving his dividends in Bob Inc. while Jim could take the cash he needs by paying a dividend to himself from Jim Inc.

¶13,325 Deferral of tax on dividends

The use of a holding company may be advisable in the situation of a non-controlling shareholder-employee of an operating company that is paying out more taxable dividends than necessary for the shareholder-employee's immediate needs. In such a case, the shareholder could transfer his or her shares in the operating company to a holding company which he or she controls. If the holding company owned more than 10% of the total voting shares and more than 10% of the fair market value of all the issued shares in the operating company, the two corporations are connected. The dividends then could be received by the holding company without attracting the Part IV tax as long as the holding company and the operating company which had no investment income or portfolio dividends were connected.

A much smaller deferral of tax (if any) is possible on dividends from non-connected corporations on which Part IV tax is payable. The Part IV tax is levied at a 33⅓% rate. Therefore, there will only be a deferral benefit when the personal combined rate of federal and provincial tax plus surtaxes exceeds 33⅓%.

¶13,330 Implementing an estate freeze

Another reason for the use of a holding company to own shares of an operating company would be to effect a planning device known as an estate freeze. To give a very simple example, the owner of an operating company may wish to freeze or stop the growth in his or her interest in the operating company to avoid further capital gains on these shares which would ultimately be triggered at his or her death. The owner could arrange to transfer his or her common shares in the operating company to a holding company in which the common shares were owned by the next generation in the family, the children. The owner could take back in return, perhaps, preferred shares with voting rights in the holding company. These preferred shares would not grow in value, but could pay a sufficient dividend to meet his or her personal needs and would maintain control over the operating company through the voting privileges.

Dividends paid on the common shares of the operating company would flow to the holding company free of Part IV tax as long as the operating company had no investment income or portfolio dividends to trigger a dividend refund while the two companies were connected. Estate planning will be discussed in greater detail in Chapter 17.

¶13,340 Qualified Small Business Corporation Shares (QSBCS)

The corporate entity referred to as a "small business corporation" (SBC) is widely used throughout the Act. For example, the term is used in connection with a small business development bond and a business investment loss and an exemption from the effects of the corporate attribution rules. Dispositions of the shares of small business corporations may qualify for the capital gains deduction.

ITA: 15.1, 39(1)(c), 74.4

A capital gains deduction to a maximum of $250,000 of taxable capital gains net of any portion of the capital gains deduction of previously claimed is available. This amount is the equivalent of a gross capital gain of $500,000. [The March 19, 2007 federal budget proposed to increase the capital gains deduction limit to $375,000, thereby increasing the total capital gains exemption to $750,000. This increase will apply to capital gains arising on dispositions on or after March 19, 2007.]

ITA: 110.6(2.1)

Since there is also an equivalent deduction for qualified farm and fishing property, these two are integrated to ensure that the maximum deduction with respect to all properties combined does not exceed $250,000 [$375,000 under the March 19, 2007 federal budget proposal].

ITA: 110.6(4)

¶13,345 Small business corporation (SBC)

A small business corporation (SBC) is defined as a Canadian-controlled private corporation of which all or substantially all of the assets, on a fair market value basis, are used principally in an active business, carried on primarily in Canada by the corporation or a related corporation. The reference to a related corporation means that assets leased or loaned to a related corporation also qualify. Alternatively, the assets meeting the "all or substantially all" test may be shares or debt in an SBC that is a connected corporation, or a combination of assets in direct use and securities of a connected corporation.

ITA: 248(1)

ITA: 186(4)

The CRA's interpretation of the phrase "all or substantially all", as stated in about 10 different Interpretation Bulletins, is that it means at least 90%. However, in a recent court case on another issue, but in respect of the phrase "all or substantially all", the Tax Court of Canada concluded that the CRA "might be hard pressed to refuse a claim where the percentage was 89%, maybe even 85% or 80% or lower". See *Wood v. M.N.R.* The court concluded that the "term 'substantially all' does not lend itself to a simple mathematical formula" like at least 90%. The court preferred the meaning given by "small unrelated amounts" reducing the total to arrive at substantially all. The word "primarily", while not defined in the Act, is generally considered to mean more than 50%. Elsewhere, the CRA states that the word "principal" is not defined in the Act but it is considered that the words "chief" and "main" are synonymous to it. While a principal or main use may be less than 50% if the use is the most of many uses, the CRA has generally interpreted the word to mean more than 50%. Exhibit 13-9 presents the definition of a small business corporation in point form.

IT-151R5, par. 31

87 DTC 312 (T.C.C.)

IT-73R6, par. 12

¶13,340

EXHIBIT 13-9
Small Business Corporation (SBC)
[ssec. 248(1)]

A Small Business Corporation is a corporation which was at any particular time:

— a Canadian-controlled private corporation, and

— all or substantially all (90% test) of the fair market value of assets (including unrecorded assets but excluding liabilities) were

    (a) used principally in an active business carried on primarily (>50%) in Canada by

        • the particular corporation, or

        • a corporation related [sec. 251] to the particular corporation; or

    (b) shares or debt

        • of a SBC that was connected [ssec. 186(4)] with the particular corporation; or

    (c) a combination of (a) and (b).

Example Problem

Maya lives in Toronto and owns 100% of Maya's Ltd. The corporation was incorporated 10 years ago, in Ontario, to operate a retail clothing establishment in Toronto. The following is the recent balance sheet for the corporation.

Maya's Ltd.
BALANCE SHEET
as at December 31, 2007

Assets
Current

Cash	$ 2,500
Marketable securities	200,000
Accounts receivable (net of reserve)	95,000
Inventory	270,000
Prepaid expenses	2,000
Total (equal to fair market value)	$ 569,500

Fixed

Land, at cost (FMV: $225,000)	150,000
Building, at net book value (FMV: $350,000)	160,000
Equipment, at net book value (FMV: $100,000)	120,500
	$1,000,000

Liabilities
Current

Accounts payable	$ 265,000
Income taxes payable	5,000
Due to shareholder	80,000
	$ 350,000
Mortgage payable	275,000
	$ 625,000

Shareholder's Equity

Share capital	1,000
Retained earnings	374,000
	$1,000,000

The goodwill of the business has been valued at $250,000.

— REQUIRED

Determine whether Maya's Ltd. is a small business corporation, assuming that the marketable securities were held:

(A) as a short-term investment of surplus cash at the low-point of the corporation's inventory cycle, and

(B) as a long-term investment to produce investment income.

— SOLUTION

In this case the critical condition in the definition of a small business corporation is the 90% test. It must be determined whether all or substantially all of the fair market value of the assets, including unrecorded goodwill, was used principally in an active business carried on primarily in Canada by Maya's Ltd. Retailing is an active business and it is being carried on exclusively in Canada in this case.

(A) If the marketable securities are held for use in the business, as would be the case if they represented a short-term investment of cash surplus, pending the build-up of inventory, then it can be concluded that all of the fair market value of the assets is used principally in an active business carried on primarily in Canada. Therefore, the company meets the 90% test and is a small business corporation.

(B) If the marketable securities are not considered to be used in the active business of retailing, then their relative value must be determined as follows:

	Fair market value	%
Cash	$ 2,500	0.17
Marketable securities	200,000	13.38
Accounts receivable	95,000	6.36
Inventory	270,000	18.07
Prepaid expenses	2,000	0.13
Land	225,000	15.06
Building	350,000	23.42
Equipment	100,000	6.69
Goodwill	250,000	16.72
Total	$1,494,500	100.00%

Since the marketable securities comprise more than 10% of the fair market value of the assets, the 90% test in the definition of a small business corporation is not met. (Note that the legislation does not quantify the term "all or substantially all". The courts may not interpret this term as meaning at least 90% as used administratively by the CRA.) Note that the definition of a small business corporation applies at a particular point in time. Therefore, if some of the marketable securities can be removed from the corporation: either sold with the proceeds used to pay off liabilities or invested in assets used in the active retailing business, the 90% test can be met after the removal or reinvestment. Thus, the corporation can be "purified" to meet the 90% test. It is not enough to convert the marketable securities into cash, if the cash is not used in an active business carried on by the corporation.

¶13,350   Basic QSBCS rules applied to a single corporation

This analysis will attempt to break down the provision into several easy-to-understand components. The first application will be to a single corporation. Next, the rules will be applied to a parent and subsidiary relationship. Application beyond two corporations becomes too complex for an introductory tax course and really requires the assistance of a tax specialist.

The term "qualified small business corporation share" of an individual is defined as follows: ITA: 110.6(1)

(a) a share of the capital stock of a corporation that is a small business corporation (SBC) at the time of disposition (i.e., the determination time) and is owned by the individual, by the individual's spouse or by a partnership related, as specifically defined for this purpose, to the individual (related party) (for determining whether a person or partnership is related to an individual);   ITA: 110.6(14)(*d*)

(b) the share was not owned by anyone, other than the individual or a person (including a personal trust) or partnership related to the individual throughout the 24-month period preceding the disposition (without exception to the 24-month period in the case of a deemed disposition caused by death);

(c) the share was, throughout that part of the 24-month period ending immediately before the disposition that the share was owned by the individual or a person or partnership related to the individual:

(i) a share of a corporation that was a Canadian-controlled private corporation, and

(ii) more than 50% of the fair market value of the corporation's assets were used principally in an active business carried on primarily in Canada by the corporation or a related corporation.

Each of the above three parts of the definition can be considered as tests which will be referred to, respectively, as:

(a) the SBC Test,

(b) the Holding Period Test, and

(c) the Basic Asset Test (50% Test).

Exhibit 13-10 presents the foregoing tests in point form for ease of reference.

EXHIBIT 13-10
Qualified Small Business Corporation Share (QSBCS)
[ssec. 110.6(1)]

Basic Tests

A Qualified Small Business Corporation Share is:

— at any time (i.e., determination time)

• typically at time of disposition or deemed disposition;

— a share that meets the following tests:

(a) SBC Test

— an SBC at determination time

— owned by:

• the individual,

• the individual's spouse, or

• a partnership related to the individual [par. 110.6(14)(*d*)];

(b) Holding Period Test

— throughout the 24 months preceding the determination time

— owned by no one other than

• the individual, or

• a person or partnership related to the individual [pars. 110.6(14)(*c*), (*d*), (*e*), (*f*)] (i.e., related party);

(c) Basic Asset Test (50% Test)

— throughout that part of the 24 months preceding the determination time while owned by the individual or related party

● share of a CCPC for which more than 50% of the fair market value of its assets were used principally in an active business carried on primarily in Canada by the corporation or by a related corporation.

Graphically, the timing factor in each of the three tests could be depicted as follows:

		Determination time
(a) SBC Test		|
(b) Holding Period Test	|← 24 months	→|
(c) Basic Asset Test	|← 24 months	→|

Example Problem

Reconsider the facts of the previous example problem. Assume that the problem raised by the marketable securities has been resolved by removing the marketable securities from the corporation. Also, assume that the relative proportion of assets held at December 31, 2007 has not changed in the last five years.

— *REQUIRED*

Determine whether the shares are eligible for the capital gains exemption, assuming:

(A) the shares were acquired on incorporation 20 years ago, and

(B) the shares were acquired from the brother of Maya in blocks of 200 shares annually for the last five years.

— *SOLUTION*

At the time of their disposition or deemed disposition, to qualify for the capital gains exemption, the shares must meet three tests. The difference between parts (A) and (B) of the Required will be seen in the application of the second test.

(1) SBC Test

The shares must be of an SBC at the time of the disposition or deemed disposition. In this case, steps have been taken to make the corporation an SBC, if it did not already qualify as such, as discussed in the previous example problem.

(2) Holding Period Test

Throughout the 24 months preceding the disposition, the shares cannot be owned by anyone other than Maya or a related party (i.e., Maya's brother).

(A) This test is met, because the shares were held for the preceding two years by Maya.

(B) Where the shares have been acquired from the related individual (i.e., Maya's brother) even within the previous 24-month period, the test is still met. If the individual from whom the shares were acquired was not related, then the shares would have to be held by the present shareholder for the full 24 months. Since the holding period test is applied to each share, a series of dispositions can be staged as the shares meet the 24-month test on a first-in, first-out basis as permitted.

ITA: 110.6(14)(*a*)

(3) Basic Asset Test (50% Test)

This test requires that throughout the 24 months preceding a disposition or deemed disposition, while the shares were held by a particular individual (i.e., Maya) or related party (i.e., Maya's brother), the shares were of a Canadian-controlled private corporation in which more than 50% of the fair market value of the assets were used principally in an active business carried on primarily in Canada by the corporation or by a related corporation. Since no other corporation is involved in this situation, the other parts of the test pertaining to a connected corporation do not apply. In this case, even with a 13.38% investment in marketable securities which may not be considered to have been used in the active business of the corporation, the 50% asset test is still met throughout

...nths preceding a contemplated disposition or deemed disposition at this time, since the ...n of marketable securities has been stable throughout those 24 months. Remember that, ...gh the securities have been disposed of to meet the SBC test, they were still assets of ...ration during the 24 months preceding the disposition.

¶13,355 Modification of the asset test (stacking rule)

Even where there are a number of connected corporations, the basic rules as described above must be applied, including the 50% basic asset test in the definition paraphrased above. If the particular corporation to be sold (i.e., a parent corporation) can meet the 50% basic active business asset test with its own active business assets, its shares will meet the asset test.

ITA: 110.6(1) "qualified small business corporation share" (c)(i)

However, where the active business assets of the parent corporation are 50% or less, then the parent corporation may still qualify by including shares and indebtedness of corporations connected with it. However, the rules are further modified to ensure that one of the two levels of corporations (i.e., parent or connected subsidiaries) meets an all or substantially all test (90%) while the other level of corporations meets a "primarily" test (50%) of the aggregate of active business assets and debts or shares of a connected CCPC.

ITA: 110.6(1) "qualified small business corporation share" (d)

Recall, from the discussion of the Part IV tax in Chapter 12, that a connected corporation is a defined term. A corporation is connected with another corporation where:

ITA: 186(4)

(a) the other corporation controls the corporation or

IA: 186(2), 186(7)

(b) the other corporation holds more that 10% of the vote and fair market value in shares of the corporation.

Thus, if the parent meets the 90% test throughout the 24-month period before the disposition with a combination of its own active business assets and shares and debt of a connected corporation, the connected subsidiary need only meet the 50% test on its assets. Alternatively, if the parent does not meet the 90% test throughout the 24-month period before the disposition, the connected subsidiary must meet the 90% test. Thus, the 50% test must be met by both corporations at all times in the 24-month period before the disposition. Furthermore, if the parent does not meet the 90% test throughout the 24-month period before the disposition, then the connected subsidiary must meet the 90% test to have its securities considered as assets of the parent company which help the parent company to meet the 50% test. This modification of the 50% test is presented in Exhibit 13-11 in point form.

Another way of stating the conclusions on the application of these tests is as follows. Where more than 50% of the assets of a particular corporation are active business assets, the Basic Asset Test (50% Test) discussed in the previous segment is met and the type of assets held by connected corporations in the chain below the particular corporation is not relevant. The modified test need not apply. It is only when the 50% Asset Test is not met by the given corporation with its own active business assets that the 90% Modified Asset Test must be used. Where the modification applies in a two-corporation chain, the given corporation and the other connected corporation below it in the chain must meet the 50% Asset Test with their own active business assets in combination with the shares and debt of connected corporations and one of the parent or the connected corporation must meet the 90% test.

EXHIBIT 13-11
Qualified Small Business Corporation Share (QSBCS)
[ssec. 110.6(1)]

Modification of the Basic Asset Test (50% Test)

— Modification of the 50% Basic Asset Test where:

- there is a corporation (subsidiary) connected [ssec. 186(4)] to a particular corporation (parent); the subsidiary must be connected, but not necessarily a SBC,

- the particular corporation (parent) does not meet the 50% Test (on its own active business assets (i.e., excluding the shares and debt of a connected corporation)).

— Conclusion on modification of Asset Test:

- throughout the 24 months ending at the determination time,

  — both the parent and the connected corporation must each meet the 50% Test with a combination of their own active business assets and shares and debt of a connected corporation;

  — one of either the parent or the connected corporation must meet the 90% Test with a combination of its own active business assets and shares and debt of a connected corporation.

— Therefore,

- conceptually, the test is

  — 90/50 for parent/connected, or

  — 50/90 for parent/connected.

If a holding company owns more than one connected subsidiary corporation, then the modified asset test applies as follows.

1. If the holding company meets the 90% test with a combination of its own active business assets and shares or debt of a connected corporation that meets the 50% test, the modified asset test is passed.

2. If the holding company meets the 50% test with a combination of its own active business assets and shares or debt of a connected corporation that meets the 90% test, the modified asset test is passed.

Example Problem

Zeto, a resident of Canada, has owned 100% of the shares of Zeto's Manufacturing Limited (ZML), a Canadian-controlled private corporation, since its incorporation 20 years ago. The corporation carries on a manufacturing business in Canada. He is presently considering the sale of his shares. The fair market value of the assets of ZML is comprised as follows:

	FMV at present	%	FMV throughout past 24 months	%
Active business assets	$200,000	40%	$160,000	40%
Shares of 100%-owned subsidiary	250,000	50	120,000	30
Investments	50,000	10	120,000	30
	$500,000	100%	$400,000	100%

The subsidiary, Zeto Wholesale Ltd. (ZWL), was incorporated by ZML 15 years ago to carry on a wholesaling business in Canada. The fair market value of its assets consists of the following:

	FMV at present	%	*FMV throughout past 24 months*	%
Active business assets	$270,000	90%	$157,500	90%
Investments	30,000	10	17,500	10
	$300,000	100%	$175,000	100%

— REQUIRED

Determine whether the shares of ZML are qualified small business corporation shares at the present time.

— SOLUTION

For the shares of ZML to be qualified small business corporation shares, the following tests must be met:

(1) SBC Test

At the time of sale the shares of ZML must be of a small business corporation (SBC). An SBC is defined to be a Canadian-controlled private corporation (CCPC) which ZML is. In addition, all or substantially all (i.e., at least 90%) of the fair market value of the assets of ZML must be used, at the present time, principally in an active business carried on primarily in Canada by ZML or a related corporation or must be shares or debt of a connected SBC. This test is met by a combination of ZML's own active business assets presently comprising 40% and the shares of the wholly owned subsidiary (ZWL) presently comprising the other 50%. The subsidiary is connected with ZML because it is controlled by ZML and the subsidiary is an SBC because 90% of the present fair market value of its assets are active business assets at the time of the sale.

ITA: 248(1)

ITA: 186(2), 186(4)

(2) Holding Period Test

Throughout the 24 months preceding the present time, the shares cannot have been owned by anyone other than Zeto or a related party. This test is met because only Zeto owned the shares since 1985.

(3) Basic Asset Test (50% Test)

Throughout the 24 months preceding the present time, the shares must be of a CCPC with more than 50% of the fair market value of its assets used principally in an active business carried on primarily in Canada. However, ZML does not meet the 50% Test based on its active business assets alone. Therefore, the Modified Asset Test must be applied.

(4) Modified Asset Test

This test requires, first, that both corporations, ZML and ZWL, must hold more than 50% of their assets in a combination of active business assets and shares or debt of a connected corporation throughout the 24 months preceding the present time. This condition is met by ZML with its 40% active business assets in combination with its 30% in shares of the subsidiary. The subsidiary meets the test with its 90% active business assets. Then, one of the corporations must meet the 90% test with a combination of its active business assets and shares or debt of a connected corporation throughout the preceding 24 months. This condition is met by the subsidiary with its active business assets.

Since all of the relevant tests have been met, the shares of ZML are qualified small business corporation shares.

¶13,360 Capital Gains Deduction

The 1985 budget introduced a lifetime cumulative deduction for net taxable capital gains (net TCGs) for individuals (other than trusts) resident in Canada. The 1992 federal budget restricted the deduction on gains from most real property disposed of after February 1992 (referred to as non-qualifying property) and the 1994 federal budget completely eliminated the deduction for dispositions of all property after February 22, 1994, except for shares of qualifying small business corporations (QSBC) and qualified farm property.

¶13,365 Overview

The current capital gains deduction applies to individuals (other than trusts) who are resident in Canada throughout the year. There is, however, a deeming provision which extends the definition of a resident, for purposes of this section only, to include individuals who were resident at any time in the year and who were resident in Canada throughout either the preceding or the following taxation year. This rule allows an individual who has either ended or commenced residence in Canada during a particular year to qualify for the deduction on a disposition.

ITA: 110.6(5)

The deduction applies to net taxable capital gains (the excess of taxable capital gains (TCGs) over allowable capital losses (ACLs)) on QSBC shares and qualified farm and fishing property. Also eligible for the deduction are capital gains reserves on dispositions of farm and fishing property or QSBC shares.

The maximum fractional capital gains deduction for qualified small business corporation shares and/or qualified farm and fishing property is $250,000 [$375,000 for dispositions on or after March 19, 2007] (i.e., ½ × $500,000 [$750,000 for dispositions on or after March 19, 2007]). Note that in this text the term "exemption" is used to refer to the full amount of a capital gain and the term "deduction" is used to refer to the fractional amount of the capital gain that gives rise to the actual deduction from taxable income of an individual.

¶13,370 Computation of deduction

The amount of the deduction is discretionary and is limited by cumulative taxable capital gains net of allowable capital losses, that is, net taxable capital gains exposed to tax over an individual's lifetime, to the extent of the maximum permissible deduction. The limit on the QSBC capital gains deduction in a particular year is set at the least of three amounts.

(a) Unused lifetime deduction — This restriction limits the deduction to $250,000 [$375,000] (½ × $500,000 [$750,000]) *minus* all previously claimed capital gains deductions adjusted to the appropriate inclusion rate for the year in which the limit is being computed.[9]

ITA: 110.6(2.1)(*a*)

(b) Annual gains limit — This amount is the lesser of the net taxable capital gains (net TCG) for the particular year and the amount of the net TCG that would be determined only taking into account dispositions of QSBC shares and qualified farm property after 1984, *minus*

ITA: 3(*b*), 110.6(1)

(i) net capital losses of other years deducted in the current year, and

(ii) the allowable business investment losses (ABILs) realized during the year whether or not they are claimed.

ITA: 3(*d*)

(c) Cumulative gains limit — This amount aggregates, without an adjustment for changing inclusion rates, *all the components* of the "annual gains limit for all years" *minus* two additional amounts:

ITA: 110.6(1)

(i) the capital gains deductions claimed in preceding years, without an adjustment for changing inclusion rates, and

(ii) the cumulative net investment loss (CNIL) — a limitation which is defined below.

---

[9] The following table shows the factor to use to convert a capital gains deduction claimed in a prior year to the inclusion rate in use after October 17, 2000:

Year capital gain deduction claimed	Inclusion rate in that year	Factor to convert to post–Oct. 17, 2000 period
1985–1987	½	no adjustments
1988–1989	⅔	½ / ⅔ = ¾
1990–Feb. 27, 2000	¾	½ / ¾ = ⅔
Feb. 28, 2000–Oct. 17, 2000	⅔	½ / ⅔ = ¾
After Oct. 17, 2000	½	

This description of the computation is relatively conceptual, rather than technical. However, it is complicated by the allowable business investment loss (ABIL) rules and the cumulative net investment loss (CNIL).

¶13,375 Allowable business investment losses

As previously discussed in Chapter 7, allowable business investment losses are deductible from all sources of income. The definition of a business investment loss includes capital losses arising from the disposition of shares and debts of a small business corporation (SBC). Reference should be made to the material on allowable business investment losses in Chapter 7. In particular, Exhibit 7-1 should be reviewed for details on the treatment of a business investment loss.

ITA: 3(*d*), 39(1)(*c*), 248(1)

¶13,380 Cumulative net investment loss (CNIL)

As previously indicated, there is a further restriction to the "cumulative gains limit" which reduces the potential availability of the capital gains deduction. This reduction is basically the excess of property expenses over property income. The purpose of this restriction is to remove the perceived double benefit of capital gains offset by a capital gains deduction and non-capital sources of income offset by excess investment expenses at the same time.

The cumulative net investment loss (CNIL) is defined as the excess of investment expenses (a defined term) over investment income (another defined term) aggregated for all years after 1987.

ITA: 110.6(1)

"Investment expense" which, generally, relates to expenses incurred to earn investment income is defined as the sum of:

(a) all property expenses, including interest (either actually incurred or deemed to have been paid by section 80.5) and carrying charges, deducted by the taxpayer in computing property income, with certain resource property exceptions;

(b) certain specific expenses, including interest and carrying charges, deducted from the income of a partnership of which the taxpayer is a specified member (basically defined as a limited partner or a member who is not actively engaged in the business or a similar business on a regular, continuous, and substantial basis);

(c)(i) losses incurred in the year from a partnership of which the taxpayer is a specified member, and

(ii) limited partnership loss carryovers deducted in the year;

ITA: 111(1)(*e*)

(d) ½ of certain resource and exploration expenses incurred and flowed through by a corporation or incurred by a partnership of which the taxpayer is a specified member;

(e) losses from all property and, specifically, rental properties (i.e., business losses from rental properties) and capital cost allowance for a certified production deducted by the taxpayer or a partnership of which he or she was an *ordinary* member; and

(f) net capital losses carried over and deducted against certain net taxable capital gains of the carryover year that were not eligible for the capital gains deduction.

"Investment income" is defined as the sum of:

ITA: 110.6(1)

(a) income from all property, including recaptured capital cost allowance that was considered to be income from property and not from a business;

(b) income from a partnership of which the taxpayer is a specified member;

(c) ½ of certain recovered exploration and development expenses;

(d) income (including recapture) from rental property of the taxpayer or partnership of which he or she was an ordinary member;

(e) the interest element of certain annuities included in income; and

ITA: 56(1)(d), 56(1)(d.1), 60(a)

(f) net taxable capital gains on certain property not eligible for the capital gains deduction.

¶13,385 Other related provisions

At this stage, there are several other provisions related to the capital gains deduction worth noting.

● An individual must file a tax return if a taxable capital gain was realized or a disposition of capital property has occurred in the taxation year.

ITA: 150(1)

● An individual who is resident in Canada for only part of a taxation year is deemed to be a resident throughout the entire year if he or she is resident in Canada throughout the immediately preceding or the following taxation year.

ITA: 110.6(5)

● A capital gains deduction in respect of a particular transaction is denied forever where the capital gain was not reported on a filed tax return or where the tax return is not filed within a one-year grace period and where the Minister can prove the taxpayer knowingly or under circumstances amounting to gross negligence did not report the gain.

ITA: 110.6(6)

● A number of anti-avoidance provisions prevent abuses of the capital gains deduction.

ITA: 110.6(7)–(12)

● An individual may elect to use the capital gains deduction in respect of qualified small business corporation shares when the corporation becomes a public corporation because its shares are listed on a prescribed stock exchange in Canada.

ITA: 48.1

Example Problem

Lenny disposed of some shares of Underground Airways Limited, a QSBC, in January 2007 and realized a taxable capital gain of $305,000. In addition, he received $13,750 in interest and incurred a net rental loss of $2,500.

Also in 2007, Lenny realized a business investment loss (before any adjustment) of $50,000.

ITA: 39(9)

Prior to 2007, Lenny received cumulative interest income of $6,875 and grossed-up taxable dividends of $1,563. He also incurred a cumulative net rental loss of $12,500 and carrying charges of $12,188. In 1999, Lenny realized taxable capital gains of $25,000 on QSBCS which he fully offset with the capital gains deduction. Lenny had no previous capital transactions.

— REQUIRED

Compute Lenny's capital gains deduction for 2007 supported by all the necessary calculations.

ITA: 110.6(2.1)

— SOLUTION

(A) Unused lifetime deduction in 2007:

Lifetime cumulative deduction limit		$250,000
Less: prior years' deductions:		
Capital gains deduction claimed in 1999	$25,000	
Less: adjustment to 2007 inclusion rate	8,333	16,667
Unused lifetime capital gains deduction available for 2007		$233,333

(B) Annual gains limit for 2007:

Net TCGs for 2007[1] ($305,000 – $16,667)		$288,333
Minus:		
Net CLs deducted in 2007	Nil	
ABILs realized in 2007[1]	$ 8,333	8,333
Annual gains limit for 2007		$280,000

(C) Cumulative gains limit for 2007:[2]

Cumulative net TCGs ($25,000 + $288,333) $313,333

Minus:

Cumulative net capital losses deducted . . . . Nil

Cumulative ABILs realized . . . . $ 8,333

Cumulative CGs deductions 25,000

Cumulative net investment loss:

Investment expenses:

Cumulative interest expenses and
carrying charges $12,188

Cumulative net rental losses
($2,500 + $12,500) 15,000

$27,188

Investment income:

Cumulative investment income
($6,875 + $1,563 + $13,750) . . . .

. . . . (22,188) $ 5,000 $ 38,333

Cumulative gains limit for 2007 . . . . $275,000

(D) Least of (A), (B), (C) $233,333

— *NOTES TO SOLUTION*

[1] Allowable business investment loss (ABIL):

BIL before reduction		$ 50,000

ITA: 39(9)

Disallowed portion — Lesser of:

(a) BIL $50,000

(b) Adjustment factor × cumulative CG
deductions of previous years
(⁴⁄₃ × $25,000) $33,333

Minus: Cumulative disallowed BIL
of prior years . . . . Nil $33,333

Lesser of (a) and (b) . . . . (33,333)

BIL after adjustment . . . . $ 16,667

ABIL (½ × $16,667) . . . . $ 8,333

Allowable capital loss (ACL):

Disallowed portion of BIL . . . . $ 33,333

ACL (½ × $33,333) . . . . $ 16,667

Net TCG for 2007:

TCG $305,000

Less: ACL 16,667

Net TCG $288,333

[2] The components of the cumulative gains limit are not adjusted for inclusion rate changes over the period of accumulation.

¶13,390   Attribution Through a Corporation

Since the attribution rules for spouses and minors have been extended to apply to loans affecting such individuals, corporations have become the obvious vehicle to attempt income splitting among family members. Consider the situation where the low-income spouse incorporates a company using a nominal amount of his or her own funds. The high-income spouse then loans to the corporation a large amount of money through a non-interest bearing note. Income earned on these loans and subsequently paid out in the form of dividends is not caught by the attribution rules since these provisions deal with individuals and trusts only. Hence, the Act contains a series of rules to attribute back to the transferor income in the form of a deemed interest receipt on property transferred or loaned to a corporation.

ITA: 74.1(1), 74.1(2)

ITA: 74.4

These rules only apply during the period in which there were "designated persons" who benefit from the transfer or loan to a corporation and the corporation was not a small business corporation (SBC) as discussed above in relation to qualified small business corporation shares. A designated person is the transferor's spouse or a minor who is either not at arm's length with the transferor or who is a niece or nephew of that individual. The designated person must also be a specified shareholder defined, generally, as a person who owns at least 10% of the shares of any class of the corporation. Note that a small business corporation is one that, by definition, would generate mostly active business income which, if earned on a direct transfer or loan of funds, would not be subject to attribution. Also, note how designated persons are the same individuals to whom direct transfers or loans would be subject to income attribution. If the corporation, with designated persons as shareholders, ceased to be a small business corporation at some point during the year, the imputed interest benefit would be prorated for the part of the year that the corporation was not a SBC. `ITA: 248(1) "designated persons"` `ITA: 74.5(5), 251` `ITA: 248(1) "specified shareholder"`

The corporate attribution rule applies where one of the main purposes of the transfer or loan may reasonably be considered to be to reduce the income of the transferor and to benefit a designated person. If this rule applies, the transferor is deemed to receive, as *interest*, the following amount: `ITA: 74.4(2)`

- interest imputed on the outstanding amount of the loan or transferred property at the basic prescribed rates in effect during the year, for the period when the corporation was not an SBC and designated persons were specified shareholders `ITA: 74.4(3); ITR: 4301(c)`

less the sum of:

- interest received by the transferor in respect of the loan or transfer,

- ⁵⁄₄ of all taxable dividends received by the transferor on shares received as consideration for the loan or transfer of property, and

- where dividends are received by the designated person and these dividends can reasonably be considered to be part of the benefit sought to be conferred then the amount included in the designated person's "split income". `ITA: 120.4`

The term "outstanding amount", which is the base for the deemed interest receipt, is defined to be the fair market value of property "transferred or loaned" to the corporation in excess of the fair market value of consideration, other than "excluded consideration", *received* from the corporation in return. The term "excluded consideration" is defined to mean debt, shares of the corporation or rights to receive debt or shares of the corporation. Note that excluded consideration does *not* reduce the base for computing the deemed interest receipt because only consideration *other than* excluded consideration reduces the outstanding amount. Consideration that reduces the outstanding amount would include, for example, cash. While debt or shares received from the corporation do not reduce the outstanding amount, interest and ⁵⁄₄ of taxable dividends paid to the transferor on the debt or shares received reduce the deemed interest receipt to the transferor, as shown by the above computational formula. `ITA: 74.4(3)` `ITA: 74.4(1)`

Note how the reduction of the deemed interest income is as a result of the payment by the corporation of actual income that would attract tax in the hands of the transferor or lender and, therefore, would reduce the benefits of income splitting. It should also be noted that the deemed interest income included in the individual's income is not allowed as a deduction to the corporation.

Example Problem

Fresser and Klutz are spouses. Fresser operates a construction company, Fresser Inc., which uses all of its assets (fair market value of $1.2 million) in its active business carried on in Calgary. Klutz received an inheritance of $100,000 which he invested in Fresser Inc. 7% preference shares on January 1, 2005. Fresser Inc. immediately used this cash to pay down a bank loan. On January 1, 2006, Fresser Inc. ceased operations and liquidated its assets leaving $200,000 of cash in the company until January 31, 2007, when the 7% preference shares were redeemed for $100,000. In each of 2005 and 2006, dividends of $5,000 were paid on the preference shares.

— *R*

D   ount attributed to Klutz over the three years, assuming that the prescribed intere   ant 9%. Ignore the effects of the leap year.

— *SC*

                would not attribute any amount to Klutz since Fresser Inc. was a "small   orporation" throughout the taxation year of Klutz. Klutz's income would include only the $5,000 of dividends paid on the preference shares. *ITA: 74.4(2)*

2006:   Fresser Inc. was not a small business corporation throughout 2006; therefore, the rule applies as follows: *ITA: 74.4(2)*

Interest imputed at 9% on the outstanding amount ($100,000 × 9%)	$9,000
Less: ⁵⁄₄ of dividends received ($5,000 × ⁵⁄₄)	(6,250)
Interest received	Nil
Amount deemed to be received by Klutz as interest	$2,750

In addition, Klutz will report the $5,000 of dividends ($6,250 grossed up) received from the company.

2007:   Fresser Inc. was not a small business corporation during that portion of the year when the shares were outstanding; therefore, the rule applies as follows: *ITA: 74.4(2)*

Interest imputed at 9% on the outstanding amount ($100,000 × 9% × ³⁰⁄₃₆₅)	$ 740
Less: ⁵⁄₄ of dividends received	Nil
Interest received	Nil
Amount deemed to be received by Klutz as interest	$ 740

Remember that there is a purpose test. It may be possible to argue that, since the purpose of the loan was to finance an active business, these attribution rules do not apply. On the other hand, it may be argued that since the money was used in the business for such a short period (13 months) that "one of the main purposes of the transfer" must have been to reduce the income of Klutz and benefit Fresser. *ITA: 74.4(2)*

¶13,400   Income-Splitting Tax ("Kiddie Tax")

A special income tax computed at the top marginal rate is levied on specified income of an individual under 18 years of age at the end of a calendar year. This income-splitting tax was discussed in Chapter 6, as an alternative to the income attribution rules, for income of a minor from business sources that is not subject to the attribution rules. *ITA: 120.4*

The tax is levied, generally, on the following types of income:

- taxable dividends and other shareholder benefits derived from unlisted shares of any corporation, received either directly or indirectly through a trust or partnership; and

- income from a trust or partnership which derives income from the business of providing property or services to a business carried on by a relative of the minor or a corporation in which the relative is a specified shareholder.

Income subject to this income-splitting tax is deductible from the Part I income of the minor, so that it is not taxed twice in the hands of the minor. Similarly, income such as the dividend income, subject to the income-splitting tax, is not subject to attribution and, therefore, not taxed additionally in the hands of the transferor of the dividend-paying shares. The only tax credits permitted in computing the income-splitting tax are the dividend tax credit and the foreign tax credit. If a parent was active in the business from which the income subject to the income-splitting tax was derived, then the parent is jointly liable for the income-splitting tax payable by the minor. *ITA: 20(1)(ww)*

The income-splitting tax is not applicable to:

- minors who have no parent who is resident in Canada at any time in the year;

- income from property inherited by a minor from a parent; and

- income from property inherited by a minor from anyone else if, during the year in which the minor receives the income, the minor is:

  - in full-time attendance at a post-secondary educational institution, or

  - eligible for the disability tax credit.

To the extent that income is subject to the "kiddie tax", that same income is not subject to the regular attribution rules. In addition, if taxable dividends are subject to "kiddie tax", then they may reduce the deemed interest penalty calculated for corporate attribution purposes. ITA: 56(5), 74.4(2)(*g*), 74.5(13)

¶13,500   GENERAL ANTI-AVOIDANCE RULE UNDER THE INCOME TAX ACT

¶13,510   The Statutory Provision

¶13,515   Purpose

The technical notes released on June 30, 1988 to explain this provision when it was first introduced made the following statement: ITA: 245

> New section 245 of the Act is a general anti-avoidance rule which is intended to prevent abusive tax avoidance transactions or arrangements but at the same time is not intended to interfere with legitimate commercial and family transactions. Consequently, the new rule seeks to distinguish between legitimate tax planning and abusive tax avoidance and to establish a reasonable balance between the protection of the tax base and the need for certainty for taxpayers in planning their affairs.

The main statement of the general anti-avoidance rule (GAAR), or provision, in essence, provides that the tax benefit that results from an avoidance transaction is denied. In order to determine the amount of the tax benefit that is denied, the provision indicates that the tax consequences of the transaction to a person will be determined as is reasonable in the circumstances. ITA: 245(2)

¶13,520   Defined terms

The term "avoidance transaction" is defined as any transaction that by itself or as part of a series of transactions (i.e., a "step transaction") results in a tax benefit, unless the transaction can reasonably be considered to have a *bona fide* purpose other than obtaining the tax benefit. The technical notes indicate that "the vast majority of business, family or investment transactions will not be affected by proposed (as it was then) section 245 since they will have *bona fide* non-tax purposes". The notes go on to state that "a transaction will not be considered to be an avoidance transaction because, incidentally, it results in a tax benefit or because tax considerations were significant, but not the primary purpose for carrying out the transaction". On the other hand, the notes indicate that: ITA: 245(3)

> Ordinarily, transitory arrangements would not be considered to have been carried out primarily for *bona fide* purposes other than the obtaining of a tax benefit. Such transitory arrangements might include an issue of shares that are immediately redeemed or the establishment of an entity, such as a corporation or a partnership, followed within a short period by its elimination.

The term "tax benefit" is defined to mean "a reduction, avoidance or deferral of tax or other amount payable under this Act or an increase in a refund of tax or other amount under this Act". According to the technical notes, "the references to 'other amount payable under this Act' and 'other amount under this Act' are intended to cover interest, penalties, the remittance of source deductions, and other amounts that do not constitute tax". The term "tax consequences" is, also, defined and is necessary, as indicated previously, to determine the amount of the benefit that will be denied. The actual determination of the tax ITA: 245(1)

ITA: 245(5)

consequences is provided by a rule which sets out some of the methods by which a benefit will be denied.

¶13,525 Limitation

A limitation on the application of the GAAR is provided. In the overview commentary on the GAAR, the technical notes make the following statement:

ITA: 245(4)

> Transactions that comply with the object and spirit of other provisions of the Act read as a whole will not be affected by the application of this general anti-avoidance rule. For example, a transaction that qualifies for a tax-free rollover under an explicit provision of the Act, and that is carried out in accordance not only with the letter of that provision but also with the spirit of the Act read as a whole, will not be subject to new section 245. However, where the transaction is part of a series of transactions designed to avoid tax and results in a misuse or abuse of the provision that allows a tax-free rollover, the rule may apply. If, for example, a taxpayer, for the purposes of converting an income gain on a sale of property into a capital gain, transfers the property, on a rollover basis to a shell corporation in exchange for shares in a situation where new section 54.2 of the Act does not apply and subsequently sells the shares, the new section could be expected to apply.
>
> The new rule applies as a provision of last resort after the application of the other provisions of the Act, including specific anti-avoidance measures.

¶13,530 Examples in the technical notes

The commentary in the technical notes states that "the application of new subsection 245 [*sic*] must be determined by reference to the facts in a particular case in the context of the scheme of the Act". The notes then provide the following three examples of planning that would not be affected by the GAAR.

ITA: 245(4)

> . . . the attribution provisions of the Act set out detailed rules that seek to prevent a taxpayer from transferring property by way of a gift and thereby transferring income to a spouse or minor children. A review of the scheme of these provisions indicates that income splitting is only of concern in transfers of property involving spouses or children under 18 years of age. The attribution rules are not intended to apply to other transfers of property such as gifts to adult children. This can be discerned from a review of the scheme of the Act, its relevant provisions and permissible extrinsic aids. Thus, a straightforward gift from a parent to his adult child will not be within the scope of section 245 either because it is made primarily for non-tax purposes or because it may reasonably be regarded as not being an abuse of the provisions of the Act. If, however, the gift is made so that the adult child acquires an investment and, through a series of transactions, disposes of it and subsequently transfers the proceeds, including any income therefrom, to the parent, proposed section 245 should apply where the purpose of the transaction is the reduction, avoidance or deferral of tax. (Note that subsection 56(4.1) deals with this type of avoidance where a *loan* is made to a related person.)
>
> As another example, "estate freezing" transactions whereby a taxpayer transfers future growth in the value of assets to his children or grandchildren will not ordinarily be avoidance transactions to which the proposed rules would apply despite the fact that they may result in a deferral, avoidance or reduction of tax. Apart from the fact that many of these transactions may be considered to be primarily motivated by non-tax considerations, it would be reasonable to consider that such transactions do not ordinarily result in a misuse or abuse given the scheme of the Act and the recent enactment of subsection 74.4(4) of the Act to accommodate estate freezes. (See also IC 88-2, paragraph 10.)
>
> Another example involves the transfer of income or deductions within a related group of corporations. There are a number of provisions in the Act that limit the claim by a taxpayer of losses, deductions and credits incurred or earned by unrelated taxpayers, particularly corporations. The loss limitation rules contained in subsections 111(4) to (5.2) of the Act that apply on a change of control of a corporation represent an important example. These rules are generally restricted to the claiming of losses, deductions and other amounts by unrelated parties. There are explicit exceptions intended to apply with respect to transactions that would allow losses, deductions or credits earned by one corporation to be claimed by related Canadian corporations. In fact, the scheme of the Act as a whole, and the expressed object and spirit of the corporate loss limitation rules, clearly permit such transactions between related corporations where these transactions are otherwise legally effective and comply with the letter and spirit of

these exceptions. Therefore, even if these transactions may appear to be primarily tax-motivated, they ordinarily do not fall within the scope of section 245 since they usually do not result in a misuse or abuse. (See also IC 88-2, paragraph 8.)

¶13,535 Administration and application

Finally, it should be noted that the Act provides rules that pertain to the administration of the legislation in the GAAR.

ITA: 245(6)–(8)

On October 21, 1988, the CRA issued an Information Circular which was intended to provide guidance on the application of the GAAR. It contains over 20 fact situations which are interpreted by the CRA in the context of the application of the GAAR.

IC 88-2

The GAAR applies, not only to a misuse or abuse of the provisions of the *Income Tax Act*, but also to the provisions of the Income Tax Regulations, the Income Tax Application Rules or a tax treaty.

A paper,[10] which resulted from a panel discussion held at the 1989 Annual Conference of the Canadian Tax Foundation, presented a "GAAR Decision Tree" to outline the logic that can be used to determine whether the GAAR would apply. Exhibit 13-12 attempts to diagram the logic used.

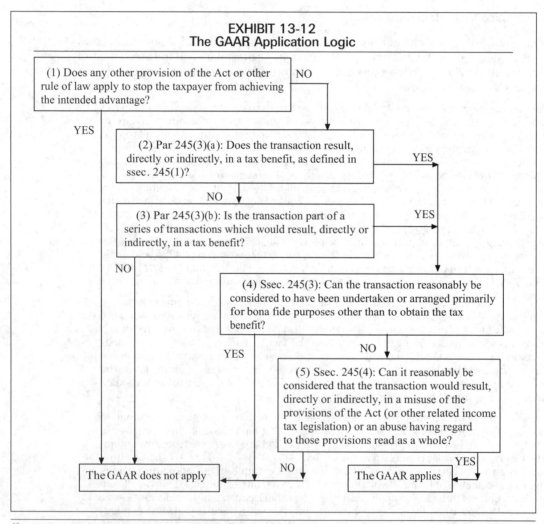

EXHIBIT 13-12
The GAAR Application Logic

(1) Does any other provision of the Act or other rule of law apply to stop the taxpayer from achieving the intended advantage? — NO

YES

(2) Par 245(3)(a): Does the transaction result, directly or indirectly, in a tax benefit, as defined in ssec. 245(1)? — YES

NO

(3) Par 245(3)(b): Is the transaction part of a series of transactions which would result, directly or indirectly, in a tax benefit? — YES

NO

(4) Ssec. 245(3): Can the transaction reasonably be considered to have been undertaken or arranged primarily for bona fide purposes other than to obtain the tax benefit?

YES — NO

(5) Ssec. 245(4): Can it reasonably be considered that the transaction would result, directly or indirectly, in a misuse of the provisions of the Act (or other related income tax legislation) or an abuse having regard to those provisions read as a whole?

The GAAR does not apply — NO — The GAAR applies — YES

---

[10] Robert D. Brown, Robert Couzin, Cy M. Fien, William R. Lawlor and William J. Strain, "GAAR and Tax Practice: More Questions than Answers", *1989 Conference Report: Report of the Proceedings of the Forty-First Tax Conference*, Canadian Tax Foundation, Toronto, 1989, pp. 11:3-4.

¶13,540 Federal Court of Appeal — OSFC Holdings Ltd.

¶13,545 The findings

The appeal by the taxpayer in *OSFC Holdings Ltd. v. The Queen* was the first decision of the Federal Court of Appeal on the GAAR.[11] After a thorough analysis of the GAAR, the court dismissed the taxpayer's appeal. It held that a series of transactions resulted in a tax benefit. The court upheld the finding of the Tax Court that the primary purpose of the transaction was to obtain a tax benefit. It also found that the transactions in question violated a clear and unambiguous general policy of the Act and, hence, concluded that the avoidance transaction resulted in an abuse of the provisions of the Act read as a whole. In June 2002, the Supreme Court of Canada refused to grant OSFC Holdings Ltd. leave to appeal.

2001 DTC 5471 (F.C.A.)

¶13,550 Application of OSFC case analytical framework

The analytical framework used in the *OSFC* case was applied in the Crown's appeal in *The Queen v. Canadian Pacific Limited*. First, the court concluded that there was a tax benefit. The court, then, upheld the Tax Court finding that the primary purpose of the transaction in question was not to minimize tax. Although the latter finding was sufficient to dismiss the Crown's appeal, the court considered the argument that there had been an abuse of the provisions of the Act read as a whole on the basis that the transaction in question contravened a policy of the Act. This argument was rejected. The court concluded that the conditions for the GAAR did not apply to the facts of this case.[12]

2002 DTC 6742 (F.C.A.)

The three-step analytical framework developed by the Federal Court of Appeal in the *OSFC* case was applied in the case of *The Queen v. Imperial Oil Limited*. The following summary of the three steps is quoted from the *Imperial Oil* case, in the indicated paragraphs.

2004 DTC 6044 (F.C.A.)

1. First, a court must determine if there is a "tax benefit", as defined. If there is not, GAAR will not apply and the inquiry ends [par. 34].

   ITA: 245(3)

2. If there is a "tax benefit", a court must take the second step and determine whether there is an "avoidance transaction", as defined. If there is no "avoidance transaction", GAAR will not apply and, again, the inquiry ends [par. 34].

   ITA: 245(3)

3. If the transaction confers a "tax benefit" and constitutes an "avoidance transaction", a court must take the third step and determine whether the transaction is a "misuse" or an "abuse". This inquiry involves taking two smaller steps [par. 35].

   ITA: 245(4)

   (a) First, a court must determine "if it may reasonably be considered that the transaction would not result directly or indirectly in a misuse" of the provisions of the Act. To determine if there has been a misuse, a court must identify the object, or underlying policy or policies, of the relevant provision or provisions of the Act, and decide if the avoidance transaction is contrary to those objectives or policies. If it is, the transaction constitutes a misuse and GAAR applies [par. 36].

   One must infer from the statutory language the policy, if any, on which the relevant provisions of the Act are unambiguously based. This exercise in statutory interpretation must be undertaken with the assistance of such extrinsic aids as: judicial statements, Hansard, ministerial or departmental statements, explanatory notes, bulletins, circulars, texts, periodicals and others [par. 49].

   (b) However, if there is no misuse, the second smaller step must be taken. This requires a court to decide if the transaction is an abuse, having regard to the provisions of the Act, other than those dealing with GAAR, when read as a whole. The question is whether the transaction contravenes any policy or policies

---

[11] An extensive commentary on this case by Thomas B. Akin appears in *Tax Topics*, Number 1546, CCH Canadian Limited, October 25, 2001, pp. 5-8.

[12] The Crown's appeals were also dismissed in the cases of *The Queen v. Produits Forestiers Donohue Inc.*, 2002 DTC 7512 (F.C.A.), and *The Queen v. Jabin Investments Ltd.*, 2003 DTC 5027 (F.C.A.). In both of these cases the OSFC framework was applied in the analysis of the applicability of the GAAR. In the latter case, the "clear and unambiguous" threshold for policy was clarified.

underlying the provisions of the Act as a whole. If it does, the transaction may constitute an abuse for the purpose of GAAR [par. 37].

While the Act does not expressly provide that the policy must be "clear and unambiguous", this is implicit in the language of the GAAR, which permits the exemption for a tax avoidance scheme where "it may reasonably be considered that the transaction would not result directly or indirectly in a misuse of the provisions of this Act or an abuse having regard to the provisions of this Act . . . read as a whole [based on former wording of the provision]." [par. 39]

ITA: 245(4)

Thus, if the scheme may reasonably be considered not to result directly or indirectly in a misuse or an abuse, GAAR does not apply: in effect, the taxpayer is given the benefit of any doubt. Consequently, for GAAR to apply it must be clear that the provisions of the Act are being misused or the Act as a whole is being abused. It is not enough that a court might reasonably consider them to be misused or abused [par. 40].

¶13,560 Supreme Court of Canada — Canada Trustco and Mathew et al.

On October 19, 2005, the Supreme Court of Canada (S.C.C.) released two decisions on the GAAR, *Canada Trustco Mortgage Co.* and *Mathew (sub nom. Kaulius) et al.*

2005 DTC 5523 (S.C.C.); 2005 DTC 5538 (S.C.C.)

¶13,565 The transactions

In the *Canada Trustco* case, the taxpayer had purchased trailers and then leased them back to the vendor. A major purpose for this transaction was to allow Canada Trustco to claim CCA on these trailers while the arrangements were structured so the taxpayer had little or no financial risk. While there are special rules in the Act to counter this type of transaction, trailers were exempt from them. The CRA reassessed under the GAAR to deny the CCA claimed.

2005 DTC 5523 (S.C.C.)

In the *Mathew* case, Standard Trust, an insolvent trust company, transferred a loan portfolio, with accrued losses of $52 million, to a partnership that had arm's length partners. The losses were then realized and allocated to these arm's length partners. The CRA reassessed under the GAAR to deny the losses claimed.

2005 DTC 5538 (S.C.C.)

¶13,570 Application of the OSFC tests and interpretations

In both cases, the Court applied the three tests set out in *OSFC Holdings* with the following results.

Test 1: There was a tax benefit.

Test 2: There was an avoidance transaction.

Test 3: The issue before the Court was whether there was a misuse of the provisions of the Act or an abuse of those provisions read as a whole.

The Supreme Court stated, at paragraph 66 of the *Canada Trustco* case,

2005 DTC 5523 (S.C.C.)

[t]he approach to s. 245 of the *Income Tax Act* may be summarized as follows.

1. Three requirements must be established to permit application of the GAAR:

   (1) A tax benefit resulting from a transaction or part of a series of transactions (s. 245(1) and (2));

   (2) that the transaction is an avoidance transaction in the sense that it cannot be said to have been reasonably undertaken or arranged primarily for a *bona fide* purpose other than to obtain a tax benefit; and

   (3) that there was abusive tax avoidance in the sense that it cannot be reasonably concluded that a tax benefit would be consistent with the object, spirit or purpose of the provisions relied upon by the taxpayer.

2. The burden is on the taxpayer to refute (1) and (2), and on the Minister to establish (3).

3. If the existence of abusive tax avoidance is unclear, the benefit of the doubt goes to the taxpayer.

4. The courts proceed by conducting a unified textual [words used], contextual [context of provision] and purposive [purpose of analysis] analysis of the provisions giving rise to the tax benefit in order to determine why they were put in place and why the benefit was conferred. The goal is to arrive at a purposive interpretation that is harmonious with the provisions of the Act that confer the tax benefit, read in the context of the whole Act.

5. Whether the transactions were motivated by any economic, commercial, family or other non-tax purpose may form part of the factual context that the courts may consider in the analysis of abusive tax avoidance allegations under s. 245(4). However, any finding in this respect would form only one part of the underlying facts of a case, and would be insufficient by itself to establish abusive tax avoidance. The central issue is the proper interpretation of the relevant provisions in light of their context and purpose.

6. Abusive tax avoidance may be found where the relationships and transactions as expressed in the relevant documentation lack a proper basis relative to the object, spirit or purpose of the provisions that are purported to confer the tax benefit, or where they are wholly dissimilar to the relationships or transactions that are contemplated by the provisions.

7. Where the Tax Court judge has proceeded on a proper construction of the provisions of the *Income Tax Act* and on findings supported by the evidence, appellate tribunals should not interfere, absent a palpable and overriding error.

The following are some of the other comments made in the *Canada Trustco* case that might shed some light on the third requirement for the application of the GAAR.

[36] The third requirement for application of the GAAR is that the avoidance transaction giving rise to a tax benefit be abusive. The mere existence of an avoidance transaction is not enough to permit the GAAR to be applied. . . .

[39] . . . Parliament could not have intended this two-step approach, which on its face raises the impossible question of how one can abuse the Act as a whole without misusing any of its provisions. We agree with the Tax Court judge, in the present case [2003 DTC 587], at para. 90, that "[i]n effect, the analysis of the misuse of the provisions and the analysis of the abuse having regard to the provisions of the Act read as a whole are inseparable." . . .

[40] There is but one principle of interpretation: to determine the intent of the legislator having regard to the text, its context, and other indicators of legislative purpose. The policy analysis proposed as a second step by the Federal Court of Appeal in *OSFC* is properly incorporated into a unified, textual, contextual, and purposive approach to interpreting the specific provisions that give rise to the tax benefit.

[41] The courts cannot search for an overriding policy of the Act that is not based on a unified, textual, contextual and purposive interpretation of the specific provisions in issue. First, such a search is incompatible with the roles of reviewing judges. The *Income Tax Act* is a compendium of highly detailed and often complex provisions. To send the courts on the search for some overarching policy and then to use such a policy to override the wording of the provisions of the *Income Tax Act* would inappropriately place the formulation of taxation policy in the hands of the judiciary, requiring judges to perform a task to which they are unaccustomed and for which they are not equipped. Did Parliament intend judges to formulate taxation policies that are not grounded in the provisions of the Act and to apply them to override the specific provisions of the Act? Notwithstanding the interpretative challenges that the GAAR presents, we cannot find a basis for concluding that such a marked departure from judicial and interpretative norms was Parliament's intent.

[42] Second, to search for an overriding policy of the *Income Tax Act* that is not anchored in a textual, contextual and purposive interpretation of the specific provisions that are relied upon for the tax benefit would run counter to the overall policy of Parliament that tax law be certain, predictable and fair, so that taxpayers can intelligently order their affairs. Although Parliament's general purpose in enacting the GAAR was to preserve legitimate tax minimization schemes while prohibiting abusive tax avoidance, Parliament must also be taken to seek consistency, predictability and fairness in tax law. These three latter purposes would be frustrated if the Minister and/or the courts overrode the provisions of the *Income Tax Act* without any basis in a textual, contextual and purposive interpretation of those provisions.

[43] For these reasons we conclude, as did the Tax Court judge, that the determinations of "misuse" and "abuse" under s. 245(4) are not separate inquiries. Section 245(4) requires a single, unified approach to the textual, contextual and purposive interpretation of the specific provisions of the *Income Tax Act* that are relied upon by the taxpayer in order to determine whether there was abusive tax avoidance.

. . .

[45] . . . An abuse may also result from an arrangement that circumvents the application of certain provisions, such as specific anti-avoidance rules, in a manner that frustrates or defeats the object, spirit or purpose of those provisions. By contrast, abuse is not established where it is reasonable to conclude that an avoidance transaction under s. 245(3) was within the object, spirit or purpose of the provisions that confer the tax benefit.

. . .

[52] In general, Parliament confers tax benefits under the *Income Tax Act* to promote purposes related to specific activities. For example, tax benefits associated with business losses, CCA and RRSPs, are conferred for reasons intrinsic to the activities involved. Unless the Minister can establish that the avoidance transaction frustrates or defeats the purpose for which the tax benefit was intended to be conferred, it is not abusive.

¶13,580   The Saga Continues — Decisions Since Canada Trustco

There have been a number of cases since *Canada Trustco* where the judges applied the findings of the highest court. It would seem that more time will be needed to obtain clarity on the application of the GAAR.

¶13,585   L Mark Evans (2005 DTC 1762 (T.C.C.))

Dr. Evans undertook an income-splitting arrangement with his children. He created special shares with high fair market value and low paid-up capital that he sold to his children. The resulting capital gain was offset by the capital gains exemption. These shares were then redeemed and the deemed dividend was taxed in the hands of his children at a very low tax rate. Effectively, Dr. Evans was able to withdraw funds from his company with very little tax paid. The CRA viewed these transactions as a surplus strip and reassessed under the GAAR.

2005 DTC 1762 (T.C.C.)

Chief Justice Bowman, at paragraph 33, stated,

I have endeavoured to find in the respondent's argument the identification of a provision or set of provisions of the *Income Tax Act* that have been misused or abused. I have been unable to do so. Counsel state that the appellant stripped surplus from 117679, thereby frustrating the scheme of the Act. In fact, he sold the shares to a partnership of which his children were partners and realized a capital gain. Dividends or deemed dividends were paid to the partnership but the reason they were not taxed in the hands of the children was that they were in a low tax bracket.

At paragraph 35, Chief Justice Bowman stated,

In light of the principles stated by the Supreme Court of Canada I have concluded that the transactions involved here are not abusive for the following reasons:

(a) Not one of the transactions defeats or frustrates the object, purpose or spirit of any of the provisions.

(b) The transactions do not lack economic substance. The transactions were real and legally effective. They were not shams. By economic substance I do not intend to import into this criterion a business purpose test. The Supreme Court of Canada did not do so. Rather, I think what was meant was that a genuine change in legal and economic relations took place as the result of the transactions.

(c) To treat the transactions as abusive so that their results can be recharacterized would not preserve but rather would destroy certainty, predictability and fairness and would frustrate Parliament's intention that taxpayers "take full advantage of the provisions of the Act that confer tax benefits".

(d) A finding of abuse cannot be warranted because it cannot reasonably be concluded that the transactions were carried out in a manner that is inconsistent with the object, spirit or purpose of the various provisions of the Act.

(e) The burden that is on the Minister to show that the object, spirit and purpose of the various provisions relied on have been defeated or frustrated has not been met. I imply no criticism of counsel for the respondent. They presented the Crown's case with great skill. The words "burden of proof" of which the Supreme Court of Canada speaks may imply an evidentiary burden but primarily they impose a requirement that the Crown identify the object, spirit or purpose of the relevant legislation that is said to be frustrated or defeated. This might be described as a "burden of persuasion" although this is not the usual sense of the expression "burden of proof". I think it would be premature for me to elaborate at any greater length on just how this burden can be met or what evidence should be adduced. This will need to be developed in future cases and in different fact situations. It is sufficient to say that nothing that has been put before the Court in this case has persuaded me either as a matter of fact or as a matter of argument that there has been any abuse of the Act read as a whole. Indeed, if there were any doubt on this point, the Supreme Court of Canada has said that the benefit of that doubt should go to the taxpayer.

It should be noted that this plan would not work under today's law, as the "kiddie tax" would cause the children to pay tax at the top personal marginal tax rate thereby eliminating the tax benefit realized by Dr. Evans.

¶13,590   Michael Overs (2006 DTC 2192 (T.C.C.))

In this case, the taxpayer structured a series of transactions that avoided the application of subsection 15(2) income inclusion of $2.3 million, and allowed him to deduct the interest on what was originally a non-deductible loan. The Tax Court judge determined that while Mr. Overs "may have obtained a tax benefit", the transactions were not avoidance transactions and, therefore, the second of the three tests was not met. Justice Little then went on to say, at paragraph 20, "In *Canada Trustco* the Supreme Court stated that the third requirement for the application of GAAR is that the avoidance transaction giving rise to a tax benefit must be abusive. In view of my findings concerning tax avoidance as noted above it may not be necessary for me to deal with this test. However, if I am not correct on my earlier comments regarding my determination that the transactions under review are not tax avoidance transactions I believe that I should also consider and comment upon the third test". At paragraphs 24 and 25, Justice Little said, "based on my understanding of the evidence before me and the applicable GAAR legislation I do not believe that any of the transactions under review could be considered to be 'abusive tax avoidance' transactions. For the reasons outlined above I have concluded that the GAAR provisions should not be applied in this situation".

2006 DTC 2192 (T.C.C.)

However, the judge did not address the "primary purpose" part of the second test. This test states that "the transaction is an avoidance transaction in the sense that it cannot be said to have been reasonably undertaken or arranged primarily for a *bona fide* purpose other than to obtain a tax benefit". It appears that while the judge did not fully apply the second test, he did address the third test anyway and concluded that the GAAR did not apply.

¶13,595   Jordan B. Lipson and Earl Lipson (2006 DTC 2687 (T.C.C.))

This is a case about the conversion of interest expense from being non-deductible to being deductible. Earl and Jordanna purchased a home for $750,000. A few months later, Jordanna borrowed $560,000 from the bank to buy shares of a family company from Earl. She and Earl then borrowed an additional $560,000 from the bank, secured by a mortgage on their new home, to pay off the original loan to buy the shares. By not electing under subsection 73(1) on the sale of shares from Earl to Jordanna, there was no gain on this transaction and the attribution rules would then cause any dividend income and interest expense to be reported in Earl's return. The judge concluded that there was a "tax benefit" and that it could not be said "to have been reasonably undertaken or arranged primarily for a *bona fide* purpose other than to obtain a tax benefit", as required by the Act.

2006 DTC 2687 (T.C.C.)

As a result, the third test of misuse or abuse was the determining factor. On this issue, the judge found, at paragraphs 31 and 32,

> This case is, in my view, an obvious example of abusive tax avoidance. Whatever commercial or other non-tax purpose, if any, is served by transferring Earl's shares to Jordanna, it is subservient to the objective of making the interest on the purchase of the house deductible by Earl.

> In this case I am not looking to any "overarching policy" that supersedes the specific provisions of the ITA. I am simply looking at the obvious purpose of the various provisions that are relied on and have concluded that those purposes have been subverted and those sections turned on their heads. I mentioned above that section 245 must itself be subjected to a textual, contextual and purposive analysis. If there ever was a case at which section 245 was aimed, it is this one.

The Federal Court of Appeal confirmed the decision of the Tax Court of Canada in the *Lipson* case.   2007 DTC 5172 (F.C.A.)

¶13,800 REVIEW QUESTIONS

(1) Mr. Smith owns a small manufacturing company that has suddenly become very profitable. This year his accountant has told him to declare a bonus to himself of approximately $150,000 in order to reduce his corporate income to the business limit. His dilemma is that he also needs the money in his business in order to finance expansion. What should he do?

(2) Mr. Jones owns a manufacturing company that is earning well over $400,000 each year. He has been declaring a bonus to himself each year but is now re-thinking this strategy. What items should he consider when deciding whether to pay the bonus or leave the money in the company? Assume that the provincial corporate is 12%.

(3) What is the range of fiscal year-ends that might be chosen to allow the owner of a company to declare a bonus and be taxed on it personally in either of two calendar years?

(4) What are the five criteria for the deductibility of bonus accruals as decided in the *Totem Disposal* case?

(5) Mr. Crunchy is the sole shareholder of Chocobar Inc. His wife's brother has just come to him and asked to borrow some money in order to start up his professional accounting practice. Mr. Crunchy has decided to have Chocobar Inc. lend his wife's brother $20,000 on October 31, 2007, with interest only for the first two years and then principal payments of $10,000 per year starting in the third year. The fiscal year-end of the company is December 31. Discuss the tax implications of the loan.

(6) Ms. Jones is the President and sole shareholder of a construction company. She has two vice-presidents who are not related to her. As part of their compensation package she has agreed that all employees of the company are entitled to an interest-free loan from the company of up to $25,000. Ms. Jones herself has taken her $25,000 loan and bought a boat. Comment.

(7) If your province of residence were to declare a tax holiday for all CCPCs, what impact would this have on compensation for your owner-manager clients?

(8) How much personal tax will a single individual pay on $30,000 of dividend income if that is his or her only source of income and his or her only non-refundable tax credit is his or her personal credit. Assume the gross-up of 25% applies.

(9) Ms. Sorry owned 10% of the shares of a small business corporation that went out of business. Six months after it ceased business she sold her shares to an arm's length person, Mr. X, for $1. When she went to claim a loss on her investment she did not know how much she could write off. In order to have the loss treated as an ABIL, the company needed to be a small business corporation at the time of sale and at that time it did not have any assets used in an active business. She has not used any of her capital gains exemption before. Can you clarify this situation for her?

(10) What does the phrase "all or substantially all" mean?

(11) A corporation that has had 40% of its assets invested in term deposits for the last two years, and the balance in active business assets, qualifies as a "small business corporation" but not a "qualified small business corporation". Do you agree or disagree? Explain.

(12) Mr. Smith incorporated his company 20 years ago for $100 of share capital. It has prospered since then and it now has some excess capital. He has decided to have his wife set up an investment holding company and his company will lend her company $100,000 of cash for her to invest and thereby split income. Will the attribution rules apply?

¶13,825 MULTIPLE CHOICE QUESTIONS

Question 1

Stan owns 100% of the shares of S Ltd. which has a December 31 year-end. He is also an employee of S Ltd. On January 1, 2007, S Ltd. loaned Stan $200,000 interest-free to assist him in purchasing a new home. Stan signed a promissory note for the loan. Under the terms of the note, the loan is to be repaid in 5 equal annual instalments commencing January 1, 2008. Such a loan is not available to other employees. Which *one* of the following statements is *true*?

(A) Stan will have $200,000 included in his income in 2007.

(B) Stan will have $160,000 included in his income in 2008.

(C) An imputed interest benefit will be calculated for 2007 using a rate not in excess of the rate in effect at January 1, 2007, as the loan was used to purchase a home.

(D) The portion of the loan not repaid by December 31, 2008, will be included in Stan's income in 2009.

Question 2

In 2007, S Ltd., which has a December 31 year-end, made the following loans to shareholders. All of the shareholders are resident in Canada and are not related to S Ltd. This was the first time that these shareholders had received a loan or had become indebted to S. Ltd. Since S Ltd. was not in the business of lending money, it was very careful, in each case, to ensure that *bona fide* arrangements were made at the time the loan was made for repayment of the loan within a reasonable time. Taking all this into consideration, which one of the following loan principal amounts will be included in the borrower's income in 2007?

(A) A loan to Mrs. A, a vice-president and 20% shareholder. The loan was made to assist Mrs. A in the purchase of newly issued shares of S Ltd. The loan was made on April 1, 2007, and repaid on April 1, 2008. No other employees have received similar loans.

(B) A loan made to B Ltd., a corporation which is a 20% shareholder of S Ltd. The loan was used to help B Ltd. repurchase some of its shares for cancellation and pay off a bank loan.

(C) A loan to Mrs. C, a vice-president and 20% shareholder. The loan was made to assist Mrs. C in the purchase of a home. The loan was made on April 1, 2007, and will be repaid on April 1, 2009. No other employees have received similar loans.

(D) A loan to Mr. D, an S Ltd. vice-president and 5% shareholder. Mr. D deals at arm's length with S Ltd. The loan was made to assist Mr. D in the purchase of a home computer for employment use. Five other employees of the company currently work at home and have received similar loans. None of the other employees are shareholders. Mr. D's loan was made on April 1, 2007, and will be repaid on April 1, 2009.

Question 3

In computing the net income on the financial statement of Fortelli Inc. for its year ended December 31, 2007, bonuses of $300,000 were accrued. On August 15, 2008, $100,000 of the bonus was paid to the owner-manager, and the remaining $200,000 of bonuses were paid to the sales staff on August 31, 2008. Which one of the following statements is *true*?

(A) If the $100,000 bonus, due to a related party, was not paid by December 31, 2008, it would be included in Fortelli Inc.'s income in the year 2010.

(B) The $100,000 bonus is not deductible in 2007, but the $200,000 bonus is deductible.

(C) An election is available to deem the bonus paid and loaned back to the corporation. This election can be used if the bonuses are not going to be paid by the appropriate deadline.

(D) The $300,000 bonus is not deductible in 2007.

Question 4

The Act contains a general anti-avoidance provision often referred to as the GAAR. Which one of the following statements concerning the GAAR is *false*?

(A) The tax benefit that results from an avoidance transaction will be denied.

(B) When the GAAR is applied, a penalty will be assessed, in addition to the tax owing plus interest.

(C) An avoidance transaction is any transaction that results in a tax benefit, unless the transaction can reasonably be considered to have a *bona fide* purpose other than obtaining the tax benefit.

(D) The GAAR applies to transactions that result in a misuse or abuse of the Act read as a whole.

Question 5

The general anti-avoidance provision, GAAR, is most likely to apply to which *one* of the following transactions?

(A) As part of an estate freeze, Bill had a trust for his adult children acquire 80% of the common shares of B Ltd. Until then, Bill had owned all the shares of B Ltd., a successful grocery retail outlet. Each year B Ltd. pays dividends to the trust which are paid to the children. The dividends are received by the children tax-free due to the dividend tax credit, since, as university students, they have no other income.

(B) Sam transferred his unincorporated Pizza business, on tax-deferred basis, to a corporation, for the sole purpose of reducing tax by claiming the small business deduction.

(C) Paul gave his son a gift of $10,000 and the son invested it in dividend-paying shares. His son does not pay tax on the dividend income as he is a 19-year old student with little other income. Paul will celebrate his 65th birthday two years after his son graduates. It is anticipated that Paul will receive a birthday gift of $10,000 from his son at that time.

(D) Mary owns all the shares of M Ltd., a CCPC which carries on an active business. For M Ltd.'s taxation year ended June 30, 2007, Mary accrued herself a bonus of $700,000 which reduced M Ltd.'s taxable income to $300,000.

Question 6

Mrs. Investor owns all the Class A common shares of a corporation which has an investment portfolio worth $500,000. The corporation has no other assets and has a December 31 year-end. On January 1 of the current year, Mr. Investor (Mrs. Investor's husband) subscribed for $1 million of Class B shares of the corporation and paid for them in cash. The purpose of this transaction was to income-split with his wife. The corporation earned $10,000 during the year and paid a $10,000 cash dividend to Mrs. Investor. Assuming the prescribed rate is 6% throughout the year, what is the minimum amount of income that Mr. Investor must report in the year in respect of his investment in the corporation?

(A) $10,000

(B) $12,500

(C) $30,000

(D) $60,000

Question 7

Ms. Prentice owns P Ltd., a Canadian-controlled private corporation with assets worth $4 million and liabilities amounting to $1 million. 60% of its assets are used in an active business carried on in Canada by the corporation and 20% are used in an active business carried on in Canada by a corporation controlled by Ms. Prentice's brother. The remaining assets (non-active business assets) earn investment income. Which of the following is the minimum amount of non-active business assets that P Co must sell in order for its shares to qualify as shares of a small business corporation? Assume that the after-tax proceeds on the sale will be used to pay off some of the corporation's liabilities.

(A) None

(B) $400,000

(C) $444,445

(D) $1,333,333

¶13,850 EXERCISES

Exercise 1

ITA: 78

Slipit Ltd. declared a bonus payable of $10,000 to Mr. Slip, its president and majority shareholder, on September 30, 2007, its fiscal year-end. If the bonus is paid it will be subject to withholding tax in the amount of $3,500.

— *REQUIRED*

(A) If the corporation is to get a deduction with no future consequences for the bonus payable, by what date must the bonus be paid?

(B) What are the consequences of not paying the bonus by this date?

(C) Assume that, instead of a bonus, the amount owing to Mr. Slip is rent, properly included on the cash basis, on the only rental property he owns and rents to the corporation:

(i) If the corporation is to get a deduction with no future consequences for the rent payable, by what date must the rent be paid?

(ii) What are the consequences of not paying the rent by this date?

(iii) How can these consequences be avoided without paying the rent?

Exercise 2

ITA: 15(2), 80.4

Mr. Leverage relocated his private business, Leverage-Lovers Limited, to Alberta from Ontario at the end of May 2007. As a result of the move, the corporation made the following loans on June 1, 2007 to Mr. Leverage, the president and majority shareholder:

(a) a $75,000 loan at 2% interest per year with a five-year term but amortized over a 25-year period to purchase a house in the new location;

(b) a $5,000 loan at 5% interest per year with no definite term to buy furniture for the new house; and

(c) a $10,000 loan with no interest but with a five-year term to buy previously unissued, fully paid shares from the corporation.

The corporation uses the calendar year as its fiscal year and by the end of 2008 the loans described were still outstanding. Any interest required to be paid on the loans at the indicated rates was paid in 2007. Assume that the prescribed rates applicable to shareholder loans during 2007 were: 1st quarter, 4%; 2nd quarter, 3%; 3rd quarter, 4%; and 4th quarter, 4%.

— *REQUIRED*

Discuss the tax consequences in 2007 of the loan described, if Mr. Leverage received the loans:

(A) by virtue of his employment;

(B) by virtue of his shareholdings.

Exercise 3

ITA: 15(2), 20(1)(*j*)

Mr. Skimit is a shareholder of Wonder-Benefits Ltd. which has a December 31 year-end. Consider the following transactions in his shareholder loan account:

Date	Loan (repayment)	Balance
Dec. 31/Year 1	—	Nil
Jan. 31/Year 2	$ 20,000	$ 20,000
Apr. 30/Year 2	25,000	45,000
June 30/Year 3	(15,000)	30,000
Sept. 30/Year 3	(17,000)	13,000
Mar. 31/Year 4	(12,000)	1,000
Nov. 30/Year 4	10,000	11,000
May 31/Year 5	(11,000)	Nil
Nov. 30/Year 5	23,000	23,000
July 31/Year 6	(14,000)	9,000
Dec. 31/Year 6	—	9,000

— REQUIRED

(A) If it is assumed that these transactions result in the conclusion that there is a series of loans and repayments, compute the principal amounts that must be included or the repayments that may be deducted for each of the years indicated according to the guidelines in IT-119R4.

(B) If there has not been a series of loans and repayments, how would the amounts differ from the above? How would you argue there was no series of loans and repayments?

Exercise 4

ITA: 15(2), 80.4; ITR: 4300

Cohber Marlach is a major shareholder and senior executive of Burlon Ltd. He was required to use a car about 60% for the duties of his employment. On April 1, under a plan available to the five other senior executives of the corporation, he was granted a loan of $35,000 at a rate of interest of 3% per annum and agreed to annual payments on the anniversary day of $7,000 for principal and monthly payments of interest at the end of each month. During the year he faithfully made the monthly interest payments for seven months, but neglected to make the interest payments for the last two months of the year.

— REQUIRED

What are the income tax consequences to the taxpayer? Assume that the prescribed rates were as follows:

first quarter	5%	third quarter	5%
second quarter	4%	fourth quarter	6%

Ignore the effects of the leap year, if applicable.

Exercise 5

ITA: 6(1)

Consider the data provided in Exhibit 13-4 on page 704.

— REQUIRED

Analyze the situation if the business use of the car is 20,000 out of 30,000 km.

Exercise 6

ITA: 82(1), 117, 121, 123–125

Payme Now is the sole shareholder and employee of Conduit Corporation Ltd. which operates a processing business in a province with a 5% corporate rate (i.e., a total corporate rate of 18.12%) on its income. The corporation has income of $20,000 before salaries and corporate taxes which is eligible for the small business deduction. Mr. Now has no other income and has federal tax credits of $2,000 and provincial tax credits of $1,290. He requires all of the income generated by the business.

— REQUIRED

Consider the following three remuneration alternatives:

(A) all salary,

(B) all dividends, and

(C) $11,000 in salary and the remainder in dividends.

Compare the net cash to Mr. Now for these alternatives ignoring employment income deductions available to an employee. Can the best of these alternatives be improved upon?

Exercise 7

ITA: 82(1), 117, 121, 123–125

I.M.A. Saver is a sole proprietor generating $80,000 in income before taxes from a processing business operating in a province with a 6% corporate rate (i.e., a total corporate rate of 19.12%). He requires $25,000 after taxes for living expenses and has federal personal tax credits of $2,000 and provincial tax credits of $1,290. He has no other source of income or deductions (except as assumed for (B)(iii) below). The business has a December 31 taxation year-end.

— REQUIRED

(A) Compute the tax that would be paid if he continues to operate the business as an unincorporated proprietorship.

(B) Compare your answer in (A) with the total tax that would be paid if he incorporates the business and remunerates himself by the following alternative methods:

(i) $29,141 in salary;

(ii) $25,000 in dividends; and

(iii) $8,435 in salary and $16,565 in dividends. (Assume that the excess federal tax credits resulting from this case can be used against tax on other income.)

Ignore deductions available to employees.

Exercise 8

ITA: 248(1)

Consider each of the following independent proportions of assets at fair market value. Assume the assets are owned by a Canadian-controlled private corporation. Active business assets refer to assets used principally in an active business carried on primarily in Canada.

	A	B	C	D
Active business assets	85%	50%	—	40%
Marketable securities	15	—	20%	20
Shares of a connected small business corporation	—	50	80	40
	100%	100%	100%	100%

— REQUIRED

Determine whether each of the above proportions meets the test of a small business corporation as defined in the Act.

Exercise 9

ITA: 110.6

Bobby Beamboy Accountant has provided you with the following information:

	2005	2006	2007
Taxable capital gains on sale of qualified small business corporation shares	$75,000	—	$300,000
Business investment loss (before ssec. 39(9) adjustment)	—	—	160,000
Interest income	—	$ 600	1,200
Grossed-up taxable dividends	—	140	—
Net rental income (loss)	—	(1,100)	(220)
Carrying charges	—	1,075	—

The 2005 taxable capital gain was fully offset by a capital gains deduction in that year. The 2007 disposition occurred prior to March 19, 2007.

— REQUIRED

Determine Bobby's capital gains deduction for 2007 supported by all the necessary calculations. Assume that there were no other capital transactions before 2005.

Exercise 10

ITA: 74.4

Mrs. Albert owns all of the outstanding common shares of a corporation, Prince Albert Inc., which operates a small retail store in Saskatoon. Her husband owns the building with a fair market value of $200,000, in which the store is located. He is planning to transfer it to Prince Albert Inc. in exchange for $80,000 of cash, a 5% demand note for $20,000 and preference shares for $100,000. The fair market value of the business assets (which are all of the assets excluding cash used to pay for the building) in the company immediately before the transfer is $600,000. Of the total space in the building, 20% is used in the retail business. The net rental income that Mr. Albert earned in the previous year was $20,000.

— REQUIRED

Determine the tax consequences, if any, to Mr. Albert for 2007, assuming the prescribed interest rate is a constant 4% and that the sale took place on January 1, 2007. The corporation's year-end is September 30. Dividends of $2,000 were paid on the preference shares in 2007.

ITR: 4301(c)

Exercise 11

ITA: 245

Gangster Production Ltd., a Canadian-controlled private corporation, paid its shareholder-manager, Herb, a salary of $250,000 which reduced the corporation's income to $399,500 for the taxation year. The amount of the salary is considered to be reasonable.

— REQUIRED

Determine whether the general anti-avoidance rule (GAAR) would apply in this situation.

¶13,875 ASSIGNMENT PROBLEMS

Problem 1

ITA: 15(1), 18(1)

Mimi Gimmee is a vice president of Pump You Up Ltd., a private corporation she started and currently owns with three of her university colleagues. Mimi has recently signed a lease for an upscale downtown condominium which she intends to move into next month. It has been agreed that Pump You Up Ltd. will pay the $2,000 monthly rental for the condominium.

— *REQUIRED*

Discuss the income tax consequences of this arrangement to Mimi and to Pump You Up Ltd.

Problem 2

ITA: 15(2), 20(1)(*j*), 20(1)(*q*), 67, 78, 80.4, 80.5, 147, 147.2

As the auditor for Skimmed Limited, a Canadian-controlled private corporation, you have discovered in your 2007 year-end audit several items that require further consideration. Mr. Skimmer is an 80% shareholder and president of the company which has a December 31 fiscal year-end.

The following items were expensed during the year:

Salary for Mr. Skimmer (assume equal to employment compensation)	$90,000
Royalty payable to Mr. Skimmer on material prepared for the corporation . . .	54,000
Contribution to registered pension plan (money purchase plan) for Mr. Skimmer whose employee contributions are being matched by the corporation	3,000

The royalty was the only item not paid during the fiscal year. In fact, it was still unpaid at the time of the audit and Mr. Skimmer indicated to you that it could not be paid until sometime in 2009 when he anticipated that the company would have sufficient cash.

The records showed that the corporation had made several loans to Mr. Skimmer or to his son, age 30, who owns the other 20% of the shares of the corporation and is, also, an employee of the corporation. Each of the following was evidenced by a separate promissory note, duly signed and approved by the Board of Directors:

(a) a $180,000 non-interest bearing loan, dated August 1, 2007, repayable in $18,000 annual instalments, to permit Mr. Skimmer's son to purchase previously unissued, fully paid shares from the corporation at their fair market value;

(b) a $270,000 3% loan, dated June 1, 2007, repayable over 15 years in equal instalments of principal payable on the anniversary date, but with interest payable monthly, to enable Mr. Skimmer to purchase a new home, a few blocks from his old home; and

(c) a $24,000 4% loan, dated October 1, 2007, with no principal repayment arrangements, but with interest paid quarterly, to permit Mr. Skimmer to purchase a car to be used in his employment with the corporation.

Mr. Skimmer had repaid $4,800 of the car loan on May 31, 2008 and expressed the intention to repay $4,800 annually for four more years.

Any interest required to be paid on the loans at the indicated rates was paid in 2007. Assume the prescribed rates for 2007 were 4% for the first and second quarters, and 5% for the third and fourth quarters.

— *REQUIRED*

(A) Discuss the deductibility of expenses contained in the foregoing information (excluding the shareholder loans).

(B) Discuss the tax implications of the shareholder loans if Mr. Skimmer and his son received the loans by virtue of being:

(i) shareholders,

(ii) employees.

Support your answer with specific calculations where appropriate and provide reasons for your conclusions.

Problem 3

ITA: 15(2), 15(2.3), 15(2.4), 15(2.6), 20(1)(*j*), 80.4; ITR: 4300(7)

In 2006, Sunshine Publishing Ltd., a book publishing company with a fiscal year-end on December 31, made a loan of $100,000 to Stuart Sunshine, the president and majority shareholder. Both Stuart and Sunshine Publishing Limited are Canadian residents.

This is the first loan that Stuart ever received from the company, and it helped him finance the purchase of a new home which was built just outside Toronto, 10 kilometres farther from the corporate headquarters than Stuart's previous home. The loan was made on May 1, 2006, and a mortgage agreement was signed on that date. This agreement requires that the $100,000 owing be repaid over five years in equal instalments of $20,000 on each anniversary date without interest. Early prepayments of principal are allowed.

Assume that the prescribed rates applicable to taxable benefits are: 6% for the first quarter of 2006, 8% for the second quarter, 9% for the third quarter, 7% for the fourth quarter and 6% for all of 2007.

— *REQUIRED*

(A) It is now December 2006 and Stuart has asked you to advise him on the tax consequences of the loan. It is not a company policy to make housing loans to employees and no other loans have been made to employees on similar conditions. What are the income tax consequences of this loan to Stuart in 2006 and 2007?

(B) If it was a company policy to make such loans to employees and other loans had been made to employees on similar terms and conditions, how would this change your answer to Part (A)?

(C) Assume the following facts: it was a company policy to make such loans to employees; other loans had been made to employees on similar terms and conditions; Stuart was a 9.5% shareholder rather than a majority shareholder; he was not related to any shareholders of the company; and the loan was to buy a rental property rather than a home. How would this change your answer to Part (B)?

Problem 4

ITA: 82(1), 117, 121, 123–125

Nancy Ball presently operates a retailing proprietorship with a December 31, year-end and makes $150,000 of net income for tax purposes annually. She is thinking of incorporating her business and has asked for your advice. She lives in a province where the provincial corporate tax rate is 5% of this type of federal taxable income. She has $2,000 of federal personal tax credits, $1,290 of provincial personal tax credits, and no other income.

— *REQUIRED*

(A) Estimate the personal taxes that Nancy would pay currently on $150,000 of business income compared with the amount of corporate and personal taxes that would be paid if she incorporated her business and only took out a salary of $50,000? Ignore all payroll taxes (e.g., Canada Pension Plan premiums) when making your estimates.

(B) Based on your calculations in (A), estimate the amount of personal tax that Nancy defers by keeping the remaining after-tax retained earnings in her company this year? [Hint: compute the additional personal tax that she would pay on a dividend equal to the corporation's after-tax retained earnings.]

Problem 5

ITA: 82(1), 117, 121, 123–125

Mrs. Entrepreneur presently operates a retailing proprietorship with a December 31 fiscal year-end. She expects net income for tax purposes of $210,000 from the business. Since the business currently requires considerable amounts of working capital, she can only afford to withdraw $50,000 annually to meet her family's needs.

She lives in a province where the provincial corporate tax rate is 7% of federal taxable income. She is married and has two children (ages 18 and 19) who will start university soon. Her husband, who looks after their home, has no income and no interest in the business.

Mrs. Entrepreneur has federal personal credits of $2,200, provincial personal tax credits of $1,419 and has no other income. She is contemplating the incorporation of her business. If she does so, she has been advised that if she makes all withdrawals from the business in the form of $50,000 salary, she will end up with enough after-tax to meet her family's needs. Although she is not considering it at present, she expects to pay dividends at a time when her other taxable income is at about the same level as it is currently.

— REQUIRED

(A) Compare the total tax that Mrs. Entrepreneur would pay in 2007 on the $210,000 earned personally with the total tax that would be paid if she incorporated her business and only took out a salary of $50,000. Ignore any Canada Pension Plan premiums payable on the income.

(B) How much personal tax does Mrs. Entrepreneur defer each year by keeping the remaining after-tax retained earnings in her company? [Hint: compute the additional personal tax that she would pay on a dividend equal to the corporation's after-tax retained earnings.]

(C) Compare the total income tax incurred by using a corporation to earn income with the personal tax incurred when the income is earned directly by Mrs. Entrepreneur. Consider the corporate tax plus the personal tax on the salary and the dividend paid out of after-tax retained earnings. What is the absolute income tax cost or savings for Mrs. Entrepreneur if she incorporates?

(D) Assuming Mrs. Entrepreneur chooses the incorporated form of business, what additional tax savings could be achieved by income splitting with her family members?

Problem 6

ITA: 82(1), 117, 121, 123-125.1

I.M. Stressed approaches you with the following information:

(a) She resides in a province with a 5% corporate tax rate (i.e., a total tax rate of 18.12%) where she owns and operates an incorporated business which generates income in the amount of $125,000 before taxes.

(b) She has federal personal tax credits of $2,300 and provincial personal tax credits of $1,484 including, among others, the marital status tax credit.

(c) She requires $40,000 after taxes for living expenses each year. This is after she makes her CPP and RRSP contributions.

(d) She wants to maximize her Canada Pension Plan contributions each year. The CPP calculations are as follows:

Pensionable earnings (salary)	$43,700
Basic exemption	(3,500)
Maximum contributory earnings	$40,200
Employee rate	4.95%
Maximum contribution	$ 1,990

(e) She wants to make the maximum RRSP contribution based on the earned income you determine she should have. Assume that her earned income for 2006 is the same as for 2007.

— REQUIRED

Determine the optimum salary/dividend combination for Ms. Stressed to achieve her goals and maximize the amount remaining in the company for future dividends. [Hint — you might want to model this in a spreadsheet to compute a required dividend of $13,197.]

Problem 7

ITA: 110.6

Karen owns all the common shares of K Ltd. which was incorporated in 1994 to hold her 85% interest in Cyber Corp. Cyber Corp. distributes computer equipment and games to retail stores in southern Ontario. Both corporations are CCPCs. The following is a balance sheet prepared as at December 31, 2007.

Cyber Corp.
Balance Sheet
as at December 31, 2007

Assets		
Cash	$	4,500
Marketable securities (FMV $700,000)		300,000
Accounts receivable (FMV $780,000)		800,000
Inventory (FMV $920,000)		920,000
Prepaid expenses (FMV $1,000)		1,000
Fixed assets (FMV $150,000)		140,000
		$2,165,500

Liabilities & Shareholders' Equity

Accounts payable and accrued liabilities	$ 600,000
Loans payable	400,000
Future income taxes	100,000
Share capital	1,000
Retained earnings	1,064,500
	$2,165,500

The relative values of Cyber Corp.'s assets have remained stable over the past three years. The marketable securities comprise Cyber Corp.'s investment portfolio which is not held as part of the corporation's business activities. The estimated value of the goodwill of the business is $200,000.

K Ltd. was recently offered $1,450,000 for the 85% interest in Cyber Corp. However, Karen has talked the prospective purchaser into buying the shares of K Ltd. instead of the shares of Cyber Corp., as she understands that by selling the shares of K Ltd. she is able to receive a tax-free $500,000 capital gain.

K Ltd. has term deposits of $100,000 in addition to the shares of Cyber Corp.

— REQUIRED

(A) Advise Karen as to whether the shares of K Ltd. are qualified small business corporation (QSBC) shares.

(B) If the shares of K Ltd. are not QSBC shares, then suggest a method for purifying K Ltd. and indicate the tax consequences of your recommendations.

Problem 8

ITA: 110.6

Rogo Dan owns all of the common shares of Julie Inc. which in turn owns all of the shares of two other companies, Opco Inc. and RE Inc. Opco Inc. carries on an active business in Sudbury. RE Inc. owns real estate, of which 100% is used by Opco Inc. in its business. All three corporations are CCPCs. The following are further details:

Julie Inc. assets:	
Shares of Opco Inc. at FMV	$850,000
Shares of RE Inc. at FMV	800,000
Portfolio investments at FMV	75,000
Opco Inc. assets and liabilities:	
Active business assets at FMV	$900,000
Term deposits	50,000
Liabilities	100,000
RE Inc. assets and liabilities:	
Land and building at FMV	$800,000
Portfolio investments at FMV	200,000
Mortgage	200,000

The proportion of assets in each of the companies has been constant over the past three years. Rogo has owned the shares of Julie Inc. for the past five years.

— REQUIRED

(A) Determine whether Julie Inc. meets each of the three tests necessary for its shares to be qualifying small business corporation shares.

(B) If the shares of Julie Inc. are not QSBC shares, then suggest ways of purifying Julie Inc. and indicate the tax consequences of your recommendations.

Problem 9

ITA: 110.6

Phil Zamboni realized taxable capital gains of $12,000 in 1999. This gain was offset by a capital gains deduction of $12,000 in that year.

In 2005, Zamboni received interest income of $825 and grossed-up taxable dividends of $200. He also incurred a net rental loss of $15,000 and carrying charges totalling $1,475 in 2005.

In 2006, Zamboni earned investment income of $200. He had a rental loss that year in the amount of $13,000 and carrying charges of $2,000. He also realized a business investment loss of $20,000 in December 2006.

In 2007 (before March 19), Zamboni sold the shares of Maps Unlimited Ltd., a qualified small business corporation, for a capital gain of $185,000 and he realized a capital loss of $21,000 on the sale of public company shares. He also received $1,650 in interest and incurred a net rental loss of $1,000 in 2007.

Zamboni had no other previous capital transactions, investment income, or investment expenses.

— *REQUIRED*

Compute Zamboni's capital gains deduction for 2007 supported by all the necessary calculations.

Problem 10

ITA: 74.4

Bob Smith incorporated Smith Inc. 20 years ago and owns all of the shares himself. Smith Inc. is a "small business corporation" which carries on an active business in Victoria, B.C. In 1994, Bob felt that he would like to involve his wife Betty in the share ownership and, on the advice of his accountant, Holdco Inc. was incorporated with Bob and Betty each owning 50 common shares which they bought for $1 each with their own funds. Bob then transferred his common shares of Smith Inc., which were worth $600,000, to Holdco Inc. on a tax-free basis. As consideration for the transfer, Bob received 6% non-cumulative preference shares with a fair market value of $600,000. On July 1, 2007, Smith Inc. sold some property that was used in the active business for net proceeds of $150,000. This amount was then paid as a dividend from Smith Inc. to Holdco Inc. on the same day. Bob and Betty plan to have the corporation invest this amount and use it as capital for their retirement. After the sale of the property and the payment of the dividend to Holdco Inc., Smith Inc. has a fair market value of $800,000 and is still a "small business corporation". Bob received $6,000 in dividends on his preferred shares of Holdco Inc.

— *REQUIRED*

Determine the tax consequences of the 2007 transactions as they relate to the corporate attribution rules. Assume that the prescribed rate for 2007 was 4%.

ITR: 4301(*c*)

Problem 11

ITA: 245

Consider each of the following independent fact situations.

(1) Adam Aref has contributed the maximum amount to an RRSP on the first business day of each year in respect of the previous year and shortly thereafter has withdrawn the funds.

(2) Bill Loadsofmoney loaned his wife $1,000,000 in 2003 through a non-interest bearing promissory note. His wife invested the funds in GICs and earned $80,000 of interest income which was properly attributed to him, except for any compound interest. Bill gave his wife another cash amount to cover the income tax on the compound interest.

(3) Wells Ltd. is owned 100% by Mrs. Hugejaysfan. Stieb Ltd. is owned by Mrs. Hugejaysfan's husband and minor children. Wells Ltd. made an interest-free loan out of its taxable surplus to Stieb Ltd. such that the corporate attribution rule does not apply. Stieb Ltd. used the proceeds of the loan to earn property income.

(4) Traub has $200,000 of investments and a mortgage on his personal home for a similar amount. Traub sold the investments, paid off the mortgage, and re-borrowed to acquire the investments.

(5) Guntandy made a loan to his adult child's corporation, Vancouver Hockey Puck Ltd., in order to avoid attribution, since the corporation used the funds to earn property income.

— *REQUIRED*

Discuss whether the general anti-avoidance rule (GAAR) applies to the above situations.

Problem 12

ITA: 245; IC 88-2

Consider each of the following independent fact situations:

(1) An individual transfers his or her unincorporated business to a corporation primarily to obtain the benefit of the small business deduction.

(2) An individual provides services to a corporation with which he or she does not deal at arm's length. The company does not pay a salary to the individual because payment of a salary would increase the amount of a loss that the company will incur in the year.

(3) A taxable Canadian corporation, which is profitable, has a wholly owned taxable Canadian corporation that is sustaining losses and needs additional capital to carry on its business. The subsidiary could borrow the monies from its bank but the subsidiary could not obtain any tax saving in the current

year by deducting the interest expense. Therefore, the parent corporation borrows the money from its bank and subscribes for additional common shares of the subsidiary and reduces its net income by deducting the interest from its business.

(4) Profitco and Lossco are taxable Canadian corporations. Lossco is a wholly owned subsidiary of Profitco. Lossco has non-capital losses that would be deductible if Lossco had income. In order to generate income in Lossco from which its non-capital losses may be deducted, Profitco borrows from its bank and uses the monies to subscribe for common shares of Lossco. Lossco lends these monies to Profitco at a commercial rate of interest. Profitco repays the bank. The amount of share subscription is not in excess of the amount of monies that Lossco could reasonably be expected to be able to borrow for use in its business on the basis solely of its credit from an arm's length lender.

(5) Each of two private corporations owns less than 10% of the common shares of a payer corporation that is to pay a substantial taxable dividend. The payer corporation will not be entitled to a dividend refund on the payment of the dividend. None of the corporations is related to any of the others. The private corporations form a corporation, Newco, transfer their shares of the payer corporation to Newco in exchange for common shares of Newco, and elect under subsection 85(1) (assume that this is done correctly to avoid tax on the transfer) in respect of the transfer. Following the transfer of the payer corporation's shares to Newco, Newco will be connected with the payer corporation. The payer corporation pays the dividend to Newco, free of Part IV tax. Newco pays the same amount to the private corporations as a dividend, free of Part IV tax. The primary purpose of the transfer of the shares is to avoid the Part IV tax which would be payable if the dividend were received directly by the private corporations.

(6) The owner of land inventory has agreed to sell the property to an arm's length purchaser. The purchaser wants to buy the property for cash, but the owner does not want to have the profits recognized in the year of sale. The owner sells the land inventory to an intermediary company deferring receipt of the proceeds of disposition of the land for several years after the date of sale. In this way, a reserve can be claimed under paragraph 20(1)(*n*). The intermediary sells the land to the third party for cash. The owner receives interest from the intermediary in respect of the monies received by the intermediary from the third party.

— *REQUIRED*

Discuss whether the part of the general anti-avoidance rule (GAAR) that asks the question "can it reasonably be considered that the transaction would not result, directly or indirectly, in a misuse of the provisions of the Act or an abuse having regard to the provisions of the Act read as a whole" applies to the above situations.

[For more problems and solutions thereto, see the CD accompanying this book.]

¶13,880 ADVISORY CASE

Aurora Collectibles

Herb Smith, the tax partner, has just talked to you about one of his clients, John Barwell. John Barwell has owned his retail store, Aurora Collectibles, for the past four years. Despite a recession, he has been able to do very well with the store by offering customers decorating advice along with the antiques and other unusual items that he sells. Last year, his store earned net income of $125,000.

When he first started the business, he set it up as a proprietorship and financed it with a loan of $100,000 from his wife, Alison, and a $75,000 bank operating loan. Currently, both of the loans remain unpaid, since both John and Alison enjoy a lifestyle that uses up all of their cash flow. Both John and Alison agree that they are going to improve their spending habits. They want John to pay off the bank operating loan from the business earnings. Once this is done, any excess cash will be used by John to invest in some property that they will eventually move the store into.

Herb wants you to identify the tax issues and tell him what analysis you propose to do to help John and Alison. He doesn't want you to get into the numbers yet.

¶13,900 SUPPLEMENTAL NOTES

(This section can be omitted without losing the continuity of the chapter. None of the review questions, multiple choice questions, exercises or assignment problems utilizes this information.)

¶13,910 General Anti-Avoidance Rule Under the Excise Tax Act

The *Excise Tax Act* (ETA) contains a general anti-avoidance rule (GAAR) almost identical in nature to the GAAR of the *Income Tax Act*. In its explanatory notes to the GST legislation, the Department of Finance made the following statement in regard to the GAAR in the ETA:

> This section introduces a general anti-avoidance rule which, like its counterpart in section 245 of the *Income Tax Act*, is intended to prevent abusive tax avoidance transactions or arrangements without interfering with legitimate commercial transactions. The comments on the income tax provisions, which are found in the explanatory notes to Bill C-139 (1988, C. 55) published in June 1988, are also generally applicable in respect of this section.

These explanatory notes should be reviewed in the context of GST. The definitions and concepts in respect of the GAAR in the ETA are based on their income tax counterparts.

As with the general anti-avoidance rule under the *Income Tax Act*, the essence of the GAAR for GST purposes is that the tax benefit that results from an avoidance transaction will be denied. In order to determine the amount of the tax benefit that will be denied, the provision indicates that the tax consequences to a person will be determined as is reasonable in the circumstances. The actual determination of the tax consequences is provided for in a provision of the ETA which sets out some of the methods by which a benefit will be denied.

The term "avoidance transaction" is defined as any transaction that by itself or as part of a series of transactions (i.e., a "step transaction") results in a tax benefit, unless the transaction can be considered to have been undertaken or arranged primarily for *bona fide* purposes other than to obtain the tax benefit. Thus, if there is a primary non-tax purpose for a transaction, it is not an avoidance transaction even if a tax benefit results.

The term "tax benefit" is defined as a reduction, avoidance, or deferral of tax or other amount payable, or an increase in a refund or rebate of tax or other amount. Thus, a tax benefit could arise if there is a deferral of tax or instalment payments. The term "tax consequences" is, also, defined as the amount of tax, net tax, input tax credit, rebate, or other amount payable by, or refundable to, the person under the legislation, or any other amount that is relevant for the purposes of computing that amount. As indicated previously, this term is necessary to determine the amount of the benefit that will be denied.

A limitation on the application of the GAAR in the ETA is provided. In the explanatory notes to the GAAR in the ETA, the Department of Finance makes the following statement:

> Subsection 274(4) recognizes that the provisions of Part IX are intended to apply to transactions with real economic substance, not to transactions intended to exploit, misuse or frustrate those provisions so as to avoid tax. It also recognizes, however, that tax benefits expressly provided for in the legislation should not be neutralized by this section in non-abusive situations.

Finally, rules that pertain to the administration of the GAAR in the ETA are provided.

ETA: 274

ETA: 274(5)

ETA: 274(3)

ETA: 274(1)

ETA: 274(4)

ETA: 274(6)–(8)

Chapter 14

Rights and Obligations Under the Income Tax Act

LEARNING GOALS

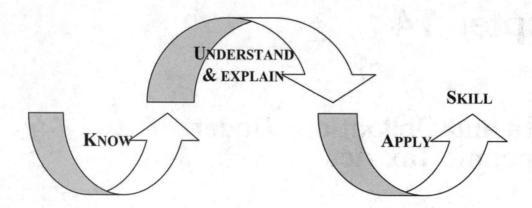

Know

By the end of this chapter you should know the basic provisions of the *Income Tax Act* and the *Excise Tax Act* that relate to the taxpayer compliance rules, the powers of the Canada Revenue Agency (CRA), and a taxpayer's rights and requirements on appeals. Completing the Review Questions (¶14,800) and Multiple Choice Questions (¶14,825) is a good way to learn the technical provisions.

Understand and Explain

You should understand and be able to explain:

- The requirements for taxpayers of income tax and registrants for GST to make payments, file returns, and, possibly, incur penalties and interest, if the taxpayer does not comply with the legislation on an accurate and timely basis;

- The powers and obligations of the CRA to assess and reassess a taxpayer's or registrant's filings;

- The rights of taxpayers and registrants to appeal within deadlines; and

- The compliance rules applicable to employers, other payers of tax, and representatives of deceased taxpayers.

Completing the Exercises (¶14,850) is a good way to deepen your understanding of the material.

Apply

You should be able to apply your knowledge and understanding of the key elements of compliance pertaining to payment of tax and filing returns and appeals to achieve a client's goals of minimizing interest and penalties in the early stages of the process. Completing the Assignment Problems (¶14,875) is an excellent way to develop your ability to apply the material in increasingly complex situations.

OVERVIEW

Canadian income tax is based on the self-assessment system. The obligation of calculating taxable income and taxes payable and of paying taxes owing is that of the taxpayer and not the CRA. The *Income Tax Act* enumerates these obligations and also specifies the rights and powers of the CRA to enforce the system. Finally, taxpayers are given the right to appeal any actions taken by the CRA.

In the interest of efficiency and enforcement, the Act shifts some of the obligations from the taxpayer to other persons. These include employers and persons paying interest, dividends, and other payments to non-residents. The obligations of these persons to report payments and/or withhold tax and remit it to the CRA will also be discussed.

Under the *Excise Tax Act*, containing the legislation pertaining to the Goods and Services Tax (GST), registrants are agents of the Crown and are responsible to collect tax on their taxable supplies. In addition, registrants are responsible to remit the net tax to the Receiver General and to meet certain reporting requirements.

The following chart outlines the major provisions of Part I, Division I of the *Income Tax Act*, pertaining to returns, assessments, payments and appeals discussed in this Chapter.

PART I — DIVISION I
RETURNS, ASSESSMENTS, PAYMENTS AND APPEALS

A	Liability for tax	150	Returns
B	Computation of income	150.1	Electronic filing
		151	Estimate of tax
C	Computation of taxable income	152	Assessment
		153-160.4	Payment of tax
D	Taxable income earned in Canada by non-residents	161	Interest
		161.1-161.2	Offset of Refund Interest and Arrears Interest
E	Computation of tax	161.3-161.4	Small amounts owing
E.1	Minimum tax	162-163.1	Penalties
F	Special rules	163.2	Misrepresentation of a tax matter by a third party
G	Deferred and other special income arrangements	164	Refunds
		165	Objections
H	Exemptions	166-167	General
I	Returns, Assessments, Payments, Appeals	168	Revocation of reg'n of certain org's
J	Appeals to the courts		

¶14,000 OBLIGATIONS OF THE TAXPAYER UNDER THE INCOME TAX ACT

¶14,010 Returns, Penalties, and Criminal Offences

¶14,015 Returns

¶14,015.10 *Filing deadlines*

The Act requires taxpayers to file returns in prescribed form and containing prescribed information, and specifies the date by which the returns must be filed as follows:

(a) Corporations — within six months after the end of the taxation year. ITA: 150(1)(*a*)

(b) Individuals — on or before April 30 of the next year, unless an individual or the individual's cohabiting spouse carried on a business in the year, in which case the filing deadline is June 15 of the following year. ITA: 150(1)(*d*)

(c) Deceased individuals — where an individual has died after October of a particular year and before the filing date for that year (April 30th or June 15th, as discussed above), the return for the particular year of the deceased must be filed by the legal representative by the later of:

(i) six months after the date of death, and

(ii) the usual filing date (i.e., April 30th or June 15th) following the particular year. ITA: 150(1)(*b*)

Where the death has occurred outside of these time limits, the normal filing dates as discussed in (b) above apply. The objective of these rules is to provide the legal representative of the deceased a minimum of six months after the date of death within which to file a return. These rules are discussed in more detail later in this chapter.

(d) Trusts or estates — within 90 days after the end of the taxation year. ITA: 150(1)(*c*)

The following summarizes the filing deadlines:

Income tax return	Filing date
Corporations	6 months
Individuals	April 30 or June 15
Deceased individuals	Later of 6 months after death and the normal due date
Trusts	90 days

¶14,015.20   *Requirements to file a return*

Note that corporations that are resident in Canada or carry on business in Canada must file for each taxation year, but individuals are only required to file if one of the following applies:

(a) a balance of tax is owing for the year;   ITA: 150(1.1)(*b*)(i)

(b) a capital property has been disposed of in the year;   ITA: 150(1.1)(*b*)(ii)

(c) a non-resident individual has a taxable capital gain (e.g., claimed a capital gains   ITA: 150(1.1)(*b*)(iii)
    reserve in the previous year);

(d) the individual's Home Buyer Plan (HBP) balance or Lifelong Learning Plan (LLP) is a   ITA: 146.01(1), 146.02(1),
    positive amount; or   150(1.1)(*b*)(iv)

(e) a return is demanded by the Minister.   ITA: 150(2)

Of course, individuals entitled to a refund due to over-withholding or refundable tax credits should file in any case. Low-income taxpayers should file to receive income-based benefits such as the GST credit, the Canada Child Tax Benefit and the Guaranteed Income Supplement. If they do not file a tax return, they are not eligible to receive these amounts.

¶14,015.30   *Electronic and other filing options*

Individuals can file their personal return electronically. The primary benefit of the   ITA: 150.1
electronic filing program for taxpayers is that processing of a tax refund can be much faster. The primary benefit to the CRA is the elimination of data inputting errors on their computer system.

Taxpayers who electronically file their tax return are not required to submit any receipts or other supporting documentation. The CRA, however, has the right to request supporting documentation, which, in fact, may delay the processing of the return.

Alternatively, taxpayers who are issued a Web Access Code by the CRA are eligible to Netfile their personal return. Simple returns can be Telefiled where the CRA has issued a Telefile Access Code.

¶14,020   Penalties

¶14,020.10   *Failure to file return*

The Act provides penalties for failure to file a tax return as and when required. The   ITA: 150(1)
penalty is 5% of the tax unpaid at the date on which the return was due to be filed. In   ITA: 162(1)(*a*)
addition, a further penalty of 1% of the unpaid tax is levied for each complete month that the   ITA: 162(1)(*b*)
return was late, for up to 12 months.

A higher penalty is imposed for a taxpayer who has already been assessed a penalty for   ITA: 162(2)
failure to file a return in any of the three preceding years. This penalty equals 10% of unpaid tax plus 2% per month, for up to 20 months.

¶14,020.20   *Failure to report an amount of income*

A penalty of 10% of the income that a taxpayer has failed to report is imposed if there   ITA: 163(1)
had been a previous failure to report in the preceding three years. However, no penalty will   ITA: 163(2)
apply where the more severe penalty for false statements or omission (below) or where the previous failure was more than three years ago.

¶14,020.30   *False statements or omission*

Where taxpayers knowingly or under circumstances amounting to gross negligence   ITA: 163(2)
under-report income, the Act imposes a penalty equal to the greater of $100 and 50% of the difference in tax liability. This provision is invoked frequently in cases involving omission of income on returns. The term "gross negligence" has been interpreted to include errors which amount to little more than careless omissions, if the taxpayer knew or should have known that

the amount was omitted.[1] This provision would not be applied to amounts excluded because of an honest dispute as to their taxability.

¶14,020.40   *Interplay of penalty provisions*

The interplay between the penalties for failure to report and for false statements or omission should be noted. On the first failure to report income, the first penalty would not apply, so the CRA could impose the penalty for false statements or omissions. On a repeated failure to report income within the three years specified, the CRA may have a choice between the failure to report penalty, which is based on 10% of income, and the false statement or omission penalty, which is based on 50% of tax. For example, if no tax is payable on unreported income, due to the availability of loss carryovers, the penalty for failure to report could be used to yield 10% of the unreported income.

ITA: 163(1), 163(2)
ITA: 163(1)
ITA: 163(2)
ITA: 163(1)
ITA: 163(2)
ITA: 163(1)

¶14,020.50   *Penalty for late or deficient instalments*

The Act imposes a penalty of 50% of the interest, charged on late or underpaid instalment payments, in excess of the greater of $1,000 or 25% of the interest calculated as if no instalments had been paid. This section applies if *any* instalment for the year is late or deficient, as discussed later in this chapter.

ITA: 161, 163.1

¶14,020.60   *Civil penalties for misrepresentation of a third-party*

The Act imposes civil penalties for misrepresentations by third parties in respect of another person's tax matters. The penalty is directed to tax professionals, appraisers and valuators and promoters of tax shelters and other tax minimization schemes. Two penalties are imposed.

ITA: 163.2

The first penalty, referred to as the planner's penalty, is a penalty that is imposed when the third-party person makes or furnishes, or participates in the making of, or causes another person to make or furnish, a statement that the person knows, or would reasonably be expected to know but for circumstances amounting to "culpable conduct" (as defined in the provision) is a false statement or omission that may be used by another person for tax purposes.

ITA: 163.2(2)

ITA: 163.2(1)

The penalty is one of two amounts. The first amount applies where a "false statement" (as defined in the provision) is made in the course of a "planning activity" or a "valuation activity" (as defined). The penalty is the greater of $1,000 and the total of the person's "gross entitlement" (as defined) in respect of the planning activity and the valuation activity calculated at the time at which the notice of assessment of the penalty is sent to the person. The second amount is $1,000, which applies in any other case of a false statement in a situation that falls outside of the definition of a "planning activity" or a "voluntary activity" or, perhaps, in which there is no gross entitlement.

ITA: 163.2(3)
ITA: 163.2(1)
ITA: 163.2(1)
ITA: 163.2(1)

The second penalty, referred to as the preparer's penalty, is a penalty imposed on a third-party person who makes, or participates in, assents to or acquiesces in the making of a false statement or omission statement to, or by or on behalf of, another person.

The statement must be established as one that the person knows, or would be reasonably expected to know but for circumstances amounting to "culpable conduct", is a false statement or omission that may be used for tax purposes by or on behalf of the other person. The penalty is the greater of two amounts. The first amount is $1,000. The second amount is, generally, the amount of tax sought to be avoided, or the amount of excess refund sought to be obtained. Additional discussion and clarification of the CRA's position on third party civil penalties, with examples, is contained in an Information Circular.

ITA: 163.2(4), 163.2(5)

IC 01-1

---

[1] See *Cowan v. M.N.R.*, 69 DTC 553 (T.A.B.), and *Nesbitt v. The Queen*, 96 DTC 6588 (F.C.A.), for cases in this area.

The following flow chart may be helpful in applying these civil penalties.

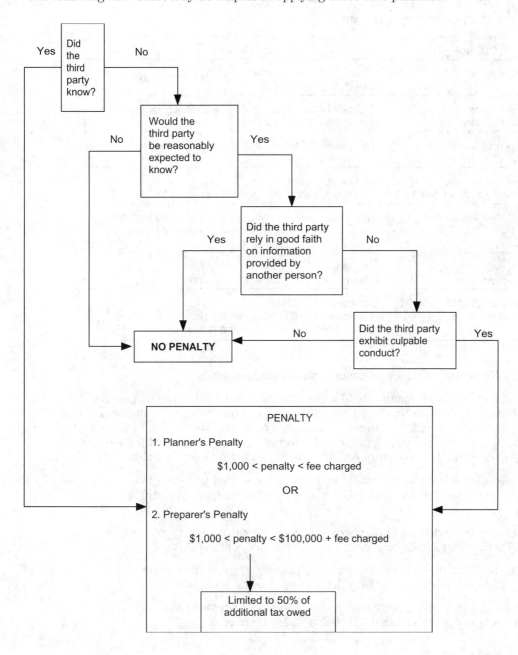

¶14,020.70 *Summary of penalties*

The following table summarizes the above penalties.

Offence	Penalty
Late-filed tax return	Balance of tax owing × 5% + 1% for each complete month late: Maximum = 17%
Late-filed tax return — repeat offender	Balance of tax owing × 10% + 2% for each complete month late: Maximum = 50%
Failure to report income — repeat offender	Income not reported × 10%
Under-reporting income — knowingly or gross negligence	Minimum = $100 Maximum = increased tax liability × 50%
Late or deficient instalments	[Interest charged–greater of (a) $1,000 and (b) 25% of interest that would have been charged if no instalments were made] × 50%
Third party civil penalty Planner's penalty	Minimum = $1,000 Maximum = Fee charged for the planning
Third party civil penalty Preparer's penalty	Minimum = $1,000 Maximum = $100,000 + Fee charged Limited to 50% × tax on unreported income

¶14,020.80 *CRA power to waive or cancel interest and penalties*

The CRA has the legislative authority to waive or cancel penalties, if the taxpayer makes a voluntary disclosure. The CRA's voluntary disclosure program is outlined in an Information Circular. Where a taxpayer makes voluntary disclosures to correct inaccurate or incomplete information or to disclose previously unreported information, the taxpayer will have to pay taxes owing plus interest, but monetary penalties and prosecution may be waived. *[ITA: 220(3.1) IC 00-1R]*

The Act also allows the CRA to cancel or waive interest and penalties in a number of other circumstances. Another Information Circular sets out three types of circumstances that would warrant a waiver. *[ITA: 230(3.1) IC 07-1]*

1. Circumstances beyond the taxpayer's or employer's control such as natural disasters, postal strikes, serious illness or accident or serious emotional or mental distress.

2. Actions of the Department such as processing delays, errors in CRA materials, errors in CRA advice, processing errors or CRA delays in providing information.

3. To facilitate collection when there is an inability to pay or where a reasonable repayment arrangement is not possible due to the heavy interest charges.

¶14,025 Criminal offences

In addition to the penalties described above, the Act prescribes a number of more serious penalties that can be imposed for a variety of offences. *[ITA: 238, 239]*

A person is liable for a fine of $1,000 to $25,000 or both the fine and imprisonment for up to 12 months on summary conviction for failing to file a return as and when required. A person convicted under this section is not liable to pay a penalty under specified sections of the Act unless that penalty was assessed before he or she was charged under this section. *[ITA: 238(3)] [ITA: 162, 227]*

On summary conviction, there is a fine of between 50% and 200% of tax sought to be evaded or both the fine and imprisonment for up to two years for: *[ITA: 239(1)]*

(a) making a false statement in a return;

(b) destroying books and records;

(c) falsifying books and records;

(d) wilfully attempting to evade compliance with the Act; and

(e) conspiring to commit any of the above four offences.

If the foregoing five offences are prosecuted by indictment at the election of the Attorney General of Canada, as indicated in the case of *The Queen v. Smythe*, a conviction can result in a fine of 100% to 200% of the tax sought to be evaded and imprisonment for up to five years. Again, a person convicted under this section is not liable for the penalty under specified sections of the Act for the same attempt to evade tax unless that penalty was assessed before charges were laid under this section.

ITA: 239(2), 239(3)

70 DTC 6382 (Ont. S.C.)

ITA: 162, 163, 163.2

¶14,030 Payments and Interest

The following is a summary of the payment deadlines.

Taxpayers	Balance-due day
Individuals	April 30
Corporations	2 months after year-end
CCPC claiming Small Business Deduction with taxable income under the business limit in the previous year	3 months after year-end
Trusts	Due date for trust return

¶14,035 Individuals

¶14,035.10 *Instalment threshold*

Individuals whose primary sources of income are wages and salary generally do not have to pay instalments because their employers are remitting withholding tax on a monthly basis. However, if the difference between the total tax liability (federal and provincial for all provinces, except Quebec) in either the current year or one of the two preceding years exceeds the amount of tax withheld at source by $2,000 ($1,200 if resident in Quebec), referred to as the instalment threshold, then the Act provides that quarterly instalments must be paid. [The March 19, 2007 federal budget proposed to increase the instalment threshold to $3,000 ($1,800 for Quebec residents), effective for the 2008 and subsequent taxation years.]

ITA: 156, 156.1(1)

¶14,035.20 *Instalment amounts and timetable*

These instalments must be paid by the 15th day of each calendar quarter (i.e., the 15th day of March, June, September, and December), with the balance of tax due the following April 30. Each instalment is computed as the least of:

(a) one-quarter of the estimated tax payable for the current year;

(b) one-quarter of the instalment base (defined for this purpose in a regulation, in essence, as tax payable excluding the effect of certain tax credits) for the immediately preceding year; and

ITR: 5300

(c) one-quarter of the instalment base for the second preceding year for the March and June instalments, and one-half of the instalment base for the preceding taxation year net of the March and June payments for the September and December instalments.

Individuals are informed by the CRA with respect to the exact amount of their instalment requirement under option (c) described previously. For example, in respect of 2007, the March and June instalments are based on one-quarter of the 2005 instalment base. The September and December instalments are equal to 50% of the excess of the individual's 2006 instalment base over 50% of the 2005 instalment base. Instalments can continue to be based on the estimated liability for the year but will be subject to interest penalties on understated amounts where an estimate is too low, as discussed below.

¶14,035.30   *Interest on deficient or late instalments*

The Act charges interest on deficient and late instalments from the day the instalment should have been made to the day the final payment of tax is due (e.g., April 30 for individuals). An instalment interest offset is available on prepaid or overpaid instalments. However, this credit offset can only be applied against instalment interest owing; it is not refundable and may not be applied against any other debts. Interest is calculated from the date the final payment is due until the amount is paid. Interest charges on deficient instalments can be avoided by computing instalments on the preceding year's instalment base even if the current year's income is likely to be higher. Interest on deficient instalments may be cancelled if the interest does not exceed $25 for a taxation year.

ITA: 161(2)
ITA: 161(2.2)
ITA: 161(1)
ITA: 161(4.01)
ITA: 161.3

The prescribed interest rate is set quarterly in relation to the average interest rate on 90-day treasury bills during the first month of the preceding quarter. Exhibit 14-1 lists the recent prescribed rates under Part XLIII of the Regulations.

EXHIBIT 14-1
Prescribed Interest Rates Under Part XLIII of Regulations

Year	Quarter	Employee or shareholder loans	CRA refunds	Unpaid tax and instalments
2005	1	3	5	7
	2	3	5	7
	3	3	5	7
	4	3	5	7
2006	1	3	5	7
	2	4	6	8
	3	4	6	8
	4	5	7	9
2007	1	5	7	9
	2	5	7	9
	3	5	7	9

The lowest prescribed rate applies to imputed interest benefit calculations on employee or shareholder loans. The basic prescribed rate is increased by two percentage points for the purpose of calculating interest on amounts, such as refunds, owed by the CRA to a taxpayer. The rate applicable to late and deficient instalments and tax payments is increased by four percentage points. Also, subject to the highest rate of interest are unpaid employee source deductions and other amounts withheld at source.

ITR: 4301

Interest paid on unpaid tax and instalments, arrears interest, is not deductible for tax purposes. However, interest received must be included in income. Refund interest accruing over a period can offset any arrears interest that accrues over the same period, to which the refund interest relates. Hence, only the excess refund interest is taxed to the individual.

ITA: 18(1)(*t*)
ITA: 161.1

The rate of interest paid on refunds is calculated at the basic rate described above plus two percentage points. However, contra-interest, as an interest offset on overpayments of tax, contains the additional four percentage points indicated for deficient payments.

ITA: 161(2.2)

Note that all interest is compounded daily, based on the quarterly prescribed rates.

ITA: 248(11)

Example Problem

Joe is self-employed. According to the CRA Instalment Remittance form, his 2007 instalments due were $1,000 for March 15 and June 15 and $1,500 for September 15 and December 15.

Due to a cash flow problem, he did not pay any instalments until September 15, 2007 when he wrote a cheque to the Receiver General for the full $5,000. On April 30, 2008, he paid the remaining balance of the tax owing. Assume that the prescribed rates, for this purpose, for 2007 are 7%, 6%, 6% and 6%, and for the first and second quarters of 2008 the prescribed interest rate is 6%.

— REQUIRED

Calculate the interest and penalty Joe will be charged on his deficient instalments. Assume that Joe pays the interest owing on April 30, 2008. Ignore the effects of the leap year.

— SOLUTION

Date	Amt. owing to CRA: opening balance[1]	Instalment due	Amt. paid	Amt. owing to RC: closing balance
Mar. 15/07	—	$1,000	—	$1,000.00
Mar. 31/07	$1,003.07	—	—	1,003.07
June 15/07	1,015.68	1,000	—	2,015.68
June 30/07	2,020.65	—	—	2,020.65
Sept. 15/07	2,046.39	1,500	$5,000.00	(1,453.61)
Dec. 15/07	(1,475.51)	1,500	—	24.49
Apr. 30/08	25.04	—	25.04	—
		$5,000	$5,025.04	

Total interest charged = $5,025.04 – $5,000 = $25.04

Penalty is nil, since $25.04 is less than $1,000. ITA: 163.1

— NOTE TO SOLUTION

[1] Calculation of opening balances above:

$$\text{Mar. 15–Mar. 31/07 (16 days):} \quad \$1,000.00 \times (1 + \frac{.07}{365})^{16} = \$1,003.07$$

$$\text{Mar. 31–June 15/07 (76 days):} \quad \$1,003.07 \times (1 + \frac{.06}{365})^{76} = \$1,015.68$$

$$\text{June 15–June 30/07 (15 days):} \quad \$2,015.68 \times (1 + \frac{.06}{365})^{15} = \$2,020.65$$

$$\text{June 30–Sept. 15/07 (77 days):} \quad \$2,020.65 \times (1 + \frac{.06}{365})^{77} = \$2,046.39$$

$$\text{Sept. 15–Dec. 15/07 (91 days):} \quad \$1,453.61 \times (1 + \frac{.06}{365})^{91} = \$1,475.51$$

$$\text{Dec. 15–Apr. 30/08 (137 days):} \quad \$24.49 \times (1 + \frac{.06}{365})^{137} = \$\quad 25.05$$

¶14,040 Corporations

¶14,040.10 *Instalment threshold and interest considerations*

Corporations must make instalment payments of their tax with the number of instalments dependent on the type of the corporation. A private corporation is permitted to reduce its monthly instalments by $1/12$ of the corporation's dividend refund on the payment of dividends for the year. A corporation is not required to make instalments if taxes payable for the current or preceding year do not exceed $1,000. [The March 19, 2007 federal budget proposed to increase the instalment threshold for corporations to $3,000, effective for 2008 and subsequent taxation years.] Corporate instalments will only be considered to have been received on time if received by the due date, i.e., postmarks will not suffice.

ITA: 157(1), 157(3)

ITA: 157(2.1)

ITA: 248(7)

The offsetting of interest on corporate tax overpayments and underpayments is permitted. This is different from the contra interest mechanism previously discussed. The provision is aimed at situations most commonly encountered by corporations with complex tax matters, where multiple taxation years may be reassessed concurrently to reallocate income and expenses from one taxation year to another. The provision allows a corporation to avoid paying non-deductible arrears interest for a period for which refund interest is being calculated in the corporation's favour. A written application will be required for the interest offset mechanism to be implemented.

ITA: 161.1
ITA: 161(2.2)

ITA: 161.1(2)

¶14,040.20   *Eligible Canadian-controlled private corporations [Proposed]*

[The March 19, 2007 federal budget proposed to allow CCPCs that are required to pay instalments to do so quarterly for taxation years that begin after 2007. These instalments will be due on the last day of each quarter of the CCPC's taxation year.

Only an eligible CCPC may pay quarterly instalments. A CCPC will be considered to be an eligible CCPC if:

(a) the corporation has a "perfect compliance history", as outlined below, at the time that the quarterly instalment is due;

(b) a small business deduction was claimed in computing the corporation's income tax payable for either the current or the previous taxation year; and

(c) the corporation has, together with any associated corporation, in either the current or the previous taxation year:

  (i) taxable income not exceeding $400,000 (i.e., the small business deduction limit), and

  (ii) taxable capital employed in Canada for the taxation year not exceeding $10,000,000.

A corporation will be considered to have a "perfect compliance history" at the time that a quarterly instalment is due if, throughout the 12-month period before that time, it has no compliance irregularities pertaining to remittance of tax and filing of returns under the *Income Tax Act* or the GST/HST portion of the *Excise Tax Act*.

Eligible CCPCs will be permitted three options to determine the amount of their quarterly instalments, computed as follows:

(a) four instalments equal to $\frac{1}{4}$ of the estimated tax payable for the current taxation year;

(b) four instalments equal to $\frac{1}{4}$ of the tax payable for the previous taxation year; or

(c)(i) a first instalment equal to $\frac{1}{4}$ of the tax payable for the second preceding year, and

  (ii) three instalments equal to $\frac{1}{3}$ of the amount by which the tax payable for the previous taxation year exceeds the first instalment paid for the current year.

This pattern of three options parallels that for quarterly instalments paid by individuals, as outline above, and for monthly instalments paid by corporations that are not eligible for quarterly instalments, to be discussed next. The only difference is in the third option, which varies with the frequency of instalments.

Interest and penalty provisions that are applicable to other corporations are discussed in the following section.

¶14,040.30   *Other corporations*

Corporations that are not eligible CCPCs must make monthly instalment payments of their tax at the end of each month. The basics of the calculation of monthly instalments, along with the liability of all corporations for interest and penalties, are illustrated by the following problem.

¶14,040.20

Example Problem

No Flab Enterprises Limited is an incorporated company involved in the sale of muscle building and physical fitness equipment. For the fiscal year ended March 31, 2004, the company generated taxes payable of $1,860,000. In fiscal 2005, taxes payable were $1,900,000.

Mr. Flab, president and controlling shareholder of the company, planned a reduced sales effort on his part for the fiscal year ended March 31, 2006. As a result, he estimated the company's taxes payable at $1,524,000 for the year and paid 12 equal monthly instalments based on this amount. By March 2006, Mr. Flab had tabulated the profits and knew that the company's taxes payable would be $2,154,000.

Since Mr. Flab had reinvested all of the profits for fiscal 2006, he did not have the cash to pay the additional $630,000 in tax, so he paid nothing further. He filed the corporation's tax return on December 31, 2006, and, in order to avoid showing the further taxes payable, he did not report income for the corporation's 2006 fiscal year, thereby reducing taxes for the year by the $630,000. He reasoned that he would declare this income in the following year and pay the taxes on that income then.

Furthermore, instead of using the corporate tax return form readily available at his local District Tax Services Office, he filed his corporation's return on some accounting paper. As a result of filing in this way, however, his return did not contain all of the information required to be filed by the corporation.

In May 2007, the corporation's file was randomly selected for a full-scale audit during which discussions with Mr. Flab revealed the omitted taxable income. He argued with the tax auditor that the added taxable income resulted from his forgetting to record the sales of 123,000 units in September 2006. He was forcefully requested to pay the added tax by June 30, 2007 which he planned to do by that date. In addition to the added tax and interest, the tax auditor decided to assess the corporation for appropriate penalties, in this case, based on the evidence on hand. These were included in the notice of assessment requiring payment by June 30, 2007.

— REQUIRED

(A) Set out the basis on which the interest that the corporation must pay on June 30, 2007 would be computed, assuming it was not eligible for the small business deduction.

ITA: 125

(B) Indicate which penalties would be imposed.

— SOLUTION

(A) Interest

Corporations, other than eligible CCPCs, must make instalments on their income tax liability at the end of each month. The corporation must compute the instalments on one, usually the least, of the following bases:

ITA: 157(1)

(i) $1/12$ of the estimated tax liability calculated at current rates on the estimated taxable income for the current year (estimated to be $1,524,000 in taxes payable for the year in this case);

(ii) $1/12$ of the instalment base (defined, in essence, as tax payable for this company) for the immediately preceding taxation year (amounting to $1,900,000 for the year in this case); or

ITR: 5301

(iii) $1/12$ of the instalment base (defined as above) for the second preceding taxation year (amounting to $1,860,000 for the year in this case) for the first two months, then for the next 10 months $1/10$ of the quantity computed as the instalment base (defined as above) for the immediately preceding taxation year minus the amount paid in instalments for the first two months.

Whichever base is used for installments, the difference between the estimate of the tax payable at the end of the fiscal period and the instalments paid must be paid two months after the end of the taxation year. However, for Canadian-controlled private corporations eligible for the small business deduction in the current or preceding year and with taxable income for an associated group of corporations under the small business deduction limit of $400,000 in the preceding year, the balance of tax is not due until three months after the end of the taxation year. Prudent financial management would suggest that a corporation use the base which allows it to

ITA: 125

pay the lowest amount in monthly instalments, while avoiding interest on a deficiency of installments. In periods of rising income, this will generally be the third alternative.

The monthly instalments of corporate tax and other amounts payable by corporations will be deemed for the rules relating to interest and penalties to have been remitted only when received by the Receiver General or his or her representative, not on the date of mailing.   ITA: 248(7)

Interest paid on a deficiency of instalments of a corporation is limited to interest on the   ITA: 161(4.1)
difference between the amount of instalments actually paid and an amount based on the least of: ITA: 157(1)

(a) the tax payable for the year (in this case $2,154,000);

(b) the instalment base for the immediately preceding taxation year (in this case $1,900,000); and

(c) the instalment base for the second preceding taxation year (in this case $1,860,000) and the immediately preceding taxation year (in this case $1,900,000).

The deficiency of instalments in this case could be set out as follows (000s omitted from chart):

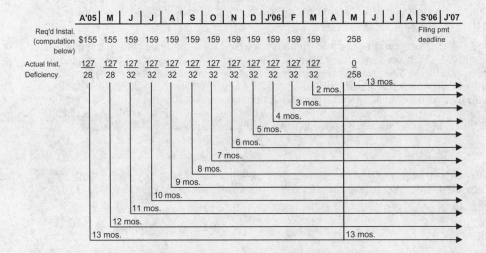

The required instalments are computed as follows:

(a) first two months: $\frac{1}{12} \times \$1,860,000 = \$155,000$

(b) next 10 months: $\frac{1}{10} \times [\$1,900,000 - (2 \times 155,000)] = \$159,000$

(c) final instalment: $\$2,154,000 - [(10 \times \$159,000) + (2 \times \$155,000)] = \$254,000$

Interest is imposed at prescribed rates on underpaid instalments. This interest runs from the   ITA: 161(2); ITR: 4301
time when the instalment payment was due to either the date of payment or the date when the   ITA: 157(1)(b)
remainder of tax payable should be paid, whichever is earlier, and is compounded daily. Interest is   ITA: 161(1)
imposed on the tax *and interest* owing on May 31, 2006 from the date the remainder of tax
payable and interest payable is due until it is paid on June 30, 2007.

(B) Penalties

A penalty is provided for failure to file the corporate tax return on September 30, 2006. The   ITA: 162(1)(a)
penalty is 5% of the tax unpaid at the date on which the return was due for filing. In this case,
since the return was not filed on time in the prescribed form, the penalty would be 5% of the
$630,000 in unpaid taxes or $31,500. In addition, the provision levies a further penalty of 1% of   ITA: 162(1)(b)
the unpaid tax per complete month that the return was past due for up to 12 months. In this case,
the penalty would be 1% of the unpaid taxes of $630,000 for three months or $18,900.

The Act imposes a penalty of $100 for failing to provide the required information on a   ITA: 162(5)
prescribed form.

Where information is provided resulting in lower tax than that under proper information, the penalty is the greater of $100 and 50% of the difference in tax liability. In this case, the penalty would be 50% of the $630,000 in reduced taxes or $315,000. *ITA: 163(2)*

Interest is charged on unpaid penalties, calculated from the date the tax return was due. *ITA: 161(11), 162, 163*

The Act imposes a penalty of 50% of the excess interest, if any, (after any interest offsets) charged on deficient instalments of tax minus the greater of $1,000 or 25% of the interest if no instalments had been paid. *ITA: 161, 163.1*

¶14,050 Books and Records

Taxpayers are required to keep adequate books and records. This requirement is for all persons carrying on a business and persons required to pay or collect taxes, among others. While the word "adequate" is not defined or illustrated, the records (including inventory documentation) must be sufficient to support a determination of income subject to tax or of amounts to be remitted. In an Information Circular, the CRA implies that basic transaction data, including invoices, receipts, contracts, bank statements and cancelled cheques, would be the minimum required. Electronic images of this data are acceptable as a method of keeping records. *ITA: 230* *IC 78-10R4*

All such books and records must be maintained at the taxpayer's place of business or residence in Canada until the taxpayer receives written permission to dispose of these materials. A set of rules prescribes a period for keeping certain records or books together with accounts and vouchers necessary to verify them and establishes a period of six years from the end of the last taxation year to which the records and books relate for all other cases not prescribed. Further subsections deal with a person who has not filed a return or a person who has a case under appeal, with a special request from the Minister and with permission to dispose of records and books before the expiration of the required period. If such materials are microfilmed to save space, guidelines for this procedure are set out in an Information Circular. *ITA: 230(4); ITR: 5800* *IC 78-10R4*

Failure to keep adequate books and records is a punishable offence. Punishable offences will be discussed later in this chapter. *ITA: 238(1)*

¶14,100 POWERS AND OBLIGATIONS OF THE CRA

While the Department of Finance formulates tax policy, the CRA controls, regulates, manages and supervises the income tax system. The duties of the Minister of National Revenue and the employees of his or her agency are set out in the Act. The Commissioner of the Canada Revenue Agency, the CRA's chief executive officer, is empowered to exercise all the powers and perform all of the duties of the Minister under the Act. *ITA: 220*

¶14,110 Assessments and Reassessments

Having made a quick check of the return in the initial assessment process for verifying the basic information and calculations, the CRA can do a detailed review of the return, subject to the time restrictions, where applicable. The CRA may assess tax, interest and penalties and, furthermore, it may reassess or make additional assessments in the following situations: *ITA: 152(4)*

(a) at any time, if the taxpayer or person filing the return has made any misrepresentation that is attributable to neglect, carelessness or wilful default or has committed any fraud in filing the return or in supplying any information under the Act;

(b) within the normal reassessment period, which is defined to be four years from the date of mailing a notice of assessment for all corporations, other than Canadian-controlled private corporations, and three years from the date of mailing of a notice of assessment for Canadian-controlled private corporations and all other taxpayers; *ITA: 152(3.1)*

(c) within three years of the expiration of the normal reassessment period, if the taxpayer was reassessed or was eligible to be reassessed. This allows the CRA to reassess, for example, for both a given year and any of the previous years to which a loss may have been carried back;

ITA: 152(6)

(d) at any time, if the taxpayer has filed, within the normal assessment period, a waiver of the statutory assessment period. A waiver might be used where the taxpayer wishes to be able to re-open a return for a year in which there was a very complex problem that is expected to take longer than the normal assessment period to sort out. The ability to reassess is *limited* to the matter(s) specified in the waiver, and the waiver can be revoked upon six months' notice.

The normal reassessment period can be summarized as follows.

Taxpayers	Normal reassessment period
Individuals	3 years
Trusts	3 years
CCPCs	3 years
Corporations other than CCPCs	4 years

The Act gives the Minister the discretion to reassess beyond "the normal reassessment period" where an application has been made by an individual or a testamentary trust for a reduction of taxes, interest and penalties. Taxpayers might make such an application where they inadvertently forget to claim a deduction or tax credit. However, it should be remembered that the provision gives the Minister the discretion to either reject or accept the application. In addition, the Minister also has the discretion to waive any assessed interest and penalties. For requests made after 2004, there is a 10-year limit on a reassessment and a waiver in these circumstances.

ITA: 152(4.2)

ITA: 220(3.1)
ITA: 152(4.2), 220(3.1)

The Minister is permitted to reassess beyond "the normal reassessment period" in situations where a reassessment within "the normal reassessment period" affects the tax liability for a year which is outside "the normal reassessment period". However, a reassessment of this type is permitted only to the extent that it relates to the change in a particular balance of a taxpayer for a particular year. For example, if the amount of a net capital loss is redetermined by a subsequent assessment within "the normal reassessment period" but impacts on the carryback or carryforward of taxation periods outside of "the normal reassessment period", then the Minister has the authority to reassess those statute-barred taxation years. Obviously, this provision can work either in favour of or to the disadvantage of the taxpayer.

ITA: 152(4.3), 152(4.4)

Where fraud or misrepresentation is alleged through the issue of a reassessment after the normal assessment period, the onus is on the CRA to prove it if the taxpayer appeals the assessment. However, having proved it, the onus shifts to the taxpayer to show that the assessment of tax resulting from the fraud or misrepresentation is incorrect. In tax matters, the taxpayer always has the burden of proving that an assessment is incorrect, since it is assumed that under our self-assessment system the taxpayer has all of the basic data under his or her own control.[2]

In the case of *M.N.R. v. Taylor*, it was established that the standard of proof need only be that of the "balance of probabilities" used in civil cases rather than the more rigourous standard of "beyond reasonable doubt" used in criminal proceedings.

61 DTC 1139 (Ex. Ct.)

It should also be noted that misrepresentation has been interpreted to include "innocent" misrepresentation, that is, a false statement made in the honest belief that it is true, but under the current wording of the Act it may be more restricted in concept. Finally, it should be noted that where the Minister reassesses beyond the normal reassessment period, the

ITA: 152(4.01), 152(5)

---

[2] This onus of proof was affirmed in the case of *Violi v. M.N.R.*, 80 DTC 1191 (T.R.B.).

¶14,110

reassessment may only be made in respect of an amount which the taxpayer failed to include in the situation under consideration either for fraud or misrepresentation or for the waiver of the normal reassessment period.

Example Problem

Mr. Don Godfather filed a personal tax return on April 30, 2007 declaring income of $2,500 for the year ended December 31, 2006. As a result of an investigation, the CRA determined that, at December 31, 2005, Mr. Godfather had total assets estimated at $125,000 and total liabilities estimated at $90,000. At December 31, 2006, the taxpayer had total assets estimated at $140,000 and total liabilities estimated at $102,500. It was also determined by the CRA that a sum of $15,500 represented personal or living expenses of the taxpayer and it was further established that the taxpayer won $1,000 from playing poker with friends during the course of the year.

— *REQUIRED*

(A) What legal right given by the Act does the CRA have to dispute Mr. Godfather's signed declaration of income?

(B) What will the CRA argue is the income of Mr. Godfather for 2006?

(C) What are the possible arguments available to him to substantiate a lower income figure?

— *SOLUTION* [*See Philippe Tremblay v. M.N.R.*, 54 DTC 132 (T.A.B.).][3]

(A) The Minister of National Revenue is not bound by a return of information supplied by or on behalf of a taxpayer, and may, notwithstanding such a return of information, assess the taxpayer. It is under this provision that the Minister of National Revenue, where he or she is dissatisfied with a return, makes what are known as arbitrary assessments, in which he or she assesses the income which he or she believes the taxpayer to have had.

ITA: 152(7)

(B) The most common method used is the "net worth" method which involves ascertaining the taxpayer's net worth at the beginning and end of the period. The income for the period is arrived at by adding the increase in net worth to his estimated non-deductible expenditures and deducting non-taxable receipts such as gifts. In the problem at hand, the following estimate of income might be made:

(i) net worth (05)	= assets (05) − liabilities (05)	
	= $125,000 − $90,000	
	= $35,000	
(ii) net worth (06)	= assets (06) − liabilities (06)	
	= $140,000 − $102,500	
	= $37,500	
(iii) increase in net worth	= $37,500 − $35,000 = $2,500	
(iv) income	= increase in net worth + personal or living expenses − windfalls	
	= $2,500 + $15,500 − $1,000	
	= $17,000	

(C) The onus is on the taxpayer to show that this assessment is incorrect. The taxpayer might, therefore, argue using appropriate evidence that:

(i) net worth (05) was actually higher than estimated because assets (05) were higher or liabilities (05) were lower;

(ii) net worth (06) was actually lower than estimated because assets (06) were lower (e.g., they belonged to a spouse) or liabilities (06) were higher;

(iii) personal or living expenses were actually lower than estimated; or

(iv) windfalls (e.g., inheritance, gambling winnings) were actually higher.

---

[3] For other cases involving the use of arbitrary assessments, see *George v. M.N.R.*, 64 DTC 516 (T.A.B.), and *Courtois v. The Queen*, 79 DTC 506 (T.R.B.), and 80 DTC 6175 (F.C.T.D.).

¶14,120   Refunds and Interest

The Act also requires the Minister to determine the amount of any refund owing to a taxpayer as a result of overpayment of tax. The Minister *may* pay the refund upon assessment but *must* pay it upon application in writing by the taxpayer within the normal reassessment period. However, the Minister is given the authority to make refunds of tax paid beyond "the normal reassessment period". After 2004, there is a 10-year limit on such refunds. As a practical matter, refund cheques are generally mailed out with notices of assessment. If the taxpayer has other tax liabilities, the Minister may apply the refund to that liability.

ITA: 152
ITA: 164

ITA: 164(1.5)

Interest, compounded daily at the prescribed rate shown in Exhibit 14-1, is paid in most cases on overpayments of tax from the latest of:

ITA: 164(3)

   (a) the day the overpayment arose;

   (b) for individuals, 30 days after the balance-due day for the year, which is April 30 of the following year;

   (c) for corporations, 120 days after the end of the taxation year; and

   (d) where the return was filed after the filing-due date, 30 days after the date the return was filed for individuals, and the day the return was filed for corporations.

Where a refund arose from a loss carryback or other provision that changed the tax payable in a previous year, no interest is payable for the period prior to the filing of the tax return for the subsequent year in which the loss was established. Similar rules are provided for other carryback provisions in the Act. The effect of the loss carryback is also ignored in computing interest charged on deficient instalments in that carryback year.

ITA: 164(5)

ITA: 164(5.1)
ITA: 161(7)

Note that any refund interest received is taxable as interest income in the year received.

¶14,200   RIGHTS OF THE TAXPAYER

¶14,210   Objections and Appeals

A taxpayer may discover that the CRA disagrees with his or her calculation of tax payable either when a CRA auditor questions particular items (more usual for large corporations which routinely undergo an audit every few years) or when a notice of assessment or reassessment is received. If matters cannot be resolved favourably through informal negotiation, the next step is to file a notice of objection. All taxpayers, except individuals, must file a notice of objection within 90 days of the mailing of the notice of assessment. The due date for the notice of objection for individuals and testamentary trusts is the later of:

ITA: 165(1)(*b*)

   (a) one year after the filing-due date of the taxpayer for the year; and

   (b) 90 days after the day of mailing of the notice of assessment.

The "filing-due date" is defined to be the day on or before which the taxpayer's return for the year is required to be filed, and is:

ITA: 248(1) "filing-due date"

   (a) for a trust, 90 days after the end of the year;

   (b) for a deceased individual who died after October of one year or before June 16 of the next year, the later of six months after the day of death and the date the return would otherwise be required to be filed; and

   (c) in any other case, April 30 of the following year or June 15 of the following year where an individual or a cohabiting spouse carried on a business in the year.

Deadlines for the filing of a Notice of Objection are summarized as follows.

Taxpayers	Notice of objection due date
Individuals & testamentary trusts	Later of – Mailing date on the Notice + 90 days – Tax return filing-due date + 1 year
Other taxpayers	Mailing date on the Notice + 90 days

Even if the dispute appears headed for a favourable resolution, taxpayers often file a notice of objection as protection if the 90-day period is about to expire. Limits are placed upon the right to object to assessments and determinations in respect of court decisions and specified provisions.

ITA: 165(1.1), 165(1.2)

A notice of objection can be delivered or mailed to the Chief of Appeals in a Tax Services Office or Taxation Centre of the CRA. The objection may be submitted on Form T400A. The use of this form is not mandatory. The only requirement is that the notice must contain the facts and reasons for the appeal. The notice of objection is limited for individuals and trusts to assessments under Part I of the Act, individual surtax and tax on Old Age Security benefits.

ITA: 165(2)

ITA: 165(2.1)

¶14,220　Amended Returns

The Act does not provide general procedures for filing an amended tax return, other than:

- situations relating to reassessments where options granted by a taxpayer are exercised in a subsequent year;

ITA: 49(4)

- a situation which requires the Minister to amend a return if a loss or tax credit is being carried back to that year; and

ITA: 152(6)

- situations relating to amendments made by a legal representative of a deceased taxpayer.

ITA: 164(6)

With respect to the carryback of a loss, it should be noted that the Minister is only required to do so if the prescribed form (e.g., the T1A for individuals or T2A for corporations) or an amended return is filed by the date the tax return for the year the loss is incurred is required to be filed.

To amend other items, if the 90-day period for filing a Notice of Objection has not expired, the return may be amended by filing the Notice of Objection. Otherwise, the CRA's administrative policy is that a return may only be amended if the taxpayer makes a written request for a refund within three years of the end of the year in question and:

IC 75-7R3

(a) the CRA is satisfied that the previous assessment was wrong;

(b) the reassessment can be made within the normal reassessment period or the taxpayer has filed a waiver;

(c) the requested decrease in taxable income assessed is not based solely on a permissive deduction such as an increased claim for capital cost allowance where the taxpayer originally claimed less than the allowable amount; and

(d) application for a refund is not based solely on a successful appeal to the courts by another taxpayer.

Often, a previous assessment was not wrong but the taxpayer wishes to amend the discretionary deductions he or she claimed (or failed to claim) in a previous year. For example, a company in a loss position may choose not to claim capital cost allowance in the loss year because unclaimed capital cost allowance can be carried forward indefinitely whereas non-capital losses expire in seven years. Two years later, the company may find itself profitable, and may wish to claim the capital cost allowance for the previous year to increase the loss carryforward.

The CRA allows such amendments to change discretionary deductions where the amendment would not alter taxes payable for that year. Where a loss is increased by claiming additional capital cost allowance, no increase in taxes payable could, of course, result.

¶14,300   OBLIGATIONS OF PAYERS AND OTHER PERSONS

¶14,310   Employers

Every person paying salary, wages, or other remuneration or any of the other amounts listed in section 153 is required to withhold prescribed amounts from the payments and remit them to the Receiver General. Where the average monthly remittances, including CPP and EI premiums, in the second preceding calendar year are between $15,000 and $50,000, tax withheld from remuneration paid in the first 15 days of a month is due on the 25th of that month, and from remuneration paid in the balance of the month on the 10th of the following month. Where the average monthly remittances in any particular month exceed $50,000, employers are required to remit up to four times a month.

A regulation relaxes these rules on an elective basis as follows:

(a) employers with average monthly remittances in the preceding calendar year of less than $15,000 are required to remit on the 15th of the month following payment; and

(b) employers with average monthly remittances between $15,000 and $50,000 for the preceding calendar year (and over $50,000 in the second preceding year) are allowed to remit on the 25th and 10th days as described above.

Small employers with average monthly withholding amounts of less than $1,000 for the second preceding calendar year and no compliance irregularities in the preceding 12 months are allowed to remit quarterly. Remittances for each quarter are due April 15, July 15, October 15 and the following January 15.

The employee completes a TD1 form listing personal credits and certain other deductible amounts, and the withholding amount is based on gross salary less these amounts. The amounts of withholding on both periodic and lump-sum payments are prescribed. The employee can elect to increase the amount withheld if he or she so chooses.

In addition, the Act provides for a reduction in the amount withheld if the amount required to be withheld would cause "undue hardship". The CRA district offices will generally approve applications by employees for reduced withholding if a *pro forma* tax return indicates that a substantial refund will be forthcoming due to substantiated deductions such as RRSP contributions or support payments.

The payer is also required to file information returns as prescribed. Employers, for example, must complete forms T4 Summary and T4 Supplementary by the last day in February, and send two copies of the T4 Supplementary to the employee.

Every person paying a fee, commission or other amount to a non-resident in respect of services rendered in Canada is required to withhold 15%. Non-residents exempt from paying Canadian tax by virtue of the Act or a tax treaty can apply for a waiver of this requirement.

Any person required to withhold by section 153 who fails to withhold tax is liable for a penalty of 10% of the tax that should have been withheld, together with interest. A second or further occurrence of failure to withhold under section 153 will result in a penalty of 20% of the tax that should have been withheld. Withholding taxes will only be considered to have been received on time if received by the due date, i.e., postmarks will not suffice. Any person who withheld tax but failed to remit it is required to pay, in addition to the tax withheld, a penalty of 10% of the amount that should have been remitted. Once again, the penalty doubles to 20% of the tax withheld for second-time offenders. If a taxpayer had tax withheld at source and the withholder did not remit the amount, the CRA cannot require the taxpayer to pay the amount. See, for example, *Lalonde v. M.N.R.*, in which the employee was paid in

IC 84-1

ITR: 108(1.1)

ITR: 108(1.11)

ITR: 108(1)

ITR: 100–200

ITA: 153(1.1)

ITR: 205

ITR: 105

ITA: 227(8)

ITA: 248(7)
ITA: 227(9)

82 DTC 1772 (T.R.B.)

cash and the employer neither remitted the tax nor provided a T4 or other documentation that tax had been withheld.

> ### Example Problem
>
> The *Toronto Gazette* employs a number of foreign correspondents who are often required to report from war zones. On September 30, 2007, "Ace" Johnson, a veteran reporter, is killed while reporting from Iraq. The *Gazette* decides to continue his monthly salary of $4,000 to his widow for the balance of 2007.
>
> — *REQUIRED*
>
> What are the obligations of the *Gazette* in terms of withholding tax under the Act?
>
> — *SOLUTION*
>
> The payer is required to withhold tax on a death benefit, which is defined as an amount received "upon or after the death of an employee in recognition of the employee's service". The amount of withholding for periodic payments of remuneration is prescribed. Remuneration is defined as including a death benefit. However, the definition of death benefit excludes the lesser of $10,000 or the amount received as the death benefit. Thus, withholding would only be required on the amount received in excess of $10,000 (i.e., $2,000 = ($4,000 × 3) – $10,000, in this case).
>
> The Regulations are silent on how the withholding should be spread, e.g., over all the payments or only once the total amount paid exceeds $10,000. If the widow has no other source of income for the year, the tax on the $2,000 would be less than her personal tax credits for the year and she could file a TD1 so that no withholding would be required. Otherwise, the CRA has suggested that the lump-sum withholding rate in Regulation 103(4) ($^{103}/_{152}$ of 10% in Ontario on amounts less than $5,000) would be satisfactory.

ITA: 153(1)(d), 248(1) "death benefit"; ITR: 102(1)

ITR: 101

¶14,320 Obligations of Other Payers, Trustees, etc.

¶14,325 Payments to residents of Canada

The Act allows the Governor in Council to make any regulations requiring "any class of person to make information returns respecting any class of information required in connection with assessment under the Act". The provisions also require any such person to supply copies of the information to the person whose income is being reported. The Minister is allowed to demand a prescribed information return, and penalties for failure to make such returns are prescribed. In addition, the offences on which penalties are imposed apply to failure to make information returns, or giving false information on such returns.

ITA: 221(1)(d)

ITA: 162(7), 233

ITA: 238, 239

Regulations prescribe which persons are required to make information returns, and other information such as filing dates. In addition to employers, these regulations affect payers of interest, dividends and royalties and persons making payments to non-residents. Other persons required to make information returns include trustees of RRSPs and other deferred income plans. Unless otherwise indicated, such returns are due the last day of February (e.g., the T5 Summary and Supplementary in respect of dividends and interest).

ITR: 200–235

Promoters of tax shelters are required to file an information return in prescribed form containing information on the persons who acquired interests and the amount paid for each interest. There are also filing requirements for partnerships, and securities dealers handling sales of shares, commodities, etc., with penalties for failure to file, as discussed earlier.

ITA: 237.1

ITR: 229, 230

¶14,330 Payments to non-residents

The Act specifies the payments on which tax must be withheld by Canadians remitting amounts to non-residents. The rate of withholding specified is 25%, but this is often reduced or eliminated by the applicable tax treaty. Such payers are also required to file information returns (e.g., NR4 Summary and Supplementary). [The March 19, 2007 federal budget proposed to eliminate the withholding tax on all arm's length payments of interest to

ITA: 212

IC 76-12R5

non-residents and to non-arm's length U.S. treaty residents with a three-year phase-out for the non-arm's length payments subject to the U.S. treaty.]

Non-residents receiving rent from real property in Canada or a timber royalty in Canada can elect to file a Canadian income tax return reporting the net rental or royalty income, rather than paying the flat withholding tax (under Part XIII) on the gross rents or royalties. There are no personal credits permitted on such returns, but the graduated tax rates do apply to individuals. A return must be filed within two years from the end of the year in which the rent or royalty was paid and is in addition to any other returns that may be required under Part I. While withholdings must still be made by the non-resident's agent on the gross rent or royalty, the election allows for a refund of excess Part XIII tax withheld, where Part I tax on the net rental or royalty income is lower.

ITA: 216

ITA: 216

ITA: 215(3)

If, in addition to the general election, the non-resident files an election on form NR6 with the CRA, committing to file a Canadian return relating to the rents or royalties, an agent for the non-resident can withhold tax on the basis of net (instead of gross) income. However, the same withholding rate applies. In this case, the tax return must be filed within six months from the end of the year that the rents or royalties are paid.

ITA: 216, 216(4)

Failure to withhold, remit, or file information returns results in the same penalties imposed on persons making payments to residents in Canada.

¶14,335   Foreign reporting requirements

The Act imposes reporting requirements on Canadian corporations with respect to transactions with non-arm's length non-residents to be filed within six months from the end of the year.

ITA: 233.1

Canadian taxpayers and partnerships are required to report certain information relating to foreign investments.

The Act requires a person who transfers or loans property to certain foreign trusts to file information returns. Certain resident taxpayers and partnerships are required to file information returns relating to foreign property held, if the cost of such property exceeds $100,000. Resident taxpayers and partnerships are required to file information returns with respect to foreign affiliates Certain Canadian entities that own a beneficial interest in a non-resident trust and are not required to file an information return for transfers or loans to a foreign trust are required to file an information return in each year they receive a distribution from or become indebted to the trust.

ITA: 233.2
ITA: 233.3

ITA: 233.4
ITA: 233.2, 233.5

Penalties for failure to file such returns and for providing false statement or omissions in these information returns are provided.

ITA: 162(7)–(10.1), 163

Example Problem

Reconsider the previous example problem.

— *REQUIRED*

If the death benefit had been paid to a resident of the U.K. instead of Canada, what would the withholding tax requirement have been?

— *SOLUTION*

A 25% withholding tax is imposed on a death benefit as defined by the Act, i.e., the amount in excess of $10,000. The Canada–U.K. Tax Convention is silent on the issue of death benefits and, thus, the 25% rate would still apply.

ITA: 212(1)(j)

¶14,340 Deceased Taxpayers

A number of special rules apply to tax returns and payment of tax for deceased taxpayers. Note that rules governing the deemed disposition of the deceased's capital property are covered in Chapter 8.

¶14,345 Tax returns

There are two provisions which govern the filing of deceased taxpayers' tax returns. Where the individual has died after October of a year and on or before the usual filing due date for the year (i.e., April 30 or June 15 of the following year), the individual's legal representative has six months or until the day the return would otherwise have to be filed, whichever is later, to file the return. Where the taxpayer has died outside of this time period, the normal filing deadline of April 30th (or June 15 where the deceased individual or his or her spouse carried on business in the year) is imposed. The key to understanding how these two provisions interact is to identify the particular tax return year to which these rules apply.

ITA: 150(1)(*b*)
ITA: 150(1)(*d*)

¶14,345.10 *Prior taxation year*

Where the taxpayer has died in the period from January 1 to the usual filing due date for the prior year, the legal representative of the taxpayer has 6 months after the date of death to file a tax return for the immediately preceding year and pay the balance of tax. For example, for a taxpayer who died on March 1, 2007 without filing his or her 2006 tax return, the return and balance would be due September 1, 2007.

ITA: 150(1)(*b*)

¶14,345.20 *Terminal return*

The legal representative of the taxpayer must also file a final or terminal return for the period in the year to the date of death (e.g., January 1 to March 1 in the above example). The deadline for the terminal return and the payment of any balance owing depends on the date of death. For those persons who have died between January 1 and October 31, the terminal return is due April 30 or June 15 of the following year. For those persons who have died between November 1 and December 15, the terminal return is due 6 months from the date of death, or in the case of an individual who carried on business in the year, June 15, and for deaths between December 16 and December 31, 6 months from the date of death. Therefore, in the example of a death on March 1, 2007, the terminal return for 2007 is due April 30 or June 15, 2008. No instalments are required in respect of a terminal return.

Amounts in respect of periodic payments, such as interest, rent, salary, etc., must be accrued on a daily basis to the date of death and reported on the terminal return.

ITA: 70(1)

The full year's personal tax credits may be claimed, although the taxpayer was alive for only part of the year. The reserves that may be claimed on a terminal return are limited.

ITA: 72

¶14,350 Rights or things

The legal representative of the taxpayer is allowed to report the income from "rights or things" of the deceased on a separate tax return. The return is due on the date that is the later of one year after death and 90 days after assessment of any return for the year of death. This alternative return is generally advantageous, since personal tax credits equal to those claimed in the terminal return may be claimed on the rights or things return as well as on the terminal return, in addition to the benefit of lower marginal tax brackets on both returns.

ITA: 70(2)
ITA: 118(1), 118(2), 118.93

Rights or things are amounts which are receivable at the date of death but have not been received such as:

- matured, uncashed bond coupons;

- declared, unpaid dividends;

- farm crops; and

- unpaid salary, commissions, vacation pay or CPP, if pertaining to pay periods *completed* before date of death.

Alternatively, the legal representative can assign, under the directions of a will, the income from "rights or things" to a particular beneficiary or beneficiaries. However, the income must be distributed to the beneficiary prior to the expiry of the deadline for the rights or things election as described above. This alternative would be advantageous where the beneficiary would be taxed at a lower rate as compared to the rights or things election for a separate return of the deceased. `ITA: 70(3)` `ITA: 70(2)`

The CRA states that where there is genuine doubt about whether the income is a periodic payment or a right or thing, its treatment is generally resolved in favour of the taxpayer. `IT-212R3`

Rights or things do not include accrued periodic amounts taxable in the terminal return. With the provision of acceptable security, tax owing on a rights or things return may be paid in up to 10 annual instalments. Of course, interest will be charged until the balance owing is paid in full. `ITA: 70(1), 159(5)` `ITA: 70(2)`

¶14,355 Other return

One other return may be used to report income of the deceased taxpayer.

Beneficiaries of a trust report their trust income based on the income earned by the trust in the trust year that ends in the taxation year of the beneficiary. Also, a testamentary trust can have a year-end other than December 31 as long as the first year-end chosen is not more than 12 months from the death of the individual who created the trust. As a result, an individual beneficiary of the trust who dies after the trust year-end will have to report not only the income from the trust (12 months), but also any further income earned by the trust after the trust year-end and before the date of death that is payable to the deceased individual. For example, assume that a testamentary trust had a year-end of March 31, 2007, and that the sole beneficiary died on July 31, 2007. On the final return, the deceased would report the 12 months of income from the trust year that ended March 31, plus the four months of income earned by the trust from March 31 to July 31. To alleviate this burden, the Act allows the representative of the deceased to file a separate return that includes the "stub period" income, being that income earned by the trust from March 31 to July 31. `ITA: 104(23)` `ITA: 104(23)(d)`

In this case, personal tax credits equal to those claimed in the terminal return may be claimed in the separate return. `ITA: 118(1), 118(2), 118.93`

This return is due on the date that is the later of six months after the date of death and April 30 or June 15 of the year following the year of death.

¶14,360 Personal tax credits

As previously noted, the personal tax credits can be claimed on all of the three tax returns. This includes the basic personal credit, the married or equivalent-to-married credit, the infirm dependant credit and the age credit. The marital status tax credit must be reduced by the income of the surviving spouse for the full year of death in excess of the threshold for that credit. For the remainder of the credits, the claim on the terminal return and the elective returns, combined, cannot exceed the credits that could have been claimed on the terminal return, if no elective returns were filed. Some credits can only be claimed on the return on which the related income is reported (e.g., pension credit, CPP and EI credits). Note that the credit for the transfer of unused credits for a spouse can only be deducted in the terminal return according to CRA administrative practice. `ITA: 118(1), 118(2)` `IT-513R, Appendix A — Terminology: "Income"` `ITA: 118.93` `ITA: 118.8; IT-350R3, par. 11`

¶14,355

¶14,400 OBLIGATIONS OF THE REGISTRANT UNDER THE EXCISE TAX ACT

¶14,410 Collection and Remittance of Tax

A registrant who makes a taxable supply in Canada is required, as an agent of the Crown, to collect any tax payable by the recipient in respect of the supply. ETA: 221(1)

Any Goods and Services Tax (GST) collected by a person is deemed to be held in trust for the Crown until it is remitted. Input tax credits that may be claimed by the person may be deducted from the amount held in trust when the GST return for the period is filed. ETA: 222(1)
ETA: 222(2)

¶14,420 Disclosure of Tax

Registrants are required to provide certain information regarding the GST content of taxable supplies made by them. Registrants may either: ETA: 223(1)

(a) indicate on the invoice or receipt issued, or on the written agreement entered into, the consideration paid or payable and the amount of GST payable in respect of that supply; or

(b) indicate on the documentation that the amount paid or payable by the recipient includes the GST payable in respect of that supply.

The Disclosure of Tax (GST/HST) Regulations (P.C. 1990-2747) prescribe a third method of fulfilling the disclosure requirements. Where a registrant includes GST in the price but does not indicate on the invoice or receipt the amount of GST payable, or that GST is included in the price, the registrant must provide a clearly visible notice at the place of supply (the business establishment) that GST is included in the price of purchases. As with the second disclosure method noted above, the purchaser is able to compute the GST content in purchases of taxable supplies by multiplying the tax-included price by 6/106.

The ETA requires that a registrant to provide, if requested by another registrant receiving a supply from that registrant, particulars of the transaction that may be necessary to substantiate an input tax credit claim. ETA: 223(2)

¶14,430 Returns and Reporting Periods

Registrants are required to file returns for each reporting period by the dates specified. The net tax for a reporting period must generally be remitted by the date on which the return is filed, as discussed in the next section. The reporting period of a registrant may be either the fiscal month, quarter or year. If a registrant's reporting period is the fiscal month, a return must be filed for each month. If the fiscal quarter is used as the reporting period, a return must be filed for each quarter. If the fiscal year is used as the reporting period, only one return must be filed for the year, although quarterly instalments must be filed, as discussed below. Conditions for these options are discussed below. ETA: 238(1)

The "fiscal year" of a person is defined as either the person's taxation year, or the period elected to be the person's fiscal year. "Taxation year" is defined in the same subsection as the person's taxation year for purposes of the *Income Tax Act*. Where the taxation year of a person is not the calendar year, the person may elect to have fiscal years that are calendar years, effective on the first day of any calendar year. "Fiscal month" and "fiscal quarter" are determined in accordance with the ETA. ETA: 123(1)

ETA: 244(1)

ETA: 243(1), 243(2)

In general, larger businesses that are registered for GST purposes are required to adopt monthly reporting periods, and thus must file GST returns on a monthly basis. A registrant's reporting period is automatically the fiscal month if the registrant's yearly revenues from taxable (including zero-rated) supplies exceeds $6 million. Revenue in these circumstances is determined by reference to the registrant's threshold amount for the fiscal year and the fiscal quarter. The threshold amount for a fiscal year and fiscal quarter refers to taxable (including zero-rated) supplies made during the preceding fiscal year or preceding fiscal quarters ETA: 245(2) ending in the current year. Thus, monthly returns are required where revenue is greater than $6 million in the preceding fiscal year or in the previous quarters ending in the current fiscal year.

Quarterly and annual reporting periods are available for smaller businesses, depending on the level of sales. Quarterly reporting is required where revenue is $6 million or less in the preceding fiscal year and in the preceding quarters ending in the current fiscal year. An election for quarterly reporting is also available in certain circumstances. An election to file on a yearly basis rather than quarterly is available where revenue in the preceding year does not exceed $500,000.[4] New registrants who qualify for annual reporting based on this threshold are automatically entitled to file on an annual basis (i.e., the election is not required).

ETA: 245(2)
ETA: 247(1)
ETA: 248

The above reporting period requirements are summarized by the following.

GST/HST Returns — Reporting periods & remittances

Annual taxable sales and revenues	Reporting period	Optional reporting periods
$500,000 or less	Annual	Monthly, quarterly
$500,001 – $6,000,000	Quarterly	Monthly
$6,000,001 or more	Monthly	Nil

Returns for monthly and quarterly filers must be filed within one month following the end of the registrant's reporting period. Persons filing on an annual basis are required to file their annual return within three months following the end of their reporting period.

Any registrant can opt to file on a monthly basis if desired. For example, exporters may wish to file on a monthly basis in order to obtain GST refunds on a more frequent basis (since exports are zero-rated). However, once a registrant has decided on the frequency of filing its GST return, it must proceed on that basis for the entire fiscal year.

ETA: 246(1)

A registrant can apply to the Minister of National Revenue to have one or more reporting periods designated for the purpose of not having to file returns. Reporting periods eligible for designation are essentially those in which the total of the GST collected (received) or collectible (receivable) for the period (plus any other amounts that are remittable for the period) does not exceed $1,000. Input tax credits or other allowable deductions are ignored for purposes of this calculation. If more than one period is to be designated, the $1,000 threshold is determined in a cumulative basis.

ETA: 238.1

Returns are generally filed on a legal-entity basis. However, where a corporation has divisions with separate accounting systems, an election can be made to file on a divisional basis. In these cases, the divisions must be identifiable by virtue of their activities or locations, and separate records must be maintained.

ETA: 239(1)

¶14,440   Remittance of Tax

In filing a return for a period, registrants are required to calculate "the net tax" for the period and to remit that tax. Where the net tax for a reporting period is a negative amount, a refund may be claimed. Net tax is determined by adding the total amount of GST that was collected (received) or became collectible (receivable) during the period plus any amount that is required to be added for that period, and then subtracting the total amount of input tax credits claimed for the period and any amount that may be deducted for the period. For example, assume $50,000 of GST has been collected, $10,000 is collectible but not yet collected, and another $5,000 must be added because a bad debt that was previously written off and deducted from net tax is recovered. Further, an input tax credit of $45,000 may be claimed and $6,000 may be deducted to reflect a refund made to a purchaser of excess GST that was previously collected. The net tax in this example is calculated as [($50,000 + $10,000

ETA: 228(1), 228(2)
ETA: 228(3)
ETA: 225(1)

---

[4] [The March 19, 2007 federal budget proposed to triple this threshold to $1.5 million, effective for fiscal years beginning after 2007.]

+ \$5,000) − (\$45,000 + \$6,000)] = \$14,000. Where net tax is owed for a reporting period, that amount must be remitted to the Receiver General by the date on which the return is due.

In determining net tax, where an amount was previously included in calculating the amount of GST that was collected or collectible for a period, it must not be included in a return for a subsequent period. Similarly, where an amount was previously claimed as an input tax credit, it may not be claimed again in a later period. These two subsections are intended to prevent double-counting.

ETA: 225(2)

ETA: 225(3)

There is a four-year time limit on claiming input tax credits. For most registrants, an input tax credit is not available unless it is claimed in a return filed within four years from the time the return in which the claim could have originally been made was required to be filed. For example, if a registrant who files GST returns on a monthly basis purchased goods to be used in commercial activities on February 1, 2005, an input tax credit could have been claimed in a return filed for that period (i.e., for the month of February), which is due March 31, 2005. If the input tax credit was not claimed at that time, the registrant has until March 31, 2009 to claim the credit before entitlement to the credit would be lost.

ETA: 225(4)

Large registrants, i.e., those with more than \$6 million in annual taxable supplies, face a two-year limit for carrying input tax credits. An input tax credit for a particular reporting period is not available to these registrants unless it is claimed in a return filed for a reporting period that ends within two years after the period in which the ITC could have first been claimed.

Where annual reporting has been elected, quarterly instalments of tax are required. The instalments are payable to the Receiver General within one month after the end of each fiscal quarter. The amount of each instalment is equal to one-quarter of the registrant's previous year's net tax. Where the instalment base for a reporting period is less than \$1,500, the instalment base for that period is deemed to be nil. [The March 19, 2007 federal budget proposed to double this threshold to \$3,000.]

ETA: 237, 248

Under the instalment base formula, a registrant is able to base instalments for the current year on an estimate of the net tax for the year, on a similar basis to income tax instalments. This is advantageous for registrants who anticipate that less tax will be payable in the current year than had been payable in the preceding year.

¶14,450 *Books and records*

Registrants are required to maintain documentation to support input tax credits, as prescribed by regulation. These requirements, which are contained in the Input Tax Credit (GST/HST) Information Regulations (P.C. 1990-2755), are not restricted in terms of form or physical characteristics. Supporting documentation may include invoices, receipts, credit card receipts, debit notes, books or ledgers of account, written contracts or agreements, computer records, and other validly issued or signed documents.

ETA: 169(4)

Depending on the value of the purchase, the information requirements vary. The relevant information and thresholds at which requirements change are summarized below.

(1) Purchases under \$30:

- the vendor's name or trading name,
- sufficient information to identify when the GST was paid or became payable, and
- the total consideration paid or payable for the supply.

(2) Purchases of \$30 or more and less than \$150:

- the above, plus
- the vendor's GST registration number, and
- the total amount of GST charged on the supply or, if prices are on a tax-included basis, a statement to this effect (however, if one document is used in respect of both taxable and exempt supplies, the tax status of each supply must be indicated).

(3) Purchases of $150 or more:

- the above, plus

- the purchaser's name or trading name,

- sufficient information to ascertain the terms of sale (e.g., cash or credit sale), and

- a description sufficient to identify the supply.

To a large extent, documents already being used to support expense deductions under the *Income Tax Act* may be used to support input tax credit claims. The retention period is also generally six years. Supporting documentation is not required for items such as a reasonable *per diem* reimbursements, or other cases where the Minister is satisfied that sufficient records are otherwise available.

ETA: 169(5)

Registrants are required to issue an appropriate document containing the requisite information if requested by a purchaser who is also a registrant.

ETA: 223(2)

Similar to the requirements under the *Income Tax Act*, adequate books and records must be kept. The following persons are required to maintain records and books of account for the CRA's audit purposes:

ETA: 286(1)

- persons who carry on business or engage in a commercial activity in Canada;

- persons who are required to file a GST return; or

- persons who make an application for a refund or rebate.

The records must be adequate to determine the amount of the person's liability under the ETA or the amount of any refund or rebate to which the person is entitled. The records must be kept in either English or French at the person's place of business in Canada, unless otherwise permitted by the Minister. As under the *Income Tax Act*, the retention period is generally six years. Chapter 15.2 of the GST/HST Memoranda Series sets out the CRA's administrative policy in respect of computerized records.

¶14,500   POWERS AND OBLIGATIONS OF THE CRA IN RESPECT OF THE EXCISE TAX ACT

While the Department of Finance has the responsibility for tax policy, the CRA is responsible for the administration and enforcement of the ETA. The duties of the Minister of National Revenue and his or her employees are set out in section 275 of the ETA. The Commissioner, the CRA's chief executive officer, is empowered to exercise all the powers and perform all of the duties of the Minister under the ETA. On imported goods, the GST is administered and enforced by the Canada Border Services Agency (CBSA).

¶14,510   Assessments and reassessments

The CRA is given broad powers to assess persons for tax remittable or payable, and for interest and penalties. Reassessments and additional assessments may also be made. The CRA may also assess or reassess rebate applications. Assessments must be made within the following time limits:

ETA: 296(1)
ETA: 297(1)
ETA: 298

(a) at any time, if the person has committed fraud or made any misrepresentation that is attributable to the person's neglect, carelessness or wilful default;

(b) within four years after the later of the day on which the return for a period was filed or the day on which it was required to be filed; or

(c) at any time if the person has filed a waiver.

The Minister of National Revenue has authority, on an *ex parte* application to the court, to obtain judicial authorization to assess and take action to recover an amount determined by the Minister to be remittable by a registrant at the time the application is heard. This gives the Minister the power to take action to recover tax before the normal due date for the registrant's remittance. Where the court is satisfied that any delay in issuing the assessment would jeopardize the collection of GST and consequently grants the authorization, the CRA will be permitted to issue the assessment and take immediate collection action.

ETA: 322.1

¶14,520   Refunds and interest

If the net tax for a reporting period is a negative amount, a refund may be claimed in the return for that period. The Minister is required to pay the refund with all due dispatch. Interest on unpaid refunds begins accruing 30 days after the tax return claiming the particular refund has been filed, provided that all required returns have been filed up to that time. Interest is payable at the prescribed rate.[5] In assessing net tax, the Minister is required to apply the amount of any net tax overpayment against any GST liability of the person for any other reporting period and refund that part of the overpayment that was not so applied.

ETA: 228(3)
ETA: 229(1)
ETA: 229(1), 229(2), 229(3)
ETA: 296(3)

Interest at the same prescribed rate used for late or deficient remittances and instalments is paid on overpayments of net tax 30 days from the later of:

(a) the day on which the return for the period was filed; and

(b) the day on which the return was required to be filed.

Interest on rebate claims is payable, provided that a rebate application has been filed; interest accrues from the 30th or 60th day after filing, depending on the nature of the rebate.

ETA: 297

Interest is compounded daily.[6] Any refund interest received is taxable under the *Income Tax Act* as interest income in the year received.

¶14,600   RIGHTS OF THE REGISTRANT

¶14,610   Objections and appeals

Where a person is unable to resolve a dispute with the CRA after receiving a notice of assessment, a notice of objection may be filed within 90 days of the mailing of the notice of assessment. As noted earlier in this chapter, taxpayers often file a notice of objection as protection if the 90-day period is about to expire, even if a favourable resolution appears likely.

ETA: 301(1.1)

If, in response to the notice of objection, the Minister confirms the assessment or reassesses, the person may appeal to the Tax Court of Canada. The appeal must be made within 90 days after notice is sent that the Minister has confirmed the assessment or has reassessed.

ETA: 302

As described earlier in this chapter, a person seeking to appeal to the Tax Court of Canada may choose to have the appeal heard under the more formal general procedure or under the informal procedure. The various time limits described earlier also apply to appeals that relate to GST.

A decision of the Tax Court of Canada may be appealed to the Federal Court of Appeal and from there, possibly to the Supreme Court of Canada.

---

[5] Subsection 229(2) provides that a net tax refund will not be paid to a person at any time until the person files all returns, of which the Minister of National Revenue has knowledge, that the person is required to file up to that time under the ETA (both GST/HST and non-GST/HST portions), the *Air Travellers Security Charge Act*, the *Excise Act, 2001*, and the *Income Tax Act*.

[6] Effective April 1, 2007, the calculation of interest rates was changed to the following:

- on amounts payable to the Minister, the 90-day treasury bill rate, adjusted quarterly, rounded up to the nearest whole percentage, plus four percentage points, and
- on amounts payable by the Minister, the 90-day treasury bill rate, adjusted quarterly, rounded up to the nearest whole percentage, plus two percentage points.

¶14,620   Amended returns and GST adjustments

The legislation does not contain any provisions regarding amendments to previously filed GST returns. The CRA's administrative guidelines regarding such adjustments are set out in Policy Paper P-149R. Registrants are advised to contact their local district office, in writing, to request adjustments to previously filed GST returns. Amounts included on previously filed GST returns may be adjusted, except where a registrant is attempting to increase the amount of input tax credits or other credit adjustments without a corresponding increase in GST liability for the same reporting period.

In certain circumstances, administrative flexibility may be exercised. For example, in the case of an annual filer who would be required to wait over 12 months in order to claim a missed input tax credit, the registrant may amend the originally submitted GST return through a request for an assessment or a reassessment of the previously filed return. Resource availability and the circumstances surrounding the registrant's request will be taken into account by the CRA in deciding whether to assess or reassess the previously filed return. Flexibility may also be exercised in situations of financial hardship where delaying a net tax refund by not making an adjustment for a missed input tax credit would have a severe negative impact on the registrant's business.

The legislation outlines the procedure for refunding GST to purchasers in certain circumstances. The ETA permits an adjustment, refund or credit of the GST in two situations.   ETA: 232
First, where an excess amount of GST has been charged or collected, and secondly, where consideration for a supply is reduced after the GST has been charged or collected and the supplier adjusts, refunds or credits the GST charged on the original consideration. Any such adjustment, refund or credit must be made within two years after the end of the supplier's reporting period in which the tax was collected or charged, or the price reduction was made. To document the tax adjustment, the supplier may issue a credit note or the recipient may issue a debit note.

¶14,700   SIMPLIFIED METHOD AND QUICK METHOD

Special simplified accounting methods have been introduced to help small businesses minimize paperwork and to reduce accounting and bookkeeping costs. These simplified accounting procedures are the Quick Method and the Simplified Method. The rules for these   ETA: 227(1)
methods are authorized in the ETA and are contained in the Streamlined Accounting (GST/HST) Regulations (P.C. 1990-2748).

The simplified method is available to small businesses with annual taxable supplies of $500,000 or less and taxable purchases (excluding zero-rated purchases) of $2 million or less (based on the preceding fiscal year). These businesses are permitted to calculate their input tax credits by simply multiplying the total amount of their GST-taxable purchases (including GST or HST, provincial sales taxes and gratuities) by a factor of 6/106 (14/114 for HST purposes). This factor also applies in the case of reimbursements for taxable expenses incurred by employees and partners.

The quick method is available to small businesses with annual taxable supplies of $200,000 or less, with some exceptions (eg. accountants, lawyers, financial consultants). Under the quick method the amount of GST/HST to remit is calculated as a percentage of taxable supplies for the period, including GST/HST, but not provincial sales tax. The percentage varies by industry and can range from 2.2% to 11%.

¶14,800   REVIEW QUESTIONS

(1) In each of the following situations indicate whether the answer is true or false and give a reference to the Act.

(a) The taxable income of Unco Inc., a corporation resident in Canada, was nil for the year. As a result, it did not have to file a corporate tax return.

(b) Mr. Lucky sold his shares in a qualified small business corporation and realized a $200,000 capital gain. The full amount of the gain was eligible for the capital gains exemption leaving his taxable income at nil. He does have to file a tax return for the year.

(c) Instalments for individuals are due on the 30th of March, June, September and December.

(2) Mr. Smith paid his first instalment on time but was unable to pay his second one on time. He paid both the second and the third instalments on September 15. Is there any way he can avoid the interest that was charged to him for the late payment on the second instalment?

(3) Badyearco Inc. has been quite profitable, but this year the corporation realized a business loss that it is going to carry back to the third preceding year. They are also hoping to collect interest from the date they filed the return for that third preceding year. What do you think?

(4) Ms. Unhappy received a Notice of Reassessment from the CRA to disallow certain expenses that she had claimed. She contacted her accountant who sent a letter to the CRA outlining the basis for the deduction. Both Ms. Unhappy and her accountant feel that the deduction will be allowed. Should she also file a Notice of Objection?

(5) Bad Luck Corp. has had a bad year. The corporation lost money for the first time in its history and some of its key employees have left. Because of all this confusion Bad Luck Corp. was late in getting its financial records in shape and it did not file its corporate tax returns until seven months after the end of the year. Bad Luck Corp. still needs the cash so it is waiting anxiously for the tax refund from the loss being carried back to the third preceding year. Do you think Bad Luck Corp. will be disappointed?

(6) Describe the different tax returns that can be filed for a deceased individual.

¶14,825   MULTIPLE CHOICE QUESTIONS

Question 1

Jane filed her tax return for the 2006 taxation year on September 15, 2007. She enclosed with the return a cheque for $10,000, the balance of tax owing. Neither Jane nor her husband carried on business in 2005. Jane will be assessed a late filing penalty of:

(A) $500

(B) $900

(C) $950

(D) $1,000

Question 2

A Canadian-controlled private corporation received a notice of assessment for its taxation year ended December 31, 2006. The date of mailing on the notice of assessment was August 15, 2007. The normal reassessment period for the corporation's 2006 taxation year ends:

(A) December 31, 2009

(B) August 15, 2010

(C) December 31, 2010

(D) August 15, 2011

Question 3

Darol disagrees with the notice of assessment he received for his 2006 tax return. The date of mailing on the notice of assessment was October 16, 2007. The tax return was filed on June 15, 2007 as Darol carried on a business in 2006. The notice of objection must be filed by:

(A) December 31, 2007

(B) January 14, 2008

(C) April 30, 2008

(D) June 15, 2008

Question 4

Bill was a lawyer with a very successful law practice. He died March 31, 2007. Which *one* of the following is the due date for his 2006 tax return?

(A) April 30, 2007

(B) June 15, 2007

(C) June 30, 2007

(D) September 30, 2007

Question 5

The controller of X Ltd., a Canadian-controlled private corporation, estimates that the company's taxes payable for its year ended December 31, 2007, will be $200,000. Taxes payable for each of the previous three years was as follows:

2004 $212,000

2005 180,000

2006 140,000 (taxable income was $600,000)

What is the minimum monthly instalment that X Ltd., which is not an eligible CCPC, must pay in the 2007 taxation year and the due date for the final balance of tax?

(A) The minimum monthly instalment is $11,667 and the due date for the final balance of tax is February 29, 2008.

(B) The minimum monthly instalment is $16,667 and the due date for the final balance of tax is February 29, 2008.

(C) The minimum monthly instalment is $16,667 and the due date for the final balance of tax is March 31, 2008.

(D) The minimum monthly instalment is $15,000 and the due date for the final balance of tax is February 29, 2008.

Question 6

Ms. Jones is a retired partner in a law firm and has taxable income of $70,000 each year from the partnership, her RRIF and her investments. She expects to pay $25,000 in tax in respect of 2007. She paid $16,400 in tax in respect of 2006 and $15,300 in respect of 2005. No tax is withheld on any of this income.

Which of the following is the minimum amount that Ms. Jones should pay for her 2007 quarterly income tax instalments, in order to avoid any unnecessary interest costs?

(A) 4 payments of $6,250

(B) 2 payments of $4,100 and 2 payments of $6,250

(C) 2 payments of $3,825 and 2 payments of $4,100

(D) 2 payments of $3,825 and 2 payments of $4,375

¶14,850 EXERCISES

Exercise 1

ITA: 150(1)

When must the tax returns for the following be filed: (a) a corporation, (b) a deceased person (terminal return only), (c) a trust, and (d) an individual?

Exercise 2

ITA: 152(4)

An individual filed her 2006 tax return on April 30, 2007. The CRA responded with a notice of assessment mailed on May 27, 2007. If the CRA wishes to make an additional assessment of tax for 2006, by what date must it issue a notice of reassessment?

Exercise 3

ITA: 153(1)

List five payments from which the payer must withhold tax.

Exercise 4

Give two examples of a windfall that would reduce an estimate of income in a net worth assessment.

Exercise 5

ITA: 156(1)

In 2007, Mr. Ordinary projects his income to be $40,000 consisting of employment income of $25,000 and income from a small business, operated as a sideline, of $15,000. He expects that his tax liability will be $6,000 on the business income. During 2005 and 2006 he paid $3,000 and $4,000, respectively, in tax on the business income. Is he required to make instalments for 2007? If so, how much must he pay in instalments during 2007 so that he does not incur interest and when must each instalment be paid?

Exercise 6

ITA: 157(1)

A corporation that is not an eligible CCPC uses the calendar year for its taxation year. In 2005, it paid tax of $158,400. By the end of March 2007, it had computed its tax for 2006 at $237,600. It estimates that it will have to pay $356,400 in tax for 2007. Is the corporation required to make instalments for 2007? If so, how much must it pay in instalments during 2007 and when must each be paid?

Exercise 7

ITA: 150(1), 162(1), 238(1)

X, Y and Z filed their tax returns on May 5, 2007, for the 2006 year. X and Y are employees and Z is a proprietorship business owner. X determined that he owed $4,700 in tax on that date and enclosed a cheque for the $4,700; Y computed a refund of $2,000; and Z included a cheque for $3,500 relating to his balance of tax. What penalties and offences might each be liable for?

Exercise 8

ITA: 161, 164

Compare the calculation and tax treatment of interest paid on amounts owing to the CRA and interest paid on refunds by the CRA.

Exercise 9

ITA: 163.2; IC 01-1

You have been engaged by Sly Coverup, a self-employed new client, to prepare an income statement and his tax return. Sly has instructed you to prepare these based on a figure for his total revenue and a list of his business expenditures, which he has provided to you. Based on your quick review of these data, you concluded that the expenditures were consistent with Sly's type of business and the amounts appeared to be reasonable. You prepared the income tax return, showing $100,000 of total revenue and $70,000 of expenses.

Subsequently, Sly's return was selected for audit. The CRA determined that many of the expenses deducted in the return could not be substantiated by adequate records. The CRA concluded that some of these expenditures may not have been made. The CRA, also, discovered that only 65% of the actual revenues of the business had been reported.

— REQUIRED

Determine whether you are at risk of being assessed under the civil penalties provisions of the Act.

ITA: 163.2

Exercise 10

ITA: 165(1), 169, 172, 180

Outline briefly the full appeal procedure indicating the time allowed between steps in the procedure.

Exercise 11

ITA: 216, 220(3)

A non-resident individual owns a rental property in Canada and has paid non-resident withholding tax on the gross rental revenue since 2002. He has heard that he may be able to recover some of this withholding tax if he files Canadian income tax returns for those years. What would you advise him?

Exercise 12

ITA: 161

Mr. Sol Proprietor's only source of income is from his dry cleaning business. In March and June of 2006, he paid instalments of $2,000 each in respect of his 2006 taxes. By September, he realized things were not going well and he would likely have a loss for the year. He, therefore, paid no further instalments.

On June 15, 2007, Sol filed his 2006 tax return claiming a loss and a refund of his $4,000 instalments. He also filed a T1A carrying the loss back to 2005. He expects a tax refund of $5,000 from the carryback.

— REQUIRED

What interest can Sol expect to receive on his tax refunds?

Exercise 13

ITA: 70, 104, 111

Sam Elder died on September 10, 2007. Discuss how the following are to be reported:

(A) $200, accrued but unpaid, interest on his bank account.

(B) $100 dividend declared on September 15, 2007 and paid on September 30 (the previous dividend was paid on March 30).

(C) CPP of $600 for August 2007, received on September 3 and $200 for the period September 1 to 10, received on October 4.

(D) Charitable donations for the period January 1 to September 10, 2007.

(E) Capital losses incurred in 2006 of $4,000, of which no amount was deducted in 2006.

(F) Income of $900 from a trust established on his wife's death, of which Sam was a beneficiary, for the year ended May 31, 2007.

(G) $50,000 in life insurance payable on Sam's death.

Exercise 14

ITA: 70, 150

After the 2006 personal tax season, the brother (Mr. Kaye) of one of your clients (Ms. Kaye) contacted you with respect to his sister. He indicated that his sister had passed away on May 2, 2007, at the age of 50.

Mr. Kaye indicated that his sister had the following income from January 1 to May 2, 2007:

(a) Salary — $22,000, of which $2,000 had not been paid at the time of her death.

(b) Bond interest payable of $950 which had not been received at the time of death.

(c) Interest in her savings/chequing account of $150.

(d) Interest of $140 on a 60-day GIC which matured on May 15, 2007.

(e) Grossed-up dividend income of $250 on 100 Flying High shares, payable on April 30, 2007, but had not been paid at the time of her death.

(f) The fair market value of Flying High shares on May 2, 2007, was $25/share. These shares had been purchased for $10/share in 2000.

(g) Her RRSP had a value of $34,000 at the date of her death. In February 2007, Ms. Kaye made an RRSP contribution, in respect of 2007, of $9,000. Her earned income for 2006 was $80,000.

— REQUIRED

Discuss the tax implications and filing requirements as a consequence of Ms. Kaye's death.

¶14,875 ASSIGNMENT PROBLEMS

Problem 1

ITA: 156, 156.1, 161, 163.1

Bert Logan's daughter Amanda is an accounting student. After a brief review of Bert's previous tax returns she advised him that he would likely have to begin making income tax instalments for 2007; however, she was uncertain about how these instalments were to be calculated and the consequences of making inadequate instalments. Amanda called one of the tax specialists at her employer firm, First and Partners, for assistance.

Amanda provided the following information:

(a) 2005 actual tax liability was $8,750;

(b) 2006 actual tax liability was $7,640; and

(c) 2007 estimated tax liability is $5,520.

— REQUIRED

You are the tax specialist. Write a memo, in point form, for partner review explaining the options available to calculate instalment payments for Bert Logan and the consequences if incorrect instalments are made.

Problem 2

ITA: 157, 162, 163, 163.1

Ruffle Limited, a public company, specializes in the games business. For their fiscal year ended October 31, 2006, the company's tax liability was $54,024. Due to the success of the board game, Run About, the company's bottom line has increased significantly, resulting in a tax liability of $69,036 for the fiscal period ended October 31, 2007.

Ruffle Limited's climb to success came to a halt in the next fiscal year. Due to increased competition, profits are expected to decline significantly and the controller of Ruffle Limited estimates the tax payable for the fiscal period ending October 31, 2008 to be $45,000.

In addition, the controller informed you that, due to cash flow problems, the actual instalments for June, July, and August 2008 were $1,050 less than the amount required. The controller also indicated that in order to compensate for this shortfall an instalment payment of $4,500 was made in October 2008 and that the remaining outstanding balance would be included in the December remittance.

— REQUIRED

The controller has asked you, his tax accountant, to provide him with the following information:

(A) The required instalments for the 2008 taxation year.

(B) Assuming that the estimated tax of $45,000 for 2008 is correct, what payment should be made on December 31, 2008 to stop further interest charges?

Assume that the prescribed interest rates on the deficient instalments are:

● last quarter of 2007: 9%

● first quarter of 2008: 8%

● second and third quarters of 2008: 7%

● last quarter of 2008: 8%.

Ignore the effects of the leap year in 2008.

Problem 3

ITA: 152, 161, 162, 163.1;
IC 00-1R

On September 1, 2007, you started in your new position as manager of taxation for Malic Corporation, a large public company with a December 31 year-end. On the second day into the job, Maureen Smythe, the VP Finance, comes into your office with a folder entitled "Outstanding Items". She tells you that the folder was found in the bottom drawer of your desk when the office was cleaned up after the previous manager of taxation left. She is concerned about the following items found in the file:

(a) Two letters from the CRA paper-clipped to the corporation's notice of assessment for the 2001 taxation year (dated September 30, 2002). One of the letters is a reassessment, dated April 30, 2007, and states that the corporation has been assessed additional tax for the 2001 taxation year in the amount of $722,500. The second letter, dated June 15, 2007, demands payment of the $722,500 within 30 days and indicates that if payment is not made, company assets will be seized.

(b) A memo to the tax files from the previous manager stating that for the 2006 taxation year minimum instalments were made for January to October, no instalment was made in November, and an instalment of $1,450,000 was made in December.

(c) A partially completed tax return for the 2006 taxation year indicating taxes payable of $10,760,000. The return had not been filed.

Ms. Smythe leaves the file with you and asks you to do the following.

— *REQUIRED*

(A) Determine the validity of the CRA letters and the threat of seizure.

(B) Determine if the corporation owes any additional tax and/or penalty with respect to the 2006 taxation year and, if so, the amount of the tax and/or penalty. Previous tax returns indicate the tax liabilities for the 2003 to 2005 taxation years were $7,500,000, $5,400,000, and $9,200,000, respectively.

Assume that the prescribed interest rate required by Regulation 4301, to be used for the purpose of computing imputed interest on employee and shareholder loans, is 6% for all of 2006 and 5% for all of 2007. Assume also that for the purposes of the section 163.1 penalty the amount of interest which would have been payable, if no instalments were paid is $350,000.

ITA: 152(4), 163, 220(3.1); IC 00-1R

Problem 4

Mr. Dishonest has approached you, on July 12, 2007, for some advice considering a reassessment notice for the 2003 year which he has received. Mr. Dishonest has misplaced the reassessment notice but assures you that it was dated June 15, 2007. In your conversation with Mr. Dishonest, he reveals that he has had considerable difficulty with the CRA in the past, and has had to pay penalties under the Act. Mr. Dishonest is positive that he has complied with the law in this situation and wishes to dispute the assessment.

ITA: 162, 163

— *REQUIRED*

(A) Determine what additional information you require from Mr. Dishonest before discussing the relative merits of the particular disputed items.

(B) Assuming you accept the engagement, what steps would you immediately take?

(C) Explain to Mr. Dishonest the penalty under section 163.

Problem 5

ITA: 163(2), 163.2

Mr. Trouble visited his accountant Ms. Back Date, on March 31, 2007, to discuss the tax consequences of a large dividend received on January 10, 2007. Mr. Trouble owns 30% of the shares of Dot.com Ltd. which paid the dividend.

Ms. Back Date explained that if he had transferred his shares of Dot.com Ltd. to a holding corporation on December 31, 2007, he could have deferred tax on the dividend until they were paid out of the holding corporation.

Ms. Back Date indicated that the documentation with respect to the transfer of the shares to the holding corporation and the payment of the dividend to the holding corporation can be back-dated to achieve the result desired.

— *REQUIRED*

What are the tax consequences of back-dating the documentation with respect to the transfer of the securities?

Problem 6

ITA: 163.2; IC 01-1

Bill, an accountant, lives in an exclusive neighbourhood where house prices are in excess of $1,000,000. He has recently become friendly with a new neighbour and in March the neighbour hired Bill to prepare his personal tax return. The neighbour gave Bill a T4 reporting $60,000 of income. Thinking that the income was on the low side, Bill asked if this was all the income he had and the neighbour replied that it was. Bill did not ask any further questions but prepared the tax return. When the neighbour's tax return was audited by the CRA, it was discovered that he had in excess of $300,000 in income for the year.

— *REQUIRED*

Advise Bill as to whether he is at risk of being assessed under the civil penalty provisions in the Act.

ITA: 163.2

Problem 7

ITA: 212(1), 215(3), 215(6), 216(1); IC 77-16R4

After several years of visiting Florida, Mr. Snowbird moved from Toronto to Florida on December 31, 2006, and became a non-resident of Canada. Mr. Snowbird decided to rent his house in Canada for the next few years. Mr. Snowbird has arranged with a relocation agency, Gone-Today-Here-Tomorrow, to collect the rent, pay all expenses and remit the balance to him quarterly. During 2007, the house was rented for $1,950 for January to June, and $2,150 for July to December. Expenses amounted to $1,550 per month.

— *REQUIRED*

Discuss withholding tax and other tax implications concerning Mr. Snowbird's rental property.

Problem 8

ITA: 153

A Canadian university hires a well-known American lecturer to lecture on American history. The work will take approximately six weeks and she is to be paid $20,000.

— *REQUIRED*

Is there any requirement to withhold Canadian tax on the $20,000?

Problem 9

ITA: 153, 162(1), 162(2), 212(1)(*d*), 233.3; ITR: 108(1.11); IC 77-16R4

On January 10, 2008, you started your new job as controller for Bordessa Corporation, a Canadian-controlled private corporation with a December 31 year-end. On your first day, the president and owner-manager of the company has asked you to follow up on some personal and corporate tax concerns that he has.

(1) The company is the exclusive Canadian manufacturer and distributor of menswear designed by a famous U.S. designer and pays the designer a royalty equal to 10% of sales each quarter. Royalty payments are due one month after each quarter end (i.e., on April 30, July 31, October 31, and January 31). The company's financial statements show a 2007 royalty expense of $60,000. The financial statements also show the amount of royalties payable at the company's December 31, 2007 year-end to be $20,000 (the comparable number for December 31, 2006 is $10,000). According to the company's 2007 cheque register, however, only $45,000 has been paid to the menswear designer and only $5,000 has been paid to the CRA. The president wants to know how much the company should remit when it makes its January 31, 2008 payment to make up for unpaid royalties and withholding taxes it owes in respect of 2007.

(2) The company accrued a $100,000 bonus payable to the President on its financial statements. This bonus was declared by way of a director's resolution at the company's Board of Directors' last 2007 meeting. The president understands that his bonus must be paid within 180 days after the year-end in order for it to be deductible in 2007 and you have verified that this is correct. This is the first time the company has accrued such a bonus and the president wants to know the deadline for the remittance of payroll deductions on the bonus. You do a quick review of payroll remittances for 2007 and 2006 and find that they amounted to about $120,000 in each year.

ITA: 78(3)

(3) The president tells you that he filed his 2006, 2005, and 2004 tax returns yesterday (January 9, 2008) after receiving a demand to file these returns in December 2007. He is expecting a net refund of $5,490 (see the schedule below). He wants to know whether he will be assessed any penalties for late filing and what the amount of the penalties will be. He tells you that his wife is a self-employed medical doctor.

	Balance due (Refund $)
2004	(20,500)
2005	10,000
2006	5,010
Net refund expected	(5,490)

(4) During 2007, the president of the company inherited U.S. stock from a distant relative who lived in the U.S. The value of the stock at the date of the relative's death was $120,000 Cdn. The president has asked you if he has to report this on his 2007 tax return. The stock is held in safekeeping at a stockbroker's office in Toronto.

— *REQUIRED*

Report your findings to the president.

Problem 10 ~~MA 60, 70, 118.93~~

ITA: 60, 70, 118.93; IT-210R2, IT-212R3, IT-326R3

In early March, you were preparing your client list with respect to the personal tax return preparation season. When you came across Mr. Ricky's name you realized that Mrs. Ricky had called you regarding her husband's death. Mr. Ricky had passed away March 1, 2007, at age 62.

value at March

Mr. Ricky owned and operated a Canadian-controlled private corporation, Shining Ltd., involved in reconditioning cars. Mr. Ricky's 100 shares had an adjusted cost base and paid-up capital of $55,000. The fair market value of the shares at the date of death was $750,000. Seventy-five per cent of the shares were left to his wife and the rest of the shares were left to his 25-year-old son.

Mr. Ricky earned $20,000 per month in salary. A bonus of $35,000 had been declared on February 15, 2007, but had not yet been paid at the time of his death. His February salary was due on the last day of the month, but was paid on March 10, 2007.

In addition to his shares, Mr. Ricky owned bonds which earned $5,500 of interest income in 2006 and accrued $917 of interest in 2007 to the date of his death. He owned another bond on which there was $500 in uncashed bond interest due on January 4, 2007, the anniversary date of that bond. Further, Mr. Ricky had owned two rental properties. Net rental income after capital cost allowance from January 1, 2006 to December 31, 2006 was $45,000 and net rental income before capital allowance was $4,000 for each of the months of January and February 2007.

Other Information:

(1) All assets of Shining Ltd. have been used in the active business of the corporation.

(2) The shares of Shining Ltd. have been owned by Mr. Ricky since 1990.

400,000
(173,750)
226,250

C shares = 6,950

(3) Mr. Ricky had earned income in 2005 and 2006 of $95,000. He contributed to his RRSP the maximum amount allowed as a deduction in 2006. His RRSP was worth $295,000 at the time of his death. Mrs. Ricky is the designated beneficiary of his RRSP.

(4) Mr. Ricky had a savings/chequing account which earned $2,500 interest in 2006 and $150 during January and February 2007.

226,250
6950
= 3269

(5) Mr. Ricky had utilized $100,000 of his capital gains exemption.

500,000 Exemption
(100,000)
400,000 ½ = 200,000 deduct.

(6) All of Mr. Ricky's other assets have been left to his wife, except for the two rental properties which are bequeathed to his 20 year-old daughter.

(7) The rental properties had a fair market value of $100,000 each. Both properties had the following details:

	Unit #1	Unit #2
Capital cost	$72,000	$83,000
UCC	50,000	52,000

— *REQUIRED*

Prepare a letter, in draft form for partner review, to Mrs. Ricky explaining the tax implications and the filing requirements in respect of Mr. Ricky's death. Calculate taxable income for 2007.

Problem 11

ETA: 169(4), 169(5), 223; 225(1)–(4), 228(1)–(3), 237(1), 238(1), 238.1, 239(1), 243, 244(1), 245(2), 246(1), 248, 286(1)

Mr. E. Entrepreneur has decided to open a small car detailing company. The individual at the name registration office suggested that Mr. Entrepreneur walk down to the CRA office and pick up the information package with respect to tax filing, etc.

Mr. Entrepreneur had anticipated that the package of information obtained at the CRA office would include information on the goods and services tax (GST). Unfortunately, this information was not included in the package obtained. Mr. Entrepreneur approached his son, Sam, who is an accountant, to explain the obligations of a registrant under the *Excise Tax Act*.

— *REQUIRED*

As Sam, provide the appropriate explanations.

[For more problems and solutions thereto, see the CD accompanying this book.]

¶14,900 SUPPLEMENTAL NOTES

(This section can be omitted without losing the continuity of the chapter. None of the review questions, multiple choice questions, exercises, or assignment problems utilizes this information.)

¶14,910 Penalties

A penalty of $100 for each failure to provide the information required on a prescribed form is imposed. It should be noted, however, that section 32 of the *Interpretation Act* provides that where a form is prescribed, deviations therefrom not affecting the substance or calculated to mislead, do not invalidate the form used.

ITA: 162(5)

The Act imposes a penalty of $100 for each failure to provide an individual's Social Insurance Number to a person required to make an information return. The penalty will not apply if the individual applies for a S.I.N. within 15 days of the request and the S.I.N. is provided to the person making an information return within 15 days after receiving it.

ITA: 162(6)

A penalty equal to the greater of $100 and $25 per day to a maximum of 100 days for failure to file, as and when required, certain information returns is imposed. Some of the more common information returns required include: partnership information returns, tax shelter information returns, transactions with related non-resident persons, and various information returns relating to foreign property.

ITA: 162(7), 162(7.1)

The Act imposes a further penalty of $100 per member of the partnership for each month or part of a month, not exceeding 24 months, during which the failure continues. This additional penalty only applies where a penalty under subsection 162(7.1) has been assessed, a demand for the return has been made, and a penalty under subsection 162(7.1) has already been assessed for one of the three preceding fiscal periods.

ITA: 162(8)

A penalty equal to the greater of $500 and 25% of any consideration received or receivable in respect of a tax shelter before correct information is provided and an identification number is obtained, for providing false or misleading information to the Minister or for selling units before an identification number is obtained is imposed.

ITA: 237.1(7.4)

The Act imposes a further penalty for each month or part of a month, not exceeding 24 months, during which the failure to file the information return of transactions with related non-resident persons continues beyond 90 days of demand. The penalty applies to persons or partnerships who knowingly or under circumstances amounting to gross negligence fail to file information returns relating to certain non-arm's length foreign investments whether or not demand has been served. The amount of the penalty is $500 per month where no demand is served and $1,000 per month where a demand is served and not complied with. In addition, the Act imposes an additional penalty where a return relating to foreign investments is more than 24 months overdue.

ITA: 162(10)

ITA: 162(10.1)

The onus of proof changes to the Minister where any penalty has been assessed under the Act. Normally, the burden of establishing the facts is initially on the taxpayer. This provision, however, reverses this initial responsibility of establishing the facts by placing that responsibility on the Minister, but only where a penalty has been assessed.

ITA: 163(3)

Late-filed or amended returns and certain specific elections are dealt with in a series of provisions. These provisions have the effect of waiving interest and penalties assessed by the Minister. The taxpayer relief provisions were designed to improve the fairness of the tax system. Administrative guidelines are contained in an Information Circular.[7]

ITA: 220(3.1)–(3.7)

IC 07-1

Example Problem

Mr. Sums, the new controller of Secret Ltd., a CCPC, is in the process of preparing the company's 2007 T2 return. He notices a section of the return asking for information about the percentage ownership of the top three shareholders of the company. Secret Ltd. is so secretive that even Mr. Sums does not know exactly how many shares the president and vice-president own.

---

[7] For a case on the exercise of Ministerial discretion under subsection 220(3.1) and the guidelines in IC 07-1 see *Floyd Estate v. M.N.R.*, 93 DTC 5499 (F.C.T.D).

He, therefore, sends the return to Mr. Close, the president. Mr. Close writes "None of your business" in that section of the return, signs it, and returns it to Mr. Sums for filing.

Mr. Sums, worried, calls you, Secret Ltd.'s tax adviser, and asks you to speak to Mr. Close. Mr. Sums says that all tax owing for the year has been paid and that the return will be filed on time.

— *REQUIRED*

What would you tell Mr. Close about the risks, if any, Secret Ltd. is running by not completing the section of the T2 return?

— *SOLUTION*

Secret Ltd. is required to file a tax return containing prescribed information. Any information asked for on a form issued by the CRA is prescribed information, since such forms are prepared and released (in theory) by order of the Minister.
ITA: 150(1)

The CRA could, therefore, take the position that Secret Ltd. failed to file a return "as required" and assess a penalty. No amount would be payable since the penalty for a first offence is 5% plus 1% per month of unpaid tax. However, should the CRA disagree with the company's calculation of tax payable, the penalty would be based on tax unpaid per the assessment or reassessment.
ITA: 162(1)

In any case, Secret Ltd. would likely be assessed the $100 minimum penalty for failing to provide complete information on a prescribed form. Since subsection 162(5) applies, subsection 162(7) would not likely be applied in this case.
ITA: 162(5)

¶14,920 Objections and appeals

The contents of a valid notice of objection are specified for large corporations (i.e., corporations having taxable capital in excess of $10,000,000). Such an objection must specify each issue to be decided, the relief sought (expressed as the change in the amount of a particular balance such as income taxes payable) and the facts and reasons relied on by the corporation for each issue. In addition, only those issues and the related relief set out in the notice of objection can be the subject of further objection or appeal to the courts. However, any new issues raised by the CRA on subsequent reassessments may be the subject of a separate objection.
ITA: 165(1.11)

If the response by the appeals section of the CRA does not satisfy the taxpayer, he or she can apply to the Minister who can extend the filing deadline for the notice of objection in certain situations. An extension is possible where:
ITA: 166.1(7)

(a) the application for the extension is made within one year after the deadline for filing the notice of objection;

(b) the taxpayer was unable to act or to instruct another to act in his or her name; and

(c) the taxpayer had a *bona fide* intention to object to the assessment.

The taxpayer must demonstrate that:

(a) it would be just and equitable for the Minister to grant his or her application; and

(b) the application was made as soon as circumstances permitted.

The Minister's decision to refuse an application can be appealed to the Tax Court of Canada. The appeal to the Tax Court of Canada must be made in writing by summarizing the facts and the grounds for appeal, the conditions of which are similar to those described above on an application to the Minister. This must be done:
ITA: 166.2

(a) within 90 days after the day on which the notification of refusal was given; or

(b) after 90 days from the mailing of the application for extension if there has been no reply to the Notice of Objection.

¶14,920

Appeals are heard by one of the judges of the Tax Court of Canada and they may be heard *in camera* (i.e., closed to the public) on request. The Tax Court of Canada can, at its discretion, award costs to the taxpayer.

Section 12(1) of the *Tax Court of Canada Act* provides that the Tax Court of Canada has exclusive jurisdiction to hear appeals under the Act and certain other federal statutes. The taxpayer is given the option of an "informal procedure" or a "general procedure".

The informal procedure may be elected when the amount of federal tax and penalties at issue for one taxation year is $12,000 or less, or the amount of the loss is $24,000 or less, or the only subject matter is interest assessed under the Act. The only requirement of the informal procedure is that the appeal is submitted in writing. Court rules of evidence are flexible and, hence, the taxpayer, other than a corporation, can represent himself/herself or be represented by an agent (i.e., any individual) who need not be a lawyer. The Minister has 45 days to reply to the appeal. The court must fix a hearing for no later than 90 days following the day the Minister files a reply to the original appeal. Judgments must be rendered within 60 days of the hearing unless exceptional circumstances prevail. If the taxpayer is more than 50% successful, the court may award costs. Normally, the taxpayer cannot appeal a Tax Court decision reached using the informal procedure and the decision cannot be used as a precedent in subsequent cases. However, there may be a judicial review by the Federal Court of Appeal on errors of law or erroneous findings of fact found in a capricious manner. If the Minister appeals to the Federal Court, the taxpayer's costs must be covered by the Minister. The introduction of the informal procedure is intended to ensure that most taxpayers can have their cases resolved quickly, simply, and at a low cost.

Where the general procedure is chosen in the Tax Court of Canada, the Court will be bound by strict rules of evidence. The taxpayer can only represent himself/herself or be represented by legal counsel. Where a case has not been heard or terminated within one year after the reply to the original appeal is filed, the case may be dismissed for delay, the appeal may be allowed, or the case may be heard based on the facts filed with the appeal. If a judgment is not rendered within 75 days, the appellant may apply for a motion for judgment. Costs are in the court's discretion. In this general procedure, the taxpayer can appeal the decision of the Tax Court to the Federal Court of Appeal and the Tax Court decision can be used as a precedent in other cases.[8]

An appeal to the Federal Court of Appeal from a decision of the Tax Court of Canada can be made by either the taxpayer or the CRA. This must be done within 30 days from the date of mailing of the decision of the Tax Court of Canada.

ITA: 180(1)

The ultimate court of appeal for tax cases in Canada is the Supreme Court of Canada. An appeal can be made to the Supreme Court only if the Federal Court of Appeal decides that the issue should be referred to the Supreme Court, or if the Supreme Court authorizes the appeal, which it will do only where there is an issue of national importance. At this level, questions of legal interpretation are raised rather than questions of fact alone.

Example Problem

Wall Talk Inc., a wallpaper manufacturing company incorporated and with its head office in the U.S., sells wallpaper in Canada through a full-time employee, Mr. Zale. He lives in the U.S. and returns there on weekends and for holidays, spending his weekdays travelling throughout Canada. He signs the contracts but all merchandise is shipped from the U.S.

The Canadian operation rents a small hotel room in Toronto on a year-round basis which is empty except for the days Mr. Zale is in town. He stores some samples there and receives some voice-mail messages there. Urgent messages go to the U.S. office. In 2006, the U.S. company bought a car for $15,000 for Mr. Zale to use in Canada.

---

[8] Prior to proclamation of the new system, the system provided for an appeal to the Tax Court of Canada under what is essentially the "general procedure" described above. An appeal of a Tax Court of Canada decision could be made to the Federal Court–Trial Division. It was also possible to bypass the Tax Court of Canada and go directly to the Federal Court–Trial Division. Appeals from the judgments of the Trial Division were heard by the Federal Court of Appeal, under the old system.

No Canadian income tax returns have ever been filed by Wall Talk Inc. However, acting on information provided by a dissatisfied customer, the CRA, on May 13, 2007, mailed a notice of assessment to the Toronto office in respect of the 2006 taxation year. The $100,000 of taxable income was based on Canadian sales figures provided in the U.S. company's financial statements. In addition to Part I tax, the notice of assessment included interest, penalties and an additional 25% Part XIV tax.

Due to a combination of business in Western Canada and his annual vacation, Mr. Zale did not return to the Toronto office and, hence, did not get the notice of assessment until August 20, 2007. Wall Talk Inc.'s U.S. accountants sent it on to you on September 1, 2007.

— REQUIRED

What steps would you take on behalf of your client? What arguments would you put forth?

— SOLUTION

Although the 90 days allowed for filing a notice of objection have expired, the Act allows you to apply to the Minister for an order extending the time limit. The Minister cannot allow such an extension:

ITA: 165(1), 166.1

(a) unless the application to extend the time for objecting or appealing is made within one year after the expiration of the time otherwise limited by this Act for objecting to or appealing the assessment in respect of which the application is made; and

(b) unless the Minister is satisfied that,

(i) an objection or appeal would have been made within the time otherwise limited by the Act for so doing,

(ii) the taxpayer was unable to act or to instruct another to act in his or her name,

(iii) the application was brought as soon as circumstances permitted it to be brought, and

(iv) there are reasonable grounds for objecting to or appealing the assessment.

If the Minister refuses Wall Talk Inc.'s application, it can appeal to the Tax Court of Canada.

In this case, the delay in receiving the notice of assessment would be a strong point in favour of the taxpayer.[9]

If the application was approved by the Minister, a notice of objection would be filed on the basis that Wall Talk Inc. was not subject to Canadian tax. Although it carries on business in Canada by virtue of having a full-time employee in Canada, soliciting orders and entering into contracts, the Canada–U.S. Tax Treaty prevents Canada from taxing Wall Talk Inc. unless it carries on business in Canada through a permanent establishment. You would argue that a hotel room irregularly occupied does not constitute a permanent establishment.

Furthermore, by the same treaty provision, the Part XIV "Branch Tax" cannot be imposed unless there was a permanent establishment.

You would also want to argue that even if the CRA considered there to be a permanent establishment, the income earned in Canada was less than $100,000, perhaps, because Mr. Zale's salary has not been deducted (assuming this was the case). In addition, branch tax is based on after-tax income after allowing for an investment allowance (e.g., the car purchase), rather than taxable income. Finally, branch tax is reduced to 5% by Article X of the Protocol to the Canada–U.S. Tax Treaty (1995).

¶14,930 Late-filed or amended elections

Part of the taxpayer relief provisions pertains to elections under the Act or Regulations that do not specifically provide for late, amended or revoked elections. The elections which are affected by these rules are set out in Regulations. Some of the provisions which have been covered in the text so far are:

ITA: 220(3.2)–(3.7)
ITR: 600

(a) capitalized interest;

ITA: 21

---

[9] For other decisions on such a request, see, for example, *Kidd v. M.N.R.*, 83 DTC 639 (T.C.C.), and *Graphics Specialties v. M.N.R.*, 83 DTC 644 (T.C.C.).

(b) replacement properties; and

ITA: 13(4), 14(6), 44(1)

(c) interspousal transfers at FMV.

ITA: 73(1)

First, acceptance by the Minister of a late-filed, an amended or a revoked election is established. For requests made after 2004, there is a 10-year limit on requests under this provision. For this purpose, designations made under the debt forgiveness rules are considered to be elections. The taxpayer or partnership must apply for a time extension or permission to amend or revoke. An Information Circular indicates that a request may be accepted if:

ITA: 80, 220(3.2)

IC 07-1

(a) the tax consequences to the taxpayer are unintended and there is evidence that the taxpayer took reasonable steps to comply with the law;

(b) the request arises out of circumstances beyond the taxpayer's control;

(c) the taxpayer acted on incorrect information provided by the Minister;

(d) the request arises from a mechanical error;

(e) the subsequent accounting of the transactions was such that the parties acted as if the election has been made; and

(f) the taxpayer was unaware of the provision and took remedial action as soon as possible.

A request will not be accepted if:

(a) it is reasonable to conclude that the request was made for retroactive tax planning;

(b) adequate records do not exist to verify the request; and

(c) the request is being made because the taxpayer was negligent or careless.

Two provisions have the effect of backdating or cancelling elections and requiring the Minister to reassess taking into account these changes.

ITA: 220(3.3), 220(3.4)

The Act provides for a penalty in situations where the taxpayer's application has been accepted. The penalty is $100 for each complete month from the due date of the election to the application date to a maximum of $8,000.

ITA: 220(3.5)

Some sections of the Act have their own penalties for late-filed or amended elections. (See, for example, subsection 85(8).) Often these elections are filed late because an audit reveals that the election was inadvertently omitted. The late-filing penalty may be substantially less than the benefit from the election.

¶14,940 Enforcement and collections

Direct contact between the taxpayer and the CRA is generally made through one of the almost 30 District Tax Services Offices. Trained assessors and special investigators who conduct desk audits of an individual's return or field audits of business returns are located in these offices.

The Head Office in Ottawa supervises and directs the activities of the District Tax Services Offices. It serves to maintain efficiency and uniformity of treatment across Canada. In addition, a number of regional Taxation Centres are maintained to do routine operations and the initial processing of all individual income tax returns.

The sweeping powers of investigation previously available to the CRA have been subjected to judicial safeguards as a result of amendments. Tax officials may enter the taxpayer's places of business, property, places where anything is done in connection with the business or places where records are kept. However, where the place where the records are kept is a "dwelling house", officials may not enter without either the permission of the occupant or a court-issued warrant. The CRA may audit the books and records, examine all property and require that assistance be given and that questions be answered. Seizure of books and records for evidence must be carried out by means of a warrant, and a taxpayer may apply to the courts to have documents returned. Finally, the Minister is allowed to demand information or

ITA: 231–231.2

documents from third parties after obtaining judicial authorization. This would include information from the files of the taxpayer's accountant, which are not protected by the confidentiality which applies to solicitor–client communications.

The primary method of collection is based on withholding of tax at the source of payment and instalment payments. However, the Act grants the CRA further powers to collect unpaid taxes. The following is a brief outline of these powers.

(1) The CRA may obtain a judgment against a tax defaulter by registering with the Federal Court a certificate showing the amount owed. If payment is not made, the judgment can be enforced by the seizure and sale of the taxpayer's property.
ITA: 223

(2) Under the power of garnishment, the CRA may order a person who owes money to a taxpayer to make a payment on account of the taxpayer's liability for tax.
ITA: 224

(3) The Act provides for the seizure and sale at public auction of certain property of the taxpayer whether or not the assessment at issue is under objection or appeal.
ITA: 225

(4) The CRA may also demand immediate payment from a taxpayer whom it believes is about to leave Canada.
ITA: 226

Taxpayers are required to pay all amounts owing forthwith upon mailing of a notice of assessment or reassessment. However, the CRA is not permitted to exercise its collection powers:
ITA: 158, 225.1

(a) for 90 days after the date of assessment, if no Notice of Objection is filed;

(b) for 90 days after an assessment is upheld following a Notice of Objection, if no appeal is made to the courts; or

(c) until the decision of the court is rendered.

For a "large corporation", the normal rules are overridden. This provision allows the Minister of National Revenue to collect ½ of any assessed amount disputed by a "large corporation". The definition of a large corporation is discussed in Chapter 11. Generally, a large corporation is defined as a corporation which is liable for large corporation tax.
ITA: 225.1(1)–(4), 225.1(7)

If an appeal to a higher court is undertaken, security may be posted in lieu of payment of taxes owing.

Collection action may be taken earlier (subject to judicial review) if a delay could reasonably jeopardize collection. Under more restricted circumstances, tax already paid may be refunded during the appeal process.

Chapter 15

Corporate Distributions, Windings-Up, and Sales

LEARNING GOALS

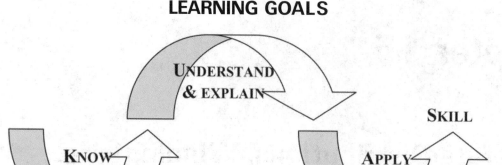

Know

By the end of this chapter you should know the basic provisions of the *Income Tax Act* pertaining to corporate surplus and its distribution in a variety of ways. Completing the Review Questions (¶15,800) and the Multiple Choice Questions (¶15,825) is a good way to learn the technical provisions.

Understand and Explain

You should understand and be able to explain:

● the tax-paid or tax-free components of corporate surplus;

● the income tax effects of distributing corporate surplus in a variety of situations; and

● the process for analyzing the tax consequences of two options for selling an incorporated business.

Completing the Exercises (¶15,850) is a good way to deepen your understanding of the material.

Apply

You should be able to apply your knowledge and understanding of the key elements of corporate surplus distributions to the analysis of the tax consequences of

● distributing a variety of types of dividends, and

● the options available on the sale of an incorporated business.

The objectives of this analysis should be to support a client's decisions and accomplish the client's goals in these areas. Completing the Assignment Problems (¶15,875) is an excellent way to develop your ability to apply the material in increasingly complex situations.

OVERVIEW

This chapter deals primarily with transactions between corporations and their shareholders involving the accumulated surplus of a corporation or the value of its shares. The discussion begins with distributions of corporate surplus. The chapter follows with a discussion of the winding-up of a corporation and the sale of a corporation in terms of assets or shares. This chapter will introduce only the general concepts and the basic calculations, rather than cover all aspects of the topics.

The following chart will help to locate the major provisions of the Act discussed in this chapter.

PART I — DIVISION B
SUBDIVISION H
CANADIAN CORPORATIONS AND THEIR SHAREHOLDERS

	DIVISION		SUBDIVISION		SECTION	
A	Liability for tax		Basic rules			
B	**Computation of income**	a	Office or employment			
C	Computation of taxable income	b	Business or property			
D	Taxable income earned in Canada by non-residents	c	Capital gains and losses			
		d	Other income			
E	Computation of tax	e	Other deductions			
E.1	Minimum tax	f	Rules relating to computation of income			
F	Special rules					
G	Deferred and other special income arrangements	g	Amounts not included in income			
H	Exemptions	**h**	**Cdn corporations and shareholders**	82	Taxable dividends	
I	Returns, assessments, payments, and appeals			83(1)	Tax-deferred dividends	
J	Appeals to the courts	i	Shareholders of non-resident corporations	83(2)-(5)	Capital dividends	
				84(1)	Deemed dividend	
		j	Partnerships	84(2)	Winding-up dividend	
		k	Trusts	84(3)	Redemption dividend	
				84(4)	PUC reduction dividend	
				84.1-84.2	NAL sale of shares	
				85	Transfer of property to a corporation	
				85.1	Share-for-share exchange	
				86	Reorg of capital	
				87	Amalgamation	
				88	Winding-up	
				89	Definitions	

¶15,000 CORPORATE SURPLUS BALANCES

¶15,010 Overview

The shareholders' equity section of a balance sheet has to be analyzed to arrive at the balances in the tax surplus accounts. The basic components are capital stock and retained earnings. Exhibit 15-1 is a schematic representation of a tax-basis balance sheet.

EXHIBIT 15-1
Tax-Basis Balance Sheet

ASSETS	LIABILITIES
	CAPITAL STOCK Paid-up Capital (PUC)
	RETAINED EARNINGS 1. Capital Dividend Account 2. Undistributed Surplus
<u>XXXX</u>	<u>XXXX</u>

Retained earnings can be subdivided into two amounts. The capital dividend account (CDA) generally represents the non-taxed portion of net capital gains and a portion of proceeds from eligible capital property. This account provides for the integration of capital gains through a private corporation as discussed in a previous chapter. The other amount might be termed "undistributed surplus" because it has no special tax surplus designation. It consists primarily of income generated and not distributed through dividends or other means.

Corporate surplus can be distributed in a variety of ways. Paid-up capital, discussed below, can be returned as a tax-free capital receipt to shareholders under certain conditions. The capital dividend account of a private corporation can be used to pay tax-free dividends through an election. Finally, most distributions of corporate surplus are made in the form of taxable dividends.

ITA: 83(2)

¶15,020 Paid-Up Capital of Shares

¶15,025 The tax concept

Paid-up capital (PUC) is an important tax concept as it is the amount which the corporation can return to the shareholder without it being reported as a dividend to the shareholder. The rationale for this tax-free return is that PUC was contributed from the after-tax funds of the shareholder on the initial investment in corporate shares. Therefore, PUC should not be taxed as a dividend on its return. However, on a *disposition* of shares by the shareholder it is the adjusted cost base, not the paid-up capital that is used to determine the gain or loss.

It should be noted that much confusion surrounds the tax term "paid-up capital" because this concept is also used in accounting and in corporate law. In accounting it is called share capital, and it reflects the capital contributed to the corporation. However, in related-party transactions, the amount recorded as share capital may be different than that recorded for tax purposes. In corporate law it is called legal stated capital and usually reflects the value of the property contributed to the corporation in exchange for shares. For example, if you were to buy shares from a corporation for $1,000, then the paid-up capital, share capital, and legal stated capital should all be the same at $1,000. However, assume that you contributed a piece of property that you have owned for some time to the corporation and received only shares in exchange. Also, assume that the fair market value of the property is $1,000 and the cost base to you is $600. In this case, the paid-up capital for tax purposes will be $1,000, the share capital for accounting purposes will be $600, and the legal stated capital will be $1,000, unless it is set at some other value. At this point, just beware of the potential for differences. Over the next few chapters you will better understand the differences.

¶15,030   Technical tax aspects

The definition of "paid-up capital" indicates that initially the paid-up capital for tax purposes is determined in accordance with the corporate law governing the particular corporation under discussion (i.e., legal stated capital (LSC)). Depending on the particular corporate law, the initial paid-up capital may refer to the stated capital of the shares, the par value of the shares or the consideration paid for the shares. However, there are a number of adjustments to the initial PUC or stated capital, some of which will be examined in subsequent chapters. Therefore, PUC for tax purposes and stated capital for accounting purposes may not be the same. These differences are seldom disclosed in the notes to the financial statements.   ITA: 89(1)

Note that paragraph (*a*) in the definition of PUC defines the paid-up capital of a share in terms of the average paid-up capital of the entire class. As a result, the paid-up capital of a particular share may not be the same amount as that paid for the share on its original issue. For example, further issues of shares from the same class at different amounts will change the paid-up capital of a particular share after such subsequent issues. Hence the paid-up capital per share is an average, over time, of issue prices of shares in a particular class.   ITA: 89(1)

Consider the following example for illustrative purposes.

Joe incorporated Smithco Inc. five years ago and paid $1,000 to the corporation for 1,000 common shares. His ACB of these shares is $1,000 and the PUC at the corporate level is $1,000.

This year Joe needed additional capital for expansion. Bill agreed to invest $100,000 for an additional 1,000 fully-paid common shares to be issued from Smithco Inc. After this transaction, Joe will still have an ACB on his 1,000 shares of $1,000. Bill will have an ACB on his 1,000 common shares of $100,000. At the corporate level the PUC will be $101,000. Since the PUC is allocated equally among the shares of that class it means that Joe's shares have a PUC of $50,500 and Bill's shares have a PUC of $50,500.

¶15,035   The effect of corporate law

Most jurisdictions in Canada now permit only shares without par value. Examples of such corporate laws are the *Canada Business Corporations Act*, the *Ontario Business Corporations Act* and the *Alberta Business Corporations Act*. With respect to corporations governed by such Acts, the PUC is the "stated capital" as determined by the directors of the corporation. Generally, this stated capital will be the fair market value of the consideration for which the shares were issued. However, these statutes provide that, in connection with certain non-arm's length transactions, the corporation may establish a stated capital amount which is less than the consideration for which the shares were issued. This reduced stated capital (i.e., less than the fair market value of the consideration received) will then be the initial amount of PUC for tax purposes. Accordingly, a corporation may, under most jurisdictions, establish shares with a low PUC and a high redemption amount (commonly referred to as "high-low shares"). In a few situations, the corporate law may not permit the creation of such shares and, in such event, it will be necessary for an alternative approach to be considered. The significance of these shares will become more evident when the topic of redemption of shares is discussed later in the chapter.

In jurisdictions which permit both par value and no par value shares to be issued, the PUC with respect to the par value shares will generally be equal to the par value of the shares.   ITA: 84(1)(*c*.3)

When such par value shares are issued for property with a fair market value greater than the par value of the shares such surplus amount (contributed surplus in accounting terms) can be converted to paid-up capital as long as the transaction(s) was (were) not accomplished on a (tax-free) rollover basis. Amounts so converted will have been contributed to the corporation with after-tax or tax-paid property and, hence, should logically be accessible on distribution to shareholders on a tax-free basis. Generally, the PUC with respect to the no par value or stated value shares will be equal to the fair market value of the property transferred to the corporation and for which the corporation issued such shares, except for certain reorganizations with non-arm's length parties, as previously mentioned.

¶15,040 Effect of PUC in a redemption of shares

Conceptually, the PUC is computed at the corporate level (not the shareholder level) by reference to all the shares of a particular class. However, the amount of paid-up capital is relevant to any shareholder on a redemption or cancellation of the shares. These events might occur when some of the shares of the corporation are redeemed or when all of the shares are, in essence, redeemed and cancelled on the winding-up of a corporation. On the other hand, the adjusted cost base is calculated only for the shares held by a particular shareholder (i.e., at the shareholder level, not the corporate level) and is relevant only where there is a disposition or deemed disposition of the shares. However, since a redemption or cancellation of shares involves a disposition of the shares held by a shareholder, any deemed dividend arising on the redemption or cancellation must be removed in calculating the resultant capital gain or loss. (Refer to the definition of proceeds of disposition.) That deemed dividend is subject to tax, as such, separately and should not be double-counted in the capital gain or loss.

ITA: 84(2), 84(3)

ITA: 54 "proceeds of disposition"

Consider the previous example of Joe and Bill. The following shows the adjusted cost base, paid-up capital, and fair market value of their shares immediately after Bill buys his 1,000 common shares. It then shows the tax implications if Joe and Bill each redeem their shares (i.e., the company uses corporate funds to buy the shares from them).

	# of Shares	ACB	PUC	FMV
Joe	1,000	$ 1,000	$50,500	$100,000
Bill	1,000	$ 100,000	$50,500	$100,000

Redemption	Joe	Bill
(A) Deemed dividend:		
Proceeds	$100,000	$ 100,000
Paid-up capital	(50,500)	(50,500)
Deemed dividend	$ 49,500	$ 49,500(A)
(B) Capital gain (loss):		
Proceeds	$100,000	$ 100,000
Deemed dividend	(49,500)	(49,500)
Adjusted proceeds	$ 50,500	$ 50,500
Adjusted cost base	(1,000)	(100,000)
Capital gain (loss)	$ 49,500	(49,500)(B)
A + B	$ 99,000	—

As you can see, Joe will recognize his full "economic gain" of $99,000 as a combination of deemed dividend and capital gain. Bill did not have an economic gain on the disposal, but, because the paid-up capital is allocated equally at the corporate level to each share of that class issued while adjusted cost base is calculated at the individual shareholder level, the nature of the income on redemption is not what you would otherwise expect. In fact, it may not be "fair" in terms of the tax implications of dividends, capital gains, and capital losses. A more detailed discussion on redemption of shares can be found later in this chapter.

¶15,045   Effect of PUC in other corporate distribution

As will be demonstrated, the Act is very protective about amounts that are added to PUC, because amounts in PUC can be distributed to shareholders without creating a deemed dividend. Therefore, amounts added to PUC must represent the value of property contributed to the corporation with after-tax or tax-paid funds. If an amount added to PUC does not represent tax-paid funds contributed to the corporation, then, usually, a deemed taxable dividend will result, so that the amount added to PUC is tax paid.

Summary	
Paid-up capital **PUC**	**Adjusted cost base** **ACB**
Calculated at the corporate level:	Calculated at the shareholder level:
• Based on capital contributed to the corporation;	• Based on amount paid for the shares;
• Averaged among all shareholders of that class based on shares held;	• Unique to each shareholder;
Can be withdrawn from the company free of deemed dividend.	Considered on the disposition of the shares.

¶15,050   Capital Dividend Account

The purpose of the capital dividend account is to complete integration of corporate and personal income tax on capital gains and similar receipts. When an individual realizes a capital gain of, say, $400, the individual pays income tax on $\frac{1}{2}$ of the capital gain or $200. The other $200 is not taxed. When a private corporation realizes the same capital gain of $400, the private corporation is taxed (including additional refundable tax and net of any dividend refund) on $200. The other $\frac{1}{2}$ or $200 is added to the private corporation's capital dividend account, to be distributed tax free to the corporation's shareholders. This is done to ensure that the integration concept applies to capital gains.

¶15,055   Components of the account

This account begins to accumulate amounts only for private corporations. For most private corporations, the period covered would be from the date of incorporation, but this cannot be earlier than January 1, 1972.

¶15,055.10   The components in concept

Conceptually, for the purposes of this chapter, this account includes five basic components:

(a) the portion of net capital gains (i.e., capital gains in excess of capital losses) not recognized in computing income for tax purposes, that is, the non-taxable portion of net capital gains, *plus*

(b) capital dividends received from another corporation, *plus*

(c) the portion of net gain not recognized in the cumulative eligible capital account, that is, the non-taxable portion of the economic gain (now $\frac{1}{2}$ of the excess of proceeds over actual original cost) on the disposition of eligible capital property, *plus*

(d) proceeds arising on death from certain life insurance policies received by the corporation net of the cost basis of the policies, *minus*

(e) capital dividends paid.

¶15,055.20　The major components technically

The balance of this account is computed for the entire period (refer to the next session for a discussion of "the period") as the sum of the following abridged amounts described here in simplified terms:

(a) *the untaxed portion of net capital gains which is computed as:*

    (i) generally, the excess, if any, of all capital gains (net of capital losses),   *ITA: 89(1) par. (a) of definition*

    minus:

    (ii) taxable capital gains (net of allowable capital losses) included in income at the appropriate inclusion rate on a disposition during the period ($\frac{1}{2}$ for gains and losses realized before 1988, $\frac{2}{3}$ for gains and losses realized in 1988 and 1989, $\frac{3}{4}$ for gains and losses realized from 1990 to February 27, 2000, $\frac{2}{3}$ for gains and losses realized from February 28, 2000 to October 17, 2000 and $\frac{1}{2}$ thereafter);

(b) *capital dividends received:* capital dividends received from another corporation;   *ITA: 83(2), 89(1) par. (b) of definition*

(c) *the untaxed portion of gains on eligible capital property:* for taxation years ending after October 17, 2000, the addition to the capital dividend account, at the end of a taxation year in which a disposition occurs, is equal to $\frac{2}{3}$ of the "economic gain" on the disposition of eligible capital property. The "economic gain" is considered to be the excess of a negative balance in the CEC pool over the cumulative CEC claims taken in prior years. This amount should be equal to the taxed portion of the negative balance. Refer to Chapter 5 for the details of the cumulative eligible capital amount. There may be other adjustments that are not addressed in this book.   *ITA: 89(1) par. (c.2) of definition*

(d) *untaxed insurance proceeds:* proceeds received, or in certain circumstances deemed to be received, as a result of death, from certain life insurance policies by the corporation in a period since it last became a private corporation, as a beneficiary of a policy, minus the adjusted cost basis of the policy;   *ITA: 89(1) par. (d) of definition*

minus (from the aggregate of the above four items)

(e) capital dividends paid or payable by the corporation.   *ITA: 89(1)*

Note that, technically, this account does not continue a balance from one year to the next with one year's opening balance being the previous year's closing balance. Each subparagraph accumulates from the beginning of "the period" to the particular time that a calculation of the balance in the account is being made. In this respect, notice that all subparagraphs except (b) require the inclusion of "the amount, *if any*, by which" the aggregate of one item exceeds another item. Thus, it is not possible to have a negative amount for these subparagraphs at a particular point in time. However, at a subsequent point in time the aggregate for one of these subparagraphs may be positive after offsetting aggregate losses or expenditures at that particular time.

¶15,060　"The period"

As indicated previously, the specific wording of the definition of the "capital dividend account" must be read very carefully (not just the above summary) when actually doing the capital dividend account calculation. The major confusion relates to the various time periods referred to. The first time period is described in clause $(a)(i)(A)$ of the definition and is referred to as "the period", as introduced above. Since only private corporations can have a capital dividend account, this concept is important when corporations can change their characteristics (e.g., a private corporation becomes a public corporation upon the listing of its shares or acquisition of control by a public corporation or a public corporation becomes a private corporation under prescribed conditions). For private corporations, which were incorporated prior to 1972, this time period starts "on the first day of the first taxation year commencing after the corporation last became a private corporation", or January 1, 1972, the day upon which the tax legislation made a distinction between public and private   *ITA: 89(1)*

      ITA: 89(1) "private corporation", "public corporation"

corporations, if that date is later. Note that the subparagraphs dealing with the disposition of eligible capital property and life insurance proceeds received, also, use the term "the period" to refer to this time condition. Hence, the balance date for the cumulative eligible capital account "at the commencement of the period" would be January 1, 1972 for corporations incorporated prior to 1972 and, as a result, would have a nil balance at that time. Similarly, private corporations incorporated after 1971 would have a nil balance in the cumulative eligible capital account on the first day they became private corporations. However, for public corporations which become private corporations, there may very well be a balance in the cumulative eligible capital account on this first day.

¶15,065 Example of disposition of eligible capital property

Facts: A Canadian-controlled private corporation with a fiscal year-end of December 31, had the following transactions.

Cost of eligible capital property on November 30, 2005	$12,000
Proceeds of disposition on January 15, 2007	20,000
Economic gain on disposition	8,000

As of January 1, 2005 the corporation had no balance in its CEC pool.

Application of the law:

CEC Account	
ECE × ¾ [$12,000 × ¾]	$ 9,000
CECA — 2005 [7%]	(630)
Balance December 31, 2005	$ 8,370
CECA — 2006 [7%]	(586)
Balance December 31, 2006	$ 7,784
ECA × ¾ [$20,000 × ¾]	(15,000)
Negative balance	$ (7,216)
Previous CECA	1,216
Final balance	$ (6,000)

Income inclusion on December 31, 2007			
Recapture of previous CECA	$ 1,216		
⅔ × final balance ($6,000)	4,000		ITA: 14(1)
Income*	$ 5,216		

Capital dividend account at December 31, 2007	
⅔ × final balance ($6,000)	$ 4,000

---

* The total of:

(a) the lesser of:
    (i) negative balance <u>$7,216</u>; and

    (ii) total CECA claimed ($630 + $586) <u>$1,216</u>

the lesser is	$ 1,216
(b) ⅔ × [$7,216 − $1,216]	4,000
Income	$ 5,216

Remember, for eligible capital property, the addition to the capital dividend account does not take place at the time of the transaction (January 15), but at the year end of the corporation (December 31).

This is equal to 50% of the economic gain on the eligible capital property i.e., 50% × [$20,000 − $12,000].

Example Problem

Surplus Accumulation Ltd. provides you with the following information:

Dispositions during the fiscal year ended December 31, 2007.

	Cost	Selling costs	Proceeds
Land	$20,000	$ 1,500	$35,000
Equipment	5,000	100	500
Securities	3,000	200	2,000

Capital dividends received in "the period"	$10,000	ITA: 83(2)
Capital dividends paid in "the period"	5,000	

In 1997, the corporation purchased goodwill for $6,000 and has deducted CECA of $2,325 to the present. In 2007, it sold an indefinite-life franchise for $19,000.

— REQUIRED

Compute the balance in the corporation's capital dividend account as at December 31, 2007.

— SOLUTION

Capital dividend account:

Untaxed fraction of net capital gains or losses:			ITA: 89(1) par. (*a*) of definition
Land			
P of D		$ 35,000	
ACB	$20,000		
Selling costs	1,500	21,500	
Capital gain		$ 13,500	
½$^{(1)}$ thereof		$ 6,750	
Equipment			
(No capital loss on depreciable property)		Nil	
Securities			
P of D		$ 2,000	
ACB	$ 3,000		
Selling costs	200	3,200	
Capital loss		$ (1,200)	
½ thereof		(600)	
Excess		$ 6,150	
Capital dividends received		10,000	ITA: 89(1) par. (*b*) of definition
Untaxed fraction of gain on eligible capital property			ITA: 89(1) par. (*c*.2) of definition
CEC balance ($6,000 × ¾$^{(2)}$ – $2,325)		$ 2,175	
Proceeds × ¾ ($19,000 × ¾)		(14,250)	
Negative balance		$(12,075)	
Recaptured CECA (income)		2,325	
		$ (9,750)	
Income (⅔$^{(3)}$ × $9,750 + $2,325)		$ 8,825	
Addition to capital dividend account (⅔$^{(3)}$ × $9,750)		$ 6,500	
		$22,650	
Less: capital dividends paid		(5,000)	ITA: 83(2)
Balance — December 31, 2007		$17,650	

The following alternative format may be useful to keep track of the transactions, particularly when they occur in different years.

		Capital dividend account					
Year	Asset	Untaxed fraction of net cap. gains	Capital dividend received	Untaxed fraction of net gain on ECP	Untaxed life ins. proceeds	Capital dividend paid	Balance
1997	Goodwill			(3,000)[4]			
2007	Land	$6,750					
	Equipment	Nil					
	Securities . . .	(600)					
	Franchise . . .			$ 9,500[4]			
	Capital dividend received		$10,000				
	Capital dividend paid . . .					($5,000)	
		$6,150	$10,000	$ 6,500		$(5,000)	$17,650

—NOTES TO SOLUTION

[1] The one-half rate represents the current untaxed portion of the capital gain which is computed in the definition of capital dividend account as the full capital gain minus the taxable capital gain at the ½ inclusion rate.

ITA: 89(1) par. (*a*) of definition

[2] On the purchase of goodwill in 1997, ¾ of the cost would have been added to the CEC balance.

[3] Because the CEC pool uses the ¾ inclusion rate, the fraction used here (⅔) brings the result to ½ (¾ × ⅔ = ½). This can be conceptually equated to the capital gains calculation by taking one-half of the economic gain into income and the other half into the capital dividend account. For example, $19,000 of proceeds − $6,000 cost = $13,000 gain.

[4] Neither the amount in respect of the cost of goodwill (in effect, ½ × $6,000 = $3,000) nor the amount in respect of the proceeds of disposition for the franchise (in effect, ½ × $19,000 = $9,500) affects the capital dividend account balance until the end of the year of the disposition, in this case, of the franchise.

¶15,100   USE OF CORPORATE SURPLUS BALANCES

¶15,110   Income Tax Treatment of Taxable Dividends Received or Deemed to be Received

¶15,115   Treatment of taxable dividends

A dividend, whether paid in cash, in stock, or in kind, or deemed to be a dividend, is treated by a shareholder like a dividend paid in cash. Where the shareholder is a corporation, the dividend is included in income for tax purposes; however, if it is declared by a Canadian corporation, the dividend is deducted in the calculation of taxable income of the recipient corporation. Depending on the circumstances, the dividend may be subject to Part IV tax on portfolio dividends.

Where the shareholder is an individual and the dividend, of whatever type, is from a Canadian corporation, the individual is subject to the gross-up and tax credit system. An "eligible dividend" to which the 45% gross-up and tax credit apply must be designated as eligible by the corporation paying or deemed to have paid the taxable dividend. The corporation must notify the shareholder in writing that all or any part of the dividend is an eligible dividend. A dividend that is not an eligible dividend is subject to the 25% gross-up and tax credit when received or deemed to be received by an individual.

¶15,120   Source of taxable dividends

A CCPC, which may have earned business income subject to the general or high rate of tax, may designate an eligible dividend to the extent of its general rate income pool (GRIP). A designation of an eligible dividend in excess of that GRIP balance that exists at the end of a taxation year will result in a 20% tax on the excessive eligible dividend.   ITA: Part III.1

Very simply, the GRIP balance is comprised of:

- the CCPC's GRIP balance at the end of the preceding year (can be nil or negative);

- the after-tax earnings, assuming a 32% corporate tax rate (or a 68% retention rate) for the year of the corporation that have not benefited from the small business deduction and are not considered to be aggregate investment income eligible for refundable tax, i.e., high-rate business income (losses of this nature reduce the GRIP balance);

- the eligible dividends received by the corporation in the taxation year;

The GRIP balance is reduced by the corporation's eligible dividends (that were not excessive eligible dividends) paid in its preceding taxation year.

Non-CCPCs could have a low rate income pool (LRIP), if the corporation receives a dividend out of the LRIP of a CCPC. A non-CCPC must pay dividends from its LRIP first to the extent of that balance. If it pays an eligible dividend when it has a LRIP, it will be subject to a penalty. A dividend received by an individual from a corporation's LRIP is subject to the 25% gross-up and tax credit.

¶15,130   Cash or Stock Dividends

Corporate surpluses are used in the process of paying dividends. Dividends may be paid in cash, stock or kind. Where a stock dividend is paid by any corporation, it will be taxed in the same manner as a taxable dividend paid in cash. The definition of "dividend" includes a   ITA: 248(1) "dividend"
stock dividend. However, the amount of the dividend will be deemed to be equal to the   ITA: 248(1) "amount"
increase in the corporation's paid-up capital as a result of the stock dividend. This amount is
used regardless of the fair market value of the shares received. This same amount will be   ITA: 52(3)(*a*)
considered to be the shareholder's cost of the shares received.

¶15,140   Dividends in Kind

It is possible for a corporation to declare a dividend to be paid neither in cash nor in shares but in assets of the corporation. Such dividends are known as dividends in kind or in *specie*. The tax effect of declaring a dividend in kind is equivalent to the corporation selling the assets for fair market value and paying a cash dividend with the proceeds of disposition. Thus, as a result of paying a dividend in kind:

(a) the corporation is deemed to have disposed of the assets at their fair market value;

(b) the shareholders are deemed to have acquired the assets at their fair market value;   ITA: 52(3)(*a*)
    and

(c) the corporation is considered to have paid and the shareholders are considered to have received a dividend equal to the fair market value of the assets distributed.

A loss to the corporation on the transfer of the assets to a controlling shareholder is   ITA: 40(3.3), 40(3.4)
denied.

¶15,150 Deemed Dividends

Generally, anything in a corporation's equity that is not PUC or a capital dividend account balance is taxable retained earnings. The only way those retained earnings can be distributed by the corporation to a shareholder is by a taxable dividend. Therefore, any distribution made by a corporation to a shareholder in excess of PUC and not elected as a capital dividend or declared as a taxable dividend will be deemed to be a dividend that will be taxable. Dividends may be deemed to have been paid in certain situations. ITA: 84

Conceptually, distributions from a corporation to a shareholder can be monitored by the following diagram of the simple equity accounts:

Simple equity		Distribution
PUC	$xxxxx	↓ Not taxable as a dividend
Capital dividend account	xxxxx	↓ Not taxable by election of capital dividend
Retained Earnings	xxxxx	↓ Taxable dividend (declared or deemed)

Amounts distributed from PUC or the capital dividend account are not taxable to the shareholders as a dividend. Once a distribution has dipped into the retained earnings pool, the part of the distribution from retained earnings will be a taxable dividend, because the only way that these retained earnings can be distributed is by a taxable dividend.

¶15,155 Deemed dividend on increase in PUC

A deemed dividend may occur where a corporation increases its paid-up capital without a corresponding increase in net assets. This situation might arise on the sale of property to a corporation (other than on a tax-free rollover basis discussed in the next chapter). In that case, the paid-up capital of the shares issued might exceed the fair market value of the property transferred to the corporation net of the value of debt issued by the corporation. The amount of the resultant deemed dividend is added to the adjusted cost base of the shareholders' shares, so that it is not taxed again as a capital gain on the disposition of the shares. The paid-up capital of a class of shares has considerable tax significance in limiting the amount that a corporation can return to its shareholders without being taxed as a dividend.[1] Thus, the Act prevents a corporation from arbitrarily increasing this limit. The provision ensures that increases in paid-up capital represent contributions of after-tax funds or tax-paid property to the corporation. However, the provision will not apply in the following situations, among others: ITA: 84(1) ITA: 53(1)(b) ITA: 84(1) ITA: 84(1)

(a) where the increase in paid-up capital results from the payment of a stock dividend because other tax consequences will result as discussed previously; ITA: 84(1)(a)

(b) where the paid-up capital is increased as a result of an equivalent or greater increase in net assets at fair market value as would be the case on the issue of shares for cash or other assets or on the issue of shares for existing debt; ITA: 84(1)(b)

(c) where the paid-up capital of one class of shares is decreased and the paid-up capital of another class is increased by an amount not greater than the decrease of the first class (i.e., where there has been no net increase in the paid-up capital of the corporation);[2] and ITA: 84(1)(c)

---

[1] While the return of capital represented by paid-up capital is not taxed as a dividend, there may still be a capital gain or loss as will be shown subsequently.

[2] Under the tax-free rollover provisions discussed in Chapters 16 and 17, there is usually no subsection 84(1) deemed dividend, because the potential paid-up capital increase is offset by an equal reduction.

(d) where a corporation converts its contributed surplus that arose on the issuance of shares into paid-up capital except those transactions which involve the tax-free rollover provisions as discussed in Chapters 16 and 17.

ITA: 84(1)(c.3)

The following numerical examples summarize these rules for a deemed dividend, showing the conditions for the exception in (b), above:

ITA: 84(1)
ITA: 84(1)(b)

	A	B	C
Facts			
Increase in FMV of net assets (cash)	$ 100	$ 90	$ 110
Increase in PUC of shares issued	$ 100	$ 100	$ 100
Results			
Deemed dividend			
Increase in paid-up capital	$ 100	$ 100	$ 100
Minus: net assets increase, if any	(100)	(90)	(110)
Excess, if any (i.e., deemed dividend)	Nil	$ 10	Nil
Contributed surplus (which can only be distributed by a taxable dividend unless converted to PUC) (see point (d) above)	Nil	Nil	$ 10

ITA: 84(1)

¶15,160 Deemed dividend on winding-up

A deemed dividend will result where a corporation distributes its assets to its shareholders on winding-up or reorganization. This process will be discussed in more detail later in this chapter and will be seen to be very similar to the results of a redemption discussed next.

ITA: 84(2)

¶15,165 Deemed dividend on redemption, acquisition, or cancellation of shares

¶15,165.10 *Basic Application*

Where a corporation redeems, acquires or cancels its shares, there will be a deemed dividend to the extent of the excess of the amount paid by the corporation on the redemption (redemption price) over the paid-up capital of the shares. The redemption price is normally the fair market value of the shares. In addition to the deemed dividend, there may also be a capital gain or loss on the transaction. However, to remove the element of double taxation, the proceeds for capital gain (loss) purposes are reduced by the amount of the deemed dividend.

ITA: 84(3)

ITA: 54 "proceeds of disposition" (j)

Example Problem

Ms. T incorporated a company with an initial capitalization of 10 common shares @ $10 per share.

During the second year of operation, the corporation entered into a transaction which resulted in an ACB reduction of $4 per share.

ITA: 53(2)

In the third year of operations, Ms. T acquired an additional 10 common shares @ $20 per share of paid-up capital equal to the fair market value.

Two years later, Ms. T caused the corporation to redeem 5 of her shares at the then fair market value of $50.

During this period, the corporation's business income has been taxed at the low rate on business income.

— *REQUIRED*

Indicate the tax consequences of the above transactions.

— SOLUTION

First year: Ms. T's shares have an adjusted cost base and paid-up capital of $10 per share.

Second year: Ms. T's shares have an adjusted cost base of $6 per share (i.e., $10 – $4) but the paid-up capital remains the same at $10 per share.

Third year: Ms. T's shares have an adjusted cost base of $13 per share:

($10 – $4) ×	10 shares = ...	$ 60
$20 ×	10 shares = ...	200
	20	$ 260

Ms. T's shares have a paid-up capital per share of $15:

$10 ×	10 shares = ...	$ 100
$20 ×	10 shares = ...	200
	20	$ 300

Fifth year:

Deemed dividend on redemption — ITA: 84(3)

Redemption price ($50 × 5 shares) = ...	$ 250
Paid-up capital ($15 × 5 shares) = ...	75
Deemed dividend	$ 175

Capital gain (loss)

Proceeds of disposition (redemption amount) (5 shares @ $50)	$ 250
Less: deemed dividend	175
Adjusted proceeds of disposition (equal to PUC)	$ 75
Adjusted cost base ($13 × 5 shares)	65
Capital gain	$ 10

ITA: 54 "proceeds of disposition" (*j*)

Reconciliation

Economic gain

Actual proceeds (5 shares @ $50)		$ 250
Cost (5 shares @ $13)		65
		$ 185
Deemed dividend	$ 175	
Capital gain	10	$ 185

ITA: 84(3)

Comments

The effect of the reduction of the ACB in the second year was a capital gain upon the ultimate disposition. — ITA: 53(2)

Assuming this redemption occurs in a province with a provincial personal tax on income rate of 17%, and a dividend tax credit rate at a low-rate income of 6 ⅔% of the grossed-up dividend, then the deemed dividend of $175 would bear tax at a top rate of 32.5% (see Note (1) below), whereas the capital gain of $10 would bear a tax rate of 23% (see Note (2) below). Therefore, given a choice, a taxpayer would prefer a capital gain on an outright sale rather than a deemed dividend. For example, if Ms. T wanted to sell one-half of her shares to one of her employees, then it would be to Ms. T's advantage to sell her shares to the employee directly, rather than to redeem her shares and then have the corporation sell treasury shares to the employee.

— NOTES TO SOLUTION

(1) $(100\% \times 1.25) \rightarrow 125\% \times [(.29 + .17) - (.1333 + .0667)] = 32.5\%$

(2) $(\frac{1}{2} \times 100\%) \rightarrow 50\% \times (.29 + .17) = 23\%$ (ignoring surtaxes)

As demonstrated in the previous example problem, on a redemption of shares, the proceeds of disposition for the calculation of the capital gain or loss will be equal to the PUC used for the calculation of the deemed dividend. This works since the adjusted proceeds for capital gains purposes is equal to the actual proceeds minus the deemed dividend which must mathematically equal the PUC. The implications of this are that where the PUC and the ACB are different there will either be a capital gain (PUC > ACB) or a capital loss (PUC < ACB).

¶15,165.20 *Denied capital loss*

If there is a capital loss on the redemption of shares, then the Act may deny the loss by what is referred to as a "stop-loss" rule. This provision applies if the shareholder and the corporation are "affiliated", as defined in the Act, immediately after the redemption. For a shareholder and the redeeming corporation to be affiliated the shareholder, his or her spouse or common law partner or a corporation that they control must control the redeeming corporation. If that is the case then the capital loss will be denied and added to the ACB of any shares that the redeeming shareholder has.

ITA: 40(3.6)
ITA: 251.1

Consider the following example for illustrative purposes.

Mr. A owns all 100 common shares and all 1,000 Class A shares of Aco Inc. The ACB and PUC of these shares are as follows:

	ACB	PUC
Common	$100	$100
Class A	$1,000	$100

If the Class A shares are redeemed for $2,000 then there will be a deemed dividend of $1,900 and a capital loss of $900. Since Mr. A owns all of the common shares he controls, and is, therefore, affiliated with Aco Inc., so the stop-loss rule would apply to deny the capital loss of $900 and add it to the ACB of Mr. A's common shares.

ITA: 40(3.6)

	ACB	PUC
Common	$1,000	$100
	($100 + $900)	

As a result, the common shares will have an ACB of $1,000 and the PUC will remain the same at $100.

¶15,165.30 *Summary*

> ### Redemption of Shares
>
> In summary, a redemption of shares involves a set of calculations that can be completed in two steps.
>
> Step 1: Deemed dividend [ssec. 84(3)]
>
> | | |
> |---|---|
> | Redemption amount . . . . | $xxx |
> | Less: PUC of shares redeemed . . . . | xxx |
> | Deemed dividend on redemption . . . . | $xxx |
>
> In the context of the simple equity diagram introduced previously, note that the deemed dividend arises because the corporation has distributed an amount that exceeds the PUC layer and, in the absence of a capital dividend account balance, dips into the retained earnings layer.

Step 2: Capital gain (loss)

Since the process of redeeming shares involves, in essence, a disposition by the shareholder, Step 2 computes first the adjusted proceeds of disposition [ssec. 84(9)] and then any capital gain or loss:

Proceeds of disposition (redemption amount) [sec. 54 "proceeds of disposition" (j)]	$xxx
Less: deemed dividend	xxx
Adjusted proceeds of disposition	$xxx
Adjusted proceeds of disposition	$xxx
Less: adjusted cost base	xxx
Capital gain (loss)	$xxx

Since a disposition includes a share redemption/cancellation, both a deemed dividend and a capital gain/loss may occur at the same time.

The deemed dividend provisions do not apply where a corporation purchases its shares on the open market in the same manner as any member of the public would purchase shares in the open market.   **ITA: 84(6)(*b*)**

In summary, the following differences between PUC and ACB of share capital should be noted.

PUC	ACB
(1) PUC is utilized in determining the deemed dividend arising from a redemption and/or cancellation of a share.	(1) ACB is utilized in determining the capital gain or capital loss on a disposition.
(2) PUC is calculated at the corporate level and attaches itself to a particular class or series of shares, not to particular shareholders. Therefore, any increase or decrease in PUC affects all shareholders equally.	(2) ACB is calculated at the shareholder level and relates to a particular class or series held by a particular shareholder and may very well be a unique amount for each shareholder. For example, the price paid by each shareholder for his or her shares in an open market purchase will normally differ in each circumstance. However, the PUC will be the same for each shareholder.

PUC and ACB have a number of separate and, in most cases, independent adjustments. PUC adjustments are scattered throughout the reorganization sections of the Act and will be discussed in the next two chapters. ACB adjustments are found in subsections 53(1) and (2) and may or may not affect each taxpayer on an identical basis.

¶15,170 Deemed dividend on reduction of PUC

The fourth type of deemed dividend would occur in the occasional situation where a corporation considers it appropriate to return some of the shareholders' capital without redeeming any of the issued shares. As an example of this situation, a corporation may divest itself of a major part of its business and pay the sale proceeds to its shareholders rather than reinvest those proceeds. Where such a payment is made by a private corporation and the paid-up capital of the shares is reduced by an amount equal to the payment, there will be no deemed dividend, but the shareholders' adjusted cost base of the shares will be reduced. A payment in excess of the paid-up capital will be a deemed dividend.   **ITA: 84(4)**   **ITA: 53(2)(*a*)(ii)**   **ITA: 84(1)(*c*)**

When a payment is made by a public corporation to reduce its paid-up capital, however, the entire payment is usually treated as a deemed dividend. [Bill C-33, November 22, 2006,   **ITA: 84(4.1)** proposed to provide an exception to this deemed dividend where the amount paid on a reduction of paid-up capital may reasonably be considered to be a distribution of proceeds realized by a public corporation from a transaction that occurred outside the ordinary course of the corporation's business and within the prior two-year period. The sale of a business unit of the corporation, for example, may be considered to give rise to proceeds eligible for distribution of paid-up capital. The distribution of normal earnings would not qualify, given these restrictions.]

That portion of the payment, which is deemed to be a dividend, does not reduce the adjusted cost base of the shares, since the amount has already been included in income.

ITA: 84(4) or 84(4.1)

For example, if a private corporation makes a distribution of capital in the amount of $8 per share on shares with a paid-up capital of $10, but reduces the paid-up capital by only $7, there will be a deemed dividend of $1. Hence, if the corporation does not reduce its paid-up capital by the full amount of the distribution, the excess distribution is considered to be from taxable surplus and is taxed as a dividend. The adjusted cost base is reduced by the amount of this paid-up capital reduction, because cost has been reduced by the amount distributed as a return of paid-up capital, that is, $7 in the example.

ITA: 84(4)

Note that where a corporation reduces its paid-up capital (without making any payments to its shareholders in excess of the actual paid-up capital) there will be no tax consequences unless the shareholder's ACB is less than the reduction in which case there is a capital gain in the amount of the excess of the reduction over ACB. In addition, such a reduction in paid-up capital may be advantageous where share redemptions are anticipated (i.e., the smaller the PUC, the greater the subsection 84(3) deemed dividend) and shareholders in a low tax bracket would prefer a dividend to a capital gain.

Consider the following example for illustrative purposes.

In an earlier illustrative example two shareholders, Joe and Bill each owned 1,000 common shares of Smithco Inc. Their share characteristics were as follows.

	# of Shares	ACB	PUC	FMV
Joe	1,000	$ 1,000	$50,500	$100,000
Bill	1,000	$100,000	$50,500	$100,000
PUC reduction				
PUC in corporation			$101,000	
PUC in reduction			(101,000)	
Deemed dividend			—	

Capital Gain	**Joe**	**Bill**
ACB	$ 1,000	$100,000
PUC reduction	(50,500)	(50,500)
Capital gain (if negative)	$(49,500)	
Revised ACB	$ —	$ 49,500

If the paid-up capital of Smithco Inc. is reduced by $101,000 there will not be a deemed dividend to either Joe or Bill since the amount of the reduction does not exceed the amount of the PUC. However, Joe will report a capital gain of $49,500 and the ACB of his 1,000 common shares will be nil. Bill will not report a capital gain, but the ACB of his 1,000 common shares will be $49,500.

Summary

To summarize the tax principles underlying the concept of a deemed dividend:

(a) a corporation may return its paid-up capital to the shareholders as a tax-free capital receipt with any excess being deemed to be a dividend; and

> (b) a corporation may not increase its total paid-up capital beyond an increase in net assets without tax consequences.

¶15,180 Capital Dividend

All dividends, whether actual or deemed, are taxable dividends unless some action is taken by the corporation prior to payment. The action that can be taken in the case of a private corporation in certain circumstances is to make an election to treat either an actual dividend or a deemed dividend as having been distributed from its capital dividend account. Such a dividend is received tax-free by the shareholder. However, an election in excess of the amount in the capital dividend account will result in a penalty tax under Part III of ³⁄₅ or 60% of the excess.

ITA: 83(2), proposed in the July 18, 2005 Draft Legislation

ITA: 83(2), 184(2) proposed in Bill C-33, Nov. 22, 2006

There are situations envisaged by the Act in which an excess election is made inadvertently. For example, a corporation may compute the balance in its capital dividend account based on the assumption that a particular transaction resulted in a capital gain, rather than business income. On this basis, the corporation may have elected to distribute a capital dividend. Later, on reassessment, it may be determined that the gain on the transaction was business income and an amount must be removed from the capital dividend account. This could make the dividend paid in excess of the reassessed balance in the capital dividend account. Recognizing this possibility, an election which allows the corporation to avoid the 60% penalty is available. This election allows the corporation to separate the dividend paid into a part that does not exceed the balance in the capital dividend account and a part that can be considered as a taxable dividend. The election must be made not later than 90 days after the day of mailing of the notice of assessment in respect of the 60% penalty.

ITA: 184(3)

Example Problem

Hum Along Records Ltd., a Canadian-controlled private corporation, has 5,000 outstanding preferred shares with a redemption and current fair market value of $6,000 and a paid-up capital value of $5,000 in total. The balance in its capital dividend account is $800. The company has decided to redeem the preferred shares at their fair market value and to properly elect a capital dividend on all preferred shares. As a result, a part of the deemed dividend on the redemption of the preferred shares will be a capital dividend.

— *REQUIRED*

What are the tax consequences to Mr. Hal Leluya who is unrelated to other shareholders and who owns 500 of the preferred shares which cost him $1.00 per share?

— *SOLUTION*

The following would be the results for the 10% shareholder:

Step 1: Deemed Dividend

Redemption amount paid (10% of $6,000)	$ 600
Less: PUC of shares redeemed (10% of $5,000)	(500)
Deemed dividend on redemption	$ 100
Capital dividend[(1)] (10% of $800)	(80)
Taxable deemed dividend	$ 20

ITA: 84(3)

ITA: 83(2)

Step 2: Capital Gain (Loss)

Proceeds of disposition (redemption amount)	$ 600
Less: deemed dividend	(100)
Adjusted proceeds of disposition	$ 500
Adjusted proceeds of disposition	$ 500
Less: adjusted cost base (500 shares × $1.00)	(500)
Capital loss	$ (Nil)
Allowable capital loss	$ Nil

ITA: 84(3)

ITA: 54 "proceeds of disposition" (j)

—NOTE TO SOLUTION

(1) Since a capital dividend can only be elected on the full amount of a dividend, an election must be made to treat the excess of $20 as a taxable dividend.

ITA: 83(2), 184(3)

¶15,200   WINDING-UP OF A CANADIAN CORPORATION

¶15,210   Disposition of Net Assets of the Corporation

On the winding-up of a corporation, the assets could be liquidated on the open market with the net proceeds, after paying the liabilities, paid to the shareholders. Alternatively, the net assets might be distributed directly to the shareholders. If the second alternative is chosen, all property of the corporation so distributed is deemed to have been distributed at its fair market value immediately before the winding-up. In either case, the disposition may result in income and losses within the corporation on the sale of current assets, such as inventory, in recapture or terminal losses on the disposition of depreciable property and in capital gains or losses on the disposition of capital property. This may result in an income tax liability and, perhaps, an increase in the refundable dividend tax on hand if the company is a private corporation. It may also result in adjustments to the "capital dividend account".

ITA: 89(1)

ITA: 69(5)

ITA: 89(1)

¶15,220   Deemed Dividend on Winding-Up

¶15,225   Timing of winding-up

The sale of the assets of a corporation need not be followed immediately by a winding-up. The proceeds from the sale of assets can be reinvested in a new set of assets to carry on a new business or in a portfolio of securities, using the corporation as a holding company. Alternatively, the proceeds from the sale of assets can be distributed to shareholders, maintaining the corporation merely as a shell with nominal assets and shares. In this situation, distributions that did not represent a tax-free reduction of paid-up capital or a tax-free distribution from the capital dividend account will be treated as taxable dividends to the shareholders. A winding-up may not be completed for several years after the sale of the assets of a corporation, because certain clearance certificates must be issued to attest to the fact that creditors' claims, including Canada Revenue Agency (CRA), have been satisfied.

¶15,230   Components of the winding-up distribution

When a distribution on a winding-up does occur, the Act establishes the portion of the amount received by the shareholders in a winding-up that is taxable in their hands. This subsection provides that any amount received in excess of the paid-up capital is deemed to be a dividend. However, as indicated in the previous part of this chapter, this winding-up dividend can be broken into separate amounts abridged to two as follows:

ITA: 84(2)

ITA: 89(1)

ITA: 88(2)(*b*)

(a) a capital dividend to the extent of the balance in the company's capital dividend account if the corporation *elects* on that amount; and

ITA: 83(2)

(b) a taxable dividend to the extent of the balance of the deemed dividend.

In the winding-up, the shareholders dispose of their shares in return for the amounts received from the corporations. For the purpose of computing the capital gain or loss on the disposition of the shares, proceeds of disposition are deemed to be actual proceeds, or amounts received from the corporation, less the amount of the deemed dividend.

ITA: 54 "proceeds of disposition" (*j*), 84(2)

Similar to the redemption of shares discussed earlier, the calculations for the winding-up can be completed in two steps.

Step 1: Deemed Dividend

Funds or property available for distribution to the shareholder(s)	$ xxx
Less: Paid-up capital	(xxx)
Deemed dividend on winding-up	$ xxx
Less: Elected amount of capital dividend	(xxx)
Deemed dividend taxable in hands of shareholder	$ xxx

ITA: 84(2)

ITA: 88(2)(*b*)(ii)

Step 2: Capital Gain or Loss

Funds or property available for distribution to the shareholder(s)	$ xxx
Less: Deemed dividend above	(xxx)
Adjusted proceeds of disposition (= PUC)	$ xxx
Adjusted cost base of shares	xxx
Capital gain	$ xxx

ITA: 54 "proceeds of disposition" (*j*)

The components of the distribution can be illustrated conceptually by Exhibit 15-2.

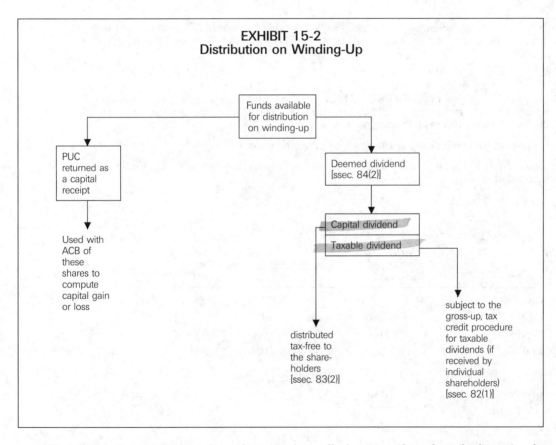

EXHIBIT 15-2
Distribution on Winding-Up

Note the similarity between the redemption/cancellation procedure described previously in the chapter and the winding-up procedure. Both provisions have the same essential purpose on the distribution of funds from a corporation to a shareholder. The provisions must differentiate between the tax-free return of capital and a taxable distribution from retained earnings. The main difference is that a redemption usually pertains to all or part of one class of shares, while a winding-up involves the redemption or cancellation of all shares. Of course, part or all of the remaining winding-up deemed dividend can be treated as an elective non-taxable capital dividend.

ITA: 84(3)

ITA: 84(2)

¶15,240   Application of the Winding-Up Rules

Example Problem

Winditup Limited is a Canadian-controlled private corporation founded in 1995 by Mr. Winditup who holds all of the shares which he purchased at that time from the company for $1,000. As of December 31, 2007, its tax balance sheet appears as follows:

Winditup Limited

BALANCE SHEET

as of December 31, 2007

Assets		Liabilities	
Cash	$ 5,000	Liabilities	Nil
RDTOH	5,000		
Land at cost (FMV $210,000)	150,000	**Shareholders' Equity**	
Building at UCC (cost $200,000; FMV $250,000)	125,000	Paid-up capital	$ 1,000
		Surplus	284,000
Total	$285,000	Total	$285,000

The surplus accounts include $50,000 in the capital dividend account. The assets are to be liquidated and the proceeds are to be distributed to Mr. Winditup on the winding-up beginning on January 1, 2008.

— *REQUIRED*

(A) Compute the amount available for distribution to the shareholder assuming the company pays corporate tax at the overall rate of 20% on the first $400,000 of active business income and 40% on all other income, before the additional refundable tax of 6⅔%.

(B) Determine the components of the distribution to the shareholder.

(C) Compute the taxable capital gain or allowable capital loss on the disposition of Mr. Winditup's shares.

— *SOLUTION*

(A)

	Actual or deemed proceeds[1]	Income generated		Capital dividend account	RDTOH
		Bus.	Invest.		
Opening balance		Nil	Nil	$ 50,000	$ 5,000
Cash	$ 5,000	Nil	Nil		
Land[2]	210,000	Nil	$30,000	30,000	
Building[3]	250,000	$75,000	25,000	25,000	
Income tax[5]	(40,667)	$75,000[4]	$55,000		14,667
RDTOH[6]	19,667				$ 19,667
	$444,000			$105,000	

(B)

Funds available for distribution to shareholder	$ 444,000	
Less: paid-up capital (return of capital)	(1,000)	
Deemed dividend on winding-up	$ 443,000	ITA: 84(2)
Less: capital dividend elected	(105,000)	ITA: 83(2), 88(2)(*b*)(i)
Deemed taxable dividend (sufficient to clear RDTOH)	$ 338,000	ITA: 88(2)(*b*)(iii)

(C) Taxable capital gain to Mr. Winditup:

Actual proceeds on winding-up	$ 444,000
Less: Deemed dividend	(443,000)
Proceeds of disposition	$ 1,000
Cost	(1,000)
Capital gain	Nil
Taxable capital gain ($\frac{1}{2}$ × Nil)	Nil[7]

ITA: 84(2), 54 "proceeds of disposition" (*j*)

— *NOTES TO SOLUTION*

[1] It should be noted that in a winding-up of this nature it is possible either to sell the assets to any purchaser for proceeds equal to the fair market value of the assets or to distribute the assets to the shareholders of the corporation. If the latter alternative is taken, proceeds of disposition are deemed to be the fair market value of the assets so distributed.

[2]		
Proceeds on sale of land		$210,000
Cost		150,000
Full increase in value		$ 60,000
Taxable capital gain ($\frac{1}{2}$ × $60,000) (Canadian investment income)		$ 30,000
Capital dividend account ($\frac{1}{2}$ × $60,000)		$ 30,000

[3]		
Actual proceeds on sale of building		$250,000
UCC		125,000
Gain		$125,000
Recapture ($200,000 – 125,000) (active business income)		$ 75,000
Capital gain ($250,000 – 200,000)		$ 50,000
Taxable capital gain ($\frac{1}{2}$ × $50,000) (Cdn. investment income)		$ 25,000
Capital dividend account ($\frac{1}{2}$ × $50,000)		$ 25,000

[4] The $400,000 business limit for the small business deduction must be prorated for the number of days in the taxation year. Since the winding-up may take some time to complete, this solution assumes that the corporation maintains its eligibility for the small business deduction in the year in which the sale of assets occurs. In this case, there would be no need to bonus down to the business limit for the small business deduction, given active business income of $75,000. The CRA's policy of not challenging the reasonableness of bonuses paid by a CCPC to an active shareholder, resident in Canada, from the normal earnings of an active business, may not apply if a bonus is paid from the sale of assets that is not part of normal business. The CRA indicated, at the 2003 Canadian Tax Foundation Annual Conference, that it is a question of fact in a specific situation whether such a bonus from non-normal business income is reasonable.

IT-73R6, par. 9

[5]		
Tax @ 20% on $75,000 of recapture	$15,000	
Tax @ 46⅔% on $55,000 of investment income	25,667	$40,667
RDTOH (26⅔% of $55,000)		$14,667

ITA: 129(3)(*a*)(i)

[6] Assumes a minimum $59,000 (i.e., 3 × $19,667) is to be distributed as a taxable dividend to produce a refund. Given the funds available for distribution, net of the capital dividend account, it can be seen, by inspection, that the taxable dividend resulting on the winding-up will exceed the minimum necessary to obtain the full refund.

ITA: 129(1)

(7) Had there been a taxable capital gain, the capital gains deduction for qualified small business corporation shares would not apply, because the shares would not meet the small business corporation test (as discussed in Chapter 13) after the assets have been sold for cash.

Summary of the Winding-Up Procedure

The winding-up procedure demonstrated above can be summarized as follows:

(a) dispose of all assets at FMV and determine any resulting income or loss and adjustments to the capital dividend account;

(b) pay the liabilities including any tax liability and bonus generated;

(c) calculate the RDTOH and assume it to be fully refunded;

(d) distribute the net proceeds to the shareholder, determining a deemed dividend as the excess, if any, of such proceeds over the paid-up capital;[3]

(e) elect on an amount not in excess of the capital dividend account. Elect that the remainder is a taxable dividend;

ITA: 83(2)
ITA: 184(3)

(f) check to see if the taxable dividend is sufficient to generate the full dividend refund that was assumed under (c); and

(g) compute the shareholder's gain or loss on the disposition of the shares.

¶15,300   SALE OF AN INCORPORATED BUSINESS

¶15,310   Assets Versus Shares

The sale of an incorporated business can be handled by two basic methods. One of these methods is selling the shares which entitles the buyer to control over the net assets of the corporation. This method results in a standard capital gains computation on the sale of shares.

The other method is selling the assets of the corporation. The proceeds from the sale of assets after taxes are paid would remain in the corporation after such a sale. The shareholder could then re-invest those net proceeds in the corporation or he or she could distribute them, perhaps, by winding up the corporation. This method, ultimately, results in the same procedure as the winding-up procedure demonstrated in the previous part of this chapter.

¶15,320   Analysis for the Decision

Example Problem

Mr. Nudge owns all of the shares of Strikeout Ltd., a Canadian-controlled private corporation, whose operations have been successful, but Mr. Nudge has little time to devote to this company. As a result he is considering an offer from a Canadian public company to buy his business as at January 1, 2008. The offer is to buy the shares for $130,000. This value for the shares reflects the fact that the purchaser will not have access to tax-free dividends from the corporation's capital dividend account. Alternatively, the public company is prepared to pay $166,000 for the assets (including an investment in cash which it will need for working capital). Strikeout's fiscal year-end is December 31.

Financial information concerning Strikeout Ltd. on December 31, 2007 was as follows:

---

[3] For the purposes of corporate law, the full distribution to the shareholders (including PUC) is done by way of a dividend, although only certain elements of the distribution will be taxed as a dividend.

Assets	Actual cost	UCC	FMV at Dec. 31, 2007
Cash	$ 4,000		$ 4,000
Accounts receivable	10,000		7,000
Inventory	30,000		37,000
Land	10,000		20,000
Buildings (Class 1)	35,000	$10,000	39,000
Equipment (Class 8)	25,000	18,000	12,000
Goodwill	Nil		47,000
			$166,000

Liabilities			
Current liabilities	$ 20,000		
Future income taxes	3,000		
Depreciation claimed	22,000		
Paid-up capital	10,000		
Retained earnings	57,000		
Reserve for doubtful accounts	2,000		

$10,000 - 7,000 + 2,000 = (1,000)$

The surplus accounts on December 31, 2007 before the sale were as follows:

Tax-paid retained earnings	$37,000
Capital dividend account	20,000

— *REQUIRED*

(A) Mr. Nudge requests your advice as to which option he should accept assuming that he would begin winding up the company immediately if assets are sold to the Canadian public company. You should assume that Mr. Nudge's marginal tax rate, federal and provincial, on income from this transaction is 46%. Cost of the shares in Strikeout Ltd. was $10,000. Assume that the corporation pays tax at the overall rate of 20% on active business income up to $400,000 and 40% initially on all other income, plus the additional refundable tax on investment income. Assume that the corporation has a nil GRIP balance at the time of the winding-up.

(B) What factors should the purchaser have considered in setting the offer price for the shares if the purchaser were: (a) another Canadian-controlled private corporation, (b) a Canadian public corporation, or (c) a non-resident corporation?

(C) Determine a selling price for the shares that results in the same after-tax net cash retained on the sale of assets and winding-up.

(D) Based on an offer of $166,000 for the assets, what is the maximum price the Canadian public company should be willing to pay for the shares of Strikeout Ltd.? Assume that the public company pays tax at a 40% rate, that it uses an after-tax discount rate of 8% and that it does not expect to sell the fixed assets of Strikeout Ltd. for a very long time.

— *SOLUTION*

Part (A): Options

Option 1 — Sale of shares for $130,000

Proceeds	$130,000
Adjusted cost base	10,000
Capital gain	$120,000
Taxable capital gain (½ × $120,000)	$ 60,000*
Tax thereon at 46% of $60,000	$ 27,600
Net proceeds ($130,000 – $27,600)	$102,400

---

* This capital gain would also be eligible for the QSBCS capital gains deduction to a maximum of $250,000 if the tests for a small business corporation are met, as discussed in Chapter 13.

Option 2 — Sale of assets and subsequent winding-up

Calculation of funds available for distribution on winding-up:

	Actual or deemed proceeds	Income generated Bus.	Income generated Invest.	Capital dividend account	RDTOH
Opening balance		Nil	Nil	$20,000	Nil
Cash	$ 4,000	Nil	Nil		
Accounts receivable(1)	7,000	$ (1,000)	Nil		
Inventory	37,000	7,000	Nil		
Land(2)	20,000	Nil	$ 5,000	5,000	
Buildings(3)	39,000	25,000	2,000	2,000	
Equipment(4)	12,000	(6,000)	Nil		
Goodwill(5)	47,000	23,500	Nil	23,500	
Current liabilities(6)	(20,000)				
Income taxes(8)	(12,967)	$ 48,500(7)	$ 7,000		$ 1,867
RDTOH(9)	1,867				$ 1,867
	$134,900(10)			$50,500	

ITA: 23(1)

Calculation of deemed taxable dividend on the winding-up:

Funds available for distribution	$ 134,900
Less: paid-up capital	(10,000)
Deemed dividend on winding-up	$ 124,900
Less: capital dividend elected	(50,500)
Deemed taxable dividend (sufficient to clear RDTOH)	$ 74,400

ITA: 84(2)
ITA: 83(2), 88(2)(*b*)(i)

Calculation of taxable capital gain on disposition of shares in the winding-up:

Actual proceeds from distribution	$ 134,900
Less: deemed dividend	(124,900)
Proceeds of disposition (also equal to PUC)	$ 10,000
Cost	(10,000)
Capital gain	Nil
Taxable capital gain	Nil

ITA: 54 "proceeds of disposition" (*j*)

These results can be verified by the use of Exhibit 15-2.

Net cash retained after sale of assets and subsequent winding-up:

Funds distributed on wind-up		134,900
Tax on incremental income from distribution:		
Deemed taxable dividend	$ 74,400	
Gross-up (1/4 × $74,400)	18,600	
Grossed-up dividend	$ 93,000	
Taxable capital gain	Nil	
Incremental taxable income	$ 93,000	
Combined federal and provincial tax @ 46%	$ 42,780	
Less: approximate combined dividend tax credit ((13 1/3% + 6 2/3%) of $93,000)	(18,600)	(24,180)
Net cash retained		$ 110,720
∴ Sell assets to retain net proceeds of		$ 110,720

—NOTES TO PART (A) SOLUTION

(1) The reserve of $2,000 must be added to income whether or not a section 22 election is used. If this election is used the excess of face amount over proceeds of $3,000 would be a business loss such that the net effect on income in this case would be a $1,000 business loss. Under section 22, the purchaser must include the difference ($3,000) between the face amount and the amount paid in income. This inclusion permits the purchaser to deduct a reasonable reserve for doubtful debts on the receivables purchased and to deduct any bad debts as they occur. Note that one of the conditions of this election is that the seller must dispose of all or substantially all of its business assets to a purchaser who must propose to carry on the business. The following are the effects of the election made jointly between the vendor and the purchaser, as discussed in Chapter 4:

ITA: 20(1)(*l*), 20(1)(*p*)

Vendor		Purchaser	
Reserve	$2,000		
Business income		$ 2,000	
Consideration	$7,000	Accounts receivable . . .	$10,000
Business loss	3,000	Consideration	$ 7,000
Accounts receivable	10,000	Income	3,000

If section 22 is not used, the $3,000 loss incurred by the vendor will be a capital loss (deductible only against capital gains) and any gain or loss realized by the purchaser on collection of the receivables will be a capital gain or loss with no reserve or write-off permitted to the purchaser.

(2) Proceeds on sale of land	$20,000
Actual cost	10,000
Full increase in value	$10,000
Taxable capital gain (½ × $10,000) (investment income)	$ 5,000
Capital dividend account (½ × $10,000)	$ 5,000

(3) Proceeds on sale of building.	$39,000
Tax value (UCC)	(10,000)
Full increase in value	$29,000
Taxable capital gain (½ × ($39K – $35K)) (investment income)	$ 2,000
Capital dividend account (½ × ($39K – $35K))	2,000
Recapture ($35K – $10K) (business income)	25,000
	$29,000

(4) Proceeds on sale of equipment	$12,000
UCC	18,000
Terminal loss (active business income offset)	$(6,000)

(5) Goodwill — increase in value	$47,000
Credit to pool (¾ of proceeds) (¾ × $47,000)	$35,250
Active business income (⅔ × $35,250)	$23,500
Capital dividend account (⅔ × (¾ × $47,000))	$23,500

ITA: 14

(6) The future income tax credit is not a liability that must be paid directly. The actual income tax liability resulting from the sale of the corporation's assets is computed below.

(7) The $400,000 business limit for the small business deduction must be prorated for the number of days in the taxation year. Since the winding-up may take some time to complete, this solution assumes that the corporation maintains its eligibility for the small business deduction in the year in which the sale of assets occurs. In this case, there would be no need to bonus down to the business limit for the small business deduction, given active business income of $48,500.

ITA: 73R6, par. 9

(8) Tax @ 20% on $48,500	$ 9,700
Tax @ 46.67% on $7,000	3,267
Total Part I tax	$12,967

(9) Refundable portion of Part I tax to RDTOH

26⅔% of investment income ($7,000) .... $ 1,867

A distribution of $5,600 (i.e., 3 × $1,867) in taxable dividends will be required to receive a dividend refund of $1,867 which clears the RDTOH account.

(10) There is no reason why Mr. Nudge could not use the net cash within the corporation to invest in securities or in another business if he wishes. In that case, the winding-up would not take place and, as a result, the RDTOH of $1,867 would not be available until dividends are paid by the corporation. On the other hand, Mr. Nudge avoids (postpones) the income taxes on the deemed dividend of $74,400. This example distributes the net proceeds in a winding-up to compare with the after-tax consequences of a sale of shares.

Part (B): Factors to be considered by the Purchaser

Theoretically, the value of a company's shares to a purchaser should be given by the present value of the expected future after-tax cash flows accruing to the purchaser when these cash flows are discounted at the purchaser's required rate of return appropriately adjusted for the risk of the situation. Tax considerations may affect the discount rate. Interest on money borrowed to acquire shares is deductible, reduces the after-tax cost of funds and, hence, it affects the discount rate used. The result of using a relatively lower discount rate is a relatively higher present value for the shares.

Tax considerations also affect the present value of the shares primarily through their effect on cash flows. The level of after-tax cash flows accruing to all purchasers will be affected by the amount of capital cost allowance that can be taken on the assets of the company whose shares have been purchased. Since, in the purchase of shares, there is no step-up in the capital cost to fair market value of the assets, the after-tax cash flows arising from capital cost allowance are not affected by the purchase of shares.

The deductibility of loss carryovers which reduce future taxes and, hence, increase future cash flows may be affected by the purchase of shares. The Act permits a corporation in which there has been an acquisition of control of shares to deduct non-capital losses if the business in which the losses were incurred continues to be carried on after the acquisition of control under restrictive conditions discussed in Chapter 11. However, the Act does not permit the carryover of net capital losses when there has been an acquisition of control of the shares. If such losses cannot be carried over, the future after-tax cash flows are reduced, thereby reducing the value of the shares to the purchaser.

ITA: 111(5)

ITA: 111(4)

(a) Considerations of a Canadian-controlled Private Corporation as Purchaser

Most of the tax advantages of the small business deduction would continue if the shares of a Canadian-controlled private corporation were acquired by another Canadian-controlled private corporation as long as the corporate group had some eligibility for the small business deduction left (i.e., active business income does not exceed the business limit of $400,000). However, it should be noted that the amount of the small business deduction for a year must be allocated within a group of associated corporations resulting in a potential reduction of the deduction for a particular corporation in the group and, therefore, increased tax and lower after-tax cash flows.

(b) Considerations of a Canadian Public Corporation as Purchaser

The small business deduction would be lost to the acquired corporation on the purchase of control of its shares by a Canadian public corporation. This will reduce future after-tax cash flows and, hence, the value of the shares to the purchaser. Amounts in the acquired company's capital dividend account are no longer available for tax-free distribution after control of the company has been purchased by a Canadian public corporation. As a result, it might be advisable to elect and pay a dividend out of the capital dividend account before the purchase of control and to reduce the selling price of the shares accordingly. While ordinary dividends would still be received by the purchasing corporation without attracting tax, such dividends paid to the shareholders of the purchasing corporation may be subject to tax, thereby reducing the value of the acquiring company's shares. This may increase the cost of funds to the acquirer, thereby increasing the required return. Also, refundable taxes would be lost on the acquisition of control by a Canadian public corporation. This would clearly reduce future cash flows.

(c) Considerations of a Non-resident Corporation as Purchaser

ITA: 18(4), 88

Again, the small business deduction would be lost to the acquired corporation on the purchase of control of its shares by a non-resident corporation. This will result in additional tax that will reduce the value of the shares. Management fees, royalties, interest, dividends and capital dividend payments paid to a non-resident purchaser will be subject to withholding tax. This will result in a cash outflow earlier than might otherwise be the case, if such tax did not have to be paid immediately, resulting in a reduction of the present value of the shares. The thin capitalization rules may operate to reduce the deductibility of interest on debt, if any, held by the non-resident corporation purchaser. This will reduce future cash flows. A rollover (as discussed in the next chapter) on the winding-up of a wholly owned Canadian corporation would not be available if the purchaser is not another Canadian corporation. If such a winding-up were contemplated it may result in higher taxes being paid earlier resulting in lower cash flows in early years after the acquisition and a lower value for the shares. Finally, the acquisition of shares by a non-resident corporation would be subject to government review. This would result in relatively higher expenses of acquisition and a lower value for the shares.

Part (C): Minimum Share Price Acceptable to Mr. Nudge

The calculation of the net proceeds in Part (A) above can be represented algebraically as:

$$P - .46 \left[\tfrac{1}{2} (P - \$10,000) \right]$$

where P = proceeds of disposition.

To equate the above expression with the net cash retained of $110,720 from the sale of assets and wind-up of the corporation, the following equation in one unknown results:

$$P - .46 \left[\tfrac{1}{2} (P - \$10,000) \right] = \$110,720$$
Solving for P,   P = $140,805

Therefore, Mr. Nudge should be willing to accept an offer of $140,805 for the shares.

A more tax-effective plan for the sale of shares would be to have Strikeout Ltd. elect to pay a tax-free dividend from its capital dividend account balance of $20,000 before the sale of the shares. This may require that the corporation borrow the cash to pay the dividend. The result would be a decrease in the value of the shares, but a saving of the tax on $20,000 which would otherwise be in the proceeds of disposition on the shares and would be taxed as a capital gain. The calculation of the net proceeds needed for the shares to equate the after-tax retention from the sale of assets would be given by the following equation:

$$\$20,000 + P - .46 \left[\tfrac{1}{2} (P - \$10,000) \right] = \$110,720.$$
Solving for P,   P = $114,831.

Part (D): Maximum Share Price Acceptable to Canadian Public Company

When shares are purchased, the purchaser, in essence, steps into the tax position of the acquired corporation. As a result, there is no step-up of cost values such as ACB and UCC to fair market value. Therefore, the purchaser assumes the eventual tax liability on accrued gains on the assets and loses the opportunity to benefit from the write-off of stepped-up costs. The increased write-offs on the purchase of assets can be thought of as reducing the net cost of the assets. Also, avoiding the assumption of inherent tax liabilities by the purchase of assets at fair market value and establishing their cost at that value can be thought of as decreasing the net cost of assets.

Consider the comparative effects of a purchaser of each asset in this case. On the purchase of accounts receivable, electing under section 22, income of $3,000 must be recorded, as shown. However, the purchaser can deduct a reserve in respect of those accounts receivable. If shares are purchased, the prior year's reserve of $2,000 must be included, but a new reserve can be deducted. Also, due to the acquisition of control, the Act requires the deduction of the loss in value of $3,000 in the deemed taxation year resulting from the acquisition of control. The net result between a purchase of assets and a purchase of shares would be about the same in this case.

ITA: 111(5.3)

On the purchase of inventory, the cost is established at fair market value of $37,000. If shares are purchased, the purchaser assumes the liability for tax on the $7,000 of income (i.e., $37,000 – $30,000) when the inventory is sold. Since inventory is likely to be sold within the year, the tax would amount to $2,800 (i.e., 40% of $7,000). Purchasing assets avoids this tax cost.

On the purchase of the land, the ACB is established at fair market value of $20,000. If shares are purchased, the purchaser assumes the inherent liability for tax on the $10,000 of capital gain accrued on the land. However, this tax is only incurred on the sale of the land by the purchaser. In this case, since the purchaser does not anticipate a sale in the foreseeable future, the present value of this future tax can be assumed to be negligible.

On the purchase of the building, the UCC and the ACB are established at fair market value of $39,000. If shares are purchased, the purchaser assumes the liability for tax on the $25,000 of recapture and $4,000 of capital gain, if this income is realized on the ultimate disposition of the building. Again, since the purchaser does not anticipate a sale of the building in the foreseeable future, the present value of this future tax can be assumed to be negligible.

However, on the purchase of the building, the purchaser can benefit from an increase in CCA relative to a purchase of shares which will shield future income from tax. The present value of the tax shield for the purchase of the building in Class NRB in this case is given by:

$$\frac{c \times d \times t}{d + r} \left[\frac{1 + r/2}{1 + r} \right]$$

$$= \frac{\$39,000 \times .06 \times .40}{.06 + .08} \left[\frac{1 + .08/2}{1 + .08} \right]$$

$$= \$6,438$$

where c = capital cost
d = CCA rate
t = tax rate
r = after-tax discount rate

If shares are purchased, the corporation continues to deduct CCA in Class 1 on a UCC base of $10,000, providing a tax shield with a present value given by:

$$\frac{c \times d \times t}{d + r}$$

$$= \frac{\$10,000 \times .04 \times .40}{.04 + .08}$$

$$= \$1,333$$

The incremental tax saved from CCA on the purchase of assets in present value terms is $5,105 (i.e., $6,438 – $1,333). This can be considered a decrease in the net cost of purchasing assets.

On the purchase of equipment at a fair market value of $12,000 (which is less than UCC of $18,000), the UCC base for future UCC is established at $12,000 and the first year's CCA after the purchase is subject to the half-year rule. However, on the purchase of shares, there is an acquisition of control which causes the UCC after the acquisition of control to be reduced to fair market value of $12,000, but the half-year rule is not applicable to the CCA in this case. As a result, there is a difference between the effect of a purchase of the equipment and a purchase of shares in this case, based on the application of the half-year rule in the calculation of CCA on the purchase of assets. The difference is negligible (i.e., $127), in this case, and will be ignored in the subsequent analysis, since it does not affect the decision.

ITA: 111(5.1)

On the purchase of goodwill at a fair market value of $47,000, the purchaser can add $35,250 (i.e., ¾ × $47,000) to its cumulative eligible capital account and it can amortize that amount at 7% on a declining balance basis. The present value of the write-off is given by:

$$\frac{c \times d \times t}{d + r}$$

$$= \frac{\$35,250 \times .07 \times .40}{.07 + .08}$$

$$= \$6,580$$

If shares are purchased, there is no balance of cumulative eligible capital to amortize. Therefore, the $6,580 is a net cost reduction on the purchase of assets.

To summarize these effects, the following is a calculation of the cost of a purchase of assets net of the cost reduction discussed above:

Cost of gross assets, per offer		$166,000
Tax savings — Present value of future CCA/CECA:		
Building	$6,438	
Goodwill	6,580	(13,018)
After-tax cost of assets		$152,982

Next, what the purchaser would pay for the shares to have an after-tax cost of the shares of $154,413 must be determined. This calculation would be as follows:

Price of shares	x =	$131,515
Liabilities assumed	$ 20,000	20,000
Tax savings — Present value of future CCA:		
Building	$ (1,333)	(1,333)
Tax costs — Present value of tax on accrued gains:		
Inventory	2,800	2,800
After-tax cost of shares	$152,982	$152,982

This price of $131,515 is the maximum amount that the Canadian public purchaser corporation should be willing to pay for the shares in this case.

Summary

The results of the analysis in Parts (C) and (D) can be summarized, in terms of pre-tax costs and equivalent values, as follows:

Purchaser's after-tax cost:

	Pre-tax		*After-tax*	
Asset purchase	$166,000	$\longrightarrow$	$152,982	⌉
Share purchase	$131,515 ◄—		$152,982 ◄	

Vendor's after-tax proceeds:

	Pre-tax		*After-tax*	
Asset sale	$166,000	$\longrightarrow$	$110,720	⌉
Share sale	$140,805 ◄—		$110,720 ◄	

This table can be further summarized by the grid as follows:

	Assets	*Shares*
Maximum that purchaser will pay	$166,000	$131,515
Minimum that vendor will accept	$166,000	$140,805

From this grid it can be seen that, if the value of the assets is in fact, $166,000, then the vendor should be willing to accept no less than $140,805 for the shares and the purchaser should be willing to pay no more than $131,515 for the shares. This establishes that, in this particular case, there is no negotiation range within which a transaction for shares may be better than a transaction for assets. For example, at the $130,000 offered for the shares, the vendor, Mr. Nudge, will retain less in after-tax proceeds than on a sale of assets. On the other side, a purchase of shares at $130,000 results in a slightly lower net tax cost than a purchase of assets with a net after-tax cost of $131,515. If both parties agree on the value of the assets at $166,000, they will transact in assets and not shares in this particular case. The vendor will have a higher after-tax retention from the sale of assets instead of shares and the purchaser will have a lower after-tax cost.

On the other hand, if the $20,000 balance in the capital dividend account is paid to Mr. Nudge as a tax-free dividend, then he requires a minimum of only $114,831 for the shares, to be indifferent between a sale of shares and a sale of assets in terms of his after-tax retention. If the minimum that he will accept for the shares is $114,831 and the maximum that the purchaser will pay is $111,515 ($131,515 − $20,000), then there is still no negotiation range within which a transaction price will make both parties better off from the sale of shares compared with the sale of assets.

¶15,400   GST AND THE WINDING-UP OF A CANADIAN CORPORATION

Where a corporation is wound up and the winding-up rules of the *Income Tax Act* apply, the supply of property on the winding-up is subject to the general rules of the GST. GST applies to all taxable supplies made in Canada. If a corporation is wound up and the corporation's property is acquired by a recipient, GST is payable by the recipient on any taxable supplies of property.

ITA: 88(2); ETA: 165(1)

An election, however, may be available, in which case the payment of GST will generally not be required. The ETA deals with the situation where a supplier makes a supply of a business or part thereof that was established or carried on by the supplier (or established or carried on by another person and acquired by the supplier). In that situation, the recipient must be acquiring ownership, possession or use of all or substantially all (i.e., 90% or more) of the property that can reasonably be regarded as being necessary for the recipient to be capable of carrying on the business. Where these conditions are met, the vendor and purchaser may jointly elect to have GST not apply to the sale. However, GST will still apply to the following supplies:

ETA: 167(1)

- a taxable supply of services to be rendered by the vendor;

- a taxable supply by way of lease, licence or similar arrangement; and

- where the purchaser is not a registrant, a taxable supply of real property by way of sale.

Reference will be made to this election repeatedly in Chapters 15 through 18, since it is an important provision in the context of various types of corporate reorganizations and other business transfers.

This provision applies to *all* types of property sold. Thus the election is available even when the corporation being wound up was involved in making exempt supplies. As well, the corporation does not have to be a registrant. However, if the corporation being wound up is a registrant, then the purchaser must also be a registrant.

ETA: 167(1)

Because businesses are entitled to claim input tax credits in respect of GST paid on purchases used in commercial activities, the use of the election in the ETA may not result in any net GST savings. However, it may result in cash flow advantages, since GST does not have to be paid and then recovered through an input tax credit.

ETA: 167(1)

¶15,800   REVIEW QUESTIONS

(1) Assuming that you are working in a province in which only par value shares can be issued, what journal entry would you use to record the issuance of 100 common shares, which had a par value of $100 each, for $30,000?

(2) In jurisdictions without par value shares, how is the paid-up capital determined?

(3) What are "high-low" shares?

(4) What are the five basic components of the capital dividend account?

(5) Calculate the effect on the capital dividend account as a result of the sale of unrecorded goodwill this year for $100,000. The only other transaction in eligible capital property took place three years ago when a customer list was purchased for $10,000. The balance in the CEC account is now approximately $6,000.

(6) Smith Co. has total PUC of $10,000. It decided to make a distribution of capital in the amount of $9,000, but when it actually paid out the $9,000, the PUC was only reduced by $8,000. What are the tax consequences?

(7) What are the three components of a distribution on the winding-up of a corporation where the only shareholder is an individual?

(8) Gone Co. is a CCPC that is in the process of being wound up under the general winding-up rule. One of its assets is a building that has an accrued terminal loss. The lawyer has suggested that subsection 13(21.2) will apply to deny the terminal loss to the corporation on winding-up. What do you think?

ITA: 88(2)

(9) Technically, on the winding-up of a corporation under the general winding-up rule, how are the proceeds of disposition of the shares calculated?

ITA: 88(2)

¶15,825 MULTIPLE CHOICE QUESTIONS

Question 1

Which one of the following statements is FALSE?

(A) A capital dividend is usually received tax-free.

(B) A corporation must elect to pay a capital dividend, not later than the day the dividend is paid.

(C) If a private corporation has had more capital gains than capital losses, it will probably have a balance in its capital dividend account.

(D) The payment of a capital dividend by a private corporation will trigger a dividend refund: one dollar refund for each three dollars of capital dividends paid.

Question 2

Mr. Andrews owned Class A special shares of Atlantis Ltd. with the following characteristics:

Fair market value	$60,000
Cost	20,000
Paid-up capital	10,000

These shares were redeemed. Which one of the following best describes the tax consequences of the redemption to Mr. Andrews?

(A) A capital gain of $40,000

(B) A dividend of $40,000

(C) A dividend of $50,000 and a capital gain of $40,000

(D) A dividend of $50,000 and a capital loss of $10,000

Question 3

X Ltd. had $40,000 available for distribution to its sole shareholder, Xavier, on winding-up. The balances in the tax accounts of X Ltd. were as follows:

Share capital (paid-up capital)	$ 2,000
RDTOH	Nil
Capital dividend account	8,000
Other surplus	30,000
	$40,000

Xavier paid $1,000 for the shares of X Ltd. when he purchased them two years ago. Which one of the following statements is TRUE?

(A) The winding-up can occur on a tax-deferred basis. Xavier will be able to defer the recognition of any income for tax purposes.

(B) Xavier will have dividend income of $30,000 which will be grossed-up to $37,500 for tax purposes. In addition, he will have a capital gain of $1,000.

(C) Xavier will have dividend income of $30,000 which will be grossed-up to $37,500 for tax purposes. In addition, he will have a capital gain of $9,000.

(D) Xavier will have a capital gain of $39,000 on the winding-up of X Ltd.

Question 4

Art, the sole shareholder of Art's Variety Inc. with a November 30 year-end, has decided to wind up the corporation, effective December 1. The balance sheet as at that date is anticipated to be as set out below.

¶15,825

Assets	
Cash	$ 45,000
Refundable dividend tax on hand	30,000
Land, at cost (FMV, $850,000)	250,000
Building, at UCC (FMV, $780,000; cost, $380,000)	180,000
	$505,000

Liabilities & Equity	
Liabilities	$ 20,000
Paid-up capital	5,000
Capital dividend account	10,000
Other surplus	470,000
	$505,000

Art's Variety Inc. is a Canadian-controlled private corporation. It pays tax at a combined federal and provincial rate of 18% on business income in the winding-up period and 45% including the additional refundable tax on investment income.

The amount available for distribution to Art on the windup will be:

(A) $485,000

(B) $1,394,000

(C) $1,557,333

(D) $1,838,333

Question 5

At the beginning of its first taxation year, Newco Ltd., a newly-incorporated company, issued 100 common shares to Mr. A for $10,000. On June 1 of the same year, Newco issued an additional 100 common shares to Mr. B for $15,000 (which is the fair value of the shares on that date). On December 30 of the same year, Mr. C acquired all of Mr. A's common shares for $20,000. At the end of this year (December 31), which of the following statements is true?

(A) The total paid-up capital of the common shares is $25,000, ½ of which is attributable to each of Mr. C and Mr. B.

(B) The total paid-up capital of the common shares is $35,000, ½ of which is attributable to each of Mr. C and Mr. B.

(C) The total paid-up capital of the common shares is $25,000, $10,000 of which is attributable to Mr. C and $15,000 of which is attributable to Mr. B.

(D) The total paid-up capital of the common shares is $35,000, $20,000 of which is attributable to Mr. C and $15,000 of which is attributable to Mr. B.

Question 6

C Co. is a Canadian controlled private corporation with a December 31 year-end. During the year it sold all its assets including goodwill. The goodwill was sold for fair market value: $1,000,000. The cost of the goodwill and the company's cumulative eligible capital account was Nil. Which of the following is a correct statement?

(A) C Co. will report a taxable capital gain of $500,000 and its capital dividend account will increase by $500,000.

(B) C Co. will report active business income of $500,000 and its capital dividend account will increase by $500,000.

(C) C Co. will report active business income of $750,000 and its capital dividend account will increase by $250,000.

(D) C Co. will report a taxable capital gain of $500,000 and its refundable dividend tax on hand account will increase by $133,335.

¶15,850 EXERCISES

Exercise 1

ITA: 89(1)

The following capital properties have been sold by a Canadian-controlled private corporation during the year ended December 31:

	A	B	C
Proceeds of disposition	$4,000	$1,000	$2,000
Cost	2,000	2,000	2,000
Selling expenses	400	100	200

— *REQUIRED*

Compute the effects of the dispositions on the capital dividend account.

Exercise 2

ITA: 89(1)

Adjusted Ltd., a Canadian-controlled private corporation, sold the following two capital properties during the fiscal year ending December 31:

	Cost	Proceeds	Selling costs
Property 1	$75,000	$110,000	$11,000
Property 2	40,000	11,000	5,500

— *REQUIRED*

Compute the effects of these sales on:

(A) the net income for tax purposes, and

(B) the balance in the capital dividend account.

Exercise 3

ITA: 83, 84

Mr. Deemed, the sole shareholder of Dividend Limited, a Canadian-controlled private corporation, requires some cash for other personal investment transactions. Dividend Limited's share capital is composed of 100 common shares with an ACB and PUC of $1 per share and 1,000 6% preferred shares with an ACB and PUC per share of $15 and a retractable value of $75 per share. Mr. Deemed is considering the following alternatives:

(a) Mr. Deemed would cause Dividend Limited to redeem 800 preferred shares at $75 per share.

(b) Mr. Deemed would cause Dividend Limited to pay a cash dividend of $60,000 on the common shares. Dividend Limited has a capital dividend account of $75,000.

(c) Mr. Deemed would cause Dividend Limited to make a non-dividend cash distribution of $60,000 on the preferred shares.

— *REQUIRED*

Discuss the tax implication of the above transactions.

Exercise 4

ITA: 54, 84(3), 248(1)

A Canadian-controlled private corporation has paid a dividend this year in the form of 10 first preference shares each having a redemption value of $1,000 and a paid-up capital value of $1.00.

— *REQUIRED*

(A) What are the tax consequences of the receipt of the dividend by an individual shareholder?

(B) What are the tax consequences to the corporation?

(C) What are the tax consequences to the individual shareholder of a sale at their fair market value of the shares received?

(D) What are the tax consequences to the individual shareholder of a redemption of the shares received?

Exercise 5

ITA: 53(1)(*b*), 53(2)(*a*), 84(1), 84(3), 84(4)

The following situations deal with Canadian-controlled private corporations and their non-arm's length shareholders. However, each transaction, described below, is separate and distinct from the other transactions unless the contrary is stated.

(a) X Ltd. issued to the daughter of its only shareholder retractable special shares (preferred shares) with a PUC of $150 and a redemption value of $1,000 for $100 cash.

(b) A, the sole shareholder of A Ltd., gave the corporation land with a FMV of $150,000.

(c) Y, the controlling shareholder of Y Ltd., converted debt of $20,000 for preferred shares with a PUC and redemption value of $2,000 plus cash of $20,000.

(d) Z, the sole common shareholder of Z Ltd., is considering causing the corporation to make a payment as a return of capital (PUC). The shares have a FMV of $50,000, PUC of $10,000 and ACB of $20,000:

(i) payment is for $5,000;

(ii) payment is for $18,000.

— *REQUIRED*

Discuss the tax consequences of the above transactions.

Exercise 6

ITA: 54, 83(2), 84(2), 88(2), 89(1)

Finished Limited is a Canadian-controlled private corporation, founded in 1992 by Mr. Finished who holds all of the outstanding shares. The following balance sheet reflects the position of the corporation after selling all assets and paying all liabilities:

Finished Limited

BALANCE SHEET

as at December 31, 2007

Cash	$ 950,000	Capital stock (PUC)	$ 625,000	
RDTOH	50,000	Capital dividend account	150,000	
		Other surplus	225,000	
			$1,000,000	
Total assets	$1,000,000			

— *REQUIRED*

(A) Determine the components of the distribution to Mr. Finished.

(B) Compute the taxable capital gain or allowable capital loss on the disposition of Mr. Finished's shares on January 1, 2008, assuming that their adjusted cost base was $350,000.

Exercise 7

ITA: 54, 83(2), 84(2), 88(2), 89(1)

Through Ltd., a CCPC, has been wound up this year and its only shareholder has surrendered her shares. She received $30,000 in total from the corporation for her shares which had a cost to her equal to their paid-up capital of $2,000. The company had elected a capital dividend on a dividend of $2,000. All business income of the CCPC has been taxed only at the low rate.

— *REQUIRED*

What are the tax consequences to the shareholder if she will be taxed on any income from the winding-up at a combined 29% federal and 17% provincial marginal rate of 46%?

Exercise 8

ITA: 54, 83(2), 84(2), 88(2), 89(1)

Downandout Limited is a Canadian-controlled private corporation which will be wound up by its only shareholder, Mr. Downer, who bought the shares at their paid-up capital value of $2,000. As at December 31, 2007, its balance sheet appears as follows:

Downandout Limited

BALANCE SHEET

as at December 31, 2007

Assets		Liabilities	
Cash	$ 20,000	Bank loan	$ 47,000
RDTOH	10,000	Wages payable	3,000
Inventories at cost (FMV: $220,000)	200,000	Total	$ 50,000
Land at cost (FMV: $70,000)	40,000	**Shareholder's Equity**	
Buildings at UCC (cost: $200,000; FMV: $300,000)	60,000	Paid-up capital	$ 2,000
Equipment at UCC (Cost: $100,000; FMV: $80,000)	40,000	Surplus	318,000
Total	$370,000	Total	$370,000

The balance in the corporation's capital dividend account was nil as at the above balance sheet date. The assets are to be liquidated, the liabilities paid and the net proceeds distributed to Mr. Downer effective January 1, 2008.

— *REQUIRED*

(A) Compute the amount available for distribution to the shareholder assuming the corporation pays corporate tax at the rate of 20% on the first $400,000 of active business income and 40% initially on any other income, plus the additional refundable tax on investment income, from the winding-up. The balance in the corporation's GRIP is nil.

(B) Determine the components of the distribution to the shareholder.

(C) Compute the taxable capital gain or allowable capital loss on the disposition of Mr. Downer's shares assuming that their adjusted cost base was $1,000.

(D) Discuss the GST implications on the wind-up of Downandout Limited.

¶15,875   ASSIGNMENT PROBLEMS

Problem 1

ITA: 89(1)

Surplus Accounts Limited, a Canadian-controlled private corporation, whose fiscal year-end is December 31, provides you with the following data concerning its tax accounts and capital transactions for 2007. The balance in its capital dividend account was nil on January 1, 2007. Ms. Tsakiris, a Canadian resident, is the sole shareholder.

Surplus Accounts Limited is considering winding up the corporation and wishes to determine the impact of the sale of all its capital assets on its tax surplus accounts. The following capital assets are recorded in the books of account:

Assets	Cost	UCC/ CEC	Estimated proceeds	Estimated selling costs
Investments	$60,000		$ 22,000	$ 500
Land	40,000		200,000	10,000
Building	70,000	$ 45,000	125,000	6,000
Equipment	35,000	Nil	8,000	400
Customer lists (Note 1)	40,000	16,000	60,000	—

Additional Information

(1) The balance in the cumulative eligible capital account reflects the purchase of the customer lists in 1997 for $40,000 less the tax write-offs for 1997 to 2006, inclusive.

(2) In addition to the above assets, there is $35,000 of goodwill which will also be sold.

— REQUIRED

Compute the effect on income and the capital dividend account balance immediately after the above transactions.

Problem 2

ITA: 89(1)

You have been asked to compute the capital dividend account of Granatstein Ltd., a Canadian-controlled private corporation incorporated in 1985. You have reviewed the tax returns of the corporation for the period January 1, 1985 to December 31, 2007, and made the following notes:

1986   Disposed of bonds resulting in a capital gain of $10,000.

1988   Received taxable dividend of $2,000 and capital dividend of $5,000.

1989   Disposed of shares resulting in a capital loss of $4,000.

1991   Disposed of equipment resulting in a capital gain of $6,000 and recapture of $3,000.

1993   Eligible capital property was purchased for $40,000.

1994   Sold vacant land and reported capital gain of $100,000.

1997   1994 capital gain of sale of vacant land was reassessed by the CRA as income. Granatstein Limited did not fight the reassessment.

2000   Sold shares resulting in a capital gain of $20,000.

2002   Received life insurance proceeds of $100,000 on a life insurance policy on the life of the company president purchased in 1994. As at January 1, 2002, the policy had an adjusted cost basis of $20,000.

2003   Paid capital dividends of $50,000.

2006   Sold a customer list for $100,000. The company's cumulative eligible capital balance at the time of the sale was $25,000.

2007   Sold shares resulting in a capital gain of $37,500.

— REQUIRED

Compute the balance in Granatstein Ltd.'s capital dividend account at the end of the 2007 taxation year. Show *all* calculations and explain why you omitted any of the above amounts in your answer.

Problem 3

ITA: 53(1)(*b*), 84

The following situations deal with a Canadian-controlled private corporation and its shareholders. Each transaction described below is separate and distinct from the other transactions.

(a) Capital Inc. issued 135 preferred shares with PUC equal to $110 each for $11,050 cash and assets with a FMV of $2,800.

(b) Paid Ltd. has shares with a FMV of $35,000 and a PUC of $5,500. Paid Ltd. is considering making the following paid-up capital reductions on these shares. Their shareholders have an ACB of $16,000 for their shares:

(i) payment of $3,750; and

(ii) payment of $8,750.

(c) Up Ltd. has 4,500 common shares with a PUC of $22,500. In March of this year the corporation declared and distributed a 15% stock dividend in common shares with a PUC of $3,375.

(d)(i) The sole shareholder of Baker Corp. Ltd. contributed assets worth $38,400 to the corporation in return for cash of $15,400 and preferred shares with a PUC of $23,000 (redemption value of $23,000).

(ii) A year later, the sole shareholder redeemed the preferred shares.

— REQUIRED

Discuss the tax consequences for deemed dividends for each of the above transactions.

ITA: 84

Problem 4

ITA: 54, 84(3), 84(6)

Ms. Chiu owns all of the 100 Class B shares issued by Chiu Ltd., a small business corporation, which was formed by Ms. Chiu in 1992. Her son owns all the Class A shares. The current fair market value of the Class B shares is $100 per share. The paid-up capital value of the shares and their adjusted cost base to Ms. Chiu is presently $5 each. Ms. Chiu would like to know the tax consequences if (a) her shares are redeemed by Chiu Ltd. for their fair market value or, alternatively, (b) she sells her shares to her son for their fair market value.

Ms. Chiu has also sold 100 common shares of Bellco Limited, a company whose shares are listed on the CDNX Stock Exchange. She has found out Bellco Limited, itself, had purchased her shares through the exchange for $4.10 each. The paid-up capital value of the shares was $1 each and their cost to Ms. Chiu three years ago was $1.25 each.

— REQUIRED

Comment on the tax implication of the above transactions.

Problem 5

ITA: 54, 83(2), 84(2), 84(2.1), 89(1)

Ms. Batt owns all the common shares of Batterup Ltd., a Canadian-controlled private corporation, which started operations in 1986. Batterup Ltd. has been quite profitable since the early 1990s. As a result, Three-Strikes Ltd., a Canadian public corporation, has offered Ms. Batt $252,500 for the assets, excluding cash, as at December 31, 2007. The offer price reflects unrecorded goodwill of $47,500. Ms. Batt wants to wind up the company after the sale of the assets.

The pro forma balance sheet of Batterup Ltd. as at December 31, 2007, is as follows:

Assets	Cost	UCC	FMV
Cash	$ 2,500		
Accounts receivable (net)	8,750		$ 7,500
Inventory	22,250		15,500
Land	11,000	—	45,000
Building	35,000	$ 7,500	95,000
Equipment	45,000	22,000	10,000
Marketable securities	14,250	—	32,000
	$138,750		$205,000

Liabilities

Current liabilities	$ 54,000
Future income taxes	5,000

Shareholder's Equity

Paid-up capital	10,000
Capital dividend account	4,000
Retained earnings	65,750
Total liabilities and equity	$138,750

Additional Information:

(1) Batterup Ltd. pays corporate tax at the overall rate of 20% on active business income eligible for the small business deduction and an initial 40% rate for investment income, plus the 6⅔% additional refundable tax on investment income. The corporation has a GRIP balance of nil.

(2) The reserve for doubtful accounts at December 31, 2007 was $1,500.

(3) Batterup Ltd. and Three-Strikes Ltd. elected under section 22.

— *REQUIRED*

(A) Compute the amount available for distribution to the shareholder.

(B) Determine the components of the distribution to the shareholder.

(C) Compute the taxable capital gain or allowable capital loss on the disposition of Ms. Batt's shares on the winding-up. (Assume the adjusted cost base of Ms. Batt's common shares is $10,000.)

(D) Explain the conditions for and advantages of using a section 22 election.

Problem 6

ITA: 54, 83(2), 84(2), 88(2), 89(1)

You have been approached by one of your clients, Mr. Sidney Chow, for help in determining what will be the tax consequences if he sells all his assets in his corporation (at their fair market value) in 2007 to someone who will continue the business. However, Mr. Chow is not sure if he should wind up his corporation at this time. The following tax balance sheet for Chow Enterprises Ltd. has been prepared as at December 31, 2007.

Chow Enterprises Ltd.

BALANCE SHEET

as at December 31, 2007

Cash		$ 10,000
RDTOH		5,000
Accounts receivable	$30,000	
Less: reserve for doubtful debts	5,000	25,000
Land		55,000
Building (Class 1) — UCC		95,000
Equipment (Class 8) — UCC		12,000
Shares in Bell Canada — cost		15,000
Goodwill — cumulative eligible capital balance		18,000
		$235,000
Liabilities		$ 35,000
Future income taxes		12,000
Common shares — PUC		20,000
Capital dividend account		8,000
Other surplus		160,000
		$235,000

Additional Information

(1) Mr. Chow owns all the common shares of the corporation, which he acquired in 1994 for $20,000 when the business was incorporated.

(2)

Assets	Cost	FMV
Accounts receivable	$30,000	$ 18,000
Land	55,000	150,000
Building — Class 1	170,000	320,000
Equipment — Class 8	30,000	3,000
Shares in Bell Canada	15,000	26,000
Goodwill	50,000	120,000

Goodwill was acquired in 1997 in connection with a similar business which was purchased that year. The fair market value reflects the goodwill for the combined businesses. The maximum amortization has been deducted for tax purposes.

(3) The corporation is taxable at a total 20% corporate tax rate for the first $300,000 of active business income and a 40% rate for any other income, plus the $6\frac{2}{3}$% additional refundable tax on investment income. The corporation has a GRIP balance of nil.

(4) The accounts receivable are to be sold to a factoring company.

— *REQUIRED*

(A) Compute the effect of the sale of the above assets on the various tax accounts in 2007, ignoring any potential normal business transactions.

(B) If Mr. Chow should decide to wind up beginning in 2008, ignoring any subsequent business transactions,

(i) determine the components of the distribution to him; and

(ii) compute the taxable capital gain or allowable capital loss on the disposition of Mr. Chow's shares.

(C) Indicate briefly the tax consequences of leaving the proceeds in the corporation and investing the money in high-yielding securities.

(D) Discuss the GST implications on the sale of assets and the subsequent winding-up.

Problem 7

ITA: 54, 83(2), 84(2), 88(2)

J. Tilkenhurst Limited (JTL) is a Canadian-controlled private corporation which was started in 1987 by Mr. Santosh Prasad with an initial investment in common shares of $18,000. Mr. Prasad has decided that it's time to retire and move to his retirement home in Saskatoon, Saskatchewan. Therefore, Mr. Prasad wishes to wind up JTL.

The following is a projected tax balance sheet prior to the sale and distribution of the assets as at the intended date of the winding-up:

J. Tilkenhurst Limited
BALANCE SHEET
as at December 31, 2007

Cash		$ 15,000
RDTOH		6,000
Accounts receivable	$60,000	
Less: reserve for doubtful accounts	5,000	55,000
Inventory		110,000
Marketable securities		26,000
Land		85,000
Building — UCC		23,000

Equipment — UCC		10,000
Customer list — CEC account balance		20,600
		$350,600
Liabilities		$ 45,000
Future income taxes		41,000
Common shares (PUC)		18,000
Capital dividend account (no unabsorbed negative amounts)		12,000
Other surplus		234,600
		$350,600

Additional Information

(1) The corporation is taxable at a total 20% corporate tax rate for the first $400,000 of active business income and an initial 40% rate for all other income, plus the $6\frac{2}{3}\%$ additional refundable tax on investment income. The corporation has a GRIP balance of nil.

(2)

Assets	Cost	FMV
Accounts receivable	$ 60,000	$52,000
Inventory	110,000	127,000
Marketable securities	26,000	26,000
Land	85,000	150,000
Building	66,000	97,000
Equipment	30,000	6,000
Customer lists*	42,453	70,000

* The customer lists were acquired in 2001 from a similar business which was acquired that year. The balance in the CEC account includes the maximum cumulative eligible capital amounts in each year.

(3) The books of account do not reflect unrecorded goodwill with an estimated fair market value of $60,000. This is in addition to the customer lists.

(4) The accounts receivable are to be sold to a factoring company.

— *REQUIRED*

Prepare an analysis of the income tax implications of the winding-up.

Problem 8

ITA: 14, 38, 82, 83(2), 117, 121, 123, 124, 129

Mr. Lotsaluck incorporated a company in 2007 in a province with a 20% corporate tax rate on active business income, a 40% total corporate tax rate on other income, before the $6\frac{2}{3}\%$ additional refundable tax, and a 46% combined personal tax rate (including a 17% personal provincial tax on income rate), taking one share with a paid-up capital value of $1 and a note representing a loan to the company of $499,999. The company, Luck Unlimited Limited, a private corporation, purchased the assets of a business in the same year for $500,000. The purchase price was allocated to the land and building of the business in the amount of $400,000 and to goodwill in the amount of $100,000. However, before the business had commenced, the company sold the assets of the business for $700,000, including $170,000 for goodwill.

— *REQUIRED*

Assume that the sale of land and building was considered to result in a *capital gain*. How much of the $700,000 received in the corporation would Mr. Lotsaluck retain, if he removed all of this amount from the corporation.

Problem 9

ITA: 54, 83(2), 84(2), 84(2.1), 89(1)

Ms. Debbie, the sole shareholder of Shining Limited, a CCPC, has been considering selling her common shares to Let's-Make-a-Deal Ltd., a CCPC. However, Ms. Debbie recalls reading somewhere that one should compare a share sale with an asset sale to determine which would result in higher after-tax cash flow.

Ms. Debbie provides you with the following information:

(1) The cost of Ms. Debbie's common shares in Shining Limited was $120,000.

(2) Shining Limited pays tax at the overall rate of 20% on the first $300,000 of active business income, 33% on additional active business income, and 40% on all other income, plus the 6⅔% additional refundable tax on investment income. The corporation has a GRIP balance of nil.

(3) Ms. Debbie's combined federal and provincial personal tax rate is 46%, including a personal provincial tax on income rate of 17%. The provincial dividend tax credit is 6⅔% of the grossed-up dividend.

(4) Financial information concerning Shining Limited on December 31, 2007 is as follows:

Assets	Book cost	UCC	FMV
Cash (required as working capital)	$ 23,000		
Marketable securities (required as working capital)	58,000		$ 54,000
Inventory	41,000		50,000
Land	154,000		210,000
Building (Note)	213,700	$195,000	440,000
Goodwill	Nil		85,000
	$489,700		$839,000

Liabilities			
Current liabilities	$ 43,000		
Future income taxes	4,800		
Paid-up capital	120,000		
Capital dividend account	48,000		
Retained earnings	273,900		
	$489,700		

(5) Shining Limited earned active business income of $50,000 during the year.

NOTE: The original cost of the building in Class 1 was $410,000. Book cost of $213,700 is net book value after accumulated amortization.

— REQUIRED

(A) If Ms. Debbie sells all of the assets, except cash, to Let's-Make-a-Deal Ltd., pays the outstanding liabilities, and then winds up Shining Limited, what would be the net amount available for distribution to her? Show all computations.

(B) Determine the components of the distribution to Ms. Debbie.

(C) Determine the amount, including principal, Ms. Debbie would retain from this distribution.

(D) Determine a selling price for the Shining Limited shares that results in the same after-tax net cash retained as the net cash from sale of assets followed by a wind-up, as determined in Part (C).

(E) Based on the indicated fair market value of the net assets, what is the maximum price a Canadian-controlled private corporation should be willing to pay for the shares of Shining Limited? Assume that the CCPC pays tax at the low rate of 20% on all of its business income, that it uses an after-tax discount rate of 10%, and that it does not expect to sell the fixed assets of Shining Limited for a very long time. Also, assume that if the purchaser bought the assets, it would have to invest $23,000 in cash to meet working capital requirements.

[For more problems and solutions thereto, see the CD accompanying this book.]

¶15,880 ADVISORY CASE

Ottawa Associates Inc.

Ottawa Associates Inc. is a business that was set up 25 years ago by Grant Carter to provide consulting services to the federal government. When the economy was good, the company was able to generate substantial profits and, even now, with a slow economy, the profits are approximately $450,000 before tax. Grant now feels that the company is worth $1,200,000 based on the income it is generating.

Grant is 50 years old this year. When he started the business, another shareholder, John Price, owned the other 50% of the shares. Each had put $10,000 of cash into the corporation as share capital. Initially, their working relationship had been excellent, but John had wanted to branch out into other areas of consulting, while Grant wanted to concentrate on government consulting. Fifteen years ago, they had agreed to go their own separate ways and Grant had bought John's shares from him for $30,000.

Grant's wife, Betty, does not work in the business directly. However, she does receive a salary for her work as secretary-treasurer of the corporation and for the time she spends on charitable activities, which is sometimes of benefit to Grant in his business. Grant would like to involve Betty in the ownership of the business, unless there are any problems with this.

Grant and Betty's two children, Scott and Kelly, are 21 and 16 years old, respectively. Scott is in university at Queen's and Kelly is in high school in Ottawa. At this point, it is not certain whether Scott and Kelly will join Grant in the business, but both are open to the possibility. Both work in the business during the summer holidays and are paid enough to cover their schooling costs.

Grant and Betty are now planning to build the cottage they have always wanted. They feel they need a place to unwind on the weekends and, also, they want a place for the children to come back to once they have left home. They see the cottage as a family gathering place. The land and construction costs are going to be approximately $200,000. Although they have that much extra cash in the corporation, they do not want to pay tax on the dividends to get the cash out. As a result, they plan to take out a mortgage to finance the cottage and pay it off over 10 years from Grant's bonus cheques.

Please provide your recommendations.

¶15,900   SUPPLEMENTAL NOTES

(This section can be omitted without losing the continuity of the chapter. None of the review questions, multiple choice questions, exercises, or assignment problems utilizes this information.)

¶15,910   GST and the Sale of an Incorporated Business

As discussed earlier in this chapter, the sale of an incorporated business can be handled by two basic methods — the sale of assets or the sale of shares. The election in the ETA discussed earlier may be available on the sale of assets of an incorporated business. As noted above, this provision of the ETA deals with the situation where a supplier sells a business (or part of a business) that it had established, carried on, or acquired. The recipient must acquire ownership, possession or use of all or substantially all of the property that is necessary to carry on that business or that is capable of being used to carry on a business. ETA: 167(1)
ETA: 167(1)

Under the election, a supplier may retain certain assets that were used in the business and lease those assets to the recipient, without disqualifying the parties from using the election. As well, the election can apply to all property sold as part of a business, including property that was used in exempt activities.

It is important to note that under the election, the parties need not be registrants; however, if the vendor is a registrant (and therefore able to claim input tax credits), the recipient must also be a registrant.

Some relief on the sale of capital personal property (see Chapter 5) is provided under certain circumstances. Where a registrant sells capital personal property that was used primarily in an exempt activity immediately before the sale, the sale is deemed to be made otherwise than primarily in the course of a commercial activity. Consequently, GST is not payable. It is important to note that the vendor must be a registrant for this provision to apply. ETA: 200(3)

A provision that may provide relief on the sale of a business (or the sale of most assets) between related parties, is found in the ETA. Where an election is made under that provision, transfers between corporations in a "closely-related group" are deemed to be supplies for no consideration. In other words, no GST applies. Corporations making this election are treated as if they are part of the same legal entity, avoiding the requirement to initially pay GST on taxable supplies and then claim a corresponding input tax credit. This election is not available for sales of real property, or for supplies that are not to be used by the recipient exclusively (i.e., 90% or more) in a commercial activity. ETA: 156

The exclusion for sales of real property, however, will generally not have any negative implications. GST need not be collected by the vendor of real property if the recipient is a registrant and the real property is not a residential complex supplied to an individual. When this applies, the purchaser is required to remit the GST payable on that real property directly to the Receiver General. However, a mechanism allows the input tax credit being claimed by the purchaser of such real property to be offset against the GST remittable in these circumstances. Consequently, no GST need be remitted on the sale of real property if it is to be used exclusively in a commercial activity. ETA: 221(2)

ETA: 228(4)

ETA: 228(6)

The definition of a closely-related group is quite detailed and is further complicated by the inclusion of additional rules in the Closely Related Corporations (GST/HST) Regulations. In basic terms, two corporations are closely related if they are registered for GST purposes and are members of a group of corporations resident in Canada with common ownership of 90% or greater. Special rules apply where the closely-related group includes a financial institution. ETA: 128(1)

If, however, the business is transferred by way of a sale of shares, the transfer has no GST consequences, since the sale of shares is an exempt supply under the GST. A "financial service" is defined to include an equity security. A "financial service" is defined in the same subsection to include the transfer of ownership of a financial instrument. Part VII of Schedule V of the ETA provides that the supply of a financial service is an exempt supply. ETA: 123(1) "financial
service" (*b*)

Where a registrant that is a corporation resident in Canada is engaged in a takeover attempt in which it is acquiring or attempting to acquire all or substantially all (i.e., 90% or more) of the voting shares of another corporation, it is entitled to claim input tax credits for GST paid on any purchases of property and services attributable to that activity. For this provision to apply, the target corporation must be engaged exclusively in commercial activities. Without this provision, GST paid in respect of the share purchase on legal fees and investment counsel fees, for example, would not be considered to be for use in a commercial activity. Consequently, the purchaser would not be entitled to an input tax credit.

ETA: 186(2)

To the extent that neither of these provisions of the ETA is applicable and GST is payable on taxable supplies made in the course of the sale, a full input tax credit will be available to the purchaser if the supplies are used exclusively in commercial activities. Any related costs, such as legal and accounting fees that are subject to GST, will also generate input tax credits under a provision that states that to the extent a person does anything in connection with the acquisition, establishment, disposition or termination of a commercial activity, that person is deemed to have been engaged in a commercial activity.

ETA: 156, 186(2)

ETA: 141.1(3)

Chapter 16

Income Deferral: Rollover on Transfers to a Corporation and Pitfalls

LEARNING GOALS

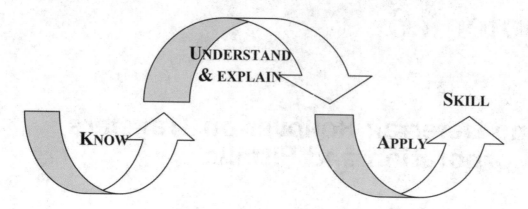

Know

By the end of this chapter you should know the basic provisions of the *Income Tax Act* pertaining to the transfer of property to a corporation, by a person who will be a shareholder of the corporation, on a tax deferred or rollover basis. Completing the Review Questions (¶16,800) and Multiple Choice Questions (¶16,825) is a good way to learn the technical provisions.

Understand and Explain

You should understand and be able to explain:

- The basic tax consequences of the transfer of property to a corporation by a shareholder on a rollover basis where applicable;

- Options for the transfer of property to a corporation;

- The means that a corporation can use to pay for the assets transferred and their tax consequences; and

- Two potential traps or pitfalls on the transfer of shares to a corporation, the cause of the issues that arise and how to avoid them.

Completing the Exercises (¶16,850) is a good way to deepen your understanding of the material.

Apply

You should be able to apply your knowledge and understanding of the key elements of the rollover on the transfer of property to a corporation in a variety of tax planning situations, including the incorporation of an unincorporated business, while avoiding the pitfalls of doing so, and in a way that accomplishes a client's goals. Completing the Assignment Problems (¶16,875) is an excellent way to develop your ability to apply the material in increasingly complex situations.

OVERVIEW

The general rule for the taxation of capital gains and losses is that all dispositions of capital property result in an immediate recognition of a capital gain or loss. This rule also applies to non-arm's length dispositions. However, in some circumstances, particularly in non-arm's length transactions, there is often no real change in the *economic interest* in the property. For example, where an individual transfers property to a wholly owned corporation,

ITA: 69

there is no real change in the individual's economic interest in the property. A "rollover" may provide, in limited circumstances, a deferral of capital gains or losses, as well as other types of income. A rollover normally provides for a transfer of property at a value that will be referred to initially as its "tax value". This term is not used in the Act, but is meant to refer to adjusted cost base, undepreciated capital cost or other tax value representing cost.

In return for the property transferred, the transferor should receive a "package" of consideration, the total fair market value of which should be equal to the fair market value of the property transferred. This fair market value exchange is done to avoid important tax complications that will be discussed later in the chapter. On the ultimate disposition of the property by the recipient or transferee, the gain or loss that was deferred at the time of the previous transfer (rollover) is included in the transferee's income. This chapter will discuss   ITA: 85 the rollover provisions in the Act pertaining to the transfer of property to a corporation by a shareholder. The chapter will also discuss two major pitfalls that can arise on the transfer of   ITA: 84.1, 55(2) shares. The final part of this chapter discusses the GST implications of the transfer of property to a corporation under the rollover. The next chapter will complete the discussion of rollovers involving corporations and their shareholders.

Refer to the chart at the beginning of Chapter 15 for the location in the Act of the major provisions discussed in this Chapter.

¶16,000   TRANSFER OF PROPERTY TO A CORPORATION BY A SHAREHOLDER

¶16,010   The Basic Concepts

Fundamentally, on the transfer of assets to a corporation, there is a disposition at fair   ITA: 85(1) market value. An election allows the transferor to choose the proceeds of disposition to defer some or all of the gain.

The provision that is most often referred to by its section number in the Act, section 85, permits a tax-free rollover of property to a corporation but only as long as the transferor accepts shares as part of the consideration for the transfer. The basic concept is that the transferor, who is now a shareholder of the transferee corporation, should be in the same economic position that he or she was in before the transfer. Therefore, the adjusted cost base of the shares that he or she receives should be exactly equal to the adjusted cost base of the asset transferred. Now, the deferred income inclusion (e.g., capital gain) will be triggered if the shares are sold in an arm's length transaction. Similarly, the corporation should retain the adjusted cost base of the transferred property. The above is the basic concept behind a pure tax-free rollover.

However, there are additional variables which add complexity to the pure concept. First, the transferor is permitted to trigger income inclusions (e.g., capital gains, recapture, etc. depending on the nature of the property) if he or she so desires. Second, the consideration can be, not only shares (common and preferred), but also debt or cash.

Therefore, this part will introduce the basic principles of a section 85 transfer of property to a corporation through three specific situations; a fourth will be added later in the chapter. Each situation will begin with the conditions or rules for the particular situation. Subsequent situations will introduce new variables so that, by the end of the third situation, some, but not all, of the basic concepts underlying section 85 should be understood. The balance of the chapter will build upon these concepts with the technical rules which add refinements to the basic concepts.

The first three situations will introduce the concepts in the following order:

- Situation One shows the necessity to make a downward adjustment to the paid-up capital (PUC) of the share consideration to equal the tax value of the asset transferred.

- Situation Two introduces the concept of a transfer price other than the tax value of the transferred asset so that income inclusions can be triggered.

- Situation Three introduces the possibility of accepting non-share consideration (e.g., debt or cash).

A fourth situation, which is introduced later in this chapter, demonstrates the concept that the FMV of the property transferred must equal the FMV of the consideration received, or adverse tax consequences will occur.

Note that the situations described are a conceptual introduction to section 85. The underlying technical rules are discussed later in the chapter. An understanding of these concepts will assist you in applying the complex technical rules that follow. Read these three initial situations carefully. In fact, you may find it helpful to revisit these concepts after you have attempted the technical readings, exercises and assignment problems.

At this point, it is important to understand the concept of "elected amount". The Act allows you to transfer assets to a corporation and "elect" your proceeds of disposition. While you cannot create a loss, you can either elect at the tax value to defer any gain or elect at some higher amount to recognize some or all of the gain on the property being transferred. This "elected amount" also becomes the cost of the property to the corporation. `ITA: 85(1)`

¶16,015 Situation one

¶16,015.10 *Conditions for transfer*

To defer any accrued gain, the assets must be transferred choosing an elected amount equal to their tax value, i.e., adjusted cost base (ACB), undepreciated capital cost (UCC), etc., depending on the type of property, so that there are no tax consequences in respect of the transfer. The consideration received on the transfer in this first situation will be common shares.

¶16,015.20 *Facts*

Ms. Ava wishes to transfer some land that is capital property to a corporation, Ava Ltd., which he presently controls through the ownership of all the Class A common shares. The land being transferred has an ACB of $10,000 and an FMV of $50,000. Ms. Ava will accept as consideration one Class B common share.

¶16,015.30 *Results*

Since Ms. Ava does not want any tax consequences from the transfer, Ms. Ava and the corporation should be in the same economic position as if the transfer did not happen.

Land

(1) The proceeds of disposition should be the elected amount of $10,000, which is the ACB of the land so that no gain is triggered.

(2) The cost of the land to Ava Ltd. should also be the elected amount of $10,000, which is Ms. Ava's ACB so that Ava Ltd. is in the same economic position (i.e., there is a potential capital gain of $40,000 upon the disposition of the land by Ava Ltd.).

Consideration — One Class B common share

(1) The ACB of the Class B common share should also be equal to Ms. Ava's ACB of the land. He is now in the same economic position as before with a potential capital gain of $40,000 on the one Class B common share. The ACB of the share represents the cost of the land which was acquired with after-tax or tax-paid funds and can be recovered on a disposition of the share.

(2) The FMV of the Class B share should be $50,000 which is equal to the underlying value of the land transferred to Ava Ltd. The result is that Ms. Ava had exchanged land with a fair market value of $50,000 for shares with a fair market value of $50,000.

(3) Logically, the paid-up capital (PUC) should be $10,000, the amount that can be withdrawn dividend-free on a redemption of the share, since this $10,000 represents the cost of the land that could be recovered tax-free on its disposition. However, under corporate law, the stated capital (the equivalent of paid-up capital for tax purposes) would normally be equal to the fair market value of the transferred property of $50,000. Therefore, the paid-up capital must be reduced to the ACB of the land of $10,000 in this particular situation. Note that this PUC *reduction* (i.e., $40,000) is exactly equal to the deferred accrued capital gain on the land (i.e., $50,000 – $10,000). Further modifications of the PUC reduction will be introduced later as additional conditions are added to the following situations.

In summary, the following has occurred.

Before transfer		After transfer	
Ms. Ava owned	*Land*	*Ms. Ava owns*	*Shares*
ACB	$10,000	ACB	$10,000
FMV	50,000	PUC	10,000
		FMV	50,000
		Corporation owns	*Land*
		ACB	$10,000
		FMV	50,000

¶16,015.40   *Conclusion*

This situation demonstrates that if an asset is transferred to a corporation at its tax value and only common share consideration is accepted, there will be no tax consequences to the transferor, Ms. Ava. Her proceeds of disposition and ACB of the consideration are exactly equal to the tax value of the transferred property. At the same time, the corporation assumes the tax value for the ACB of its newly-acquired property. The PUC of the common share must also be the tax value of the transferred asset. If this is not the case under corporate law, then the paid-up capital must be reduced for tax purposes.

¶16,020   Situation two

¶16,020.10   *Conditions for Transfer*

The assets can now be transferred with proceeds chosen at any elected amount between the tax value (ACB, etc.) and the FMV of the particular asset. This range of elected amounts will permit the taxpayer to trigger the appropriate amount of taxable capital gains or other income (e.g., recapture) to offset loss carryforwards and the allowable capital losses in the transfer year. Again, the consideration received on the transfer in this situation will be common shares.

¶16,020.20   *Facts*

Ms. Elizabeth wishes to transfer land and a building to a corporation, Elizabeth Ltd., which she presently controls through the ownership of all of the Class A common shares.

Land — ACB	$ 10,000
— FMV	50,000
Building — cost	95,000
— UCC	75,000
— FMV	110,000

Ms. Elizabeth will accept as consideration for the transfer of the land and building, Class B common shares. Ms. Elizabeth has a net capital loss carried forward from the preceding year (½ inclusion rate year) of $10,000 which she wishes to utilize on the transfer.

¶16,020.30   *Results*

Since Ms. Elizabeth wishes to utilize the net capital loss of $10,000 on the transfer, she must first decide on which asset she will trigger the taxable capital gain and what the elected amount will be. If she chooses the building, then at the same time she will trigger recapture as well as a capital gain. Since there is no evidence that she has a business loss for this year or non-capital losses, this course of action is not recommended. In respect of the land, she can choose an elected transfer price between $10,000 and $50,000. If she chooses an elected amount of $30,000, a taxable capital gain of $10,000 will result [i.e., ($30,000 – $10,000) × ½] which will offset the net capital loss.

Therefore, the recommended elected amounts would be:

Land	$ 30,000
Building	75,000

Land

(1) The proceeds of disposition for Ms. Elizabeth will be $30,000, the elected amount as discussed above.

(2) The cost of the land to Elizabeth Ltd. should also be $30,000, the elected amount, so that the remaining accrued gain of $20,000 (i.e., $50,000 – $30,000) will not be triggered on the transfer, but will be included in Elizabeth Ltd.'s income on the ultimate disposition of the land.

Building

On the assumption that no additional income (i.e., recapture and/or a capital gain) should be triggered, the elected amount chosen should be the tax value or UCC of $75,000.

(1) The proceeds of disposition for Ms. Elizabeth, therefore, will be the elected amount of $75,000, resulting in no recapture or capital gain.

(2) The UCC of the building for Elizabeth Ltd. will also be the elected amount of $75,000 which was the UCC for Ms. Elizabeth. In addition, Elizabeth Ltd. will assume Ms. Elizabeth's capital cost of the building of $95,000 so that the corporation will be responsible for the potential recapture of $20,000 and capital gain of $15,000.

Consideration — Class B common shares

(1) The ACB of the Class B common shares should logically be the sum of:

(a) ACB of the land	$ 10,000
(b) the capital gain triggered on the land transfer	20,000
(c) UCC of the building	75,000
	$105,000

Another way of looking at it would be the sum of the elected amounts:

Land	$ 30,000
Building	75,000
	$105,000

(2) The FMV of the Class B shares should be $160,000, the underlying fair market values of the land and building transferred to Elizabeth Ltd.

(3) As previously mentioned in Situation One, the stated value of the Class B shares for accounting and corporations law purposes would be $160,000. (Remember that the starting point for determining paid-up capital is the accounting or corporations law stated value.) However, the paid-up capital should be reduced to $105,000, which represents the ACB and UCC of the land and building, respectively, for Elizabeth Ltd. (i.e., $10,000 and $75,000) plus the accrued capital gain recognized and included in income on the transfer of the land (i.e., $20,000). This paid-up capital reduction of $55,000 should be exactly equal to the stated

value of the Class B shares ($160,000) minus the elected amount ($105,000) [i.e., FMV ($160,000) minus Elizabeth Ltd.'s tax values ($30,000 + $75,000)]. The PUC after the reduction should reflect the tax-paid cost values of the assets of $105,000 (i.e., ($10,000 + $20,000) + $75,000).

In summary, the following has occurred:

Before transfer			*After transfer*	
Ms. Elizabeth owned	*Land*	*Building*	*Ms. Elizabeth owns*	*Shares*
ACB/Cost	$10,000	$ 95,000	ACB	$105,000
UCC	n/a	75,000	PUC	105,000
FMV	50,000	110,000	FMV	160,000

Ms. Elizabeth had a net capital loss carryforward of $10,000.			Taxable capital gain of $10,000 offset by net capital losses.

Corporation owns	*Land*	*Building*
ACB/Cost	$30,000	$ 95,000
UCC	n/a	75,000
FMV	50,000	110,000

¶16,020.40   *Conclusion*

As long as the transferor (Ms. Elizabeth) elects an amount for the transferred asset(s) within the range between tax value (ACB, UCC, etc.) and the FMV, this elected amount will be:

(a) the proceeds of disposition of the transferor (Ms. Elizabeth);

(b) the tax value (i.e., ACB, UCC, etc.) of the transferred asset to the transferee corporation (Elizabeth Ltd.);

(c) the ACB of the common share consideration received by the transferor (Ms. Elizabeth); and

(d) the paid-up capital of the common shares held by the transferor (Ms. Elizabeth) after the paid-up capital reduction which will be equal to the remaining deferred gain of $55,000 (i.e., $160,000 – $105,000), resulting in a PUC of $105,000 (i.e., $160,000 – $55,000).

¶16,025   Situation three

¶16,025.10   *Conditions for transfer*

The asset(s) can be transferred at any amount between the tax value and FMV of the particular asset. However, in this situation, the consideration can be a mixture of common shares and non-share consideration (referred to as "boot") such as cash or debt, including debt attached to the transferred property (assumed debt). The inclusion of non-share consideration, however, imposes a further limitation — namely, that the non-share consideration or boot cannot exceed the elected amount without adverse tax consequences which are discussed below.

¶16,025.20   *Facts*

Mr. Benjamin wishes to transfer land to a corporation, Benjamin Ltd., which he presently controls through the ownership of all the Class A common shares.

Land — ACB	$10,000
— FMV	50,000

The land has an outstanding mortgage of $4,000 attached to it. Mr. Benjamin will accept as consideration for the transfer:

(a) a promissory note of $14,000 from Benjamin Ltd.;

(b) the assumption of the mortgage of $4,000 by Benjamin Ltd.; and

(c) the balance of the FMV of the land in Class B common shares.

Mr. Benjamin has $6,000 of net capital losses arising in 1999 which he wishes to utilize on the transfer.

¶16,025.30   *Results*

Since Mr. Benjamin wishes to utilize the $4,000 ($6,000 × ⅓ × ½) of net capital losses, he must elect at an amount which will trigger a capital gain of $8,000, yielding a taxable capital gain of $4,000. Therefore, he should elect at $18,000 ($10,000 ACB plus $8,000 capital gain). Since he has accepted, as part of his consideration, boot of $18,000 (a $14,000 note plus the assumed mortgage of $4,000) he has not violated the condition that the boot cannot exceed the elected amount (i.e., $18,000).

Land

(1) The proceeds of disposition to Mr. Benjamin is the elected amount of $18,000 which will trigger a capital gain of $8,000 to offset the net capital loss of $4,000 (i.e., ½ × $8,000).

(2) The cost of the land to Benjamin Ltd. will be the elected amount of $18,000 so that the corporation will only be liable for the remaining capital gain of $32,000.

Consideration

(1) The ACB of the Class B common shares will be the elected amount minus the FMV of the boot.

Elected amount		$18,000
Boot — note	$14,000	
— mortgage	4,000	18,000
Excess		Nil

∴ ACB of the shares is nil.

This result is logical since Mr. Benjamin has recovered from the corporation $18,000 of debt consideration equal to the full amount of the ACB of land ($10,000) plus the realized capital gain of $8,000. When the debt is repaid by the corporation, there will be no further tax consequences since the repayment amount reflects the tax-paid cost of the land transferred after the realization of $8,000 of capital gain.

(2) The PUC should logically be nil since Mr. Benjamin has recouped all of his invested cost in the land in the form of boot. If Mr. Benjamin had not accepted boot as part of the consideration package, then the PUC would have been equal to the tax-paid cost of the transferred land (i.e., $18,000) as demonstrated in Situations One and Two. However, in this situation Mr. Benjamin has recovered all of the tax cost of the land (i.e., note of $14,000 and a mortgage of $4,000). Therefore, the stated value of the Class B common shares (i.e., FMV of $32,000) must be reduced by $32,000 to give a paid-up capital of nil.

Another way of arriving at the PUC of nil is:

Stated capital (FMV of land ($50,000) – Boot ($18,000))		$32,000
Minus: elected amount	$18,000	
Less: boot	18,000	Nil
PUC reduction		$32,000
∴ PUC = (FMV ($32,000) – PUC reduction ($32,000))		Nil

Thus the PUC of nil reflects the fact that all of the tax-paid cost of the land has been recovered through boot, leaving no more tax-paid cost to be recovered in the shares on their redemption.

Note how this result differs from Situation Two where only Class B common shares were accepted as consideration. The ACB and the paid-up capital were not reduced to nil in Situation Two, since Ms. Elizabeth had not extracted from the corporation any non-share consideration (i.e., cash or debt).

In summary, the following has occurred:

Before transfer		After transfer			
Mr. Benjamin owned	Land	*Mr. Benjamin owns*	Debt	*Corporation owns*	Land
ACB	$ 10,000	ACB	$ 14,000	ACB	$ 18,000
FMV	50,000	FMV	14,000	FMV	50,000
Mr. Benjamin owed $4,000 on a mortgage.		*Mr. Benjamin owns*	*Shares*	*Corporation owes to:*	
		ACB	Nil	Mr. Benjamin	$ 14,000
Mr. Benjamin had a net capital loss carryforward of $4,000 (adjusted).		PUC	Nil	Mortgage	4,000
		FMV	$ 32,000		
		Mr. Benjamin no longer owes $4,000 on a mortgage.			
		Taxable capital gain of $4,000 offset by net capital losses.			

¶16,025.40 Conclusion

The elected amount of $18,000 in this situation was used to determine the following values:

(a) proceeds of disposition to Mr. Benjamin of $18,000, triggering a capital gain of $8,000;

(b) an ACB of the Class B common shares of nil, since all of the elected amount was assigned to the boot of $18,000;

(c) a cost of the land to Benjamin Ltd. of $18,000 since the corporation is responsible for the remaining capital gain of $32,000; and

(d) a paid-up capital of the Class B common shares of nil since all of the elected amount has been extracted from Benjamin Ltd. through the boot consideration.

Finally, the non-share consideration or boot did not result in any adverse tax consequences, since the total boot (debt of $14,000 and the assumption of Mr. Benjamin's liability of $4,000) did not exceed the elected amount of $18,000.

¶16,025.50 *Boot consideration in excess of elected amount*

If Mr. Benjamin had forgotten the assumed mortgage of $4,000 was part of the non-share/boot consideration and had taken back a promissory note of $18,000 (equal to the elected amount), the following would be the tax consequences.

(1) The elected amount would be bumped automatically by the $4,000 which is the excess boot over the elected amount (i.e., ($18,000 + $4,000) – $18,000) to arrive at a new elected amount of $22,000.

(2) The proceeds of disposition to Mr. Benjamin would be the *new* elected amount of $22,000, triggering a taxable capital gain of $6,000 ($\frac{1}{2} \times$ ($22,000 − $10,000)) of which only $4,000 would have been offset by the net capital loss (as adjusted).

(3) The cost of the land to Benjamin Ltd. would be the *new* elected amount of $22,000.

(4) The ACB of the Class B common shares would still be nil, computed as:

New elected amount		$22,000
Less: boot:		
(a) note	$18,000	
(b) mortgage	4,000	22,000
ACB of Class B shares		Nil

(5) The paid-up capital of the Class B common shares would still be nil since the entire elected amount of $22,000 would be recovered through boot.

PUC Reduction		
Stated value of shares*		$28,000
Minus: elected amount	$22,000	
Less: boot	22,000	Nil
Reduction		$28,000
∴ PUC = ($28,000 − $28,000)		Nil

---

* FMV of land transferred of $50,000 minus the boot or non-share consideration of $22,000 ($4,000 + $18,000).

¶16,030   Basic Technical Rules on the Transfer

¶16,035   Use of the rollover

Section 85 provides for the transfer of "eligible" property, as defined, to a corporation by a person who, after the transfer, is a shareholder. The provision is applicable on many transfers of property to a corporation, including transfers on the incorporation of a proprietorship, a partnership, or an investment portfolio and transfers to a subsidiary. Section 85 is also applicable on the transfer by an individual of shares in one corporation to another corporation, perhaps, to effect one form of estate freeze to be discussed more fully in the next chapter. The party transferring property (i.e., the transferor) can be an individual, a trust, a corporation or a partnership (discussed in more detail in Chapter 18), either resident or non-resident in Canada.   *ITA: 85(1.1)*

¶16,040   Conditions for the rollover to apply

In order for the rollover to apply, the following conditions must be met:

(a) the corporate transferee must be a taxable Canadian corporation as defined;   *ITA: 89(1)*

(b) the consideration received by the transferor must include shares (i.e., at least one share or a fraction of a share, although a more literal interpretation of the provision might suggest two or more shares or fractions thereof for each type or class of asset) of the corporation;   *IC 76-19R3, par. 8*

(c) the property transferred must be eligible property defined to include capital property (including both depreciable and non-depreciable capital property, but usually not real or immovable property owned in any manner by a non-resident), eligible capital property, a resource property, or inventory (other than real or immovable property, an interest therein or an option in respect thereof); and   *ITA: 85(1.1)*

(d) the taxpayer(s) and the corporation must jointly elect to have these rollover provisions apply (form T2057 for transfers from an individual, trust, or corporation or T2058 for transfers from a partnership) on or before the first time for filing a tax return of any person, who was a party to the election, for the year in which the property was transferred. A late election may be filed within three years of the due date. There is a penalty equal to the lesser of ¼ of 1% of the deferred gain and $100 for each month that the election is late to a maximum penalty of $8,000. The Minister may accept new elections or amendments to previous elections filed after the three-year deadline in cases where this would be just and equitable.

ITA: 85(6)

ITA: 85(7), 85(8)

ITA: 85(7.1)

¶16,045 Elected transfer price

The importance of filing the election with complete and correct information is evident from the case of *Deconinck v. The Queen* (affirmed by the Federal Court of Appeal), in which the taxpayer failed to refer to four of the five properties he intended to transfer in his rollover election. The Federal Court–Trial Division held that section 85 provides a significant advantage to the taxpayer, but to take advantage of that provision, the information provided must be correct. Intention of the taxpayer is not sufficient. As a result, the four properties were not subject to the rollover and were considered to be transferred at their fair market value.

88 DTC 6410 (F.C.T.D.),
aff'd 90 DTC 6617
(F.C.A.)

The price at which property is transferred may be elected within a range set out in Exhibit 16-1. This elected transfer price is very important because it is used to solve the following four problems that arise on the transfer:

(a) proceeds of disposition to the transferor;

ITA: 85(1)(*a*)

(b) the cost of the property to the corporation.

ITA: 85(1)(*a*)

(c) the cost of the package of consideration taken by the transferor from the corporation in return for the assets transferred to the corporation; and

ITA: 85(1)(*f*), 85(1)(*g*),
85(1)(*h*)

(d) a part of the calculation of paid-up capital for tax purposes of the share consideration received.

ITA: 85(2.1)

In order to defer the maximum capital gain or income, the elected transfer price should be the minimum in the range. To ensure that the absolute minimum is selected, it is necessary to make sure that consideration other than shares, e.g., debt, cash, etc. ("boot" or non-share consideration) taken from the corporation is no more than the lesser or least of two or three amounts at the bottom of the appropriate column in Exhibit 16-1. It should be recognized that the amount of this non-share consideration taken from the corporation is the only decision variable in establishing the limits on the elected transfer price range. The other items such as fair market value and tax value of the property transferred are fixed, although often not with great precision, at the time of the transfer and cannot be varied on the transfer.

EXHIBIT 16-1
Restrictions on Elected Transfer Price

	Inventory* or capital property other than depreciable property [par. 85(1.1)(a), (f)]	Depreciable capital property [par. 85(1.1)(a)]	Eligible capital property [par. 85(1.1)(e)]
UPPER LIMIT	FMV of property transferred [par. 85(1)(c)]	FMV of property transferred [par. 85(1)(c)]	FMV of property transferred [par. 85(1)(c)]
LOWER LIMIT [par. 85(1)(e.3)]	*Greater of:* FMV of non-share consideration received [par. 85(1)(b)]	*Greater of:* FMV of non-share consideration received [par. 85(1)(b)]	*Greater of:* FMV of non-share consideration received [par. 85(1)(b)]
	and	and	and
	Lesser of [par. 85(1)(c.1)]:	*Least of [par. 85(1)(e)]:*	*Least of [par. 85(1)(d)]:*
	(1) FMV of property**	(1) FMV of property**	(1) FMV of property**
	(2) ACB of property if capital property or tax value of	(2) UCC of class of property	(2) $\frac{4}{3}$ of the cumulative eligible capital balance
	property if inventory	(3) cost of property to transferor	(3) full or actual cost of property to transferor

* Other than real property (i.e., land and buildings) held as inventory.

** The fair market value of the property restriction prevents the creation of an artificial loss. Further restricted by subsection 13(21.2) for depreciable capital property, to be discussed subsequently, and by subsection 14(12) for eligible capital property.

¶16,050 Non-share consideration or boot

Although it is not necessary to take non-share consideration, it will usually be beneficial to take the maximum amount of "boot" that will still permit a transfer of the property at an amount which will fully defer the accrued gains on the property. The benefits of receiving cash as "boot" without triggering tax on the accrued gains are obvious. Even if debt of the corporation is received as "boot", the debt can be redeemed for cash later without any adverse tax consequences. However, there is a pitfall on the transfer of shares, as discussed later, and taking the maximum "boot" in that situation will not be beneficial.

ITA: 84.1

One of the most common errors in the application of section 85 is to forget to include in "boot" the debts of the transferor which are assumed by the corporation. Where the maximum new debt has already been exchanged on the transfer, this omission will cause unwanted income inclusions through an automatic bump in the elected amount for the excess boot (i.e., the assumed debts).

If the fair market value of non-share consideration received ("boot"), labelled as the lower limit, is greater than the fair market value of property transferred to the corporation, labelled as the upper limit, then the transfer price will be the latter amount. This will create other problems which will subsequently be discussed in more detail.

ITA: 85(1)(c)

¶16,060   Application of the Basic Rules

Exhibit 16-2 presents three basic alternative combinations of the three key variables: fair market value (FMV) of the property transferred, tax value (TV) of the property transferred, and non-share consideration (boot) received. The rules summarized in Exhibit 16-1 are applied to these three cases on the assumption that there is, at least, nominal share consideration (e.g., one cent) to meet the requirement in the rollover provision. Other possible cases will be discussed later.

ITA: 85(1)

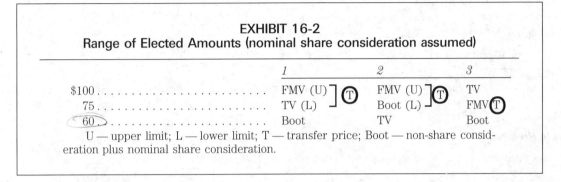

In Case 1 of Exhibit 16-2, the range of elected amounts is between the TV (the lower limit of $75) and the FMV (the upper limit of $100). Since the boot of $60 is below the TV of $75, it does not affect the lower limit. In Case 2, the range of elected amounts is still between $75 and $100. However, the boot of $75 is the lower limit in this situation and would result in a capital gain of $15 (i.e., $75 − $60). In Case 3, there is no range of elected amounts, but only one amount which is both the upper and lower limit.

In Case 1 of the Exhibit, if the objective was to fully defer the accrued gain on the property of $25 (i.e., $100 − $75) on the transfer, the elected transfer price should be $75. Taking "boot" of up to $75 as consideration would not jeopardize the lower limit on the transfer price of $75. Since "boot" is considered to be "hard" consideration like cash or debt which can be repaid in cash without tax consequences, taking the maximum of $75 in this case is most beneficial. To take less than $75 of "boot" in Case 1 will still permit a full deferral of the accrued gain on the property transferred, but it wastes an opportunity to receive consideration without tax consequences. The reason that $75 of "boot" can be received as consideration without tax consequences, is that the $75 represents the cost of the asset transferred. The cost was incurred by expending after-tax funds. Therefore, it should be recovered on a disposition of the property without tax consequences. Hence, the maximum "boot" of $75, in this case, allows a tax-free recovery of the cost of the property transferred.

In Case 2 of the Exhibit, the lower limit is the boot of $75 rather than the TV of $60, as was the situation in Case 1. This result is because the taxpayer has extracted from the corporation $75 of boot which is $15 more than the tax value of the asset transferred (i.e., $60). Since the elected amount is the proceeds of disposition to the transferor, a capital gain of $15 is triggered (i.e., $75–$60). Under the technical rules of section 85, this result is accomplished by automatically bumping the elected amount by the excess of the boot over the cost amount. In Case 3 of the Exhibit, it would have been possible to receive boot of $75, i.e., the fair market value of the asset transferred, without adverse tax consequences. Only where boot exceeds fair market value, does this problem arise.

ITA: 85(1)(*c*)

Consider the following numerical example of the application of the rules on the transfer of capital property having an adjusted cost base of $1,000 and a fair market value of $1,500:

| | *Alternatives* | | |
Consideration	*A*	*B*	*C*
Cash, etc.	0	$ 1,000	$ 1,300
Preferred shares (FMV and legal stated capital)	$ 1,000	300	180
Common shares (FMV and legal stated capital)	500	200	20
Total	$ 1,500	$ 1,500	$ 1,500
Election range:			
high[1]	$ 1,500	$ 1,500	$ 1,500
low[2]	$ 1,000	$ 1,000	$ 1,300
Election price (assumed at lowest)	$ 1,000	$ 1,000	$ 1,300
Adjusted cost base	1,000	1,000	1,000
Capital gain	Nil	Nil	$ 300
Taxable capital gain at ½ inclusion rate	Nil	Nil	$ 150

NOTE: (1) Fair market value of property transferred.

(2) Fair market value of consideration received other than shares, limited further in Case A by the adjusted cost base of the property transferred.

Example Problem

Mr. Sole Proprietor owns the following assets in a business that he wants to incorporate:

	*Tax value**	*Fair market value*
Short-term investments	$ 15,000	$ 18,000
Inventory	45,000	46,000
Machinery (cost: $54,375)	26,250	38,500
Goodwill	—	30,000
	$ 86,250	$132,500
Liabilities	10,000	10,000
	$ 76,250	$122,500

* Cost values for tax purposes used to describe the lowest limit of the elected transfer price range in Exhibit 16-1.

As fair market value consideration, he wants $70,000 in new debt, $35,000 in preferred shares and the balance in common shares to total the fair market value of the net assets transferred to the corporation. Also, the corporation will assume the existing debt of the proprietorship.

— *REQUIRED*

Indicate the appropriate elected amounts which should be used to defer any taxation upon the incorporation of the proprietorship.

— *SOLUTION*

				FMV of consideration[2]				
	Tax value	*Fair market value*	*Elected transfer price*	*Assumed debt*[3]	*New debt*[3]	*Preferred shares*	*Common shares*	*Income*
Short-term investments[1]	$ 15,000	$ 18,000	$ 15,000	$ 10,000	$ 5,000	$ 3,000	$ —	Nil
Inventory	45,000	46,000	45,000	—	45,000	1,000	—	Nil
Machinery	26,250	38,500	26,250	—	20,000	18,500	—	Nil
Goodwill	Nil	30,000	1[4]	—	—	12,500	17,500	$0.50
	$ 86,250	$132,500	$ 86,251[5]	$ 10,000	$70,000	$35,000	$17,500	

— *NOTES TO SOLUTION*

[1] Short-term investments should only be transferred to the corporation if they can be considered assets used in the active business of the corporation, in this case. If they are investment assets, they may jeopardize the status of the corporation's shares as qualifying small

business corporation shares (QSBCS). Here, it is assumed that the short-term investments represent the investment of temporarily surplus cash needed for active business operations.

(2) The order of the allocation of debt and share consideration, as shown in this example, is arbitrarily made in the order that the assets are listed in the facts. This particular method, while not required by the legislation, allows for a systematic allocation, first of the "boot", including assumed debt, up to the maximum, if desired, and, then, of the share consideration.

(3) Note that the debt, as non-share consideration, can be set at any level, but the amount taken affects the minimum elected transfer price. It is the only consideration that has an effect on that minimum elected transfer price and must be selected to meet the transferor's objective of, in this case, deferring any taxation on the transfer. In this situation, the maximum new debt consideration or boot (i.e., $76,251) was not taken in order to demonstrate certain effects. However, the transferor might be advised to take debt consideration, including assumed debt, to a total of $86,251 which is equal to the desired minimum elected amount. By not receiving the maximum debt consideration, where financially feasible, the transferor is wasting an opportunity to recover, at the time of the transfer to the corporation, his cost in the property transferred on a tax-free basis. The share consideration, which has no effect on the elected amount, is used to balance the fair market value of the total consideration received, including "boot" and shares, with the total fair market value of all property transferred to the corporation. Under the rollover, this balancing of fair market value is necessary to avoid the problems which will be discussed later.

Note, however, that preferred shares generally have a fixed value (i.e., redemption value or retraction value), whereas common shares have a floating value which absorbs the fair market value of the property transferred net of the other consideration (i.e., boot and preferred shares).

(4) To have a valid election the minimum elected transfer price must be a nominal amount (i.e., $1.00). IC 76-19R3

(5) The elected amount is used as proceeds of disposition to the transferor, as the cost of the property to the corporation and as adjusted cost base of the consideration received by the transferor from the corporation.

¶16,070 The Corporation's Position

As previously indicated, the elected transfer price becomes the corporation's cost of the property. For depreciable property, the Act provides that the capital cost of the property to the corporation will be deemed to equal the capital cost of the property to the transferor. The corporation will be deemed to have claimed capital cost allowances equal to the amount by which the capital cost exceeds the transfer price. In essence, the corporation steps into the transferor's tax position in all respects on transfer of the assets of the corporation at undepreciated capital cost. The corporation takes capital cost allowance from undepreciated capital cost and it is liable for recapture up to the transferor's original capital cost. ITA: 85(1)(*a*)
ITA: 85(5)(*a*)
ITA: 85(5)(*b*)

Note that the half-year rule for calculating capital cost allowance in the year of acquisition of an asset does not apply in this election if two conditions apply: ITR: 1100(2.2); ITA: 85(1)

- the transferor was not dealing at arm's length with the corporation at the time of the transfer; and

- the property was owned continuously by the transferor for the period from at least 365 days before the end of the taxation year of the corporation in which the asset was acquired to the date of the election.

Similarly non-arm's length transfers of depreciable property retain the same capital cost allowance class. For example, a Class 3 asset (building) acquired by a non-arm's length party, as would be the case where the property is transferred to a corporation controlled by the transferor or a person related to the transferor, would be placed in Class 3. In an arm's length acquisition, the asset would be placed in Class 1 [or Class NRB (non-residential building), under a proposal of the March 19, 2007 federal budget]. ITR: 1102(14)

¶16,070

¶16,080 The Shareholder's Position

For the shareholder, the elected transfer price is basically allocated to become the cost of the property received (i.e., boot or shares) as consideration in exchange for the property transferred in the following order:

(a) property other than shares (i.e., boot or non-share consideration) up to the fair market value of that property as long as that fair market value does not exceed the fair market value of the assets transferred to the corporation; ITA: 85(1)(*f*)

(b) preferred shares up to the fair market value of those shares after the transfer as long as that fair market value does not exceed the proceeds of disposition (elected amount) minus the fair market value of the non-share consideration received; and ITA: 85(1)(*g*)

(c) common shares to the extent that proceeds of disposition (elected amount) exceed the sum of the fair market value of the non-share consideration and the cost allocated to the preferred shares above (non-negative amounts only). ITA: 85(1)(*h*)

The Act defines a preferred share as a share other than a common share. A common share is defined as a share the holder of which is not precluded from participating in the assets of the corporation beyond the amount paid up on that share plus a fixed premium and a defined rate of dividend. ITA: 248(1) "common share", "preferred share"

The shares received as consideration are deemed to be capital property of the recipient of the shares where all or substantially all of the assets transferred to the corporation were used in an active business carried on by the transferor. This rule ensures that where a transfer is made in contemplation of the sale of the shares received as consideration, the latter sale of shares will be treated as a capital transaction. Where the seller of the shares is an individual, the sale may qualify for the capital gains deduction for QSBC shares. ITA: 54.2

Recall the three-alternative example starting on page 857, involving the transfer of the single capital property. Applying these rules, the following shows the cost of the *consideration* received under each alternative:

| | Alternatives | | |
Consideration	A	B	C
Elected transfer price	$ 1,000	$ 1,000	$ 1,300
Cost after ssec. 85(1):			
First — Cash, etc.	—	$ 1,000	$ 1,300
Second — Preferred shares	$ 1,000	Nil	Nil
Third — Common shares	Nil	Nil	Nil
	$ 1,000	$ 1,000	$ 1,300

Example Problem

Reconsider the previous example problem starting on page 858.

— *REQUIRED*

Compute the cost of the consideration taken from the corporation for the net assets transferred.

— SOLUTION

Elected transfer price		$ 86,251
Allocation to cost of non-share consideration:		
Liabilities assumed	$10,000	
New debt	70,000	80,000
Allocation to preferred shares (up to their FMV)		$ 6,251
Allocation to common shares		Nil

Note that the $86,251 of elected amount represents the tax-paid cost in the assets transferred to the corporation, that is, $86,250 of tax value and $1 elected on goodwill and included in income. The cost of the consideration received for these assets reflects that tax-paid cost. The $10,000 of liabilities are assumed without any tax consequences on the transfer or in the future. The new debt of $70,000 can be repaid without tax consequences in the future. The preferred shares have a cost of $6,251 which can be recovered tax free in the future. The common shares have a cost of nil, because all of the tax-paid cost in the assets transferred to the corporation has been recovered in the debt and preferred shares received.

¶16,090 Paid-Up Capital Reduction on Shares Issued as Consideration

¶16,095 The issue in concept

Recall the discussion of paid-up capital of shares in the previous chapter. Where shares have no par value or stated value under corporate law, their paid-up capital value normally reflects the fair market value of the property for which the shares were issued. In the previous example problem (on page 858) this legal stated capital (LSC) was $35,000 for the preferred shares and $17,500 for the common shares, since, on the issue of the shares, the fair market value of net assets of the corporation increased by a total of $52,500 (i.e., $132,500 – ($10,000 + $70,000)). This value of $52,500 is also the fair market value of all the shares issued and reflects, in part, the accrued income on the inventory, machinery and goodwill deferred on the transfer of those assets to the corporation. Since the adjusted cost base of the preferred shares is $6,251 and that of the common shares is nil, a capital gain would result from an arm's length sale of the shares. This capital gain may be eligible for the QSBC share capital gains deduction while the original income deferred on the transfer would not have been. Similarly, if the shares were redeemed by the corporation for their fair market value, there would be no deemed dividend, because their fair market value is equal to their paid-up capital value. As a result, on the redemption there would be a capital gain which, again, may be eligible for the QSBC share capital gains deduction. Finally, if the individual shareholder were to continue to hold indefinitely the shares received as consideration, the paid-up capital could be removed on a tax-free basis through a payment that would result in a PUC reduction that would not be subject to deemed dividend rules.

ITA: 84(3)

ITA: 84(4), 84(4.1)

¶16,100 The technical solution

The QSBC share capital gains deduction has apparently necessitated an anti-avoidance rule which provides for a reduction (often referred to in practice as a "grind") in the paid-up capital of a *particular* class of shares of a corporation after the disposition of property equal to:

ITA: 85(2.1)(*a*)

$$(A - B) \times \frac{C}{A}$$

where A = the increase in legal stated capital of all shares of the corporation after the disposition under section 85;

B = the excess, if any, of the corporation's cost of the property (i.e., the elected amount) *over* the fair market value of the non-share consideration (i.e., the "boot");

C = the increase in legal stated capital of a particular class of shares on the transfer of property to the corporation.

If the amount (A – B) is negative, it is deemed to be nil.   ITA: 257

¶16,105   Illustration of application

To better understand the effects of the PUC reduction, consider a capital asset with the   ITA: 85(2.1)
following features:

Tax value	$10,000
Fair market value	15,000

If this property is sold in an arm's length transaction, there will be either business income or a capital gain, depending on the nature of the asset, in the amount of $5,000. Hence, of the $15,000 of proceeds received, $5,000 is income subject to tax in some form and the other $10,000 is a recovery of the cost (i.e., tax value) of the asset on a tax-free basis, because the asset was purchased with after-tax funds.

Now consider a transfer of the above asset to a corporation using the rollover as follows: ITA: 85(1)

Elected amount (equal to tax value)	$10,000
Fair market value of non-share consideration ("boot")	10,000
Fair market value and LSC of share consideration	5,000
Adjusted cost base of share consideration	Nil

ITA: 85(1)(g) or 85(1)(h)

If the share consideration received from the corporation is subsequently sold in an arm's length transaction for its current fair market value, a capital gain of $5,000 would result in most circumstances. This capital gain is equal to the gain that had accrued on the asset transferred to the corporation. If the asset was a capital property that would have resulted in a capital gain on its arm's length disposition, the usual capital gain on the disposition of the share consideration would provide the equivalent treatment, that is, taxation of one-half of the gain.

However, if the asset was inventory that would have resulted in business income on its arm's length disposition, a transfer to a corporation in the manner described would potentially convert the business income into a capital gain on the ultimate sale of the share consideration. Shares accepted as consideration on a disposition to a corporation are deemed   ITA: 54.2, 248(1)
to be capital property of the transferor. The provision requires, however, that all or substan-   "business"
tially all of the assets, used in an active business by the transferor, must be disposed of to the corporation. Note that the definition of a business specifically excludes an adventure in the nature of trade for their purpose.

On the other hand, if the share consideration received from the corporation is subse-   ITA: 85(2.1)
quently redeemed by the corporation, the PUC reduction will have an effect. First, the rule will reduce (or grind) the paid-up capital for tax purposes of the share consideration to nil as follows:

LSC of share consideration before reduction		$5,000
Less: reduction in PUC		
(1) increase in LSC of all shares on the transfer to the corporation	$5,000 (A)	
(2) elected amount $10,000		
less: boot 10,000		
excess if any	Nil (B)	
total reduction (A − B)		5,000*
Tax PUC of share consideration after reduction		Nil

ITA: 85(2.1)

*This PUC reduction equals the untaxed gain (i.e., the deferred gain) on the transfer of the property to the corporation.

Since only one class of shares was assumed to have been received as consideration, there is no need to apply the prorating component of the formula.

PUC of New Shares Received

Note how the tax PUC of the share consideration after the reduction is nil. This PUC value for tax purposes represents the amount of the original cost of the asset transferred (i.e., $10,000) that has not been recovered through "boot". Since the "boot" of $10,000 in this case can be thought of as a full recovery of the original cost of the asset transferred, there is no further amount of that cost to be recovered on a tax-free basis and, hence, the tax PUC value should be nil. Recall that PUC represents an amount that can be returned to a shareholder on a tax-free basis, because it represents a contribution to the capital of the corporation made with after-tax funds. In this case, the "funds" contributed to the corporation consisted of a property with an untaxed, accrued capital gain. This conceptual approach to determining the tax value of the PUC of shares can be used to predict or to check the application of the technical formula.

ITA: 85(2.1)

¶16,110 The effect

Assume the shares received as consideration are now redeemed for their fair market value of $5,000. The following compares the effects of the PUC reduction on the results of a redemption if the PUC reduction had not been added to the legislation:

ITA: 85(2.1)

	With PUC reduction	*Without PUC reduction*	
Proceeds on redemption	$5,000	$5,000	
Less: PUC	Nil	5,000	
Deemed dividend	$5,000	Nil	ITA: 84(3)
Proceeds on redemption	$5,000	$5,000	
Less: deemed dividend	5,000	Nil	ITA: 84(3)
Proceeds of disposition	Nil	$5,000	ITA: 54
Less: adjusted cost base	Nil	Nil	
Capital gain	Nil	$5,000	

Note that a *redemption* of the shares, received as consideration under the rollover transfer, results in a deemed dividend, rather than a capital gain that might have been eligible for the QSBC share capital gains deduction. In other words, the PUC reduction converts what would have been a taxable capital gain into a deemed dividend if the corporation is redeeming the shares.

ITA: 85(1)

ITA: 85(2.1)

The foregoing analysis illustrates the effects of the PUC reduction as an anti-avoidance rule which prevents the conversion of an amount that might have been taxed as property income into a potentially tax-free capital gain on the *redemption* of shares received as consideration.

ITA: 85(2.1)

Example Problem

Reconsider the previous example problem on page 858.

— *REQUIRED*

Compute the paid-up capital for tax purposes of the preferred and common shares received from the corporation.

— *SOLUTION*

	Preferred shares	Common shares
Reduction in PUC:		
(1) increase in LSC of *all* shares on the transfer to the corporation . . . . $52,500 (A)		
(2) elected amount . . . . $ 86,251		
less: non-share consideration 80,000		
excess, if any . . . . 6,251 (B)		
total reduction (A – B) . . . . $46,249⁽¹⁾		
(3) increase in LSC of a class of shares issued . . . . $35,000 (C)		$17,500 (C)

Reduction in each class $[(A - B) \times \frac{C}{A}]$

Preferred shares:	$46,249 \times \dfrac{\$35,000}{\$52,500}$	(30,833)	
Common shares: $46,249 \times \dfrac{\$17,500}{\$52,500}$			(15,416)
PUC (for tax purposes) of each class		$ 4,167	$ 2,084

ITA: 85(2.1)

This PUC reduction will have no tax consequences unless and until the shares are *redeemed* by the corporation. Arm's length sales are unaffected by the PUC reduction. On redemption for fair market value of the shares, the following will occur:

	Preferred shares	Common shares
Redemption amount (FMV)	$ 35,000	$17,500
Less: PUC (tax)	4,167	2,084
Deemed dividend	$ 30,833	$15,416
Redemption amount	$ 35,000	$17,500
Less: deemed dividend	30,833	15,416
Proceeds of disposition	$ 4,167	$ 2,084
Proceeds of disposition	$ 4,167	$ 2,084
Less: adjusted cost base	6,251	Nil
Capital gain (loss)	$ (2,084)	$ 2,084

ITA: 84(3)

ITA: 54

ITA: 85(1)

Note that, had the PUC not been reduced, there would not have been a deemed dividend, because redemption proceeds would have been equal to PUC. The result would have been a capital gain on the preferred shares of $28,749 (i.e., $35,000 – $6,251) and on the common shares of $17,500 (i.e., $17,500 – Nil). Therefore, the PUC reduction converts, at least in part, what might have been a taxable capital gain into a taxable deemed dividend.

— *NOTE TO SOLUTION*

(1) Again, this PUC reduction appears to be the untaxed gain (i.e., the deferred gain) on the transfer of property with a fair market value of $132,500 at an elected amount of $86,251 for a deferred gain of $46,249 (i.e., $132,500 – $86,251). The resultant PUC for tax purposes of $6,251

(i.e., $4,167 + $2,084) represents the tax value or cost (that has not been eroded by a decline in fair market value below cost) that has not been recovered through debt consideration, including assumed debt. Of the $86,251 of tax value in the assets originally transferred, $80,000 (i.e., $10,000 + $70,000) has been recovered through "boot" received on the transfer. The remainder of unrecovered tax value is $6,250 (i.e., $86,250 – $80,000) which differs from the tax value of PUC by the $1 included in income from the required elected amount on the goodwill.

From the foregoing example problem, it can be seen that if property is transferred to a corporation utilizing the provisions of section 85 and, in consideration, the corporation issues common shares without par value, the fair market value of the shares will reflect to some degree the fair market value of the assets transferred. The adjusted cost base of the shares will depend upon the elected transfer price and the PUC will be determined as has been previously mentioned. Therefore, it can be seen that each of these three amounts, that is, the fair market value, adjusted cost base and PUC can and sometimes will all be different as each is determined independently.

¶16,120　Other Rules Applicable in the Rollover

¶16,125　Depreciable capital property

¶16,125.10　*Ordering of dispositions within a class*

When a transfer involves a number of items of eligible capital property or depreciable property of the same prescribed class, the taxpayer must designate the order of disposition. Otherwise the Minister will make the designation. By having separate, sequential dispositions, the undepreciated capital cost or cumulative eligible capital balance will be reduced after each separate disposition for the purpose of determining the minimum transfer price. For example, consider the following case:

	Depreciable property	
	1	*2*
Capital cost	$7,000	$14,000
Fair market value	9,000	12,000
UCC of class	$13,000	
Possible elected amounts	7,000	12,000

ITA: 85(1)(*e*)

Were it not for the ordering rule, the total elected amount of $19,000 for both assets would be subtracted from the balance in the class resulting in a credit balance of $6,000 (i.e., $19,000–13,000) which would be included in income as recapture. However, using the ordering rule, property 1 could be transferred first at its elected amount of $7,000. Proceeds of disposition would, thus, be $7,000 and this would be subtracted from the balance of $13,000 in the class to leave an undepreciated capital cost balance of $6,000. Then, property 2 would be transferred. Using the minimum elected transfer price rule, the elected amount cannot be less than the least of: fair market value of the property transferred ($12,000), undepreciated capital cost of the class of the property transferred ($6,000), and cost of the property transferred ($14,000). Thus, the elected transfer price would be established at $6,000 which would become proceeds of disposition. When this is subtracted from the undepreciated capital cost balance of $6,000 the new balance becomes nil and no recapture results.

ITA: 85(1)(*e*.1)

ITA: 85(1)(*e*)

¶16,125.20　*Terminal losses*

A terminal loss generally occurs where there is a positive balance in a depreciable capital property class and the taxpayer no longer owns any property in that class. Although depreciable capital property can be transferred under section 85, there is no advantage in doing so in the case of an individual transferring depreciable capital property with an unrealized terminal loss and subjecting the transfer to all the conditions imposed under section 85 (i.e., taking back share consideration, etc.). Therefore, it is recommended that depreciable capital property with an unrealized terminal loss should not be transferred under section 85, but should be sold to the corporation at fair market value, taking back debt consideration.

A stop-loss rule denies a terminal loss on a transfer of depreciable capital property by an individual, corporation, trust or partnership to a corporation, among others, with which the transferor is affiliated, as defined. Section 85 does not apply to the transfer in these situations. The amount of the unrealized terminal loss is held in the capital cost allowance class from which the property came and the transferor subject to these rules will be allowed to claim capital cost allowance on that class. On the occurrence of one of several specified events in the future, involving a disposition or deemed disposition of the property by the transferee corporation, the remaining UCC can be written off as a terminal loss by the transferor. The recipient corporation is allowed to deduct capital cost allowance on a UCC equal to the FMV of the property at the time of the transfer. The recipient corporation will be liable for recapture up to the original capital cost of the property to the transferor. (A parallel set of rules applies to the transfer of eligible capital property.)

ITA: 13(21.2), 251.1

ITA: 14(12)

¶16,125.30 *Limitations on transferee's cost basis for CCA*

Where depreciable property with an accrued capital gain (and, perhaps, an undepreciated capital cost equal to or only slightly less than capital cost) is transferred to a corporation with which the transferor does not deal at arm's length, there may be a temptation to elect at fair market value on the transfer to trigger the accrued capital gain. The capital gain would be only ½ taxable, and the corporation would be deemed to have acquired depreciable property at full fair market value which would become the base for the future undepreciated capital cost in the corporation. The prospect of such a transfer probably resulted in the introduction of a rule which, conceptually, restricts any step-up of the original capital cost, in respect of a non-arm's length transfer, to the *taxable* capital gain realized.

ITA: 13(7)(e)

Consider the transfer by an individual to a corporation, which he or she controls, of a depreciable capital property, the only asset in the class, with an undepreciated capital cost of $50,000, a capital cost of $55,000 and a fair market value of $95,000. If the individual can offset all of the accrued taxable capital gain with net capital losses, and he or she elects, under the rollover, to transfer the property at fair market value of $95,000, the following taxable income would result for the individual:

ITA: 85(1)

Recapture ($55,000 – $50,000)	$ 5,000
Taxable capital gain [½ × ($95,000 – $55,000)]	20,000
Income	$25,000

Where the cost of the property to the corporation (i.e., the elected amount of $95,000) exceeds the capital cost of the property to the transferor (i.e., $55,000) on a non-arm's length transfer of depreciable property, the capital cost of the property to the corporation is deemed to be equal to the aggregate of:

ITA: 13(1)(e)(i)

(a) The capital cost of the property to the transferor		$55,000
(b) The transferor's proceeds of disposition (i.e., the elected amount)	$ 95,000	
Less: the capital cost (ACB) of the property to the transferor	55,000	
Excess, if any	$ 40,000	
½ of excess		20,000
Deemed capital cost to the corporation		$ 75,000

This technical calculation can be summarized as follows:

Sum of:	
(a) transferor's original capital cost	$ 55,000
(b) taxable capital gain [½ × ($95,000 – $55,000)]	20,000
Deemed capital cost	$ 75,000

This deemed capital cost of $75,000 will be the base for future capital cost allowance for the corporation and the limit of recapture on a future disposition. Hence, only an amount that has been fully taxed to the transferor is eligible for the CCA base which will give rise to fully deductible CCA However, for the purposes of future capital gains, the capital cost will be the $95,000 elected amount which is not affected by the limitation on capital cost for that purpose.

ITA: 85(1)(*a*)
ITA: 13(7)(*e*)(i)

¶16,125.40   *Limitations on transferee's cost base for CECA*

As with depreciable property, where eligible capital property is transferred in a non-arm's length transaction, the purchaser may not be able to claim CECA on 75% of the full purchase price.

While a full discussion of this issue can be found in Chapter 5, we will consider this in the context of a section 85 election. On the transfer of the assets of a business to a corporation, there is often a fair market value determined for goodwill. At the same time, since the goodwill is internally generated, there is no CEC balance, since no intangibles had been purchased. One of the conditions of section 85 is that an "amount" be elected. Since zero is not considered to be an amount for tax purposes, a nominal election of $1 is usually made. As a result, there is an income inclusion to the vendor of $0.50 ($1 × 75% × ⅔). The purchaser (the corporation) might have expected to claim CECA on $0.75 ($1 × 75%), but if the purchaser and the vendor are not dealing at arm's length, then the purchaser will only be able to claim CECA on $0.50 ($1 × 75% − 50% × $0.50). As a result, the non-arm's length purchaser can only claim CECA on the amount that the vendor included in income.

ITA: 14(5), variable A in the definition of "cumulative eligible capital" [as proposed by Bill C-33, Nov. 22, 2007]

¶16,130   Transfer of non-depreciable capital property with unrealized capital losses to affiliated persons

The legislation imposes restrictions on a capital loss arising from property that is transferred to certain non-arm's length persons, referred to as "affiliated persons". Some of the restrictions depend upon the type of the affiliated person (i.e., individual, corporation, etc.); others are common to all affiliated persons. These provisions are often referred to as the "stop-loss" rules.

¶16,130.10   *Definition of Affiliated Persons*

In order to understand the definition of "affiliated person", a few additional rules should be noted at the outset. Persons are considered to be affiliated with themselves, and a person includes a partnership. The following terms are defined:

ITA: 251.1(1)
ITA: 251.1(3)
ITA: 251.1(3)

(a) an "affiliated group of persons" refers to a group each member of which is affiliated with every other member; and

(b) "controlled" means controlled, directly or indirectly in any manner whatever, and, hence, includes *de facto* control as defined, discussed in a previous chapter.

ITA: 256(5.1)

Two individuals are considered to be affiliated only when they are spouses of each other, including common-law partner as defined.

ITA: 248(1) "common-law partner", 251.1(1)(*a*)

A corporation is described as being affiliated with three types of persons:

ITA: 251.1(1)(*b*)

(a) a person by whom the corporation is controlled (as defined above);

(b) each member of an affiliated group (as defined above) by which the corporation is controlled; and

(c) the spouse of a person in either of the first two categories above.

Very generally, for example, a corporation affiliated with an individual transferor, as contemplated by section 85, is one which is controlled by the individual or the individual's spouse.

Consider the following example. A, an individual who is not married, controls A Ltd., A and two other individuals, B and C, own an equal number of shares and votes in ABC Ltd. B and C are married to each other.

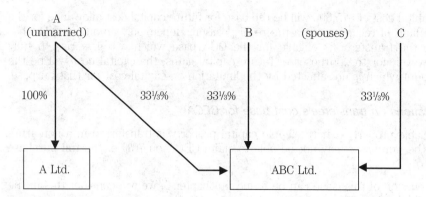

A is not affiliated with any individual, since he is not married. B and C are affiliated, because they are spouses. A Ltd. is affiliated with A since A controls it. ABC Ltd. is affiliated with both B and C, since they are members of an affiliated group that controls (i.e., owns 66⅔% of) ABC Ltd. ABC Ltd. is not affiliated with A unless A has some form of non-voting *de facto* control.

¶16,130.20   *Unrealized Capital Losses*

The stop-loss provisions deny the immediate recognition of the capital loss in all situations where the transferee is affiliated with the transferor. However, the subsequent treatment of the capital loss will depend upon the type of non-depreciable asset that is transferred and the type of person which is the transferor and/or transferee.

(i) Individual Transferors

For individual transferors, the denied capital loss (except for certain share transfers discussed below) is added to the adjusted cost base of the property held by the corporate transferee. For individuals, the capital loss denial is achieved through the interaction of two provisions: the definition of a "superficial loss" and the superficial loss denial. The definition of a "superficial loss" includes any capital loss arising on a transfer of capital property by individuals to an affiliated person.

ITA: 53(1)(*f*)

ITA: 40(2)(*g*), 54
ITA: 251.1

For example, if Ms. X transfers to her wholly owned corporation land which has an unrealized capital loss of $10,000 (e.g., FMV of $90,000 and ACB of $100,000), then the capital loss of $10,000 will be added to the FMV of the land of $90,000 resulting in a $100,000 adjusted cost base of the transferred land held by the corporation. In essence, the corporation will hold the land with an ACB of $100,000 and a FMV of $90,000, as Ms. X did before the transfer. To accomplish the transfer, it is not necessary to elect under section 85 with its conditions. A simple sale at fair market value for consideration like debt of equal fair market value is all that is necessary in the case of an individual transferor.

(ii) Corporate, Trust, and Partnership Transferors

For corporations, trusts and partnerships, the denied capital loss (except for certain share transfers, discussed below) is subject to stop-loss rules which cause the affected capital loss to be retained by the transferor and its recognition by the transferor to be deferred until the earliest of the following events:

(a) a subsequent disposition of the transferred property to a person that is not the transferor or a person affiliated with the transferor (provided that neither acquires (or holds a right to acquire) the transferred property (or identical property) within 30 days after the subsequent disposition);

(b) a deemed disposition on leaving Canada and changing residence; or

ITA: 128.1

(c) an acquisition of control of the corporation.

(iii) All Transferors

For all taxpayers, another stop-loss rule denies a capital loss arising from the redemption of shares of a corporation where the corporation is affiliated with the transferor immediately after the transfer. In this situation, the denied capital loss is added to the adjusted cost base of any shares held by the transferor in the transferee corporation. For example, if the transferor transfers *all* its shares to the issuing corporation (i.e., all of the shares are redeemed) and, as a result, the transferor is no longer affiliated, then the loss is recognized because the transferor is no longer affiliated with the transferee corporation. If, however, the transferor (or another affiliated shareholder) controls the corporation after the transfer, then the loss is denied and the denied loss is added to the adjusted cost base of the remaining shares held by the transferor. However, if the transferor does not hold any shares after the transfer, but is still affiliated, the denied loss is lost.

ITA: 40(3.6)

¶16,135 Summary of stop-loss rules

The loss denial or stop-loss rules discussed above are summarized in Exhibit 16-3.

EXHIBIT 16-3
Stop-loss Rules

Transferor is a corporation, trust or partnership	Transferor is an individual
Capital loss on transfer	**Capital loss on transfer**
• to an affiliated purchaser [sec. 251.1]	• to an affiliated purchaser [sec. 251.1]
• capital loss is denied [ssec. 40(3.4)]	• capital loss is denied as a superficial loss [sec. 54, par. 40(2)(*g*)]
• capital loss is kept with the transferor until the transferee sells the asset to a non-affiliated person	• denied loss is added to the cost of the asset to the transferee
Terminal loss	**Terminal loss**
• on transfer to an affiliated purchaser [sec. 251.1]	• same as for corporations, trusts or partnerships
• terminal loss is denied [ssec. 13(21.2)]	
• terminal loss is kept with the transferor until the transferee sells the asset to a non-affiliated person	
• transferee records the asset with a cost equal to the cost to the transferor and an addition to UCC equal to FMV [par. 13(7)(*e*)]	
Capital loss on redemption	**Capital loss on redemption**
• affiliated [sec. 251.1] immediately after the redemption	• same as for corporations, trusts or partnerships
• capital loss is denied [ssec. 40(3.6)]	
• capital loss is added to the ACB of any other shares owned by the transferor; if no other shares owned, but the transferor is still affiliated, then capital loss is lost	

¶16,140 Benefits Conferred on Shareholders and Related Persons

Throughout the chapter so far, it has been emphasized that the fair market value of the consideration taken back by the transferor must equal the fair market value of the property transferred. Now the adverse tax consequences of not adhering to this principle will be examined.

The topic will be introduced, first, conceptually. Then, the technical rules will be examined in two situations:

(a) where the consideration package is valued at less than the fair market value of the property transferred; and

(b) where the consideration package is valued at greater than the fair market value of the property transferred.

¶16,145   Conceptual example

¶16,145.10   *Conditions for transfer*

The assets can be transferred at any amount between the tax value and the fair market value of the particular asset. The consideration in this situation will be preferred shares with a specific redemption value or retraction value (shares are redeemed at the option of the corporation and retracted at the option of the shareholder). Remember that common shares, as used in the previous situations, will automatically pick up the FMV of the asset transferred net of any boot or non-share consideration. This is not true for preferred shares unless the retraction or redemption value is fixed exactly equal to the FMV of the property transferred net of any boot. Therefore, as long as the FMV of the property transferred is exactly equal to the FMV of the consideration (i.e., boot plus preferred shares) there will be no negative tax consequences as demonstrated below.

¶16,145.20   *Facts*

Mr. Philip wishes to transfer land to a corporation, Philip Ltd., which his daughter presently controls through the ownership of all the common shares.

Land — ACB	$ 30,000
— FMV	150,000

Mr. Philip is considering three different consideration packages:

(a) a promissory note of $30,000 plus non-voting preferred shares with a retraction and stated value of $120,000 for a total FMV equal to the FMV of the land;

(b) a promissory note of $10,000 and non-voting preferred shares with a retraction and stated value of $20,000 for a total FMV which is less than the FMV of the land; or

(c) a promissory note of $200,000 and non-voting preferred shares with a retraction and stated value of a nominal amount for a total FMV which is greater than the FMV of the land.

Package (a) is on-side and there are no adverse tax consequences. However, Packages (b) and (c) are off-side and result in adverse tax consequences.

Mr. Philip and Philip Ltd. are going to choose an elected amount of $30,000 equal to the ACB of the land.

¶16,145.30   *Results*

The *first* consideration package is on-side and will not have any adverse tax consequences since the FMV of land (i.e., $150,000) equals the FMV of the consideration (i.e., $30,000 of boot plus preferred shares retractable at $120,000). Note that the boot is also on-side since it does not exceed the elected amount of $30,000. The $30,000 of boot, which will be received ultimately tax-free, reflects the tax-paid cost of the land. See Situation Three where the boot is off-side.

¶16,145

In summary, the following has occurred:

Before transfer		After transfer			
Mr. Philip owned	*Land*	*Mr. Philip owns*	*Debt*	*Corporation owns*	*Land*
ACB	$ 30,000	ACB	$ 30,000	ACB	$ 30,000
FMV	150,000	FMV	30,000	FMV	150,000
		Mr. Philip owns	*Shares*	*Corporation owes to:*	
		ACB	Nil	Mr. Philip	$ 30,000
		PUC	Nil		
		FMV	$120,000		

The *second* consideration package is off-side since Mr. Philip has accepted consideration which, in total, is less than the FMV of the land (i.e., ($10,000 + $20,000) compared to $150,000). Mr. Philip is deemed to have conferred a benefit (gift) on his daughter of $120,000 (i.e., the FMV of the land ($150,000) – the FMV of the consideration ($10,000 + $20,000)). Since the daughter is the common shareholder, this $120,000 difference (contributed surplus in accounting terms) will increase the FMV of the common shares. In essence, Mr. Philip has attempted to pass $120,000 of the accumulated growth in the land which should be taxed in his hands to his daughter. The tax consequences of this off-side transaction will be as follows:

(1) The original elected amount of $30,000 will be bumped by the amount of the gift (i.e., $120,000) to $150,000 which is exactly equal to the FMV of the land (i.e., $150,000) and a capital gain of $120,000 will be triggered in Mr. Philip's hands since his proceeds of disposition are now $150,000.

(2) The ACB of the land now held by Philip Ltd. will be the new elected amount of $150,000.

(3) Since the ACB of the preferred shares cannot exceed their retraction amount of $20,000 (the fair market value), a downward adjustment must be made. The ACB of the preferred shares of $20,000 is determined as the original elected amount of $30,000 (not the new elected amount of $150,000) minus the $10,000 allocated to the boot. This ACB of $20,000 is now equal to the retraction amount. However, there is an inherent, but hidden penalty in the daughter's common shares, since they retain their original ACB while the value has increased by $120,000 as a result of the gift. Therefore, she will realize a capital gain of $120,000 upon the ultimate disposition of her shares. This is analogous to the one-sided adjustments in section 69, discussed in Chapter 8, on non-arm's length transfers which can result in a double-counting of income.

(4) The PUC of Mr. Philip's preferred shares, however, will be calculated with the *increased* elected amount of $150,000 as calculated below:

Stated capital*		$ 20,000
Less: elected amount (new)	$150,000	
less: boot	10,000	140,000
PUC reduction		Nil
∴ PUC		$ 20,000

This $20,000 represents the remaining cost of the land transferred (i.e., $30,000) after taking out boot in the form of a promissory note (i.e., $10,000).

---

*Note that under the *Canada Business Corporations Act* (CBCA), normally the stated value of the share consideration must equal the fair market value of the property transferred (i.e., $150,000, the FMV of the land). However, for non-arm's length transactions, the stated value can, at the discretion of the corporate directors, be set at less than the fair market value (i.e., $20,000).

In summary, the following has occurred:

Before transfer		*After transfer*			
Mr. Philip owned	*Land*	*Mr. Philip owns*	*Debt*	*Corporation owns*	*Land*
ACB . . . . $ 30,000		ACB . . . . $ 10,000		ACB $150,000	
FMV 150,000		FMV 10,000		FMV 150,000	
		Mr. Philip owns	*Shares*	*Corporation owes to:*	
		ACB . . . . $ 20,000		Mr. Philip . . . . $ 10,000	
		PUC 20,000			
		FMV 20,000			
		Mr. Philip has a capital gain of $120,000 to include in her income.		*The value of the corporation's common shares held by the daughter has increased by $120,000 with no ACB increase.*	

The *third* consideration package is also off-side since Mr. Philip has accepted consideration which, in total, is more than the FMV of the land (i.e., $150,000 compared to $200,000 boot plus preferred shares with a retraction and stated value of a nominal amount). The tax consequences are as follows:

(1) The boot of $200,000 exceeds the elected amount of $30,000; hence, the elected amount is bumped to $150,000 triggering a capital gain of $120,000. Note that the elected amount can never exceed the FMV of the transferred property (i.e., land with a FMV of $150,000 in this case).

(2) There will be a benefit conferred on Mr. Philip as a shareholder: ITA: 15(1)

FMV of consideration

Boot	$200,000	
Retraction value of preferred shares	nominal	$200,000
Less: FMV of land		150,000
Benefit		$ 50,000

ITA: 15(1)

This benefit of $50,000 will be added to the cost of the boot consideration received. Since the elected amount of $150,000 becomes the initial cost of boot, the ACB of the boot is increased to $200,000 (i.e., the $150,000 of the elected amount allocated to the boot plus the subsection 15(1) benefit of $50,000).   ITA: 52(1)

(3) The cost to the corporation of the land will be the *new* elected amount of $150,000.

(4) The ACB of the preferred shares will be:

Elected amount (new)	$150,000
Less: boot	200,000
Excess	Nil

(5) The PUC will be reduced to nil as follows:

Stated value		nominal
Less: elected amount (new)	$ 150,000	
boot	(200,000)	Nil
Reduction		nominal
∴ PUC = (nominal – nominal)		Nil

All of the tax-paid cost of $200,000 is represented in the value of the boot which will be repaid without further tax cost in the future. Therefore, nothing is left to recover tax free in the PUC of the shares on their redemption. In this situation, after the transfer, there is a total tax-paid cost of $200,000 derived from:

¶16,145.30

Cost of the original land	$ 30,000
Capital gain triggered on the section 85 transfer (i.e., $150,000 – $30,000)	120,000
Benefit	50,000
	$200,000

ITA: 15(1)

This tax-paid cost is reflected in the ACB of the boot (i.e., the $200,000 demonstrated above).

In summary, the following has occurred:

Before transfer		After transfer			
Mr. Philip owned	*Land*	*Mr. Philip owns*	*Debt*	*Corporation owns*	*Land*
ACB	$ 30,000	ACB	$200,000	ACB	$150,000
FMV	150,000	FMV	200,000	FMV	150,000
		Mr. Philip owns	*Shares*	*Corporation owes to:*	
		ACB	Nil	Mr. Philip	$200,000
		PUC	Nil		
		FMV	Nil		

Mr. Philip has income from a capital gain of $120,000 and property income of $50,000.

¶16,145.40   *Conclusion*

This situation clearly demonstrates that as long as the FMV of the consideration received equals the FMV of the property transferred there will be no adverse tax consequences. Where these two amounts are not equal then income inclusions will be triggered.

¶16,150   Benefit conferred on a related person — Technical rules

A benefit is deemed to have been conferred on a related person:

(a) where the fair market value of the property, immediately before it is transferred to the corporation, exceeds the greater of:

(i) the fair market value immediately after the transfer of all consideration (including shares or rights to receive shares) received from the corporation, and

(ii) the elected amount; and

(b) where it is reasonable to regard any part of that excess as a benefit conferred by the taxpayer on a person related to the taxpayer (including the transferee corporation itself unless it is wholly owned by the transferor).

The result is that the elected amount or transfer price is increased by that part of the excess that is a benefit, but there is no increase in the cost of the share consideration received.

ITA: 85(1)(e.2)

For example, consider a capital property that has a cost of $100 and a fair market value of $200. To defer maximum capital gains, the transfer price is elected at $100. Consideration from the corporation consists of cash in the amount of $100 and preferred shares with a fair market value of $40. In this case, an asset worth $200 is transferred to a corporation for consideration worth $140. The $60 discrepancy in fair market value would form part of taxable surplus (contributed surplus)[1] and would be taxed eventually as a dividend. The tax implications of the benefit of $60 depends upon who is the recipient of the benefit, as described below.

If the transferor owned none of the common shares of the company after the transfer and persons related to the transferor owned the common shares, it may be argued that the transferor has given the other shareholders a benefit equal to the excess of fair market value

---

[1] The right to convert this contributed surplus to paid-up capital would be denied since the amount arose under section 85. See page 815 in Chapter 15.

of the property transferred ($200) over the consideration received ($140). This argument is based on the principle that common shareholders own the residual equity, including contributed surplus, in a corporation. Thus, the elected amount or transfer price would be increased by $60 (i.e., $200–$140) for the purpose of determining the proceeds of disposition to the transferor and the cost of the property to the corporation.

However, as a penalty, the cost of the shares received as consideration by the transferor would remain at nil. Thus, there will be recognition of income on the transfer but no parallel increase in the cost base of the shares received as consideration. Furthermore, the fair market value of the common shares held by other shareholders will increase by $60, but there will be no offsetting increase in the adjusted cost base of the shares held by those shareholders. Therefore, the $60 capital gain will be taxed potentially in the hands of the other shareholders when they dispose of their shares. The penalty inherent in this "benefit" rule is similar to the one where there is an arm's length transfer between related individuals. In this case, a non-arm's length rule evokes a one-sided adjustment and as a result the capital gain is taxed twice.

ITA: 69(1)(b)

To avoid the pitfall of this benefit rule, the transferor should always take as consideration from the corporation a package with a total fair market value equal to the fair market value of the property transferred to the corporation.

An alternative might be to first gift $60 worth of property to the related shareholders who could then transfer the gifted property to the corporation. The other shareholder could then transfer the $140 of property to the corporation for consideration with a total fair market value of $140. However, the potential effects of the GAAR should be evaluated before making this suggestion.

In the above example, if the transferor owned 100% of the shares of the corporation, there would be no benefit, because of the exception in that case. If the transferor owns some but not all of the common shares, then the benefit would be prorated between the transferor and the related common shareholders, with the amount allocated to the related shareholders comprising the benefit.

ITA: 85(1)(e.2)

¶16,155 Subsection 15(1) benefit conferred on a shareholder — Technical rules

This benefit rule provides for what is, in essence, a penalty where the fair market value of the property transferred to a corporation is less than the fair market value of the non-share consideration received from the corporation. In these circumstances, the Act encourages a balancing of the fair market value of the total consideration with the fair market value of the property transferred. The excess consideration will result in a benefit conferred on a shareholder which is taxed as income to the transferor.

ITA: 15(1)

Exhibit 16-4 presents an analysis similar to that in Exhibit 16-2. Here, three more alternative combinations of the following three key variables are used: fair market value of the property transferred, adjusted cost base (or other tax value) of the property transferred, and non-share consideration "boot" received. Note that in each case, the "boot" exceeds the fair market value of the property transferred, resulting in a shareholder benefit.

ITA: 15(1)

EXHIBIT 16-4
Range of Elected Amounts
(nominal share consideration assumed)

	1	*2*	*3*
$100	boot┐	boot┐	ACB
75	Ⓣ FMV┘ Ⓘ	ACB ┐Ⓘ	boot┐Ⓘ
60	ACB	Ⓣ FMV┘	Ⓣ FMV┘

T — transfer price; I — income (ssec. 15(1)); boot — non-share consideration.

Now consider the following numerical example involving the transfer of a capital property having an adjusted cost base of $1,000 and a fair market value of $1,500:

Consideration

Debt		$ 1,800
Preferred shares (FMV and LSC)		nominal[1]
Common shares (FMV and LSC)		nominal[1]
Total		$ 1,800
Election range:		
high[2]		$ 1,500
low		$ 1,500
Election price (no choice; deemed) [par. 85(1)(c)]		$ 1,500
Adjusted cost base		1,000
Capital gain		$ 500
Taxable capital gain at ½ inclusion rate		$ 250
Income inclusion [ssec. 15(1)]:		
FMV of "boot"		$ 1,800
FMV of shares issued		nominal[1]
		$ 1,800
FMV of assets transferred		(1,500)
Benefit amount [ssec. 15(1)][3]		$ 300

NOTE: [1] A nominal amount, in this case, could be one cent or even ¹/₁₀ of a cent.

[2] The upper limit of the elected transfer price is restricted to the fair market value of the property transferred to the corporation [par. 85(1)(c)].

[3] The income amount computed would be added to the cost of the debt to raise it from $1,500, the elected amount, to $1,800, its fair market value. Note, however, that the adjusted cost base of the asset will remain at $1,500, the elected amount [ssec. 15(1), ssec. 52(1)].

¶16,160 Summary of Rules

Exhibit 16-5 presents a schematic summary of the major rules of the rollover and their consequences for a case involving property with an accrued gain at the time of the transfer.

ITA: 85(1)

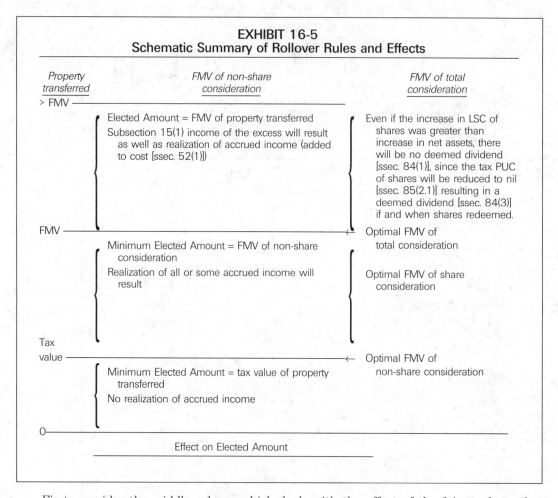

EXHIBIT 16-5
Schematic Summary of Rollover Rules and Effects

Property transferred	FMV of non-share consideration	FMV of total consideration
> FMV		
	Elected Amount = FMV of property transferred	Even if the increase in LSC of shares was greater than increase in net assets, there will be no deemed dividend [ssec. 84(1)], since the tax PUC of shares will be reduced to nil [ssec. 85(2.1)] resulting in a deemed dividend [ssec. 84(3)] if and when shares redeemed.
	Subsection 15(1) income of the excess will result as well as realization of accrued income (added to cost [ssec. 52(1)])	
FMV		← Optimal FMV of total consideration
	Minimum Elected Amount = FMV of non-share consideration	
	Realization of all or some accrued income will result	Optimal FMV of share consideration
Tax value		← Optimal FMV of non-share consideration
	Minimum Elected Amount = tax value of property transferred	
	No realization of accrued income	
0		

Effect on Elected Amount

First, consider the middle column which deals with the effect of the fair market value (FMV) of non-share considerations (i.e., boot) on the elected amount. If the fair market value of the boot is less than the tax value of the asset transferred, the lower limit on the elected transfer price range will be the tax value and none of the accrued income on the property will be triggered on the transfer. If the fair market value of the boot is greater than the tax value of the property transferred, the lower limit on the elected transfer price range will be equal to the fair market value of the boot and part or all of the accrued income on the property transferred will be realized and subjected to tax. The optimal fair market value of the boot, therefore, is equal to the tax value of the property transferred. This is optimal, because it permits the maximum amount of non-share consideration with the maximum accrued income deferred. Since non-share consideration will typically involve either cash or debt of the corporation which can be repaid in cash without tax consequences, taking the maximum boot is worthwhile.

Now consider the third column dealing with the fair market value of *total* consideration. If the optimal fair market value of boot (equal to the tax value of the property transferred) is taken, then the fair market value of share consideration when added to the fair market value of boot should equal, in total, the fair market value of the property transferred. To take less share consideration may result in the benefit rule being invoked. To take more share consideration will result in a deemed dividend, if and when the shares are redeemed. Therefore, it is usually best to take back from the corporation share consideration with a fair market value

ITA: 85(1)(e.2)
ITA: 84(3)

which, when added to the fair market value of boot, totals the fair market value of the property transferred to the corporation.

¶16,170 Fair Market Value

From the foregoing discussion, the importance of the role of fair market value should be apparent. The fair market value of property transferred to a corporation must be established in order to determine the fair market value of both non-share and share consideration to receive from the corporation. The valuation of common shares of a privately-held corporation, in particular, can present problems.

The term "fair market value" is mentioned more than 600 times in the Act. In addition to the requirements of section 85, determinations of fair market value are most commonly required pursuant to the following sections:

- Subsection 52(2) — payment of dividends in kind
- Section 69 — non-arm's length transactions
- Section 70 — deemed dispositions on death
- Subsection 104(4) — deemed disposition of trust property after 21 years
- Section 160 — certain transfers between spouses.

Historically, the Canada Revenue Agency (CRA) has provided little guidance as to what was required of taxpayers to support valuations required for these sections. Business valuations are generally not filed with the CRA as part of typical transaction documentation. In order to ensure that a subsequent review of fair market values by the CRA does not result in a one-sided adjustment causing double taxation, many taxpayers avail themselves of a price adjustment clause.

A price adjustment clause, however, can ensure that if the CRA determines that a sale price does not reflect fair market value, the price will be adjusted appropriately. Case law indicates that a price adjustment clause will only be recognized if the parties have reasonably, and in good faith, attempted to determine transaction prices that equal fair market values.[2]

IT-169

An Information Circular provides a detailed listing of specific factors that should be considered and analyzed in business valuations. The Circular discusses the conventional approaches to business valuations, being the assets and the earnings methods, and also deals with such sophisticated areas as options, buy–sell agreements and the concepts of family and group control.

IC 89-3

The CRA undertakes sophisticated reviews of fair market value determinations. Undoubtedly, the income tax practitioner must be aware of these requirements in order to ensure compliance with the various sections of the Act as illustrated by section 85 where fair market value determinations are required.

IC 89-3

¶16,180 Section 22 Election

Where there is a potential capital loss on the transfer of accounts receivable to a corporation by an affiliated person, the rollover should not be used. Accounts receivable are capital property, and any capital loss triggered on any transfer (not just a section 85 election) to an affiliated corporation would be denied, as discussed previously. For an individual transferor, this capital loss would be passed on to the corporation through a bump in the adjusted cost base of the accounts receivable. For other transferors, the recognition is deferred in a different manner, as discussed previously. The better alternative is to use an election under section 22 on the transfer of accounts receivable in order to qualify them for a reserve for doubtful debts and bad debt write-off in the corporation.

ITA: 85(1)

ITA: 53(1)(*f*)

Form T2022

---

[2] *Guilder News Co. (1963) Ltd. et al. v. M.N.R.*, 73 DTC 5048 (F.C.A.).

One of the main requirements for the deduction of a reserve or a bad debt is that the transaction that gave rise to the debt must have been included previously in the taxpayer's income. If the corporation buys the receivables and one subsequently goes bad, it cannot meet this test. Section 22 covers this situation in a case where a person has sold all or substantially all the property (including receivables) used in a business to a purchaser who proposes to continue the business. The CRA indicates that where 90% of the assets of the business carried on in Canada are sold, "all or substantially all" of the assets of such business will be considered sold. If the vendor and purchaser jointly execute and file an agreement in the prescribed form, a future reserve for doubtful debts and bad debt write-offs will be permitted to the purchaser.

ITA: 20(1)(l) or 20(1)(p)(ii)

IT-188R, par. 1

Consider the following set of facts:

1. the accounts receivable have a face amount of $6,000;

2. they have a fair market value of $4,700; and

3. last year, the allowance for doubtful accounts was $500.

In this case the following entries would be made:

Proprietor (Vendor)		
Reserve	$ 500	
Income [(par. 12(1)(d)]		$ 500
Consideration	4,700	
Loss from business	1,300	
Accounts receivable ...		6,000
— Note that loss offsets income.		

Corporation (Purchaser)		
Accounts receivable	$6,000	
Consideration		$4,700
Income		1,300
— Can take reserve at year-end.		
— Can write off bad debts.		

If the section 22 election is not made, the vendor will still have to include last year's reserve in income ($500 in this case), but the loss in this case would be a capital loss. This loss would be denied on the transfer to the corporation by an individual under paragraph 40(2)(g) and would be added to the adjusted cost base of the accounts receivable in the corporation. The purchaser will have acquired the accounts receivable as capital property at the transferor's cost, i.e., FMV plus the denied capital loss. If the corporation recovers less than adjusted cost base, it will have a capital loss. The purchaser would not be eligible to take a reserve for doubtful accounts or a bad debt write-off for tax purposes on the accounts acquired without the election under section 22.

ITA: 40(2)(g), 53(1)(f)

The decision tree in Exhibit 16-6 may be useful in providing an approach to problems dealing with transfer of property to a corporation.

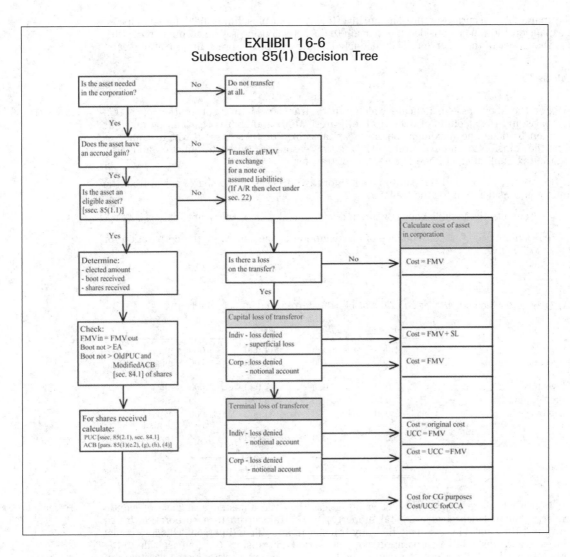

EXHIBIT 16-6
Subsection 85(1) Decision Tree

¶16,190 Application

Example Problem

Rollmeover operates an unincorporated business having the following balance sheet stated in tax values at its taxation year-end:

	Tax value	Fair market value	
Cash	$ 1,000	$ 1,000	✗
Marketable securities	11,000	15,000	✓
Accounts receivable	5,500	4,700	22
Inventory	7,000	7,000	✓
Prepaid rent	3,000	3,000	✗
Land	42,000	31,000	✗ — CAP SUPERFICIAL
Buildings (capital cost — $46,000)	28,000	50,000	→ RECAPTURE
Equipment (capital cost — $20,000)	8,000	3,000	✗ — CAP BUSINESS LOSS
Goodwill	—	47,000	
Total assets	$105,500	$161,700	
Liabilities		8,000	
		$153,700	

The marketable securities represent an investment of surplus funds held for anticipated future expansion and can be considered to pertain to the active business. The accounts receivable figure is shown net of the reserve of $500 deducted at the end of the preceding taxation year.

— *REQUIRED*

(A) For the above assets, indicate which can be transferred to a corporation on a tax-deferred basis and the amounts of debt (to the nearest $100) and shares that can be taken as consideration to defer the maximum possible capital gain. For those assets which cannot or should not be transferred under the rollover, state the reasons for this determination and, also, indicate the tax implications of another method of transfer.

ITA: 85(1)

(B) Compute the cost and the paid-up capital for tax purposes of the shares taken from the corporation as consideration for the transfer.

(C) (i) Compute the taxable capital gain on a subsequent sale of the shares at $73,000.

(ii) Compute the tax consequence of a redemption of the shares by the corporation for $73,000.

— *SOLUTION*

(A) (i) Items which *cannot* or *should not* be transferred under ssec. 85(1):

	Tax value	Fair market value	Transfer price	New debt	Income effect
Cash[1]	$ 1,000	$ 1,000	$ 1,000	$ 1,000	nil
Accounts receivable[2]	6,000	4,700	4,700	4,700	business loss allowed
Inventory[3]	7,000	7,000	7,000	7,000	nil
Prepaid rent[1]	3,000	3,000	3,000	3,000	nil
Land[4]	42,000	31,000	31,000	31,000	capital loss denied
Equipment[5]	8,000	3,000	3,000	3,000	terminal loss denied
Total	$67,000	$49,700	$49,700	$49,700	

Note that where the fair market value is less than the adjusted cost base of capital property (but not depreciable capital property) to be transferred to a corporation by an individual, the capital loss is denied for any transfer to an affiliated person. This loss denial applies to all transfers to a corporation, not just section 85 transfers (e.g., a cash sale to the corporation). The denied loss, however, is added to the corporation's adjusted cost base of the transferred asset. This puts the corporation in exactly the same tax position as an individual transferor was in prior to the transfer. As a result, capital property with accrued losses should not be transferred to the corporation under section 85 since there is no gain to defer. For example, land, in this case, can be sold at fair market value in return for boot like any of the above assets.

ITA: 40(2)(*g*), 54 "superficial loss", 251.1

ITA: 53(1)(*f*)

(ii) Items transferred on a tax-deferred basis:

ITA: 85(1)

	Tax value	Fair market value	Elected transfer price	FMV of consideration			Income Effect
				Assumed debt[9]	New debt	Shares	
Marketable securities[6]	$11,000	$ 15,000	$11,000	$8,000	$ 3,000	$ 4,000	Nil
Buildings	28,000	50,000	28,000	—	28,000	22,000	Nil
Goodwill[7]	Nil	47,000	1	—	—	47,000	$ 0.50
	$39,000	$112,000	$39,001[8]	$8,000	$31,000	$73,000	

Note that if the transferor had a net capital loss available, the securities could have been transferred at an elected amount of $15,000 to trigger the $4,000 of accrued capital gains which would not be taxed after using the net capital loss. This would allow debt consideration of $15,000 which can be repaid by the corporation later without any tax consequence. Furthermore, the corporation would be deemed to have acquired the marketable securities at an adjusted cost base of $15,000 for future capital gain purposes.

If an election is made on the building at fair market value of $50,000 to trigger the accrued capital gain of $4,000, the capital cost to the corporation would be restricted to only $48,000 (i.e., the original capital cost of $46,000 plus the taxable capital gain of $2,000 ($\frac{1}{2} \times$ ($50,000 – $46,000))). The transferor would also trigger recapture of $18,000 (i.e., capital cost of $46,000 minus UCC of $28,000). The latter election on the building, therefore, would probably not be beneficial, unless the transferor had some non-capital losses to offset the recapture.

ITA: 13(7)(*e*)(i)

An election, at up to $47,000, for the goodwill would have resulted in business income, which could be offset by a non-capital loss or a current business loss (an alternative which is not available in this example). In this case, there is a potential business income of up to $23,500 (i.e., $\frac{2}{3} \times \frac{3}{4} \times$ $47,000). This would, also, have allowed debt consideration of $47,000. The corporation (a non-arm's length purchaser) would have been deemed to have made an eligible capital expenditure of $23,500 which could be written off. The actual amount that would be added to the cumulative eligible capital account would have been $23,500 (i.e., $\frac{3}{4} \times$ $47,000 – $\frac{1}{2} \times$ $23,500). Since the transfer to a controlled corporation would be a non-arm's length transaction, the usual addition of $\frac{3}{4}$ of the purchase price is reduced by $\frac{1}{2}$ of the transferor's income. The effect of the reduction is to add, in a non-arm's length transaction, an amount to the cumulative eligible capital account that will provide a base for the deduction of amortization. The added amount is only equal to the income of the transferor that was included in income. A similar adjustment is made to undepreciated capital cost in a non-arm's length transfer of depreciable property. In this case, the amount to be amortized would be $23,500 ($\frac{3}{4} \times$ $47,000 – $\frac{1}{2} \times$ $23,500).

ITA: 14(1)(*a*)(v)

ITA: 20(1)(*b*)

ITA: 14(1)(*b*), 14(5) variable A in the definition of "cumulative eligible capital" [as proposed by Bill C-33, Nov. 22, 2007]

ITA: 13(7)(*e*)

(B) The cost of shares would be:

Elected transfer price of assets (in total)		$ 39,001
Deduct:		
Debt issued	$31,000	
Liabilities assumed[(9)]	8,000	39,000
ACB of the common shares		$ 1

The tax PUC of the shares would be:

LSC of share consideration before reduction			$ 73,000
Less: reduction in PUC:			
(i) increase in LSC of all shares on the transfer to the corporation		$73,000 (A)	
(ii) elected amount	$39,001		
less: non-share consideration	39,000		
excess, if any		1 (B)	
(A – B)		$72,999	
(iii) increase in LSC of a class of shares issued on the transfer		$73,000 (C)	

ITA: 85(2.1)

ITA: 85(1)

Reduction: (A – B) $\times \dfrac{C}{A} = \$72,999 \times \dfrac{\$73,000}{\$73,000}$ $72,999

Tax PUC of share consideration	$ 1

(C) (i) Taxable capital gain

Proceeds of disposition	$ 73,000
ACB of shares	1
Capital gain	$ 72,999
Taxable capital gain ($\frac{1}{2} \times$ $72,999)	$ 36,500

¶16,190

(ii) Tax consequence of redemption of all the shares

Redemption amount	$ 73,000	
Less: tax PUC	1	
Deemed dividend	$ 72,999	ITA: 84(3)

Redemption amount	$ 73,000	
Less: deemed dividend	72,999	
Proceeds of disposition	$ 1	ITA: 54
Less: adjusted cost base	1	
Capital gain/loss	Nil	

Note how the net economic effect of $72,999 of deemed dividend on the redemption is the same as the capital gain in (c)(i) above and is equal to the gain on the assets deferred by the rollover on their transfer to the corporation.

ITA: 85(1)

— NOTES TO SOLUTION

[1]Cash and prepaids (i.e., prepaid rent) are not normally capital property. Therefore, these two assets cannot be transferred under section 85. However, they can be loaned to the corporation at their FMV, taking back debt consideration.

[2]Accounts receivable are capital property; hence, any capital loss arising on the transfer would be denied and, for an individual transferor, as discussed in Part (A)(i) of this solution, added to the adjusted cost base of the transferred accounts receivable. If, however, Rollmeover and the corporation jointly elect under section 22, then:

(a) the loss of $1,300 (i.e., $5,500 tax value net of reserve + $500 reserve taken into income – $4,700 fair market value) is deemed to be a business loss, rather than a capital loss; and

(b) the business loss of Rollmeover must be taken into the corporation's income. This action will permit the corporation to write off any uncollectible accounts receivable and to set up a reserve in respect of doubtful accounts receivable.

[3]A transfer of the inventory under the rollover is not recommended, because there is no income to defer on the transfer and the transfer would be subject to all of the section 85 restrictions.

ITA: 85(1)

[4]A transfer of the land under the rollover is not recommended, because there is no gain to defer on the transfer and the transfer would be subject to all of the section 85 restrictions. The capital loss will be denied on the transfer, as noted in Part A(i) of this solution. However, the accrued loss would be preserved in the ACB of $42,000 in the corporation.

ITA: 85(1)

[5]A transfer of the equipment under the rollover is not recommended. Although the terminal loss would not be recognized by the transferor using the rollover, the transfer would be subject to all the section 85 restrictions. The simpler alternative is to sell the equipment directly to the corporation and take back debt equal to the fair market value.

ITA: 85(1)

[6]Shares should be taken as consideration to bring the total consideration up to the fair market value of the property transferred. Before transferring the short-term investments to the corporation, it should be ascertained that they can be considered assets used in an active business, to preserve the QSBCS status of the corporation's shares.

(7)Goodwill must be transferred at least at a nominal amount of $1.00 so that it is listed in the election. Since the courts have consistently determined that Nil is not an amount, the CRA would apply the non-arm's length transfer rule to deem the sale at the fair market value which would trigger an income inclusion of $23,500 ($2/3 \times 3/4 \times$ $47,000). Note that it is permissible to take $1 in debt, but the instruction was to take debt only to the nearest $100.

ITA: 85(1)
ITA: 69

ITA: 14(1); IC 76-19R3, par. 4, 6

(8)The elected transfer price becomes the proceeds of disposition for each property to the transferor, the cost of each property to the corporation and the adjusted cost base of the consideration received from the corporation by the transferor.

(9)Consider the liabilities assumed by the corporation as part of the consideration other than shares received from the corporation against part of the property transferred, thereby reducing the amount of new debt to be taken. According to the CRA, the most common error made in using the rollover election is to forget that assumed liabilities are part of the "boot" received. Note that the $8,000 of liabilities could have been assumed by the corporation in return for the assets not transferred under the rollover, instead of in return for the assets transferred under the rollover.

ITA: 85(1)

¶16,200   TRANSFER OF SHARES

¶16,210   Non-Arm's Length Sale of Shares

¶16,215   The situation: QSBC shares

Consider the case of Mr. Strip. He incorporated a company Strippit Limited in 1990 having paid-up capital of $1,000. These shares, all of which are owned by Mr. Strip, currently have a fair market value of $200,000. If Mr. Strip sold the shares in an arm's length transaction, he would realize a capital gain of $199,000. Perhaps more important, Mr. Strip would receive, at least, part of the capital gain tax free by offsetting it with, say, $99,000 of available QSBC share capital gains exemption. Actually, Mr. Strip does not want to sell his shares and give up the business, but the prospect of receiving of $99,000 of the accrued gain tax free is attractive. Alternatively, he may simply want to implement an estate freeze, as discussed in the next chapter. In either case, if Mr. Strip continues to own the shares, the only way that he can receive the surplus represented by the $200,000 value is to receive a taxable dividend of $199,000.

To achieve this objective without losing control of the corporation, Mr. Strip decides to set up a holding company, Holdit Ltd., and to transfer his shares in Strippit Ltd. to Holdit Ltd. using the provisions of section 85. He chooses to transfer his shares at an elected amount of $100,000 to realize $99,000 of capital gains on the transfer. As consideration for these shares, he can take from Holdit Ltd. up to $100,000 in debt or shares as long as he takes at least one share to qualify the transfer under section 85 and as long as the total non-share consideration does not exceed $100,000 to avoid capital gains subject to tax on the transfer. It should be easy to see that if he takes, for example, cash of $100,000 from Holdit Ltd. which borrowed these funds, he will have received $99,000 of the accrued gain on the shares of Strippit Ltd. tax free.

If, in fact, Holdit Ltd. had borrowed the funds, the loan could be repaid by having Strippit Ltd., which Holdit Ltd. now owns, pay a dividend to Holdit Ltd. which, in turn, would be used to repay the borrowed funds. This dividend would be received by Holdit Ltd. free of Part I tax and, normally, free of Part IV tax, since Strippit Ltd. is connected with Holdit Ltd. Other variations of this scheme are possible using debt or shares of Holdit Ltd. issued to Mr. Strip. The general situation can be diagrammed as shown in Exhibit 16-7.

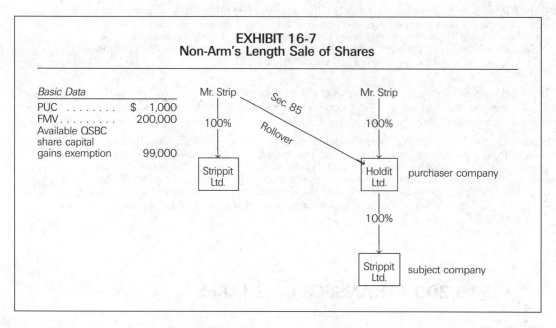

EXHIBIT 16-7
Non-Arm's Length Sale of Shares

Basic Data	
PUC	$ 1,000
FMV	200,000
Available QSBC share capital gains exemption	99,000

Recognize that if the shares of Strippit Ltd. are not sold at arm's length, the only way that Mr. Strip could realize the surplus which creates the values shown for the shares is through a dividend or a deemed dividend on redemption, both of which would be taxable. Thus, the process illustrated by Exhibit 16-7 is an attempt to convert what might otherwise have been paid out as a taxable dividend into a tax-free capital gain, without giving up control of the shares. The resultant capital gain is received tax free, because it is protected through the qualified small business corporation share (QSBCS) capital gains deduction. This process is often referred to as "dividend stripping" and, historically, such attempts have been popular whenever capital gains were taxed at a lower rate than taxable dividends.

A provision will be shown to turn capital gains derived by the process described back into taxable deemed dividends under certain conditions. It appears to be the non-arm's length nature of the sale of shares, in which the benefits of owning the shares are effectively maintained, that offends the legislation. Any other type of asset, such as land, buildings or eligible capital property, transferred to a corporation under similar conditions is not affected by this provision. ITA: 84.1

¶16,220 Conditions for section 84.1 to apply

The following conditions, as set out at the beginning of the provision, must exist in order for the rules of section 84.1 to apply: ITA: 84.1(1)

(a) the disposition must be made by a taxpayer resident in Canada other than a corporation;

(b) the subject shares (the shares being transferred) must be shares of a corporation resident in Canada and must be capital property to the taxpayer;

(c) the disposition must be made to a corporation with which the taxpayer does not deal at arm's length within the standard meaning of the phrase under subsection 251(1);[3] and

---

[3] The definition of non-arm's length is extended to include groups of persons under certain circumstances [par. 84.1(2)(b) and ssec. 84.1(2.2)].

¶16,220

(d) the subject corporation must be connected with the purchaser corporation immediately after the disposition, i.e., the purchaser corporation must control (as defined specifically) the subject corporation, or the purchaser corporation must own more than 10% of the voting shares and more than 10% of the fair market value of all of the issued shares of the subject corporation.

ITA: 186(2), 186(4)

¶16,225 The basic rules formulated

¶16,225.10 *PUC reduction*

84.1(1)(a)

The rules provide for a reduction in the paid-up capital of the shares issued by a purchaser company.[4] The following formula computes a reduction in paid-up capital for all new shares of the corporation issued and, then, allocates a part of the reduction to each class of shares.

PUC reduction:

(1) Increase, if any, in legal stated capital (LSC) of purchaser corporation . . . . xxx (A)

Less:

(2) Greater of:

(a) PUC of shares transferred xxx

(b) modified ACB of shares transferred (based on adjusted actual cost ignoring any increase in the ACB as a result of the capital gains exemption) xxx

} xxx

Less: Fair market value of non-share consideration received ("boot") . . . . (xxx)

Excess, if any . . . . xxx (B)

Total PUC reduction of all shares (A – B) xxx

PUC reduction of shares of any particular class for which increase in LSC was C:

$$(A - B) \times C/A$$

Note how the adjusted cost base of the shares transferred (i.e., the subject shares) is modified for use in the PUC reduction formula, above. The usual adjustments to be made to cost are those found in section 53. The adjusted actual cost is referred to as modified ACB here.

ITA: 84.1(2)(a), 84.1(2)(a.1)

Adjustments to cost base are made in one situation for the purposes of the coverage of this book. If the ACB of the shares includes an amount claimed as the capital gains exemption by that person or a related person, then the modified ACB will be determined by deducting the capital gains exemption claimed from the ACB of the shares otherwise determined.

Recognize that a reduction in paid-up capital has no tax consequences unless and until the shares received as consideration are redeemed by the issuing corporation.

ITA: 84.1(1)(a)

> Conceptually, the PUC of the shares after the reduction will be equal to their "hard" cost (i.e., the greater of PUC and modified ACB) that has not been recovered by the boot received in the transfer.

---

[4] Note that the PUC reduction in subsection 85(2.1) will not apply at the same time as the PUC reduction in section 84.1 (see the condition in the preamble of ssec. 85(2.1)).

¶16,225.20   *Deemed dividend*

ITA: 84.1(1)(*b*)

The rules provide for an immediate deemed dividend to the transferor of subject shares. The following formula computes the deemed dividend.

Deemed dividend:

Sum of:
(1) Increase, if any, in LSC of purchaser corporation . . . .   xxx (A)

(2) Fair market value of non-share consideration received ("boot") . . . . .   xxx (D)

(A + D)   xxx

Less sum of:
(3) Greater of:

(a) PUC of shares transferred   xxx

(b) modified ACB of shares transferred (based on adjusted actual cost ignoring any increase in the ACB as a result of the capital gains exemption.)   xxx

} xxx (E)

(4) Total PUC reduction . . . .   xxx (F)

ITA: 84.1(1)(*a*)

(E + F) . . . .   (xxx)

Deemed dividend . . . .   (A + D) – (E + F)   xxx

> Conceptually, the deemed dividend will usually be equal to the boot received in the transaction in excess of the "hard" cost of the shares (i.e., the greater of their PUC and their modified ACB).

¶16,230   Application of rules

Recall the case of Mr. Strip on page 883 with the following basic data:

Paid-up capital and cost of shares transferred (Strippit)	$ 1,000
Fair market value of shares transferred	200,000
Elected amount under ssec. 85(1)	100,000
Available QSBC share capital gains exemption	99,000

Exhibit 16-8 shows the application of these rules to the situation if Mr. Strip takes one of two consideration packages from Holdit Ltd. on the transfer of the above shares. Case A uses the "optimal" package of consideration from the point of view of using the rules in section 85 to advantage as discussed previously and Case B uses no non-share consideration.

ITA: 84.1

EXHIBIT 16-8
Examples of Section 84.1 Application

Consideration received by individual on transfer of shares	A	B
Cash, notes or other non-share consideration	$100K	Nil
Common shares (LSC and FMV)	100K	$200K
Total FMV	$200K	$200K
PUC reduction [par. 84.1(1)(a)]		
(1) Increase in LSC of purchaser corporation . . . . (A)	$100K	$200K
Less		
(2) Greater of:		
(a) PUC of shares transferred	$ 1K	$ 1K
(b) Modified ACB of shares transferred	1K	1K
Less: FMV of non-share consideration received	100K	Nil
Excess, if any . . . . (B)	Nil	$ 1K
PUC reduction . . . . (A – B)	$100K	$199K
PUC after reduction	Nil	$ 1K
Deemed dividend [par. 84.1(1)(b)]		
Sum of:		
(1) Increase in LSC of purchaser corporation . . . . (A)	$100K	$200K
(2) FMV of non-share consideration received . . . . (D)	100K	Nil
(A + D)	$200K	$200K
Less sum of:		
(3) Greater of:		
(a) PUC of shares transferred	$ 1K	$ 1K
(E)		
(b) Modified ACB of shares transferred	1K	1K
(4) PUC reduction [par. 84.1(1)(a)] . . . . (F)	100K	199K
(E + F)	$101K	$200K
Deemed dividend . . . . (A + D) – (E + F)	$ 99K	Nil

---

In Example A, note how the PUC of the shares received as consideration is reduced to nil, because all of the hard cost of the old shares (i.e., $1,000) has been recovered through the receipt of boot. Note, also, how the deemed dividend of $99,000 is equal to the excess of boot of $100,000 over the $1,000 of hard cost. In Example B, since there is no boot consideration, the PUC after the reduction is $1,000, exactly equal to the hard cost, and there is no deemed dividend. Hence, the rules in section 84.1 only permit the immediate tax-free recovery of hard cost in the transaction that meets the conditions for the rules to apply.

To generalize, the deemed dividend can be avoided, as in example B, by limiting the fair market value of non-share consideration to the greater of:

(a) the paid-up capital of the subject shares transferred, and

(b) the modified adjusted cost base of the subject shares transferred.

In order to fully comprehend the effects of these provisions, it is necessary to do some further analysis beyond the rules in section 84.1. Exhibit 16-9 illustrates the effect of the deemed dividend on the use of the elected amount as proceeds of disposition of the subject shares. Note how the deemed dividend is excluded from the proceeds of disposition of the subject shares. This procedure is similar to the one used in Chapter 15 in determining the proceeds of disposition for capital gains purposes on the redemption of shares where the deemed dividend is deducted. Since the definition of "proceeds of disposition" is of general application within Subdivision c, this exclusion will occur whether or not section 85 is used for the transfer of subject shares to the purchaser corporation. The result may be a capital loss on the subject shares, as in Case A, which will be denied as a superficial loss, where Mr. Strip, an affiliated person, still controls Holdit Ltd., the purchaser corporation, after the disposition of the Strippit Ltd. shares, whether or not the transfer is made pursuant to section 85. Therefore, an outright sale at fair market value of shares to a non-arm's length holding company, without a section 85 election, will have the same effect under section 84.1 as that discussed here.

ITA: 84.1

ITA: 84.1(1)(*b*)

ITA: 54 "proceeds of disposition" (*k*)

ITA: 84(3)

ITA: 40(2)(*g*)

EXHIBIT 16-9
Calculation of ACB of Purchaser Corporation (Holdit Ltd.) Shares

	A	B
Elected amount under ssec. 85(1) (proceeds of disposition)	$ 100K	$100K
Less: sec. 54 exclusion from proceeds for sec. 84.1 deemed dividend	99K	Nil
Adjusted proceeds of disposition for transferred shares	$ 1K	$100K
ACB of transferred shares	1K	1K
Capital gain (capital loss may be denied by par. 40(2)(*g*))*	Nil	$99K
Capital gain utilized	Nil	99K
Effect on taxable income	Nil	Nil
Cost and ACB of purchaser (Holdit Ltd.) shares after ssec. 85(1)**		
(a) Elected amount ($100) – Boot ($100)	Nil	
(b) Elected amount ($100) – Boot (Nil)		$100K

   * Loss denial, if any, depends on whether the corporation was controlled by an affiliated person, e.g., the transferor, the transferor's spouse or corporation(s) controlled by the transferor or the spouse. If the loss is denied, it is added to the ACB of the Strippit Ltd. shares held by Holdit Ltd. [par. 53(1)(*f*)].

   ** Note that for the purposes of the section 85 rule which determines the adjusted cost base of the purchaser corporation's shares by allocating the elected amount (i.e., proceeds of disposition under section 85), the exclusion of the deemed dividend does not apply [sec. 54, par. (*k*) of definition of "proceeds of disposition"]. That exclusion applies only where the term "proceeds of disposition" is being used in Subdivision c to compute a capital gain or loss. It does not apply, therefore, to the use of the term in paragraph 85(1)(*h*).

In summary, in Case A, the provision deemed the transferor to have received a taxable dividend of $99,000 on the transfer (Exhibit 16-6). Thus, the attempt to strip the $99,000 taxable surplus by converting it into an exempt capital gain, resulted in the same amount of taxable dividend as the amount of surplus that would otherwise have been converted. Note, in particular, that no capital gain resulted from the transfer of the shares to the holding company (Exhibit 16-7), although a capital gain was the objective of electing on the transfer at $100,000. In essence, the deemed dividend removed the capital gain by adjusting the proceeds, leaving nothing available against which to use the QSBC share capital gains deduction.

ITA: 84.1(1)(*b*)

In Case B, where non-share consideration did not exceed $1,000, there was no deemed dividend and the ACB of the holding company shares reflected the elected amount in excess of non-share consideration. This higher ACB would reduce a future capital gain on the disposition of the holding company shares, thereby resulting in a benefit from utilizing the QSBC share capital gains deduction on the original transfer and election of $100,000. Therefore, if non-share consideration is limited in this manner, section 84.1 will not prevent the "crystallization" of an individual's QSBC share capital gains deduction through the transfer of shares to a holding company. Section 84.1 discourages the removal of non-share consideration in excess of PUC or adjusted actual cost on the transaction.

To complete the analysis of the consequences of section 84.1, Exhibit 16-10 shows the results of a redemption of the purchaser corporation shares for their fair market value at the time of their issue as shown in Exhibit 16-8. Note that the amount of the "net economic effect" is equal to the gain in excess of the utilized capital gains exemption on the original subject shares. However, recognize that the components of that net economic effect are taxed differently and at different times. In both cases shown in Exhibit 16-10, the total deemed dividend is equal to the full accrued gain on the original subject shares at the time of their transfer to the purchaser corporation. The advantage of Case B over Case A is that there is no immediate taxable deemed dividend on the transfer to the purchaser corporation in Case B. The capital loss shown for Case B is equal to the accrued gain that is offset by the available capital gains exemption on the transfer of the original subject shares. Of course, to obtain the tax shield effect from that capital loss, a capital gain must be realized. Note that if the original subject shares had themselves been redeemed, there would not have been a capital loss of $99,000, only a deemed dividend of $199,000.

EXHIBIT 16-10
Hypothetical Redemption of Purchaser's (Holdit Ltd.'s)
Shares for Fair Market Value
(based on the facts and results in Exhibits 16-8 and 16-9)

	A	*B*
Deemed dividend on redemption		
Redemption amount	$ 100K	$ 200K
Less: PUC after reduction [par. 84.1(1)(*a*)]	Nil	1K
Deemed dividend [ssec. 84(3)]	$ 100K	$ 199K
Capital gain (loss) on redemption		
Redemption amount	$ 100K	$ 200K
Less: Deemed dividend [ssec. 84(3)]	100K	199K
Adjusted proceeds of disposition	Nil	$ 1K
ACB (Exhibit 16-9)	Nil	100K
Capital gain (capital loss)	Nil	$ (99K)*
Summary of income effects		
Sec. 84.1 deemed dividend (Exhibit 16-8)	$ 99K	Nil
Ssec. 84(3) deemed dividend (above)	100K	$ 199K
Capital gain on disposition of Strippit Ltd. shares (Exhibit 16-9)	Nil	99K
Capital gains exemption utilized (Exhibit 16-9)	Nil	(99K)
Capital loss on redemption of Holdit Ltd. shares	Nil	(99K)
Net economic effect	$ 199K	$ 100K

* The capital loss is not denied, because Mr. Strip redeemed all of his shares in Holdit Ltd. and, therefore, he is no longer affiliated with Holdit Ltd.

As an alternative to disposing of the purchaser corporation shares by redemption, Exhibit 16-11 shows the results of an arm's length sale, if this is possible in the circumstances, for their fair market value at the time of their issue as shown in Exhibit 16-8. While the net economic effect is, again, equal to the gain on the shares in excess of the utilized capital gains exemption, part of that effect for Case A is an immediate deemed dividend that occurred on the original transfer of the subject shares. Of course, the results for Case B are the same as they would have been if the original subject shares had been sold in an arm's length transaction. Thus, Case B represents a method of avoiding the adverse consequences of section 84.1 if a non-arm's length transfer of shares is necessary, perhaps, to implement an estate freeze as will be discussed in the next chapter.

EXHIBIT 16-11
Hypothetical Sale of Purchaser's Shares for Fair Market Value
(based on the facts and results in Exhibits 16-8 and 16-9)

	A	*B*
Capital gain (loss) on sale		
Proceeds of disposition	$ 100K	$ 200K
ACB	Nil	(100K)
Capital gain (loss)	$ 100K	$ 100K
Summary of income effects		
Sec. 84.1 deemed dividend (Exhibit 16-8)	$ 99K	Nil
Capital gain on disposition of Strippit Ltd. shares (Exhibit 16-9)	Nil	99K
Capital gains exemption utilized (Exhibit 16-9)	Nil	(99K)
Capital gain (loss) on sale of Holdit Ltd. shares (above)	100K	$ 100K
Net economic effect	$ 199K	$ 100K

Conclusions

The results illustrated by the foregoing analysis can be summarized as follows:

(1) The paid-up capital reduction is for tax purposes only and has effect only if and when the shares of a purchaser corporation are redeemed. The amount of PUC after the reduction will represent the amount of hard cost in the old shares that has not been recovered through boot.

ITA: 84.1(1)(*a*)

(2) The deemed dividend which arises immediately on transfer of the subject shares and which is the penalty inherent in section 84.1 caused by receiving boot in excess of the hard cost in the old shares, can be avoided by limiting the fair market value of non-share consideration to the greater of:

ITA: 84.1(1)(*b*)

(a) paid-up capital of the subject shares transferred; and

(b) modified adjusted cost base (based on actual cost with section 53 adjustments made to it) of the subject shares transferred.

(3) A subsequent redemption of the shares of the purchaser corporation will result in a deemed dividend and a capital loss. On the redemption, the overall "net economic effect" is income equal to the gain in excess of the utilized capital gains exemption on the subject shares. However, this effect consists of:

ITA: 84(3)

(a) a possible immediate deemed dividend (which can be avoided);

(b) a deemed dividend at the time of redemption; and

(c) a capital loss at the time of redemption.

Of course, taxable dividends are taxable in one manner (through the gross-up and tax credit procedure) and capital losses can only be used to offset capital gains taxable in another manner. There are, also, time value of money consequences, since the immediate deemed dividend will not occur at the same time as the deemed dividend and capital loss on redemption. Also, capital gains to offset the capital loss may not be realized at the same time as the capital loss on redemption. If the immediate deemed dividend is avoided, the results on redemption of the purchaser corporation shares are no different than the results for a redemption of the original subject shares would have been.

(4) A subsequent disposition of the shares of the purchaser corporation by an arm's length sale, if this is possible in the circumstances, will result in the realization of the gain in excess of the utilized capital gains exemption on the subject shares, on a "net economic effect" basis. However, this gain may be taxed as:

(a) a possible immediate deemed dividend (which can be avoided); and

(b) a capital gain at the time of sale of the purchaser corporation shares.

Again, the tax consequences and their timing will differ, but if the immediate deemed dividend is avoided, the results on the arm's length sale of the purchaser corporation shares are the same as they would have been on the arm's length sale of the original subject shares.

Example Problem

Ms. Annalen owns all of the common shares of Margen Ltd. The shares have a PUC and a cost of $10,000. Their current fair market value is $100,000. She transferred these shares to a holding company, Howal Ltd., receiving as consideration controlling shares of Howal Ltd. having an LSC value of $75,000 and debt with a principal amount of $25,000. She elected under section 85 at $25,000 in order to use $15,000 of her available QSBC share capital gains exemption.

— REQUIRED

(A) Indicate conceptually the immediate tax consequences of the transfer.

(B) Provide a technical explanation and computations to support your conclusions in Part (A).

(C) Assume that Ms. Annalen has $90,000 of QSBC share capital gains exemption available and that she sells her shares of Margen Ltd. to Howal Ltd., in which she already owns controlling shares, for their fair market value of $100,000, receiving as consideration $100,000 of debt from Howal Ltd. No subsection 85(1) election is made. Determine the immediate tax consequences of the sale.

(D) Assume, again, that Ms. Annalen has $90,000 of QSBC share capital gains exemption available and that she sells her shares of Margen Ltd. to Howal Ltd., which she controls, for their fair market value of $100,000, receiving as consideration $100,000 of preferred shares of Howal Ltd. No section 85 election is made. The preferred shares are subsequently redeemed for $100,000. Determine the tax consequences of the sale of Margen Ltd. shares and the ultimate redemption of the Howal Ltd. preferred shares.

— SOLUTION

Verify that all of the conditions for section 84.1 to apply are met:

(a) the share disposition was made by a taxpayer resident in Canada, Ms. Annalen, other than a corporation;

(b) the subject shares, shares of Margen Ltd., are shares of a corporation resident in Canada and are capital property to Ms. Annalen;

(c) Ms. Annalen and Howal Ltd. are not dealing at arm's length, since Ms. Annalen controls Howal Ltd.; and

ITA: 251(2)(*c*)(i)

(d) the subject corporation, Margen Ltd., is connected with the purchaser corporation, Howal Ltd., since Howal Ltd. controls Margen Ltd.

ITA: 186(4)(*a*)

(A)

The following tax consequences should occur on the application of section 84.1:

(a) the PUC of the Howal Ltd. shares should be nil since Ms. Annalen has taken back debt ($25,000) which is greater than the PUC and modified ACB of the Margen Ltd. shares ($10,000);

(b) there will be a deemed dividend of $15,000 because the debt received ($25,000) exceeds the greater of the PUC and modified ACB of the Margen Ltd. shares ($10,000); and

(c) the proceeds of disposition on the transfer of the Margen Ltd. shares will be reduced by the deemed dividend of $15,000.

(B)

PUC reduction:

ITA: 84.1(1)(*a*)

    (1) increase in LSC of Howal Ltd. . . . . $75,000 (A)

    less

    (2) greater of:

        (a) PUC of Margen Ltd. shares $10,000

                                                      $10,000

        (b) Modified ACB of Margen Ltd. shares $10,000

           Less: FMV of "boot"   25,000

           Excess, if any . . . .   Nil   (B)

    PUC reduction (A – B) $75,000

    PUC of Howal Ltd. after reduction

        ($75,000 – $75,000) . . . .   Nil

While this PUC reduction occurs on the transfer, because all of the $10,000 hard cost of the Margen Ltd. shares was recovered in the boot received from Howal Ltd., the reduced PUC has no effect unless and until the shares of Howal Ltd. are redeemed. There will also be a deemed dividend immediately, as a result of the transfer, because the $25,000 of boot received exceeds the $10,000 hard cost of the Margen Ltd. shares transferred, computed as follows:

Deemed dividend:

ITA: 84.1(1)(*b*)

Sum of:

    (1) increase in LSC of Howal Ltd.

        shares . . . . $ 75,000 (A)

    (2) FMV of "boot" . . . .   25,000 (D)

    (A + D) $100,000

Less sum of:

    (3) greater of:

        (a) PUC of Margen Ltd. shares $10,000

                                                 $10,000 (E)

        (b) Modified ACB of Margen Ltd. shares $10,000

    (4) PUC reduction . . . .   75,000 (F)

ITA: 84.1(1)(*a*)

    (E + F)   85,000

    Deemed dividend (A + D) – (E + F) . . . . $ 15,000

This particular case involves an attempt, which is thwarted by section 84.1, to convert $15,000 of surplus in Margen Ltd., which could otherwise be realized only through a taxable dividend, into an exempt capital gain on the transfer. The result is a deemed taxable dividend of $15,000 and, as is shown below, no capital gain eligible for the QSBC share exemption. The case, also, involves an increase in PUC from the $10,000 that existed in Margen Ltd. to the $75,000 of LSC shares issued from Howal Ltd. However, the individual only has an entitlement to recover the $10,000 in PUC on a tax-free basis, since that is all that was originally contributed on an after-tax basis. Since the $10,000 was recovered in debt from Howal Ltd. on a tax-free basis, the PUC of the Howal Ltd. shares issued should be reduced to nil for tax purposes, reflecting the fact that no more of the PUC of Margen Ltd. is left to be recovered on a tax-free basis.

The adjusted cost base of the Howal Ltd. shares held by Ms. Annalen would be computed as follows:

Elected amount	$ 25,000	ITA: 85(1)
Less: non-share consideration (debt)	25,000	
ACB of Howal Ltd. shares after rollover	Nil	ITA: 85(1)

The capital gain or loss on the disposition of the Margen Ltd. shares would be determined as follows:

Elected amount — Proceeds of disposition of Margen Ltd. shares	$ 25,000	ITA: 85(1) ITA: 54 "proceeds of disposition" (*k*)
Less: exclusion from proceeds for sec. 84.1 deemed dividend	15,000	
Adjusted proceeds of disposition for Margen Ltd. shares	$ 10,000	
ACB of Margen Ltd. shares	(10,000)	
Capital gain (capital loss denied by par. 40(2)(*g*))	Nil	

In this case there is no denied superficial loss on the disposition of the transferred shares to add to the ACB of the Howal Ltd. shares owned. There is, also, no capital gain on the disposition of the Margen Ltd. shares and, hence, nothing against which to use the capital gains exemption.

ITA: 40(2)(g)

(C)

Note how the conditions of section 84.1 also apply to this sale of shares at their fair market value. Shares of a corporation resident in Canada (Margen Ltd.), held as capital property by an individual (Ms. Annalen), are sold to a non-arm's length corporation (Howal Ltd., controlled by Ms. Annalen). Since Howal Ltd. will control all of the shares of Margen Ltd. the corporations are connected.

Since no new shares of Howal Ltd. were issued in this transaction, there is no PUC reduction. However, there will be an immediate deemed dividend, because the $100,000 of boot received exceeds the $10,000 of hard cost in the Margen Ltd. shares, computed as follows:

Deemed dividend:			ITA: 84.1(1)(*b*)
Sum of:			
(1) increase in LSC of Howal Ltd. shares		Nil (A)	
(2) FMV of "boot"		$100,000 (D)	
(A + D)		$100,000	
Less sum of:			
(3) greater of:			
(a) PUC of Margen Ltd. shares	$10,000		
(b) Modified ACB of Margen Ltd. shares	$10,000	$10,000 (E)	
(4) PUC reduction		Nil (F)	ITA: 84.1(1)(*a*)
(E + F)		10,000	
Deemed dividend (A + D) − (E + F)		$ 90,000	

Proceeds of disposition for the Margen Ltd. shares will be reduced, so that there will be no capital gain against which to offset the capital gains deduction, as follows:

ITA: 54 "proceeds of disposition" (k)

Proceeds of disposition (i.e., debt received)	$100,000	
Less: exclusion from proceeds for sec. 84.1 deemed dividend	90,000	
Adjusted proceeds of disposition	$ 10,000	
ACB of Margen Ltd. shares	(10,000)	
Capital gain	Nil	

When the $100,000 of debt is repaid by Howal Ltd. there will be no further tax consequences, since all of the gain in the shares has been taxed on their sale to Howal Ltd.

(D)

Again the conditions of section 84.1 would be met by this transaction. There would be a PUC reduction computed as follows:

PUC reduction:　　　　　　　　　　　　　　　　　　　　　　　　　　　　　　ITA: 84.1(1)(*a*)
 (1) increase in LSC of Howal Ltd. . . . .　$100,000 (A)

 less

 (2) greater of:
　(a) PUC of Margen Ltd. shares . . . .　$10,000
　　　　　　　　　　　　　　　　　　　　　　　　　　　　　　　$10,000
　(b) Modified ACB of Margen Ltd. shares . . . .　$10,000

　Less: FMV of "boot" . . . .　Nil

　Excess, if any . . . .　10,000 (B)

 PUC reduction (A – B) . . . .　$ 90,000

PUC of Howal Ltd. after reduction ($100,000 – $90,000) . . . .　$ 10,000

Note how the PUC of the Howal Ltd. shares is reduced to $10,000 despite there being no boot. The $10,000 of PUC of the Howal Ltd. shares reflects the $10,000 of PUC of the Margen Ltd. shares transferred. The result is no increase in the PUC entitlement to a tax-free recovery of hard cost.

Since no "boot" was received, there will be no deemed dividend, as shown by the following:

Deemed dividend:　　　　　　　　　　　　　　　　　　　　　　　　　　　　　ITA: 84.1(1)(*b*)
Sum of:
 (1) increase in LSC of Howal Ltd. shares . . . .　$100,000 (A)
 (2) FMV of "boot" . . . .　Nil　(D)
　(A + D) . . . .　$100,000
Less sum of:
 (3) greater of:
　(a) PUC of Margen Ltd. shares . . . .　$10,000
　　　　　　　　　　　　　　　　　　　　　　　　　　　　　　　$10,000 (E)
　(b) Modified ACB of Margen Ltd. shares . . .　$10,000

 (4) PUC reduction . . . .　90,000 (F)　ITA: 84.1(1)(*a*)
　(E + F) . . . .　100,000

Deemed dividend (A + D) – (E + F) . . . .　Nil

Since there is no deemed dividend, proceeds of disposition for the Margen Ltd. shares are equal to the $100,000 of preferred share consideration received from Howal Ltd. The result is the following:

Proceeds of disposition for Margen Ltd. shares . . . .　$100,000
ACB . . . .　(10,000)

Capital gain . . . .　$ 90,000

Taxable capital gain (½ × $90,000) . . . .　$ 45,000
Less: QSBC share capital gains deduction . . . .　45,000

Effect on taxable income of Ms. Annalen . . . .　Nil

On the ultimate redemption of all of the Howal Ltd. preferred shares, the following will result:

(1) Deemed dividend on redemption:
　Redemption proceeds . . . .　$ 100,000
　Less: PUC after reduction . . . .　10,000　ITA: 84.1(1)(*a*)
　Deemed dividend . . . .　$ 90,000　ITA: 84(3)

(2) Proceeds of disposition	$ 100,000	
Less: Deemed dividend	90,000	ITA: 84(3)
Adjusted proceeds of disposition	$ 10,000	ITA: 54
ACB of Howal Ltd. shares (equal to FMV of property sold for preferred shares)	(100,000)	
Capital loss	$ (90,000)	

The net economic effect of the redemption is seen to be nil, but in reality the deemed dividend of $90,000 cannot be offset by the capital loss of $90,000.

In this case, the sale of the Margen Ltd. shares for preferred shares of Howal Ltd. resulted in the successful crystallization of the $45,000 QSBC share capital gains deduction (i.e., ½ × $90,000 capital gains deduction). The crystallization effect is found in the increased ACB of the Howal Ltd. shares which results in a capital loss on their redemption. That capital loss can be used to offset capital gains from other property, thereby gaining the benefit of the capital gains deduction in the future.

¶16,240   Sale of Shares by a Corporation to an Unrelated Person

¶16,245   Situation addressed by section 55

These rules form a set of anti-avoidance provisions which prevent a Canadian-resident corporate shareholder from converting a capital gain on the disposition of shares held in another corporation into a dividend that would not be taxable under Part I or under Part IV due to the connected corporation exemption. This conversion is referred to as capital gains stripping and is opposite to the dividend stripping prevented by section 84.1. **ITA: 55(1)–(6)** **ITA: 112, 186(1)**

A typical set of transactions which would be caught by section 55 is described below.

Facts:

(a) Corp. B is a wholly owned subsidiary of Corp. A.

(b) Corp. A wishes to dispose of the shares of Corp. B to Corp. C but does not wish to trigger a capital gain on the sale.

(c) Corp. C is not related to Corp. A and Corp. B.

Avoidance transactions:

(a) Prior to the sale of the Corp. B shares, Corp. A causes Corp. B to declare a large dividend the funds for which are obtained by a short-term bank loan.

(b) The shares of Corp. B are sold to Corp. C.

(c) Corp. C injects enough cash into Corp. B to pay off the bank loan.

Results of the avoidance transactions:

(a) The inter-company dividend is not taxed:

(i) under Part I because of the deduction in the calculation of taxable income, or **ITA: 112**

(ii) under Part IV because of the connected corporation rules. **ITA: 186(1), 186(4)**

(b) The fair market value of the Corp. B shares will drop by the amount of the dividend and should, with good planning, eliminate the capital gain on the sale of the Corp. B shares.

Effects of section 55:

(a) The offensive dividend is deemed not to be a dividend but proceeds of disposition for capital gains purposes, thereby re-establishing the capital gain which Corp. A tried to avoid.

(b) However, the offensive dividend is reduced by any post-1971 income (referred to as "safe income") and/or dividends subject to Part IV tax.

Subsection 55(2) applies to any dividend received by a corporation as part of a transaction or a series of transactions[5] that resulted in a disposition of any property to a person with whom the corporation was not related. It also applies if the transaction resulted in an unrelated person gaining a significant increase in ownership interest in the corporation receiving the dividend.

ITA: 55(3)(*a*), 248(10)

The term "related person" is defined generally in the Act, and related persons in the general definition include brothers and sisters. However, as an exception to these general rules, brothers and sisters are deemed not to be related to each other such that the "not related" condition in subsection 55(2) would apply to transactions between corporations which they control. Furthermore, if an attempt is made to escape subsection 55(2) by transactions which cause two or more persons to be related, these persons shall be deemed not to be related to each other.

ITA: 251, 55(4)
ITA: 55(5)(*e*)

ITA: 55(4)

¶16,250 Illustration of the effect of section 55

Consider the case of corporation X that owns a controlling interest in the shares of corporation Y. Corporation X has an adjusted cost base on its shares of corporation Y of $1.00 each and the current fair market value of these shares is $20.00 each. Corporation X wishes to dispose of its interest in the shares of corporation Y. One method of doing so would be to sell the shares for their fair market value resulting in a capital gain of $19.00 per share (i.e., $20 − $1). In that case, of the $20 received per share, $1 would be a tax-free return of cost and the other $19 would be a capital gain of which one-half would be subject to tax.

Alternatively, since corporation X controls corporation Y, it could cause corporation Y to pay a dividend of $19 per share. If corporation Y has no refundable taxes, the dividend would be received by corporation X without tax consequences under Part I or Part IV of the Act. With the payment of a $19 dividend, the fair market value of the shares of corporation Y should fall to $1.00 each. These shares could then be sold to an unrelated purchaser for their fair market value which is now equal to their adjusted cost base of $1.00 with no tax consequences. The result of this alternative would be to convert what would have been a $19 capital gain subject to tax into a $19 dividend not subject to tax in corporation X on the disposition of its shares in corporation Y.

However, to the extent that the $19 dividend cannot reasonably be considered to be attributable to income earned or realized by corporation Y after 1971 and before the dividend was received by corporation X, it will be deemed not to be a dividend received by corporation X. Then the provision will deem the $19 amount received in the transaction to be part of the proceeds of disposition of the shares. If that is the case, total proceeds of disposition will be $20 resulting in a capital gain of $19 (i.e., $20 − $1) which is the same outcome as the original sale of the shares for proceeds of disposition of $20. The following calculation would be made:

ITA: 55(2)(*a*)

ITA: 55(2)(*b*)

Dividend received		$19
Less: dividend attributable to post-1971 income (designated as a separate dividend)	Nil	
dividend subject to Part IV tax	Nil	(Nil)
Deemed proceeds of disposition		$19
Add: actual proceeds of disposition		1
Total proceeds of disposition		$20
Less: adjusted cost base		(1)
Capital gain		$19

ITA: 55(5)(*f*)

ITA: 55(2)(*b*)

---

[5] For a discussion of the meaning of the phrase "part of a transaction or series of transactions or events" *see Meager Creek Holdings Limited v. the Queen*, 98 DTC 2073 (T.C.C.). For a discussion of whether a series exists at common law, see the case of *The Queen v. Canadian Utilities Limited et al.*, 2004 DTC 6475 (F.C.A.).

Now consider another alternative for corporation X to dispose of its shares of corporation Y. Corporation X could transfer its shares in corporation Y to a purchaser corporation, selecting an elected amount of the $1.00 adjusted cost base of the shares transferred. As consideration for this transfer, corporation X could receive shares of the purchaser corporation with a paid-up capital and redemption/retraction value of $20 which represents the fair market value of the shares of corporation Y transferred. The paid-up capital value of the shares received after the reduction would be $1.00. The adjusted cost base of the shares received as consideration by corporation X would be $1.00, the elected amount, since the transaction did not involve boot. If the appropriate number of shares (votes and value test) are received as consideration, corporation X may be connected with the purchaser corporation (i.e., more than 10% of the votes and value of all the outstanding shares). *[ITA: 85(1)]* *[ITA: 85(2.1)]*

The purchaser corporation could then redeem its shares held by corporation X for $20 each. This would result in a deemed dividend to the extent that the redemption price of $20 exceeds the paid-up capital of $1.00 of the shares redeemed. This deemed dividend of $19 would not be taxable under Part I or Part IV of the Act. Furthermore, corporation X would be deemed to have disposed of its shares of the purchaser corporation for proceeds of disposition equal to the excess of the redemption price of $20 over the deemed dividend of $19. This would result in proceeds which are equal to the adjusted cost base of the shares of $1.00 such that there is no capital gain on the disposition of the shares. *[ITA: 84(3)]*

Again, the provision would apply in this case with the same result as that in the previous illustration. Thus, the deemed dividend of $19 would be deemed not to be a dividend and, therefore, would be part of the proceeds of disposition of the shares in corporation Y. Using the two-step redemption procedure outlined previously, the following would result: *[ITA: 55(2)]*

Step 1 — Deemed dividend on redemption

Redemption amount paid	$20	
Less: PUC	1	
Deemed dividend on redemption	$19	*[ITA: 84(3)]*
Less: part of dividend designated as a separate dividend attributable to post-1971 income ...... Nil		*[ITA: 55(5)(f)]*
part of dividend subject to Part IV tax ...... Nil	Nil	
Part of dividend deemed not to be a dividend	$19	*[ITA: 55(2)]*

Step 2 — Capital gain or loss on disposition of shares

Redemption amount paid	$20	
Less: designated part of dividend (see above)	Nil	*[ITA: 84(3)]*
Proceeds of disposition	$20	
Less: adjusted cost base	1	
Capital gain	$19	

¶16,255 Exceptions to the application of section 55

It should be emphasized that section 55 is not applicable where the entire dividend, in either of the transactions described by the foregoing illustrations, can reasonably be considered to be attributable to income, referred to as "safe income" earned or realized on a tax basis by corporation Y after the later date of acquisition of the shares and 1971 and before the dividend was received by corporation X. In this situation, the dividend is not deemed to be proceeds of disposition of the shares disposed of by corporation X. Therefore, it does not offend this legislation to pay a tax-free intercorporate dividend from "post-1971 earnings". The provision permits the separation of the total dividend resulting from the transaction into a part that would not be affected by subsection 55(2) because it was attributed to post-1971[6] realized earnings and a part that would be subject to the deemed proceeds of disposition rules of subsection 55(2). Alternatively, the same effect would be achieved by actually declaring *[ITA: 55(5)(f)]*

---

[6] For the CRA's view on the calculation of post-1971 income, see John R. Robertson, "Capital Gain Strips: A Revenue Canada Perspective on the Provisions of Section 55", *1981 Conference Report*, Canadian Tax Foundation, pp. 88-91 and Michael A. Hiltz, "Section 55: An Update," *1984 Corporate Management Tax Conference*, Canadian Tax Foundation, pp. 45-46. For the courts' views on the calculation of "safe income", see the cases of *The Queen v. Nassau Walnut Investments Inc.*, 97 DTC 5051 (F.C.A.), *The Queen v. Kruco Inc.*, 2003 DTC 5506 (F.C.A.), *VIH Logging Ltd. v. The Queen*, 2004 DTC 2090 (T.C.C.), and *729658 Alberta Ltd. et al. v. The Queen*, 2004 DTC 2909 (T.C.C.). These cases illustrate a divergence by the courts from the CRA's administrative position.

and paying a separate dividend equal to post-1971 earnings before any other transaction is made. Note that the post-1971 income of a corporation, earned or realized *after* the transaction or series of transactions that gave rise to the dividend in question, cannot be used to reduce the tax liability under subsection 55(2).

Therefore, in the previous numerical examples, if corporation Y had post-1971 income of, for example, $15, the capital gain would have been only $4 in both cases.

If the dividend received by corporation X in the foregoing illustrations had been subject to Part IV tax either because corporation X was not connected with the corporation paying the dividend or because that payer corporation had refundable taxes, then that dividend received would also not be subject to the deemed proceeds of disposition rules of subsection 55(2). However, for this exception to apply, the Part IV tax paid cannot be refunded as a consequence of the payment of a dividend to a corporation as part of a series of transactions or events.

Finally, a rule provides an exemption for *bona fide* corporate reorganizations including an estate freeze and what is known in practice as a "butterfly" transaction. The latter typically involves the breaking up of a corporation with the assets of the corporation being distributed to holding companies owned by the shareholders of the corporation being broken up. The specifics of these transactions are beyond the scope of this text.

ITA: 55(3)(*b*)

Key signals:

Here are four key factors which may signal an application of section 55:

(a) a dividend(s), ordinary or deemed, has occurred;

(b) the dividend is a part of a transaction or a contemplated series of transactions usually involving the corporate reorganization provisions;

(c) one of the main purposes was to effect a significant reduction of the potential capital gain; and

(d) the dividend is followed by the disposition of shares of a corporation to an arm's length party.

¶16,800 REVIEW QUESTIONS

(1) In tax terms, what does the word "rollover" mean and how does it impact on both the transferor and the transferee?

(2) Della Inc. is a corporation that was incorporated in Delaware, U.S.A., in 1965 and has been resident in Canada since 1973 when its sole shareholder, Mr. Della, moved to Canada. During this year, Mr. Della wanted to transfer some land and a building, that was capital property to him, to Della Inc. for use in the business. He did transfer the property to the corporation and used section 85 to defer the accrued gain. Comment on whether there is any technicality that would not allow him to use section 85.

(3) When using section 85, the elected price is very important since it is used in the determination of four things that arise on the transfer. What are they?

(4) Since the tax value and the fair market value are usually fixed, what is the one decision variable that you can use that will have an effect on the limits of the elected transfer price range?

(5) When using section 85, what is the maximum amount of "boot" that should be taken in order to maximize the deferral?

(6) Ms. Smith heard at a party last night that she can avoid the "half-year rule" for CCA by first purchasing the equipment personally and then selling it shortly thereafter to her corporation and electing under section 85. She thinks that the corporation will then be able to claim the full CCA in the first year instead of only one half. What do you think and why? ITR: 1100(2)

(7) How is the cost of the consideration taken back by the transferor in a section 85 transfer determined?

(8) Bar Ltd., a CCPC, owns shares in Loser Ltd., a small business corporation, that have gone down in value. Bar Ltd.'s problem is that it cannot sell the shares because there is no market. Bar Ltd. then decides that it will sell the shares to a company owned by the wife of the sole shareholder of Bar Ltd., called Spouse Ltd., claim an ABIL and at least be able to withdraw from Spouse Ltd. the fair market value of the shares of Loser Ltd. Bar Ltd. does not own any shares in Spouse Ltd. Since there is no gain to defer, they will not elect under section 85. Comment on this strategy.

(9) Using section 85, what is the amount that determines how much the transferor can withdraw from the company on a tax-free basis?

(10) Ms. Smith has decided to transfer some portfolio shares to her wholly owned company in exchange for more shares of the company. The shares have a cost of $5,000 and a fair market value of $8,000. She plans to elect at $8,000 and take back shares with a PUC and redemption amount of $10,000. What are the tax consequences to Ms. Smith and her company?

(11) If the optimal value of the boot is equal to the tax value of the property transferred under section 85, what will the ACB and PUC of the shares taken back be?

(12) Given that FMV is often not easily arrived at when transferring assets under section 85, what protection can you use to avoid a one-sided adjustment by the CRA if their value is different than yours?

(13) What is the purpose behind section 84.1?

(14) Mr. Big got a good deal a few years ago on the shares of a company that he just bought. He paid $10,000 for the shares even though the PUC of the shares is $100,000. Today the company is worth $100,000 again thanks to his hard work. Mr. Big has never used his QSBC share capital gains exemption. How can he get money out of the company without paying any personal tax?

...sset to a corporation owned by her husband. The characteristics

. . . .	$3,000
. . . .	2,200
. . . .	800

...wing statements is *true*?

...be deferred due to the spousal rollover since the corporation is owned by
Pa...

(B) ...ould file a section 85 election and elect at $2,200 to defer the tax on the sale.

(C) Pauli... should file a section 85 election and elect at $800 to defer the tax on the sale.

(D) If a section 85 election is not made, the capital cost and UCC of the asset to the corporation will be $3,000.

Question 2

Steve plans to sell a non-depreciable asset which has a mortgage of $15,000 to S Ltd. S Ltd. is a taxable Canadian corporation. Steve owns all the shares. Steve and S Ltd. will file an election under section 85. S Ltd. will assume the mortgage. For proceeds, Steve would like to receive a non-interest bearing note for the maximum amount possible without incurring adverse tax consequences. The balance of the consideration will be in shares of S Ltd. Steve considers any tax incurred an adverse consequence. The asset has the following characteristics:

FMV	$100,000
ACB	40,000

What is the maximum amount of the note that Steve should take?

(A) $100,000

(B) $85,000

(C) $40,000

(D) $25,000

Question 3

Susan sold a Class 1 depreciable asset to a corporation that she controls in exchange for a non-interest bearing demand loan of $100,000 and preferred shares redeemable for $80,000 in total. Susan and the corporation filed a section 85 election electing for the transfer to take place at $120,000. The characteristics of the asset were as follows:

FMV	$180,000
Capital cost	100,000
ACB	100,000
UCC	75,000

The capital cost of the asset to the corporation is:

(A) $120,000

(B) $110,000

(C) $90,000

(D) $75,000

Question 4

Sylvia is the sole shareholder of Strained Ltd., a taxable Canadian corporation. Sylvia transferred a non-depreciable capital property having an adjusted cost base of $40,000 and a fair market value of $50,000 to Strained Ltd. in exchange for the following package of consideration.

Cash	$ 3,000
Debt	2,000
Preferred shares (FMV and legal stated capital)	15,000
Common shares (FMV and legal stated capital)	30,000
	$50,000

Sylvia and Strained Ltd. made a joint election under section 85, electing a transfer price of $40,000.

The cost to Sylvia of the common shares received as consideration is:

(A) $35,000

(B) $23,000

(C) $23,333

(D) $20,000

Question 5

Which one of the following is an advantage for a vendor and purchaser using a section 22 election to transfer accounts receivable rather than electing under section 85?

(A) The vendor will realize a loss that may be a superficial loss.

(B) The vendor will realize a loss that is a capital loss.

(C) The vendor will not be required to add the prior year's doubtful debts reserve to income.

(D) The purchaser will be able to take a doubtful debts reserve on the accounts receivable.

Question 6

Rebecca transfers land to R Co and makes a joint election with R Co under section 85 of the *Income Tax Act* in the amount of $50,000. The land has a cost of $50,000 and a fair market of $210,000. Rebecca takes back a demand promissory note of $60,000 and redeemable, retractable preference shares worth $150,000 in value. The tax consequences of this transaction are that:

(A) Rebecca is deemed to dispose of the land for proceeds of $50,000.

(B) R Co.'s cost of the land is $50,000.

(C) Rebecca's cost of the preference shares is $150,000.

(D) R Co.'s cost of the land is $60,000.

EXERCISES

...... the transfer of capital assets to a corporation for considera-
...... boot".

	A	B	C	D	E	F	G	
....	$120	$100	$ 80	$100 *UP* 110	$100	$ 80	FMV
....	N/A	75	N/A	75	N/A	75	N/A	
....	100	N/A	100	N/A *LL* 100	N/A	100	CC
....	200	N/A	50	N/A	150	N/A	50	TV
....	~~170~~	~~N/A~~	~~110~~	~~N/A~~	~~140~~	~~N/A~~	~~110~~	
....	150	200	80	50	80	90	20	BOOT

(margin: 901)

(A) ..... the minimum elected amount possible given these data.

(B) Compute the effects on income given these data.

(C) Indicate the maximum "boot" that should be taken in each case to maximize the deferral of taxation.

Exercise 2

Dee transferred capital property to Dee Ltd. The capital property had an adjusted cost base of $5,000 and a fair market value of $10,000. Dee could receive any of the following packages of considera-tion:

	A	B	C
Notes at fair market value	$5,000	$2,500	$4,000
Preferred shares at fair market value and LSC	4,500	7,500	—
Common shares (LSC)	500	—	6,000

— *REQUIRED*

(A) Given an elected amount of $5,000, what would be the cost of each item of consideration under each possible package of consideration?

(B) What will be the PUC for tax purposes under each possible package of consideration?

Exercise 3

Last year Mr. Goodroll purchased a business location including land for $150,000 and a brick building for $436,224. He operated the business as a sole proprietorship for a year taking maximum capital cost allowance on the building. On your advice, this year he incorporated the business using section 85 to transfer the land and building to the corporation without triggering any of the gain that had accrued on these assets during the year. The following is a summary of the transfer under section 85.

	Tax value	Appraised FMV	Elected amount	Consideration Assumed mortgage	New debt	Common shares	
Land.............	$150,000	$375,000	$150,000	$150,000	—	$225,000	ACB=0
Building (UCC).....	427,500	525,000	427,500	97,500	$330,000	97,500	ACB=330
	$577,500	$900,000	$577,500	$247,500	$330,000	$322,500	PUC

— *REQUIRED*

(A) What are the tax consequences of electing a transfer price of $577,500 as indicated?

(B) (i) Compute the cost of the consideration received from the corporation.

(ii) Compute the PUC for tax purposes of the common shares.

(C) (i) What are the tax consequences to Mr. Goodroll if the corporation redeems the debt issued by the corporation for $330,000 and he sells his shares in the corporation for $425,000?

(ii) What are the tax consequences to Mr. Goodroll if the corporation redeems the common shares for $425,000?

Exercise 4

ITA: 85(1)(*e*.2), 85(2.1)

Mother owned some debt securities which she transferred to a corporation in which Daughter (age 29) owns all of the common shares. These securities cost Mother $100,000 in 2004 and had a fair market value at the time of transfer of $125,000. Section 85 was used to transfer the securities at an elected amount of $100,000. As consideration for the securities transferred, Mother received a note having a value of $100,000 and a preferred share having a fair market value and an LSC of $1,000.

— *REQUIRED*

What are the tax consequences of this transaction and how could they have been avoided?

Exercise 5

ITA: 85(1)(*e*.1), 85(2.1)

Rancid Rollover, who owns 100% of Rollover Ltd., has come to you concerning transferring some additional assets to the corporation. The following facts relate to the transfer:

Asset #1	
Capital cost	$10,000
Undepreciated capital cost	5,000
Fair market value	20,000
Asset #2	
Adjusted cost base	$ 8,000
Fair market value	14,000

Rancid wishes to take back one no par value common share and $18,000 cash.

— *REQUIRED*

Discuss the tax implications of the proposed transaction.

ITA: 22, 85

Exercise 6

Mrs. Designer has provided you with the following balance sheet and additional information relative to her unincorporated ladies' fashion business.

Mrs. Designer

(A Proprietorship)

BALANCE SHEET

May 31, 2007

Cash		$ 4,000	Accounts payable		$ 14,000
Short-term investments		10,000	Mortgage payable		
Accounts receivable	$ 12,000		(current maturity) . . .		6,000
Allowance for doubtful					$ 20,000
accounts	(2,000)	10,000			
Inventory		5,000			
Prepaid insurance		500			
		$ 29,500			
			Mortgage payable	$ 60,000	
Building cost	$ 80,000		Current portion	(6,000)	$ 54,000
Accumulated			Proprietor's equity		47,500
depreciation	(18,000)	$ 62,000			$101,500
Land, cost		30,000			$121,500
		$ 92,000			
		$121,500			

Additional Information

(1) Incomes for tax and financial accounting purposes have always been the same.

(2) All assets were acquired after 1971.

(3) The May 31, 2007 fair market value of various assets owned by the proprietorship are:

Short-term investments	$ 5,000
Accounts receivable	9,000
Inventory	25,000
Prepaid insurance	400
Building	60,000
Land	26,500
Goodwill	44,000

Effective June 1, 2007, Mrs. Designer wants to transfer her business assets to a corporation (Hi-Fashion Co. Ltd.) in which her husband owns 100% of the common shares.

She has indicated that, provided the company assumes the business debts, she would receive the balance in debt and preferred shares (stated value $100) as full consideration.

— *REQUIRED*

(A) Determine which assets should not be transferred to the corporation under section 85 and those that should not be transferred at all and give reasons.

(B) Determine the amounts to be elected on the various assets to avoid any taxes.

(C) Determine the consideration to be received without any tax consequences.

(D) Determine the adjusted cost base of the consideration in part (C) above.

(E) Determine the tax PUC of the preferred shares received.

(F) Determine the cost/capital cost of the transferred assets for the corporation, Hi-Fashion Co. Ltd.

Exercise 7

ITA: 13(7)(*e*), 85(1), 85(2.1), 110.6

In 2007, Ms. Kvetch transferred a depreciable capital property (the only one in its class) to a corporation which she controls. The property had an undepreciated capital cost of $27,000, a capital cost of $30,000 and a fair market value of $100,000. She elected to transfer the property under section 85 at $80,000 in order to offset the resultant taxable capital gain with a 1999 net capital loss of $37,500. As consideration for the property, she received a note for $80,000 and common shares with a stated value of $20,000.

— *REQUIRED*

What are the income tax implications of this transaction?

Exercise 8

ITA: 84(3), 84.1, 85

Mr. Nailed, a Canadian resident, owned all of the common shares with a paid-up capital value and cost of $75,000 in an operating company, Opco Ltd. He transferred these shares under section 85 to a company, Broco Ltd., owned by his brother at a time when the value of the Opco Ltd. shares was $800,000. As consideration for the shares transferred he received a note with a principal amount of $500,000 and preferred shares with a paid-up capital and fair market value of $300,000 such that an elected amount of $500,000 was possible under section 85. Mr. Nailed offset all of the resultant $425,000 of capital gain with his available QSBC share capital gains exemption. Both Opco Ltd. and Broco Ltd. are Canadian-controlled private corporations.

— *REQUIRED*

(A) What are the tax consequences of the transfer to Mr. Nailed?

(B) What are the tax consequences if the preferred shares received from his brother's corporation are redeemed by that corporation for their fair market value?

(C) What are the tax consequences if the preferred shares are sold in an arm's length transaction for their fair market value?

Exercise 9

ITA: 54, 84(3), 84.1

Ms. Erin owns all of the common shares of Davpet Ltd. The shares have a PUC and cost of $1,000. Their current fair market value is $300,000. The shares are qualified small business corporation shares and she is anxious to crystallize her capital gains exemption on the accrued gain in these shares. Her father owns all of the common shares of Lenmeag Ltd., a Canadian-controlled private corporation, and is willing to use that corporation to assist her in her plans.

— *REQUIRED*

(A) Determine the immediate tax consequences, if Ms. Erin sells her common shares in Davpet Ltd. to Lenmeag Ltd. for their fair market value, receiving a $300,000 note from Lenmeag Ltd. which will ultimately be repaid in cash. Her father will allow her to continue to manage Davpet Ltd. and she will ultimately inherit the shares of Lenmeag Ltd. to reacquire control of Davpet Ltd.

(B) Determine the tax consequences, alternatively, if she sells her shares of Davpet Ltd. to Lenmeag Ltd. for their fair market value of $300,000, receiving $300,000 of the common shares of Lenmeag Ltd. No section 85 election is made.

Exercise 10

ITA: 55(1)–(6)

Vendco Ltd. owns all of the shares of Preyco Ltd. The shares of Preyco have a total adjusted cost base of $100,000 and a fair market value of $1,000,000. Since 1971 Preyco has realized and retained $700,000 of income and has no refundable taxes.

Vendco wishes to sell its shares in Preyco to Purchco. It causes Preyco to borrow $900,000 from the bank and to pay a dividend on its shares of $900,000. This reduces the fair market value of Preyco's shares to $100,000 and Purchco buys the shares for this amount.

— *REQUIRED*

What are the tax consequences of these transactions?

¶16,875 ASSIGNMENT PROBLEMS

Problem 1

ITA: 85(1)

The following assets are to be transferred under section 85 for consideration including common shares plus "boot" as indicated below:

	Fair market value	ACB/ Capital cost/ ECE	UCC/ CEC	Boot
Land	$ 75,000	$60,000	—	$50,000
Marketable securities	65,000	55,000	—	60,000
Building*	95,000	85,000	$70,000	55,000
Equipment	50,000	65,000	40,000	45,000
Furniture and fixtures	10,000	15,000	7,000	5,000
Licence**	100,000	82,500	60,000	15,000

* Only asset in class.
** Indefinite life.

— REQUIRED

(A) Compute the minimum possible elected amounts.

(B) Compute the effects on income.

(C) Indicate the maximum "boot" that should be taken to maximize the deferral of taxation.

Problem 2

ITA: 85(1)

Pete Handyman is the sole proprietor of a hardware store, The Handyman Shop. Pete has decided to incorporate the business but wishes to minimize any income inclusions on the transfer of his business to the new corporation.

The Handyman Shop has the following assets:

	Tax value	FMV
Cash	$22,000	$22,000
Inventory (cost: $44,000)	39,500	39,500
Furniture and fixtures (cost: $12,000)	6,000	8,000
Building ($75,000 cost)	45,000	55,000
Land	8,000	30,000

As consideration for the transfer of the above assets, Pete would like to take back the maximum amount of debt and the balance in the form of common shares. There is no goodwill value in the business.

— REQUIRED

Determine the appropriate transfer price under section 85 for the assets which can and should be transferred. Determine the amount of debt and share consideration that Pete can accept without any adverse tax consequences. Compute the adjusted cost base and the PUC for tax purposes of the common shares received as consideration.

Problem 3

ITA: 84(3), 85

Ms. Hart, a Canadian resident, has provided you with the following balance sheet and additional information concerning her unincorporated active retail clothing business. Effective November 10, 2007, she wishes to transfer all of her business assets and liabilities to a corporation (Hart Ltd.) in which her husband owns 100% of the common shares. She wants to minimize her personal tax on the transaction and insists on receiving the following package of consideration:

(1) The maximum amount of debt (to the nearest $100); and

(2) Voting, redeemable, retractable preferred shares for the balance of the consideration with a legal stated capital equal to their fair market value.

The following financial information concerning the business as of November 10, 2007, was provided:

	Tax value	Fair market value
Shares in public companies (note 1)	$ 11,000	$ 6,000
Accounts receivable (note 2)	13,000	10,000
Inventory	8,000	9,000
Land (held as inventory)	100,000	220,000
Prepaid property insurance	600	600
Building (Class 1, cost $90,000).............	70,000	50,000
Land (capital property)	140,000	160,000
Goodwill	nil	80,000

Additional Information:

1. The shares are capital property to Ms. Hart. Ms. Hart owns less than 1% of each public company.

2. The tax reserve for doubtful debts taken in the previous year was $1,000. The original cost of the accounts receivable before deducting the reserve was $14,000.

3. The unincorporated business has liabilities of $60,000 which are to be assumed by Hart Ltd.

— REQUIRED

(A) Prepare an analysis, with explanations as necessary, of the income tax consequences of selling the assets to Hart Ltd. without electing under section 85 or section 22. Show all calculations whether or not relevant to the final answer.

(B) Recommend a more tax-effective manner in which to achieve Ms. Hart's objectives. Explain your recommendation in detail, including the income tax implication for Hart Ltd., as well as for Ms. Hart.

(C) What are the tax consequences if Ms. Hart sells her preferred shares to a third party for their fair market value?

(D) What will be the tax consequences if Hart Ltd. redeems Ms. Hart's preferred shares for their fair market value?

Problem 4

ITA: 85

Joe Schmaltz has carried on a retail business since 1987. He intends to transfer the business assets and liabilities to a corporation, Schmaltz Enterprises Ltd. (SEL), in which he will own all of the voting preferred shares. His three children, all in their 20's, have already subscribed for all of the common shares in equal numbers. The balance sheet of the proprietorship and certain additional information are provided as follows:

Assets	Balance sheet, April 30, 2007	Fair market value April 30, 2007
Cash	$ 12,000	$ 12,000
Accounts receivable	120,000	102,000
Reserves for doubtful debts[1]	(10,000)	—
Inventories......................	90,000	100,000
Shares of Supplyco Ltd.[2]	36,000	40,000
Shares of Clientco Ltd..............	1,000	100
Land	96,000	103,000
Buildings[3]	48,000	144,000
Equipment[3]	72,000	40,000
1987 Oldsmobile[3]	3,000	5,000
Goodwill	—	90,000
	$468,000	$636,100

Liabilities[4]		
Bank loan	$ 30,000	
Accounts payable	31,000	
Accrued liabilities	6,000	
Mortgage on land and building	84,000	
	$151,000	
Proprietor's equity	317,000	
	$468,000	

Notes to Balance Sheet

(1) The reserve for doubtful debts represents the closing reserve for the previous fiscal period.

(2) These shares represent a 2% ownership in the common shares of Supplyco Ltd. which is a small business corporation.

(3) Fixed assets are recorded at original cost less accumulated financial accounting depreciation. Tax data follow:

	Original cost	UCC
Buildings	$ 95,000	$42,000
Equipment	110,000	57,000
1987 Oldsmobile	18,000	1,000

No single piece of equipment was fairly valued in excess of its cost at April 30, 2007.

(4) Liabilities are to be assumed by the corporation. In addition, Joe Schmaltz will receive as consideration for the transfer of assets under section 85 the maximum in notes payable by the corporation to permit the maximum deferral of taxation on the transfer and voting retractable preferred shares.

— *REQUIRED*

(A) Indicate which assets should not be transferred to the corporation at all.

(B) Indicate which assets should be transferred to the corporation, but cannot or should not be transferred under section 85 and explain why.

(C) Assuming that the appropriate procedure has been adopted to take advantage of the provisions of section 85 of the Act, indicate the elected amounts which should be used in order to defer any taxation upon the transfer of the business to the company and the effect of the consideration package as expressly requested by your client. He has $4,500 of net capital losses (arising in 1999) that he would like to use on the transfer.

(D) What is Joe's cost on the consideration and the PUC for tax purposes of the shares he receives for the transfer of assets?

(E) Without re-doing all of the calculations, indicate the tax consequences of having the corporation issue the maximum debt, as indicated above, but only $150,000 of voting, retractable preferred shares.

(F) What are the tax consequences, if on a subsequent assessment the CRA determines that the value of the goodwill was $120,000? What protection from this eventuality can be implemented?

Problem 5

ITA: 85

Mr. Schminkie, the sole proprietor of a small manufacturing business wishes to have his wife involved in the business on an equal basis. Mr. Schminkie's barber advised him that this is possible by incorporating a company and having Mr. and Mrs. Schminkie subscribe for all the common shares equally. Then, Mr. Schminkie could transfer all the assets of the business to the newly formed company, taking back Class A and Class B non-voting preference shares as consideration. Mr. Schminkie thought this was a wonderful idea and proceeded with incorporating the company.

The assets and liabilities of the proprietorship and certain additional information are provided as follows:

Assets	Balance sheet Dec. 31/07	Fair market value Dec. 31/07
Cash	$ 20,000	$ 20,000
Accounts receivable(1)	90,000	85,000
Inventories	86,000	86,000
Shares in Public Co.	50,000	20,000
Land — Parcel I(3)	200,000	339,000
Building(2)	15,000	75,000
Land — Parcel II(4)	20,000	45,000
Equipment(2)	35,000	5,000
Auto(2)	10,000	12,000
Goodwill	—	60,000
	$526,000	

Liabilities[5]

Bank loan	$169,000
Accounts payable	43,000
Mortgage on building	30,000
	$242,000
Proprietor's equity	284,000
	$526,000

Notes to Balance Sheet

[1] The accounts receivable are net of a $6,000 reserve for doubtful accounts which represents the closing reserve for the previous fiscal period.

[2] Fixed assets are recorded at original cost less accumulated financial accounting depreciation. Tax data is as follows:

	Original cost	UCC
Building	$60,000	$15,000
Equipment	80,000	35,000
Auto	16,000	11,000

[3] Parcel I of land is the property upon which the building used in the business is sited.

[4] Parcel II of land was acquired in 2006. Mr. Schminkie purchased it with the intention to sell as soon as the fair market value exceeded $50,000. Mr. Schminkie speculates this will occur by April 19, 2008, at which point he will sell for the quick profit.

[5] Liabilities are to be assumed by the corporation.

— REQUIRED

(A) Indicate which assets should not be transferred to the corporation at all.

(B) Indicate which assets should be transferred to the corporation, but cannot or should not be transferred under section 85 and briefly explain why.

(C) For the assets which can be transferred under section 85 to the corporation, indicate the maximum amount of debt in addition to the shares that can be taken as consideration to defer all possible capital gains, losses, other income and other available adverse tax consequences given the consideration to be taken. The corporation will issue a maximum of $200,000 Class A retractable non-voting preference shares with a dividend rate of 8% and the remainder of the share consideration will be Class B retractable, non-voting preference shares with no dividend entitlement.

(D) What is Mr. Schminkie's cost of the consideration and the PUC for tax purposes of the preferred shares that he receives for the transfer of assets?

(E) Compute the tax consequences of a redemption in 2008 of the preferred shares of the corporation at their fair market value after the transfer of assets to the corporation.

(F) What could be done to avoid a benefit problem, if the Class B consideration is limited to an authorized share capital amount of only $50,000 and the Class A consideration remains the same?

Problem 6

ITA: 84.1, 85(1)

Mrs. Andrews, a Canadian resident, set up VonTrapp Holdings Limited (VHL) to hold all of her shares in Plummer Enterprises Inc. (Plummer) in order to crystallize her remaining $400,000 capital gains exemption for qualified small business corporation shares.

Mrs. Andrews owns 100% of the outstanding common shares of Plummer. Plummer is a small business corporation and meets all the tests for the shares to be qualified small business corporation shares. Plummer and VHL are both Canadian resident corporations. She purchased the Plummer shares in 1986 from an unrelated third party for their then fair market value of $200,000.

The fair market value of the Plummer shares today is $1,000,000. The paid-up capital of these shares is $1,000.

Mrs. Andrews will jointly elect under section 85 with VHL and will take back the following consideration:

(a) non-interest bearing note for $200,000, and

(b) 6% voting preference shares with a retractable and fair market value equal to the balance of the fair market value of the Plummer common shares.

— *REQUIRED*

Discuss the tax implications of the proposed transaction, supported by your computations.

Problem 7

ITA: 84(3), 84.1, 85

Mrs. Diet owns all 100 common shares of Low-Cal Caterers Inc. (Low-Cal), a Canadian-controlled private corporation with a December 31 year-end. Low-Cal was incorporated in 1983 when Mrs. Diet invested $250,000 in common shares with a paid-up capital of the same amount. The Low-Cal shares are now valued at $2,000,000.

Mrs. Diet would like to freeze the present value of Low-Cal so that any future increase in value would accrue to her 20-year old son, Slim. She proposes that Slim incorporate a new corporation, Slim Pickings Holdings Ltd. (Slim Pickings), with $100 of his own money by acquiring all the common shares of the new corporation.

Mrs. Diet would then transfer her common shares in Low-Cal to Slim Pickings using a section 85 election in order to defer the inherent gain on these shares. Mrs. Diet would like to receive as consideration a non-interest bearing note for $750,000 and the balance of the fair market value for 1,000 8% non-cumulative, voting preference shares with a retraction value, fair market value and paid-up capital of $1,250,000. Since she would also like to use all her capital gains exemption (of $500,000 for QSBC shares), she proposes that the elected amount under section 85 be $750,000. You have determined that both Low-Cal and Slim Pickings are small business corporations at the present time and that Low-Cal meets all the conditions for QSBC shares.

— *REQUIRED*

(A) Describe the tax consequences to Mrs. Diet of the proposed section 85 transfer of the Low-Cal common shares to Slim Pickings.

(B) How would you change the above proposed consideration package so that Mrs. Diet achieves her objectives as stated above?

(C) What would be the tax consequences if Mrs. Diet sold to Slim Pickings for cash or debt just enough of the 100 common shares of Low-Cal common shares to realize a capital gain of $500,000 in order to utilize her capital gains exemption as described above?

(D) Indicate the tax consequences for parts (A) and (B) if Mrs. Diet:

(i) redeems all the preference shares in Slim Pickings for their fair market value; or

(ii) sells all the preference shares in Slim Pickings to an arm's length party for their fair market value.

Problem 8

ITA: 55(1)–(6)

Strip Limited has received an offer from an unrelated corporation, Corporate Raider Inc., to purchase all of Strip's common shares in a wholly owned subsidiary, Profits Galore Ltd. All three corporations are Canadian-controlled private corporations and have December 31 year-ends.

The common shares of Profits Galore Ltd. have an adjusted cost base and paid-up capital of $500,000 and a fair market value of $2,400,000. Profits Galore Ltd. has realized and retained income for tax purposes of $900,000 since 1971. All of this realized income was derived from active business assets.

Strip Limited has come to you for your comments on two acquisition alternatives proposed by Corporate Raider Inc.

Plan A would first have Profits Galore Ltd. borrow from the bank $1,900,000 and, then, immediately pay a dividend to its parent corporation, Strip Limited, for the same amount. Corporate Raider Inc. would then purchase the common shares of Profits Galore Ltd. from Strip Limited for the residual fair market value of $500,000. Then, Corporate Raider would inject $1,900,000 into Profits Galore Ltd. through a common share subscription so that the bank loan could be repaid.

Plan B would have Strip Limited transfer its common shares in Profits Galore Inc. to Corporate Raider Inc. on a tax-free basis by jointly electing under section 85 at a transfer price of $500,000. Strip Limited Inc. would accept as consideration only special shares of Corporate Raider Inc. with a paid-up capital of $500,000 and a redemption/retraction value of $2,400,000. These shares would represent 15% of all the voting rights and fair market value of Corporate Raider Inc. Strip Limited would, then, retract the special shares which it holds in Corporate Raider.

— REQUIRED

Describe the tax implications of the above acquisition alternatives supported by any relevant calculations.

[For more problems and solutions thereto, see the CD accompanying this book.]

¶16,900   SUPPLEMENTAL NOTES

(This section can be omitted without losing the continuity of the chapter. None of the review questions, multiple choice questions, exercises, short questions or assignment problems utilizes this information.)

¶16,910   GST and Section 85 Rollovers

If the property that is the subject of the section 85 rollover, was used by the taxpayer in a commercial activity, the rollover will be a taxable transaction for GST purposes. For example, if a sole proprietorship or partnership transfers property on incorporation, the transfer will be subject to GST. However, an election may be available to cancel any potential GST liability. As discussed in Chapter 15, the election is available where a supplier makes a supply of a business, an acquired business, or part thereof that was established or carried on by the supplier or previous owner. The recipient must acquire ownership, possession or use of all or substantially all (i.e., 90% or more) of the property that can reasonably be regarded as being necessary for the recipient to be capable of carrying on the business or part thereof as a business. If an election is made under this subsection, tax is generally not payable in respect of the supply.

ETA: 167(1)

On a section 85 rollover, the election for closely-related groups (see Chapter 15) will only be available if the transferor and transferee are both corporations and the other criteria for the use of the election are met.

ETA: 156

If neither of the elections are available, the transfer of property under section 85 of the *Income Tax Act* will be subject to the general rules of the GST. To the extent the transfer of property is a taxable supply, GST will be payable on the consideration paid or payable for the property, and the elected amount under section 85 will not be relevant. The value of the consideration received will be deemed to be equal to the fair market value of the consideration at the time of transfer. Thus, the value of the consideration will be deemed to be equal to the fair market value of the share and non-share consideration received. If the transferred property is for use in commercial activities, the recipient may claim an input tax credit for any GST paid or payable on the transfer, to the extent the property is for use in such activities. If, on the other hand, the property will be used exclusively in making exempt supplies, an input tax credit cannot be claimed. The issuance of shares is an exempt financial service and, hence, not subject to GST.

ETA: 153(1)(*b*), 156, 167(1)

If advisory fees such as legal and accounting fees are incurred by the transferor, the ETA provides that anything done by a person in connection with the acquisition, establishment, disposition or termination of a commercial activity is deemed to be part of the commercial activity. Consequently, these fees will also generate input tax credits. The transferee is not entitled to claim input tax credits in respect of GST paid on advisory fees that relate to the making of exempt supplies, i.e., the issuance of shares. However, other fees that relate to the acquisition of property (taxable supplies) to be used in a commercial activity will qualify for an input tax credit.

ETA: 141.1(3)

Chapter 17

Income Deferral: Other Rollovers and Use of Rollovers in Estate Planning

LEARNING GOALS

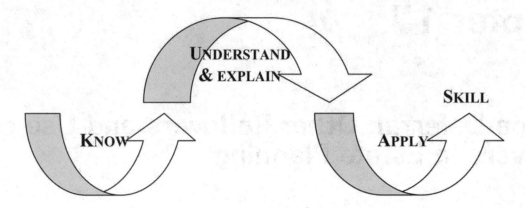

Know

By the end of this chapter you should know the basic provisions of the *Income Tax Act* pertaining to various corporate rollovers that are useful in many planning situations. Completing the Review Questions (¶17,800) and Multiple Choice Questions (¶17,825) is a good way to learn the technical provisions.

Understand and Explain

You should understand and be able to explain the tax consequences of:

• the various rollovers discussed,

• their use in various planning situations, and

• applying some of them in the estate freeze planning opportunity.

Completing the Exercises (¶17,850) is a good way to deepen your understanding of the material.

Apply

You should be able to apply your knowledge and understanding of the key elements of corporate rollovers to implement:

• a basic corporate capital reorganization, amalgamation, or winding-up of subsidiary into a parent; and

• a basic estate freeze in a way that accomplishes a client's goals.

The Assignment Problems (¶17,875) are an excellent way to develop your ability to apply the material in increasingly complex situations.

OVERVIEW

This chapter completes the discussion of rollovers which permit the deferral of income on transactions between corporations and their shareholders. The chapter also discusses the application of some of the rules presented in this and previous chapters to the planning technique known as "estate freezing". The final part of this chapter will discuss the GST consequences of the income tax rollovers presented in the chapter.

For a chart that locates the major provisions discussed in this Chapter, refer to the beginning of Chapter 15.

¶17,000   ROLLOVERS INVOLVING CORPORATIONS AND THEIR SHAREHOLDERS

¶17,010   Share for Share Exchange

¶17,015   The concept

The Act permits a tax-free rollover to a shareholder of a corporation who exchanges his or her shares for shares of another corporation. The provision is most often used in a business combination or take-over situation where a shareholder of one corporation exchanges his or her shares for shares of the purchasing corporation. While the application of this provision is automatic, this deferral of the potential capital gains or losses is conditional on a set of very specific rules that must be adhered to in order to avoid immediate tax consequences.

ITA: 85.1

For example, Mr. Investor owns shares of A Ltd. Another company B Ltd., wants to acquire his A Ltd. shares in exchange for shares in B Ltd. Where Mr. Investor exchanges his A Ltd. shares for new shares of B Ltd., the inherent capital gain or loss on the shares of A. Ltd. is deferred. The adjusted cost base to Mr. Investor, now holding the new shares from B Ltd., is the adjusted cost base of the original A Ltd. shares. Therefore, Mr. Investor is in the same tax position that existed prior to the exchange.

However, unlike other rollover provisions, this provision deems that the cost of A Ltd. shares, now held by B Ltd., is the lesser of the fair market value and the paid-up capital of A Ltd. shares prior to the exchange. If the fair market value of the A Ltd. shares has increased above the PUC of those shares, establishing their cost to B Ltd. at their PUC will be disadvantageous to B. Ltd. on the future sale of the A Ltd. shares. Establishing cost to the purchaser at this lesser amount is mandatory and is independent of whether the vendor chose to defer the gain on the exchange of A Ltd. shares.

ITA: 85.1

¶17,020   The conditions

The provision envisages a situation where a taxpayer, referred to as the "vendor", exchanges shares in a corporation for shares in another corporation, referred to as the "purchaser".

(1) The transferred shares of the taxpayer/vendor must be capital property.

ITA: 54 "capital property"

(2) The purchaser must be a Canadian corporation. The provision allows for foreign share for share exchanges but this topic is beyond the scope of this book.

ITA: 85.1(5), 85.1(6), 89(1) "Canadian corporation"

(3) In respect of the exchanged shares the only consideration, given by the purchaser to the taxpayer/vendor, must be previously unissued shares of any particular class. Therefore, the consideration is restricted to shares of only one class.

ITA: 85.1(2)(d)

(4) Immediately prior to the exchange, the vendor and the purchaser must be dealing with each other at arm's length.

ITA: 85.1(2)(a)

(5) Immediately after the exchange, the vendor/taxpayer, along with non-arm's length persons, must not:

(a) control the purchaser; or

(b) own more than 50% of the fair market value of all the outstanding shares.

ITA: 85.1(2)(b)

(6) The vendor and the purchaser cannot have elected under the rollover available on a transfer of property to a corporation in respect of the exchanged shares.

ITA: 85(1), 85(2), 85.1(2)(c)

(7) The vendor cannot have recognized any portion of the potential capital gain or loss in respect of the exchanged shares through any other provision.

ITA: 85.1(1)(a)

¶17,025 The consequences

If the above conditions are met on the exchange, then the vendor is deemed to have disposed of the shares for an amount equal to their adjusted cost base and to have acquired the purchaser's shares for the same amount. The cost of the exchanged shares to the purchaser is deemed to be the lesser of fair market value and the paid-up capital of the vendor's shares immediately before the exchange.

ITA: 85.1(1)(*a*)

ITA: 85.1(1)(*b*)

Furthermore, the PUC of the exchanged shares of the purchaser, acquired by the vendor, will be limited to the amount of the PUC of the vendor's shares through a PUC reduction or grind mechanism.

ITA: 85.1(2.1)

¶17,030 Other issues

If any of the above conditions are not met, the vendor will not receive the benefit of a deferral of the capital gain or loss on exchange. As a result, the exchange would take place for proceeds equal to fair market value.

In situations where the paid-up capital of the vendor's shares is less than their cost, section 85 should be considered as an alternative to avoid the deemed cost restriction described above. The elected amount becomes the transferee corporation's cost and the capital gain is thereby deferred. The subsection 85(1) alternative may not be practical if the vendors hold shares in a public corporation and the transfer requires literally hundreds of section 85 elections. However, the deemed cost restriction under the share-for-share exchange rollover, described above, may not be important if the purchaser is anticipating a subsequent amalgamation or wind-up of a subsidiary, as described later in the chapter.

ITA: 85.1(1)(*b*)

ITA: 87, 88

Finally, the condition that the consideration be only shares of any particular class of shares of the purchaser does not preclude another separate and distinct transaction which includes non-share consideration and/or shares of a different class.

Example Problem

Nat owns common shares in Nat's Trading Corporation Limited with the following values:

FMV	$950,000
ACB	100,000
PUC	10,000

Elaine's Pubco Ltd., a widely-held Canadian public company, has acquired all of the common shares of Nat's Trading Corporation Limited owned by Nat. In exchange for these common shares, Elaine's Pubco Ltd. has issued its common shares for a total fair market value of $950,000, representing 10% of the fair market value of all of its shares.

Nat would like to defer the realization of the capital gain accrued on his shares.

— *REQUIRED*

What are the tax consequences of applying the share-for-share exchange rollover in this case?

ITA: 85.1

— *SOLUTION*

As long as Nat (the vendor) does not include in his income any portion of the gain on the shares he has given up in the exchange, all of the conditions of the rollover appear to apply. The tax consequences of the rollover, which applies automatically, to Nat will be as follows:

ITA: 85.1

Proceeds of disposition for Nat's Trading Corporation Limited shares....	$100,000
ACB of Nat's Trading Corporation Limited shares	(100,000)
Capital gain	Nil

ACB of Elaine's Pubco Ltd. shares acquired on exchange $100,000

As a result, the ACB of the shares given up becomes the ACB of the shares acquired in the exchange and the accrued capital gain is deferred.

The ACB of the Nat's Trading Corporation Limited shares to Elaine's Pubco Ltd. (the purchaser) will be equal to $10,000 being the lesser of:

FMV of Nat's Trading Corporation Limited shares before exchange $950,000

PUC of Nat's Trading Corporation Limited shares before exchange . . . . . $ 10,000

The rules will apply to limit the addition to the PUC of Elaine's Pubco Ltd. on the issue of its shares in the exchange to the amount of the PUC of Nat's Trading Corporation Limited (i.e., $10,000) through a PUC "grind" mechanism.   ITA: 85.1(2.1)

Nat may not receive non-share consideration from Elaine's Pubco Ltd. for his shares. If this restriction on the use of section 85.1 is a concern, then a subsection 85(1) election can be made, as an alternate method of accomplishing a deferral of the accrued gain in the exchange. Thus, Nat and the purchaser corporation could jointly elect to transfer Nat's shares at an elected amount of $100,000. Nat could receive as consideration boot for up to the $100,000 ACB of these shares and shares of Elaine's Pubco Ltd. for the remaining $850,000 (i.e., $950,000 – $100,000) of value.   ITA: 85.1(2)(*d*)

An election under section 85 may not be feasible when the exchange involves widely dispersed share holdings held by many diverse shareholders who must elect. In these cases, the automatic nature of section 85.1 is more advantageous.

¶17,040   Reorganization of Capital

¶17,045   Overview

In the course of a reorganization of capital of a corporation, a class of outstanding shares may be changed into another newly-authorized class of shares[1] and, perhaps, there may also be non-share consideration. Such reorganization will be accomplished by way of amendment to the articles or letters patent of the corporation. Such an amending document is referred to as articles of amendment or supplementary letters patent, respectively. Of course, the governing corporate law must permit the desired changes to be effected.

Such capital reorganizations might involve the exchange of common shares for special (preferred) shares, for example, to allow for an estate freeze discussed later in this chapter or to facilitate the purchase of a business. In such a reorganization the outstanding common shares would be exchanged for newly-authorized special shares with, usually, a fixed dividend rate and a provision with respect to the redemption/retraction amount of the share. Newly-authorized common shares would be issued and these might be subscribed for by, say, trusts for the children in the case of an estate freeze or by the purchaser where the business is being sold. Other examples of capital reorganizations might involve an exchange of voting shares for a new class of voting shares and another new class of non-voting shares on the reorganization of control of the corporation or a reorganization of an existing class of shares into two new classes, one of which would have a lower unit value in order to facilitate an employee share purchase program.

Generally, the rollover on a capital reorganization provides for a deferral of any accrued gain on the shares held immediately prior to the reorganization as long as the sum of the fair market value of the non-share consideration (boot) and the paid-up capital of the share consideration which are received as part of the reorganization does not exceed the paid-up capital of the existing shares. The PUC of the new shares will normally be equal to the PUC of the old shares less any non-share consideration.   ITA: 86

---

[1] There is no statutory definition of the phrase "in the course of a reorganization of capital"; nor have the Canadian courts addressed this issue. Conservative planning for a section 86 reorganization would require a change in the articles of incorporation to authorize completely new shares for the exchange.

¶17,050 Conditions

In order for the rollover to apply, the following conditions must be met:

(a) the shares are capital property to the shareholder;

(b) all of the shares of a particular class owned by the shareholder are exchanged; and

(c) property receivable by the shareholder on the exchange includes other shares.

The exchange need not apply to all shareholders who hold a particular class of shares for the rollover to apply. Only one class of shares need be the subject of the exchange. A class of shares also includes a subclass or what is referred to as a "series of shares".   ITA: 248(6)

Note that section 86 will not apply if a rollover in section 85 has been used.   ITA: 86(3)

¶17,055 A conceptual view of the rollover for a reorganization of capital

A capital reorganization rollover involves, in essence, the issuance of new shares and the redemption or cancellation of old shares. Therefore, the capital reorganization rollover consists of two transactions and related calculations.   ITA: 86

SECTION 86 — OVERVIEW

(a)   Issuance of new shares
Calculate:
- PUC of the new shares; and
- ACB of the new shares.

(b)   Redemption of old shares
Calculate:
- deemed dividend on the redemption of the old shares; and
- capital gain or loss on the disposition of the old shares.

Note:
- To fully defer the unrealized gain on the old shares, i.e., for a full rollover, non-share consideration (boot) exchanged for the old shares should not exceed their PUC.
- To avoid the benefit rule, balance the fair market value of the old shares with the total fair market value of the package of consideration received.

(a) *Issuance of New Shares*

Calculate:

- PUC of the new shares; and

- ACB of the new shares.

On the issuance of new shares under the rollover there is an initial downward adjustment to the paid-up capital of the new shares in order to avoid the triggering of a deemed dividend. In the end, the PUC of the new shares issued should reflect the PUC in the old shares that has not been recovered in non-share consideration received on the exchange.   ITA: 86 / ITA: 84(1)

The cost and, hence, the initial adjusted cost base of the new shares received in the exchange are computed by first allocating the adjusted cost base of the existing share to the non-share consideration received, if any, up to its fair market value and, then, allocating the remainder to the new shares. If more than one class of new shares is received, the remaining adjusted cost base allocation must be made to each class in the proportion that the fair market value of the shares of a given class received is to the fair market value of all classes of shares received.   ITA: 86(1)(a), 86(1)(b)

¶17,050

(b) *Redemption of Old Shares*

Calculate:

- deemed dividend on the redemption of the old shares (proceeds – PUC); and

- capital gain or loss on the disposition of the old shares (adjusted proceeds – ACB).

In Chapter 15, the redemption proceeds were only cash or debt and usually resulted in a deemed dividend plus a capital gain or loss. The mandatory inclusion of shares in the exchange transaction adds additional complexity. ITA: 84(3)

The proceeds of the redemption of the old shares under the capital reorganization rollover will be the sum of any boot consideration plus the PUC of the newly issued shares. On the other hand, the proceeds of disposition for capital gains purposes will equal the sum of the FMV of the boot consideration plus the cost of newly issued shares (see above). ITA: 84(5)(*d*), 86

In certain circumstances, the rules in section 86 may result in a capital loss being realized. If this happens, then the loss is denied and added to the adjusted cost base of any shares owned by that person immediately after the transaction. The capital loss will only likely occur if the PUC of the old shares was less than the adjusted cost base of those shares and the boot exceeds that PUC. ITA: 40(3.6), 53(1)(*f.2*)

If, during the reorganization, a benefit is conferred on a related person, then a different calculation of the capital gain or loss must be completed, as discussed later in this chapter.

Exhibit 17-1 uses a simple numerical example to summarize all of the steps in the calculation that must be done when the rollover is used. Note that a balancing of the fair market value of the shares given up with the fair market value of the total package of consideration received on the exchange is essential. Also, note from the facts that the exchange will not result in the realization of income through a redemption deemed dividend because the total of non-share consideration plus the reduced PUC of the new shares does not exceed the PUC of the old shares. Therefore, the consideration in this case allows for a perfect rollover. ITA: 86

ITA: 84(3)

EXHIBIT 17-1
Summary of Calculation Procedure for Section 86

Facts:

Old shares given up		Package of consideration received		
FMV	$ 150	Boot — FMV	$ 100	⎤
ACB	100			⎥ $ 150
PUC	100	New shares — FMV	50	⎦
		— LSC	50	

Calculation Procedure:

Issuance of New Shares

(1) Reduced PUC [par. 86(2.1)(*a*)]:

LSC increase for new shares		$ 50
Less: PUC of old shares	$ 100	
Less: boot	100	Nil
PUC reduction		$ 50
Reduced PUC ($50 – $50)		Nil

(2) Cost of new shares received [par. 86(1)(*b*)]:

ACB of old shares	$ 100
Less: FMV of non-share consideration	100
Cost of new shares (allocate if more than one class)	Nil

Cost of non-share consideration (boot) received (equal to its FMV)
[par. 86(1)(*a*)] . . . . $ 100

[*Exhibit 17-1 — continued*]

Redemption of Old Shares

(1) Proceeds on redemption of old shares [par. 84(5)(*d*)]:

Reduced PUC of new shares	Nil
FMV of non-share consideration (boot)	$ 100
Redemption proceeds	$ 100

Deemed dividend on redemption [ssec. 84(3)]:

Redemption proceeds (above)	$ 100
PUC of old shares	(100)
Deemed dividend on redemption [ssec. 84(3)]	Nil

(2) Proceeds of disposition of old shares for capital gains purposes [par. 86(1)(*c*)]:

Cost of new shares (above)	Nil	
FMV of boot	$ 100	$ 100
Less: deemed dividend on redemption [ssec. 84(3)]		Nil
Proceeds of disposition of old shares		$ 100

Capital gain (loss) on old shares:

Proceeds of disposition	$ 100
ACB	(100)
Capital gain (loss) (may be denied [ssec. 40(3.6)], but, if so, add to cost base of new shares [par. 53(1)(*f*.2)])	Nil

Net Economic Effect:

Deemed dividends on redemption [ssec. 84(3)]		Nil
Capital gain (loss) on sale of old shares		Nil
Accrued capital gain on new shares:		
Fair market value	$ 50	
ACB — Cost of new shares	Nil	$ 50
Net economic effect (equal to accrued gain on old shares)		$ 50

PUC of new shares will be Nil since all of the original PUC of $100 has been recovered through the boot of $100 [par. 86(2.1)(*a*)].

Example Problem 1

Trebor Maeb owns a controlling interest in Six Sixty-One Ltd. and, therefore, is not at arm's length with the corporation. His present common shares have a PUC and adjusted cost base of $2,500 and a fair market value of $3,700. The corporation is in the process of reorganizing its capital structure and will exchange these shares for the following package of consideration:

Notes (at fair market value)	$1,000
New preferred shares (fair market value and legal stated capital)	2,700
Total	$3,700

— REQUIRED

Determine the tax consequences to Mr. Maeb as a result of the capital reorganization.

— SOLUTION

Calculation Procedure:

Issuance of new shares

(1) Reduced PUC: ITA: 86(2.1)(*a*)

LSC increase for new preferred shares		$ 2,700
Less: PUC of old common shares	$ 2,500	

Less: boot	1,000	1,500
PUC reduction...		$ 1,200
Reduced PUC ($2,700 − $1,200)		$ 1,500

The primary objective of this calculation is to show that the PUC reduction will avoid the triggering of a deemed dividend. ITA: 84(1)

(2) Cost of preferred shares received: ITA: 86(1)(*b*)

Adjusted cost base of old shares	$ 2,500
Less: fair market value of non-share consideration	1,000
Cost of preferred shares received	$ 1,500
Cost of the notes received (equal to their fair market value)	$ 1,000

ITA: 86(1)(*a*)

Redemption of old shares ITA: 84(5)(*d*)

(1) Proceeds on redemption of old shares:

FMV of boot	$ 1,000
Reduced PUC — New preferred shares (as determined in (1) above) ...	1,500
Redemption proceeds	$ 2,500
Proceeds on redemption — above	$ 2,500
PUC — Old common shares	2,500
Deemed dividend on redemption.............................	Nil

ITA: 84(3)

(2) Proceeds of disposition of old shares for capital gains purposes: ITA: 86(1)(*c*)

Cost of all new shares (as determined in (2) above)	$ 1,500
Plus: cost of all non-share considerations	$ 1,000
Proceeds of disposition of old shares	$ 2,500
Less: deemed dividend on redemption	Nil
Proceeds of disposition of old shares	$ 2,500
Proceeds of disposition of old shares	$ 2,500
ACB — Old shares	2,500
Capital gain/loss	Nil

ITA: 84(3)

Net Economic Effect: ITA: 84(3)

Deemed dividend on redemption..............................		Nil
Capital gain (loss) on sale of old shares		Nil
Accrued capital gain on new shares:		
Fair market value	$ 2,700	
ACB — Cost of new shares	1,500	$ 1,200
Net economic effect (equal to accrued gain on old shares)...........		$ 1,200

Comments:

(1) The reduced PUC of the preferred shares of $1,500 reflects the fact that only $1,000 of the original PUC of $2,500 of the old common shares has been recovered through boot consideration. The receipt of boot up to $2,500 is tax free both on the exchange and in the future, if the boot is debt that is repaid later.

(2) Since the reduced PUC of the preferred shares ($1,500) plus the boot ($1,000) is less than or equal to the PUC of the old common shares ($2,500) there can be no deemed dividend. ITA: 84(1)

(3) No deemed dividend is triggered on the redemption of the old common shares since the proceeds on redemption (the reduced PUC of $1,500 plus the boot of $1,000) is equal to the PUC of the old common shares. ITA: 84(3)

(4) There is no capital gain or loss since the proceeds of disposition for capital gains purposes (cost of the new shares of $1,500 plus the boot of $1,000) is exactly equal to the ACB of the old common shares of $2,500.

(5) The final PUC of $1,500 reflects the unrecovered portion of the PUC of the old common shares as indicated in (1) above. The addition to final PUC does not appear to have a general application to all cases. ITA: 86(2.1)(*b*)

(6) If the new preferred shares are sold immediately, there would be a capital gain of $1,200, exactly equal to the accrued capital gain on the old common shares.

New preferred shares: P of D ($2,700) − cost ($1,500) = $1,200

Old common shares: FMV ($3,700) − ACB ($2,500) = $1,200

Example Problem 2

Ms. Oasis owns some of the common shares of Capital Structure Ltd. with an adjusted cost base and paid-up capital of $1,200 and a fair market value of $3,700. In the course of a capital reorganization, Ms. Oasis exchanged all of her shares for the following package of consideration:

Cash	$ 500
Notes (at fair market value)	1,500
New preferred shares (at fair market value and LSC)	1,000
New common shares (at fair market value and LSC)	700
Total	$3,700

— *REQUIRED*

Determine the tax consequences to Ms. Oasis as a result of the capital reorganization.

— *SOLUTION*

Calculation Procedure:

Issuance of new shares

(1) Reduced PUC: ITA: 86(2.1)(*a*)

LSC increase for all new shares		$ 1,700
Less: PUC of old commons	$ 1,200	
Less: boot ($500 + $1,500)	2,000	Nil
PUC reduction in total		$ 1,700

Proration of PUC reduction:

(a) Preferred shares: $1,700 × $\dfrac{\$1,000}{\$1,700}$ = $1,000

(b) Common shares: $1,700 × $\dfrac{\$ 700}{\$1,700}$ = $700

	Preferred shares	Common shares
LSC increase by class of share	$ 1,000	$ 700
Less: PUC reduction by class of share	1,000	700
Reduced PUC	Nil	Nil

(2) Cost of preferred and common shares received: ITA: 86(1)(*b*)

Adjusted cost base of old shares	$ 1,200
Less: fair market value of non-share consideration	2,000
Cost of preferred and common shares received	Nil

Allocation of cost of new shares:

Preferred shares:

$$\dfrac{\text{FMV of preferred shares}}{\text{FMV of all shares}} \times \text{total cost of new shares}$$

$$\dfrac{\$1,000}{\$1,000 + \$700} \times \text{Nil} \quad\quad\quad\quad\quad\quad\quad\quad\quad \text{Nil}$$

Common shares:

$$\dfrac{\text{FMV of common shares}}{\text{FMV of all shares}} \times \text{total cost of new shares}$$

$$\dfrac{\$700}{\$1,000 + \$700} \times \text{Nil} \quad\quad\quad\quad\quad\quad\quad\quad\quad \text{Nil}$$

Cost of the cash and notes received at FMV		$ 2,000	ITA: 86(1)(*a*)

Redemption of old shares

(1) Proceeds on redemption: — ITA: 84(5)(*d*)

Boot — Cash	$ 500	
— Notes	1,500	$ 2,000
Reduced PUC — New preferreds	Nil	
— New commons	Nil	Nil
		$ 2,000

Deemed dividend on redemption: — ITA: 84(3)

Proceeds on redemption	$ 2,000
PUC of old common shares	1,200
Deemed dividend on redemption	$ 800	ITA: 84(3)

(2) Proceeds of disposition:

Cost of boot		$ 2,000
Cost of shares		
— Preferred shares	Nil	
— Common shares	Nil	
		$ 2,000
Less: deemed dividend on redemption		800	ITA: 84(3)
Proceeds of disposition of old shares		$ 1,200

Capital gain (loss) on old shares:

Proceeds of disposition of old shares	$ 1,200
Less: ACB of old shares	1,200
Capital gain (loss[1])	Nil

Net Economic Effect:

In the foregoing case, the "net economic effect" can be aggregated as a conceptual illustration as follows:

Deemed dividend on redemption		$ 800	ITA: 84(3)
Accrued capital gain on new shares:		
Fair market value	$1,700	
ACB (total)	Nil	1,700
Net economic effect equal to accrued gain on old common shares (i.e., $3,700 - $1,200)		$ 2,500

Comments:

The final PUC of Nil for both the new common and preferred shares is logical since all of the PUC of the old common shares ($1,200) has been removed in the form of boot (i.e., cash of $500 and notes of $1,500).

The redemption deemed dividend was caused by taking back a non-share consideration — ITA: 84(3) package (i.e., boot comprised of cash of $500 and notes of $1,500) in excess of the PUC of the old shares (i.e., $1,200). The deemed dividend could have been avoided by taking back less boot to reflect the $1,200 of PUC in the old shares that can be received tax free.

—NOTE TO SOLUTION

[1] If a capital loss is triggered, the resultant tax treatment depends on whether the corporation, after the exchange, is affiliated with the shareholder. If, for example, the shareholder or the — ITA: 40(3.6), 53(1)(*f*.2) shareholder's spouse still controls the corporation and, hence, the corporation is affiliated with the shareholder, then the capital loss is denied and added to the remaining shares, including the exchanged shares owned by the shareholder after the transaction.

¶17,060 Benefit rule

There is a benefit rule provided (similar to the one in section 85) to reduce the effect of a — ITA: 86(2), 85(1)(*e*.2) deferral where a reorganization is used to confer a benefit on a related person. The benefit is any part of the excess of the fair market value of the old shares over the cost of the non-share consideration received plus the fair market value of the new shares that can reasonably be regarded as a benefit conferred on a person related to the taxpayer who disposed of old shares in the reorganization.

Where there is a benefit, the proceeds of disposition of the old shares for capital gains purposes are different from the non-benefit situation previously outline. Proceeds of disposition will be deemed to be the lesser of: ITA: 86(1)

(a) the fair market value of the non-share consideration plus the amount of the gift determined by the excess above; and

(b) the fair market value of the old shares.

Where a capital loss is created, the loss is deemed to be nil. The cost of the new shares will be reduced by the fair market value of the non-share consideration plus the benefit. ITA: 86(2)(*d*)

Example Problem

Adam owns all of the Class A common shares of BJay Ltd. His son, Stieb, owns all of the Class B common shares and is active in the management of the corporation. Adam is now prepared to pass all of the future growth in the corporation to his son. To do so, Adam will give up all of his Class A common shares which have a fair market value of $500,000, an adjusted cost base of $100,000 and a paid-up capital value of $100,000. In return, he will receive $100,000 in cash and preferred shares with a fair market value of $350,000 and a legal stated capital of $350,000. Stieb will then own all of the only class of common shares outstanding and, thereby, will receive all of the future growth of BJay Ltd.

— REQUIRED

What are the income tax consequences under the capital reorganization rollover to Adam on the proposed transaction? ITA: 86

— SOLUTION

The benefit rule will apply in this case, because the $500,000 fair market value of Adam's Class A common shares is greater than the sum of the $100,000 of cash and $350,000 fair market value of the preferred shares received on the reorganization. Furthermore, it is reasonable to regard the $50,000 excess as a benefit that Adam desired to have conferred on a related person, his son. ITA: 86(2)

The following are the consequences of the transaction:

Issuance of new shares

(1) Reduced PUC:		
LSC increase for new shares		$ 350,000
Less: PUC of old shares	$100,000	
Less: boot	100,000	Nil
PUC reduction		$ 350,000
Reduced PUC ($350,000 – $350,000)		Nil

ITA: 86(2.1)(*a*)

(2) Cost of preferred shares received:		
ACB of Class A shares		$ 100,000
Less: cost (equal to FMV) of non-share		
consideration	$100,000	
benefit	50,000	150,000
Cost of preferred shares (excess, if any)		Nil
Cost of non-share consideration (equal to its FMV)		$ 100,000

ITA: 86(2)(*e*)

mption of old shares

Proceeds on redemption of old shares:

Reduced PUC of preferred shares	Nil
FMV of non-share consideration	$ 100,000
Proceeds on redemption	$ 100,000

Deemed dividend on redemption: ITA: 84(3)

Redemption proceeds	$ 100,000
PUC of Class A shares	(100,000)
Deemed dividend on redemption	Nil

ITA: 84(3)

(2) Proceeds of disposition of Class A shares: ITA: 86(2)(c)
Lesser of:

(a) cost (equal to FMV) of non-share consideration . . .	$ 100,000	
Plus: benefit	50,000	
	$ 150,000	
(b) FMV of Class A shares	$ 500,000	
Proceeds of disposition		$ 150,000

Capital gain (loss) on Class A shares:

Proceeds of disposition	$ 150,000
ACB	(100,000)
Capital gain	$ 50,000

Net Economic Effect:

Deemed dividend on redemption		Nil
Capital gain on sale of Class A shares		$ 50,000
Accrued gain on preferred shares:		
FMV	$ 350,000	
ACB	Nil	350,000
Total (equal to the accrued gain on the old shares)		$ 400,000

ITA: 84(3)

The final PUC of the new shares reflects the fact that, of the $100,000 of the PUC of the old shares, all $100,000 has been recovered in boot. Therefore, the final PUC of the new shares is logically nil.

Note the total net economic effect in this case. In addition to the immediate capital gain of $50,000, there is an accrued gain on the new shares of $350,000 to be realized on ultimate disposition. This $400,000 reflects the gain that had accrued on the Class A shares (i.e., $500,000 – $100,000) before the reorganization. However, it should be recognized that Adam has given up shares with a value of $500,000 for a package of consideration worth a total of only $450,000. From another point of view, he has paid tax on $50,000 of capital gain on the Class A shares and he has received consideration with a total cost value of $100,000 in non-share consideration ($100,000, from (2) under "Issuance of New Shares" above) and preferred shares (nil, from (2) under "Issuance of New Shares" above) in return for the Class A shares which had a cost of $100,000. As a result, he has incurred a tax-paid cost that he cannot recover.

Furthermore, the fair market value of the common shares held by the son, Stieb, will increase in value by the $50,000 benefit without any offset in the cost base of the common shares. Therefore, the $50,000 of accrued gain will be taxed on the disposition of the common shares. This potential $50,000 gain to be taxed in the hands of the common shareholder, along with the lost opportunity for Adam to recover the $50,000, is the penalty inherent in subsection 86(2).

To avoid this penalty the fair market value of the total package of consideration received in the reorganization should be equal to the fair market value of the shares given up in the exchange.

¶17,070 Statutory Amalgamations

¶17,075 Overview

This rollover provision applies automatically at both the corporate level and the shareholder level in an amalgamation situation. First, it should be emphasized that a statutory amalgamation is distinct from business combination accounting. In a statutory amalgamation, two or more corporations are merged into one with the result being a single legal entity with one charter. In business combination accounting, for which consolidated financial statements are usually prepared, the original companies continue to exist as separate legal entities and are taxed separately.

¶17,080 Conditions

The provision sets out several conditions for the rollover to apply:

ITA: 87(1)

(a) the predecessor corporations must be taxable Canadian corporations;

(b) all of the property and liabilities of the predecessor corporations, except inter-company accounts, must belong to the new corporation by virtue of the amalgamation;

(c) all shareholders of the predecessor corporations, other than predecessor corporate shareholders, must receive shares of the new corporation by virtue of the amalgamation; and

(d) the transfer of property cannot occur as the result of a normal purchase of such property or the distribution on a winding-up of a corporation.

¶17,085 Two levels of rollover

The rollover for a statutory amalgamation deals with:

(a) the transfer of capital property from the predecessor corporation to the successor or amalgamated corporation to permit a deferral of accrued capital gains transferred at the corporate level; and

(b) the exchange of shares of a predecessor corporation by its shareholders for shares of the successor corporation to permit a deferral of capital gains at the shareholder level.

¶17,090 Income tax consequences

The amalgamated corporation is treated, for many purposes, as a continuation of the predecessor corporations. The effect would be like placing the balance sheets of two corporations side by side and adding together the similar accounts on each balance sheet based on the tax values such as adjusted cost base or undepreciated capital cost of each asset. The result would be a single balance sheet based on those tax values with no realization of capital gains or losses or recapture.

ITA: 87

While the new corporation is considered by most Corporations Acts to be a continuation of the predecessor corporations, for tax purposes a new corporation is deemed to have been formed and the predecessor corporations are deemed to have a year-end immediately before the amalgamation.[2] Thus, any provision of the tax legislation that counts taxation years will be affected by the amalgamation. As a result, the following could occur:

- one short taxation year will be counted in respect of unpaid amounts subject to treatment under section 78;

- capital cost allowance will be claimed on a declining balance basis;

- the amount of the business limit ($400,000) allocated for the small business deduction will also be prorated for a short taxation year; and

- non-capital losses carried forward by a predecessor corporation will be deductible in the short taxation year, but that taxation year will count as one of the carryforward years available. (Note that for non-capital losses incurred in a taxation year that ends after March 22, 2004, the carryforward period is 10 years, and for those incurred after 2005, the carryforward period is 20 years.)

---

[2] Paragraph 9 of IT-474R states that "the effective date of amalgamation is governed by corporate law and is generally the date of issuance of letters patent or the date shown or set forth in the certificate of amalgamation, as the case may be. The time of the amalgamation is the earliest moment on that date in the absence of a particular time specified in the certificate of amalgamation".

The new corporation begins its first taxation year on the date of amalgamation. It may choose any year-end it wishes, but in this first year it will be liable for instalments of tax based on the instalment bases of the predecessor corporations adjusted for a twelve-month equivalent in the case of a short taxation year.

Consider the case of Corporation A with a December 31 year-end and Corporation B with a June 30 year-end. Assume that an amalgamation took place on October 1, 2007, and that the amalgamated corporation, Amalco, chooses a December 31 year-end. This situation can be diagrammed as follows:

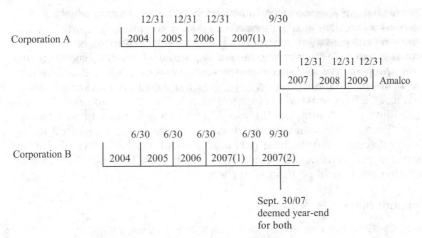

Exhibit 17-2 summarizes the effect of the major rollover provisions.

ITA: 87

EXHIBIT 17-2
Major Rollover Provisions of Section 87

Paragraph	Item	Rollover effect
	Assets and Reserves	
Par. 87(2)(*b*)	Inventory	at cost amount
Par. 87(2)(*d*)	Depreciable capital property	at UCC[1]
Par. 87(2)(*e*)	Non-depreciable capital property	at ACB
Par. 87(2)(*f*)	Eligible capital property	at 4/3 of CEC balance[2]
Par. 87(2)(*g*)	Reserves	flowed through
	Loss Carryforwards	
Ssec. 87(2.1)	Non-capital losses	flowed through[3]
Ssec. 87(2.1)	Net capital losses	flowed through
Ssec. 87(2.1)	Restricted farm losses	flowed through
Ssec. 87(2.1)	Farm losses	flowed through
	Tax Accounts	
Par. 87(2)(*z*.1)	Capital dividend account	flowed through[4]
Par. 87(2)(*aa*)	Refundable dividend tax on hand	flowed through[4]

Note: [1] The new corporation will be liable for recapture in the same manner that a predecessor corporation would have been liable for such recapture.

[2] This amount becomes an eligible capital expenditure of the amalgamated corporation, which would add ¾ of the ECE to its CEC balance under item A of the definition of "cumulative eligible capital" [ssec. 14(5)]. In this way, the amalgamated corporation steps into the tax position of the predecessor corporation on this property.

---

(3) The limitations regarding the carrying on of the loss business on a previous acquisition of control of a predecessor corporation will apply after the amalgamation to losses previously subject to those limitations in the predecessor corporation. Note that there is not necessarily an acquisition of control on amalgamation itself (e.g., the relative shareholdings have not changed from those of the predecessor corporations). The deemed year-end of a predecessor corporation on amalgamation will be counted as one of the seven years available for the carryforward of non-capital losses.

(4) These accounts which pertain only to private corporations would be lost if one of the predecessor corporations were a public corporation.

¶17,095   Availability of a "bump" on vertical amalgamation

Where a parent corporation and one or more subsidiary corporations are amalgamated, in what is commonly known as a "vertical amalgamation", an added advantage is available. The new corporation formed on amalgamation can increase its cost of certain capital property acquired by it on the amalgamation. This increase in cost is permitted without triggering any of the unrealized gain on the property at the time of the amalgamation. This "bump" in cost, therefore, places the new corporation in a position to recover more cost on a tax-free basis on the ultimate sale of the assets. The provision refers to the rules in subsection 88(1) which provides the same opportunity for a "bump" on the winding-up of a subsidiary into its parent. A discussion of how the "bump" works and the reasons for its existence is deferred to the winding-up of a subsidiary discussion in the next part of this chapter. Also, a formula for the calculation for the parent of proceeds of disposition for the shares of the subsidiary, which uses the rules in subsection 88(1), will be discussed there.

ITA: 87(11)

¶17,100   Planning opportunities

Planning opportunities involving the use of an amalgamation might include:

- the utilization of prior-year losses that might not be absorbed by the income of a predecessor corporation;

- the utilization of current-year losses in one predecessor corporation against the income of another predecessor corporation; or

- the faster utilization of capital cost allowance in a high-rate or rapid write-off class.

Other planning opportunities might involve the following:

- where a parent corporation has been amalgamated with one or more wholly owned subsidiary corporation, i.e., a vertical amalgamation, losses realized subsequent to the amalgamation the amalgamated corporation may be carried back and applied to the income of the predecessor *parent* corporation;

ITA: 87(2.11)

- it might also be possible to effect an improvement in the manufacturing or processing tax credit (which may be more important for provincial tax) through an amalgamation; and

- an amalgamation might facilitate a change in fiscal year-end which would ordinarily require the consent of the Canada Revenue Agency (CRA), although an Information Circular pertaining to the general anti-avoidance rule (GAAR) indicates that if an amalgamation is undertaken with a shell corporation solely to effect a year-end change, the GAAR would be applied (as discussed in a previous chapter).

ITA: 245; IC 88-2, par. 21

¶17,105   Effects of the rollover at the shareholder level

At the shareholder's level, the shareholder is deemed to have disposed of his or her shares for proceeds equal to their adjusted cost base and to have acquired the new shares of the amalgamated corporation at that same adjusted cost base. The conditions for this rollover to apply to the shareholder's position are:

ITA: 87(4)

(a) that he or she receive no consideration for his or her shares other than shares of the successor corporation or its Canadian parent corporation (i.e., no "boot" can be received);

(b) that the original shares are capital property to the shareholder; and

(c) the amalgamation does not result in a deemed gift to a person related to the shareholder.

Note that the potential problem of a deemed dividend exists if the paid-up capital of the amalgamated corporation increases on the issue of shares by more than the increase in the fair market value of the net assets transferred to that corporation.

ITA: 84(1)

¶17,110 Winding Up a Subsidiary

¶17,115 Overview

This provision sets out rules for an automatic rollover where a taxable Canadian corporation of which at least 90% of each class of shares is owned by another Canadian corporation, is wound up into its parent corporation under appropriate corporate law. These rules are very similar to those for a statutory amalgamation that could take place between a parent company and its subsidiary, i.e., a "vertical amalgamation". They generally avoid the recognition of accrued capital gains on the transfer of assets from a subsidiary to its parent in a winding-up. The major difference between such a winding-up and an amalgamation arises in the area of the parent's utilization of the loss carryforwards of the subsidiary, as discussed below.

ITA: 88(1)

Again, there are two components to the rollover. The first deals with the transfer of property to the parent in which the subsidiary is deemed to have disposed of its assets for proceeds equal to:

(a) nil, in the case of a resource property; and

(b) the cost amount to the subsidiary, in the case of any other property.

ITA: 88(1)(a), 248(1) "cost amount"

¶17,120 Availability of a "bump" and other effects on the parent

The parent is deemed to have acquired the property at a cost equal to the deemed proceeds of the subsidiary. However, when the adjusted cost base of the subsidiary's shares held by the parent exceeds the tax values of the net assets of the subsidiary transferred on the winding-up, there is a possible increase or "bump" in the adjusted cost base of some non-depreciable capital property received from the subsidiary. The amount of the increase cannot raise the adjusted cost base of an asset above the fair market value at the time when the parent acquired control of the subsidiary.

This "bump" or "step-up" in adjusted cost base is calculated as follows:

ITA: 88(1)(d)

Parent's adjusted cost base of the subsidiary's shares *minus* the sum of:

(a) the cost amount of the subsidiary's assets plus cash net of liabilities and certain reserves; and

(b) dividends (including both taxable and capital dividends) paid to the parent on its shares of the subsidiary.

The "bump" may be allocated to any non-depreciable capital property owned by the subsidiary continuously from the time when the parent acquired control of the subsidiary to the date of the winding-up.

¶17,125 Illustration

Consider the case of a subsidiary with the following balance sheet immediately before the winding-up:

Cash	$ 5,000	Accounts payable	$ 5,000
Land	160,000	Paid-up capital	20,000
Depreciable property	60,000	Retained earnings	200,000
	$225,000		$225,000

Other relevant facts include the following:

Parent's adjusted cost base of the subsidiary's shares	$300,000
FMV of the land when the parent acquired control of the subsidiary . . .	200,000
Dividends paid by the subsidiary to the parent	10,000

Note that the only item of non-depreciable capital property is the land. Exhibit 17-3 illustrates the application of the bump to this set of facts. The adjusted cost base of the land will be increased from $160,000 to $200,000. Although a total "bump" of $70,000 was available, there were no other non-depreciable capital assets available to absorb the remaining $30,000 which is lost.

ITA: 88(1)(*d*)

EXHIBIT 17-3
Conceptual Application of Paragraph 88(1)(d)

BEFORE WIND-UP

PARENT

Shares of subsidiary at ACB	$300,000
Dividends from subsidiary (recovery of cost)	(10,000)
Net cost	$290,000

SUBSIDIARY

Cost amount of net assets ($225K – 5K)	$220,000

Potential "bump":
$70,000 (i.e., $290,000 – $220,000)

AFTER WIND-UP

PARENT

Cost amount of net assets of former subsidiary . . .	$220,000
Addition to ACB of former subsidiary's land	40,000*
Total cost amount	$260,000

* Limit of "bump" on land:		
FMV of land at time parent acquired control of subsidiary	. . . . .	$ 200,000
ACB of land at time of wind-up	. . .	(160,000)
Limit	. .	$ 40,000

Note how the shares of the subsidiary, held as assets in the parent, are replaced by the cost amounts of the subsidiary's net assets. Conceptually, the net cost of the subsidiary's shares to the parent is reduced by dividends, either taxable or capital, received from the subsidiary. However, the result is that the parent replaces assets having a net cost of $290,000 with assets having a net cost of $220,000. The "bump" is meant to help the parent recover some of the difference in cost.

The same rule applies for the same reasons, in a vertical amalgamation. While there are differences under corporate law, conceptually, a vertical amalgamation and a winding-up of a subsidiary into its parent have the same effect. Therefore, it is reasonable for the tax treatment to be the same.

ITA: 87(1)(*a*)

In the case of depreciable property, the parent corporation is deemed to have a capital cost for the property equal to that of the subsidiary and, thus, becomes potentially liable for recapture.

¶17,130 Loss utilization

On the winding-up of a subsidiary into its parent, there is no deemed year-end for either corporation, as is the case for an amalgamation. The subsidiary, simply, ceases to exist on completion of the winding-up, since it has no assets and no shares outstanding, and the parent corporation continues with its same year-end that it had been using. Consider the case of Parentco with a December 31 year-end and Subcorp with a June 30 year-end. Assume that a winding-up commences October 1, 2007, when the net assets of Subcorp are transferred to

Parentco. Subcorp continues to exist until it is formally dissolved some time later. This situation can be diagrammed as follows:

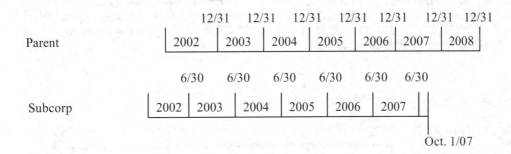

When a subsidiary is wound up into its parent, the deductibility by the parent of the subsidiary's non-capital losses, restricted farm losses, farm losses, limited partnership losses and net capital losses is limited as follows: *ITA: 88(1.1), 88(1.2)*

(a) the losses that have not been deducted by the subsidiary are first deductible by the parent in its taxation year following the taxation year in which the winding-up began; and

(b) the losses are only deductible by the parent to the extent that they would have been deductible to the subsidiary in any taxation year following that in which the winding-up began (if it is assumed that the subsidiary had such a taxation year); that is, the losses could not have expired in the taxation year following that of the winding-up, if the subsidiary had a taxation year then.

When the subsidiary has a taxation year different from that of the parent, the subsidiary's losses will be deemed to have occurred in the parent's taxation year which includes the taxation year-end of the subsidiary. The following illustrates this rule schematically:

Losses of the subsidiary for its fiscal year ended	losses of the parent for its fiscal become year ended	Available for deduction by parent for fiscal years ended December 31														
		2007	2008	2009	2010	2011	...	2014	2015	2016	2017*	...	2026	2027	2028
June 30/07	Dec. 31/07*	X	√	√	√	√	...	√	√	√	√	...	√	√	expired
June 30/06	Dec. 31/06*	X	√	√	√	√	...	√	√	√	√	...	√	expired	
June 30/05	Dec. 31/05*	X	√	√	√	√	...	√	√	expired					
June 30/04	Dec. 31/04	X	√	√	√	√	...	√	expired						
June 30/03	Dec. 31/03	X	√	√	√	expired									
June 30/02	Dec. 31/02	X	√	√	expired										
June 30/01	Dec. 31/01	X	√	expired											
June 30/00	Dec. 31/00	X	expired												

↳ losses not available in year of wind-up

* Note that for non-capital losses incurred in a taxation year that ends after March 22, 2004, the carryforward period is 10 years. The carryforward period is extended to 20 taxation years for taxation years that end after 2005.

The above assumes that the winding-up commences on October 1, 2007, such that none of the losses would be available to the parent until its 2008 taxation year. The 2000 loss of the subsidiary, which would have been deductible by the subsidiary in its 2007 taxation year if it had such a taxation year, will not be available to the parent. This represents an application of the rule that the parent cannot use a subsidiary's losses in the winding-up year. This rule on a winding-up provides a somewhat similar effect to the rule on an amalgamation which provides for a deemed year-end which may result in a short year counting as one taxation year for loss carryforwards of the loss corporation before they become available to the new corporation.   *ITA: 88(1.1)*

For cases where control of a parent or subsidiary has changed, the Act provides rules restricting the availability of non-capital losses or farm losses that are similar to the restrictions discussed in Chapter 11.   *ITA: 88(1.1)(e), 111(5)*

¶17,135   Planning opportunities

The planning opportunities involving the use of a winding-up will generally include the same opportunities as those considered for an amalgamation. A winding-up will usually be preferred if the timing of loss carryforwards will result in greater deductibility of such losses. It should be recognized, however, that a winding-up is considerably more expensive and time-consuming to implement than an amalgamation.

¶17,140   Disposition by parent of subsidiary's shares

The second component of the rollover deals with the disposition or cancellation of shares by the parent on the winding-up. The parent corporation is deemed to have disposed of the shares of the subsidiary for proceeds equal to the greater of:

(a) the lesser of:

   (i) the paid-up capital of the shares of the subsidiary, and

   (ii) the aggregate of the cost amounts of the assets of the subsidiary received, net of any liabilities, and certain tax reserves assumed; and

(b) the adjusted cost base of the shares of the subsidiary held by the parent immediately   ITA: 88(1)(*b*)
before the winding-up.

In the foregoing example, the parent corporation would be deemed to have disposed of the subsidiary for proceeds equal to the greater of:

(a) the lesser of:

(i) the paid-up capital of the shares of the subsidiary	$ 20,000	
(ii) the cost amounts of the net assets immediately before the winding-up	$220,000	
the lesser amount		$ 20,000
(b) the adjusted cost base of the shares of the subsidiary held by the parent		$300,000

Proceeds of disposition would be established at the greater amount, i.e., $300,000. Since this amount is equal to the ACB, no capital gain or loss will result.

As a result of this rule, the parent may realize, in fairly rare circumstances, a gain on the liquidation of its subsidiary, but it may not realize a capital loss because the deemed proceeds of disposition of the shares of the subsidiary cannot be less than their adjusted cost base to the parent. In most situations, the parent will obtain, in effect, a rollover on the disposition of the shares in the subsidiary.

The same rule with the same formula applies in the determination of proceeds of   ITA: 87(11)(*a*)
disposition to the parent for shares of the subsidiary in a vertical amalgamation.

¶17,200   ROLLOVERS INVOLVING SHARES OR CORPORATE SECURITIES

¶17,210   Convertible Properties

Convertible properties are commonly issued in the form of shares, bonds or notes of a corporation. These securities can be exchanged for shares of the corporation under specific conditions at the option of the holder. In essence, the securities held are given up on the conversion in return for share capital. Note how this rollover differs from section 86. This rollover does not require newly-authorized shares whereas section 86 appears to require, in the course of a capital reorganization, new shares created by a change in authorized capital through the articles of incorporation. A conversion of shares can be made by shares that are already authorized.   *ITA: 51*

The Act permits a deferral of the inherent gain on the exchanged securities, but only if the following conditions are met: *ITA: 51*

(a) only shares are issued for the exchanged securities;

(b) the exchanged securities are capital property to the taxpayer; and

(c) the exchanged securities, other than shares, must have a conversion right attached to the particular security.

The provision is not elective but is automatic if the above conditions are met. However, the application of section 51 is denied if section 85 or 86 has been applied to the exchange transaction.   *ITA: 51(4)*

When the holder of a convertible property exercises the conversion privilege and as a result acquires the shares of one class of the capital stock of the corporation, the exchange is deemed not to have been a disposition of property. The adjusted cost base of the shares acquired on conversion is deemed to be the adjusted cost base of the convertible security before the exchange. The effect is to defer any capital gain accrued on the convertible security prior to the exchange until such time as the new shares are sold. For example, a taxpayer purchased a $1,000 bond, the terms of which conferred upon the holder the right of conversion into five common shares. The adjusted cost base of the bond is $1,000. If the bond is converted into the five shares when those shares have a value of $225, the taxpayer will not realize the accrued gain on the bond which should have a fair market value of $1,125 (i.e., 5 × $225). Instead the $1,000 cost base of the bond will flow through to the five shares such that each share will have a cost base of $200 (i.e., $1,000/5). If shares of more than one class are received on the conversion, the adjusted cost base of the convertible security before the exchange would be allocated among the classes of shares received on the conversion in proportion to their respective fair market values after the exchange.

A penalty provision applies where a benefit has been conferred on a related person and is similar in effect to the capital reorganization benefit rule. Subsection 51(3), which determines the paid-up capital of the newly issued shares, has a formula which is practically identical to subsection 86(2.1) as previously discussed.   *ITA: 51(2)*

A similar provision covers the case where a bondholder acquires a new bond of the same debtor in exchange for the original bond. There is a similar flow-through of the adjusted cost base of the original bond to the new bond and of any tax-free zone position on the original bond.   *ITA: 51.1*

¶17,220   Inter-Spousal Transfers

To defer the recognition of a capital gain or loss on the transfer of property between spouses or to a qualifying trust in favour of one spouse, an automatic rollover is available. The Act does not allow the recognition of the gain or loss unless the taxpayer elects not to have the rollover apply. This rollover applies when capital property is transferred between living spouses (*inter vivos*) either by way of sale at any price or gift. A qualifying trust is one created by the taxpayer under which the spouse is entitled to receive all the income of the trust that arises before the spouse's death and no person except the spouse may receive or obtain the use of any of the trust property before the spouse's death. Also, the spouse or trust must be resident in Canada at the time of the property transfer. The topic of spousal trusts will be discussed more fully in a subsequent chapter.

The Act provides that the property is deemed to have been sold by one spouse and acquired by the other spouse or trust for an amount equal to its adjusted cost base in the case of capital property such as shares. As indicated above, the provision allows an election to transfer such property at its fair market value.

ITA: 73(1)

A similar rollover applies on a transfer of the same property at death through a will. This rollover, like that between living spouses, is applied automatically, although an election can be made to use the general rules applicable at death to recognize capital gains and losses. For example, a husband may bequeath shares having a cost of $100 and a fair market value at the time of death of $250. If the rollover is used, the shares will be deemed to have been transferred at their adjusted cost base of $100 such that no gain or loss is realized on the transfer. However, if the election is made, the transfer will take place at $250, thereby realizing a capital gain of $150. Again, similar rules apply to depreciable property.

ITA: 70(6), 70(6.2), 73(1)

ITA: 70(6.2)

¶17,300   USE OF ROLLOVERS IN ESTATE FREEZING

¶17,310   Objectives

The tax planning area of estate freezing has been alluded to in previous discussions of the advantages of the use of corporations to hold sources of income from business or investments. The purpose of this section of the chapter is not to deal with the topic exhaustively, but to illustrate briefly and conceptually the application as planning tools of some of the provisions discussed in this and the previous chapters.

The primary purpose of estate freezing is to freeze all or part of the value of growing assets at their current fair market value, such that future growth in these assets accrues to the next generation of family members. The result will be that this future growth will not be taxed in the hands of the taxpayer on a disposition or at his or her death. In the process of implementing an estate freeze, some of the following secondary objectives may be addressed:

- The taxpayer contemplating an estate freeze will not likely wish to incur any immediate tax cost in implementing the freeze, but may want to establish the amount of the tax liability that will arise on his or her death.

- The taxpayer will often wish to maintain control over the assets the value of which is being frozen even though their future growth in value is being passed to the next generation. At the same time, the taxpayer may wish to retain a source of income from the assets to maintain himself or herself.

- The implementation of an estate freeze may coincide with planning to split income with low tax-rate family members, although great care must be taken to avoid the adverse tax consequences of the attribution rules and the income-splitting tax imposed on minors, discussed in previous chapters.

- In the process of implementing an estate freeze, it may be possible to realize capital gains sufficient to use up a taxpayer's capital gains deduction on the disposition of the shares of a small business corporation, as discussed in a previous chapter.

- Through their ownership of common shares, the estate freeze will have the effect of placing the beneficiaries of an estate freeze in a position to generate sufficient future capital gains on those common shares to use their own capital gains deduction.

The focus of the discussion of techniques to accomplish these objectives will be on three principal methods of exchanging growth assets for non-growth assets, which can be termed:

holdco freeze, internal freeze and reverse or asset freeze. The intention is only to provide a conceptual overview without dealing with the details of implementation.

¶17,320   Holdco Freeze

This type of estate freeze uses section 85 as its primary planning device. In this case, a holding company is incorporated and the growing assets are transferred to the corporation, using the rollover to avoid incurring an immediate tax cost. Growing assets subject to the freeze may include: shares of an operating company, assets of an unincorporated business or a portfolio of securities. The estate freeze is implemented by the taxpayer's taking, as consideration from the new corporation for the growing assets transferred, debt and preferred shares. The preferred shares can have voting rights attached to them to meet the objective of maintaining control over the assets transferred. Both types of security can provide income to their holder. However, neither type of security, if properly issued with appropriate features, will grow in value as the assets of the corporation grow. In structuring the consideration received from the holding company, care must be taken to avoid the adverse tax consequences of dividend stripping, as discussed previously.

ITA: 85

ITA: 84.1

The future growth in the assets of the new corporation will be reflected in the value of the common shares of the corporation. These common shares can be subscribed for by the children in the family. Of course, care must be taken not to invoke the corporate or regular attribution rules and the income-splitting tax imposed on minors, as previously discussed. This problem is of particular concern if a small business corporation is not involved in the estate freeze.

ITA: 248(1) "small business corporation"

The process of this type of estate freeze can be illustrated schematically by the following diagram:

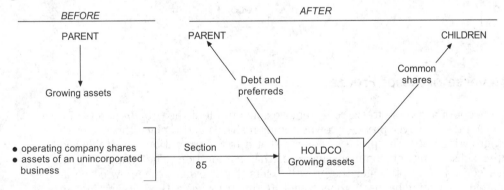

¶17,330   Internal Freeze

A capital reorganization of an existing corporation is the basis of this type of estate freeze. A taxpayer who owns common shares of a corporation may cause the corporation to undertake a capital reorganization. The taxpayer gives up the common shares in return for debt and newly-authorized preferred shares of the corporation, using section 86 to defer any accrued gains on the common shares given up. Again, the preferred shares may have voting rights to maintain control over the corporation. Both the debt and preferred shares can provide the taxpayer with a source of income. The children can subscribe for new common shares to which the future growth in the value of the corporation's assets will accrue.

This method of estate freeze has several advantages over the holdco freeze.

- First, a new company need not be incorporated, thereby avoiding the costs associated with incorporating and maintaining the additional corporation.

- Second, the rollover provision in section 86 is applied automatically without any need for an election to be made.

- Finally, the rules in section 84.1 are not applicable, thereby avoiding a potentially serious problem. However, extreme care must be taken to structure the paid-up capital of the new shares to avoid a deemed dividend problem.   ITA: 84(3) ITA: 84(1)

Note that the internal freeze cannot generate a capital gain for purposes of crystallization as demonstrated earlier in the chapter.   ITA: 86

A final note of warning in respect of both the holdco and the internal freeze, is that careful planning is required to ensure that the corporate attribution rules are not triggered. As long as the respective corporations are small business corporations (i.e., meet the 90% active business asset rule), then the corporate attribution rules will not apply.   ITA: 74.4

The following diagram provides a conceptual illustration of an internal freeze:

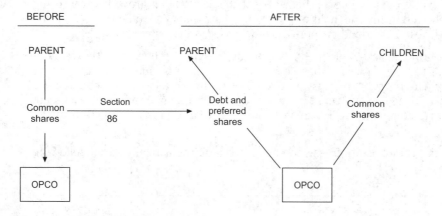

¶17,340   Reverse or Asset Freeze

The basic concept of a reverse freeze is to remove some or all of the *growth* assets of a corporation in which the taxpayer presently owns common shares and replace those growth assets with non-growth assets. The process requires that a new corporation be established with the children subscribing for common shares of that corporation. The taxpayer then causes his or her corporation to transfer the growth assets that it owns to the new corporation. Again, section 85 would be used to accomplish the transfer without incurring an immediate tax cost. Since assets, other than shares of a subject corporation, are being transferred, section 84.1 will not apply. If the preferred shares taken back have voting rights, the taxpayer can maintain control over the assets transferred to the new corporation through the exercise of control over his or her corporation, which owns the voting preferred shares. His or her corporation can also earn income for his or her benefit on the debt and preferred shares it owns. However, the value of the common shares held by the taxpayer in his or her original corporation will not grow in the future if the only assets of that corporation are the non-growth debt and preferred securities of the new corporation. On the other hand, the common shares of the new corporation held by the children will grow in value as the assets transferred to that corporation grow.

One of the advantages of the reverse freeze technique is that selected growth assets can be transferred, such that the children will only participate in the future growth of the selected assets transferred. Furthermore, if different children are to participate in the future growth of different assets and each child subscribes for the common shares of a different new corporation, selected assets can be transferred to the benefit of each child as desired. Unlike the previous types of freezes, the attribution rules do not apply in the case of a reverse freeze, because the transferor or lender is not an individual.   ITA: 56(4.1), 74.1, 74.2, 74.4(2)

The following diagram illustrates conceptually a basic reverse freeze:

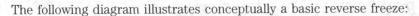

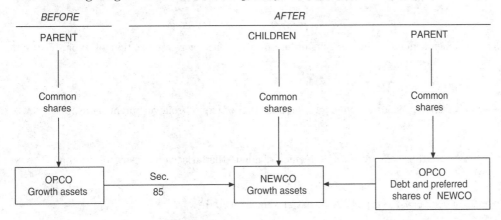

¶17,800   REVIEW QUESTIONS

(1) What legal documents need to be filed in order to accomplish a reorganization of capital rollover?   ITA: 86

(2) What are some of the occasions on which a reorganization of capital rollover might be used?   ITA: 86

(3) What adjustments are there as a result of a deemed dividend that arises on a reorganization of capital rollover?   ITA: 86

(4) Legally, what happens to two corporations that are amalgamated?

(5) At the time of amalgamation there is a deemed year-end for tax purposes. What are some of the other tax rules that are impacted by this deemed year-end?   ITA: 87(2)(a)

(6) Acme Co. is a CCPC with a January 31 year-end. The owners want to change the year-end of the company to July 31 to allow bonuses to be paid either in this year or the next. It is now July and they do not have time to receive clearance from the CRA so they incorporate another company and amalgamate it with Acme on July 31 to create a new year-end. Do you have any problems with this tactic?

(7) In order for subsidiary wind-up rollover to apply, what ownership criteria need to be met?   ITA: 88(1)

(8) Ms. Switch purchased 1,000 convertible preferred shares at a total cost of $10,000. These shares gave her the right to convert each preferred share into 2 common shares. She exercised her conversion right at a time when the common shares were trading at $10 each. What is the ACB of her new common shares?

(9) What is the primary purpose of estate freezing?

(10) What might be some of the secondary objectives of an estate freeze?

(11) What are the three principal methods of freezing the value of growth assets?

(12) What are the basic steps involved in doing a Holdco freeze?

(13) When doing an estate freeze on the shares of a small business corporation in favour of a spouse, what is one of the biggest dangers? Assume that the freeze was done correctly.

(14) Describe when a "reverse or asset freeze" would be used and the steps you would take to accomplish it.

¶17,825   MULTIPLE CHOICE QUESTIONS

Question 1

P Ltd. is a profitable taxable Canadian corporation with a December 31 fiscal year-end. It has a wholly owned subsidiary, L Ltd., with a June 30 fiscal year-end. L Ltd. has a significant 2004 non-capital loss balance. Therefore, consideration is being given to either amalgamating P Ltd. and L Ltd. or winding up L Ltd. into P Ltd. in order to utilize the loss. The amalgamation or the winding-up will take place on November 1, 2007. Which *one* of the following statements is *true*?

(A) The newly amalgamated corporation can utilize the non-capital loss in its deemed year ended October 31, 2007.

(B) The newly amalgamated corporation cannot utilize the non-capital loss until its taxation year commencing one year after the amalgamation.

(C) If a winding-up takes place, P Ltd. can utilize the non-capital loss in its taxation year commencing January 1, 2008.

(D) If a winding-up takes place, P Ltd. can utilize the non-capital loss in its taxation year ended December 31, 2007.

Question 2

On September 1, 2004, X Ltd. acquired all the shares of Y Ltd. for $500,000. At that time, Y Ltd. had land with a fair market value of $130,000 and a cost of $100,000. On September 1, 2007, a winding-up of Y Ltd. into X Ltd. took place. At the time of the winding-up, the tax values of Y Ltd.'s assets totalled $420,000. The fair market value of the land at this time was $300,000. X Ltd. received $15,000 of dividends from Y Ltd. between September 1, 2004 and September 1, 2007. The adjusted cost base of the land after the winding-up cannot exceed:

(A) $100,000

(B) $130,000

(C) $165,000

(D) $180,000

Question 3

In the course of the reorganization of the capital of A Ltd., Chris exchanged all his common shares of A Ltd. (which are capital property to him) for the package of consideration outlined below.

Cash	$ 135
Preferred shares (50 shares redeemable at $100 each)	5,000
	$5,135

At the time of the exchange, Chris' common shares had an ACB of $2,000 and a FMV of $5,135. Which one of the following best describes the tax consequences to Chris as a result of the exchange?

(A) Chris will have no capital gain on the disposition of his common shares and the ACB of his preferred shares is $2,000.

(B) Chris will have no capital gain on the disposition of his common shares and the ACB of his preferred shares is $1,865.

(C) Chris will have a capital gain of $3,135 on the disposition of his common shares and the ACB of his preferred shares is $5,135.

(D) Chris will have a capital gain of $135 on the disposition of his common shares and the ACB of his preferred shares is $2,135.

Question 4

Shelly exchanged her shares of Simpsons for shares of Hudson's Bay when Simpsons was taken over by Hudson's Bay. Her shares of Simpsons had the following characteristics:

FMV $12,000

ACB 7,000

PUC 5,000

Section 85.1 is often used in take-over situations. Which one of the following statements with respect to the rollover in this case is FALSE?

(A) When there are many diverse shareholders, a share-for-share exchange rollover is easier to accomplish than a subsection 85(1) rollover because there is no need for each shareholder to file an election.   ITA: 85.1

(B) The ACB of Shelly's shares of Hudson's Bay is $7,000.

(C) The ACB of the Simpsons' shares acquired by Hudson's Bay from Shelly is $5,000.

(D) Non-share consideration, up to the PUC of the exchanged shares, $5,000, could have been received by Shelly without any adverse tax consequences to her.

Question 5

Mr. Wise owns 100% of the shares of ABC Co., a small business corporation. He would like to freeze the value of this company for tax purposes at today's value and transfer future growth to his children without giving up control over the company. He does not want to pay tax any sooner than he has to. His will currently leaves everything to his wife. Which of the following plans will achieve his objectives?

(A) His children should subscribe to common shares of a holding company and he should transfer his shares of ABC to this holding company, electing under section 85 at tax cost and taking back voting redeemable retractable preferred shares as consideration.

(B) He should change his will to leave his shares of ABC to his children rather than his wife.

(C) He should gift the ABC shares to his children during his lifetime.

(D) He should sell the ABC shares to his children at fair market value, taking back debt as consideration.

Question 6

Which of the following techniques will allow Mr. Successful to use up his $500,000 capital gains exemption on the accrued gain on shares of a qualified small business corporation? The shares were issued to him 20 years ago for $1 and are worth $1 million now.

(A) A reverse asset freeze.

(B) An internal freeze.

(C) A holdco freeze, taking back boot of $1.

(D) A holdco freeze, taking back boot of $500,001.

¶17,850 EXERCISES

Exercise 1

ITA: 85.1

Magnamous Publico Ltd., a widely-held public corporation, has offered to exchange its common shares, currently trading on the CDNX Stock Exchange at $4.70 per share, for the common shares of Targetco Ltd., another widely-held public corporation. The shares of Targetco Ltd. trade currently on the CDNX Stock Exchange in the range of $2.00 to $2.25 each. Magnamous Publico Ltd. has offered to exchange one of its common shares for every two common shares tendered by shareholders of Targetco Ltd.

Mr. Sucker owns 1,000 shares of Targetco Ltd. which he bought several years ago for $1.25 each. Their paid-up capital value is $1.00 per share. On the announcement of the exchange offer their value on the market rose to $2.35. Mr. Sucker is interested in the exchange offer, but does not wish to realize any of the accrued gain on his shares of Targetco Ltd. Upon taking up the exchange offer, Mr. Sucker indicates that he will never own more than 10% of the shares of Magnamous Publico Ltd.

— *REQUIRED*

What are the tax consequences to Mr. Sucker and to Magnamous Publico Ltd. of taking up the exchange offer?

Exercise 2

ITA: 86

Abig Roller owned some Class A preferred shares of a corporation that reorganized its capital structure. He exchanged all these shares which had an adjusted cost base and paid-up capital of $2,000 and a fair market value of $3,000 for the following consideration:

Cash.	$ 675
Fair market value of Class B preferred shares (LSC: $1,000)	1,755
Fair market value of common shares (LSC: $325)	570

— *REQUIRED*

What are the tax consequences to Mr. Roller as a result of this exchange?

Exercise 3

ITA: 86(2)

Mrs. Janna and her daughter Rayna, respectively, own 75% and 25% of the 100 common shares of Adam Ltd. The total fair market value of all the shares of the corporation is $600,000. The shares were acquired by both individuals at a total cost of $1,000 on incorporation in 1990.

Mrs. Janna is now prepared to freeze the future growth of her ownership in the corporation, so that the future growth will be passed on to her daughter. Mrs. Janna will give up all of her common shares for preferred shares of Adam Ltd. having a legal stated capital of $750 and a fair market value of $350,000. As a result, Rayna will own all of the common shares.

— *REQUIRED*

What are the tax consequences under section 86 to Mrs. Janna on the proposed transaction?

Exercise 4

ITA: 87, 88(1)

Mergem Limited owns all of the shares of Acquisition Limited. The cost of the shares to Mergem was $75,000 and they now have a fair market value of $100,000. Acquisition's only asset is land which cost it $50,000. The land had a fair market value of $90,000 when the shares of Acquisition were purchased by Mergem (at a bargain price!) and the land now has a fair market value of $100,000.

— *REQUIRED*

Determine the income tax consequences to Mergem Limited and Acquisition Limited of using either an amalgamation or a winding-up of a subsidiary to combine.

ITA: 87, 88

Exercise 5

ITA: 51

Convertit owns $10,000 of debentures of Convertibles Ltd. They were purchased several years ago at their face value and are convertible into 16 common shares of the corporation for each $100 of debentures owned at the option of the holder. When the common shares traded on the market at $100 each, Convertit exercised the conversion privilege.

— *REQUIRED*

What are the tax consequences of this conversion?

¶17,875   ASSIGNMENT PROBLEMS

Problem 1

ITA: 85, 85.1

Jason purchased all of the common shares of Quality Appliances Ltd., a Canadian-controlled private corporation, in 1988 for $50,000. The paid-up capital of the shares was $25,000. These shares have recently been valued at $125,000.

Big Distributors Ltd., a Canadian, arm's length corporation, has offered to buy all of Jason's shares. The following alternatives have been presented to Jason:

(a) $25,000 in cash and $100,000 of FMV in common shares of Big Distributors Ltd.

(b) $125,000 of FMV in Big Distributors Ltd.'s common shares.

Jason is at arm's length with Big Distributors Ltd. and, after acquiring its shares, will neither control Big Distributors Ltd. nor own more than 50% of the FMV of its shares.

— *REQUIRED*

(A) What are the tax consequences to Jason if these transactions are conducted using the provisions of section 85.1?

(B) What are the tax consequences to Jason if these transactions are conducted using the provisions of section 85?

Problem 2

ITA: 84(1), 84(3), 86

Matt owns common shares of Maeb Inc. The adjusted cost base and paid-up capital of these shares is $300,000 and the FMV is $900,000. In the course of a capital reorganization, the following two packages of consideration were offered in exchange for the shares:

(a)	Cash	$ 10,000
	Bond	80,000
	FMV* and LSC of Class A preferred shares	600,000
	FMV and LSC of Class B preferred shares	210,000
(b)	Cash	$500,000
	FMV* and LSC of Class A preferred shares	300,000
	FMV and LSC of Class B preferred shares	100,000

* Equal to retraction and/or redemption value.

— *REQUIRED*

Indicate the tax consequences to Matt as a result of the above proposed reorganizations.

Problem 3

ITA: 86(2)

Mr. Fresser, age 67, owns 80% of the common shares of Fresser Ltd., a CCPC. The other 20% is owned by his daughter, Elana, who has worked in the business with Mr. Fresser for the past 22 years.

When the business was incorporated and capitalized, the 1,000 common shares were issued to Mr. Fresser and his daughter for $62,500 in total. They now have a fair market value of $625,000. Mr. Fresser proposes a capital reorganization in which he would give up his common shares in return for $90,000 in cash and $300,000 in retractable voting preferred shares with a legal stated capital of $300,000 which he could redeem at his convenience. As a result, Elana could own all of the outstanding common shares.

— *REQUIRED*

(A) What are the tax consequences to Mr. Fresser of section 86 on the proposed transaction?

(B) What are the tax consequences to Mr. Fresser of subsequently redeeming the preferred shares for their fair market value?

Problem 4

ITA: 87, 88(1)

Jonsub Ltd. is a wholly owned subsidiary of Normpar Ltd. Normpar Ltd. plans to merge the two companies, either by amalgamating with the subsidiary or by winding up the subsidiary. The balance sheet of Jonsub Ltd. immediately before the merger is as follows:

ITA: 87, 88(1)

Assets:
Cash	$ 80,000
Marketable securities at cost (FMV $950,000)	300,000
Accounts receivable (net of $30,000 reserve)	800,000
Inventory at cost (FMV $920,000)	920,000
Land at cost (FMV $2,000,000)	1,200,000
Building at UCC (FMV $500,000)	300,000
Equipment at UCC (FMV $150,000)	200,000
Total current assets	$3,800,000

Liabilities and shareholder's equity:
Accounts payable and accrued liabilities	709,000
Loans payable	1,000,000
Share capital	1,000
Retained earnings	2,090,000
	$3,800,000

Other Information

(1) Normpar Ltd. acquired all of the shares of Jonsub Ltd. for $4,000,000 in 1995. The total amount of dividends paid by Jonsub Ltd. to Normpar Ltd. during the period of ownership is $500,000.

(2) The same marketable securities were owned by Jonsub Ltd. at the time Normpar Ltd. acquired control but the marketable securities had a fair market value of only $800,000 at that time. Normpar Ltd. plans to sell the marketable securities in the next few years.

(3) The fair market value of the land and building at the time Normpar Ltd. acquired control were $1,900,000 and $400,000 respectively.

(4) The fair market value of goodwill developed by Jonsub Ltd. (i.e., not purchased) was $300,000 at the time Normpar Ltd. acquired control and $500,000 immediately before the merger.

— REQUIRED

What are the tax consequences to both Jonsub and Normpar on either an amalgamation or a winding-up?

ITA: 87, 88(1)

Problem 5

ITA: 87(2.1), 88(1.1)

Loser Limited is a wholly owned subsidiary of Bigbucks Limited. Loser has generated the following losses which it has not been able to absorb in a carryover year and it is not likely to generate sufficient income to absorb them in the foreseeable future.

	Non-capital	
Taxation year of loss	*loss*	*Net capital loss*
2006	$43,000	$14,000
2005	7,000	10,000
2004	6,000	Nil
2000	4,000	5,000

Loser's fiscal year-end is December 31.

Bigbucks has a January 31 fiscal year-end and expects to generate sufficient business income and taxable capital gains to absorb any of Loser's losses that might be made available to it. As a result, Bigbucks is considering either an amalgamation or a winding-up effective June 30, 2007. After the reorganization, the January 31 fiscal year-end will be retained.

ITA: 87, 88(1)

— REQUIRED

Determine the availability to Bigbucks of the losses of its subsidiary under both alternatives being considered. Should any other factors be considered in the choice between the alternatives?

Problem 6

ITA: 84.1, 85, 86

Ms. Knight owns all of the common shares of Knight Manufacturing Limited (KML) that she acquired 20 years ago from an arm's length person. These shares have a paid-up capital of $100,000 and their adjusted cost base is $400,000. Their current fair market value is $1,800,000 and it is anticipated that this value will continue to grow rapidly. Ms. Knight is considering freezing the value of KML at $1,800,000 by holding non-growth debt and preferred shares and having her adult children own the common shares. Ms. Knight would like to use up her remaining (QSBC share) capital gains exemption of $400,000.

— REQUIRED

(A) One method of freezing the future growth of her KML common shares is to transfer her present common shares to a newly-formed holding company, Knight Holdings Ltd. (KHL). She would take from the holding company as consideration for the shares, debt in the amount of $800,000 and voting preferred shares with a legal stated capital and fair market value of $1,000,000. What are the tax consequences of this plan and how can the adverse tax consequences be avoided? Show all calculations.

(B) What are the tax consequences if the preferred shares in KHL received in (A) are:

(i) sold in an arm's length transaction for their fair market value?

(ii) redeemed by the corporation for their fair market value?

(C) As an alternative, Ms. Knight is considering a capital reorganization of KML in which she would receive $800,000 in debt and $1,000,000 in voting preferred shares in return for her common shares. The $1,000,000 amount of preferred shares represents their legal stated capital, fair market value and retractable value. What are the tax consequences to Ms. Knight on the reorganization? How can the adverse tax consequences be avoided?

(D) What are the consequences if the shares received by Ms. Knight on the reorganization in (C) are:

(i) sold in an arm's length transaction for their fair market value?

(ii) redeemed by the corporation for their fair market value?

(E) Compare the alternatives in (B) and (D) in terms of their total "net economic effects":

(i) with the adverse tax consequences of the plan as outlined, and

(ii) with the tax consequences of the plan that avoids these adverse tax consequences.

[For more problems and solutions thereto, see the CD accompanying this book.]

¶17,880 ADVISORY CASES

Case 1: Orillia Resorts Inc.

Orillia Resorts Inc. is a company established by Gil George about 20 years ago to operate a tourist resort. Gil had originally contributed $100 for 100 shares of the company, which is now worth $1.4 million as a result of the increase in the value of lake-front property.

Gil has found that he is no longer able to look after the resort, now that he is 68 years old. Also, he and his wife, Ruth, feel that they would like to spend their summers travelling, instead of working 14 hours a day. He has had discussions with his lawyer and, on her recommendation, is now in the process of transferring the business to his daughter, Dale. He is going to accomplish this transfer by taking the following steps.

1) He will exchange his common shares of Orillia Resorts Inc. for non-voting preference shares with a value of $1.4 million.

2) He will then transfer these preference shares of Orillia Resorts Inc. to a holding company (Holdco) in exchange for preference shares of Holdco that are worth $900,000 plus cash of $500,000. On this transfer, he will elect under section 85 at a value of $750,000 to use up his capital gain exemption.

3) Both Gil and Ruth will be the common shareholders of Holdco so Gil can pay dividends to Ruth in their retirement years. In addition, he will have Holdco charge a management fee to Orillia Resorts Inc. while he is still active in the business.

The plan is that Orillia Resorts Inc. will pay a 7% dividend each year to Holdco and then Gil and Ruth will decide how much they will take out of Holdco to live on. This will give them some investment assets outside of the business to provide some security for them in retirement.

Gil and Ruth would like your advice on the tax implications of their situation.

Case 2: Whyte Co. Inc.

Whyte Co. Inc. is a manufacturing company started by Bill and Betty Whyte about 25 years ago when they each paid $50 for 50 shares in the company. Since that time, it has grown significantly and now competes on a global basis.

Bill is 60 years old and Betty is 59 years old. They are both actively involved in the business and each owns 50% of the shares. However, they now want to start winding down their involvement in the business, so they can spend some time travelling together while they are still young. Betty and Bill have three children, Sandra (age 32), Paul (age 29), and Joan (age 26).

Sandra is actively involved in the business and is vice president, Operations. She is married to Jason and they have no children. Neither Paul nor Joan is involved in the business, nor do they plan to be. They each have their own career.

Betty and Bill are financially well off. Their personal net worth is as follows:

Cash	$ 10,000
Marketable securities	180,000
Loans to Whyte Co.	100,000
Residence	300,000
Florida condo	120,000
RRSP	450,000
Real estate used in Whyte Co.	2,800,000
Whyte Co shares	4,500,000
Total	8,460,000
Mortgage on real estate	150,000
Net worth	$ 8,310,000

Bill and Betty have thought about estate planning and feel that their children will be well taken care of. They want to be fair to each of them, so they are going to leave everything equally among them. They have group life insurance through the company for $200,000 each. Otherwise, they do not like to spend money on life insurance. When they think about retirement, they think they will need after-tax income of about $100,000 per year to do the things they want to do.

Bill and Betty would like your advice on the tax implications of their objectives.

¶17,900   SUPPLEMENTAL NOTES

(This section can be omitted without losing the continuity of the chapter. None of the review questions, multiple choice questions, exercises or assignment problems utilize this information.)

¶17,910   GST Consequences of Rollovers Involving Corporations and Their Securities

Often businesses will engage in a reorganization of their affairs into separate corporations, wind up a corporation for income tax or other reasons, or undertake some other form of rollover transaction without considering the GST consequences. Under the GST, a number of these transactions trigger a liability, while other transactions involving reorganizations or rollovers have no GST consequences.

¶17,915   Share for share exchange

Where a share for share exchange under section 85.1 of the *Income Tax Act* is undertaken, there will be no GST consequences in respect of the exchange. The definition of "financial instrument" includes, among other things, an equity security. "Financial service" is defined in the same subsection to include, among other things, the issue, granting, variation or transfer of ownership of a financial instrument. Thus, the exchange of shares will qualify as a financial service, which is exempt pursuant to Part VII of Schedule V of the ETA.
    ETA: 123(1)

Any GST that is paid in respect of services related to the share for share exchange, such as legal or investment counsel fees, will not be recoverable as an input tax credit, except to the extent allowed under the ETA. As discussed in Chapter 15, where a registrant that is a corporation resident in Canada is engaged in a takeover attempt in which it is acquiring or attempting to acquire all or substantially all (i.e., 90% or more) of the voting shares of another corporation, it is entitled to claim input tax credits for GST paid on any purchases of property and services attributable to that activity. For this provision to apply to a share for share exchange, one corporation must acquire or attempt to acquire 90% or more of the shares of the other corporation. Also, where the share for share exchange is considered to be a financial service that relates to the registrant's commercial activities, the registrant is not required to apportion the inputs.
    ETA: 185, 186
    ETA: 186(2)
    ETA: 185(1)

¶17,920   Reorganizations

A reorganization of capital under section 86 of the *Income Tax Act* does not have GST consequences. The variation of existing shares would qualify as an exempt financial service. Any GST that is paid in respect of services related to the capital reorganization, however, will generally not be recoverable as an input tax credit.

Relief may be available in limited circumstances. Where a parent corporation resident in Canada has an investment in shares of the capital stock of a related corporation and the related corporation is engaged exclusively in commercial activities, the parent may claim an input tax credit in respect of any tax on the supply of property or services acquired by it that may reasonably be considered to relate to those shares. Thus, the parent must have acquired the services in respect of the reorganization and paid GST on those services in order to obtain relief. Also, where the reorganization of capital is considered to be an incidental financial service of the registrant, the registrant is not required to apportion the inputs.
    ETA: 185(1), 186(1)
    ETA: 186(1)
    ETA: 185(1)

¶17,925 Statutory amalgamations

The *Excise Tax Act* deals specifically with amalgamations. Where two or more corporations (referred to as predecessors) are merged or amalgamated to form a single corporation, the new corporation is generally treated as being a person separate from each of the predecessor corporations. No supplies are considered to have been made in respect of property transferred on the merger or amalgamation and, hence, there are no GST consequences. However, the new corporation will be deemed to be the same corporation as, and a continuation of, each predecessor for the purposes of the ETA, and for other prescribed purposes. Section 231 of the ETA deals with bad debts while section 249 of the ETA covers threshold amounts for purposes of the new corporation's reporting requirements (see Chapter 14). The new corporation will report the appropriate deduction from, or addition to, net tax, as the case may be, in relation to an amount owed to a predecessor that is written off as a bad debt or recovered after the amalgamation. The new corporation's threshold amounts under the ETA are calculated by reference to supplies made by the predecessor corporations. For example, if the predecessor corporations previously reported on a quarterly basis because their individual threshold amounts for the fiscal year were $4 million and $3 million, respectively, the new corporation will be required to report on a monthly basis because its threshold amount exceeds $6 million by reference to the supplies made by the two predecessors. The Amalgamations and Windings-Up Continuation (GST/HST) Regulations prescribe additional provisions of the ETA where the new corporation is deemed to be the same corporation as, and a continuation of, the predecessor corporations.

ETA: 231, 271

ETA: 231, 249

ETA: 249

Section 271 of the ETA does not apply where the merger or amalgamation occurs as the result of the acquisition of property of one corporation by another corporation pursuant to the purchase of the property by the other corporation or as the result of the winding-up of the other corporation.

Special rules are provided for amalgamations that involve financial institutions.

ETA: 149(2)

¶17,930 Winding up a subsidiary

The ETA deals specifically with wind-ups where 90% or more of the issued shares of each class of the capital stock of the wound-up corporation were, immediately before that time, owned by another corporation. This provision is similar to section 271 of the ETA which applies to amalgamations. On the wind-up, the transfer of assets to the parent is deemed not to be a supply.

ETA: 272

The parent will be deemed to be the same corporation as, and a continuation of, the subsidiary, and for other prescribed purposes. As explained above in the context of amalgamations, any amount that is owed to the subsidiary that is written off as a bad debt or recovered after the amalgamation is to be reported by the parent in its calculation of net tax. Similarly, in determining the parent's threshold amount for reporting purposes of the ETA (see Chapter 14), any taxable supplies made by the subsidiary prior to the wind-up are deemed to be made by the parent. The Amalgamations and Windings-Up Continuation (GST/HST) Regulations prescribe additional provisions of the ETA where the parent corporation is deemed to be the same corporation as, and a continuation of, the subsidiary.

ETA: 231, 249

ETA: 249

¶17,935 Convertible properties

Where section 51 of the *Income Tax Act* applies to the exchange of convertible properties for shares, the exchange will be an exempt financial service. The transfer of the convertible properties by the holder and the issuance of shares by the corporation are both exempt for GST purposes. The definition of "financial instrument" includes, among other things, debt and equity securities. Thus, shares, bonds or notes of a corporation are considered to be financial instruments. "Financial service" is defined in the same subsection to include, among other things, the issue, granting, variation or transfer of ownership of a financial instrument. The exchange would qualify as a financial service, which is exempt pursuant to Part VII of Schedule V. Any GST paid on expenses incurred on the exchange will only be eligible for an input tax credit if the requirements of subsection 186(1) or (2) or subsection 185(1), as discussed above, are satisfied.

ETA: 123(1)

Chapter 18

Partnerships and Trusts

LEARNING GOALS

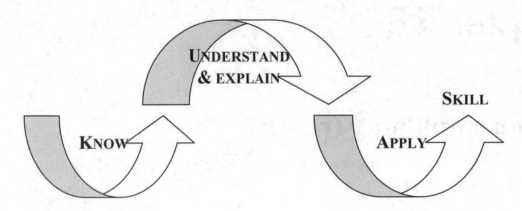

Know

By the end of this chapter you should know the basic provisions of the *Income Tax Act* that relate to partnerships and trusts. Completing the Review Questions (¶18,800) and Multiple Choice Questions (¶18,825) is a good way to learn the technical provisions.

Understand and Explain

You should understand and be able to explain how a partnership and a trust are established, how income earned within a partnership or trust is computed and how this income is taxed. Completing the Exercises (¶18,850) is a good way to deepen your understanding of the material.

Apply

You should be able to apply your knowledge and understanding of partnerships and trusts to apply them in a way that accomplishes a client's goals. Completing the Assignment Problems (¶18,875) is an excellent way to develop your ability to apply the material in increasingly complex situations.

OVERVIEW

This chapter is intended to provide only an overview of the provisions dealing with partnerships. The chapter will deal, in general terms, with the computation of partnership income, the concept of a partnership interest, and some of the rollover provisions affecting partnerships.

The chapter will also introduce some basic concepts in the taxation of trusts and illustrate some of the ways in which trusts are used in tax planning. There are two types of trusts for tax purposes: the personal trust and the commercial trust. This chapter will focus, in general, on the provisions of the Act as they relate to personal trusts. Certain types of trusts which are provided for specifically in the Act, such as registered pension plans, registered retirement savings plans and deferred profit sharing plans have already been introduced and will not be dealt with here.

The following chart will help locate in the Act the major provisions discussed in this Chapter pertaining to partnerships and trusts.

SUBDIVISION J & K
PARTNERSHIPS & TRUSTS

DIVISION		SUBDIVISION		SECTION	
A	Liability for tax				
B	Computation of income		Basic rules		
C	Computation of taxable income	a	Office or employment		
D	Taxable income earned in Canada by non-residents	b	Business or property		
		c	Capital gains and losses		
E	Computation of tax	d	Other income	96	General rules
E.1	Minimum tax	e	Other deductions	97	Contributions to a partnership
F	Special rules	f	Rules relating to computation of income	98	Partnership ceases
				98.1	Residual interests
G	Deferred and other special income arrangements			98.2	Transfers on death
		g	Amounts not included in income	99	Fiscal periods
				100	Disposition of partnership interests
H	Exemptions	h	Cdn corporations and shareholders	101	Farmland
I	Returns, Assessments, payments, appeals	i	Shareholders of non-resident corporations	102	Definition of Canadian partnership
J	Appeals to the courts			103	Agreement to share income
		j	**Partnerships**		
		k	**Trusts**	104	General rules
				105	Benefits under a trust
				106	Income interests
				107	Capital interests
				107.1-107.4	Special trusts
				108	Definitions

¶18,000   PARTNERSHIPS

¶18,010   Nature of a Partnership

¶18,015   What is a partnership?

The term "partnership" is not defined in the Act. The Act merely outlines the tax consequences if a partnership exists. In order to determine whether a particular relationship is a partnership, reference must be made to the definitions contained in the various provincial Partnership Acts. Generally, these statutes define a partnership as a legal relationship existing between two or more persons who carry on a business in common for the purpose of profit. Partnerships can be formed by individuals, corporations or a combination of individuals and corporations. In addition, two other factors generally suggest the existence of a partnership:

(a) joint and several liability with respect to debts incurred by the partnership; and

(b) an agreement indicating the method by which profits and losses are to be shared.

The Canada Revenue Agency (CRA), has issued an Interpretation Bulletin which sets out the factors it considers in determining whether a partnership exists.   IT-90

Partners may set out their interests in partnership property and their rights and duties in relation to the partnership by written agreement. In the absence of a written agreement, the interests of the partners may be implied from all of the surrounding circumstances. If there is no agreement, express or implied, then the Partnership Acts generally provide that all the partners are entitled to share equally in the capital, profits and losses of the partnership.

¶18,020   Partnership versus joint venture

A partnership is to be distinguished from a joint venture. The tax consequences of being a partner or co-venturer (a member of a joint venture) are quite different. A partnership is a separate entity. Therefore, unless a rollover provision applies, transfers of property by the partner to the partnership take place at fair market value. On the other hand, a co-venturer generally retains title to any property used in the joint venture. If the co-venturer should contribute property to the joint venture, this is not a taxable transaction, as the contribution to a joint venture is not a disposition; there has been no change in ownership. Also, in a partnership net income is computed at the partnership level. Therefore, capital cost allowance is deducted at the partnership level. Each partner does not have the discretion to deduct capital cost allowance independently of the other partners. In a joint venture, each co-venturer computes net income separately. Therefore, each co-venturer is able to deduct capital cost allowance independently of the other co-venturers.

Whether a particular relationship is a partnership or a joint venture is a question of fact. It is not easy to determine. The fact that an agreement refers to a relationship as a partnership or a joint venture is not determinative of that relationship. The true nature of the relationship must be determined from all the facts.

A Canadian tax case, *Woodlin Developments Ltd. v. M.N.R.*, has stated that the following are indicators of a joint venture: 86 DTC 1116 (T.C.C.)

(a) joint property interest in the subject-matter of the venture;

(b) a right of mutual control and management of the enterprise; and

(c) generally, a limitation of the objective to a single undertaking or a limited number of undertakings.

¶18,000

¶18,030 Partnership Income

¶18,035 General rules

A partnership is not a person, nor is it deemed to be a person for the purposes of the Act. However, the Act provides that the income of a partner is computed as if the partnership was a separate person resident in Canada. So, for example, deductions such as capital cost allowance are taken at the partnership level.

ITA: 96(1)

Each taxable capital gain and allowable capital loss from the disposition of property owned by the partnership and the amount of any income or loss of the partnership from such sources as business or property will be calculated for each fiscal period of the partnership. However, this income under Division B is not taxed at the partnership level but is allocated to the partners according to the terms of the partnership agreement. The partners then include their share of the partnership income in their income for the year. If, in computing income, the partnership deducts amounts that, for purposes of the Act, are deductions either from taxable income or from taxes payable, these amounts are added back to the partnership income before they are allocated to the partners.

¶18,035.10 *Nature of income retained*

The income that flows through to each partner retains its original character or source, thereby enabling the partner to benefit, for example, from the dividend tax credit, the foreign tax credit and the capital gains deduction in respect of qualified farm property or qualified shares of a small business corporation. The income of the partnership will be combined on each partner's tax return with the partner's non-partnership income or losses. For example, non-partnership capital losses of an individual partner may be offset against that partner's share of partnership capital gains, since these gains are allocated to the partner. Similarly, a partner's share of rental income allocated by the partnership may be used to offset rental losses created by capital cost allowance on the partner's own rental property. Taxable income is computed by each partner, and each partner reports his or her partnership income on his or her own return and pays tax. The partnership itself does not file a tax return.

The taxation year of the partnership is the fiscal period of the partnership. The fiscal period of a partnership of which a member is an individual must end on December 31.

ITA: 249.1

¶18,035.20 *Reporting*

The partnership is required to provide an information return to each partner as follows:

ITR: 229

(a) where all of the partners are corporations, five months from the end of the fiscal period;

(b) where all the partners are individuals, the last day of March in the calendar year following the calendar year in which the fiscal period of the partnership ended; and

(c) in every other case, the earlier of five months after the end of the fiscal period and the last day of March following the calendar year in which the fiscal period of the partnership ended.

Failure to file a partnership information return on time will result in penalties.

Example Problem

The following income statement was prepared for the Alpha Beta Partnership, a partnership comprised of two individuals that carries on an active business:

Alpha Beta Partnership
INCOME STATEMENT
For the year ended December 31, 2007

Gross revenue $350,000
Less:

Office salaries	$29,000	
Rent	42,000	
Office supplies	8,950	
Depreciation on office furniture	3,375	
Charitable donations	3,000	86,325
		$263,675

Gain on sale of securities	$50,000	
Dividends received from taxable Canadian corporations	4,000	54,000
Net income		$317,675

The partners drew a total of $67,000 in "salaries".

The dividends were received from a CCPC, all of whose income was eligible for the small business deduction.

— *REQUIRED*

Compute the partnership income for the year and the income to be allocated to the partners for income tax purposes. Assume that the office furniture is included in Class 8 for capital cost allowance purposes. The capital cost allowance available in respect of the office furniture is $2,750, based on an undepreciated capital cost of $13,750.

— *SOLUTION*

Partnership's net income for financial accounting purposes[1]	$317,675
Deduct: Gain on sale of securities	(50,000)
Capital cost allowance	(2,750)
Add: Depreciation on office furniture	3,375
Charitable donations[2]	3,000
Taxable capital gain (½ × $50,000)	25,000
Income to be allocated (Division B)	$296,300

	Partnership
Nature of income:	
Taxable capital gain (½ × $50,000)	$ 25,000
Dividends	$ 4,000
Active business income	267,300
	$ 296,300

— *NOTES TO SOLUTION*

[1] Salaries paid by a partnership to its members do not constitute a business expense but are a method of distributing partnership income to members of the partnership.

[2] Charitable donations are not deductible in computing Division B income. Instead, they are allocated to the partners and are used as the basis for computing the charitable donations tax credit for an individual partner.

¶18,040 Limitation on deduction of partnership losses

Generally, business or property losses may be deducted by a limited partner only to the extent that the partner's investment in the partnership and share of the partnership's profit (known as the partner's "at-risk" amount) exceeds any amount owing to the partnership by the partner and any guaranteed return in respect of the partnership interest, guaranteed buy-

ITA: 96(2.1), 96(2.2)

back of the partnership interest and so on. To the extent that the business or property losses otherwise allocable to the limited partner are restricted in the manner described above, they are added to the limited partner's "limited partnership loss" in respect of the partnership for the year and are deductible only to the extent that the partner has an "at-risk" amount in future years in respect of the partnership that gave rise to the loss.

A limited partner is generally a partner whose only interest in the partnership is financial. If a limited partner takes part in the management of the partnership's business then, under provincial partnership law, that partner will lose status as a limited partner. Nevertheless, that partner may continue to be a limited partner for purposes of the "at-risk" rules.

Unlike a limited partner of a limited partnership, a member of limited liability partnership (LLP) can be liable for the general debts and obligations of a limited liability partnership. However, a member of a limited liability partnership is not liable for the debts of the partnership, or any member of the partnership, arising from negligent acts or omissions that another partner or an employee, agent or representative of the partnership commits in the course of the partnership business. The Act excludes from the "at -risk" rules members of limited liability partnerships where a partner's liability is limited by operation of a statutory provision of Canada or a province that limits the member's liability.

ITA: 96(2.4)(*a*)

¶18,045 Partnership allocations: Anti-avoidance

The partnership agreement will set out how the partners have agreed to allocate any income or loss among themselves. An anti-avoidance provision applies to a situation where the partnership agreement to share income or loss is considered to result in a reduction or postponement of tax that might otherwise have been payable. For example, the income allocated between partners may reflect more of a desire to split income or to allocate losses in an arbitrary way than a desire to reward each partner for his or her respective contribution. An anti-avoidance provision permits the partnership's income sharing arrangement to be set aside for tax purposes. The amounts would then be reallocated to the partners in a manner which is reasonable in the circumstances.

ITA: 103(1)

ITA: 103(1.1)

Where the partners do not deal at arm's length, specific rules are provided to determine a reasonable allocation of profit. Each partner's capital contribution and work performed, together with any other relevant factor, will be considered.

ITA: 103(1.1)

¶18,050 Computation of taxable income

Charitable gifts made by the partnership provide a deduction for partners who are corporations. A partner who is an individual includes a his or her share of the donation with their own total charitable gifts for purposes of calculating the personal tax credit. These donations are flowed through to a partner according to the partner's share of partnership income.

ITA: 110.1(1)(*a*)
ITA: 118.1(3)

Taxable capital gains generated by a partnership retain their character as part of the net income of the partnership flowed out to the partners. As a result, these taxable capital gains may provide individual partners with eligibility for the capital gains deduction available for qualified farm property and qualified small business corporation shares and provide partners with an opportunity to utilize personal net capital losses.

Since there is no computation of taxable income at the partnership level, losses carried forward and backward are not deductible by the partnership. Losses of the partnership are allocated to the partners at the end of each fiscal period. Any losses that are not utilized by a partner in the year incurred are carried forward or backward by the partner and deducted by the partner in the computation of that partner's taxable income. However, as already stated, in certain circumstances the ability of a limited partner to deduct an amount may be restricted by the partner's at-risk amount.

ITA: 111

¶18,055   Personal tax credits generated by the partnership

Charitable gifts made by the partnership entitle the individual partners to a tax credit. These gifts and the corresponding credits are flowed through to a partner according to the partner's share of partnership income.   ITA: 118.1(8)

Dividend income of the partnership maintains its source characteristics when allocated to the partners. An individual who is a member of a partnership will be entitled to claim a dividend tax credit in respect of the partner's share of any taxable dividend received by the partnership from a taxable Canadian corporation during a fiscal period of a partnership. When dividend income is allocated to a partner who is an individual, the dividend allocated to the partner must be grossed up by the usual rules, when it is included in the partner's income.   ITA: 121   ITA: 82(1)

Similarly, the partner may deduct any foreign tax credits on foreign income allocated to the partner by the partnership. Also, political contributions made by a partnership are allocated to each partner and, thus, provide each partner with a tax credit. The investment tax credit is treated on a similar basis. However, in certain circumstances, the ability of a limited partner to deduct an amount in respect of the investment tax credit may be restricted by the partner's at-risk amount.   ITA: 126   ITA: 127(4.2)   ITA: 127(8)   ITA: 127(8.1)–(8.5)

Example Problem

Refer to the previous example problem concerning Alpha Beta Partnership. Mrs. Alpha and Mrs. Beta share income equally.

— *REQUIRED*

Compute Mrs. Alpha's taxable income for 2007, assuming she has no other income.

— *SOLUTION*

Income to be allocated (Division B)	$296,300
Dividends (½ × $4,000)	$ 2,000
TCG (½ × $25,000)	12,500
ABI (½ × $267,300)	133,650
	$148,150
Dividend gross-up (¼ × $2,000)	500
Taxable income	$148,650

— *NOTE TO SOLUTION*

Mrs. Alpha will be eligible for a dividend tax credit of $333 (⅔ × $500) and a charitable donation credit computed on ½ of the partnership's charitable donations in computing her basic federal income tax.

¶18,060   Partnership Interest

¶18,065   The concept

As indicated previously, the property of a partnership is owned by the partnership, not the individual partners. Thus, any gains or losses on the disposition of that property are included in the computation of the net income of the partnership. The property owned by the partnership must be distinguished from each partner's interest in the partnership, which is a separate property owned by each partner. A taxpayer's "partnership interest" represents his or her total rights and obligations as a partner. It may be bought and sold by the partner. In this respect, a partnership interest is analogous to the share held by a shareholder of a corporation. A person acquires a partnership interest by becoming a member of a partnership and disposes of a partnership interest when he or she withdraws from the partnership.

Generally, a partnership interest is a capital property. As a capital property, a partnership interest has an adjusted cost base. The gain or loss from the disposition of a partnership interest is calculated as the difference between the adjusted cost base of the partnership interest and the partner's proceeds of disposition. The taxable capital gain or allowable capital loss arising on the disposition of the partnership interest is included in a partner's income. The basic computation made on the disposition of a partnership interest is illustrated by Exhibit 18-1.

EXHIBIT 18-1

Gain or Loss on Disposal of a Partnership Interest

		Case 1		*Case 2*
Proceeds received by partner for his or her interest		$22,750		$12,750
Less: Adjusted cost base of his or her interest	$16,000		$16,000	
Selling expenses	1,750	17,750	1,750	17,750
Partner's capital gain (loss)		$ 5,000		$ (5,000)
Taxable capital gain (allowable capital loss)		$ 2,500		$ (2,500)

¶18,070   Adjusted cost base (ACB)

The adjusted cost base of a partner's partnership interest is basically the partner's net investment in the partnership business. Each partner's adjusted cost base is the original cost of the partnership interest with adjustments for earnings, drawings and other similar transactions between a partner and the partnership.

¶18,070.10   *Additions to ACB*

Generally, items which increase a partner's net investment in the partnership are added to the adjusted cost base of the partnership interest. The following are some of the more common items added to the adjusted cost base:

(a) the partner's share of income of the partnership for each fiscal period, except that 100% of any gains on the disposition of capital property owned by the partnership is added to the adjusted cost base, instead of the inclusion percentage;   ITA: 53(1)(*e*)(i)

- This income will be taxed in the partner's hands and, therefore, represents the amount of tax-paid income that can be withdrawn from the partnership tax-free.

(b) the partner's share of any capital dividends received on shares of the capital stock of a corporation which were owned by the partnership;   ITA: 53(1)(*e*)(ii), 83(2)

- Capital dividends are not taxable, so they should be able to be withdrawn from the partnership without further tax to the partners. If this was not added to the ACB, then when the funds are withdrawn, a negative ACB would be created with an eventual capital gain higher than it should be.

(c) the partner's share of the net proceeds on death of life insurance policies received by the partnership after 1971;   ITA: 53(1)(*e*)(iii)

- Life insurance proceeds are not taxable, so they should be able to be withdrawn from the partnership without further tax to the partners. If this was not added to the ACB, then when the funds are withdrawn, a negative ACB would be created with an eventual capital gain higher than it should be.

(d) the partner's contributions of capital to the partnership after 1971.   ITA: 53(1)(*e*)(iv)

- Clearly capital contributions should increase the ACB to allow them to be withdrawn at a later date tax-free.

¶18,070.20 *Deductions from ACB*

Generally, items which reduce or erode a partner's net investment in the partnership are deducted from the adjusted cost base of the partnership's interest. The following are some of the more common items deducted from the adjusted cost base:

(a) the partner's share of any loss of the partnership for each fiscal period (other than limited partnership losses), except that 100% of losses on the disposition of capital property owned by the partnership is deducted from the adjusted cost base, instead of the inclusion percentage;
    ITA: 53(2)(*c*)(i)

- Consistent with the treatment of income explained above, partnership losses are deductible by the partners on their individual or corporate returns, and any tax refunds come to the partners. As a result of receiving this benefit, the losses reduce the ACB.

(b) the partner's share of any charitable gifts or political contributions made by the partnership;
    ITA: 53(2)(*c*)(iii)

- The partners, as individuals or corporations, receive the tax benefits of the charitable gifts and political donations allocated to them. This is like them receiving a cash distribution from the partnership and then making the donation themselves. The result is a reduction in the ACB of their partnership interest.

(c) the partner's drawings of his or her share of partnership income or capital;
    ITA: 53(2)(*c*)(v)

- As capital contributions increase the partner's ACB, so drawings of any kind reduce the ACB.

(d) the amount of any investment tax credit used by the partner in respect of expenditures made by the partnership.
    ITA: 53(2)(*c*)(vi)

- The ITC is a credit reported on the partner's tax return, so it is treated in a similar fashion to the charitable and political donations.

¶18,070.30 *Summary of ACB adjustments*

Exhibit 18-2 summarizes the most common adjustments to the ACB of a partnership interest.

EXHIBIT 18-2

SUMMARY
PARTNER'S ACB IN A PARTNERSHIP

Capital

Add	Capital contributions
Deduct	Capital withdrawals

Income

Add	Partner's share of the partnership's income
Deduct	Partner's share of the partnership's losses
Add	Partner's contributions to finance partnership losses
Deduct	Partner's drawings from partnership income
Add	Untaxed portion of any capital gain (The TCG is included in income that has been added above to the ACB.)
Deduct	Untaxed portion of any capital losses

Add	Partner's share of capital dividends (These dividends are in the partnership, but not in the income, so they need to increase the ACB. Then, their withdrawal will not cause a negative ACB, since the withdrawal is of funds that should be received tax-free.)

Other

Add	Partner's share of life insurance proceeds received by the partnership (These proceeds are in the partnership, but not in the income, so they need to increase the ACB. Then their withdrawal will not cause a negative ACB, since the withdrawal is of funds that should be received tax-free.)
Deduct	Partner's share of charitable donations or political contributions (Since partnerships do not pay tax, it is the partners who use the charitable donations. This adjustment recognizes that the funds, while not deductible, have been paid out of the partnership.)
Deduct	Partner's share of any investment tax credit earned by the partnership.

¶18,070.40 *Negative ACB*

The adjusted cost base of a partnership interest may be a negative amount. A negative adjusted cost base in respect of all other capital property other than a partnership interest is deemed to be a capital gain as soon as it arises even when there is no actual disposition of the property at the time. The deemed capital gain does not apply where a negative adjusted cost base arises in a partnership interest. As long as there is no actual disposition of his or her interest by the partner, a negative adjusted cost base will not be taxed as a capital gain. However, this special treatment for partnership interests does apply to a negative adjusted cost base of limited and certain other passive partners. This represents an extension of the at-risk rules and its implementation affects film tax shelters, in particular.

ITA: 40(3)

ITA: 40(3.1)

Where a taxpayer disposes of only part of his or her partnership interest, an equivalent proportion of the adjusted cost base as calculated at that particular time is deducted from the proceeds of disposition in computing the taxpayer's gain or loss.

If the adjusted cost base of the partnership interest is negative at the time of disposition, the negative amount (or, in a partial disposition, an equivalent portion of the negative amount) is added to the gain otherwise determined. Exhibit 18-3 illustrates this treatment.

ITA: 40(1), 100(2)

EXHIBIT 18-3
Treatment of Negative Adjusted Cost Base

Assumptions: Partner sells a partnership interest for proceeds of disposition of $5,000. The selling expenses total $250. The partner's adjusted cost base of the partnership interest is a negative $1,250.

Proceeds of disposition received	$5,000
Deduct: selling expenses	250
Gain otherwise determined	$4,750
Add: negative adjusted cost base at date of sale	1,250
Partner's capital gain	$6,000
Taxable capital gain (½ × $6,000)	$3,000

¶18,080 Reorganization of Partnerships

The provisions which deal with the reorganization of partnerships parallel the tax-free corporate rollover discussed in the preceding chapters. Conceptually, the problems encountered in the partnership scenario are similar in nature to those in the context of a corporation. The major difference is that on a transfer of property to a partnership the consideration received by the transferor must include a "partnership interest" as compared to "share capital". Both types of reorganizations can include non-partnership interest consideration or "boot" and the amount of "boot" is restricted to prevent the stripping of accrued gains on the entity's assets.

¶18,085   Transfer of partnership property to a corporation

The partners of the partnership may wish to incorporate the partnership's assets. The eligible assets of the partnership can be transferred to a Canadian corporation for consideration, including shares of the corporation. These shares then become the assets of the partnership. The partnership must only be a Canadian partnership if the property that is being transferred is real property that is capital property, or an interest or option in respect of real property. This rollover parallels directly the rollover available to a person transferring property to a corporation. A joint election is required by the corporation and all of the members of the partnership.

ITA: 85(2)

ITA: 85(1)

It may be desirable to subsequently wind up the partnership and have the former partners hold the shares of the corporation directly. This transaction is accomplished on a tax-deferred basis. In order for the rollover to apply, the only partnership assets must be cash or shares received from the corporation as consideration for the transfer of partnership property to the corporation. Also, the partnership must be wound up within 60 days of the transfer. This rollover is automatic and there are no filing requirements.

ITA: 85(3)
ITA: 85(3)(c)

ITA: 85(3)(b)

Example Problem

The partners of ABC Partnership wish to incorporate the partnership's asset. The partnership's asset is land which was purchased in 1996 for $12,000. The fair market value of the land is now $48,000 and the land is capital property. On the transfer of the land to the corporation the partnership receives the following from the corporation:

Cash	$12,000
Preferred shares (FMV)	12,000
Common shares (FMV)	24,000
Total	$48,000

One month after the transfer of the land to the corporation, the partnership is wound up.

ITA: 85(3)

— *REQUIRED*

What is the position of Mr. Aleph who received a ⅔ share of each asset distributed by the partnership on the winding-up? The adjusted cost base of his partnership interest is $12,000.

— *SOLUTION*

Cost of preferred shares:		
Lesser of:		
(a) fair market value of shares (⅔ × $12,000)		$ 8,000
(b) ACB of partnership interest less FMV of consideration other than shares ($12,000 – ⅔ × $12,000)		$ 4,000
Cost of common shares:		
ACB of partnership interest		$12,000
Less: FMV of non-share consideration	$8,000	
cost of preferred shares	4,000	12,000
		Nil

ITA: 85(3)(e)

ITA: 85(3)(f)

Proceeds of disposition of partnership interest:	
Deemed cost of preferred shares	$ 4,000
Deemed cost of common shares	Nil
Other consideration	8,000
Total proceeds	$12,000

ITA: 85(3)(g)

Since the proceeds for the partnership interest equal its adjusted cost base, there is no gain or loss on the disposition of the partnership interest. As a general rule, as long as the "boot" received by the partner does not exceed his or her ACB there will not be a gain.

¶18,090 Transfer of property to a partnership

¶18,090.10 *Rollover available*

Generally, when a partner transfers property to a partnership, the partner is deemed to dispose of the property for proceeds equal to its fair market value and the partnership is deemed to acquire the property for the same amount. This rule may result in gains or losses where there is no actual change in economic interest in the property. To prevent this inequity, a rollover is provided where a Canadian partnership acquires property from a person who immediately after the transfer is a partner. To qualify, the partnership must be a Canadian partnership immediately after the transfer, and all partners must elect to have the rollover apply. The types of property that can be transferred are limited to capital property (including depreciable capital property), eligible capital property, inventory (including land inventory) and certain resource properties. *ITA: 97(1)* *ITA: 97(2)*

A Canadian partnership is defined as a partnership all the members of which are resident in Canada at the particular time. *ITA: 102*

The partners elect an agreed amount on a form which is filed with the CRA. The agreed amount is the proceeds of disposition of the property to the partner and the cost of the property to the partnership. In essence, the same rules apply for establishing the elected amount range for transfers of property to a partnership as are applicable to transfers of property to a corporation. At the upper limit, the agreed amount at which the property can be transferred is the fair market value of that property. At the lower limit, the agreed amount can be set at the fair market value of consideration, other than a partnership interest, received for the property transferred, if that amount is not less than the lesser of the fair market value and the tax value of the property transferred. Any excess of the agreed amount over the fair market value of the consideration other than a partnership interest received is added to the adjusted cost base of the partnership interest of the partner.

¶18,090.20 *Terminal loss*

A loss-denial rule applies where the fair market value of depreciable property is less than both its cost and its undepreciated capital cost (terminal loss) and the transferor is a person (i.e., an individual, a corporation or a trust), or partnership. Where the transferor or certain affiliated persons hold the property 30 days after the disposition, no loss is recognized on the transfer. Instead, the accrued terminal loss is retained by the transferor in the same CCA class. The recognition of the loss by the transferor will generally be deferred until such time as the depreciable property is transferred to a person who is not an affiliated person. *ITA: 13(21.2)* *ITA: 251.1*

¶18,090.30 *Non-arm's length transfer*

An adjustment must be made where depreciable property is transferred to the partnership by a non-arm's length person or partnership (the transferor), and the capital cost of the property to the transferor is less than the cost of the property to the partnership. The partnership is deemed to have a capital cost equal to the cost of the property to the transferor plus the person's or partnership's taxable capital gain inclusion. The deemed capital cost is for purposes of computing capital cost allowance, not future capital gains or losses. *ITA: 13(7)(e)*

¶18,090.40   Capital loss

Where the transferor is a corporation, trust or partnership (but not an individual), a capital loss arising on the transfer of non-depreciable capital property to a partnership of which the transferor is a majority-interest partner is denied. A majority-interest partner as defined is a partner who is entitled to more than one-half of the partnership's income from all sources in the immediately preceding year or would be entitled to more than one-half of the amount paid to all members of the partnership if it were wound up at the time. The loss is retained by the transferor and not recognized until the earliest of several events. Where the taxpayer is an individual who is a majority-interest partner, the superficial loss rule will apply to deny the loss and add it to the cost of the property in the partnership.

ITA: 40(3.3), 40(3.4)

ITA: 248(1)

ITA: 40(2)(g)(i), 54

¶18,090.50   Capital cost of depreciable property

On the transfer of depreciable capital property, the partnership generally assumes the position of the transferor with respect to the capital cost of the property for the determination of capital gains and recapture when the partnership eventually disposes of the property.

¶18,090.60   Reallocation of deferred income

Recognize that, as a result of the rollover, part of the deferred income may, in effect, be transferred to the other partners. Each partner will include his or her proportionate share of the income when the partnership disposes of the property.

ITA: 97(2)

Example Problem

Mr. Black and Mr. Red operate accounting practices as sole practitioners. They wish to form a partnership in which Mr. Black will hold a 60% share and Mr. Red a 40% share. The relevant financial data for the separate practices as at December 31, 2007 are as follows:

	Mr. Black		Mr. Red	
	Cost	FMV	Cost	FMV
Cash	$ 94,000	$ 94,000	$ 60,000	$ 60,000
Marketable securities	20,000	10,000	10,000	5,000
Land (capital property)	5,000	50,000	—	—
Accounts receivable	130,000	130,000	40,000	40,000
Furniture and fixtures	80,000	80,000	30,000	34,000
Leasehold improvements	30,000	40,000	20,000	—
Goodwill	20,000	50,000	—	—
	$379,000	$454,000	$160,000	$139,000
Accounts payable		$120,000		$130,000

The tax values of the following assets are:

	Mr. Black	Mr. Red
Furniture and fixtures (UCC)	$70,000	$24,000
Leasehold improvements (UCC)	30,000	—
Balance of cumulative eligible capital	9,000	—

— *REQUIRED*

(A) Compute the values at which the assets should be transferred to defer any immediate tax consequences of the transfer assuming the accounts payable are not transferred to the partnership and no consideration other than a partnership interest is received.

(B) Compute the adjusted cost bases of the partnership interests of Mr. Black and Mr. Red.

(C) Indicate the tax effects of having the partnership assume the accounts payable of Mr. Black and Mr. Red.

(D) Indicate the tax consequences to Mr. Black and Mr. Red of having the partnership dispose of the land in 2007 for proceeds of disposition of $50,000. Assume that the land is capital property to the partnership, and that no consideration, other than a partnership interest, is received by the partners.

— *SOLUTION*

(A)

	Mr. Black	Mr. Red
Cash	$ 94,000	$ 60,000
Marketable securities	10,000[(1)]	5,000[(2)]
Land	5,000	—
Accounts receivable	130,000	40,000
Furniture and fixtures	70,000	24,000
Leasehold improvements	30,000	—
Goodwill ($^4/_3 \times$ $9,000)	12,000	—
	$351,000	$129,000

(B)

Adjusted cost base:

	Mr. Black	Mr. Red
Transfer value of assets	$351,000	$129,000

(C) If Mr. Black's accounts payable are transferred to the partnership, the transfer value of his net assets would be $231,000 ($351,000 – $120,000) resulting in an adjusted cost base for his partnership interest of $231,000. In Mr. Red's case there will be a gain of $1,000. This results from the requirement that the elected transfer price be no less than the non-partnership interest consideration received (which in this case would be $130,000). Since the proceeds of disposition are $130,000 and the adjusted cost base of the assets is $129,000 there would be a gain of $1,000. Since the proceeds of disposition of the property do not exceed the fair market value of the non-partnership interest consideration received the adjusted cost base of the partnership interest to Mr. Red would be nil.

(D)

Proceeds of disposition	$50,000
Adjusted cost base	5,000
Capital gain	$45,000
Taxable capital gain (½ of $45,000)	$22,500
Income to be allocated	$22,500

	Mr. Black	Mr. Red
Share of income	$ 13,500	$ 9,000
Adjusted cost base of partnership interest	$351,000	$129,000
Add: share of capital gain (i.e., income from taxable capital gain + untaxed fraction of capital gain)	27,000	18,000
	$378,000	$147,000

On the transfer of the land to the partnership, Mr. Black deferred the recognition of a $45,000 capital gain. When the partnership disposed of the land, it realized a capital gain of $45,000 and a taxable gain of $22,500. A portion of that capital gain was allocated to each partner as his share of the partnership income for the year. Because a portion of the taxable capital gain was allocated to Mr. Red, as well as Mr. Black, part of the deferred gain ($18,000) and the tax liability on that gain was essentially transferred from Mr. Black to Mr. Red. The partnership agreement could have been structured to require the full amount of this gain to be allocated to Mr. Black to avoid this inequity.

(1) Under the definition of "superficial loss", Mr. Black will have a superficial loss, since the partnership is a person that is affiliated with him. Accordingly, the loss is deemed to be nil. The amount of the denied loss will be added to the adjusted cost base of the marketable securities to the partnership.

ITA: 54, 251.1(1)(*e*)
ITA: 53(1)(*f*)

(2) Since Mr. Red is not a majority interest partner he is not denied the loss.

¶18,100   Fiscal Period of Terminated Partnership

The fiscal period of a terminated partnership is deemed to have ended on the date the partnership ceases.

ITA: 99

Where an individual is a member of a partnership, the individual may elect to have the fiscal period terminate on the date it would have normally ended had the partnership not ceased to exist. The election is only valid if the individual is resident in Canada on the date the fiscal period of the partnership normally would have ended.

The purpose of these provisions is to permit a partner to spread his or her income over two years rather than have two fiscal years' income (i.e., more than 12 months of income) included in the same taxation year of the individual partner.

The Act, which requires a December 31 fiscal year-end for a partnership of which an individual is a member, renders this rule generally unnecessary, because the termination of a partnership cannot cause more than 12 months of income to be reported in the same year. If an off-calendar year and the alternative method are used, by the partnership, then section 99 may have some application.

ITA: 249.1(4)

¶18,200   TRUSTS

¶18,210   Nature of Trust

¶18,215   General

¶18,215.10   *Definition of trust*

Before dealing with the taxation of a trust one must understand what a trust is. The law of trusts is a separate area of law just as the law relating to land and the law relating to contracts are separate areas of law.

A trust is not a contract. In a contract there are mutual covenants (or promises) where one person promises to do something in return for the other person promising to do something. It is enforceable only by the parties and is dependent upon "consideration".[1] A trust is a relationship whereby a person (who is called a trustee) is bound to deal with property over which he or she has control (which is called the trust property) for the benefit of persons (who are called the beneficiaries) any of whom may enforce the obligation.[2]

A trust is created when a person (called the settlor) transfers the title of a property to the trustee who holds it for the benefit of the income and capital beneficiaries. Therefore for a trust to exist, there must be three certainties present.

(1) There must be certainty of intention; the settler must have intended to establish a trust.

(2) There must be a certainty of subject matter; there must be a specific property given to the trustee.

(3) There must be certainty of objects; it must be clear who the income and capital beneficiaries are.

---

[1] J. Wardlaw, "Inter Vivos Trusts: A Base Primer," *Estates and Trusts Quarterly*, Vol. 5, 1980-81, p. 298.

[2] Underhill and Hayton, *Law Relating to Trusts and Trustees*, 14th ed., 1987, p. 3.

One of the fundamental characteristics of a trust is the separation of title-holding and the management of property from its enjoyment. For example, assume that a parent wants to provide an income for a child in order to pay that child's personal living expenses. That parent may also be prepared to transfer income — earning property to the child when he or she has reached a certain age. Until that time, however, the parent does not want the child to control the property. A trust may be used to accomplish all of these objectives. The investments would be transferred to a trustee. The trust agreement would provide for the distribution of income to the child annually and the distribution of the investments to the child when the child reaches a specific age.

The following diagram illustrates the relationship among the settlor, trustees and beneficiaries.

TAXATION OF TRUSTS – OVERVIEW

Settlor ⟶ (3 certainties) **Trustee**
(Gives property to **Executor/Executrix**
the trustee/executor(trix)) (owns and controls the property
Living settlor – *inter vivos* for the benefit of the beneficiaries)
Deceased settlor – testamentary

Powers given to Trustee:
Discretionary

Non discretionary

**Estate
or
Trust**

Beneficiaries
Income
Capital

Trusts are particularly useful when the beneficiaries are minors. Generally, with certain limited exceptions, a minor cannot enter into a binding contract. All other contracts are voidable at the option of the minor. This means that they cannot be enforced unless ratified by the minor when he or she reaches the age of majority. As a result, those dealing with minors don't want to transfer property to or contract with them. Instead they would prefer to deal with a trustee who holds property or enters into contracts for the benefit of the minor.

¶18,215.20 *Taxation of trusts*

A trust is considered to be a taxpayer separate and distinct from its settlor, trustees or beneficiaries. As a separate taxpayer, the trust is deemed to be an individual. Therefore, the income of the trust is generally computed in the same way as is the income of any individual.

ITA: 104(2)

¶18,215.30 *Residency of trusts*

Determining the residency of a trust is an important tax issue. If the trust is resident in Canada, it will be taxed on its worldwide income. If it is not resident in Canada, it will be taxed in Canada as a non-resident.

There is still some uncertainty as to the rules that determine the residence of a trust. The leading Canadian case on the question of the residence of a trust is *Thibodeau Family Trust v. The Queen*. In that case, one trustee was resident in Canada. Two other trustees were residents of Bermuda. The assets and administration of the trust were in Bermuda. Under the provisions of the trust agreement, the trustees had the power to act by a majority.

78 DTC 6376 (F.C.T.D.)

Evidence suggested that the trustees in Bermuda had exercised independent judgment and had at times declined to accept the suggestion of the Canadian trustee. Some of the beneficiaries were resident in the U.S. while others were resident in Canada.

The court held that the trust was solely resident in Bermuda. The decision was based on two facts: the majority of the trustees were resident in Bermuda and the trust document permitted a majority decision on all matters of trustees' discretion.

The decision provides little assistance in situations where a majority of trustees do not reside in one jurisdiction or situations where trustees must act unanimously. The decision may also not be helpful where the trustee is a corporation resident in several jurisdictions.

The CRA indicates that in its view a trust is generally considered to reside where the trustee, executor, administrator, heir or other legal representative who manages the trust or controls the trust's assets resides. The CRA will consider a number of factors in deciding who has management and control of the trust. Where there is more than one trustee, the trust will be considered by the CRA to reside in the jurisdiction in which the trustee who exercises a more substantial portion of management and control resides. Where several trustees exercise equal control and trustees exercising more than 50% of control reside in one jurisdiction, the trust will reside in that jurisdiction. *[IT-447]*

¶18,220   Types of trust

¶18,220.10   *Inter vivos and testamentary*

A testamentary trust arises as the consequence of the death of an individual. An *inter vivos* trust is created while the settlor is still alive and it is defined in the Act to be a trust other than a testamentary trust. *[ITA: 108(1)]*

A testamentary trust can be "tainted" and, hence, no longer a testamentary trust, if property is contributed to the trust otherwise than as a result of the individual's death. For example, if some other individual contributes property to the trust, the trust loses its testamentary status and becomes an *inter vivos* trust. A trust can also lose its testamentary trust status if it borrows money from a beneficiary or someone not dealing at arm's length with a beneficiary. This borrowing restriction was put in place to prevent income splitting through this type of trust to take advantage of the graduated tax rates. *[ITA: 108 "testamentary trust" (b)]* *[Proposed in Bill C-33, Nov. 22, 2006]*

¶18,220.20   *Discretionary and non-discretionary*

Trusts may be discretionary or non-discretionary. In a discretionary trust, the trustee is given the power of choice. The trustee may be given the power to determine the date of the distribution of trust property, whether income is to be paid to a beneficiary, how much is to be paid to a beneficiary and in what proportions among a group of beneficiaries it is to be paid. For example, by using their discretionary powers trustees may, in certain circumstances, allocate income to taxpayers with a lower marginal tax rate. The trustee may also be given the discretion to decide when a trust is to be terminated. The flexibility provided by the discretionary trust has made it a useful tool in tax planning. With a non-discretionary trust, the trustee does not have the power of choice. The trust document sets out certain decisions which the trustees are obliged to implement.

¶18,220.30   *Personal trust and commercial trust*

A "personal trust" is either a testamentary trust or an *inter vivos* trust, where no beneficial interest in the trust was acquired for consideration paid either to the trust or to a person who made a contribution to the trust. The term "commercial trust" is not defined in the Act. *[ITA: 248(1) "personal trust"]*

The term "commercial trust" is generally used to describe a trust that is not a personal trust. A commercial trust may include a "specified investment flow-through trust" (SIFT trust), often referred to as an income trust. A SIFT trust is a trust that is resident in Canada with its units listed publicly and that holds one or more non-portfolio investment properties. This no-portfolio income of such a trust is to bear a special tax on its distribution. *[ITA: 122.1 [proposed in Dec. 21, 2006 Draft Legislation]]*

¶18,220.40 *Spousal trust*

A spousal trust is one which meets certain conditions set out in the Act. The conditions for an *inter vivos* spousal trust are provided in the Act. The conditions for a testamentary spousal trust are also set out in the Act. In either case, under the trust:

ITA: 73(1)
ITA: 70(6)

(i) the spouse must be entitled to receive all of the income of the trust that arises before the spouse's death; and

(ii) no person except the spouse may, before the spouse's death, receive or otherwise obtain the use of any of the income or capital of the trust.

In addition, for an *inter vivos* trust to qualify as a spousal trust, both the settlor and trust must be resident in Canada at the time of transfer. In the case of a testamentary trust there is a further requirement that the property must vest in the trust within 36 months after the death of a taxpayer, or a later period where a written application has been made to the Minister.

If all of the conditions for a spousal trust have been satisfied, property is transferred to the trust for proceeds equal to its tax cost. For example, non-depreciable capital property may be transferred to the trust at its adjusted cost base, while depreciable capital property may be transferred to a trust at the property's proportionate amount of undepreciated capital cost of the class. The trust is deemed to acquire the property at a cost equal to the tax cost of the property to the transferor. The tax consequences apply automatically. No election need be filed.

An election can be made not to have the rollover provisions apply. If this election is made, the general rules apply and the property will be deemed to have been disposed of for proceeds of disposition equal to its fair market value.

ITA: 70(6.2), 73(1)

¶18,220.50 *Alter-ego trust*

Alter-ego trusts were created to allow an individual to create a trust for him or her self. The concept is that an individual would transfer property to a trustee who would hold the property for the individual's benefit until the individual asked for the property back or died. The idea was to allow people to organize their financial affairs well in advance of death or disability. The trust document would indicate who would receive the property on the individual's death thus acting as a will. In addition, the trustee would continue to manage the property in the event of the individual's incapacity thus acting as the individual's power of attorney. The issue was, could the property be transferred to the trustee without causing a deemed disposition. These rules allow individuals to rollover property to an alter-ego trust as long as the following conditions are met:

ITA: 248(1) "alter ego trust"

(i) the taxpayer was entitled to receive all the income for the trust that arose before the taxpayer's death;

(ii) no person, except the taxpayer could, before the taxpayer's death, receive or otherwise obtain the use of any of the income or capital of the trust;

(iii) the individual who establishes the trust must be 65 years of age; and

(iv) the trust is created after 1999.

This type of trust does not avoid the deemed disposition on death. That event occurs at the same time that it would have happened if no trust had been established, on the death of the taxpayer that established the trust.

¶18,220.60 *Joint spousal or common-law partner trust*

Joint spousal or common-law partner trusts are very similar in purpose and rules to the alter-ego trust. The concept is to allow an individual to transfer property to a trust in which he and his spouse or common-law partner are the beneficiaries. The property is managed in the trust until either the property is withdrawn or the individual and the spouse or

ITA: 248(1) "joint spousal or common-law partner trust"

common-law partner have died and the property is distributed to the beneficiaries. Property can be rolled over to this type of trust as the following conditions are met:

(i) the taxpayer who created the trust and/or the taxpayer's spouse or common-law partner are entitled to receive all the income of the trust that was earned prior to the later of the death of the taxpayer and the spouse or common-law partner;

(ii) that taxpayer who created the trust and/or the taxpayer's spouse or a common-law partner must be the only persons able to receive income or capital of the trust prior to the later death of the taxpayer and spouse or the common-law partner;

(iii) at the time of the trust's creation, the taxpayer creating the trust was alive and had attained 65 years of age; and

(iv) the trust was created after 1999.

This type of trust does not avoid the deemed disposition on death either. The deemed disposition occurs at the same time it would have happened if no trust had been established, on the death of the surviving spouse or common-law partner.

¶18,230 Settlement of Trust

As a general rule, capital property is transferred to the trust at fair market value. Therefore, if a settlor transfers capital property to a trust with accrued income and gains, these amounts will be taxed in the hands of the settlor. The trust will acquire the assets at a cost equal to their fair market value. As already noted, there are exceptions to the general rule for a qualifying spousal trust, an alter-ego trust or a joint spousal or common-law partner trust.

¶18,240 Computation of Income

¶18,245 Income of trust

As already discussed, the net income of the trust is computed in generally the same way as is the income of any individual.

¶18,250 Income payable to beneficiary

A trust is entitled to deduct in computing its net income, income that is paid or payable to a beneficiary. In this way, the trust is not taxed on such income, but acts as a conduit for its beneficiaries. An amount is considered to be payable to a beneficiary in a taxation year if he or she is entitled in the year to enforce payment thereof. ITA: 104(6), 104(24)

The income deducted from the trust's net income is taxed in the hands of the beneficiary as income from property unless it falls within certain categories specified in the Act. In this case, the income retains its source for the purposes of calculating the taxable income and tax payable of the beneficiary. This special treatment applies to the following sources of income: ITA: 108(5)

(a) taxable dividends from a Canadian corporation (which enables the beneficiary to utilize the dividend tax credit); ITA: 104(19)

(b) non-taxable dividends (which are then excluded from the computation of taxable income); ITA: 104(20)

(c) net taxable capital gains (net capital losses do not flow through to the beneficiary); and ITA: 104(21)

(d) foreign income and its related foreign tax paid (which enables the beneficiary to take full advantage of the foreign tax credit). ITA: 104(22)

Net taxable capital gains of a trust that are allocated to individual beneficiaries and designated by the trust are eligible for the capital gains deduction available in respect of qualified farm property and qualified shares of a small business corporation. In order to qualify, the trust must be resident in Canada throughout the year. ITA: 104(21.2), (21.3)

A trust is allowed to deduct less than the amount of income paid or payable to a beneficiary in computing its income. This provision enables a trust to utilize its loss carryforwards without having to reduce its current income distributions. Where the trust is a testamentary trust, income splitting can be achieved, thereby allowing income to be taxed at the graduated rates, notwithstanding the fact that income has been distributed to the beneficiaries. A similar rule is provided for taxable capital gains.

ITA: 104(13.1)

ITA: 104(13.2)

Example Problem

The income of a trust for the year is $6,000 of dividends from resident Canadian public corporations. The sole beneficiary of the trust is the spouse of the deceased settlor. The trustee paid $5,000 to the beneficiary.

— *REQUIRED*

What is the taxable income of the trust and the spouse?

— *SOLUTION*

(A) Trust

Income from dividends	$6,000
Deduction of amount paid to beneficiary	5,000
Net dividend income	$1,000
Gross-up (45%)	450
Taxable income	$1,450

ITA: 104(6)

(B) Spouse

Income (designated)	$5,000
Gross-up (45%)	2,250
Taxable income	$7,250

ITA: 104(19)

¶18,255 Attribution

As a general rule, where an individual has transferred or loaned property to a trust for the benefit of a non-arm's length person or a niece or nephew under the age of 18, or for the benefit of the spouse, the appropriate attribution rules will operate to include the income from the property in the income of the transferor. These rules are applicable only where the trust income would otherwise be taxed in the hands of a beneficiary. The attribution rules will also apply to any property substituted for the property originally loaned or transferred to the trust. The accumulating income (other than the income that is the subject of a preferred beneficiary election, discussed subsequently) will be subject to tax in the trust. It will not be attributed back to the transferor.

ITA: 74.3

Taxable capital gains and allowable capital losses realized by an *inter vivos* spousal trust and allocated out of the trust to be taxed in the hands of the beneficiary spouse will be attributed to the individual who loaned or transferred the property to the spousal trust. For any other *inter vivos* trust, any property income earned in the trust and allocated out to "designated persons" will be subject to attribution.

ITA: 74.2, 74.3

ITA: 74.1, 74.5(5) "designated person"

The amount to be attributed is determined by the Act. Only the income and capital gains earned by spouses and the income earned by non-arm's length persons and nieces or nephews under 18 ("designated persons") from loaned or transferred property are subject to the attribution rules.

ITA: 74.3

The amount of income of a person, who is a designated person, from property loaned or transferred to a trust to be attributed to the transferor is the lesser of:

ITA: 74.3(1)(*a*)

(a) the income of that person from the trust; and

(b) the income earned by the trust from loaned or transferred funds multiplied by the fraction where the numerator is the total income of the designated person from the trust and the denominator is the aggregate income from the trust of all designated persons.

The amount of taxable capital gains of a spouse beneficiary of a trust to be attributed is the lesser of: *ITA: 74.3(1)(b)*

(a) the amount designated by the trust to be a taxable capital gain of the beneficiary spouse; and   *ITA: 104(21)*

(b) the net taxable capital gains for the year from the disposition by the trust of the property.

The exceptions to the general attribution rules as discussed in a previous chapter also apply to trusts.   *ITA: 74.5*

Loans of property by an individual to a non-arm's length individual or indebtedness between such individuals are also subject to the attribution rules. Income will be taxed in the hands of the transferor if it may reasonably be considered that one of the main reasons for the loan was to reduce or avoid tax by having the income taxed in the transferee's hands. This rule will also apply where the loan is made to an individual or the indebtedness arises by means of a trust.   *ITA: 56(4.1)*

Example Problem

Assume that this year John Smith makes a non-interest bearing loan of $1,000 to a trust. The trust acquires a $1,000 bond. The trust has four beneficiaries: Betty Smith, John's wife, and their three children, one of whom is under 18. The income of the trust for the year prior to claiming any deductions for amounts paid or payable to the beneficiaries is $240 of which $100 is interest from the bond. All income is payable to the beneficiaries.

— *REQUIRED*

How much income is attributed to John Smith in the year?

— *SOLUTION*

There are two designated beneficiaries, Betty Smith and the child who is under 18.

The income attributed to John Smith for each designated beneficiary is determined as follows:

A = income of the designated person from the trust

$= \frac{1}{4} \times \$240 = \$60$

B = income of all designated persons from the trust

$= \$120$

C = income from the loaned property

$= \$100$

$$\frac{A}{B} \times C = \frac{\$60}{\$120} \times \$100 = \$50$$

Therefore, the total income attributed to John Smith is $50 × 2 = $100.

Two aspects of the formula should be noted. First, the income of a designated beneficiary is deemed to be received first from the income derived from property acquired with the loan. Second, the amount of income attributed in respect of the spouse or minor cannot exceed the amount of that person's income from the trust.

¶18,260   Tax on split income or "kiddie tax"

"Kiddie tax" was introduced to discourage income splitting with minor children. This tax is levied at the top marginal rate and is imposed on certain income of individuals age 17 or under. The types of income which are taxed in this way are:

ITA: 120.4

- taxable dividends and other shareholder benefits of unlisted Canadian and foreign companies received directly or through a trust or partnership; and

- income from a partnership or trust where the income is derived by the partnership or trust from the business of providing goods or services to a business carried on by a relative of the child or in which the relative participates.

The income subject to this tax is not eligible for any deductions or credits other than the dividend tax credit and foreign tax credit. Income taxed in this way is not subject to the regular attribution rules. In addition, income that is subject to kiddie tax reduces the deemed interest benefit assessed under the corporate attribution rules.

ITA: 56(5), 74.5(13)

ITA: 74.4(2)(*g*)

¶18,265   Accumulating income and preferred beneficiary election

In certain circumstances, a trust is entitled to a deduction in computing income for accumulated income for which an election was filed in respect of a beneficiary that is a preferred beneficiary. The preferred beneficiary election is a joint election made within 90 days of the trust's year-end by both the trustees and a preferred beneficiary. As a consequence of making the election, the beneficiary is required to include in income his or her share of the accumulating income of the trust. The income in the trust, having been taxed, is not subject to tax when it is actually distributed to the beneficiaries. This feature of having the income taxed in the hands of the beneficiary yet leaving the cash in the trust can be a very effective way of taxing the income in the hands of a beneficiary in a low tax bracket without the trustees giving up control over the money.

ITA: 104(14)

A preferred beneficiary is a resident of Canada who is a beneficiary of the trust and who is either the settlor of the trust, spouse or common-law partner (or former spouse or common-law partner) of the settlor, or a child, grandchild or great grandchild of the settlor of the trust (or spouses thereof) and who is entitled to the tax credit for mental or physical impairment.

ITA: 108(1), 118(3.1)

¶18,270   Computation of Tax

¶18,275   Fiscal years

The fiscal year-end of an *inter vivos* trust is December 31. The taxation year of a testamentary trust does not have to be at the end of the calendar year basis; however, it cannot exceed 12 months. The fiscal year can be based on the year for which accounts have ordinarily been made up. The first fiscal period of a testamentary trust must end no later than one year from the death of the settlor. Whatever the fiscal year of the trust, tax returns must be filed within 90 days of the end of the trust's fiscal period.

ITA: 104(23)(*a*), 249.1(1)(*b*)(i.1)

ITA: 150(1)(*c*)

A beneficiary includes in income the amount paid or payable by the trust during the year. The beneficiary includes that amount in income in the calendar year in which the trust's taxation year ends.

ITA: 104(13)

¶18,280   Tax rate

¶18,280.10   *General*

The Act provides that trusts are to be taxed as individuals. *Inter vivos* trusts are subject to a federal rate of 29%.

ITA: 122(1)

Testamentary trusts are subject to the same marginal rates of tax as individuals.

¶18,280.20   *Special tax on a SIFT trust*

To make the tax on the business income of a SIFT or income trust equitable with the tax on the same type of income earned by a corporation, a SIFT trust will be subject to a special tax. The rate of tax on the distributed non-portfolio or, in essence, business income of a SIFT trust will be the basic federal corporate rate net of the federal abatement, plus a rate of 13% to proxy a provincial corporate tax rate. This type of income will not be deducted by the trust and the after-tax distribution will be taxed in the hands of the investors as a dividend. This dividend may not be taxable immediately if the investors are pension funds or may not be taxed at all in Canada if they are non-residents.

¶18,285   Tax credits

No deduction may be made for personal credits in computing the tax payable by a trust for a taxation year. However, trusts are still entitled to claim other credits such as the dividend tax credit and the foreign tax credit.

ITA: 122(1.1)

¶18,290   Minimum tax

Trusts are subject to the minimum tax in respect of income that is not paid or payable to beneficiaries.

The $40,000 exemption from the minimum tax is available only to a testamentary trust. The $40,000 exemption must be shared by all trusts that arose as a consequence of contributions to the trust by the same individual.

Where income is accumulated in the trust and a preferred beneficiary election has been made, any amounts that are non-deductible for minimum tax purposes and that were deducted in computing the trust's income must be separately identified and allocated to the trust's beneficiaries.

¶18,300   Family Planning Uses of a Trust

The foregoing discussion of trusts would suggest a number of planning opportunities for their use in family situations. While some of these opportunities provide an income tax advantage, others may provide non-tax advantages.

¶18,305   Uses of a trust for income tax advantages

Income tax can be saved by the following uses of a trust in family planning situations.

(i) Income tax savings — A testamentary trust, which is taxed on its income with the graduated rates applicable to an individual, may attract less tax on its income than the same income taxed in the hands of an individual in a high tax bracket. Furthermore, provincial surtaxes on individuals in higher tax brackets can be reduced where the income can be taxed in a testamentary trust. This would support leaving inheritances in a testamentary trust instead of to the individual beneficiary directly.

(ii) Capital gains deduction utilization — A trust that realizes capital gains on qualifying small business corporation shares (QSBCS) can allocate such gains to the capital beneficiaries who can then use their own capital gains deduction. This sprinkling of the capital gains on such shares results in multiple use of the capital gains deduction.

(iii) Family income splitting — Where family income splitting is possible, and attribution can be avoided, on a transfer of income-producing and or gains-producing property to a family member, the same income splitting benefits can be achieved with the use of a trust. At the same time, the use of a trust may have additional advantages, as discussed below.

¶18,310 Uses of a trust for non-tax advantages

Trusts can be used to achieve advantages that are not directly related to income tax considerations in family planning situations.

(i) Control and management — Family members can be provided with a source of income as beneficiaries of a trust without allowing them to control the assets that produce the income. The original owner of the property can maintain control over the assets through the appointment of the trustees. Assets can be managed for the benefit of the beneficiaries where those beneficiaries are not considered to be capable or do not have the time or expertise to manage the assets on their own. Income and capital can be distributed at the appropriate time and in the appropriate manner, according to the objectives of the plan.

(ii) Asset protection — Assets held in a trust are generally owned by the trust, as distinct from an individual. These assets held in a trust are, in essence, "creditor proofed" and, generally, not accessible to the creditors of an individual. The assets held in a trust may not be subject to equalization in a marital breakdown situation.

(iii) Facilitation of distributions on death — Property held in a trust is not part of an estate subject to a will that must be probated. This may avoid probate fees. Property transferred to a trust prior to death can be transferred in private and not be subject to a public probating of a will or be contested, as a distribution under a will can be.

¶18,800   REVIEW QUESTIONS

(1) What does the term "partnership" mean and where would you find the definition?

(2) A limited partner can deduct in full losses allocated to that partner by the partnership. True or false? Explain.

(3) An older man, Dadd, and his son, Ladd, wish to carry on a business as a partnership. Dadd is going to contribute land, building and equipment and cash while Ladd is going to contribute energy. They have agreed that they will split the profit from the business on a 50/50 basis; however, they would allocate any capital gain on the land and building fully to Dadd. In addition, any losses in the first five years are to be allocated fully to Dadd. What are your comments on the allocation of the gains and losses?

(4) Assume that you are a partner in a partnership and you are entitled to 25% of the income. How would your income allocation and adjusted cost base be affected by a $1,200 capital gain realized by the partnership?

(5) Assume that you are a partner in a partnership and you are entitled to 25% of the income. How would your income allocation and adjusted cost base be affected by a $100,000 receipt from a life insurance policy on the death of one of your partners?

(6) Ms. Jones is about to become a partner in a partnership and she wants to contribute some property on a rollover basis. There are 13 other partners involved although one of them has just moved to the U.S. for a four-year assignment. Should Ms. Jones have any concerns about the availability of the rollover?   ITA: 97(2)

(7) What is a trust?

(8) Comment on this statement: "Trusts are taxed in much the same way as partnerships; they are both conduits of income and neither is liable to pay tax".

(9) How is a testamentary and an *inter vivos* trust created?

(10) What is a discretionary trust and how does it work?

(11) One method of transferring the tax liability from the trust to the beneficiary is to either pay out the income or make it payable to the beneficiaries. What types of income retain their source for purposes of calculating the taxable income and tax payable of the beneficiary?   ITA: 104(6)

(12) Ms. Betty is the sole beneficiary of a trust that arose on the death of her father. He died on March 15, 2006. March 15 is the year-end chosen for the trust. When does the trust file a tax return for the fiscal period ended March 15, 2007? When does Ms. Betty report the income that is allocated to her by the trust in fiscal 2007?

(13) Mr. Bill had an income interest in a trust set up on his father's death. He now finds that he needs some capital to pay off gambling debts, so he is selling his income interest to his sister for $30,000. What are the tax implications to Mr. Bill and his sister?

(14) Ms. Daisy had a capital interest in a trust set up on her father's death. She now finds that she needs some capital to pay off shopping debts, so she is selling her interest in the trust to her chauffeur for $45,000. What are the tax implications to Ms. Daisy and her chauffeur?

¶18,825 MULTIPLE CHOICE QUESTIONS

Question 1

Bert & Ernie
Partnership Income Statement
For the year ended December 31, 2007

Income:

Consulting fees		$300,000
Dividends received from low-rate income of a CCPC		40,000
Gain of sale of shares of taxable Canadian corporations		120,000
		$460,000

Expenses:

Salaries to staff	$50,000	
Capital cost allowance on equipment	15,000	
Office rent	10,000	
Charitable donations	20,000	$ 95,000
Net income		$365,000

The dividends were received from a CCPC whose income was eligible for the small business deduction.

Bert and Ernie each took drawings of $30,000 in the year.

Bert and Ernie share income from the partnership equally. Bert has no other source of income in 2007. Bert will have taxable income in 2007 of:

(A) $182,500

(B) $187,500

(C) $167,500

(D) $171,500

Question 2

On January 1, 2007, Ann and Bob formed a partnership to provide window cleaning services. The partners each contributed $5,000 and agreed that all income and losses would be shared equally. For the fiscal period January 1 to December 31, 2007, the following information is available.

(1) The partnership earned income for tax purposes of $200,000. Included in this amount is a taxable capital gain of $40,000.

(2) The partnership made charitable donations of $12,000.

(3) Ann took draws totalling $70,000.

(4) Ann contributed additional capital of $14,000 to the partnership.

The adjusted cost base of Ann's partnership interest at January 1, 2008, is:

(A) $33,000

(B) $43,000

(C) $63,000

(D) $69,000

Question 3

Al Smith settled a trust in favour of his two children on May 1, 2007. He settled the trust with marketable securities worth $50,000. His adjusted cost base for the marketable securities was $20,000. Al, his wife, and a family friend were named as trustees. His two children are ages five and six. Which one of the following statements is FALSE?

(A) The tax return for the first year of the trust is due March 30, 2008.

(B) The trust is entitled to a deduction in computing its income for amounts paid to the children during the year.

(C) Income in the trust will be subject to a 29% federal rate of tax.

(D) Al can defer the recognition of the capital gain on the transfer of the securities to the trust.

Question 4

The James Stewart family trust was created on and as a consequence of the death of James Stewart on May 1, 2007. Which one of the following statements with respect to the trust is TRUE?

(A) The trust must have a December 31 year-end.

(B) The income in the trust will be subject to the same graduated rates of tax applicable to individuals.

(C) The trust return is due six months after the year-end of the trust.

(D) The trust is not entitled to claim a dividend tax credit for dividends received and retained in the trust.

Question 5

Which of the following types of trusts has a deemed disposition of all its assets at fair market value on the settlor's death?

(A) An *inter vivos* trust

(B) A joint partner trust

(C) An alter ego trust

(D) A discretionary trust

Question 6

Which of the following is **not** an advantage of providing for testamentary trusts in your will for each of your children with a giftover to your grandchildren on each child's death?

(A) Income-splitting using the available designations.   ITA: 104(13.1), 104(13.2)

(B) Avoiding a deemed disposition of assets at fair market value on the child's death that would result if the assets were left directly to the child.

(C) Avoiding the deemed disposition of trust assets at fair market value at the end of 21 years.

(D) Providing your children with beneficial ownership over their inheritances, but giving control over their inheritances to the trustees of each trust.

¶18,825

¶18,850 EXERCISES

Exercise 1

ITA: 96, 110.1, 118.1, 121

The following income statement was prepared for Bob and Stan Tax Services, a partnership of two individuals who share income equally:

Bob and Stan Tax Services

INCOME STATEMENT

for the year ended December 31, 2007

Gross revenue from operations		$400,000
Less: Depreciation on office furniture	$ 3,750	
Donations to charities	5,500	
Dues to Canadian Tax Foundation	550	
Employees' salaries	67,220	
Fringe benefits for employees	11,500	
Heat, light and water	2,400	
Interest expense	725	
Membership in fitness club	1,250	
Office rent	9,000	
Office supplies	2,250	
Repairs and maintenance	575	104,720
		$295,280
Dividends received from a taxable Canadian corporation		4,000
Capital gain		5,000
Net income		$304,280

Additional Information

(1) Maximum capital cost allowance on the furniture for the year is $4,300.

(2) The partners each took drawings of $54,000 in the year.

(3) The dividends were received from a CCPC, all of whose income was eligible for the small business deduction.

— REQUIRED

Bob is your client. He has received personal investment income consisting of $3,500 in Canadian-source dividends and $1,200 in interest income. Determine his taxable income for 2007 and analyze the nature of his income.

Exercise 2

ITA: 53(1)(*e*), 53(2)(*c*)

Early in 2002, a partnership was formed between David and Katie to carry on a professional accounting practice. Both partners made an initial contribution of $50,000 at that time agreeing to make equal drawings and to share equally in the profits and losses of the practice. The following data pertain to the partnership business during the period from its inception to the present:

Income of the partnership during the period	$450,000
Losses of the partnership during the period	15,000
Net taxable capital gains included in the above income (2005)	20,000
Drawings by the partners in the period	176,000
Capital dividends received by the partnership	4,000
Charitable donations made by the partnership	27,000
In 2007, Katie will retire from the partnership and will receive in full settlement of her partnership interest	250,000

— REQUIRED

What are the tax consequences to Katie of the disposition of her partnership interest in 2007?

Exercise 3

ITA: 104

On January 1, 2007, Mr. Ruester settled a trust for the benefit of his two children, Rebecca and Robert, both over the age of 18, neither of whom has other income. Robert attends, for eight months a year, a university in Canada where tuition is $3,500 per year. All tuition for 2007 was paid in respect of that year. Under the terms of the trust, the trustees have complete discretion to allocate the accumulated income to the beneficiaries in any manner they wish. The trust earned income from cash transferred to the trust by Mr. Ruester. For the 2007 taxation year, the trust received the following income:

Interest	$11,500
Dividends	9,000
Capital gain	9,000

The trustees paid the income, and made the appropriate designations as follows:

	Interest	Divi-dend	Capital gain
Rebecca	$5,500	$3,000	$3,000
Robert	1,500	3,000	3,000
Total paid	$7,000	$6,000	$6,000
Total income accumulated in trust	$4,500	$3,000	$3,000

The remaining income was accumulated in the trust.

The dividends were received from a CCPC, all of whose income was eligible for the small business deduction.

— REQUIRED

Compute the taxable income and the federal taxes payable of the trust and each beneficiary.

¶18,875   ASSIGNMENT PROBLEMS

Problem 1

ITA: 53(1)(*e*), 53(2)(*c*)

The following income statement was prepared for Ludlum, Clancy, Follet & Associates, a partnership comprised of four partners who share income equally:

Ludlum, Clancy, Follet & Associates
INCOME STATEMENT
for the year ended December 31, 2007

Gross revenue		$994,250
Less:		
Professional staff employee salaries	$229,000	
Office salaries	74,000	
Rent	42,000	
Office supplies	17,000	
Client entertainment	5,075	
Capital cost allowance	16,222	
Donations to charities	250,000	633,297
		$360,953
Gain on sale of securities of public companies	$100,000	
Dividend income:		
Dividends received from taxable Canadian corporations	25,000	
Capital dividends	5,000	130,000
Net income for accounting purposes		$490,953

The adjusted cost base to Mr. Clancy of his partnership interest was $45,792 at the beginning of the year. His drawings for the year were $77,500.

The dividends were received from a CCPC, all of whose income was eligible for the small business deduction.

— *REQUIRED*

(A) Compute the partnership income for the year, the income to be allocated to Mr. Clancy and the nature of the income.

(B) Compute Mr. Clancy's taxable income and tax payable for 2007 assuming a marginal federal tax rate of 29% and a provincial marginal tax rate of 17%.

(C) Compute the adjusted cost base to Mr. Clancy of his partnership interest.

Problem 2

ITA: 53(1)(*e*), 53(2)(*c*)

Early in 2002, Guiseppe, Cristina, Giovanni and Brunco formed a partnership to carry on a snow removal and landscape business. All the partners, except Cristina, made an initial contribution of $40,000. Cristina made an initial contribution of $80,000. Each agreed to share in the profits and losses of the practice based on their initial capital contribution. At the end of the 2007 fiscal year of the partnership, Cristina and Brunco decided to go their separate ways. Brunco received $125,000 for his partnership interest, while Cristina received $250,000. The tax records for the five years ended December 31, 2006 reflected the following cumulative amounts:

Income (before capital gains) from operations for tax purposes	$750,000
Losses	80,000
Capital gains (2002-2006)	10,000
Drawings by the partners	730,000*
Charitable donations (added back to Division B income for tax purposes)	15,000

* Cristina, $170,000; Guiseppe, $150,000; Brunco, $250,000; and Giovanni, $160,000.

Financial results for the year ended December 31, 2007, are as follows:

Net income per financial statements	$60,000
Charitable donations (deducted from accounting income)	2,000
Drawings:	
Cristina	10,000
Brunco	5,000
Guiseppe	5,000
Giovanni	4,000

Other Information

(1) Cristina is single, and has interest income of $2,500 for the year 2007.

(3) Brunco is divorced, has interest income of $6,600, and paid his former spouse $16,000 for her support in 2007. He has made an RRSP contribution in 2007 of $2,700 (his 2006 earned income was $15,000).

— *REQUIRED*

(1) Compute the partnership income for the year ended December 31, 2007, and the income to be allocated to the partners.

(2) What are the tax consequences to Brunco and Cristina as a result of the disposition of their partnership interests in 2007?

(3) Compute Brunco's and Cristina's taxable income and tax payable for 2007 using the hypothetical provincial tax rate table presented in Chapter 10.

Problem 3

ITA: 22, 97(2)

Adam and Amit formed a partnership this year to operate a retail store specializing in gag gifts. Adam, who has been in the business since 1991 as a sole proprietor, owned the following assets:

	Cost amount	Fair market value
Accounts receivable	$17,500	$ 17,000
Inventory	22,000	22,000
Store fixtures (cost: $17,500)	16,000	19,500
Leasehold improvements (cost: $37,500)	33,500	35,000
Goodwill	—	40,000
	$89,000	$133,500

Adam transferred these assets to the partnership on February 1, 2007, in exchange for a 60% partnership interest. Amit contributed $59,000 in cash and marketable securities with a fair market value of $30,000 in return for a 40% interest. The marketable securities were purchased in 1996 at a cost of $25,000.

— *REQUIRED*

(A) How can Adam's assets be transferred to the partnership without immediate tax consequences? What is the cost to the partnership of Adam's assets?

(B) What is the maximum non-partnership consideration that Adam can receive without adverse tax consequences?

(C) What is the adjusted cost base of his partnership interest to Adam, assuming that the only consideration received for the transferred assets is a partnership interest?

(D) What is the adjusted cost base of his partnership interest to Amit, assuming that (i) the only consideration received for the transferred assets is a partnership interest and (ii) Amit and the partnership elected jointly to have the rollover provisions apply to the transfer?

ITA: 97(2)

Problem 4

Part A

ITA: 117(2), 122, 248(1)

Identify the federal rate of tax payable by each of the following trusts settled by Mrs. A:

(a) On June 1, 2007, Mrs. A settled a maple leaf gold coin on her daughters, B and C, in trust for her grandchildren.

(b) Mrs. A's will provides that her shares of ABC Co. are to be held in trust for her grandchildren.

(c) Same as (b) above; however, subsequent to Mrs. A's death, Mrs. A's daughter, B, transfers assets to the trust.

Part B

ITA: 70(6)

Mr. B died on March 15, 2007. Mr. B's will provides that the residue of his estate is to be transferred to a trust for the benefit of his wife, Mrs. B, a resident of Canada. The will provides that the income of the trust is to be paid to Mrs. B. The will also provides for a liberal power to encroach on capital for the benefit of Mrs. B. On Mrs. B's death, the trust's assets are to be distributed to the Bs' children. Mr. B's assets include shares of ABC Inc. which were purchased in 1981 for $10 and have a fair market value at his death of $1,000.

— *REQUIRED*

(A) What are the tax consequences to Mr. B arising out of the transfer of the ABC Inc. shares to the trust for Mrs. B?

(B) How would your answer to (A) be different if Mr. B's will provided the trustees with the power to encroach on capital for the benefit of the Bs' children?

Part C

ITA: 104(13.1), 104(13.2), 108(1)

Mrs. Jones died in 2001. Under the terms of her will, an investment portfolio was settled on Mr. Shrewd and Mrs. Clever, as trustees, for the benefit of her daughter, Hilary Jones. In 2007, the trust will have substantial income comprised almost exclusively of capital gains. The trust has a non-capital loss carryforward which arose three years ago.

— *REQUIRED*

Hilary's income from other sources is substantial with the result that any allocation of income from the trust to her will increase her overall tax liability. Is there any strategy that can be adopted by the trustees in order to reduce the taxes payable in respect of a distribution to Hilary?

Problem 5

ITA: 104

On January 1, 2005, Mr. Bucks settled a trust for his daughter Jane, who became age 17 in 2005. The trust was documented by a written agreement. There are three trustees, Mr. Bucks, Mrs. Bucks and a long-time family friend. Among other important provisions, the trust provided that the trustees had complete discretion to distribute any portion of the capital or annual income of the trust to the beneficiary.

Mr. Bucks transferred the following assets into the trust on January 1, 2005:

(a) $250,000 cash; and

(b) 1,500 shares of Successful Retailers Ltd., a corporation that is incorporated in Canada and is a CCPC. The original cost of the shares in 1984 when they were purchased by Mr. Bucks was $17 per share. At the date of transfer the fair market value was $20 per share.

The trust purchased a residential rental property with the $250,000 cash early in January 2005. The value of the property was allocated 55% to the land and 45% to the building. The rental income before capital cost allowance but after all other expenses is estimated to be $12,000 per annum.

The amount of dividends paid on the Successful Retailers Ltd. shares for each of 2005 and 2006 is $7,500. The estimated dividend to be paid in 2007 is $7,500. The dividends were received only from income eligible for the small business deduction.

On July 1, 2007, the trust sold the rental property for $350,000, allocating 60% to the land and 40% to the building.

¶18,875

In each year, the trust is to "accumulate" 60% of the income earned and pay out the remainder before capital cost allowance to the beneficiary to meet her financial needs.

— *REQUIRED*

(A) Outline the income tax consequences to Mr. Bucks of the transfer of property to the trust in 2005.

(B) Calculate the amount of net income allocable to each of Mr. Bucks, Jane and the trust in 2005, 2006, and 2007, assuming that no elections under the Act have been utilized.

(C) What steps could have been taken when the trust was established to minimize the income allocable to Mr. Bucks?

(D) Calculate the taxes payable by Jane and the trust in 2007. Use the hypothetical individual tax rate table presented in Chapter 10.

Problem 6

ITA: 84(1), 85, 86, 104, 129(6)

Mr. Wealthy is 55 years old. He is the President and sole shareholder of Amazing Results Inc. ("Amazing"). Amazing was incorporated in 1984. At the time of incorporation, Mr. Wealthy subscribed for 100 common shares without par value for subscription proceeds of $100. These are still the only shares that are issued and outstanding.

Amazing has been involved in the lobbying business and achieves results for its clients which are considered to be simply amazing. Amazing has just been involved in a very successful high-profile lobbying effort. Business is booming. Amazing has been a very profitable company. It is estimated that the fair market value of the shares is $1,000,000 today. Mr. Wealthy believes that the value of the shares of Amazing will increase dramatically over the next two years to about $3,000,000.

Included in Amazing's assets is land and building (the "real estate") which is located steps away from the provincial legislature. The real estate was purchased in 1987 for $200,000 and is estimated to be worth about $700,000 today. The cost and value of the real estate is allocated 50/50 between land and building. The undepreciated capital cost of the building as at today's date is $35,000. It is estimated that the property will be worth about $1,200,000 within five years.

Mr. Wealthy is divorced with three children. Wendy is 30 years old and very active in the business. Her intention is to make a career out of Amazing. Wayne, who is 25 years old, is an artist with no interest in Amazing. Winona, who is 15 years old, is a high school student with no income. She has stated her intention is to become a doctor. She attends a private school to which Mr. Wealthy pays $4,000 tuition annually.

Mr. Wealthy would like to retire from active involvement in Amazing within the next 10 years. He estimates that he will continue to require an income of $50,000 per year thereafter. He wants to take action now so that, in the event of his death, he will not be taxed on the expected growth of Amazing in the next five years.

Mr. Wealthy has decided that a plan should be implemented to ensure that Wendy will benefit from the future growth of Amazing. At the same time, Mr. Wealthy wants to be fair to Wayne and Winona by providing them with some benefits from the growth of his estate in the future. He wants to maintain sufficient control over Amazing during his life in the event that Wendy does not fulfil his expectations of her involvement in the business. Mr. Wealthy tells you that his neighbour has "frozen" everything in favour of his children as a means of saving taxes. Mr. Wealthy would like to freeze everything too. Mr. Wealthy has never claimed a capital gains exemption.

— *REQUIRED*

(A) Advise Mr. Wealthy of the tax consequences and merits of the following proposals to achieve his objectives:

    (i) Mr. Wealthy would transfer the shares of Amazing, using section 85, to a corporation (Holdco) of which Wendy holds the common shares. Mr. Wealthy would receive as consideration preferred shares with a PUC of $100 and a redemption value of $600,000.

    (ii) The same as in (i); however, the consideration for the transfer would be a promissory note of Holdco for $500,000 and fixed-value preferred shares of Holdco with a redemption value and legal stated capital of $500,000.

    (iii) Mr. Wealthy would exchange the shares of Amazing for a newly-created class of fixed-value preferred shares of Amazing. Mr. Wealthy has been advised that under corporate law the stated capital of the fixed-value preferred shares can be $1,000,000. He would like the paid-up capital to be $1,000,000 since he understands that paid-up capital can be returned to him tax-free.

(iv) Mr. Wealthy would cause Amazing to transfer its land and building to a new corporation in exchange for preferred shares of the new corporation having a fair market value of $700,000 and then lease the real estate back from the new corporation. The common shares of the new corporation would be owned by Wayne and Winona.

(B) Suggest to Mr. Wealthy an alternative to his plans, taking into consideration his age and objectives.

[For more problems and solutions thereto, see the CD accompanying this book.]

¶18,880   ADVISORY CASE

Cora Dusk

Cora Dusk owns 100% of the common shares of a corporation, Cee Ltd. These shares have an original cost of $1,000, a paid-up capital of $1,000 and a fair market value of $1,800,000. At the current time, the common shares are the only shares of Cee Ltd. that are issued and outstanding.

Cora is a Canadian resident, 70 years old and a recent widow. She wants to freeze the value of her common shares of Cee Ltd. in favour of a trust for her children and grandchildren. Cora has a 40 year-old daughter, Jordan, and a 35 year-old daughter, Susanne. All of Cora's grandchildren are under the age of 10. Her current will leaves these shares equally to Jordan and Susanne.

Cee Ltd. carries on a real estate rental business and has nine full-time employees throughout the year, including Cora, Jordan and Susanne. The company qualifies as a small business corporation and the shares which Cora owns meet all the tests to be qualified small business corporation (QSBC) shares.

Cora's plan is to settle one trust for her daughters and grandchildren with $100. The trust would use the $100 to subscribe and pay for 100 common shares of a holding company (Holdco Inc.) at a cost of $1 each. The trustees of the trust will be Jordan, Susanne and the family's lawyer and decisions would be made by a majority of trustees. The trust agreement would allow the trustees discretion as to the allocation of income to beneficiaries on an annual basis. The trust agreement would provide that, at the end of 21 years, the trust capital would be distributed equally to the children of Jordan and Susanne.

Cora would then sell her common shares of Cee Ltd. to Holdco Inc. Since she wants to crystallize the $400,000 remainder of her lifetime QSBC capital gains exemption when she freezes the value of her shares, she plans to make an election under section 85 of the Act in the amount of $401,000. She will receive $401,000 of debt, with the balance of the consideration being Holdco Inc. shares with a fair market value and legal stated capital of $1,399,000 from Holdco Inc. in return for her common shares of Cee Ltd.

Cora currently pays tax at the top marginal rate, but Jordan and Susanne do not because of child care expenses, RRSP contributions and other deductions and tax credits.

Cora has asked you for your comments on her stated plans and whether you have any ideas for improvement or alternatives for her to consider.

¶18,900 SUPPLEMENTAL NOTES

(This section can be omitted without losing the continuity of the chapter. None of the review questions, multiple choice questions, exercises or assignment problems utilizes this information.)

¶18,910 Partnerships

¶18,915 Corporate partnerships

A partnership may have, as its partners, a number of corporations. At one time, corporate partnerships were used as a means of multiplying the use of the small business deduction. The Act now provides that corporate partners must share the benefit of a single annual small business deduction by allocating one annual business limit ($400,000) among them with respect to the partnership income as discussed in Chapter 12. This limitation applies whether or not the corporations are associated. However, partners, who are not associated, may have additional active business income from sources other than the partnership. This income may be added to the annual business limit allocated to them from the partnership income up to the maximum of $400,000 in total.

There are a number of anti-avoidance rules in the Act to prevent the multiplication of the small business deduction. Where a corporation or an associated corporation is a member of more than one partnership and it may reasonably be considered that one of the main reasons for the separate existence of the partnership is to increase the amount of the small business deduction of any corporation, the specified partnership income of the corporation for the year will be the income from the partnership with the greatest income. The income of all other partnerships will be deemed to be nil for the purpose of determining that corporation's specified partnership income. For example, suppose A Co. Ltd. is a partner of ABC partnership and BCA partnership. The specified partnership income of ABC partnership is $300 and the specified partnership income of BCA partnership is $100. For purposes of this rule, the specified partnership income of A Co. Ltd. in respect of ABC partnership is $300; the specified partnership income of A Co. Ltd. in respect of BCA partnership is nil. ITA: 125(7)(f), 125(6)

Where a corporation is a member of a partnership which is itself a member of a partnership, there is a look-through rule which ensures that a corporation that is a member of a partnership is deemed to be the member of the second partnership. ITA: 125(6.1)

Example Problem

A partnership of two unassociated corporations A Ltd. and B Ltd. earns $500,000 of active business income in the year. In addition, A Ltd. earns $50,000 of active business income from a second business venture.

— REQUIRED

Determine how much income of A Ltd. and B Ltd. is eligible for the small business deduction if they allocate equally their entitlement to the small business deduction on partnership income.

— SOLUTION

A Ltd. —Specified partnership income equal to the lesser of:

(a) share of partnership income (50% of $500,000)	$250,000	
(b) share of business limit (50% of $400,000)	$200,000	$200,000
Income from other venture		50,000
Income entitled to small business deduction..................		$250,000
B Ltd. —Specified partnership income as computed above.............		$200,000

The remaining $50,000 of income of the partnership for each partner is subject to the higher corporate rates of tax discussed in previous chapters.

¶18,920 Transfer of property from a partnership

¶18,920.10 *Cessation of a partnership*

Under the general rules, if a partnership transfers property to one of the partners, there is a deemed disposition of that property at fair market value. However, in the situation where a partnership ceases to exist, there is an opportunity for a Canadian partnership to transfer the property to a partner on a tax-deferred basis.

ITA: 98(3)

The partnership is deemed to have disposed of each property at its tax cost. Each partner is deemed to acquire an undivided interest in each property equal to his or her percentage of the cost amount to the partnership of the property.

Each partner must take an undivided interest in each property distributed under the rollover. This means that each former partner will own an interest in each property of the former partnership equal to his or her interest in the partnership. This will prevent partners in a low tax bracket from taking property with high accrued income and partners in a high tax bracket from taking property with low accrued income to minimize the ultimate tax consequences of the liquidation. As a result each partner will share in the tax consequences inherent in the accrued capital gains or recapture on each property.

Each partner is deemed to have disposed of his or her partnership interest for proceeds equal to the greater of:

(a) the adjusted cost base of his or her partnership interest; or

(b) cash plus his or her share of the cost amount to the partnership of property distributed. ("Cost amount" is defined.)

ITA: 248(1) "cost amount"

The cost to each partner of his or her share of property distributed to him or her can be increased by the excess of (a) over (b) above. The excess can be added to non-depreciable capital property up to the fair market value of that property. If any excess remains after the allocation to non-depreciable capital property, it cannot be allocated to any other property.

ITA: 98(3)(c)

The assumption of partnership liabilities by a partner prior to the cessation of the partnership is a contribution of capital to the partnership that increases the adjusted cost base to him or her of his or her partnership interest.

ITA: 53(1)(e)(iv)

Example Problem

Debits and Credits, Chartered Accountants, is a partnership that was formed several years ago. At that time Ms. Debit contributed $60,000 cash as consideration for her ¾ partnership interest. The adjusted cost base of Ms. Debit's partnership interest is now $75,000.

The partnership is going to cease to exist with both partners taking an undivided interest in each property. The attributes of the partnership property at the date of the cessation of the partnership are the following:

Property	Cost amount	FMV
Supplies inventory	$24,000	$35,000
Land	15,000	20,000
Building	33,000	40,000
	$72,000	$95,000

— REQUIRED

What are the tax consequences to Ms. Debit on dissolution of the partnership?

— *SOLUTION*

Proceeds of disposition of partnership interest

ITA: 98(3)(*a*)

Greater of:
(a) partner's share of cost amount (¾ × $72,000) $54,000
(b) ACB of partnership interest 75,000

Since the proceeds of disposition ($75,000) equals the adjusted cost base to Ms. Debit of her partnership interest, there is no gain or loss to her on the cessation of the partnership. However, because the cost to Ms. Debit of her partnership interest exceeds her share of the cost amount to the partnership of the property distributed to her ($54,000), the excess ($21,000) can be added to non-depreciable capital property up to the fair market value of that property, as follows:

	Undivided interest ¾ *of cost amount*	*Par. 98(3)(c) allocation*	*Increased cost*
Supplies inventory	$18,000	—	$18,000
Land	11,250	$3,750	15,000
Building	24,750	—	24,750
	$54,000	$3,750	$57,750

The potential bump to the adjusted cost base of the land is limited to ¾ of the fair market value of the land (i.e., ¾ × $20,000). The excess of $17,250 (i.e., $21,000 – $3,750) cannot be allocated to any other property.

¶18,920.20 *Sole proprietorship*

If one of the partners continues to operate the business as a sole proprietorship within 3 months of the dissolution of the partnership (the "proprietor"), an automatic rollover is available to the proprietor. This rollover applies to the partnership assets that are used by the proprietor to carry on the business. The partnership must be a Canadian partnership.

ITA: 98(5)

The partnership is deemed to have disposed of the partnership assets to the proprietor for proceeds of disposition equal to their cost amount. The cost to the proprietor of each property received by him or her is equal to its cost amount. The proprietor is deemed to have disposed of his or her partnership interest for proceeds of disposition equal to the greater of:

(a) the adjusted cost base of his or her partnership interest; and

(b) the cost amount to the partnership of property received by him or her used to carry on the business plus the fair market value of any property distributed to him or her but not used to carry on the business.

Note that, because the deemed proceeds of disposition are at least equal to the adjusted cost base of his or her partnership interest, the proprietor may realize a capital gain on the disposition of his or her partnership interest, but not a capital loss.

The cost to the proprietor of each property received by him or her can be increased by the excess of (a) over (b). The excess can be added to non-depreciable capital property up to the fair market value of that property. If any excess remains after the allocation to non-depreciable capital property, it cannot be allocated to any other property.

ITA: 98(5)(*c*)

In the event of a loss on property transferred to the partnership, the rules permit an allocation within limits of the potential loss to the assets received for the continuation of the business.

Example Problem

Schlemeel and Schlemozzle have operated a partnership for 10 years. Schlemozzle plans to retire this year while Schlemeel carries on the partnership business on his own. The following partnership property will be used in Schlemeel's business:

Property	Cost amount	FMV
Inventory	$ 5,000	$ 6,000
Land	24,000	26,000
Building	40,000	46,000
	$69,000	$78,000

In addition Schlemeel is to receive other consideration having a fair market value of $5,000 for his partnership interest.

Schlemeel's partnership interest has an adjusted cost base of $80,000.

—REQUIRED

What are the tax consequences to Schlemeel?

—SOLUTION

Deemed proceeds of disposition of partnership interest

ITA: 98(5)(*a*)

Greater of:
  (a) cost amount of property plus other consideration
      ($69,000 + $5,000) $74,000
  (b) ACB of partnership interest 80,000

Since the proceeds of disposition ($80,000) equal the cost to Schlemeel of his partnership interest, there is no gain or loss to him on the transfer of the partnership assets to the proprietorship. However, because the cost to Schlemeel of his partnership interest exceeds the cost amount of the partnership property used by him in the proprietorship and other consideration ($74,000), the excess ($6,000) can be added to non-depreciable capital property up to the fair market value of that property, as follows:

Property	Cost amount	Par. 98(5)(c) allocation	Cost
Inventory	$ 5,000	—	$ 5,000
Land	24,000	$2,000	26,000
Building	40,000	—	40,000
	$69,000	$2,000	$71,000
Other consideration			$ 5,000

Note the fair market value upper limit on the allocation of the loss for capital property. The excess ($4,000) cannot be allocated to any other property.

¶18,920.30 *Continuation of partnership*

A partner may withdraw from the partnership and the remaining partners may continue to carry on the business in a new partnership. Depending on the terms of the partnership agreement, the withdrawal of a partner may result in a dissolution of the original partnership. Under the general rules this would result in the disposition of the partnership property by the partnership and the partnership interests by the remaining partners. However, a specific rollover provision allows the new partnership to be a continuation of the original partnership. Any member's partnership interest in the new partnership is deemed to be a continuation of his or her partnership interest in the original partnership. All of the property of the original partnership must be transferred to the new partnership and all of the members of the new partnership must have been members of the original partnership. This provision applies only to Canadian partnerships.

ITA: 98(6)

The partners of the new partnership must consist only of partners who were members of the old partnership. Therefore, it does not apply to the situation where one or more new partners are admitted to the new partnership. However, in such a case, the original partnership could be dissolved using a rollover provision and the remaining partners, along with any new partners, could use another rollover to transfer property to the new partnership. A similar combination of the rollovers would have to be used to merge two or more existing partnerships into one new partnership such that all transfers involved could be made on a tax-deferred basis. This is the subject of discussion in an Interpretation Bulletin. Note, however, that the provisions in these rollovers apply only to Canadian partnerships and that a joint election is required where partners are contributing property to a partnership.

ITA: 98(6)

ITA: 98(3)
ITA: 97(2)

IT-471R
ITA: 97(2)

¶18,930 Dispositions from Trust

¶18,935 Disposition of capital property

¶18,935.10 *Deemed dispositions*

All capital properties held by a trust are deemed to be disposed of 21 years after:

ITA: 104(4)

(a) the surviving spouse's death in the case of a spousal trust;

(b) the later of the trust's inception date and January 1, 1972 for all non-spousal trusts; or

(c) the previous date of deemed disposition for all trusts.

For deemed dispositions of depreciable capital property under the 21-year rule discussed below, the trust is deemed to dispose and reacquire the depreciable property at its fair market value. However, where the capital cost prior to the disposition was greater than the deemed proceeds (i.e., the FMV), then the original capital cost will still be the capital cost for capital cost allowance purposes and the difference will be deemed to be capital cost allowance subject to future potential recapture by the trust.

ITA: 104(5)

For non-depreciable property, the trust is deemed to have disposed of, and reacquired the assets at fair market value. It is then taxed upon the applicable capital gains or losses arising from the difference between the fair market value and adjusted cost base of each asset.

ITA: 104(4)

¶18,935.20 *Actual dispositions*

When a trust disposes of capital property through an actual transaction, it is subject to tax on the difference between the proceeds of disposition and the adjusted cost base for each property. The difference is a capital gain or a capital loss, as the case may be.

¶18,940 Disposition of income interest

A person has an income interest in a trust when he or she has a right as a beneficiary under the trust to receive all or any part of the income of the trust. A taxpayer with an income interest in a trust having income which is currently payable to him or her is currently liable to pay tax on that income.

On disposition of an income interest to a third party, the Act requires the beneficiary to include the full proceeds of disposition in income. The cost of this income interest and any income currently payable to him or her by the trust are fully deductible against the proceeds of disposition. The income interest is not a capital property.

ITA: 106(2)(*a*)

Distributions of property by the trust to the beneficiary in satisfaction of his or her income interest are deemed to have been acquired by the beneficiary at fair market value. There are no income tax consequences to the beneficiary. The trust, however, will be deemed to dispose of the property at fair market value. This may, depending on the circumstances, trigger capital gains and recapture.

¶18,945   Disposition of capital interest

A capital interest in a personal trust is a right of the taxpayer as a beneficiary under the trust to receive all or any part of the capital of the trust. This interest is a capital property.

Disposition of a capital interest, like other capital property, may result in either a capital gain or capital loss to the beneficiary. Capital gains are computed as the excess, if any, of proceeds of disposition over the greater of:

ITA: 107(1)(*a*)

(a) adjusted cost base of capital interest; and

(b) "cost amount" to the beneficiary.

"Cost amount" is defined as the beneficiary's proportionate interest of the tax cost of the trust's assets less its liabilities. Capital losses on disposition of a capital interest are computed by deducting the proceeds of disposition from the adjusted cost base, as for any capital property.

In general, if the beneficiary of the personal trust receives a distribution of property from the trust in satisfaction of all or part of his or her capital interest, the trust is deemed to dispose of the property for its cost amount and the beneficiary is deemed to acquire the property at its cost amount.

ITA: 107(2)

It is not possible to defer a gain by a commercial trust on a disposition of its property in satisfaction of a capital interest.

¶18,950   GST and Partnerships

¶18,955   Treatment of partnerships under the Excise Tax Act

The term "partnership" is not defined in the ETA. Consequently, the problems that arise for income tax purposes in determining whether a partnership exists also arise for GST purposes. The discussion earlier in this chapter on the nature of a partnership should be reviewed in the context of GST.

Unlike the treatment of partnerships under the *Income Tax Act*, for GST purposes, partnerships are treated as if they are separate legal entities and there is no flow-through to partners. Commercial activities engaged in by the members of a partnership are deemed to be commercial activities of the partnership. Consequently, partnerships are required to register and collect GST on taxable supplies. Individual partners are not required to register separately for GST purposes.

ETA: 272.1

Generally, it is the partnership, rather than the individual partners, that is entitled to claim input tax credits for GST paid on purchases of property and services used in the commercial activities of the partnership. However, members (other than individuals) of a partnership are entitled to claim input tax credits for GST paid by them on purchases used in the commercial activities of the partnership. This provision applies to members of a partnership that are corporations, trusts or other partnerships.

ETA: 272.1(2)

Where a partnership pays a reasonable allowance to a partner for travel and other expenses incurred in Canada on which the partner has paid GST, the partnership may claim an input tax credit equal to 6/106 of the allowance. This provision was referred to in Chapter 4 in the context of employer allowances.

ETA: 174

Similarly, where a partner incurs an expense that is reimbursed by the partnership, any GST included in the reimbursement is deemed to have been paid by the partnership. As a result, the partnership may claim an input tax credit under this provision, provided that the partner has not claimed a credit.

ETA: 175, 272.1(2)

A rebate of GST may be claimed by partners in certain circumstances. This rebate is similar to the rebate available to employees, as discussed in Chapter 3. The rebate is available to individual members of a partnership who incur expenses outside the partnership that are subject to GST and that are deductible in computing the individual's income from the partnership (an individual is defined to mean a natural person). This rebate is also available in respect of capital cost allowance claimed in respect of a motor vehicle, aircraft or a musical instrument, provided the purchase of the property was subject to GST. As well, the rebate is available in respect of leases of musical instruments, motor vehicles or aircraft, and in respect of an importation of any property. The rebate is calculated as 6/106 of the amount deducted for income tax purposes (including GST and provincial sales tax). For income tax purposes, the portion of the rebate that relates to expenses other than capital cost allowance will be added to the partner's income, while the amount in respect of capital cost allowance will reduce the capital cost under subsection 13(7.1) of the *Income Tax Act*.

ETA: 253, 123(1)

As discussed in Chapter 3 in the context of employees, a partner is also not entitled to claim a GST rebate under this provision in respect of expenses for which the partner has received an allowance, unless the partnership certifies that it did not consider the allowance to be reasonable for income tax purposes at the time it was paid (the test of reasonableness is based on the assumption that the partner was an employee for the purposes of the allowance.

ITA: 6(1)(b)(v), 6(1)(b)(vi), 6(1)(b)(vii), 6(1)(b)(vii.1)

The amount of the rebate that may be claimed is limited to the amount that would qualify as an input tax credit if the expenses had been incurred, and GST paid thereon, by the partnership. Thus, the GST rebate is not available to partners to the extent that the expense relates to an activity that is not a commercial activity. Thus, if the partnership is engaged in making exempt supplies, such as a medical or dental practice, the individual partners are not entitled to claim a rebate for GST paid personally on purchases that relate to that activity.

ETA: 253(2)

The application for a rebate must be filed within four years after the end of the year to which the rebate relates. Generally, the rebate will be filed when the partner files his or her income tax return.

ETA: 253(3)

¶18,960   The partnership interest

The definition of "financial instrument" includes, among other things, an interest in a partnership or any right in respect of such an interest. The definition of "financial service" in the same subsection includes, among other things, the issue or transfer of ownership of a financial instrument. Pursuant to Part VII of Schedule V, financial services are exempt supplies. Therefore, no GST will be payable on the issue or transfer of ownership of a partnership interest.

ETA: 123(1)

Advisory services, however, such as legal and accounting services, will be subject to GST. Input tax credits will only be available for GST paid on these fees if they are incurred in the course of the partnership's commercial activities. Anything done by a person in connection with the acquisition, establishment, disposition or termination of a commercial activity will be deemed to be part of the commercial activity. In other words, these fees will only generate input tax credits if they are incurred in connection with the acquisition, establishment, disposition or termination of the partnership's commercial activities and not in connection with the issuance or transfer of ownership of the partnership interest.

ETA: 141.1(3)

¶18,965   Transfer of property to a partnership

Notwithstanding the rollover available under the *Income Tax Act*, the transfer of property to a partnership will generally be subject to GST, with certain exceptions. If the partners contribute cash to the partnership, there are no GST implications since the definition of "property" specifically excludes money. The transfer of debt and accounts receivable are considered to be exempt financial services and, hence, not subject to GST. Furthermore, if the partners were not previously engaged in commercial activities and the property was not used in such activities, GST will not be payable on the transfer. For example, GST will not be payable on the transfer of property to a medical or dental partnership, since doctors and dentists are engaged in making exempt supplies and are not engaged in commercial activities.

ITA: 97(2)

ETA: 123(1)

If the transfer of property to the partnership is subject to GST, partial relief may be available by using an election. As discussed in Chapter 15, this election is available where:

ETA: 167(1)

(a) a supplier makes a supply of a business or part thereof that was established or carried on by the supplier (or established or carried on by another person and acquired by the supplier); and

(b) the recipient is acquiring ownership, possession or use of all or substantially all (i.e., 90% or more) of the property that can reasonably be regarded as being necessary for the recipient to be capable of carrying on the business or part thereof as a business.

Because businesses are entitled to claim input tax credits in respect of GST paid on purchases used in commercial activities, the use of this election may not result in any net GST savings. However, it may result in cash flow advantages, since GST does not generally have to be paid and then recovered through an input tax credit.

A partner who transfers property to a partnership, will also be entitled to claim an input tax credit for GST paid on expenses related to the transfer, such as legal and accounting fees. As discussed above, the ETA states that to the extent a person does anything in connection with the acquisition, establishment, disposition or termination of a commercial activity, the person is deemed to have done that thing in the course of commercial activities. Thus, an input tax credit will be available.

ETA: 141.1(3)

¶18,970   Transfer of property from a partnership

On the cessation of a partnership, the transfer of property to the partners may be subject to GST. If the partnership was not a registrant, for example, because it was engaged in making exempt supplies, GST would not be payable on the transfer. If the partnership was a registrant and is transferring the business as a going concern, the election, as discussed above, may be available. If this election is not available, the general rules relating to the sale of property used in a commercial activity will apply.

ETA: 167(1)

Where a partnership disposes of partnership property to a partner or prospective partner, or to a person who is ceasing to be a partner, the partnership is deemed to have made a supply of the property for consideration equal to the total fair market value of the property (including the fair market value of the person's interest in the property). The consideration is deemed to become due at the time the property is disposed of.

ETA: 272.1(4)

¶18,975   Joint and several liability

Partners and former partners (other than a member who is a limited partner and not a general partner) are jointly and severally liable with the partnership for the payment or remittance of all GST amounts that become payable or remittable by the partnership before or during the period in which the person is a member of the partnership. Where the person was a member of the partnership at the time the partnership was dissolved, the liability also applies to amounts that become payable or remittable after the dissolution of the partnership. However, the liability for amounts that became payable or remittable before the person became a partner is limited to the property and money of the partnership, as determined under provincial law (relating to partnerships).

ETA: 272.1(5)

In all cases, the joint liability is discharged to the extent of the payment or remittance by the partnership or by any member of an amount in respect of the liability.

Partners and former partners are also jointly and severally liable for all other obligations for which the partnership is liable, such as filing returns.

¶18,980 Continuation of partnership

Where a partnership would otherwise be regarded as having ceased to exist (i.e., because of the addition or departure of a partner), the partnership is not deemed to have ceased to exist until the registration of the partnership is cancelled.

ETA: 272.1(6)

Special rules apply to certain partnership reorganizations, such as the dissolution of a partnership into two separate partnerships. Where a majority of the members of the predecessor partnership (i.e., that together had more than a 50% interest in the capital of the predecessor partnership) comprise more than half of the members of a new partnership, and those members transferred all or substantially all of the property distributed to them in settlement of their capital interests in the predecessor partnership, the new partnership is deemed to be a continuation of the predecessor partnership. However, this rule does not apply if the new partnership applies for registration.

ETA: 272.1(7)

¶18,990   GST and Trusts

¶18,995 Treatment of trusts under the Excise Tax Act

A trust is included in the definition of "person". Consequently, a trust that is engaged in commercial activities is required to register and collect GST on taxable supplies.

ETA: 123(1)

The definition of "financial instrument" includes, among other things, an interest in a trust or any right in respect of such an interest. The definition of "financial service" in the same subsection includes the transfer of ownership of a financial instrument. Consequently, the sale of an interest in a trust is an exempt financial service pursuant to Part VII of Schedule VII of the ETA.

ETA: 123(1)

The GST rules relating to trusts also apply to estates of deceased individuals.

¶18,996 Settlement of trust

For GST purposes, where property is settled through the use of an *inter vivos* trust (within the meaning of the *Income Tax Act*), the settlor and the trust are deemed to have sold and purchased the property, respectively, for consideration equal to the amount determined under the *Income Tax Act* to be the proceeds of disposition of the property. Consequently, the supply is generally treated as having been made at fair market value and GST is payable on supplies that are taxable. As previously noted, the definition of property specifically excludes money.

ETA: 268

ITA: 123(1)

¶18,997 Distributions of property

Where the trust distributes property, the distribution is deemed to be a supply of property made by the trust for consideration equal to the amount determined under the *Income Tax Act* to be the proceeds of disposition. In this regard, reference should be made to the discussion earlier in this chapter on trust distributions.

ETA: 269

¶18,998 Liability of trustees

Each trustee is liable to satisfy every obligation imposed on the trust, such as the obligation to file returns. However, where one trustee satisfies a particular obligation, the liability of the other trustees is discharged.

ETA: 267.1(2)

Joint and several liability is imposed on trustees for the payment or remittance of all GST amounts that become payable or remittable by the trust while the trustee acts as trustee. This liability is extended to periods before which the trustee began to act as a trustee. However, it applies only to the extent of the property and money of the trust under the control of the trustee. The payment or remittance by the trust or trustee of an amount in respect of the liability discharges the joint liability to the extent of that amount.

ETA: 267.1(3)

Appendix I

Discussion Notes for Review Questions

CHAPTER 2
Liability for Tax

(1) Canadian individuals are taxed based on residency and not their citizenship. Canadian residents are taxed on their world income. ITA: 2(1)

(2) He or she will be deemed to be a resident only if he or she sojourned in Canada for 183 or more days during the year. ITA: 250(1)

(3) You need to look at other factors to determine where they have a "continuing state of relationship", such as family and social ties and other personal property. The Interpretation Bulletin categorizes the type of facts that can be used to establish residential ties. IT-221R3

(4) He or she would be considered to be a non-resident of Canada throughout the year. However, since he or she carried on business in Canada during the year while a non-resident, he or she would be taxable in Canada on his or her Canadian business profits for the year. ITA: 2(3)

(5) If he or she is establishing a "fresh start" in Canada on March 31 then he or she becomes resident on that date and is taxed in Canada on his or her world income from that date. The sojourning rules would not apply since they only apply to non-residents who are in Canada on a temporary basis.

(6) The residency of a corporation is either determined by the common law test of "central management and control", or a corporation is deemed to be a Canadian resident if it is incorporated in Canada after April 26, 1965, or it meets the tests outlined in the Act if it was incorporated before that date. ITA: 250(4)

(7) A corporation is deemed to be resident in Canada if it was incorporated in Canada after April 26, 1965. Reference to the tax treaty would be the next step but Canada does not have a tax treaty with Bermuda. Therefore, it would be resident in Canada and taxable in Canada on its world income. ITA: 250(4)(a)

(8) Any company which was incorporated in Canada before April 27, 1965 and which carried on business in Canada in any year after that date is deemed to be resident in Canada. An extended meaning of carrying on business includes soliciting orders in Canada. The facts fit the meaning because of the continuity of the order solicitation over a period of years. Therefore, the company would be resident in Canada and taxable in Canada on its world income. ITA: 250(4)(a) ITA: 253(b)

(9) Subsection 2(3) refers to "employed in Canada in the year or a previous year". Therefore, section 115 of Division D requires the income from an office or employment to be taxed in Canada. ITA: 115(2)(c)

(10) While the income would be business income, it would not be income from "carrying on" business under normal circumstances, since this term implies some ongoing activity which does not exist in this case. However, since the land was offered for sale in Canada it may fit into the extended definition of carrying on business in Canada, but this is unlikely since, in order to fit into this "extended" definition, he or she first has to be "carrying on business" which he or she is not. Therefore, the transaction cannot be included in the extended definition and would not be taxable in Canada. ITA: 253

(11) The U.S. company is soliciting orders in Canada and, therefore, is carrying on business in Canada. The corporation is, thus, taxable in Canada on the profits related to these sales. ITA: 2(3), 115, 253

(12) Under the extended meaning of carrying on business, the company would be resident in Canada. However, under the Canada–U.S. tax treaty, the U.S. company would not have a permanent establishment in Canada and, therefore, would not be taxable here.   ITA: 253

(13) Yes, a person can be a resident of more than one country since residency is determined under the laws of each country. Article IV of the Canada–U.S. tax treaty provides rules for resolving who collects the tax where a person is a resident of both the U.S. and Canada.

(14) Under Article VII of the Canada–U.S. tax treaty, it will only be subject to tax on the income attributable to that permanent establishment.

(15) Article XIV of the Canada–U.S. tax treaty will cause him to be taxed in the U.S. only if he has a "fixed base regularly available to him" in the U.S. Therefore, he will only pay tax in Canada on this income.

CHAPTER 3
Employment Income

(1) The personal tax return (T1 General) does not include RPP contributions, union and professional dues and other paragraph 8(1)(*i*) deductions in the calculation of employment income. These are included under the heading "Net Income" in the personal tax return. It would be misleading to use the personal tax return format for this specific purpose, because certain deductions are limited to the amount of employment income in the year, such as the home office expense deduction.

(2) An employee can only deduct those expenses that are specifically allowed under section 8 whereas a self-employed individual may deduct all expenses incurred to earn business and property income as permitted by Subdivision b. Both the employee and the self-employed individual are subject to the reasonableness test.   ITA: 67

(3) No one test is conclusive in itself. All tests should be considered together before a conclusion is reached.

(4) The control subtest in the economic reality or entrepreneur test determines whether one person is in a position to order or require not only what is to be done but how it is to be done. Where such control, by the business over the individual, does exist, an employer–employee relationship is implied.

(5) The integration or organization test examines the degree of economic dependence of the individual on the organization. Where the individual is financially dependent on the organization, then an employer-employee relationship is implied.

(6) The specific result test looks at the expected results of the work performed. An employee–employer relationship usually contemplates the employee putting his or her personal services at the disposal of his or her employer during a given period of time without reference to a specified result and, generally, envisages the accomplishment of work on an ongoing basis. On the other hand, where a party agrees that certain specified work will be done for the other, it may be inferred that an independent contractor relationship exists.

(7) The Act uses the word "received" to determine the timing of the taxation of employment income. In this case, she will be considered to have received her bonus in the year she received the cheque. Just because she chose not to cash the cheque does not change the timing of when she received the payment.   ITA: 5

(8) The Act uses the word "received" to determine the timing of the taxation of employment income. The voluntary deferment of an unconditional right to receive the bonus is not an acceptable method of deferring income.   ITA: 5
Blenkarn v. M.N.R., 63 DTC 581 (T.A.B.)

(9) Employers cannot deduct all of the taxable benefits reported on the employee's T4. Items such as deemed interest benefits and standby charges for automobiles are not deductible to the employer since they are not expenses that are incurred for the purpose of earning income.   ITA: 80.4

(10) If the employer makes *any* of the premium payments then the benefit payments received will likely be taxable.   ITA: 6(1)(*f*); IT-428

(11) The CRA follows normal commercial practice such that the first day of the contract is counted and the last day is excluded for purposes of determining the number of days of interest. In this case the number of days from June 2 to June 29 inclusive will be used to determine the benefit, that is, 28 days.

(12) A reimbursement is a payment by an employer to an employee for expenses of the employer which have been paid by the employee and which are substantiated by receipts. This is normally accomplished by submitting an expense report. An allowance is a fixed amount which is paid to an   IT-522R, pars. 40, 50

employee in excess of his or her salary without the requirement that the employee be accountable for the amount expended.

(13) The standby charge is calculated as follows:

$$\frac{20,004}{20,004} \times 2\% \times 12 \times (\$40,000 + \$3,200 + \$2,400) = \$10,992.$$

(14) The five conditions that a salesperson must meet in order to be able to deduct expenses are: *ITA: 8(1)(f)*

(a) he or she must be employed in the year in connection with the selling of property or negotiating of contracts for his or her employer;

(b) under the terms of his or her contract of employment he or she must be required to pay his or her own expenses;

(c) he or she must be ordinarily required to carry on his or her duties away from his or her employer's place of business;

(d) he or she is remunerated in whole or in part by commissions or other similar amounts fixed by reference to the volume of the sales made or the contracts negotiated; and

(e) he or she was not in receipt of a reasonable allowance for travelling expenses in respect of *ITA: 6(1)(b)(v)* the taxation year that was not included in computing his or her income.

(15) The four conditions that must be met to allow an employee to deduct travelling expenses, *ITA: 8(1)(h)* other than car expenses, are:

(a) he or she is ordinarily required to carry on his or her duties away from his or her employer's place of business or in different places;

(b) under his or her employment contract, he or she is required to pay the travelling expenses incurred by him or her in the performance of his or her duties;

(c) he or she was not in receipt of a reasonable allowance for travelling expenses that was not *ITA: 6(1)(b)(v),* included in computing his or her income; and *6(1)(b)(vi), 6(1)(b)(vii)*

(d) he or she did not claim any deduction for railway company employees, salespersons, or *ITA: 8(1)(e), 8(1)(f),* transport company employees. *8(1)(g)*

(16) There is nothing in paragraph 6(1)(b) that would exclude this allowance from income. However, another rule would apply to cause this receipt to be exempt from tax. In order to be exempt *ITA: 81(3.1)* under this provision, the allowance must meet the following tests:

(a) he must deal at arm's length with his employer;

(b) he must have other employment or business income (not necessary in this case, since he is employed as a professor or teacher at a designated educational institution);

(c) the amount received must be reasonable and must relate only to travel to and from part-time employment; and

(d) the part-time location must be at least 80 km away from both the employee's ordinary place of residence and his principal place of employment or business.

(17) Neither word is defined in the Act. However, an Interpretation Bulletin interprets the word *IT-352R2, par. 2* "principally" as more than 50%. Therefore, as long as the employment-use of the work space is its main or chief purpose, the test is met. "Exclusively" is not defined in the tax law, so reference is made to other sources. *Webster's English Dictionary* defines "exclusively" as "to the exclusion of all others" which is a much more onerous test.

(18) The Act deems that taxes withheld have been received at the time the bonus was paid. *ITA: 153(3)* Therefore, even though the company still had the government's portion of the bonus, tax cannot be deferred on it. In addition, if the amount withheld in respect of the tax was not deemed to have been received by Ms. Smith, then she would not have received credit for the payment of this tax on her personal tax return.

CHAPTER 4
Income from Business: General Concepts and Rules

(1) This type of transaction is commonly referred to as an "adventure in the nature of trade" and would result in business income, if the facts of the situation indicate that it has the "badges of trade".

One of the indicators that a transaction is an adventure in the nature of trade is that the taxpayer has specialized knowledge in respect of the transaction. Mr. Flip is a real estate salesperson and, hence, on the surface appears to meet this test. Since "business" is defined in subsection 248(1) to include "an adventure in the nature of trade", this transaction would be classified as business income.

(2) There is no requirement in the Act to use GAAP for tax purposes. The courts have, on occasion, rejected conformity between income for accounting and tax purposes, particularly in cases where GAAP is at variance with the court's concept of ordinary commercial trading and business principles and practices or common law principles. However, GAAP profits are usually used as the starting point for the calculation of net income for tax purposes.

(3) No. Since the performance of this contract would have been income to Opco if the customer had completed it, the damages received would also be treated as business income.

(4) The agreement was of such importance to Aco Ltd. that it would constitute a large part of the company's total business structure. As a result, the receipt may be treated as a capital transaction on the sale of eligible capital property with no cost base. Thus, 50% of the receipt is included in business income. (See Chapter 5.)

(5) No. Income from illegal activities is taxable. Subsection 9(1) does not impose conditions on how the profit is earned. See IT-256R for the CRA's position. See, also, the cases listed in the text on this issue.

(6) The subsidy is taxable as if it were an expense reduction to Opco. Refer to IT-273R2 for the CRA's position.

(7) There are a number of limitations that restrict the deductibility of expenses even though they may have been incurred to earn income. Expenditures that are not deductible include:

ITA: 18

- capital outlay or loss;

ITA: 18(1)(*b*)

- use of recreational facilities and club dues;

ITA: 18(1)(*l*)

- political contributions; and

ITA: 18(1)(*n*)

- limitations on interest and property taxes.

ITA: 18(2), 18(3.1)

(8) A provision specifically prohibits the deduction of any amount paid or payable under the Act. As a result, the interest paid to the Receiver General will not be deductible.

ITA: 18(1)(*t*)

(9) Not necessarily. Section 67 also places a limitation on the amount of an outlay or expense. It can only be deducted to the extent that it is "reasonable in the circumstances."

(10) If the replacement of the roof served to restore it to its original condition then the cost should be fully deductible in the year incurred. If the replacement roof was superior to the old roof, the cost could be considered capital in nature. This would result in an addition to the undepreciated capital cost pool. Then, the cost would be deductible over a number of years. An Interpretation Bulletin comments on the issue of income *versus* capital expenditures.

IT-128R

(11) No. Airplane, train, or bus fares are specifically excluded from the 50% limitation.

ITA: 67.1(4)(*a*)

(12) The reserve is only allowed if the company is the manufacturer of the product and pays an arm's length party to take over the obligations of the warranty for the company.

ITA: 20(1)(*m.1*)

(13) Yes. The deduction of certain expenditures of a capital nature made in Canada that are in respect of scientific research and experimental development is permitted. These expenditures do not include land.

ITA: 37(1)(*b*)

CHAPTER 5
Depreciable Property and Eligible Capital Property

(1) The full amount of the capital cost is added to the CCA class. The half-year rule makes a separate adjustment for purposes of calculating CCA in the year of acquisition, but this adjustment does not affect the capital cost.

ITR: 1100(2)

(2) A terminal loss is allowed only when the asset sold is the last asset in the class. Otherwise, the proceeds are credited to the UCC of the class under the definition of "undepreciated capital cost" and CCA is claimed on the remaining balance.

ITA: 13(21), 20(16)

(3) "Cost amount" reflects the tax value of an asset at a particular moment in time. With respect to depreciable property, cost amount is that proportion of the UCC that the capital cost of the asset is of the capital cost of all the assets in the class. Capital cost is not defined, but as used here, it means the laid-down cost which includes the actual cost plus all costs of preparing the asset for use.

ITA: 248(1) "cost amount"

ITA: 13(21)

(4) The "capital cost" is the amount that is added to the CCA class when the asset is first acquired [item A in the definition of "undepreciated capital cost"]. See (3) above for a broadly worded definition.

ITA: 13(21)

(5) Certain exceptions to the half-year rule are found in the Regulations. However, regulations for leaseholds and for classes like Classes 24 and 27 provide their own version of the half-year rule.

ITR: 1100(2)
ITR: 1100(1)(b), 1100(1)(t), 1100(1)(ta)

(6) The half-year rule is a simple, arbitrary adjustment that is made to reflect a period of ownership during the year. It is a simpler alternative to prorating CCA for the number of days the asset is owned during the year.

(7) Normally, the statement is true. However, the "available-for-use" rules do not allow CCA to be claimed until the asset is available for use by the taxpayer.

ITA: 13(26)–(32)

(8) An Information Circular provides the CRA's position on when the CCA claim for prior years can be changed. If the change results in a lower taxable income for the year, it must be requested within the normal time limits for appeals (see Chapter 14). If the change does not result in a lower taxable income, as, for example, the case of a loss year, the change will be allowed.

IC 84-1, par. 9, 10

(9) A regulation provides for this daily proration in the case of the short taxation year of a business, as might occur, for example, in the start-up year.

ITR: 1100(3)

(10) Normally, this statement is true. However, a regulation allows a CCA claim equal to one-half the normal CCA in the year of disposition, as compensation for the inability to claim a terminal loss on the disposal of a Class 10.1 automobile. To qualify, the taxpayer must have sold an auto that was in Class 10.1 and that was owned by him or her at the end of the preceding year.

ITR: 1100(2.5)

(11) Your client is correct. The Act reduces the capital cost of depreciable property for grants, subsidies, forgivable loans, deductions from tax, investment allowances or other assistance received on the acquisition of the property.

ITA: 13(7.1)

(12) There are four choices available for the legal costs of obtaining the patent:

(a) deduct them as expenses of representation;

ITA: 20(1)(cc)

(b) deduct the costs equally over 10 years;

ITA: 20(9)

(c) capitalize them in Class 14 by an election not to include them in Class 44 and depreciate them over the life of the patent; or

ITR: 1103(2h)

(d) capitalize the costs in Class 44 and depreciate them at a 25% declining-balance rate.

Any deduction under paragraph 20(1)(cc) or subsection 20(9) is subject to recapture.

ITA: 13(12); IT-99R5

(13) There is only *one* CEC pool for all eligible capital expenditures for each business. Since Mrs. Smith is only carrying on one business within her corporation, the additions to the company's CEC account in the year will be 75% of $10,800.

(14) He is able to deduct the full CEC balance as a business loss in the year that he ceased to carry on business.

ITA: 24

CHAPTER 6
Income from Property

(1) The principal would be separated from the accrued interest and cause the interest to be included in Billy's income as interest income. The purchaser can deduct the same amount that the vendor included in income.

ITA: 20(14)(a)
ITA: 20(14)(b)

(2) Interest accrued annually to the anniversary date of the bond is taxable, requiring tax to be paid from some other source of funds, since no interest will be received on the compound interest bond. Your client may wish to invest in the type of Canada Savings Bonds that pay interest annually. Note that the annual accrual rules may not present a cash flow problem if the holder of the bond is not taxable on the accrued interest due to a low level of total income.

ITA: 12(4)

(3) Attribution would not appear to apply to cause any income allocated to Mrs. Soleprop to be reallocated to her husband since there is no attribution of business income. (It should be noted that, if she is not actively involved in the business, then she will not be a specified member of the partnership and the income from the partnership will be deemed to be income from property.) | ITA: 74.1(1)

ITA: 248(1), 96(1.8)

(4) Although the corporation is carrying on a business, Mrs. Smith is not. She will be earning property income (i.e., dividends on the shares), so the exception to the attribution rules for business income does not apply. Attribution as a result of guarantees would only cause the attribution rules to apply if the loan was not at commercial rates. If the bank is charging commercial interest rates, then the attribution rules will not apply. | ITA: 74.5(7)

ITA: 74.5(1)

(5) The interest on the 10 acres would be capitalized since it is not used in business and there is no revenue from the land. | ITA: 18(2)

(6) CCA cannot be claimed to create or increase a loss on rental property. However, those loss limitation rules do not apply to a corporation whose principal business was the leasing, rental, development or sale, or any combination thereof, of real property owned by it. In this case, Rent Co. will be able to claim CCA to create or increase a loss. | ITR: 1100(11)–(14)

(7) No interest is deductible if Ms. Cautious is considered to realize a capital gain on the sale of the gold. Since capital gains are not income from business or property, she does not meet the requirements and cannot deduct the interest. Also, there is no provision that would allow her to capitalize the interest to the cost of the gold. On the other hand, if the gain on the sale of the gold is considered to be income from business or property, the interest would be deductible. Note that the CRA would allow her to choose income treatment for these transactions. | ITA: 9(3)

ITA: 20(1)(c)

ITA: 53

IT-346R, par. 8

(8) In the *Attaie* case, the Federal Court–Trial Division agreed that the interest expense was deductible. However, the Federal Court of Appeal reversed this decision and decided that the interest was not deductible, since there was not a direct link between the borrowed funds and the income from property. | 87 DTC 5411 (F.C.T.D.)

90 DTC 6413 (F.C.A.)

(9) Under the proposed plan, the interest would not be deductible since the money is not being used to earn income. However, if your client were to borrow from the bank the $100,000 needed to loan to the purchaser in order to complete the sale of his existing house, then at least the interest would be deductible up to 8%. The purchaser would then be in a position to pay the full purchase price for the new residence.

(10) Since the corporation that your client invested in has gone out of business, there is no longer a possibility of earning income from business or property. However, the amount of the lost capital would be deemed to continue to be borrowed for the purpose of earning income and, hence, would allow the interest in this case to continue to be deductible. Refer to IT-533, paragraph 19. | ITA: 20.1(1)

CHAPTER 7
Capital Gains: An Introduction

(1) The transaction will probably be an income receipt. The partnership appears to have been set up specifically to buy and hold the land. The partnership agreement seems to confirm that their primary intention was to make a profit, since the agreement specifically states how the income is to be split. If, after five years, they still have done nothing to develop the land to earn rental or other income, then it would appear to be a speculation gain and, therefore, income.

(2) The transaction will probably be an income receipt. Rachel has used her specialized knowledge, derived from her normal occupation, to make the large profit. This factor, combined with her trading history, would weigh heavily in favour of income treatment.

(3) Normally, stock market transactions are treated as capital gains or losses. However, his intention seems to be to make a profit in trading shares, thereby indicating an income receipt. He may elect to have these transactions treated as capital gains. However, Winston should be careful that the CRA does not subsequently deem him to be a "trader" and thereby revoke his election. | ITA: 39(4), 39(5)

(4) The transaction would probably be an income receipt. Her primary intention is to develop the shopping centre for sale which would be an income transaction. Therefore, the sale of the land prior to development would also be an income transaction.

(5) Capital receipt (not taxable). Doug's $15,000 net winnings should not be treated as income because his actions are more in the nature of a hobby, not making a profit. If this was his business, the profits would be taxable. | IT-334R2, par. 10

(6) "Proceeds of disposition" is defined to include the principal amount of the mortgage that is owed to the mortgage company. This transaction may trigger recaptured CCA or a terminal loss.

ITA: 13(1), 13(21.1), 20(16), 54 "proceeds of disposition" (*h*)

(7) Whenever the adjusted cost base becomes negative there will be an immediate capital gain. The only exception to this rule is for a partnership interest in a general partnership (but not a limited partnership).

ITA: 40(3)

(8) Until the end of 1981 each individual could own and claim a principal residence. After that time the principal residence exemption is restricted to one residence per family. The rules provide the framework for deciding which residence should be claimed for which years in order to maximize the exemption. Mr. Confused and his wife must choose one residence or the other for the exemption.

ITA: 54 "principal residence" (*c*)
ITA: 40(2)(*b*)

(9) The cottage is considered to be "personal-use property" (PUP). Any loss on the disposal of PUP cannot be deducted. The losses are considered to arise as a result of normal personal use over time.

ITA: 40(2)(*g*)(iii), 54

(10) For the purpose of calculating the capital gain or loss on any disposal of PUP the taxpayer's cost is deemed to be the greater of the adjusted cost base of the property and $1,000. Similarly, the taxpayer's proceeds of disposition are deemed to be the greater of actual proceeds and $1,000. Listed personal property (LPP) is defined to be a subset of PUP; therefore, the $1,000 rule also applies to LPP.

ITA: 46(1)
ITA: 54

(11) The dividend should be included with the gross-up in income. The amount of the dividend before the gross-up will increase the cost base of the shares and effectively reduces the capital gain or increase the capital loss when the shares are sold.

ITA: 53(2)

(12) The result of the taxable capital gains minus the allowable capital losses cannot be negative. Any negative amount is a "net capital loss" that can be carried back three years or forward indefinitely.

ITA: 3(*b*) of Div. B; 111(1)(*b*), 111(8) of Div. C

(13) You would be deemed to have acquired the prize at a cost equal to its fair market value at the time you received it.

ITA: 52(4)

(14) The car has a cost base equal to the $35,000 benefit included in her income as a shareholder benefit.

ITA: 15(1), 52(1)

CHAPTER 8
Capital Gains: The Finer Points

(1) The loss on foreign currency is a capital loss. However, as an individual, she must deduct $200 from the loss in arriving at her capital loss. In this case her capital loss is $2,300.

ITA: 39(2)(*b*)

(2) One way to approach this question is to assume that the cost was allocated equally to each acre. Therefore, the cost of the three acres sold would be ½ of the original cost of the six acres or $12,000. However, the CRA, in applying the law, may consider that $12,000 is too high an amount to be "reasonably regarded as attributable to that part," since the lake-front portion would usually be more valuable than the non-lake-front property assuming that access is still available to both parcels. This, then, becomes a valuation issue.

ITA: 43

(3) He has to replace the land before the end of the second taxation year after the initial year. If they finally agreed to the price in 2007 then he has until December 31, 2009 to replace the property. The initial year is the year that the "amount has become receivable as proceeds of disposition", i.e., 2007 in this case.

ITA: 44(1)(*c*)
ITA: 44(1), 44(2)

(4) Yes. In order for these rules to apply the destroyed equipment must be either property that was stolen, destroyed or expropriated or a "former business property". The definition of former business property only refers to real property which has a common law definition of "land and building." Equipment is not included in that definition. However, if the property is stolen, destroyed or expropriated, it only has to meet the definition of "property." In this case the equipment meets this definition and the replacement property rules can apply. Of course, any potential recapture would be offset, by the normal rules, because the purchase of the new machine was made in the year of loss.

ITA: 248(1) "former business property"

(5) Under the definition of "former business property" the advice she received was incorrect. This building qualifies as a former business property, since it is rented to a related corporation and is used in the related corporation's business.

ITA: 248(1) "former business property", 251

(6) A change in use does not include a transfer of property from one income-producing use to another. In this case the property is being transferred from earning property income to earning business income. As a result there is no income to report on July 1 of last year when zoning was applied for. However, when the property is eventually sold an assessment will need to be done at July 1 of last year since the increase in value up to that point will be a capital gain and any profit after that date will be business income from the sale of the condominiums.

ITA: 13(7), 45(1); IT-218R

(7) If Mrs. Smith did not make any structural changes to the house, then there will not be any change in use. The house will still remain her principal residence. She will have to declare the rental income and can deduct the expenses that relate to it.

IT-120R6, par. 30

(8) Since she was moved by her employer nine years ago and was still employed by that employer when she moved back this year, the Act modifies paragraph (*d*) of the definition of "principal residence" to allow her to continue to claim her house as her principal residence for more than the 4 years generally allowed on a normal change in use under the definition. All years qualify since she was still resident in Canada, as required. She still has to make the election not to have a change in use in the year they moved. As a result, on the sale of the house, she will be able to claim the full principal residence exemption.

ITA: 45(2), 54, 54.1
ITA: 40(2)(*b*)

(9) The Act causes a deemed disposition on all her property other than certain property and certain items that are subject to withholding tax. In this case the term deposits will be deemed to be disposed of, but since there is no capital gain, there would not be any tax.

ITA: 128.1(4)

(10) Mr. State will be excepted from the deemed disposition rules on the shares of his U.S. employer since he was in Canada less than 60 months in the past 10 years.

ITA: 128.1(4)

(11) The Act generally treats the sale of this option as a disposition with the cost base being nil. Therefore, the capital gain will be equal to the proceeds and will be taxed in the year the option is sold.

ITA: 49(1)

(12) On the granting of an option there is a disposition and the ACB is deemed to be nil. He does not have the alternative of reducing the cost base.

ITA: 49(1)

(13) Ms. Sorry can elect to have disposed of her note when it is established to have become uncollectible. This will result in a capital loss equal to $100,000 and the note will then have a cost equal to nil. All or some of this loss can then be carried back under Division C to be applied against the previous capital gain. If the original property disposed of was personal-use property then the debt would have been "personal-use property". Then the Act allows a capital loss only to the extent of the capital gain on the original disposition.

ITA: 50(1), 54 "personal-use property"

ITA: 50(2)

(14) A rollover on the exchange of the common shares for the debentures is provided as long as the debenture had the conversion feature built into its terms and no cash was received. The shares will have a cost base of $10 each, so the accrued gain of $10 per share will be deferred until the common shares are sold.

ITA: 51

(15) If a person sells something to someone with whom he or she does not deal at arm's length then the proceeds will be deemed to be the fair market value. Related parties do not deal at arm's length, but in this case the two are not related. However, it is a question of fact whether persons not related to each other are dealing at arm's length. In this case there is no evidence of hard bargaining and the transaction is obviously not at fair market value. Therefore, it would be unlikely that they would be considered to be dealing at arm's length and the proceeds would likely be deemed to be $100,000. Her friend will have a cost base equal to what she paid for the land of $50,000. As a result there will be double taxation.

ITA: 69, 251, 251(1)(*c*)

(16) At the time of the gift, Bill will be deemed to have sold the shares at their fair market value. Scott will be deemed to have received the shares at a cost to him equal to the fair market value at the time of the gift. Since the shares were a gift, the attribution rules applicable to an income-splitting loan will not apply.

ITA: 69(1)(*b*), 69(1)(*c*)

ITA: 56(4.1)

CHAPTER 9
Other Sources of Income and Deductions in Computing Income

(1) The payment was made to Ms. Tired "upon or after retirement of a taxpayer from an office or employment in recognition of her long service" and as such should qualify as a retiring allowance and be included in income. An Interpretation Bulletin states that "the cessation of employment for any reason is considered as being retirement or loss of employment." Therefore, even though she quit, this amount should still qualify as a retiring allowance.

ITA: 56(1)(*a*)(ii), 248(1) "retiring allowance"
IT-337R4, par. 2

(2) The accumulated sick days will qualify as a "retiring allowance" and be taxed as such. However, the unused vacation days will not qualify under this definition, according to the Interpretation Bulletin, and will be taxed as employment income.

ITA: 6(3), 56(1)(*a*)(ii), 248(1) "retiring allowance"; IT-337R4 par. 5

(3) Since the $3,000 per month is contained in the written agreement and the $1,200 mortgage payment is part of the "allowance," the full amount should be deductible. However, the deductibility for the mortgage payment is limited to ⅕ of the original principal. In this case, ⅕ × $120,000 = $24,000. After 20 months ($24,000/$1,200), Charles will no longer be able to deduct the payments related to the mortgage and Dee will no longer have to take them into income.

ITA: 60.1(2)

(4) Under this agreement, the $500 in monthly fees paid to the financial institution will qualify as an allowance since Mark does have the discretion as to where the $500 is paid. In addition, this amount is part of the monthly spousal maintenance payment specified in the agreement.

(5) The loan would have to be included in employment income when received. Such amounts are not awards and are not subject to the rules for scholarships and research grants. As a result, neither the full exemption for scholarships nor research expenses are available as deductions. Any repayment of this repayable award is deductible provided the conditions of that paragraph are met.

ITA: 5(1), 6(3), 8(1)(*n*); IT-340R
ITA: 56(1)(*n*), 56(1)(*o*)

(6) The OAS Supplement would fall into the category of "social assistance payments" since it is based on an income test. As a result, the payments are included in net income, but there is a corresponding deduction to exclude it from taxable income. The effect of these two provisions is to raise Mrs. Smith's income to a point that no one can claim her as a dependant, but at the same time not to make Mrs. Smith taxable on this amount.

ITA: 56(1)(*u*), 110(1)(*f*)

(7) The $15,000 will be taxed in Mr. Slippery's hands on an indirect payment and not in Mrs. Slippery's hands.

ITA: 56(2)

(8) Defined benefit pension plans are approved by and registered with the CRA. Once the CRA has agreed to the terms of the plan, the amount that the company can deduct is determined by an actuary who certifies the amount that is necessary to fund the accruing benefits of the plan.

(9) The maximum benefit that may be provided to an individual under a defined benefit plan is 2% of the individual's average best 3 years of remuneration times the number of years (normally a maximum of 35 years) of pensionable service, with a dollar limit of $77,770 in 2007.

(10) Under a defined benefit plan, the benefit that is to be paid is defined, usually in regard to a certain percentage of an employee's earnings in the last few years of employment, regardless of the cost to the employer or the earnings experience of the plan. The benefit that is tax-assisted is limited to an annual maximum pension of $77,770 in 2007. Under a money purchase plan, the contribution that is required by the employer and the employee is defined rather than the benefit. The retirement benefit of the employee is based on the amount accumulated in the plan at retirement and the annuity that this amount can buy at that time.

(11) The "18%" part of the limit for RRSP contributions was arrived at as follows:

(a) it is assumed that $9 of contributions buys $1 of annual pension income,

(b) pension income is limited to 2% of income per year up to an effective maximum of 35 years,

therefore, to get $1 of pension income in the future you will need a contribution of 18% (9 × 2%) of current income.

(12) The "$19,000" part of the RRSP limit was arrived at as follows:

(a) it is assumed that $9 of contributions buys $1 of annual pension income,

(b) pension income is limited to 2% of income per year up to an effective maximum of 35 years,

(c) the maximum pension available out of a defined benefit plan is $73,885 for 2006,

(d) the maximum number of years that are eligible for the defined benefit calculation is normally 35 years at the 2% rate,

this amounts to $73,885/35 years = $2,111 per year. Thus, to fund the maximum pension of $73,885, a contribution of $2,111 × 9 = $19,000 is needed.

(13) The explanation is based on the fact that the two pension systems are integrated and the integration is based on how rich your pension plan is. The richness of your pension plan is determined by the Pension Adjustment calculation. For this system to work, the pension calculation has to come first. So, your maximum pension contribution is based on your current income. Then, early in the following year your pension adjustment (PA) is calculated. Finally, your RRSP limit is determined, based on your earned income and PA, both of which relate to the prior year.

(14) Using the assumptions given in the question, the calculation would be as follows:

(a) $2,000 compounded at 10% for 15 years within the RRSP minus 46% tax on withdrawal equals $4,511.

(b) $2,000 compounded at 5.4% after tax for 15 years outside the RRSP equals $4,402.

If the rate of return was only 8% the funds would have to be left in the plan for about 18.5 years:

(a) $2,000 compounded at 8% for 18.5 years within the RRSP minus 46% tax on withdrawal equals $4,485.

(b) $2,000 compounded at 4.32% after tax for 18.5 years outside the RRSP equals $4,374.

(15) The Regulations set the withholding rates based on the amount of the withdrawal — 10% of the amount if it is $5,000 or less; 20% if the amount is between $5,000 and $15,000; and 30% if the amount exceeds $15,000. The rates are one-half of these amounts in Quebec. Based on this formula, the withholdings would be 30% of $20,000 or $6,000. Instead, if she were to withdraw four payments of $5,000, then the tax withheld would amount to only 10% of $20,000 or $2,000. In both cases the $20,000 withdrawn will have to be included in her income for the year and the same amount of ultimate tax will have to be paid. The tax will have to be funded from other sources to allow for the $20,000 to be spent for the car. Alternatively, the withdrawal will have to be increased for the amount of the tax to be paid. The necessary withdrawal would be $20,000/(1 − t), where t is her marginal tax rate. ITR: 103(4), 103(6)

(16) Since he left his RRSP to an adult child, the estate will have to pay tax on the basis that the full amount of the RRSP was included in income in the year of death. At a 50% tax rate, this will amount to $75,000 of tax which will come out of the residue or Jim's share of the estate. As a result, Kim will receive $150,000 of cash and Jim will receive the residue of the estate minus the $75,000 of tax and any other tax that may be payable. Mr. Mort should have calculated the division of property based on the after-tax values to the estate.

(17) The following items would show up on her personal tax return:

(a) the $40,000 would be included in income as a retiring allowance;

(b) $35,000 could be deducted as a transfer of a retiring allowance in respect of pre-'96 years of service to an RRSP; and ITA: 60(j.1)

(c) $5,000 of the $8,000 of legal fees could be deducted. ITA: 60(o.1)

The full amount of the legal fees was deductible; however, the deduction is limited to the net of the retiring allowance less the amount transferred to the RRSP and deducted. She should have only contributed $32,000 to her RRSP from the retiring allowance. ITA: 60(j.1)

CHAPTER 10
Computation of Taxable Income and Taxes Payable for Individuals

(1) Within section 111 there is no ordering that is required to be followed when choosing among the different kinds of losses, except that the oldest losses are always applied first. Generally, the rule of thumb is that the most restricted losses are claimed first. The factors that would have to be taken into account in making this decision are as follows: ITA: 111(3)(b)

(a) Does she have the kind of income needed to offset the losses? She would need net taxable capital gains to offset net capital losses.

(b) Which losses are going to expire first? Net capital losses can be carried back 3 years and forward indefinitely and non-capital losses can be carried back 3 years and forward 10 years for taxation years ending after March 22, 2004, and 20 years for taxation years that end after 2005.

(c) What is the likelihood that she will realize the type of income needed in future years to offset those losses she decides not to claim this year? If she uses up her non-capital losses this year and not her net capital losses, what is the likelihood that she will have a taxable capital gain in the future?

(2) His marginal tax rate on dividend income would be:

Cash dividend	$10,000
Gross-up	4,500
Taxable dividend	$14,500
Federal tax @ 29%	$ 4,205
Dividend tax credit @ 19% of $14,500	(2,755)
Basic federal tax	$ 1,450
Provincial tax @ 17% of $14,500	2,465
Provincial dividend tax credit @ 12% of $14,500	(1,740)
Total tax	$ 2,175

His marginal tax rate on these dividends is $2,175/$10,000 = 21.75%.

(3) His marginal tax rate on interest income would be:

Interest earned	$10,000
Federal tax @ 29%	$ 2,900
Provincial tax @ 17% of $10,000	1,700
Total tax	$ 4,600

His marginal tax rate on this interest is $4,600/$10,000 = 46%.

(4) Her marginal tax rate on capital gains would be:

Capital gain	$10,000
Taxable capital gain (½)	$ 5,000
Federal tax @ 29%	$ 1,450
Provincial tax @ 17% of $5,000	850
Total tax	$ 2,300

Her marginal tax rate on this capital gain is $2,300/$10,000 = 23%.

(5) The Act allows an artist to designate the proceeds of the piece of art that is not established to be cultural property at anywhere between the cost and the fair market value, in this case between $200 and $8,000. Looking at the two alternatives: ITA: 118.1(7)

    (a) if she designates $200 she will report no net income since her proceeds equal her cost. However, she will receive a donation receipt for $200 which is worth a federal credit of $200 × 15.5% = $31;

    (b) if she designated $8,000 as the proceeds, she would report an additional $7,800 in income and pay an additional federal tax of $7,800 × 15.5% = $1,209. However, she will also receive a donation receipt for $8,000 which will generate a federal credit of $200 × 15.5% + $7,800 × 29% = $2,293. On a net basis she would have a net federal credit from this alternative of $2,293 − $1,209 = $1,084.

On a net basis, she would be further ahead to designate the full $8,000 as the proceeds. She would receive an incremental benefit of $1,053 (i.e., $1,084 − $31) plus the provincial tax credit.

The Act deems the artist to have received proceeds of disposition equal to the cost of the work of art that is a cultural gift. However, the legislation would entitle the artist to a credit based on the certified fair market value of the work. As a result, no income needs to be reported on the disposition and a credit based on the full value is available. ITA: 118.1(7.1)
ITA: 118.1(1)

(6) Ms. Hurry will receive a personal credit of 15.5% times the maximum CPP contribution for the year of $1,990. The excess $1,990 will be refunded to her since it will be an overcontribution. She will not have any liability for CPP on her self-employed earnings since the full amount has been paid by her and the matching employer contributions. ITA: 118.7

(7) Given the short-term nature of the move, the fact that his family does not move with him, and the fact that he will be moving back to Canada within 15 months indicate that he will continue to be a resident of Canada for income tax purposes and he will be taxable in Canada on his worldwide income. However, since he is a Canadian resident, was employed by a Canadian resident corporation and was working outside Canada on a construction contract for more than 6 months, Mr. Jones will be entitled to a tax credit. The credit for 2007 will be equal to: ITA: 122.3

    the lesser of:

        (a) $80,000 × 365/365 = $80,000   } $80,000
        (b) 80% × $120,000 = $96,000
    divided by $120,000
    times the tax otherwise payable.

As a result, he will receive a credit for $80,000/$120,000 or 66⅔% of his tax otherwise payable on his personal tax return for 2007. In 2008, the same calculation would be made prorating the $80,000 for the 90-day period abroad and another credit would be claimed.

CHAPTER 11
Computation of Taxable Income and Tax after General Reductions for Corporations

(1) Charitable donations are tax credits only on personal tax returns. On corporate tax returns they are deductions under Division C. Donations up to 75% of net income plus 25% of the amount of a taxable capital gain and 25% of recapture in respect of gifts of capital property with appreciated value can be deducted in the year. If the charitable donations are in excess of this amount then the excess can be carried forward for 5 years.

ITA: 110.1

(2) Income can be increased in the current year by not claiming some of the optional deductions for tax purposes. For example, the deductions for the allowance for bad debts, CCA, CECA or scientific research and experimental development expenditures can be foregone in order to increase income. These deductions will be available in future years and will not be lost. Also, the CRA will allow the revision of some permissive deductions for prior years. In addition, the company could consider the sale of any redundant assets to generate income through recapture and/or capital gain.

IC 84-1

(3) Where there has been an acquisition of control, the corporation cannot carry over its net capital losses. To the extent that the corporation has *net* taxable capital gains in the year, it may take an optional deduction of net capital losses which may in turn increase the amount of non-capital losses. Accrued capital losses are deemed to be realized in the deemed year-end immediately preceding the acquisition of control. However, there may be some relief because the corporation is allowed to trigger, on an elective basis, enough unrealized accrued capital gains to use up the net losses that are going to expire.

ITA: 111(4), 111(8)

ITA: 111(4)
ITA: 111(8)

(4) The first restriction is on the type of income against which the loss carryover can be deducted, and the second restriction is on the number of years a loss can be carried over.

Net Capital Losses: Applied against taxable capital gains only; carried back 3 years and forward indefinitely.

Non-capital Losses: Applied against all sources of income; carried back 3 years and forward 20 taxation years.

Restricted Farm Losses: Applied only against farm income; carried back 3 years and forward 20 taxation years.

Farm Losses: Applied against all sources of income; carried back 3 years and forward 20 taxation years.

(5) The deemed year-end applies whenever there is an acquisition of control even if the company acquired is not a loss company. Mr. Magoo will not be able to claim a full year of CCA since CCA is prorated for a short fiscal year.

ITR: 1100(3)

(6) The three main objectives are:

(a) alleviate double taxation;

(b) prevent the avoidance of tax through the use of a corporation; and

(c) provide tax incentives to corporations.

See the text under the heading II.A. of Chapter 11 for details.

(7) The gross revenue from that sale will be attributed to Alberta since, even though the sale was handled from Ontario, the order was delivered to a province in which the company had a permanent establishment.

ITR: 402(4)(*a*)

(8) The theory is that the country where the income is earned has the first right to tax the income. Then, in order to prevent double taxation when Canada also taxes this income, a credit is given in Canada for the foreign taxes paid.

(9) Investment income may be taxed in the foreign country even though there is no permanent establishment in that country. Canada assumes that this investment income, other than from real property, is earned through its permanent establishment in Canada and, therefore, considers this income to be earned in a province for purposes of section 124. Foreign business income, on the other hand, is assumed to be earned in a permanent establishment in the foreign country and, therefore, is not eligible for the federal abatement.

(10) Since Lossco does not have any net income or Canadian income tax, it cannot claim a foreign tax credit. No carryover is allowed for non-business income tax. However, the corporation can deduct the foreign taxes which will increase its loss for the year. This deduction will at least provide the benefit of the foreign taxes being carried forward as part of the non-capital losses.

ITA: 126(1)
ITA: 20(12)

CHAPTER 12
Integration for Business and Investment Income of the Private Corporation

(1) The purpose of integration is to avoid the double taxation of income earned through a corporation. Integration should cause the total tax paid by a corporation and its shareholders to be equal to the total tax paid by an individual who carries on the same economic activity directly and not through a corporation. The system should be neutral as to the form of organization used.

(2) Ideal integration depends on:

(a) When the corporation itself pays tax, the shareholder must include in income and pay tax on the full pre-tax income earned by the corporation and then get a full credit for all the income tax paid by the corporation.

(b) All after-tax income would have to be either paid out as dividends in the year earned or taxed in some manner at the shareholder level in that year to avoid the indefinite deferral of tax that might otherwise be available if the corporate rates were lower than individual tax rates. This would equate the position of the shareholder with the position of the proprietor, partner or owner of investments who must pay tax on income from his or her economic activity whether or not it is distributed.

(3) The gross-up is intended to add to the dividend received by the individual shareholder an amount equal to the total income tax paid by the corporation on the income that gave rise to the dividend. Thus, the grossed-up dividend is intended to represent the corporation's pre-tax income. The shareholder will pay tax on the grossed-up dividend at his or her personal rate. The tax credit is intended to give the shareholder credit for the total tax paid by the corporation on the shareholder's behalf. This procedure is intended to equalize the tax paid on the income that is flowed through the corporation to its shareholders with the tax paid on the same income that is earned directly. When the gross-up is 25% and the total (i.e., federal and provincial) corporate tax rate is 20%, integration is theoretically perfect. When the gross-up is 45% and the total (i.e., federal and provincial) corporate tax rate is 31%, integration is, also, theoretically perfect.

(4) Its purpose is to help small CCPCs retain capital in order to expand their businesses. This is accomplished by using a relatively low corporate tax rate after the small business deduction to defer tax until the income is paid out as a dividend.

(5) There is a deemed year-end on July 15 as a result of the acquisition of control and he is deemed to acquire control at the commencement of that day. Mr. Smith can now choose any year-end he wants and the company should qualify as a CCPC throughout the year.

ITA: 249(4), 256(9)

(6) Paragraph 125(1)(*a*) deals with Division B income (net of expenses) while paragraph 125(1)(*b*) starts off with taxable income. Therefore, if there are Division C deductions such as donations or loss carryforwards then paragraph 125(1)(*b*) could be lower.

(7) The concept is that foreign income which is not taxed in Canada because of a foreign tax credit should be removed from the base amount on which the small business deduction is calculated.

A $^{10}/_3 \times$ factor is applied to the non-business foreign tax credit in order to estimate the foreign non-business income. This is based on the theory that the corporate rate is 30%.

A $3 \times$ factor is applied to the business foreign tax credit in order to estimate the foreign business income. This is based on the theory that the corporate rate is 40% less the general tax reduction of 7% on foreign business income. The abatement is not applied since it is assumed that the income is attributable to a permanent establishment outside of Canada.

(8) Some advantages of incorporation are:

- limited liability except for personal guarantees;

- tax savings if the combined corporate tax rate is under 20%;

- tax deferral;

- income splitting with family members as employees or shareholders (beware of the attribution rules and the tax on split income);

- estate freezing;

- availability of registered pension plans to the owner;

- separation of business and personal activities;

- greater flexibility as to the timing of income received personally;

- continuity of separate legal entity;

- deferral of accrued capital gains on transfer of shares to a spouse;

- access to financing

- availability of capital gains exemption on QSBCS; and

- availability of deferral of capital gains on shares of a SBC.

(9) Some disadvantages of incorporation are:

- tax cost if combined corporate tax rate is over 20%;

- a prepayment of tax at lower levels of personal income on business income not eligible for the small business deduction;

- additional costs including provincial capital tax; and

- inability to deduct losses against personal income. This disadvantage may be offset somewhat by the availability of the ABIL.

(10) He will not be able to get the M&P profits deduction on income eligible for the small business deduction. In addition, the question does not indicate whether this venture is incorporated. If it is not, then these deductions are not available since they are only available to incorporated businesses. ITA: 125.1(1)(*a*)

(11) Part IV tax of 33⅓% on portfolio dividends prevents a significant deferral of tax.

(12) (a) Refundable Part I tax;

   (b) Part IV tax;

   (c) Dividend gross-up and tax credit;

   (d) Refundable dividend tax on hand; and

   (e) Dividend refund.

(13) The gross-up is intended to place the shareholder in an income position equivalent to that of the corporation before it paid corporate taxes. At an assumed corporate tax rate of 20% or 31%, the 25% or 45% gross-up, respectively, represents the underlying corporate tax. This is added to the after-tax dividend to tax, theoretically, the pre-tax corporate profits in the hands of the individual shareholder.

(14) The dividend tax credit is intended to give the shareholder credit against his or her taxes for the taxes paid by the corporation on the income from which the dividend was paid. Since the gross-up theoretically takes the dividend up to the pre-tax corporate income level, the dividend tax credit is needed to reduce the individual tax by the theoretical amount of corporate tax already paid on that income. At a corporate tax rate of 20%, for example, tax of $20 would be paid on corporate income of $100. The gross-up of 25% would take the individual's income on that dividend of $80 back up to the $100 of corporate pre-tax income level. Assuming a provincial dividend tax credit of 6⅔% the total dividend tax credit would be 20% of the grossed-up dividend or $20. Thus the dividend tax credit represents the underlying corporate tax paid on the dividend.

(15) Of the $1,000 capital gain, $500 is not taxable and is allocated to the capital dividend account to be passed out to the shareholders tax-free as a capital dividend. This provides for the tax-free receipt of this $500 whether the capital gain is realized in the corporation or by the individual directly. ITA: 82(3)

The remaining $500 is theoretically taxed at an approximate initial rate of Part I tax of 40%. An additional refundable tax of 6⅔% is also levied and added to this account. Then, 26⅔% of the income is classified as refundable Part I tax and added to the refundable dividend tax on hand account. Dividend payments result in a return to the corporation of $1 for every $3 of dividends that are paid. This would leave an effective tax rate in the corporation on taxable capital gains of 20% which is the level at which integration works.

(16) Ordinarily the interest would be taxed at the full rate of 38% plus the 6⅔% additional refundable tax under Part I with part of this being classified as refundable Part I tax and added to the refundable dividend tax on hand account. However, since the two companies are associated and the interest is being deducted against the active business income of Opco, the deeming rules will deem the interest income to be active business income and not eligible for the refundable tax treatment.

ITA: 129(6)

(17) While A Ltd. does not have more than 10% of the votes and value of B Ltd., A Ltd. does have control, since A Ltd. and the son of the only shareholder are related and do not deal at arm's length. Thus, over 50% of the voting shares belong to a person with whom A Ltd. does not deal at arm's length.

ITA: 186(2)

(18) The factors to be considered are:

- the same non-capital losses cannot be deducted under both provisions;

- the normal corporate tax rates under Part I are usually higher than the 33⅓% Part IV tax;

- the Part IV tax is a refundable tax and not a permanent tax like Part I tax;

- the non-capital losses would otherwise expire without any value; and

- the corporation is not expected to pay a dividend to claim the refund until years in the future.

CHAPTER 13
Planning the Use of a Corporation and Shareholder-Manager Remuneration

(1) Mr. Smith can pay the bonus within the 179-day limit and loan the net after-tax amount back to the company. If he actually does this, he should consider charging interest to the company in order to reduce payroll taxes by converting his salary into interest income. This will also protect his ability to claim a capital loss or an ABIL in the event the company was unable to repay the loan. He should also consider securing the loan.

ITA: 78(4)

(2) (a) If he leaves the money in the company, the income over $400,000 will not be eligible for the small business deduction, but it will be eligible for the general rate reduction. The marginal tax rate will be 34.12% (i.e., 38% − 10% + 1.12% − 7% + 12%).

(b) If he declares and pays the bonus the personal marginal tax rate will be 46% (i.e., 29% + 17%).

(c) He can defer approximately 10.4% (see Exhibit 13-8) of tax by leaving the income in the company to be taxed.

(d) If he leaves the income in the company to be taxed, he will have to pay tax on the dividend when he eventually pays it out. The combined tax rate at that point, assuming the 45% dividend tax credit, will be approximately 48.4% which is slightly above the 46% personal tax cost of paying out the bonus now.

(e) Calculation:

Corporate income	$1,000
Corporate tax	(341)
After-tax income	$ 659
Dividend paid	$ 659
Gross-up (45%)	297
Taxable dividend	$ 956
Tax @ 46%	$ 440
Dividend tax credit	(297)
Net personal tax	$ 143
Net cash after tax	$ 516
Total tax ($341 + $143)	$ 484

(3) If he or she chooses a fiscal year-end on or after July 6 and before December 31, then the bonus can be paid within the 179 days in either this calendar year or on January 1 of the next calendar year.

ITA: 78(4)

(4) The following are the five criteria for the deductibility of bonus accruals as decided in the *Totem Disposal* case:

- reasonableness of the bonus in relation to profit and services rendered;

- payment for real and identifiable service;

- some justification for expecting a bonus over regular salary (e.g., a company policy);

- reasonableness of the time between determining profit and establishing the bonus; and

- a legal obligation to pay the accrued bonus.

(5) Mr. Crunchy is related to his brother-in-law. Therefore, they are deemed not to deal with each other at arm's length and the brother-in-law is connected with Mr. Crunchy. As a result, the conditions in the shareholder loan rule are met and none of the exceptions are met. Therefore, the brother-in-law will be required to take the full amount of the loan into income in 2007 since none of it was repaid by December 31, 2008. In 2009 and 2010, the brother-in-law will be able to deduct the principal repayments. The imputed interest benefit included in his 2007 tax return can be removed through an amended return to eliminate the benefit.

ITA: 15(2.1), 251(2)
ITA: 15(2), 15(2.4)
ITA: 20(1)(*j*)

ITA: 80.4(3)(*b*)

(6) Since Ms. Jones is a shareholder and received a loan, the shareholder loan rules apply. Although Ms. Jones is an employee, the boat does not fit into one of the exceptions. Therefore, Ms. Jones will have to take the $25,000 into income unless she repays it within one year from the end of the taxation year in which she received the loan. If she has to include the principal in income then the imputed interest rules will not apply.

ITA: 15(2)
ITA: 15(2.4)(*b*)–(*d*), 15(2.6)
ITA: 80.4, 80.4(3)(*b*)

(7) This provincial tax holiday would bring the combined corporate tax rate on income eligible for the small business deduction down below 20% and would provide a tax incentive to flowing active business income through a corporation, paying corporate tax and then paying dividends. Thus, there would then be an advantage to paying dividends instead of salary to the owner due to the fact that the dividend tax credit is greater than the underlying corporate tax.

(8) With the dividend gross-up his taxable income would be $37,500. The federal tax would be $5,744 less the dividend tax credit of $5,000 and the personal credit of $1,384 (in 2007) leaving basic federal tax of nil. Provincial tax on $37,500 would be $3,757, less the provincial dividend tax credit of $2,500 (i.e., 6⅔ % of $37,500) and the provincial personal tax credit of $893 (i.e., ($1,384/.155) × .10), leaving provincial tax of $364.

(9) It is true that in order to claim an ABIL the shares need to be shares in a small business corporation. However, the definition of small business corporation allows the status as a small business corporation to continue for 12 months for purposes of the ABIL provisions. Since she sold the shares within six months she should be able to claim the loss as an ABIL.

ITA: 248(1)
ITA: 39(1)(*c*)

(10) In several Interpretation Bulletins, the CRA states that the phrase means at least 90%. It should be noted that this phrase has not been specifically determined by the courts and it is unclear whether the courts would allow 85% or require 95% as the percentage necessary to meet this test. Practitioners generally use 90%.

IT-151R5, par. 31 (for example)

(11) This corporation is neither, since in order to meet the definition of "small business corporation" it has to meet the 90% test at the determination time. Since the corporation does not meet this test it is neither an SBC nor a QSBC.

(12) The preamble to the corporate attribution rule refers only to situations where "individuals have transferred or loaned property." In this case his corporation has loaned the funds to her corporation. It could not even be said that he did it indirectly since he has not loaned or transferred any money to his own corporation. Therefore, even though her corporation is not an SBC, the corporate attribution rules should not apply. However, GAAR should be considered.

ITA: 74.4(2)

CHAPTER 14
Rights and Obligations under the Income Tax Act

(1) (a) False. All corporations resident in Canada have to file tax returns within six months of the end of the year.

ITA: 150(1)(*a*)

(b) True. An individual is required to file a tax return if he or she "has disposed of a capital property". Even if there is no taxable income or tax liability a return must be filed. In addition, Mr. Lucky may lose his capital gains deduction in respect of this transaction, if he does not file the return.

ITA: 110.6(6), 150(1)

(c) False. Instalments must be paid on the 15th of each of those months.

ITA: 156(1)

(2) An instalment interest offset is available on prepaid or overpaid instalments. However, this credit offset can only be applied against instalment interest owing; it is not refundable and may not be applied against any other debt. To benefit, he would have to pay the December 15 instalment on September 15 which would offset the fact that the June 15 instalment was three months late. In

ITA: 161(2.2)

addition, the prescribed interest rate for the last quarter would have to be equal to or greater than the prescribed interest rate for the second quarter.

(3) They will not be able to collect interest for the last three years. Interest will not be paid for the period prior to the filing of the tax return for the year in which the request is made to carry the loss back. ITA: 164(5)

(4) Since the accountant sent a letter to the CRA, it may take some time before a reply is received. If the reply is received late and there is disagreement, it may be too late to file a Notice of Objection. Therefore, it may be prudent to file the Notice of Objection in the first place unless the matter is a minor one. ITA: 165(1)

(5) In order to amend the tax returns for the third preceding year the company would have had to file form T2A by the time the corporate tax returns are due for the loss year which is six months after the fiscal year-end. However, Bad Luck did not meet this deadline since it did not file until seven months after the year-end. Therefore, the CRA will not have to let the corporation carry the loss back at all. However, the loss will still be available to be carried forward. ITA: 152(6)

(6) The following are the three returns that can be filed:

(a) Terminal return — This return reports the income for the period in the year before the date of death and includes any gain or loss on the deemed disposition on death. Full personal credits may be claimed. ITA: 70(1)

(b) Rights or things — "Rights or things" can be reported on a separate return to take advantage of the lower marginal tax brackets. Also, the full personal tax credits allowed can be claimed again. ITA: 70(2), 118(1), 118(2)

(c) Trust return — Similar rules to those in (c) above apply to those situations that have more than one trust year-end in the same calendar year. This would only apply in the case of a testamentary trust since they are the only ones that can have an off-calendar year-end. Again, the lower marginal tax rates and the personal tax credits are available. ITA: 104(23)(d)

CHAPTER 15
Corporate Distributions, Windings-Up, and Sales

(1) Dr.: Cash $30,000
    Cr.: Share capital $10,000
    Cr.: Contributed surplus $20,000

(2) In these jurisdictions, the paid-up capital is the "stated capital" as determined by the directors of the corporation. Generally, this stated capital will be the fair market value of the consideration for which the shares were issued. However, these statutes provide that, in connection with certain non-arm's length transactions, the corporation may establish an amount which is less than the consideration for which the shares were issued as the stated capital and such amount as so determined will then be the amount of PUC for tax purposes.

(3) In no par value jurisdictions, in certain non-arm's length situations, the stated capital (PUC) can be set at less than the fair market value of the consideration received by the corporation. In these situations, the PUC may be kept low to avoid certain penalty provisions of the Act. This will result in the redemption value of the shares being high to represent the value of the assets transferred and the PUC being low to avoid tax penalties or to benefit from a deemed dividend on redemption rather than a capital gain, since the tax on dividends is lower than the tax on an equal amount of capital gain. This ignores the capital gains exemption.

(4) The five basic components of the capital dividend account are:

(a) the non-taxable portion of net capital gains;

(b) capital dividends received from other corporations;

(c) the untaxed portion of the proceeds of eligible capital property;

(d) proceeds from life insurance policies net of their adjusted cost base; and

(e) capital dividends paid, which reduce the account.

(5)

CEC balance	$6,000
Proceeds (¾ × $100,000)	(75,000)
	$(69,000)
Previous CECA claims ((¾ × $10,000) – $6,000)	1,500
	$(67,500)
Income ((⅔ × $67,500) + $1,500)	$46,500
Capital dividend account (⅔ × $67,500)	$45,000

Even though the goodwill may not relate to the customer list, the two are both included in the same calculation as long as they both relate to the same business.

(6) The $8,000 reduction in capital will not cause a deemed dividend. However, the extra $1,000 of payment will be a deemed dividend since it is considered to be a distribution out of taxable surplus.   ITA: 84(4)

(7) The three components of a distribution are: ITA: 88(2)

(a) paid-up capital which is returned tax-free;

(b) a capital dividend to the extent of the capital dividend account and the election of a capital dividend; and   ITA: 83(2)

(c) a taxable dividend to the extent of the balance.

(8) On the winding-up of the corporation, subsection 13(21.2) does not apply. Therefore, the terminal loss will be allowed as a deduction to the corporation.   ITA: 69(5)(d)

(9) The Act provides the definition of "proceeds of disposition" for purposes of the calculation of capital gain or loss. The proceeds do not include the deemed dividend on the winding-up distribution. Therefore, the proceeds are calculated as the amount distributed less the deemed dividend.   ITA: 54
ITA: 84(2)

CHAPTER 16
Income Deferral: Rollover on Transfers to a Corporation and Pitfalls

(1) In general, a rollover allows for a partial or complete deferral of the recognition of income on the transfer of property from one person to another. The transferor, in return for the property transferred, should receive a package of consideration, the total fair market value of which should be equal to the fair market value of the property transferred. The transferor is the one who is deferring the recognition of income. The transferee usually steps into the position of the transferor in terms of the tax value of the asset received. Therefore, on the ultimate disposition of the asset by the transferee, the income will be recognized. Examples of rollovers include subsections 73(1), 85(1), 88(1) and sections 51 and 86.

(2) In order to use section 85, the corporation must be a "taxable Canadian corporation" which is defined to be a "Canadian corporation" that is not exempt from tax. A "Canadian corporation" is defined to include a company that is resident in Canada and was either incorporated in Canada or resident in Canada since before June 18, 1971. In this case, Della Inc. has been resident in Canada only since 1973 and, therefore, is not a Canadian corporation and not a taxable Canadian corporation. Although the real estate is capital property to Mr. Della and, thus, it is "eligible property", this property cannot be transferred using section 85 since the transferee is not a taxable Canadian corporation.   ITA: 85(1.1)
ITA: 89(1)

(3) The following are the four uses of the elected price:

(a) it is the proceeds of disposition to the transferor;

(b) it is the cost of the property to the corporation;

(c) it is used to determine the ACB of the package of consideration taken by the transferor from the corporation in return for the assets transferred to the corporation; and

(d) it is used to calculate the paid-up capital of the shares taken as consideration by the transferor from the corporation.

(4) On the transfer, the only decision variable you have is the non-share consideration or boot. If the boot is higher than the lower limit for the particular asset transferred, then the lower limit is increased. The boot cannot, however, raise the upper limit above fair market value.   ITA: 85(1)(b), 85(1)(c)

(5) The maximum "boot" that should be taken in order to maximize the deferral is the lower limit on the election range as determined by the tax value, unless the FMV is lower. This will cause a problem if the asset being transferred is shares and section 84.1 applies. This problem could occur if the shares being transferred were QSBCS. and an amount was elected to trigger a gain equal to the available exemption. When section 84.1 applies, the maximum boot should be the greater of the PUC and the arm's length cost, not a higher elected amount.

(6) The Regulations would still apply. She may have heard about another regulation which allows the transferee to avoid the half-year rule as long as the transferor was not dealing at arm's-length with the corporation at the time of the transfer (which is true in this situation) and the property was owned continuously by the transferor (Ms. Smith) for the period from at least 364 days before the end of the taxation year of the corporation in which the asset was acquired to the date of the election. If the taxation year of the corporation occurs at least 364 days after the purchase of the equipment, then the condition is met. ITR: 1100(2), 1100(2.2)

(7) The elected transfer price is equal to the total cost of the consideration taken back. This elected amount is allocated among the different types of consideration in the following manner:

First: to non-share consideration (boot) up to the FMV of that property as long as that FMV does not exceed the FMV of the assets transferred to the corporation; ITA: 85(1)(*f*)

Second: to preferred shares up to the FMV of those shares after the transfer but only to the extent that there is a balance left after the boot has been deducted from the elected amount; and ITA: 85(1)(*g*)

Third: to common shares to the extent that the elected amount exceeds the FMV of the boot and the cost allocated to the preferred shares. ITA: 85(1)(*h*)

(8) Normally, the sale of shares in an SBC would allow Bar Ltd. to claim the loss as a business investment loss. However, the ABIL is denied, since it must sell to an arm's length person. Bar Ltd. and Spouse Ltd. do not deal at arm's length since they are related. Therefore, the loss would be an ordinary capital loss. ITA: 39(1)(*c*) ITA: 251

However, in this case, Bar Ltd. is transferring the shares to a corporation controlled by the sole shareholder's wife, an affiliated person; therefore, the superficial loss will be denied to Bar Ltd. However, Spouse Ltd. can take advantage of the ability to add the loss to the cost base of the Loser Ltd. shares now owned by Spouse Ltd. An election under section 85 is not required in order to apply. The rule applies whenever a taxpayer disposes of capital property to an affiliated person, including a corporation that was controlled, directly or indirectly in any manner whatever, by the taxpayer, by the spouse of the taxpayer or by other affiliated persons. ITA: 53(1)(*f*), 54, 251.1 ITA: 40(2)(*g*) ITA: 40(2)(*g*)

(9) The "elected amount" determines how much can be withdrawn tax-free since this is the starting point for determining the ACB and the PUC of the shares. In addition, it is the amount that is used to determine how much boot to take back on the transaction to fully defer the accrued income.

(10) The elected amount is correct since the upper limit is the FMV of $8,000. Ms. Smith will realize a capital gain of $3,000. The company will have a cost in the portfolio shares of $8,000 which is the elected amount. There will be a paid-up capital reduction to reduce the PUC to $8,000. Thus, on redemption, she will have a deemed dividend for $2,000 (i.e., $10,000 of redemption value – $8,000 of PUC). ITA: 85(1)(*b*) ITA: 85(2.1)

(11) If boot is equal to the elected amount and equal to the tax value of the property being transferred, then the ACB and PUC of the shares will be nil. However, if the transaction results in a capital loss, the stop-loss rules may deny the loss. The capital loss can then be added to the adjusted cost base of the property held by the transferee corporation. If the benefit rule applies, then the PUC will exceed the ACB by the amount of the benefit. If section 84.1 applies, then the ACB will exceed the PUC by the amount of the PUC reduction. ITA: 40(2)(*g*), 54 "superficial loss" ITA: 53(1)(*f*) ITA: 85(1)(*e.2*)

(12) Price adjustment clauses are often used to provide for an adjustment to the consideration taken back in the event that the assessed value is different than what was originally used. The courts have determined that the price adjustment clause will only be recognized if the parties have reasonably and in good faith attempted to determine fair market value. The CRA's position on them is outlined in an Interpretation Bulletin. IT-405

(13) The provision is designed to prevent an individual from stripping the fair market value in excess of the greater of his or her arm's length cost or the PUC out of the company without selling the shares in an arm's length transaction (i.e., a share redemption).

(14) He can reduce the PUC of the shares by $100,000. This will cause his ACB in the shares to become negative $90,000 which will give rise to an immediate capital gain. Alternatively, he can transfer his shares to a holding company under section 85 and take back a note for $100,000 and one share with a nominal value of, say, one cent. Section 84.1 will not give rise to a deemed dividend, since the boot ITA: 40(3), 84(4)

does not exceed the greater of the arm's length cost and the PUC. In either case, he can use his capital gains exemption to shelter the gain.

CHAPTER 17
Income Deferral: Other Rollovers and Use of Rollovers in Estate Planning

(1) Either articles of amendment or supplementary letters patent need to be filed with the incorporating jurisdiction in order to reorganize the capital of the corporation. Nothing needs to be filed with the CRA.

(2) Some of the uses of a reorganization of capital rollover include:

    (a) an estate freeze to allow the children to benefit from future capital appreciation;

    (b) a reduction in the value of the common shares to allow a purchaser to buy common shares for a nominal amount; and

    (c) a reduction in the value of the common shares to allow employees to buy shares at a reduced value.

ITA: 86

(3) A deemed dividend may arise under the reorganization of capital rollover where the redemption proceeds (the reduced PUC of the new shares plus the non-share consideration) exceeds the paid-up capital of the old shares. The deemed dividend results in an adjustment to the proceeds of disposition. As a result, the proceeds will be reduced by any deemed dividend.

ITA: 54 "proceeds of disposition" (*j*), 84(3), 86
ITA: 84(3)
ITA: 84(3), 86(1)(*c*)

(4) For corporate law purposes, the two predecessor corporations are deemed to continue to exist as an amalgamated corporation. The amalgamated corporation is deemed to have existed previously as the predecessor corporations. Property owned by the predecessor corporations continues to be the property of the new amalgamated corporation. Liabilities enforceable against the predecessor corporations are now enforceable against the new amalgamated corporation.

(5) The deemed year-end as a result of an amalgamation has an impact on:

    (a) unpaid amounts — the deemed year-end will count for purposes of section 78;

    (b) CCA will have to be prorated;

ITR: 1100(3)

    (c) the small business deduction business limit ($400,000) will have to be prorated for a short taxation year; and

ITA: 125(5)

    (d) the short taxation year will count as one of the carryforward years available.

ITA: 111

(6) The CRA has indicated that, if an amalgamation is undertaken with a shell corporation solely to effect a year-end change, the GAAR would be applied. Therefore, this is considered to be an offensive transaction as far as the CRA is concerned.

IC 88-2
ITA: 245

(7) In order for the rollover on winding up a subsidiary to apply, not less than 90% of the issued shares of each class of the capital stock of the subsidiary need to be owned by the parent, which is a taxable Canadian corporation, and all of the shares of the subsidiary that were not owned by the parent immediately before the winding-up were owned at that time by persons with whom the parent was dealing at arm's length.

ITA: 88(1)

(8) Her new ACB is the total ACB she had on her preferred shares divided by the total number of new common shares. In this case her new ACB on the common shares would be $10,000 divided by 2,000 or $5 per share.

ITA: 51

(9) The primary purpose of estate freezing is to freeze all or part of the value of growing assets at their current fair market value, such that future growth in these assets accrues to someone else, usually the next generation of family members. The result will be that this future growth will not be taxed in the hands of the taxpayer on a disposition or at his or her death.

(10) Some secondary objectives of an estate freeze would be to:

    (a) defer any immediate tax cost on the freeze transaction and establish the amount of the tax liability on death;

    (b) maintain control over the asset that has been frozen;

    (c) maintain a source of income from the asset being frozen;

    (d) split income with low tax-rate family members; and

(e) use up the QSBC share capital gains exemption on the asset being frozen (holdco freeze only).

(11) The three principal methods of freezing the value of growth assets are:

(a) holdco freeze;

ITA: 85

(b) internal freeze; and

ITA: 86

(c) reverse or asset freeze between corporations.

ITA: 85

Refer to the text for details of these methods.

(12) The basic steps involved in a Holdco freeze are:

(a) incorporate the holding company;

(b) transfer the shares of an operating corporation to the holding corporation using section 85 to avoid incurring an immediate tax cost; and

(c) have the transferor take back, as consideration for the growth asset, debt and preferred shares of the holding company. The preferred shares will have certain characteristics to achieve the freezor's objectives including a fixed retraction value which will freeze the value. Other features would revolve around desired voting control, income and security.

(13) One of the biggest dangers of doing an estate freeze on the shares of an SBC in favour of a spouse or minor children is that the corporation will subsequently lose its SBC status and the corporate attribution rules will apply to deem an interest benefit on the transferor. Remember that the corporation only has to accumulate over approximately 10% of the FMV of its assets in non-active business assets in order to fall offside. This may be done easily if the company is generating excess cash and invests it. Keep in mind that the corporate attribution rules only apply if "one of the main purposes of the transfer or loan may reasonably be considered to be to reduce the income of the individual and to benefit, either directly or indirectly, by means of a trust or by any other means whatever, a person who is a designated person in respect of the individual." Thus, before the corporate attribution rule applies, this purpose test must be met.

ITA: 74.4(2)

ITA: 74.4(2)

(14) A "reverse or asset freeze" would be used to transfer some or all of the growth assets of a corporation in which the taxpayer owns common shares to a new corporation owned by family members who will benefit from the future growth through their ownership of the new corporation's common shares. The consideration taken back on the transfer will usually consist of non-growth assets such as debt and preferred shares with a fixed retraction value. For example, an operating company owns land and building that are used in the business and the present shareholders want the increase in value of the land and building to go to their adult children.

The steps that would be taken are as follows:

(a) a new company would be incorporated with the adult children subscribing for the common shares usually for a nominal amount;

(b) the existing corporation would then transfer the growth assets to the new corporation using section 85 to defer any tax; and

(c) the transferor corporation will take back, as consideration for the growth assets, debt and preferred shares of the new corporation. The preferred shares will have certain characteristics to achieve the freezor's objectives including a fixed retraction value which will freeze the value. Other features would revolve around desired voting control, income and security.

CHAPTER 18
Partnerships and Trusts

(1) The term "partnership" is not defined in the *Income Tax Act*. The term "partnership" is defined in the provincial Partnership Acts. The Ontario *Partnership Act*, for example, provides that a "partnership is a relation that subsists between persons carrying on a business in common with a view to profit."

(2) False. The amount of losses a limited partner can deduct in computing income in respect of losses allocated by the limited partnership is limited. The losses can only be deducted to the extent of the limited partner's "at-risk amount" as defined. Generally, the losses may be deducted by a limited partner only to the extent that the total of his or her investment in the partnership plus his or her share of the partnership profit exceeds any amount owing to the partnership by him or her and any guaranteed return as a result of a buy-back of the partnership interest, guaranteed buy-back and so on. To the extent that limited partnership losses are restricted, they can be carried forward indefinitely and

ITA: 96(2.1)
ITA: 96(2.2)

deducted under paragraph 111(1)(*e*), but only against income from the limited partnership that gave rise to the loss.

(3) Because Dadd and Ladd do not deal at arm's length, the anti-avoidance rule must be considered. The issue is whether the allocation is reasonable in the circumstances having regard to the capital invested in or work performed for the partnership by the members thereof, or such other factors as may be relevant. For example, the allocation of the capital gain to Dadd may be reasonable given that it was his property in the first place. Since Dadd is the only one with capital and cash invested in the partnership, any losses may be his losses, as the losses impair his capital in the partnership. Arguments can be made that the allocation is reasonable in the circumstances.

ITA: 103(1.1)

Because the decision has been made to allocate income on a 50/50 basis but to allocate all of the losses to Dadd, reference should also be made to another anti-avoidance rule. There should be no problem with this allocation on the basis that the principal reason for the allocation cannot reasonably be considered to be the reduction or postponement of the tax otherwise payable under the Act.

ITA: 103(1)

(4) Income is calculated at the partnership level and then allocated to the partners. A $600 taxable capital gain would be included in the income of the partnership, of which your share is $150 (25% × $600). Your adjusted cost base will be increased by $300, being your share of the taxable capital gain of $150 and your share of the non-taxable portion of $150.

ITA: 53(1)(*e*)

(5) Income is calculated at partnership level and then allocated to the partners. A $100,000 receipt would not be included in the partnership's income, since life insurance proceeds are not taxable. The adjusted cost base of your partnership interest will be increased by your share or $25,000.

ITA: 53(1)(*e*)

(6) A rollover is available only on a transfer to a Canadian partnership. This is defined to include only those partnerships where all the members are resident in Canada at the particular time. In this case, Ms. Jones will need to determine whether the partner in the U.S. is still considered a resident of Canada for purposes of the Act. If not, the rollover will not be available.

ITA: 97(2)
ITA: 102

(7) A trust is a relationship whereby a person (who is called a trustee) is bound to deal with property (which is called the trust property) over which he or she has control for the benefit of persons (who are called the beneficiaries) any of whom may enforce the obligation according to the terms of the trust document. A trust is created when a person (called the settlor) transfers property to a trustee.

(8) While it is true that trusts are conduits by allowing certain types of income to flow through to the beneficiaries and retain their character for tax purposes (for example, dividends, capital gains, foreign income), the income of a trust may be subject to tax. Trusts are taxed as an individual on any income that is not paid or payable to the beneficiaries. The rate of tax paid depends on whether the trust is an *inter vivos* trust or a testamentary trust.

ITA: 104(2), 104(6)

(9) A testamentary trust is created as a consequence of the death of an individual. An *inter vivos* trust is one that is created during the lifetime of an individual. An *inter vivos* trust may also be created for tax purposes where a person other than the deceased has contributed property to a testamentary trust.

(10) A discretionary trust is a trust where the trustee is given the power of choice. The trustee may be given the power to determine the date of distribution of trust property, whether income or capital is to be paid to a beneficiary, how much is to be paid to a beneficiary and in what proportions among a group of beneficiaries it is to be paid. This feature gives the trust a great deal of flexibility and is a very useful planning tool for income splitting and estate equalization purposes.

(11) The special treatment applies to the following types of income:

(a) taxable dividends from a Canadian corporation which allows the beneficiary to use the dividend gross-up and tax credit;

ITA: 104(19)

(b) net taxable capital gains which are eligible for the capital gains deduction available in respect of qualified shares of a small business corporation and qualified farm property (note that net capital losses do not flow through to the beneficiary);

ITA: 104(21)–(21.3)

(c) non-taxable dividends which are excluded from the computation of taxable income;

ITA: 104(20)

(d) foreign income and related foreign tax paid to allow the beneficiary to claim the foreign tax credit; and

ITA: 104(22)

(e) superannuation and pension benefits.

ITA: 104(27), 104(28)

(12) The trust would file a tax return for the fiscal period ending on March 15, 2007 on or before June 13, 2007 (that is, 90 days after the end of the trust's year). She would report the income in the calendar year in which the fiscal year-end of the trust fell. For example, in 2007 Ms. Betty would report the income that is allocated to her out of the trust for the period ended March 15, 2007.

ITA: 104(13), 104(14)

(13) An income interest in a trust is not a capital property. The sale by Mr. Bill will cause the full amount of the proceeds to be included in his income. His sister will have a $30,000 cost of her income interest. She will benefit from that addition to the cost when she sells this interest, or receives future income from the trust.

ITA: 106(2)(*a*)

(14) A capital interest in a trust is a capital property. As a result, a disposition of a capital interest in a trust to a third party will give rise to a capital gain or loss. In this case she will have a capital gain. It will be calculated as the excess of the proceeds over the greater of:

ITA: 107(1)(*a*)

(a) the adjusted cost base of the capital interest (in this case nil); and

(b) the "cost amount" to the beneficiary which is defined as the beneficiary's proportionate interest of the tax cost of the trust's assets less its liabilities. In this case we do not know what this "cost amount" is.

Her chauffeur will have a cost base for his capital interest in the trust equal to $45,000. This will be recognized if he were to sell the interest. However, if he were to receive a capital distribution from the trust then he would receive the assets tax-free with a potential bump (or step-up) in adjusted cost base for his cost of the interest.

ITA: 107(2)

Appendix II

Solutions to Multiple Choice Questions

CHAPTER 2
Liability for Tax

Question 1

(B) is correct. Since X Ltd. is not incorporated in Canada, it is not deemed to be resident in Canada. Since the directors are not resident in Canada, X Ltd. is not resident in Canada under the common law "central management and control" rule. ITA: 250(4)

(A) is incorrect because X Ltd. is deemed to be resident. ITA: 250(4)(*a*)

(C) is incorrect because X Ltd. is resident under the common law "central management and control" rule.

(D) is incorrect because X Ltd. is deemed to be resident; the common law "central management and control" rule would also apply. ITA: 250(4)(*c*)

Question 2

(C) is correct. Generally, the CRA will consider the individual not to have severed residential ties within Canada if he has a dwelling available for occupancy. IT-221R3, par. 6

(A) is incorrect, because taking his wife and children with him to Germany is not feasible, since the couple is legally separated and the children are not dependent on him for support. IT-221R3, par. 7

(B) is incorrect, because giving up Canadian citizenship has little relevance in determining residency.

(D) is incorrect. Although putting all his household furniture and personal effects into storage in Canada is a residential tie, the tie is a weaker one than that cited in (C). IT-221R3, par. 8

Question 3

(B) is correct. Only the $50,000 of employment income earned in Canada would be reported on Mr. N's Canadian personal income tax return for the year. ITA: 2(3), 115

(A) is incorrect. The $10,000 interest, earned by the non-resident, is not taxable under Part I. However, the interest would be subject to Part XIII tax withheld at source.

(C) is incorrect for the same reason as (A).

(D) is incorrect, because only residents of Canada are subject to Canadian income tax on their worldwide income. ITA: 2(1)

Question 4

(C) is correct. Because Jerry Dykopf ceased to be a resident of Canada on April 30 of the year, only his worldwide income during the first four months of the year ($26,000 = $25,000 + $1,000) is subject to tax in Canada under Part I and would be reported on his Canadian personal income tax return for the year.   ITA: 2(1), 114

(A) includes income earned while not a resident of Canada: $58,000 = $25,000 + $1,000 + $30,000 + $2,000. The $30,000 of employment income earned in Israel and the $2,000 of Canadian interest earned from May 1 to December 31 of the year are not subject to Part I tax because Jerry is not resident in Canada at that time. The $2,000 of Canadian interest is subject to tax under Part XIII, not Part I. Tax is withheld at source under Part XIII — no return is filed.   ITA: 2(1), 114

(B) includes the salary earned in Israel: $56,000 = $25,000 + $1,000 + $30,000. As in (A) above, the $30,000 of employment income earned in Israel is not subject to tax in Canada.

(D) excludes the worldwide income earned while Jerry was a resident in Canada. As discussed in (A) above, this would be reported on his Canadian personal income tax return for the year.   ITA: 2(1), 114

Question 5

(B) is correct. Judy is a non-resident. She seems to have severed her residential ties to Canada (moving her belongings) and established new ties to London, England (buying a house).

(A) is incorrect. James is still a resident of Canada. There is no indication that James has severed his residential ties to Canada or established ties to London, England.

(C) is incorrect. Since ERT Limited was incorporated in Canada after April 26, 1965, it is deemed to be a resident of Canada.   ITA: 250(4)(a)

(D) is incorrect. Doug is deemed to be a resident of Canada because he is a member of the Canadian armed forces.   ITA: 250(1)(b)

Question 6

(C) is correct.

Sales (taxable at 7%)	$250,000
Purchase of supplies from a registrant	30,000
	$220,000 × 7% = $15,400.

(A) incorrectly takes a deduction for salaries which is an exempt supply: $250,000 – $30,000 – $70,000 = $150,000. $150,000 × 7% = $10,500.

(B) incorrectly takes a deduction for interest expense: $250,000 – $30,000 – $20,000 = $200,000. $200,000 × 7% = $14,000.

(D) incorrectly includes exports (which are zero-rated) and takes a deduction for interest expense (an exempt supply): $250,000 + $100,000 – $30,000 – $20,000 = $300,000. $300,000 × 7% = $21,000.

CHAPTER 3
Employment Income

Question 1

(A) is correct: 12 × 2% × $34,500 = $8,280.   ITA: 6(2)

(B) and (C) are wrong because the operating cost benefit is computed as: 22 cents × 15,000 personal use km = $3,300. Part (B) incorrectly computes the operating cost benefit as: 15,000/20,000 × $3,300 = $2,475. Part (C) incorrectly computes the operating cost benefit as: 20 cents × 15,000 personal use km = $3,000.   ITA: 6(1)(k); ITR: 7305.1

(D) is wrong because he does not have more than 50% employment use.   ITA: 6(1)(k)(iv)

Question 2

(B) is correct: $50,000 salary + $3,500 allowance – $3,000 automobile expenses = $50,500. The car allowance is taxable because it is not based solely on kilometres driven. Since the car allowance is   ITA: 6(1)(b)(x), 8(1)(f), 8(1)(h.1)(iii) taxable, the automobile expenses can be deducted. The entertainment expenses are not deductible because she has no commission income.

(A) incorrectly excludes a deduction for automobile expenses: $53,500 = $50,000 salary + $3,500 allowance. The automobile expenses are deductible because the allowance is included in income.

ITA: 8(1)(*h*.1)
ITA: 6(1)(*b*)

(C) incorrectly includes a deduction for entertainment expenses: $49,500 = $50,000 salary + $3,500 allowance – $3,000 automobile expenses – $1,000 entertainment expenses. The entertainment expenses (50% × $2,000) are not deductible because she has no commission income or income from negotiating contracts.

ITA: 8(1)(*f*)

(D) incorrectly excludes the car allowance and the deduction for automobile expenses and incorrectly includes a deduction for entertainment expenses: $49,000 = $50,000 salary – $1,000 entertainment expenses.

Question 3

(A) is correct. Susanne Denholm can claim home office expenses because she is required by contract to maintain an office in her home and she works principally in her home (i.e., "most of the time"). The $500 correct amount of deductible home office expenses is calculated as follows:

ITA: 8(1)(*i*)(iii), 8(13)(*a*)(i)

$$\text{Heat, hydro \& maintenance: } \$5,000 \times 10\% = \$500$$

(B) incorrectly includes a deduction for property taxes and insurance: $1,100 = $500 + $200 insurance + $400 property taxes. The insurance (10% × $2,000) and property taxes (10% × $4,000) are not considered to be supplies. However, if Susanne had commission income, 10% of her insurance and property taxes would be deductible.

IT-352R2, par. 6
ITA: 8(1)(*i*)(iii)
ITA: 8(1)(*f*)

(C) incorrectly includes deductions for insurance, property taxes and the general telephone line: $1,400 = $500 + $200 insurance + $400 property taxes + $300 general telephone line. The insurance, property taxes and the cost of the general telephone line (50% × $600) are not deductible. If Susanne had commission income, the cost of the general telephone line would still not be deductible — only a special phone line and/or long distance calls would be deductible.

IT-352R2, pars. 6, 10(a)
ITA: 8(1)(*i*)(iii)

(D) incorrectly includes insurance, property taxes, the general telephone line and mortgage interest: $3,800 = $500 + $200 insurance + $400 property taxes + $300 general telephone + $2,400 mortgage interest. The insurance, property taxes, the cost of the general telephone line and mortgage interest (10% × $24,000) are not considered to be supplies. If Susanne had commission income, the mortgage interest would still not be deductible since the Act limits interest expense of an employee to interest on automobiles and planes.

IT-352R2

ITA: 8(1)(*i*)(iii)
ITA: 8(1)(*j*)

Question 4

(A) is correct. The loan qualifies as a home relocation loan. The benefit is computed using the lower of the prescribed interest rate at the time of the loan (4%) and the prescribed interest rate during the year (3%). Therefore the employment benefit is $1,000 (3% × $100,000 – 2% × $100,000 interest paid).

ITA: 6(9), 80.4(1), 80.4(4)

(B) incorrectly computes the employment benefit using 4%: $2,000 = 4% × $100,000 – 2% × $100,000.

(C) incorrectly ignores the 2% interest paid in the computation of the interest benefit: $3,000 = 3% × $100,000.

(D) incorrectly computes the employment benefit using 4% rather than 3%. The 2% interest paid is not deducted: 4% × $100,000.

Question 5

(D) is correct. The stock option benefit is ($40 – $30) × 1,000 shares = $10,000. She meets the conditions for deferral because the option price was greater than the fair market value at the date of grant ($19 per share) in March 2006. She can therefore defer the employee benefit until she sells the shares. The benefit is therefore $10,000 in 2007.

(A) incorrectly reports the benefit in 2006 rather than 2007 and incorrectly subtracts a deduction (½ × $10,000) in computing the benefit ($10,000 – $5,000). This deduction is a Division C deduction.

ITA: 110(1)(*d*)

(B) and (C) incorrectly compute the benefit based on the sales price of $38,000 ($38,000 – $30,000 = $8,000) rather than the price of the stock at the time of purchase. The benefit is $10,000. The $2,000 subsequent decline in value of the stock is a capital loss.

Question 6

(B) is correct.

Meals and entertainment (50% × $14,000)	$ 7,000
Driving costs (90% × $10,000)	9,000
Expenses eligible for deduction	$16,000

ITA: 8(1)(*f*)

Tim can either claim a deduction for these amounts to the extent of his commission income ($5,000) or he can claim a deduction for his automobile costs ($9,000) alone, without the commission limitation. The maximum deduction is therefore $9,000.

ITA: 8(1)(*f*) 8(1)(*h*.1)

(A) is incorrect because it is the commission-limited amount.

ITA: 8(1)(*f*)

(C) is incorrect because it is the full meals and entertainment amount ($14,000) and ignores the $5,000 commission limitation.

ITA: 67.1

(D) is incorrect because it represents the expenses eligible as a salesperson ($16,000) but ignores the $5,000 commission limitation.

ITA: 8(1)(*f*)

CHAPTER 4
Income from Business: General Concepts and Rules

Question 1

(D) is correct. A deduction for interest and penalties on late income tax payments is denied.

ITA: 18(1)(*t*)

(A) is a deductible item. A deduction for amounts paid for landscaping business premises is allowed.

ITA: 20(1)(*aa*)

(B) is a deductible item. A deduction for interest on money borrowed to finance the purchase of a factory for use in its business is allowed.

ITA: 20(1)(*c*)

(C) is a deductible item. If the beneficiary of a $100,000 term life insurance policy on an employee is the employee's family, the cost of the insurance premium is part of the cost of the employee's remuneration package. As such, it is not denied as it is incurred for the purpose of earning income.

ITA: 18(1)(*a*)

Question 2

(C) is correct. The entire $15,000 spent on three social events for all employees at a particular location is deductible as long as the number of events does not exceed six.

ITA: 67.1(2)(*f*)

(A) The deduction for $11,000 of accrued legal fees for a pending law suit is not allowed, because it is a contingent liability. There is no legal liability to pay this amount.

ITA: 18(1)(*e*)

(B) The deduction for $4,000 of donations to registered charities is denied because it is not incurred for the purpose of earning income. The donations would be deductible in the computation of taxable income.

ITA: 18(1)(*a*), 110.1(1)(*a*)

(D) The deduction of $1,500 for golf club membership dues for employees is denied.

ITA: 18(1)(*l*)

Question 3

(D) is correct, because the Act provides an exception to the 50% rule for the cost of meals and entertainment relating to a fund-raising event the primary purpose of which is to benefit a registered charity.

ITA: 67.1(2)(*b*)

(A) is incorrect since donations to political parties are not deductible. The federal political donation would be eligible for a tax credit.

ITA: 18(1)(*n*), 127(3)

(B) is incorrect, because accrued bonuses are not deductible if they are unpaid 180 days after year-end.

ITA: 78(4)

(C) is incorrect, because the deduction for a financial accounting reserve for warranty expenses is denied.

ITA: 18(1)(*e*)

Question 4

(A) is the correct answer. The $13,000 to be added back is computed as follows:

Legal expenses related to the purchase of an investment in shares..........	$ 5,000
Legal expenses incurred to dispute a tax assessment	0
Legal expenses related to the issuance of debt........................	4,000
Accounting fees in connection with the preparation of a prospectus........	4,000
	$13,000

ITA: 18(1)(*b*)
ITA: 60(*o*)
ITA: 20(1)(*e*)
ITA: 20(1)(*e*)

(B) incorrectly adds back $4,000 (instead of $5,000) for the legal expenses related to the purchase of an investment in shares: $12,000 = $4,000 + $4,000 + $4,000.

(C) incorrectly adds back nothing for either the legal expenses related to the issuance of debt or the accounting fees in connection with the preparation of a prospectus: $9,000 = $5,000 + $4,000.

(D) incorrectly adds back only the $5,000 legal expenses related to the purchase of an investment in shares.

Question 5

(D) is correct. Most of the facts support capital gains treatment: the nature of the asset (real estate), its use and intended use (rental), the 10-year holding period and the unsolicited offer for sale. As a result, the gain on the sale of the land will likely be treated as a capital gain for income tax purposes.

(A) is incorrect. Because Sam is a real estate agent, the CRA may argue that the gain on the sale of the land is business income (not a capital gain).

(B) is incorrect. The fact that the land has been held for 10 years supports capital gains treatment, not business income treatment.

(C) is incorrect. The unsolicited offer for sale supports capital gains treatment, not business income treatment.

Question 6

(A) is correct. Legal fees to defend a lawsuit brought by a customer would be deductible.

ITA: 18(1)(*a*)

(B) and (C) are incorrect because these items (accounting losses on the sale of capital property and the principal amount of a mortgage) are on account of capital and therefore not deductible.

ITA: 18(1)(*b*)

(D) is incorrect because personal and living expenses are not deductible.

ITA: 18(1)(*h*)

CHAPTER 5
Depreciable Property and Eligible Capital Property

Question 1

(C) is correct. The maximum CCA is: ½ × 30% × $30,000 = $4,500.

ITA: 13(7)(*g*); ITR: 7307(1)

(A) incorrectly uses the $50,000 cost of the vehicle to compute CCA: ½ × 30% × $50,000 = $7,500.

(B) incorrectly ignores the half-year rule: 30% × $30,000 = $9,000.

(D) incorrectly uses the pre-2001 maximum Class 10.1 cost of $27,000: ½ × 30% × $27,000 = $4,050.

Question 2

(A) is correct. $10,000 is the lesser of ⅕ × $80,000 = $16,000 and $80,000/8 = $10,000. For 2007, the year the cost was incurred, the maximum CCA = 50% of $10,000 = $5,000.

ITR: 1100(1)(*b*), Sch. III

(B) is incorrect. It is 50% of the $16,000 amount calculated in (A).

(C) is incorrect because the $10,000 figure does not take into account the 50% rule.

ITR: 1100(1)(*b*)

(D) is incorrect for the reasons outlined for (B) and (C) combined.

Question 3

(D) is correct. The maximum CECA claim is: 75% × $100,000 × 7% = $5,250.

(A) is incorrect: $100,000/40 = $2,500. Forty years is the maximum period for amortization of goodwill for accounting purposes only.

(B) is incorrect: ½ × $100,000 × 7% = $3,500. The ½ rate does not apply for purposes of additions to the CEC pool.

(C) is incorrect: 7% × $100,000 = $7,000. Only 75% of the cost is used before multiplying by 7%.

Question 4

(B) is correct because the remaining lease term in 2007 is 3 years and the first renewal period is 3 years. The maximum CCA claim is $5,000, calculated as follows:

Lesser of: (i) 1/5 × $60,000   = $12,000
           (ii) $60,000/(3 + 3)   = $10,000

For 2007, the year the cost was incurred, the maximum CCA is: 50% of $10,000 = $5,000.   ITR: 1100(1)(*b*)

(A) is incorrect, because it uses the initial 5-year term of the lease in the calculation in place of the remaining lease term of 3 years: $60,000/(5 + 3) = $7,500 × 50% = $3,750.

(C) is incorrect, because the greater ($12,000), as opposed to the lesser ($10,000), of the two amounts calculated has been used: $6,000 = 50% × $12,000.

(D) is incorrect, because it uses the initial 5-year term of the lease in the calculation in place of the remaining lease term of 3 years and ignores the 50% rule in Regulation 1100(1)(*b*): $60,000/(5 + 3) = $7,500.

Question 5

(B) is correct. Under the Regulations, dies and moulds and software are not excepted from the half net-amount rule, but the other Class 12 items are: linens are listed in paragraph (*g*), cutlery and dishes are listed in paragraph (*b*) and kitchen utensils costing less than $500 are listed in paragraph (*c*). ½ ($1,200 + $600) + $15,000 + $400 = $16,300.   ITR: 1100(2)

(A) is incorrect because it uses the half net-amount rule on all Class 12 assets: ½ ($1,200 + $600 + $15,000 + $400) = $8,600.

(C) is incorrect because it ignores the half net-amount rule on the dies and moulds: $1,200 + ½ × $600 + $15,000 + $400 = $16,900.

(D) is incorrect because it ignores the half net-amount rule on the dies and moulds and software: $1,200 + $600 + $15,000 + $400 = $17,200.

Question 6

(D) is not available, since the property is not eligible capital property.

(A), (B), and (C) are all options for the treatment of patent costs.

CHAPTER 6
Income from Property

Question 1

(B) is correct. The calculation is as follows:

Grossed up dividend ($12,000 × 1.25)	$15,000
Combined tax rate	× 46%
	$ 6,900
Dividend tax credit	(3,000)
Net tax	$ 3,900

(A) incorrectly ignores provincial tax: $15,000 × 29% – $3,000 = $1,350.

(C) incorrectly ignores the dividend tax credit:

$$\$15,000 \times 46\% = \$6,900$$

(D) incorrectly ignores the gross-up and the dividend tax credit: $\$12,000 \times 46\% = \$5,520$.

Question 2

(B) is the correct answer. The calculation is as follows:

	Property			
	1	*2*	*3*	*Total*
UCC at Jan. 1st	$100,000	$75,000	$150,000	
Rental revenue for the year	$ 58,000	$22,000	$ 20,000	
Expenses for the year	50,000	20,000	20,000	
Income before CCA	$ 8,000	$ 2,000	(Nil)	$10,000
4% × UCC	$ 4,000	$ 3,000	$ 6,000	$13,000
Maximum CCA [Reg. 1100(11)]				$10,000

(A) is incorrect. $13,000 is the CCA calculation ignoring the rental property restriction.   ITR: 1100(11)

(C) is incorrect. $7,000 is the maximum CCA calculation on the first two buildings only. This calculation ignores the fact that the CCA on the third property can be claimed against the net rental income on the first two properties.

(D) is incorrect. It is one-half of the $13,000 calculated in (A) above.

Question 3

(B) is the correct answer. The $12,000 of dividend income will be attributed to Mr. P. Mabel and Mr.   ITA: 56(4.1)
P are related and it can reasonably be considered that one of the main reasons for making the loan was to reduce tax.

(A) is incorrect. The $3,000 of interest income will not be attributed. Peter is not under 18 years of age and, therefore, attribution does not apply. If it had been a loan, instead of a gift, subsection 56(4.1)   ITA: 74.1(2)
would apply and may attribute the income.

(C) is incorrect. Even though an interest-free loan was made to which attribution would apply,   ITA: 56(4.1)
there is no property income from the cottage to attribute.

(D) is incorrect. Even though a gift was made to a spouse to which attribution would apply, there is   ITA: 74.1(1)
no property income from the chequing account to attribute.

Question 4

(B) is correct. The premium paid on a $100,000 term life insurance policy on the taxpayer's life   ITA: 20(1)(e.2)
which is required as collateral for a $100,000 bank loan used to purchase a $100,000 investment in common shares is deductible.

(A) is incorrect because commissions paid on the purchase of an investment in common shares are   ITA: 18(1)(b)
capitalized as part of the cost of the shares.

(C) is incorrect because the Act does not allow a deduction for interest expense on a loan to invest   ITA: 18(11)(b)
in a registered retirement savings plan.

(D) is incorrect because commissions paid on the sale of an investment in common shares are a selling cost deducted in computing the capital gain on the sale of the shares. One-half of a capital gain is a taxable capital gain which is computed under Subdivision c of Division B of Part I of the Act, whereas income from business or property is computed under Subdivision b.

Question 5

(D) is correct: $\$20,000 \times 1.25 + \$8,500 + \$1,500$ tax withheld = $35,000.   ITA: 82(1)

(A) is incorrect because it ignores the gross-up on the dividend and the foreign income: $20,000.

(B) is incorrect because it ignores the gross-up on the dividend and the foreign tax withheld: $20,000 + $8,500 = $28,500.

(C) is incorrect because it ignores the gross-up on the dividend: $20,000 + $8,500 + $1,500 = $30,000.

Question 6

(D) is correct.

(A) is incorrect because the tax on split income only applies to taxpayers under age 18 throughout the year. Since Ron is 18, the tax on split income will not apply. ITA: 120.4 "specified individual"

(B) is incorrect because the only exemption regarding inherited shares is for shares inherited from a parent. If Ron had been under 18 at any time in the year, the tax on split income would have applied to dividends received on the shares. ITA: 120.4 "excluded amount"

(C) is incorrect because the tax on split income does not apply to capital gains. ITA: 120.4 "split income"

CHAPTER 7
Capital Gains: An Introduction

Question 1

(B) is correct. The gain is: $600,000 – $100,000 = $500,000. The maximum 2007 reserve is computed using the lesser of the percentage of proceeds payable after the end of the year ($510K/$600K or 85%, in this case) and four fifths ($^4/_5$). Since the lesser amount is four fifths, the reserve is $400,000 ($^4/_5 \times $500,000) and the capital gain is therefore $100,000 ($500,000 – $400,000). The minimum taxable capital gain is therefore $50,000 ($^1/_2$). ITA: 40(1)(a)

(A) is incorrect, because the capital gain must be multiplied by $^1/_2$ to compute the taxable capital gain.

(C) is incorrect, because it uses the 85% figure to compute the reserve and does not multiply the result by $^1/_2$: $500,000 – 85% × $500,000 = $75,000.

(D) is incorrect, because it uses the 85% figure to compute the reserve: $75,000 × $^1/_2$.

Question 2

(C) is correct. The loss on the automobile is not allowed since it is personal-use property (PUP). The $1,000 rule means that the gain on the boat (which is PUP) is $500, the gain on the painting (which is listed personal property (LPP)) is $300, and the loss on the jewellery (which is LPP) is $400. Since the deductible portion of the $400 LPP loss is limited to the LPP gain in the year ($300), the capital gain is: $500 + $300 – $300 = $500. The $100 LPP loss can be carried over against LPP gains. ITA: 2, 41(1), 46(1), 54

(A) is incorrect, because it ignores the $1,000 rule and computes the gain on the boat (PUP) as $900, the gain on the painting (LPP) as $700, and the loss on the jewellery (LPP) as $1,200. The LPP gain is then offset by a portion of the LPP loss, leaving the $900 gain.

(B) is incorrect, because it does not subtract the deductible portion of the LPP loss from the LPP gain: $500 + $300 = $800.

(D) is incorrect, because it deducts the full LPP loss ($400) against all the gains: $500 + $300 – $400 = $400.

Question 3

(A) is correct since only the gift to the son will result in a taxable capital gain.

The ACB of Mike's stock is:

100 × $3.11 plus $39 commission (incl. sec. 7 benefit)	$350	
100 × $4 plus $50 commission	450	
200	$800	= $4 ACB per share.

ITA: 47, 53(1)(i)

His taxable capital gain on the gift to his son is: $^1/_2$ ($6 – $4) × 100 = $100.

There is no taxable capital gain on the gift to his wife, because the transfer occurs at his $4 ACB since no special election was filed. ITA: 73(1)

(B) incorrectly excluded brokerage commissions from the ACB of his shares as: ½ ($6 − $711/200) × 100 = $122.

(C) incorrectly computes a capital gain on the gift to Mike's wife: ½ ($6 − $4) × 200 shares = $200.

(D) is incorrect, because it incorrectly computes a capital gain on the gift to his wife and does not apply the ½ fraction to compute the taxable portion of the gain: ($6 − $4) × 200 = $400.

Question 4

(B) is the correct answer. Since Amanda had no capital gain on her house, she must have designated it as her principal residence for all but one of the years 1998 to 2006. She therefore has 2 years to designate in respect of the cottage: one of the years not used on the house (say, 2006) plus 2007. Since she owned the cottage 8 years (2000 to 2007), the principal residence exemption for the cottage is: ⅜ × $80,000 = $30,000 (3 = 2 years designated + "one-plus rule"). Therefore, Amanda's taxable capital gain is $25,000 (½ × ($80K − $30K principal residence exemption)).

(A) is incorrect, because $80,000 is the capital gain before the exemption.

(C) is incorrect, because it uses ⅖ × $80,000 = $20,000 as the principal residence exemption: ½ × ($80K − $20K) = $30,000.

(D) is incorrect, because $50,000 is the capital gain, not the taxable capital gain.

Question 5

(B) is correct. The amount of the dividend is $4, the increase in the paid-up capital, and this is also the cost of the shares (ssec. 53(3)). However, the individual's net income would increase by $5.80, since it is a taxable dividend: $4 × 1.45 gross-up = $5.80.

ITA: 82(1)

(A) is incorrect because although $4 is the amount of the dividend, the amount included in net income is the grossed-up dividend (1.45 × $4 = $5.80).

(C) is incorrect because the amount of the dividend is not based on the $10 fair market value of the share.

(D) is also incorrect because the amount of the dividend is not based on the $10 fair market value of the share and the amount included in income is the increase in paid-up capital grossed up by 1.45, not the fair market value grossed up by 1.45.

Question 6

(C) is correct.

Shares		$1,600
Personal-use property		700
Listed personal property	$500	
Listed personal property	(140)	
Listed personal property losses of prior year	(100)	260
Shares		(820)
Personal-use property		Nil
Capital gain		$1,740
Taxable capital gain (½)		$ 870

(A) is incorrect because it deducts the $1,000 personal use property loss: ½ ($1,740 − 1,000) = $370.

(B) is incorrect because it deducts the $1,000 personal use property loss and does not multiply by the ½ fraction: ($1,740 − $1,000) = $740.

(D) is incorrect because it does not deduct the listed personal property loss of other years: ½ × ($1,740 + $100) = $920.

CHAPTER 8
Capital Gains: The Finer Points

Question 1

(D) is the correct answer. Since the expropriation is an involuntary disposition, the property must be replaced by the later of two years and 24 months from the end of the taxation year in which the disposition took place. Since the relevant taxation year was May 31, 2008, the two-year deadline is May 31, 2010.   ITA: 44(1)(c)

(A) incorrectly uses the one-year deadline which is applicable for voluntary dispositions.

(B) incorrectly uses two years from the disposition date as the deadline.

(C) incorrectly uses two years from the end of the calendar year of the disposition as the deadline.

Question 2

(A) is correct.   ITA: 74.1(2)

(B) is incorrect, because capital gains or losses do not attribute on loans or gifts to minors.

(C) is incorrect, because there will be a capital gain on the gift.   ITA: 69

(D) is incorrect. $100,000 is the capital gain. The taxable capital gain is:

½ × $100,000 = $50,000.

Question 3

(C) is correct. There is a superficial loss because Ms. Y has incurred a loss and an affiliated person (Mr. Y) acquired the shares within 30 days of the disposition.   ITA: 40(2)(g), 54

(A) is incorrect, because it ignores the superficial loss rule and computes the loss as ½ × ($800K – $900K).

(B) is not correct, because Ms. Y elected out of the interspousal rollover.   ITA: 73(1)

(D) is not correct. There is no attribution because she elected out of the subsection 73(1) rollover and received fair market value consideration (i.e., $800,000 cash).   ITA: 74.5

Question 4

(B) is correct, because the taxable capital gain is computed as follows: listed shares of a public corporation resident in Canada (= ½ × ($40,000 – $10,000) = $15,000) + painting (= ½ ($10,000 – $6,000) = $2,000) = $17,000.

The rental real estate in Canada and the registered retirement savings plan are specifically exempted from the deemed disposition rules.   ITA: 128.1(4)

(A) incorrectly excludes the taxable capital gain on the painting.

(C) incorrectly includes ½ of the gain on the RRSP ($10,000).

(D) incorrectly includes a $25,000 taxable capital gain on the rental real estate in Canada.

Question 5

(C) is correct. The calculation is as follows:

	Division B income
Toronto home (no capital gain; principal residence)	—
Rental property in London, Ontario	
— Land: ½ ($100,000 – 50,000)	$25,000
— Building: recapture = $25,000 – $2,000	23,000
Taxable capital gain = ½ ($35K – $25K)	5,000
Mutual fund units: ½ ($60K – $12K)	24,000
Shares of a public company: ½ ($100K – $90K)	5,000
	$82,000

(A) incorrectly ignores recapture: $82,000 – $23,000 = $59,000.

(B) incorrectly multiplies the recapture by the ½ taxable capital gains fraction: $25,000 + ½ × $23,000 + $5,000 + $24,000 + $5,000 = $70,500

(D) incorrectly includes a capital gain on the principal residence: $82,000 + ½ × ($240K – $100K) = $152,000

Question 6

(B) is correct. Because Gary made the election to be deemed not to have changed the use in respect of the property, there is deemed to be no change in use in 2001. The only disposition occurs in 2007 on the date of sale. The Act allows Gary to designate the property as his principal residence for up to 4 years where the election was made. The gain on the property is $200,000 ($250K – $50K) and the total years of ownership were 18 (1990 to 2007) and the maximum number of years that can be designated is 16 (1990 to 2001 plus 4). Therefore, the principal residence exemption is [(16 + 1)/18] × $200,000 or $188,888. The capital gain is therefore $11,112 ($200K – $188,888) and the taxable capital gain is $5,556 (½ × $11,112).

ITA: 45(2)

ITA: 54
ITA: 45(2)

(A) is incorrect because there is a taxable capital gain to report in 2007 because not all years of ownership qualify as years eligible for a principal residence. The extension of the four-year rule does not apply, because Gary did not move back into the residence before it was sold.

ITA: 54.1

(C) incorrectly calculates taxable capital gains of $50,000 in 2001 [½ ($150K – $50K)] and 2007 [½ ($250K – $150K)]. The timing is wrong because there is no deemed disposition in 2001 because of the election. The amount is also wrong because 12 years (1990–2001) can be designated in respect of the residence.

ITA: 45(2)

(D) correctly calculates the gain in 2007 as $200,000 without claiming any principal residence exemption, thus resulting in a taxable capital gain of $100,000 (½ × $200,000).

CHAPTER 9
Other Sources of Income and Deductions in Computing Income

Question 1

(B) is the correct answer and is calculated as follows:

ITA: 60(j.1)

21 years employed before 1996 (1975 – 1995) × $2,000	$42,000
14 years employed before 1989 when no RPP or DPSP benefits vested (1975 – 1988) × $1,500	21,000
	$63,000

(A) incorrectly ignores the $1,500 rule for pre-89 years where RPP or DPSP benefits have not vested.

(C) incorrectly includes 1996 and 1989: 22 × $2,000 + 15 × $1,500 = $66,500.

(D) incorrectly counts 1996 to 2007 in the calculation: 33 × $2,000 + 15 × $1,500 = $88,500.

Question 2

(C) is correct. The $6,000 is calculated as follows:

The lesser of:		
the 2007 RRSP dollar limit		$19,000
18% of earned income:		
Income from employment	$44,000	
RPP contributions	1,000	
Support received	3,600	
Real estate rental income	1,400	
	$50,000 × 18%	$ 9,000
The lesser amount	$ 9,000	
minus 2006 PA	(4,000)	
add unused deduction room	1,000	
	$ 6,000	

(A) incorrectly uses $44,000 as earned income: 18% × $44,000 – $4,000 PA + $1,000 = $4,920.

(B) incorrectly excludes the unused deduction room: $9,000 – $4,000 = $5,000.

(D) incorrectly ignores the earned income calculation: $19,000 – $4,000 + $1,000 = $16,000.

Question 3

(A) is correct. The calculations are as follows:

	Meg	*James*	
Salary	$46,000		
Employment expenses	(2,800)		ITA: 8
Business income	—	$18,000	
Interest income	800	1,500	
Net income	$44,000	$19,500	
Earned income	$46,000	$18,000	ITA: 63

Since James has the lower net income ($19,500), he must claim the deduction, which is the least of:

(a) Eligible child care expenses: $15,000 + ($100 × 2 weeks) $15,200

(b) Eligible children:
    $4,000 × 1 = $4,000
    $7,000 × 2 = 14,000 . . . . $18,000

(c) ⅔ × James' earned income: ⅔ × $18,000 . . . . $12,000

Since Joanne is age 17, she is not an eligible child. The deduction for the overnight camp for Susie   ITA: 63(3)
is restricted to $100 per week.

(B) is incorrect, because Meg cannot claim the deduction, since she has the higher net income.

(C) and (D) are incorrect because they are not the least amount calculated in (A) above.

Question 4

(B) is correct and is calculated as follows:

Moving van to transport household effects		$ 5,000
Travelling cost — self, spouse and two children		
Meals — flat rate ($51 × 4 persons × 5 days)	$ 1,020	
Car — flat rate (4,430 kms × $0.485)	2,149	
Hotel ($100 × 5 nights)	500	3,669
Legal fees — Vancouver house		900
Legal fees — Toronto house		1,100
Hotel costs while waiting for Vancouver house — $100 per day		
for 15 days (max.)		1,500
		$12,169

(A) incorrectly excludes the legal fees on the houses and uses $3,000 as travel costs:
$12,169 – $2,000 – $3,669 + $3,000 = $9,500.

(C) incorrectly includes all the hotel costs: $12,169 + 1,500 = $13,669.

(D) incorrectly includes all the hotel costs and the house hunting trip and uses $3,000 as travel
costs: $12,169 + $1,500 + $800 – $3,669 + $3,000 = $13,800.

Question 5

(D) is correct. The earned income that should be used to calculate her RRSP deduction for 2007 is her 2006 earned income, which is: ITA: 146(1)

	2006	
Salary	$100,000	
Taxable benefits	8,000	ITA: 6, 7
Travel expenses	(3,000)	ITA: 8
Business losses	(1,000)	
Rental income (net of expenses and CCA)	3,200	
Spousal support paid	(12,600)	
2006 Earned income	$ 94,600	ITA: 146(1)

(A) and (C) are incorrect. The earned income that should be used to calculate her child care   ITA: 63(3)
expense deduction for 2007 is $118,000:

	2007	
Salary	$110,000	
Taxable benefits	8,000	ITA: 6, 7
Earned income	$118,000	ITA: 63(3)

(A) incorrectly includes 2007 salary only ($110,000).

(C) is the 2007 net income under Division B which includes amounts for travel expenses, RPP   ITA: 63(3)
contributions, business losses, rental income and spousal support which are not part of the earned
income calculation for the child care expense deduction.

(B) is Sahar's 2007 earned income for computing her 2008 RRSP deduction: ITA: 146(1)

	2007	
Salary	$110,000	
Taxable benefits	8,000	ITA: 6, 7
Travel expenses	(2,000)	ITA: 8
Business losses	(1,200)	
Rental income (net of expenses and CCA)	3,600	
Spousal support paid	(12,000)	
Net income under Division B	$106,400	

Question 6

(D) is correct. Deductible moving costs are: ITA: 62(3)

Moving van		$2,600
Travelling costs to move Natalie and family		
Meals — flat rate ($51 × 4 persons × 3 days)	$ 612	
Car — flat rate (1,000 kms × $0.455)	455	
Hotel ($100 × 2 nights)	200	1,267
Cost of maintaining vacant former residence (maximum amount)		5,000
Cost of changing address on legal documents		100
		$8,967

(A) which totals $25,700 incorrectly includes all expenses listed, including only $900 for travelling costs.

(B) which totals $15,967 incorrectly includes the actual cost of maintaining the former residence (an additional $4,000) plus the $3,000 house hunting trip.

(C) which totals $12,600 incorrectly includes all actual cost of maintaining the former residence (an additional $4,000) and uses only $900 for travel.

CHAPTER 10
Computation of Taxable Income and Taxes Payable for Individuals

Question 1

(C) is correct. Since BL is a CCPC and is at arm's length with Brad, the stock option benefit will be included in Brad's income in the year of sale (along with Brad's taxable capital gain). The stock option benefit is $3,000 (($5 − $2) × 1,000). Brad's taxable capital gain is $1,000 (½ × ($7 − $5) × 1,000). Since Brad held the shares for at least 2 years, he can claim a Division C deduction of $1,500 (½ × his $3,000 option benefit).

ITA: 7(1.1)

ITA: 110(1)(d.1)

(A) incorrectly includes the section 7 benefit in 2005 and ignores the deduction.

(B) incorrectly includes the employment benefit and the incorrectly calculated Division C deduction (at ¼ of the $3,000 benefit) in 2005.

ITA: 7, 110(1)(d.1)

(D) incorrectly ignores the Division C deduction.

ITA: 110(1)(d.1)

Question 2

(C) is correct and is calculated as follows:

Basic	$ 8,929		ITA: 118(1)(c)
Age: $5,177 − 15% × ($47,500 − $30,936)	2,692		ITA: 118(2)
Pension	2,000		ITA: 118(3)
Employment	1,000		ITA: 8(10)
	$14,621 × 15.5% =	$2,266	
Dividend tax credit: 19% × $2,500		475	ITA: 121
		$2,741	

(A) incorrectly ignores the dividend tax credit: ($8,929 + $2,692 + $2,000 + $1,000) × 15.5% = $2,266.

ITA: 121

(B) incorrectly ignores the pension credit and the employment credit: ($8,929 + $2,692) × 15.5% + $475 = $2,276.

ITA: 118(3), 118(10)

(D) incorrectly ignores the income restriction on the age credit: ($8,929 + $5,177 + $2,000 + $1,000) × 15.5% + $475 = $3,126.

ITA: 118(2)

Question 3

(C) is correct. Shabir's net income and taxable income is calculated as follows:

Scholarship income (exempt)	$ Nil
Employment income	9,000
Moving expenses:	
to McGill University (limited to scholarship income)	Nil
to Toronto	(200)
	$ 8,800

Since Shabir's income is less than $8,929, his entire tuition fee, education, and textbook credits can be transferred to his parent (up to a maximum of $5,000).

ITA: 118.9

Tuition fee	$3,900
Education credit: 8 × $400	3,200
Textbook credit: 8 × $65	520
	$7,620; max. $5,000 × 15.5% = $775

(A) incorrectly computes the credit base on tuition only ($3,900 × 15.5% = $605).

(B) incorrectly includes the scholarship in income and claims the full moving costs to McGill: $1,100 + $9,000 − $500 − $200 = $9,400. Since this income exceeds $8,929 ($9,400 − $8,929 = $471), then $4,529 ($5,000 − $471) can be transferred resulting in a credit of $702 to a parent.

(D) incorrectly ignores the $5,000 limit: $7,620 × .155 = $1,181.

Question 4

(A) is correct.

Salary	$ 60,000
Cdn dividends ($20K × 1.45)	29,000
Stock option benefit	200,000
Taxable capital gain (½ × $200K)	100,000
Net income	$389,000
Stock option deduction (½ × $200K)	(100,000)
Taxable income	$289,000

Tax:	
1st $120,887	$ 26,040
balance @ 29% of $168,113	48,753
Basic personal amount ($8,929 × 15.5%)	(1,384)
Transfer of tuition, education, and textbook credits (15.5% × $5,000 × 3) . . .	(2,325)
Employment (15.5% of $1,000)	(155)
Dividend tax credit (19% of $29,000)	(5,510)
Federal tax	$ 65,419

(B) incorrectly omits the gross-up on the dividend and the dividend tax credit: $65,419 – (29% × $9K) + $5,510 = $68,319

(C) incorrectly omits the dividend tax credit: $65,419 + $5,510 = $70,929

(D) incorrectly omits the stock option deduction: $65,419 + 29% × $100K = $94,419

Question 5

(A) is correct.

Taxable income	$289,000
Add:	
30% of capital gain	60,000
3/5 of the stock option deduction	60,000
Deduct:	
Gross-up on dividends	(9,000)
Adjusted taxable income	$400,000
Less: Basic Exemption	(40,000)
Net	$360,000
Minimum tax before minimum tax credit ($360,000 × 15.5%)	$ 55,800
Basic personal amount ($8,929 × 15.5%)	(1,384)
Employment ($1,000 × 15.5%)	(155)
	$ 54,261

(B) incorrectly deducts the $2,325 transfer of tuition and education credits: $54,261 – $2,325 = $51,936.

(C) incorrectly omits the adjustment to add back the stock option deduction: $54,261 – 15.5% × $60K = $44,961.

(D) incorrectly omits the adjustment to add back the tax-free portion of the capital gain and the stock option deduction: $54,261 – 15.5% × $120K = $35,661.

CHAPTER 11
Computation of Taxable Income and Tax after General Reductions for Corporations

Question 1

(B) is correct. Loss Co may select any date, within the 53-week period commencing February 1, 2007, as its new year-end.   ITA: 249(4)(b), 249(4)(d)

(A) is incorrect, as the taxation year is deemed to have ended immediately before control was acquired. Since control was acquired on February 1, 2007, the year is usually deemed to have ended January 31, 2007. (Technically, it is possible to have an acquisition of control occur at a specific time, say, 10 am, on February 1, in which case, the taxation year can be deemed to have ended on February 1 at 9:59 am. Usually, a time is not specified, in which case, the taxation year is deemed to end the day before.) ITA: 249(4)(*a*)

(C) is incorrect because the corporation is deemed not to have established a fiscal period yet. This being the case, the corporation is free to select any year-end, within the 53-week limitation. ITA: 249(4)(*d*)

(D) is incorrect for the same reason as (C).

Question 2

(C) is correct. The ACB of the land is reduced from $200,000 to $140,000, its FMV. The $60,000 reduction is deemed to be a capital loss for the taxation year ended May 14, 2007. ITA: 111(4)(*c*), 111(4)(*d*)

(A) is incorrect as it includes the $25,000 accrued loss on the building which is depreciable property. Depreciable property is specifically excluded. ITA: 111(4)(*c*)

(B) is incorrect as it includes the $20,000 accrued loss on the inventory which is not a capital property.

(D) is incorrect, because the $60,000 accrued loss on the land was reduced by the $10,000 accrued gain on the marketable securities. The recognition of the accrued gain on the marketable securities is not required. An election is available to recognize the accrued gain, if it is desirable. ITA: 111(4)(*e*)

Question 3

(C) is correct. The UCC of the Class 45 computer equipment is reduced by $5,000, from $38,000 to $33,000. The UCC of the Class 8 office furniture and equipment is reduced by $10,000, from $58,000 to $48,000. The total of the two reductions, $15,000, is deemed to have been claimed as CCA in the year ended March 31, 2007. ITA: 111(5.1)

(A) is incorrect as this amount adjusts the UCC of all the classes to the FMV of the classes. This amount includes an adjustment of $8,000 to increase the UCC of the Class 10 automobiles and the Class 12 assets to the FMV of the respective classes. The $8,000 is then subtracted from the $15,000 reduction calculated in (C). This is incorrect. The adjustment applies only to the classes where the UCC is higher than the FMV. ITA: 111(5.1)

(B) is incorrect as it includes only 72% of the adjustment calculated in (C).

(D) is incorrect for the same reason as (A). The difference between (A) and (D) is that in (D) the positive and negative adjustments have been totalled, whereas in (A) they have been netted.

Question 4

(D) is correct. For its year ending December 31, 2007, Loss Co will be able to deduct non-capital losses of $15,000 (maximum), provided the widget retailing business is carried on throughout the taxation year ended December 31, 2007 with a reasonable expectation of profit. ITA: 111(5)(*a*)

(A) is incorrect as net capital losses incurred prior to the acquisition of control expire on the date control is acquired. ITA: 111(4)(*a*)

(B) is incorrect. Non-capital losses realized prior to an acquisition of control cannot be deducted against taxable capital gains incurred after the acquisition of control. Non-capital losses are only deductible against income from the business in which the losses were incurred and income from a similar products or services. ITA: 111(5)(*a*)

(C) is incorrect. The non-capital loss deduction has been limited to the income from a similar products or services net of the loss from the widget business. The netting of the widget business loss is not required. ITA: 111(5)(*a*)

Question 5

(D) is correct.

Net income for tax purposes	$600,000	
Canadian dividends	(100,000)	
Charitable donations		– not exceeding $450,000
	(200,000)	(75% of net income)
	$300,000	

ITA: 112

(A) incorrectly makes no adjustments: $600,000.

(B) incorrectly omits the deduction for charitable donations: $600,000 – $100,000 = $500,000.

(C) incorrectly omits the section 112 deduction for Canadian dividends: $600,000 – $200,000 = $400,000.

Question 6

(C) is correct.

Taxable income as per the answer to Question 5	$300,000
Part I tax on taxable income	
Tax @ 38% on $300,000	$114,000
Deduct: Federal tax abatement (10% × 90% × $300,000)	(27,000)
	$ 87,000
Add: Corporate surtax (1.12% of $300,000)	3,360
Deduct: M&P deduction (7% of $250,000)	(17,500)
Deduct: 7% rate reduction on income not eligible for the M&P deduction: 7% × [$300K – $250K]	(3,500)
Total federal tax	$ 69,360

(A) incorrectly applies the rate reduction to all income, including that eligible for the manufacturing and processing profits deduction: $69,360 + $3,500 – 7% × $300K = $51,860.

(B) incorrectly calculates the surtax as 4% × 21% × $300K rather than 4% × 28% × 300K. $69,360 – $3,360 + $2,520 = $68,520.

(D) incorrectly omits the 7% rate reduction: $69,360 + 3,500 = $72,860.

CHAPTER 12
Integration for Business and Investment Income of the Private Corporation

Question 1

(B) $18,400 is correct. It is calculated as follows:

Least of:	(a)	income from an active business carried on in Canada	$120,000
		net of loss from an active business carried on in Canada	(0)
			$120,000
	(b)	taxable income	$132,000
	(c)	business limit: $400,000 – $285,000	$115,000

The least is (c): $115,000 × 16% = $18,400

(A) $16,000 is incorrect. The foreign business loss of $20,000 has been netted against the $120,000 of Canadian business income.

(C) $19,200 is incorrect. This amount is 16% of the Canadian active business income.

(D) $21,120 is incorrect. This amount is 16% of the taxable income.

Question 2

(D) is correct. M Ltd. is carrying on an active business. The business is not a personal services business as the services are provided to an associated corporation. M Ltd. and ACC Ltd. are associated. M Ltd. is not a specified investment business as the principal purpose is not to derive income from property. Thus, by default, it is carrying on an active business.

ITA: 125(7)
ITA: 256(1)(d)

(A) is incorrect. M Ltd. is not carrying on a personal services business for the reasons outlined above.

(B) is incorrect. M Ltd. is not carrying on a personal services business for the reasons outlined above.

(C) is incorrect. M Ltd. is not carrying on a specified investment business as the principal purpose is not to derive income from property.

Question 3

(A) Nil is correct. Cdn. M&P profits are less than ABI eligible for the SBD.

(B) $1,400 is incorrect. This amount is 7% of taxable income in excess of $400,000.

(C) $23,170 is incorrect. This amount is 7% of Cdn. M&P profits in excess of the SBD of $64,000.

(D) $27,650 is incorrect. This amount is 7% × Cdn. M&P profits.

Question 4

(C) $68,000 is correct.

ITA: 186(1), 186(4)

Dividend received from non-connected corporation, C Ltd.:	
$120,000 × ⅓	$40,000
70% of $40,000 dividend refund received by connected corporation, B Ltd.	28,000
	$68,000

B Ltd is connected to A Ltd., because of *de jure* control and because A Ltd. holds more than 10% of the issued share capital in both votes and value.

ITA: 186(2), 186(4)

(A) $60,000 is incorrect. This amount is 70% and 8% of the dividend refunds received by B Ltd. and C Ltd., respectively.

(B) $64,000 is incorrect. This amount applies the Part I tax rate on investment income, 26⅔%, to the total dividends received.

(D) $80,000 is incorrect. This amount is ⅓ × the dividends received and ignores the special rules for connected corporations.

Question 5

(D) is correct because (A), (B) and (C) are all correct.

(A) and (B) are correct because Joanne controls J Co. and her spouse controls D Co. Two corporations are associated under paragraph 256(1)(c), if related persons control each corporation and either person owns at least 25% of the shares of the related persons' corporation. Spouses are related by marriage.

ITA: 251(6)(b)

(C) is correct because if a trust for their twin daughters controls a third company, T Co., those shares are deemed to be owned by the beneficiaries. In addition, because those beneficiaries are minors, their shares are deemed to be owned by each of Joanne and Doug. Therefore, J Co. and T Co. are associated because they are deemed to be controlled by the same person (Joanne). The same is true for D Co. and T Co. (each deemed to be controlled by Doug). The two corporations are associated with each other unless an election is made to deem the third corporation (T Co.) to have a business limit of nil.

ITA: 256(1.2)(f)(ii), 256(1.3)
ITA: 256(1)(a)

ITA: 256(2)

Question 6

(C) is correct. X Ltd. and Y Ltd. are not associated because although X Ltd. is controlled by a person who is related to each member of the various groups of persons (i.e., an pair of the two daughters

ITA: 256(1)(d)

and one son or all three) who controls Y Ltd., there is no cross-ownership of at least 25%. Thus, X Ltd. and Y Ltd. are not associated.

(A) is not correct. X and Y are associated. The same group (Rod and Patrick) controls both corporations. This group controls X Ltd., despite the fact that Patrick himself controls X Ltd. It does not matter that the individuals are not related.

ITA: 256(1)(*b*)
ITA: 256(1.2)(*b*)(i)

(B) is not correct because X Ltd. and Y Ltd. are associated because they are controlled by related persons (a parent and son are related by blood) and one of the persons owns not less than 25% of the shares of both companies.

ITA: 256(1)(*c*)
ITA: 251(6)(*a*)

(D) is not correct because the corporations in (A) are associated.

CHAPTER 13
Planning the Use of a Corporation and Shareholder-Manager Remuneration

Question 1

(A) is correct. The entire loan will be included in Stan's income in 2007, the year he received the loan. He does not meet the criterion for exclusion, as the loan will not be repaid within one year after the end of the taxation year of the lender in which the loan was made. He does not meet the other criteria for exclusion. Since such a loan is not available to other employees, it is not reasonable to conclude that he received the loan because of his employment.

ITA: 15(2)
ITA: 15(2.6)
ITA: 15(2.4)

(B) is incorrect. If the loan is not repaid within one year of the end of the year of S Ltd. in which the loan was made, then $200,000 must be included in the year of the loan. Repayments are deductible in the year of the repayment.

(C) is incorrect. There is no imputed interest benefit when the loan is included in income. If there was an imputed interest benefit the prescribed rate protection rule would not apply as the loan was not received because of his employment.

ITA: 80.4(1), 80.4(3)(*b*), 80.4(4)

(D) is incorrect. One year after the end of the calendar year in which the loan is received has no significance. The shareholder loan rule includes the loan in income in the year it is *received* unless it is repaid by one year after the end of the taxation year of the *lender* in which the loan was made, or the loan meets one of the specific exclusions.

ITA: 15(2)

Question 2

(C) is the correct answer. The shareholder loan rule would include the principal amount of the loan in Mrs. C's income in 2007 because none of the exception tests are met.

ITA: 15(2.2), 15(2.3), 15(2.4), 15(2.6)

(1) The exception test in subsection 15(2.2) does not apply because Mrs. C is resident in Canada.

(2) The exception in subsection 15(2.3) does not apply since the money is not lent in the ordinary course of money lending business.

(3) None of the exceptions for employees in subsection 15(2.4) are met, because it is not reasonable to conclude that the loan is received because of employment since no other employees have received similar loans.

(4) The exception in subsection 15(2.6) does not apply since the debt was repaid on April 1, 2009, which is more than one year from the end of S Ltd.'s December 31, 2007 fiscal year.

The loan in (A) would not be included in Mrs. A's income because the one-year repayment exception test applies: the debt is repaid on April 1, 2008, which is within one year from the end of S Ltd.'s December 31, 2007 fiscal year. Note, however, that the imputed interest benefit rule would apply to compute a deemed interest benefit on the loan.

ITA: 15(2.6)

ITA: 80.4(2)

The loan in (B) would not be included in B Ltd's income because the shareholder loan rule does not apply to corporate shareholders resident in Canada.

ITA: 15(2)

The loan in (D) would not be included in Mr. D's income because one of the exceptions for employees is met: Mr. D is not a specified employee and it is reasonable to conclude that the loan is received because of employment, since the computer is for employment use and other employees currently working at home have received similar loans. Since Mr. D is not a specified employee, the loan does not have to be for any specified purpose. A specified employee is an employee who is either a specified shareholder (i.e., generally, a person who owns at least 10% of the shares of any class of the

ITA: 15(2.4), 248(1)

corporation) or a person who does not deal at arm's length with the corporation. Since Mr. D owns only 5% of the shares of S Ltd. and deals at arm's length with the corporation, he is not a specified employee.

Question 3

(D) is correct. Since the $300,000 bonus is unpaid on the 180th day after the end of the taxation year of Fortelli Inc. in which the expense was incurred, it is not deductible until 2008, the taxation year in which it is actually paid.

ITA: 78(4)

(A) is incorrect. This amount refers to the rules in subsection 78(1) for unpaid amounts due to related persons, other than pension benefits, retiring allowances, salary, wages, or other remuneration.

(B) is incorrect. Subsection 78(4) does not distinguish between amounts owed to related and unrelated persons.

(C) is incorrect for the same reason as (A).

Question 4

The correct answer is (B). There is no penalty. The tax benefit that would otherwise have been enjoyed is denied.

ITA: 245(2)

(A) is incorrect as it is true in accordance with subsection 245(2).

(C) is incorrect as it is true in accordance with subsection 245(3).

(D) is incorrect as it is true in accordance with subsection 245(4).

Question 5

(C) is correct. The purpose of the transaction seems to be the reduction or avoidance of tax on the income earned on the $10,000 gift. This transaction goes against the spirit of the Act, read as a whole, and falls within the definition of an avoidance transaction. Note that an attribution rule would apply if it was a loan instead of a gift.

ITA: 245(3)
ITA: 56(4.1)

(A) is incorrect. The transaction is an estate freeze which can reasonably be considered to have been undertaken for *bona fide* purposes other than to obtain the tax benefit. This transaction does not result in a misuse or abuse of the Act, read as a whole.

IC 88-2, par. 10

(B) is incorrect. The incorporation of a business and the claiming of a small business deduction by a CCPC is specifically provided for in the Act. This transaction does not result in a misuse or abuse of the Act, read as a whole.

IC 88-2, par. 11

(D) is incorrect. The Act will deny the deduction of the bonus to the extent it is in excess of a reasonable amount. To the extent the transaction is reasonable, it does not result in a benefit. Corporate tax will be reduced by the accrual, but Mary will pay tax on the income personally.

ITA: 67; IC 88-2, par. 18

Question 6

(D) is correct. All the conditions for corporate attribution are met. As a result, Mr. Investor is deemed to have income of 6% × $1 million = $60,000.

ITA: 74.4

(A) incorrectly attributes the cash dividend received by Mrs. Investor to Mr. Investor: $10,000.

(B) incorrectly attributes the grossed up dividend received by Mrs. Investor to Mr. Investor: $12,500.

(C) incorrectly computes the attributed amount to Mr. Investor based on $500,000: 6% × $500,000 = $30,000.

ITA: 74.4

Question 7

(C) is correct. In order to be a small business corporation, the percentage of assets used in an active business by the corporation and the corporation controlled by Ms. Prentice's brother must be at least 90%. It is now 80% (60% + 20%) or $3.2 million.

ITA: 248(1) "small business corporation"

Therefore total assets must be $3.2 million/90% or $3,555,555.

Therefore $444,445 ($4 million – $3,555,555) of the non-active business assets must be sold.

(A) is incorrect because the corporation does not currently meet the 90% test.

(B) incorrectly assumes that 10% of the assets must be sold: 10% × 4 million = $400,000.

(D) incorrectly ignores the assets used by the related corporation and calculates that since active business assets are $2.4 million (60% × $4M), total assets must be $2.4 million/90% or $2,666,666 to meet the 90% test. As a result, $1,333,333 ($4 million − $2,666,666) of the non-active business assets must be sold.

CHAPTER 14
Rights and Obligations under the Income Tax Act

Question 1

(B) is correct. The penalty is $900. The initial penalty rate of 5% is increased by 1% for each *complete* month after April 30, 2007 that the return was not filed to a maximum penalty of 5% + 4% = 9%. ITA: 162(1)

(A) is incorrect as it includes only the initial penalty of 5% of the unpaid tax.

(C) is incorrect as it includes ½% for the half month of September. Only complete months should be counted for purposes of the penalty.

(D) is incorrect as it includes 1% for the month of September. Only complete months should be counted for purposes of the penalty.

Question 2

(B) August 15, 2010 is correct. The normal reassessment period for a CCPC ends 3 years after the day of mailing of a notice of assessment for the year. ITA: 152(3.1)

(A) December 31, 2009, 3 years after the end of the taxation year, is incorrect. The 3-year period commences with the date of mailing of the notice of assessment, not the last day of the fiscal year.

(C) December 31, 2010, 4 years after the end of the taxation year, is incorrect.

(D) August 15, 2011, 4 years after the day of mailing of a notice of assessment for the year, is incorrect. It would be correct if the taxpayer were a corporation other than a CCPC. ITA: 152(3.1)

Question 3

(D) June 15, 2008 is correct. The notice of objection filing due date is one year after Darol's filing-due date for 2006. ITA: 165(1)

(A) December 31, 2007, being one year after the end of the taxation year, is incorrect.

(B) January 14, 2008, being 90 days after the date of mailing of the notice of assessment, is incorrect in this case. For an individual and a testamentary trust, the due date is the later of this date and one year after the filing-due date for the tax return.

(C) April 30, 2008, being one year after the filing-due date for 2006 for an individual *not* carrying on a business, is incorrect. Darol's filing-due date for 2006 was June 15, 2007, as he carried on business in 2006.

Question 4

The correct answer is (D) September 30, 2007, being 6 months after the date of death. ITA: 150(1)(b)

(A) is incorrect. It is the most common due date for 2006 personal tax returns. This date is not correct for two reasons: first, he has income from carrying on business, and second, he died after October 2006. ITA: 150(1)(a)(i)

(B) is incorrect. It is the date the return would have been due if he had not died. ITA: 150(1)(a)(ii)

(C) is incorrect as it is 6 months after the end of the year for which the return is being filed.

Question 5

(A) is correct. ⟨...⟩ n monthly instalment is the least of:

− ¹⁄₁₂ of the e⟨...⟩ ayable: ¹⁄₁₂ × $200,000 = $16,667

– ¹/₁₂ of the prior year's taxes payable: ¹/₁₂ of $140,000 = $11,667

– ¹/₁₂ of the second prior year's taxable payable (¹/₁₂ of $180,000 = $15,000) for 2 months and 10 payments of $11,000 (³/₁₀ × [$140K – 2 × $15,000]).

The least of these is either the prior year method or the second prior year method. Only the prior year method ($11,667 per month) is listed as a choice in this question. Because X Ltd. had taxable income in the prior year of more than the small business deduction limit, it must pay its final balance due within two months of year end (February 29, 2008).

(B) and (C) incorrectly base the instalments on estimated taxes payable. (B) has the correct final due date. (C) incorrectly uses the balance-due day that is 3 months after the end of the year which is applicable only for Canadian-controlled private corporations that have taxable income that is less than the small business deduction limit in the prior year.

(D) incorrectly uses the amount for the first two payments of the second prior year method for all 12 payments but has the correct final due date for the balance due. (D) would have been a correct answer had it indicated that the payments for the last 10 months would be $11,000 per month.

Question 6

(D) is correct (2 payments of $3,825 and 2 payments of $4,375). The minimum monthly instalment is the least of:

– ¹/₄ of the estimated taxes payable: ¹/₄ × $25,000 = $6,250

– ¹/₄ of the prior year's taxes payable: ¹/₄ of $16,400 = $4,100

– ¹/₄ of the second prior year's taxable payable (¹/₄ of $15,300 = $3,825) for 2 months and 2 payments of $4,375 (¹/₂ × [$16,400 – 2 × $3,825]).

(A) is incorrect because 4 payments of $6,250 is not the minimum payment.

(B) is incorrect because 2 payments of $4,100 and 2 payments of $6,250 is not the minimum amount. Four payments of $4,100 would result in the minimum amount.

(C) is incorrect because 2 payments of $3,825 and 2 payments of $4,100 is not the minimum amount. If the first 2 payments are $3,825, the last 2 payments must be $4,375. Alternatively, 4 payments of $4,100 can be made.

CHAPTER 15
Corporate Distributions, Windings-Up, and Sales

Question 1

(D) is false. Only taxable dividends paid are included in the computation of dividend refunds.   ITA: 129(1)

(A) is true.   ITA: 83(2)(*b*)

(B) is true.   ITA: 83(2)

(C) is true.   ITA: 89(1) "capital dividend account" (*a*)

Question 2

(D) is correct.

Redemption amount	$ 60,000	
PUC	(10,000)	
Dividend	$ 50,000	ITA: 84(3)
Redemption amount	$ 60,000	
Dividend	(50,000)	
Proceeds of disposition	$ 10,000	ITA: 54
ACB	(20,000)	
Capital loss	$(10,000)	

(A) is incorrect. This amount ignores the redemption deemed dividend.   ITA: 84(3)

(B) is incorrect. This amount calculates the dividend using the cost as opposed to the PUC.

(C) is incorrect. The dividend has not been subtracted from the redemption amount to arrive at the proceeds of disposition.

Question 3

(B) is correct.

Funds available for distribution	$ 40,000	
PUC	(2,000)	
Deemed dividend	$ 38,000	ITA: 84(3)
Elected amount of capital dividend	(8,000)	
Taxable dividend	$ 30,000	
Funds available for distribution	$ 40,000	
Deemed dividend	(38,000)	
Proceeds of disposition	$ 2,000	ITA: 54
ACB	(1,000)	
Capital gain	$ 1,000	

(A) is incorrect. Only subsidiaries in which the parent company owns at least 90% of the shares can wind up on a tax-deferred basis.

(C) is incorrect. The capital dividend has not been subtracted in the calculation of the proceeds.

(D) is incorrect. The ACB has been subtracted from the funds available to arrive at a $39,000 capital gain. The general winding-up rule and the deemed dividend on winding-up have been ignored.   ITA: 84(2), 88(2)

Question 4

(C) $1,557,333 is correct.

	Deemed proceeds	Business income	Investment income	CDA	RDTOH
Opening balance		Nil	Nil	$ 10,000	$ 30,000
Cash	$ 45,000				
Land	850,000		$300,000	300,000	
Building	780,000	$200,000	200,000	200,000	
	$1,675,000		$500,000	$510,000	
Liabilities	$ (20,000)	× 18%	× 45%		
Tax	(261,000)	$ 36,000	$225,000		$133,333
RDTOH	163,333				$163,333
	$1,557,333				

(A) $485,000 is incorrect. The liabilities of $20,000 have been subtracted from the asset total of $505,000 on the balance sheet.

(B) $1,394,000 is incorrect. The RDTOH has been omitted.

(D) $1,838,333 is incorrect. The liabilities and the income tax have not been deducted in the computation of the amount available for distribution.

Question 5

(A) is correct. The total paid-up capital of the common shares is $25,000, ½ of which is attributable to Mr. C and ½ is attributable to Mr. B. The total paid-up capital of the common shares is

100 common shares issued to Mr. A	$10,000
100 common shares issued to Mr. B	15,000
	$25,000

(B) and (D) are incorrect. The total paid-up capital of the common shares is not $35,000. The sale by Mr. A to Mr. C for $20,000 does not affect the paid-up capital of the shares.

(C) is incorrect because the $25,000 total paid-up capital of the common shares is split equally among the shares and is not based on the issue price of the shares.

Question 6

(B) is correct. The $^3/_4$ × the proceeds would be deducted from the CEC pool which would cause it to have a negative balance of $750,000. The Act states that this negative balance should be multiplied by $^2/_3$, which makes it $500,000. The definition of the capital dividend account requires the tax-free portion of the gain ($500,000) to be included in the capital dividend account.

ITA: 14(1)(*b*)
ITA: 89(1) "capital dividend account" (*c*.2)

(A) and (D) are incorrect because there is no taxable capital gain on the sale of goodwill. As well, the reference in (D) to the refundable dividend tax on hand account is incorrect. The account is not affected.

(C) is incorrect as it does not take into consideration the business income inclusion or paragraph (*c*.2) of the definition of "capital dividend account".

ITA: 14(1)(*b*), 89(1)

CHAPTER 16
Income Deferral: Rollover on Transfers to a Corporation and Pitfalls

Question 1

(C) is correct. Electing at $800, the UCC of the transferred asset, will defer recapture as well as the capital gain.

ITA: 85(1)(*e*)

(A) is incorrect. The spousal rollover applies to transfers to a spouse or a spousal trust, but never to a corporation.

ITA: 73(1)

(B) is incorrect. Electing at $2,200 will defer the capital gain, but recapture of $1,400 will be incurred.

(D) is incorrect. Since the corporation will have acquired the depreciable asset from a non-arm's length individual, $2,600 (i.e., $2,200 + ½ ($3,000 − $2,200) is the maximum amount that the capital cost could be.

ITA: 13(7)(*e*)

Question 2

(D) $25,000 is correct. In order to defer the gain, Steve will elect at $40,000, the ACB of the asset. The elected amount cannot be less than the non-share consideration. Since S Ltd. assumed the mortgage of $15,000, an additional $25,000 of non-share consideration is the maximum that can be taken.

ITA: 85(1)

(A) $100,000 is incorrect. This amount would result in a capital gain of $60,000 as well as a shareholder benefit of $15,000.

ITA: 15(1)

(B) $85,000 is incorrect. This amount would result in a capital gain of $60,000.

(C) $40,000 is incorrect. This amount would result in a capital gain of $15,000.

Question 3

(B) $110,000 is correct. Since the corporation has acquired the depreciable property from a non-arm's length individual, the capital cost is limited to the transferor's capital cost, $100,000 plus the taxable capital gain on the transfer, $10,000. This totals $110,000.

ITA: 13(7)(*e*)

(A) $120,000, the elected transfer price, is incorrect for the same reason that (B) is correct.

(C) $90,000, the transferor's UCC plus the taxable capital gain on the transfer, is incorrect. The starting point is the transferor's capital cost, not UCC.

ITA: 13(7)(*e*)

(D) $75,000, the transferor's UCC, is incorrect for the same reason that (B) is correct.

Question 4

(D) $20,000 is correct.

Elected transfer price $40,000

Allocated to non-share consideration:

Cash	$3,000	
Debt	2,000	$ 5,000
Allocated to the preferred shares, up to their FMV		15,000
Allocated to the common shares, remainder		20,000
		$40,000

ITA: 85(1)(*g*)
ITA: 85(1)(*h*)

(A) $35,000 is incorrect. The elected amount, in excess of the non-share consideration, has all been allocated to the common shares.

(B) $23,000 is incorrect. None of the elected amount has been allocated to the cash.

(C) $23,333 is incorrect. The allocation between the preferred and common shares has been done based on proportionate values.

Question 5

(D) is correct because a section 22 election ensures that the purchaser will be able to take a doubtful debts reserve on the accounts receivable.

(A) and (B) are incorrect because a section 22 election ensures that the loss to the vendor is a business loss rather than a capital loss or superficial loss. If no section 22 election is made, the vendor will realize a loss that is a capital loss. Further, if the vendor and purchaser are affiliated persons, the loss will be denied and will be a superficial loss.

ITA: 54

(C) is incorrect because the vendor is always required to add the prior year's doubtful debts reserve. It does not matter whether or not a section 22 election is made.

ITA: 12(1)(*d*)

Question 6

(D) is correct. Because the promissory note is $60,000, the elected amount is deemed to be $60,000. The elected amount determines the proceeds of disposition to Rebecca, R Co.'s cost of the land, the cost of the consideration to Rebecca, and the paid-up capital of the shares issued as consideration after the paid-up capital reduction.

ITA: 85(2.1)

(A) is incorrect because the proceeds to Rebecca are deemed to be $60,000 not $50,000 as discussed above.

(B) is incorrect because R Co.'s cost of the land is deemed to be $60,000, not $50,000 as discussed above.

(C) is incorrect because Rebecca's cost of the preference shares is zero. It is calculated as the elected amount minus the boot ($60,000 – $60,000 demand note).

ITA: 85(1)(*g*)

CHAPTER 17
Income Deferral: Other Rollovers and Use of Rollovers in Estate Planning

Question 1

(C) is correct. On winding-up, the losses of the subsidiary are not available to the parent, until the parent's taxation year commencing after the commencement of the winding-up. Thus, the losses of L Ltd. would first be available to P Ltd. in its taxation year commencing January 1, 2008.

ITA: 88(1.1)

(A) is incorrect. The predecessor corporations are deemed to have a year-end immediately before the amalgamation, October 31, 2007. The amalgamated corporation first exists on November 1, 2007.

(B) is incorrect. The amalgamated corporation can utilize the losses in its first taxation year commencing November 1, 2007.

ITA: 87(2.1)

(D) is incorrect for the reasons (C) is correct.

Question 2

(B) is correct.

X Ltd's adjusted cost base of the shares of Y Ltd	$500,000

Less: Cost amount of Y Ltd.'s assets	(420,000)	
Dividends paid to X Ltd.	(15,000)	
Potential bump	$ 65,000	ITA: 88(1)(*d*)

The ACB of the land can be bumped by $30,000, up to its FMV at the time X Ltd. acquired control of   ITA: 88(1)(*d*)
Y Ltd., $130,000.

(A) is incorrect. The bump available on a winding-up has not been applied.   ITA: 88(1)(*d*)

(C) is incorrect. The full amount of the bump available has been allocated to the land. The ACB of   ITA: 88(1)(*d*)
the land cannot be bumped above the FMV of the land when X Ltd. acquired control of Y Ltd.

(D) is incorrect for the same reason as (C). In addition, the potential bump has not been reduced
by the dividends received from X Ltd.

Question 3

(B) is correct. Since Chris exchanged all his common shares as part of a reorganization of capital,   ITA: 86(1)(*b*)
the rollover applies automatically. The cost of the preferred shares is equal to the cost of his common
shares, less the non-share consideration: $2,000 – $135 = $1,865. For purposes of calculating the capital   ITA: 86(1)(*c*)
gain on the disposal of the common shares, proceeds are defined as the cost of the new shares, plus
non-share consideration received: $1,865 + $135 = $2,000. As the proceeds equal his ACB, there is no
capital gain.

(A) is incorrect. The ACB of the preferred shares has not been reduced by the non-share consideration received.

(C) is incorrect. The tax deferral provisions have been ignored.

(D) is incorrect. A capital gain equal to the non-share consideration has been recognized.

Question 4

(D) is correct as it is false. The provision specifically states that subsection 85.1(1) does not apply   ITA: 85.1(2)
where consideration other than shares of the particular class of the purchaser was received by the
vendor. Therefore, in the absence of any other election being made, Shelly would have a capital gain of
$5,000 on the exchange if she received any non-share consideration.

(A) is incorrect as it is true. Section 85.1 is automatic; no election is required.

(B) is incorrect as it is true.   ITA: 85.1(1)(*a*)

(C) is incorrect as it is true.   ITA: 85.1(1)(*b*)

Question 5

(A) is the correct answer because this plan will freeze the value of his interest in ABC for tax
purposes (since preferred shares don't grow in value) and transfer future growth to his children
(because common shares do grow in value) without giving up control (because the preferred shares are
voting). There will be no tax on the transfer since he will be electing at tax cost.

(B) is incorrect because changing his will to leave his shares of ABC to his children does not
achieve his objective of freezing the value of his interest and having no tax on the transfer.

(C) is incorrect because gifting the ABC shares to his children results in the loss of control and   ITA: 69
immediate tax on the accrued capital gain because the gift results in a deemed disposition at fair market
value.

(D) is incorrect because, although a sale at fair market value taking back debt as consideration will   ITA: 40
defer tax somewhat because of the 10-year reserve available for such transfers, there will be tax on the
accrued gain payable over the 10-year period and there is a loss of control.

Question 6

(C) is correct, assuming an election is made at $500,001. The boot must be limited to $1 because   ITA: 84.1(1)
the Act will cause any boot in excess of this amount to be a deemed dividend not a capital gain. That is
why (D) is incorrect.

(A) is incorrect because a reverse asset freeze involves a transfer by a company rather than an
individual. Hence, the $500,000 capital gains exemption cannot be used.

(B) is incorrect because an internal freeze involves an automatic rollover. Hence, the $500,000   ITA: 86
capital gains exemption cannot be used.

CHAPTER 18
Partnerships and Trusts

Question 1

(C) $167,500 is correct.

Net income per financial statement		$ 365,000
Add: Donations		20,000
Sale of shares — Taxable capital gain	$ 60,000	
— Accounting gain	(120,000)	(60,000)
		$ 325,000
Bert's share		× ½
		$ 162,500
Dividend gross-up: $20,000 × ¼		5,000
Taxable income		$ 167,500

(A) $182,500 is incorrect. All of the adjustments have been ignored: donations, net accounting/tax gain, and the dividend gross-up.

(B) $187,500 is incorrect. The only adjustment that was made was for the dividend gross-up.

(D) $171,500 is incorrect. All adjustments were made except for the dividend gross-up, which, at 45%, was incorrect on dividends from a CCPC out of its LRIP.

Question 2

(C) $63,000 is correct.

Contributions — initial	$ 5,000
— additional	14,000
Share of profit	100,000
Share of non-taxable portion of capital gain	20,000
Share of charitable donations	(6,000)
Drawings	(70,000)
ACB	$ 63,000

(A) $33,000 is incorrect. The capital gain has been excluded completely.

(B) $43,000 is incorrect. The non-taxable portion of the capital gain has not been included.

(D) $69,000 is incorrect. The ACB has not been reduced by Ann's share of the charitable donations.

Question 3

(A) is true. The tax return is due 90 days after the year-end of the trust. *Inter vivos* trusts are   ITA: 150(1)(c), 249(1)(b)
taxed on a calendar year basis.

(B) is true. The trust is entitled to the deduction.   ITA: 104(6)

(C) is true. The tax rate is 29%.   ITA: 122(1)

(D) is false. Al is deemed to have received proceeds equal to the fair market value of the marketable   ITA: 69(1)(b)
securities transferred to the trust. Therefore, Al is required to recognize the $30,000 capital gain.

Question 4

(B) is true. Testamentary trusts are taxed as individuals.   ITA: 104(2)

(A) is false. The taxation year of a testamentary trust does not have to be on a calendar year basis.   ITA: 104(23)

(C) is false. The trust return is due 90 days after the end of the fiscal period of the trust.   ITA: 150(1)(c)

(D) is false. The trust is entitled to claim a dividend tax credit for dividends received from taxable Canadian corporations.

ITA: 104(2), 121

Question 5

(C) is correct. An alter ego trust has a deemed disposition on the settlor's death.

ITA: 248(1)

(A) is incorrect. An *inter vivos* trust generally has a deemed disposition at fair market value at the end of 21 years, unless it is a joint partner trust (described in (B)), in which case the deemed disposition takes place on the partner (ie., spouse or common-law partner) beneficiary's death.

(D) is incorrect. A discretionary trust would always have a deemed disposition at fair market value at the end of 21 years, since it cannot be a joint partner trust (which, by definition, must pay the income out to the beneficiary and, therefore, cannot be discretionary).

Question 6

(C) Avoiding the 21-year rule is not an advantage. You cannot avoid it unless the trust is a joint partner trust.

ITA: 104(4)

(A) is incorrect because income-splitting using the available designations is an advantage.

ITA: 104(13.1), 104(13.2)

(B) is incorrect, because avoiding the deemed disposition on the child's death is an advantage.

(D) is incorrect, because providing your children with beneficial ownership but not control over their inheritance is an advantage.

Appendix III

Solutions to Exercises

CHAPTER 1
Introduction

Exercise 1

The following summary is discussed in more detail below:

Case	Topic	Part	Division	Subdivision	Provision
(A)	Taxable capital gain	I	B	c	paragraph 38(*a*)
(B)	Membership dues	I	B	a	subparagraph 8(1)(*i*)(i)
(C)	Personal injury award	I	B	g	paragraph 81(1)(*g*.1)
(D)	Expense limit	I	B	f	section 67
(E)	Parent	XVII	—	—	subsection 252(2)
(F)	*Inter vivos* trust	I	B	k	subsection 108(1)
(G)	Filing deadline	I	I	—	paragraph 150(1)(*b*)
(H)	Shareholder benefit	I	B	b	subsection 15(1)
(I)	Non-arm's length	I	B	f	paragraph 69(1)(*b*)
(J)	Investment fees	I	B	b	paragraph 20(1)(*bb*)

(A) Part I, Division B, Subdivision c, paragraph 38(*a*): — Most definitions applicable to the Taxable Capital Gains and Allowable Capital Losses subdivision of Part I, Division B are found in section 54. However, this definition is set out at the beginning of Subdivision c. Definitions of terms used throughout the Act are found in subsection 248(1). If a term is not specifically defined in subsection 248(1) or in a section elsewhere in the Act, judicial precedents should be consulted for the meaning of the word.

(B) Part I, Division B, Subdivision a, subparagraph 8(1)(*i*)(i): — Employment income and deductions are set out in sections 5 to 8 of Part I, Division B, Subdivision a of the Act. All deductions from this source appear in section 8 with the major list of deductions occurring in subsection 8(1) and further explanation or restriction of these deductions appearing in subsections 8(2) to 8(11).

(C) Part I, Division B, Subdivision g, paragraph 81(1)(*g*.1): — Income from property acquired as personal injury award is one in a limited list of items found in section 81 which are not included in computing income.

(D) Part I, Division B, Subdivision f, section 67: — Inclusions and deductions in the computation of income are generally found in Part I, Division B, Subdivisions a, b, c, d or e. In this case, however, the rule is found in Subdivision f dealing with general rules relating to the computation of income from all sources.

(E) Part XVII, subsection 252(2): — The word "parent" appears throughout the Act, so the definition is most likely to be in Part XVII on "Interpretation."

(F) Part I, Division B, Subdivision k, subsection 108(1): — Trusts and their beneficiaries are dealt with in Subdivision k of Part I, Division B. The definitions section for this subdivision is section 108.

(G) Part I, Division I, paragraph 150(1)(*b*): This is a procedural matter generally handled in Division I of Part I of the Act dealing with Returns, Assessments, Payment and Appeals.

(H) Part I, Division B, Subdivision b, subsection 15(1): — A benefit received by a shareholder, if it is to be taxed, would likely be income from property which is handled in Subdivision b of Division B of Part I. Inclusions from that source are generally listed in sections 12 to 17.

(I) Part I, Division B, Subdivision f, paragraph 69(1)(*b*): — This provision can be found in the set of general rules pertaining to the computation of income in Subdivision f of Division B of Part I because it affects the computation of income from a variety of sources.

(J) Part I, Division B, Subdivision b, paragraph 20(1)(*bb*): — Investments provide income from property and deductions from such income are generally listed in subsection 20(1).

Exercise 2

DIVISION B

Par. 3(*a*)	*Subdivision a*				
	Sec. 5	Salary		$ 60,000	
	Par. 6(1)(*c*)	Director's fees		5,000	
	Ssec. 6(9)	Imputed interest		3,000	$ 68,000
	Less:				
	Par. 8(1)(*i*)	Professional engineering fees		$ 300	
	Par. 8(1)(*m*)	Registered pension plan contributions		4,000	4,300
					$ 63,700
	Subdivision b				
	Sec. 9	Business income — share of partnership tax profits		$ 10,000	
	Par. 12(1)(*c*)	Canadian bank interest		3,000	13,000
	Subdivision d				
	Par. 56(1)(*a*)	Retiring allowance			20,000
		Total par. 3(*a*) income			$ 96,700
Par. 3(*b*)	*Subdivision c*				
	Par. 38(*a*)	Taxable capital gain		$ 20,000	
	Par. 38(*b*)	Allowable capital loss		(2,000)	18,000
					$114,700
Par. 3(*d*)	*Subdivision b*				
	Ssec. 9(2):	Rental loss			
		Rental revenue		$ 25,000	
		Less: Expenses			
		Par. 20(1)(*c*)	Mortgage interest	(23,000)	
		Par. 18(1)(*a*)	Taxes and insurance	(4,500)	
		Par. 18(1)(*a*)	Maintenance	(1,500)	(4,000)

Division B income				$110,700
Par. 110(1)(*j*)	Home relocation interest deduction		$ 1,000	
Par. 111(1)(*a*)	Non-capital loss		3,000	
Par. 111(1)(*b*)	Net capital loss		5,000	(9,000)
Taxable income				$101,700

Federal tax after credits			
Tax before credits			$ 21,051
Sec. 118	Personal credits		(2,559)
Sec. 118.7	CPP contributions credit		(308)
Sec. 118.7	EI premium credit		(112)
Sec. 118.5	Tuition credit		(68)
Sec. 118.6	Education and textbook credit transfer		(80)
Sec. 118.1	Charitable donation credit		(550)
Basic federal tax			$ 17,374

CHAPTER 2
Liability for Tax

Exercise 1

(A) Alpha is a part-time resident of Canada until August 27 of the year when he appears to have made a "clean break" with Canada. While in Canada he would not have been sojourning, so the deeming rule would not apply.

ITA: 250(1)(*a*)

(B) Beta has no residential ties with Canada. Citizenship is not a determining factor in establishing such ties.

(C) Gamma is a non-resident of Canada and is taxable only on employment income earned in Canada.

ITA: 2(3)(*a*), 115(1)(*a*)(i)

(D) Delta is either a part-time resident of Canada or a non-resident employed in Canada, depending on the facts of his stay in Canada. He is also taxable under paragraph 2(3)(*c*) because the shares are taxable Canadian property.

ITA: 115(1)(*b*)(iv)

(E) Epsilon is deemed a resident of Canada because of his relationship to his mother.

ITA: 250(1)(*c*)(i), 250(1)(*f*)

(F) Mu is not deemed to be a resident of Canada by any of the deeming rules. She has never been resident in Canada. Therefore, she is not a resident of Canada.

ITA: 250(1)

Exercise 2

[See: *MacDonald v. M.N.R.*, 68 DTC 433 (T.A.B.).]

(A) The full-time residence alternative→taxed in Canada on worldwide income for full year:

ITA: 2(1)

Criterion: residence is a question of fact dependent on the degree of permanency in the relationship between a person and a place;

Evidence:

(i) factors indicating this relationship between the appellant and Canada,

    1. he sold his house in the United States and paid an American capital gains tax for not buying another residence,

    2. his wife, upon arriving in Canada, rented premises pending the purchase of a house,

    3. she and the children, whom the appellant was supporting to the extent of $600 per month, stayed in Canada all year-round,

    4. he stayed in Canada when he was off-duty to the extent of 166 out of 180 days in 1964,

      — full-time presence is not necessary,

    5. other non-determining factors,

      — joint account in Canada where pay cheques were deposited during his vacations,

      — joint ownership of a car with New Brunswick registry,

      — citizenship irrelevant;

(ii) factors detracting from a relationship with Canada,

    1. a few rooms, without exclusive use, made available for him at his sister's house in the United States,

      — not a permanent abode,

      — an individual can have more than one residence,

    2. U.S. citizen and previously and subsequently resided in the United States with a stated intention to return,

      — but only 1964 in question on the facts,

        — stated intention must be supported by behavioural facts,

      — worked for a U.S. company and paid in U.S. currency,

— but not determining because a Canadian resident can be involved in such a situation, providing employment services abroad for a non-Canadian company,

— memberships and investments including bank accounts, securities and pension plan in United States,

— factors may indicate U.S. residence, but not determining and also possible for a person resident in Canada,

— no Canadian memberships or investments and no application for family allowances,

— not determining factors and also possible of a Canadian resident,

— children living in United States,

— married and apparently not dependent,

— phone in wife's name in Canada,

— a factor, but hardly determining,

— neither employed in Canada nor carrying on business in Canada,

— not necessary condition for full-time residence.

(This list of factors is longer but there is more substance for full-time residence.)

(B) The deemed residence alternative→taxed in Canada on worldwide income for full year: ITA: 2(1)

Criterion: the condition of sojourning an aggregate of 183 days or more;   ITA: 250(1)

Evidence: his total stay in Canada in the year was only for 166 days; therefore, the condition is not met.

(C) The part-time residence alternative→taxed in Canada on worldwide income for part of the   ITA: 2(1), 114, 118.91
year resident in Canada with deductions applicable to the period of part-time residence and non-refundable tax credits either prorated for or applicable to the period of part-time residence (as long as not resident in Canada during some other part of the year);

Criterion: clean break or fresh start during 1964;

Evidence: neither occurred.

(D) The non-residence alternative→taxed in Canada on income earned in Canada: ITA: 2(3)

Criteria: employed in Canada, carried on business in Canada or disposed of taxable Canadian property in the year;

Evidence: none of these conditions occurred in the year.   ITA: 2(3)

(E) Conclusion: if the taxpayer is to be found a resident it must be as a full-time resident:

— the major factors indicate a relationship with Canada which would warrant a conclusion of such resident status.

Exercise 3

(A) Inch Incorporated is resident in Canada by virtue of the common law principle of central   ITA: 250(4)
management and control. The corporation cannot be deemed resident in Canada because it was not incorporated in Canada.

(B) Foot Limited is deemed resident in Canada because it was incorporated in Canada after   ITA: 250(4)(a)
April 26, 1965.

(C) Yard Incorporated is not resident this year by virtue of the common law principle of central management and control. Furthermore, the corporation cannot be deemed resident in Canada because it was not incorporated in Canada.

(D) Mile Limited is resident in Canada. The corporation was incorporated in Canada before   ITA: 250(4)(c)
April 27, 1965 and after that time it was resident by virtue of the central management and control rule.

CHAPTER 3
Employment Income

Exercise 1

[See: *Isaac v. M.N.R.*, 70 DTC 1285 (T.A.B.)]

The following tests are applied to determine whether R.N. is an employee or an independent contractor.

Economic Reality or Entrepreneur Test

In applying the control subtest, the question is whether Canadian Forces Hospital, Halifax controlled not only what was done by R.N. but how it was done. In this case the Hospital exercised control over R.N. in connection with dividing up the patients to be cared for among the available nurses and imposing routine rules and regulations with regard to the administration of drugs and other medications. On the other hand, the Hospital did not exercise any control over the method in which R.N. did her work, which requires special knowledge, skill, and judgment. Accordingly, it does not appear that the Hospital exercised sufficient control to conclude that R.N. was an employee on the basis of this test alone.

However, the application of the other subtests is particularly revealing. R.N. does not run the risk of financing the equipment, supplying other assistants necessary to carry out her duties in the Hospital or seeking out clients. R.N. used the equipment and supplies furnished by the Hospital. She neither hired nor fired any of the nursing assistants who worked under her. She could only request that the Hospital hire additional staff to assist her. The clients were patients of the Hospital. R.N. was not in a position to substitute the services of another nurse if she was unable to perform her duties. All this evidence tends to establish that from an economic reality point of view R.N. was an employee, but this test may not be definitive in this case.

Integration or Organization Test

The Hospital deducted Canada Pension Plan contributions from her pay as they did with the nurses who were employed full-time by the Hospital. R.N. appeared to be economically dependent on the hospital, although she was not precluded from offering her services elsewhere. R.N. was subject to co-ordinational control of the hospital in terms of where to perform her services and when to do so. On the other hand, R.N. was not eligible for the regular benefits of a full-time nurse such as holidays, sick pay, retirement plan, etc. She was hired on a day-to-day basis at a *per diem* rate of pay. Her services could be terminated on 24 hours notice if full-time nurses became available. On the weight of the evidence it can be argued that R.N. is an employee of the Hospital based on the integration test.

Specific Result Test

On the one hand, it was R.N.'s personal services that were at the disposal of the Hospital. Her work was done on a continuous day-to-day basis without there being any limited or specified amount of work that she had, by contract, to accomplish. She could not substitute another person to perform her duties if she was unable to do so. On the other hand, R.N. was not a full-time nurse for any specified period of time. Her time was made up on a weekly basis in advance. She could be laid off on 24 hours notice. On balance, it appears that the evidence leads to the conclusion that, by applying the specific result test, R.N. was an employee. This conclusion is consistent with that for the integration or organization test.

Conclusion

The application of the control subtest of the economic reality or entrepreneur test leads to the conclusion that R.N was not an employee of the Hospital. The application of the other subtests of the economic reality test, the integration test and the specific result test leads to the inference that R.N. was an employee of the Hospital. (Your own conclusion after weighing all of these tests.)

Exercise 2

(A) Specifically exempted. ITA: 6(1)(*a*)

(B) Taxable; only private medical plan premiums and provincial health service levies are exempted. ITA: 6(1)(*a*)

(C) and (D) Exempted, since the premium was paid to a private medical plan. ITA: 6(1)(*a*)

(E) Taxable. The Interpretation Bulletin only exempts tuition fees where the course is primarily for the benefit of the employer. ITA: 6(1)(*a*), IT-470R, par. 18, 19

(F) Normally, taxable, but since the payment meets the conditions, namely that the Christmas gift is under $500 and is not cash or near cash, the CRA's position is that the gift is not a taxable benefit. ITA: 6(1)(*a*)

(G) Partly taxable: The CRA takes the position that there will be no benefit if William had reimbursed the company the actual cost ($420). Since William did not completely reimburse the company for the actual costs, then the benefit would be calculated by taking the difference between the actual costs ($420) and the amount paid by William ($200) for a taxable benefit of $220.

ITA: 6(1)(a); IT-470R, par. 28

(H) Taxable, but the CRA takes the position that the amount would not be taxable if the membership was principally for the employer's advantage rather than the employee's.

ITA: 6(1)(a); IT-470R, par. 34

(I) Taxable unless the financial counselling was in respect of re-employment or retirement.

ITA: 6(1)(a), 6(1)(a)(iv)(B)

Exercise 3

The $6,000 merchandise discount is a taxable benefit. Administrative practice reflected in the Interpretation Bulletin does exempt discounts on merchandise, but they must be offered to all employees and not to just select groups. If there was an overall discount of 10% to all employees, it would seem reasonable in the circumstances to include only 25% in income; however, the Interpretation Bulletin is silent on this point.

IT-470R

IT-470R, par. 27

Exercise 4

The entire $5,500 is a taxable benefit. The exclusion for an eligible housing loss does not apply, because the loss was not incurred in an eligible relocation. The Interpretation Bulletin does provide some relief in this area, but only when an employee moves because he or she:

ITA: 6(1)(a), 6(19), 6(20), 248(1) "eligible relocation", IT-470R, par. 35

(a) has been transferred from one establishment of the employer to another; or

(b) has accepted another position at a location other than his or her former location.

If either of the above situations had existed, there would be no taxable benefit. Note that on the sale of the house, the loss cannot be greater than the actual loss to the employee, calculated as the amount by which the cost of the house exceeds the net selling price received.

IT-470R, par. 37

Exercise 5

Premiums paid:

(A) Provincial medical plan premiums paid by an employer are a taxable benefit; however, a provincial health service levy paid by an employer is not a taxable benefit.

ITA: 6(1)(a)

(B) and (C) The extended health care and dental care plans are private medical plans; hence, the premiums paid by the employer are not employment income.

ITA: 6(1)(a)

(D) Since the sickness or accident income protection plan is a group plan, premiums paid by the employer are exempt from employment income.

ITA: 6(1)(a)

Conclusion:

The following rearrangement would result in a lower tax cost:

(A) Company should pay for 100% of the extended health care and dental plan.

(B) Employees should pay the provincial medical plan premiums since company payments would be taxable benefits.

(C) Employees should consider paying the sickness or accident income protection premium themselves.

When an employer pays *any* portion of the premium for this type of plan, amounts that are paid out of the plan are taxable as employment income, less the employee's contribution to date. Conversely, if the employee pays all of the premiums, none of the amounts paid out of the plan are taxable. Since this particular plan has benefits of only 50% of the wages, the employee would be in a relatively poor cash position. The imposition of tax, even though at a lower rate, would certainly result in extreme hardship if the illness is prolonged.

ITA: 6(1)(f)

Exercise 6

Benefit would be the sum of:

ITA: 6(9), 80.4

(A) Car loan — prescribed rates

1st quarter	7% × $15,000 × 90/365 = $259	
2nd quarter	6% × $15,000 × 91/365 = 224	
3rd quarter	8% × $15,000 × 92/365 = 302	
4th quarter	7% × $15,000 × 92/365 = 265	$ 1,050

(B) Home purchase loan[1]
The lesser of the prescribed rate at the time of the loan (i.e., 7%) and the prescribed rate per quarter.

1st	7% × $100,000 × 90/365	= $ 1,726		
2nd	6% × $100,000 × 91/365	= 1,496		
3rd	7% × $100,000 × 92/365	= 1,764		
4th	7% × $100,000 × 92/365	= 1,764	6,750	

(C) Other loan

1st	7% × $ 10,000 × 90/365	= $ 173		
2nd	6% × $ 10,000 × 91/365	= 150		
3rd	8% × $ 10,000 × 92/365	= 202		
4th	7% × $ 10,000 × 92/365	= 176	701	
			$ 8,501	

Less amounts paid[2]

(a) 6% × $ 15,000 × 365/365	$ 900	
(b) 4% × $100,000 × 365/365	4,000	
(c) 7% × $ 10,000 × 365/365	700	5,600
		$ 2,901

The Act would deem $150 of the car loan interest ($1,050 – $900) to be paid in the year and, therefore, eligible for an interest deduction, since the interest was deemed to be paid within 30 days of the year-end, as required. — ITA: 80.5 / ITA: 8(1)(j), 80.4(1)(c)

An Interpretation Bulletin indicates that the deemed interest expense must be prorated for employment use. — IT-522R, par. 27

$$\frac{27,000 \text{ km}}{45,000 \text{ km}} \times \$150 = \$90$$

The interest deduction provision would deny a prorated deduction of the $900 paid on January 15 of the following year, since it was not paid in the taxation year in question. However, this amount would be eligible for a deduction in the following taxation year to the extent of the business use. — ITA: 8(1)(j)

The interest limitation restricts the interest to the lesser of (a) $90 and (b) $300 × $^{365}/_{30}$ × 27,000/45,000 = $2,190. — ITA: 67.2

— *NOTES TO SOLUTION*

[1] If this loan had been as a consequence of an employment relocation, Division C of the Act would have provided a deduction for five years, equal to the imputed interest benefit on the first $25,000 of the "home relocation loan", as defined. As a result, in this particular case, the overall benefit on the housing loan would have been reduced by $1,688 (i.e., $25,000/$100,000 of $6,750). See Chapter 10 for a complete discussion of this provision. The "lesser of" comparison is made on a quarter-by-quarter basis. — ITA: 110(1)(j), 248(1)

[2] The interest benefit is calculated on an aggregate basis. Any excess interest payment on one loan effectively reduces the deemed interest benefit on the other loans. — ITA: 80.4

Exercise 7

Year 1 — No tax effect.

Year 4 — No tax effect.

Year 5 — No tax effect, since the employer is a Canadian-controlled private corporation.

Year 6 — Must take into employment income under Division B the following: — ITA: 7(1.1)

$$50,000 \text{ shares} \times (\$3 - \$1) = \underline{\$100,000}$$

— Will have a capital gain of

$$50,000 \text{ shares} \times (\$6 - \$3) = \underline{\$150,000}$$

— May be eligible for the capital gains deduction for qualifying small business corpo- ration shares.

ITA: 110.6(1), 248(1)

— Since Katrina sold these shares within two years after the date of acquisition, she is not entitled to a deduction of one half of the subsection 7(1.1) inclusion. She is also not entitled to a general deduction since the exercise price of $1.00 was less than fair market value ($1.50) at the date the option was granted.

ITA: 110(1)(*d*), 110(1)(*d*.1)

Exercise 8

(a) Car benefit if business–use kilometres are 10,000

Standby charge

ITA: 6(1)(*e*), 6(2)

$$\frac{20,004 \text{ km}^{(1)}}{20,004 \text{ km}} \times [2\% \times (\$20,000 \times 12)] = \dots \dots \dots \dots \dots \quad \$4,800$$

Operating costs[2] (12,000 km × $0.22) 2,640 $7,440

ITA: 6(1)(*k*)(v)

Less: amount reimbursed 1,800

Total car benefit if business-use kilometres are 10,000 $5,640

(b) Car benefit if business-use kilometres are 20,000

Standby charge

ITA: 6(1)(*e*), 6(2)

$$\frac{12,000 \text{ km}^{(3)}}{20,004 \text{ km}} \times [2\% \times (\$20,000 \times 12)] = \dots \dots \dots \dots \dots \quad \$2,879$$

Operating costs[4] (50% × $2,879) = 1,440 $4,319

ITA: 6(1)(*k*)(v)

Less: amount reimbursed 1,800

Total car benefit if business-use kilometres are 20,000 $2,519

NOTES

[1] The employee does not qualify for the standby charge reduction since the car is not used more than 50% in the performance of employment duties when the business use is only 15,000 km. Therefore, in this outcome, the value of A in the formula (i.e., 12,000 km) is deemed equal to the value of B in the formula (i.e., 1,667 × 12 rounded).

[2] The election method is not available to the employee, since the car is not used more than 50% for business.

ITA: 6(1)(*k*)(iv)

[3] When the business-use kilometers is 20,000, the employee qualifies for the standby charge reduction and the numerator becomes the lesser of (a) 12,000 km, and (b) 1,667 km × 12 months.

[4] The operating benefit election at 50% of the standby charge is less than $0.22¢ × 12,000 km = $2,640. The election method is available since employment kilometres comprise more than 50% of the total.

Exercise 9

The Act would appear to deny any deduction in respect of Calvin's work space in the home. In order for Calvin to avoid the restrictions, one of two conditions must be met, neither of which appear to be adhered to. The first alternative condition is that the work place in the home must be where the individual principally performs the employment duties. The second alternative condi- tion is even more stringent, namely, that the work place must be used exclusively for employment income purposes and that the work place must be used on a regular and continuous basis as a meeting place for employment-connected persons.

ITA: 8(13)

If Calvin had met one of the conditions, then he would be able to deduct some of the expenses indicated as long as he met the conditions of paragraph 8(1)(*i*). First Calvin must have a contract with his employer indicating that he must pay for office rent and supplies and the employer completes and signs a T2200. However, of the expenses indicated, only the maintenance expense, including fuel, electricity, light bulbs, cleaning materials and minor repairs, on a pro- rated basis will be permitted. The imputed rent of $1,000 is not deductible; this position was confirmed in the *Thompson* case by the Federal Court–Trial Division.

ITA: 8(13)

IT-352R2, par. 2, 3

89 DTC 5439 (F.C.T.D.)

Exercise 10

Allowances and related expenses: There are two conditions that must be met in order to permit the allowance to be excluded from income:

ITA: 6(1)(*b*)(vii)

(a) the allowance must relate to travel outside of the municipality in which the employer's office is situated;

(b) the allowance must be a reasonable amount.

The $10,000 accommodation allowance is a taxable allowance, since the amount is an unreasonable amount on the assumption that the incurred expenses of $12,000 were reasonable. Therefore, she is entitled to a deduction, since she meets the other conditions of this paragraph; namely, she ordinarily travels in respect of her employment duties and is required by her employment contract to pay for her own expenses.

ITA: 6(1)(*b*)(vii), 8(1)(*h*)

Total accommodation expenses	$12,000
Less: disallowed meal portion (50% × $4,500)	2,250
	$ 9,750

ITA: 67.1(1)

The car expenses are deductible since she meets the conditions of this paragraph which are quite similar to paragraph 8(1)(*h*), described above, to the extent of the following calculations:

ITA: 8(1)(*h.*1)

Gas	$1,500
Maintenance	500
Capital cost allowance (½ × 30% × $30,000 × 1.12)	5,040
Insurance	1,200
Licences	90
Interest — lesser of:	

(a) $4,000

$$(b) \ \$300 \times \frac{361 \text{ days}}{30} = \$3,610$$ 3,610

$11,940

Deductible car expenses:

$$\frac{15,000 \text{ km}}{21,000 \text{ km}} \times \$11,940 = \$8,529$$

Exercise 11

6/106 of the sum of:

(a) Deductible expenses including GST and PST but excluding exempt supplies:[1]	
Accommodation and meals	$ 9,750
Gas and maintenance	1,429[2]
	$11,179
(b) Capital cost allowance	3,600[3]
	$14,779
(c) Less: any expenses for which a reasonable allowance was received	Nil
	$14,779
Rebate (6/106 of $14,779)	$ 837

Par. 6(8)(*c*) Employment income inclusion in year of receipt of rebate:

$$\frac{\$11,179}{\$14,779} \times \$837 = \underline{\$633}$$

Par. 6(8)(*d*) Capital cost reduction under ssec. 13(7.1) in year of receipt:

$$\frac{\$ 3,600}{\$14,779} \times \$837 = \underline{\$204}$$

— NOTES TO SOLUTION

$^{(1)}$ Exempt supplies: insurance, licences and interest in respect of car.

$^{(2)} \dfrac{15,000 \text{ km}}{21,000 \text{ km}} \times (\$1,500 + \$500) = \underline{\underline{\$1,429}}$

$^{(3)} \dfrac{15,000 \text{ km}}{21,000 \text{ km}} \times \$5,040 \qquad = \underline{\underline{\$3,600}}$

CHAPTER 4
Income from Business: General Concepts and Rules

Exercise 1

[See *Hiwako Investments Limited v. The Queen*, 78 DTC 6281 (F.C.A.)]

The intention of the taxpayer corporation in this case can only be inferred from the facts of the case. The nature of the asset involved in the transaction is of prime importance in this case. It was an income-producing asset that would have been regarded as a fixed capital asset had it been held longer. Normally, the increase in value on the sale of a capital asset is taxed as a capital gain. The gain represents an enhancement of value by realizing a security in the same sense that a growth stock may be sold for a gain that is regarded as a capital gain. Thus, the prospect of an increase in value does not, by itself, characterize the gain as income from business.

The nature of the activity surrounding the transaction could characterize it as an adventure in the nature of trade. However, it could be argued that an income-producing property was purchased as an investment and circumstances changed such that the investment had to be sold. This would not necessarily be regarded as a gain made in an operation of business in carrying out a scheme for profit-making.

The court indicated that the concept of "secondary intention" does no more than refer to a practical approach for determining certain questions that arise in connection with "trading cases". If property is acquired where there is no business or the purchaser has not considered how he or she will use it, then the sale may be regarded as an adventure in the nature of trade, supporting a secondary intention to sell at a profit. However, where the property in question is an active, profit-producing property, it may be more difficult to conceive of its having been held as a speculation in the sense of an adventure in the nature of trade.

The fact that the principal shareholder of the corporation had a long history of trading in real estate does not necessarily mean that his intention in the transaction at hand was to trade. That fact could be outweighed by the income-producing capital nature of the particular property in question.

The court held that the gain was not income from a business, based on the foregoing reasons. However, some believe that the arguments for business income are stronger in this case and that the decision in this case should be limited to its specific facts.

Exercise 2

The $225,000 would be considered a capital receipt based on the *Parsons-Steiner Limited v. M.N.R.* case. 62 DTC 1148 (Ex. Ct.)

The following paraphrased excerpt from that case will help explain the conclusion:

On the whole therefore having regard to the importance of the franchise to Unloadum's business, the length of time the relationship had subsisted, the extent to which the appellant's business was affected by its loss both in decreased sales and by reason of its inability to replace it with anything equivalent, and the fact that from that time the appellant was in fact out of business, leads to a conclusion that this was a capital transaction. The payment in question was to replace "a capital asset of an enduring nature". It was one which Unloadum had built up over the years and which on the termination of the franchise they were obliged to relinquish. The payment received in respect of its loss was accordingly a capital receipt.

Exercise 3

Since actual cost is known it must be used. Therefore, an assumption about cost is not appropriate. Market value is probably best reflected in net realization value for this inventory. The following calculation of inventory values could be used:

Item	Actual cost	Reg. 1801 Market	Ssec. 10(1) Each item at lower of cost or market
Mufflers	$1,120.00	$ 992.00	$ 992.00
Tailpipes	745.75	706.50	706.50
Exhaust system	633.75	604.50	604.50
Shock absorbers	4,979.20	5,056.00	4,979.20
Brackets	1,304.80	1,211.60	1,211.60
Clamps	1,134.90	1,396.80	1,134.90
Total		$9,967.40	$9,628.70

Either the $9,967.40 value can be used or the $9,628.70 value can be used. However, the ending valuation method used in a particular year must be the same as that used for the end of the preceding year.

ITR: 1801
ITA: 10(1), 10(2.1)

Exercise 4

(A) The deduction of these costs are prohibited, notwithstanding the argument that the lodge was used to produce income from client business.

ITA: 18(1)(l)

(B) The deduction of costs are allowed if they were incurred in the ordinary course of the company's business of providing the property for rent. The facts of this case *may* fit this exception.

ITA: 18(1)(l)

Exercise 5

(A) — contribution may be made within 120 days of the end of 2007,

— an employer contribution to a defined-benefit RPP is deductible where it is made on the recommendation of an actuary in whose opinion the contribution is required so that the plan will have sufficient assets to provide benefits in accordance with its terms as registered,

— in this case, both the current service contribution and the lump-sum amount based on an actuarial valuation would be deductible in 2007, if they are in accordance with the plan.

(B) A full deduction of an amount paid in the year is permitted — or a taxpayer may elect to write it off in equal amounts over the 10-year period beginning in the current year.

ITA: 20(1)(cc)
ITA: 20(9)

(C) The deduction of the full amount of utilities connection costs is permitted. Since the taxpayer does not own the gas lines but the utilities company does, the amount is not eligible for capital cost allowance.

ITA: 20(1)(ee)

(D) Salary of an owner-employee's spouse is an allowable deduction to a corporation as long as it is reasonable in the circumstances. While $7,000 per month for full-time secretarial work is probably not reasonable, some lesser, reasonable amount would be deductible in this case. The amount in excess of a reasonable amount will not be deductible to the corporation, but will be included in the recipient's income from employment.

Exercise 6

Only ½ of the discount of $108.10 may be deducted because the bond was issued at less than 97% even though within the ⁴⁄₃ × 9% or 12% yield range.

ITA: 20(1)(f)

Given that the discount is paid effectively on maturity when the principal amount is repaid, then the $54.05 is deductible in 2007.

Exercise 7

Net income per financial statements			$150,000
Add: Items deducted in financial statements but not deductible for tax purposes:			
Par. 18(1)(e)	Provision for income taxes — current	25,000	
	— future	130,000	
Par. 18(1)(b)	Depreciation expense	40,000	
Par. 18(1)(t)	Non-deductible interest — re interest on late taxes	2,500	
Par. 18(1)(b), (e)	Bond discount	7,500	

Ssec. 10(1)	Inventory (closing) to FIFO basis		10,000
			$365,000

Deduct: Items not deducted in financial statements but deductible for tax
purposes:

Par. 20(1)(*aa*)	Landscaping costs	$12,000	
Ssec. 10(1)	Inventory (opening) to FIFO basis	15,000	(27,000)
Net Income for tax purposes before CCA			$338,000

Exercise 8

This transaction would likely involve a receipt of income because the intention is likely to make a profit on the purchase and sale of land. This would be substantiated by the frequency of transactions in land or, at least, the indication of an adventure in the nature of trade. During the year of sale the following income would be computed:

			Reference
Revenue from the sale of land		$250,000	
Less: cost of land	$107,500		
real estate commission	12,500	120,000	
Income from the sale of land		$130,000	Sec. 9
Less: reserve for amount not due until later year*			Spar. 20(1)(*n*)(ii)
$\dfrac{\$130,000}{\$250,000} \times (\$250,000 - \$110,000)$		72,800	
Income after reserve	$ 57,200		

---

* The reserve is not available, unless the sale occurred within 36 months of the end of the year in which a reserve is to be taken.   ITA: 20(8)(*b*)

Note that the minimum two-year repayment period does not apply on the sale of land which qualifies for the reserve. In the next year, the reserve of $72,800 would be taken into income.   ITA: 12(1)(*e*)(ii), 20(1)(*n*)(ii)

Exercise 9

Since Mr. Flogger has sold substantially all of his business assets to a person who intends to carry on the business, a section 22 election is available. Note that Mr. Flogger and Mr. Sucker must elect jointly in prescribed form [T2022] to have section 22 apply. Mr. Flogger must include last year's doubtful debt reserve in income. Then, Mr. Flogger may deduct, as a business loss, the difference between the face value of the accounts ($45,000) and the consideration paid by Mr. Sucker which should be equal to their fair market value ($36,000). Hence, Mr. Flogger will have a deduction of $9,000. Mr. Sucker must include the same $9,000 difference in his business income for the taxation year of the purchase. However, Mr. Sucker will now be put in a position to deduct an appropriate reserve for doubtful debts at the end of the taxation year or to write off any of the accounts that can be established to have become bad debts, since an amount has been included in income in respect of these receivables.   ITA: 20(1)(*l*)   ITA: 12(1)(*d*)   ITA: 22(1)(*a*), 22(1)(*b*)   ITA: 20(1)(*l*), 20(1)(*p*)   ITA: 22(1)(*c*)

		Income Effect
Mr. Flogger		
Last year's reserve		$ 6,500
Loss on sale: Proceeds	$36,000	
Face amount	(45,000)	(9,000)
Net effect		($2,500)
Mr. Sucker		
Mr. Flogger's loss on sale included in income		$ 9,000
Face amount of receivables		$45,000

If the election in section 22 is not used, the loss of $9,000 would be a capital loss, only ½ deductible as an allowable capital loss. Furthermore, an allowable capital loss can only be offset against a taxable capital gain.

Exercise 10

Since the corporation is carrying on business, it is engaged in a commercial activity. Therefore, the corporation is required to register and collect GST on its supplies, i.e., sales of goods, which are "taxable supplies." As a registrant, the corporation is entitled to a full input tax credit (ITC) in respect of GST paid or payable on goods and services that it purchases exclusively for use in its commercial activity. If GST collected or collectible on its sales exceeds its ITCs, the corporation must remit the difference. On the other hand, if ITCs exceed GST collected or collectible, a refund of the excess is available.

ETA: 123(1)

ETA: 169(1)

The following is the appropriate GST treatment of the items listed:

(a) Net income per financial statements would have been increased by GST charged which is included in revenue and reduced by GST paid or payable which is included in costs. GST charged net of ITCs from GST paid or payable must be remitted.

(b) There are no GST implications for the provision for income taxes.

(c) GST paid on the purchase of depreciable property provides an ITC, as discussed in Chapter 5. When the cost of the asset is subsequently written off through depreciation or capital cost allowance, there are no further GST implications.

The following costs would involve payment of GST on taxable supplies and, hence, would give rise to an ITC:

(a) inventory of goods purchased, and

(b) landscaping goods and services.

The following costs would not involve the payment of GST, since they are for exempt supplies:

(a) interest paid on income tax due results from a financial service, and

(b) bond interest also results from a financial service.

CHAPTER 5
Depreciable Property and Eligible Capital Property

Exercise 1

The overpass is not eligible for capital cost allowance, since the owners have no title to the land on which the footings are placed and capital cost allowance cannot be claimed on assets that are not owned (see *Saskatoon Community Broadcasting Co. Ltd. v. M.N.R.*). The cost of the overpass qualifies as an eligible capital expenditure.

58 DTC 491 (T.A.B.)

Exercise 2

No terminal loss can be deducted for an automobile in Class 10.1. The special "half-year rule" to compute capital cost allowance in the year of disposition applies to Class 10.1.

ITA: 20(16.1);
ITR: 1100(2.5)

(A)	Jan. 1/07		UCC (Class 10.1)	$ 18,475
	2007		CCA (½ × .30 × $18,475)	(2,771)[1]
			Proceeds of disposition	(12,000)
			Terminal loss of $3,704 denied	Nil
(B)	2007		Purchase ($36,000) (new Class 10.1) max.	$ 34,200[2]
	Dec. 31/07		UCC before adjustment	$ 34,200
			One-half of net amount (½ × $34,200)	(17,100)
			UCC before CCA	$ 17,100
			CCA @ 30% of $17,100	(5,130)[3]
			Add: ½ net amount	17,100
	Jan.1/2008		UCC	$ 29,070

— *NOTES TO SOLUTION*

[1] Note that 75% of $2,771 or $2,078 is the deduction based on business use.

[2] Limited to $30,000 plus PST (8%) and GST (6%) or $34,200, since it was acquired after 2000.

(3) Note that 75% of $5,130 or $3,848 is deductible, since CCA claimed is not subject to the limitation on sales/negotiating person's expenses.

ITA: 8(1)(*f*), 8(1)(*j*)

Exercise 3

	Cl. 1: 4%	Cl. 8: 20%	Cl. 10: 30%	Cl. 13: S.L.	Cl. 14: S.L.	Cl. 43: 30%
Jan. 1/07						
UCC	$120,000	$75,000	$40,000	$42,000	$54,400	Nil
2007 Purchases:						
— mfg. equip.						$50,000
— off. equip.		10,000				
Disposals:						
— building	(100,000)(1)					
— equip.						
Dec. 31/07						
UCC before adjustment	$ 20,000	$85,000	$40,000	$42,000	$54,400	$50,000
½ net-amount	Nil	(5,000)	Nil	Nil	N/A	(25,000)
UCC before CCA	$ 20,000	$80,000	$40,000	$42,000	$54,400	$25,000
CCA	(800)	(16,000)	(12,000)	(1,250)(2)	(3,400)(3)	(7,500)
½ net-amount	Nil	5,000	Nil	Nil	N/A	25,000
Jan. 1/2008						
UCC	$ 19,200	$69,000	$28,000	$40,750	$51,000	$42,500

— NOTES TO SOLUTION

(1) Capital gain on disposition of building of $50,000.

(2) Lesser of: (a) ⅕ of $50,000 .... $10,000

(b) $50,000/40 (max.) .... $ 1,250   } $1,250

— not reduced by ½ because not first year of ownership.

(3) $\dfrac{\$68,000}{(20 \times 365)} \times 365 = \$3,400$

Exercise 4

	Cl. 3: 5%
Jan. 1, 2006 UCC	$ 221,000
Disposal(1)	
lesser of:	
(a) capital cost $300,000	
(b) proceeds $295,000	(295,000)
Dec. 31, 2006 UCC	$ (74,000)
Recapture	74,000
Jan. 1, 2007 UCC	Nil

Aug. 2007 File an amended return for 2006 as follows:

ITA: 13(4)

Jan. 1, 2006 UCC	$ 221,000
Deemed proceeds	
lesser of:	
(a) capital cost $300,000	
(b) proceeds .... $295,000 → $295,000	

ITA: 13(4)(*c*)

reduced by lesser of:

(a) recapture ($295K – $221K) . . .	$ 74,000 → $ 74,000	
(b) replacement cost $400,000		$(221,000)

Dec. 31, 2006	UCC		Nil
	Recapture		Nil
Jan. 1, 2007	UCC		Nil

Cl. NRB: 6%[2]

2007	Purchase of new building	$400,000		
	Less: reduction above	74,000	$ 326,000	ITA: 13(4)(c)
Dec. 31, 2007	UCC		$ 326,000	
	CCA @ 6% of [$326,000 – (½ × $326,000)]		(9,780)	
Jan. 1, 2008	UCC		$ 316,220	

— NOTES TO SOLUTION

[1] The CRA appears to require that even if a replacement property is purchased before the tax return for the year of disposition must be filed (i.e., within six months of the taxation year-end), the recapture must be reported in the year of disposition. The taxpayer can request a reassessment if and when the replacement is purchased within the specified time limits. In lieu of paying tax initially on the recapture, the CRA will take acceptable security until the final determination of tax is made.

IT-259R3, par. 3

[2] Note how the rules allow for a replacement with an asset of another class.

ITA: 13(4)

Exercise 5

The change in use rules could be applied as follows:

ITA: 13(7)(d)

Cl. 10:[1] *30%*

2005	Purchase (85% of $14,600)	$12,410
Dec. 31, 2005	UCC	$12,410
	CCA @ 30% of [($12,410 – (½ × $12,410)]	(1,862)
Jan. 1, 2006	UCC	$10,548
2006	Disposal (5% of $12,200)[2]	(610)
Dec. 31, 2006	UCC	$ 9,938
	CCA @ 30% of $9,938	(2,981)
Jan. 1, 2007	UCC	$ 6,957
2007	Purchase (10% of $9,800)[3]	980
Dec. 31, 2007	UCC	$ 7,937
	CCA @ 30% of [$7,937 – (½ × $980)]	(2,234)
Jan. 1, 2008	UCC	$ 5,703

In practice, however, the following calculation of capital cost allowance might be made:

		Cl. 10: 30%	*Business deduction of CCA*
2005	Purchase	$14,600	
Dec. 31, 2005	UCC	$14,600	
	CCA @ 30% of ½ × $14,600	(2,190)	85% of $2,190 = $1,862
Dec. 31, 2006	UCC	$12,410	
	CCA @ 30%	(3,723)	80% of $3,723 = $2,978
Dec. 31, 2007	UCC	$ 8,687	
	CCA @ 30%	(2,606)	[80% + ½ (90% – 80%)][4] of $2,606 = $2,215
Jan. 1, 2008	UCC	$ 6,081	

— *NOTES TO SOLUTION*

(1) Since the automobile cost less than the prescribed limit, it is placed in Class 10.   ITA: 13(7)(*g*)

(2) Lesser of proceeds at fair market value and capital cost.

(3) Since fair market value is less than cost, the increase in capital cost is based on fair market value.

(4) An increase in use for business represents an addition to the class which is subject to the half-year rule. In practice, the CCA may be computed simply as 90% of $2,606 or $2,345.

Exercise 6

The cumulative eligible capital account would be affected as follows:

Year	Opening balance	Par. 20(1)(b) deduction[1]	Ssec. 14(1) business income inclusion	Closing balance
1995	$ 8,100	$ 567		$7,533
1996[2]	7,533	527		7,006
2006	7,006	490		6,516
2007	6,516	—	$18,684[3]	
Total . . .		$1,584		

2007 Opening balance	$ 6,516
Sale (¾ × $45,000)	(33,750)
Negative balance	(27,234)
Minus: previous CECA claims	1,584
Balance	($25,650)
Income inclusion:	
Previous CECA claims	$ 1,584
⅔ × $25,650	17,100
Total	$ 18,684

— *NOTES TO SOLUTION*

(1) 7% of the declining balance.

(2) No amortization deductions taken in the 1997–2005 period because of business losses.   ITA: 20(1)(*b*)

(3) The sale in 2007 would result in $18,684 of business income which is equal to the sum (rounded) of par. 20(1)(*b*) deductions ($1,584) plus ½ of the gain of $34,200 ($45,000 – $10,800).

Exercise 7

Jan. 1, 1999	Purchase of goodwill (¾ × $40,000)	$ 30,000
Dec. 31, 1999	Cumulative eligible capital amount @ 7%	(2,100)
Jan. 1, 2000	Cumulative eligible capital	$ 27,900
Dec. 31, 2000	Cumulative eligible capital amount @ 7%	(1,953)
Jan. 1, 2001	Cumulative eligible capital	$ 25,947
June 1, 2001	Purchase of license (¾ × $50,000)	37,500

	Cumulative eligible capital	$ 63,447
Dec. 31, 2001	Cumulative eligible capital amount @ 7%	(4,441)
Jan. 1, 2002	Cumulative eligible capital	$ 59,006
Dec. 31, 2002	Cumulative eligible capital amount @ 7%	(4,130)
Jan. 1, 2003	Cumulative eligible capital	$ 54,876
Mar. 1, 2003	Purchase of trademark (¾ × $20,000)	15,000
	Cumulative eligible capital	$ 69,876
Dec. 31, 2003	Cumulative eligible capital amount @ 7%	(4,891)
Jan. 1, 2004	Cumulative eligible capital	$ 64,985
Nov. 1, 2004	Purchase of goodwill (¾ × $50,000)	37,500
	Cumulative eligible capital	$ 102,485
Dec. 31, 2004	Cumulative eligible capital amount @ 7%	(7,174)
Jan. 1, 2005	Cumulative eligible capital	$ 95,311
Sept. 7, 2005	Sale of goodwill (¾ × $100,000)	(75,000)
	Cumulative eligible capital	$ 20,311
Dec. 31, 2005	Cumulative eligible capital amount @ 7%	(1,422)
Jan. 1, 2006	Cumulative eligible capital	$ 18,889
Dec. 31, 2006	Cumulative eligible capital amount @ 7%	(1,322)
Jan. 1, 2007	Cumulative eligible capital	$ 17,567
Aug. 3, 2007	Sale of license (¾ × $150,000)	(112,500)
	Sale of trademark (¾ × $200,000)	(150,000)
Dec. 31, 2007	Cumulative eligible capital	$(244,933)
	Business income	172,433
	Non-taxed ⅓ of "gain" [⅓ × ($244,933 − 27,433)]	72,500
Jan. 1, 2008	Cumulative eligible capital	$ Nil

ITA: 14(1)

The business income in 2007 is calculated as:

The total of:

(a) the lesser of:

(i) the negative amount .... $ 244,933

and

(ii) the total of: ....

all cumulative eligible capital deductions ...... $ 27,433

less: all recaptured deductions in prior years ... Nil

$ 27,433

The lesser is $ 27,433

and

(b) ⅔ of negative amount less recaptured deductions above [⅔ × ($244,933 − 27,433)]   145,000*

Business income $172,433

* This is the same as:

Proceeds ($100,000 + $150,000 + $200,000)	$ 450,000
Cost ($40,000 + $50,000 + $20,000 + $50,000)	(160,000)
Gain	$ 290,000
½ = ...	$ 145,000

CHAPTER 6
Income from Property

Exercise 1

(A) In its June 30, 2007 taxation year, the corporation would be required to include in income the interest received March 31, 2007 for the period October 1, 2006 to March 31, 2007 plus interest accrued from April 1 to June 30, 2007. Accrued interest from October 1, 2006 to January 1, 2007 (the period prior to acquisition), which was purchased with the bond, would give rise to a deduction.

ITA: 12(3), 20(14)

(B) The Act would require accrued interest from November 1, 2007 to October 31, 2008 to be included in income in 2008.

ITA: 12(4)

(C) The anniversary day would be December 31, 2007. Accrued interest from the date of purchase to December 31, 2007 would be included in 2007 income.

(D) The first anniversary day would occur October 31, 2008 and accrued interest would be included at that time. The CRA has, in the past, administratively allowed Canada Savings Bond interest to be accrued on a "bond year" basis. The Act gives legislative effect to this practice.

IT-396R, par. 25;
ITA: 12(4)

(E) The $80 received each year would be included in income. On November 30, 2007, there will be an anniversary day, but all of the interest accrued to that day will have been included in income as interest received in the year.

ITA: 12(1)(c)

Exercise 2

(A) (i) The Act would attribute the income on the bond to him even though she is legally entitled to receive it, since a gift is considered to be a transfer and is not a fair market value exchange which would be exempt.

ITA: 74.1(1), 74.5(1)

    (ii) Since a sale is also considered to be a transfer, attribution would apply except that, in this case, the transfer would be exempt because it was for fair market value consideration, as long as they elect jointly not to have the rollover apply.

ITA: 74.1(1), 74.5(1)(a), 73(1)

    (iii) This situation still involves a sale directly between husband and wife and is, therefore, a transfer subject to the attribution of income. A non-interest bearing demand note would not qualify for the exception because a commercial rate of interest was not charged.

ITA: 74.1(1), 74.5(1)(b)

    (iv) The loan of funds would result in attribution, because the exception would not apply since a commercial rate of interest was not charged on the loan.

ITA: 74.1(1), 74.5(2)

(B) If the loan was to a non-arm's length minor or a niece or nephew who is also a minor, then attribution would apply to transfers or loans by means of a trust to or for the benefit of a minor in the same way as spousal attribution applied in part (A) above. However, there are special rules pertaining to transfers or loans to a trust which will be discussed in Chapter 18.

ITA: 74.1(2)
ITA: 74.1(1)

(C) Attribution of income does not apply to a transfer involving an individual who is 18 or older. However, another provision might apply to transactions (iii) and (iv) involving loans. The key condition for this rule to apply is that one of the main reasons for the loan was to reduce or avoid tax on income from property or substituted property. A loan bearing a commercial rate of interest would be exempt from attribution.

ITA: 74.1(2)
ITA: 56(4.1)

Exercise 3

(i) The deductibility of carrying charges is not limited because the land is being used in the course of the hotel business.

ITA: 18(2)

(ii) The Act will limit the deductibility of carrying charges to 75% of their total (i.e., to the amount of the net revenues) so as not to create a loss by their deduction, unless the land is owned by a corporation whose principal purpose is the rental of real property (i.e., land and building) owned by it. This is not the principal purpose of a hotel corporation.

ITA: 18(2)(e)

ITA: 18(2)(f)

(iii) The deductibility of carrying charges may be limited in the same manner as in (ii), above, until the property is used in the business.

ITA: 18(2)

Exercise 4

	Class 1:4% Building 1	Class 1: 4% Building 2[1]	Class 8: 20%	Total
UCC, January 1	$148,000	—	$25,000	
Purchases	—	$137,500	—	
UCC, December 31	$148,000	$137,500	$25,000	
CCA	5,920	2,750[2]	4,350[3]	$13,020
UCC, January 1	$142,080	$134,750	$20,650	

— NOTES TO SOLUTION

[1] Separate class for rental building costing $50,000 or more.　　　　　ITR: 1101(1ac)

[2] 4% of [$137,500 − (½ × $137,500)].

[3] Net rental income before CCA ($9,270 + 3,750) $13,020

CCA on rental building and leasing properties (i.e., furniture and fixtures) limited to $13,020 [$13,020 − ($5,920 + $2,750) = $4,350] . . . .　(13,020)

Net income from rental properties . . . .　Nil

Note that where less than maximum capital cost allowance is taken, the less than maximum amount should be taken in classes with relatively higher CCA rates, so that the UCC carried forward to the following year is eligible for CCA at the higher rate in that subsequent year.

Exercise 5

(A)

	Property A	Property B	Total
UCC, January 1	$330,000	$480,000	
Disposal	(336,000)	—	
UCC, December 31	$ (6,000)	$480,000	
Recapture	6,000		
CCA @ 5% (Class 3) — see below	—	(12,000)	
UCC forward	Nil	$468,000	
Revenue	$ 13,500	$ 22,500	$36,000
Recapture	6,000	—	6,000
Expenses before CCA	(11,250)	(18,750)	(30,000)
Net	$ 8,250	$ 3,750	$12,000
CCA (5% of $480,000 = $24,000; limited to net above)			(12,000)
Net income from property			Nil

(B)　The rule to defer recapture applies on a voluntary disposition of a "former business property". A rental property is excluded from the definition and, hence, the deferral rule does not apply.　ITA: 13(4), 248(1)

CHAPTER 7
Capital Gains: An Introduction

Exercise 1

Step 1: Determine gain per year of ownership

	City home		Cottage		
P of D		$ 247,000		$ 164,000	ITA: 40(2)(*b*)
ACB	$ 180,000		$ 90,000		
SC	12,000	(192,000)	6,000	(96,000)	
Gain		$ 55,000		$ 68,000	
Gain per year	$\dfrac{\$55,000}{16 \text{ years}}$ = $ 3,438		$\dfrac{\$68,000}{11 \text{ years}}$ = $ 6,182		

Step 2: Assignment of no-option years

In the five taxation years 1992 to 1996, Peter owned only the city home. Therefore, there is no option in those years but to designate the city home as his principal residence.

Step 3: Gain determined   ITA: 40(2)(*b*)

The gain per year of ownership for the cottage ($6,182) exceeds that for the city home ($3,438). If all 11 years are assigned to the cottage, however, one year will be wasted. Hence, the city home should be designated for one of the years 1997 to 2007.

	City home	Cottage
Gain	$ 55,000	$ 68,000
Exemption	(24,063)[1]	(68,000)[2]
Capital gain	$ 30,937	Nil

—NOTES TO SOLUTION

[1] $\dfrac{1 + 5 + 1}{16}$ × $55,000 = $24,063; years designated — 1992–96 and one of 1997–2007

[2] $\dfrac{1 + 10}{11}$ × $68,000 = $68,000; years designated — all but one of 1997–2007

Exercise 2

	Painting		Antique clock		Outboard motor		Gold coin	
P of D		$2,000		$1,200		$1,000		$1,000
ACB	$1,000		$1,000		$1,000		$1,000	
SC	100	(1,100)	20	(1,020)	15	(1,015)	10	(1,010)
CG (CL)		$ 900		$ 180		$ (15)		$ (10)

Net taxable capital gain:

LPP — Painting	$ 900
— Gold coin	(10)[1]
	$ 890
— ½	$ 445
PUP — Antique clock (½ × $180)	90
	$ 535

— NOTE TO SOLUTION

[1] Listed personal property losses, whether current or carried-over, are applied at the full capital gain (capital loss) amount.

Exercise 3

(A) P of D 200 shares @ $25			$5,000
ACB 200 shares @ $33[1]			$6,600
SC		75	(6,675)
CL[2] (Superficial loss of $1,675)			Nil

(B) Adjusted cost base of shares

$$
\begin{array}{rl}
50 \text{ shares @ \$33} & = \$1,650 \\
200 \text{ shares @ \$26} & = 5,200 \\
\text{superficial loss} & \underline{1,675} \\
& \underline{\$8,525} \div 250 \text{ shares} = \underline{\$34.10}
\end{array}
$$

— NOTES TO SOLUTION

[1]
$$
\begin{array}{rl}
100 \text{ shares @ \$30} & = \$3,000 \\
150 \text{ shares @ \$35} & = \underline{5,250} \\
& \underline{\$8,250} \div 250 \text{ shares} = \underline{\$33}
\end{array}
$$

[2] Since Ivan acquired additional shares of Solid Investments within the 30-day period.

Exercise 4

Adjusted cost base:	
1,000 shares @ $35	$35,000
brokerage	500
1984 — stock dividend (50 shares × Nil)	Nil
1990 — stock dividend — 105 shares (10% × 1,050) × $10	1,050
2004 — stock dividend — 231 shares (20% × 1,155) × $10	2,310
	$38,860

Shares (1000 + 50 + 105 + 231) = 1,386
ACB per share: $38,860 ÷ 1,386 = $28.04

Exercise 5

2006:	Capital gain allocated	$ 96.37
	Taxable capital gain (½ × $96.37)	$ 48.19

The taxable capital gain of $48.19 must be included in her income for 2006.

2007:	P of D (25 units)	$ 718.00
	ACB (25 units @ $27.38[1])	(684.50)
	CG	$ 33.50
	TCG (½ × $33.50)	$ 16.75

— NOTE TO SOLUTION

[1] Adjusted cost base of units:

72.788	units	$2,000.00
3.774	units @ $25.535	96.37
76.562	units	$2,096.37

Weighted average: $2,096.37 ÷ 76.562 = $27.38

Exercise 6

		2006	*2007*
Par. 3(*a*)	Income from non-capital sources (non-negative):		
	Employment income	$25,000	$30,000
	Property income	10,000	—
	Business income — other	8,000	—
		$43,000	$30,000

Par. 3(*b*)   Net taxable capital gains (non-negative):

Taxable capital gain — personal-use property (½ × $8,000)		$ 4,000	—
Plus			
Listed personal property gain	$4,000		—
Less: LPP loss carryforward — 2003	(1,000)		
LPP loss carryback — 2007	(1,500)		
	$1,500		
Taxable net gain — ½ thereof	1,750		
		$ 4,750	
Public corporation — allowable capital loss...........	(4,750)	Nil[1]	
— taxable capital gain			$ 4,500[2]
		$43,000	$34,500

Par. 3(*d*)	Losses from non-capital sources:		
	Property loss................................	—	(4,000)
	Business loss	—	(9,000)
	Allowable business investment loss	(3,000)[3]	(1,000)[4]
	Division B income	$40,000	$20,500

— NOTES TO SOLUTION

[1] Of the $6,000 allowable capital loss (½ × $12,000), $1,250 cannot be claimed in 2006 and will be carried back or forward under Division C as a "net capital loss" to be discussed in Chapter 10.

[2] ½ × $9,000

[3] ½ × $6,000

[4] ½ × $2,000

CHAPTER 8
Capital Gains: The Finer Points

Exercise 1

Sale of car

P of D — Canadian dollars ($10,000 ÷ .87)	$11,494
ACB — Canadian dollars	(4,000)
CG	$ 7,494
TCG (½ × $7,494)	$ 3,747

Currency
P of D — Canadian dollars received	$11,765
ACB — Canadian dollars at time of sale	(11,494)
Gain	$ 271
Exempt portion	(200)
CG	$ 71
TCG (½ × $71)	$ 36

Exercise 2

(A) During the years prior to the settling of the claim, Tax Processing Ltd. is deemed to own the   ITA: 44(2)
destroyed asset. Hence the company can continue to take capital cost allowance.

		Class 10: 30%
UCC before the fire		$17,150
CCA — 2005	$ 5,145	
CCA — 2006	3,601	(8,746)
UCC before proceeds received		$ 8,404

(B) In the second year after the fire (2007) when the company received the proceeds, the company would be deemed to have sold the computer for $60,000 with the following tax consequences:

Taxable capital gain:
P. of D		$60,000
ACB		(50,000)
CG		$10,000
TCG (½ × $10,000)		$ 5,000

Recapture:
UCC before proceeds received		$ 8,404
Less the lesser of:		
(i) Capital cost	$50,000	
		(50,000)
(ii) P of D	$60,000	
Recapture		$41,596

(C) In the year of purchase of the new computer (2008), which is within the 24-month time limit for an involuntary disposition, Tax Processing Ltd. would file an amended return for the 2007 year in which the taxable capital gain and recapture were recognized.

Taxable capital gain:
½ of the lesser of:			
(i) capital gain (see above)		$10,000	
(ii) P of D	$60,000		= Nil
less replacement cost	70,000	Nil	

ACB of new computer in 2008: ($70,000 – $10,000) = $60,000   ITA: 44(1)(*f*)

Recapture: ITA: 13(4)

		Class 10: 30%	
UCC before proceeds received (see above calculation)		$ 8,404	
Less deemed disposal:			
lesser of (i) cost ($50,000)	$50,000		
(ii) P of D ($60,000)			
Less the lesser of:			
(i) the recapture			
($8,404 – $50,000)	$41,596		
(ii) replacement cost	70,000	41,596	8,404

ITA: 13(4)(*c*)

UCC after proceeds received, Dec. 31, 2007	Nil

Class CE: 55%

2008 addition:		
Capital cost of replacement property	$70,000	
Less reduction for deferred gain	10,000	ITA: 44(1)(*f*)
Deemed capital cost	$60,000	
Less reduction for deferred recapture	41,596	ITA: 13(4)(*d*)
UCC before CCA	$18,404	
CCA (55% of ½ × $18,404)	(5,061)	
UCC after CCA	$13,343	

Exercise 3

When Howard rents his home, he is deemed to have changed the use of the home and a capital gain may be triggered. However, Howard can designate the home with the appropriate number of years and should not be taxed on the gain. Under this course of action, Howard would now have a rental property from which he must declare the income less all his expenses. However, a rental loss could not be generated with capital cost allowance on the home and equipment therein.   ITA: 45(1)   ITR: 1100(15))

Alternatively, Howard could elect to defer the gain until he either sells the home or rescinds his election. Note that the CRA normally permits a retroactive election at the time of sale. In this situation, Howard would not be allowed to claim any capital cost allowance on the home or the election to be deemed not to have changed the use would be invalid.   ITA: 45(2)   IT-120R6   ITA: 45(2)

The election would permit Howard to designate his Vancouver home as his principal residence for at least four extra years depending upon whether he is self-employed or employed.   ITA: 45(2)

(A) Self-employed

Paragraph (*d*) in the definition of a "principal residence" permits Howard to designate his Vancouver home as his principal residence for four years, while it is being rented, if he elects to be deemed not to have changed the use according to paragraphs (*b*) and (*d*) of the definition.   ITA: 54   ITA: 45(2)

Howard might consider rescinding his election after the fourth year. This course of action would enable Howard to claim capital cost allowance after the fourth year subject to the loss restrictions discussed above.

(B) Employed

The Act waives the four-year restriction discussed above if Howard (or his wife) has moved at least 40 km closer to his new work location. Howard then can designate his Vancouver home as his principal residence during all the rental years if: ITA: 54.1

   (i) Howard subsequently resumes ordinary habitation of his home while employed with the same employer; or

   (ii) Howard subsequently resumes ordinary habitation of his home within one year from the end of the year in which he terminates employment with that employer; or

   (iii) Howard dies.

Note that "ordinarily inhabited" means any time during the year according to the CRA, but Howard cannot temporarily move back in order to qualify for this exemption.   IT-120R6

Exercise 4

Capital property A

  (A) If Mr. Emigrant departs prior to June 1, 2007, there will be no capital gain on the capital asset which he brought from the U.S. by virtue of the 60-month short-term exemption.   ITA: 128.1(4)

  (B) If he departs subsequent to June 1, 2007, there will be a taxable capital gain on ½ of the excess of the proceeds of disposition ($12,000) over the fair market value at the time of entry ($5,000), namely, $3,500.

Capital property B

(A) First, it is necessary to determine whether the capital property acquired in Canada is exempt from immediate departure tax but will be taxed on its ultimate disposition. ITA: 2(3)

(B) If the property is not exempted then the taxpayer will be taxed at the time of exit from Canada.

Exercise 5

Doctor Quick

July 1, 2006 — acquired an option (capital property) with an adjusted cost base of $5,000.

Feb. 1, 2007 — transaction resulted in a capital loss of $3,000 (i.e., $2,000 – $5,000) of which only $1,500 would be recognized since 50% of the option was for a principal residence.

Doctor Slow

Feb. 1, 2007 — acquired an option with an adjusted cost base of $2,000.

May 1, 2007 — acquired a property with an adjusted cost base and a capital cost of $102,000 ($100,000 + $2,000).

Devalued Properties Ltd.

July 1, 2006 — received business income of $5,000; not a capital gain.

May 1, 2007 — received business income of $100,000; not a capital gain. May subtract the cost of property inventory to arrive at income for tax purposes.

— note that section 49 is not applicable if the gain is not a capital gain.

Exercise 6

(A) Since they are related by marriage, they are not at arm's length. ITA: 251(2)(a), 251(6)(b)

(B) Since they are not considered to be related by blood, they are at arm's length. ITA: 251(6)(a)

(C) Since they are still legally married, they are not at arm's length.

(D) The facts of a situation can determine that two unrelated persons are not at arm's length. ITA: 251(1)(b)

Exercise 7

	James *(seller or transferor)*	*Hayden* *(purchaser or transferee)*
(A) sale at $2,000	has proceeds of $2,000 and, hence, a capital gain of $800 (i.e., $2,000 – $1,200)	deemed [par. 69(1)(a)] to have acquired at $1,500 resulting in potential double-counting of $500 gain
(B) sale at $1,200	deemed [par. 69(1)(b)] to have proceeds of $1,500 and, hence, a capital gain of $300	acquired at $1,200 resulting in potential double-counting of $300 gain
(C) gift	deemed [par. 69(1)(b)] to have proceeds of $1,500	deemed [par. 69(1)(c)] to have acquired at $1,500

Exercise 8

(A) (i) Since a gift is a transfer, the interspousal rollover would automatically deem that Alice's proceeds of disposition are equal to her adjusted cost base ($12,000), resulting in no capital gain. ITA: 73

(ii) Alice would be subject to the income attribution rules on any dividends from the shares, because a gift would not meet the exception, since the fair market value of the property transferred exceeded the fair market value of the consideration received and an election out of the interspousal rollover was not made. ITA: 74.1, 74.5(1)(a)

ITA: 73(1)

(iii) Alice would also be subject to capital gains attribution for the same reason as discussed in part (A)(ii) above. There would be full capital gains attribution on all substituted property. ITA: 74.2; IT-511R, par. 27

(B) (i) Since Alice does elect out of the interspousal rollover, the non-arm's length transfer rule, with which the transaction conforms, will apply, since the cash consideration ($15,000) was equal to the fair market value of the property transferred. A capital gain of $3,000 would be triggered. ITA: 73(1)
ITA: 69(1)(b)(ii)

(ii) There would be no income or capital gains attribution, because Alice has conformed with the attribution rule exception. The fair market value of the property transferred did not exceed the fair market value of the consideration received and an election out of the interspousal rollover was made.

ITA: 74.5(1)(*a*)

ITA: 73(1)

(C) (i) Unless Alice elects not to have the provisions of the interspousal rollover apply, there will be no capital gain triggered on the transfer to her husband.

ITA: 73

(ii) Although Alice has received consideration (debt) with a face value ($15,000) equal to the fair market value of the property transferred, the interest rate must be at least equal to the prescribed rate at the time or a commercial rate. In addition, the Act requires that Alice elect out of the interspousal rollover. Therefore, Alice will be subject to both income and capital gains attribution.

ITA: 74.5(1)(*b*)(i)

74.5(1)(*c*)

(D) The result would be the same as in (A) above since the shares would be considered substituted property for a transfer of cash for no consideration.

(E) The result would be the same as in (C) above since the shares would be considered substituted property.

Exercise 9

If section 22 is not used, Mr. Flogger must still include in income last year's reserve of $6,500. However, the loss of $9,000 will be regarded as a capital loss which is only fractionally deductible and can be offset only against taxable capital gains. Since Mr. Sucker has not included any amount as income in respect of these accounts receivable, he will not be allowed a deduction for a reserve or for bad debts because the conditions of the reserve for doubtful debts or the bad debt expense rules will not be met. If Mr. Sucker collects more than the $36,000 fair market value, the excess will be a capital gain and, if he collects less than $36,000, the difference will be a capital loss.

ITA: 20(1)(*l*), 20(1)(*p*)

CHAPTER 9
Other Sources of Income and Deductions in Computing Income

Exercise 1

The $200 monthly payments made for Ursalla's support prior to November 1st are income to Ursalla and deductions to Uriah as long as the agreement provides for their being considered as part of the agreement and the agreement makes a specific reference to subsection 56.1(3). The payments of $200 for November and December are income to Ursalla and deductions to Uriah.

ITA: 56(1)(*b*), 60(*b*)

The mortgage payments of $400 would qualify as income to Ursalla and deductions for Uriah since they are considered to be an allowance as referred to in the legislation, as long as the conditions of these provisions are met. Conceivably, if the payments are recognized in the agreement, then the conditions would be met.

ITA: 56.1(2), 56(1)(*b*),
60(*b*), 60.1(2)

The $700 monthly support payments for the children and the medical expense payments are neither income to Ursalla nor deductions for Uriah, since they are child support amounts.

ITA: 56.1(4)

Exercise 2

The maximum amount that Don is able to deduct in respect of a spousal RRSP is his annual contribution limit, less any contributions made to his own RRSP in respect of the year.

Don's annual contribution limit for 2007 is calculated as the lesser of 18% of his 2006 earned income (i.e., $11,916 as calculated below) and the RRSP dollar limit for 2007, which is $19,000, less the PA reported by his employer in respect of 2006 of $6,084.

Don's earned income for 2006 is calculated as:

ITA: 146(1)

Employment income — Subdivision a	$68,400	
Add: RPP contribution	2,800	$71,200
Rental loss		(5,000)
Earned income		$66,200
18% thereof		$11,916

Therefore, Don is able to deduct $5,832 (i.e., $11,916 – $6,084) of RRSP contributions in 2007. Since he has already contributed $5,000 to a spousal RRSP, he can either contribute $832 to his own RRSP, or an additional $832 to the spousal RRSP for 2007.

Exercise 3

Mr. Retired is able to contribute $17,300 to an RRSP for 2007 [(lesser of 18% of his earned income from 2006 (i.e., 18% of $120,000) and $19,000) less his 2006 PA of $700]. He may make this annual contribution to either his own or a spousal RRSP, as long as the total of the contributions does not exceed $17,300. These contributions may be made in the year or within 60 days of December 31, 2007.

He does not have to include the lump-sum transfer from his RPP in his income nor does he get an offsetting deduction, as long as it is eligible to be transferred.

ITA: 147.3(4), 147.3(9)

Mr. Retired is able to transfer $44,000 to his RRSPs in respect of his retiring allowance. Since all of his employer's contributions have vested, he is able to contribute $2,000 for each of the 22 pre-'96 years of employment, including the part year for 1974. Since he is able to make such a transfer in the year or within 60 days of the year, he may make an additional contribution of $4,000 ($44,000 less his initial contribution of $40,000) in the first 60 days of 2008 and he will be able to deduct the full $44,000 in his 2007 return.

ITA: 60(*j*.1)

Mr. Retired may also make a one-time additional $2,000 contribution to his RRSP for 2007 without incurring penalties. He will not receive a deduction for this additional contribution, but as long as he has enough earned income in 2008 to deduct at least $2,000 in respect of 2009, the year prior to the year in which he must remove the funds from the plan (i.e., at the end of the year in which he turns 71, which is 2012), he will not be double-taxed on the funds when they are withdrawn from the plan. This will be the case if, instead of making a $2,000 contribution in 2009, he uses the carryforward rules to deduct the $2,000. It may also be worthwhile for Mr. Retired to contribute the additional $2,000 in 2007 if he expects to have enough earned income in 2009 to make a $2,000 contribution in 2010. Although he is not able to make a contribution to his RRSP in 2011, since his RRSP matured at the end of 2010, he is able to take an RRSP deduction in 2010 using the carryforward rules.

Exercise 4

Allowable moving expense deduction

(A) 2007

Travelling cost — air fare	$ 1,300	ITA: 62(3)(*a*)
Household effects — transporting	1,000	ITA: 62(3)(*b*)
Selling costs of Vancouver residence		ITA: 62(3)(*e*)
— legal fees	500	
— real estate commission	10,000	
Allowable purchase cost of Montreal residence		ITA: 62(3)(*f*)
— legal fees	1,000	
— Quebec transfer tax	300	
Total potential deductions	$14,100	
Less		
Amount paid by the employer not included income	$ 5,000	ITA: 62(1)(*c*)
	$ 9,100	
Deduction restricted to income from new work location — 2007	$ 7,000	ITA: 62(1)(*f*)

(B) 2008

Balance deductible from income from the new location only in 2008	2,100	ITA: 62(1)
	$ 9,100	

Exercise 5

This problem situation does not involve a single parent attending a qualifying education program or both parents attending a qualifying education program at the same time, as the legislation requires. Therefore, the limits for these situations are not applicable.

ITA: 63(2.2)
ITA: 63(2.3)

Cathy Childcare's maximum deduction is the lesser of: ITA: 63

(A) the least of:

   (i) amount paid in the year
     ($200 × 52) $10,400

   (ii) 1 × $4,000 = $ 4,000

      2 × $7,000 = $14,000 . . . . . $18,000

   (iii) ⅔ × earned income
       (⅔ × ($47,000
         + $4,000)) $34,000

   least amount . . . . $ 10,400

(B) the sum of:

   (i) $175 × 2 = $350

   (ii) $100 × 1 = 100

           $450 × 30 weeks = $13,500

   Lesser amount $10,400

Charles Childcare's maximum deduction is the least of: ITA: 63

   (a) $200 × 52 weeks = $10,400

   (b) 1 child × $4,000 = $ 4,000

                                         $10,400

      2 children × $7,000 = $14,000 $18,000

   (c) ⅔ × earned income ($23,850)[1] = $15,900

minus amount deducted by Cathy   10,400

                                                      Nil

— NOTE TO SOLUTION

   [1] Earned income
      Gross salary $23,000
      Taxable benefits   850
      Scholarship (fully exempt)   Nil
                        $23,850

Note that earned income for child care expenses is defined differently than earned income for a   ITA: 63(3), 146(1)
registered retirement savings plan.

CHAPTER 10
Computation of Taxable Income and Taxes Payable for Individuals

Exercise 1

(A)

	2005	2006	2007	
Income from non-capital sources (≥0):				ITA: 3(a)
Property income	$ 1,000	Nil	$ 2,000	
Net taxable capital gains (≥0).				ITA: 3(b)
Taxable capital gains				
(see Schedule 1, Part (A) below)	$18,750	$25,000	$ 5,625	
Allowable capital losses	(7,500)	Nil	(11,250)	
	$11,250	$25,000	Nil	
Total income	$12,250	$25,000	$ 2,000	ITA: 3(b)
Losses from non-capital source and ABIL:				ITA: 3(d)

	2005	2006	2007
Property loss	Nil	$(7,000)	Nil
ABIL	Nil	(15,000)	Nil
Division B income	$12,250	$ 3,000	$ 2,000
(B) Deduct: Net capital losses (see Schedule 1, Part (B) below for maximum)	(4,102)	(Nil)	Nil
Non-capital losses	Nil	Nil	Nil
Taxable income (max. equal to personal tax credit base)	$ 8,148	$ 3,000	$ 2,000

ITA: 3(*e*)

SCHEDULE 1

	2005	2006	2007
(A) Net taxable capital gains — Net TCG (Net allowable capital losses — Net ACL)			
Taxable capital gains (TCG)	$18,750	$ 25,000	$ 5,625
Allowable capital losses (ACL)	(7,500)	—	(11,250)
	$11,250	$ 25,000	$ (5,625)

ITA: 111(1)(*b*),
111(1.1)(*a*),
111(8)(*a*)

(B) Net capital losses.

	2005	2006	2007
Lesser of:			
(i) Net TCGs for the year	$11,250	$25,000	Nil
(ii) Total of adjusted net CLs	$ 7,500	$ 9,023	$9,023
Lesser amount	$7,500	$9,023	Nil

(C) Loss continuity schedule

	2003	2007	Total
Net CL	$ 7,500	$5,625	$13,125
Utilized in 2005	(4,102)	N/A	(4,102)
Available in 2008	$ 3,398	$5,625	$ 9,023

Exercise 2

(A) Personal tax credits

ITA: 118

Basic personal tax credit base	$ 8,929	ITA: 118(1)(*a*)
Dolly's tax credit base: $8,929 – $3,000	5,929	ITA: 118(1)(*a*)
Child amount ($2,000 × 2)	4,000	ITA: 118(1)(*b*.1)
Don:[1] over 18 years old and not infirm	Nil	ITA: 118(1)(*d*)
Dave's tax credit base:[2] $4,019 – ($3,200 – $5,702)	4,019	ITA: 118(1)(*d*)
Mother's tax credit base:[3] $4,019 – ($6,000 – $5,702): claim	Nil	ITA: 118(1)(*d*)
Alternative caregiver credit[3]	4,019	ITA: 118(1)(*c*.1)
Total tax credit base[4]	$29,896	
Total personal tax credits @ 15.5%	$ 4,633	

— *NOTES TO SOLUTION*

[1] Don's father may claim the transferred tuition fee, education, and textbook tax credits, since Don's income tax will be completely offset by his basic personal tax credit.

ITA: 118.9(1)

⁽²⁾ The alternative caregiver tax credit would have the same base of $4,019.

⁽³⁾ The alternative caregiver tax credit would have a higher base of $4,019, since it would not be reduced, because the mother's income is under $13,726.

⁽⁴⁾ An impairment tax credit of $1,068 ($6,890 × 15.5%) is also available in respect of the mother and son Dave, if their impairment is certified by a medical doctor.   ITA: 118.3(1)

Exercise 3

(A) Optimum personal tax credit:

Jack's tax credit base:

— Jack	$ 8,929	ITA: 118(1)(*a*)
— Jill: $8,929 – $9,600	Nil⁽¹⁾	
ETM	Nil⁽²⁾	ITA: 118(1)(*b*)
	$ 8,929	
Jack's tax credit @ 15.5%	$ 1,384	

Jill's tax credit base:

— Jill	$ 8,929	ITA: 118(1)(*b*)(i)
— one of Jill's children⁽³⁾	8,929	ITA: 118(1)(*b*)(ii)
— child amount⁽⁴⁾	4,000	ITA: 118(1)(*b*.1)
	$21,858	
Jill's tax credits @ 15.5%	$ 3,388	

(B) In 2008, Jack and Jill could each claim a basic personal tax credit. Neither is eligible for the equivalent-to-married tax credit.

— *NOTES TO SOLUTION*

⁽¹⁾ All income of a spouse during the year of marriage is used in determining a spousal tax credit.   ITA: 118(1)(*a*)(ii)

⁽²⁾ Jack does not have the option of claiming either of the children as ETM since they were not related to nor living with him at the time during the year that he was single.   ITA: 118(1)(*b*)

⁽³⁾ Jill has the option of claiming either Jack (however, his income is too high in this fact situation) or one of her children as ETM since she falls into both paragraphs. It would appear that Jack and Jill cannot both claim each other at the same time according to a court decision which determined that spouses cannot simultaneously support each other. (See *The Queen v. Robichaud*.)   ITA: 118(1)(*a*)
ITA: 118(1)(*b*); IT-513R, par. 27
83 DTC 5265 (F.C.T.D.)

⁽⁴⁾ It appears from the legislation that Jill can claim both children for the child amount even though she is claiming one as equivalent-to-married.

Exercise 4

$300 contribution is an employment deduction.   ITA: 8(1)(*m*)
$800 is pension income.   ITA: 56(1)(*a*)
Nil; a pension credit is not available since the amount is not from a life annuity, as required in the definition of "qualified pension income".   ITA: 118(3), 118(7)

Exercise 5

(A) Division B and taxable income	$5,000
Federal tax @ 15.5% of $5,000	$ 775
Less: basic personal tax credit	1,384
Federal tax payable	Nil

Credits available for transfer:

Tuition fee tax credit (15.5% of $1,800)	$ 279
Education tax credit (15.5% of $400 × 8)	496
Textbook tax credit (15.5% of $65 × 8)	81
Total	$ 856

Amount deductible by qualified transferee:

Lesser of:

(a) $775
(b) student's tuition fee, education, and textbook tax credits — $856   } $ 775

Less: amount of tax credit required to reduce student's tax payable to nil	Nil
Net amount deductible by transferee	$ 775

Note that the Employment Insurance premium and CPP contribution tax credits cannot be transferred.

(B) If Sammy was married, his wife could deduct the $775 in tuition fee, education, and textbook tax credits, since Sammy's federal tax, after his personal tax credit, is nil. Sammy's parent or grandparent can deduct all or some part of the $775 as a tax credit, if Sammy so designates.   ITA: 118.7

Exercise 6

Tax payable by Tina:

Division B income and taxable income		$ 9,105
Federal tax 15.5% of $9,105		$ 1,411
Less: basic personal tax credit	$1,384	
other tax credits (age, pension)	856	2,240
Federal tax payable		Nil

Transferable tax credits available:		
Age credit (15.5% of $5,177)		$ 802
Pension credit (15.5% of $350)		54
Total credits available to Tina's husband		$ 856
Less: federal tax payable net of basic personal tax credit ($1,411 − $1,384)		27
		$ 829

Exercise 7

Income increased by grossed-up dividend			$1,305
Increase in federal tax @ 29% of $1,305			$ 378
Less increase in tax credits:			
Married credit with election [15.5% of ($8,929 − nil)]	$ 1,384		
Married credit without election [15.5% of ($8,929 − $1,305)]	(1,182)	$ 202	
Dividend tax credit (19% of $1,305)		248	450
Net federal tax reduction			$ 72

ITA: 82(3)

Therefore, the election should be made in this case.   ITA: 82(3)

Exercise 8

Federal foreign tax credit

lesser of:

(i) $225

(ii) $\dfrac{\$1,500}{\$156,800 - \$6,000} \times (\$34,715 + \$83^*) = \underline{\$348}$ } $225

---

* The dividend tax credit is equal to 19% of the grossed-up dividend of $435 (i.e., 1.45 × $300).

Exercise 9

	Regular Part I Tax		Minimum Tax	
(A) $100 interest	($100 × .29) =	$29	($100 × .155) =	$16
(B) $100 cash dividend				
($145 grossed up)	$145 × .29 = $42		($100 × .155)=	$16
	DTC (28)	$14		
(C) $100 capital gains				
($50 taxable capital				
gains)	($50 × .29)	$15	($50 + $30) × .155	$12

Exercise 10

Taxable income	$100,000
Add: CCA loss on resource property shelter	103,500
	$203,500
Less: gross-up of dividends	(13,500)
Adjusted taxable income	$190,000
Less: basic exemption	(40,000)
	$150,000
Minimum tax before minimum tax credit (15.5% of $150,000)	$ 23,250

Less basic minimum tax credits:

Basic personal (15.5% × $8,929)	$1,384	
Employment Insurance premiums	112	
CPP contributions	308	
Employment	155	1,959
Minimum amount		$ 21,291

Betty Bucks' Part I tax will be her minimum amount of $21,291 and $10,906 ($21,291 − $10,385) can be carried forward and applied to reduce tax payable in a subsequent year.

CHAPTER 11
Computation of Taxable Income and Tax after General Reductions for Corporations

Exercise 1

	2006		2007		2008	
Income under Division B	$(7,350)		$22,050		$14,700	
Deduct: charitable donations						
limited by 75% of						
income above						
— carried forward	Nil		$ 2,625		Nil	
— current	Nil	Nil	4,700	(7,325)	$11,025[1]	(11,025)
unlimited charitable						
donation						
— carried forward	Nil		—		$ 3,675	
— current	Nil	Nil	$14,725[2]	(14,725)	—	(3,675)[3]
non-capital loss from						
2006[4]		Nil		Nil		Nil
Taxable income		Nil		Nil		Nil

— *NOTES TO SOLUTION*

(1) $975 is available to carry forward to 2009 and an additional four years to 2013.

(2) If the donation of the land gave rise to a capital gain, the taxable portion would be included in the amount of income under Division B.

(3) $1,300 is available to carry forward to 2009 to 2012.

(4) $7,350 is available to carry forward from 2007 to 2026 (20 taxation years).

Exercise 2

	2005	2006	2007
Alternative A: Claiming maximum charitable donations			
Income before CCA	$ 100,000	$115,000	$132,250
CCA	(200,000)	(101,667)[(1)]	(116,917)
Income (loss) under Division B	$(100,000)	$ 13,333	$ 15,333
Charitable donations:			
— Carried forward	Nil	(10,000)[(1)]	(11,500)[(1)]
— Current	Nil	Nil	Nil
Non-capital loss carried forward from 2005	n/a	(3,333)	(3,833)[(2)]
Taxable income	Nil	Nil	Nil
Alternative B: Non-capital loss utilization			
Income before CCA	$100,000	$115,000	$132,250
CCA	(107,167)[(3)]	(86,333)	(132,250)
Income (loss) under Division B	$ (7,167)	$ 28,667	Nil
Charitable donations:			
— carried forward	Nil	(21,500)	Nil
— current	Nil	Nil	Nil
Non-capital loss carried forward from 2005	n/a	(7,167)[(3)]	Nil
Taxable income	Nil	Nil	Nil
Alternative C: Maximum donation and non-capital loss utilization			
Income before CCA	$100,000	$115,000	$132,250
CCA	(107,166)	(101,667)	(116,917)
Income (loss) under Division B	$ (7,166)	$ 13,333	$ 15,333
Charitable donations:			
— Carried forward	Nil	(10,000)[(4)]	(11,500)[(4)]
— Current	Nil	Nil	Nil
Non-capital loss carried forward from 2005	n/a	(3,333)	(3,833)
Taxable income	Nil	Nil	Nil

● *Summary*	*Alternatives*		
	A	B	C
Total donations claimed	$ 21,500	$ 21,500	$ 21,500
Total CCA claimed	418,584	325,750	325,750
Unclaimed non-capital loss	92,834	Nil	Nil

— *NOTES TO SOLUTION*

(1) CCA amount selected to provide sufficient Division B income for a deduction of charitable donations (maximum of 75% of Division B income for 2005 and subsequent years). The 2001 charitable donations would, otherwise, expire after 2006.

(2) $92,834 of non-capital loss from 2005 remains.

(3) Determined by looking forward to 2006 and creating the maximum non-capital loss in 2005 that can be fully utilized in 2006.

(4) Uses the five-year carryforward of charitable donations to the maximum — i.e., the $11,500 donations of 2002 may be carried forward to 2007, as in Alternative A.

Exercise 3

Sum of: loss from business		$129,000
allowable business investment loss		8,000
dividends deductible under sec. 112		10,750
net capital loss deducted [½ × ($46,400 – $12,000)]		17,200[1]
		$164,950
Less: income from property	$32,250	
net taxable capital gains [½ × ($46,400 – $12,000)]	17,200[1]	(49,450)
Non-capital loss for the year		$115,500

— NOTE TO SOLUTION

[1] The corporation may deduct the net capital loss from income even though it has no impact on the taxable income. However, the deduction is restricted to the net taxable capital gain for the year. Once deducted, the net capital loss can be included in the non-capital loss computation.

Exercise 4

Allowable capital loss (excluding ABIL)	$ 51,750
Less: taxable capital gain	(4,700)
Net	$ 47,050
Add: unutilized allowable business investment loss in respect of which the carryover period expires in the year (i.e., the 10th carryforward year)	Nil
Net capital loss for the year	$ 47,050

Exercise 5

	Alternative A[1]	*Alternative B*[1]
Income from business	$55,500	$55,500
Taxable capital gains	37,000	37,000
Income under Division B	$92,500	$92,500
Less: net capital losses	(37,000)[2]	(10,000)[2]
non-capital losses	(55,500)	(82,500)
Taxable income	Nil	Nil
Summary:		
Unutilized non-capital losses	$27,000	Nil
Unutilized net capital losses	3,000[2]	$30,000[2]

—NOTES TO SOLUTION

[1] In Alternative A, maximum net capital losses are claimed before non-capital losses. In Alternative B, maximum non-capital losses are claimed before net capital losses.

[2]	*Alternative A*	*Alternative B*
1999 Net capital losses available	$60,000	$60,000
Adjusted to 2007 ($60,000 × ½ / ¾)	40,000	40,000
Utilized in 2007 (limited to TCG)	(37,000)	(10,000)
Available to carryforward	$ 3,000	$30,000

Exercise 6

Part (a)

Because of the acquisition of control by Holdco Ltd., Loser Ltd. is deemed to have a taxation year-end on March 9, 2007. This taxation year will be only 69 days long, having commenced on January 1, 2007. The exception does not apply, since the date of the acquisition of control is more than seven days after the last year-end.

ITA: 249(4), 256(9)

ITA: 249(4)(c)

Loser Ltd. will be required to make certain adjustments as of March 9, 2007. The adjustments will increase the company's business losses of $3,000 to $48,000, as follows:

Business losses	$ 3,000
Excess of UCC ($70,000) over fair market value ($40,000) of assets in Class 8 [ssec. 111(5.1)]	30,000
Accrued inventory losses	Nil
Doubtful accounts receivable deemed to be actual bad debts [ssec. 111(5.3)]	15,000
Losses from non-capital sources (all from business)	$48,000

The balance in the CEC account is not affected by the acquisition of control, because there was no unrealized loss at the time of the acquisition of control (i.e., $\frac{3}{4}$ of the fair market value of $68,000 = $51,000 which is greater than the $50,000 CEC account balance).

Division B income for the deemed taxation year ended March 9, 2007 would be computed as follows:

Par. 3(a):	Income from non-capital sources		Nil
Par. 3(b):	Net taxable capital gains:		
	Election under par. 111(4)(e) on land ($\frac{1}{2} \times$ $56,000)	$28,000	
	Allowable capital losses	Nil	$28,000
Par. 3(c):	Par. 3(a) + par. 3(b)		$28,000
Par. 3(d):	Losses from non-capital sources (above)		(48,000)
	Division B income and taxable income		Nil

Since the net capital losses of $30,000 will expire on March 10, 2007, if nothing is done, the corporation should deduct the net capital losses of $30,000. Although the taxable income will be unaffected, the non-capital losses can be increased by this amount.

The non-capital loss for the deemed year ending March 10, 2007, would be:

Losses from business sources	$48,000
Add: net capital losses deducted at $\frac{1}{2}$ inclusion rate ($30,000 $\times$ $\frac{4}{3}$ $\times$ $\frac{1}{2}$)	20,000
	$68,000
Less: par. 3(c) income determined above	28,000
Non-capital loss for deemed year	$40,000

The adjusted cost base of the land will be increased by the amount of the gain elected to $256,000 (i.e., $200,000 + $56,000) on March 10, 2007.

ITA: 111(4)(e)

The undepreciated capital cost in Loser's Class 8 will be reduced from $70,000 to $40,000 as at March 10, 2007. Loser Ltd. will be deemed to have deducted the $30,000 as capital cost allowance for taxation years ending before March 10, 2007; thereby, making Loser Ltd. liable for recapture on that amount if the assets are subsequently sold.

ITA: 111(5.1)

Similarly, the corporation will be deemed to have made a claim for bad debts totalling $15,000. Accordingly, Loser Ltd.'s accounts receivable will be $225,000 as at March 10, 2007, the start of its next taxation year.

ITA: 20(1)(p), 111(5.3)

Loser Limited will be allowed the deduction of the 2006 $600,000 non-capital losses in any year up to 2026 including the short deemed taxation year (if the corporation reverts to a December 31 year-end) after which they will expire. However, in order to be deducted, the widget manufacturing business must be carried on by Loser Ltd. for profit or with a reasonable expectation of profit throughout each of those taxation years. Similarly, the $40,000 non-capital losses of the March 9, 2007 taxation year will be eligible for carryforward 20 years, under the same conditions, to December 31, 2026 if the company reverts to a December 31 year-end. It appears that this condition will be met, since Holdco Ltd. will provide capital and management to turn Loser's business around. The non-capital losses may be deducted in a carryforward year from the incomes of the widget manufacturing business and a business with similar products in that year.   ITA: 111(5)

Part (b)

Loser Limited would still have business losses of $3,000 plus the deemed business loss on the Class 8 assets of $30,000 and the loss on the accounts receivable of $15,000, which gives a total of $48,000 of losses from business sources. In addition, Loser Limited has a property loss of $10,000.

The 1999 net capital loss of $30,000 is $20,000 when converted from a ¾ to a ½ inclusion rate.

The minimum designated proceeds or deemed proceeds would be as follows: ITA: 111(4)(e)

Deemed proceeds = 2 × ($20,000 net capital losses plus $10,000 property losses)
plus ACB of the land of $200,000
= $260,000

Now, the Division B and taxable income for the deemed taxation year ended March 9, 2007 would be:

Par. 3(a)	Income from non-capital sources		Nil
Par. 3(b)	Net taxable capital gains:		
	Election under par. 111(4)(e) —		
	($260,000 – $200,000) × ½	$30,000	
	Less allowable capital losses	Nil	$30,000
Par. 3(c)	. . . .		$30,000
Par. 3(d)	Losses from non-capital sources:		
	Business losses	$48,000	
	Property losses	10,000	(58,000)
Division B income			Nil
Division C deductions:			
Net capital losses			$20,000
Taxable income			Nil

Note how just enough paragraph 3(c) income was created (i.e., $30,000) to offset the property loss of $10,000 plus the net capital loss of $20,000, both of which are about to expire.

The non-capital loss balance for the deemed year ended March 9, 2007 would be:

Par. 3(d) losses	$58,000
Add: net capital losses deducted	20,000
	$78,000
Less: par. 3(c) income	(30,000)
Total non-capital loss for the year ended March 9, 2007	$48,000

The non-capital loss of $48,000 for the year ended March 9, 2007 would be added to the 2006 non-capital loss balance to give a total of $648,000 to be deducted in the future. If Loser Limited reverts to a December 31 year-end, these could be deducted in any year that the loss business is carried on against income of the business that generated the loss or against business income from the sale of similar products up to:

2006 non-capital loss	2025
March 2007 non-capital loss	2026

The adjusted cost base of the land will now be increased to $260,000.

Exercise 7

		2006		2007
Net income (loss) per financial accounting statements		$ (53,000)		$126,000
Add total of items not deductible for tax purposes		127,700		240,700
		$ 74,700		$366,700
Less CCA ($7,900 less in 2006)		51,700		51,670
Income for tax purposes		$ 23,000		$315,030
Inter-company dividends	$23,000		$23,000	
Charitable donations (max. 75% of income):				
Carried over	—		15,000	
Current	Nil		15,000	
Non-capital loss carryover	—	23,000	18,000	71,000
Taxable income		Nil		$244,030
Taxable income originally computed		Nil		$245,610

Conclusion:

This calculation produces better results. All of the inter-company dividends are fully deductible in 2006 with the reduction of the capital cost allowance by $7,900. Both alternatives allowed, in total, an equal amount of non-capital losses and donations to be claimed over the two-year period. Although the original calculation enabled $6,320 (i.e., $59,600 + $50,090 − $51,700 − $51,670) more capital cost allowance to be claimed in total over the two years, the original calculation could not utilize $7,900 of the potential dividend deduction. This alternative increases the future CCA write-offs by $6,320 as shown below.

Capital cost allowances were computed as follows:		Building Class 1: 4%	Equipment Class 8: 20%
2007:	UCC, January 1, 2007	$ 356,250	$ 187,100*
	CCA (total deduction: $51,670)	(14,250)	(37,420)
2008:	UCC, January 1, 2008	$ 342,000	$ 149,680
	UCC originally computed	$ 342,000	$ 143,360

* $179,200 + $7,900.

Exercise 8

Division B income			$116,850
Less: charitable donations limited to 75% of $116,850 or $87,638			
— carried forward		$10,250	
— current		77,388[1]	(87,638)
dividends from taxable Canadian corporations			(12,300)
subtotal			$ 16,912
non-capital losses[2]			(16,912)
net capital losses[2] (not to exceed the taxable capital gains for the year)			(Nil)
Taxable income			Nil

— NOTES TO SOLUTION

(1) The balance of $2,612 in current charitable donations may be carried forward to the next five years.

(2) These carried-over losses may be claimed in a different sequence and in different amounts from that shown. For example, if there is little prospect of future capital gains, the corporation might make the following deductions:

subtotal	$16,912
net capital losses ($41,000 × ½ / ¾)	(27,333)
non-capital losses	Nil
taxable income	Nil

The balance of the net capital losses may be carried forward indefinitely.

Net capital losses claimed are added to the non-capital loss balance carried forward.

Exercise 9

Income from Japan in Canadian dollars (77,515,723 yen × .00954)		$ 739,500
Total income under Division B ($2,500,000 + $739,500)		$3,239,500
Less: Dividends deductible under sec. 112	$100,000	
Net capital losses carried forward (adjusted to current year inclusion rate)	25,000	125,000
Taxable income		$3,114,500
Tax @ 38%		$1,183,510
Less: general tax reduction @ 7% of 3,114,500		218,015
Net tax		$ 965,495

Foreign Business Tax Deduction

Least of: (a) amount paid (31,006,289 yen × .00954)	$ 295,800

$$\text{(b)} \quad \frac{\text{income from Japan}}{\substack{\text{Div. B income minus s. 112 ded.} \\ \text{and net capital loss ded.}}} \times \substack{\text{tax otherwise} \\ \text{payable before} \\ \text{abatement plus surtax}}$$

$$= \frac{\$739,500}{\$3,239,500 - (\$100,000 + 25,000)} \times \substack{(\$965,495 + \\ \$34,882^*)} = \qquad \$\ 237,527$$

(c) Part I tax otherwise payable plus surtax minus foreign non-business tax credit ($965,495 + $34,882 – nil)	$1,000,377

Therefore, the foreign tax deduction is $237,527.

* 1.12% of $3,114,500.

Exercise 10

Income under Division B		$2,645,000
Less: Charitable donations	$ 69,000	
Taxable dividends deductible under sec. 112	517,500	
Non-capital losses	127,600	714,100
Taxable income		$1,930,900
Tax @ 38%		$ 733,742
Less: Federal tax abatement (10% of 86% of $1,930,900)		166,057
		$ 567,685
Add: Surtax (1.12% of $1,930,900)		21,626
Total		$ 589,311

Less: Non-business foreign tax credit (see Schedule 1) ...... $ 25,875

Business foreign tax credit (see Schedule 2) 36,800

Manufacturing and processing profits deduction (7% of
$1,495,000) 104,650

Tax reduction (see Schedule 3) 30,513

Federal political contributions tax credit (max.) 650 198,488

Part I tax payable .... $ 390,823

Schedule 1: Non-business foreign tax credit

Lesser of: (a) amount paid .... $ 25,875

(b) $\dfrac{\text{foreign non-business income}}{\substack{\text{Div. B income minus s. 112 ded.}\\ \text{and net capital loss ded.}}} \times \substack{\text{tax otherwise payable}\\ \text{after abatement plus}\\ \text{surtax minus general tax}\\ \text{reduction}}$

$= \dfrac{\$172,500}{\$2,645,000 - (\$517,500 + 0)} \times \$558,798^{(1)}$ .... $ 45,308

Schedule 2: Business foreign tax credit

Least of: (a) amount paid .... $ 36,800

(b) $\dfrac{\text{foreign business income}}{\substack{\text{Div. B income minus s. 112 ded.}\\ \text{and net capital loss ded.}}} \times \substack{\text{tax otherwise payable}\\ \text{before deductions plus}\\ \text{surtax minus general}\\ \text{tax reduction}}$

$= \dfrac{\$115,000}{\$2,645,000 - (\$517,500 + 0)} \times \substack{(\$733,742 + \$21,626\\ - 30,513)}$ $ 39,181

(c) $733,742 + $21,626 − $30,513 − $25,875 .... $698,980

Schedule 3: Tax reduction

Taxable income $1,930,900

Less M&P profits deduction ÷ .07 ($104,650 ÷ .07) 1,495,000

Net .... $ 435,900

7% of $435,900 .... $ 30,513

— NOTE TO SOLUTION

(1) $733,742 − $166,057 + $21,626. − $30,513 (Schedule 3)

Exercise 11

The total investment tax credit is 10% of $900,000 = $90,000.

Taxable income before CCA on eligible property $300,000

Less: CCA on qualified property (½ × 4% of $900,000) 18,000

Taxable income $282,000

Net federal tax: @ 22.12% of $282,000 .... $ 62,378

Less: fed. pol. contributions tax credit .... $ 500

investment tax credit (limited to ($62,378 − $500)) .... 61,878 $(62,378)

Part I tax payable .... Nil

Note that the $61,878 of investment tax credit will reduce the balance of UCC in Class 1 in the following year. The remainder of $28,122 (i.e., $90,000 − $61,878) of ITC may be carried back three taxation years and forward 20 taxation years. Any amount used to reduce tax in a particular carryover year will reduce the UCC in the year following the year of use or the year following the purchase, whichever is later.

Exercise 12

Earned investment tax credit of 10% of $3,500,000 = $350,000

Income under Division B before CCA on eligible property		$2,645,000
Less: CCA on eligible property ($\frac{1}{2} \times .30 \times \$3,500,000$)		525,000
Income under Division B.		$2,120,000
Less: charitable donations	$ 69,000	
taxable dividends deductible under sec. 112	517,500	
non-capital losses	127,600	714,100
Taxable income		$1,405,900
Tax @ 38%		$ 534,242
Less: federal tax abatement (10% of 86% of $1,405,900)		120,907
		$ 413,335
Add: surtax[1] (1.12% of $1,405,900)		15,746
Total		$ 429,081
Less: manufacturing and processing profits deduction (see Schedule 1)	$67,900	
non-business foreign tax credit (see Schedule 2)	25,875	
business foreign tax credit (see Schedule 3)	36,800	
Tax reduction (see Schedule 4)	30,513	
federal political contribution tax credit	500	161,588
Part I tax payable before investment tax credit		$ 267,493
Investment tax credit		(267,493)
Part I tax payable		Nil

The remaining investment tax credit of $82,507 (i.e., $350,000 – $267,493) can be carried forward 20 years.

The UCC balance in Class 43 will be reduced by $267,493 in the following year and by the amount of the $82,507 remainder in subsequent years, if that amount is deducted.

Schedule 1: Manufacturing and processing profits deduction

manufacturing and processing profits before CCA on eligible property		$1,495,000
less: CCA on eligible property ($\frac{1}{2} \times .30 \times \$3,500,000$)		525,000
manufacturing and processing profits		$ 970,000
7% of $970,000		$ 67,900

Schedule 2: Non-business foreign tax credit

Lesser of:

(a) amount paid		$25,875
(b) $\dfrac{\$172,500}{\$2,120,000 - \$517,500} \times \$398,568^{(1)}$		$42,904

Schedule 3: Business foreign tax credit

Least of:

(a) amount paid		$ 36,800

(b) $\dfrac{\$115,000}{\$2,120,000 - \$517,500} \times (\$534,242 + \$15,746 - \$30,513)$ $\underline{\$37,279}$

(c) $\$534,242 + \$15,746 - \$30,513 - \$25,875$ .... $\underline{\$493,600}$

Schedule 4: Tax reduction

Taxable income	$1,405,900
Less 100/7 M&P profits deduction (100/7 × $67,900)	970,000
Net	$ 435,900
7% of $435,900	$ 30,513

— *NOTE TO SOLUTION*

(1) $534,242 – $120,907 + $15,746 – $30,513 (Schedule 4).

CHAPTER 12
Integration for Business and Investment Income of the Private Corporation

Exercise 1

[Note: The facts of this case are those of *The Queen v. Rochmore Investments Ltd.* However, the legislation under which the case was decided did not contain a definition of "active business" or "specified investment business".]

76 DTC 6156 (F.C.A.)

Under the current legislation, "active business" is defined to exclude "a specified investment business" in such a way that if a business is not a specified investment business (and is not a personal service business), it is an active business. Note that the definition includes an adventure in the nature of trade and is only applicable in respect of the small business deduction.

ITA: 125(7), 248(1)

In this particular case, the facts indicate that it is carrying on a specified investment business. It would appear that the principal purpose of the corporation's business is to derive income from interest on mortgage loans. It does not appear to be carrying on the business of a credit union and it is not in the business of leasing movable property. If it did, the corporation would be considered to be carrying on an active business. Since the corporation had no full-time employees, it cannot escape the definition of a specified investment business, to be treated as an active business, through paragraph (a) of the definition, which requires more than five full-time employees.

ITA: 125(7)

The only possibility for escape is in paragraph (b) of the definition of "specified investment business". If the taxpayer company did not have more than five full-time employees because another corporation associated with it provided the services to the taxpayer corporation that would otherwise be performed by its own full-time employees, then the taxpayer corporation could be considered as carrying on an active business. In this case, the two principal operators of the taxpayer corporation own and manage a number of other companies. Further facts are required to determine if any of these other corporations are associated with the taxpayer corporation and if such an associated corporation provides services that would otherwise be provided by more than five full-time employees of the taxpayer corporation. This seems unlikely given the facts outlined in the case.

ITA: 125(7)

The taxpayer corporation, therefore, is likely carrying on a specified investment business. It is not carrying on a personal services business because it is not likely that the principals of the taxpayer corporation would reasonably be regarded as employees of the persons to whom the mortgage loans were made.

Exercise 2

(A) (i)   Mr. Beta is at arm's length with the corporation because his 25% ownership does not give him control. However, paragraph 251(1)(b) could always apply if the facts indicate that the non-related persons are not dealing at arm's length at a particular moment in time.

ITA: 251(2)(b)

(ii)   Mr. Beta and his brother are not at arm's length with the corporation. Mr Beta and his brother form a related group; since they are siblings, each is related by blood.

ITA: 251(2)(b)(ii), 251(6)(a)

(iii) Mr. Delta is not at arm's length with the corporation because of the share purchase option. This provision deems Mr. Delta to control Alpha Corp. unless the exceptions in this subparagraph are met. `ITA: 251(5)(b)(i)`

(iv) Mr. Epsilon is at arm's length with the corporation because of the exception, which is contingent on the death of Mr. Beta, unless paragraph 251(1)(b) applies, as described in (i) above. `ITA: 251(5)(b)(i)`

(B) (i) The corporations are not at arm's length. This subparagraph applies where Lambda Corp. is controlled by a person (i.e., A) and Tau Corp. is controlled by a related group (i.e., A and B). A is related to himself for purposes of share ownership and to his brother. `ITA: 251(2)(c)(iii), 251(5)(c), 251(6)(a)`

(ii) The corporations are at arm's length because subparagraph 251(2)(c)(iv) does not apply where there is an unrelated group of persons controlling one corporation, unless the person controlling the other corporation is related to each member of the unrelated group. For example, if two first cousins control one corporation and their grandfather controls the other, the two corporations would be related. Of course, factual non-arm's length can always apply as described in (A)(i) above.

(iii) The corporations are related and, hence, they are not at arm's length. This provision deems two corporations to be related where each corporation is related to another common corporation. `ITA: 251(3)`

Exercise 3

(A) Jay-one Ltd. and Jay-two Ltd. are associated, both being controlled by the same person. Jay-one Ltd. and Jay-three Ltd., are associated. Since Janna has voting control of Jay-one Ltd. and Jay-one Ltd. in turn has voting control of Jay-three Ltd., then Janna controls Jay-three Ltd. Therefore, all three corporations are controlled by the same person. As a result of this application of the association rule in paragraph 256(1)(b), the election under subsection 256(2) is not available to Jay-one Ltd., because Jay-three Ltd. and Jay-two Ltd. are associated without subsection 256(2). `ITA: 251(1)(b), 256(1)(a), 256(1)(b)`

(B) Benco Ltd. and Rayco Ltd. are associated. Benco Ltd. is controlled by Rayna's mother and Rayco Ltd. is controlled by Rayna. Rayna and her mother are related. Rayna owns at least 25% of the shares, which are not of a specified class, of both corporations. `ITA: 256(1)(a), 256(1)(c)`

(C) Adamco Ltd. and Kidco Ltd. are associated. Adamco Ltd. is controlled by Adam. Kidco Ltd. is controlled by the group consisting of Adam, his daughter and his son-in-law. Adam is related to himself, to his daughter and to his son-in-law. Adam owns at least 25% of the shares which are not of a specified class of Kidco Ltd. `ITA: 252(1)(e), 256(1)(d), 256(1.5), 251(6)(a), 251(6)(b)`

(D) Since both corporations are controlled by a group, paragraph 256(1)(e) is the only possibility for association. However, while Sisco Ltd. is controlled by a related group of sisters, Cousco Ltd. is not controlled by a related group. The two sisters as a group do not control Cousco Ltd. One sister and her daughter do not control the company. Finally, cousins and aunts and nieces are not related by the rules. Therefore, the condition in paragraph 256(1)(e) fails and the two corporations are not associated unless subsection 256(5.1) can be used with the argument that control in fact is exercised by Sister One and Sister Two through direct or indirect influence on their daughters or unless subsection 256(2.1) is invoked on the basis that one of the main reasons for the separate existence of the two corporations is to reduce taxes. `ITA: 251(6)(a)` `ITA: 251, 252`

Exercise 4

Taxit and Sibling are associated: `ITA: 256(1)(c)`

— each corporation is controlled by one person;

— the person who controlled one was related to the person who controlled the other;

— one of these persons owned not less than 25% of the shares which are not of a specified class of each corporation.

Since the two corporations are associated, they must share the small business deduction on a maximum of $400,000 of active business income. The Act requires that the corporations file an agreement, in prescribed form, allocating the $400,000 business limit. If an agreement is not filed within the time period indicated in subsection 125(4), that subsection empowers the Minister to make an allocation. `ITA: 125(3)`

They could each gain their eligibility for the small business deduction on a full $400,000 by having Beta reduce her holdings in Taxit to below 25% or by having Beta convert her holdings in Taxit to shares of a specified class (i.e., in essence, non-voting preferred shares). However, this strategy would work only as long as there are no factors present of the kind that would enable the deeming provisions to apply. `ITA: 256(2.1)`

Exercise 5

Since neither corporation is controlled by one person, and both corporations are not controlled by the same group of persons, the only provision in subsection 256(1) that can potentially apply is paragraph 256(1)(*e*). That paragraph sets out three conditions, each of which must be met by the facts of the case for association.

(1) Each corporation must be controlled by a related group. — The group of brothers controlling Chutzpah Enterprises Limited is related. The group consisting of Bett and Dalled Chutzpah controlling Schlock Sales Limited are related as brother-in-law and sister-in-law or by paragraph 251(6)(*a*) and paragraphs 252(2)(*b*) and (*c*). Therefore, the condition is met.

ITA: 251(2)(*a*), 251(6)(*a*)
ITA: 251(6)(*b*)

(2) Each of the members of one of the related groups was related to all of the members of the other related group. — Consider the group consisting of Aleph and Bett Chutzpah which is a related group controlling Chutzpah Enterprises Limited and the group Bett and Dalled Chutzpah which is a related group controlling Schlock Sales Limited. Aleph is related to his brother Bett, as discussed above, and to Dalled. Bett is related to himself and his sister-in-law, Dalled, as discussed above. Therefore, the condition is met.

ITA: 251(2)(*a*), 251(6)(*a*), 256(1.5)

(3) One or more members of both related groups must own, either alone or together, not less than 25% of the issued shares of any class, other than a specified class, of shares of the capital stock of the other corporation. — Bett, who is a member of both related groups, owns alone the minimum 25% of the shares necessary to meet this condition. Common shares are not shares of a specified class.

ITA: 256(1.1)

Exercise 6

Part I tax payable

Part I Tax on Taxable Income

Taxable income		$ 79,700
Tax @ 38% on $79,700		$ 30,286
Deduct: Federal tax abatement (10% of $79,700)		7,970
Net		$ 22,316
Federal surtax @ 1.12% of $79,700		893
Additional refundable tax (ART) — 6⅔% × lesser of:		
(a) AII	$ 7,000	
(b) TI – SBD amount (Schedule 1)	$ 3,500	
6⅔% of $3,500		233
Total		$ 23,442
Deduct: Non-business foreign tax credit (assumed)	$ 1,050	
Small business deduction (see Schedule 1).........	12,192	
Manufacturing and processing profits deduction		
(M&P profits less than inc. eligible from SBD)	Nil	
General reduction (see Schedule 2)	Nil	13,242
Part I federal tax payable		$ 10,200
Provincial tax @ 5.5% of $79,700		4,384
Total tax payable		$ 14,584

Schedule 1: *Small Business Deduction*

16% of the least of:

Income from an active business		$110,000(I)
Taxable income	$79,700	
Less: ¹⁰⁄₃ × foreign non-business tax credit (see above) (¹⁰⁄₃ × $1,050)	3,500	$ 76,200(II)
Business limit		$400,000(III)

Small business deduction — 16% of $76,200 = $12,192

Schedule 2: *General Reduction*

taxable income		$ 79,700
less: M&P profits deduction ÷ .07	$ Nil	
$^{100}/_{16}$ of the small business deduction	76,200	
AII	7,000	(83,200)
net		Nil
7% of Nil		Nil
Total		$ Nil

Exercise 7

Paragraph 186(1)(*b*) requires that Part IV tax be calculated as follows:

$$\frac{\$90,000}{\$120,000} \times \$18,000 = \$13,500$$

Exercise 8

(A) *Computation of Taxable Income*

Net income for income tax purposes		$186,250
Deduct: taxable dividends	$18,750	
non-capital losses	37,500	
net capital losses ($68,750 × ½ / ¾; limited to TCG)	37,500	93,750
Taxable income		$ 92,500

Part I Tax on Taxable Income

Tax @ 38% of $92,500		$ 35,150
Deduct: federal tax abatement (10% of $92,500)		9,250
Net		$ 25,900
Add: surtax @ 1.12% of $92,500		1,036
Additional refundable tax (ART) — 6⅔% of lesser of:		
(a) AII ($37,500 + $45,000 + $18,750 – $37,500 – $18,750) = $45,000		
(b) TI – SBD amount ($92,500 – $85,000) = $7,500		500
		$ 27,436
Deduct: small business deduction (see Schedule 1)	$13,600	
General reduction	Nil	$ 13,600
Part I tax payable (federal)		$ 13,836
Provincial tax @ 8% of $92,500		7,400
Total tax payable		$ 21,236

Schedule 1: *Small Business Deduction*

Income from active business	$ 85,000(I)
Taxable income (no foreign tax credits)	$ 92,500(II)
Business limit	$400,000(III)
16% of the least of amounts (I), (II) and (III)	$ 13,600

(B) *Refundable Portion of Part I Tax*

Least of:		
(a) 26⅔% × aggregate investment income (26⅔% × ($45,000 + $37,500 + $18,750 – $37,500 – $18,750))		$ 12,000
(b) Taxable income	$ 92,500	
Less: Amount eligible for the SBD	(85,000)	
26⅔% × $7,500 =		$ 2,000
(c) Part I tax – surtax ($13,836 – $1,036)		$ 12,800
Refundable portion of Part I tax — the least amount		$ 2,000

Part IV Tax on Taxable Dividends Received

Taxable dividends subject to Part IV tax × ⅓ ($18,750 × ⅓)	$ 6,250
Deduct: non-capital loss claimed for Part IV × ⅓ (all claimed under Part I)	Nil
Tax	$ 6,250

Refundable Dividend Tax on Hand

Refundable dividend tax on hand at end of last year	Nil	
Deduct: dividend refund for last year	Nil	
	Nil	
Add: refundable portion of Part I tax	$ 2,000	
Part IV tax	6,250	$ 8,250

Dividend Refund

Taxable dividends paid in the taxation year ($112,500 × ⅓)	$ 37,500(VI)
Refundable dividend tax on hand	$ 8,250(VII)
Dividend refund — lesser of (VI) and (VII)	$ 8,250

Exercise 9

(A) *Part I Tax on Taxable Income*

Tax @ 38% of $130,000		$ 49,400
Deduct: federal tax abatement (10% of 95% of $130,000)		12,350
Net		$ 37,050
Add: surtax @ 1.12% of $130,000		1,456
Additional refundable tax (ART) — 6⅔% of lesser of:		
(a) AII ($50K + $30K + $20K + $50K – $20K – $50K) = $80,000		
(b) TI – SBD amount ($130K – $90K) = $40,000		2,667
Total		$ 41,173
Deduct: non-business foreign tax credit (given)	$ 4,000	
business foreign tax credit (given)	1,000	
small business deduction (see Schedule 1)	14,400	
General reduction	Nil	19,400
Part I tax payable (federal)		$ 21,773
Provincial tax @ 7% of 95% of $130,000		8,645
Total tax		$ 30,418

Schedule 1: *Small Business Deduction*

16% of least of:

Income from active business			$ 90,000(I)
Taxable income		$130,000	
Deduct: non-business foreign tax credit × ¹⁰⁄₃	$13,333		
business foreign tax credit × 3	3,000	16,333	$113,667(II)
Business limit			$400,000(III)
Small business deduction — 16% of $90,000			$ 14,400

(B) *Refundable Portion of Part I Tax*

Least of:

(a) 26⅔% × aggregate investment income (26⅔% × $80,000)			$ 21,333
Less: non-business foreign tax credit	$4,000		
minus: 9⅓% × foreign investment income (9⅓% × $30,000)	(2,800)	(1,200)	$ 20,133

(b) Taxable income $130,000

Less: amount eligible for SBD................... (90,000)

$^{25}/_9$ × non-business FTC ($4,000) .... (11,111)

3 × business FTC ($1,000) .... (3,000)

26⅔% × $25,889 = $ 6,904

(c) Part I tax – surtax ($21,773 – $1,456)...................... $ 20,317

Refundable portion of Part I tax — The least......................... $ 6,904

Part IV Tax on Taxable Dividends Received

Taxable dividends subject to Part IV tax:

Non-connected corporations × ⅓ ($30,000 × ⅓) .... $ 10,000

Connected corporations to the extent of share of dividend refund to payer 4,000

Total Part IV tax payable .... $ 14,000

Refundable Dividend Tax on Hand

RDTOH at end of last year .... Nil

Deduct: Dividend refund for last year .... Nil   Nil

Add: Refundable portion of Part I tax .... $ 6,904

Part IV tax 14,000

RDTOH at end of year .... $ 20,904

Dividend Refund

Taxable dividends paid in year ($70,000 × ⅓) .... $ 23,333(VI)

RDTOH at end of year .... $ 20,904(VII)

Dividend refund — lesser of (VI) and (VII) .... $ 20,904

Exercise 10

(A) Splitinc Limited and Husband Ltd. are associated. Husband Ltd. is controlled by one person, Mr. Split. He is related to each member of the group, Husband Ltd. and Wife Ltd. that controls Splitinc Limited, because he is related to Husband Ltd. which he controls and he is related to Wife Ltd., which is controlled by his wife. Also, he owns not less than 25% of the shares of Splitinc Limited through his ownership of shares in Husband Ltd. These shares are not specified shares. By a similar analysis, Splitinc Limited and Wife Ltd. are associated.

ITA: 256(1)(*d*)

ITA: 251(2)(*b*)(i), 251(2)(*b*)(iii)

ITA: 256(1.2)(*d*)

Since the rental income would be deductible as an expense from the income of an active business of an associated payer, it will not be income from property of the recipient. It will be deemed to be income from an active business of the recipient, Husband Ltd. Since Husband Ltd. has only dividend income it will be eligible for the small business deduction in respect of the rental income as long as it is allocated a part of the business limit of the associated corporations.

ITA: 129(6)(*a*)(i)

ITA: 129(6)(*b*)(i)

ITA: 125(1)

(B) Since Splitinc is connected with both holding companies there will be no Part IV tax liability unless Splitinc gets a dividend refund as a result of the dividends it pays. However, Splitinc earns only active business income which is not subject to refundable taxes and dividend refunds.

Exercise 11

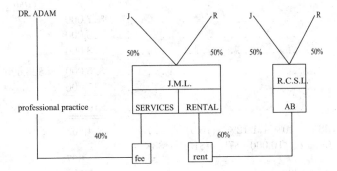

(A) Rent from RCSL:

   (i) RCSL is associated with JML;

   (ii) RCSL deducts the rent from its active business.

ITA: 256(1)(*b*)

Therefore, the rent is deemed to be income of JML from an active business, eligible for the small business deduction.

ITA: 125(1), 129(6)(*b*)(i)

(B) Services fee from Dr. Adam:

   (i) JML's income from providing services would be considered income from an active business unless further facts indicate that it is carrying on a personal services business;

   (ii) the business of providing services would be a personal services business if one or both of the shareholders of JML, who are specified shareholders (because they own at least 10% of the shares of JML), performed the services and would be regarded as an employee of the professional practice of Dr. Adam.

Therefore, if the services fee is considered income from an active business, it would qualify for the small business deduction.

Exercise 12

Interest income		$ 7,000
Dividends grossed up ($\frac{5}{4} \times \$15,000$)		18,750
Taxable capital gains ($\frac{1}{2} \times \$6,000$)		3,000
Incremental taxable income		$28,750

Federal tax on total taxable income of $48,750		
(i.e., $28,750 incremental + $20,000 other income):		
Tax on first $37,178	$ 5,763	
Tax on next $11,572 @ 22%	2,546	$ 8,309
Less: dividend tax credit ($13\frac{1}{3}$% of $18,750)	$ 2,500	
other personal tax credits	1,400	3,900
Basic federal tax		$ 4,409
Provincial tax		
Tax on first $37,178	$ 3,718	
Tax on next 11,572 @ 12%	1,389	
		$ 5,107
Less: dividend tax credit ($6\frac{2}{3}$% of $18,750)	$ 1,250	
other personal tax credits	900	(2,150)
Total tax on taxable income of $48,750		$ 7,366

Taxation of Income from Investment Portfolio through a Corporation

		Available cash
Corporation		
Interest income	$ 7,000	
Dividends	15,000	
Taxable capital gains	3,000	
Income	$25,000	$25,000[1]
Less: dividends [sec. 112]	15,000	
Taxable income	$10,000	
Tax under Part I @ 44.62% (38% − 10% + 1.12% + 15.5%)	$ 4,462	
Additional refundable tax at 6⅔% of $10,000 ($7K + $15K + $3K − $15K)	667	
Tax under Part IV @ 33⅓% of $15,000	5,000	10,129
Retained in corporation[1]		$14,871
Refundable tax:		
Part I (26⅔% of ($7K + $15K + $3K − $15K))	$ 2,667	
Part IV (33⅓% × $15,000)	5,000	7,667
Available for distribution to shareholders as taxable dividend		$22,538[2]
Shareholder		
Taxable dividend (per requirements)		$15,000
Gross-up (¼ × $15,000)		3,750
Incremental taxable income		$18,750
Federal tax on total taxable income of $38,750		
(i.e., $18,750 incremental + $20,000 other income):		
Tax on first $37,178	$5,763	
Tax on next $1,572 @ 22%	346	$ 6,109
Less: dividend tax credit (13⅓% of $18,750)	$2,500	
other personal tax credits	1,400	(3,900)
Basic federal tax		$ 2,209
Provincial tax		
Tax on first $37,178	$3,718	
Tax on next 1,572 @ 12%	189	
	3,907	
Less: dividend tax credit (6⅔ of $18,750) ... $1,250		
other personal tax credits ... 900	2,150	1,757
Total tax on taxable income of $38,750		$ 3,966
Total Taxes Paid		
Through corporation:		
Corporation after refund on $15,000 of dividends paid		
($10,129 − ⅓ × $15,000)		$ 5,129
Shareholder		3,966
Total[3]		$ 9,095
Received directly		$ 7,366

— *NOTES TO SOLUTION*

[1] Ignores the non-taxable portion of capital gain which can be distributed tax free.

[2] Note that a dividend of $22,538 will result in a dividend refund of only $7,513 (i.e., $22,538 × ⅓), not the $7,667 that was added to the RDTOH for the year. This deficiency results from imperfections in the tax rates. A larger dividend of $23,000 (i.e., 3 × $7,667) would have to be paid, using other

sources of funds, to clear the RDTOH. Alternatively, the maximum dividend that can be paid in this case is $22,307, determined algebraically, as follows:

$$
\begin{aligned}
R &= \tfrac{1}{3}\,D \\
D &= N - T + R \\
  &= N - T + \tfrac{1}{3}\,D \\
  &= (N - T) \times \tfrac{3}{2} \\
  &= (\$25{,}000 - \$10{,}129) \times \tfrac{3}{2} \\
  &= \$22{,}307 \\
R &= \$7{,}436
\end{aligned}
\qquad
\begin{aligned}
\text{where: } R &= \text{dividend refund} \\
D &= \text{dividend} \\
N &= \text{Division B net income} \\
T &= \text{total tax}
\end{aligned}
$$

Note that if the combined federal and provincial corporate tax rate had been 40%, before the additional refundable tax and the dividend refund, the amount available for dividends would be sufficient to clear the RDTOH.

[3] This amount is higher because not all of the corporate tax has been refunded as yet, and because the provincial corporate tax is 5.5% higher than the theoretical rate of 10%.

CHAPTER 13
Planning the Use of a Corporation and Shareholder-Manager Remuneration

Exercise 1

(A) The bonus must be paid on or before 179 days from the end of the year in which it was deducted. In this case, it must be paid on or before March 28, 2008. (Administrative practice would allow payment on the 180th day). IT-109R2, par. 10

(B) If the bonus is not paid on or before March 28, 2008, the corporation may not deduct the bonus in its 2007 taxation year. The bonus may only be deducted when it is paid.

(C) (i) The rent must be paid within two years from the end of the year in which it was deducted. In this case, it must be paid by September 30, 2009.

(ii) If the rent is not paid by September 30, 2009, the corporation must add the $10,000 to its income for its 2010 taxation year beginning October 1, 2009. This does not cancel the payable, such that if the rent is ever paid, the shareholder will declare the rental income, but there will be no deduction for the corporation.

(iii) An election can be filed before the date on which the corporation must file its tax return for 2010. In this case, that date is March 31, 2011. If such an election is filed, Mr. Slip will be deemed to have income of $10,000 and to have loaned that amount back to the corporation on October 1, 2009. When the loan is repaid to Mr. Slip, there are no tax consequences since the amount of the loan has already been taxed. The election can be filed late. However, $2,500 (effectively, a late-filing penalty) will be added back to the income of the corporation for its 2010 fiscal year. Mr. Slip's tax position is not affected by this late-filed election. ITA: 78(1)(b) ITA: 78(3)

Exercise 2

(A) *Employee*

Principal-Amount

— Note that the shareholder loan rule applies in this case because he is a shareholder. ITA: 15(2)

(a) House Loan

The Act would exempt the principal amount of this loan from income since Mr. Leverage received the loan in his capacity as an employee (i.e., by virtue of his employment), the purpose of the loan was to purchase a house and *bona fide* arrangements were made for repayment of the loan within a reasonable time; ITA: 15(2.4)(b)

— however, an interest benefit on a "home purchase loan" would be included in income as shown in the calculation below. ITA: 80.4

(b) Furniture Loan

There is no exemption from income for this loan because it was not repaid within one year of the 2007 taxation year of the corporation; ITA: 15(2.3), 15(2.4), 15(2.6)

— since the loan is included in income in 2007, it is an exception for the purposes of the imputed interest benefit and, hence, there is no interest benefit. ITA: 15(2), 80.4(3)(b)

(c) Share Purchase Loan

This loan is exempt from income because Mr. Leverage received the loan in his capacity as an employee and *bona fide* arrangements were made to repay the loan within a reasonable time;   ITA: 15(2.4)(c)

— since this type of loan is not an exception to the imputed interest rules, there is an interest benefit as shown in the calculation below.   ITA: 80.4

Interest Benefit

(a) interest on "home purchase loan" made to an officer or employee computed, at lesser of: (i) the prescribed rate in effect during the period in the year that the loan was outstanding, and (ii) the prescribed rate in effect at the time the loan was made. This "lesser of" choice can be made on a quarter-by-quarter comparison of tax rates. In this case, the 3% prescribed rate in June 2007, when the loan was received, is less than the rate for the other two quarters of 2007 in which the loan was outstanding. Therefore, the benefit would be based on the following calculation: ITA: 80.4(1)(a), 80.4(4)

June–Dec. 2007: 3% of $75,000 $\times$ $^{214}/_{365}$ $1,319

(b) interest on share purchase loan computed at prescribed rates in effect
during the period in the year that the loan was outstanding   ITA: 80.4(1)(a)
June 2007: 3% of $10,000 $\times$ 30/365 = $ 25
July–Sept. 2007: 4% of $10,000 $\times$ 92/365 = 101
Oct.–Dec. 2007: 4% of $10,000 $\times$ 92/365 = <u> 101</u>   227

Subtotal $1,546
(c) Less: interest paid on above loans (2% of $75,000 $\times$ 214/365) . . . . <u> 879</u>

Benefit calculated under ssec. 80.4(1) and included in employment income $ 667   ITA: 61(1)(a), 6(9)
Less: deduction for imputed interest on loan to buy shares . . . . <u> 227</u>   ITA: 20(1)(c), 80.5

Net benefit under Division B . . . . $ 440

Since the loan to purchase the house is a "home relocation loan", the Act provides for a deduction from taxable income in Division C, calculated as the least of: ITA: 248(1). 110(1)(j)

(a) the net imputed interest on the home purchase loan computed
under paragraph 80.4(1)(a) as the lesser amount above $1,319
less: interest paid in respect of the year, ...   879 $ 440

(b) interest on $25,000 computed under paragraph 80.4(1)(a) as
the lesser amount above ($25,000/$75,000 $\times$ $1,319) . . . . $ 440

(c) benefit deemed received under section 80.4 for the year . . . . . . $ 667

Therefore, the deduction would be $440.   ITA: 110(1)(j)

(B) *Shareholder*

If Mr. Leverage received the loans by virtue of being a shareholder, then all the loans would be included in income in the year that the loans were received, unless the loans were repaid by the end of the fiscal year in which the loans were made. Where a loan is outstanding in the year in which the loan was made, there would be an imputed interest inclusion. However, the inclusion would be reversed on the filing of the amended return for the loan inclusion.   ITA: 80.4(2)
ITA: 15(2)

For imputed interest, the main difference is that the benefit on the loan to purchase the house would be based only on the prescribed rate in effect during the period in the year that the loan was outstanding and reduced by the amount of interest paid on the loan by the shareholder in the period not later than 30 days after the corporation's year-end. This is because the calculation of the imputed interest benefit by virtue of shareholdings does not take into account the special rules for a "home purchase loan" or a "home relocation loan". Therefore, there would also not be a deduction available.   ITA: 80.4(2), 80.4(7), 248(1)
ITA: 110(1)(j)

Exercise 3

(A) The Department indicates that it examines the balance in the account at the end of each year of the lender considering a net increase as a loan to be included in the income of the borrower and a net decrease as a repayment to be deducted from the income of the borrower. This approach would result in the following:

IT-119R4, par. 34-35

Lender's year end	Change from previous year	Income [ssec. 15(2.6)] or repayment [par. 20(1)(j)]
Year 2	$45,000	income
Year 3	(32,000)	repayment
Year 4	(2,000)	repayment
Year 5	12,000	income
Year 6	(14,000)	repayment

(B) If there is no series of loans and repayments, then repayments are considered to apply first to the oldest loan out-standing unless the facts clearly indicate otherwise. Applying this approach would result in the following:

IT-119R4, par. 27

Lender's year end	Net inclusion (or deduction)	Explanation
Year 2	$25,000	— only the $20,000 borrowed in year 2 is repaid within one year of year 2; the $25,000 loan was not fully repaid within one year, so it must be taken into income in year 2
Year 3	(12,000)	— repayment of $12,000 of the $25,000 year 2 loan previously included
Year 4	(12,000)	— repayment of part of balance of year 2 loan
	Nil	— Nov. 30/year 4 loan repaid within one year of year 4
Year 5	(1,000)	— repayment of remainder of April 30/year 2 loan
	23,000	— full amount of Nov. 30/year 5 loan, since not fully repaid within one year of year 5
Year 6	(14,000)	— repayment of $14,000 of year 5 loan

Note that these methods of calculation are based on administrative practice and are not stipulated by the Act. Note that based on these methods, while total inclusions net of deductions over the period amount to $9,000 under each alternative, the time pattern of net inclusion is more favourable in this case if there is no series of loans and repayments considered.

If the loans are all part of a single running loan account, they are likely a series of loans and repayments. However, if the loans are for separate purposes, with differing repayment or other terms, and the repayments relate to specific loans, the facts might suggest there was no series of loans and repayments.

Exercise 4

Since he is a shareholder of the corporation, the shareholder loan rule applies and the loan that was received by the taxpayer should be included in income. However, the Act provides an exclusion for the $35,000 principal amount of the loan because:

ITA: 15(2)

ITA: 15(2.4)(d)

— the taxpayer is an employee of the lender;

— the loan is to enable him to acquire a motor vehicle to be used by him in the performance of his employment duties;

— the taxpayer received the loan because of his employment, not because of his share-holdings, since other employees were eligible for a loan; and

— *bona fide* arrangements were made, at the time the loan was made, for repayment within a reasonable time.

Since the loan is a low-interest loan, the imputed interest benefit rule applies to impute an interest benefit calculated as follows: ITA: 80.4(1)

April 1 to June 30: $^{91}/_{365} \times$ 4% of $35,000 = ...	$ 349
July 1 to Sept. 30: $^{92}/_{365} \times$ 5% of $35,000 = ...	441
Oct. 1 to Dec. 31: $^{92}/_{365} \times$ 6% of $35,000 = ...	529
Total	$1,319
Less: interest *paid* (not payable) ($^{214}/_{365} \times$ 3% of $35,000)	616
Net interest benefit	$ 703

The Act deems the imputed interest benefit of $703 to have been paid in the year. As a result, a part of the interest will qualify as a deduction of interest *paid* limited as follows: ITA: 80.5
ITA: 8(1)(*j*), 67.2

Lesser of:

(a) interest deemed paid	$703	
interest *paid* ($^{214}/_{365} \times$ 3% of $35,000)	616	$1,319
(b) $\dfrac{\$300}{30} \times 214$ days of interest paid.....................		$2,140
Lesser amount $\times$ 60% business usage (60% of $1,319).....................		$ 791

Exercise 5

Shareholder-Manager Pays Tax on Benefit

Benefit from use of car:		
standby charge[1] (10,000km/20,004km $\times^2/_3 \times$ $6,000)	2,000	
value of operating costs of personal use[2]	1,000	ITA: 6(1)(*e*)
Incremental taxable income	$ 3,000	
Tax @ 46% on $3,000 of incremental taxable income..................	$ 1,380	

Shareholder-Manager Leases Car Personally	
Incremental taxable income ($2,880 + $6,000)......................	$ 8,880
Less: deduction for business use of car [66⅔% of ($6,000 + $2,880)]	(5,920)
Add: GST rebate (6.5/106.5 $\times$ $5,920)[3]	361
Incremental taxable income	$ 3,321
Tax @ 46% on $3,321 of incremental taxable income..................	$ 1,528
Tax net of GST rebate.....................................	$ 1,167

Notice that the second alternative is the better by $213.

—NOTES TO SOLUTION

[1] This calculation assumes that business usage of 80% meets the test that the primary distance travelled was for business. Generally, the term "primarily" has been interpreted by the CRA to mean more than 50%.   ITA: 6(2)

[2] The election includes a benefit of 50% of the standby charge of $2,000 (i.e., $1,000) which is less than 22¢ $\times$ 10,000km or $2,200.   ITA: 6(1)(*k*)

[3] In reality, the GST rebate would have to be taken into income in the following year. Note that the present value considerations on the rebate have been ignored. Also, ignored is the effect of the input tax credit (ITC) received by the corporation if it incurs the annual lease and operating costs. If the corporation pays additional salary equal to its net costs for these items after ITC and, hence, if the shareholder manager must pay the GST from other sources, it can be shown that the shareholder-manager's after-tax retention is reduced by the after-tax equivalent of the GST costs. This would reduce the advantage of the second alternative.

Exercise 6

Corporation	Salary	Dividends	Combination
	Remuneration alternatives		
Income before salary and taxes	$ 20,000	$20,000	$ 20,000
Salary	(20,000)	—	(11,000)
Taxable income	Nil	$20,000	$ 9,000
Tax @ 18.12% (i.e., 38% – 10% + 1.12% – 16% + 5%).................	—	(3,624)	(1,631)
Available for dividends	Nil	$16,376	$ 7,369
Shareholder			
Employment income (ssec. 8(1) deductions not considered)	$ 20,000	—	$ 11,000
Grossed-up dividends (⁵/₄ × dividend) ...	—	$20,470	9,211
Taxable income	$ 20,000	$20,470	$ 20,211
Federal tax before dividend tax credit ...	$ 3,100	$ 3,173	$ 3,132
Dividend tax credit (13⅓% of grossed-up dividend)	—	(2,729)	(1,228)
Personal tax credits	(2,000)	(2,000)	(2,000)
Basic federal tax*	$ 1,100	$ Nil	$ Nil
Provincial tax....................	2,000	2,047	2,021
Provincial dividend tax credit (6⅔% of grossed-up dividend)	—	(1,365)	(614)
Provincial personal tax credits	(1,290)	(1,290)	(1,290)
Total tax*	$ 1,810	Nil	$ 117
Summary			
Income before salary and taxes	$ 20,000	$20,000	$ 20,000
Less: tax paid by corporation	Nil	(3,624)	(1,631)
tax paid by shareholder	(1,810)	Nil	(117)
Net cash to shareholder	$ 18,190	$16,376	$ 18,252
Excess federal dividend and personal tax credits ($3,173 – $2,729 – $2,000)		$ 1,556	

---
* Cannot be negative.

Effect of additional $100 of salary on all-dividend alternative at the corporate level when all of the income is distributed:

Increase in salary expense	$ 100.00
Decrease in corporate tax @ 18.12%	(18.12)
Decrease in amount available for dividend	$ 81.88

Effect of additional $100 in salary on all-dividend alternative at shareholder level:

Increase in salary	$ 100.00
Decrease in dividend	(81.88)
Decrease in gross-up	(20.47)
Decrease in taxable income	$ (2.35)
Decrease in federal tax @ 15.5% of $2.35	$ (.36)
Decrease in federal dividend tax credit (13⅓% of ⁵/₄ × $81.88)	13.65
Increase in tax	$ 13.29

Additional salary to eliminate $1,556 in excess tax credit ($1,556/.1329) ... $ 11,708

Corporation:

Income before salary	$ 20,000
Salary	(11,708)
Taxable income	$ 8,292
Corporate tax @ 18.12%	(1,503)
Available for dividend	$ 6,789

Shareholder:

Income from salary	$ 11,708
Income from dividend	6,789
Gross-up	1,697
Taxable income	$ 20,194
Federal tax	$ 3,130
Dividend tax credit (13⅓% of ⁵/₄ × $6,789)	(1,131)
Personal tax credits	(2,000)
Net federal tax (cannot be negative)	Nil
Provincial tax	2,019
Provincial dividend tax credit	(566)
Provincial personal tax credits	(1,290)
Total tax	$ 163

Net cash to shareholder ($20,000 – $1,503 – $163) .... $ 18,334

Improvement ($18,334 – $18,252) .... $ 82

Exercise 7

(A)   *Taxation of Income from Sole Proprietorship*

Income from business and taxable income $80,000

Federal tax		
Tax on first $74,357	$13,942	
Tax on next $5,643 @ 26%	1,467	$15,409
Personal tax credits		(2,000)
Basic federal tax		$13,409
Provincial tax (15% of ($80,000 – $74,357) + $8,179)		9,025
Provincial personal tax credits		(1,290)
Total tax paid		$21,144

(B)   *Taxation of Income through a Corporation*

	Remuneration alternatives		
	All salary	All dividends	Combination
Corporation			
Income before salary and taxes	$ 80,000	$ 80,000	$ 80,000
Salary	(29,141)	—	(8,435)[3]
Taxable income	$ 50,859	$ 80,000	$ 71,565
Tax @19.12% (i.e., 38% – 10% + 1.12% – 16% + 6%)	(9,724)	(15,296)	(13,683)
Available for dividend	$ 41,135	$ 64,704	$ 57,882
Shareholder			
Salary[1] .... (A)	$ 29,141	—	$ 8,435

	Remuneration alternatives		
	All salary	*All dividends*	*Combination*
Dividend . . . . (B)	—	$ 25,000	16,565
Gross-up @ ¼ of dividend	—	6,250	4,141
Income	$ 29,141	$ 31,250	$ 29,141
Federal tax	$ 4,517	$ 4,844	$ 4,517
Dividend tax credit (13⅓% of grossed-up dividend)	—	(4,167)	(2,761)
Personal tax credits	(2,000)	(2,000)	(2,000)
Basic federal tax	$ 2,517	Nil	(244)[4]
Provincial tax	2,914	3,125	2,914
Provincial dividend tax credit	Nil	(2,083)	(1,380)
Provincial personal tax credits	(1,290)	(1,290)	(1,290)
Total tax . . . . (C)	$ 4,141	Nil	Nil
Disposable income (A + B − C)	$ 25,000	$ 25,000	$ 25,000
Total Taxes paid			
Through corporation:			
Corporation	$ 9,724	$ 15,296	$ 13,683
Shareholder	4,141	Nil	Nil
Total	$ 13,865	$ 15,296	$ 13,683
Paid directly by proprietor	$ 21,144	$ 21,144	$ 21,144
Tax Saving (maximum[2])	$ 7,279	$ 5,848	$ 7,461

— NOTES TO SOLUTION

[1] Assumes no deductions available to employee.

[2] Assumes amount retained in the corporation can be distributed as taxable dividends in amounts that will not attract tax after personal tax credits.

[3] Note that the marginal analysis used in Example Problem 2 on page 709 of the book can be used to derive this amount. The excess tax credits in the all-dividend alternative amount to $1,571 (i.e., $4,844 − $4,167 − $2,000 + $3,125 − $2,083 − $1,290), assuming that all excess federal credits can be used on other income, as required in this problem. Since only part of the corporate income is being distributed, the focus is on the shareholder-manager. If salary is increased by $100, the following would occur:

Increase in salary	$ 100.00
Decrease in dividend	(100.00)
Decrease in gross-up	(25.00)
Decrease in taxable income	$ (25.00)
Decrease in tax @ 25.5% (i.e., 15.5% federal and 10% provincial) of $25.00	$ (6.38)
Decrease in dividend tax credit (20% of 5/4 × $100.00)	25.00
Increase in tax	$ 18.62
Increase in salary to eliminate $1,571 of excess tax credits ($1,571/.1862)	$ 8,437

[4] Negative allowed only due to assumption in the required.

Exercise 8

In each of the cases, the test to be applied to the facts is whether all or substantially all (i.e., at least 90%) of the fair market value of the assets are:

(a) used principally in an active business carried on primarily in Canada by the corporation (or a related corporation);

(b) shares or debt of a connected SBC; or

(c) a combination of (a) and (b).

(A) This situation depends on whether the marketable securities are used in the active business or are passive investments not necessary to the active business. If the marketable securities are used in the active business, then the 90% test is met. This would be the case, for example, if the marketable securities represented a short-term investment of cash surpluses, awaiting the purchase of inventory for the next season.

(B) In this situation, the 90% test is met with a combination of active business assets and shares in a connected SBC.

(C) In this case, the marketable securities cannot be considered to be used in an active business, because the corporation has no other active business assets to carry on such a business. Since the shares of a connected SBC represent only 80% of the total fair market value of the corporation's assets, the 90% test is not met.

(D) Again, this case fits the definition of an SBC if the marketable securities are considered to be used in an active business. If the facts of this case so indicate, then the 90% test is met by a combination of active business assets (including the marketable securities) and the shares of a connected SBC.

Exercise 9

(A) Unused lifetime deduction in 2007:

Lifetime cumulative deduction limit [prior to March 19, 2007]		$ 250,000
Less: prior years' deductions:		
Capital gains deduction claimed in 2005		75,000
Capital gains deduction available for 2007		$ 175,000

(B) Annual gains limit for 2007:

Net taxable capital gains for 2007[1]		$ 225,000
Minus:		
Net capital losses deducted in 2007	Nil	
ABILs realized in 2007[1]	5,000	5,000
Annual gains limit for 2007		$ 220,000

(C) Cumulative gains limit for 2007:

Cumulative net taxable capital gains ($75,000 + $225,000)			$ 300,000
Minus:			
Cumulative net capital losses deducted		Nil	
Cumulative ABILs realized	$	5,000	
Cumulative capital gains deductions		75,000	
Cumulative net investment loss:			
Investment expenses —			
Cumulative carrying charges	$ 1,075		
Cumulative net rental losses			
($1,100 + $220)	1,320		
	$ 2,395		
Investment income —			
Cumulative interest income			
($600 + $1,200)	(1,800)		
Cumulative grossed-up dividends	(140)	455	80,455
Cumulative gains limit for 2007			$ 219,545

(D) Least of (A), (B), (C) . . . . $ 175,000

— NOTE TO SOLUTION

(1) Allowable business investment loss (ABIL):

BIL before ssec. 39(9) reduction			$ 160,000
Disallowed portion — Lesser of:			
(a) BIL	$ 160,000		
(b) Adjustment factor × cumulative CG deductions of previous years (2 × $75,000)	$150,000		
Minus: Cumulative disallowed BIL of prior years	Nil	$ 150,000	
Lesser of (a) and (b)			(150,000)
BIL after adjustment			$ 10,000
ABIL (½ × $10,000)			$ 5,000

Allowable capital loss (ACL):

Disallowed portion of BIL	$ 150,000
ACL (½ × $150,000)	$ 75,000

Net TCG for 2007:

TCG	$ 300,000
Less: ACL	75,000
Net TCG	$ 225,000

Exercise 10

The disposition of the real estate is a transfer for tax purposes in 2007. The facts do not provide enough details on the cost base to determine the tax effect of the disposition.

In this case it can likely be established that one of the main purposes of the transfer of the building may reasonably be considered to be to reduce the income of Mr. Albert and to benefit Mrs. Albert who is a designated person and a specified shareholder. Had Mr. Albert kept the building himself he would have earned $20,000 of rental income on which he would have been taxable. Instead, he will receive $1,000 of interest and $2,000 of dividends. Mrs. Albert benefited from the rental income since this will accrue to the common shares of the corporation. Therefore, it may be argued that the purpose test will have been met.

Furthermore, the corporation will no longer be a "small business corporation", since the fair market value of the assets of the corporation will be as follows: ITA: 248(1)

Retail assets, 75%	$600,000
Building, 25%	200,000
Total	$800,000

Even if 20% of the building (FMV $40,000) is classified as an active business asset, the corporation will still not be a small business corporation since all or substantially all of the fair market value of the assets are not used principally in an active business carried on primarily in Canada.

Mr. Albert's attributed amount	
FMV of the building transferred	$200,000
Less: cash received	(80,000)
Outstanding amount	$120,000
Interest imputed at 4%	$4,800
Less: interest received (5% of $20,000)	(1,000)
⁵/₄ of dividends received	(2,500)
Attributed amount	$1,300
Mr. Albert would also have	
Interest income	1,000
Taxable dividends ($2,000 × 1.25)	2,500
Total income	$4,800

Exercise 11

The following comments are based on the application of the logic presented in Exhibit 13-11 to the facts of this situation.

(1) Does any other provision of the Act or other rule of law apply to stop the taxpayer from achieving the intended advantage? No, the amount paid is considered to be reasonable and, hence, is not prohibited. Remuneration is considered to be an expense incurred to produce income from business and, thus, is not prohibited.

ITA: 67

ITA: 18(1)(a)

(2) Does the transaction result, directly or indirectly, in a tax benefit, i.e., a reduction, avoidance or deferral of tax or an increase in a refund? On the one hand, corporate tax is reduced, but on the other hand the individual receives income subject to tax at approximately the same rate. However, the reduction of income to the corporation reduces the potential for double taxation on income taxed at more than a 20% rate in the corporation which may be considered to be a tax benefit. If it is concluded that there is no tax benefit, GAAR should not apply.

ITA: 245(1)

(3) Is the transaction part of a series of transactions, which would result, directly or indirectly, in a tax benefit? If the answer to question 2 is yes, then proceed directly to question 4.

(4) Can the transaction reasonably be considered to have been undertaken or arranged primarily for *bona fide* purposes other than to obtain the tax benefit? No, a tax reduction for the corporation was probably the primary purpose. On the other hand, it might be argued that, since the amount paid was reasonable, it is necessary remuneration.

(5) Can it reasonably be considered that the transaction would result directly or indirectly in a misuse of the provisions of the Act or an abuse having regard to the provisions of the Act read as a whole? No, "the Act recognizes the deductibility of reasonable business expenses."

IC 88-2, par. 18

CHAPTER 14
Rights and Obligations under the Income Tax Act

Exercise 1

Subsection 150(1):

(a) corporations — within 6 months from the end of the taxation year;

(b) deceased persons — for a tax return of a given year where the individual died after October 31 of the given year and before the normal filing due date for that year, on or before the later of 6 months after the day of death and the day the return would otherwise be due; in all other cases by April 30 (or June 15, if the deceased individual or his or her spouse carried on a business in the year of death) following the year of death (i.e., if the death occurs in the first 10 months of a year, the return is due by April 30 or June 15 of the next year);

(c) trust — within 90 days from the end of the taxation year;

(d) individual — on or before April 30 of the next calendar year unless the individual or his or her spouse carried on a business, in which case the deadline is June 15 of the next year.

Exercise 2

Subsection 152(4):

— No limit if fraud or misrepresentation in the 2006 return can be established or on a matter for which the taxpayer has filed a waiver of the limit by May 27, 2010;

— Otherwise, the reassessment must be made within 3 years of May 27, 2007.

Exercise 3

Subsection 153(1):

(a) salary or wages or other remuneration from employment;

(b) a superannuation or pension benefit;

(c) a retiring allowance;

(d) a death benefit for long service from an employer;

(e) an Employment Insurance benefit;

(f) a benefit under a supplementary unemployment benefit plan;

(g) an annuity payment;

(h) a benefit from a deferred profit sharing plan;

(i) fees, commissions and other amounts for services;

(j) a payment under a registered retirement savings plan;

(k) certain amounts resulting from an income averaging annuity;

(l) a payment from a registered retirement income fund.

Exercise 4

Inheritance, gambling winnings, lottery prize, etc.

Exercise 5

As his net tax owing in the current year and one of the two preceding years is in excess of $2,000 [$3,000 under a proposal of the March 19, 2007 federal budget, effective for 2008 and subsequent taxation years], he is required to make instalments.

Instalments of $750 ($\frac{1}{4} \times$ $3,000) must be paid by March 15 and June 15 and instalments of $1,250 (i.e., ($4,000 – 2 × $750) × $\frac{1}{2}$) must be paid by September 15 and December 15. The balance of the tax liability must be remitted by the balance-due date of April 30, 2008.

Exercise 6

As the corporation's estimated taxes payable for the current year and the taxes paid for the preceding year exceed $1,000, instalments are required.

The Act would allow the following: ITA: 157(1)(*a*)(iii)

January 31 and February 29, 2007 — $\frac{1}{12}$ of $158,400 or $13,200;

Last day of March to December 2007 — $\frac{1}{10}$ of ($237,600 – 2 × $13,200) or $21,120;

Balance on the last day of the third month after the taxation year-end, where a small business deduction was taken by virtue of section 125 in the current or preceding year and the corporation and associated corporations' aggregate taxable incomes for the preceding year did not exceed the small business deduction limit of $400,000, or, in this particular case, the last day of February 2008, as applicable to any other case.

Exercise 7

Subsection 150(1):

Y and Z will incur no penalties; furthermore, Y is not required to file since no tax is payable, unless he disposed of capital property.

Subsection 162(1):

Failure to file when required — 5% of unpaid tax plus 1% of unpaid tax per complete month past due for a first offence:

X — 5% of $4,700 or $235 plus 1% of $4,700 × nil = $235.

Y — 5% of nil or nil.

Z — no penalty as the return is not due until June 15. Interest charges on the unpaid tax from April 30 will, however, apply.

Subsection 238(1):

Failure to file as or when required — liable on summary conviction to a fine of $1,000 to $25,000 or a fine and imprisonment for up to 12 months;

— Y could be fined if there has been a demand to file under subsection 150(2).

Exercise 8

The Act computes interest at a basic prescribed rate plus 4% on amounts owing to the CRA from the earliest date the amount was due until the date it was paid;   ITA: 161

— the interest is not tax deductible.

Interest is computed at the same basic prescribed rate plus 2% on refunds by the CRA;   ITA: 164(3)

— the interest is taxable;

— if the interest relates to instalments, an interest offset is computed using the 4% addition,   ITA: 161(2.2)
against interest owing on late instalments for interest earned on early instalments.

Both interest calculations are based on daily compounding.

Interest on the overpayment of taxes for individuals will start to accrue 30 days after the later of the balance due day for the return (i.e., April 30, 2008 for 2007 returns) or the date the return is filed.

An individual's refund interest accruing over a period can be offset by any arrears interest that accrues over the same period, to which the refund interest relates. Hence, only the excess refund interest is taxed to the individual.

Exercise 9

The following comment on this situation is provided by the CRA: IC 01-1

There was nothing in the income statement that would have made the accountant question the validity of the information provided to him. Therefore, he could rely on the good faith defence and would not be subject to the preparer penalty.

Use of the flowchart presented in the chapter may be helpful in analyzing this situation and reaching this conclusion.

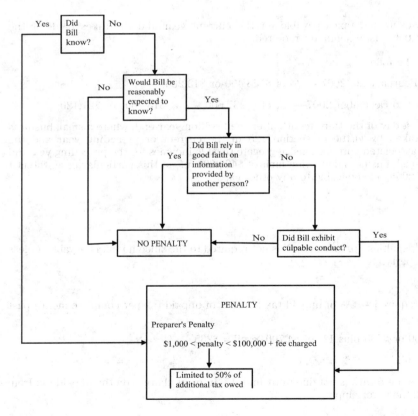

Exercise 10

(a) Notice of objection: ITA: 165(1)

— to be filed by *individual* taxpayers by the later of:

(i) one year after the filing-due date, which is normally April 30 or June 15 except for trusts and deceased persons, and   ITA: 248(1)

(ii) the 90th day after the mailing date of the notice of assessment;

— to be filed within 90 days of mailing of notice of assessment for all other taxpayers;

— a prescribed form is not required.

(b) Appeal to the Tax Court of Canada: ITA: 169

— after 90 days of date of decision on notice of objection or 90 days after the mailing of the notice of objection if there has been no response to it;

— may be able to elect informal procedure under subsection 18(1) of the *Tax Court of Canada Act*.

(c) Appeal to the Federal Court of Appeal (section 17.6 of the *Tax Court of Canada Act*):

— within 30 days from date of mailing of decision of the Tax Court of Canada only if that taxpayer chose the general procedure in the Tax Court of Canada.

(d) Appeal to Supreme Court of Canada:

— on recommendation of Federal Court of Appeal;

— with permission of Supreme Court of Canada.

Exercise 11

A tax return may be filed by a non-resident within two years after the end of the year that rents were paid;. In that return, rental income for the year, net of expenses, would be reported and any withholding tax paid in the year in respect of rental revenue would be considered taxes paid for the year.   ITA: 216

This individual is eligible to file this return for 2005, 2006, and 2007. The 2002, 2003, and 2004 rents do not fall into the eligible filing period. However, the Minister may extend the time for filing a return. The individual may consider requesting such an extension.   ITA: 216   ITA: 220(3.2)

Exercise 12

Sol will receive interest on the $9,000 only from 30 days after June 15, 2007 (i.e., July 15, 2007) to the date the cheque was mailed. When he determined he had paid excess instalments, he could consider requesting that the instalments be transferred to his employer remittance account, if he has employees from whom he withholds tax.

Exercise 13

(A) The accrued interest is a periodic payment to be reported on the terminal T1 return, due April 30, 2008.   ITA: 70(1)

(B) Since the dividend is not payable until declared, it does not have to be accrued. Because it was declared after death, it is not a right or thing. Therefore, it is income of his estate.   ITA: 70(1), 70(2)

(C) The $800 of CPP would be reported on the terminal T1 return, since no amount was unpaid at the date of death that related to a *completed* pay period. Hence, CPP earned from September 1 to the date of death on September 10 is not considered to be a right or thing, since it is not legally receivable for a completed pay period on the date of death.

(D) The donations are creditable, to the extent of 100% of net income reported, on all the year of death returns combined or in the preceding year's return. Only personal tax credits may be deducted on each of the separate returns for the year of death.   ITA: 118(1), 118(2)   ITA: 118.93

(E) Net capital losses are deductible from any source of income in the year of death and the preceding year.   ITA: 111(2)

(F) Trust income of $900 for the year ended May 31, 2007 must be reported on the terminal return. An election is permitted to report the trust income payable to Sam for the stub period, June 1, 2007 to September 10, 2007 on a separate return, also due April 30, 2008. The personal tax credits can be deducted on this return.   ITA: 104(23)(*d*)   ITA: 118(1), 118(2)

(G) Life insurance proceeds received on death are not taxable.

Exercise 14

Ms. Kaye's 2007 terminal personal tax return is required to be filed by April 30, 2008. In Ms. Kaye's 2007 return all accrued income earned on a periodic basis during the period January 1 to May 1, 2007 should be included. In addition, all capital property (such as her Flying High shares) is deemed to have been disposed of at the fair market value. A claim for the full personal tax credits can be made on the terminal return even though Ms. Kaye died on May 2, 2007. The RRSP contribution of $9,000 is deductible on her 2007 terminal return, since it is less than the maximum amount (i.e., lesser of $19,000 and 18% of $80,000).

ITA: 150(1)(*d*)
ITA: 70(1)
ITA: 70(5)

Ms. Kaye's 2007 terminal return will include the following:

Salary	$22,000
Bond interest	950
Savings account interest	150
GIC interest	140
Dividend income	250
Taxable capital gain [½ ($25–$10)×100]	750
RRSP accumulation	34,000
RRSP contribution	(9,000)
Taxable income	$49,240

Ms. Kaye's legal representative can report amounts which were receivable but not received at the date of death, on a separate tax return, called a "rights or things" return, instead of on the terminal return.

ITA: 70(2)

The unpaid salary of $2,000, interest payable of $950 and $250 of grossed-up dividend income would qualify as income from "rights or things." Personal tax credits equal to the amounts claimed in the terminal return may be claimed again on the "rights or things" return. This return is due on the date that is the later of one year after death and 90 days after assessment of any return for the year of death.

Alternatively, the legal representative can assign the income from "rights or things" to a particular beneficiary.

ITA: 70(3)

CHAPTER 15
Corporate Distributions, Windings-Up, and Sales

Exercise 1

	A	B	C
Proceeds of disposition	$ 4,000	$ 1,000	$ 2,000
Less: adjusted cost base	(2,000)	(2,000)	(2,000)
selling expenses	(400)	(100)	(200)
Capital gain (loss)	$ 1,600	$(1,100)	$ (200)
Adjustment to CDA (½ × capital gain (loss))	$ 800	$ (550)	$ (100)

Exercise 2

(A) Net income for tax purposes	*Property 1*		*Property 2*	
Proceeds of disposition		$110,000		$ 11,000
Less: ACB	$75,000		$40,000	
selling costs	11,000	86,000	5,500	45,500
Capital gain (loss)		$ 24,000		$(34,500)
Taxable capital gain (allowable capital loss)		$ 12,000		$(17,250)
(B) Adjustment to CDA (½ × capital gain (loss))		$ 12,000		$(17,250)

Exercise 3

(A) Where Dividend Limited redeems the preferred shares, Mr. Deemed will have a deemed dividend equal to: $\qquad$ ITA: 84(3)

Redemption amount	$60,000
Less: PUC (800 × $15)	12,000
Deemed dividend	$48,000

ITA: 84(3)

Mr. Deemed will not have a capital gain on the transactions because the adjusted proceeds of disposition equals the ACB of shares as demonstrated below:

Proceeds of disposition	$60,000
Deemed dividend	48,000
Adjusted proceeds of disposition	$12,000
Less: ACB (800 shares × $15)	12,000
Capital gain	Nil

ITA: 84(3)

ITA: 54 "proceeds of disposition" (*j*)

(B) The dividend payment of $60,000 will be a taxable dividend unless Dividend Limited makes an election to treat the cash dividend as a distribution from the capital dividend account. Where this election is made, the dividend will be tax-free to Mr. Dividend.

ITA: 83(2)

(C) A non-dividend distribution to Mr. Deemed in excess of the PUC of the preferred shares will result in a deemed dividend of $45,000 (i.e., $60,000 – $15,000). The ACB of the shares will be reduced by the non-taxed portion of the payment of $15,000. The PUC of the shares must be reduced by the $15,000 in this case to reflect the tax-free distribution of PUC If PUC is not reduced by $15,000 in this transaction, an additional $15,000 will be treated as a deemed dividend.

ITA: 84(4)
ITA: 53(2)(*a*)(ii)
ITA: 84(4)(*a*)

Exercise 4

(A) The amount of the stock dividend is $1.00 per share and must be grossed up and included in income of the shareholder. Thus, income would total $12.50 (^{5}⁄$_4$ × $1.00 × 10 shares). The dividend tax credit would be available on the $1.00 amount of the stock dividend or about $.25 total (including provincial tax effect) per share. The adjusted cost base of the shares on the acquisition date would be $10.00 in total (i.e., $1.00 per share).

(B) The corporation will be deemed to have paid a dividend of $10.00 for determining its dividend refund and other amounts dependent on dividends paid.

(C)	P of D (10 shares @ $1,000 FMV)		$10,000
	ACB (see (A) above)		(10)
	Capital gain		$ 9,990
	Taxable capital gain (eligible for capital gains deduction)		$ 4,995
(D)	(i)	Redemption amount (10 shares @ $1,000)	$10,000
		PUC (10 shares @ $1.00)	(10)
		Deemed dividend on redemption	$ 9,990
	(ii)	Proceeds of disposition (above)	$10,000
		Less: deemed dividend	(9,990)
		Adjusted proceeds of disposition	$ 10
		ACB	(10)
		Capital gain	Nil

ITA: 84(3)

ITA: 54 "proceeds of disposition" (*j*)

Exercise 5

(a) This transaction would cause an immediate deemed dividend of $50 since the daughter could immediately retract the shares and receive $150 tax free whereas the price paid for the shares was only $100.

ITA: 84(1)

Deemed dividend			ITA: 84(1)
PUC increase		$150	
PUC decrease		(Nil	
		$150	
Increase in net assets		(100)	
Deemed dividend		$ 50	ITA: 84(1)

This $50 deemed dividend would be added to the ACB of the preferred shares acquired by the daughter.

In addition, there would be a subsection 84(3) deemed dividend on the ultimate redemption of the preferred shares as calculated below:

Redemption of shares			
Redemption amount		$1,000	
PUC — Special share		(150)	
Deemed dividend on redemption		$ 850	ITA: 84(3)
Proceeds of disposition		$1,000	
Less: deemed dividend		850	ITA: 54 "proceeds of disposition" (j)
Adjusted P of D		$ 150	
ACB			
— original cost	$100		
— ssec. 84(1) deemed dividend	50	(150)	ITA: 53(1)(b)
Capital gain		Nil	

Economic consequences		
Redemption amount		$1,000
Actual price paid		(100)
Economic gain on redemption		$ 900

Tax results:			
Deemed dividend		$ 50	ITA: 84(1)
Deemed dividend		850	ITA: 84(3)
Total gain taxed ($1,000 – $100)		$ 900	

(b) As long as there is no capital gain or loss triggered on the transfer, the gift of land to the corporation should have no other immediate tax consequences. The accounting and tax records would show an increased balance in the contributed surplus account. However, the withdrawal of this contributed surplus can only be in the form of taxable dividend subject to the gross-up and tax credit mechanism. However, the Act permits the capitalization of the contributed surplus into PUC as long as the amount did not arise under one of the corporate tax-free rollover provisions, discussed in the next few chapters.

ITA: 84(1)(c.3)

(c) Y has received $2,000 more in consideration than the cancelled debt (i.e., $2,000 + $20,000 versus $20,000); therefore, Y will have an income inclusion of:

PUC increase	$2,000	
Net asset increase ($20,000 – $20,000)	Nil	
Deemed dividend	$2,000	ITA: 84(1)

The cost of the shares is nil since the $20,000 cash cancelled the debt; however, there will be an increase in ACB equal to the deemed dividend of $2,000.

ITA: 53(1)(b)

(d) (i) Since the payment of $5,000 is less than the PUC of the outstanding share(s) (i.e., $10,000), there are no immediate tax consequences because this payment is a return of the original investment in the corporation with tax-paid funds. However, the adjusted cost base of the shares is reduced to $15,000 (i.e., $20,000 – $5,000) by the amount of the return of capital which would result in a potential higher capital gain on the ultimate disposition of the shares.

ITA: 53(2)(a)(ii)

Deemed dividend		ITA: 84(1)
PUC before distribution	$10,000	
PUC after distribution	(5,000)	
PUC decrease (not an increase)	$ 5,000	
Adjusted cost base		
ACB prior to distribution	$20,000	
Distribution amount	(5,000)	
New ACB	$15,000	

(ii) Since the payment of $18,000 exceeds the PUC of the outstanding share(s), there will be a deemed dividend of $8,000. However, the ACB of the share(s) will only be reduced by the non-taxed portion of the payment to $10,000.   ITA: 84(4)

Exercise 6

(A) Funds available for distribution to shareholder	$1,000,000	
Less: paid-up capital	(625,000)	
Deemed dividend on winding-up	$ 375,000	ITA: 84(2)
Less: capital dividend elected	(150,000)	ITA: 83(2), 88(2)(*b*)(i)
Taxable dividend (sufficient to clear RDTOH)	$ 225,000	
(B) Taxable capital gain (allowable capital loss) to Mr. Finished:		
Proceeds on winding-up	$1,000,000	
Less: deemed dividend	(375,000)	ITA: 54 "proceeds of disposition" (*j*)
Proceeds of disposition	$ 625,000	
ACB	350,000	
Capital gain	$ 275,000	
Taxable capital gain (½)	$ 137,500	

Exercise 7

Funds available for distribution	$30,000	
Less: paid-up capital	(2,000)	
Deemed dividend or winding-up	$28,000	ITA: 84(2)
Less: capital dividend elected	(2,000)	ITA: 83(2), 88(2)(*b*)(i)
Deemed taxable dividend	$26,000	
Capital gain or loss on disposition of shares:		
Actual proceeds from distribution	$30,000	
Less: deemed dividend	(28,000)	ITA: 54 "proceeds of disposition" (*j*)
Proceeds of disposition	$ 2,000	
Cost	(2,000)	
Capital gain (loss)	Nil	
Taxable capital gain	Nil	

Net cash retained:

Funds distributed		$30,000
Tax on incremental income from distribution:		
Deemed taxable dividend.	$26,000	
Gross-up (¼ × $26,000)	6,500	
Taxable capital gain	Nil	
Incremental taxable income	$32,500	
Combined federal and provincial tax @ 46%	$14,950	
Less: combined dividend tax credit in province @ (6⅔% + 13⅓) × ⁵⁄₄ × $26,000	(6,500)	8,450
Net cash retained		$21,550

Exercise 8

(A)

	Proceeds	Income Bus.	Income Invest.	C.D. a/c	RDTOH
Opening balances		Nil	Nil	Nil	$ 10,000
Cash	$ 20,000	Nil	Nil		
Inventories	220,000	$ 20,000	Nil		
Land[1]	70,000	Nil	$ 15,000	$15,000	
Buildings[2]	300,000	140,000	50,000	50,000	
Equipment[3]	80,000	40,000	Nil		
Liabilities	(50,000)				
Income taxes[5]	(70,333)	$200,000[4]	$ 65,000		17,333
RDTOH[6]	27,333				$ 27,333
	$597,000		$65,000		

(B)
Funds available for distribution to shareholder.	$597,000	
Less: paid-up capital	2,000	
Deemed dividend on winding-up	$595,000	ITA: 84(2)
Less: capital dividend elected	65,000	ITA: 83(2)
Deemed taxable dividend (clears RDTOH)	$530,000	

(C) Taxable capital gain to Mr. Downer
Actual proceeds on winding-up	$597,000
Less: deemed dividend	595,000
Proceeds of disposition	$ 2,000
Cost	(1,000)
Capital gain.	$ 1,000
Taxable capital gain (½ × $1,000)	$ 500

(D)

Where a corporation is wound up and the general winding-up rules of the Act apply, the supply of property on the wind-up is subject to GST. GST is payable on any taxable supplies of property. However, an election may be available, in which case the payment of GST is not required. In order to qualify, a registrant must have sold or transferred all or substantially all of the assets used in a commercial activity that is part of a business carried on. Since Downandout Ltd. is being wound up by Mr. Downer it would qualify for this election.

ITA: 88(2)

ETA: 167(1)

— *NOTES TO SOLUTION*

[1]	Proceeds on sale of land	$ 70,000
	Cost	40,000
	Capital gain.	$ 30,000
	Taxable capital gain (½ × $30K) (investment income)	$ 15,000
	Capital dividend account (½ × $30K)	$ 15,000

(2) 　Actual proceeds on sale of building $300,000
　　　UCC . . . . 　60,000

　　　Gain $240,000

　　　Recapture ($200K – $60K) (business income) $140,000

　　　Taxable capital gain (½ × ($300K – $200K)) (investment income) . . . . $ 50,000

　　　Capital dividend account (½ × ($300K – $200K)) . . . . $ 50,000

(3) 　Actual proceeds on sale of equipment . . . . $ 80,000
　　　UCC . . . . 　40,000

　　　Gain . . . . $ 40,000

　　　Recapture ($80K – $40K) — fully accounts for gain
　　　　(business income) . . . . $ 40,000

(4) 　The $400,000 business limit for the small business deduction must be prorated for the number of days in the taxation year. Since the winding-up may take some time to complete, this solution assumes that the corporation maintains its eligibility for the small business deduction in the year in which the sale of assets occurs. In this case, there would be no need to bonus down to the business limit for the small business deduction, given active business income of $200,000. 　*IT-73R6, par. 9*

(5) 　Income taxes
　　　20% × ABI ($200,000) $40,000
　　　46⅔% × investment income ($65,000) . . . . 　30,333　　$ 70,333

　　　RDTOH (26⅔% of $65,000) . . . . 　　　　$ 17,333

(6) 　Assumes a minimum $81,999 (i.e., 3 × $27,333) is to be distributed as a taxable dividend to produce a refund of the full RDTOH.

CHAPTER 16
Income Deferral: Rollover on Transfers to a Corporation and Pitfalls

Exercise 1

	A	B	C	D	E	F	G
(A) Minimum elected amount or deemed proceeds	$120	$100	$ 80	$ 75	$100	$ 90	$ 50
(B) Proceeds	$120	$100	$ 80	$ 75	$100	$ 90	$ 50
Cost	100	75	100	75	100	75	100
Capital gain	$ 20	$ 25	Nil*	Nil	Nil	$ 15	Nil
Taxable capital gain (½)	$ 10	$ 13	Nil	Nil	Nil	$ 8	Nil
Lesser of cost or proceeds	$100		$ 80		$100		$ 50
UCC of class	200		50		150		50
Recapture	Nil		$ 30		Nil		Nil
Income	$ 30	$100	Nil	Nil	Nil	Nil	Nil
(C) Maximum "boot"	$100	$ 75	$ 50	$ 75	$100	$ 75	$ 50

ITA: 15(1)

---

* No capital loss on depreciable property.

Exercise 2

	A	B	C
(A) Cost of consideration received:			
Elected transfer price	$5,000	$5,000	$5,000
Allocated to note up to FMV	5,000	2,500	4,000
Allocated to preferred up to FMV	Nil	$2,500	Nil
Allocated to common shares	Nil	Nil	$1,000

	A	B	C
(B)			
LSC before reduction	$5,000	$7,500	$6,000

Reduction in PUC   ITA: 85(2.1)

		A	B	C
(a) Increase in LSC of all shares		$5,000 (A)	$7,500 (A)	$6,000 (A)
(b) Elected amount	$5,000			
Less: boot............	5,000			
Excess, if any		Nil (B)	$2,500 (B)	$1,000 (B)
Total reduction in PUC (A – B)		$5,000	$5,000	$5,000

For B: Elected amount $5,000, Less: boot 2,500, Excess $2,500 (B)
For C: Elected amount $5,000, Less: boot 4,000, Excess $1,000 (B)

(c) Allocation of reduction to different classes:

Preferred shares

$$\$5,000 \times \frac{\$4,500}{\$5,000} = \$4,500$$

Common shares

$$\$5,000 \times \frac{\$500}{\$5,000} = \$\ 500$$

Tax PUC

	A	B	C
Preferred shares......	Nil	$2,500	
Common shares	Nil		$1,000

Note how the PUC after reduction is equal to the amount of the $5,000 ACB of the original capital property that has not been recovered through the notes received as consideration.

Exercise 3

(A) The elected amount becomes the proceeds of disposition of the assets transferred by Mr. Goodroll. Since his adjusted cost base on the land and his undepreciated capital cost on the building are equal to these proceeds, there will be no capital gain on that land and no recapture on the building. The corporation is deemed to acquire these assets at a cost equal to the elected amount. On the building, the corporation is deemed to have a capital cost of $436,224 and to have taken capital cost allowance of $8,724 making it liable for future recapture and for a potential future capital gain if ultimate proceeds exceed $436,224. This places the corporation in the same position as Mr. Goodroll was in with respect to the building prior to the transfer.

(B) (i) The cost of the debt and shares taken as consideration would be computed as follows:

Elected transfer price...		$577,500
Allocated to debt:		
— mortgage assumed	$247,500	
— new debt issued	330,000	577,500
Allocated to shares..		Nil

(ii) LSC before reduction $322,500

Reduction in PUC   ITA: 85(2.1)

(1) Increase in LSC of all shares	$322,500 (A)	
(2) Elected amount	$577,500	
less: boot ($247,500 + $330,000)	577,500	
Excess, if any...........................	Nil (B)	
Total PUC reduction (A – B)		(322,500)
Tax PUC after reduction...................................		Nil

(C) (i) If the new debt is redeemed for $330,000, given its adjusted cost base in Mr. Goodroll's hands of $330,000, there would be no gain or loss. However, on the disposition of the shares, the following would result:

Proceeds of disposition	$425,000
Adjusted cost base	Nil
Capital gain	$425,000
Taxable capital gain	$212,500

(ii)

Redemption amount	$425,000	
Less: PUC	Nil	
Deemed dividend	$425,000	ITA: 84(3)
Redemption amount	$425,000	
Less: deemed dividend	425,000	
Proceeds of disposition	Nil	ITA: 54 "proceeds of disposition" (*j*)
Less: adjusted cost base	Nil	
Capital gain	Nil	

Exercise 4

The benefit rule would apply. The amount of the benefit would be equal to: ITA: 85(1)(*e*.2)

Fair market value of property transferred		$125,000
Less greater of:		
(a) fair market value of all consideration received	$101,000	101,000
(b) elected amount	$100,000	
Benefit		$ 24,000

The proceeds of disposition of the securities to Mother would be increased by the amount of the benefit, $24,000, to $124,000 resulting in a capital gain of $24,000 on the transfer. The cost of the property to the corporation would also be increased by $24,000 to $124,000. However, the cost of the consideration received would be as follows:

Elected amount	$100,000
Allocated to note (up to FMV)	100,000
Allocated to preferred share	Nil

Thus, the cost of the consideration received or of the shares owned by Daughter, which would increase in value by $24,000, is not increased by the amount of the benefit resulting in potential double taxation.

The $1,000 LSC of the preferred share would not be reduced and would equal tax PUC.

Reduction in PUC   ITA: 85(2.1)

(a) Increase in LSC		$ 1,000 (A)
(b) Elected amount (as increased by benefit)	$124,000	
Less: boot	100,000	
Excess, if any		24,000 (B)
Total PUC reduction (A – B)		Nil

ITA: 257

To avoid the problem of the $24,000 benefit being potentially taxed twice, Mother should have taken more share consideration in the amount of $24,000 such that the fair market value of all consideration received was equal to the fair market value of the property transferred. The PUC of these shares will be reduced to nil by the above formula, but this will not have any immediate tax consequences.   ITA: 85(2.1)

Exercise 5

Elected amount	*Range*
Asset #1	$5,000 — $20,000
Asset #2	$8,000 — $14,000

However, the Act forces the minimum elected amount to be $18,000 because of the non-share consideration taken in that amount.   ITA: 85(1)(*b*)

Assign the elected amount as follows:

Asset #1	$ 5,000
Asset #2	13,000
	$18,000

Note that the minimum amount is assigned to the depreciable asset to avoid recapture being fully taxed.

Income

Asset #1	P of D	$ 5,000
	ACB	10,000
	CL	Nil
Asset #2	P of D	$13,000
	ACB	8,000
	CG	$ 5,000
	TCG	$ 2,500

Under corporate law[1], the paid-up capital of the one common share would be equal to the net fair market value of the assets transferred to the corporation. In this case, the PUC would be $16,000 (i.e., $20,000 + $14,000 – $18,000). However, the Act will reduce the PUC as follows: ITA: 85(2.1)

(a)	Increase in legal PUC of all shares on the transfer to the corporation		$16,000 (I)
(b)	Elected amount	$18,000	
	Less: non-share consideration ("boot")	18,000	
	Excess, if any		Nil (II)
	Total PUC reduction (I – II)		$16,000

Since there is only one class of shares issued, there is no prorating of this reduction. As a result, the PUC of the share will be reduced to nil (i.e., $16,000 – $16,000) for tax purposes. The PUC is reduced to nil, because all of the tax-paid cost in UCC of $5,000 and ACB of $8,000 has been recovered through cash.

— NOTE TO SOLUTION

[1] Where the transferor and the corporation do not deal at arm's length, the legal stated capital (the initial PUC) can be less than the fair market value of the transferred assets at the discretion of the corporate directors.

Exercise 6

(A) Items not transferred under subsection 85(1):

Cash	$ 4,000	(not capital property)
Short-term investments	5,000	(superficial loss denied)
Accounts receivable	9,000	(use section 22[1])
Prepaid insurance	400	(business loss of $100)
Building	60,000	(terminal loss of $2,000 denied)
Land	26,500	(superficial loss denied)
Total	$104,900	(assume proprietorship debt of $74,000 and take back new debt for the balance of $30,900.)

The building may be transferred using the rules in section 85, but there is no advantage to doing so, because of the unrealized terminal loss. A stop-loss rule applies to deny the loss. The corporation will acquire the building with a UCC of $60,000 which is equal to its fair market value and the amount paid by the corporation.   ITA: 13(21.2

If the short-term investments can be considered assets used in the active business of the corporation, they can be transferred to the corporation. However, the capital loss will be considered to be a superficial loss because the corporation is affiliated with the transferor, Mrs. Designer. Therefore, a stop-loss rule will deny the loss to Mrs. Designer. The amount of the loss will be added to the cost of the investments to the corporation, such that the corporation's ACB of the investments will be $10,000.   ITA: 54   ITA: 40(2)(*g*), 53(1)(*f*)

Section 85 need not be used when there is no accrued income to defer. If the short-term investments cannot be considered as assets used in an active business, then they should not be transferred to the corporation, because it will seriously jeopardize the qualification of the shares of the corporation as QSBCS.

The land need not be transferred under section 85 for the same reasons as the short-term investments, because of the accrued capital loss. While the loss will be denied to Mrs. Designer, the corporation will acquire the land for $26,500 of consideration, but hold it with an ACB of $30,000 which was Mrs. Designer's tax position in the land before the transfer.

(B) and (C) Items transferred under subsection 85(1) and consideration:

				Consideration			
	Tax value	FMV	Elected amount	Assumed debt[2]	New debt	Pref. shs.	Income
Inventory	$ 5,000	$25,000	$ 5,000	Nil	$ 5,000	$20,000	Nil
Goodwill	Nil	44,000	1	Nil	Nil	44,000	$0.50
	$ 5,000	$69,000	$ 5,001	Nil	$ 5,000	$64,000	

Since the corporation will qualify as a small business corporation, the Act will not apply to attribute income or capital gains back to Mrs. Designer.   ITA: 74.4, 248(1)

(D) Elected transfer price.			$ 5,001
Allocated to debt consideration:			
debt assumed		Nil	
new debt		5,000	5,000
Allocated to ACB of preferred shares			$ 1
(E) LSC before reduction.			$64,000

Reduction in PUC   ITA: 85(2.1)

(i) Increase in LSC of all shares.	$64,000 (A)		
(ii) Elected amount	$ 5,001		
Less: boot	5,000		
Excess, if any		1 (B)	
Total PUC reduction (A – B)		(63,999)	
Tax PUC after reduction		$ 1	

The $1 of PUC after the reduction represents the amount of tax-paid cost that has not been recovered through boot received from the corporation. The $1 of income resulting from the transfer of the goodwill is a tax-paid cost. A total of $5,000 of total tax-paid cost was recovered through boot.

(F) For those assets *not* transferred under subsection 85(1) and not subject to the specific provisions discussed below, the cost for tax purposes to the corporation would be equal to the fair market value of the consideration:

Cash	$ 4,000
Prepaid insurance	400
Building	60,000
	$64,400 = debt consideration

Under section 22, the purchaser, Hi-Fashion, would record the accounts receivable at their face value of $12,000 which would be their adjusted cost base for tax purposes. Under the conditions of section 22, the corporation must include in its income the business loss of $3,000 recognized by the transferor (i.e., difference between the face value ($12,000) and the fair market value ($9,000)). Hi-Fashion is now entitled to set up a reserve to offset any potential doubtful debts (i.e., $3,000), plus an amount equal to any further decline in value. In addition, the corporation is now eligible to write off any realized bad debts since it has included an amount in income in respect of these receivables.

The ACB of the short-term investments and the land to the corporation will be their fair market value plus the denied superficial loss. Therefore, the ACB of the short-term investments will be $10,000 ($5,000 FMV + $5,000 denied loss) and that of the land will be $30,000 ($26,500 FMV + $3,500 denied loss). This puts the corporation in the same tax position on these assets as Mrs. Designer was in before the transfer.

The capital cost and, therefore, the ACB of the building in the corporation is $80,000.

For the inventory that has been transferred under subsection 85(1), the cost base would be the elected amount (i.e., inventory — $5,000). The goodwill, which is eligible capital property, would have a cost base of 75 cents (i.e., ¾ × $1.00).

—NOTES TO SOLUTION

(1) Reserve of $2,000 from last year must be brought into income this year. There will be a full business loss of $3,000 (i.e., face value of $12,000 less fair market value of $9,000) using section 22.

(2) The $104,900 of debt consideration for the assets not transferred under subsection 85(1) could include all assumed liabilities of $74,000, leaving none to be assumed in the subsection 85(1) transfer.

Exercise 7

An elected transfer price of $80,000 will result in the following: ITA: 85(1)

Recapture ($27,000 – $30,000)		$ 3,000
Taxable capital gain [½ ($80,000 – $30,000)]		25,000
Income		$28,000
Less: 1999 net capital loss ($37,500 × ½ / ¾ to adjust to 2007		25,000
Incremental taxable income		$ 3,000
ACB of consideration received:		
Note		$80,000
Common shares		Nil

PUC of common shares: ITA: 85(2.1)
LSC of shares issued $20,000
Less: PUC reduction   ITA: 85(2.1)

(a) increase in LSC		$20,000 (A)	
(b) elected amount	$80,000		
boot	80,000		
excess, if any	Nil	(B)	
(A – B)		$20,000	
PUC for tax purposes		Nil	

Capital cost of transferred property to corporation for CCA and recapture purposes is equal to the aggregate of:

(a) capital cost to transferor $30,000

(b) proceeds of disposition to transferor	$80,000	
less: capital cost of property transferred	30,000	
excess, if any	$50,000	
½ of excess	25,000	
Deemed capital cost to corporation	$55,000	ITA: 13(7)(*e*)(i)

The capital cost used for future CCA write-offs, which shield business income from full tax, will be increased by the taxable capital gain triggered, but not, in effect, the untaxed portion of the capital gain.

Capital cost of the depreciable property for future *capital gains* purposes (equal to elected amount) is $80,000.

Exercise 8

Part (A)

Section 84.1 applies because Mr. Nailed is a Canadian resident and is not at arm's length with his brother who controls the corporation to which the Opco shares were transferred. Therefore, Mr. Nailed is not at arm's length with the corporation. In addition, Opco Ltd. is connected with Broco Ltd., since Broco owns all of its outstanding common shares.

ITA: 251(2)(*b*)(iii)
ITA: 186(2)

PUC reduction:

ITA: 84.1(1)(*a*)

(a) Increase in LSC of brother's corporation		$ 300,000 (A)	
Less:			
(b) Greater of:			
(i) PUC of operating company shares	$75,000		
(ii) Modified ACB* of operating company shares	$75,000	$ 75,000	
Less: FMV of boot	500,000		
Excess, if any		Nil (B)	
PUC reduction (A – B)		$ 300,000	
PUC after reduction		Nil	

The PUC after reduction is nil because all of the $75,000 hard cost in the operating company shares has been recovered in boot from the brother's corporation.

Deemed dividend:

ITA: 84.1(1)(*b*)

Sum of:			
(a) Increase in LSC of brother's corporation		$ 300,000 (A)	
(b) FMV of boot		500,000 (D)	
(A + D)		$ 800,000	
Less sum of:			
(c) Greater of:			
(i) PUC of operating company shares	$ 75,000		
(ii) Modified ACB* of operating company shares	$ 75,000	$ 75,000 (E)	
(d) PUC reduction	300,000 (F)		ITA: 84.1(1)(*a*)
(E + F)		375,000	
Deemed dividend (A + D) – (E + F)		$ 425,000	

* Adjusted actual cost.

This deemed dividend is equal to the excess of the $500,000 in boot received from the brother's corporation over the $75,000 of hard cost in the operating company shares transferred.

Capital gain or loss on disposition of Opco Ltd. shares:

Elected amount and proceeds of disposition for operating company shares	$ 500,000	ITA: 85(1)
Less: deemed dividend	425,000	ITA: 54 "proceeds of disposition" (*k*)
Adjusted proceeds of disposition for operating company shares	$ 75,000	
Less: ACB of operating company shares	75,000	
Capital gain (loss) if any, (not denied*)	Nil	ITA: 40(2)(*g*)

ACB of Broco Ltd. shares received:

Cost of shares of Broco Ltd. after allocation of $500,000 elected amount to "boot"	Nil	ITA: 85(1)(*g*)

---

* He is not affiliated with Broco Ltd. by the definition of "affiliated person" in section 251.1, since he does not control, directly or indirectly, Broco Ltd.

Part (B)

Ultimate redemption of shares of brother's corporation

Redemption amount	$ 300,000	
Less: PUC	Nil	
Deemed dividend on redemption	$ 300,000	ITA: 84(3)
Proceeds of disposition	$ 300,000	
Less: deemed dividend on redemption	300,000	ITA: 84(3)
Adjusted proceeds of disposition	Nil	ITA: 54 "proceeds of disposition" (*j*)
Less: adjusted cost base	Nil	
Capital gain (loss)	Nil	

Summary of income effects:

Sec. 84.1 deemed dividend	$ 425,000	
Redemption deemed dividend	300,000	ITA: 84(3)
Capital gain (loss) on transfer	Nil	ITA: 85(1)
Capital gain (loss) on redemption	Nil	
Net economic effect	$ 725,000	

Note that $725,000 represents the accrued gain on the Opco Ltd. shares at the time of the transfer.

Part (C)

Ultimate arm's length sale of shares of brother's corporation

Proceeds of disposition	$ 300,000	
Less: adjusted cost base	Nil	
Capital gain	$ 300,000	

Summary of income effects:

Sec. 84.1 deemed dividend	$ 425,000	
Capital loss on transfer	Nil	ITA: 85(1)
Capital gain on arm's length sale	300,000	
Net economic effect	725,000	

Again, the $725,000 represents the accrued gain in the Opco Ltd. shares at the time of the transfer.

Exercise 9

For either alternative involving the sale of the Davpet Ltd. shares, the conditions of section 84.1 are met. Davpet Ltd. is a corporation resident in Canada and its shares are held as capital property by Ms. Erin, a Canadian resident. These shares are sold to a non-arm's length corporation, Lenmeag Ltd., since

Ms. Erin is related to her father who controls Lenmeag Ltd. The two corporations are connected, since all of the shares of Davpet Ltd. are owned by Lenmeag Ltd. after the sale.

(A) Since no new shares of Lenmeag Ltd. were issued in this alternative, there is no PUC reduction. However, there will be an immediate deemed dividend computed as follows:

Deemed dividend: ITA: 84.1(1)(*b*)

Sum of:

(a)	Increase in LSC of Lenmeag Ltd. shares..............	Nil	(A)
(b)	FMV of "boot"..................................	$300,000	(D)
	(A + D)	$300,000	

Less sum of:

(c)	Greater of:			
	(i) PUC of Davpet Ltd. shares	$1,000		
			$1,000 (E)	
	(ii) Modified ACB of Davpet Ltd. shares	$1,000		
(d)	PUC reduction		Nil (F)	
	(E + F)..		1,000	
	Deemed dividend (A + D) − (E + F)		$299,000	

ITA: 84.1(1)(*a*)

This deemed dividend represents the excess of the $300,000 in boot received from Lenmeag Ltd. over the $1,000 in PUC of the Davpet Ltd. shares.

Proceeds of disposition for the Davpet Ltd. shares will be reduced so that there will be no capital gain against which to offset the QSBC share capital gains deduction, as follows: ITA: 54 "proceeds of disposition" (*k*)

Consideration in debt received on sale	$300,000
Less: sec. 84.1 deemed dividend	299,000
Adjusted proceeds of disposition..................................	$ 1,000
ACB of Davpet Ltd. shares	(1,000)
Capital gain	Nil

ITA: 54 "proceeds of disposition"(*k*)

When the $300,000 debt is repaid by Lenmeag Ltd., there will be no further tax consequences. However, the plan is ineffective, because Ms. Erin will have to pay tax on a deemed dividend of $299,000 at the time of the sale of her shares instead of the intended capital gains.

(B) In this alternative, there will be a PUC reduction, computed as follows:

PUC reduction: ITA: 84.1(1)(*a*)

(a)	Increase in LSC of Lenmeag Ltd.		$300,000	(A)
	Less:			
(b)	Greater of:			
	(i) PUC of Davpet Ltd. shares..........	$1,000		
			$ 1,000	
	(ii) Modified ACB of Davpet Ltd. shares	$1,000		
	Less: FMV of "boot"		Nil	
	Excess, if any		1,000	(B)
	PUC reduction (A − B)		$299,000	
	PUC of new Lenmeag Ltd. shares after reduction ($300,000 − $299,000).....................		$ 1,000	

The PUC of $1,000 after reduction represents the $1,000 of hard cost in the Davpet Ltd. shares transferred. None of that $1,000 of cost was recovered through boot on this transfer.

Since no "boot" was received, there will be no deemed dividend. As a result, proceeds of disposition for the Davpet Ltd. shares are equal to the $300,000 common share consideration received from Lenmeag Ltd. The result is the following:

Proceeds of disposition for Davpet Ltd. shares	$300,000
ACB	1,000
Capital gain	$299,000
Taxable capital gain (½ × $299,000)	$149,500
Less: Capital gains deduction for QSBCS	149,500
Effect on taxable income of Ms. Erin	Nil

The ACB of the Lenmeag Ltd. shares acquired by Ms. Erin will be equal to the $300,000 fair market value of the shares in Davpet Ltd. given up. As a result, when the shares of Lenmeag Ltd. are either sold or redeemed the $300,000 ACB of the shares will shield an equal amount from being taxed as a capital gain and the objective of crystallizing the QSBC share capital gains exemption will be accomplished without an immediate capital gain or deemed dividend on the sale of the Davpet Ltd. shares.

Exercise 10

Of the $900,000 dividend received by Vendco, $700,000 can be attributed to post-1971 earnings of Preyco and, therefore, can be received by Vendco without tax consequences under Part I and Part IV of the Act. The other $200,000 of the total dividend received will be deemed not to be a dividend received and will be deemed to be part of the proceeds of disposition of the shares sold to Purchco. As a result, the following capital gain on the disposition of the shares would be computed:

Actual proceeds on the disposition of the shares to Purchco	$100,000
Deemed proceeds of disposition ($900,000 – $700,000)	200,000
Total proceeds of disposition	$300,000
ACB	100,000
Capital gain	$200,000

ITA: 55(2)(*b*)

These results are equivalent to Vendco's receiving a dividend from Preyco, of $700,000 without tax consequences and then selling the shares of Preyco to Purchco for their fair market value of $300,000 (i.e., $1,000,000 – $700,000). With an adjusted cost base of $100,000 for the shares, a capital gain of $200,000 would result.

CHAPTER 17
Income Deferral: Other Rollovers and Use of Rollovers in Estate Planning

Exercise 1

Section 85.1 applies because shares of a Canadian corporation (Magnanimous, the purchaser) are being issued to a taxpayer (Mr. Sucker, the vendor) in exchange for capital property (shares of Targetco) of Mr. Sucker. Since Mr. Sucker wishes to fully defer the accrued gains in his shares he should not include any amount in his income on the disposition of his Targetco shares as a result of the exchange. Mr. Sucker and Magnanimous are at arm's length before the exchange. Furthermore, Mr. Sucker will neither control nor own more than 50% of the fair market value of all of the outstanding shares of Magnanimous after the exchange.

The tax consequences to Mr. Sucker will be as follows:

Proceeds of disposition for Targetco shares ($1.25 × 1,000)	$1,250
ACB of Targetco shares	(1,250)
Capital gain	Nil
ACB of Magnanimous shares received by Mr. Sucker in exchange	$1,250

As a result, the ACB of the 1,000 shares of Targetco given up by Mr. Sucker becomes the ACB of the 500 shares acquired in the exchange and the accrued capital gain on the Targetco shares is deferred. The ACB per share of the Magnanimous shares held by Mr. Sucker will be $2.50 (i.e., $1,250/500).

Magnanimous will have acquired the 1,000 Targetco shares from Mr. Sucker at an ACB equal to the lesser of:

FMV of Targetco shares before exchange (1,000 × $2.35)	$2,350
PUC of Targetco shares before exchange (1,000 × $1.00)	$1,000

The provision will apply to limit the addition to the PUC of Magnanimous shares on their issue in exchange to the amount of the PUC of the Targetco shares received (i.e., $1.00 per share).

ITA: 85.1(2.1)

Exercise 2

There is no deemed dividend, because the redemption amount paid, consisting of cash for $675 and total reduced PUC of the new shares for $1,325, does not exceed the PUC of the old shares of $2,000. (See calculations (4) and (5) below.)

ITA: 84(3)

Issuance of New Shares

(1) Reduced PUC:

ITA: 86(2.1)(a)

LSC increase for all new shares		$1,325
Less: PUC of old class A preferred shares	$2,000	
Less: boot	675	1,325
PUC reduction		Nil
Total reduced PUC (class B preferreds, $1,000; commons, $325)		$1,325

(2) Cost of class B preferred and common shares received:

Adjusted cost base of old shares	$2,000
Less: fair market value of non-share consideration	675
Cost of Class B preferred and common shares received	$1,325
Cost of non-share consideration (boot) received (equal to FMV)	$ 675

ITA: 86(1)(c)

Allocation of cost of new shares:

Class B preferred shares:

$$\frac{\text{FMV of class B preferred shares}}{\text{FMV of all shares}} \times \text{cost of new shares}$$

$$= \frac{\$1,755}{\$1,755 + \$570} \times \$1,325 = \underline{\$1,000}$$

Common shares:

$$\frac{\text{FMV of common shares}}{\text{FMV of all shares}} \times \text{cost of new shares}$$

$$= \frac{\$570}{\$1,755 + \$570} \times \$1,325 = \underline{\$325}$$

Redemption of Old Shares

(1) Proceeds on redemption of old shares:

ITA: 84(5)(d)

Boot or non-share consideration	$ 675
Reduced PUC of the new shares — see above	1,325
Redemption proceeds	$2,000

ITA: 84(5)(d)

Deemed dividend on redemption:			ITA: 84(3)
Redemption proceeds		$2,000	
Less: PUC of old shares		2,000	
Deemed dividend on redemption		Nil	ITA: 84(3)

(2) Proceeds of disposition of old shares:				ITA: 86(1)(c)
Cost of all new shares (above)	$1,325			
Plus: cost of all non-share consideration (equal to FMV)	675	$2,000		
Less: ssec. 84(3) deemed dividend		Nil		ITA: 84(3)
Proceeds of disposition of old shares		$2,000		
Capital gain or loss on disposition of old shares:				
Proceeds of disposition of old shares		$2,000		
Adjusted cost base of old shares		2,000		
Capital gain (loss)[1]		Nil		

Net economic effect:			
Deemed dividends on redemption		Nil	ITA: 84(3)
Capital gain (loss) on disposition of old shares		Nil	
Accrued capital gain on new shares:			
FMV ($1,755 + $570)	$2,325		
ACB	(1,325)	$1,000	
Net economic effect		$1,000	

This $1,000 reflects the accrued gain (i.e., $3,000 – $2,000) on the old shares before the reorganization.

—NOTE TO SOLUTION

[1] Capital losses on a redemption are denied where the corporation is still affiliated with the shareholder (e.g., where the shareholder or the shareholder's spouse still controls the corporation after the exchange).

ITA: 40(3.6)

Exercise 3

The benefit rule will apply in this case because the FMV of Mrs. Janna's common shares ($450,000, i.e., 75% of $600,000) is greater than the FMV of the preferred shares received on the reorganization ($350,000) and it is reasonable to regard the $100,000 excess as a benefit that Mrs. Janna desired to have conferred on a related person, her daughter.

ITA: 86(2)

There is no deemed dividend, as shown by the following:

ITA: 84(3)

Issuance of New Shares

(1) Reduced PUC:				ITA: 86(2.1)(a)
LSC increase for new preferred shares			$750	
Less: PUC of old common shares		$750		
Less: boot		Nil	750	
PUC reduction			Nil	
Reduced PUC ($750 – Nil)			$750	

(2) The cost of the preferred shares received will be equal to:				ITA: 86(2)(e)
ACB of common shares			$ 750	
Less: cost of non-share consideration		Nil		
benefit		$100,000	100,000	
Cost of preferred shares			Nil	

Since no boot was taken back on the exchange the final PUC of the preferred shares will be $750.

Redemption of Old Shares

(1) Redemption amount:

Non-share consideration	Nil	
PUC of preferred shares received	$ 750	$ 750
Less: PUC of common shares given up		(750)
Deemed dividend on redemption		Nil	ITA: 84(3)

(2) The deemed proceeds of disposition of Mrs. Janna's common shares will be equal to the lesser of: ITA: 86(2)(c)

(a) Cost (equal to FMV) of non-share consideration		Nil
Plus: benefit		$100,000
		$100,000
(b) FMV of common shares given up		$450,000

There will be a capital gain on the disposition by Mrs. Janna of her common shares equal to:

Deemed proceeds of disposition (lesser of (a) and (b) above)	$100,000
ACB of common shares (75% of $1,000)	(750)
Capital gain	$ 99,250

The following net economic effect can be aggregated from the foregoing:

Deemed dividend on redemption		Nil	ITA: 84(3)
Capital gain on disposition of common shares		$ 99,250
Accrued capital gain on preferred shares:		
FMV	$350,000	
ACB	Nil	350,000
Net economic effect		$449,250

This $449,250 reflects the accrued gain (i.e., 75% of ($600,000 – $1,000)) on the common shares held by Mrs. Janna, before the reorganization. Note how $99,250 is realized immediately on the reorganization and the remainder will be realized on the disposition of the preferred shares.

Furthermore, Mrs. Janna has lost the ability to recover $100,000 in tax-paid cost, because the cost of the preferred shares is nil, having been reduced by the benefit. The $100,000 is tax-paid cost because it reflects the $750 of cost in the common shares, plus $99,250 of capital gain realized on the disposition of those shares and included in income. At the same time, Rayna has had the benefit of a $100,000 increase in the value of her shares without any increase in their adjusted cost base. Therefore, the $100,000 of gain will be taxable in her hands on the disposition of her common shares.

Exercise 4

If either section 87 or subsection 88(1) is used:

(A) Acquisition Limited will be deemed to have proceeds of disposition on the land of $50,000, so the capital gain will be deferred.

(B) Mergem will be able to "bump" the cost base of the land on its books

— the "bump" would be computed as follows: ITA: 88(1)(d)

Mergem's ACB of Acquisition's shares		$75,000
Less the sum of:		
(I) cost amount of Acquisition's assets	$50,000	
(II) dividends paid by Acquisition to Mergem	Nil	50,000
Increase in ACB of land		$25,000

— this "bump" cannot exceed:

fair market value of the land at the time control was acquired	$90,000
less: ACB of the land	50,000
maximum "bump"	$40,000

— therefore, the ACB of the land to Mergem will be $75,000 after a "bump" of $25,000.

Exercise 5

Adjusted cost base of common shares equal to adjusted cost base of the debentures at the time of conversion	$10,000

Adjusted cost base of each common share:

Number of shares received on conversion ($\frac{\$10,000}{\$100} \times 16$)	1,600
ACB of each share ($10,000/1,600)	$ 6.25

CHAPTER 18
Partnerships and Trusts

Exercise 1

Partnership's net income for financial accounting purposes		$304,280
Deduct: Capital gain		5,000
		$299,280
Add: Depreciation on office furniture	$ 3,750	
Donations	5,500	
Membership in fitness club	1,250	
Taxable capital gain (½ × $5,000)	2,500	13,000
		$312,280
Deduct: Capital cost allowance		4,300
Income to be allocated (Division B)		$307,980
Bob's share of income from partnership		$153,990
Add: Gross-up of Bob's share of partnership dividends (¼ × $4,000 × ½)	$ 500	
Grossed-up personal dividends	4,375	
Personal interest income	1,200	6,075
Bob's net income (Division B) and taxable income		$160,065

Analysis of Bob's income:

	Personal	Partnership	Total
Grossed-up dividends	$4,375	$ 2,500	$ 6,875
Interest	1,200	—	1,200
Taxable capital gains	—	1,250	1,250
Business income		150,740	150,740
Total	$5,575	$154,490*	$160,065

* $153,990 + $500 gross-up

Notes:

(1) Drawings taken by the members of a partnership do not constitute a business expense but are a method of distributing partnership income to members of the partnership.

(2) Charitable donations are not deductions in computing the income of a partnership but are used as the basis for computing the charitable donations tax credit for an individual partner.

(3) Fees paid to a fitness club are non-deductible expenses.

ITA: 18(1)(*l*)

(4) Bob will be eligible for the following federal dividend tax credit:

— on share of partnership dividends (13⅓% of ⁵⁄₄ × ½ × $4,000)	$ 333
— on personal dividends (13⅓% of ⁵⁄₄ × $3,500)	583
Total.	$ 916

Exercise 2

Adjusted cost base of Katie's partnership interest:

Contributions		$ 50,000
Add: Share of profits excluding taxable capital gain (½ × ($450,000 – $20,000))	$215,000	
Share of full capital gain (½ × $20,000 × ²⁄₁)	20,000	
Share of capital dividends (½ × $4,000)	2,000	237,000
		$287,000
Deduct: Share of losses (½ × $15,000)	$ 7,500	
Drawings (½ × $176,000)	88,000	
Share of donations (½ × $27,000)	13,500	109,000
ACB of partnership interest		$178,000

Capital gain on disposition of partnership interest:

Proceeds of disposition	$250,000
ACB	178,000
Capital gain	$ 72,000
Taxable capital gain (½ of $72,000)	$ 36,000

Exercise 3

	Trust	Rebecca	Robert
Income			
Interest	$4,500	$ 5,500	$ 1,500
Taxable capital gain	1,500	1,500	1,500
Taxable dividends	3,750	3,750	3,750
Net income/taxable income	$9,750	$10,750	$ 6,750
Federal tax (@ 29% for trust and 15.5% for individuals)	$2,828	$ 1,666	$ 1,046
Personal tax credit @ 15.5% of $8,929	—	(1,384)	(1,384)
Tuition credit and education credit	—	—	Nil
Dividend tax credit @ 13⅓% of $3,750	(500)	(500)	—
Total tax.	$2,328	$ Nil	Nil

Note: None of the tuition and education tax credits were claimed by Robert. Federal tuition and education tax credits of $775[1] are transferable to a parent, or the unused amount of $1,039 less any amount transferred to a supporting person may be carried forward. The definition of tax payable and the ordering rules require that the personal, tuition and education tax credits be deducted before the dividend tax credit which is lost in this case.

ITA: 118.9(1)
ITA: 118.61

ITA: 118.81, 118.92

—*NOTE TO SOLUTION*

(1) Lesser of:

(a) $775 (federal) = <u>$775</u>

(b) (15.5% × $3,500) + (15.5% of ($400 × 8)) = <u>$1,039</u>

$ 775

Minus ($1,046 – $1,384) . . . .   Nil

Net amount transferred to parent . . . . $ 775

Topical Index